ASIA
MAPS 46 – 67

AFRICA
MAPS 68 – 81

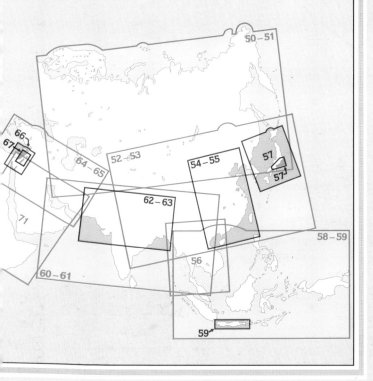

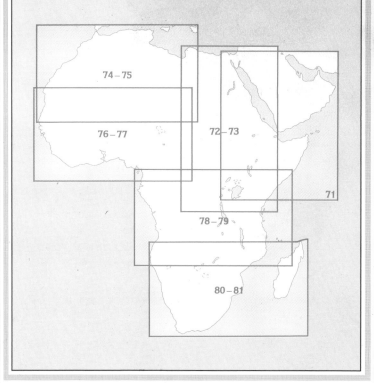

Continued on Back Endpaper

COLLINS
ATLAS
OF THE
WORLD

COLLINS
ATLAS
OF THE
WORLD

COLLINS

LONDON · GLASGOW · SYDNEY · AUCKLAND · TORONTO · JOHANNESBURG

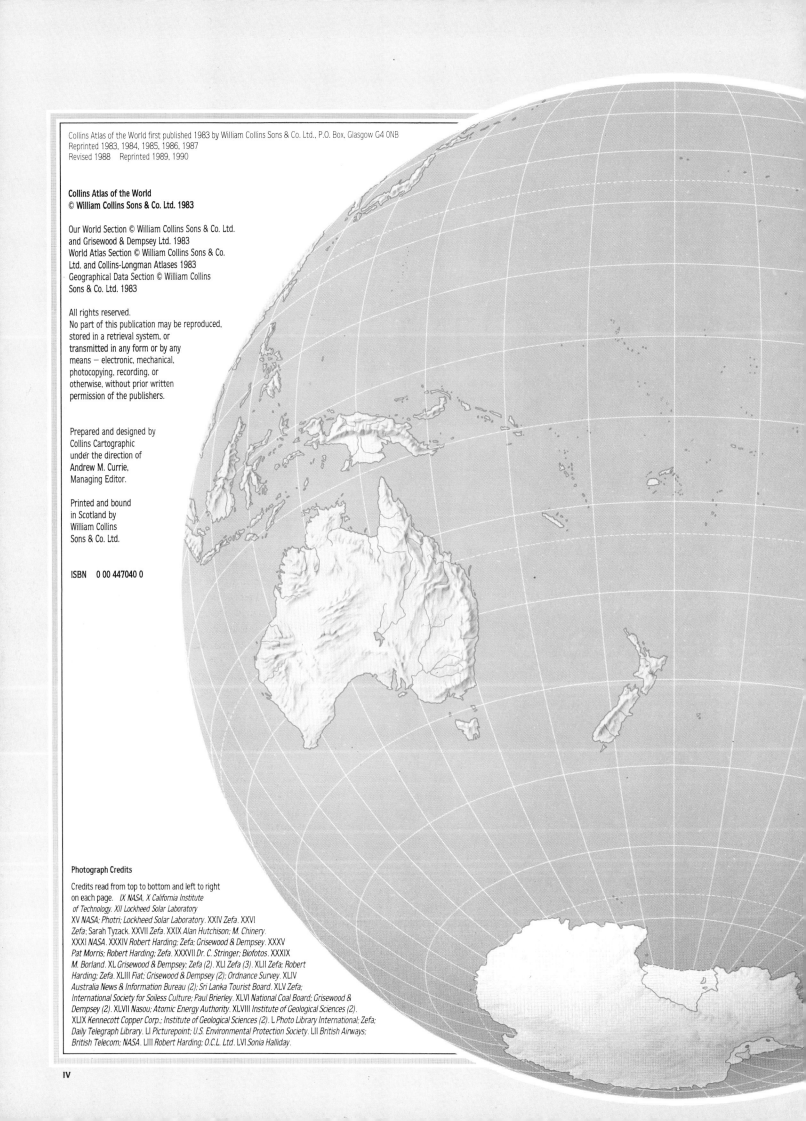

Collins Atlas of the World first published 1983 by William Collins Sons & Co. Ltd., P.O. Box, Glasgow G4 0NB
Reprinted 1983, 1984, 1985, 1986, 1987
Revised 1988   Reprinted 1989, 1990

Prepared and designed by
Collins Cartographic
under the direction of
Andrew M. Currie,
Managing Editor.

Printed and bound
in Scotland by
William Collins
Sons & Co. Ltd.

ISBN   0 00 447040 0

Photograph Credits

Credits read from top to bottom and left to right
on each page.   *IX NASA. X California Institute
of Technology. XII Lockheed Solar Laboratory*
XV *NASA; Photri; Lockheed Solar Laboratory.* XXIV *Zefa.* XXVI
Zefa; Sarah Tyzack. XXVII *Zefa.* XXIX *Alan Hutchison; M. Chinery.*
XXXI *NASA.* XXXIV *Robert Harding; Zefa; Grisewood & Dempsey.* XXXV
Pat Morris; Robert Harding; Zefa. XXXVII *Dr. C. Stringer; Biofotos.* XXXIX
M. Borland. XL *Grisewood & Dempsey; Zefa (2).* XLI *Zefa (3).* XLII *Zefa; Robert
Harding; Zefa.* XLIII *Fiat; Grisewood & Dempsey (2); Ordnance Survey.* XLIV
Australia News & Information Bureau (2); Sri Lanka Tourist Board. XLV *Zefa;
International Society for Soiless Culture; Paul Brierley.* XLVI *National Coal Board; Grisewood &
Dempsey (2).* XLVII *Nasou; Atomic Energy Authority.* XLVIII *Institute of Geological Sciences (2).*
XLIX *Kennecott Copper Corp.; Institute of Geological Sciences (2).* L *Photo Library International; Zefa;
Daily Telegraph Library.* LI *Picturepoint; U.S. Environmental Protection Society.* LII *British Airways;
British Telecom; NASA.* LIII *Robert Harding; O.C.L. Ltd.* LVI *Sonia Halliday.*

FOREWORD

MAPS, as essential aids in the understanding of the world around us, would appear to have been made ever since man first moved about the Earth. To begin with they were relatively primitive plans of very limited areas, carved in wood or painted on rock, bark or skins. Later, the highly organized peoples of the ancient civilizations, in conducting their everyday life, made many functional maps on such materials as clay tablets, papyrus and eventually paper.

However, the first attempt to map the whole of the known world, as opposed to producing local plans of small areas, is attributed to the famous Greek cosmographer, Ptolemy (AD 87 – 150). The many maps of the classical world that accompanied his celebrated manuscript *Geographia* – itself to be regarded as the standard geographical reference work for many centuries – represent the forerunner of the atlas as we know it today.

ATLASES, in the modern sense of systematic collections of maps of uniform size, were born, much later still, in the Netherlands of the 16th century, during the world's great age of exploration. Indeed, it was the eminent Flemish cartographer Mercator (1512 – 1594) who first so used the word Atlas; taking the the name of the ancient Greek mythological titan who symbolically supported the world on his shoulders.

Since the time of these early atlases our knowledge of the world has been greatly increased through continued exploration and scientific discovery. Today, the fast developing space age technology allows man to survey our planet, and beyond, in the most precise detail. The resulting mass of geographical and astronomical data is such that the non-specialist atlas user could easily be overwhelmed. This current information explosion, combined with a new awareness of our world brought about by the views of our planet from space, improved communications, greater opportunity for leisure and travel, and increased media exposure, we believe, calls for a new type of atlas that, presents to the general reader, not only an up-to-date collection of well-documented maps, but also an illuminating and readily accessible record of the latest findings and essential facts about our world.

COLLINS ATLAS OF THE WORLD is published with the explicit aim of meeting this need for a convenient and moderately priced reference atlas, that places at our fingertips an accurate, authoritative, comprehensive and clearly presented picture of the world as it is known today. To achieve this objective, Collins, building on its traditions and experience of over one hundred years' innovative atlas publishing, assembled a talented team of geographers, cartographers, designers, editors and writers. Working to a carefully devised plan, this team has brought together in a single volume a new and complete set of maps, a compendium of contemporary geographical data, and an illustrated and information-packed survey of our world's structure, organization and human environment from the innermost core of our planet to the furthest known extent of the universe.

As a result of the detailed process of research, compilation and design, together with the latest cartographic techniques, which have gone into the production of *Collins Atlas of the World*, we believe that our readers will have the best and most up-to-date atlas available in its class. In terms of cartographic presentation, geographical knowledge and visual elegance, the publication of *Collins Atlas of the World* represents a major step forward, which we hope will contribute to a better awareness and understanding of our fascinating and fast changing world as we approach the 21st century.

Andrew M. Currie
Managing Editor

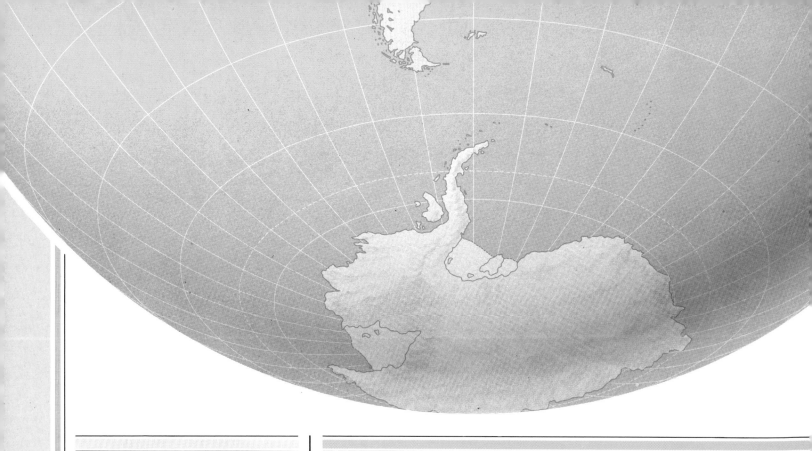

OUR WORLD

WORL

CONTENTS

TLAS

GEOGRAPHICAL DATA

GUIDE TO THE ATLAS

COLLINS ATLAS OF THE WORLD consists of three self-contained but interrelated sections, as is clearly indicated in the preceding list of contents. First, under the title of OUR WORLD there is an authoritative illustrated survey of the most recent scientific knowledge of the world's origin, development and current state. Next, the WORLD ATLAS section, comprising 128 pages of newly created maps, using the most modern cartographic techniques and up-to-date sources, forms the core of this book. Finally, the maps, diagrams and text of these first two sections, are complemented by a detailed compendium of GEOGRAPHICAL DATA.

OUR WORLD

This concise encyclopaedia section, by use of stimulating illustration and informative text, brings together many of the latest scientific discoveries and conclusions about our world; our place in the universe, our neighbours in space, the origin, structure and dynamics of our planet, the evolution of life, the distribution of peoples and resources, and the increasingly significant effects of man on his environment. Each double-page opening has been carefully designed to highlight an important facet of our world as we know it today. As a special feature, every subject presentation includes a *Factfinder* panel, to which quick and easy reference can be made in order to find out particularly notable facts. All statistics quoted in this section are presented in metric terms in accordance with the System International d'Unites (S.I. units).

WORLD ATLAS

The main section of 128 pages of maps has been carefully planned and designed to meet the contemporary needs of the atlas user. Full recognition has been given to the many different purposes that currently call for map reference.

Map coverage extends to every part of the world in a balanced scheme that avoids any individual country or regional bias. Map areas are chosen to reflect the social, economic, cultural or historical importance of a particular region. Each double spread or single page map has been planned deliberately to cover an entire physical or political unit. Generous map overlaps are included to maintain continuity. Following two world maps, giving separate coverage of the main political and physical features, each of the continents is treated systematically in a subsection of its own. Apart from being listed in the contents, full coverage of all regional maps of each continent is also clearly depicted in the *Key to Maps* to be found on the front and back endpapers. Also at the beginning of each continental subsection, alongside a special *Global View* political map, all map coverage, country by country, is identified in an additional handy page index. Finally as a further aid to the reader in locating the required area, a postage stamp key map is incorporated into the title margin of each map page.

Map projections have been chosen to reflect the different requirements of particular areas. No map can be absolutely true on account of the impossibility of representing a spheroid accurately on a flat surface without some distortion in either area, distance, direction or shape. In a general world atlas it is the equal area property that is most important to retain for comparative map studies and feature size evaluation and this principle has been followed

wherever possible in this map section. As a special feature of this atlas, the *Global View* projections used for each continental political map have been specially devised to allow for a realistic area comparison between the land areas of each continent and also between land and sea.

Map scales, as expressions of the relationship which the distance between any two points of the map bears to the corresponding distance on the ground, are in the context of this atlas grouped into three distinct categories.

Large scales, of between 1:1 000 000 (1 centimetre to 10 kilometres or 1 inch to 16 miles) and 1:2 500 000 (1 centimetre to 25 kilometres or 1 inch to 40 miles), are used to cover particularly dense populated areas of Western Europe, United States, Canada and Japan, as well as a special detailed map of the Holy Land.

Medium scales, of between 1:2 500 000 and 1:7 500 000 are used for maps of important parts of Europe, North America, Australasia, India, China, etc.

Small scales, of less than 1:7 500 000 (e.g. 1:10 000 000, 1:15 000 000, 1:25 000 000 etc.) are selected for maps of the complete world, continents, oceans, polar regions and many of the larger countries.

The actual scale at which a particular area is mapped therefore reflects its shape, size and density of detail, and as a basic principle the more detail required to be shown of an area, the greater its scale. However, throughout this atlas, map scales have been limited in number, as far as possible, in order to facilitate comparison between maps.

Map measurements give preference to the metric system which is now used in nearly every country throughout the world. All spot heights and ocean depths are shown in metres and the relief and submarine layer delineation is based on metric contour levels. However, all linear scalebar and height reference column figures are given in metric and Imperial equivalents to facilitate conversion of measurements for the non-metric reader.

Map symbols used are fully explained in the legend to be found on the first page of the World Atlas section. Careful study and frequent reference to this legend will aid in the reader's ability to extract maximum information.

Topography is shown by the combined means of precise spot heights, contouring, layer tinting and three-dimensional hill shading. Similar techniques are also used to depict the sea bed on the World Physical map and those of the oceans and polar regions.

Hydrographic features such as coastlines, rivers, lakes, swamps and canals are clearly differentiated.

Communications are particularly well represented with the contemporary importance of airports and road networks duly emphasized.

International boundaries and national capitals are fully documented and internal administrative divisions are shown with the maximum detail that the scale will allow. Boundary delineation reflects the 'de facto' rather than the 'de jure' political interpretation and where relevant an undefined or disputed boundary is distinguished. However there is no intended implication that the publishers necessarily endorse or accept the status of any political entity recorded on the maps.

Settlements are shown by a series of graded

town stamps, each representing a population size category, based on the latest census figures.

Other features, such as notable ancient monuments, oases, national parks, oil and gas fields, are selectively included on particular maps that merit their identification.

Lettering styles used in the maps have been chosen with great care to ensure maximum legibility and clear distinction of named feature categories. The size and weight of the various typefaces reflect the relative importance of the features. Town names are graded to correspond with the appropriate town stamp.

Map place names have been selected in accordance with maintaining legibility at a given scale and at the same time striking an appropriate balance between natural and man-made features worthy of note. Name forms have been standardized according to the widely accepted principle, now well established in international reference atlases, of including place names and geographical terms in the local language of the country in question. In the case of non-Roman scripts (e.g. Arabic), transliteration and transcription have either been based on the rules recommended by the Permanent Committee on Geographical Names and the United States Board of Geographical Names, or as in the case of the adopted Pinyin transcription of Chinese names, a system officially proposed by the country concerned. The diacritical signs used in each language or transliteration have been retained on all the maps and throughout the index. However the English language reader's requirements have also been recognised in that the names of all countries, oceans, major seas and land features as well as familiar alternative name versions of important towns are presented in English.

Map sources used in the compilation of this atlas were many and varied, but always of the latest available information. At each stage of their preparation the maps were submitted to a thorough process of research and continual revision to ensure that on publication all data would be as accurate as practicable. A well-documented data bank was created to ensure consistency and validity of all information represented on the maps.

GEOGRAPHICAL DATA

This detailed data section forms an appropriate complement to the preceding maps and illustrated texts. There are three parts, each providing a different type of essential geographical information.

World Facts and Figures Drawn from the latest available official sources, these tables present an easy reference profile of significant world physical, political and demographic as well as national data.

Glossary of Geographical Terms This explains most of the foreign language and geographical terms which are to be found incorporated in the place names on the maps and in the index.

World Index This concluding part of the atlas lists in alphabetical order all individual place names to be found on the maps, which total about 40,000. Each entry in the index is referenced to the appropriate map page number, the country or region in which the name is located and the position of the name on the map, given by its co-ordinates of latitude and longitude. A full explanation of how to use the index is to be found on page 140.

OUR WORLD

The Space Age, which began in 1957 with the triumphant launch of the Russian satellite Sputnik I, has already greatly enriched our understanding of the Solar System. It has also afforded us a new perspective on our own planet, not least through photographs taken by astronauts that remind us that the Earth is a mere speck in space. These photographs have dispelled the dangerous notion that our world is boundless in extent, with limitless resources. To view our planet from space is to recognize its finite nature and that we misuse it at our peril.

The Earth is a dynamic planet, with an ever-changing face. Movements in the restless atmosphere and hydrosphere are plain to see, while cataclysmic volcanic eruptions and earthquakes testify to the massive forces that operate beneath the Earth's crust. Continental drift is slowly but inexorably changing the world map, creating new ocean basins and lofty mountain ranges.

Change ensures that the Earth's resources are constantly renewed. But nature works slowly, while our exploitation of those resources increases year by year — a consequence of a massive population explosion, which is most marked in the poorer nations, where malnutrition and short average life expectancies are features of everyday life. For example, an expanding population must be fed. But in many areas, over-intensive farming and over-grazing can rapidly transform once lush farmland into bleak desert.

Many question marks hang over the future of mankind, divided as it is by race, religion, language and political philosophies. And the plunder of our planet home is threatening many other life forms with extinction. One contribution we can all make to the survival of our world is to study and comprehend the delicate and infinitely varied environments that make Earth such a fascinating planet on which to live. Perhaps then our world can be preserved as, in the words of astronaut Neil Armstrong, 'a beautiful jewel in space'.

THE STARS AND GALAXIES

To appreciate how insignificant our world is in space, we must remember that the Sun, an average-sized star, is only one of the 100,000 million stars that are held together by gravity in the spiral Milky Way galaxy. And the Milky Way galaxy is only one of millions of galaxies that can be oberved through large telescopes. Distances in space are so vast that they are measured in light-years – one light-year being the distance travelled by light in one year. Because light travels at a rate of 300,000 kilometres per second, one light-year is the equivalent of nearly 10 million million kilometres.

A star is a hot, glowing ball of gas that produces tremendous energy. Its life cycle begins when huge clouds of hydrogen and other elements begin to contract and the dense centre becomes so hot that it starts to glow. Thermonuclear reactions begin and the hydrogen starts to turn into helium. The reactions may continue for thousands of millions of years. But when the core of the dead helium becomes too big, the star starts to collapse, producing energy that causes it to swell into a red giant star that sheds its outer layers. Finally, the remainder cools, shrinks

and becomes an extremely dense, planet-sized white dwarf star.

On clear nights, about 6000 stars can be seen from Earth with the naked eye, about 2000 being observable from any one place. The brightest stars have special names, while others are grouped in constellations. Constellations are patterns of stars, many of which were named in ancient times after animals, such as the Great Bear, objects, such as the Lyre, people, such as the Archer, and classical heroes, such as Perseus. According to an international agreement in 1928, 88 constellations are recognized. Each has a Latin and English name, as listed in the keys to the star charts, below. Astronomers use constellations to pinpoint the positions of other heavenly bodies, while they are used by navigators to measure latitude and directions.

Constellations appear to move across the sky. The constellations in the northern hemisphere seem to circle around the Pole Star (Polaris), which is almost directly above the North Pole and so it appears to be stationary. There is no equivalent star above the South Pole.

Above: The diagram shows the flat spiral formation of the Milky Way galaxy as it would appear side on (top) and from above (bottom). The red arrow indicates the Sun, one of about 100,000 million stars in our galaxy.

Below: The Andromeda galaxy, which can be seen in the Andromeda constellation, is the nearest spiral galaxy to our galaxy. The Milky Way galaxy would probably look much like this if it was viewed from space.

The star chart shows the constellations that can be seen in the northern hemisphere.

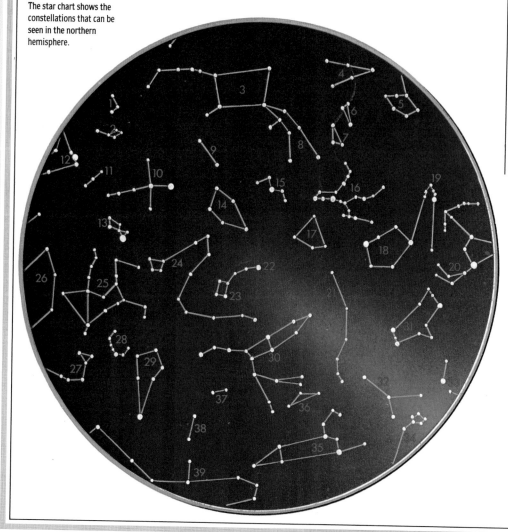

Constellations of the Northern Hemisphere

1 Equuleus, Colt
2 Delphinus, Dolphin
3 Pegasus, Flying Horse
4 Pisces, Fishes
5 Cetus, Sea Monster
6 Aries, Ram
7 Triangulum, Triangle
8 Andromeda, Chained Maiden
9 Lacerta, Lizard
10 Cygnus, Swan
11 Sagitta, Arrow
12 Aquila, Eagle
13 Lyra, Lyre
14 Cepheus, King
15 Cassiopeia, Lady in Chair
16 Perseus, Champion
17 Camelopardus, Giraffe
18 Auriga, Charioteer
19 Taurus, Bull
20 Orion, Hunter
21 Lynx, Lynx

22 Polaris, Pole Star
23 Ursa Minor, Little Bear
24 Draco, Dragon
25 Hercules, Kneeling Giant
26 Ophiuchus, Serpent-bearer
27 Serpens, Serpent
28 Corona Borealis, Northern Crown
29 Boötes, Herdsman
30 Ursa Major, Great Bear
31 Gemini, Twins
32 Cancer, Crab
33 Canis Minor, Little Dog
34 Hydra, Sea Serpent
35 Leo, Lion
36 Leo Minor, Little Lion
37 Canes Venatici, Hunting Dogs
38 Coma Berenices, Berenice's Hair
39 Virgo, Virgin

The shapes of galaxies vary. There are three main kinds. Elliptical galaxies (1) have a ball-like shape. They contain old stars and resemble the nucleus of a spiral galaxy. Spiral galaxies, the commonest types, include the loose, small-hubbed type (2). Older stars lie at the centre, with newer stars in the spiral arms. Some galaxies, however, are irregular in shape (3).

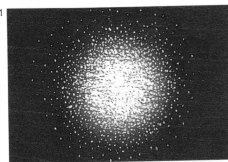

1

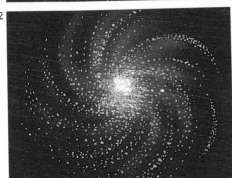

2

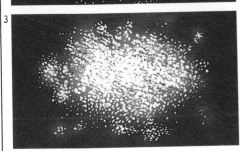

3

FACTFINDER

Brightest star in the sky: Sirius (the Dog Star) in the constellation Canis Major. Magnitude: −1·46. Distance from the Sun: 8·7 light-years.

Nearest star to the Sun: The faint Proxima Centauri (4·3 light-years distant). The nearest star visible to the naked eye is Alpha Centauri in the constellation Centaurus. It is 4·3 light-years away from the Sun.

Size of the Milky Way galaxy: Diameter: 100,000 light-years. Thickness: at the centre, 13,000 light-years; in the spiral arms, about 5000 light years.

Stars in the Milky Way galaxy: 100,000 million.

Age of the Milky Way galaxy: About 12,000 million years.

Position of the Solar System: About 27,000 light-years from the centre of the Milky Way galaxy.

Largest star in the Milky Way galaxy: IRS5 in Perseus constellation, with a diameter of about 15,000 million km or about 10,770 times as large as the Sun.

Nearest external galaxy: The Magellanic Clouds, 160,000 light-years away.

Number of galaxies: About 100 million galaxies are within reach of the larger telescopes.

Andromeda galaxy: Distance from the Sun: 2·2 million light-years. It appears as a fuzzy patch in the Andromeda constellation. The Andromeda galaxy is about the same size as the Milky Way galaxy but contains about 300,000 million stars.

The star chart shows the constellations that can be seen in the southern hemisphere.

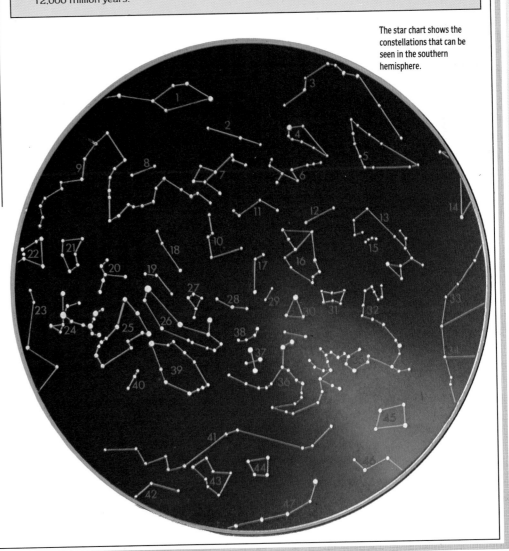

Constellations of the Southern Hemisphere

1 Cetus, Sea Monster
2 Sculptor, Sculptor
3 Aquarius, Water-bearer
4 Piscis Austrinus, Southern Fish
5 Capricornus, Sea Goat
6 Grus, Crane
7 Phoenix, Phoenix
8 Fornax, Furnace
9 Eridanus, River Eridanus
10 Hydrus, Little Snake
11 Tucana, Toucan
12 Indus, Indian
13 Sagittarius, Archer
14 Aquila, Eagle
15 Corona Austrinus, Southern Crown
16 Pavo, Peacock
17 Octans, Octant
18 Dorado, Swordfish
19 Pictor, Painter's Easel
20 Columba, Dove
21 Lepus, Hare
22 Orion, Hunter

23 Monoceros, Unicorn
24 Canis Major, Great Dog
25 Puppis, Poop
26 Carina, Keel
27 Volans, Flying Fish
28 Chamaeleon, Chameleon
29 Apus, Bird of Paradise
30 Triangulum Australe, Southern Triangle
31 Ara, Altar
32 Scorpio, Scorpion
33 Serpens, Serpent
34 Ophiuchus, Serpent-bearer
35 Lupus, Wolf
36 Centaurus, Centaur
37 Crux, Southern Cross
38 Musca, Fly
39 Vela, Sails
40 Pyxis, Compass Box
41 Hydra, Sea Serpent
42 Sextans, Sextant
43 Crater, Cup
44 Corvus, Crow
45 Libra, Scales
46 Virgo, Virgin

THE SOLAR SYSTEM

The Solar System rotates once around the centre of the Milky Way galaxy every 200 million years. The Solar System consists principally of the Sun and the nine planets that orbit around it, but it also includes moons and much debris, such as the spectacular rings of Saturn, and asteroids, which are called minor planets because they measure up to about 1000 km across. Other rocky matter and frozen gas form comets, which are even more numerous than asteroids. Comets have extremely elongated orbits, the farthest point of which may be in the vicinity of the outer planets. The path of one is shown by the red line in the diagram below. As the comets near the Sun, the frozen matter vaporizes to form a tail that is millions of kilometres long. If the orbit of a comet crosses that of the Earth, loose particles may be ejected into the atmosphere. There, they burn up in meteor showers. Fragments large enough to reach Earth are called meteorites.

Many solar systems probably exist in the Universe. In 1982 Russian astronomers

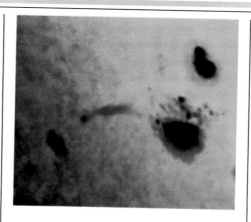

Groups of sunspots are dark areas on the Sun's surface that are around 1000° cooler than surrounding areas. The largest recorded sunspot covered 10,000 million km². Sunspots probably result from magnetic fields that cause local cooling. Sunspots may last for months, but small ones vanish after a few days.

estimated that 130 solar systems similar to our own lie within the observable part of the Milky Way galaxy. But their presence can only be inferred.

Our Sun probably began to form about 4600 million years ago from the solar nebula, a huge cloud of dust and gas. The planets formed somewhat later from the debris that was left over. The Sun consists mainly of hydrogen that is being turned into a central core of helium. The reactions involved in this process generate energy, giving the Sun a surface temperature of 6000°C. Prominences, eruptions of gas from the surface, may reach 50,000°C or more. They are often associated with sunspots, cooler patches possibly caused by strong magnetic fields that block the outward flow of heat. The Sun is surrounded by a thin atmosphere, the corona, which can be seen during a total eclipse. Eventually, the Sun, like all stars, will use up most of its hydrogen and will become a red giant star, engulfing the Solar System. But this will not occur for another 5000 million years.

The Inner Planets

The planets differ in many ways in their makeup, appearance, size and temperature. The four inner planets are the cratered Mercury, whose surface resembles that of our Moon; Venus, which is swathed by a cloudy atmosphere containing much carbon dioxide; Earth; and Mars, which also has a cratered surface. These four, comparatively small, rocky bodies are called terrestrial planets.

The Outer Planets

Most of the asteroids in the Solar System lie between Mars, the outermost of the terrestrial planets, and Jupiter, the innermost of the outer planets. The outer planets include three others – the ringed Saturn, Uranus and Neptune – which, like Jupiter, are huge balls of gas, mainly hydrogen and its compounds, with nitrogen (giving ammonia), carbon (giving methane) and helium. Rocky cores may exist beneath the gases. Pluto, which was discovered in 1930, is probably a rocky body with a methane-type atmosphere.

FACTFINDER

		Mean distance from the Sun (millions of km)	Equatorial diameter (km)	Period of rotation on axis	Surface °C temp- erature	Mass (Earth = 1)	Sidereal Period
1	Sun	—	1,392,000	25d 9h	6000°	333,434.00	—
2	Mercury	58	4,850	58d 14h	350/−170°	0·04	88d
3	Venus	108	12,104	243d	480°	0·83	225d
4	Earth	149·5	12,756	23h56m	22°	1·00	1y
5	Mars	228	6,790	24h 37m	−50°	0·11	1y 322d
6	Jupiter	778·5	142,600	9h 50m	−150°	318.00	11y 315d
7	Saturn	1427	120,000	10h 14m	−180°	95.00	29y 167d
8	Uranus	2870	52,000?	24h(?)	−210°	15.00	84y 6d
9	Neptune	4497	48,000?	22h(?)	−220°	17.00	164y 288d
10	Pluto	5900	3,000?	6d 9h	−230°?	0·06	247y 255d

Number of satellites: Mercury and Venus – 0; Earth – 1; Mars – 2; Jupiter – 14?; Saturn – 17?; Uranus – 5; Neptune – 2; Pluto – 1.

Orbital inclination: Mercury – 7°; Venus – 3°24′; Mars – 1°51′; Jupiter – 1°18′; Saturn – 2°29′; Uranus – 0°46′; Neptune – 1°46′; Pluto – 17°06′.

THE MOON

The Moon, our nearest neighbour in space, has been studied to a degree that is out of all proportion to its importance in the Solar System. From the late 1950s, space probes began to explore the Moon from close range and, in July 1969, the American astronaut Neil Armstrong became the first man to set foot on it. Subsequent missions conducted scientific experiments and collected rocks from a range of sites. Most of these Moon rocks proved to be between 3300 and 4400 million years old, demonstrating that the surface features of the Moon are extremely old by comparison with those on Earth. The oldest rocks dated back 4600 million years, which supports the theory that the Moon was formed in the same way and at the same time as the rest of the Solar System.

The Moon contains several distinctive features. The maria, or 'seas', were so called because early astronomers thought that they contained water. In fact, they are plains smoothed out by vast lava flows, such as the

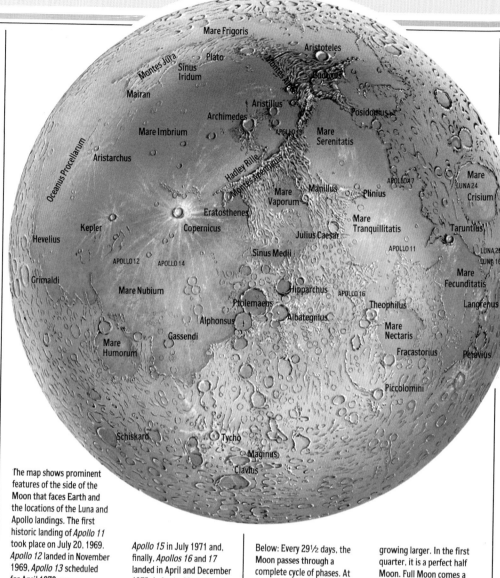

The map shows prominent features of the side of the Moon that faces Earth and the locations of the Luna and Apollo landings. The first historic landing of *Apollo 11* took place on July 20, 1969. *Apollo 12* landed in November 1969, *Apollo 13* scheduled for April 1970, was abandoned after an explosion in the service module. *Apollo 14* landed in February 1971.

Apollo 15 in July 1971 and, finally, *Apollos 16* and *17* landed in April and December 1972. Left: the Moon's diameter is about the same as the distance across Australia.

Below: Every 29½ days, the Moon passes through a complete cycle of phases. At new Moon, it cannot be seen (if the line-up is perfect a solar eclipse occurs). A thin crescent is soon visible, growing larger. In the first quarter, it is a perfect half Moon. Full Moon comes a week later. The Moon then wanes through the last quarter to the next new Moon.

Mare Serenitatis (Sea of Serenity). The most typical features are probably the craters which have given the Moon a pock-marked face. Most of these craters were created by the impacts of meteorites, but some are of volcanic origin. The largest craters may be as big as 240 km across and 6100 metres deep. Other features of the lunar landscape are mountain ranges, such as the Montes Apenninus, and rilles, such as Hadley Rille. Straight rilles are probably downfaulted depressions, like rift valleys on Earth. All the features of the Moon have been unchanged for 3000 million years, untouched by crustal disturbances or erosion.

The Moon has no atmosphere or weather, because its gravity is insufficient to hold any gases. Consequences of its lack of atmosphere are an absence of sound and enormous differences between night and daytime temperatures.

Phases of the Moon

Waxing gibbous

First quarter

Waxing crescent

Full Moon

Earth

New Moon

Waning gibbous

Last quarter

Waning crescent

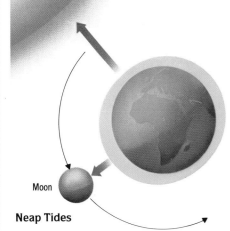

Spring Tides

Neap Tides

FACTFINDER

Diameter of the Moon: 3476 km.

Axial inclination: 6½°.

Density: 3·34 times that of water.

Mass: 0·012 times that of Earth.

Force of gravity at the surface: 0·16 times that of Earth. The Moon's gravity is too weak for this lifeless body to hold an atmosphere.

Escape velocity: 2·4 km/sec, less than a quarter that on Earth.

Mean velocity in orbit: 1 km/sec.

Surface temperatures: 100°C at noon; −150°C at night.

Lunar month: 29 days, 13 hours (measured from new Moon to new Moon). It is also called the synodic month. The lunar month is not the same as a calendar month, because there is no relationship between the rotation of the Moon around the Earth and the rotation of the Earth around the Sun.

Mean distance from Earth: 384,400 km. Every time the Moon completes an orbit of the Earth, it also completes one revolution on its axis. Hence, it always shows the same face to Earth.

Tides occur because of the gravitational pull of the Moon and Sun on the oceans. The lowest high tides (neap) occur when the Moon, Earth and Sun form a right angle. The gravitational pull of the two bodies is then opposed. Highest high (spring) tides occur when the Sun, Moon and Earth are in a straight line. The gravitational pull of the two bodies is then combined.

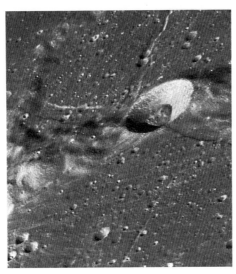

Left: The surface of the Moon is pitted with craters, which are the result of meteoric impacts or of volcanic activity many millions of years ago.

Below left: In a lunar eclipse, the Moon passes through the Earth's shadow. In a solar eclipse, the Moon's shadow is cast on to the Earth's surface. Below: The brownish colour of the photograph of a lunar eclipse is caused by sunlight filtering through the Earth's atmosphere. Bottom: In total eclipses of the Sun, the corona becomes visible.

Lunar eclipse

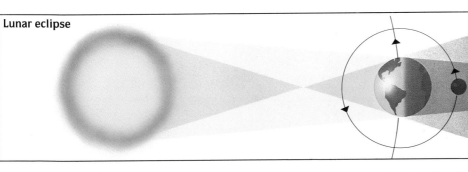

Solar eclipse

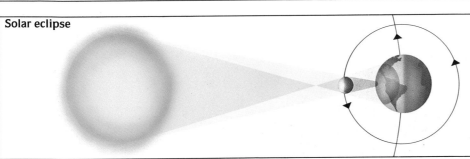

THE WHIRLING EARTH

The Earth moves in three ways: it spins on its axis; it orbits the Sun; and it moves around the Milky Way galaxy with the rest of the Solar System. As it spins on its axis, the Sun appears to move around the sky once every 24 hours. This, the mean solar day, is slightly longer than the sidereal day of 23 hours, 56 minutes and 4 seconds. The difference between the two is explained by the fact that the Earth is orbiting the Sun while it spins on its axis, with the effect that it must rotate 1/365th of a revolution more than a sidereal day in order that the same meridian exactly faces the Sun again.

As the Earth spins on its axis, the time at any point on the surface is calculated from the position of the Sun in the sky. This is called the local or apparent time. Because the Earth rotates 360° in 24 hours, local time changes by one hour for every 15° of longitude or 4 minutes for every 1° of longitude. For practical purposes, however, we use standard or zone time, so that the times are fixed over extensive north-south zones that also take account of national boundaries. By an international agreement in 1884, time zones are measured east and west of the prime meridian (0° longitude) which passes through Greenwich, London. Because clocks are advanced by 12 hours 180° east of Greenwich, but put back by 12 hours 180° west of Greenwich, there is a time difference of 24 hours at the International Date Line. This is approximately 180°W or E, although internationally agreed deviations prevent confusion of dates in island groups and land areas.

People crossing the International Date Line from west to east gain a day. Those going from east to west lose a day.

The Seasons
Because the Earth's axis is tilted by 23½°, the Sun appears to travel in a higher or lower path across the sky at various times of the year, giving differing lengths of daylight. The diagram at the top of the page shows that, at the spring equinox in the northern hemisphere (March 21), the Sun is overhead at the Equator. After March 21, the overhead Sun moves northwards as the northern hemisphere tilts towards the Sun. On June 21, the summer solstice in the northern hemisphere, the Sun is overhead at the Tropic of Cancer (latitude 23½° North). By September 23, the Sun is again overhead at the Equator. By about December 21, the Sun is overhead at the Tropic of Capricorn (23½° S). This is the winter solstice in the northern hemisphere. The seasons are reversed in the southern hemisphere.

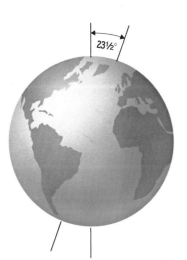

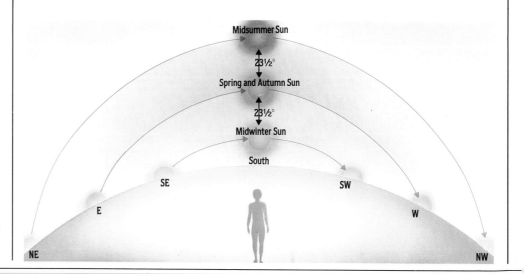

Above: The Earth's axis (joining the North and South poles via the centre of the Earth) is tilted by 23½°. The Earth rotates on its axis once every 23 hours, 56 minutes and 4 seconds. The tilt of the axis remains constant as the Earth orbits the Sun.

Right: The path of the Sun across the sky is highest on Midsummer Day, the longest day, and lowest at midwinter (December 21), the shortest day. The total variation in altitude is 47°, which is twice the angle by which the Earth's axis is tilted.

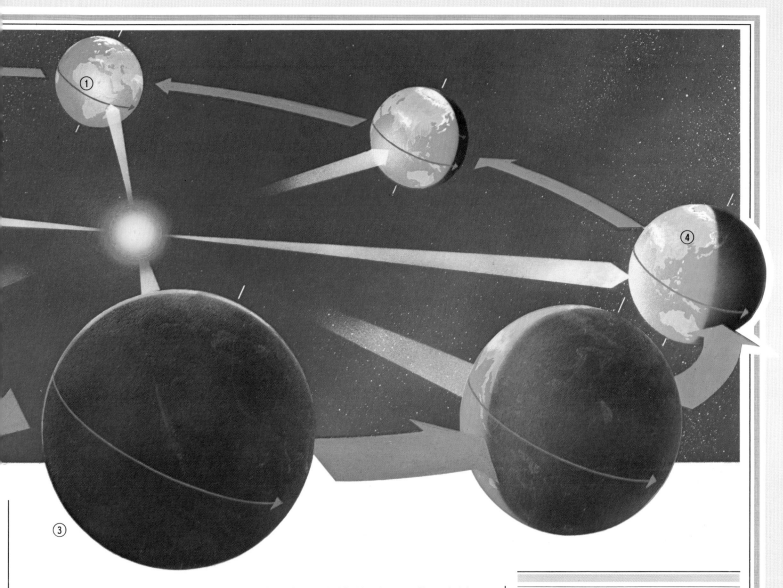

Above: Because the Earth's axis is tilted during its annual orbit of the Sun, there are variations in solar radiation that cause seasons. On March 21, the spring or vernal equinox in the northern hemisphere, the Sun is overhead at the Equator (1). On June 21, it is overhead at the Tropic of Cancer, the summer solstice (2). On September 23, it is overhead at the Equator, the autumn solstice (3). On December 21, it is overhead at the Tropic of Capricorn, the winter solstice (4).

Below: The world is divided into time zones. The standard time at Greenwich (0° longitude) on the map is 12.00 Greenwich Mean Time (not British Summer Time). East of Greenwich, standard times are ahead of GMT, while west of Greenwich, they are behind it. Ideally, time zones should be longitudinal bands of 15° or 7½° (representing time differences of 1 hour or 30 minutes). But time zones are irregular in shape to prevent small countries having two standard times.

FACTFINDER

Length of day: Mean solar day, 24 hours. Sidereal day (measured against fixed stars) 23·93 hours.

Speed of the Earth's rotation on its axis: At the Equator, it is rotating at 1660 km/h. It is less away from the Equator: at 30°N and S, it is 1438 km/h; at 60° N and S, it is 990 km/h.

Equinoxes: The vernal equinox is on March 21, and the autumn equinox on September 23 in the northern hemisphere. The equinoxes are reversed in the southern hemisphere.

Solstices: In the northern hemisphere, the summer solstice is on June 21 and the winter solstice on December 21. The reverse applies in the southern hemisphere.

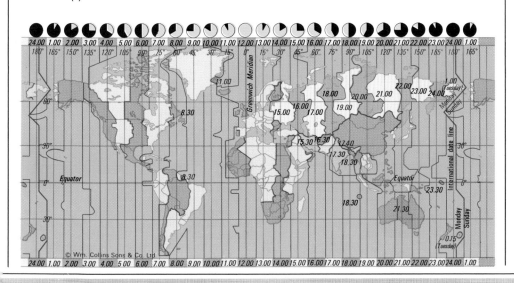

© Wm. Collins Sons & Co. Ltd

THE EARTH'S STRUCTURE

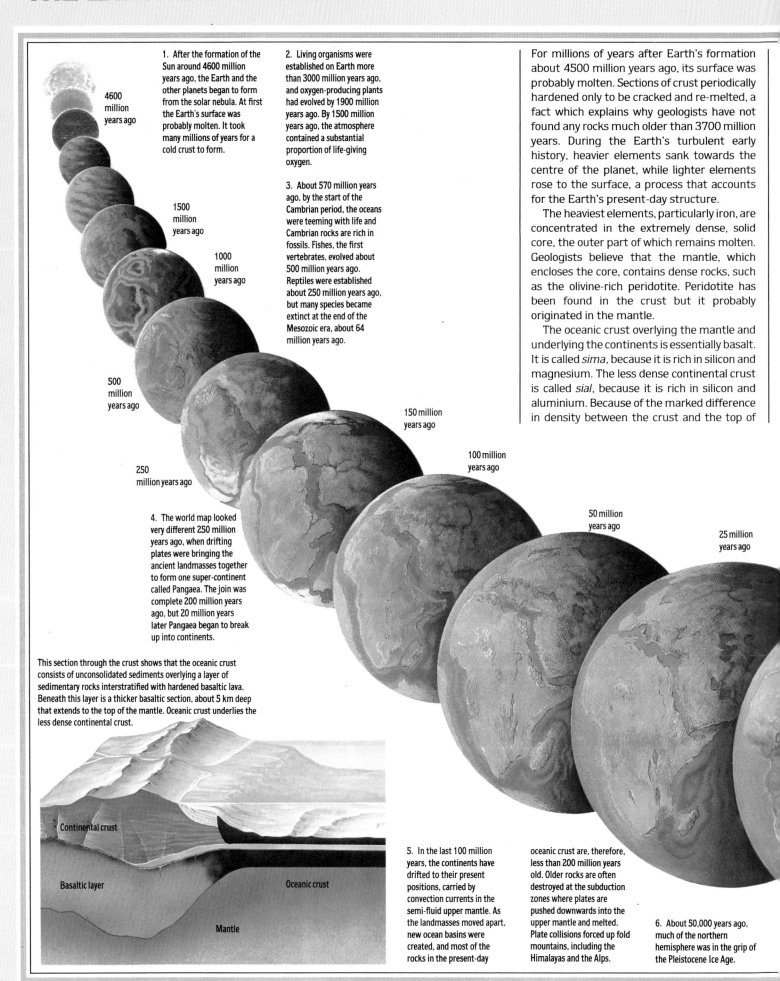

1. After the formation of the Sun around 4600 million years ago, the Earth and the other planets began to form from the solar nebula. At first the Earth's surface was probably molten. It took many millions of years for a cold crust to form.

2. Living organisms were established on Earth more than 3000 million years ago, and oxygen-producing plants had evolved by 1900 million years ago. By 1500 million years ago, the atmosphere contained a substantial proportion of life-giving oxygen.

3. About 570 million years ago, by the start of the Cambrian period, the oceans were teeming with life and Cambrian rocks are rich in fossils. Fishes, the first vertebrates, evolved about 500 million years ago. Reptiles were established about 250 million years ago, but many species became extinct at the end of the Mesozoic era, about 64 million years ago.

4600 million years ago

1500 million years ago

1000 million years ago

500 million years ago

250 million years ago

150 million years ago

100 million years ago

50 million years ago

25 million years ago

4. The world map looked very different 250 million years ago, when drifting plates were bringing the ancient landmasses together to form one super-continent called Pangaea. The join was complete 200 million years ago, but 20 million years later Pangaea began to break up into continents.

This section through the crust shows that the oceanic crust consists of unconsolidated sediments overlying a layer of sedimentary rocks interstratified with hardened basaltic lava. Beneath this layer is a thicker basaltic section, about 5 km deep that extends to the top of the mantle. Oceanic crust underlies the less dense continental crust.

Continental crust

Basaltic layer

Oceanic crust

Mantle

5. In the last 100 million years, the continents have drifted to their present positions, carried by convection currents in the semi-fluid upper mantle. As the landmasses moved apart, new ocean basins were created, and most of the rocks in the present-day oceanic crust are, therefore, less than 200 million years old. Older rocks are often destroyed at the subduction zones where plates are pushed downwards into the upper mantle and melted. Plate collisions forced up fold mountains, including the Himalayas and the Alps.

6. About 50,000 years ago, much of the northern hemisphere was in the grip of the Pleistocene Ice Age.

For millions of years after Earth's formation about 4500 million years ago, its surface was probably molten. Sections of crust periodically hardened only to be cracked and re-melted, a fact which explains why geologists have not found any rocks much older than 3700 million years. During the Earth's turbulent early history, heavier elements sank towards the centre of the planet, while lighter elements rose to the surface, a process that accounts for the Earth's present-day structure.

The heaviest elements, particularly iron, are concentrated in the extremely dense, solid core, the outer part of which remains molten. Geologists believe that the mantle, which encloses the core, contains dense rocks, such as the olivine-rich peridotite. Peridotite has been found in the crust but it probably originated in the mantle.

The oceanic crust overlying the mantle and underlying the continents is essentially basalt. It is called *sima*, because it is rich in silicon and magnesium. The less dense continental crust is called *sial*, because it is rich in silicon and aluminium. Because of the marked difference in density between the crust and the top of

FACTFINDER

The Earth's crust: The oceanic crust averages 6 km thick; density, 3·0 g/cm³. The continental crust averages 35–40 km, reaching 60–70 km under high mountains; density 2·7 g/cm³.

Mantle: About 2900 km thick; density, 3·4–4·5 g/cm³.

Core: Diameter 6740 km. Outer core 2000 km thick, molten iron and nickel. Inner core, a solid metal ball, 1370 km thick. Density of core, 10–13 g/cm³. Temperature at 2700°C, under pressure of 3800 tonnes per sq cm.

Surface area of the Earth: 510,066,000 km². About 148,326,000 km², or just over 29 per cent of the Earth's surface, is land.

Mass: 5976 million million million tonnes.

Shape and size: Oblate spheroid, slightly flattened at the poles and bulging at the Equator. So, at sea level, the diameter of the Earth between the poles is 12,713 km, as compared with a diameter of 12,756 km, across the plane of the Equator. Similarly, the equatorial circumference of 40,075 km is greater than the polar circumference of 40,007 km.

the mantle, the crust cannot sink. It is split into large, rigid plates that 'float' on the denser mantle. Plate movements cause earthquakes, mountain building and volcanic activity – occurrences that remind us of the restless nature of our world.

About 85 per cent of the top 16 km of the crust are either igneous rocks (rocks formed from molten magma) or metamorphic rocks (igneous or sedimentary rocks that have been changed by heat, pressure or, sometimes, chemical action). However, sedimentary rocks cover 75 per cent of the surface of landmasses. Many sedimentary rocks are clastic (formed from eroded rock fragments), some, such as coal, are organic, and some are formed by chemical action, such as rock salt precipitated from water.

Below are eight rocks found in the Earth's crust. There are three main kinds of rocks: igneous, sedimentary and metamorphic. Igneous rocks, including obsidian and granite, are forms of hardened magma. Many sedimentary rocks, such as sandstone and conglomorate, are composed of worn fragments of other rocks, while coal is compressed plant remains. Metamorphic rocks, such as marble and slate, are formed when great heat and pressure alter igneous or sedimentary rocks.

Obsidian is a glassy, extrusive igneous rock, formed on the surface.

Granite is a coarse-grained, intrusive igneous rock, which forms in huge underground masses.

Marble is formed by the action of great heat and pressure on limestone.

Slate is usually formed by the metamorphism of shale.

Coal is a fossil fuel formed in ancient swamps.

Limestones are sedimentary rocks composed mainly of calcium carbonate.

Sandstone contains grains of quartz and other minerals bound together by tough mineral cements.

Conglomerates contain pebbles cemented in a fine silt or sand matrix.

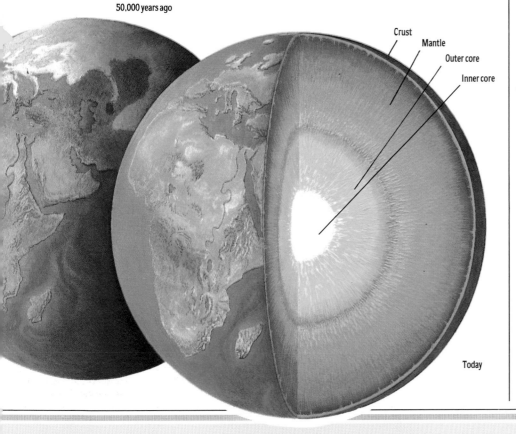

50,000 years ago

Crust
Mantle
Outer core
Inner core

Today

THE VIOLENT EARTH

Ever since the Earth formed, volcanic activity has continued ceaselessly. It was responsible for releasing pockets of gas from the rocks to form an atmosphere and water vapour to fill the oceans. It was molten magma that formed the Earth's first, fragile, potentially life-supporting crust and, even today, newly formed volcanic soils are among the world's most fertile.

Most volcanoes lie near plate edges. Some, including Surtsey – a volcanic island that appeared off Iceland in 1963 – are on the ocean ridges where new crustal rock is being created as magma wells up from the interior (see pages xxii–xxiii). Other volcanoes are near subduction zones where descending plates are melted to produce pockets of magma. A few volcanoes are far from plate edges. They are apparently situated above radioactive heat sources in the mantle.

Magma, molten rock at temperatures around 1100°C to 1200°C, reaches the surface as lava. Gases in thick, pasty lava cannot easily escape; they expand, shatter and eject the lava in fragments, called *pyroclasts*, ranging in size from loaf-shaped volcanic bombs to fine dust and ash. Quiet volcanoes, however, emit thin, runny lava, usually basalt, from which gases escape easily. Quiet eruptions build up flattish, shield mountains, contrasting with the ash cones of explosive eruptions. Most volcanoes are intermediate, sometimes erupting explosively, sometimes quietly.

Magma may also emerge from long fissures and build up huge plateaux, such as the Deccan Plateau in India. Other magma solidifies underground in huge batholiths and laccoliths, or in thin dykes and sills. In some areas, where volcanic activity has almost ceased, fumaroles (holes from which steam and gases emerge under pressure), hot springs, geysers and boiling mud pools still testify to past activity.

Most volcanoes in populated areas are now carefully observed for signs of activity, including changes in pressure and temperature, earth tremors, tilts of slopes caused by magma swelling below, and changes in the composition of gases from fumaroles. But prediction of eruptions remains inexact.

FACTFINDER

Greatest volcanic eruption: Thera or Santorini in the Aegean Sea, in about 1470 BC. The explosion, 130 times more powerful than the greatest H-bomb detonation, removed 62 km³ of rock.

Greatest recent explosion: Krakatoa, in 1883. The explosion had about one fifth of the power of the Thera explosion. Over 36,000 people on nearby Java and Sumatra were drowned by a tsunami caused by the explosion.

Greatest amount of material discharged: Tambora, a volcano on the island of Sumbawa, Indonesia, discharged nearly 152 km³ of rock in an eruption in 1815.

Active volcanoes: 535, of which 80 are on the seabed. On average only about 20–30 volcanoes erupt a year.

Largest volcanic crater: Mount Aso, Kyushu, Japan, 27 km by 16 km; circumference 114 km.

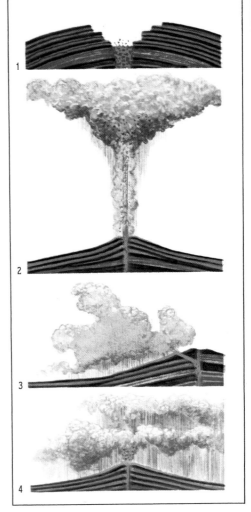

Below: The section through a volcanic landscape shows a large pocket of magma (1) in the crust. Periodically, magma rises under pressure through a vent (2) and spills out as lava (3). This volcanic cone is made up of alternating layers of hardened lava and compacted ash. Magma is also injected into rock layers to form dykes (4) that cut across existing rock layers and sills (5), which are sheets of hardened magma that are parallel to the rock strata. Large, dome-shaped intrusions of magma, like those that underlie mountain ranges, are called batholiths. They extend over hundreds of square kilometres and appear to replace rather than displace the invaded rocks. They are revealed when the overlying rocks have been worn away. Small batholiths, or laccoliths (6), arch up overlying strata. Magma sometimes flows on to the surface through long fissures and spreads over huge areas (8). In volcanic regions, where activity is declining, high temperatures still produce hot springs and geysers (7). Extinct volcanoes may contain large lakes in their craters (9). These lakes are known as *calderas*, from the Spanish word for kettle.

Right: Types of Volcanic Eruptions
1. Quiet volcanoes, as in Hawaii, discharge little gas so there are no explosive eruptions. They emit fluid lava streams that flow a long way before they harden. Hence, in cross-section, they are gently sloping.
2. Explosive volcanoes are characterized by sudden, violent eruptions in which the magma is shattered into hot dust, ash and volcanic bombs. These pyroclasts are hurled high into the air. Explosive volcanoes are often said to be Plinian in type, after the Roman writer Pliny who witnessed the explosive eruption of Mount Vesuvius in southern Italy in AD 79.
3. Peléan volcanoes, named after Mount Pelée in Martinique in the West Indies, which erupted in 1902, produce *nuées ardentes*, or 'glowing clouds' of hot gas and ash that roll downhill, burning all in their path.
4. Vesuvian volcanoes are intermediate in type. Although intermediate volcanoes may erupt explosively, lava streams accompany most eruptions.

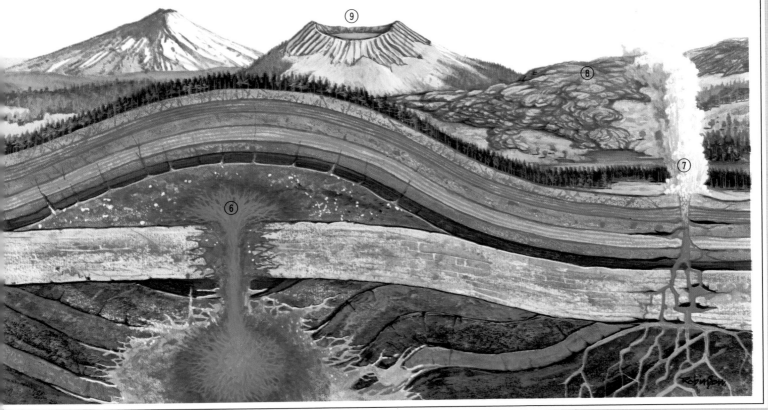

THE DRIFTING CONTINENTS

In the early 20th century, the German meteorologist Alfred Wegener and the American scientist F. B. Taylor both advanced the theory of continental drift. The idea sprang from the similarities between the shapes of the continents on either side of the Atlantic Ocean and studies showed that there were many similar rock structures and fossils found in landmasses that are now separated by thousands of kilometres.

The study of the ocean floor after World War II produced much evidence to support the theory. Mapping of the oceans revealed that there were enormous mountain ranges, called oceanic ridges, running through the oceans. These ridges were zones of seismic activity and temperature studies showed a concentration of heat along the rift valleys that run through the centre of the ridges. Further, the youngest rocks always came from the centre of the ridges and rocks

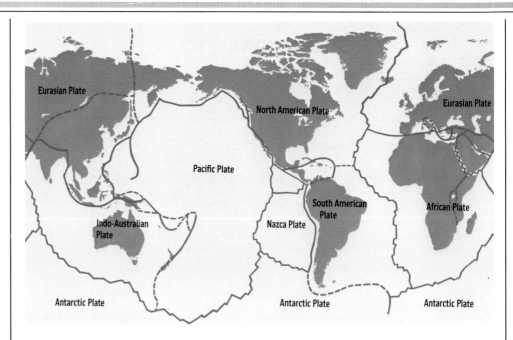

increased in age in both directions away from the ridges.

This and other evidence suggested that molten rock is welling up beneath the ridges from the semi-molten asthenosphere. This molten rock is spreading out under the crust, flowing considerable distances before cooling and sinking again. These convection currents are pulling the two sides of the ocean apart, while magma wells up to form new crustal rock along the ridges to fill the gap.

The oceanic ridges, therefore, contain breaks in the crust between rigid blocks on either side. The blocks are known as plates.

The oceans are being widened by between one and 10 cm per year, but the Earth is not growing any larger, and so there must be places where crustal rock is destroyed. These places are at the bottom of deep oceanic trenches, where the advancing edge of one plate is thrust under another in a subduction zone. As it descends into the asthenosphere, the plate is melted and magma rises through volcanoes in the overlying plate. Some plate edges are collision zones, which are former subduction zones where the plates continue

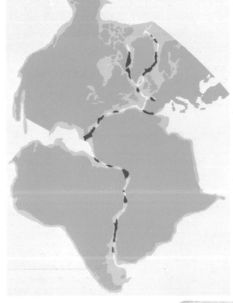

Top right: The map shows the chief plates into which the Earth's crust is divided. Plate edges are zones of intense seismic and volcanic activity.
Above: The similarity between the shapes of the landmasses on either side of the Atlantic Ocean suggests that they were once joined together. The map, which takes as the continental edge an underwater line, 1000 metres below sea level, reveals an even better fit than coastlines, which are not the true edges of the continents.

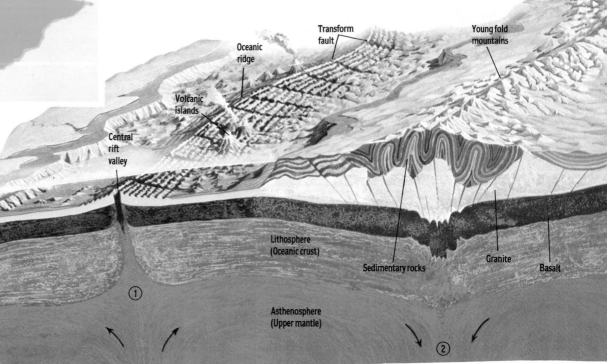

FACTFINDER

Pre-Cambrian time: From the formation of the Solar System, 4600 million years ago, to 600 million years ago.

Palaeozoic era: This era contains six periods:.

Cambrian	600–500 million yrs ago
Ordovician	500–440 million yrs ago
Silurian	440–395 million yrs ago
Devonian	395–345 million yrs ago
Carboniferous	345–280 million yrs ago
Permian	280–225 million yrs ago

Note: In the USA the Carboniferous is divided into the Mississippian period (345–300 million yrs ago) and the Pennsylvanian period (300–280).

Mesozoic era: This era, when reptiles dominated the Earth, consists of:

Triassic period	225–200 million yrs ago
Jurassic period	200–135 million yrs ago
Cretaceous period	135–65 million yrs ago

Cenozoic era: This era consists of:

Tertiary period (comprising 5 epochs)

Palaeocene epoch	65–55 million yrs ago
Eocene epoch	55–40 million yrs ago
Oligocene epoch	40–25 million yrs ago
Miocene epoch	25–5 million yrs ago
Pliocene epoch	5–2 million yrs ago

Quaternary period (comprising 2 epochs)

Pleistocene epoch	million–10,000 yrs ago
Holocene epoch	10,000 yrs ago–present

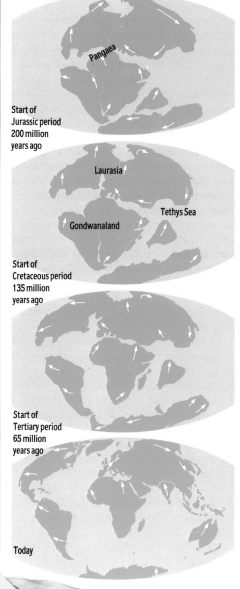

Start of Jurassic period 200 million years ago

Start of Cretaceous period 135 million years ago

Start of Tertiary period 65 million years ago

Today

to push against each other. Plates sliding alongside each other are transform faults.

The study of plate tectonics has greatly increased our understanding of many phenomena, including vulcanicity, seismology and orogenesis. It has also thrown light on the changing face of the Earth, particularly since the start of the Jurassic period, 200 million years ago. (In Earth history, periods are subdivisions of longer eras, epochs are subdivisions of periods, and ages are subdivisions of epochs.)

Below: Convection currents in the semi-molten asthenosphere (the upper mantle) pull plates apart along the oceanic ridges. Magma wells up (1) to fill the gap along the central rift valley in the ridge. This process is called ocean spreading. Lateral movements of plates cause plate collisions. The force of two plates pushing against each other can force up sedimentary rocks on intervening sea beds into new fold mountains until,

finally, the plates become locked together in a collision zone. (2). In subduction zones (3), the edge of one plate is thrust beneath another along an oceanic trench. Pressure, friction and heat melt the descending plate edge, and magma rises to the surface (4). Oceanic ridges, collision zones and subduction zones are types of plate edges. The fourth is the transform fault (5), like the San Andreas Fault in California. Here plates move alongside each other.

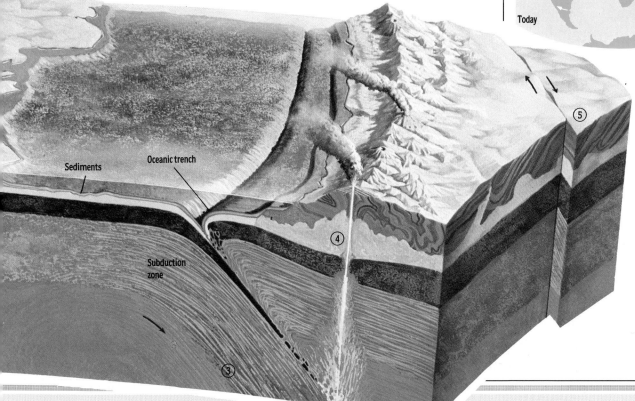

Sediments

Oceanic trench

Subduction zone

Above: About 200 million years ago, there was one super-continent, called Pangaea, or 'all Earth'. About 180 million years ago, Pangaea began to break up into the northern Laurasia and the southern Gondwanaland. The map of 135 million years ago shows that a plate bearing India had broken away from Gondwanaland and was drifting northwards. This movement continued as other landmasses drifted to their present positions. Around 53 million years ago, the Indian Plate was pushing against Asia. Sedimentary rocks on the intervening bed of the Tethys Sea were squeezed up to form the lofty Himalayas. The Indian and Eurasian Plates are now interlocked.

THE RESTLESS EARTH

Plate movements keep the Earth's crust on the move. But the movements are not smooth, because the rough plate edges become jammed. The tension mounts until the rocks snap and the plates lurch forward in sudden, violent jerks, causing earthquakes. An earthquake's point of origin is the focus, while the spot on the Earth's surface directly above it is the epicentre. Vibrations spreading outwards from the focus, are sometimes so intense that buildings collapse, fires start and destructive waves (tsunami) are generated in the sea. The intensity of the vibrations decreases away from the focus, but faint seismic waves can be detected by seismographs on the other side of the world.

The most violent earthquakes occur near plate edges, but they can occur anywhere where rocks move along faults, or where the ground is shaken by avalanches, explosions or landslides. Ways of predicting earthquakes are being sought and some successes have been claimed, but much research remains to be done.

Plate collisions are responsible for crustal deformation, when horizontal sedimentary rock layers are folded, squeezed and fractured. Intensely folded ranges include the Himalayas, which have been compressed by as much as 650 km, and the Alps. The Alps were raised up in the last 26 million years as the African plate pushed a small plate bearing Italy against the Eurasian Plate. Fracturing produces major fault lines along which horizontal and vertical movements occur. Vertical movements raise up horsts, such as the Vosges and Harz mountains, and even larger block mountains, such as the Ruwenzori range in East Africa. The Ruwenzoris overlook the world's largest rift valley, a trough formed between plate systems of roughly parallel faults. The East African Rift Valley runs from Syria in the Middle East to Mozambique in the south.

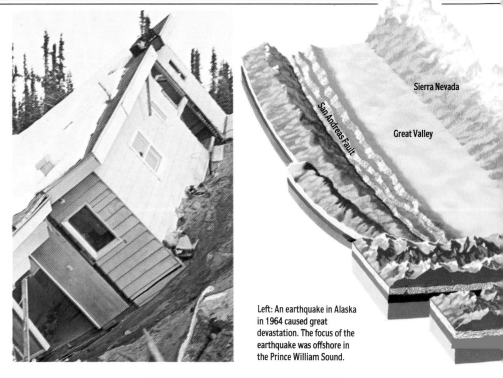

Left: An earthquake in Alaska in 1964 caused great devastation. The focus of the earthquake was offshore in the Prince William Sound.

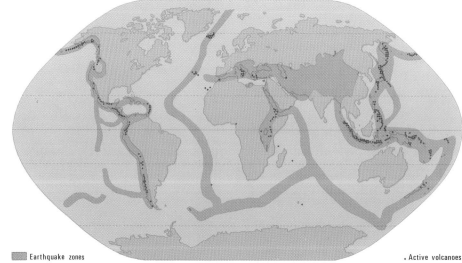

Earthquake zones · Active volcanoes

Above: Earthquakes may occur anywhere, but the main earthquake zones are near plate edges, the geologically active parts of the Earth's crust. The greatest concentration of volcanoes is in Indonesia, which has more than 160 active volcanoes and frequent earthquakes.

Enormous lateral pressure caused by plate collisions can squeeze horizontal layers of rocks into folds. A simple upfold is an anticline and a simple downfold is a syncline. If a large anticline contains a number of small folds, it is called an anticlinorium. Overfolds in which the axial plane is sharply inclined are called recumbent folds. Recumbent folds are sometimes sheared away and forced long distances. These folds are called nappes.

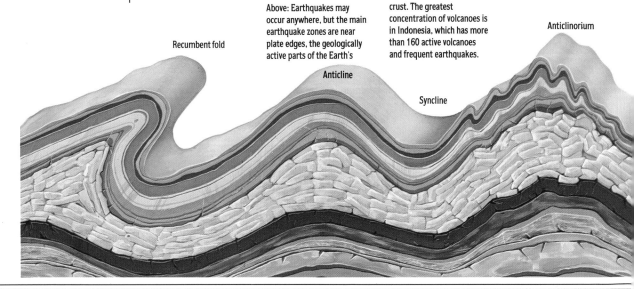

Recumbent fold

Anticline

Syncline

Anticlinorium

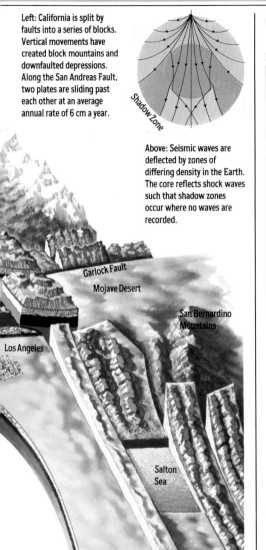

Left: California is split by faults into a series of blocks. Vertical movements have created block mountains and downfaulted depressions. Along the San Andreas Fault, two plates are sliding past each other at an average annual rate of 6 cm a year.

Shadow Zone

Above: Seismic waves are deflected by zones of differing density in the Earth. The core reflects shock waves such that shadow zones occur where no waves are recorded.

Garlock Fault
Mojave Desert
San Bernardino Mountains
Los Angeles
Salton Sea

FACTFINDER

SOME DEVASTATING EARTHQUAKES

Concepción, Chile: An earthquake south of Concepción in 1960 was the most massive ever recorded, ranking 9·5 on the revised Richter scale (in use since 1977). Death toll: 2000.

Lisbon, Portugal: The earthquake of 1775 was one of the world's greatest. Caused by sudden fault movements and fissuring on the seabed to the west and south, there were three major shocks. Fires and tsunami destroyed the city. Lakes in Norway swayed. Death toll: about 60,000.

Prince William Sound, Alaska: The 1964 earthquake (9·2 on the revised Richter scale) generated a 67-metre tsunami that battered Alaska's southern coasts. Death toll: 114. (The highest recorded tsunami appeared off Ishigaki Island in the Ryukyu chain in 1971. It was 85 metres high).

Sagami Bay, Japan: An earthquake in Sagami Bay in 1923 was the world's most destructive. On the Kwanto Plain, in nearby Tokyo and Yokohama, about 570,000 houses were destroyed. The cost of the damage was estimated at £1000 million (it would now be more than four times that figure). Death toll: 143,000.

Shaanxi (formerly Shensi) province, China: An earthquake in 1556 was the world's greatest killer. In widespread landslides and floods, more than 800,000 people perished.

Tangshan, China: An earthquake in 1976 was the greatest killer of recent times. Death toll: about 750,000.

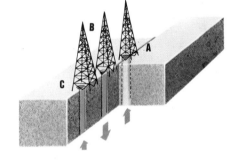

Above: The diagram shows a transform fault which is a plate edge, like California's San Andreas Fault. Movements along the fault are jerky. Sudden jerks cause earthquakes.

Below: Plate movements create tension in the crust some way from the plate edges. Such tension can fracture rocks and produce long fault lines. Tugging movements cause some blocks of land to slip down between roughly parallel faults to create graben, or rift valleys. Other blocks are squeezed up to form steep-walled horsts, or block mountains.

Above: Earthquake prevention is an important area of scientific research. American scientists have found that water lubricates faults and causes rock slippages. This principle might be applied along the San Andreas Fault. To relieve the mounting tension before a violent earthquake occurs, scientists propose that a series of wells be drilled along the fault. By pumping water *out* of wells A and C, the fault would become locked at these points. Water could then be pumped *into* the intervening well B, lubricating the fault and causing a small earthquake. Such small movements made along the entire fault might prevent a disaster.

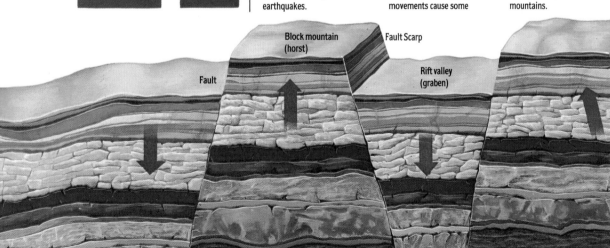

Fault
Block mountain (horst)
Fault Scarp
Rift valley (graben)

THE SCULPTURED EARTH

Natural erosion is a slow process and landscapes do not appear to change much in a person's lifetime. But even as mountains rise, natural forces, including weathering, wear them down. Weathering can be mechanical or chemical. In cool, moist areas, mechanical weathering includes action by frost. As water freezes it expands. Frost forming in cracks in the rocks exerts pressure which eventually splits the rocks apart. In hot, dry regions, the Sun's heat expands the outer layer of rocks which peel away, a process called exfoliation.

Chemical weathering includes the dissolving of minerals by water, and hydrolysis, when minerals react with water to produce new compounds, such as kaolin from potash feldspars in granite. Carbonation occurs because rainwater is a weak carbonic acid, which reacts with calcium carbonate, the chief constituent of limestone, wearing the limestone away to create karst scenery and limestone caves.

Major sculptors of the landscape are ice, the wind and running water. Although ice sheets and valley glaciers are now confined to polar and mountain regions, large parts of the northern hemisphere were sculpted by ice during the Pleistocene Ice Age. Glaciers, which form from compacted snow, contain rocks frozen into the bottom and sides. These jagged rocks give the moving ice a powerful cutting-edge, enabling it to deepen the basins and valleys that it occupies. Glaciated features include knife-edged arêtes, basins called cirques, pointed horns, and U-shaped valleys. The moraine carried by the ice ranges from boulders to fine clay. Some moraine is dumped in ridges of terminal moraine. Some is washed out by melt water and spread out as glaciofluvial deposits.

The chief agent of erosion in hot deserts is the wind. Wind-blown sand can undercut cliffs, carve rocks into the shape of mushrooms, and scour out deep hollows. Sand covers about one-fifth of the world's hot deserts; migrating dunes are a constant threat to human settlements at oases.

Valley glaciers flow from snowfields where glacier ice is formed from compressed snow. The rate of flow is determined by the rate of ice formation at the source.

Above: Glaciated lowlands contain features formed both by glacial erosion and deposition. Many lakes occupy ice-worn hollows (1) or basins dammed by moraine. Ice-scoured rocks are striated (scratched) in the direction of the ice flow. Roches moutonneés (2) are rocks that have been smoothed by the ice on the upstream side, but are jagged on the downstream side. Moraine forms winding ridges called eskers (3) and hummocks called drumlins (4). Long ridges of terminal moraine (5) mark the snouts of ancient glaciers. Beyond, melt water has spread eroded material over a glacial outwash plain (6).

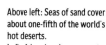

Left: Glaciated uplands contain several typical features, including pointed peaks, or horns (1), which are formed when three or more cirques (steep-sided basins, 2) form back to back. Cirques are separated by knife-edged ridges called arêtes (3). Overdeepening of the main valleys by glaciers creates truncated spurs (4) and typical U-shaped valleys (5). Tributary valleys (6) are left hanging above the overdeepened main valleys.

Above left: Seas of sand cover about one-fifth of the world's hot deserts.
Left: A barchan is a crescent-shaped sand dune formed in regions with winds that blow constantly from the same direction.

Below: Sand dunes usually accumulate around some irregularity or obstacle. Once formed, they advance in the direction of the prevailing wind as sand is blown up the windward side and down the leeward side.

Direction of wind

The Karst district of Yugoslavia has given its name to limestone landscapes in general. Typical features are gorges formed when the roofs of caves collapse.

Limestone is eroded by carbonation, caused by the reaction of the rock with rainwater containing carbon dioxide. Vertical cracks (1) are enlarged into grikes, which enclose blocks called clints (2). Streams plunge into sink or swallow holes (3). Pot-holers may enter limestone caves through dry swallow holes (4). They find dry galleries (5) and underground streams (6), which surface at resurgences (7). Limestone caves often contain features formed from calcite deposited from dripping water, including stalactites (8), stalagmites (9), plate stalagmites (10), balcony stalagmites (11) and fir cone stalagmites (12). Pillars (13) form when stalactites and stalagmites meet. Balconies (14) are deposited from water dripping over a ledge.

WATER SHAPES THE LAND

On fine summer days, mountain streams and sea waves may seem harmless enough. But when the streams are in flood and the waves are whipped up by strong winds, both become powerful sculptors of the landscape.

River Action and Valley Development

Rivers are the leading agent of erosion, transportation and deposition in moist, temperate regions. Their power depends on their speed, a function of the gradient, and their volume. Rivers have three distinct sections. The youthful stage includes the steepest gradients and is often marked by waterfalls and rapids which form where the river crosses resistant rocks. A youthful river in flood becomes a torrent, capable of further deepening its V-shaped valley. In the mature stage, the volume of water is increased, although the gradients are gentler. The river remains vigorous and sweeping meanders constantly broaden the valleys. In the old age stage, the river flows over the flattest part of its course. Little erosion occurs, but the water carries huge loads of sediment, worn by attrition into fine particles. The Mississippi sweeps an estimated 700 million tonnes of sediment past New Orleans every year. Some is dumped in the advancing delta. The rest spreads over the floor of the Gulf of Mexico. River profiles are slowly flattened, but if the land is uplifted, steeper gradients rejuvenate the river. For example, the Colorado River in the United States has been rejuvenated by the uplift of the Colorado Plateau, which was formerly a nearly flat coastal plain. With its steadily increasing gradient, the Colorado River eroded the magnificent Grand Canyon.

Power of the Sea

Sea waves constantly batter coasts by lifting up shingle and hurling it at the shore. Wave erosion is most marked during storms. The sea also dissolves some rocks and shatters others by compressing air in cracks. Wave erosion carves out bays in softer rocks, but it also slowly wears away headlands of resistant rock. The sea also has a constructive side. Eroded material is carried along the shore by waves and currents. At points where the land changes direction, the water often drops the material to form low shingle ridges called spits. Spits are often curved because waves deflect their growth towards the shore. Sometimes, spits extend from one headland to another, sealing off a bay or lagoon. Such spits are called baymouth bars. Some bars are built up offshore and are not attached to land. Tombolos are spits linking the mainland to offshore islands, such as the Tombolo di Feniglio and the Tombolo di Gianetta in Italy. Chesil Beach in southern England links the former Isle of Portland to the mainland.

Opposite: Glaciers (1) are one of the sources of rivers. Here melt water feeds a lake (2), which is drained by a river. The youthful stage of a river is marked by deep, V-shaped valleys (3) eroded by the river in flood. Waterfalls (4) and rapids occur where the river passes over particularly hard rock outcrops. Gorges (5) are other features usually associated with youthful rivers, especially in semi-arid regions where there is little weathering of the valley sides. The mature stage of a river is characterized by vigorous meanders (6). The river's power here is concentrated on lateral erosion so that the valley is widened rather than deepened. Lateral erosion sometimes undercuts the banks along the necks of meanders until the river straightens its course. The abandoned meander then becomes a stagnant oxbow lake (7). In the old age stage, the sluggish river lacks erosive power as it winds over a nearly flat flood plain (8). But large amounts of sediment are suspended in the water. This sediment may accumulate in deltas (9), or currents may sweep it out to sea where it settles on the seabed to form new sedimentary rocks (10).

FACTFINDER

Power of rivers: At speeds of 0·5 km/h, rivers move fine sand; at 10 km/h, small stones are transported; at 30 km/h, rivers shift large boulders.

Greatest flow of any river: Amazon River discharges an average of 120,000 m³/sec. In full flood, nearly 1·66 times as much water is emptied into the Atlantic Ocean.

Largest river canyon: Grand Canyon, Arizona, United States; length: 349 km; width: 6–20 km; depth: up to 2133 metres.

Longest river: River Nile, northeast Africa, Length: 6695 km.

Highest waterfall: Angel Falls, Venezuela has a drop of 979m It is on a branch of the River Carrao and was discovered by an American pilot, Jimmy Angel, in 1935.

Largest delta: Ganges-Brahmaputra delta, area: 75,000 km².

Highest sea cliffs: Molokai Island, Hawaii, 1005 metres.

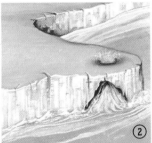

Above: Sea waves undercut headlands, forming caves which may be linked to the surface by blowholes (1). Caves on either side of a headland may unite to form a natural arch (2). When the arch collapses, only a stack (3) remains.

Above: A bar of sand and shingle encloses a lagoon on the coast of Tanzania.

Below: Sand and shingle are moved along the shore in a series of zig-zags.

Below: Spits and bars are features of the Baltic coast of northern Germany.

Above: This stack is being undercut along its bedding planes (lines of weakness).

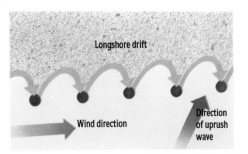

Longshore drift

Wind direction

Direction of uprush wave

Baltic Sea

THE ATMOSPHERE & CLOUDS

The atmosphere is a thin skin of gases, chiefly nitrogen and life-giving oxygen, that encircles and protects the Earth. It moderates temperatures, preventing enormous diurnal changes in heating that would destroy life on Earth. And, in the stratosphere, one of the five main layers of the atmosphere, is a belt of ozone that absorbs most of the Sun's dangerous ultraviolet radiation. The depth of the atmosphere cannot be defined precisely, because it becomes increasingly rarefied with height. But more than 99 per cent of its mass is within 40 km of the surface.

Air Pressure

Air has weight and the total weight of the atmosphere is about 5000 million million tonnes. However, we do not feel the constant pressure of about one tonne of air on our shoulders, because there is an equal air pressure inside our bodies. Air pressure varies, a major factor in weather. Generally, pressures are lower in warm, expanding air which tends to rise, as at the doldrums. It is higher in cold, dense air which sinks downwards, as at the high pressure horse latitudes.

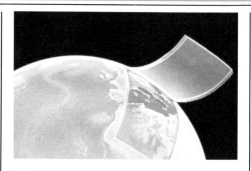

The Earth is surrounded by a thin layer of gases, known as the atmosphere.

This section through the atmosphere shows its five main layers.

EXOSPHERE, which begins at about 500 km above the surface, is extremely rarefied and composed mainly of hydrogen and helium. The exosphere merges into space.

IONOSPHERE, between 80 and 500 km, contains gas molecules that are ionized, or electrically charged, by cosmic or solar rays. Disturbances in the ionosphere cause glowing lights, called aurorae. Temperatures rise steadily with height from about −80°C at 80 km to 2200°C at 400 km.

MESOSPHERE, between 50 and 80 km, is marked by a fall in temperature from 10°C at 50 km to −80°C.

STRATOSPHERE, stretches above the tropopause (the name for the upper boundary of the troposphere) to 50 km height. It has a layer of ozone (oxygen with three rather than two atoms) that filters out most of the Sun's ultraviolet rays. Temperatures rise from −55°C to 10°C at 50 km. The noctilucent clouds are probably composed of meteoric dust.

TROPOSPHERE is the lowest 18km of the atmosphere over the Equator, the lowest 10 to 11 km in the middle latitudes, and the lowest 8 km over the poles. It contains most of the atmosphere's mass. Temperatures fall with height, but stabilize at the tropopause.

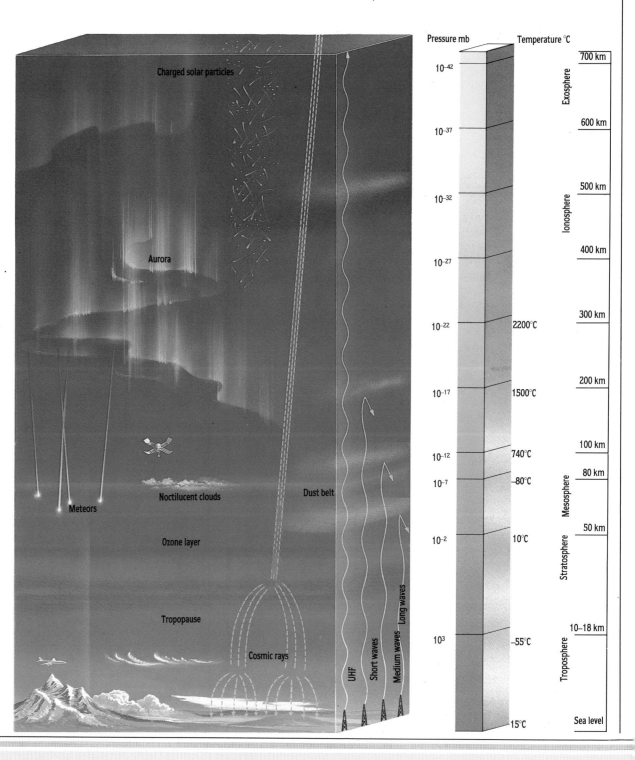

Charged solar particles

Aurora

Meteors

Noctilucent clouds

Dust belt

Ozone layer

Tropopause

Cosmic rays

UHF

Short waves

Medium waves

Long waves

Pressure mb	Temperature °C	
10^{-42}		700 km
10^{-37}		600 km
10^{-32}		500 km
10^{-27}		400 km
10^{-22}	2200°C	300 km
10^{-17}	1500°C	200 km
10^{-12}	740°C	100 km
10^{-7}	−80°C	80 km
10^{-2}	10°C	50 km
10^{3}	−55°C	10–18 km
	15°C	Sea level

Exosphere

Ionosphere

Mesosphere

Stratosphere

Troposphere

The clouds on this photograph reveal a hurricane, a rotating low pressure air system.

FACTFINDER

Composition of the air: Nitrogen (78·09 per cent); oxygen (20·95 per cent); argon (0·93 per cent).
Other gases include carbon dioxide, helium, hydrogen, krypton, methane, neon, ozone, and xenon.

Average surface pressure: 1013 mb.

Atmospheric level reached by radio waves (wavelengths in kilocycles):
Below 500 kc, 50 km;
500–1500 kc, 95 km;
1500–30,000 kc (by day), 200 km;
1500–30,000 kc (by night), 280 km.
Very short wavelengths (UHF) penetrate all layers.

Cloud Formation

All air contains water vapour, but warm air holds much more than cold air. When air is cooled it can hold less water vapour. At dew point, it is saturated, containing all the water vapour it can at that temperature. Further cooling causes water vapour to condense around specks of dust or salt in the air to form tiny, visible water droplets or ice crystals, masses of which form clouds.

Circulation of Air

Air is invisible but, powered by energy from the Sun, it is always moving. Generally, winds blow from areas of high air pressure, such as the horse latitudes, towards areas of low pressure, such as the doldrums. Winds are deflected by the Coriolis effect, which is caused by the Earth's rotation. Local factors, such as mountains, also affect winds. Monsoons are seasonal reversals of winds. For example, over northern India in winter, cold, dense air masses develop, from which winds blow outwards. But heating in summer creates low air pressure and moist winds are sucked on to the land.

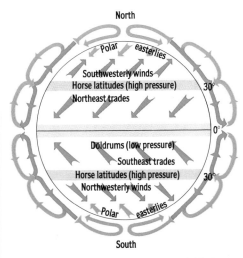

Above: The diagram shows the main movements of air in the atmosphere and across the surface in the prevailing wind systems. Winds generally blow towards low pressure regions, such as the doldrums, and outwards from high pressure systems at the horse latitudes and the poles.

Cloud Types

High Clouds

Cirrus
Cirrostratus
Cirrocumulus
6100 m
Medium Clouds
Altostratus
Altocumulus
2500 m
Stratocumulus
Cumulonimbus
Low Clouds
Cumulus
Nimbostratus
Stratus
Sea level

High Clouds
High clouds form above 6100 metres above ground level, as follows:
CIRRUS is a delicate feathery cloud, sometimes called mares' tails or ice banners. It is often the first sign of an approaching depression.
CIRROSTRATUS is a thin layer cloud, with ripples and rounded masses. It veils but does not block out the Sun.
CIRROCUMULUS is a patchy cloud composed of small white balls. Formed from ice crystals, it is often called mackerel sky.

Medium Clouds
Medium clouds occur between about 2500 and 6100 metres, as follows:
ALTOSTRATUS is a greyish or bluish layer cloud that may become so thick that it blocks out the Sun. It is a sign of an advancing depression.
ALTOCUMULUS resembles a mass of tiny clouds. It indicates unsettled weather.

Low Clouds
Low clouds form below 2500 metres above ground level as follows:
STRATOCUMULUS is a greyish-white cloud, consisting of rounded masses.
NIMBOSTRATUS is a dark cloud, associated with rain and snow, which often occurs along the warm fronts of depressions.
CUMULUS is a white, heap cloud, usually with a flat base and a dome-shaped top. In summer, fluffy cumulus is a feature of fine weather. Heavy cumulus can develop into cumulonimbus cloud.
STRATUS is a grey layer cloud that often forms ahead of warm fronts in depressions where warm air is rising fairly slowly over cold air. Such clouds bring drizzle, rain and snow.
CUMULONIMBUS is a dark, heavy cloud. It may rise 4500 metres or more from its ragged base to its often anvil-shaped top. It is associated with thunder, lightning, rain and snow.

Cloud Classification. There are three main types of cloud shapes: feathery cirrus; heap or cumuliform clouds; and layer or stratiform clouds.

WEATHER & CLIMATE

Weather is the hour to hour condition of the atmosphere, while climate is the average or usual weather of a place based on information collected over a long period. The world's climates can be classified in several ways, but most classifications used today are based on the system devised by the Russian meteorologist Vladimir Köppen. His system highlights the importance of temperature, rainfall and seasonal variations in them.

Weather and climate have a great influence on people's way of life, although modern technology now enables us to live comfortably anywhere, even in heated homes in Antarctica. Agriculture is the industry most affected by weather and climate. For instance, floods and droughts can cause havoc, especially in the developing world. In developed countries, detailed weather forecasts now play an important part in everyday life. Advance warnings of likely frosts or hailstorms can enable farmers to take steps to protect their crops. The most destructive storms are hurricanes and tornadoes, but even more common are thunderstorms. The variable weather in the middle latitudes, however, results from the development of low pressure air systems, called depressions.

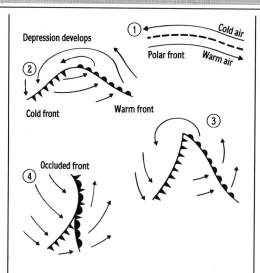

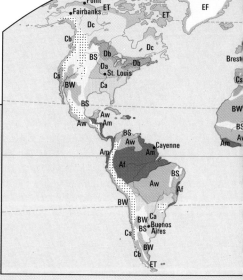

Development of a Depression

The diagram above shows how depressions form along the polar front, where sub-tropical air meets up with polar air. The advancing edge of the warm air forms a warm front, while the front edge of the cold air flowing in from behind is the cold front. A rotating air system develops in which the fronts are cloud belts formed as warm air rises above cold air (see diagram above right).

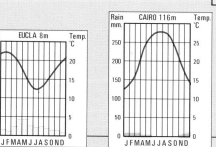

Right: The world climatic regions are based on Vladimir Köppen's classification. His basic code consists of: **A**, tropical rainy; **B**, dry climates; **C**, middle latitude or warm temperate climate; **D**, cold, snowy climates; **E**, the polar climates; and **H**, the mountain climates.

Climate Types

Cayenne, in Guiana has an **Am** climate, that is a tropical rainy monsoon type, with a fairly dry season between the months of August and October.

Bombay, in western India, has an **Aw** climate – a tropical rainy climate but with a dry winter (**w**). Summer rain is brought by southwest, monsoon winds.

Eucla, in southwestern Australia, has a **BS** climate, a dry climate with just enough rainfall to support steppeland (represented by the code **S**).

Cairo, in Egypt, has a dry climate with the code **BW**, **B** meaning a dry climate, and **W** signifying desert conditions. Temperatures are high.

Cape Town, South Africa, has a Mediterranean (**Cs**) climate, **s** denoting a dry summer, the feature of Mediterranean regions that makes them tourist centres.

Buenos Aires, Argentina, has a humid sub-tropical climate classified as **Ca**. The code **a** means that the warmest month is always above 22°.

Rainforest (Af/Am)	Savanna (Aw/As)
TROPICAL HUMID	CLIMATES

Steppe (BS)	Desert (BW)
DRY CLIMATES	

Mediterranean (Cs)	Humid Subtropical (Ca)
WARM	TEMPERATE

FACTFINDER

Cold air

METEOROLOGICAL TERMS

Rain forms from water droplets in clouds or from ice crystals that grow in size by colliding with supercooled water droplets.

Hail Hard pellets of ice.

Frost Frozen moisture caused by condensation at temperatures below 0°C.

Snow Precipitation of ice crystals.

Fog A mass of water droplets, like a cloud, at ground level.

Thunderstorm A storm associated with cumulonimbus clouds formed by fast-rising warm air currents.

Depression A low pressure air system, also called a cyclone; associated with unsettled weather.

Anticyclone A high pressure air system associated with settled weather.

Cyclone A depression (see above). But a *tropical* cyclone is another name for a hurricane or a typhoon.

Tornado A small but violent storm (West Africa); a whirlwind (USA).

CLIMATIC RECORDS

Highest rainfall in one year: 26,461 mm at Cherrapunji, India, 1860–61.

Driest place: Calama, Atacama Desert; no rain for several hundred years.

Highest shade temperature: 58°C at Al Aziziyah, Libya, 1922.

Lowest screen temperature: −88·3°C, at Vostok, Antarctica, 1960.

Most destructive hurricane: Hurricane *Betsy* in 1965 caused insurance payments of $715 million in the United States.

Highest surface wind speed: 371 km/h, on Mount Washington, New Hampshire, United States, 1934.

Lightning: A single bolt of lightning hit a hut in Zimbabwe in 1975, killing 21 people.

Right: A key to the climatic graphs, below. The graphs, arranged on the zero-line, themselves depict a wide range of climatic types found around the world, each of the stations being identified on the map. The data on the graphs represents averages of temperatures and rainfall recorded over long periods.

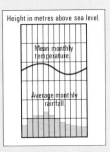

Height in metres above sea level.

Mean monthly temperature.

Average monthly rainfall.

Limits of the Monsoon

Fairbanks, Alaska, has cool summers and severe winters.

Barrow Point, in northern Alaska, has an **ET** or polar climate of the tundra (treeless) type. This means that there is a brief growing period in the summer months.

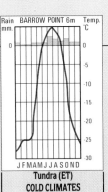

Addis Ababa, Ethiopia, has a mountain (**H**) climate. Its altitude of 2450 metres has the moderating effect of giving it a mild climate, although it is situated in the tropics.

BREST 17m

ST. LOUIS 173m

MOSCOW 154m

FAIRBANKS 134m

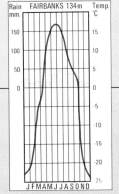

BARROW POINT 6m

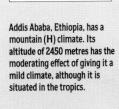

Brest on the Atlantic coast of western France, has a mild and moist maritime climate, which can be classified as **Cb**, the code **b** denoting a warm summer.

St Louis, in the United States, has a continental **Da** climate, with severe winters. **D** denotes cool temperate and the **a** signifies that the warmest month is above 22°C.

Moscow, in the USSR, has a continental **Db** climate, **b** signifying warm summers.

| Maritime (Cb/Cc) MATES | Continental Warm (Da) COOL | Continental Cool (Db) TEMPERATE | Subarctic (Dc) CLIMATES | Tundra (ET) COLD CLIMATES | Mountain (H) MOUNTAIN CLIMATES |

THE WATER OF LIFE

In some countries, people take their regular supply of fresh water for granted, while elsewhere, in desert lands, it is a prized commodity. Water reaches us, in one way or another, through the hydrological, or water, cycle, whereby land areas are supplied with precipitation that originates in the saline oceans, where more than 97 per cent of the world's water is found.

Another vital resource, also taken for granted in many places, is the soil, the character of which is largely determined by the climate. The delicate balance between climate, water, and plant life is something that we disturb at our peril.

Soil is the thin layer of loose material derived from and overlying the bedrock. Soils vary in thickness. Mineral grains, the product of weathering, make up more than 90 per cent of most dry soils. Soil also contains humus, including the remains of dead plants and animals. About 40 per cent of moist soils is made up of spaces, occupied by air or water. Soils vary according to the climate, for example, soils in tropical rainy regions are leached by heavy rain. By contrast, some soils in arid regions contain mineral salts deposited by water rising *upwards* towards the surface.

Plant life shows remarkable adaptations to a vast variety of environments. The main vegetation zones are largely determined by climate. But, like climatic regions, vegetation zones have no marked boundaries; they merge imperceptibly with one another.

Vegetation zones usually refer to the original plant cover, or optimum growth, before it was altered by human activity. Human interference with nature can be disastrous. For example, semi-arid grasslands have been ploughed up. Prolonged droughts have reduced the exposed soil to a powdery dust which is removed by the wind, creating dust bowls and encouraging the spread of deserts. The destruction of tropical forests, such as in Brazil, is a matter of concern today. Plants that have never been identified are being destroyed for ever, when they might be sources of new drugs. A massive forest clearance might change world climates.

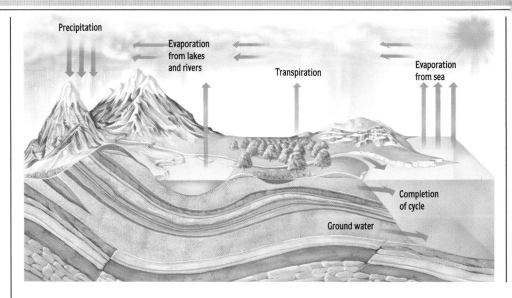

Above: The water cycle provides landmasses with fresh water. The water comes mainly from moisture evaporated from the oceans, to which the water eventually returns.

Right: The map shows the world's chief vegetation zones.

Below: The photographs show major vegetation regions:
1. Tundra is the name for treeless regions near the poles and near the tops of high mountains that are snow-covered for most of the year. But mosses, lichens and some flowering plants flourish in the short summer.
2. Coniferous forests, or taiga, cover a broad belt south of the tundra in the northern hemisphere. The shapes of conifers prevent their being overloaded by snow. The needle-like leaves reduce transpiration, while the thick bark and pitch-like sap reduce evaporation.
3. Broadleaf, or deciduous, forests grow in warm temperate regions. By shedding their leaves, deciduous trees are better able to survive the winter.
4. Scrub and semi-arid grasslands cover large areas of the world. They are highly susceptible to soil erosion if the vegetation cover is removed. Scrub, called maquis, fynbos, chaparral and mallee scrub, are typical of Mediterranean lands where the original forest cover has been destroyed.
5. Tropical grassland includes the llanos of Venezuela. The palm trees in the photograph are growing in a swamp. Tropical grassland is also called campos or savanna.
6. Evergreen tropical rain forest flourishes in regions which are hot and have ample rain throughout the year.

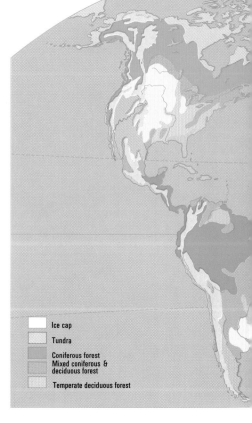

Ice cap

Tundra

Coniferous forest
Mixed coniferous & deciduous forest

Temperate deciduous forest

1

2

3

FACTFINDER

Water distribution: 97·2% is in the oceans (about 1360 million km³); 2·15% is frozen in bodies of ice; 0·625% is ground water; 0·171% is in rivers and lakes; 0·001 is water vapour in the atmosphere.

Average daily water consumption: In the United States: about 200 litres (flushing toilet, washing and bathing, 78%; kitchen use, 6%; drinking, 5%; other, 11%). In many hot countries, the daily per capita water consumption is less than 4 litres.

Common soils: Laterites (leached soils in tropical rainy regions); grey marginal soils (deserts); chestnut-brown soils (arid grasslands); brown forest earths (Mediteranean lands); podsols (cold temperate regions).

Vegetation: Ice covers about 10% of the world's land surfaces and hot deserts 20%. The largest forest is the coniferous forest of the northern USSR, which covers 1100 million hectares — 27% of the world's total forests.

Below: Well-developed soils have three layers, called the A, B and C horizons, overlying the parent rock.

Right: Prairie soils occur in regions that are wet enough in places to support woodland. The A horizon contains much humus, but it is also much leached by seeping water.

Woodland and mixed grasses

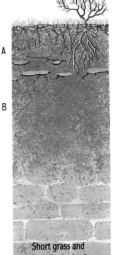

Chernozem soils, sometimes called black earths, contain much humus (mainly decomposed grass). They occur in steppelands which have less rainfall than prairies.

Tall bunch grass

Chestnut-brown soils are typical of particularly arid grasslands. They occur south of the Russian steppes and in the drier parts of Argentina, South Africa and the United States.

Short grass and xerophytic shrubs

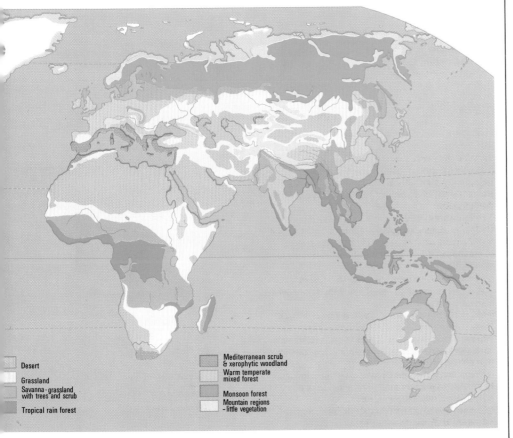

Desert

Grassland

Savanna - grassland with trees and scrub

Tropical rain forest

Mediterranean scrub & xerophytic woodland

Warm temperate mixed forest

Monsoon forest

Mountain regions – little vegetation

4

5

6

THE EVOLUTION OF LIFE

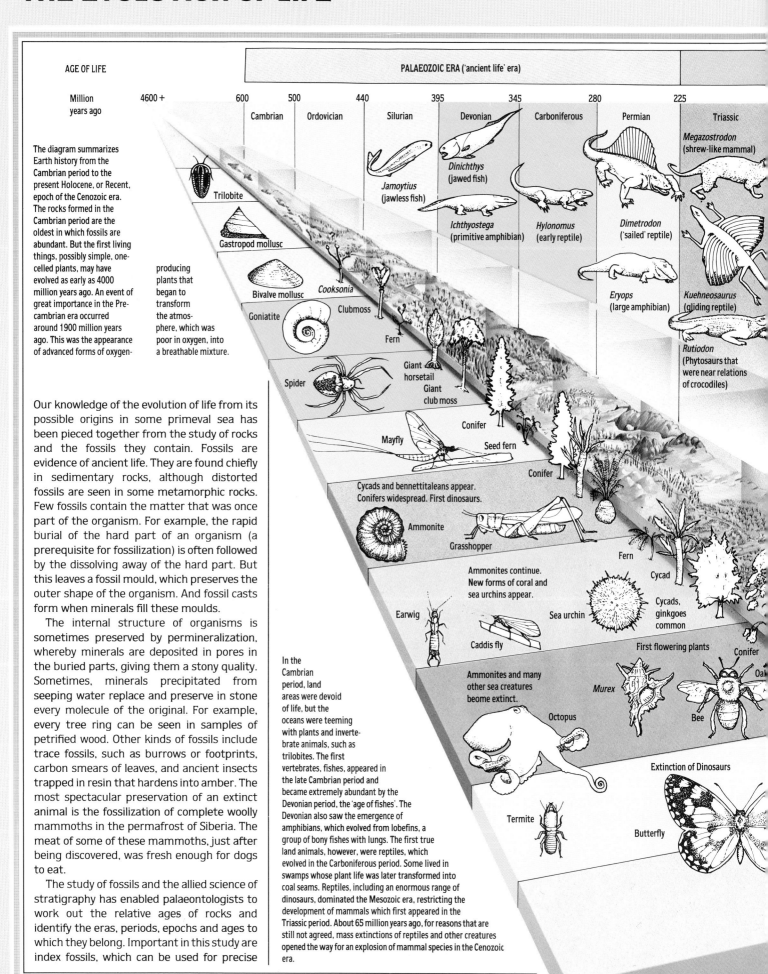

AGE OF LIFE

PALAEOZOIC ERA ('ancient life' era)

Million years ago | 4600 + | 600 | 500 | 440 | 395 | 345 | 280 | 225

Cambrian | Ordovician | Silurian | Devonian | Carboniferous | Permian | Triassic

The diagram summarizes Earth history from the Cambrian period to the present Holocene, or Recent, epoch of the Cenozoic era. The rocks formed in the Cambrian period are the oldest in which fossils are abundant. But the first living things, possibly simple, one-celled plants, may have evolved as early as 4000 million years ago. An event of great importance in the Pre-cambrian era occurred around 1900 million years ago. This was the appearance of advanced forms of oxygen- producing plants that began to transform the atmos-phere, which was poor in oxygen, into a breathable mixture.

Our knowledge of the evolution of life from its possible origins in some primeval sea has been pieced together from the study of rocks and the fossils they contain. Fossils are evidence of ancient life. They are found chiefly in sedimentary rocks, although distorted fossils are seen in some metamorphic rocks. Few fossils contain the matter that was once part of the organism. For example, the rapid burial of the hard part of an organism (a prerequisite for fossilization) is often followed by the dissolving away of the hard part. But this leaves a fossil mould, which preserves the outer shape of the organism. And fossil casts form when minerals fill these moulds.

The internal structure of organisms is sometimes preserved by permineralization, whereby minerals are deposited in pores in the buried parts, giving them a stony quality. Sometimes, minerals precipitated from seeping water replace and preserve in stone every molecule of the original. For example, every tree ring can be seen in samples of petrified wood. Other kinds of fossils include trace fossils, such as burrows or footprints, carbon smears of leaves, and ancient insects trapped in resin that hardens into amber. The most spectacular preservation of an extinct animal is the fossilization of complete woolly mammoths in the permafrost of Siberia. The meat of some of these mammoths, just after being discovered, was fresh enough for dogs to eat.

The study of fossils and the allied science of stratigraphy has enabled palaeontologists to work out the relative ages of rocks and identify the eras, periods, epochs and ages to which they belong. Important in this study are index fossils, which can be used for precise

In the Cambrian period, land areas were devoid of life, but the oceans were teeming with plants and inverte-brate animals, such as trilobites. The first vertebrates, fishes, appeared in the late Cambrian period and became extremely abundant by the Devonian period, the 'age of fishes'. The Devonian also saw the emergence of amphibians, which evolved from lobefins, a group of bony fishes with lungs. The first true land animals, however, were reptiles, which evolved in the Carboniferous period. Some lived in swamps whose plant life was later transformed into coal seams. Reptiles, including an enormous range of dinosaurs, dominated the Mesozoic era, restricting the development of mammals which first appeared in the Triassic period. About 65 million years ago, for reasons that are still not agreed, mass extinctions of reptiles and other creatures opened the way for an explosion of mammal species in the Cenozoic era.

Trilobite
Gastropod mollusc
Bivalve mollusc
Goniatite
Cooksonia
Clubmoss
Fern
Spider
Mayfly
Ammonite
Grasshopper
Earwig
Caddis fly
Octopus
Termite
Giant horsetail
Giant club moss
Conifer
Seed fern
Conifer
Murex
Butterfly

Jamoytius (jawless fish)
Dinichthys (jawed fish)
Ichthyostega (primitive amphibian)
Hylonomus (early reptile)
Dimetrodon ('sailed' reptile)
Megazostrodon (shrew-like mammal)
Eryops (large amphibian)
Kuehneosaurus (gliding reptile)
Rutiodon (Phytosaurs that were near relations of crocodiles)

Cycads and bennettitaleans appear. Conifers widespread. First dinosaurs.

Ammonites continue. New forms of coral and sea urchins appear.

Sea urchin
Cycad
Cycads, ginkgoes common

First flowering plants

Conifer
Oak
Bee

Ammonites and many other sea creatures beome extinct.

Fern

Extinction of Dinosaurs

135   65   1·8   Present

Jurassic   Cretaceous   Tertiary   Quaternary

Australopithecus
(Man-like creature,
lived between the
Pliocene and
Pleistocene epochs)

The first apes

Pteranodon
(gliding reptile)

Archaeopteryx
(the first bird,
though it retained
reptilian features)

Phororhacus
(giant bird)

Archelon
(largest of the
turtles)

Diplodocus
(Sauropod, plant-
eating dinosaur)

Sperm whale

Triceratops
(armoured, three-
horned dinosaur)

Eohippus
('draw horse',
ancestor of the
modern horse)

Woolly mammoth
(now extinct)

Cherry

lar

Pleistocene
Ice Age

FACTFINDER

Oldest known fossil: Blue-green algae found in Zimbabwe, in rocks dating back 3100 million years.

First vertebrates: Fragments of plates and scales of fishes have been found in late Cambrian rocks in the United States.

First land plants: Silurian period.

First amphibians: Devonian period.

First reptiles: Carboniferous period.

First mammals: Triassic period.

dating, because they represent evidence of organisms that lived only for a comparatively short period. Absolute dating of rocks had to await the discovery of radioactivity. The principle that radioactive substances decay at a constant rate has enabled geologists to date rocks containing traces of radioactive substances by comparing the relative amounts of the mineral and its end product created by decay. Absolute datings in Earth history are periodically revised as more specimens become available and are dated.

Right: This skull of a Neanderthal man was found in a quarry in Gibraltar in 1848. Its significance was not realized until other remains were found in 1856 in the Neander valley, east of Düsseldorf in Germany. Neanderthal man was extinct at the end of the Pleistocene epoch.

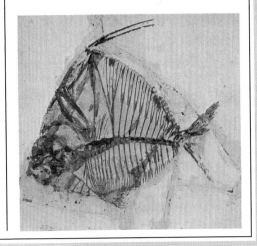

Right: This fossil fish came from rocks of the Tertiary period. Fishes have been around for 510 million years. This is the age of rocks containing fragments of primitive fishes found in Wyoming, in the United States, in the late 1970s. The first complete fish fossils date from the Ordovician period.

THE POPULATION EXPLOSION

One of the world's most serious problems is the population explosion and the difficulties that can be foreseen in feeding the people of the world in the future. On an average estimated rate of population increase of 1·8 per cent a year between 1970 and 1975, the world's population will double in the next 39 years, although recent data suggests that the rate in the 1970s is less than that in the 1960s. The problems arising from the population explosion are most marked in the developing world and least in the industrial nations where people see advantages in population control.

Population explosions occur when average birth rates far exceed death rates. In recent years, death rates have everywhere declined mainly because of improved medical care. In industrial countries, birth rates have also fallen so that a growing proportion of people is in the senior age groups. But while such countries must finance retirement pensions, developing nations have the highest expenditures on health and other children's services, because 40 per cent or more of their population is under 15. This contrast between developing and developed nations is also illustrated by the average life expectancies of 52 years in India and 74 years in the United States.

The distribution of people throughout the world is uneven, because few people live in the vast hot and cold deserts, mountain regions and rain forests. In the world's most densely populated areas, the proportions of urban dwellers is increasing quickly. Urban growth is also a problem in developing nations where unqualified youngsters flock to the cities only to become unemployed occupants of unhealthy shanty towns.

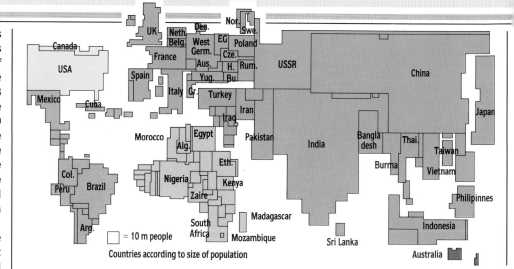

Countries according to size of population

☐ = 10 m people

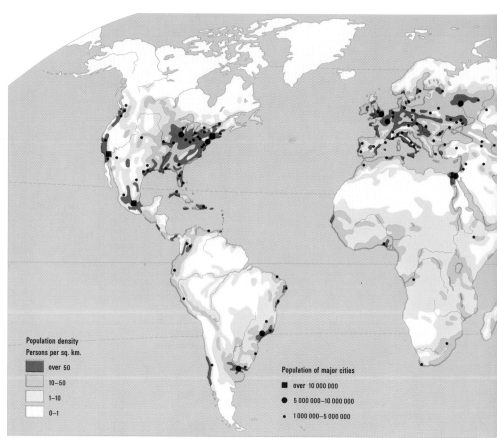

Population density
Persons per sq. km.
- over 50
- 10–50
- 1–10
- 0–1

Population of major cities
- ■ over 10 000 000
- ● 5 000 000–10 000 000
- • 1 000 000–5 000 000

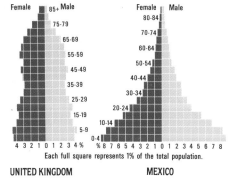

Each full square represents 1% of the total population.

UNITED KINGDOM   MEXICO

Left: The graphs depict the population structures of two nations according to sex and age. Developed nations, such as the United Kingdom (left), have a high proportion of older people, while developing nations such as Mexico (right) have a young population, with as many as 40 per cent of the people being under 15 years of age.

Above: The map shows the uneven distribution of the world's population, a feature that is emphasized by the cartogram, top, which represents the size of nations by their populations rather than by their areas.

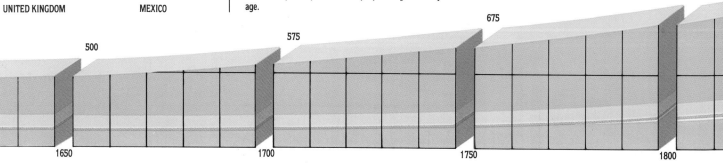

FACTFINDER

XXXIX

Population distribution: The mainly developed continents of North America, Europe and Oceania and the USSR contain 23% of the world's people. The rest live in the mainly developing continents of Africa, Latin America and Asia.

Urbanization: Ranges from 2% in Burundi to 90% in the United Kingdom (1980).

Population density: Gibraltar had 5333 people per sq km in 1979, as compared with 2 per sq km in Australia.

Largest country: USSR (by area); China (by population).

Largest metropolitan area: New York 16,479,000.

The world's population was around 300 million in AD 1000. It passed the 1000 million mark around 1850, but the Industrial Revolution led to an acceleration of population growth. The 2000 million mark was passed in the 1920s and the 4000 million mark in the 1970s. By the year 2000, if the present growth rates of 1·8% per year continue, there will be more than 6000 million people on Earth. (for the purposes of this graph, the Americas have been divided into Anglo-Saxon – and Spanish-speaking America).

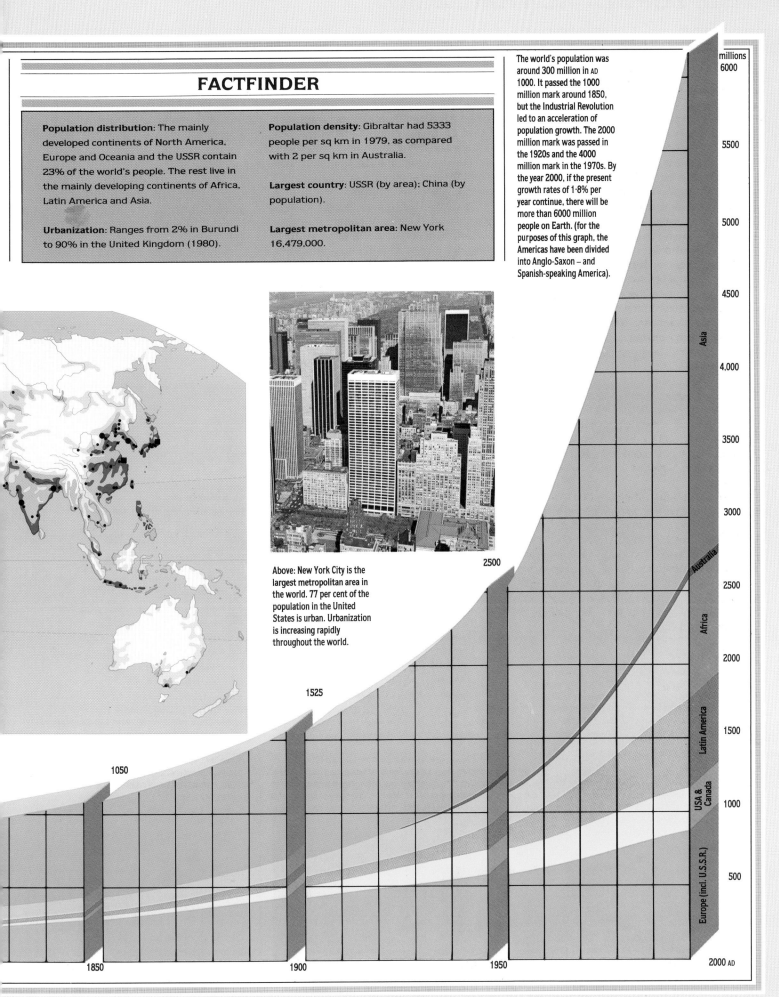

Above: New York City is the largest metropolitan area in the world. 77 per cent of the population in the United States is urban. Urbanization is increasing rapidly throughout the world.

PEOPLES OF THE WORLD

Scientifically, there is only one form of modern man – that is, *Homo sapiens*, and only one race – the human race. But anthropologists distinguish three main sub-groups: Caucasoid, Mongoloid and Negroid.

The Caucasoids originated in Europe, northern Africa, southwestern Asia and the Indian sub-continent. In Europe, the early Mediterraneans include the Basques, while the generally long-headed Mediterranean people include Arabs, Italians, Portuguese and Spaniards. To the north are the stocky Alpine people who live in a belt running from France through central Europe to Russia. North again are tall, blond Nordic people, although intermarriage between all these groups has blurred the physical divisions between them. In the northeast, the East Baltic peoples include Estonians, Finns, Latvians, Lithuanians, Poles and many Russians. The Lapps form a separate group. The Irano-Afghans

extend from Iran to northwestern India. In India are people of the 'Mediterranean' type and the darker southern Indians. The Berbers of North Africa and Semitic groups in the Horn of Africa are also Caucasoids. Mixed Caucasoid groups include the Polynesians, the Veda of South India and Sri Lanka, the Ainu of Japan, and the Australian Aborigines. The main Caucasoid language family is the Indo-European.

The Mongoloid group includes 'classic' Mongoloids, including Eskimos, Japanese, Koreans and Northern Chinese; the Turkic people of central Asia; Tibetans; Indonesian Malays, including Burmese, Southern Chinese, Filipinos and Thais; and American Indians.

The Negroid people of Africa are divided into broad language groups, including the Sudanic, Niger-Congo and Bantu families. The Bushmen and Hottentots in southern Africa are sometimes classified as a separate Khoi-

san group. Smaller Negroid groups include Papuans in Papua New Guinea and Negritos in Malaysia and many Pacific islands. American blacks are descendants of Africans, but many have intermarried with Caucasoids.

Hinduism, the most ancient of the world's

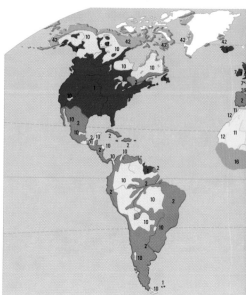

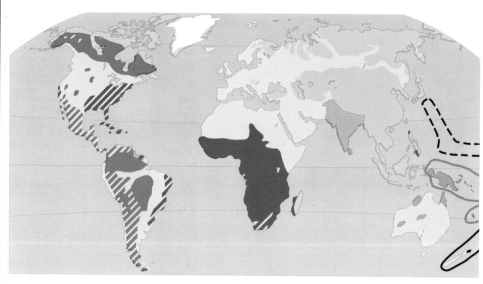

Above: The map shows the distribution of the main races. The American Indians are Mongoloids, while the Asian Indians are Cauacasoids.

This map, however, does not indicate the many multi-racial cities that are commonplace in today's world of increased mobility.

- Caucasoid
- Asian Indian
- Australoid
- Negroid
- Mongoloid
- American Indian
- Melanesian
- Polynesian
- – – Micronesian

Above: The map shows the distribution of the world's main languages.

1	Germanic
2	Romance
3	Slavonic
4	Irano-Armenian
5	Indo-Aryan
6	Greek
7	Celtic
8	Baltic
9	Albanian

Indo-European

10	American Indian
11	Semitic
12	Hamitic
13	Chadic
14	Nilo-Saharan
15	Bantu
16	West & Central African
17	Khoisan
18	Finno-Ugrian
19	Samoyed

Erythraic

Uralic

Below: Examples of Caucasoid peoples include a blue-eyed European (1), an Indian Asian (2) and an Australian Aborigine (3), a mixed or Archaic Caucasoid.

1

2

3

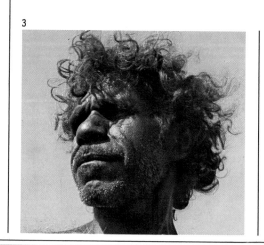

main religions, embraces the worship of many gods, although it acknowledges a supreme god. Judaism was an early monotheistic religion, which influenced Christianity and Islam. All three religions arose in south-western Asia.

FACTFINDER

Number of languages and dialects: about 5000, of which 840 are Indian. The number of languages varies widely because there are disagreements concerning what constitutes a language or dialect.

Largest language family: Indo-European, followed by Sino-Tibetan, which includes Chinese.

Most spoken languages: Northern, or Mandarin, Chinese, spoken by about 600 million people in 1980. The second language, English, was used by about 395 million people in 1980. Russian and Hindustani are spoken by about 200 million people.

Largest racial sub-groups: Caucasoid; Mongoloid; Negroid. No precise figures exist for these groups.

Oldest religion: Hinduism.

Religions: Christianity has an estimated 800 million followers; the world's largest religious organization is the Roman Catholic Church, which has its head-quarters in Vatican City, an enclave in the city of Rome. Estimated adherents of other religions include Islam (450 million), Buddhism (400 million), Confucianism and Taoism (400 million) and Hinduism (300 million).

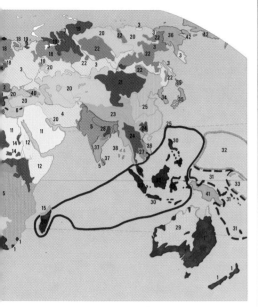

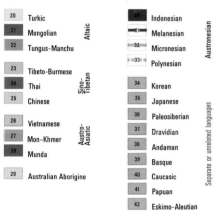

20	Turkic	Altaic
21	Mongolian	
22	Tungus-Manchu	
23	Tibeto-Burmese	Sino-Tibetan
24	Thai	
25	Chinese	
26	Vietnamese	Austro-Asiatic
27	Mon-Khmer	
28	Munda	
29	Australian Aborigine	

30	Indonesian	Austronesian
31	Melanesian	
32	Micronesian	
33	Polynesian	
34	Korean	
35	Japanese	
36	Paleosiberian	Separate or unrelated languages
37	Dravidian	
38	Andaman	
39	Basque	
40	Caucasic	
41	Papuan	
42	Eskimo-Aleutian	

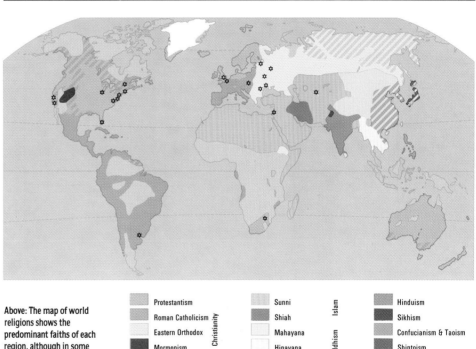

Above: The map of world religions shows the predominant faiths of each region, although in some areas many religions are practised.

Christianity		Islam			
Protestantism	Sunni	Hinduism
Roman Catholicism	Shiah	Sikhism
Eastern Orthodox	Mahayana	Confucianism & Taoism
Mormonism	Hinayana	Shintoism
Judaism	Lamaism	Tribalism & Primitive

Below: The African girl (4) is a member of the Negroid family, while the Mongoloid group includes the Chinese (5) and the North American Indians (6).

4

5

6

HUMAN ACTIVITY

Before the invention of agriculture, about 8000 years ago, people lived by hunting animals and gathering fruits and roots. Hunting and gathering life styles still survive among such peoples as African pygmies and Bushmen, Australian Aborigines, Eskimos and South American Indians. But such people form a dwindling minority, because they are now either being absorbed into modern society or they are being destroyed by it, like the Amazonian Indians, who lack resistance to diseases introduced from the outside.

Agriculture

Today, more than two fifths of the world's population work in agriculture, although in the developing world the proportion is 58·4 per cent compared with 12 per cent in the developed world. The developing world is characterized by its massive subsistence sector, in which people labour hard to provide food for their families, with little left over for sale.

Industry

In the developed world, on the other hand, the majority of population has been released from direct labour on the land and are wage-earners in a variety of jobs. One consequence of the Industrial Revolution was the fast increase in employment in mining and manufacturing. Mining is also important in the economies of many developing nations, but it employs few people. In many developed countries, industry employs two fifths or more of the workforce.

New Technology

However, an even more important trend in most rich nations is the rise in the importance of service industries, which now employ more people than manufacturing in many Western nations. Another contrast between developed and developing nations is the increasing use, in developed nations, of computers, microprocessors and automation, including the use of robots in mass production. The effect of these new techniques, after the initial upheavals that will result from lower manpower requirements in practically every walk of life, will be to increase the leisure time of people in developed nations. The economic and social differences between subsistence and developed economies are, therefore, likely to continue to increase.

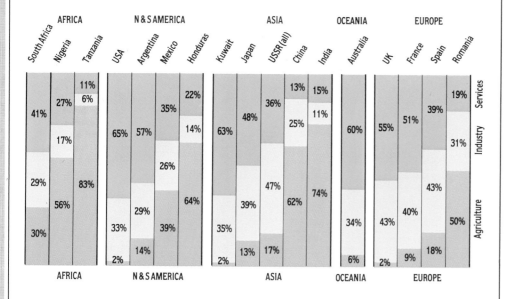

The chart showing the employment structures of several nations reveals contrasts in their economies. The chief activities in developing nations is agriculture. In many developed nations, it is service industries.

Below: Before the invention of agriculture, people lived much like the modern Bushmen of southern Africa as hunters and gatherers (1). Nomadic pastoralism (2) is important in many semi-arid regions, but many grasslands have been converted into arable farms, as in the Mid-West of the United States (3). Industry covers a multitude of disciplines. Fishing (4) is a major industry in many countries. Textile industries (5) exist in most countries. A high proportion of the workforce in industrial nations is employed in offices (6).

Right: The economic map, in distinguishing between subsistence and commercial economies, justifies the distinction made recently by economists between the relatively developed, rich 'North' and the less developed, poor 'South'.

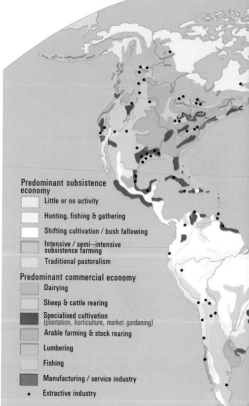

Predominant subsistence economy
- Little or no activity
- Hunting, fishing & gathering
- Shifting cultivation / bush fallowing
- Intensive / semi—intensive subsistence farming
- Traditional pastoralism

Predominant commercial economy
- Dairying
- Sheep & cattle rearing
- Specialised cultivation (plantation, horticulture, market gardening)
- Arable farming & stock rearing
- Lumbering
- Fishing
- Manufacturing / service industry
- • Extractive industry

FACTFINDER

Proportions of the workforce employed in agriculture (1981): World 44·7 per cent; Africa 64·7 per cent; Asia 57·0 per cent; Latin America 33·3 per cent; Oceania 21·7 per cent; Eastern Europe and the USSR 19·2 per cent; Western Europe 10·1 per cent; North America 2·3 per cent.

Motor vehicle producers (1980): Japan (46·6 per cent of world production); United States (21·0 per cent); France and West Germany (10 per cent each).

Steel-producing countries: USSR (20·3 per cent of the world's crude steel production); Japan (15·7 per cent); United States (13·8 per cent); West Germany (6 per cent); China (1980 figs unavailable); Italy (3·6 per cent).

Producers of electrical energy (1980): United States (2,356,140 million kWh); USSR (1,295,004 million kWh); Japan (514,032 million kWh); West Germany (368,772 million kWh).

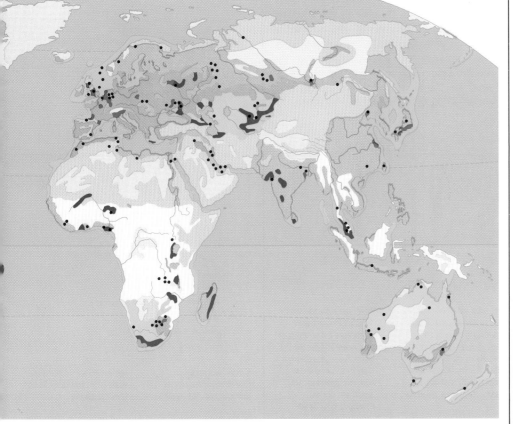

Above: Automated assembly lines are now used in many factories, as here to produce cars. Automation reduces costs but it also threatens employment.

Below: The diagram shows the shift in employment patterns in the United States from the early pioneering days, when agriculture was dominant, to today when service industries (service and commerce) employ two thirds of the workforce.

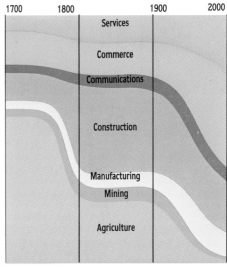

1700   1800   1900   2000

Services

Commerce

Communications

Construction

Manufacturing

Mining

Agriculture

4

5

6

FEEDING THE WORLD

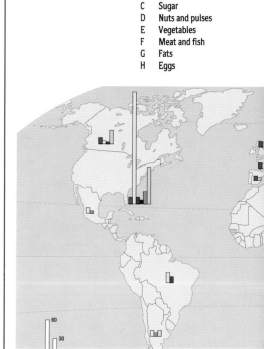

The basic human activity is agriculture. There are two main kinds of agriculture: arable and pastoral. Arable land covers nearly 10 per cent of the world's land area, and meadows and pastures another 20 per cent. In terms of producing food, arable farming is more efficient than pastoral farming. For instance, a given area of cereals will produce six times as many food calories as the milk obtained from dairy cattle grazing on an equal area of grass. Hence, pastoral farming is generally practised on land that is unsuitable for arable farming.

Cereals, the chief food crops, now grow on two-thirds of the world's cultivated land. The main cereals in temperate regions are barley, oats, rye and wheat, and in warmer areas maize, millet, rice (the staple food of more people than any other) and sorghum.

Another important food crop, sugar, is made from sugarcane in tropical regions and from sugar beet in temperate regions. Fruit and vegetables also vary according to the climate. An important group of plants, including groundnuts, oil palms and olives, are grown to make cooking oils, while other crops are grown to make beverages or to produce fibres. Pastoral farming may be extensive, as in the vast cattle or sheep ranches of Argentina, Australia, the United States and the USSR, or intensive as in the factory farming of chickens. Methods of farming vary greatly as do crop yields. For instance, average yields of arable farms in North America are more than three times as high as those of Africa.

Because of the population explosion, agriculture has to provide food for an increasing number of people every year. This involves improving methods of farming and increasing yields. Better farming methods include the use of fertilizers, land conservation and land reclamation. To raise yields, selective breeding of animals and plants will continue. In the last thirty years, many new plant varieties have been developed to raise yields in developing nations.

Another important source of food for the future may come from fish farming in inland and coastal waters. Despite all the modern fishing vessels, fishing is still primitive compared with agriculture. However, yields could probably be increased greatly by breeding young fish in fish farms and then releasing them into nutrient-rich and penned-off parts of the continental shelves.

Key to the diagrams
A Cereals
B Starchy foods, such as potatoes
C Sugar
D Nuts and pulses
E Vegetables
F Meat and fish
G Fats
H Eggs

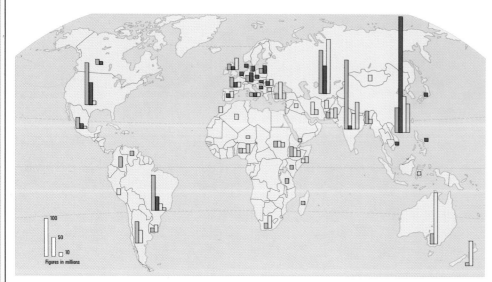

Above: The map shows the chief producers of live-stock. The leading exporters are in the southern hemisphere, with importers in the northern hemisphere.

Figures in millions
100
50
10

Major Animal Food Resources
Cattle   Pigs
Sheep   Goats

Above: The map shows the chief producers of cereals. North America stands out as the leading source of maize while South and East Asia grow mainly rice.

Figures in millions of tonnes
60
30
6

Below: Cattle ranching is extensive in semi-arid regions. Wheat (2) is the chief food in many temperate areas. Tea (3) is grown in tropical countries.

1

2

3

The diagrams compare the diets of people in developed nations, left, with those in the developing world, below. They show that people in the developed nations enjoy far more balanced diets with plenty of proteins and vitamins. In developing nations, protein-deficiency diseases, such as kwashiorkor in children, are common.

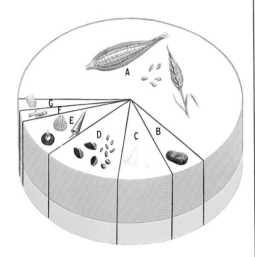

FACTFINDER

Major net exporters of food and livestock: United States, Australia, Netherlands, Brazil, Denmark.

Major net importers of food and livestock: Japan, West Germany, United Kingdom, Italy, USSR.

Yields of cereals (1981): World 2248 kilogrammes/hectare; North America 3860 kg/ha; Western Europe 3659 kg/ha; Asia 2152 kg/ha; Latin America 1991 kg/ha; Eastern Europe and the USSR 1801 kg/ha; Africa 1045 kg/ha.

Leading cereal producers (1980): **Barley**: USSR (27 per cent of the total); France (7 per cent); Canada (7 per cent); United Kingdom (6 per cent). **Maize**: United States (43 per cent); China (15 per cent); Brazil (5 per cent); Romania (3 per cent). **Rice**: China (36 per cent); India (21 per cent);

Indonesia (7 per cent); Bangladesh (5 per cent). **Rye**: USSR (37 per cent); Poland (24 per cent); West Germany (8 per cent); China (7 per cent). **Wheat**: USSR (22 per cent); United States (14 per cent); China (12 per cent); India (7 per cent).

Livestock producers (1980): **Cattle**: India (15 per cent); USSR (9 per cent); United States (9 per cent); Brazil (8 per cent). **Sheep**: USSR (13 per cent); Australia (12 per cent); China (9 per cent); New Zealand (6 per cent).

Beverage crops (1980): **Cocoa**: Ivory Coast (21 per cent); Brazil (19 per cent); Ghana (16 per cent); Nigeria (11 per cent). **Coffee**: Brazil (22 per cent); Colombia (16 per cent); Ivory Coast (5 per cent); Indonesia (5 per cent). **Tea**: India (31 per cent); China (17 per cent); Sri Lanka (10 per cent); USSR (7 per cent).

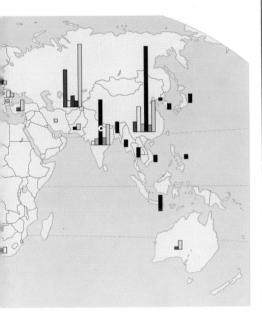

Major Cereal Food Resources

■ Barley	Millet	■ Rice	Sorghum
Maize	■ Oats	■ Rye	Wheat

Below: New food-producing methods include oyster farming (4), hydroponics (growing plants in water, 5) and making protein-rich meat substitutes from soya beans (6).

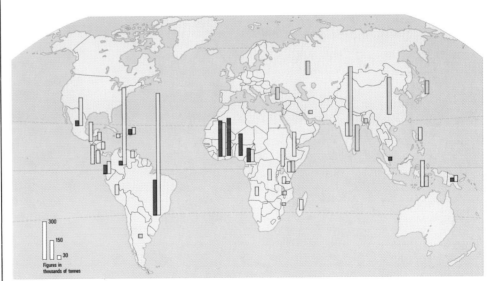

300
150
30
Figures in thousands of tonnes

Above: The map shows the chief producers of the world's leading beverages which are grown in the tropics or subtropics mainly as cash export crops.

Major Beverage Cash Crops

■ Cocoa		Tea
Coffee		

4

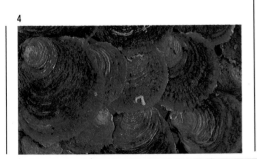

5

6

ALTERNATIVE ENERGY

All forms of energy come directly or indirectly from the Sun. Prehistoric people had only their own labour, but as life styles changed and technology developed, draught animals, the burning of wood, windmills, waterwheels and sails to propel ships were all employed. With the onset of the Industrial Revolution, another abundant source of energy, the fossil fuel coal, was used to power 'the age of steam'. And recently, oil and natural gas have become the main fossil fuels, chiefly because they are fairly cheap to extract, easy to transport, and weight for weight they are more heat-efficient than coal. In consequence, world coal production has remained roughly stable over the last thirty years, although in some industrial nations, such as France, West Germany and the United Kingdom, it has declined. And yet coal may again become important if the existing reserves of oil start to run out, as predicted on current levels of consumption, in the early 21st century.

Despite the recent pre-eminence of oil and natural gas, alternative forms of energy that could replace fossil fuels have been successfully developed, notably hydro-electricity and, in the last thirty years, nuclear power. Hydro-electricity is now the chief form of electrical energy in such countries as Norway, where it supplies 100 per cent of the nation's electrical supply, Brazil (93 per cent), Switzerland (79 per cent) and Canada (70 per cent). But hydro-electricity is clearly unsuited to flat nations, such as the Netherlands.

Nuclear power, using the heat of nuclear fission, can be generated anywhere and, in several Western nations, including the United States and the United Kingdom, it already supplies more than one tenth of the total electrical supply. Uranium, the raw material used in nuclear fission, is generally abundant, and is produced in the West by the United States, South Africa and Canada.

But nuclear power is surrounded by controversy, particularly concerning the disposal of radioactive nuclear wastes. This factor, together with the finite nature of fossil fuel reserves, have led conservationists to explore many other possible forms of energy, employing the latest modern technology. The diagram, right, summarizes the main possibilities that are currently under investigation, including the harnessing of solar radiation, the power of winds and moving water, and the exploitation of the heat that exists not far beneath the Earth's surface.

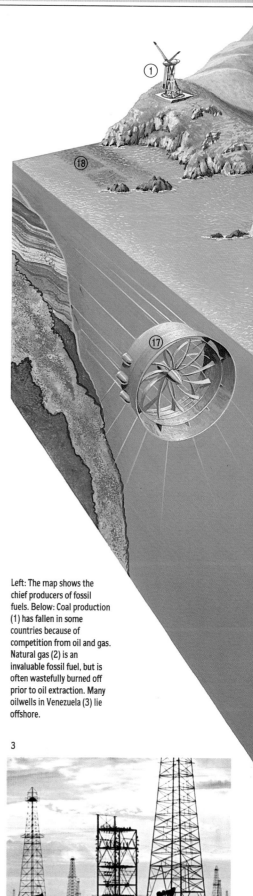

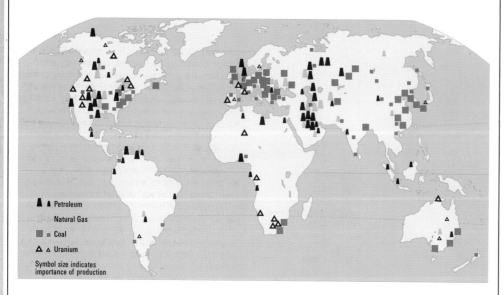

- ▲ ▲ Petroleum
- Natural Gas
- ■ Coal
- △ △ Uranium

Symbol size indicates importance of production

Left: The map shows the chief producers of fossil fuels. Below: Coal production (1) has fallen in some countries because of competition from oil and gas. Natural gas (2) is an invaluable fossil fuel, but is often wastefully burned off prior to oil extraction. Many oilwells in Venezuela (3) lie offshore.

1

2

3

FACTFINDER

Energy consumption (per capita, in equivalents of kg of coal, 1980): Africa 370; Far East 544; Middle East 1123; Oceania 3247; Western Europe 4204; North America 10,394.

Largest oil producers (1981): USSR (21 per cent of world production); Saudi Arabia (17 per cent); United States (17 per cent); Rest of Middle East (9 per cent); Mexico (4 per cent); Venezuela (4 per cent); United Kingdom (3 per cent).

Oil reserves (1978): Saudia Arabia (20 per cent); Kuwait (13 per cent); USSR (10 per cent); Iran (8 per cent); Iraq (6 per cent); United Arab Emirates (6 per cent); Mexico, United States and Malaysia (5 per cent each).

Nuclear power: Belgium (25 per cent of its electrical energy production in 1978); Sweden (22 per cent); Bulgaria (20 per cent); Switzerland (17 per cent); United Kingdom (14 per cent).

Left: Alternative energy sources include improved windmills (1) and pump storage reservoirs (2), into which water is pumped when energy is abundant and then used to drive turbine generators. Hydro-electric stations (3) are important in many countries, while solar power stations, powered by concentrated sunlight, could get microwave energy beamed from a satellite (4) or from banks of angled mirrors or heliostats (5). Decaying waste (6) is a source of heat, as are geysers (7) in volcanic areas. Mud (8) can be used to store heat, while greenhouses (9) are familiar ways of utilizing solar energy. Shallow solar ponds (10) produce heated water to drive generators, and solar houses (11) are self-supporting. Geothermal energy (12) comes from heat inside the Earth. Tidal power stations (13) have much potential, and wave power (14) could be harnessed by moving floats ('bobbing ducks'). Ordinary powered ships might use aluminium sails (15) as an extra form of energy. Floating thermal stations (16) could tap heat under the sea, while huge underwater turbines (17) could be driven by ocean currents. Even kelp (18), a seaweed, could be cultivated as a plant fuel. Solar furnaces (19) can produce temperatures of 4000°C by concentrating the Sun's rays with a paraboloid mirror.

Below: Hydro-electricity is a major alternative to fossil fuels in upland areas with abundant rivers that can be dammed (4). Nuclear power stations (5), a recent development, now supply a substantial proportion of the total electrical energy in several developed nations.

4

5

MINERAL WEALTH

In the Stone Age, people used flint and obsidian tools and, around 10,000 years ago, copper implements were first made. The invention of bronze, an alloy of copper and tin about 5000 years ago, was a major breakthrough. But modern history began with the start of the Iron Age, around 3300 years ago. Since then, metal technology has expanded greatly. For example, since the early 19th century, aluminium, which is obtained from bauxite, has become important, because it is light, strong and corrosion-resistant. And today new alloys are invented to meet all modern needs.

Scientists have identified nearly 3000 minerals, but only about 100 are of economic importance. Iron ore, from which a wide range of ferro-alloys is made, incorporating such metals as chromium, cobalt, manganese, molybdenum, nickel, tungsten and vanadium, remains the leading metallic ore. Various light and base metals, including aluminium, copper, lead, tin and zinc, are also important. The Earth's crust also yields gold, silver and platinum, such precious stones as diamond, emerald, ruby and sapphire, and non-metallic resources, such as phosphate rock which is used as a fertilizer.

Economic minerals – those that can be mined at a profit – are unevenly distributed. Nations with a wide range of minerals and fuels, such as the United States and the USSR have become rich and powerful, while those with few minerals have largely subsistence economies. Some developing countries have rich reserves of one or more minerals, such as copper-rich Zambia and bauxite-rich Guinea in Africa. But many such countries lack the other resources, capital and the skilled manpower to develop industries based on their mineral riches. Instead, they export most of their production to industrial nations. Minerals with strategic value influence political decisions. For example, the United States import manganese. But the chief producers of manganese are the Soviet Union and South Africa. Hence, calls to the United States to boycott South African exports of manganese are likely to be disregarded.

The demand for economic minerals has increased greatly as a result of the population explosion. Today, as the diagram below indicates, the economic reserves of some ores are close to exhaustion. New reserves must be prospected and new methods devised to mine in places where it is now uneconomic to do so. For example, many minerals, such as gold, are dissolved in seawater, but the extraction of these minerals, apart from bromine, magnesium and salt, is currently too expensive. On parts of the seabed are enormous numbers of manganese nodules, potato-like lumps also containing cobalt, copper, iron, nickel and other metals, but again the problem is how to extract them economically. One important source of metals, before we start thinking about mining on the Moon, is the waste products of our society. The recycling of old cars and other junk could be a major factor in overcoming the inevitable shortages in the future.

Sources of Minerals

- ■ ▪ Iron
- ● ● Ferro–alloy Metals
  Chromium, Cobalt, Manganese, Nickel, Tungsten
- ▽ ▽ Base Metals
  Copper, Lead, Mercury, Tin, Zinc
- △ △ Light Metals
  Aluminium, Beryllium, Lithium, Titanium
- ○ ○ Precious Metals
  Gold, Platinum, Silver
- ◇ ◇ Precious Stones
  Diamonds
- ▢ ▢ Industrial Minerals
  Asbestos, Nitrates, Phosphates, Potash, Rock salt, Sulphur

Symbol size indicates importance of source .

Below: Several methods have been proposed for mining the manganese nodules that litter parts of the seabed. The ship on the left is using the suction pump shown below and the ships in the middle are moving a series of dredge buckets. Remote-controlled collectors, right and bottom, shuttle between a surface platform and the seabed.

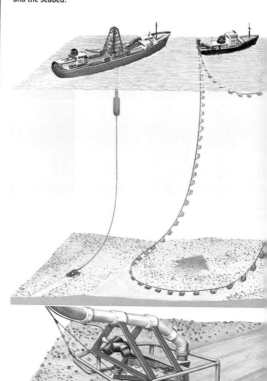

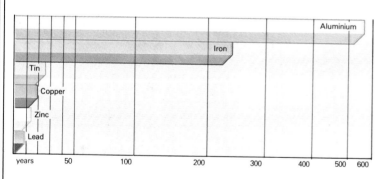

Left: The two leading metals used in construction, aluminium and iron, are abundant and the diagram shows that known reserves of other important metals, including tin, copper, zinc and lead, could run out in twenty to thirty years.

Malachite and azurite are major ores of copper.

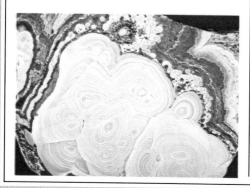

Galena is the chief ore from which lead is extracted.

FACTFINDER

Major mineral exporters (excluding fuels): United States, Canada, Australia, USSR.

Major mineral importers (excluding fuels): Japan, Italy, United Kingdom, France.

Leading metal producers (1980): **Copper**: United States (15 per cent of the total); USSR (15 per cent); Chile (14 per cent). **Iron Ore**: USSR (28 per cent); Australia (11 per cent). **Tin**: Malaysia (26 per cent); Thailand (14 per cent); Bolivia (14 per cent). **Zinc**: Canada (17 per cent); USSR (16 per cent); Peru (8 per cent).

Deepest mine: Western Deep Levels Mine, South Africa; 3582 metres deep.

Largest excavation: Bingham Canyon Copper Mine. Utah, United States. Area: over 7 km²; depth: over 775 metres.

Structural Regions

- Pre–Cambrian shield
- Old fold mountains (Hercynian & Caledonian)
- Young fold mountains (Mesozoic & Alpine)
- Sedimentary basins (Tertiary & Quarternary)

Above: The map shows the locations of the producers of the most important metal ores, precious stones and other minerals needed by the industrialized world.

Right: The world's largest excavation is the open-cast Bingham Canyon Copper Mine, south of Salt Lake City, in Utah in the western United States.

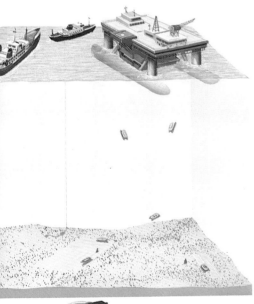

The mineral calcite is used in smelting metallic ores.

Quartz, a common mineral, is used in watchmaking.

ENVIRONMENT IN DANGER

Because of the population explosion and the industrial and technological developments of the last 200 years, great damage has been done to the environment in many areas by the disruption of the balance of nature.

Pollution has become a major problem particularly in modern industrial societies. For example, air pollution in the form of smog has made cities unpleasant and unhealthy. It causes bronchitis and various other respiratory diseases – the London smog of 1952 killed an estimated 4000 people.

Water pollution by sewage and industrial wastes has fouled rivers, lakes and even seas, notably parts of the almost tideless Mediterranean. The flora and fauna have been destroyed and people's health has been directly affected as at Minamata in Japan in the 1950s. Here perhaps as many as 10,000 people suffered death, deformity or acute illness after eating fish poisoned by acetaldehyde waste pumped into the sea by a chemical company.

The land, too, has been polluted in many ways. For example, the pesticide DDT was once regarded as a means of raising food production. But it has also wiped out large populations of birds and, because of its persistence, it has damaged the fragile ecology of soils by weakening the micro-organisms in it.

Steps have been taken in many places to control the dangers of smog, Minamata disease and DDT. But many other, perhaps even more serious, problems lie ahead if the balance of nature is disturbed. For example, if jet airliners and rocket discharges damage the ozone layer in the stratosphere, it could expose the Earth to the Sun's broiling ultraviolet rays. And no one is sure of the consequences of the rising content in the air of carbon dioxide, which increased by seven per cent between 1958 and 1980. One estimate is that it could double by the year 2030. The atmosphere would then increasingly block long-wave radiation from the Earth, like the glass roof of a greenhouse, and temperatures would rise by an average of 3°C. Climatic zones would change and ice sheets would melt, submerging coastal plains and cities.

Radioactive fallout from nuclear weapons' tests (1) pollutes the air, as do kerosene combustion products, soot and unburned fuel expelled by aircraft (2). The build-up of carbon dioxide in the air (3), caused mainly by the burning of fossil fuels and the cutting down of forests may have a greenhouse effect, causing the atmosphere to overheat.

Aerial crop spraying (4) can introduce poisons into the soil that can disturb its ecology for years, while nuclear power stations (5) may discharge radioactive coolants, and thermal power stations (6) and city air conditioning systems may cause thermal and chemical pollution.

Below: Rubbish dumps for cars (1), open-cast mines (2) and oil spillages (3) that foul beaches are all examples of pollution.

1

2

3

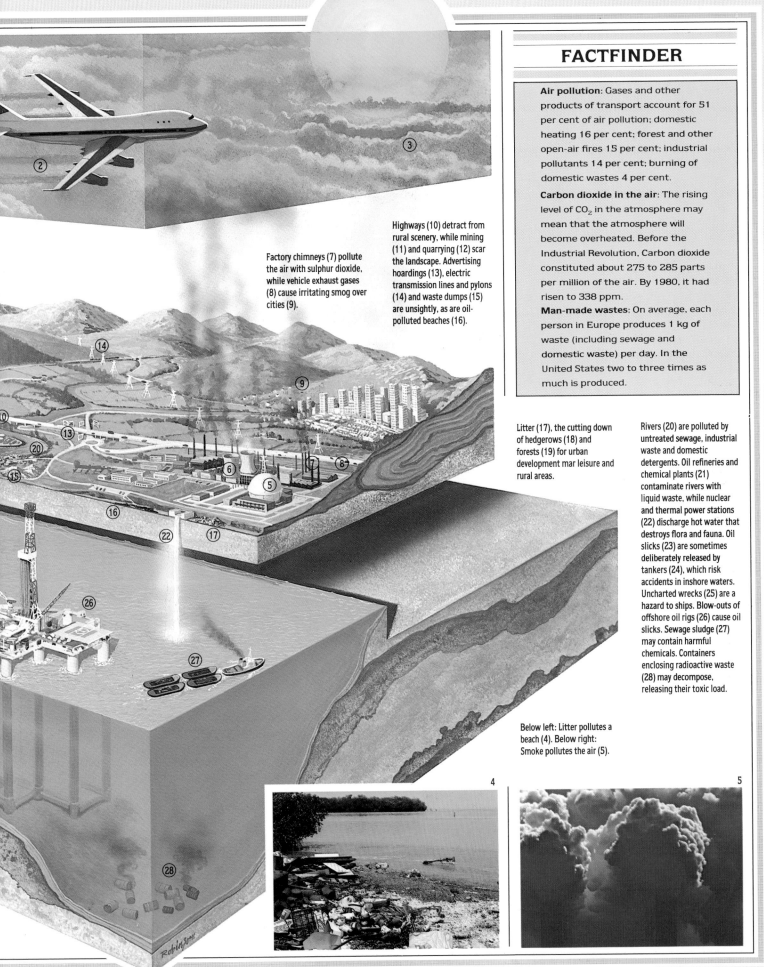

FACTFINDER

Air pollution: Gases and other products of transport account for 51 per cent of air pollution; domestic heating 16 per cent; forest and other open-air fires 15 per cent; industrial pollutants 14 per cent; burning of domestic wastes 4 per cent.

Carbon dioxide in the air: The rising level of CO_2 in the atmosphere may mean that the atmosphere will become overheated. Before the Industrial Revolution, Carbon dioxide constituted about 275 to 285 parts per million of the air. By 1980, it had risen to 338 ppm.

Man-made wastes: On average, each person in Europe produces 1 kg of waste (including sewage and domestic waste) per day. In the United States two to three times as much is produced.

Factory chimneys (7) pollute the air with sulphur dioxide, while vehicle exhaust gases (8) cause irritating smog over cities (9).

Highways (10) detract from rural scenery, while mining (11) and quarrying (12) scar the landscape. Advertising hoardings (13), electric transmission lines and pylons (14) and waste dumps (15) are unsightly, as are oil-polluted beaches (16).

Litter (17), the cutting down of hedgerows (18) and forests (19) for urban development mar leisure and rural areas.

Rivers (20) are polluted by untreated sewage, industrial waste and domestic detergents. Oil refineries and chemical plants (21) contaminate rivers with liquid waste, while nuclear and thermal power stations (22) discharge hot water that destroys flora and fauna. Oil slicks (23) are sometimes deliberately released by tankers (24), which risk accidents in inshore waters. Uncharted wrecks (25) are a hazard to ships. Blow-outs of offshore oil rigs (26) cause oil slicks. Sewage sludge (27) may contain harmful chemicals. Containers enclosing radioactive waste (28) may decompose, releasing their toxic load.

Below left: Litter pollutes a beach (4). Below right: Smoke pollutes the air (5).

THE SHRINKING WORLD

Photographs taken from the Moon emphasize that the Earth and its resources are finite. They remind us that, if we squander those resources or make the planet uninhabitable through ecological blunders or nuclear war, we have as yet nowhere else to go.

The Space Age has enabled scientists to achieve major advances in communications, which, with the revolution in transport which began in the late 17th century, has made the world shrink. Only 500 years ago, before Columbus made his epic journey across the Atlantic Ocean, the world seemed boundless, with new continents awaiting discovery. Columbus took five weeks to sail from the Canary Islands to the Bahamas, but today a trans-Atlantic crossing in a supersonic airliner takes 3½ hours.

The increasing speed of all forms of transport has given us much greater mobility. However, problems lie ahead. For example, unless alternative fuels are invented, shortages of petroleum-based fuels in the early 21st century will probably restrict the use of private transport. Instead, public systems, operated by alternative engines, will be the main forms of transport, carrying enormous numbers of passengers at speeds of thousands of kilometres per hour. In cities, computer-controlled passenger cars will pick up people and drop them at their destinations. A world shortage of petroleum will probably render the diesel locomotive obsolete. Instead, trains will be electric and will probably employ the already known principles of air-cushion vehicles. They will be capable of speeds of 800 km/h.

Telecommunications have also undergone a revolution. As late as 1860, the Pony Express was carrying messages between Missouri and California in the United States, but we can now communicate, via wire and microwave radio links or communications satellites, with people on the other side of the world. Powered by sunlight, communications satellites are located in geo-synchronous orbit over the Equator, such that they move at the same speed as the rotation of the Earth. Although they have a limited lifespan, their lofty positions enable them to transmit signals to any place on Earth without interference from the Earth's curvature. More powerful communications satellites will allow simultaneous intercontinental television broadcasts directly to home aerials, without the need for ground stations.

Opposite: Modern highways, like this road on a dyke across the IJsselmeer in the Netherlands, have speeded up private travel.

Below: Air transport has come within the range of many people in the rich developed nations in the last thirty years.

Opposite: The use of prepacked containers makes the loading and unloading of cargo ships much faster and more efficient.

Right: The space age has given us a new perspective on our planet Earth. Teams of astronauts in Skylab (1), an American space station launched into orbit at 435 km above the Earth in 1973, were able to observe our planet's surface. The development of the American shuttle *Columbia* makes the establishment of similar stations economically feasible. Various weather satellites, including *Nimbus* (2), have advanced our knowledge of the atmosphere and provided much data for weather forecasters. Communications satellites (3), in stationary orbit over the Equator at about 35,900 km, can transmit telecommunications and television signals to any part of the world. Landsat earth science satellites (4) orbit the Earth from pole to pole at heights of about 920 km. They obtain detailed survey pictures. They also monitor crop growth and pollution, and obtain information used in mineral prospecting.

Below: Viewphones using satellite communications may become commonplace in the next twenty years, although they may look different from this model.

FACTFINDER

Transport speeds: Before the Industrial Revolution, stage wagons travelled at about 5 km/h, while horse transport and sailing boats reached 16 km/h. The 'age of steam' which began in the 18th century, led to speeds of 100 km/h by steam locomotives and 50 km/h by steamboats. Piston-engined aircraft flew at 500—600 km/h after World War II. Jet airliners now fly at more than 1000 km/h, while supersonic airliners reach 2250 km/h. On land, high-speed trains reach 210 km/h.

Air travel: The British Handley Page (1932) carried 38 passengers at 170 km/h; the British Bristol Britannia (1955) carried 110 passengers at 650 km/h; the Boeing 747 now carries up to 500 passengers at 950 km/h or more.

Shipping: Until 1800, it took a month or more to cross the Atlantic. In 1827 the first crossing by a power vessel took 22 days from Rotterdam to the West Indies. In 1952 the *United States* made the fastest crossing of 3 days, 10 hours and 40 minutes from New York City to Le Havre.

Car ownership: In 1912, there were 600,000 motor vehicles in the United States. By 1940, there were 32 million. In 1979, there were 159·4 million vehicles that covered 2,454,000 million km (or 330 km per week per driver).

Highest traffic density: Hong Kong (1977) had 191,146 vehicles on 1091 km of roads — a density of 5·7 metres per vehicle (as compared with the United Kingdom, 19·4 metres per vehicle in 1979).

Telecommunications: First successful launch of international communications satellite (Comsat or Syncom), 1963.

LIFE IN SPACE

With the Earth facing problems arising from overpopulation, overexploitation of resources, and pollution, scientists have already begun to think about colonizing space, starting possibly in the early 21st century.

Solving Problems

One important question about life in space concerned the ability of the human body to withstand the stresses involved in take-off and the weightlessness experienced in orbit. Missions by American astronauts and Russian cosmonauts, including Valentin Lebedev and Anatoly Berezovoy who spent 211 days in the Salyut-Soyuz space station in 1982, have shown that life in space is possible.

Another problem concerned the transport of materials from the Earth, and possibly the Moon, in order to build space stations. The test flights of the American space shuttle *Columbia* in the early 1980s have demonstrated that this, too, is possible. Shuttles could transport cylindrical modules into orbit, where they could be linked to form space stations. These stations, which would orbit the Earth at heights of several hundred kilometres, would be the springboards for creating large space habitats.

Space Habitats

Space habitats could be situated at a Langrangian point – that is, at a distance of about 350,000 kilometres from both the Earth and the Moon, such that the gravitational pull of these two bodies would 'lock' the habitat in position.

Above: Future space habitats may be built in a simple torus or wheel shape that rotates around a central hub, which houses solar power and docking facilities.

Two basic designs for space habitats have been proposed. One consists of a pair of cylinders that rotate in order to simulate gravity. The other, which seems to offer the most benefits, is of a wheel or torus shape. This NASA design would contain a hollow tube, about 130 metres across, formed into a ring with a diameter of about 1800 metres. The ring would be linked to a central hub, housing docking bays, industrial modules, aerial arrays and radiators to remove excess heat. A large mirror above the hub would reflect light into the tube, where intensive agriculture would be practised. The ring would rotate at one revolution per minute in order to create the centrifugal force needed to hold everything in place. Such a colony could house and support an estimated 10,000 people.

FACTFINDER

SOME SPACE FIRSTS

1957 The first satellite, Russian *Sputnik 1* was launched on October 4.

1959 Russian *Luna 2* probe crash-landed on the Moon.

1961 On April 12, Yuri Gagarin on *Vostok 1* became the first traveller in space, orbiting the Earth once.

1962 First successful interplanetary probe, the American *Mariner 2*, passes near Venus.

1967 The Russian *Venera 3* made a successful landing on Venus.

1969–72 Six successful American Apollo landings on the Moon.

1973 American *Pioneer 10* probe took close-up photographs of Jupiter.

1974 American *Mariner 10* took close-up photographs of Mercury.

1976 American *Viking 1* lands on Mars.

1980–81 *Voyager* spacecraft sent back much information about Jupiter's moons and Saturn's rings and moons.

1981–2 Test flights of the American space shuttle *Columbia*.

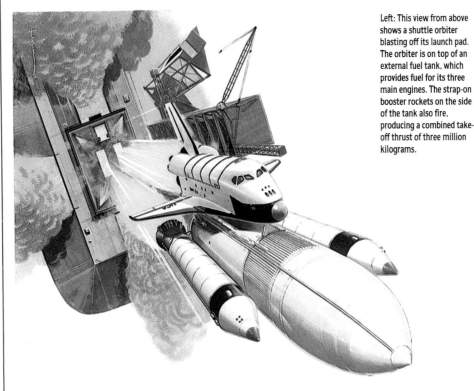

Left: This view from above shows a shuttle orbiter blasting off its launch pad. The orbiter is on top of an external fuel tank, which provides fuel for its three main engines. The strap-on booster rockets on the side of the tank also fire, producing a combined take-off thrust of three million kilograms.

Left: The inside of the outer tube of a torus space habitat gets its light from mirrors that reflect it from the hub. The centrifugal force set up by the rotation of the torus around the hub creates artificial gravity.

Right: Having shed its booster rockets and external fuel tank, the orbiter floats in orbit. Its open cargo bay can hold loads that are 18 metres long by 4·6 metres across. Here, a remote-controlled manipulating arm is launching a large satellite from the cargo bay.

HEALING THE WOUNDS

The problems that face mankind are truly monumental. According to the United Nations Environment Programme (UNEP), a recently established agency, soil erosion and soil degradation were still widespread in the early 1980s, and one third of the world's arable land was at risk of becoming desert because of human misuse. Tropical forests were disappearing at an estimated rate of 50 hectares a minute — a rate that, if it continues, will eliminate all tropical forests in forty years. One plant or animal species was also being lost per day — a rate that was accelerating. And in human terms, UNEP estimated that every day some 40,000 infants or young children were dying from hunger or from a pollution-related disease.

Disease and malnutrition are features of everyday life in the developing world and, despite all the aid that goes to developing nations, the economic gap between them and the developed world is enormous and increasing. In 1980, the per capita gross national products of the United Kingdom, United States and Switzerland were, respectively, US $7920, $11,360 and $16,440. By contrast, the per capita GNPs of Chad, Burma and India were $120, $170 and $240. A world split into two sectors — one rich and one poor — is a world fraught with danger. And the population explosion, which is most marked in the poorest countries, could cause global chaos.

The world's problems must be tackled with a real understanding of all the factors involved. People once talked of 'taming' Nature, as if Nature were hostile towards and separate from them. However, in recent years, we have begun to realize that the key to our future lies not in 'taming' but in comprehending Nature, particularly the highly complex ecological relationships that exist between us, the Earth and the millions of animals and plant species that the Earth supports. A view from space has made us realize that damage has been and is still being done. But hopefully it is not too late for us to heal the wounds we have inflicted.

WORLD ATLAS

SYMBOLS

Relief

Symbol		Feet	Relief	Metres
⬭	Land contour	16404		5000
▲ 8848	Spot height (metres)	9843		3000
⋈	Pass	6562		2000
▭	Permanent ice cap	3281		1000
		1640		500
		656		200
		0 Land Dep.		Sea Level
		656		200
		13123		4000
		22966		7000

Hydrography

⬭	Submarine contour
▼11034	Ocean depth (metres)
(217)	Lake level
~~	Reef
～	River
～	Intermittent river
～	Falls
～	Dam
～	Gorge
⊢⊢⊢⊢	Canal
⬭	Lake/Reservoir
⬭	Intermittent lake
～	Marsh/Swamp

Communications

⋯Tunnel⋯	Main railway
✈	Main airport
– – – –	Track

Road representation varies with the scale category.

═══	Principal road	} 1:1M-1:2½M
────	Other main road	
───	Principal road	} 1:2½M-1:7½M
────	Other main road	
───	Principal road	1:7½M or smaller

Administration

────	International boundary
– – –	Undefined/Disputed international boundary
········	Cease-fire line
–·–·–	Internal division : First order
–··–··–	Internal division : Second order
▨ ◉ ▣ / ◉ ▢ ▪	National capitals

Settlement

Each settlement is given a town stamp according to its population size and scale category.

	1:1M-1:2½M	1:2½M-1:7½M	1:7½M or smaller
▨	over 1 000 000	over 1 000 000	over 1 000 000
◉	500 000-1 000 000	500 000-1 000 000	500 000-1 000 000
◎	100 000-500 000	100 000-500 000	100 000-500 000
⊙	25 000-100 000	25 000-100 000	under 100 000
○	10 000-25 000	under 25 000	—
•	under 10 000		—
⬗	Major urban area (1:1M-1:2½M only)		

The size of type used for each settlement is graded to correspond with the appropriate town stamp.

Other features

∴	Ancient monument
⌣	Oasis
⬭	National Park
▲	Oil field
△	Gas field
─·─·─	Oil/Gas pipeline

Lettering

Various styles of lettering are used-each one representing a different type of feature.

ALPS	Physical feature	KENYA	Country name
Red Sea	Hydrographic feature	IOWA	Internal division
Paris	Settlement name	(Fr.)	Territorial administration

© Wm. Collins Sons & Co. Ltd.

THE WORLD : Political

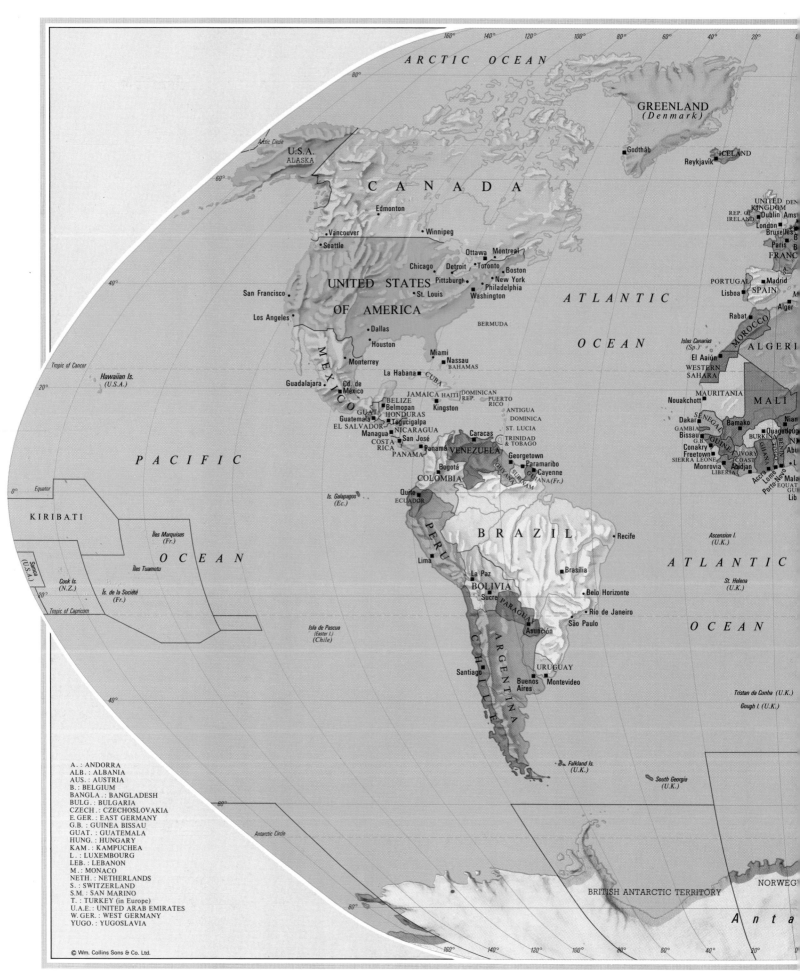

ARCTIC OCEAN

GREENLAND
(Denmark)

Godthåb

Reykjavík ICELAND

Arctic Circle

U.S.A.
ALASKA

C A N A D A

Edmonton

Vancouver Winnipeg

Seattle

Ottawa Montreal
Chicago Detroit Toronto
Boston
UNITED STATES Pittsburgh New York
Philadelphia
San Francisco St. Louis Washington

OF AMERICA

Los Angeles

BERMUDA

Dallas

Houston

Miami
Nassau
Monterrey BAHAMAS

La Habana CUBA

Guadalajara Cd. de
México

JAMAICA HAITI DOMINICAN
REP. PUERTO
RICO

BELIZE
GUAT. Belmopan ANTIGUA
Guatemala HONDURAS Kingston DOMINICA
EL SALVADOR Tegucigalpa ST. LUCIA
Managua NICARAGUA Caracas TRINIDAD
COSTA San José & TOBAGO
RICA Panamá VENEZUELA
PANAMA Georgetown
Bogotá Paramaribo
COLOMBIA Cayenne
GUIANA(Fr.)

Quito
ECUADOR

Is. Galapagos
(Ec.)

PACIFIC

KIRIBATI

PERU

B R A Z I L Recife

Lima

Îles Marquises
(Fr.)

OCEAN

La Paz Brasília

Samoa
(U.S.A.) BOLIVIA
Cook Is. Îles Tuamotu Sucre Belo Horizonte
(N.Z.)
Îs. de la Société PARAGUAY Río de Janeiro
(Fr.)
Tropic of Capricorn São Paulo
Asunción

Isla de Pascua
(Easter I.)
(Chile)

ARGENTINA URUGUAY
CHILE
Santiago Buenos Montevideo
Aires

Equator

Tropic of Cancer

Hawaiian Is.
(U.S.A.)

UNITED
KINGDOM
REP. OF Dublin Amst
IRELAND
London
Bruxelles
Paris B
FRANC

PORTUGAL Madrid
Lisboa SPAIN

Rabat Alger

MOROCCO ALGERI
Islas Canarias
(Sp.)
El Aaiún
WESTERN MAURITANIA
SAHARA
Nouakchott MALI
SENEGAL Bamako
Dakar Nian
GAMBIA Ouagadougo
Bissau G.B. BURKINA
GUINEA IVORY N
Conakry GHANA COAST Abu
Freetown TOGO
SIERRA LEONE Abidjan BENIN
Monrovia Accra Lomé
LIBERIA Porto-Novo
EQUAT. GU
Lib

ATLANTIC

OCEAN

Ascension I.
(U.K.)

ATLANTIC

St. Helena
(U.K.)

OCEAN

Tristan da Cunha (U.K.)
Gough I. (U.K.)

Falkland Is.
(U.K.)

South Georgia
(U.K.)

Antarctic Circle

BRITISH ANTARCTIC TERRITORY NORWEG

Anta

A. : ANDORRA
ALB. : ALBANIA
AUS. : AUSTRIA
B. : BELGIUM
BANGLA. : BANGLADESH
BULG. : BULGARIA
CZECH. : CZECHOSLOVAKIA
E. GER. : EAST GERMANY
G.B. : GUINEA BISSAU
GUAT. : GUATEMALA
HUNG. : HUNGARY
KAM. : KAMPUCHEA
L. : LUXEMBOURG
LEB. : LEBANON
M. : MONACO
NETH. : NETHERLANDS
S. : SWITZERLAND
S.M. : SAN MARINO
T. : TURKEY (in Europe)
U.A.E. : UNITED ARAB EMIRATES
W. GER. : WEST GERMANY
YUGO. : YUGOSLAVIA

© Wm. Collins Sons & Co. Ltd.

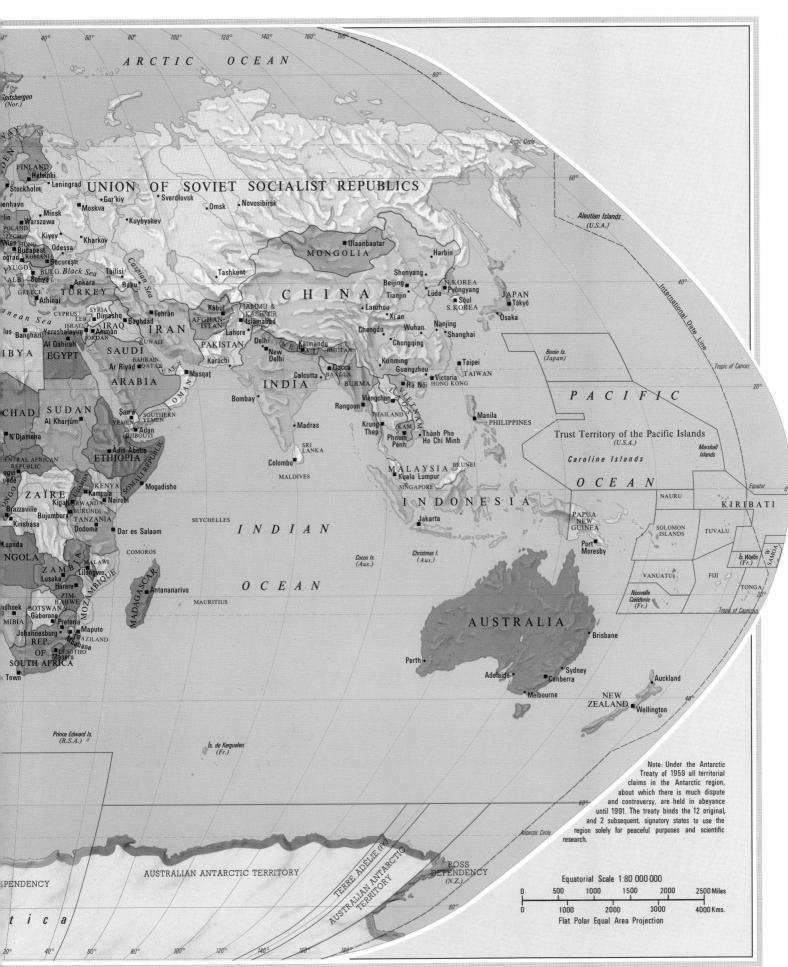

ARCTIC OCEAN

Spitsbergen
(Nor.)

FINLAND
Helsinki
Stockholm   Leningrad   Gor'kiy
enhavn   Minsk   Moskva   Sverdlovsk
lin   Warszawa   Kuybyshev   Omsk   Novosibirsk
ZECH   Kiyev   Kharkov   Odessa

UNION OF SOVIET SOCIALIST REPUBLICS

ograd   Budapest   ROMANIA
YUGO   BULG.   București
ALB.   Sofiya   Black Sea   Tbilisi   Baku
GREECE   TURKEY   Ankara   Tashkent
Athinai   Caspian Sea
ean Sea   CYPRUS   SYRIA   Dimashq   Tehrān
LEB.   ISRAEL   Baghdād   Kābul   JAMMU &
lus   Banghāzī   Yerushalayim   Amman   AFGHAN-   KASHMIR
JORDAN   IRAQ   IRAN   ISTAN   Islāmābād
IBY A   EGYPT   SAUDI   KUWAIT   PAKISTAN   Lahore   Delhi
Ar Riyāḍ   QATAR   Karāchi   New
CHAD   SUDAN   ARABIA   BAHRAIN   U.A.E.   Masqaṭ   Delhi
Al Khartūm   Ṣan'ā   OMAN   INDIA   Calcutta
CENTRAL AFRICAN   SOUTHERN   Bombay
N'Djamena   REPUBLIC   YEMEN   Ādan
ngui   ETHIOPIA   Ādis Ābeba   DJIBOUTI   Madras
ONGO   ZAIRE   KENYA   Kampala   Nairobi   Mogadishu
nde   Kigali   RWANDA   SRI
BURUNDI   LANKA
Brazzaville   Bujumbura   TANZANIA   Dodoma   Colombo
Kinshasa   Dar es Salaam   MALDIVES

Ulaanbaatar
MONGOLIA   Harbin
Shenyang
Beijing   N.KOREA
CHINA   Tianjin   Lüda   Pyŏngyang
Lanzhou   Xi'an   Sŏul
Chengdu   Wuhan   Nanjing   S.KOREA
Chongqing   Shanghai
Kunming   Guangzhou   Taipei
Kātmāndu   Victoria   TAIWAN
NEPAL   BHUTAN   Hà Nôi   HONG KONG
Dacca   BURMA   Viangchan
BANGLA.   Rangoon   THAILAND
Krung   KAM.   Thành Pho
Thep   Phnum   Ho Chí Minh
Pénh
MALAYSIA   BRUNEI
Kuala Lumpur
SINGAPORE

JAPAN
Tōkyō
Ōsaka

Arctic Circle

Aleutian Islands
(U.S.A.)

International Date Line

PACIFIC

Bonin Is.
(Japan)

Tropic of Cancer

Manila
PHILIPPINES
Trust Territory of the Pacific Islands
(U.S.A.)
Caroline Islands

Marshall
Islands

OCEAN

Equator

NGOLA
Luanda   MALAWI
ZAMBIA   Lilongwe
Lusaka   Hárare
adhoek   ZIM-
BABWE   MOZAMBIQUE
MIBIA   BOTSWANA
Gaborone   Pretoria
Johannesburg   Maputo   SWAZILAND
REP.   Mbabane   LESOTHO   Maseru
OF
SOUTH AFRICA
Town

SEYCHELLES

COMOROS

MADAGASCAR
Antananarivo
MAURITIUS

INDIAN

OCEAN

INDONESIA
Jakarta

Cocos Is.
(Aus.)

Christmas I.
(Aus.)

NAURU

PAPUA
NEW
GUINEA
Port
Moresby

SOLOMON
ISLANDS

VANUATU

Nouvelle
Calédonie
(Fr.)

KIRIBATI

TUVALU

Ïs. Wallis   W.
(Fr.)   SAMOA

FIJI

TONGA

Tropic of Capricorn

AUSTRALIA

Brisbane

Perth
Adelaide   Sydney
Canberra
Melbourne   NEW
ZEALAND   Auckland
Wellington

Prince Edward Is.
(R.S.A.)

Îs. de Kerguelen
(Fr.)

Note: Under the Antarctic
Treaty of 1959 all territorial
claims in the Antarctic region,
about which there is much dispute
and controversy, are held in abeyance
until 1991. The treaty binds the 12 original,
and 2 subsequent, signatory states to use the
region solely for peaceful purposes and scientific
research.

Antarctic Circle

PENDENCY

AUSTRALIAN ANTARCTIC TERRITORY

TERRE ADÉLIE (Fr.)

AUSTRALIAN ANTARCTIC
TERRITORY

ROSS
DEPENDENCY
(N.Z.)

tica

Equatorial Scale 1:80 000 000

0   500   1000   1500   2000   2500 Miles
0   1000   2000   3000   4000 Kms.

Flat Polar Equal Area Projection

3

THE WORLD : Physical

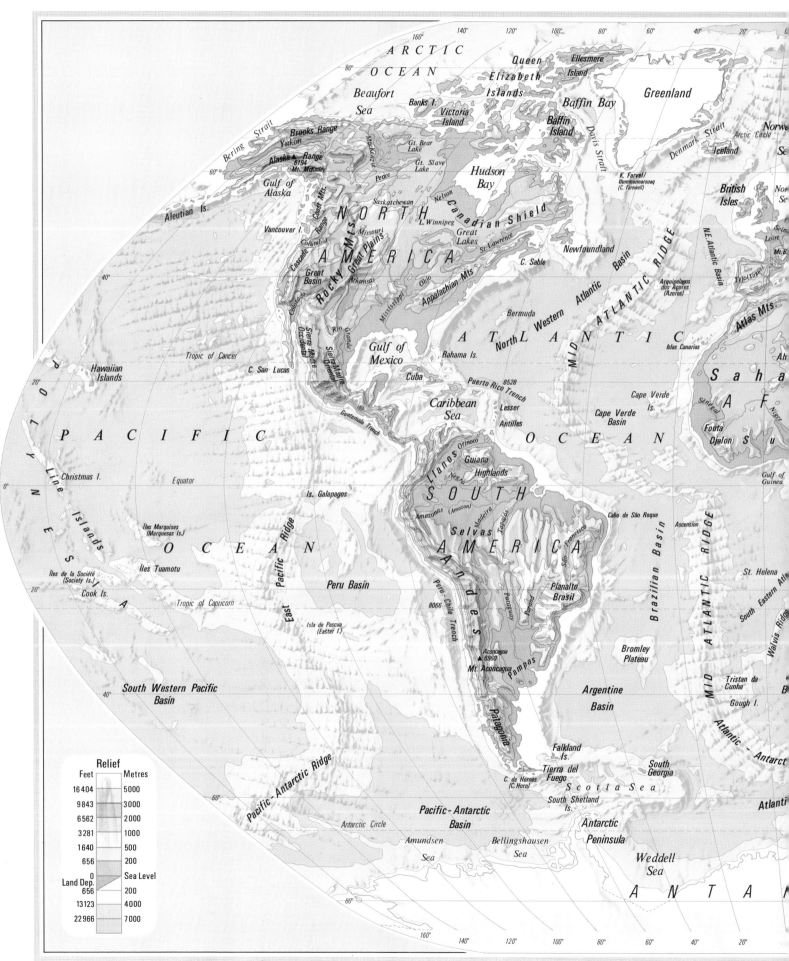

Relief

Feet	Metres
16 404	5000
9843	3000
6562	2000
3281	1000
1640	500
656	200
0	Sea Level
Land Dep.	
656	200
13 123	4000
22 966	7000

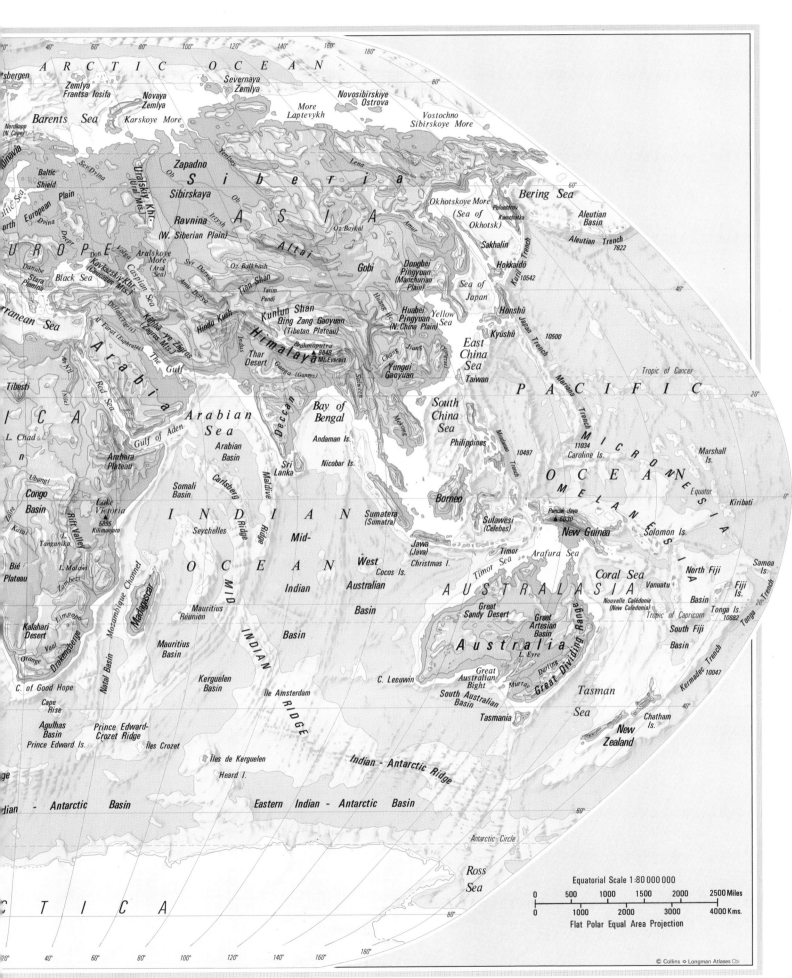

ARCTIC OCEAN

Spitsbergen
Zemlya
Frantsa Iosifa
Novaya
Zemlya
Severnaya
Zemlya
Novosibirskiye
Ostrova
80°

Nordkapp
(N. Cape)
Barents
Sea
Karskoye More
More
Laptevykh
Vostochno
Sibirskoye More

Baltic
Shield
Sev. Dvina
Zapadno
Sibirskaya
S I B E R I A
S I A

Okhotskoye More
(Sea of
Okhotsk)
Poluostrov
Kamchatka
Bering Sea
Aleutian
Basin
60°

Scandinavia
North
European
Plain
Ob
Ural'skiy Khr.
(Ural Mts.)
Ravnina
(W. Siberian Plain)
Altai
Oz. Baykal
Amur
Sakhalin
Hokkaidō
Aleutian Trench
7822

Baltic Sea
Dnepr
Don
Volga
Aral'skoye
More
(Aral
Sea)
Caspian Sea
Irtysh
Ob
Oz. Balkhash
Syr Darya
Gobi
Dongbei
Pingyuan
(Manchurian
Plain)
Sea of
Japan
Kuril Trench
10542
40°

EUROPE
Danube
Stara
planina
Black Sea
Kavkazskiy Khr.
(Caucasus Mts.)
Amu Darya
Tian Shan
Tarim
Pendi
Huang He
Huabei
Pingyuan
(N. China Plain)
Yellow
Sea
Honshū
Japan Trench
10500

Mediterranean Sea
Köhha-ye Zagros
(Zagros Mts.)
al Furat (Euphrates)
The Gulf
Hindu Kush
Kunlun Shan
Qing Zang Gaoyuan
(Tibetan Plateau)
Himalaya
Chang
Jiang
Yungui
Gaoyuan
East
China
Sea
Kyūshū
Mariana
Trench
20°

A R A B I A
Tibesti
(Nile)
Red Sea
Dijla (Tigris)
Thar
Desert
Brahmaputra
8848
Mt. Everest
Ganga (Ganges)
Salween
Taiwan
P A C I F I C
Tropic of Cancer

AFRICA
L. Chad
Amhara
Plateau
Gulf of Aden
Arabian
Sea
Deccan
Bay of
Bengal
Andaman Is.
South
China
Sea
Philippines
10497
11034
Caroline Is.
Mariana Trench
Marshall
Is.
M I C R O N E S I A
20°

Ubangi
Congo
Basin
Lake
Victoria
5895
Kilimanjaro
Somali
Basin
Carlsberg Ridge
Maldive Ridge
Arabian
Basin
Sri
Lanka
Nicobar Is.
Seychelles
Sumatera
(Sumatra)
Borneo
Sulawesi
(Celebes)
Puncak Jaya
5030
New Guinea
Solomon Is.
Kiribati
O C E A N
M E L A N E S I A
Equator

Kasai
Tanganika
Bié
Plateau
L. Malawi
Zambezi
I N D I A N
Mid-
Indian
West
Australian
Cocos Is.
Christmas I.
Jawa
(Java)
Timor
Timor
Sea
Arafura Sea
AUSTRALASIA
Coral Sea
Vanuatu
North Fiji
Basin
Samoa
Is.
Fiji
Is.
20°

Kalahari
Desert
Vaal
Limpopo
Mozambique Channel
Madagascar
Mauritius
Réunion
O C E A N
Ridge
Basin
Great
Sandy Desert
Great
Artesian
Basin
Nouvelle Calédonie
(New Caledonia)
Tonga Is.
10882
Tonga Trench
South Fiji
Basin
Tropic of Capricorn

Drakensberge
Orange
Natal Basin
Mauritius
Basin
Kerguelen
Basin
Île Amsterdam
M I D
I N D I A N
R I D G E
Basin
A u s t r a l i a
L. Eyre
Great
Australian
Bight
Darling
Murray
Great Dividing Range
Tasman
Sea
Chatham
Is.
40°

C. of Good Hope
Cape
Rise
Agulhas
Basin
Prince Edward Is.
Prince Edward-
Crozet Ridge
Îles Crozet
Îles de Kerguelen
Heard I.
C. Leeuwin
South Australian
Basin
Tasmania
New
Zealand

Antarctic Basin
Eastern Indian - Antarctic Basin
Indian - Antarctic Ridge
60°

Antarctic Circle

ANTARCTICA
Ross
Sea
80°

Equatorial Scale 1:80 000 000

| 0 | 500 | 1000 | 1500 | 2000 | 2500 Miles |

| 0 | 1000 | 2000 | 3000 | 4000 Kms. |

Flat Polar Equal Area Projection

© Collins ◇ Longman Atlases Cbi

40° 60° 80° 100° 120° 140° 160° 180°

20° 40° 60° 80° 100° 120° 140° 160° 180°

North America

ARCTIC OCEAN

Spitsbergen
(Nor.)

Barents
Sea

Novaya
Zemlya
(U.S.S.R.)

Denmark Strait

Arctic Circle

ICELAND

Reykjavik

NORWAY

SWEDEN

FINLAND

Helsinki

Leningrad

U.S.S.R.

Bergen

Oslo

Göteborg

Stockholm

Moskva

Gor'kiy

North
Sea

Århus

København

Minsk

(in Europe)

Kubyshev

REP.
OF
IRE.

Dublin

UNITED
KINGDOM

DENMARK

Birmingham

Hamburg

Berlin

POLAND

London

NETH.

EAST
GERMANY

Warszawa

Amsterdam

Leipzig

Łódź

Kiyev

Kharkov

B.

Bruxelles

Bonn

LUX.

Praha

Brno

CZECH.

WEST
GERMANY

Wien

Odessa

ATLANTIC

OCEAN

Bay
of
Biscay

Paris

Zürich

L.

AUSTRIA

Budapest

HUNGARY

Bern

SW.

Milano

Zagreb

ROMANIA

Beograd

București

FRANCE

Lyon

Oporto

AN.

S.S.M.

ITALY

YUGOSLAVIA

Sofiya

Black Sea

Caspian Sea

Lisboa

PORTUGAL

Madrid

M.

Corse
(Fr.)

Roma

Tirana

BULGARIA

ALB.

Istanbul

SPAIN

Barcelona

Sardegna
(It.)

T.

Thessaloniki

Is.
Baleares
(Sp.)

MALTA

Sicilia

GREECE

Athínai

Madeira
(Port.)

Islas Canarias
(Sp.)

Tropic of Cancer

Mediterranean Sea

Kriti

Africa

ATLANTIC

OCEAN

Equator

ATLANTIC

OCEAN

Tropic of Capricorn

South America

ALB. : ALBANIA
AN. : ANDORRA
B. : BELGIUM
CZECH. : CZECHOSLOVAKIA
L. : LIECHTENSTEIN
LUX. : LUXEMBOURG
M. : MONACO
NETH. : NETHERLANDS
REP. OF IRE. : REPUBLIC OF IRELAND
S.M. : SAN MARINO
SW. : SWITZERLAND
T. : TURKEY (in Europe)

© Wm. Collins Sons & Co. Ltd.

EUROPE

EUROPE

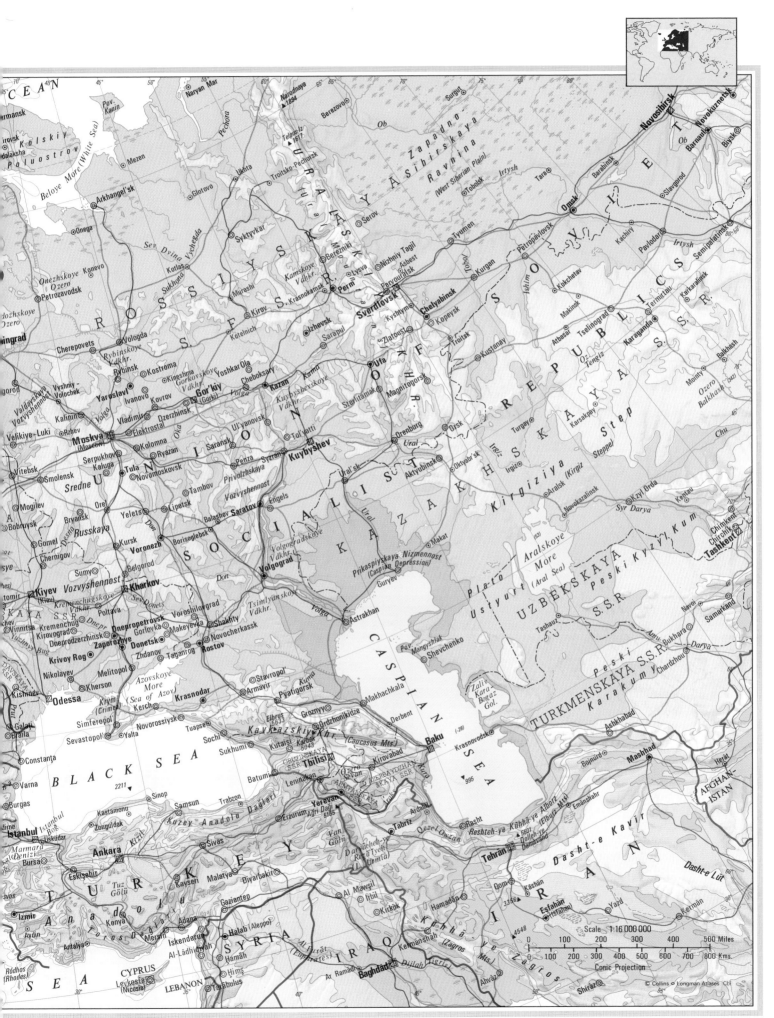

BRITISH ISLES

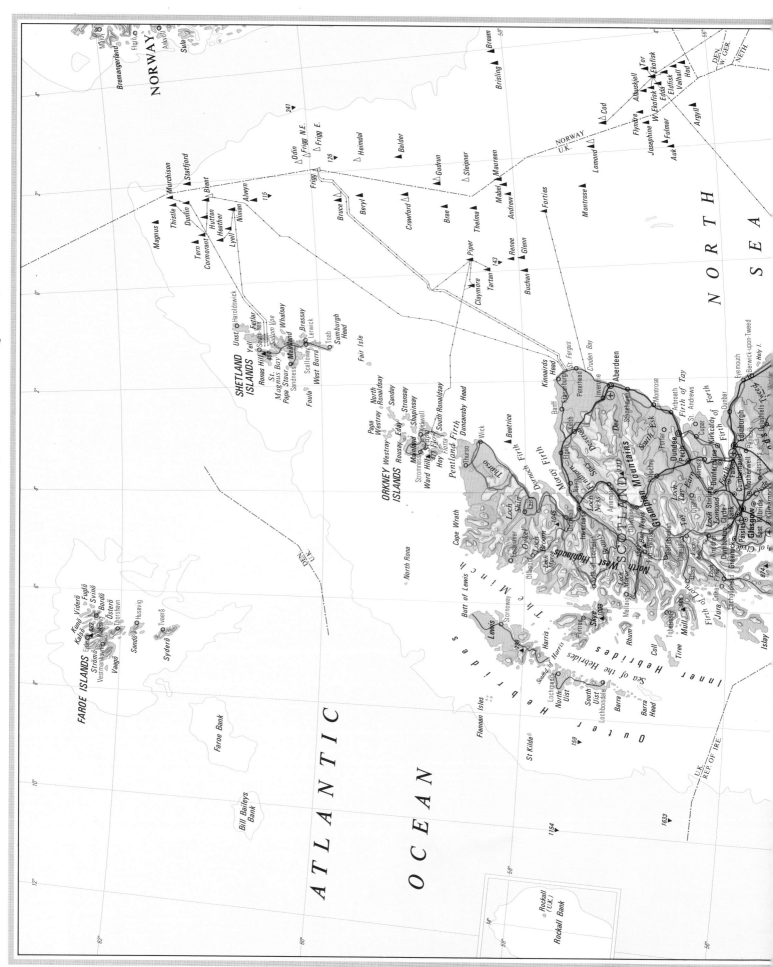

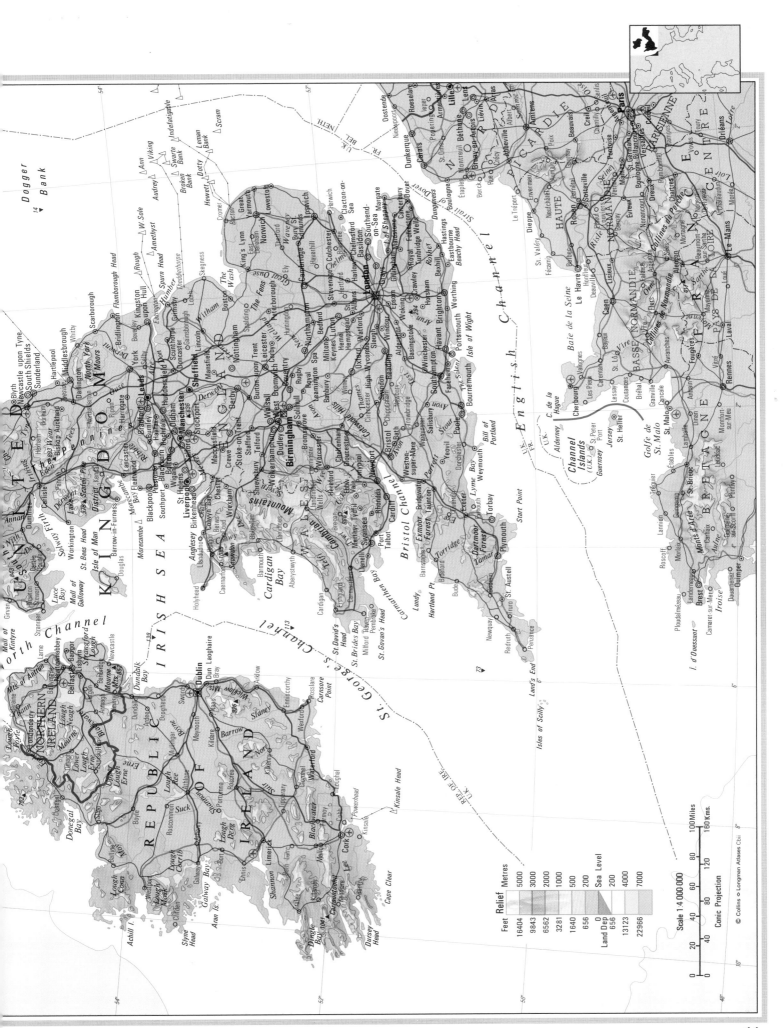

ENGLAND AND WALES

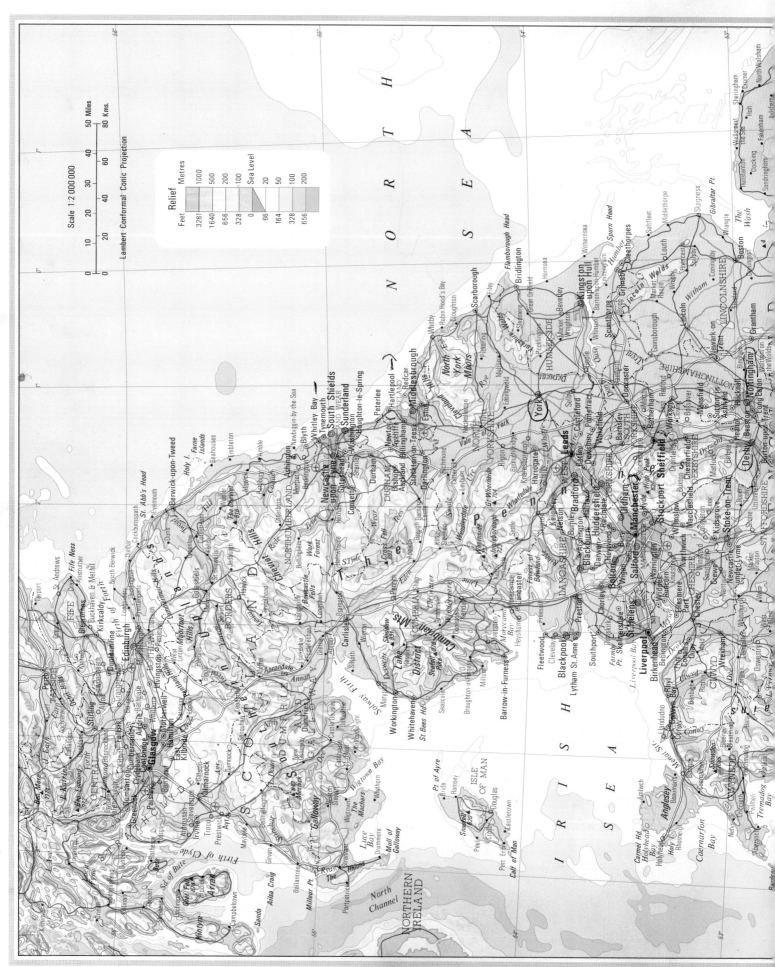

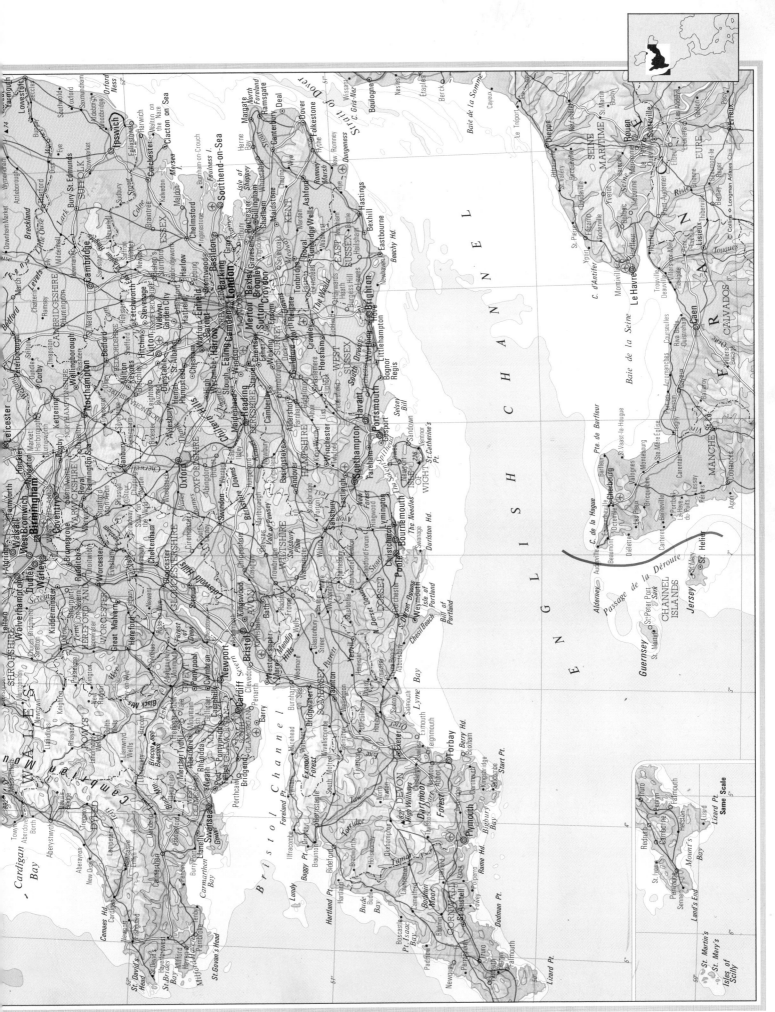

SCOTLAND

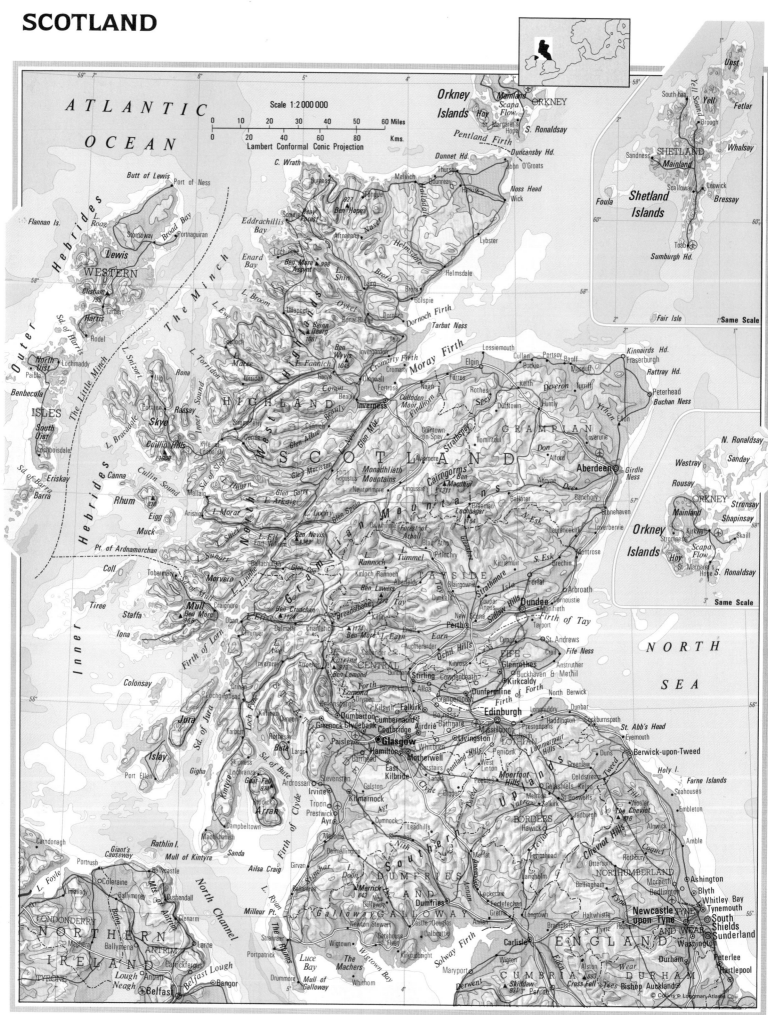

IRELAND

THE LOW COUNTRIES

Scale 1:2 000 000

0 10 20 30 40 50 60 Miles
0 20 40 60 80 Kms.

Conic Projection

Relief

Feet		Metres
16 404		5000
9843		3000
6562		2000
3281		1000
1640		500
656		200
0	Sea Level	
Land Dep.		
656		200
13123		4000
22966		7000

N O R T H

S E A

Ostfriesische Inseln
Norderney   Langeoog   Minsen
Juist   Juist   Norddeich   Dornum   Esens
Borkum   Norden   Meerhusener   Jever
Borkum   Moor   Wilhelmshaven
Aurich   Ens-Jade   Kanal   Zetel   Varel

Waddeneilanden
Schiermonnikoog
Ameland   Nes
Terschelling   Bordiep
W. Terschelling
Oost   Holwerd   Zoutkamp   Uithuizen   Delfzijl
Vlieland   Dokkum   Winsum   Appingedam   Dollard
Vlieland   Franeker   Leeuwarden   Bedum   GRONINGEN   Groningen   Emden
De Cocksdorp   Harlingen   FRIESLAND   Marum   Veendam   Winschoten   Papenburg
Texel   Workum   Sneek   Drachten   Assen   Stadskanaal   Bunde   Leer   Zwischenahn
Den Helder   Hippolytushoef   Staveren   Heerenveen   Smilde   Musselkanaal   Dörpen   Lorup   Oldenburg
Hoogezand   DRENTHE   Börger   NIEDERSACHSEN
Fluessen   Lemmer   Beilen   Rütenbrock   Sögel   Cloppenburg
Schagen   Medemblik   Noordoost-   Steenwijk   Emmen   Haren   Löningen   Bersenbrück
Bergen   Enkhuizen   Emmeloord   Hoogeveen   Coevorden   Meppen   Quakenbrück
NOORD   Urk   Nagele   Vollenhove   Meppel   Hardenberg   Lingen   Fürstenau   Freren
Alkmaar   Hoorn   Markerwaard   Kampen   Ommen   Neuenhaus   Bramsche
Heiloo   Oosthuizen   Zwolle   Hardenberg   Nordhorn   Mittelland-Kanal   Ibbenbüren
Beverwijk   Oostelijk-   Heerde   Raalte   Almelo   Rheine   Osnabrück
IJmuiden   Zaandam   Flevoland   Epe   Holten   Hengelo   Emsdetten   Burgsteinfurt   Lengerich
HOLLAND   Marken   Harderwijk   Deventer   Goor   Enschede   Gronau
Velsen   Amsterdam   Zuidelijk-   Veluwe   Apeldoorn   Lochem   Ahaus   Steinfurt   Greven
Haarlem   Amstelveen   Flevoland   Huizen   NETHERLANDS   Borghorst   Telgte   Warendorf
Heemstede   Diemen   Hilversum   Zutphen   Winterswijk   Gescher   Münster
Hillegom   Bussum   GELDERLAND   Rheden   Groenlo   Lichtenvoorde   Coesfeld   Warendorf
Katwijk aan Zee   Lisse   Woerden   Utrecht   Amersfoort   Barneveld   Dieren   Berkel   Stadtlohn   Hiltrup
Oegstgeest   Aalsmeer   Veenendaal   Ede   Arnhem   Doetinchem   Bocholt   Dülmen   Ahlen
Wassenaar   Leiden   Zeist   UTRECHT   Rhenen   Renkum   Zevenaar   Anholt   Borken   Lüdinghausen   Beckum
Scheveningen   Voorburg   Oude Rijn   Wageningen   Nijmegen   Kleve   Brünen   Haltern   Dülmen
's Gravenhage   Voorburg   Gouda   Tiel   Waal   Emmerich   Rhein   Dorsten   Marl   Beckum
(The Hague)   Delft   Rijswijk   ZUID   Gorinchem   's Hertogenbosch   Goch   Xanten   Wesel   Lippe   Dorsten   Herten   Gladbeck   Recklinghausen
Hoek van Holland   Maassluis   Oude   IJssel   Zaltbommel   Vught   Kalkar   Kamp   Gelsenkirchen   Herne   Dortmund
Maasluis   Vlaardingen   Schiedam   Rotterdam   Ridderkerk   Sliedrecht   Oss   Bergheim   Straelen   Geldern   Lintfort   Voerde   Oberhausen   Bottrop   Essen   Bochum   Witten   Hagen
Hellevoetsluis   HOLLAND   Dordrecht   Maas   Waalwijk   Kevelaer   Moers   Duisburg   Mülheim   Hattingen   Hagen   Iserlohn
Ouddorp   Brouwershaven   Middelharnis   Oosterhout   Tilburg   Oisterwijk   Venray   Krefeld   NORDRHEIN   Velbert   Wuppertal   Werdohl
Schouwen   Overflakkee   NOORD   Boxtel   Veghel   Helmond   Blerick   Viersen   Mönchen-   Neuss   Remscheid   Lüdenscheid
Duiveland   Steenbergen   Breda   BRABANT   Venlo   Tegelen   Gladbach   Rheydt   Düsseldorf   Solingen
Domburg   Tholen   Roosendaal   Oudenbosch   Eindhoven   Deurne   Roermond   WESTFALEN   Hückeswagen   Gummersbach
Noord   Goes   Bergen op Zoom   Baarle   Geldrop   Maaseik   Geilenkirchen   Bergheim   Bergisch Gladbach   Wiehl
Beveland   Middelburg   ZEELAND   Kalmthout   Weert   Neerpelt   Rotem   Sittard   Jülich   Elsdorf   Köln   Siegen
Vlissingen   Zuid   Kalmthout   Turnhout   LIMBURG   Leopoldsburg   Maaseik   Geleen   Brunssum   (Cologne)   Porz   Waldbröl   Morsbach
(Flushing)   Beveland   Breskens   IJzendijke   Mol   Lommel   Genk   Heerlen   Kerkrade   Eschweiler   Kerpen   Troisdorf   Bonn   Siegburg   Betzdorf
Westerschelde   Terneuzen   Brasschaat   Merksem   Geel   Bree   LIMBURG   Hasselt   Maastricht   Aachen   Düren   Brühl   Bonn   Bad Honnef   Altenkirchen
Knokke   Sluis   Hulst   Antwerpen   Deurne   Wilrijk   Lier   Gt. Nete   Demer   Sittard   Brunssum   Bergheim   Hennef   Rheinbach   Neuwied
Zeebrugge   Oostmalle   Wijnegem   Hoboken   Mechelen   Diest   Hückelhoven   Grevenbroich   Erkelenz   Zülpich   Bornheim   Montabaur
Blankenberge   Aardenburg   Lokeren   St. Niklaas   Dijle   Demer   Genk   Geilenkirchen   Bergheim   Euskirchen   Freilingen
Oostende   Brugge   Assebroek   Zelzate   Gent   Wetteren   Aarschot   Leuven   St. Truiden   Tongeren   Visé   Eupen   Schleiden   WEST   Bad Neuenahr   Andernach
(Ostend)   St. Andries   Eeklo   OOST   Dendermonde   Gete   Landen   Hannut   Herstal   Liège   Limburg   Verviers   Hellenthal   Ahrweiler   Koblenz
Westende   Torhout   Koekelare   VLAANDEREN   Vilvoorde   Schaerbeek   Bruxelles   Seraing   LIEGE   Batrange   692   GERMANY   Nürburg   Mayen
Nieuwpoort   Diksmuide   Tielt   Deinze   Brussel   Anderlecht   Tervuren   Wavre   St. Georges   Jodoigne   Namur   Malmedy   689   Kelberg   Cochem
Dunkerque   Veurne   WEST   Roeselare   Aalst   Ninove   Halle   Waterloo   Gembloux   Ramillies   Mariembourg   Stavelot   St. Vith   696   Gerolstein   Polch   Mosel
Hoogstade   Bergues   VLAANDEREN   Gerardsbergen   Enghien   Genappe   Hannut   Leuze   Andenne   Meuse   Ardennes   Prüm   EIFEL   Bad Kreuznach
Poperinge   Ieper   Oudenaarde   Ninove   Nivelles   Leuze   Namur   Ciney   Lierneux   La Roche   816   Montabaur
FLANDERS   Menen   Kortrijk   Mouscron   RONSE   BRABANT   Soignies   La Louvière   Gembloux   Dinant   Marche   Houffalize   Kyllburg   Wittlich   Simmern   Bingen
Armentières   Roubaix   Tourcoing   Berchem   HAINAUT   Ath   Binche   Jumet   Châtelet   NAMUR   Rochefort   La Roche   Bastogne   Bitburg   Bernkastel   Idar-Oberstein
Marcq-en-Baroeul   Lille   Orchies   Condé   Mons   Charleroi   Sambre   Thuin   Ohey   Havelange   Clervaux   Prüm   Trarbach   Kirn   Kirchenbolanden
Béthune   Lens   St. Amand   Valenciennes   Bavay   Beaumont   Philippeville   Mariembourg   Wellin   St. Hubert   Longchamps   Kyllburg   Zell   Bernkastel   Bad Kreuznach
Lievin   Hénin   Denain   Le Quesnoy   Solesmes   Avesnes   Chimay   Couvin   Wellin   LUXEMBOURG   Wiltz   Bitburg   Traben   Morbach   Kirn   Nahe
Arras   Cambrai   Landrecies   Le Cateau   La Capelle   Rocroi   Libramont   Süre   Ettelbrück   Diekirch   Echternach   Konz   Mosel   Idar-Oberstein
Beaumetz   Bapaume   Somme   Bohain   St. Quentin   Hirson   Charleville   Vresse   Neufchâteau   Martelange   Habay   Wasserbillig   Trier   Birkenfeld   Glan
Albert   Combles   Péronne   La Fère   Mézières   LUXEMBOURG   Merzig   Kösel   Köhl
Bucquoy   FRANCE   Origny   Guiscard   Marle   Serre   Montcornet   Sedan   Arlon   Luxembourg   Pétange   Dudelange   Remich   St. Wendel   Kaiserslautern
Montdidier   Chaulnes   Ham   Tergnier   Crépy   Laon   Aisne   PICARDIE   Montmédy   Esch   SAARLAND   Merzig
Maignelay   Noyon   Chauny   Coucy   CHAMPAGNE   ARDENNE   Virton   Longwy   Merzig

Collins ◇ Longman Atlases Cbiii

FRANCE

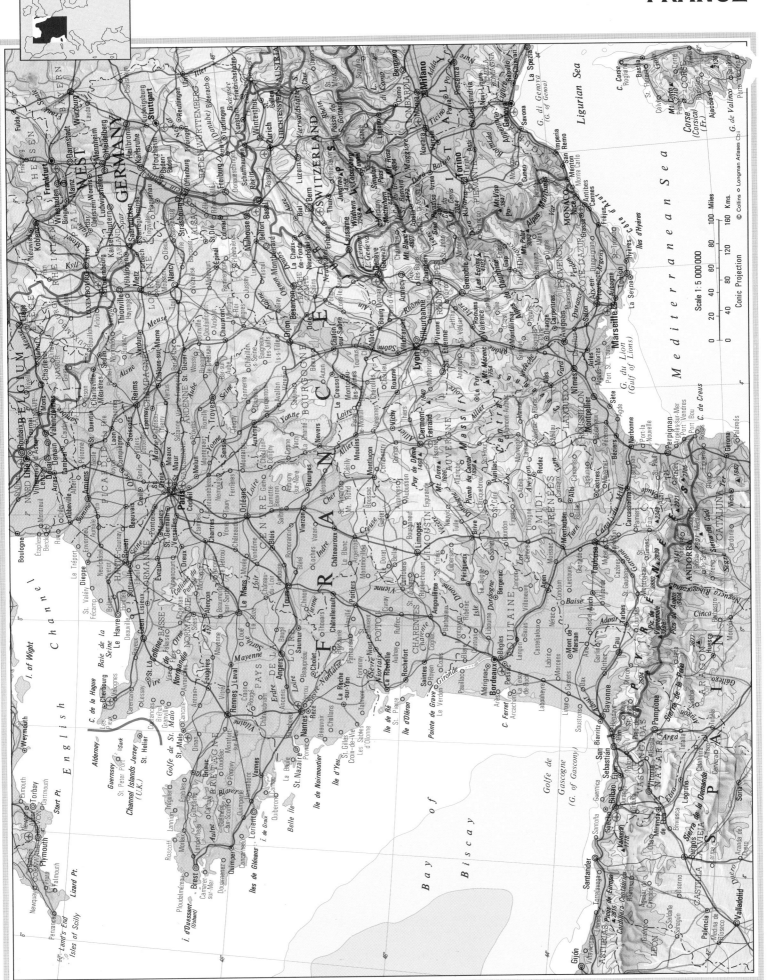

Scale 1:5 000 000
Conic Projection

© Collins ◇ Longman Atlases Cbii

17

NORTHERN FRANCE

Scale 1:2 500 000

Feet	Relief	Metres
16404		5000
9843		3000
6562		2000
3281		1000
1640		500
656		200
0		Sea Level

Land Dep.
656		200
13123		4000
22966		7000

Scale 1:2 500 000

| 0 | 25 | 50 | 75 | 100 Miles |
| 0 | 50 | 100 | 150 Kms. |

Conic Equidistant Projection

© Wm. Collins, Sons & Co. Ltd.

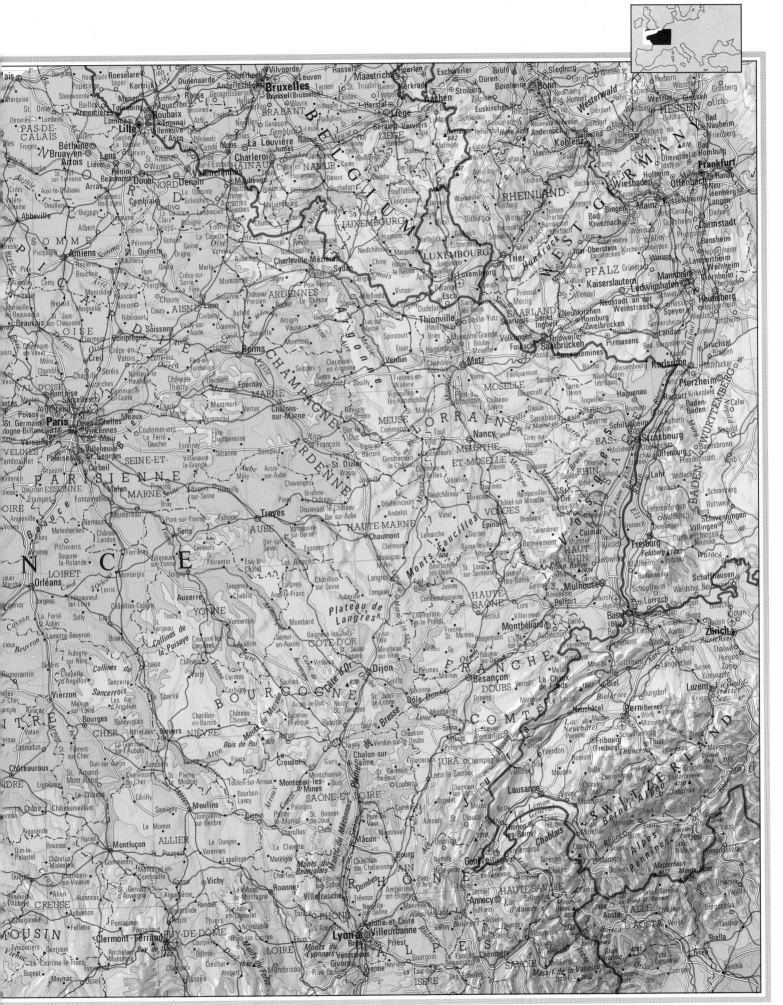

SOUTHERN FRANCE

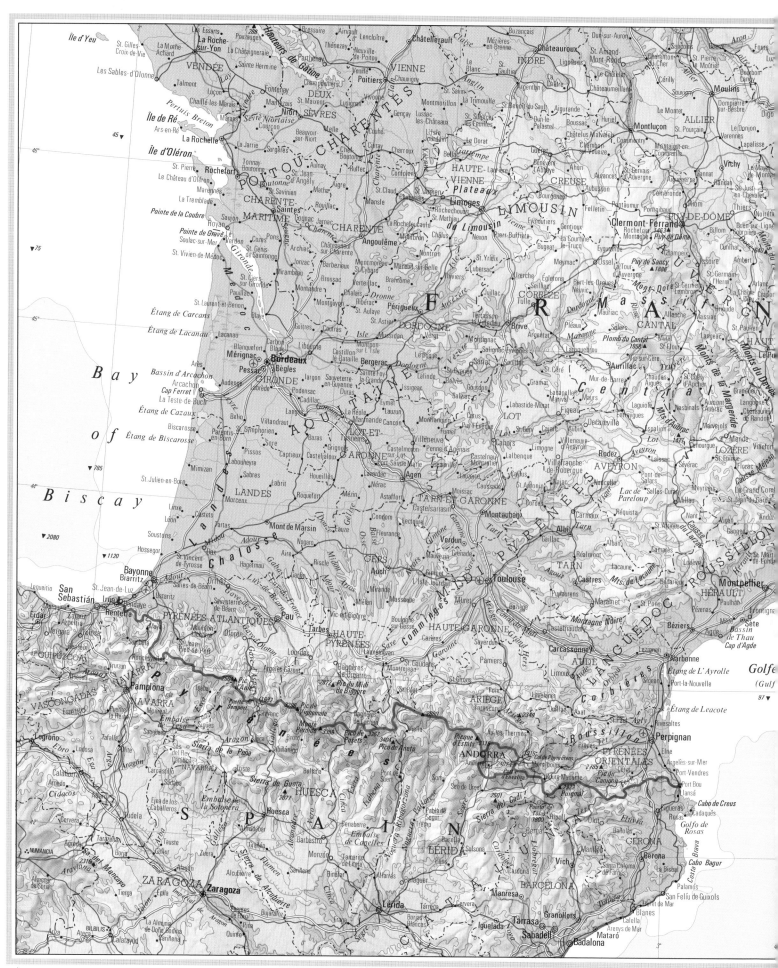

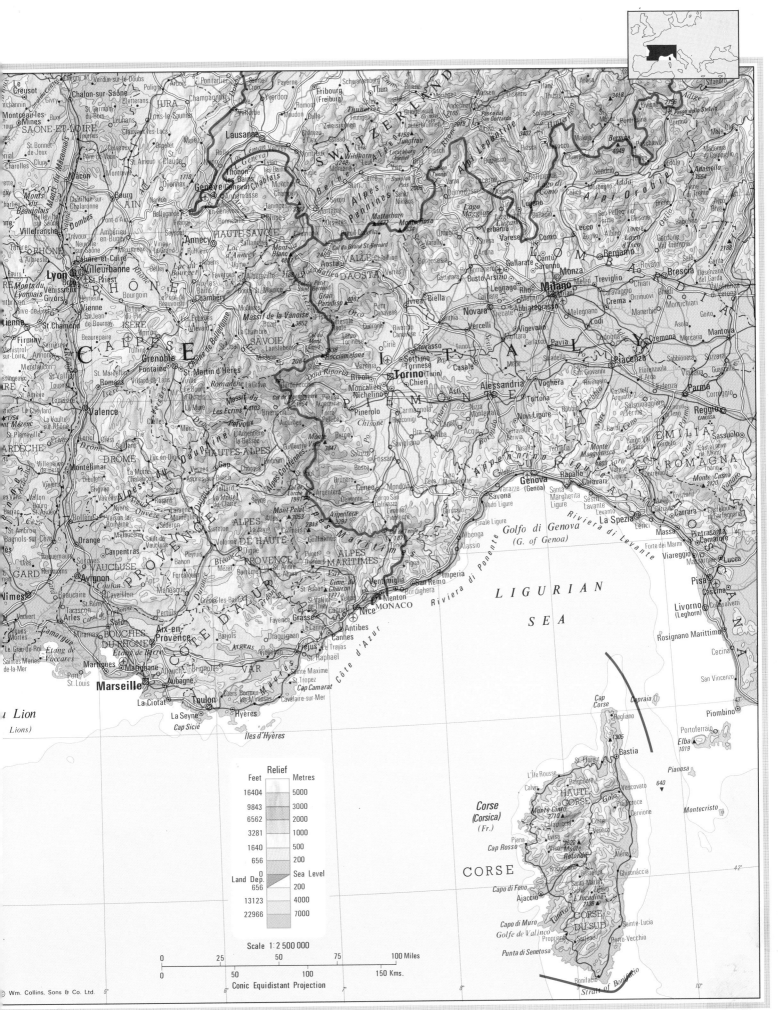

MEDITERRANEAN LANDS

23

IBERIAN PENINSULA

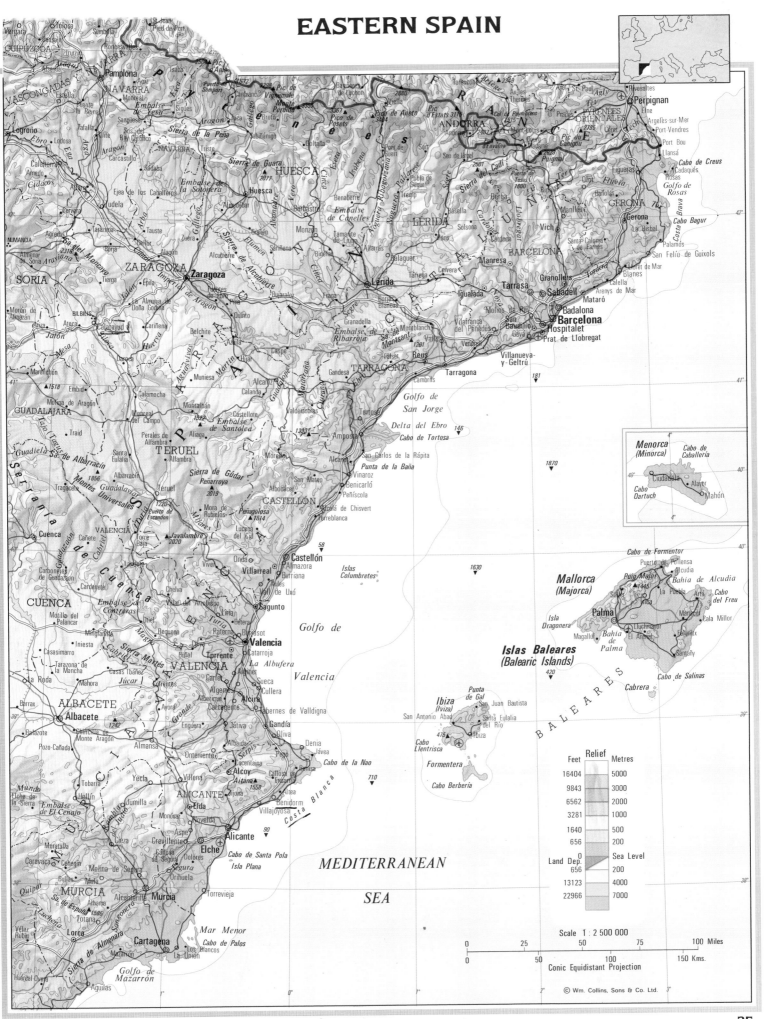

EASTERN SPAIN

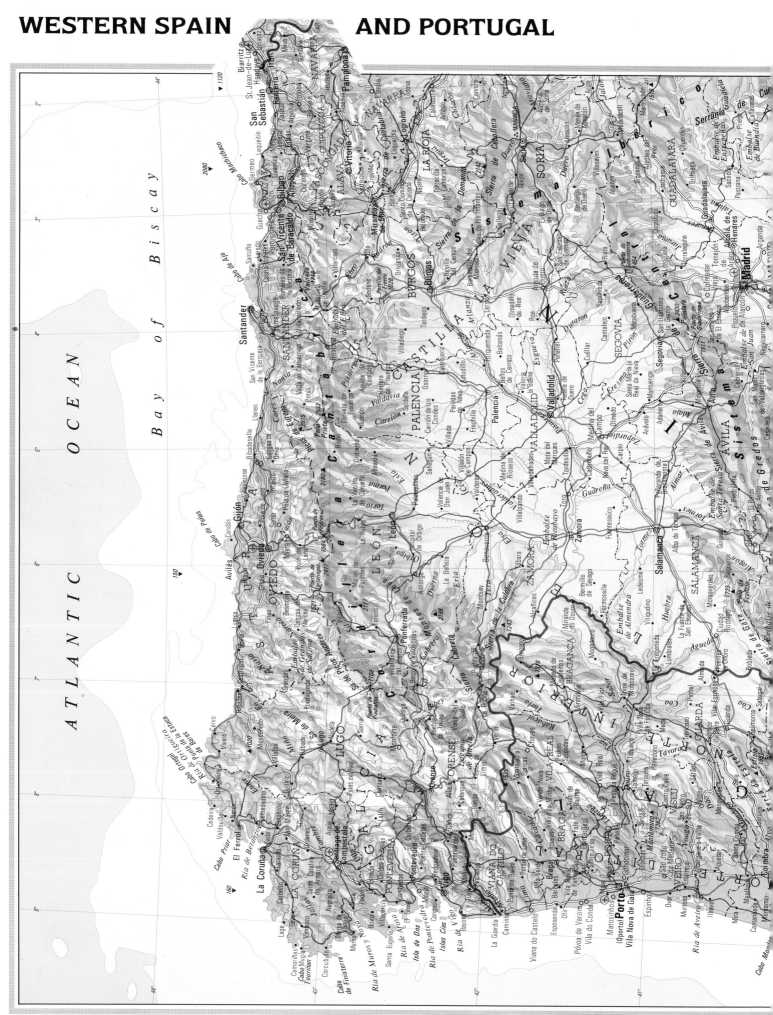

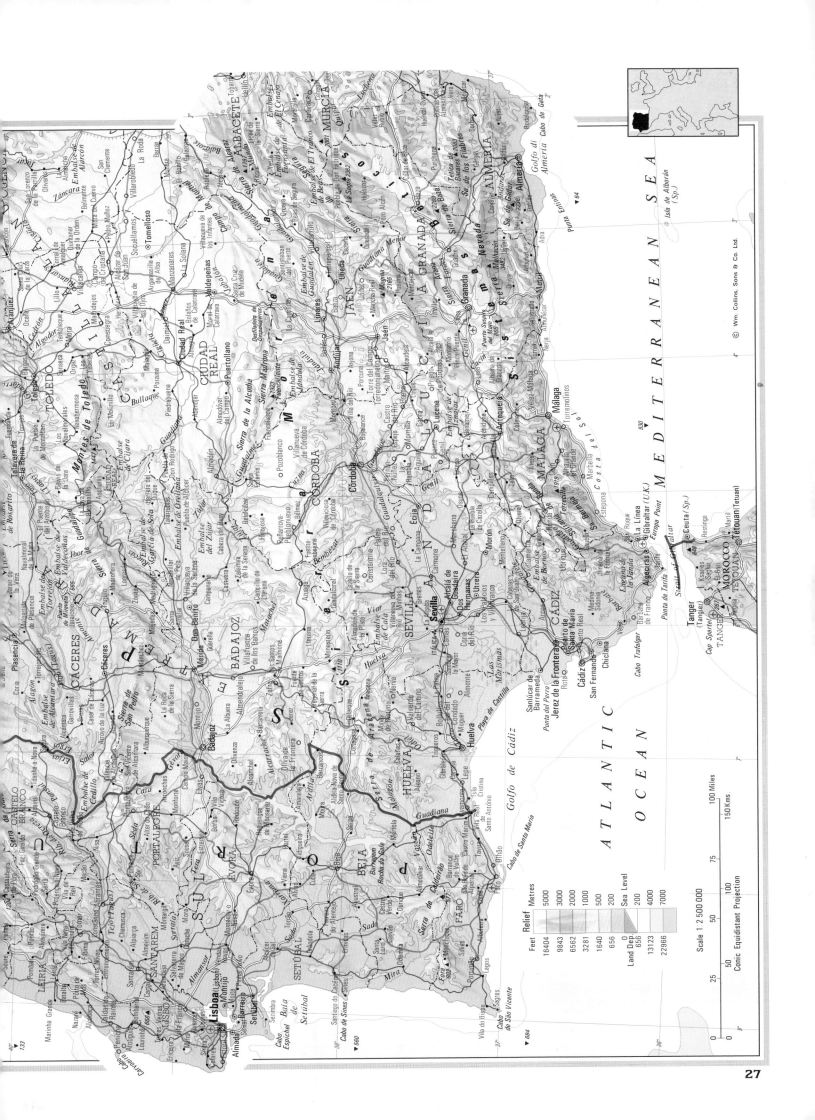

ITALY AND THE BALKANS

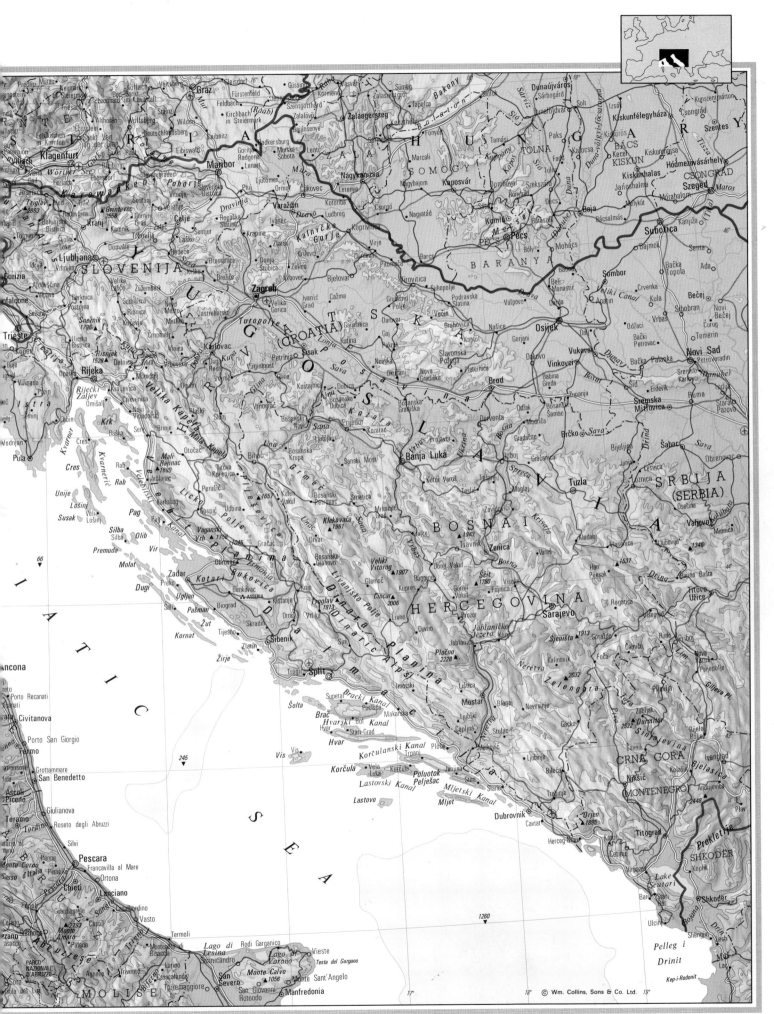

31

GREECE AND ALBANIA

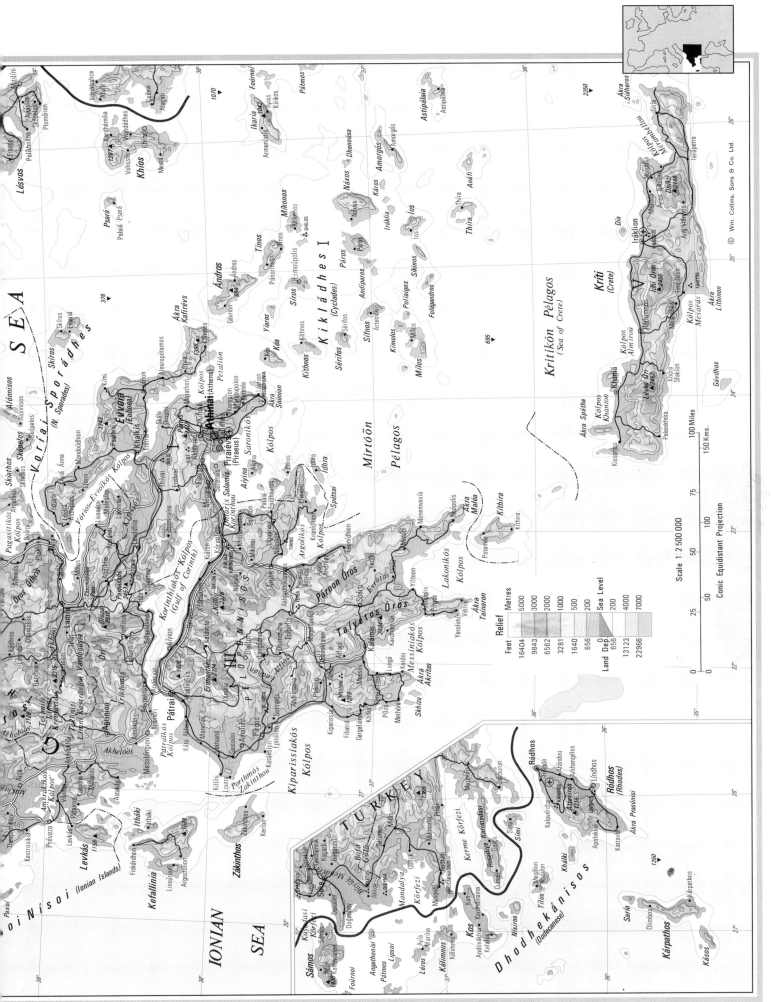

CENTRAL EUROPE

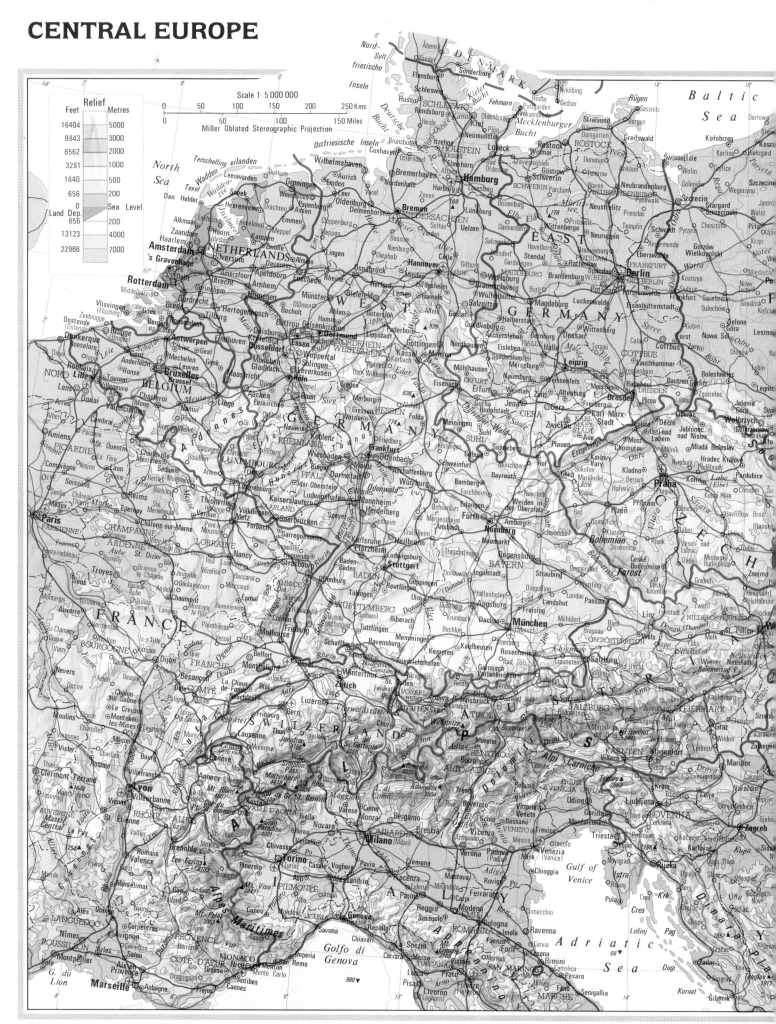

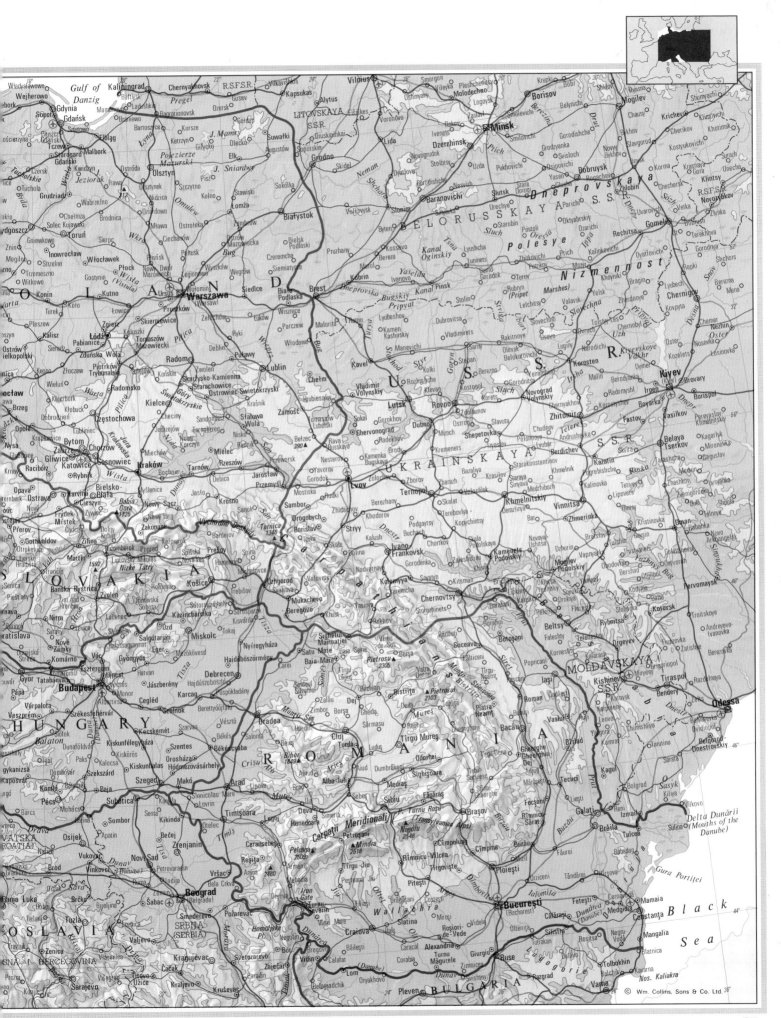

GERMANY AND SWITZERLAND

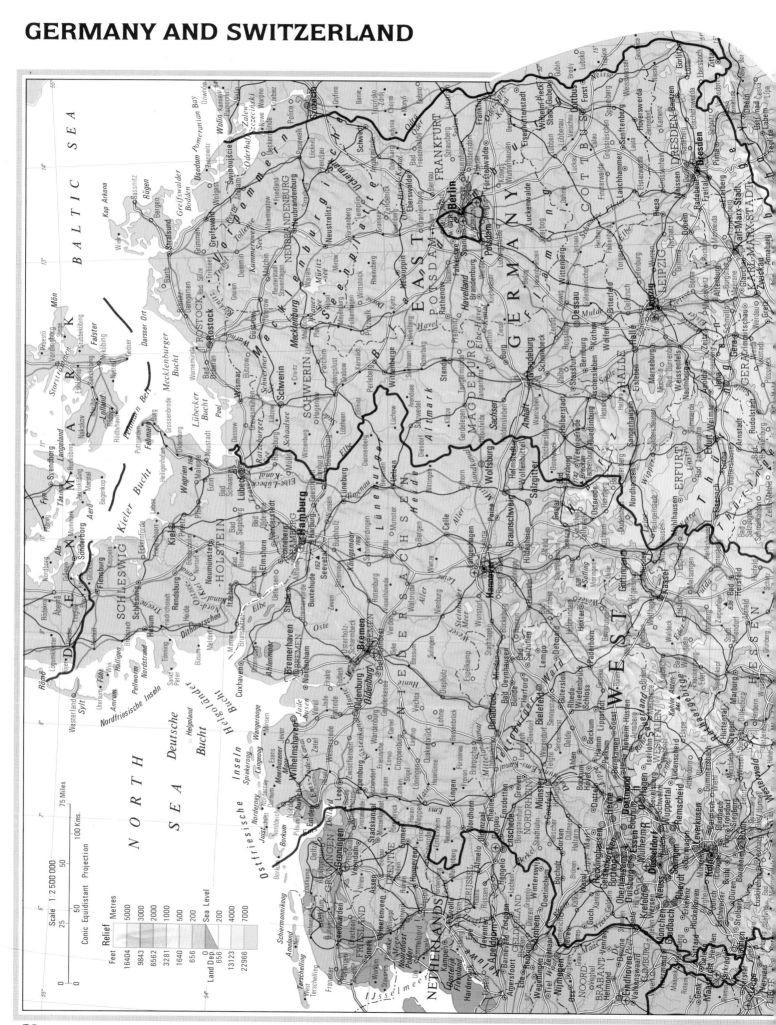

39

SCANDINAVIA AND BALTIC LANDS

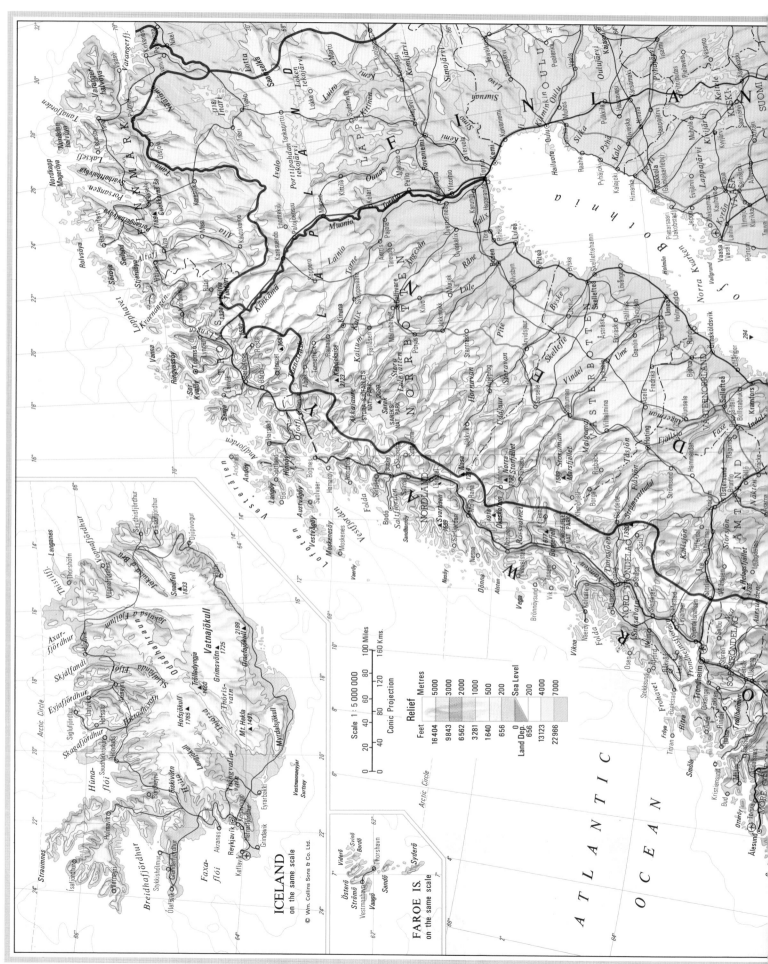

ICELAND
on the same scale

© Wm. Collins Sons & Co. Ltd.

FAROE IS.
on the same scale

Scale 1 : 5 000 000
Conic Projection

Relief

Feet	Metres
16 404	5000
9843	3000
6562	2000
3281	1000
1640	500
656	200
	Sea Level
Land Dep.	200
656	13123	4000
	22986	7000

SOUTHERN SCANDINAVIA

Relief

Feet		Metres
16 404		5000
9843		3000
6562		2000
3281		1000
1640		500
656		200
0		Sea Level
Land Dep.		
656		200
13 123		4000
22 966		7000

Scale 1 : 2 500 000

0	25	50	75	100 Miles
0	50	100		150 Kms.

Conic Equidistant Projection

© Wm. Collins Sons & Co. Ltd.

U.S.S.R. IN EUROPE

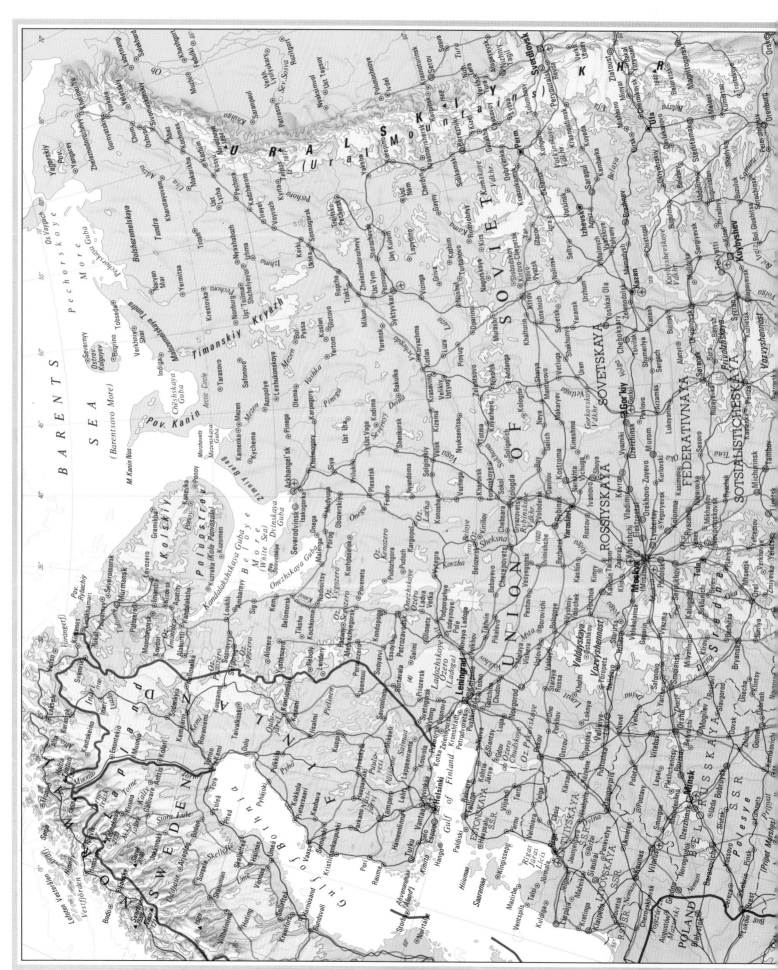

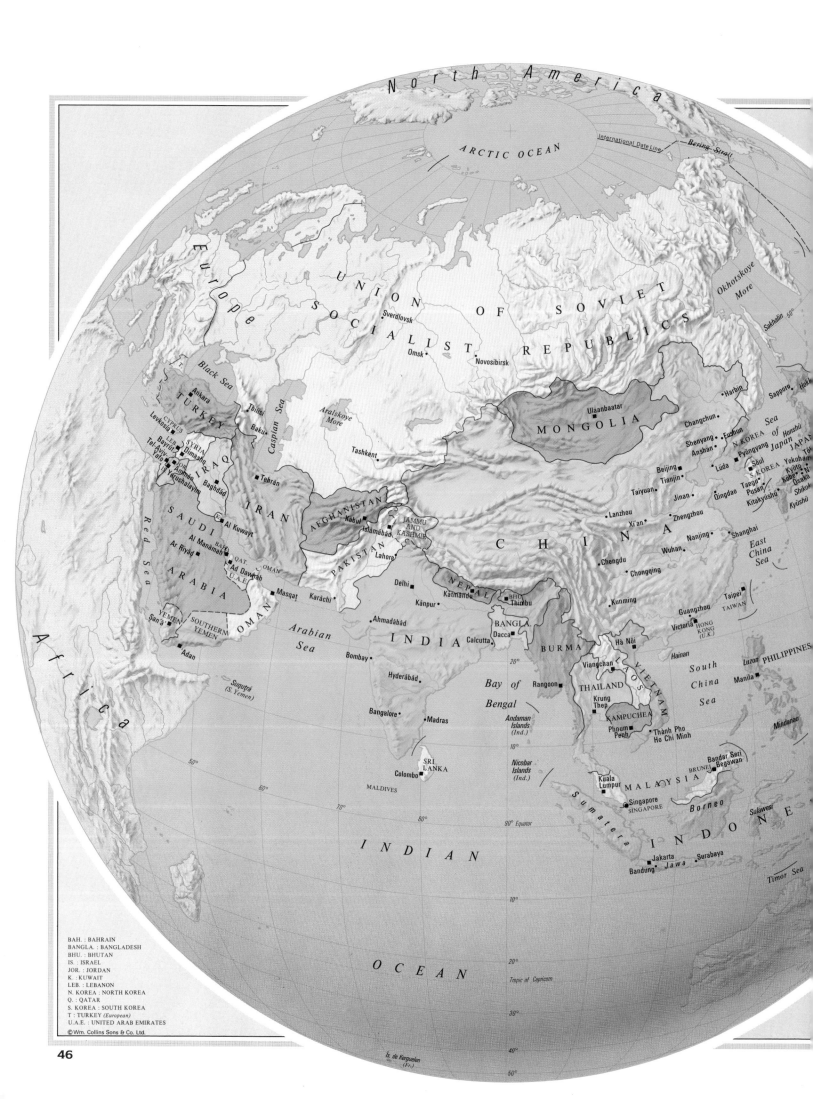

North America

ARCTIC OCEAN

International Date Line

Bering Strait

Europe

UNION OF SOVIET

SOCIALIST REPUBLICS

Okhotskoye More

Sakhalin

50°

Black Sea

Sverdlovsk

Omsk

Novosibirsk

Ankara

TURKEY

Tbilisi

Aralskoye More

Harbin

Sapporo

Hok

CYPRUS

Levkosia

Baku

Tashkent

Ulaanbaatar

MONGOLIA

Changchun

Fushun

Sea of

Honshū

JAPAN

SYRIA

Dimashq

Shenyang

N.KOREA

Bayrūt

LEB.

Anshan

Pyŏngyang

Tōk

Tel-Aviv

IS.

JOR.

Ammān

Baghdād

Beijing

Lüda

Sŏul

Kyōto

Kōbe

N

Yerushalayim

IRAQ

Tehrān

Tianjin

S.KOREA

Pusan

Shikoku

SAUDI

AFGHANISTAN

Kābul

JAMMU AND KASHMIR

Taiyuan

Jinan

Taegu

Kitakyūshū

Kyūshū

K.

Al Kuwayt

Islāmābād

Lanzhou

Xi'an

Zhengzhou

ARABIA

Al Manāmah

BAH.

QAT.

PAKISTAN

Lahore

CHINA

Nanjing

Shanghai

Ar Riyāḍ

Ad Dawḥah

U.A.E.

OMAN

Delhi

NEPAL

Kātmandu

BHU.

Thimbu

Chengdu

Chongqing

Wuhan

East China Sea

Masqat

Karāchi

Kânpur

Kunming

Guangzhou

Taipei

Red Sea

YEMEN

Ṣanā'

SOUTHERM YEMEN

OMAN

Arabian Sea

Ahmadābād

INDIA

BANGLA.

Calcutta

Dacca

BURMA

Hà Nôi

Hainan

TAIWAN

Victoria

HONG KONG

(U.K.)

PHILIPPINES

Africa

Adan

Suquṭrā

(S. Yemen)

Bombay

Hyderābād

Bay of

Bengal

Rangoon

Viangchan

LAOS

VIETNAM

South China Sea

Luzon

Manila

THAILAND

Krung Thep

Bangalore

Madras

Andaman Islands

(Ind.)

Phnum

Penh

KAMPUCHEA

Thành Pho

Ho Chi Minh

Mindanao

50°

SRI LANKA

Colombo

Nicobar Islands

(Ind.)

Kuala

Lumpur

BRUNEI

Bandar Seri

Begawan

60°

MALDIVES

70°

80°

90° Equator

Singapore

SINGAPORE

MALAYSIA

Borneo

Sulawesi

INDONE

Sumatera

INDIAN

Jakarta

Bandung

Jawa

Surabaya

Timor Sea

10°

OCEAN

20°

Tropic of Capricorn

30°

46

Îs. de Kerguelen

(Fr.)

40°

50°

ASIA

ASIA AND INDIAN OCEAN

INDONESIA

Molucca

Seram (Ceram)
Laut Banda
Buru
Laut Seram
Sulawesi (Celebes)

Timor

Flores
Sumba
Kupang
8453

Balikpapan
Ujung Pandang
Banjarmasin

Borneo

Kalimantan

Kuching

MALAYSIA

Singapore
Kuala Lumpur

Medan
Banda Aceh
Sumatera (Sumatra)
Kep. Mentawai
Padang
Jambi
Palembang
Telukbetung

Jakarta
Bandung
Semarang
Surabaya
Malang
Jawa (Java)
Laut Jawa

7352
Carpenter Ridge

of Malacca

MALDIVES

Chagos Archipelago (U.K.)

Maldive Ridge

5243

Seychelles Basin

Madingley Rise

Mascarene Ridge

Mascarene Basin

Mascarene Is.

Réunion (Fr.)

MADAGASCAR

Antananarivo (Tamanarive)

Comoros

Mozambique Channel

Majunga

Bassas da India

Europa

Tropic of Capricorn

Tromelin

Mauritius Is.

MAURITIUS

Rodrigues

Nazareth Trough

Mascarene Ridge

Mauritius Basin

6400
2152

1603

Durban

Natal Basin

Agulhas Basin

Cape Rise

5716

INDIAN OCEAN

INDIAN MID-OCEAN RIDGE

West Australian Basin

INDIAN OCEAN

Mid-Indian Basin

Ninety-East Ridge

1787

Cocos Is. (Aus.)

Christmas I. (Aus.)
6459

Java Trench
7450

Timor Sea

AUSTRALIA

Melville I.
Darwin
Wyndham
Derby
Port Hedland

Mount Magnet
Geraldton

Perth
Albany

Kalgoorlie
Nullarbor Plain
Great Australian Bight

Alice Springs
Macdonnell Ras.

Adelaide
Port Lincoln
Kangaroo I.

Bass Strait
Tasmania

South Australian Basin

S.W. Australian Ridge

S.E. Indian Basin
6857

1011

South-East Indian Ridge

2719

Indian Ridge

South-West Indian Ridge

I. Amsterdam (Fr.)
I. St. Paul (Fr.)

Kerguelen Basin

5605

5441

Is. de Kerguelen (Fr.)

Kerguelen-Gaussberg Ridge

Heard I. (Aus.)
188

Crozet Ridge
Is. Crozet (Fr.)

Prince Edward Ridge
Prince Edward Is. (R.S.A.)

Eastern Indian-Antarctic Basin

Indian-Antarctic Ridge
5565

Atlantic-Indian-Antarctic Basin

Antarctic Circle

Antarctica

Scale 1 : 45 000 000

Lambert Azimuthal Equal Area Projection

0   400   800   1200 Miles
0   400   800 1200 1600 2000 Kms.

© Wm. Collins Sons & Co. Ltd.

49

U.S.S.R.

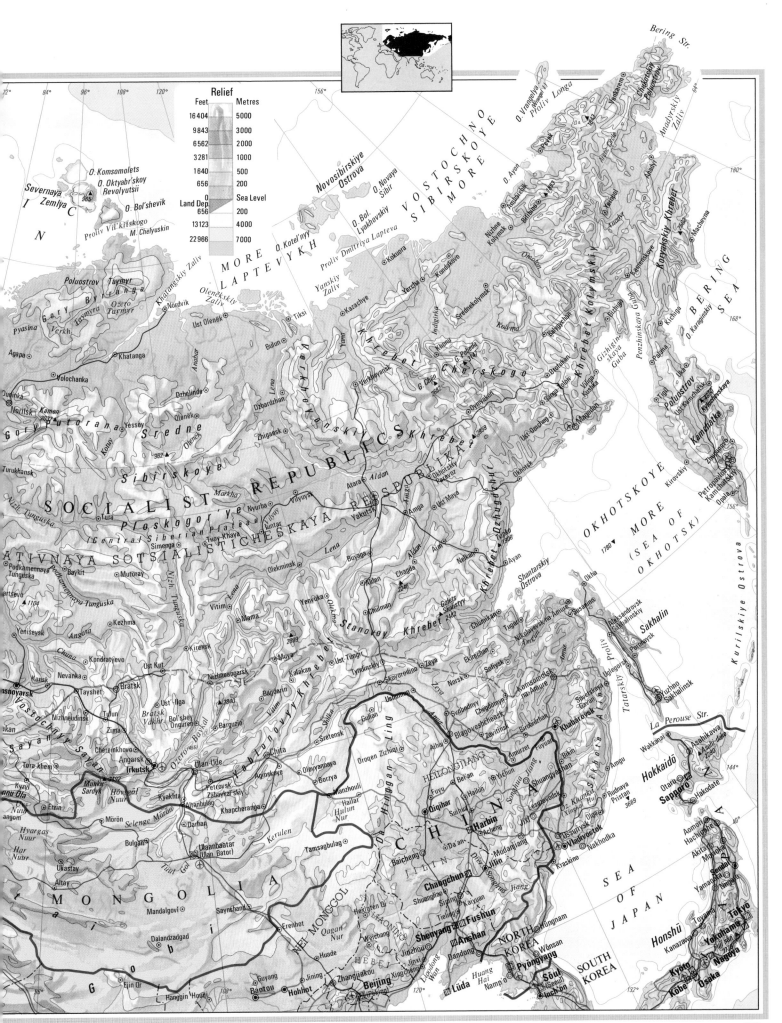

EAST ASIA

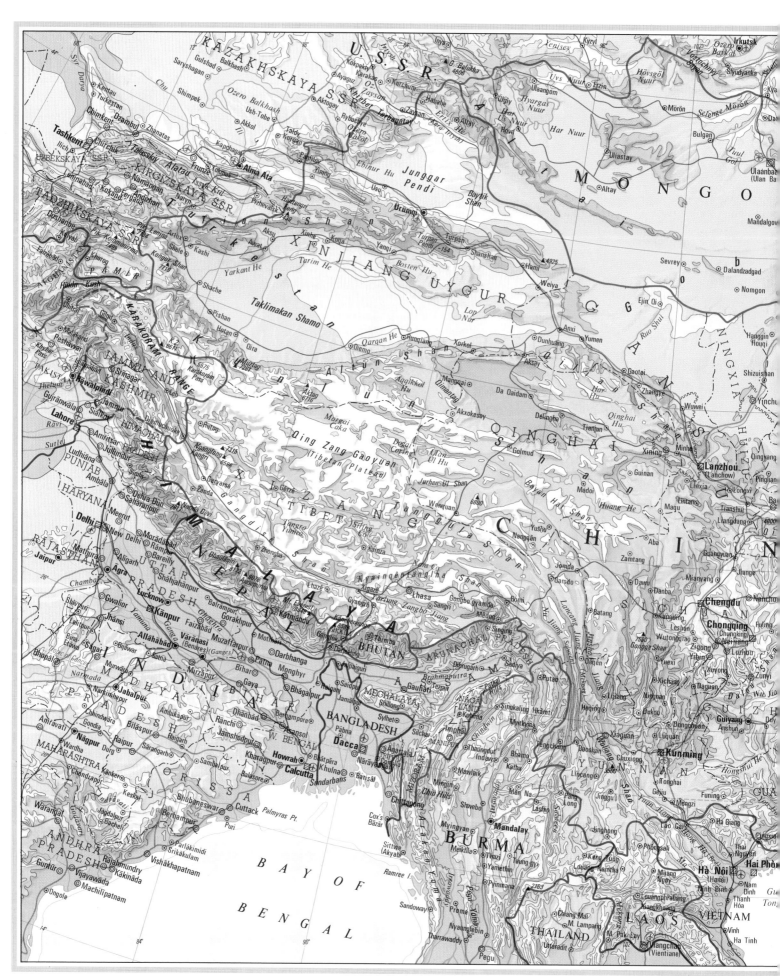

53

EAST CHINA

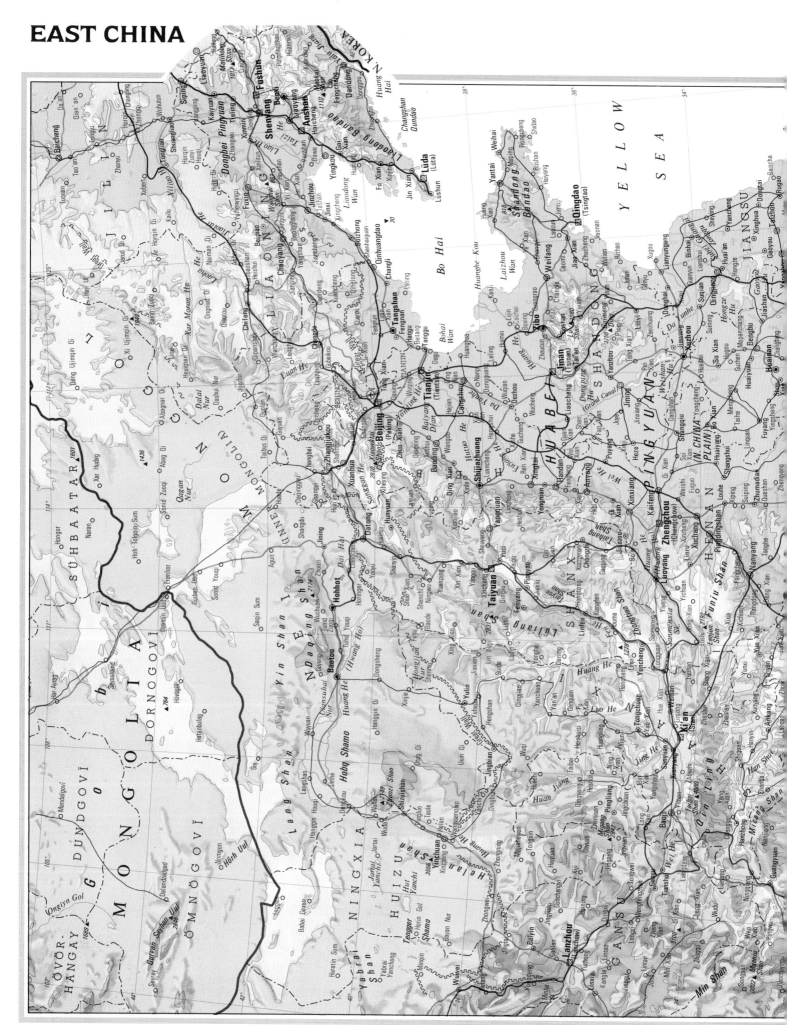

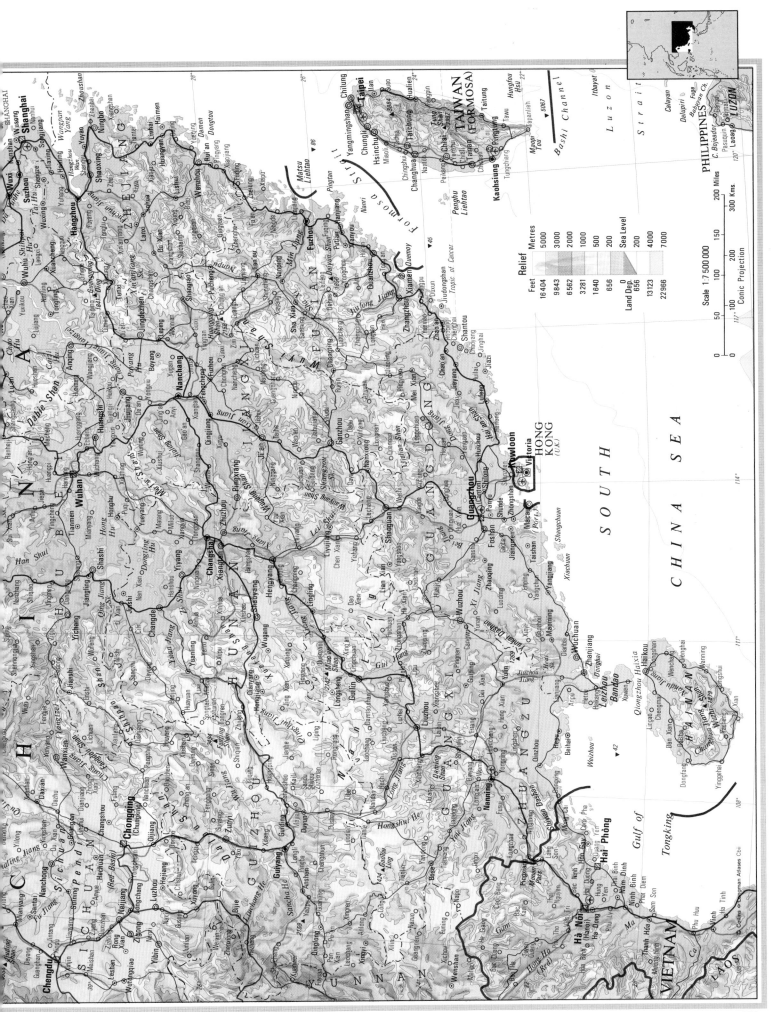

SHANGHAI
Wusong
Kunshan
Shanghai
Wuxi
Suzhou
Hangzhou
ZHEJIANG
Ningbo
Shaoxing
Wenzhou
Fuzhou
FUJIAN
Xiamen
Quanzhou
Matsu
Liehtao
TAIWAN
(FORMOSA)
Taipei
Chilung
Taichung
Hsinchu
Chiai
Tainan
Kaohsiung
Pingtung
Penghu
Liehtao
Formosa Strait
Bashi Channel
Luzon Strait
PHILIPPINES
LUZON
Wuhan
HUBEI
HUNAN
Nanchang
JIANGXI
Changsha
Ganzhou
HONG KONG
(U.K.)
Kowloon
Victoria
Guangzhou
Canton
Macau
(Port.)
GUANGDONG
Shaoguan
Shantou
GUANGXI ZHUANGZU
Nanning
Liuzhou
Guilin
Wuzhou
Xi Jiang
Zhanjiang
Leizhou
Bandao
HAINAN
Haikou
Qiongzhou Haixia
Gulf of
Tongking
SOUTH
CHINA
SEA
Hà Nôi
(Hanoi)
Hai Phòng
VIETNAM
LAOS
Chengdu
SICHUAN
Chongqing
(Chungking)
GUIZHOU
Guiyang
YUNNAN
CHINA

Relief
Metres
Feet

Scale 1:7 500 000
Conic Projection

200 Miles
300 Kms.

55

INDO-CHINA

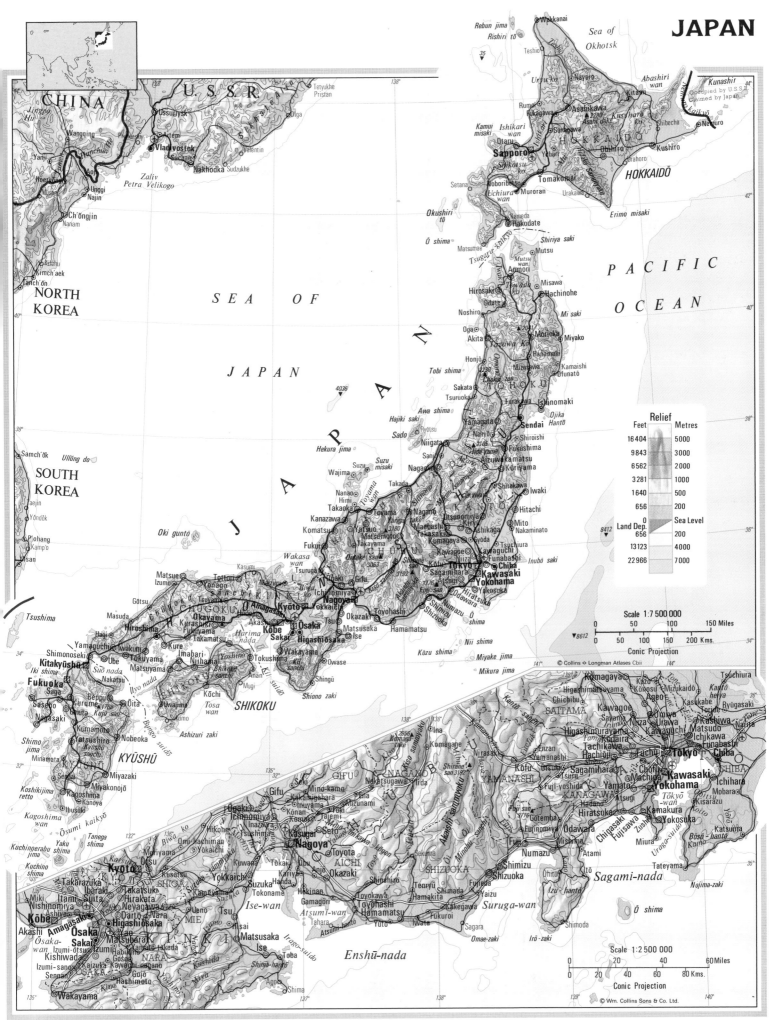

JAPAN

SEA OF OKHOTSK

PACIFIC OCEAN

SEA OF JAPAN

CHINA

U.S.S.R.

NORTH KOREA

SOUTH KOREA

HOKKAIDŌ

KYŪSHŪ

SHIKOKU

Relief

Feet		Metres
16 404		5000
9843		3000
6562		2000
3281		1000
1640		500
656		200
0	Sea Level	0
Land Dep.		
656		200
13123		4000
22 966		7000

Scale 1:7 500 000

0   50   100   150 Miles

0   50   100   150   200 Kms.

Conic Projection

© Collins · Longman Atlases Cbii

Scale 1:2 500 000

0   20   40   60 Miles

0   20   40   60   80 Kms.

Conic Projection

© Wm. Collins Sons & Co. Ltd.

57

SOUTHEAST ASIA

CHINA
Nanning
Guangzhou (Canton)
Kowloon
HONG KONG
Victoria (U.K.)

BURMA
Ramree I.
Sandoway
Prome
Myanaung
Henzada
Insein
Pegu
Thaton
Rangoon
Syriam
Pyapon
Bassein
Irrawaddy Delta
Gulf of Martaban
Moulmein

Great Coco
Little Coco
Preparis

Chiang Mai
M. Chiang Mai
M.Nan
M.Lampang
M.Phrae

Hai Phòng
Hà Nội (Hanoi)
Hai Duong
Nam Dinh
Ninh Binh
Gulf of Tongking

Dongfang
HAINAN
Haikou
Yacheng
Ya Xian

SOUTH CHINA SEA

Paracel Is.

THAILAND
Nakhon Sawan
Nakhon Ratchasima
Ayutthaya
Nakhon Pathom
Krung Thep
Thonburi
Phet Buri
Chon Buri
Bang Saphan

Uttaradit
Nong Khai
Udon Thani
Nakhon Phanom
M. Khon Kaen
Ubon Ratchathani
Surin

LAOS
Louangphrabang
Vientiane
Savannakhét
Pakse

Vinh
Ha Tinh
Dong Hoi
Quang Tri
Hue
Da Nang
Hoi An
Tam Ky
Quang Ngai

VIETNAM
Kontum
Plei ku
Qui Nhon
Binh Dinh
Nha Trang
Cam Ranh
Phan Rang
Phan Thiet

KAMPUCHEA
Kâmpóng Cham
Phnum Pénh
Phnom Penh
Kâmpóng Saôm
Kâmpôt

Da Lat
Loc Ninh
Bien Hoa
Cholon
Thành Pho Ho Chi Minh (Ho Chi Minh City)
My Tho
Vung Tau
Rach Gia
Can Tho
Bac Lieu
Con Son

ANDAMAN SEA
Port Blair
Andaman Islands (India)
Little Andaman

Ten Degree Channel
Car Nicobar
Nicobar Islands (India)
Katchall
Little Nicobar
Great Nicobar

Mergui Archipelago
Tenasserim
Prachuap Khiri Khan
Chumphon
Ranong
Isthmus of Kra
Phangnga
Ko Phuket
Phuket
Krabi
Trang

Ko Phangan
Ko Samui
Surat Thani

Gulf of Thailand

Phu Quoc
Long Xuyen
Quan Long
Mekong Delta
Mui Ca Mau

SOUTH CHINA SEA
Thitu
Nanshan
Spratly

Puerto Princesa
Brookes Poir
Palaw
Balabac
Balabac Str.
Banggi

Thale Luang
Songkhla
Pattani
Narathiwat
Yala
Kota Baharu
Pasir Puteh

Langkawi
Alor Setar
George Town
P. Pinang
Butterworth
Taiping
PENINSULAR MALAYSIA
Kuala Trengganu
Kuala Dungun
Chukai
Kuantan

MALAYSIA

Kudat
Kota Belud
Kinabalu
Kota Kinabalu
Ranau
Labuan
Bandar Seri Begawan
BRUNEI
Miri
Niah
Marudi

Banda Aceh
Sigli
Lhokseumawe
ACEH
Meulaboh
Peureulak
Langsa
Binjai
Medan
Tebingtinggi
Tapaktuan
Pematangsiantar
Tanjungbalai
Telok Anson
Ipoh
Kuala Lipis
Jerantut
Mentakab
Kuala Lumpur
Kelang
Seremban
Melaka
Muar
Batu Pahat
Mersing
Keluang
Johor Bahru

P. Tioman
Kep. Anambas

Bunguran
Bunguran Selatan

Tanjung Datu
Paloh
Kuching
Satikei
Simanggang
Singkawang

Mukah
Bintulu

BORNEO
KALIMANTAN TIMUR
G. Balu
G. Murud
Kapit
Longnawan
Tanjungredeb
G. Niapa
Tarakan
Maratua
Sangkulirang
Muarakaman
Samarinda
Donggal
Bontang
Balikpapan

SUMATERA UTARA
Tanjungtinggi
Tarutung
Sibolga
Danau Toba
Gunungsitoli
Nias
Rantauparapat
Dumai
Bagansiapiapi

Simeule

Kep. Banyak
Singkil
SUMATERA
Bukittinggi
Padangpanjang
Pariaman
Padang
RIAU
Pakanbaru
Rengat
Painan

Kep. Batu
Silogu
Sipura
Siberut Kep.
Mentawai
Pagai Utara
Pagai Selatan
Enggano

Selat Malacca

Sungaipakning
Bahari
SINGAPORE
Bintan
Kep. Riau
Lingga
Singkep

Kampa
Kep. Riau

Palembang
Perabumulih
Lahat
Baturaja
Bengkulu
Kotabumi
Manna
Telukbetung
Tanjungkarang

Jambi
Tempino
Muarabungo
Muaratembesi
JAMBI
SUMATERA SELATAN
Talangbetutu
Muntok
Pangkalpinang
Bangka
Toboali

Tanjungpandan
Belitung

Sukadana
Ketapang
Matua
Sukaraja
Kumai
Sampit
KALIMANTAN TENGAH
Palangkaraya
Kandangan
Amuntai
Martapura
Banjarmasin
Muaratewe
Kualakapuas
KALIMANTAN SELATAN

Pontianak
KALIMANTAN BARAT
Sintang
Nangapinoh
Pegunungan Schwaner
Tayan
Maya

INDONESIA

LAUT JAWA (JAVA SEA)
Tanjung Puting
Tanjung Selatan
Laut

Ujung Pandang
Sungguminasa

Pinrang
Parepare
Kep. Kangean
Madura
Pamekasan

Serang
Jakarta
Bogor
Bandung
Cirebon
Tegal
Pekalongan
Semarang
Rembang
Muryo
Kudus
JAWA TENGAH
Magelang
Madiun
Surabaya
Pasuruan
Malang
Bawean

Sukabumi
Tasikmalaya
Garut
JAWA BARAT
Cilacap
Surakarta
Yogyakarta
Kediri
Jember
Banyuwangi
BALI
Singaraja

JAWA (JAVA)

Nusa Tenggara (Lesser Sunda)
Denpasar
Mataram
Lombok
Sumbawa
Membero

Selat Sunda
Kalianda

Christmas I. (Austl.)
Java Trench

INDIAN OCEAN

Scale 1:15 000 000
0   100   200   300   400   500 Miles
0   200   400   600   800 Kms.
Bonne Projection
95°   © Collins • Longman Atlases Cbi   100°

Inset Map (top)

JAKARTA

Tanjung Tua
1281 ▲
Tanjung
Cina
Selat Sunda
Anyer Serang JAKARTA Krawang Pamanukan Indramayu Bawean
Labuan Rangkasbitung Jatinegara Cikampek
Pandeglang Purwakarta Cirebon Tegal Pekalongan Muryo 1602 ▲
Tanjung 2019 ▲ Jonggol Cimahi Sumedang Brebes Pemalang Demak Jepara Kudus Kragan Tuban Madura Ketapang Kep.
Cangkuang Labuanratu JAWA BARAT Bandung Kuningan Slamet Pati Blora Rembang Lamongan Gresik Pamekasan Kangean
Kulon Garut Ciamis Purwokerto JAWA TENGAH Semarang Purwodadi Bojonegoro Cepu Jombang SURABAYA Sampang Sumenep
Pameungpeuk Tasikmalaya Kroya Magelang Salatiga Ngawi Madiun Pasuruan Bangil Laut Bali
Cijulang Pangandaran Cilacap Purworejo YOGYAKARTA Surakarta Ponorogo Kediri Malang Probolinggo Bondowoso (Bali Sea)
YOGYAKARTA Pacitan Trenggalek Blitar Tulungagung Mohomeru Situbondo Singaraja Tejakula
JAWA Mohomeru 3676 ▲ TIMUR Banyuwangi Bali Agung
Negara Denpasar
JAWA (JAVA)
Selat Bali
Balikpapang

Scale 1 : 7 500 000
0   50   100   150 Miles
0 50 100 200 Kms.
Mercator Projection
© Collins ◇ Longman Atlases Cbii

Main Map

TAIWAN (FORMOSA)

Batan Is
Luzon Strait
Babuyan Is
C. Engaño
Aparri
Tuguegarao
2928 ▲
LUZON
Ilagan
Baguio Bayombong
Cabanatuan
Quezon City
Manila
San Pablo Daet
PHILIPPINES
Lucena Catanduanes
Napa Virac
Mindoro Legazpi
Burias Irosin
Looc Bulan Catarman
Masbate Calbayog Oras
Panay Roxas Catbalogan Samar
Iloilo Cadiz Ormoc Tacloban Guiuan
Bacolod Cebu Leyte
Negros Bohol Siargao
Tanjay Tagbilaran Surigao
Dumaguete Mindanao Sea Butuan
Dipolog Cagayan de Oro San Juan
Siocon Iligan MINDANAO
Zamboanga Moro Pagadian Davao
Basilan Basilan Lebak Piang Mati
Jolo Jolo General Santos
Sulu Arch.

Philippine

Cape Johnson
Depth 10497 ▼

Dinagat

Davao Trench

PACIFIC

OCEAN

Nero Deep
37 ▼

Challenger Depth
11034 ▼

Yap

Gaferut

Faraulep

Pigailoe

Sorol Lamotrek

Ifalik

BELAU Koror Eauripik

Caroline Islands
(U.S. Trust Territory)

Sonsorol

Merir

Tobi Helen Reef

Kep.
Mapia

Equator

Relief

Feet	Metres
16 404	5000
9843	3000
6562	1000
3281	500
1640	200
656	Sea Level
0	
Land Dep.	200
656	4000
13123	7000
22966	

CELEBES SEA

Karakelong Bulu
Tahuna Kep. Talaud
Sangihe
Siau Kep. Sangihe
Manado Sopi Morotai
Kema Tondano Tobelo
2207 ▲ Belang Akelamo
Kuandang Jailolo Halmahera
Gorontalo 1970 ▲ Ternate Soasiu Weda
Laut Maluku (Molucca Sea) Labuha
Kep. Togian Wosi
Poso Pot Waigeo Wakre
Tokala Tuli Bacan Sorong Klamono Arfak 3000 ▲
Peleng Taliabu Obi Sesepe Lenmalu Misoöl Jazirah Doberai (Vogelkop)
Teluk Tolo Kep. Sula LAUT SERAM (CERAM SEA) Kokas Teluk Berau Inanwatan Wasian
Manui Buaja Wahai Bula Faktak Weri Kaimana
Kendari Wamsasi Namlea Seram (Ceram) Tum Adi Wanapiri
Kolaka Buru Ambon Kamana Kokonau
Raha MALUKU Banda
Wowoni Kep. Kai
Muna Butung Kep. Tukangbesi Kep. Aru Dobo Wokam
Kabaena Baubau LAUT BANDA (BANDA SEA) Kobroör Kep. Aru Rebi Trangan
Kabia
FLORES Nila Teun Kep. Tanimbar
(FLORES SEA) Damar Tepa Yamdena Saumlaki Selaru
Wetar Wesiri Romang Kep. Babar Sermata
Labao Kalabahi Tutuala Kep. Leti
NUSA TENGGARA Alor Dili Viqueque
Maumere TIMOR TIMUR Atapupu
Ende Nikiniki Timor
Laut Sawu (Sawu Sea) Kupang
Sawu Roti

MANOKWARI Korim Kep. Schouten
Biak Bosnik
Warkopi Mokmer
Yapen Serui Sarmi Ansudu
Pegunungan Van Rees Jayapura Vanimo
Teluk Cendrawasih Mamberamo Taritatu Dagua Aitape Wewak
IRIAN JAYA Pegunungan Maoke Sepik Mapik Angoram Bogia
Pegunungan Sudirman Pegunungan Jayawijaya Puncak Jaya 5030 ▲ PAPUA NEW GUINEA Wabag Mt. Hagen Goroka
Puncak Jaya Pk. Wilhelm 4763 ▲ Mendi Mt. Wilhelm Kainantu
Mindiptana NEW GUINEA GUINEA Tanahmerah Lake Murray Kikori Baimuru
Kepi Mappi Digul Fly Aramia Kerema
Pulau Yos Sudarsa (Kolepom) Kimaän Okaba Kikori Kerema
Tanjung Vals Merauke Sebidiro Daru Gulf of Papua
Mulgrave I. Banks I. Port Moresby Kila Kila
Torres Str. Thursday I. Pogomajua
C. York
Prince of Wales I.

ARAFURA SEA

Coral Sea

Manus
Lorengau
Admiralty Is
Karkar I.
Bismarck Sea
Madang
Huon Pen.
Finschhafen
Morobe

SOUTH ASIA

© Collins ◇ Longman Atlases Cbi

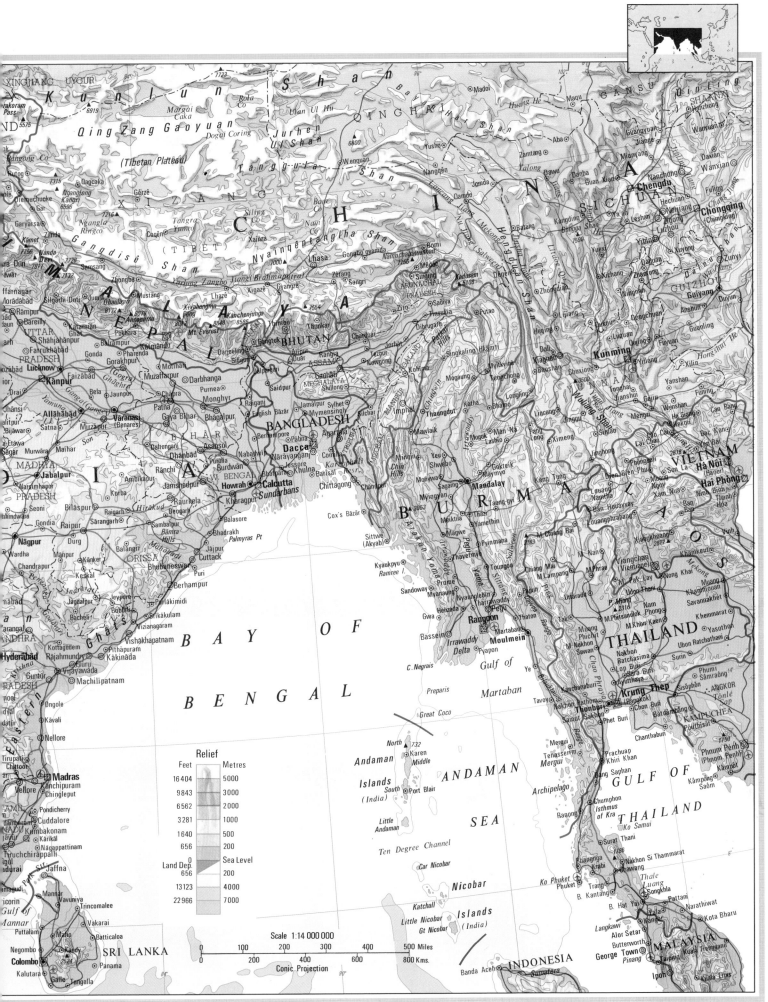

NORTHERN INDIA, PAKISTAN AND BANGLADESH

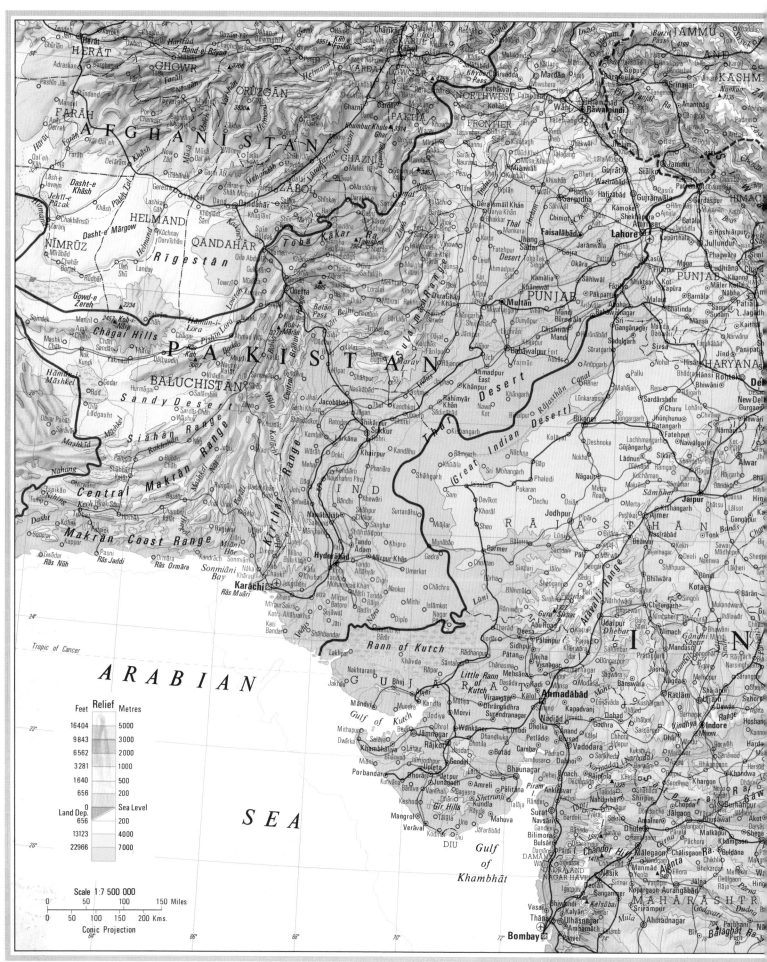

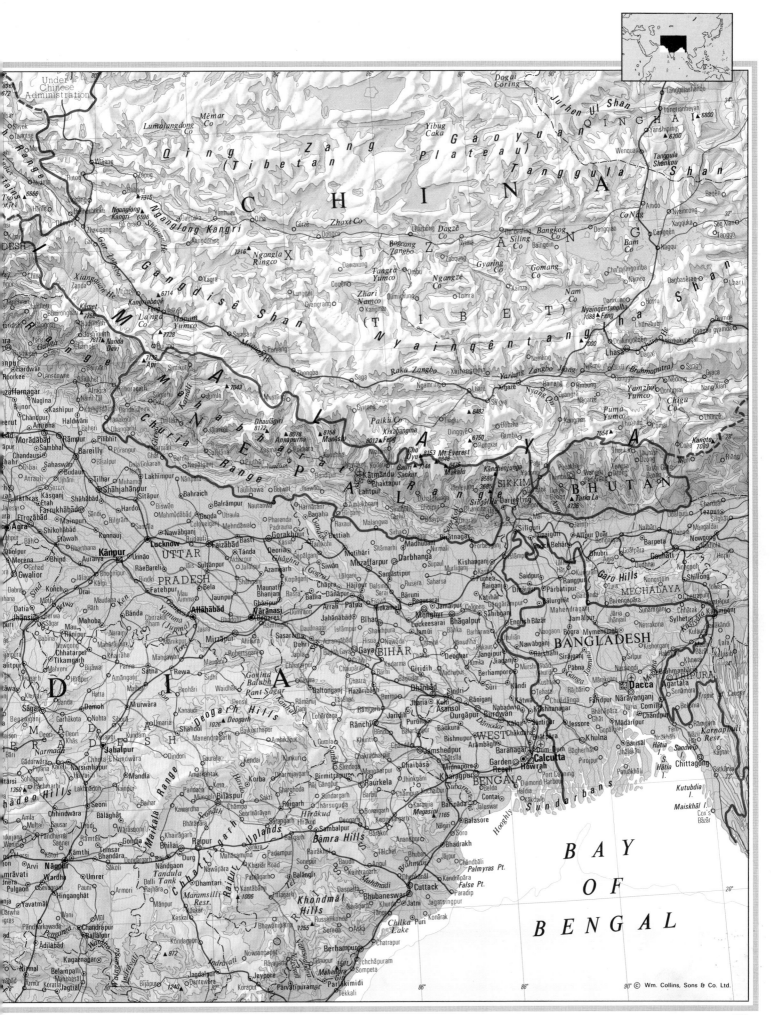

SOUTHWEST ASIA

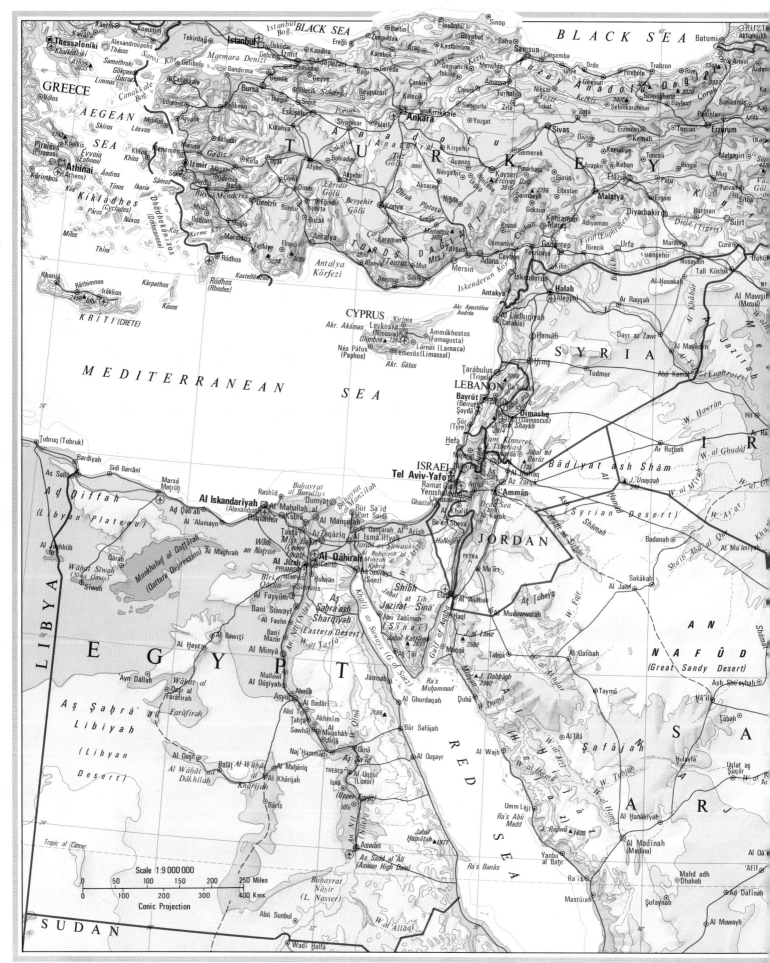

Scale 1:9 000 000

0	50	100	150	200	250 Miles

0	100	200	300	400 Kms.

Conic Projection

THE LEVANT

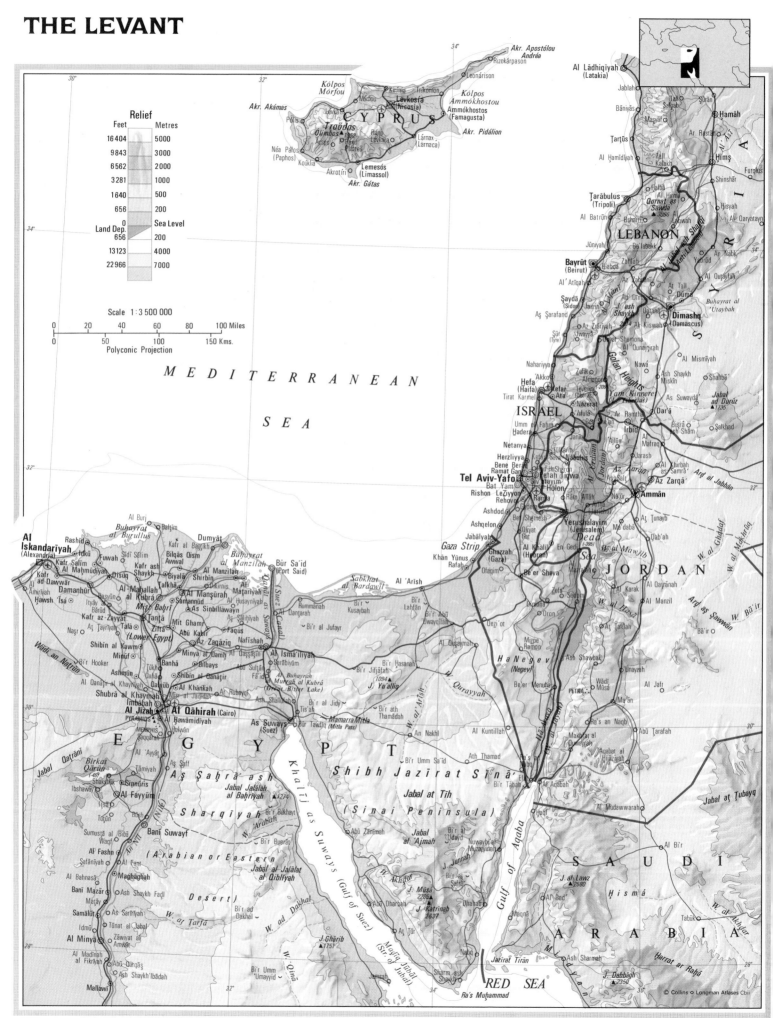

THE HOLY LAND

Scale 1:1 000 000

© Wm. Collins, Sons & Co. Ltd.

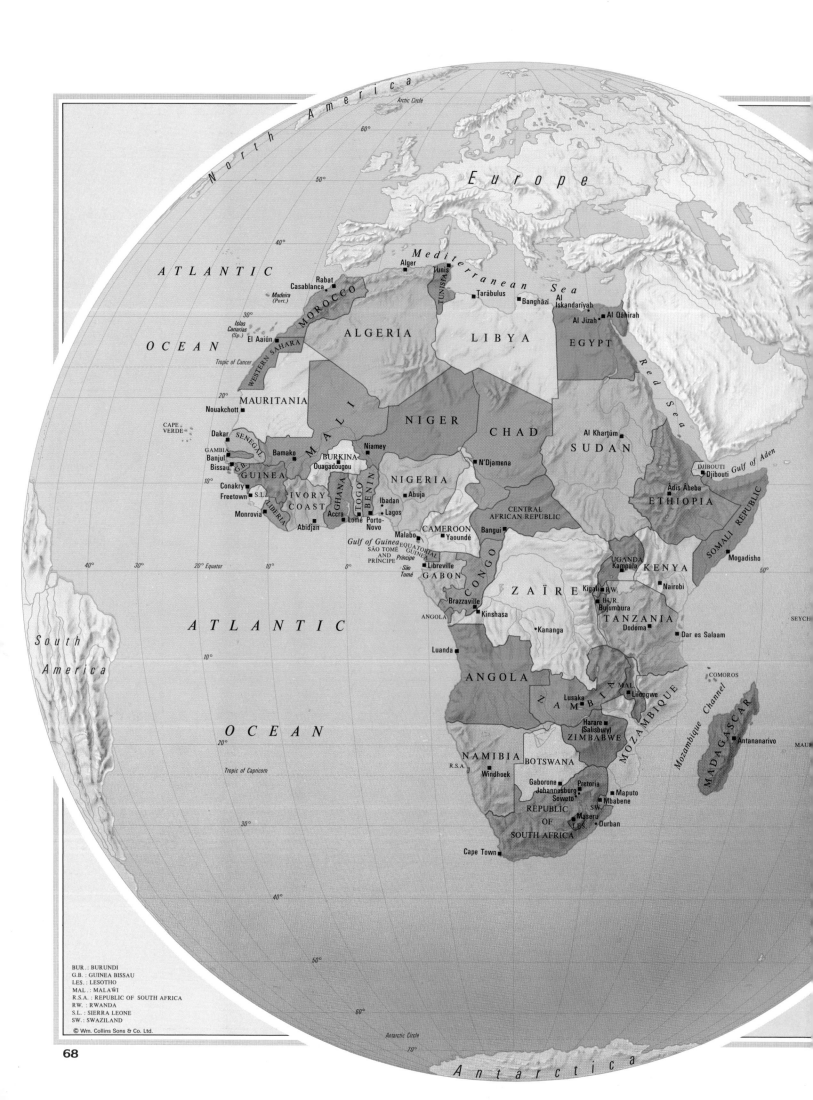

North America

Arctic Circle

60°

50°

Europe

ATLANTIC

40°

Mediterranean Sea

Alger

Tunis

TUNISIA

Tarābulus

Banghāzi

Al Iskandariyah

Al Jizah

Al Qāhirah

Rabat

Casablanca

MOROCCO

Madeira
(Port.)

30°

OCEAN

Islas
Canarias
(Sp.)

El Aaiún

Tropic of Cancer

WESTERN SAHARA

ALGERIA

LIBYA

EGYPT

Red Sea

20°

MAURITANIA

Nouakchott

MALI

NIGER

CHAD

SUDAN

Al Khartūm

CAPE
VERDE

Dakar

SENEGAL

Bamako

Niamey

N'Djamena

DJIBOUTI
Djibouti

Gulf of Aden

GAMBIA

Banjul

Bissau

G.B.

BURKINA

Ouagadougou

Ādis Abeba

ETHIOPIA

SOMALI REPUBLIC

GUINEA

NIGERIA

Abuja

CENTRAL
AFRICAN REPUBLIC

Conakry

Freetown

S.L.

IVORY
COAST

GHANA

TOGO

BENIN

Ibadan

Lagos

Mogadisho

Monrovia

LIBERIA

Accra

Lomé

Porto-
Novo

Malabo

CAMEROON

Yaoundé

Bangui

UGANDA

Kampala

KENYA

Nairobi

Gulf of Guinea

EQUATORIAL
GUINEA

SÃO TOMÉ
AND
PRÍNCIPE

Príncipe

São
Tomé

Libreville

GABON

CONGO

ZAÏRE

Kigali

RW.

BUR.

Bujumbura

40°

30°

20°

Equator

10°

0°

Brazzaville

ANGOLA

Kinshasa

TANZANIA

Dodoma

Dar es Salaam

SEYCH

ATLANTIC

Kananga

South

America

10°

Luanda

ANGOLA

ZAMBIA

MAL.

Lilongwe

COMOROS

OCEAN

20°

Tropic of Capricorn

Lusaka

Harare
(Salisbury)

ZIMBABWE

MOZAMBIQUE

Mozambique Channel

MADAGASCAR

Antananarivo

MAUR

NAMIBIA

BOTSWANA

R.S.A.

Windhoek

Gaborone

Johannesburg

Soweto

Pretoria

Maputo

Mbabene

SW.

30°

REPUBLIC
OF
SOUTH AFRICA

Maseru

LES.

Durban

Cape Town

40°

50°

Antarctic Circle

70°

Antarctica

AFRICA

ian
a

70°   80°   90°

INDIAN

OCEAN

AFRICA

ATLANTIC OCEAN

INDIAN OCEAN

Mediterranean Sea

Black Sea

Caspian Sea

RED SEA

Gulf of Guinea

Gulf of Aden

Mozambique Channel

The Gulf

Countries and regions:

FRANCE · SPAIN · PORTUGAL · ITALY · ROMANIA · YUGOSLAVIA · BULGARIA · ALBANIA · GREECE · TURKEY · U.S.S.R. · CYPRUS · LEBANON · SYRIA · ISRAEL · JORDAN · IRAQ · IRAN · KUWAIT · SAUDI ARABIA · UNITED ARAB EMIRATES · QATAR · BAHRAIN · YEMEN · SOUTHERN YEMEN

MOROCCO · WESTERN SAHARA · ALGERIA · TUNISIA · LIBYA · EGYPT · MALTA · MAURITANIA · MALI · NIGER · CHAD · SUDAN · SENEGAL · GAMBIA · GUINEA BISSAU · GUINEA · SIERRA LEONE · LIBERIA · IVORY COAST · BURKINA · GHANA · TOGO · BENIN · NIGERIA · CAMEROON · CENTRAL AFRICAN REPUBLIC · EQUATORIAL GUINEA · SÃO TOMÉ & PRÍNCIPE · GABON · CONGO · ZAÏRE · UGANDA · KENYA · ETHIOPIA · SOMALI REPUBLIC · DJIBOUTI · RWANDA · BURUNDI · TANZANIA · ANGOLA · ZAMBIA · MALAWI · MOZAMBIQUE · ZIMBABWE · NAMIBIA · BOTSWANA · SWAZILAND · LESOTHO · REP. OF SOUTH AFRICA · MADAGASCAR · COMOROS

Selected cities / labels:

Lisboa (Lisbon) · Madrid · Barcelona · Roma (Rome) · Napoli (Naples) · Palermo · Tiranë · Sofiya (Sofia) · Beograd (Belgrade) · Athínai (Athens) · Istanbul · Ankara · Bursa · Izmir · Samsun · Batumi · Yerevan · Tehrān · Halab (Aleppo) · Bayrūt · Dimashq (Damascus) · Baghdād · Esfahān · Yerushalayim · Ammān · Al Iskandarīyah (Alexandria) · Al Qāhirah (Cairo) · Al Jīzah · Ar Riyāḍ (Riyadh) · Al Madīnah (Medina) · Jiddah · Makkah (Mecca) · Ṣanʻā' · Adan · Mogadisho · Casablanca · Rabat · Fès · Meknès · Oran · Alger (Algiers) · Constantine · Annaba · Tunis · Sfax · Tarābulus (Tripoli) · Banghāzī (Benghazi) · Al Bayḍā · Nālūt · Marzūq · Aswān · Dunqulah · Bür Südän · Al Khartūm (Khartoum) · Umm Durmān · Nyala · Al Muglad · Wāw · Asmera · Mesewa · Ādīs Abeba · Djibouti · Berbera · Nouadhibou · Nouakchott · Tidjikdja · Dakar · Banjul · Bissau · Conakry · Freetown · Monrovia · Abidjan · Accra · Lomé · Porto-Novo · Lagos · Kano · Kaduna · Ibadan · Abuja · Enugu · Onitsha · Port Harcourt · Douala · Yaoundé · Bata · Malabo · Libreville · Port Gentil · São Tomé · Brazzaville · Kinshasa · Pointe Noire · Cabinda · Matadi · Kananga · Mbuji Mayi · Kisangani · Bukavu · Kigali · Bujumbura · Kampala · Nairobi · Mombasa · Dodoma · Dar es Salaam · Zanzibar · Luanda · Lobito · Benguela · Lubango · Lusaka · Lilongwe · Blantyre · Harare · Bulawayo · Maputo · Beira · Windhoek · Gaborone · Pretoria · Johannesburg · Soweto · Maseru · Mbabane · Durban · Cape Town (Kaapstad) · Port Elizabeth · East London · Kimberley · Bloemfontein · Antananarivo (Tananarive)

Physical features:

Atlas Mts · Sahara · Ahaggar · Tibesti · Libyan Desert · Nubian Desert · L. Chad · L. Nasser (Buhayrat Nāsir) · Niger · Congo Basin · Zaïre · L. Albert · L. Victoria · L. Turkana · Kilimanjaro · Mt Kenya · Mt Elgon · Ruwenzori · L. Tanganyika · L. Malawi · L. Mweru · Kalahari Desert · Namib Desert · Orange · Limpopo · Zambezi · Victoria Falls · C. of Good Hope · C. Agulhas · Madeira (Port.) · Islas Canarias (Sp.) · Tenerife · Sardegna (It.) · Sicilia · Kríti · Corse (Fr.)

Relief

Feet	Metres
16404	5000
9843	3000
6562	2000
3281	1000
1640	500
656	200
0	Sea Level

Land Dep.

656	200
13123	4000
22966	7000

Scale 1:37 000 000

0 200 400 600 800 1000 Miles

0 400 800 1200 1600 Kms.

Lambert Azimuthal Equal Area Projection

© Collins ◇ Longman Atlases Cbi

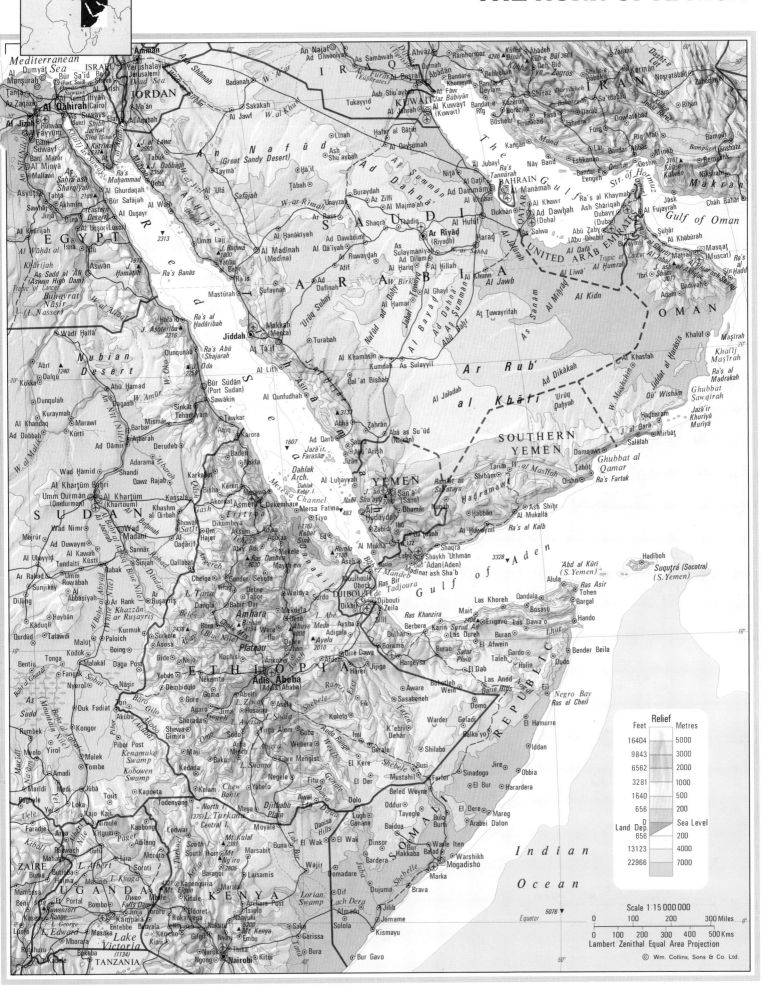

THE HORN OF AFRICA

71

NILE VALLEY

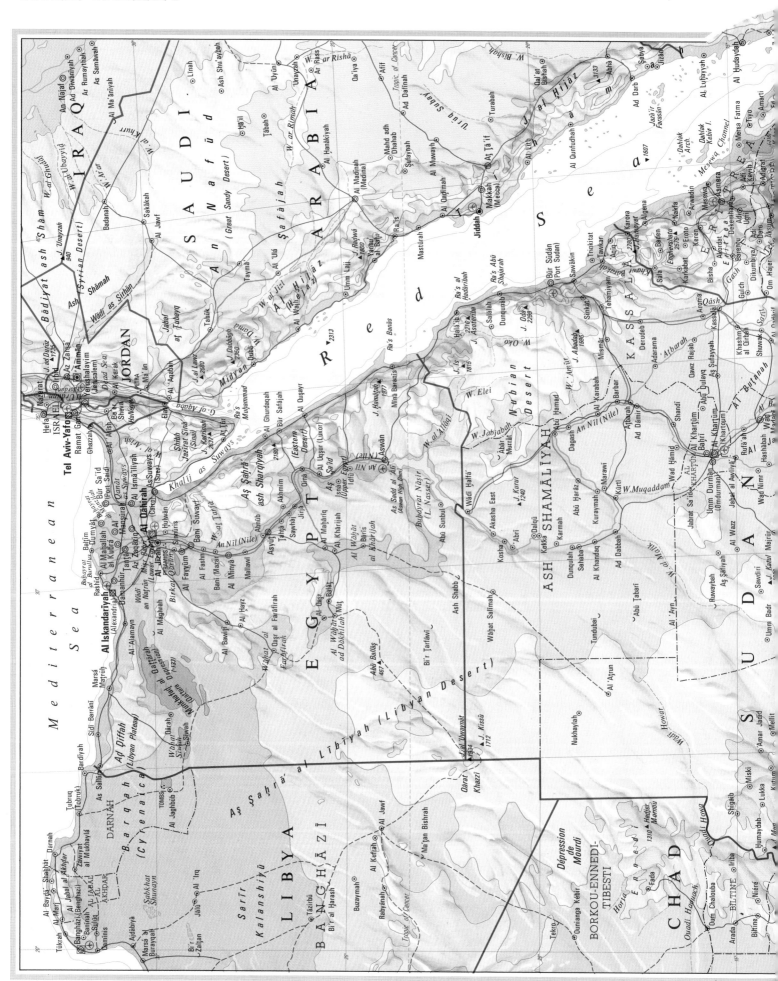

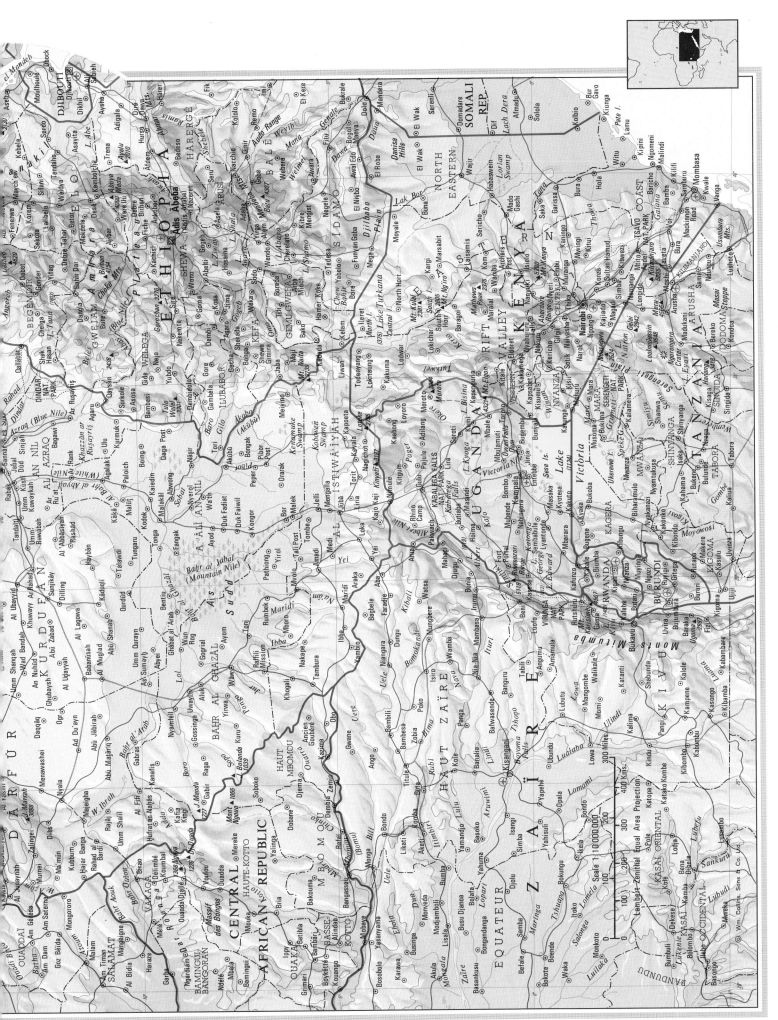

73

NORTHWEST AFRICA

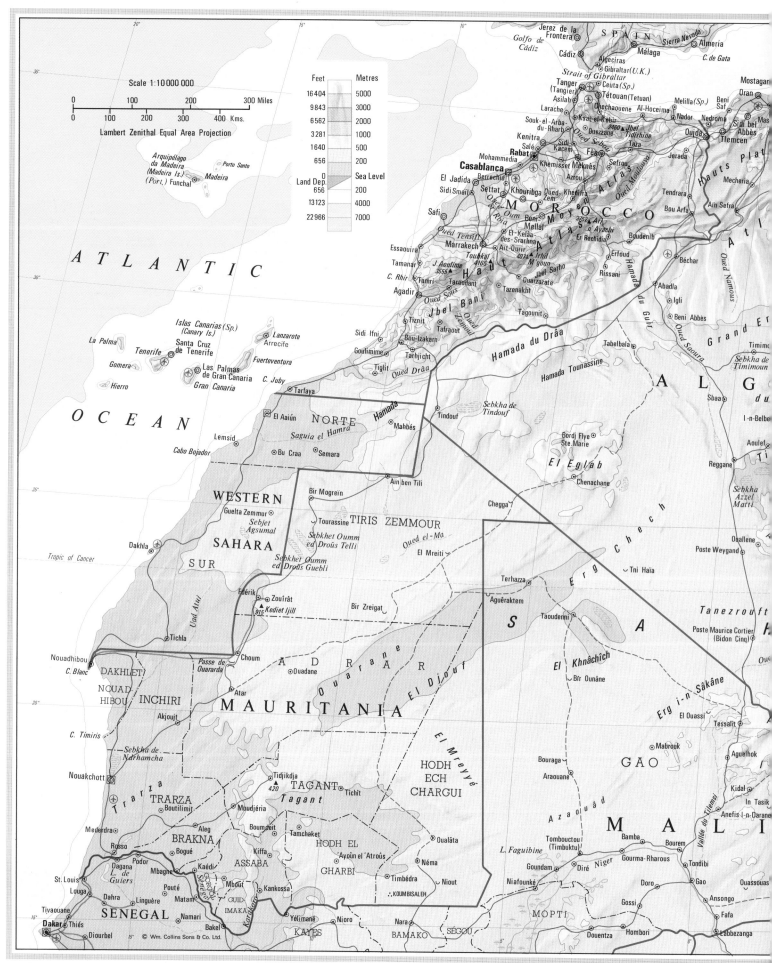

ATLANTIC

OCEAN

Scale 1:10 000 000

0   100   200   300 Miles
0 100 200 300 400 Kms.
Lambert Zenithal Equal Area Projection

Feet	Metres
16 404	5000
9843	3000
6562	2000
3281	1000
1640	500
656	200
0	Sea Level
Land Dep.	
656	200
13 123	4000
22 966	7000

Arquipélago da Madeira (Madeira Is.) (Port.) Funchal   Porto Santo   Madeira

Islas Canarias (Sp.) (Canary Is.)
La Palma   Santa Cruz de Tenerife   Lanzarote Arrecife
Tenerife   Fuerteventura
Gomera   Las Palmas de Gran Canaria   C. Juby
Hierro   Gran Canaria

Tropic of Cancer

SPAIN
Jerez de la Frontera   Sierra Nevada   Almería   C. de Gata
Golfo de Cádiz   Cádiz   Málaga   Mostagan
Algeciras   Gibraltar (U.K.)   Strait of Gibraltar
Tanger (Tangier)   Ceuta (Sp.)   Melilla (Sp.)   Oran
Asilah   Tétouan (Tetuan)   Al-Hoceima   Nador   Beni Saf
Larache   Chechaouene   Nedroma   Sidi bel Abbès
Souk-el-Arba-du-Rharb   Ksar-el-Kebir   Jbel Tidirhine 2460   Taza   Oujda   Tlemcen
Kenitra   Ouezzane   Jerada   Hauts Plat
Salé   Sidi Kacem   Fès   Sefrou   Boudenib
Rabat   Meknès   Azrou   Oued Moulouya   Mecheria
Mohammedia   Khemisset   Ain Sefra
Casablanca   Berrechid   Khouribga   Oued Zem   Kenifra   Tendrara
El Jadida   Settat   Beni Mellal   Bou Arfa
Sidi Smail   Oued Oum er Rbia   El-Kelâa-des-Srarhna   Moyen Atlas   Er Rachidia   Béchar
Safi   Marrakech   Ait-Ourir   Ayachi   Boudenib   Oued Namous
Essaouira   Oued Tensift   Toubkal 4165   M'goun   Jbel Sarho   Abadla   Igli
Tamanar   J. Aoulime 3555   Ouarzazate   Rissani   Beni Abbès
C. Rhir   Tamri   Tazenakht   Erfoud   Grand Er
Agadir   Oued Souss   Tagounit   Hamada du Guir
Jbel Bani   Tiznit   Oued Zemoul   Tabelbala   Timimo
Sidi Ifni   Bou-Izakarn   Hamada du Drâa   Sebkha de Timimoun
Goulimime   Tarhjicht   Hamada Tounassine
Tiglit   Oued Drâa   ALG
Tarfaya   Hamada   Sbaa   I-n-Belber
El Aaiún   NORTE   Tindouf   Sebkha de Tindouf
Lemsid   Saguia el Hamra   Mahbés   Bordj Flye Ste.Marie   Aoulef
Cabo Bojador   Bu Craa   Semara   El Eglab   Reggane
    Ain ben Tili   Chenachane   Sebkha Azzel Matti
WESTERN   Bir Mogrein   Chegga
Guelta Zemmur   Tourassine   TIRIS ZEMMOUR   Erg Chech
SAHARA   Sebjet Agsumal   Oued el-Ma
SUR   Sebkhet Oumm ed Drôus Telli   El Mreiti   Poste Weygand
Dakhla   Sebkhet Oumm ed Drôus Guebli   Tni Haïa
Fdérik   Zouîrât   Terhazza   Erg   Tanezrouft
Tichla   Kediet Ijill 915   Bir Zreigat   Taoudenni   Poste Maurice Cortier (Bidon Cinq)
Nouadhibou   Passe de Ouararda   Choum   A D R A R   S   El Khnâchîch   A H
C. Blanc   DAKHLET   Ouadane   Ouarane   El Djouf   Bîr Ounâne   Erg i-n Sâkâne
NOUAD HIBOU   INCHIRI   Atar   MAURITANIA   Erg i-n-Sâkâne   El Ouassi   Tessalit
Akjoujt   El Mreyyé   Mabrook   Tessalit
C. Timiris   Bouraga   GAO   Aguelhok
Sebkha de Ndrhamcha   HODH ECH CHARGUI   Araouane   Kidal
Nouakchott   Tidjikdja   Azaouâd   In Tasik
Trarza   TAGANT 420   Tichît   Anefis i-n-Daran
TRARZA   Tagant   Tombouctou (Timbuktu)   Bamba   MALI
Boutilimit   Moudjéria   M
Mederdra   Aleg   Boumdeit   Oualâta   L. Faguibine   Bourem
Rosso   BRAKNA   Tamchaket   Gourma-Rharous
Bogué   Kiffa   HODH EL   Néma   Niger   Diré   Gao
Dagana   Podor   ASSABA   Ayoûn el Atroûs   Timbédra   Goundam   Ouassou
St. Louis   L. de Guiers   Kaédi   GHARBI   Nioro   Niafounké   Ansongo
Louga   Mbagne   Mbout   Kankossa   KOUMBISALEH   Doro   Tondibi
Dahra   Pouté   GUID   Yélimané   Nara   Gossi   Fafa
Tivaouane   Matam   IMAKA   Nioro   Vallée du Tilensi
SENEGAL   Namari   Kaïkor   Niout   MOPTI   Douentza   Labbezanga
Dakar   Thiés   Bakel   Ségou   Homberi
Diourbel   Linguère   KAYES   BAMAKO   Hombori
© Wm. Collins Sons & Co. Ltd.

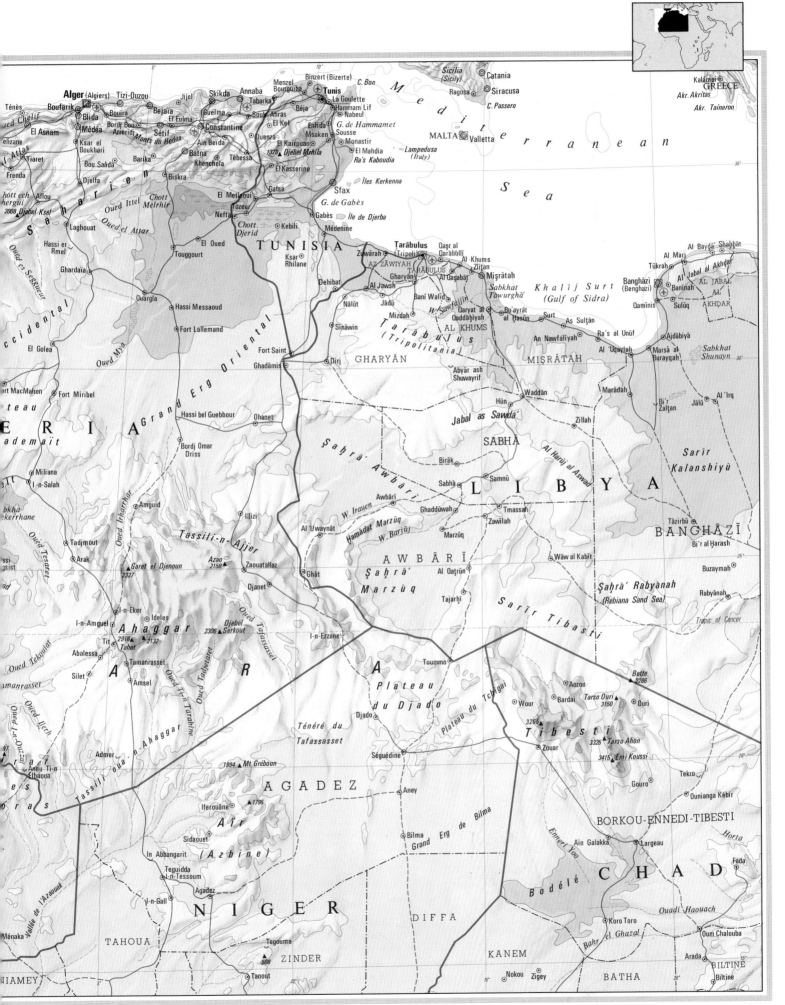

WEST AFRICA

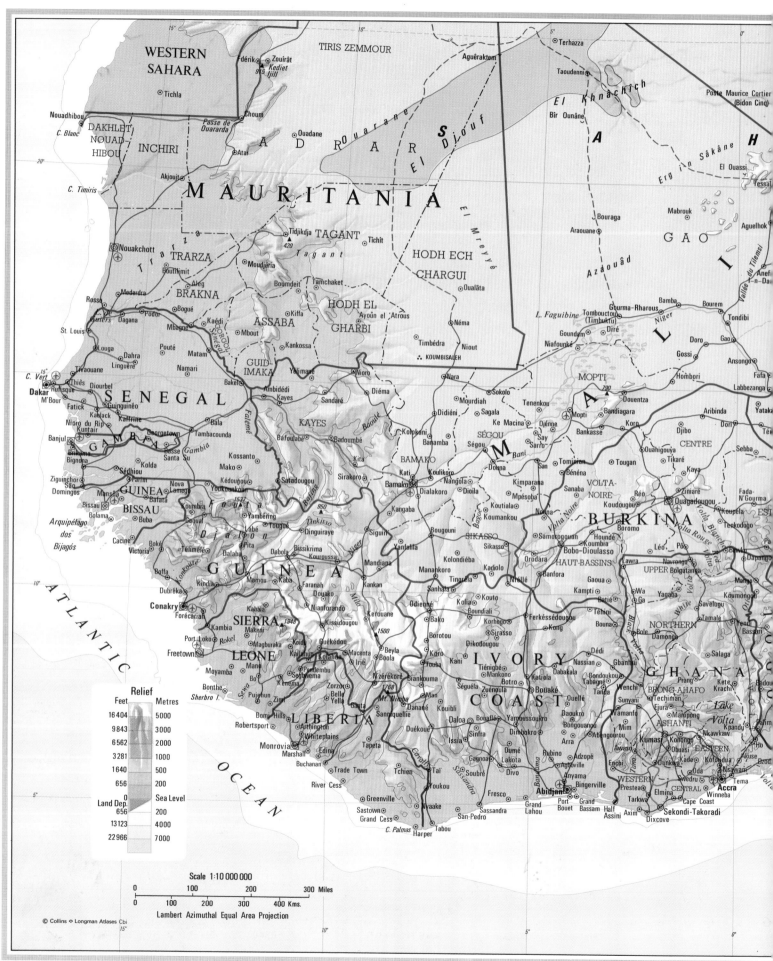

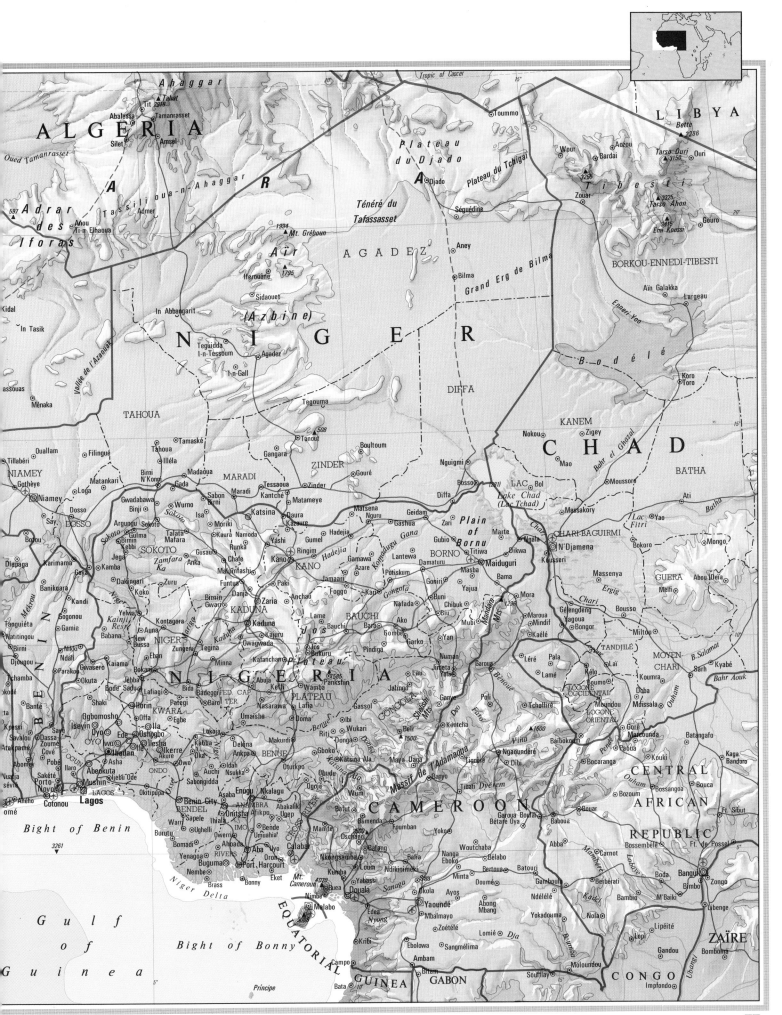

CENTRAL AND EAST AFRICA

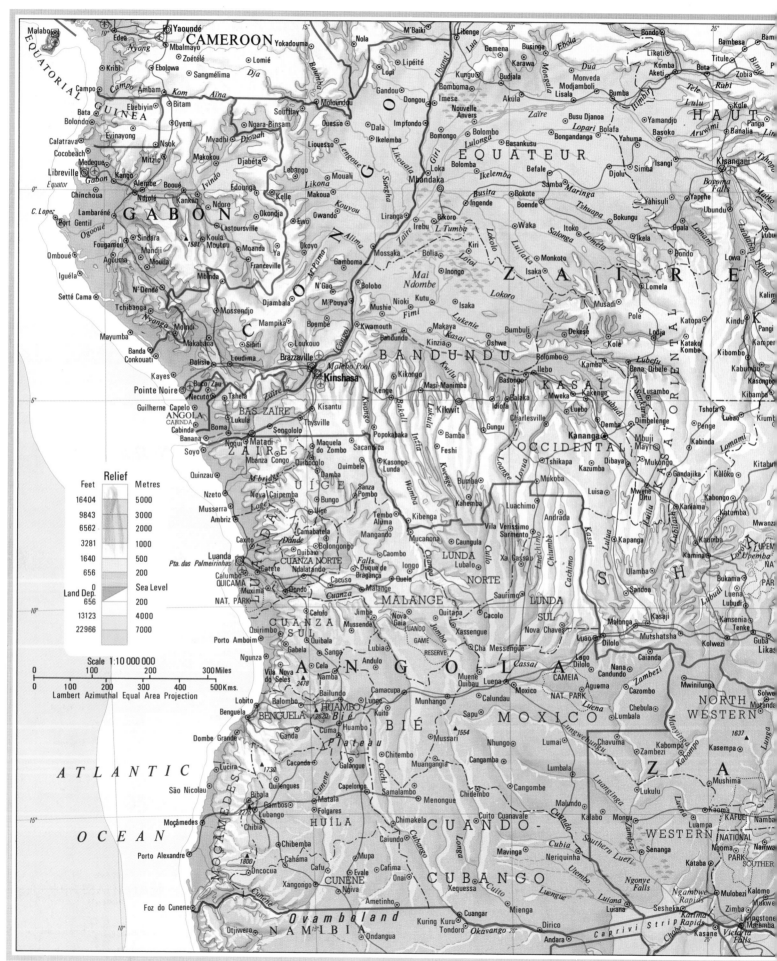

SOUTHERN AFRICA AND MADAGASCAR

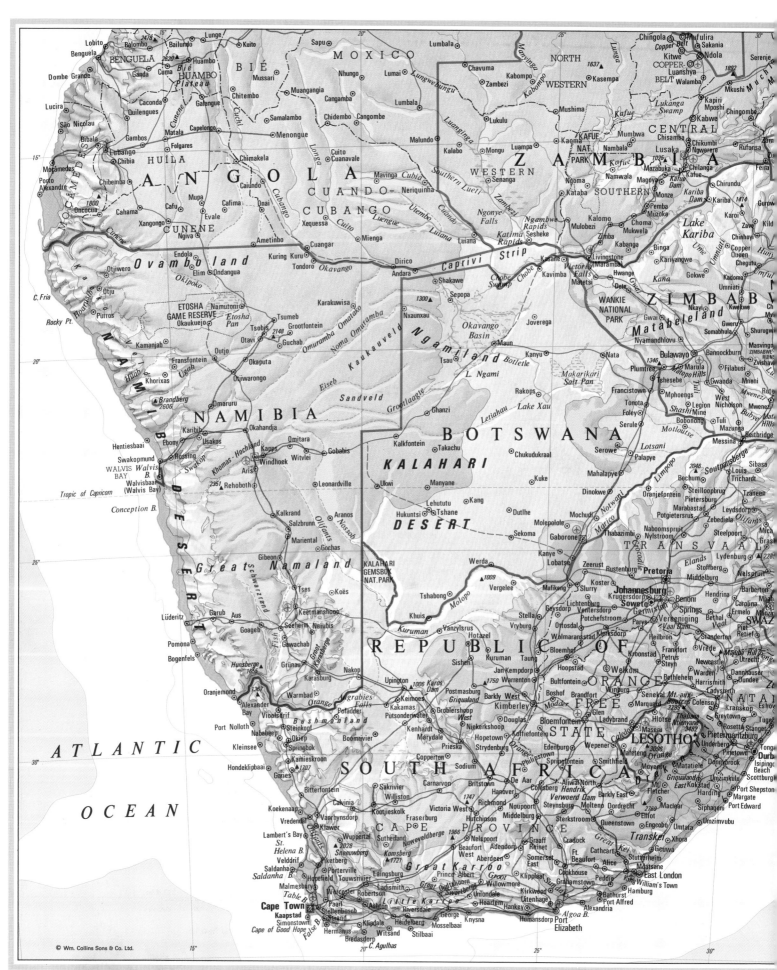

INDIAN

OCEAN

Mozambique Channel

C. d'Ambre
Antsiranana
Nosy Be
Ambilobe
Hell-Ville
Vohimarina
Anorotsangana
Ambanja
Massif de
Tsaratanana
2876
Sambava
Analalava
Bealanana
Antalaha
Antsohihy
Befandriana
Maroantsetra
Mandritsara
Mahajanga
Port-Bergé
Mitsinjo
Mampikony
Mananara
C. Masoala
Soalala
Ambato-Boeni
Tsaratanana
Soanierana-
Ivongo
Besalampy
Marovoay
Maevatanana
Nosy
Boraha
Juan de Nova
Kandreho
Maningory
Ambodifototra
Tambohorano
Morafenoro
Andriba
Fenoarivo
Atsinanana
Maintirano
Fenoarivo
Ankazobe
Anjozorobe
L. Alaotra
Antsalova
Tsiroanomandidy
Arivonimamo
Ambohidratrimo
Anivorano
Vohibinany
Andevoranto
Miarinarivo
Manjakandriana
Soavinandriana
Antananarivo
Moramanga
Belo-sur-Tsiribihina
Miandrivazo
(Tananarive)
Vatomandry
Mandoto
Faratsiho
Ambatolampy
Morondava
Betafo
Antsirabé
Mahanoro
Malaimbandy
Fandriana
Marolambo
Mahabo
Ambatofinandrahana
Ambositra
Nosy-Varika
Mandabe
Ambohimahasoa
Ambohimanga du Sud
Fianarantsoa
Mananjary
Manja
Ifanadiana
Befandriana
Berotoka
Ambalavao
Fort Carnot
Morombe
Ankaramena
Manakara
C. St. Vincent
Ihosy
Vohipeno
Ankazoabo
1761
Ivohibe
Vondrozo
Ihosy
Ranohira
Farafangana
Manombo
Iakoro
Betroka
Vangaindrano
Toliary
Tongobory
Midongy-Sud
Bekily
Tsivory
Benenitra
Bétioky
Manantenina
Ampanihy
Tranoroa
1956
Behara
Androka
Tsihombé
Faradofay
Ambovombe
C. Ste. Marie

MADAGASCAR

Metangula
Maniamba
Namecala
Ancuabe
Nkhotakota
Guerra
Marrupa
Montepuez
Pemba
Kagungu
Lichinga
Balama
Mecufi
Chipata
NIASSA
Nungo
Lurio
Dowa
Ft. Maguire
Belem
Maua
Chaonde
Simuco
Lilongwe
Massangulo
Vatiua
Intute
Memba
Dedza
Mangochi
Malema
Ribaué
Nacala
Balaka
Cuamba
NAMPULA
Mossuril
Chipera
Cabora Bassa
Matope
Zomba
Gurúe
Nampula
Meconta
Moçambique
Cabora Bassa Dam
Zobue
Blantyre
Namarroi
Alto
Mulocue
Moçambique
Magué
Moatize
Mulanje
Errego
Mutala
Namaponda
Tete
Chirkwawa
Milange
Lugela
Giló
Angoche
Chióco
ZAMBEZIA
Mocuba
Moma
Tambara
Chemba
Chiromo
Nsanje
Namacurra
Vila da
Maganja
Pebane
Mt. Darwin
Nyamapanda
Mungari
Moebase
Mungari
Vila de
Sena
Inhaminga
Quelimane
Macheke
Maringué
Mopêia Velha
Rusape
Marromeu
Luabo
Manica
Chimoio
Mazamba
Chinde
Chimanimani
Dondo
SOFALA
Conceição
Chipinge
Mt. Binga
2436
Machece
Espungabera
Gorongosa
Beira
Nova
Sofala
Buzi
Macobere
Bartolomeu
Dias
Save
Chiredzi
Maave
Maputo
Massangena
Inhassoro
I. do Bazaruto
Chicualacuala
Mapinhane
Vilanculos
INHAMBANE
Chigubo
Nhachengue
Pomene
GAZA
Mabalane
Cubo
Homoine
Massinga
Massingir
Estivane
Marão
Morrumbene
Inharrime
Inhambane
C. das Correntes
Chibuto
Jangamo
Nhacoongo
Magude
Chicomo
Quissico
Macia
Chidenguele
Xai-Xai
Manhiça
Marracuene
MAPUTO
Bela Vista
Zitundo
Catuane
Mseleni

Relief

Feet		Metres
16 404		5000
9843		3000
6562		2000
3281		1000
1640		500
656		200
0		Sea Level
Land Dep.		
656		200
13123		4000
22966		7000

Scale 1:10 000 000

0   100   200   300 Miles

0   100   200   300   400   500 Kms.

Lambert Azimuthal Equal Area Projection

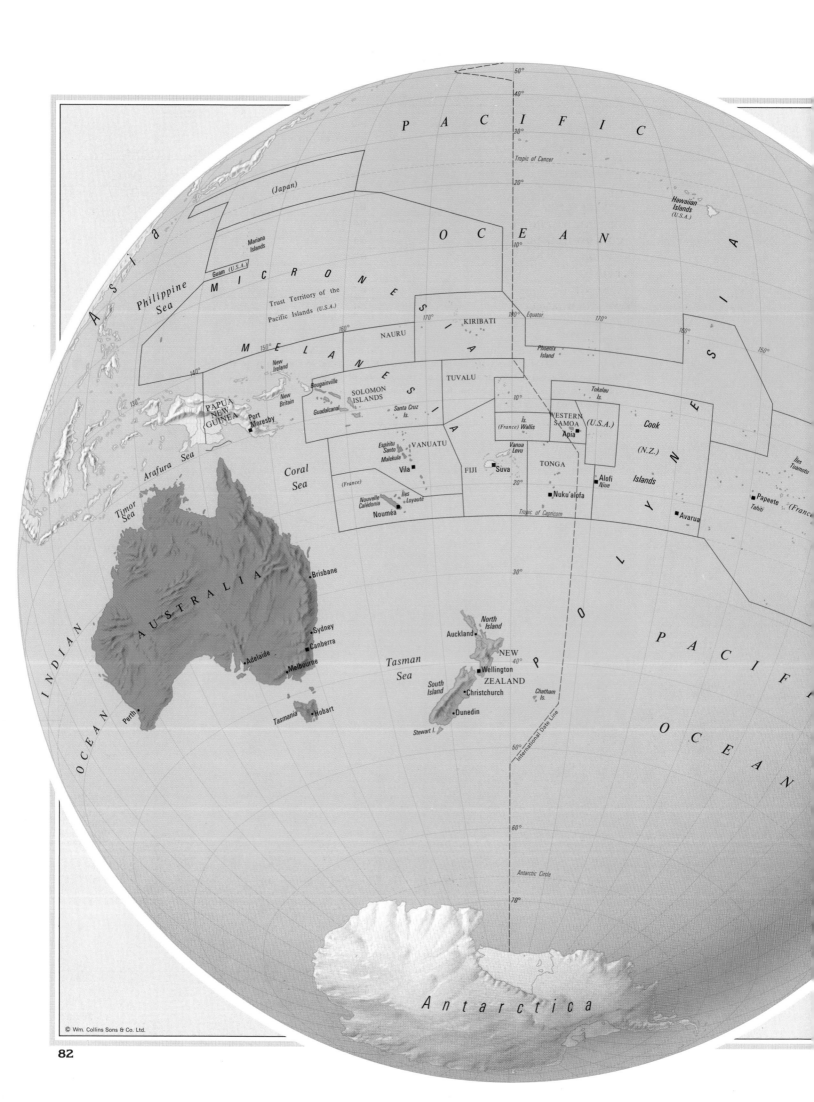

PACIFIC

OCEAN

Tropic of Cancer

50°
40°
30°
20°
10°

(Japan)

Hawaiian
Islands
(U.S.A.)

Mariana
Islands

A

S

I

A

Philippine
Sea

Guam (U.S.A.)

M I C R O N E

Trust Territory of the
Pacific Islands (U.S.A.)

S

Equator

KIRIBATI

170°
180°
170°
160°
150°

160°

NAURU

M E L A N E S

Phoenix
Island

150°

140°

New
Ireland

New
Britain

Bougainville

TUVALU

Tokelau
Is.

130°

PAPUA
NEW
GUINEA

SOLOMON
ISLANDS

Santa Cruz
Is.

I

WESTERN
SAMOA

(U.S.A.)

Cook

Îles
Tuamotu

Guadalcanal

Port
Moresby

A

Is.
(France) Wallis

Apia

(N.Z.)

Espíritu
Santo

VANUATU

Vanua
Levu

Islands

Y

Malekula

Papeete

Tahiti

(France

Coral
Sea

Vila

FIJI

Suva

TONGA

Alofi
Niue

Arafura
Sea

(France)

Îles
Loyaute

Tropic of Capricorn

Nuku'alofa

Avarua

Timor
Sea

Nouvelle
Calédonia

Nouméa

30°

I
N
D
I
A
N

Brisbane

P
A
C
I
F

AUSTRALIA

Sydney

Adelaide

Canberra

Melbourne

North
Island

Auckland

NEW

Tasman
Sea

Wellington

40°

O
C
E
A
N

Perth

Tasmania

Hobart

South
Island

Christchurch

ZEALAND

Chatham
Is.

O
C
E
A
N

Dunedin

50°

Stewart I.

International Date Line

60°

Antarctic Circle

70°

Antarctica

© Wm. Collins Sons & Co. Ltd.

OCEANIA

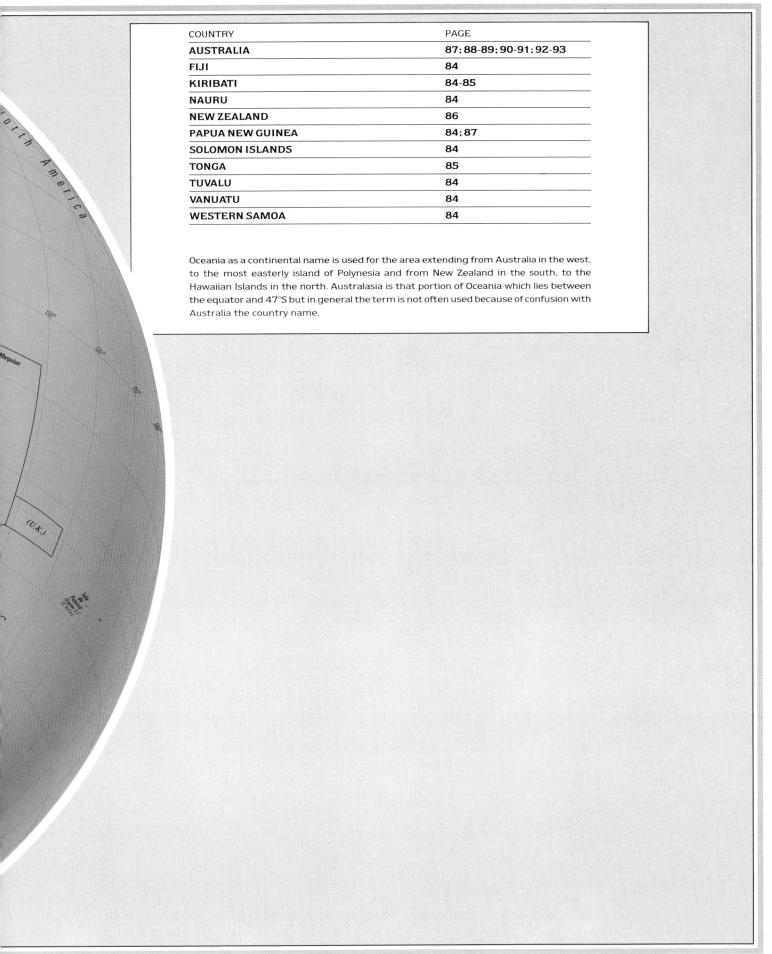

Oceania as a continental name is used for the area extending from Australia in the west, to the most easterly island of Polynesia and from New Zealand in the south, to the Hawaiian Islands in the north. Australasia is that portion of Oceania which lies between the equator and 47°S but in general the term is not often used because of confusion with Australia the country name.

PACIFIC OCEAN

SAMOA ISLANDS
Scale 1:7 500 000

Falealupo Aopo Fagamalo
Salailua Puapua
Savai'i Matautu Upolu
Matautu Tiavea
WESTERN Apia
SAMOA Salani
Pago Pago Samoa Manua Is.
(U.S.A.) Ofu Olosega
Tutuila Steps Pt. Tau

FIJI
Gt. Sea Reef
Undu C.
Lambasa Vanua Levu
Mbua Mbutha
Taveuni
Koro Yathata
Lautoka Viti Ngau Koro
Nandi Levu Sea
Singatoka Suva
Kandavu Passage Lau
Kandavu Group
Scale 1:15 000 000

RAROTONGA
(N.Z.)
Avatiu Avarua
Pokoinu Matavera
Arorangi Ngatangiia
Te Manga Muri
Titikaveka
Scale 1:500 000

NIUE
(N.Z.)
Hikutavake Mutalau
Toi Lakepa
Makefu Tuapa
Alofi Motutapu Liku
Bay Alofi
Avatele Vaiea Hakupu
Tepa Pt.
Scale 1:1 000 000

GUAM
(U.S.A.)
Ritidian Pt.
Philippine Pati Pt.
Sea Mt. Santa Rosa
Agana Catalina Pt.
Orote Yona
Pen. Talofofo
Merizo Malofos
Inarajan
Scale 1:2 000 000

VANUATU AND NEW CALEDONIA
Banks Is.
C. Cumberland C. Quiros
Espíritu Oba
Santo I. Maewo
Luganville Pentecost I.
Malekula Ambrim
Coral Epi Shepherd
Sea Islands
VANUATU Emae Tongoa
Vila Efate
Récifs Eromanga
d'Entrecasteaux
Grand Passage Tana
Grand Récif Lenakel
de Cook Aneityum
Koumac Île Uvéa Îles Loyauté
Voh Lifou (Loyalty Is)
Koné Houailou
Bourail Île Maré
Nouvelle Yaté
Calédonie Île des
(New Caledonia) Pins
(Fr.) Nouméa
Scale 1:15 000 000

© Wm. Collins Sons & Co. Ltd.

84

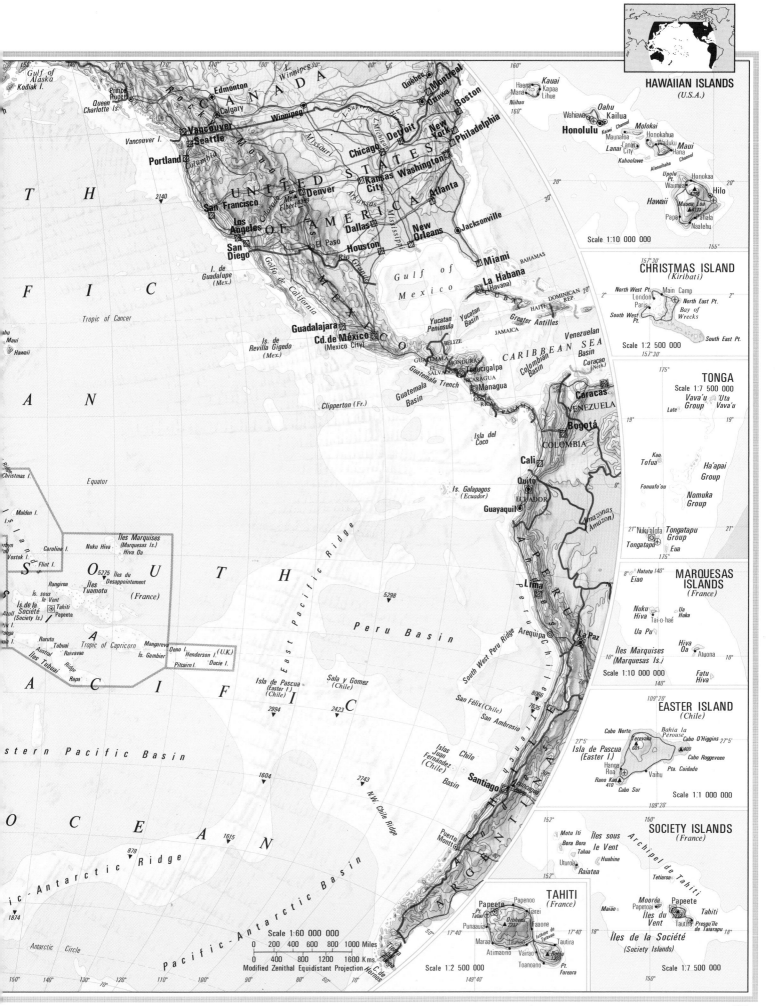

HAWAIIAN ISLANDS
(U.S.A.)

Kauai
Haena
Mana
Kapaa
Lihue
Niihau

Oahu
Wahiawa
Honolulu
Kailua
Kaneohe
Kaiwi Channel
Molokai
Maunaloa
Honokahua
Wailuku
Lanai
Lanai City
Hana
Maui
Kahoolawe
Alenuihaha

Upolu Pt.
Waimea
Honokaa
Hilo
Hawaii
Mauna Loa
4171
Papa
Pahala
Naalehu

Scale 1:10 000 000

CHRISTMAS ISLAND
(Kiribati)

North West Pt.
London
Paris
South West Pt.
Main Camp
North East Pt.
Bay of Wrecks
South East Pt.

Scale 1:2 500 000

TONGA
Scale 1:7 500 000

Vava'u Group
Late
'Uta Vava'u

Kao
Tofua
Ha'apai Group

Fonuafo'ou
Nomuka Group

Nuku'alofa
Tongatapu Group
Tongatapu
Eua

MARQUESAS ISLANDS
(France)

Hatutu
Eiao

Nuku Hiva
Tai-o-haé
Ua Huka

Ua Pu

Îles Marquises
(Marquesas Is.)
Hiva Oa
Atuona

Fatu Hiva

Scale 1:10 000 000

EASTER ISLAND
(Chile)

Cabo Norte
Bahía la Pérouse
Terevaka
601
Cabo O'Higgins
Isla de Pascua
(Easter I.)
Cabo Roggeveen
400
Hanga Roa
Pta. Cuidado
Rano Kao
410
Vaihu
Cabo Sur

Scale 1:1 000 000

SOCIETY ISLANDS
(France)

Motu Iti
Bora Bora
Tahaa
Îles sous le Vent
Uturoa
Huahine
Raiatea

Tetiaroa

Mooréa
Papetoai
Maiao
Papeete
Îles du Vent
Tahiti
Tautira
Presqu'île de Taiarapu
Îles de la Société
(Society Islands)

Scale 1:7 500 000

TAHITI
(France)

Papeete
Papenoo
Pt. Tataa
Arei
Punaauia
Orohena
2237
Faaone
Maraa
Faatau
Isthme de Taravao
Tautira
Atimaono
Vairao
Toanoano
Pt. Fareara

Scale 1:2 500 000

Map labels (main map)

Gulf of Alaska
Kodiak I.
Prince Rupert
Queen Charlotte Is.
Vancouver I.
Vancouver
Seattle
Portland

CANADA
Edmonton
Calgary
Winnipeg
L. Winnipeg
Quebec
Montreal
Ottawa
Boston
New York
Philadelphia

Rocky Mountains
2140

UNITED STATES OF AMERICA
San Francisco
Denver
Mt. Elbert 4399
Los Angeles
San Diego
El Paso
Dallas
Houston
Kansas City
Washington
Chicago
Detroit
Atlanta
Jacksonville
New Orleans
Miami

Columbia
Missouri
Mississippi
Arkansas
Rio Grande
Colorado

I. de Guadalupe (Mex.)
Golfo de California
Tropic of Cancer

Is. de Revilla Gigedo (Mex.)
Guadalajara
Cd. de México
(Mexico City)

MEXICO

BAHAMAS
Gulf of Mexico
La Habana (Havana)
HAITI
DOMINICAN REP.
Greater Antilles
JAMAICA
CARIBBEAN SEA
Colombian Basin
Curaçao (Neth.)
Venezuelan Basin

Yucatan Peninsula
Yucatan Basin
BELIZE
GUATEMALA
Guatemala Trench
EL SALVADOR
HONDURAS
Tegucigalpa
NICARAGUA
Managua
Guatemala Basin
COSTA RICA
PANAMA

Caracas
VENEZUELA
Bogotá
COLOMBIA
Cali

Isla del Coco
Is. Galapagos (Ecuador)
Quito
ECUADOR
Guayaquil

Clipperton (Fr.)

Equator

Christmas I.
Malden I.
Vostok I.
Caroline I.
Flint I.

SOUTH
Penrhyn I.

Îles Marquises (Marquesas Is.)
Nuku Hiva
Hiva Oa
5275
Îles du Désappointement
(France)

Rangiroa
Îles Tuamotu
Is. sous le Vent
Is. de la Société (Society Is.)
Tahiti
Papeete

Rurutu
Tubuai
Raivavae
Austral
Îles Tubuai
Ridge
Rapa
Mangareva
Is. Gambier
Oeno I.
Henderson I. (U.K.)
Pitcairn I.
Ducie I.

Tropic of Capricorn

PACIFIC OCEAN

Isla de Pascua (Easter I.) (Chile)
2994
Sala y Gomez (Chile)
2423
San Félix (Chile)
San Ambrosio
Islas Juan Fernández (Chile)
Chile Basin

East Pacific Ridge
5298
Peru Basin
South West Peru Ridge
Peru-Chile Trench
8066
7635
Arequipa
La Paz
Lima

PERU
BOLIVIA

1604
N.W. Chile Ridge
2743
1615
878
Pacific-Antarctic Ridge
1874

Southeastern Pacific Basin
Pacific-Antarctic Basin

Santiago
Aconcagua
Valparaíso
Puerto Montt

ARGENTINA
CHILE
Andes

Antarctic Circle

Scale 1:60 000 000
0 200 400 600 800 1000 Miles
0 400 800 1200 1600 Kms.
Modified Zenithal Equidistant Projection

85

NEW ZEALAND

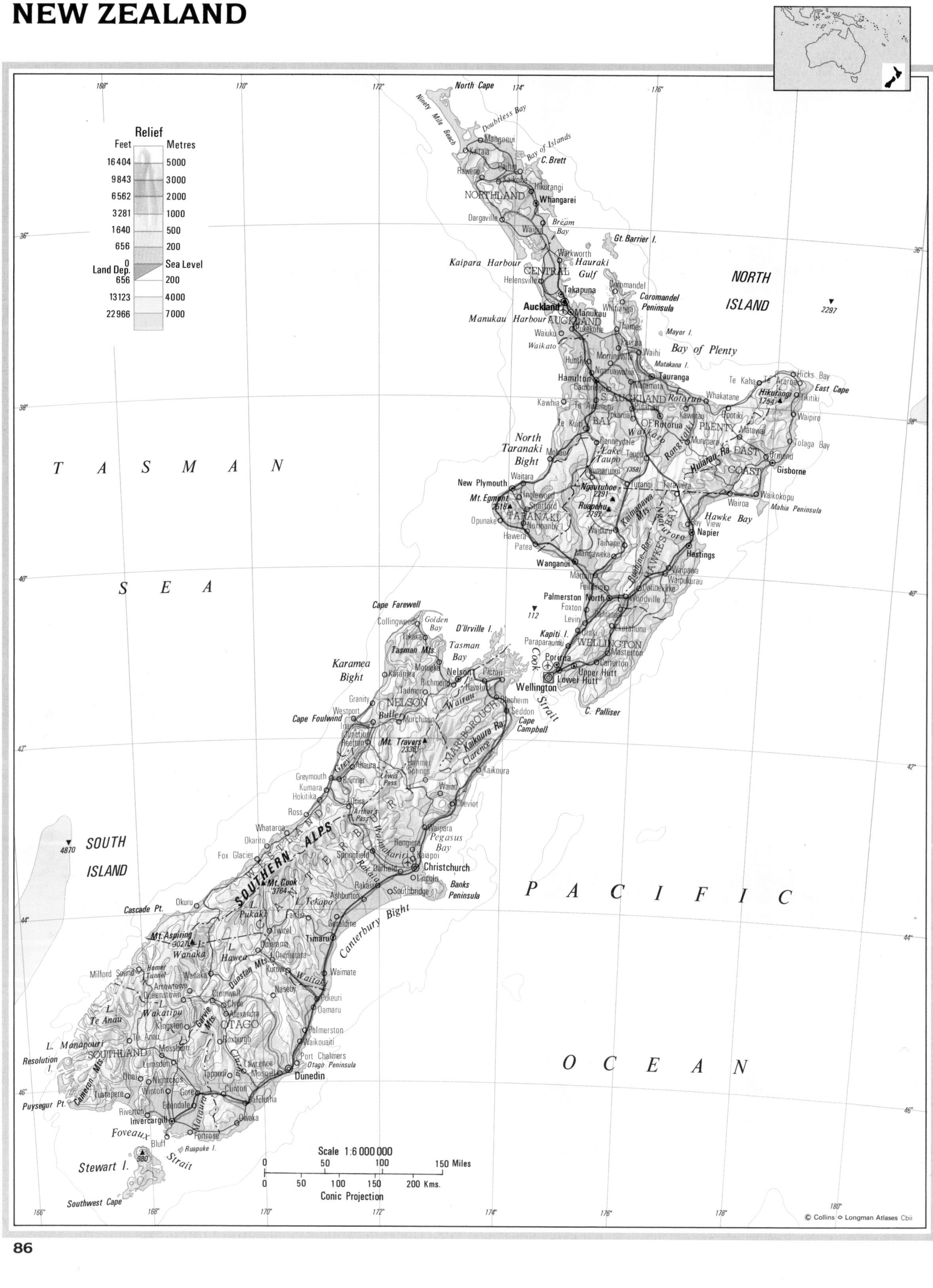

Relief
Feet
Metres
16404 5000
9843 3000
6562 2000
3281 1000
1640 500
656 200
0 Sea Level
Land Dep.
656 200
13123 4000
22966 7000
T A S M A N
S E A
P A C I F I C
O C E A N
NORTH ISLAND
SOUTH ISLAND
North Cape
Ninety Mile Beach
Doubtless Bay
Bay of Islands
C. Brett
Mangonui
Kaitaia
Rawene
Paihia
Kaikohe
Hikurangi
NORTHLAND
Whangarei
Dargaville
Bream Bay
Gt. Barrier I.
Kaipara Harbour
Warkworth
Hauraki Gulf
CENTRAL
Helensville
Takapuna
Coromandel
Coromandel Peninsula
Auckland
Manukau
Manukau Harbour
AUCKLAND
Whitianga
Thames
Pukekohe
Waiuku
Waikato
Mayor I.
Bay of Plenty
Paeroa
Waihi
Matakana I.
Huntly
Morrinsville
Ngaruawahia
Tauranga
Hamilton
Cambridge
Te Kaha
Hicks Bay
East Cape
Hikurangi 1754
Whakatane
Tikitiki
Kawhia
Te Awamutu
Putaruru
S. AUCKLAND
Rotorua
Opotiki
Waipiro
Te Kuiti
BAY
Tokoroa
OF PLENTY
Kawerau
Rotorua
North Taranaki Bight
Benneydale
Murupara
Matawai
Tolaga Bay
Mokau
Lake Taupo
Taupo
Huiarau Ra.
EAST
Ormond
COAST
Gisborne
New Plymouth
Waitara
Taumarunui
Ngauruhoe 2291
Turangi
Mt. Egmont 2518
Inglewood
Stratford
Ruapehu 2797
Kaimanawa Mts.
Waikokopu
Wairoa
Mahia Peninsula
TARANAKI
Opunake
Hawera
Patea
Normanby
Waiouru
Taihape
Hawke Bay
Bay View
Napier
Hastings
Wanganui
Mangaweka
HAWKE'S BAY
Ruahine Ra.
Waipawa
Waipukurau
Marton
Feilding
Palmerston North
Dannevirke
Woodville
Foxton
Levin
Pahiatua
Eketahuna
Kapiti I.
Paraparaumu
Otaki
WELLINGTON
Masterton
Carterton
Porirua
Upper Hutt
Lower Hutt
Wellington
C. Palliser
Cook Strait
2297
112
Cape Farewell
Collingwood
Golden Bay
Takaka
D'Urville I.
Tasman Mts.
Tasman Bay
Karamea Bight
Karamea
Motueka
Nelson
Picton
Richmond
Havelock
Tadmor
Granity
NELSON
Blenheim
Westport
Cape Foulwind
Buller
Murchison
Wairau
Seddon
Cape Campbell
Inangahua Junction
MARLBOROUGH
Kaikoura Ra.
Reefton
Mt. Travers 2338
Clarence
Hanmer Springs
Ahaura
Kaikoura
Greymouth
Kumara
Hokitika
Brunner
Lewis Pass
Waiau
Cheviot
Otira
Arthur's Pass
Ross
Whataroa
Okarito
Waipara
Pegasus Bay
Rangiora
Kaiapoi
Fox Glacier
Springfield
Darfield
Christchurch
Lincoln
Rakaia
Southbridge
Banks Peninsula
SOUTHERN ALPS
Mt. Cook 3764
Okuru
Cascade Pt.
L. Pukaki
L. Tekapo
Ashburton
Fairlie
Geraldine
Canterbury Bight
Twizel
Timaru
Mt. Aspiring 3027
L. Wanaka
L. Hawea
Omarama
Otematata
Milford Sound
Homer Tunnel
Wanaka
Dunstan Mts.
Kurow
Waitaki
Waimate
Arrowtown
Queenstown
Cromwell
Naseby
L. Wakatipu
Clyde
Alexandra
Oamaru
L. Te Anau
Kingston
Garvie Mts.
OTAGO
Te Anau
Roxburgh
Palmerston
Waikouaiti
L. Manapouri
Mossburn
Resolution I.
SOUTHLAND
Lumsden
Lawrence
Port Chalmers
Otago Peninsula
Dunedin
Ohai
Nightcaps
Tapanui
Mosgiel
Cameron Mts.
Winton
Gore
Clinton
Tuatapere
Edendale
Balclutha
Puysegur Pt.
Riverton
Invercargill
Owaka
Mataura
Foveaux Strait
Bluff
Fortrose
Ruapuke I.
Stewart I.
980
Southwest Cape
4870
Scale 1:6 000 000
0 50 100 150 Miles
0 50 100 150 200 Kms.
Conic Projection
166° 168° 170° 172° 174° 176° 178° 180°
36° 38° 40° 42° 44° 46°
© Collins ◇ Longman Atlases Cbii

AUSTRALIA

Scale 1:20 000 000

| 0 | 100 | 200 | 300 | 400 | 500 Miles |

| 0 | 200 | 400 | 600 | 800 Kms. |

Lambert Azimuthal Equal Area Projection

© Collins ◇ Longman Atlases Cbi

WESTERN AUSTRALIA

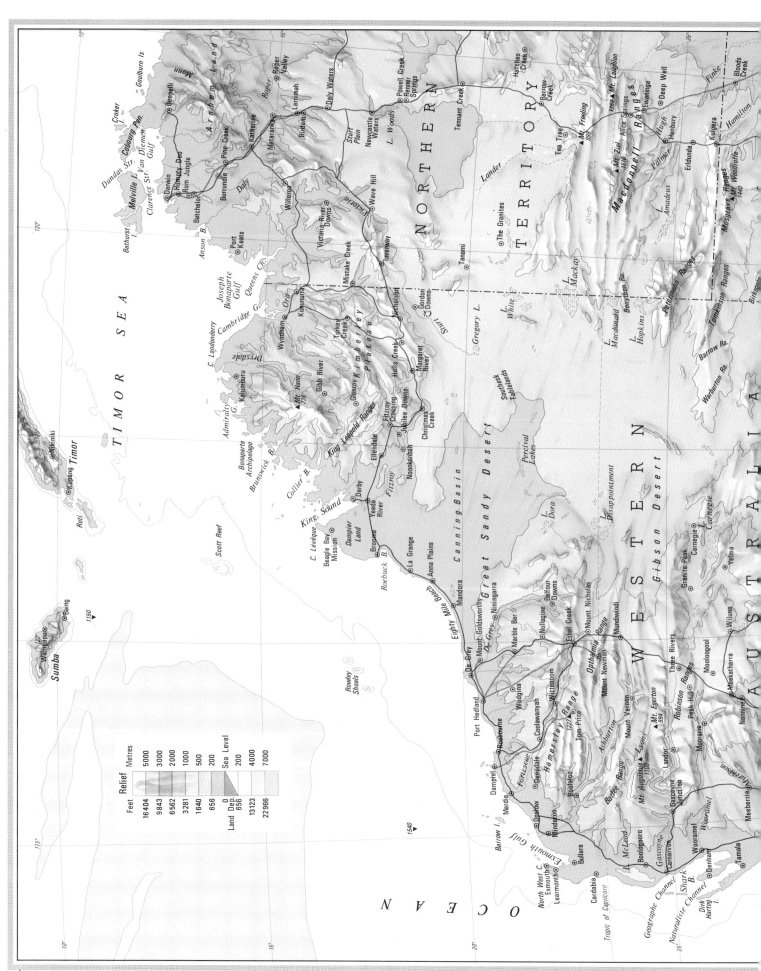

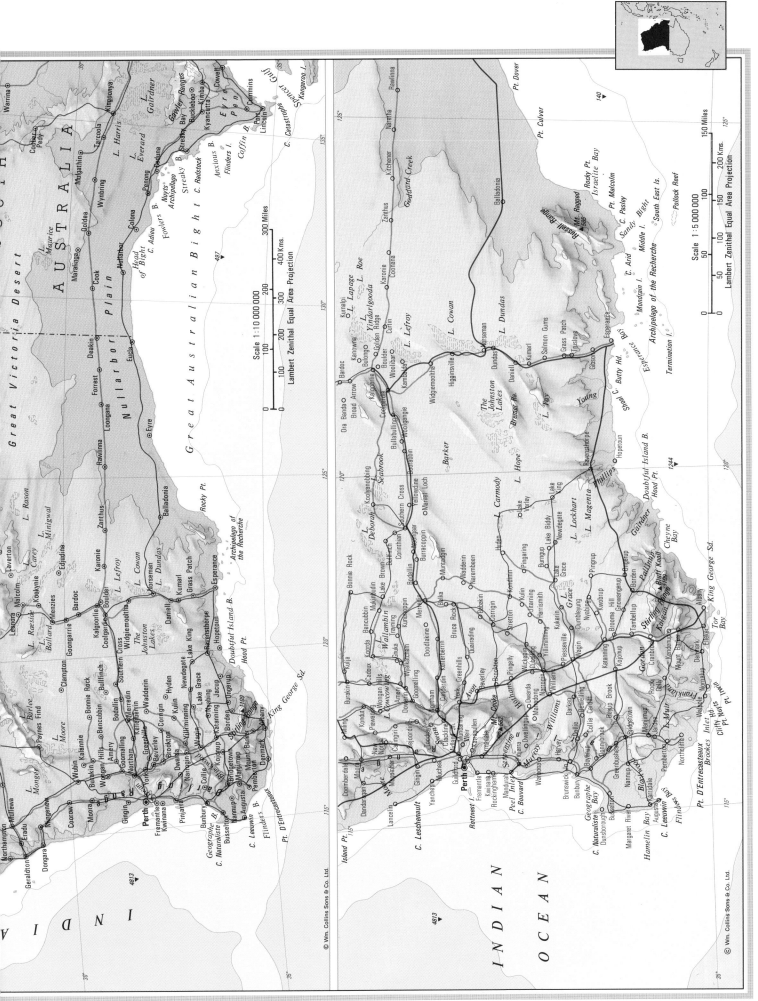

EASTERN AUSTRALIA

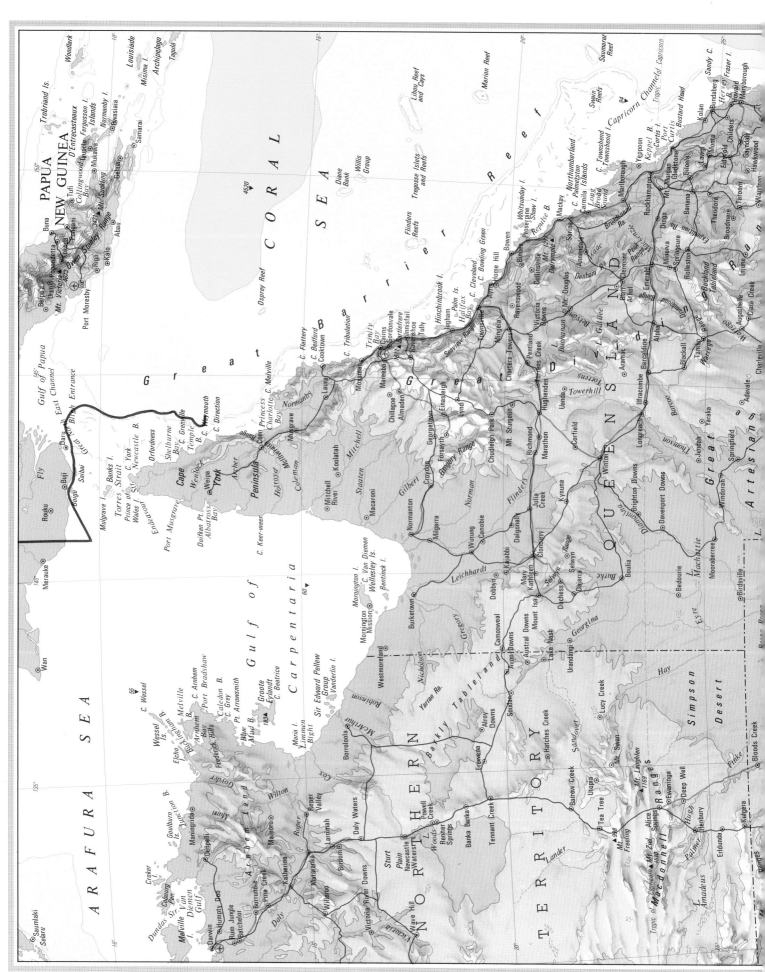

SOUTHEAST AUSTRALIA

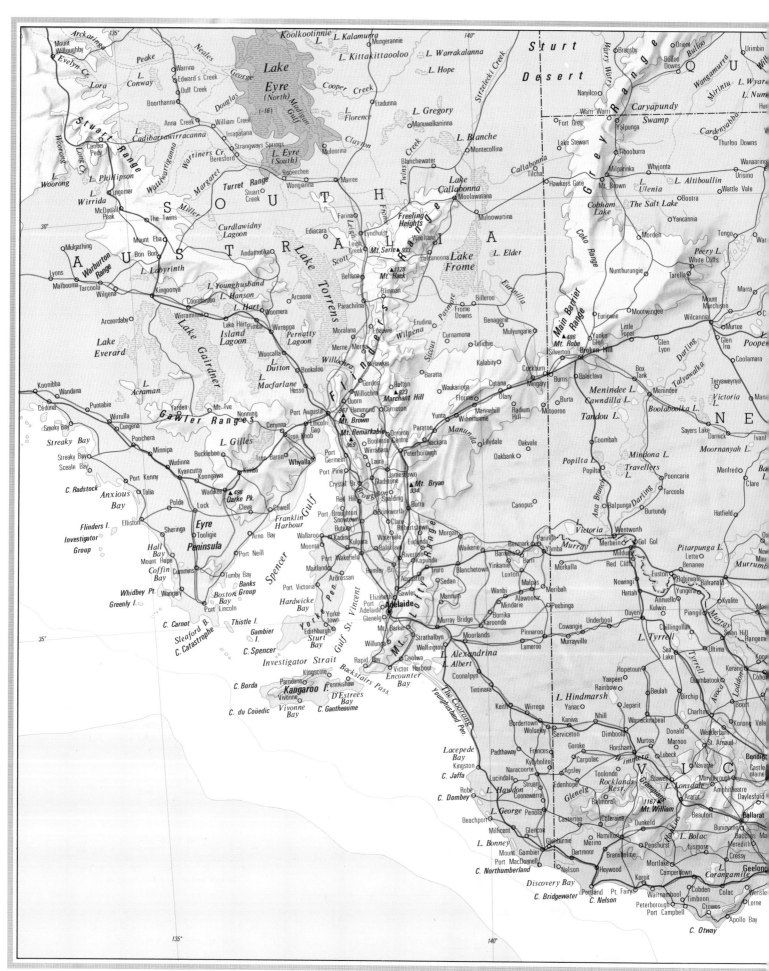

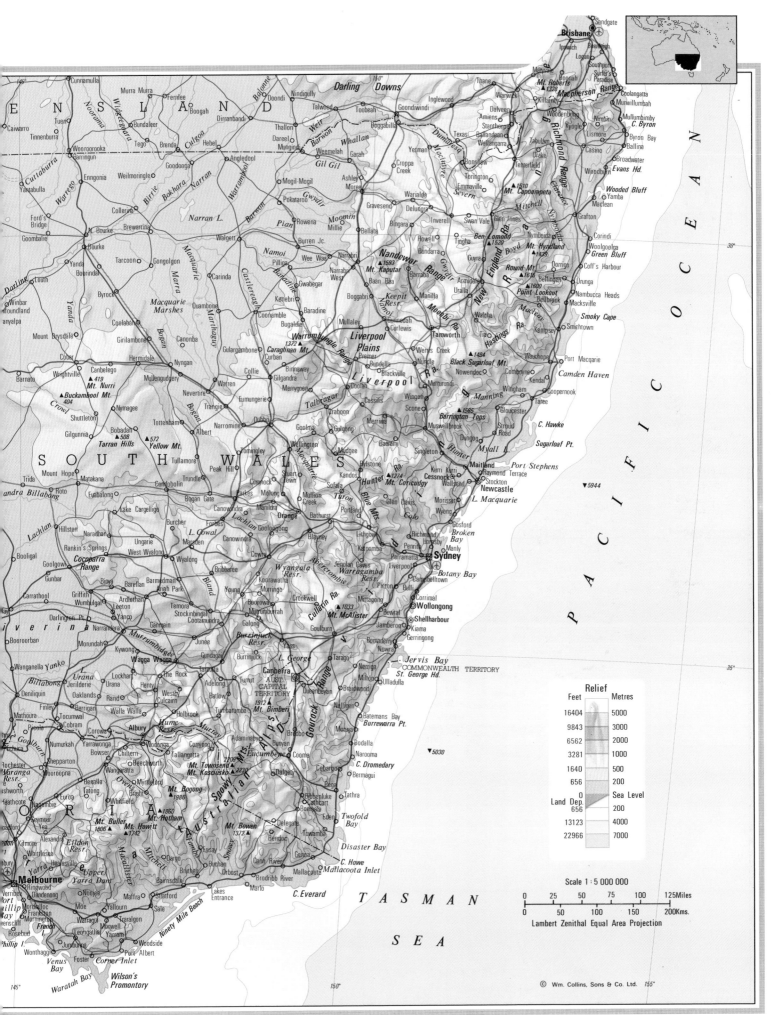

Asia

Europe

ARCTIC OCEAN

Ellesmere I.

GREENLAND (Den.)

Denmark Strait
Arctic Circle

Parry Islands

Baffin Bay

Baffin Island

Bering Strait

ALASKA
U.S.A.

Anchorage

Victoria Island

Godthåb/ Nuuk

Hudson Bay

CANADA

Newfoundland

International Date Line

50°

Edmonton

PACIFIC

Seattle

Vancouver

Winnipeg

Quebec
Montreal
Ottawa
Toronto
Buffalo
Hamilton
Paterson
Boston

40°

Portland

UNITED STATES

Milwaukee
Chicago
Detroit
Cleveland
Pittsburgh
Newark
New York

OF

Indianapolis
Cincinnati
Baltimore
Washington
Philadelphia

San Francisco

180°

San Jose

Denver

Kansas City

St. Louis

BERMUDA

Honolulu

Los Angeles
San Diego

San Bernadino

AMERICA

30°

Hawaiian Islands (U.S.A.)

Tijuana

Dallas

Atlanta

170°

I. de Guadalupe (Mex.)

Ciudad Juárez

Houston

New Orleans

BAHAMAS

Tropic of Cancer

20°

Monterray

Gulf of Mexico

Miami

160°

Is. de Revilla Gigedo (Mex.)

León

Guadalajara

MEXICO

Havana

CUBA

Santiago de Cuba

PUERTO RICO

HAITI DOM. REP.
San Juan

DOMINIC

ANT

150°

Ciudad de México

Belmopan
BELIZE

JAMAICA

Kingston

Port-au-Prince

Santo Domingo

Caribbean Sea

Guadeloupe

Martinique

ST. LUCIA

ST. V. AND G

10°

GUA

GUA
Guatemala

HONDURAS
Tegucigalpa

(Neth.)

GRENADA

140°

San Salvador
EL SAL.

Managua

NICARAGUA

OCEAN

COSTA RICA

San José

PANAMÁ

Panamá

130° Equator

120°

110°

100°

90°

So

Am

10°

20°

Tropic of Capricorn

30°

DOM. REP. : DOMINICAN REPUBLIC
EL SAL. : EL SALVADOR
GUA. : GUATEMALA
ST. V. AND G. : ST. VINCENT AND THE GRENADINES
© Wm. Collins Sons & Co. Ltd.

NORTH AMERICA

NORTH AMERICA

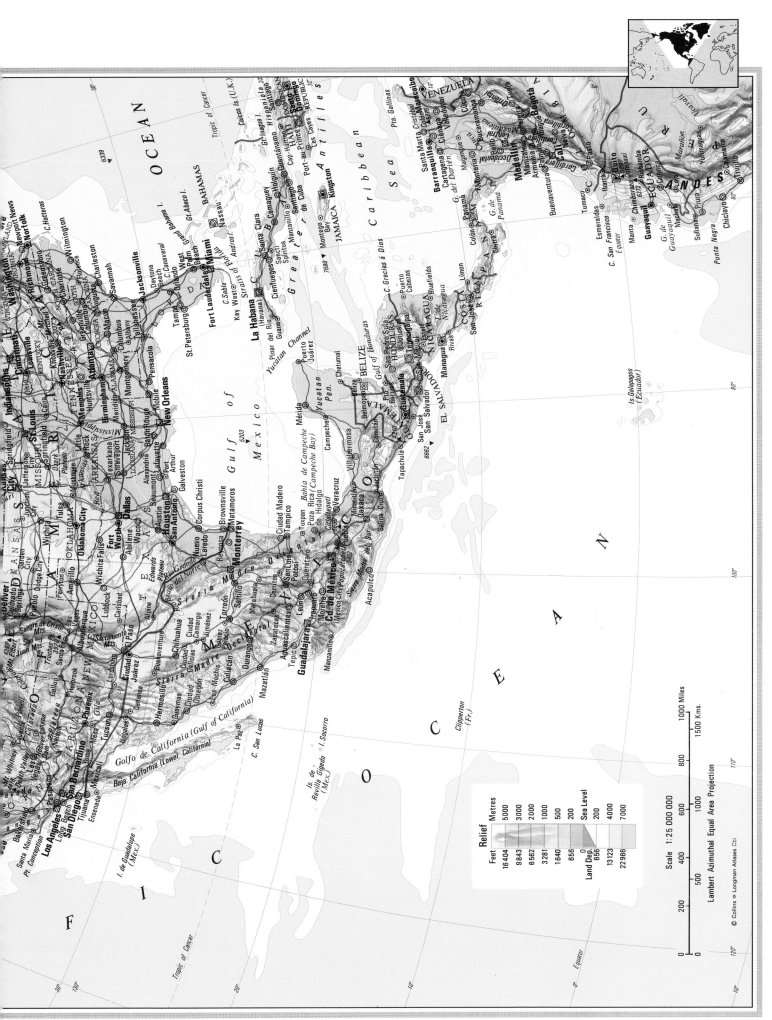

OCEAN

Tropic of Cancer

6339▼

BAHAMAS
Caicos Is. (U.K.)
Gt. Inagua I.
Gt. Abaco I.
Grand Bahama I.
Nassau

Washington
Newport News
Norfolk
VIRGINIA
Richmond
C. Hatteras
Wilmington
NORTH CAROLINA
Greensboro
Charlotte
SOUTH CAROLINA
Florence
Columbia
Augusta
Charleston
Savannah
Jacksonville
Daytona Beach
Orlando
C. Canaveral
Tampa
West Palm Beach
St. Petersburg
Fort Lauderdale
Miami
C. Sable
Key West of Florida I.
Straits of Florida
Key West (Havana)
Andros I.

Cincinnati
KENTUCKY
Louisville
Nashville
Knoxville
TENNESSEE
Memphis
Huntsville
Chattanooga
Birmingham
ALABAMA
Montgomery
MISSISSIPPI
Meridian
GEORGIA
Columbus
Albany
Macon
Atlanta
Tallahassee
Pensacola
Mobile
FLORIDA
New Orleans

Indianapolis
Springfield
St. Louis
MISSOURI
Springfield
Cairo
Paducah
ARKANSAS
Little Rock
Ozark Plateau
Jackson
Vicksburg
LOUISIANA
Baton Rouge
Alexandria
Shreveport
Texarkana
Port Arthur
Beaufort
Lafayette
Galveston

La Habana
(Havana)
Pinar del Río
Guane
Santa Clara
Cienfuegos
Sancti Spíritus
Santiago
Camagüey
Holguín
Manzanillo
Cap-Haïtien
HAITI
Port-au-Prince
Les Cayes
Santiago
Santo Domingo
DOMINICAN REPUBLIC
Hispaniola
Guantánamo
JAMAICA
Kingston
Montego Bay
7680▼

Greater Antilles

Caribbean Sea

Lesser Antilles

Gulf of Mexico

Mexico

5203▼

Yucatan Channel
Puerto Juárez
Yucatán Pen.
Chetumal
Mérida
Bahía de Campeche (Campeche Bay)
Campeche
Villahermosa
Ciudad del Carmen

Corpus Christi
Brownsville
Matamoros
Reynosa
Nuevo Laredo
Ciudad Madero
Tampico
Poza Rica de Hidalgo
Tuxpan
Veracruz
Córdoba
Orizaba
Puebla
Cd. de México
Mexico City
Popocatepetl 5452▲
Oaxaca
Salina Cruz
Tehuantepec
Gulf of Tehuantepec
6662▲
Tapachula

BELIZE
Belize
Belmopan
GUATEMALA
Guatemala
San José
EL SALVADOR
San Salvador
San Miguel
HONDURAS
Tegucigalpa
San Pedro Sula
Gulf of Honduras
C. Gracias á Dios
Puerto Cabezas
NICARAGUA
Managua
L. de Nicaragua
Rivas
COSTA RICA
San José
Limón
Puerto Limón

C A R I B B E A N   S E A

Pta. Gallinas
Maracaibo
VENEZUELA
Santa Marta
Barranquilla
Cartagena
Colón
G. del Darién
Monteria
Colombia
COLOMBIA
Cúcuta
Bucaramanga
Medellín
Manizales
Pereira
Armenia
Ibagué
Bogotá
Cali
Buenaventura
Pasto
Tumaco
Esmeraldas
San Francisco
Quito
ECUADOR
Chimborazo 6272▲
Guayaquil
G. de Guayaquil
Manta
Portoviejo
Cuenca
Machala
Tulcán
Ibarra
Ambato
Riobamba
Cotopaxi
ANDES

PERU
Tumbes
Sullana
Piura
Paita
Punta Negra
Chiclayo
Trujillo
Marañón

Bucaramanga
Panamá
PANAMA
G. de Panamá
G. de Chiriquí

Denver
COLORADO
Colorado Springs
Pueblo
Sangre de Cristo Mts.
Dodge City
Garden City
KANSAS
Wichita
OKLAHOMA
Oklahoma City
Tulsa
Wichita Falls
Amarillo
Lubbock
Abilene
Fort Worth
Dallas
Waco
Austin
San Antonio
Houston
TEXAS
Brazos
San Angelo
Midland
Odessa
Carlsbad
El Paso
Ciudad Juárez
Alpine
Del Rio
Edwards Plateau
Chihuahua

NEW MEXICO
Albuquerque
Santa Fe
Gallup
Sacramento Mts.
4989▲
San Juan Mts.

Phoenix
Mesa
Tucson
ARIZONA
Nogales
Hermosillo
Guaymas
Ciudad Obregón
Los Mochis
Culiacán
Mazatlán
La Paz
C. San Lucas
Golfo de California (Gulf of California)
Baja California (Lower California)
Ensenada
Mexicali
Tijuana
MEXICO
Sierra Madre Occidental
Sierra Madre Oriental
Sierra Madre del Sur
Monterrey
Saltillo
Torreón
Gómez Palacio
Durango
Zacatecas
Aguascalientes
San Luis Potosí
Guanajuato
León
Querétaro
Morelia
Guadalajara
Colima
Manzanillo
Tepic
Acapulco
Matehuala
Ciudad Victoria
Camargo
Jiménez
Delicias
Ciudad Camargo

Los Angeles
Long Beach
San Diego
San Bernardino
Pasadena
Santa Ana
Bakersfield
Mt. Whitney
Death Valley
Las Vegas
Santa Maria
Pt. Conception
I. de Guadalupe (Mex.)

Is. de Revilla Gigedo (Mex.)
I. Socorro

Clipperton (Fr.)

P A C I F I C   O C E A N

Is. Galapagos (Ecuador)

Equator

Tropic of Cancer

Relief	Metres	Feet
	5000	16 404
	3000	9843
	2000	6562
	1000	3281
	500	1640
	200	656
	Sea Level	0
Land Dep.	200	656
	4000	13 123
	7000	22 986

Scale 1:25 000 000

0 200 400 600 800 1000 Miles
0 500 1000 1500 Kms.

Lambert Azimuthal Equal Area Projection

© Collins ◇ Longman Atlases Cbi

CANADA AND ALASKA

BERING SEA

BEAUFORT SEA

PACIFIC OCEAN

Relief

Feet		Metres
16404		5000
9843		3000
6562		2000
3281		1000
1640		500
656		200
0		Sea Level
Land Dep.		
656		200
13123		4000
22966		7000

Scale 1 : 17 000 000

0	100	200	300	400	500 Miles

0	100	200	300	400	500	600	700	800 Kms.

Bonne Projection

WESTERN CANADA

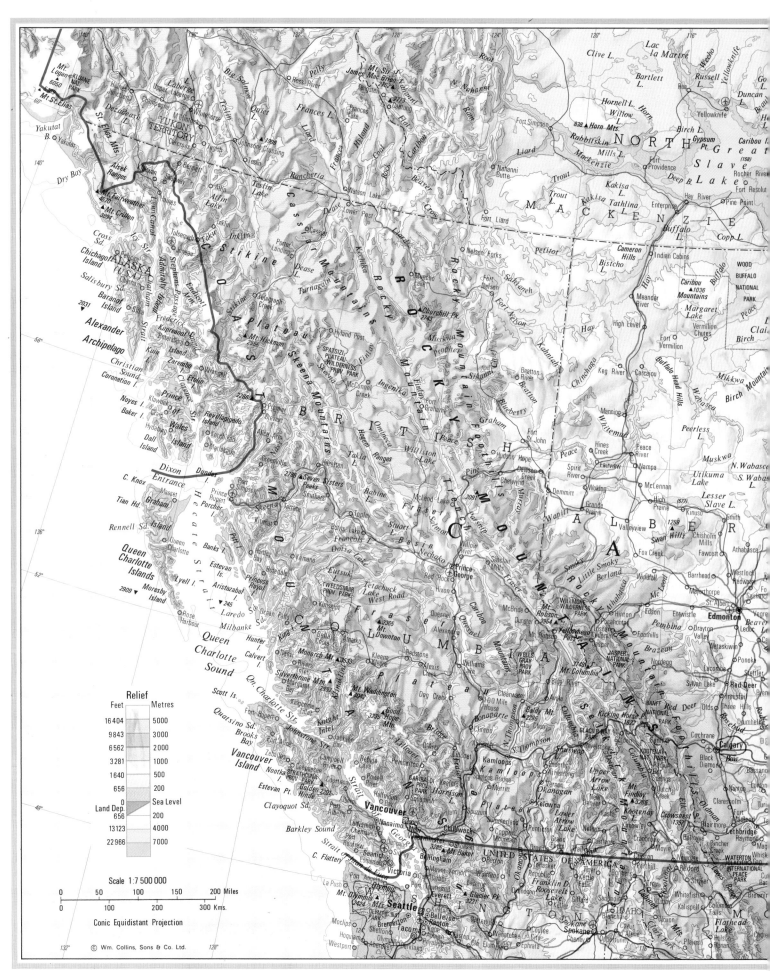

Relief

Feet		Metres
16 404		5000
9843		3000
6562		2000
3281		1000
1640		500
656		200
0	Sea Level	
Land Dep.		
656		200
13 123		4000
22 966		7000

Scale 1:7 500 000

0   50   100   150   200 Miles

0   100   200   300 Kms.

Conic Equidistant Projection

© Wm. Collins, Sons & Co. Ltd.

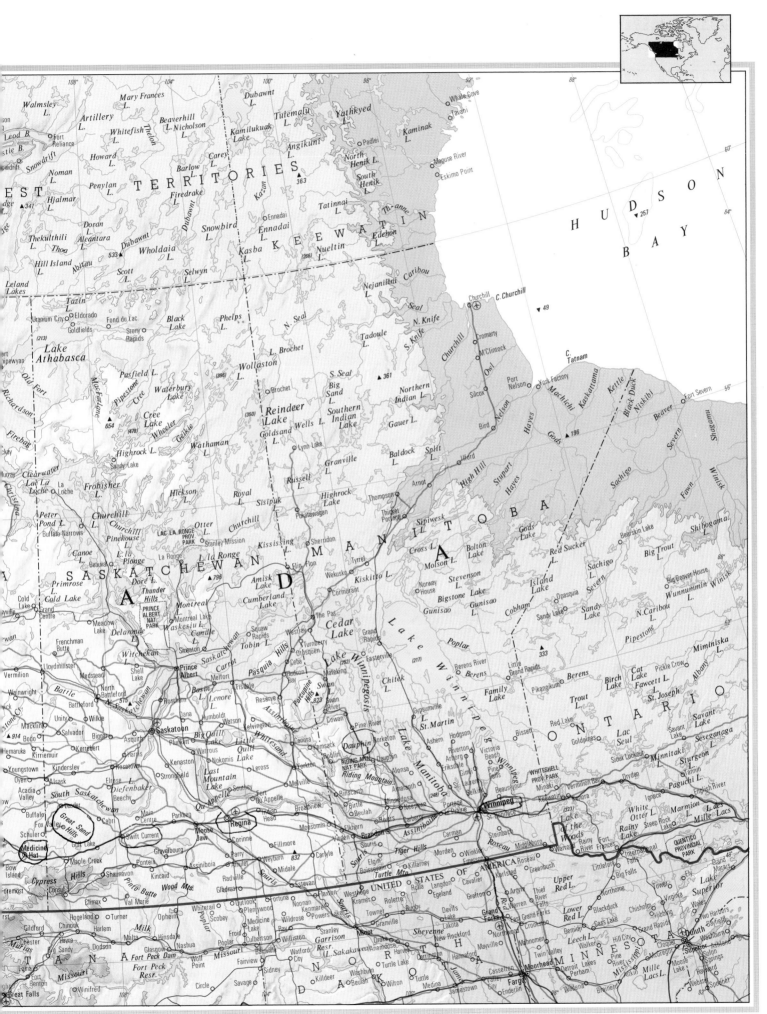

EASTERN CANADA

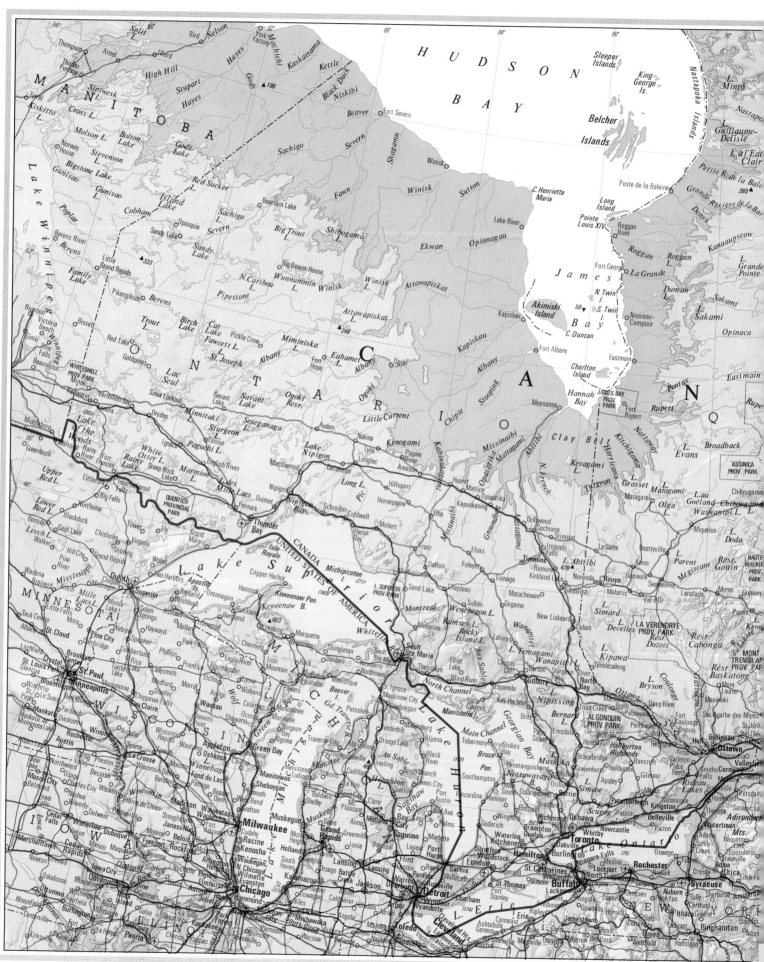

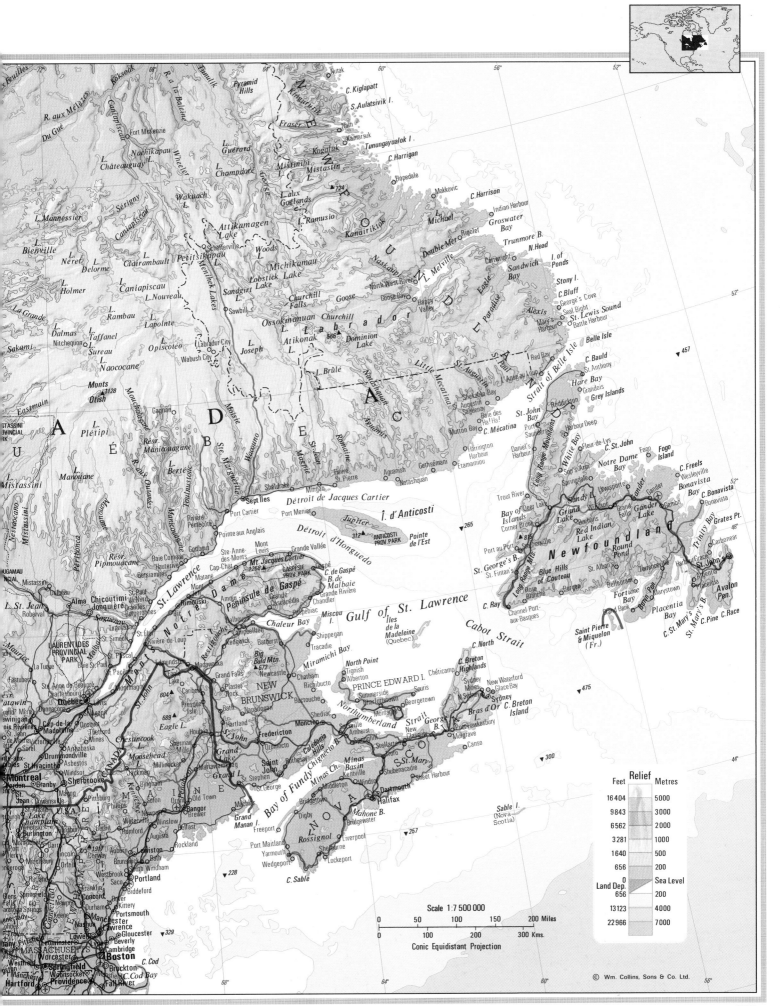

Scale 1:7 500 000

0	50	100	150	200 Miles

0	100	200	300 Kms.

Conic Equidistant Projection

Feet	Relief	Metres
16 404		5000
9843		3000
6562		2000
3281		1000
1640		500
656		200
Land Dep. 0		Sea Level
656		200
13 123		4000
22 966		7000

© Wm. Collins, Sons & Co. Ltd.

103

SOUTH CENTRAL CANADA

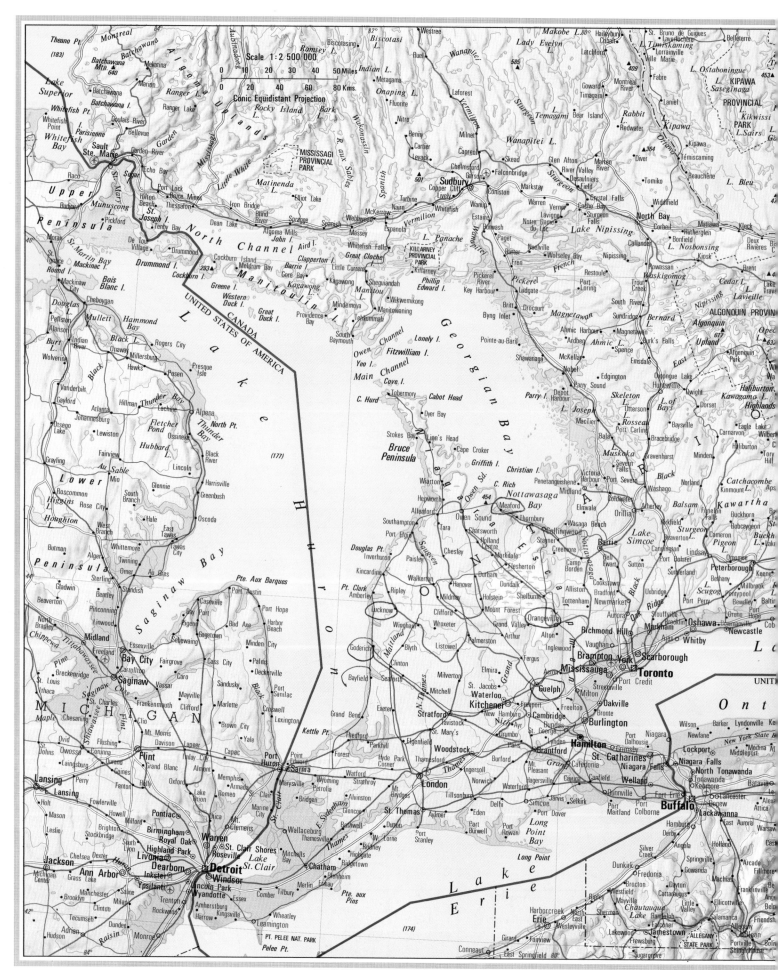

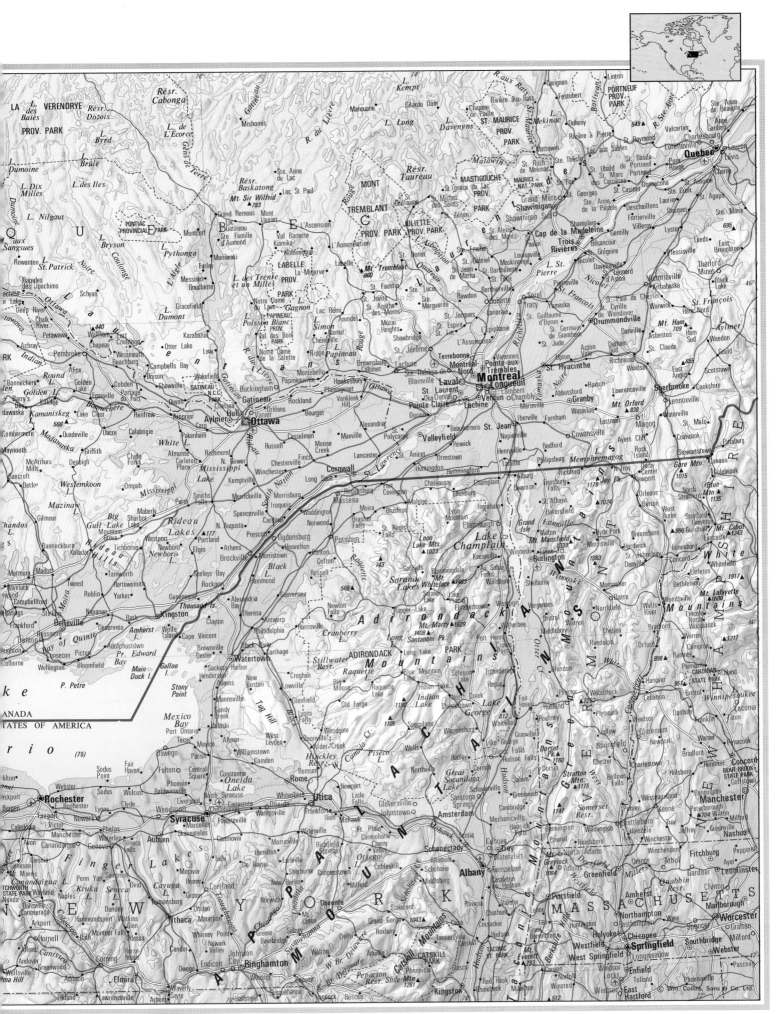

105

UNITED STATES

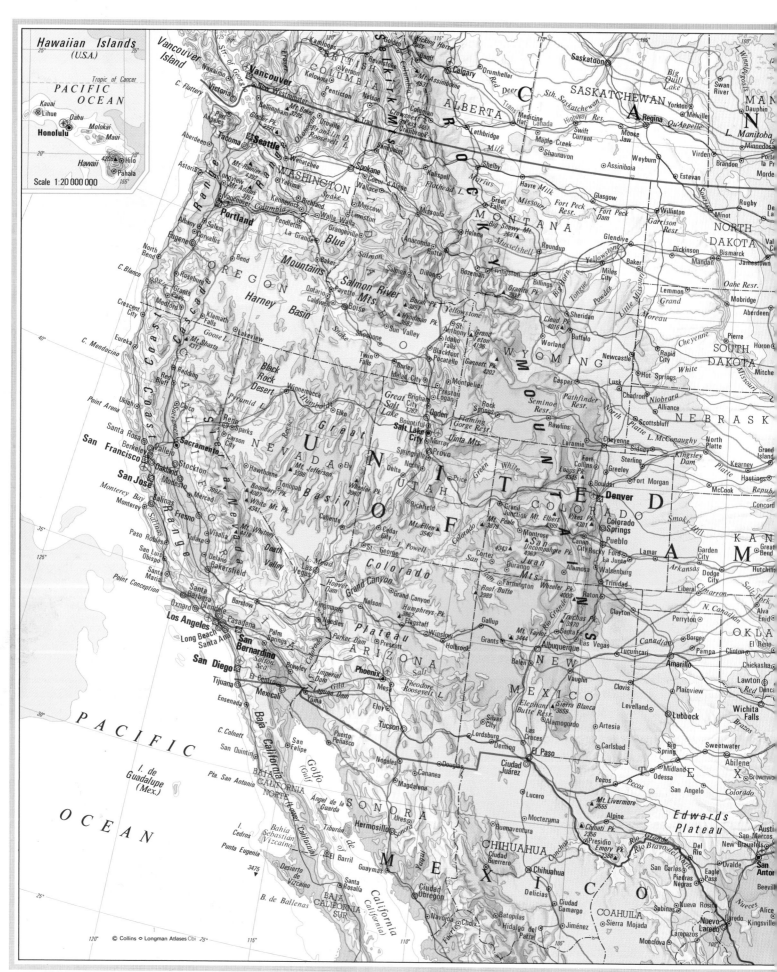

© Collins ◇ Longman Atlases Cbi

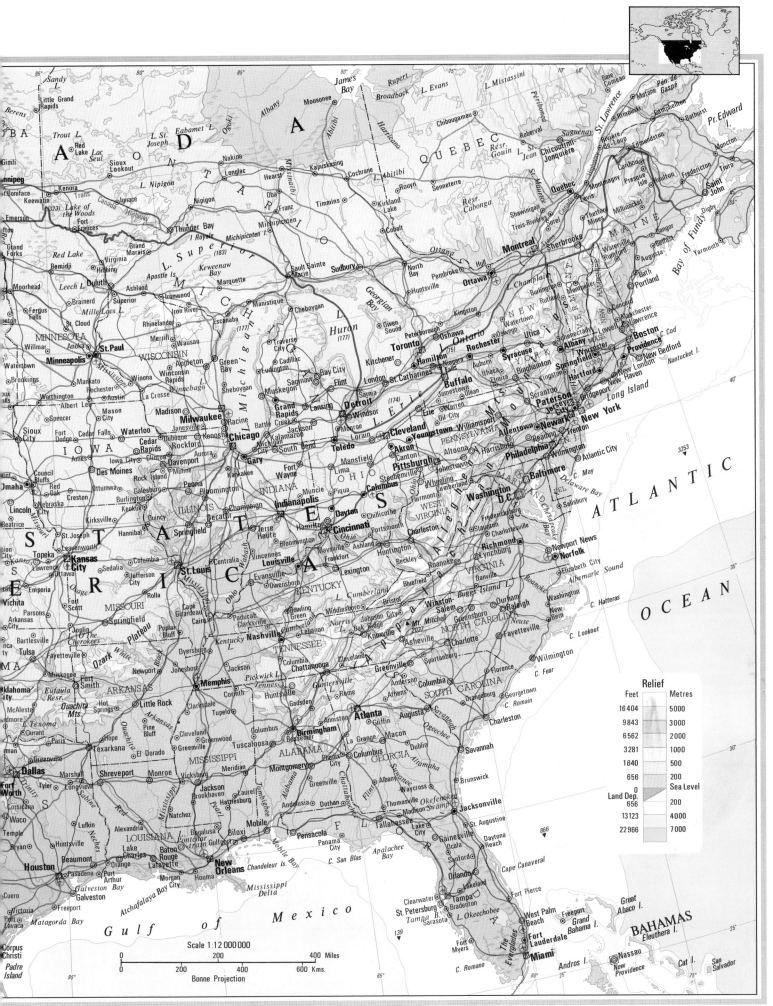

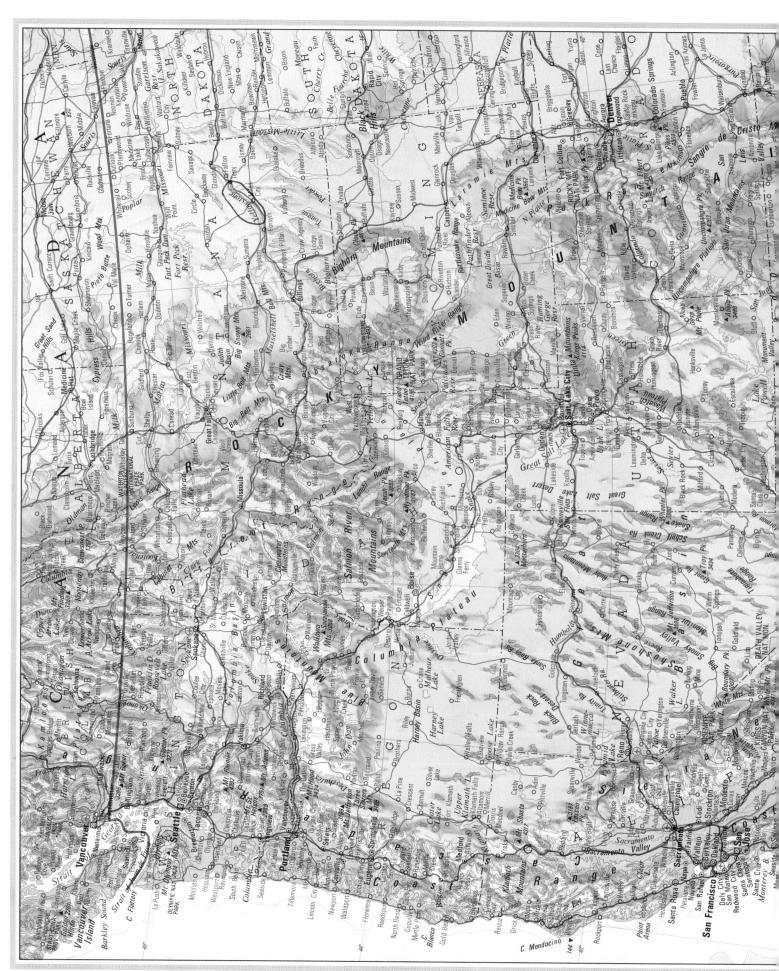

CENTRAL UNITED STATES

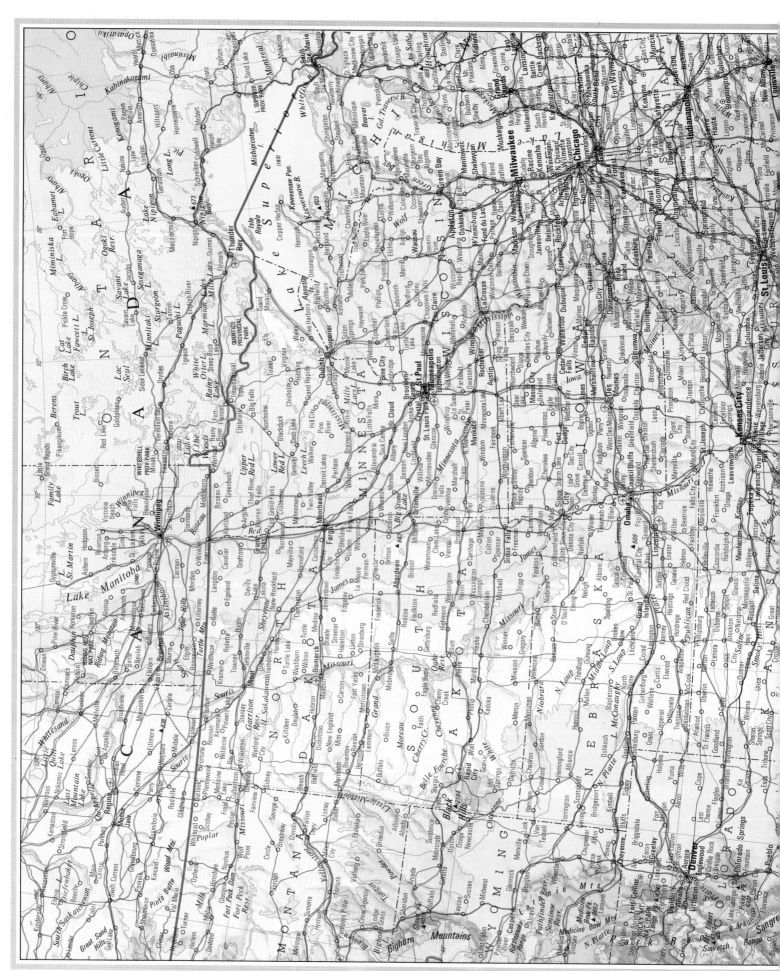

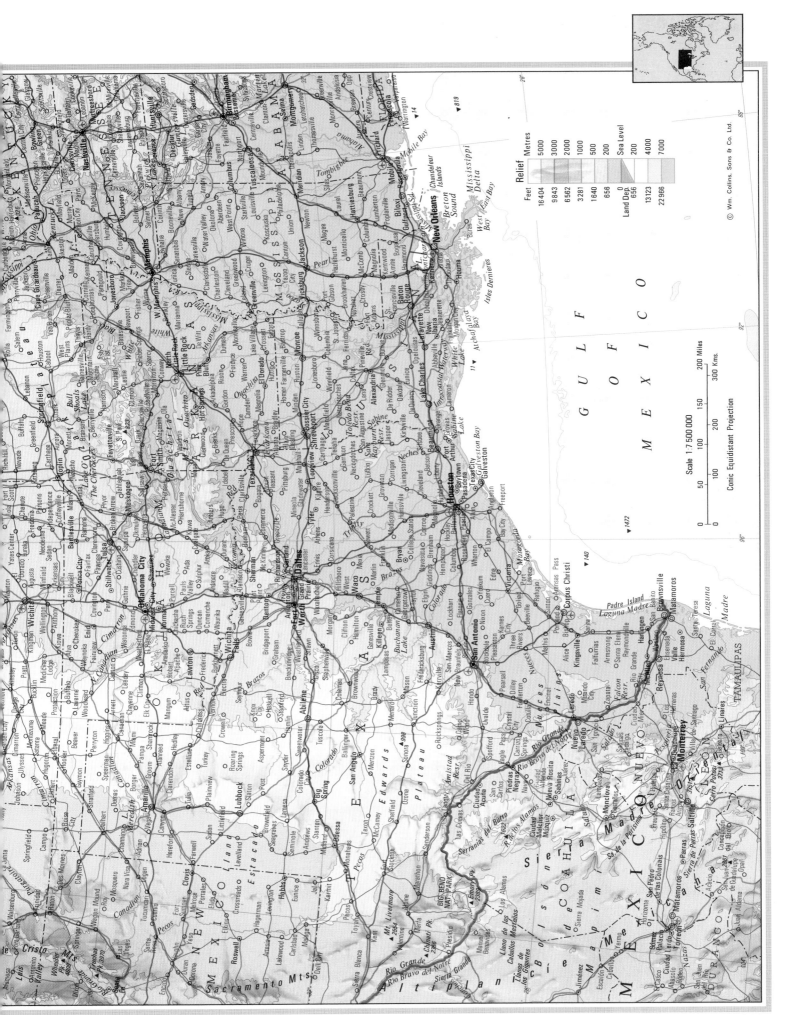

EASTERN UNITED STATES

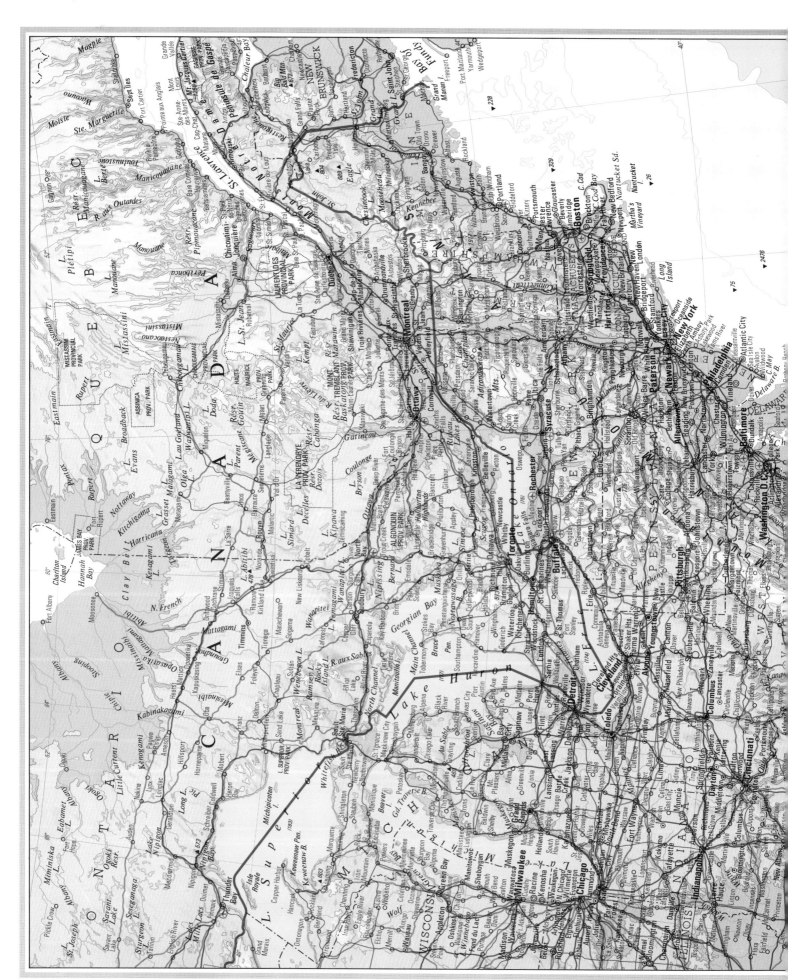

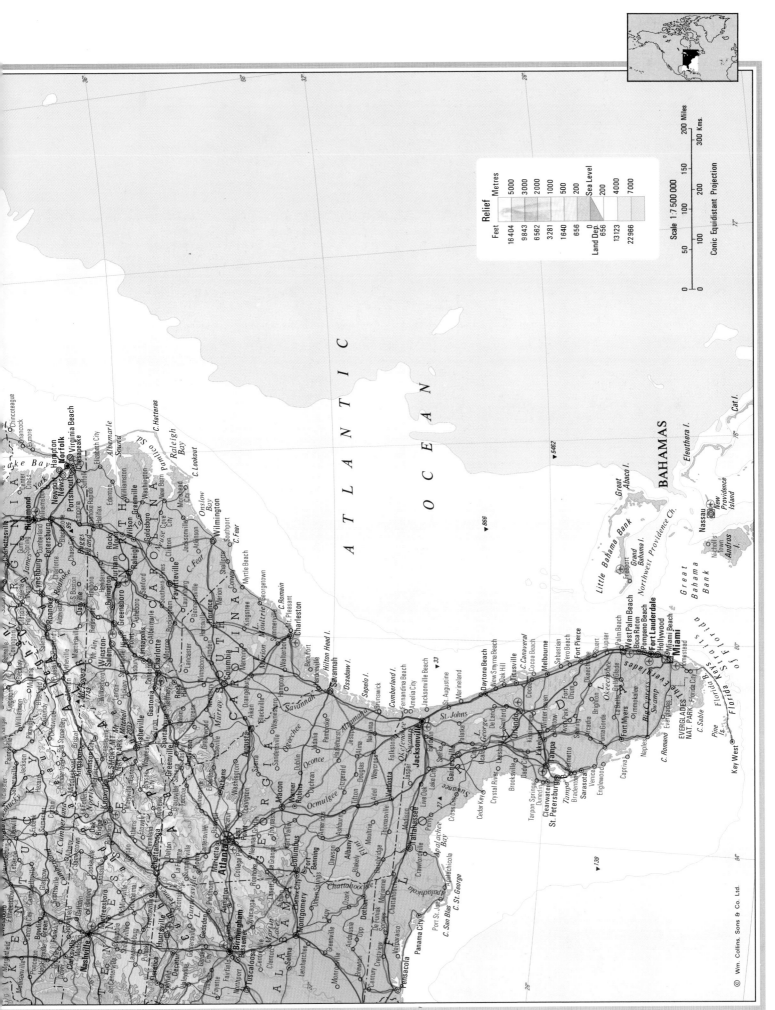

Relief

Feet	Metres
16 404	5000
9843	3000
6562	2000
3281	1000
1640	500
656	200
0	Sea Level
Land Dep.	
656	200
13 123	4000
22 966	7000

Scale 1:7 500 000

Conic Equidistant Projection

200 Miles
300 Kms.
150
200
100
50
100
0
0

© Wm. Collins, Sons & Co. Ltd.

A T L A N T I C   O C E A N

BAHAMAS

Eleuthera I.
Cat I.

Great Abaco I.
Marsh Harbour
Grand Bahama I.
Freeport

Little Bahama Bank

New Providence Island
Nassau

Northwest Providence Ch.

Andros
Nicholls Town

Great Bahama Bank

▼5462
▼866

VIRGINIA
Richmond
Petersburg
Lynchburg
Roanoke
Danville

Chincoteague
Accomac
Onancock
Exmore
Cape Charles
Chesapeake Bay
Hampton
Newport News
Norfolk
Portsmouth
Virginia Beach
Chesapeake
Suffolk
York
James

NORTH CAROLINA
Raleigh
Durham
Greensboro
Winston-Salem
Charlotte
Gastonia

Elizabeth City
Albemarle Sound
Edenton
Roanoke Rapids
Williamston
Washington
New Bern
Greenville
Goldsboro
Wilson
Rocky Mount
Kinston
Jacksonville
Morehead City
C. Hatteras
Raleigh Bay
C. Lookout
Onslow Bay
Wilmington
Southport
C. Fear
Cape Fear
Pamlico Sound

SOUTH CAROLINA
Columbia
Charleston

Fayetteville
Lumberton
Florence
Myrtle Beach
Georgetown
C. Romain
Mt. Pleasant
Moultrie

GEORGIA
Atlanta
Macon
Columbus
Savannah
Augusta

Hilton Head I.
Beaufort
Ossabaw I.
Sapelo I.
Brunswick
Cumberland I.
Amelia City

FLORIDA
Jacksonville
Gainesville
Orlando
Tampa
St. Petersburg
Clearwater
Sarasota
Fort Myers
Fort Lauderdale
Miami
Miami Beach
West Palm Beach
Boca Raton
Pompano Beach
Hollywood
Palm Beach
Fort Pierce
Vero Beach
Melbourne
Cocoa Beach
C. Canaveral
Titusville
Daytona Beach
New Smyrna Beach
St. Augustine
Jacksonville Beach
Marineland

L. Okeechobee
EVERGLADES NAT. PARK
The Everglades
Big Cypress Swamp
Key West
Straits of Florida
Florida Keys

TENNESSEE
KENTUCKY
ALABAMA
Birmingham
Montgomery
Tuscaloosa
Pensacola
Panama City
Tallahassee
Nashville
Chattanooga
Knoxville
Asheville

▼139
▼33
▼27

113

NORTHEASTERN UNITED STATES

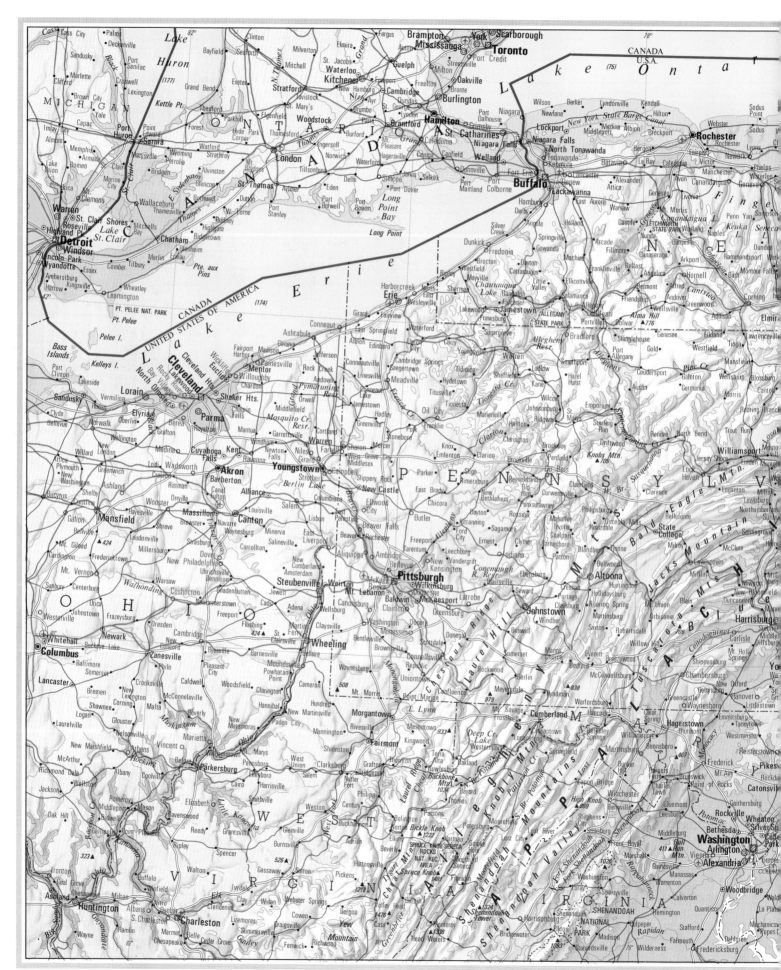

CENTRAL AMERICA AND THE CARIBBEAN

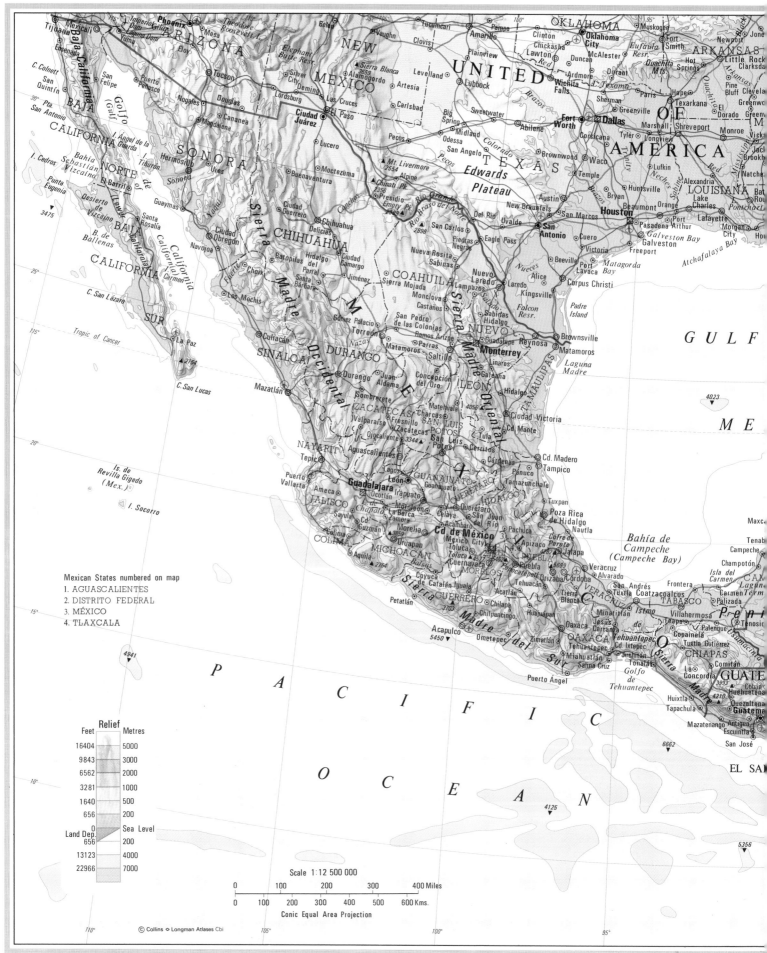

Mexican States numbered on map
1. AGUASCALIENTES
2. DISTRITO FEDERAL
3. MÉXICO
4. TLAXCALA

Relief
Feet		Metres
16404		5000
9843		3000
6562		2000
3281		1000
1640		500
656		200
0		Sea Level
Land Dep.		
656		200
13123		4000
22966		7000

Scale 1:12 500 000

0   100   200   300   400 Miles

0   100   200   300   400   500   600 Kms.

Conic Equal Area Projection

© Collins ◊ Longman Atlases Cbi

TENNESSEE
Asheville NORTH
Columbia Chattanooga Cleveland CAROLINA Charlotte Fayetteville New Bern
Greenville Spartanburg C. Lookout
Corinth Huntsville Anderson SOUTH CAROLINA Wilmington
Gadsden Rome Athens Columbia Florence
TATES Anniston Atlanta Augusta C. Fear
Birmingham Bessemer Griffin Orangeburg C. Romain
ALABAMA La Grange Macon Charleston
Columbus Dublin Savannah
GEORGIA
Montgomery Phenix City
Andalusia Albany Waycross Brunswick
Dothan Thomasville
Mobile Madison Lake City Jacksonville
Pensacola Tallahassee St. Augustine
Panama Gainesville Ocala Daytona Beach
City Apalachee Bay Sanford Cape Canaveral

ATLANTIC
OCEAN

Orlando
Lakeland
Clearwater Tampa Fort Pierce
St. Petersburg Bradenton West Palm Beach
Sarasota Lake Okeechobee
Fort Myers Freeport Grand Bahama I. Great Abaco
Fort Lauderdale
Eleuthera I.
C. Romano New Providence Rock Sound
Nicolls Town Nassau Cat I.
C. Sable Andros Town San Salvador
Key West Florida Keys The Bight
Andros I. Rolleville Rum Cay
Straits Gt. Exuma Long I. Samana Cay
of Florida Plana Cays
Crooked I. Acklin's I. Mayaguana I.
Little Turks and Caicos Is.
Inagua (U.K.)
La Habana Caicos Is. Turks Is.
(Havana) Cárdenas
Matanzas Archo. de Sabana Archo. de Camaguey
Marianao Sagua Great
Pinar del Río Guines Santa Clara Caibarien Inagua Matthew
Guane Cienfuegos Sancti Ciego de Avila Town Île de
Golfo de Spíritus Morón la Tortue Puerto Plata
Batabanó Trinidad Nuevitas Port-de-Paix
Nueva CUBA Camagüey Holguín Banes Cap-Haïtien San Francisco
Gerona Victoria Baracoa de Macorís Samaná
Isla de Pinos de las Tunas Bayamo G. de la Valverde Santiago
Jardines de la Manzanillo S. Luis Guantánamo Gonâve La Vega DOMINICAN San Juan
Reina Sa. Maestra Santiago Jérémie Île de REP. Bayamón
Little C. Cruz Turquino de Cuba Gonâve HAITI Azua Santo La Romana Arecibo
Cayman Cayman Brac 1971 Port-au- S. Cristóbal Domingo S. Pedro PUERTO
Prince Barahona de Macorís RICO
Grand Cayman Les Saona (U.S.A.)
Georgetown Cayes Hispaniola Mona Mayagüez Ponce Caguas
Cayman Is.
(U.K.) Montego Bay St. Ann's Bay
Black River May Pen Port Antonio Antilles
JAMAICA Kingston

North America

ATLANTIC

40°

30°

Tropic of Cancer

20°

OCEAN

Caribbean Sea

Barranquilla

Maracaibo   Caracas

TRINIDAD
AND TOBAGO

VENEZUELA

10°

Medellín

Bogotá

Georgetown

Paramaribo

Cayenne

GUYANA

SURINAM

GUIANA
(Fr.)

Cali

COLOMBIA

Quito

Belém

40°

ECUADOR

30°   Equator

Islas
Galápagos
(Ec.)

90°

Guayaquil

BRAZIL

Fortaleza

100°

P
E
R
U

Recife

110°

Lima

10°

La Paz

Brasília

Salvador

BOLIVIA

120°

Sucre

Belo
Horizonte

130°

PARAGUAY

Río de
Janeiro

São Paulo

Santo André

PACIFIC

San Félix (Chile)
San Ambrosio

Asunción

Curitiba

Tropic of Capricorn

20°

140°

A
R
G
E
N
T
I
N
A

Córdoba

Pôrto
Alegre

Islas
Juan
Fernández
(Chile)

Valparaíso

Santiago

Rosario

URUGUAY

30°

Buenos
Aires

La Plata

Montevideo

C
H
I
L
E

OCEAN

OCE

40°

Falkland
Is. (U.K.)

South
Georgia
(U.K.)

50°

Tierra del
Fuego

60°

Antarctic Circle

70°

International Date Line

Antarctica

© Wm. Collins Sons & Co. Ltd.

118

SOUTH AMERICA

South America as a continental name is used for the land area extending south from the Isthmus of Panama to Cape Horn and lying between 34°W and 82°W. Latin America is a term widely used to cover those parts of the Americas where Spanish, or Portuguese as in Brazil, are the adopted national languages, and thus refers to an area that includes all of South America, Central America, Mexico and the Caribbean, except for the few English, French and Dutch speaking countries and dependencies.

SOUTH AMERICA

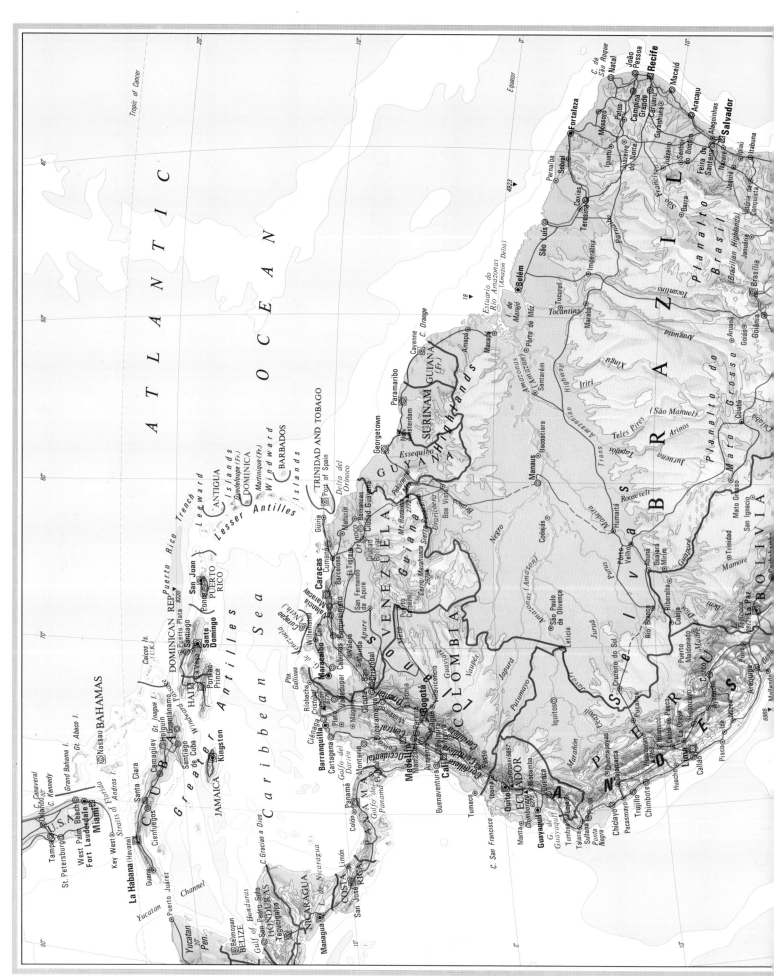

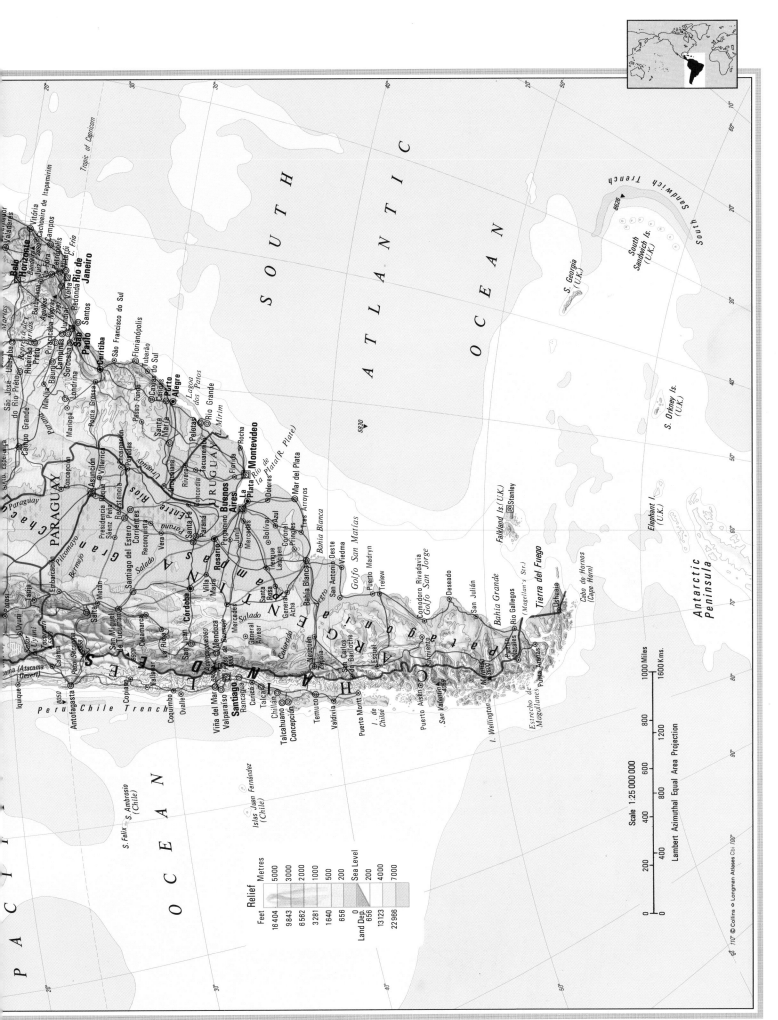

PACIFIC OCEAN

SOUTH ATLANTIC OCEAN

Relief

Metres	Feet
5000	16404
3000	9843
2000	6562
1000	3281
500	1640
200	656
Sea Level	0
Land Dep.	656
200	
4000	13123
7000	22966

Scale 1:25 000 000

1000 Miles
1600 Kms.

800   1200
400   600   800
200   400

Lambert Azimuthal Equal Area Projection

Tropic of Capricorn

Belo Horizonte
Rio de Janeiro
São Paulo
Santos
Curitiba
Porto Alegre
Pelotas
Rio Grande
Montevideo
Buenos Aires
La Plata
Rio de la Plata (R. Plate)
Mar del Plata
Bahía Blanca
Golfo San Matías
Puerto Madryn
Trelew
Golfo San Jorge
Comodoro Rivadavia
Deseado
San Julián
Bahía Grande
Río Gallegos
Tierra del Fuego
Cabo de Hornos (Cape Horn)
Ushuaia
Estrecho de Magallanes (Magellan's Str.)
Punta Arenas
Puerto Natales

PARAGUAY
Asunción
URUGUAY
ARGENTINA
Córdoba
Rosario
Santa Fe
Paraná
Santiago
Valparaíso
Concepción
Valdivia
Puerto Montt
I. de Chiloé
Bariloche
Esquel
A N D E S

Gran Chaco
Paraguay
Pilcomayo
Bermejo

Atacama (Atacama Desert)
Antofagasta
Peru/Chile Trench
Iquique
Coquimbo

Islas Juan Fernández (Chile)
S. Félix S. Ambrosio (Chile)

Falkland Is. (U.K.)
Stanley

Elephant I. (U.K.)
Antarctic Peninsula

S. Georgia (U.K.)
S. Orkney Is. (U.K.)
South Sandwich Is. (U.K.)
South Sandwich Trench

© Collins ○ Longman Atlases Cbi 100°

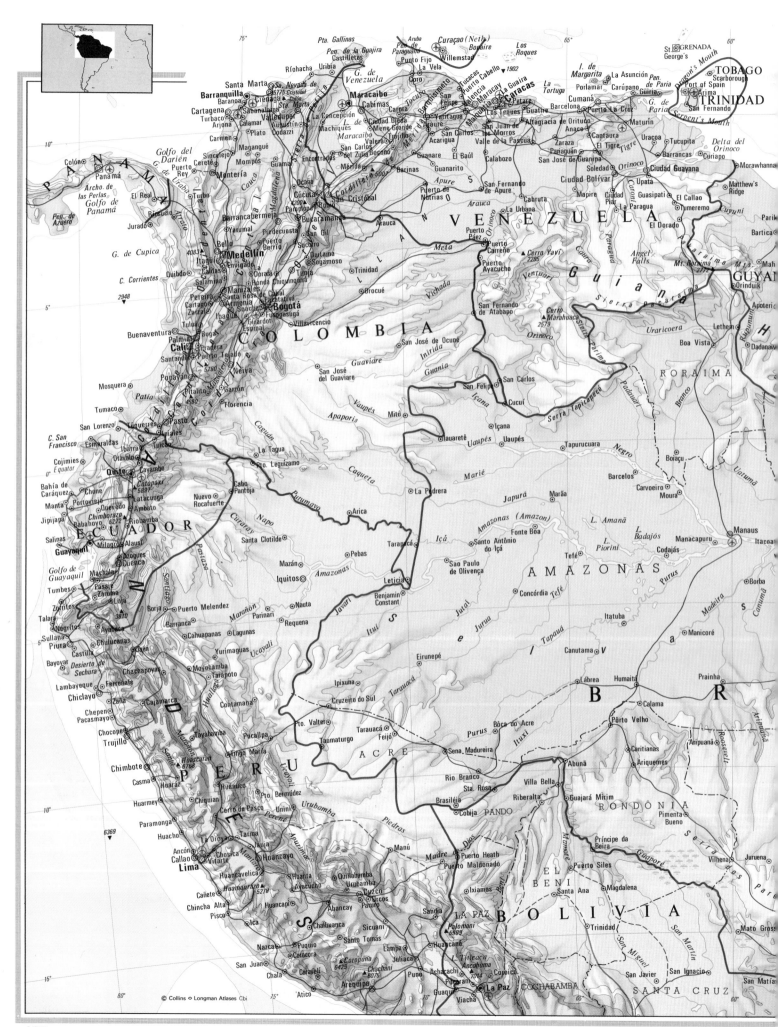

Relief

Feet	Metres
16 404	5000
9843	3000
6562	2000
3281	1000
1640	500
656	200
0	Sea Level
Land Dep.	
656	200
13123	4000

Scale 1:12 500 000

Lambert Azimuthal Equal Area Projection

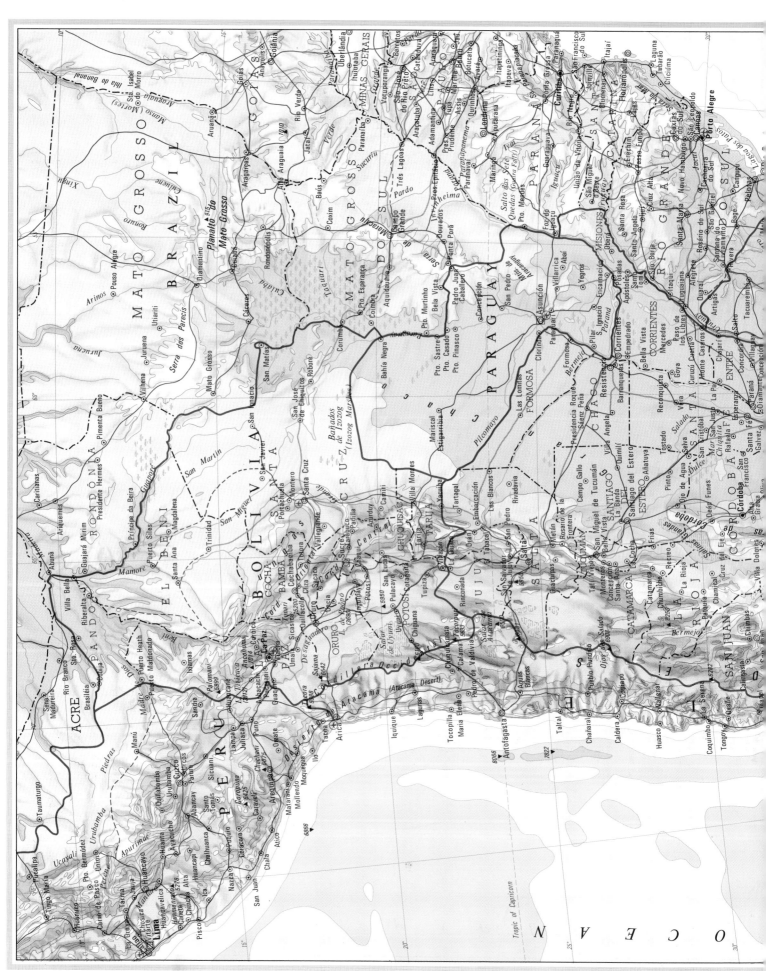

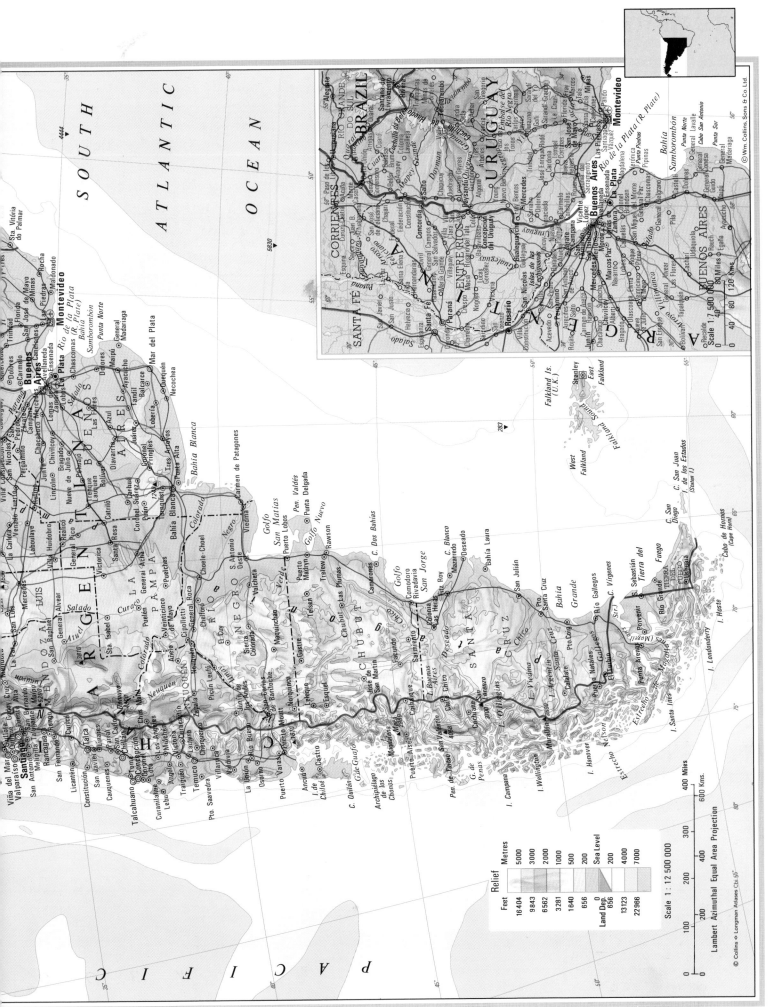

BRAZIL

BOLIVIA

PARAGUAY

ARGENTINA

URUGUAY

MATO GROSSO

MATO GROSSO DO SUL

GOIÁS

MINAS GERAIS

SÃO PAULO

PARANÁ

SANTA CATARINA

RIO GRANDE DO SUL

BAHIA

ESPÍRITO SANTO

RIO DE JANEIRO

DISTRITO FEDERAL

SANTA CRUZ

FORMOSA

CHACO

SANTIAGO DEL ESTERO

SANTA FÉ

CORRIENTES

MISIONES

ENTRE RIOS

BUENOS AIRES

PAMPA

CÓRDOBA

LA PAMPA

SALTA

Planalto do Mato Grosso

Serra dos Parecis

Planalto Brasil

Brazilian Highlands

Belo Horizonte

Brasília

Goiânia

São Paulo

Rio de Janeiro

Niterói

Curitiba

Florianópolis

Pôrto Alegre

Montevideo

Buenos Aires

La Plata

Rosario

Asunción

Santa Cruz

Cuiabá

Campo Grande

Uberlândia

Uberaba

Tropic of Capricorn

Relief

Feet	Metres
16 404	5000
9 843	3000
6 562	2000
3 281	1000
1 640	500
656	200
0	Sea Level
Land Dep.	
656	200
13 123	4000

Scale 1:12 500 000

0   100   200   300   400 Miles

0   100 200 300 400 500 600 Kms.

Lambert Azimuthal Equal Area Projection

Scale 1:7 500 000

0   40   80 Miles

0   40   80   120 Kms.

© Collins ◇ Longman Atlases Cbi

© Wm. Collins Sons & Co. Ltd.

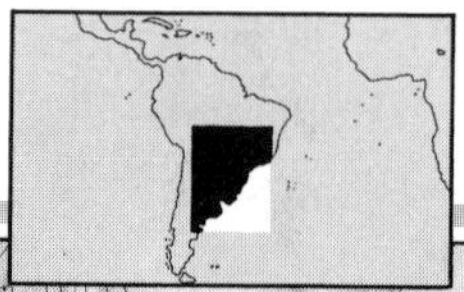

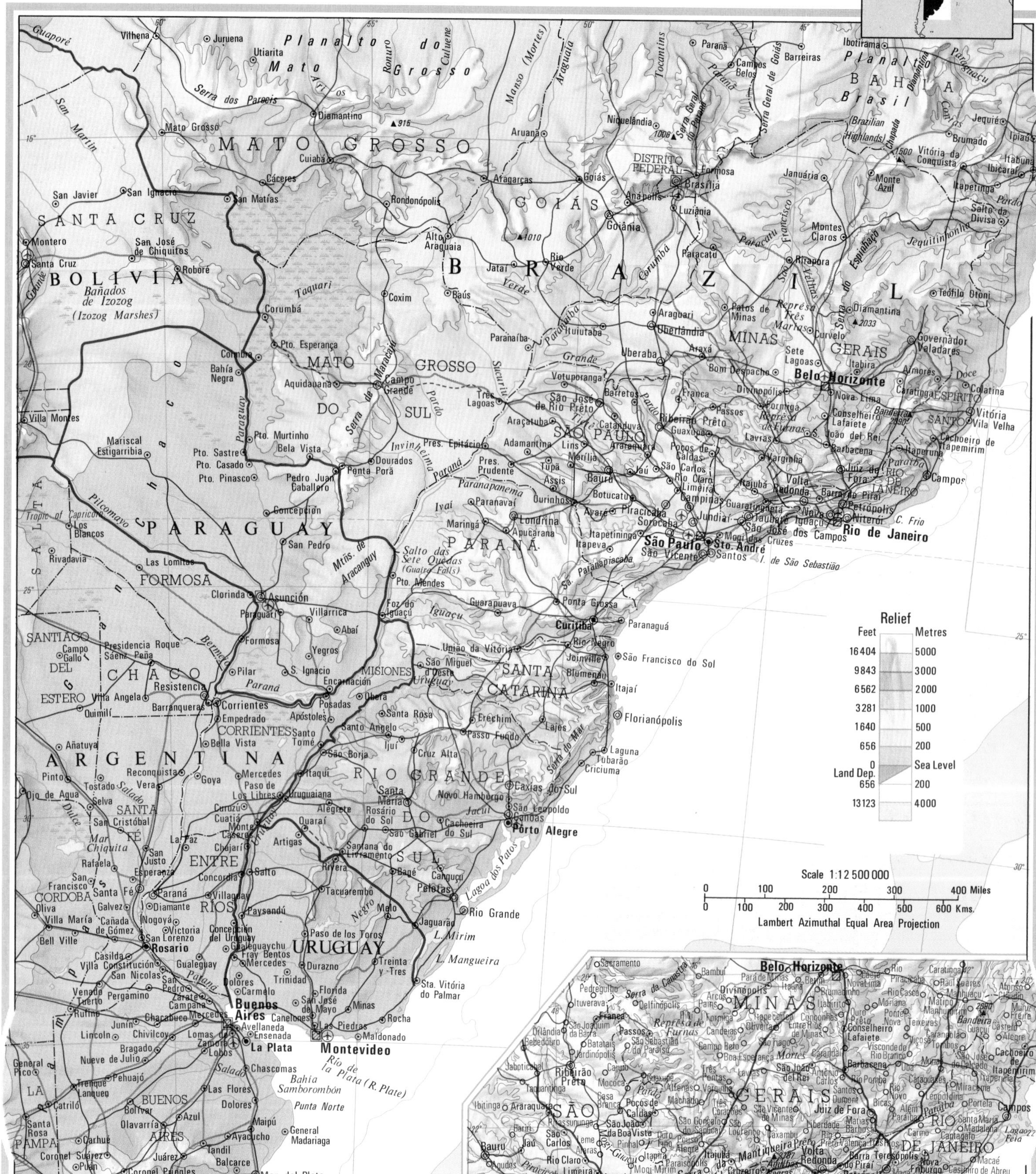

ATLANTIC OCEAN

BERMUDA
Scale 1:1 000 000

St. George's I.
St. George
St. David's I.
Ireland I.
Castle Harbour
Somerset I.
Great Sound
Flatts Village
Hamilton

CANARY ISLANDS (Spain)
Scale 1:10 000 000

Lanzarote
Arrecife
La Palma
Fuerteventura
Los Llanos de Aridane
Tenerife
Santa Cruz de Tenerife
Gomera
La Orotava
Arucas
Las Palmas de Gran Canaria
Hierro
Maspalomas
Gran Canaria
Islas Canarias (Canary Isles)
WESTERN SAHARA

MADEIRA ISLANDS
Scale 1:4 000 000 (Portugal)

Porto Santo
Porto Moniz
Santana
Madeira
Paúl do Mar
Sta. Cruz
Funchal
Arquipélago da Madeira (Madeira Is.)
Deserta Grande

CANADA
Hudson B.
Hudson Str.
Davis Strait
GREENLAND
Denmark Str.
Arctic Circle
Faroe Is. (Den.)
Bergen
ICELAND
Reykjavík
K. Farvel / Uummannarsuaq (C. Farewell)
Rockall Bank
UNITED KINGDOM
North Sea
NORWAY
SWEDEN
Oslo
Fort Chimo
Nain
Labrador
Goose Bay
Newfoundland
Labrador Basin
REP. OF IRELAND
Glasgow
Birmingham
BEL
NETH
Quebec
Ottawa
Montreal
Sept Iles
G. of St. Lawrence
Dublin
London
Bruxelles
Paris
Pittsburgh
Halifax
C. Race
Brussel
FRANCE
Cincinnati
Boston
Nantes
Lyon
Memphis
UNITED
New York
Philadelphia
Bordeaux
B. of Biscay
Marseille
Dallas
STATES
Washington
C. Finisterre
Barcelona
Madrid
Houston
OF
Birmingham
PORTUGAL
Valencia
SPAIN
New Orleans
AMERICA
C. Hatteras
Atlantic
Lisboa
Alger
Mobile
Arquipélago dos Açores (Azores) (Port.)
Sevilla
Mediterranean Sea
Algiers
La Habana (Havana)
Jacksonville
Oran
Tanger
Rabat
Atlas Mts.
Gulf of Mexico
Miama
Bermuda Rise
Casablanca
MOROCCO
Tropic of Cancer
BERMUDA
Marrakech
Nassau
BAHAMAS
265
El Aaiún
In Salah
ALGERIA
LIBYA
Yucatán
CUBA
Sargasso
Western
Basin
WESTERN SAHARA
Ahaggar
Tibesti
Mexico
Greater
North
Sea
Madeira (Port.)
Sahara
Honduras
Cayman Trough
Basin
Islas Canarias (Canary Is.) (Sp.)
Air
Bodélé
SUDAN
HAITI
Puerto Rico Trench
West Indies
Cape Verde Basin
MAURITANIA
MALI
NIGER
CHAD
HONDURAS
JAMAICA
DOM. REP.
Nouadhibou
Tombouctou
Agadez
L. Chad
N'Djamena
NICARAGUA
Caribbean Sea
PUERTO RICO
Nouakchott
Gao
Niamey
Maiduguri
COSTA RICA
Barranquilla
Colombian Basin
Guadeloupe (Fr.)
Martinique (Fr.)
CAPE VERDE
Dakar
SENEGAL
Bamako
BURKINA
Ouagadougou
Kano
NIGERIA
Jos
CENTRAL AFRICAN REPUBLIC
PANAMA
Maracaibo
Venezuelan Basin
Lesser Antilles
BARBADOS
GRENADA
TRINIDAD AND TOBAGO
GAMBIA
GUINEA BISSAU
GUINEA
Conakry
IVORY COAST
Bouaké
GHANA
Ibadan
BENIN
Lagos
Enugu
Port Harcourt
CAMEROON
Panama
Caracas
Ciudad Bolívar
Georgetown
Freetown
SIERRA LEONE
Monrovia
LIBERIA
Abidjan
Accra
Lomé
Porto-Novo
Yaoundé
Douala
EQUAT. GUINEA
Medellín
COLOMBIA
Orinoco
GUYANA
Paramaribo
SURINAM
Cayenne
GUIANA (Fr.)
Gulf of Guinea
Libreville
GABON
CONGO
ZAIRE
Bogotá
VENEZUELA
Guiana Highlands
São Tomé
Annobón
Congo Basin
Cali
ECUADOR
Quito
Negro
Guinea Basin
Brazzaville
Kinshasa
Kananga
Guayaquil
Putumayo
Branco
St. Paul Rocks
6040
Cabinda
Ubangi
Lima
PERU
Amazonas
Manaus
Amazonas (Amazon)
Belém
São Luís
Rocas
Fernando de Noronha
6537
Ascension (U.K.)
Luanda
Cuzco
Selvas
Madeira
Juruá
Fortaleza
C. de São Roque
Lobito
ANGOLA
Huambo
Arequipa
BRAZIL
Recife
Brazilian Basin
6013
Moçâmedes
La Paz
Titicaca
BOLIVIA
Planalto do Mato Grosso
Planalto
Salvador
St. Helena (U.K.)
NAMIBIA
Windhoek
Arica
Sucre
Santa Cruz
Cuiabá
Goiânia
Brasília
Brasil
Martin Vaz (Brazil)
SOUTH
Walvis Bay
BOTSWANA
Antofagasta
PARAGUAY
Ribeirão Prêto
Belo Horizonte
892
Kalahari Desert
Tropic of Capricorn
San Miguel de Tucumán
São Paulo
Niterói
Rio de Janeiro
ATLANTIC
Walvis Ridge
Kimberley
Córdoba
Asunción
Curitiba
Florianópolis
Bromley Plateau
South Eastern Atlantic Basin
REP. OF SOUTH AFRICA
Santa Fe
Pôrto Alegre
Pelotas
URUGUAY
638
OCEAN
514
Cape Town
Kaapstad
C. of Good Hope
Port Elizabeth
Santiago
Rosario
Mar del Plata
Montevideo
Río de la Plata
Tristan da Cunha (U.K.)
Cape Basin
Concepción
ARGENTINA
Buenos Aires
Agulhas Basin
Bahía Blanca
Argentine Basin
5585
Gough I. (U.K.)
411
Comodoro Rivadavia
6212
Atlantic-Antarctic Ridge
Peurto Montt
Falkland Is. (U.K.)
Stanley
S. Georgia (U.K.)
Bouvetøya (Norway)
ASCENSION (U.K.)
Scale 1:1 000 000
Georgetown
The Peak
S.E. Head
Portland Pt.
Punta Arenas
Tierra del Fuego
Scotia Sea
S. Sandwich Is. (U.K.)
8428
Settlement of Edinburgh
2160
Tristan da Cunha
Cabo de Hornos (Cape Horn)
5552
Scotia Ridge
South Sandwich Trench
S. Orkney Is. (U.K.)
Atlantic-Indian-Antarctic Basin
Inaccessible I.
TRISTAN DA CUNHA (U.K.)
ST. HELENA (U.K.)
Scale 1:1 000 000
Flagstaff
Jamestown
Longwood
Diana's Peak
Gill Pt.
Sandy B.
SW. Pt.
Pacific-Antarctic Basin
Antarctic Peninsula
Scale 1:60 000 000
500   1000   1500 Miles
500 1000 2000 2500 Kms.
Zenithal Equal-Area Projection
© Wm. Collins Sons & Co. Ltd.
Antarctic Circle
Nightingale I.
Scale 1:1 000 000

127

POLAR REGIONS

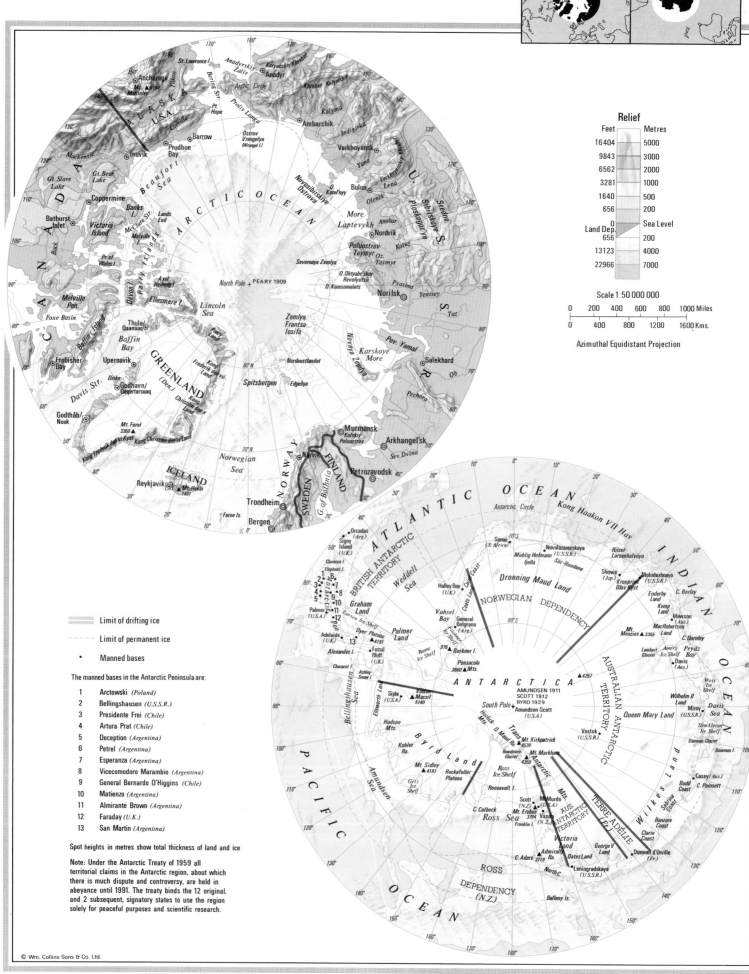

Relief

Feet		Metres
16404		5000
9843		3000
6562		2000
3281		1000
1640		500
656		200
0 Land Dep.		Sea Level
656		200
13123		4000
22966		7000

Scale 1:50 000 000

0 200 400 600 800 1000 Miles

0 400 800 1200 1600 Kms.

Azimuthal Equidistant Projection

Limit of drifting ice

Limit of permanent ice

• Manned bases

The manned bases in the Antarctic Peninsula are:

1 Arctowski *(Poland)*
2 Bellingshausen *(U.S.S.R.)*
3 Presidente Frei *(Chile)*
4 Artura Prat *(Chile)*
5 Deception *(Argentina)*
6 Petrel *(Argentina)*
7 Esperanza *(Argentina)*
8 Vicecomodoro Marambio *(Argentina)*
9 General Bernardo O'Higgins *(Chile)*
10 Matienzo *(Argentina)*
11 Almirante Brown *(Argentina)*
12 Faraday *(U.K.)*
13 San Martin *(Argentina)*

Spot heights in metres show total thickness of land and ice

Note: Under the Antarctic Treaty of 1959 all territorial claims in the Antarctic region, about which there is much dispute and controversy, are held in abeyance until 1991. The treaty binds the 12 original, and 2 subsequent, signatory states to use the region solely for peaceful purposes and scientific research.

GEOGRAPHICAL DATA
Part 1

WORLD
FACTS
AND
FIGURES

WORLD PHYSICAL DATA

Earth's Dimensions

Superficial area	510 066 000 km²
Land surface	148 326 000 km²
Water surface	361 740 000 km²
Equatorial circumference	40 075 km
Meridional circumference	40 007 km
Volume	1 083 230x10⁶ km³
Mass	5.976x10²¹ tonnes

Oceans and Sea Areas

Pacific Ocean	165 384 000 km²
Atlantic Ocean	82 217 000 km²
Indian Ocean	73 481 000 km²
Arctic Ocean	14 056 000 km²
Mediterranean Sea	2 505 000 km²
South China Sea	2 318 000 km²
Bering Sea	2 269 000 km²
Caribbean Sea	1 943 000 km²
Gulf of Mexico	1 544 000 km²
Okhotskoye More (Sea of Okhotsk)	1 528 000 km²
East China Sea	1 248 000 km²
Hudson Bay	1 233 000 km²
Sea of Japan	1 008 000 km²
North Sea	575 000 km²
Black Sea	461 000 km²

River Lengths

An Nīl (Nile); Africa	6695 km
Amazonas (Amazon); South America	6570 km
Mississippi - Missouri; North America	6020 km
Chang Jiang (Yangtze); Asia	5471 km
Ob-Irtysh; Asia	5410 km
Huang He (Hwang Ho); Asia	4840 km
Zaïre; Africa	4630 km
Amur; Asia	4416 km
Lena; Asia	4269 km
Mackenzie; North America	4240 km
Niger; Africa	4183 km
Mekong; Asia	4180 km
Yenisey; Asia	4090 km
Murray - Darling; Oceania	3717 km
Volga; Europe	3688 km

Lake and Inland Sea Areas

Some areas are subject to seasonal variations.

Caspian Sea; U.S.S.R. / Iran	371 795 km²
Lake Superior; U.S.A. / Canada	82 413 km²
Lake Victoria; East Africa	69 485 km²
Aralskoye More (Aral Sea); U.S.S.R.	66 457 km²
Lake Huron; U.S.A. / Canada	59 596 km²
Lake Michigan; U.S.A.	58 016 km²
Lake Tanganyika; East Africa	32 893 km²
Great Bear Lake; Canada	31 792 km²
Ozero Baykal (Lake Baikal); U.S.S.R.	30 510 km²
Great Slave Lake; Canada	28 930 km²
Lake Malaŵi; Malaŵi/Mozambique	28 490 km²
Lake Erie; U.S.A. / Canada	25 667 km²
Lake Winnipeg; Canada	24 514 km²
Lake Ontario; U.S.A. / Canada	19 529 km²
Ladozhskoye Ozero (Lake Ladoga); U.S.S.R.	18 390 km²

The Continents

Asia	44 391 162 km²
Africa	30 244 049 km²
North America	24 247 038 km²
South America	17 821 028 km²
Antarctica	13 338 500 km²
Europe	10 354 636 km²
Oceania	8 547 000 km²

Island Areas

Greenland; Arctic / Atlantic Ocean	2 175 597 km²
New Guinea; Indonesia / Papua New Guinea	828 057 km²
Borneo; Malaysia / Indonesia / Brunei	751 929 km²
Madagascar; Indian Ocean	587 042 km²
Baffin Island; Canada	476 068 km²
Sumatera (Sumatra); Indonesia	422 170 km²
Honshū; Japan	230 455 km²
Great Britain; United Kingdom	229 867 km²
Ellesmere Island; Canada	212 688 km²
Victoria Island; Canada	212 199 km²
Sulawesi (Celebes); Indonesia	179 370 km²
South Island; New Zealand	150 461 km²
Jawa (Java); Indonesia	126 500 km²
North Island; New Zealand	114 688 km²
Cuba; Caribbean Sea	114 525 km²

Mountain Heights (Selected)

Everest; Nepal / China	8848 m
K2; Jammu & Kashmir / China	8611 m
Kānchenjunga; Nepal / India	8586 m
Dhaulāgiri; Nepal	8172 m
Annapurna; Nepal	8078 m
Aconcagua; Argentina	6960 m
Ojos del Salado; Argentina / Chile	6908 m
McKinley; Alaska U.S.A.	6194 m
Logan; Canada	6050 m
Kilimanjaro; Tanzania	5895 m
Elbrus; U.S.S.R.	5633 m
Kenya; Kenya	5200 m
Vinson Massif; Antarctica	5139 m
Puncak Jaya; Indonesia	5030 m
Blanc; France / Italy	4807 m

Volcanoes (Selected)

	Last Eruption	Height
Cameroun; Cameroon	1922	4070 m
Cotopaxi; Ecuador	1975	5897 m
Elbrus; U.S.S.R.	extinct	5633 m
Erebus; Antarctica	1979	3794 m
Etna; Sicilia, Italy	1981	3340 m
Fuji san (Fujiyama); Japan	extinct	3776 m
Hekla; Iceland	1981	1491 m
Kilimanjaro; Tanzania	extinct	5895 m
Mauna Loa; Hawaii	1978	4171 m
Ngauruhoe; New Zealand	1975	2291 m
Popocatépetl; Mexico	1920	5452 m
St. Helens; U.S.A.	1981	2949 m
Stromboli; Italy	1975	926 m
Tristan da Cunha; Atlantic Ocean	1962	2160 m
Vesuvio (Vesuvius); Italy	1944	1277 m

WORLD POLITICAL DATA

National Areas

Union of Soviet Socialist Republics; Asia / Europe	22 402 000 km²
Canada; North America	9 976 000 km²
China; Asia	9 596 961 km²
United States; North America	9 363 123 km²
Brazil; South America	8 511 965 km²
Australia; Oceania	7 686 848 km²
India; Asia	3 287 590 km²
Argentina; South America	2 766 889 km²
Sudan; Africa	2 505 813 km²
Algeria; Africa	2 381 741 km²
Zaïre; Africa	2 345 409 km²
Greenland; North America	2 175 600 km²
Saudi Arabia; Asia	2 149 690 km²
Mexico; North America	1 972 547 km²
Indonesia; Asia	1 904 345 km²
Libya; Africa	1 759 540 km²
Iran; Asia	1 648 000 km²
Mongolia; Asia	1 565 000 km²
Peru; South America	1 285 216 km²
Chad; Africa	1 284 000 km²

National Populations

China; Asia	976 230 000
India; Asia	650 982 000
Union of Soviet Socialist Republics; Asia / Europe	265 542 000
United States; North America	227 640 000
Indonesia; Asia	131 000 000
Brazil; South America	123 032 000
Japan; Asia	115 870 000
Bangladesh; Asia	84 643 000
Pakistan; Asia	79 838 000
Nigeria; Africa	77 082 000
Mexico; North America	71 911 000
West Germany; Europe	61 658 000
Italy; Europe	57 140 000
United Kingdom; Europe	55 945 000
France; Europe	53 780 000
Vietnam; Asia	52 742 000
Philippines; Asia	46 580 000
Thailand; Asia	46 142 000
Turkey; Asia / Europe	44 312 000
Egypt; Africa	41 995 000

World Cities

New York; United States	16 479 000
Ciudad de México (Mexico City); Mexico	13 994 000
Tōkyō; Japan	11 695 000
Shanghai; China	10 820 000
Los Angeles; United States	10 607 000
Paris; France	9 863 000
Buenos Aires; Argentina	8 436 000
Moskva (Moscow); U.S.S.R.	8 011 000
Chicago; United States	7 664 000
Beijing (Peking); China	7 570 000
São Paulo; Brazil	7 199 000
Calcutta; India	7 031 000
Sŏul (Seoul); South Korea	6 879 000
London; United Kingdom	6 696 000
Bombay; India	5 971 000

Major International Organisations

United Nations - On December 1981 the United Nations had 157 members. Independent states not represented include Liechtenstein, Monaco, Nauru, North Korea, San Marino, South Korea, Switzerland, Taiwan, Tonga.

Commonwealth

Australia	Bahamas	Bangladesh	Barbados
Belize	Botswana	Canada	Cyprus
Dominica	Fiji	Gambia	Ghana
Grenada	Guyana	Hong Kong	India
Jamaica	Kenya	Kiribati	Lesotho
Malaŵi	Malaysia	Malta	Mauritius
Nauru	New Zealand	Nigeria	Papua New Guinea
St. Lucia	St. Vincent	Seychelles	Sierra Leone
Singapore	Solomon Islands	Sri Lanka	Swaziland
Tanzania	Tonga	Trinidad & Tobago	Tuvalu
Uganda	United Kingdom	Vanuatu	Western Samoa
Zambia	Zimbabwe		

OAU - Organisation of African Unity

Algeria	Angola	Benin	Botswana
Burundi	Cameroon	Cape Verde	Central African Rep.
Chad	Comoros	Congo	Djibouti
Egypt	Equatorial Guinea	Ethiopia	Gabon
Gambia	Ghana	Guinea	Guinea Bissau
Ivory Coast	Kenya	Lesotho	Liberia
Libya	Madagascar	Malaŵi	Mali
Mauritania	Mauritius	Morocco	Mozambique
Niger	Nigeria	Rwanda	São Tomé & Príncipe
Senegal	Seychelles	Sierra Leone	Somali Rep.
Sudan	Swaziland	Tanzania	Togo
Tunisia	Uganda	Upper Volta	Zaïre
Zambia	Zimbabwe		

OAS - Organisation of American States

Argentina	Barbados	Bolivia	Brazil
Chile	Colombia	Costa Rica	Dominica
Dominican Rep.	Ecuador	El Salvador	Grenada
Guatemala	Haiti	Honduras	Jamaica
Mexico	Nicaragua	Panama	Paraguay
Peru	St. Lucia	Surinam	Trinidad & Tobago
United States	Uruguay	Venezuela	

EEC - European Economic Community

Belgium	Denmark	France	Greece
Ireland	Italy	Luxembourg	Netherlands
United Kingdom	West Germany		

EFTA - European Free Trade Association

Austria	Finland (assoc.)	Iceland	Norway
Portugal	Sweden	Switzerland	

COMECON - Council for Mutual Economic Assistance

Bulgaria	Cuba	Czechoslovakia	East Germany
Hungary	Mongolia	Poland	Romania
U.S.S.R.	Vietnam	Yugoslavia (assoc.)	

ASEAN - Association of Southeast Asian Nations

Indonesia	Malaysia	Philippines	Singapore
Thailand			

ECOWAS - Economic Community of West African States

Benin	Cape Verde	Gambia	Ghana
Guinea	Guinea Bissau	Ivory Coast	Liberia
Mali	Mauritania	Niger	Nigeria
Senegal	Sierra Leone	Togo	Upper Volta

CARICOM - Caribbean Community and Common Market

Antigua	Barbados	Belize	Dominica
Grenada	Guyana	Jamaica	Monserrat
St. Kitts - Nevis	St. Lucia	St. Vincent	Trinidad & Tobago

NATIONS OF THE WORLD

COUNTRY	AREA sq. km.	POPULATION total	POPULATION per sq. km.	FORM OF GOVERNMENT	CAPITAL CITY	MAIN LANGUAGES	CURRENCY
AFGHANISTAN	647 497	15 540 000	24	democratic republic	Kābul	Pushtu, Dari (Persian)	afghani
ALBANIA	28 748	2 734 000	95	socialist people's republic	Tiranë	Albanian	lek
ALGERIA	2 381 741	18 594 000	8	republic	Alger (Algiers)	Arabic	dinar
ANDORRA	453	34 000	75	principality	Andorra	Catalan	French franc, Spanish peseta
ANGOLA	1 246 700	7 078 000	5.6	people's republic	Luanda	Portuguese	kwanza
ANTIGUA AND BARBUDA	442	74 000	167	independent political entity	St John's	English	East Caribbean dollar
ARGENTINA	2 766 889	27 863 000	10	federal republic	Buenos Aires	Spanish	peso
AUSTRALIA	7 686 848	14 727 000	1.9	monarchy (federal)	Canberra	English	dollar
AUSTRIA	83 849	7 507 000	89	federal republic	Wien (Vienna)	German	schilling
BAHAMAS	13 935	223 000	16	constitutional monarchy	Nassau	English	dollar
BAHRAIN	622	364 000	585	emirate	Al Manāmah	Arabic	dinar
BANGLADESH	143 998	86 656 000	601	people's republic	Dacca	Bengali	taka
BARBADOS	431	250 000	580	independent political entity	Bridgetown	English	dollar
BELGIUM	30 513	9 859 000	323	constitutional monarchy	Bruxelles/Brussel (Brussels)	French, Dutch, German	franc
BELIZE	22 965	145 000	6.3	constitutional monarchy	Belmopan	English	dollar
BENIN	112 622	3 567 000	31	people's republic	Porto-Novo	French	CFA franc
BHUTAN	47 000	1 298 000	27	monarchy (Indian protection)	Thimbu	Dzongkha	Indian rupee, ngultrum
BOLIVIA	1 098 581	5 600 000	5	republic	La Paz/Sucre	Spanish	peso
BOTSWANA	600 372	819 000	1.3	republic	Gaborone	English, Tswana	pula
BRAZIL	8 511 965	123 032 000	14	federal republic	Brasília	Portuguese	cruzeiro
BRUNEI	5 765	213 000	37	sultanate (U.K. protectorate)	Bandar Seri Begawan	Malay	dollar
BULGARIA	110 912	8 862 000	79	people's republic	Sofiya (Sofia)	Bulgarian	lev
BURMA	676 552	35 289 000	52	federal republic	Rangoon	Burmese	kyat
BURUNDI	27 834	4 512 000	162	republic	Bujumbura	French, Kirundi	franc
CAMEROON	475 442	8 503 000	17	republic	Yaoundé	French, English	CFA franc
CANADA	9 976 139	23 941 000	2.4	monarchy (federal)	Ottawa	English, French	dollar
CAPE VERDE	4 033	314 000	78	republic	Praia	Portuguese, Creole	escudo
CENTRAL AFRICAN REPUBLIC	622 984	2 370 000	3.8	republic	Bangui	French, Sango	CFA franc
CHAD	1 284 000	4 524 000	3.5	republic	N'Djamena	French	CFA franc
CHILE	756 945	11 104 000	15	republic	Santiago	Spanish	peso
CHINA	9 596 961	982 550 000	102	people's republic	Beijing (Peking)	Mandarin	yuan
COLOMBIA	1 138 914	27 520 000	24	republic	Bogotá	Spanish	peso
COMOROS	2 171	320 000	147	federal republic	Moroni	Comoran, Arabic, French	CFA Franc
CONGO	342 000	1 537 000	4.4	republic	Brazzaville	French	CFA franc
COSTA RICA	50 700	2 245 000	44	republic	San José	Spanish	colon
CUBA	114 524	9 833 000	86	people's republic	La Habana (Havana)	Spanish	peso
CYPRUS	9 251	629 000	68	republic	Levkosía (Nicosia)	Greek	pound
CZECHOSLOVAKIA	127 869	15 312 000	119	federal socialist republic	Praha (Prague)	Czech, Slovak	koruna
DENMARK	43 069	5 124 000	119	constitutional monarchy	København (Copenhagen)	Danish	krone
DJIBOUTI	22 000	119 000	5.4	republic	Djibouti	French, Somali, Afar	franc
DOMINICA	751	81 000	108	republic	Roseau	English, French	East Caribbean dollar
DOMINICAN REPUBLIC	48 734	5 431 000	111	republic	Santo Domingo	Spanish	peso
EAST GERMANY	108 178	16 737 000	155	people's republic	Berlin	German	mark
ECUADOR	283 561	8 354 000	29	republic	Quito	Spanish	sucre
EGYPT	1 001 449	41 995 000	41	republic	Al Qāhirah (Cairo)	Arabic	pound
EL SALVADOR	21 041	4 813 000	228	republic	San Salvador	Spanish	colón
EQUATORIAL GUINEA	28 051	363 000	13	republic	Malabo	Spanish	ekuele
ETHIOPIA	1 221 900	31 065 000	25	provisional military government	Ādīs Ābeba (Addis Ababa)	Amharic	birr
FIJI	18 272	631 000	34	monarchy (federal)	Suva	English, Fijian, Hindustani	dollar
FINLAND	337 009	4 788 000	14	republic	Helsinki	Finnish, Swedish	mark
FRANCE	547 026	53 788 000	98	republic	Paris	French	franc
GABON	267 667	551 000	2.1	republic	Libreville	French	CFA franc
GAMBIA	11 295	601 000	53	republic	Banjul	English	dalasi
GHANA	238 537	11 450 000	48	republic	Accra	English	cedi
GREECE	131 944	9 599 000	72	republic	Athínai (Athens)	Greek	drachma
GREENLAND	2 175 600	50 000	0.1	overseas territory (Denmark)	Godthåb/Nuuk	Danish, Greenlandic	kroner
GRENADA	344	97 000	281	independent political entity	St George's	English	East Caribbean dollar
GUATEMALA	108 889	7 262 000	66	republic	Guatemala	Spanish	quetzal
GUIANA	91 000	64 000	0.6	overseas department (France)	Cayenne	French	franc

NATIONS OF THE WORLD

COUNTRY	AREA sq. km.	POPULATION total	POPULATION per sq. km.	FORM OF GOVERNMENT	CAPITAL CITY	MAIN LANGUAGES	CURRENCY
GUINEA	245 857	5 014 000	20	republic	Conakry	French	syli
GUINEA BISSAU	36 125	777 000	22	republic	Bissau	Portuguese	peso
GUYANA	214 969	884 000	4.1	republic	Georgetown	English	dollar
HAITI	27 750	5 009 000	180	republic	Port-au-Prince	French, Créole	gourde
HONDURAS	112 088	3 691 000	32	republic	Tegucigalpa	Spanish	lempira
HONG KONG	1 045	5 068 000	4 850	colony (U.K.)		English, Chinese	dollar
HUNGARY	93 030	10 711 000	115	republic	Budapest	Magyar	forint
ICELAND	103 000	228 000	2.2	republic	Reykjavík	Icelandic	króna
INDIA	3 287 590	683 810 000	208	republic	New Delhi	Hindi	rupee
INDONESIA	1 904 345	147 383 000	77	republic	Jakarta	Bahasa Indonesia	rupiah
IRAN	1 648 000	37 447 000	22	islamic republic	Tehrān	Persian	rial
IRAQ	434 924	13 084 000	30	republic	Baghdād	Arabic	dinar
IRELAND, REPUBLIC OF	70 023	3 365 000	48	republic	Dublin	English, Irish	punt
ISRAEL	20 770	3 871 000	186	republic	Yerushalayim (Jerusalem)	Hebrew	shekel
ITALY	301 225	57 140 000	189	republic	Roma (Rome)	Italian	lira
IVORY COAST	322 462	7 973 000	25	republic	Abidjan	French	CFA franc
JAMAICA	10 991	2 192 000	199	constitutional monarchy	Kingston	English	dollar
JAPAN	372 313	117 057 000	314	monarchy	Tōkyō	Japanese	yen
JORDAN	97 740	2 779 000	28	monarchy	'Ammān	Arabic	dinar
KAMPUCHEA	181 035	8 872 000	49	people's republic	Phnum Pénh (Phnom Penh)	Cambodian, Khmer	riel
KENYA	582 646	16 402 000	28	republic	Nairobi	Swahili, English	shilling
KIRIBATI	886	63 000	71	republic	Bairiki	English, Gilbertese (I-Kiribati)	Australian dollar
KUWAIT	17 818	1 356 000	76	sheikdom	Al Kuwayt (Kuwait)	Arabic	dinar
LAOS	236 800	3 721 000	15	people's republic	Viangchan (Vientiane)	Lao	kip
LEBANON	10 400	3 161 000	304	republic	Bayrūt (Beirut)	Arabic	pound
LESOTHO	30 355	1 339 000	44	monarchy	Maseru	English, Sesotho	loti
LIBERIA	111 369	1 873 000	16	republic	Monrovia	English	dollar
LIBYA	1 759 540	2 977 000	1.6	republic	Țarābulus (Tripoli) / Banghāzī (Benghazi)	Arabic	dinar
LIECHTENSTEIN	157	26 000	166	constitutional monarchy	Vaduz	German	Swiss franc
LUXEMBOURG	2 586	364 000	140	constitutional monarchy	Luxembourg	Letzeburgish, French, German	franc
MADAGASCAR	587 041	8 742 000	14	republic	Antananarivo	Malagasy	Malagasy franc
MALAWI	118 484	5 968 000	50	republic	Lilongwe	English, Chichewa	kwacha
MALAYSIA	329 749	13 436 000	40	constitutional monarchy	Kuala Lumpur	Malay	ringgit
MALDIVES	298	143 046	480	republic	Malé	Divehi	rupee
MALI	1 240 000	6 906 000	5.5	republic	Bamako	French, Bambara	franc
MALTA	316	369 000	1 167	republic	Valletta	Maltese, English	pound
MAURITANIA	1 030 700	1 634 000	1.5	republic	Nouakchott	French, Arabic	ouguiya
MAURITIUS	2 045	924 000	452	independent political entity	Port Louis	English, Creole	rupee
MEXICO	1 972 547	71 911 000	35	federal republic	Ciudad de México (Mexico City)	Spanish	peso
MONACO	1.5	26 000	17 333	constitutional monarchy	Monaco	French	French franc
MONGOLIA	1 565 000	1 595 000	1.1	people's republic	Ulaanbaatar (Ulan Bator)	Mongol	tugrik
MOROCCO	446 550	20 242 000	44	monarchy	Rabat	Arabic	dirham
MOZAMBIQUE	783 000	12 130 000	13	people's republic	Maputo	Portuguese	escudo
NAMIBIA	824 292	852 000	1.1	South African mandate	Windhoek	Afrikaans, English	R.S.A. rand
NAURU	21	8 000	381	republic	Nauru	Nauruan, English	Australian dollar
NEPAL	140 797	14 010 000	99	monarchy	Kāthmāndu	Nepali	rupee
NETHERLANDS	40 844	14 220 000	348	constitutional monarchy	Amsterdam	Dutch	guilder
NEW ZEALAND	268 676	3 164 000	12	monarchy	Wellington	English	dollar
NICARAGUA	130 000	2 703 000	20	republic	Managua	Spanish	córdoba
NIGER	1 267 000	5 305 000	4.1	republic	Niamey	French	CFA franc
NIGERIA	923 768	77 082 000	83	federal republic	Abuja	English	naira
NORTH KOREA	120 538	17 914 000	148	people's republic	Pyŏngyang	Korean	won
NORWAY	324 219	4 092 000	13	constitutional monarchy	Oslo	Norwegian	krone
OMAN	212 457	891 000	4.1	sultanate	Masqaţ (Muscat)	Arabic	rial
PAKISTAN	803 943	82 441 000	103	federal republic	Islāmābād	Urdu, Punjabi, English	rupee
PANAMA	75 650	1 837 000	24	republic	Panamá	Spanish	balboa
PAPUA NEW GUINEA	461 691	3 082 000	6.7	republic	Port Moresby	English	kina
PARAGUAY	406 752	3 067 000	7.5	republic	Asunción	Spanish, Guaraní	guaraní

NATIONS OF THE WORLD

COUNTRY	AREA sq. km.	POPULATION total	per sq. km.	FORM OF GOVERNMENT	CAPITAL CITY	MAIN LANGUAGES	CURRENCY
PERU	1 285 216	17 780 000	14	republic	Lima	Spanish	sol
PHILIPPINES	300 000	48 400 000	161	republic	Manila	Pilipino	peso
POLAND	312 677	35 815 000	115	people's republic	Warszawa (Warsaw)	Polish	zloty
PORTUGAL	92 082	9 933 000	107	republic	Lisboa (Lisbon)	Portuguese	escudo
PUERTO RICO	8 897	3 188 000	358	commonwealth (U.S.A.)	San Juan	Spanish, English	dollar
QATAR	11 000	220 000	20	emirate	Ad Dawḥah (Doha)	Arabic	riyal
ROMANIA	237 500	22 201 000	93	socialist republic	Bucureşti (Bucharest)	Romanian	leu
RWANDA	26 338	5 046 000	191	republic	Kigali	Kinyarwanda, French	franc
ST KITTS - NEVIS	266	62 000	233	associated state (U.K.)	Basseterre	English	East Caribbean dollar
ST LUCIA	616	113 000	183	independent political entity	Castries	English, French	East Caribbean dollar
ST VINCENT AND THE GRENADINES	389	96 000	247	independent political entity	Kingstown	English	East Caribbean dollar
SAN MARINO	61	21 000	344	republic	San Marino	Italian	Italian lira
SÃO TOMÉ AND PRÍNCIPE	964	82 750	86	republic	São Tomé	Portuguese, Creole	dobra
SAUDI ARABIA	2 149 690	8 367 000	3.8	monarchy	Ar Riyāḍ (Riyadh)	Arabic	riyal
SENEGAL	196 192	5 661 000	28	republic	Dakar	French	CFA franc
SEYCHELLES	280	61 900	221	republic	Victoria	English, French	rupee
SIERRA LEONE	71 740	3 474 000	48	republic	Freetown	English	leone
SINGAPORE	602	2 391 000	3 972	republic	Singapore	Malay, English, Chinese, Tamil	dollar
SOLOMON ISLANDS	28 446	221 000	7.8	constitutional monarchy	Honiara	English	dollar
SOMALI REPUBLIC	637 657	3 645 000	5.7	republic	Mogadisho	Arabic, Italian, English, Somali	shilling
SOUTH AFRICA, REPUBLIC OF	1 221 037	29 285 000	23	federal republic	Cape Town (Kaapstad)/Pretoria	Afrikaans, English	rand
SOUTH KOREA	98 484	37 605 000	382	republic	Sŏul (Seoul)	Korean	won
SOUTHERN YEMEN	332 968	1 969 000	5.9	people's republic	'Adan (Aden)	Arabic	dinar
SPAIN	504 782	37 430 000	74	constitutional monarchy	Madrid	Spanish	peseta
SRI LANKA	65 610	14 738 000	225	republic	Colombo	Sinhala, Tamil	rupee
SUDAN	2 505 813	18 681 000	7.4	republic	Al Kharṭūm (Khartoum)	Arabic	pound
SURINAM	163 265	352 000	2.1	republic	Paramaribo	Dutch, English	guilder
SWAZILAND	17 363	547 000	31	monarchy	Mbabane	English, Siswati	R.S.A. rand, lilangeni
SWEDEN	449 964	8 320 000	18	constitutional monarchy	Stockholm	Swedish	krona
SWITZERLAND	41 288	6 329 000	153	federal republic	Bern (Berne)	German, French, Italian, Romansh	franc
SYRIA	185 180	8 979 000	48	republic	Dimashq (Damascus)	Arabic	pound
TAIWAN	35 961	17 479 000	486	republic	Taipei	Mandarin	dollar
TANZANIA	945 087	17 982 000	19	republic	Dar es Salaam/Dodoma	Swahili	shilling
THAILAND	514 000	46 455 000	90	monarchy	Krung Thep (Bangkok)	Thai	baht
TOGO	56 000	2 699 000	48	republic	Lomé	French	CFA franc
TONGA	699	97 000	139	monarchy	Nuku'alofa	Tongan, English	dollar
TRINIDAD AND TOBAGO	5 128	1 156 000	225	republic	Port of Spain	English	dollar
TUNISIA	163 610	6 363 000	39	republic	Tunis	Arabic	dinar
TURKEY	780 576	45 218 000	57	republic	Ankara	Turkish	lira
TUVALU	24	7 000	292	constitutional monarchy	Funafuti	Tuvalu, English	dollar
U.S.S.R.	22 402 200	265 542 000	12	federal socialist republic	Moskva (Moscow)	Russian	rouble
UGANDA	236 036	13 225 000	56	republic	Kampala	English	shilling
UNITED ARAB EMIRATES	83 600	1 040 000	12	self-governing union		Arabic	dirham
UNITED KINGDOM	244 046	55 945 000	229	constitutional monarchy	London	English	pound
UNITED STATES OF AMERICA	9 363 123	227 640 000	24	federal republic	Washington	English	dollar
UPPER VOLTA	274 200	6 908 000	25	republic	Ouagadougou	French	CFA franc
URUGUAY	177 508	2 899 000	16	republic	Montevideo	Spanish	peso
VANUATU	14 763	112 000	7.6	republic	Vila	English, French	Vatu
VENEZUELA	912 050	13 913 000	15	federal republic	Caracas	Spanish	bolívar
VIETNAM	333 000	52 742 000	158	people's republic	Hà Nôi (Hanoi)	Vietnamese	dong
WEST GERMANY	248 577	61 658 000	248	federal republic	Bonn	German	mark
WESTERN SAHARA	266 000	135 000	0.5		El Aaiún	Arabic	peseta
WESTERN SAMOA	2 842	156 000	55	constitutional monarchy	Apia	Samoan, English	tala
YEMEN	195 000	5 926 000	30	republic	Şan'ā	Arabic	riyal
YUGOSLAVIA	255 804	22 471 000	87	socialist federal republic	Beograd (Belgrade)	Serbo-Croat, Macedonian, Slovene	dinar
ZAÏRE	2 345 409	28 291 000	12	republic	Kinshasa	French, Lingala	zaïre
ZAMBIA	752 614	5 680 000	7.5	republic	Lusaka	English	kwacha
ZIMBABWE	390 580	7 360 000	18	republic	Harare	English	dollar

GEOGRAPHICAL DATA
Part 2

GLOSSARY
OF
GEOGRAPHICAL
TERMS

GLOSSARY

Introduction to Glossary

The Glossary of Geographical Terms lists in alphabetical order a selection of foreign language names and geographical terms, inclusive of any abbreviations, which are found in the names on the maps and in the index. The terms occur either as separate words (e.g. côte which means coast) or as parts of compound words (e.g. - oog in Langeoog which means island). A term preceded by a hyphen usually appears as an ending of a name on the map (e.g. -vesi in Puulavesi; -holm in Bornholm). Each term is followed by its language which is identified by abbreviations in brackets. A complete list of the language abbreviations used in the glossary is found below.

Language Abbreviations

Afr.	Afrikaans	*Fin.*	Finnish	*Man.*	Manchurian
Alb.	Albanian	*Fr.*	French	*Mon.*	Mongolian
Ar.	Arabic	*Gae.*	Gaelic	*Nor.*	Norwegian
Ba.	Baluchi	*Ger.*	German	*Per.*	Persian
Ber.	Berber	*Gr.*	Greek	*Pol.*	Polish
Blg.	Bulgarian	*Heb.*	Hebrew	*Port.*	Portuguese
Bur.	Burmese	*Hin.*	Hindi	*Rom.*	Romanian
Cat.	Catalan	*I.-C.*	Indo-Chinese	*Rus.*	Russian
Cbd.	Cambodian	*Ice.*	Icelandic	*S.-C.*	Serbo-Croat
Ch.	Chinese	*It.*	Italian	*Sp.*	Spanish
Cz.	Czechoslovakian	*Jap.*	Japanese	*Swe.*	Swedish
Dan.	Danish	*Kor.*	Korean	*Th.*	Thai (Siamese)
Dut.	Dutch	*Lao.*	Laotian	*Tur.*	Turkish
Est.	Estonian	*Lat.*	Latvian	*Ur.*	Urdu
Fae.	Faeroese	*Mal.*	Malay	*Viet.*	Vietnamese

Glossary of Geographical Terms

A

āb (*Per.*)	water
ada (*Tur.*)	island
adrar (*Ber. Ar.*)	mountain region
ákra, akrotírion (*Gr.*)	cape
alb (*Rom.*)	white
alin (*Man., Mon.*)	mountain range
alpes (*Fr.*)	alps
alpi (*It.*)	alps
alt/o/a (*It., Sp., Port.*)	high
-an (*Swe.*)	river
ao (*Ch., Th.*)	bay, gulf
arquipélago (*Port.*)	archipelago
-ås, -åsen (*Swe.*)	hills

B

bāb (*Ar.*)	gate
backe (*Swe.*)	hill
bādiya/t (*Ar.*)	desert
baelt (*Dan.*)	strait
b., bahía (*Sp.*)	bay
baḥr (*Ar.*)	great river/lake
baía (*Port.*)	bay
b., baie (*Fr.*)	bay
ban (*Hin., Ur.*)	forest
ban (*I.-C.*)	village
bañados (*Sp.*)	marshes
bandao (*Ch.*)	peninsula

bassin (*Fr.*)	basin
baṭha (*Ar.*)	plain
beloyy (*Rus.*)	white
ben, beinn (*Gae.*)	mountain
bereg (*Rus.*)	shore
berg/en (*Ger., Swe.*)	mountain/s
biq'at (*Heb.*)	valley
birkat (*Ar.*)	lake
bog., boğazi (*Tur.*)	strait
bois (*Fr.*)	wood/s
bol., bol'shaya (*Rus.*)	big
bory (*Pol.*)	forest
bredning (*Dan.*)	bay
brú (*Ice.*)	bridge
bucht (*Ger.*)	bay
bugt (*Dan.*)	bay
buḥayrat (*Ar.*)	lake
bukt/en (*Nor., Swe.*)	bay
burnu (*Tur.*)	cape
busen (*Ger.*)	bay
büyük (*Tur.*)	big

C

c., cabo (*Sp., Port.*)	cape
campo (*Sp.*)	field
c., cap (*Fr.*)	cape
capo (*It.*)	cape
causse (*Fr.*)	upland
cerro (*Sp.*)	mountain

chaco (*Sp.*)	jungle region
chaîne (*Fr.*)	chain
chapada (*Port.*)	hills
chott (*Ar.*)	salt lake
cime (*Fr.*)	summit
co (*Ch.*)	lake
co (*Viet.*)	mountain
col (*Fr.*)	pass
colline/s (*Fr.*)	hill/s
con (*Viet.*)	islands
cordillera (*Sp.*)	mountain range
costa (*Sp.*)	coast
côte (*Fr.*)	coast

D

d., daği, dağlari (*Tur.*)	mountain, mountain range
dake (*Jap.*)	peak
dal/en (*Nor., Swe.*)	valley
danau (*Mal.*)	lake
daqq (*Per.*)	salt flat
darya (*Per., Rus.*)	river
daryācheh (*Per.*)	lake
dasht (*Per.*)	desert
denizi (*Tur.*)	sea
desierto (*Sp.*)	desert
détroit (*Fr.*)	strait
dhiórix (*Gr.*)	canal
dian (*Ch.*)	lake
-dijk (*Dut.*)	dyke

ding (Ch.)	mountain	hory (Cz.)	mountain
do (Kor.)	island	hu (Ch.)	lake
		-huk (Swe.)	cape

E

eiland/en (Afr., Dut.)	island/s
embalse (Sp.)	reservoir
'emeq (Heb.)	valley
erg (Ar.)	sand desert
estrecho (Sp.)	strait
estuario (Sp.)	estuary
étang (Fr.)	pond

F

feng (Ch.)	peak
firth (Gae.)	strait
fjället (Swe.)	mountain
fjell (Nor.)	mountain
fj., fjorden (Dan., Nor., Swe.)	fjord
fjördhur (Fae., Ice.)	fjord
flói (Ice.)	bay
fonn (Nor.)	glacier

G

gau (Ger.)	district
gave (Fr.)	torrent
gebirge (Ger.)	mountains
ghubbat (Ar.)	bay
gji (Alb.)	bay
gobi (Mon.)	desert
gol (Mon.)	river
g., golfe (Fr.)	gulf
g., golfo (Sp., It.)	gulf
gölü (Tur.)	lake
golyam (Blg.)	great
g., gora/y (Rus.)	mountain/s
gorje (S.-C.)	mountain range
gross (Ger.)	great
guba (Rus.)	bay
guntō (Jap.)	island group
guoyuan (Ch.)	plateau
gura (Rom.)	mouth

H

hai (Ch.)	sea
haixia (Ch.)	strait
ḥajar (Ar.)	mountain range
halvö (Dan.)	peninsula
halvöya (Nor.)	peninsula
hāmūn (Per.)	plain
hantō (Jap.)	peninsula
har (Heb.)	mountain range
hauteurs (Fr.)	hills
hav (Dan., Nor., Swe.)	sea
hawr (Ar.)	lake
he (Ch.)	river
heiya (Jap.)	plain
hoch (Ger.)	high
hohe (Ger.)	height
höj (Dan.)	high, height
-holm (Dan.)	island
holt (Nor.)	wood

I

î., îs., île/s (Fr.)	island/s
ilha/s (Port.)	island/s
insel/n (Ger.)	island/s
i., is., isla/s (Sp.)	island/s
isola/e (It.)	island/s
istmo (Sp.)	isthmus
iztochni (Blg.)	eastern

J

j., jabal (Ar., Per.)	mountain
jarvi (Fin.)	lake
jaure (Swe.)	lake
jawb (Ar.)	basin, waterhole
jazā 'ir (Ar.)	island
jezero (S.-C., Cz.)	lake
jezioro (Pol.)	lake
jiang (Ch.)	river
jima (Jap.)	island
jökulen (Nor.)	glacier
jökull (Ice.)	glacier
jūras līcis (Lat.)	gulf, bay

K

kaikyō (Jap.)	strait
kaise (Swe.)	mountain range
kamm (Ger.)	ridge
k., kanal (Ger., Pol., Rus., S.-C., Swe.)	canal
kap (Ger.)	cape
kapp (Nor.)	cape
kep (Alb.)	cape
kep., kepulauan (Mal.)	archipelago
khalīj (Ar., Per.)	gulf, bay
khazzān (Ar.)	dam
khr., khrebet (Rus.)	mountain range
kladenets (Blg.)	well
klong (Th.)	canal, creek
ko (Jap.)	lake, bay
ko (Th.)	island
-kogen (Jap.)	plateau
koh (Per.)	mountains
kólpos (Gr.)	gulf
kör., körfezi (Tur.)	gulf, bay
kou (Ch.)	estuary
kryazh (Rus.)	ridge
kūh/ha (Per.)	mountain/s
kul (Rus.)	lake
kuppe (Ger.)	hilltop
kyst (Dan.)	coast

L

lac (Fr.)	lake
lacul (Rom.)	lake
l., lago (It., Sp.)	lake
lagoa (Port.)	lagoon
laguna (Sp.)	lagoon, lake
laut (Mal.)	north, sea

(M continued)

liedao (Ch.)	islands
liehtao (Ch.)	islands
l., límni (Gr.)	lake
ling (Ch.)	mountain range
llanos (Sp.)	plains
l., loch (Gae.)	lake
lora (Ba.)	stream
l., lough (Gae.)	lake
lule (Swe.)	eastern

M

maa (Est., Fin.)	land
mae (Th.)	river
mar/e (It., Port., Sp.)	sea
marsch (Ger.)	marsh
meer (Afr., Dut.)	lake, sea
mer (Fr.)	sea
mifraż (Heb.)	bay
misaki (Jap.)	cape
mont (Fr.)	mountain
montagne (Fr.)	mountain
mont/e/i (It., Port., Sp.)	mountain/s
moor (Ger.)	swamp, moor
more (Rus.)	sea
mörön (Mon.)	river
mui (Viet.)	point
mull (Gae.)	headland
munkhafaḍ (Ar.)	depression
munti/i (Rom.)	mountain/s
m., mys (Rus.)	cape

N

nada (Jap.)	sea, bay
nafūd (Ar.)	sandy desert
najd (Ar.)	pass
nam (I.-C., Kor.)	southern
nes (Ice., Nor.)	promontory
ness (Gae.)	promontory
nevada (Sp.)	snow-capped mountains
ngoc (Viet.)	mountain
nísoi (Gr.)	islands
nizh., nizhne, nizhniy (Rus.)	lower
nizmennost' (Rus.)	depression
nord (Dan., Fr., Ger., Nor., Swe.)	northern
nur (Ch.)	lake, salt lake
nusa (Mal.)	island
nuur (Mon.)	lake

O

occidental (Sp.)	western
odde (Dan., Nor.)	headland
ojo/s (Sp.)	spring/s
oki (Jap.)	bay
-oog (Ger.)	island
óros, óri (Gr.)	mountain, mountains
oriental/e (Sp.)	eastern
ort (Ger.)	settlement
o., os., ostrov/a (Rus.)	island/s
ost (Ger.)	eastern
oued (Ar.)	dry river bed
öy, öya (Nor.)	island
oz., ozero (Rus.)	lake

GLOSSARY

P

pampa/s (*Sp.*)	plain/s
parbat (*Ur.*)	mountain
passo (*It.*)	pass
peg., pegunungan (*Mal.*)	mountain range
pélagos (*Gr.*)	sea
pelleg (*Alb.*)	bay
peña (*Sp.*)	cliff
pendi (*Ch.*)	depression
péninsule (*Fr.*)	peninsula
pertuis (*Fr.*)	strait
peski (*Rus.*)	sand
phanom (*I.-C., Th.*)	mountain
phou (*Lao.*)	mountain
phu (*Th.*)	mountain
pic (*Fr.*)	peak
pico (*Sp.*)	peak
pik (*Rus.*)	peak
pingyuan (*Ch.*)	plain
plaine (*Fr.*)	plain
plana (*Sp.*)	plain
planalto (*Port.*)	plateau
pl., planina (*Blg., S.-C.*)	mountain range
plato (*Afr., Blg., Rus.*)	plateau
platosu (*Tur.*)	plateau
platte (*Ger.*)	plateau, plain
playa (*Sp.*)	beach
ploskogor'ye (*Rus.*)	plateau
pohorie (*Cz.*)	mountain range
pointe (*Fr.*)	promontory
pojezierze (*Pol.*)	lakeland
poleseye (*Rus.*)	area of marsh
polje (*S.-C.*)	plain, basin
pov., poluostrov (*Rus.*)	peninsula
porthmós (*Gr.*)	strait
porți (*Rom.*)	entrance
portillo (*Sp.*)	gap
proliv (*Rus.*)	strait
puig (*Cat.*)	peak
pulau (*Mal.*)	island
pta., punta (*It., Sp.*)	point
puy (*Fr.*)	peak

Q

qā' (*Ar.*)	salt flat
qanāt (*Ar., Per.*)	canal
qolleh (*Per.*)	mountain
qu (*Ch.*)	canal, stream
qūr (*Ar.*)	buttes, ridge

R

ramlat (*Ar.*)	dunes
rann (*Hin.*)	swampy region
ras, ra's, rãs (*Per., Ar.*)	cape
ravnina (*Rus.*)	plain
reprêsa (*Port.*)	reservoir
reshteh (*Per.*)	mountain range
retto (*Jap.*)	island group
ria, ría (*Port., Sp.*)	mouth of river
rijeka (*S.-C.*)	river
r., rio, río (*Port., Sp.*)	river
riviera (*It.*)	coast, river

r., rivière (*Fr.*)	river
rocca (*It.*)	rock
rücken (*Ger.*)	ridge
rūd (*Per.*)	river

S

sable/s (*Fr.*)	sand/s
sadd (*Ar.*)	dam
sāgar (*Hin., Ur.*)	lake
şaḥrā (*Ar.*)	desert
şa'īd (*Ar.*)	highland
saki (*Jap.*)	cape
salar (*Sp.*)	salt flat
salina/s (*Sp.*)	salt marsh
sammyaku (*Jap.*)	mountain range
san (*Jap., Kor.*)	mountain
-sanchi (*Jap.*)	mountains
see (*Ger.*)	lake
seenplatte (*Ger.*)	lakeland
selat (*Mal.*)	strait
selatan (*Mal.*)	southern
selkä (*Fin.*)	ridge
selseleh (*Per.*)	mountain range
selva (*Sp.*)	forest
serra (*Port.*)	mountain range
serranía (*Sp.*)	ridge
sev., severo, severnyy (*Rus.*)	north
sha'īb (*Ar.*)	ravine, wadi
shamo (*Ch.*)	desert
shan (*Ch.*)	mountain
shankou (*Ch.*)	mountain pass
shaṭṭ (*Ar.*)	large river
shibh jazīrat (*Ar.*)	peninsula
shima (*Jap.*)	island
shotō (*Jap.*)	island group
shui (*Ch.*)	river
sa., sierra (*Sp.*)	mountain range
-sjon (*Swe.*)	lake
skog (*Nor., Swe.*)	forest
skov (*Dan.*)	forest
slieve (*Gae.*)	mountain
sor (*Rus.*)	salt flat
sör (*Nor.*)	southern
spitze (*Ger.*)	peak
sredne (*Rus.*)	central
step (*Rus.*)	steppe
stora (*Fae.*)	large
strath (*Gae.*)	valley
stretto (*It.*)	strait
suidō (*Jap.*)	strait
şummān (*Ar.*)	escarpment
sund (*Dan., Ger., Ice., Nor., Swe.*)	sound
svart (*Nor., Swe.*)	black

T

take (*Jap.*)	peak
tall (*Ar.*)	mountain
tanjung (*Mal.*)	cape
tau (*Rus.*)	mountain
teluk (*Mal.*)	bay
testa (*It.*)	head
thale (*Th.*)	lagoon, sea
tierra (*Sp.*)	land, territory

tind (*Nor.*)	sharp peak
tō (*Jap.*)	island, eastern
tônlé (*Cbd.*)	lake
träsk (*Swe.*)	marsh
tunturi (*Fin.*)	treeless mountain

U

'urūq (*Ar.*)	dunes
utara (*Mal.*)	northern
uul (*Mon., Rus.*)	mountain range

V

väin (*Est.*)	strait
val (*Fr., It.*)	valley
vand (*Dan.*)	water
vatn (*Ice., Nor.*)	lake
vatnet (*Nor.*)	lake
vatten (*Swe.*)	lake
veld (*Afr.*)	field
veliki (*S.-C.*)	large
verkh., verkhne, verkhniy (*Rus.*)	upper
-vesi (*Fin.*)	lake
vest, vester (*Dan., Nor.*)	west
vidda (*Nor.*)	plateau
-viken (*Nor., Swe.*)	gulf, bay
vdkhr., vodokhranilishche (*Rus.*)	reservoir
volcán (*Sp.*)	volcano
vostochno, vostochnyy (*Rus.*)	eastern
vozvyshennost (*Rus.*)	uplands
vrata (*Blg.*)	gate
vrh (*S.-C.*)	peak

W

wāhāt (*Ar.*)	oasis
wald (*Ger.*)	forest
wan (*Ch., Jap.*)	bay

Y

yam (*Heb.*)	sea
yama (*Jap.*)	mountain
yanchi (*Ch.*)	salt lake
yarimadasi (*Tur.*)	peninsula
yazovir (*Blg.*)	dam
yoma (*Bur.*)	mountain range
yumco (*Ch.*)	lake
yunhe (*Ch.*)	canal
yuzhnyy (*Rus.*)	south

Z

zaki (*Jap.*)	cape, peninsula
zaliv (*Rus.*)	bay
zan (*Jap.*)	mountain range
zangbo (*Ch.*)	stream, river
zapadno, zapadnyy (*Rus.*)	western
zatoka (*Pol.*)	bay
zemlya (*Rus.*)	land
zhou (*Ch.*)	island
zuid (*Dut.*)	south

GEOGRAPHICAL DATA
Part 3

WORLD
INDEX

WORLD INDEX

Introduction to World Index

The Index includes an alphabetical list of all names appearing on the maps in the World Atlas section. Each entry indicates the country or region of the world in which the name is located. This is followed by a page reference and finally the name's location on the map, given by latitude and longitude co-ordinates. Most features are indexed to the largest scale map on which they appear, however when the name applies to countries or other extensive features it is generally indexed to the map on which it appears in its entirety. Areal features are generally indexed using co-ordinates which indicate the centre of the feature. The latitude and longitude indicated for a point feature gives the location of the point on the map. In the case of rivers the mouth or confluence is always taken as the point of reference.

Names in the Index are generally in the local language and where a conventional English version exists, this is cross referenced to the entry in the local language. Names of features which extend across the boundaries of more than one country are usually named in English if no single official name exists. Names in languages not written in the Roman alphabet have been transliterated using the official system of the country if one exists, e.g. Pinyin system for China, otherwise the systems recognised by the United States Board on Geographical Names have been used.

Names abbreviated on the maps are given in full in the Index. Abbreviations are used for both geographical terms and administrative names in the Index. All abbreviations used in the Index are listed below.

Abbreviations of Geographical Terms

b., B.	bay, Bay
c., C.	cape, Cape
d.	internal division e.g. county, region, state.
des.	desert
est.	estuary

f.	physical feature e.g. valley, plain, geographic district or region
g., G.	gulf, Gulf
i., I., is., Is.	island, Island, islands, Islands
l., L.	lake, Lake
mtn., Mtn.	mountain, Mountain

mts., Mts.	mountains, Mountains
pen., Pen.	peninsula, Peninsula
Pt.	Point
r.	river
resr., Resr.	reservoir, Reservoir
Sd.	Sound
str., Str.	strait, Strait

Abbreviations of Country / Administrative Names

Afghan.	Afghanistan
A.H. Prov.	Alpes de Haut Provence
Ala.	Alabama
Alas.	Alaska
Alta.	Alberta
Ariz.	Arizona
Ark.	Arkansas
Baja Calif. Norte	Baja California Norte
Baja Calif. Sur	Baja California Sur
Bangla.	Bangladesh
B.C.	British Columbia
B.S.S.R.	Belorusskaya Sovetskaya Sotsialisticheskaya Respublika
B.-Würt.	Baden-Württemberg
Calif.	California
C.A.R.	Central African Republic
Char. Mar.	Charente Maritime
Colo.	Colorado
Conn.	Connecticut
C.P.	Cape Province
Czech.	Czechoslovakia
D.C.	District of Colombia
Del.	Delaware
Dom. Rep.	Dominican Republic
E. Germany	East Germany
Equat. Guinea	Equatorial Guinea
Fla.	Florida
Ga.	Georgia
Guang. Zhuang.	Guangxi Zhuangzu
H.-Gar.	Haute Garonne
Himachal P.	Himachal Pradesh
H. Zaïre	Haut Zaïre
Ill.	Illinois
Ind.	Indiana
Kans.	Kansas
K. Occidental	Kasai Occidental
K. Oriental	Kasai Oriental
Ky.	Kentucky
La.	Lousiana
Liech.	Liechtenstein
Lit. S.S.R.	Litovskaya Sovetskaya Sotsialisticheskaya Respublika
Lux.	Luxembourg
Madhya P.	Madhya Pradesh
Man.	Manitoba

Mass.	Massachusetts
Md.	Maryland
Mich.	Michigan
Minn.	Minnesota
Miss.	Mississippi
Mo.	Missouri
Mont.	Montana
M.-Pyr.	Midi-Pyrénées
M.S.S.R.	Moldavskaya Sovetskaya Sotsialisticheskaya Respublika
N.B.	New Brunswick
N.C.	North Carolina
N. Dak.	North Dakota
Nebr.	Nebraska
Neth.	Netherlands
Nev.	Nevada
Nfld.	Newfoundland
N.H.	New Hampshire
N. Ireland	Northern Ireland
N.J.	New Jersey
N. Korea	North Korea
N. Mex.	New Mexico
Nschn.	Niedersachen
N.S.W.	New South Wales
N. Trönd.	Nord Tröndelag
N.-Westfalen	Nordrhein-Westfalen
N.W.T.	Northwest Territories
N.Y.	New York State
O.F.S.	Orange Free State
Okla.	Oklahoma
Ont.	Ontario
Oreg.	Oregon
P.E.I.	Prince Edward Island
Penn.	Pennsylvania
Phil.	Philippines
P.N.G.	Papua New Guinea
Poit.-Char.	Poittou-Charente
Pyr. Or.	Pyrénées Orientales
Qld.	Queensland
Que.	Québec
Raj.	Rājasthān
Rep. of Ire.	Republic of Ireland
Rhein.-Pfalz	Rheinland-Pfalz
R.I.	Rhode Island
R.S.A.	Republic of South Africa

R.S.F.S.R.	Rossiyskaya Sovetskaya Federativnaya Sotsialisticheskaya Respublika
S.A.	South Australia
Sask.	Saskatchewan
S.C.	South Carolina
Sch.-Hol.	Schleswig-Holstein
S. Dak.	South Dakota
S. Korea	South Korea
S. Mar.	Seine Maritime
Sogn og Fj.	Sogn og Fjordane
Somali Rep.	Somali Republic
Switz.	Switzerland
S. Yemen	Southern Yemen
Tas.	Tasmania
Tenn.	Tennessee
Tex.	Texas
T.G.	Tarn-et-Garonne
Tk. S.S.R.	Turkmenskaya Sovetskaya Sotsialisticheskaya Respublika
Trans.	Transvaal
U.A.E.	United Arab Emirates
U.K.	United Kingdom
Ukr. S.S.R.	Ukrainskaya Sovetskaya Sotsialisticheskaya Respublika
U.S.A.	United States of America
U.S.S.R.	Union of Soviet Socialist Republics
Uttar P.	Uttar Pradesh
U. Volta	Upper Volta
Va.	Virginia
Vic.	Victoria
Vt.	Vermont
W.A.	Western Australia
Wash.	Washington
W. Bengal	West Bengal
W. Germany	West Germany
Wisc.	Wisconsin
W. Sahara	Western Sahara
W. Va.	West Virginia
Wyo.	Wyoming
Xin Uygur	Xinjiang Uygur
Yugo.	Yugoslavia

For **Upper Volta** *read* **Burkina**

Aa to Akjoujt

A

Aa *r.* France **19** 51.01N 2.06E
Aachen W. Germany **38** 50.47N 6.05E
Aalen W. Germany **39** 48.50N 10.05E
A 'ālī an Nīl *d.* Sudan **73** 9.00N 32.00E
Aalsmeer Neth. **16** 52.17N 4.46E
Aalst Belgium **16** 50.57N 4.03E
Äänekoski Finland **40** 62.36N 25.44E
Aarau Switz. **39** 47.23N 8.03E
Aarburg Switz. **39** 47.19N 7.54E
Aardenburg Neth. **16** 51.16N 3.26E
Aare *r.* Switz. **39** 47.37N 8.13E
Aarschot Belgium **16** 50.59N 4.50E
Aba China **61** 32.55N101.42E
Aba Nigeria **77** 5.06N 7.21E
Aba Zaïre **73** 3.52N 30.14E
Abā as Su'ūd Saudi Arabia **71** 17.28N 44.06E
Abadab, Jabal *mtn.* Sudan **72** 18.53N 35.59E
Ābādān Iran **65** 30.21N 48.15E
Abadan, Jazīreh-ye *i.* Iran **65** 30.10N 48.30E
Ābādeh Iran **65** 31.10N 52.40E
Abadla Algeria **74** 31.01N 2.44W
Abaetetuba Brazil **123** 1.45S 48.54W
Abagnar Qi China **54** 43.58N116.02E
Abag Qi China **54** 43.53N114.33E
Abaí Paraguay **124** 26.01S 55.57W
Abajo Peak *mtn.* U.S.A. **108** 37.51N109.28W
Abakaliki Nigeria **77** 6.17N 8.04E
Abakan U.S.S.R. **51** 53.43N 91.25E
Abalessa Algeria **75** 22.54N 4.50E
Abancay Peru **124** 13.35S 72.55W
Ābār Murrāt *wells* Sudan **72** 21.03N 32.55E
'Abasān Egypt **67** 31.19N 34.21E
Abashiri wan *b.* Japan **57** 44.02N144.17E
Abasolo Mexico **111** 25.18N104.40W
Abau P.N.G. **90** 10.10S148.40E
Ābay *r. see* Azraq, Al Baḩr al Ethiopia **72**
Abay U.S.S.R. **50** 49.40N 72.47E
Abaya, L. Ethiopia **73** 6.20N 37.55E
Abba C.A.R. **77** 5.20N 15.11E
Abbadia San Salvatore Italy **30** 42.53N 11.41E
Abbasanta Italy **32** 40.08N 8.50E
Abbekås Sweden **43** 55.24N 13.36E
Abbeville France **19** 50.06N 1.50E
Abbeville La. U.S.A. **111** 29.58N 92.08W
Abbeville S.C. U.S.A. **113** 34.10N 82.23W
Abbiategrasso Italy **30** 45.24N 8.54E
Abbotsbury U.K. **13** 50.40N 2.36W
Abbotsford Canada **105** 45.27N 72.55W
Abbottābād Pakistan **62** 34.09N 73.13E
'Abd al Kūrī *i.* S. Yemen **71** 12.12N 52.13E
Abdēra *site* Greece **34** 40.59N 24.58E
Abdulino U.S.S.R. **44** 53.42N 53.40E
Abe, L. Ethiopia **73** 11.06N 41.50E
Abéché Chad **72** 13.49N 20.49E
Abéjar Spain **26** 41.48N 2.47W
Abelti Ethiopia **73** 8.10N 37.37E
Abengourou Ivory Coast **76** 6.42N 3.27W
Abenójar Spain **26** 38.53N 4.21W
Åbenrå Denmark **42** 55.02N 9.26E
Abensberg W. Germany **39** 48.49N 11.51E
Abeokuta Nigeria **77** 7.10N 3.26E
Aberayron U.K. **13** 52.15N 4.16W
Abercrombie *r.* Australia **93** 33.50S149.10E
Aberdare U.K. **13** 51.43N 3.27W
Aberdare Range *mts.* Kenya **79** 0.20S 36.40E
Aberdeen R.S.A. **80** 32.28S 24.03E
Aberdeen U.K. **14** 57.08N 2.07W
Aberdeen Md. U.S.A. **115** 39.30N 76.14W
Aberdeen Miss. U.S.A. **111** 33.49N 88.33W
Aberdeen Ohio U.S.A. **112** 38.39N 83.46W
Aberdeen S. Dak. U.S.A. **110** 45.28N 98.29W
Aberdeen Wash. U.S.A. **108** 46.59N123.50W
Aberdovey U.K. **13** 52.33N 4.03W
Aberfeldy U.K. **14** 56.37N 3.54W
Abergavenny U.K. **13** 51.49N 3.01W
Abersoch U.K. **12** 52.50N 4.31W
Aberystwyth U.K. **13** 52.25N 4.06W
Abetone Italy **30** 44.08N 10.40E
Abez U.S.S.R. **44** 66.33N 61.51E
Abhā Saudi Arabia **72** 18.13N 42.30E
Abhar Iran **65** 36.09N 49.13E
Abidjan Ivory Coast **76** 5.19N 4.01W
Abilene Kans. U.S.A. **110** 38.55N 97.13W
Abilene Tex. U.S.A. **111** 32.27N 99.44W
Abingdon U.K. **13** 51.40N 1.17W
Abisko Sweden **40** 68.20N 18.51E
Abitau *r.* Canada **101** 59.53N109.03W
Abitibi *r.* Canada **102** 51.03N 80.55W
Abitibi, L. Canada **102** 48.42N 79.45W
Abiy Adi Ethiopia **73** 13.36N 39.00E
Abnūb Egypt **64** 27.16N 31.09E
Åbo *see* Turku Finland **41**
Abohar India **62** 30.08N 74.12E
Abomey Benin **77** 7.14N 2.00E
Abong Mbang Cameroon **77** 3.59N 13.12E
Abou Deïa Chad **77** 11.20N 19.20E
Aboyne U.K. **14** 57.05N 2.48W
Abrantes Portugal **27** 39.28N 8.12W
'Abrī Sudan **72** 20.48N 30.20E
Abring Jammu & Kashmir **62** 33.42N 76.35E
Abrud Romania **37** 46.17N 23.04E
Abruzzi *d.* Italy **31** 42.35N 13.38E
Abruzzo, Parco Nazionale d' *Nat. Park* Italy **31** 41.45N 13.45E
Absaroka Range *mts.* U.S.A. **108** 44.45N109.50W
Absecon U.S.A. **115** 39.26N 74.30W
Abtenau Austria **39** 47.33N 13.21E
Abū 'Arīsh Saudi Arabia **71** 16.58N 42.50E
Abū Baḩr *f.* Saudi Arabia **71** 21.30N 48.15E
Abū Ballāş *hill* Egypt **72** 24.26N 27.39E
Abu Dhabi *see* Abū Z̧aby U.A.E. **65**
Abū Dharbah Egypt **66** 28.29N 33.20E
Abū Dulayq Sudan **72** 15.54N 33.49E
Abū Ḩamad Sudan **72** 19.32N 33.19E
Abū Ḩarāz Sudan **72** 19.04N 32.07E
Abuja Nigeria **77** 9.12N 7.11E
Abū Jābirah Sudan **73** 11.04N 26.51E
Abū Kabīr Egypt **66** 30.44N 31.40E
Abū Kamāl Syria **64** 34.27N 40.55E
Abū Madd, Ra's *c.* Saudi Arabia **64** 24.50N 37.07E
Abū Maţāriq Sudan **73** 10.58N 26.17E
Abunã Brazil **122** 9.41S 65.20W
Abū Qashsh Jordan **67** 31.57N 35.11E
Abū Qurqāş Egypt **66** 27.56N 30.50E
Abu Road *town* India **62** 24.29N 72.47E
Abū Shajarah, Ra's *c.* Sudan **72** 21.04N 37.14E
Abū Shanab Sudan **73** 10.47N 29.32E
Abū Sulţān Egypt **66** 30.25N 32.19E
Abū Sunbul Egypt **64** 22.18N 31.40E
Abū Ţabarī *well* Sudan **72** 17.35N 28.31E
Abū Ţarafah Jordan **66** 30.00N 35.56E
Abū Tīj Egypt **64** 27.06N 31.17E
Abuya Mexico **109** 24.16N107.01W
Abuye Meda *mtn.* Ethiopia **73** 10.28N 39.44E
Abū Zabad Sudan **73** 12.21N 29.15E
Abū Z̧aby U.A.E. **65** 24.27N 54.23E
Abū Zanīmah Egypt **66** 29.03N 33.06E
Abwong Sudan **73** 9.07N 32.12E
Åby Sweden **43** 58.40N 16.11E
Abyaḑ Sudan **72** 13.46N 26.28E
Abyaḑ, Al Baḩr al *r.* Sudan **72** 15.38N 32.31E
Abyār ash Shuwayrif *wells* Libya **75** 29.59N 14.16E
Åbybro Denmark **42** 57.09N 9.45E
Abyei Sudan **73** 9.36N 28.26E
Acacio Mexico **111** 24.50N102.44W
Acadia Valley *town* Canada **101** 51.08N110.13W
Acámbaro Mexico **116** 20.01N101.42W
Acapulco Mexico **116** 16.51N 99.56W
Acará Brazil **123** 1.57S 48.11W
Acarigua Venezuela **122** 9.35N 69.12W
Acatlán Mexico **116** 18.12N 98.02W
Accra Ghana **76** 5.33N 0.15W
Accrington U.K. **12** 53.46N 2.22W
Aceh *d.* Indonesia **58** 4.00N 97.30E
Acerra Italy **33** 40.57N 14.22E
Acevedo Argentina **125** 33.46S 60.27W
Achacachi Bolivia **124** 16.03S 68.43W
Achalpur India **63** 21.16N 77.31E
Achar Uruguay **125** 32.25S 56.10W
Acheng China **53** 45.32N126.59E
Achern W. Germany **39** 48.37N 8.04E
Achill I. Rep. of Ire. **15** 53.57N 10.00W
Āchīn Afghan. **62** 34.08N 70.42E
Achinsk U.S.S.R. **50** 56.10N 90.10E
Achray Canada **105** 45.52N 77.45W
Acireale Italy **33** 37.37N 15.10E
Acklin's I. Bahamas **117** 22.30N 74.10W
Aconcagua *mtn.* Argentina **124** 32.39S 70.00W
Açores, Arquipélago dos *is.* Atlantic Oc. **127** 38.30N 28.00W
Acquapendente Italy **30** 42.44N 11.52E
Acqui Italy **30** 44.41N 8.28E
Acraman, L. Australia **92** 32.02S135.26E
Acre *d.* Brazil **122** 8.50S 71.30W
Acri Italy **33** 39.29N 16.23E
Acton Canada **104** 43.37N 80.02W
Acton Vale Canada **105** 45.39N 72.34W
Açu Brazil **123** 5.35S 36.57W
Acuña Argentina **125** 29.54S 57.57W
Ada U.S.A. **111** 34.46N 96.41W
Ada Yugo. **31** 45.48N 20.08E
Adaba Ethiopia **73** 7.07N 39.20E
Adair, Bahía de *b.* Mexico **109** 31.30N113.50W
Adair, C. Canada **99** 71.24N 71.13W
Adaja *r.* Spain **26** 41.32N 4.52W
Adam Oman **71** 22.23N 57.32E
Adamantina Brazil **126** 21.42S 51.04W
Adamaoua, Massif de l' *mts.* Cameroon / Nigeria **77** 7.05N 12.00E
Adamello *mtn.* Italy **30** 46.09N 10.30E
Adaminaby Australia **93** 36.04S148.42E
Adamintina Brazil **124** 21.42S 51.04W
Adams Mass. U.S.A. **115** 42.37N 73.07W
Adams N.Y. U.S.A. **112** 43.49N 76.01W
Adams, Mt. U.S.A. **108** 46.12N121.28W
'Adan S. Yemen **71** 12.50N 45.00E
Adana Turkey **64** 37.00N 35.19E
Adanero Spain **26** 40.56N 4.36W
Adapazari Turkey **64** 40.45N 30.23E
Adarama Sudan **72** 17.05N 34.54E
Adare, C. Antarctica **128** 71.30S171.00E
Adavale Australia **90** 25.55S144.36E
Adda *r.* Italy **30** 45.08N 9.53E
Aḑ Ḑab'ah Egypt **64** 31.02N 28.26E
Ad Dabbah Sudan **72** 18.03N 30.57E
Ad Dafīnah Saudi Arabia **64** 23.18N 41.58E
Ad Dahnā' *des.* Saudi Arabia **65** 26.00N 47.00E
Ad Dāmir Sudan **72** 17.35N 33.58E
Ad Dammām Saudi Arabia **65** 26.23N 50.08E
Ad Darb Saudi Arabia **72** 17.44N 42.15E
Ad Dawādimī Saudi Arabia **65** 24.29N 44.23E
Ad Dawḩah Qatar **65** 25.15N 51.34E
Aḑ Ḑiffah *f.* Africa **64** 30.45N 26.00E
Ad Dikākah *f.* Saudi Arabia **71** 19.25N 51.30E
Ad Dilam Saudi Arabia **65** 23.59N 47.10E
Ad Dīmās Syria **66** 33.35N 36.05E
Addis Ababa *see* Ādīs Ābeba Ethiopia **73**
Addison U.S.A. **114** 42.06N 77.14W
Ad Dīwānīyah Iraq **65** 31.59N 44.57E
Ad Du'ayn Sudan **73** 11.26N 26.09E
Ad Duwaym Sudan **72** 14.00N 32.19E
Adel U.S.A. **113** 31.07N 83.27W
Adelaide Australia **92** 34.56S138.36E
Adelaide Pen. Canada **99** 68.09N 97.45W
Adelong Australia **93** 35.21S148.04E
Aden *see* 'Adan S. Yemen **71**
Aden, G. of Indian Oc. **71** 13.00N 50.00E
Adena U.S.A. **114** 40.13N 80.53W
Adendorp R.S.A. **80** 32.18S 24.31E
Adi *i.* Indonesia **59** 4.10S133.10E
Adi Daro Ethiopia **72** 14.27N 38.16E
Adieu, C. Australia **89** 31.59S132.09E
Adigala Ethiopia **73** 10.25N 42.17E
Adige *r.* Italy **30** 45.10N 12.20E
Adigrat Ethiopia **72** 14.18N 39.31E
Adi Keyih Ethiopia **72** 14.49N 39.23E
Ādilābād India **63** 19.40N 78.32E
Adilang Uganda **79** 2.44N 33.28E
Adin U.S.A. **108** 41.12N120.57W
Adirondack Mts. U.S.A. **115** 44.00N 74.00W
Adirondack Park U.S.A. **115** 43.28N 74.23W
Ādīs Ābeba Ethiopia **73** 9.03N 38.42E
Adi Ugri Ethiopia **72** 14.55N 38.53E
Adiyaman Turkey **64** 37.46N 38.15E
Adjud Romania **37** 46.04N 27.11E
Admer *well* Algeria **75** 20.23N 5.27E
Admiralty G. Australia **88** 14.20S125.50E
Admiralty I. U.S.A. **100** 57.50N134.30W
Admiralty Is. P.N.G. **59** 2.30S147.20E
Admiralty Range *mts.* Antarctica **128** 72.00S164.00E
Adolphustown Canada **105** 44.04N 77.00W
Adour *r.* France **20** 43.32N 1.32W
Adra Spain **27** 36.44N 3.01W
Adrano Italy **33** 37.40N 14.50E
Adrar *d.* Mauritania **74** 21.00N 10.00W
Adrar des Iforas *mts.* Mali / Algeria **75** 20.00N 2.30E
Adraskan Afghan. **62** 33.39N 62.16E
Adria Italy **30** 45.03N 12.03E
Adrian Mich. U.S.A. **104** 41.54N 84.02W
Adrian Mo. U.S.A. **110** 38.24N 94.21W
Adrian Tex. U.S.A. **111** 35.16N102.40W
Adrian W.Va. U.S.A. **114** 38.54N 80.17W
Adriatic Sea Med. Sea **31** 43.30N 14.30E
Ādwa Ethiopia **72** 14.12N 38.56E
Adzopé Ivory Coast **76** 6.07N 3.49W
Adzwa *r.* U.S.S.R. **44** 66.30N 59.30E
Aegean Sea Med. Sea **34** 37.00N 25.00E
Aerö *i.* Denmark **42** 54.53N 10.20E
Aëtos Greece **35** 37.15N 21.50E
Afándou Greece **35** 36.18N 28.12E
Āfdem Ethiopia **73** 9.26N 41.02E
Afghanistan Asia **62** 32.45N 65.00E
'Afīf Saudi Arabia **64** 23.53N 42.59E
Afikpo Nigeria **77** 5.53N 7.55E
Afjord Norway **40** 63.57N 10.12E
Aflou Algeria **75** 34.07N 2.06E
Afmadu Somali Rep. **79** 0.27N 42.05E
Afobaka Surinam **123** 5.00N 55.05W
Afognak I. U.S.A. **98** 58.15N152.30W
Afonso Cláudio Brazil **126** 20.05S 41.06W
Africa 70
Afsluitdijk *f.* Neth. **16** 53.04N 5.11E
'Afula Israel **67** 32.36N 35.17E
Afyon Turkey **64** 38.46N 30.32E
Agadez Niger **77** 17.00N 7.56E
Agadez *d.* Niger **77** 19.25N 11.00E
Agadir Morocco **74** 30.26N 9.36W
Agalak Sudan **73** 11.01N 32.42E
Agana Guam **84** 13.28N144.45E
Agano *r.* Japan **57** 37.58N139.02E
Agapa U.S.S.R. **51** 71.29N 86.16E
Agar India **62** 23.42N 76.01E
Agaro Ethiopia **73** 7.50N 36.40E
Agartala India **63** 23.49N 91.16E
Agaru Sudan **73** 10.59N 34.44E
Agboville Ivory Coast **76** 5.55N 4.15W
Agde France **20** 43.19N 3.28E
Agde, Cap d' *c.* France **20** 43.16N 3.30E
Agen France **20** 44.12N 0.37E
Ageo Japan **57** 35.58N139.36E
Agger *r.* W. Germany **16** 50.45N 7.06E
Aghada Rep. of Ire. **15** 51.50N 8.13W
Agia India **63** 26.05N 90.32E
Aginskoye U.S.S.R. **51** 51.10N114.32E
Agira Italy **33** 37.39N 14.32E
Agly *r.* France **20** 42.47N 3.02E
Agnew Australia **89** 28.01S120.30E
Agnone Italy **31** 41.48N 14.22E
Ago Japan **57** 34.17N136.48E
Agordo Italy **30** 46.17N 12.02E
Agouma Gabon **78** 1.33S 10.08E
Agout *r.* France **20** 43.47N 1.41E
Āgra India **63** 27.11N 78.01E
Agra *r.* Spain **24** 42.12N 1.43W
Agraciada Uruguay **125** 33.48S 58.15W
Agreda Spain **25** 41.51N 1.56W
Agri *r.* Italy **33** 40.13N 16.44E
Ağri Turkey **64** 39.44N 43.04E
Agri Bavnehöj *hill* Denmark **42** 56.14N 10.33E
Ağri Daği *mtn.* Turkey **65** 39.45N 44.15E
Agrigento Italy **32** 37.18N 13.35E
Agrínion Greece **35** 38.37N 21.24E
Agropoli Italy **33** 40.21N 15.00E
Agryz U.S.S.R. **44** 56.30N 53.00E
Agsumal, Sebjet *f.* W. Sahara **74** 24.21N 12.52W
Agua Caliente, Cerro *mtn.* Mexico **109** 26.27N106.12W
Aguanish Canada **103** 50.16N 62.10W
Aguanus *r.* Canada **103** 50.12N 62.10W
Agua Prieta Mexico **109** 31.18N109.34W
Aguas *r.* Spain **27** 37.09N 1.49W
Aguas Blancas Chile **124** 24.13S 69.50W
Aguascalientes Mexico **116** 21.51N102.18W
Aguascalientes *d.* Mexico **116** 22.00N102.00W
Aguasvivas *r.* Spain **25** 41.20N 0.25W
Agudos Brazil **126** 22.27S 49.03W
Águeda Portugal **26** 40.34N 8.27W
Águeda *r.* Spain **26** 41.02N 6.56W
Aguelhok Mali **74** 19.28N 0.52E
Aguema Angola **78** 12.03S 21.52E
Aguêraktem *well* Mali **74** 23.07N 6.12W
Aguilar Spain **27** 37.31N 4.39W
Aguilar de Campóo Spain **26** 42.47N 4.15W
Aguilas Spain **25** 37.24N 1.35W
Aguit China **54** 41.42N113.20E
Agulaa Ethiopia **72** 13.42N 39.35E
Agulhas, C. R.S.A. **80** 34.50S 20.00E
Agulhas Basin *f.* Indian Oc. **49** 45.00S 28.00E
Agulhas Negras *mtn.* Brazil **126** 22.20S 44.43W
Agung, Gunung *mtn.* Indonesia **59** 8.20S115.28E
'Agur Israel **67** 31.41N 34.54E
Ahaggar *f.* Algeria **75** 23.36N 5.50E
Ahar Iran **65** 38.25N 47.07E
Ahaura New Zealand **86** 42.21S171.33E
Ahaus W. Germany **16** 52.04N 7.01E
Ahirli Turkey **35** 38.37N 26.31E
Ahklun Mts. U.S.A. **98** 59.15N161.00W
Ahlen W. Germany **38** 51.46N 7.53E
Ahlenmoor *f.* W. Germany **38** 53.40N 8.45E
Ahmadābād India **62** 23.02N 72.37E
Aḩmadī Iran **65** 27.56N 56.42E
Ahmadnagar India **62** 19.05N 74.44E
Ahmadpur East Pakistan **62** 29.09N 71.16E
Ahmadpur Siāl Pakistan **62** 30.41N 71.46E
Ahmad Wāl Pakistan **62** 29.25N 65.56E
Ahmar Mts. Ethiopia **73** 9.15N 41.00E
Ahmic Harbour Canada **104** 45.39N 79.42W
Ahmic L. Canada **104** 45.37N 79.42W
Ahoada Nigeria **77** 5.06N 6.39E
Ahr *r.* W. Germany **16** 50.34N 7.16E
Ahram Iran **65** 28.52N 51.16E
Ahraura India **63** 25.01N 83.01E
Aḩsā', Wāḩat al *oasis* Saudi Arabia **65** 25.37N 49.40E
Ähtäri Finland **40** 62.34N 24.06E
Ahun France **20** 46.05N 2.05E
Åhus Sweden **43** 55.55N 14.17E
Ahvāz Iran **65** 31.17N 48.44E
Ahvenanmaa *d.* Finland **43** 60.15N 20.00E
Ahvenanmaa *is.* Finland **41** 60.15N 20.00E
Aichach W. Germany **39** 48.28N 11.08E
Aichi *d.* Japan **57** 35.02N137.15E
Aigle Switz. **39** 46.19N 6.58E
Aigre France **20** 45.54N 0.01E
Aigueperse France **20** 46.01N 3.12E
Aigues *r.* France **21** 44.07N 4.43E
Aigues-Mortes France **21** 43.34N 4.11E
Aiguilles France **21** 44.47N 6.52E
Aigurande France **19** 46.26N 1.50E
Aiken U.S.A. **113** 33.34N 81.44W
Ailette *r.* France **16** 49.35N 3.09E
Ailsa Craig *i.* U.K. **14** 55.15N 5.07W
Aim U.S.S.R. **51** 58.50N134.15E
Aimorés Brazil **126** 19.30S 41.04W
Ain *d.* France **21** 46.05N 5.20E
Ain *r.* France **21** 45.48N 5.10E
Aïna *r.* Gabon **78** 0.38N 12.47E
Ainaži U.S.S.R. **41** 57.52N 24.21E
Aïn Beïda Algeria **75** 35.50N 7.27E
Aïn ben Tili Mauritania **74** 26.00N 9.32W
Aïn Draham Tunisia **32** 36.47N 8.42E
Aïn Galakka Chad **75** 18.04N 18.24E
Aïn Sefra Algeria **74** 32.45N 0.35W
Aïr *mts.* Niger **77** 18.30N 8.30E
Aird I. Canada **104** 46.08N 82.25W
Airdrie U.K. **14** 55.52N 3.59W
Aire France **20** 43.42N 0.16W
Aire *r.* France **19** 49.19N 4.49E
Aire *r.* U.K. **12** 53.42N 0.54W
Airolo Switz. **39** 46.32N 8.37E
Airvault France **18** 46.50N 0.08W
Aisch *r.* W. Germany **39** 49.46N 11.01E
Aisne *d.* France **19** 49.30N 3.30E
Aisne *r.* France **19** 49.26N 2.50E
Aitana *mtn.* Spain **25** 38.40N 0.16W
Aitape P.N.G. **59** 3.10S142.17E
Aitkin U.S.A. **110** 46.32N 93.43W
Aitolikón Greece **35** 38.27N 21.22E
Aït Ourir Morocco **74** 31.38N 7.42W
Aitutaki Atoll Cook Is. **85** 18.52S159.46W
Aiud Romania **37** 46.19N 23.44E
Aix-en-Provence France **21** 43.32N 5.26E
Aix-les-Bains France **21** 45.42N 5.55E
Aíyina Greece **35** 37.44N 23.27E
Aíyina *i.* Greece **35** 37.46N 23.26E
Aiyínion Greece **34** 40.30N 22.33E
Aíyion Greece **35** 38.15N 22.05E
Aizpute U.S.S.R. **41** 56.43N 21.38E
Aizuwakamatsu Japan **57** 37.30N139.58E
Ajaccio France **21** 41.55N 8.44E
Ajanta Range *mts.* India **62** 20.15N 75.30E
Ajax Canada **104** 43.51N 79.02W
Ajdābiyā Libya **72** 30.46N 20.14E
Ajdovščina Yugo. **31** 45.53N 13.53E
Ajibar Ethiopia **73** 10.41N 38.37E
'Ajlūn Jordan **67** 32.20N 35.45E
'Ajmah, Jabal al *f.* Egypt **66** 29.12N 33.58E
'Ajmān U.A.E. **65** 25.23N 55.26E
Ajmer India **62** 26.27N 74.38E
Ajnāla India **62** 31.51N 74.47E
Ajo U.S.A. **109** 32.22N112.52W
Ajo, Cabo de *c.* Spain **26** 43.31N 3.35W
Akaishi sammyaku *mts.* Japan **57** 35.20N138.10E
Akámas, Akrotírion *c.* Cyprus **66** 35.06N 32.17E
'Akasha East Sudan **72** 21.05N 30.43E
Akashi Japan **57** 34.38N134.59E
Akbarpur India **63** 26.25N 82.33E
Akbulak U.S.S.R. **45** 51.00N 55.40E
Akelamo Indonesia **59** 1.35N129.40E
Akershus *d.* Norway **42** 60.05N 11.25E
Aketi Zaïre **78** 2.46N 23.51E
Akhaltsikhe U.S.S.R. **64** 41.37N 42.59E
Akharnaí Greece **35** 38.05N 23.44E
Akhḑar, Al Jabal al *mts.* Libya **72** 32.30N 21.30E
Akhḑar, Al Jabal al *mts.* Oman **65** 23.10N 57.25E
Akhḑar, Wādī *r.* Egypt **66** 28.42N 33.41E
Akhḑar, Wādī al *r.* Saudi Arabia **66** 28.30N 36.48E
Akhelóös Greece **29** 38.20N 21.04E
Akhelóös *r.* Greece **35** 38.36N 21.14E
Akhisar Turkey **29** 38.54N 27.49E
Akhladhókambos Greece **35** 37.31N 22.35E
Akhmīm Egypt **64** 26.34N 31.44E
Akhtyrka U.S.S.R. **45** 50.19N 34.54E
Akimiski I. Canada **102** 53.00N 81.20W
Åkirkeby Denmark **43** 55.04N 14.56E
Akita Japan **57** 39.44N140.05E
Akjoujt Mauritania **74** 19.44N 14.26W

Akkajaure to Almagro

Akkajaure *l.* Sweden **40** 67.40N 17.30E
'Akko Israel **67** 32.55N 35.05E
Akkol U.S.S.R. **52** 45.04N 75.39E
Akkoy Turkey **35** 37.29N 27.15E
Aklavik Canada **98** 68.12N135.00W
Ako Nigeria **77** 10.19N 10.48E
Åkobo *r.* Ethiopia **73** 8.30N 33.15E
Akola India **62** 20.44N 77.00E
Akordat Ethiopia **72** 15.35N 37.55E
Akot India **62** 21.11N 77.04E
Akpatok I. Canada **99** 60.30N 68.30W
Åkrafjorden *est.* Norway **42** 59.46N 6.06E
Akranes Iceland **40** 64.19N 22.05W
Åkrehamn Norway **42** 59.16N 5.11E
Akrítas, Ákra *c.* Greece **35** 36.43N 21.54E
Akron Colo. U.S.A. **110** 40.10N103.13W
Akron Ohio U.S.A. **114** 41.05N 81.31W
Akrotíri Cyprus **66** 34.36N 32.57E
Aksaray Turkey **64** 38.22N 34.02E
Aksarka U.S.S.R. **50** 66.31N 67.50E
Aksay China **52** 39.28N 94.15E
Aksay U.S.S.R. **45** 51.24N 52.11E
Akşehir Turkey **64** 38.22N 31.24E
Aksu China **52** 42.10N 80.00E
Åksum Ethiopia **72** 14.08N 38.48E
Aktag *mtn.* China **52** 36.45N 84.40E
Aktogay U.S.S.R. **52** 46.59N 79.42E
Aktyubinsk U.S.S.R. **45** 50.16N 57.13E
Akūbū Sudan **73** 7.47N 33.01E
Akūbū *r.* see Åkobo Sudan **73**
Akula Zaïre **78** 2.22N 20.11E
Akure Nigeria **77** 7.14N 5.08E
Akureyri Iceland **40** 65.41N 18.04W
Akuse Ghana **76** 6.04N 0.12E
Akxokesay China **52** 36.48N 91.06E
Akyab see Sittwe Burma **56**
Ål Norway **41** 60.38N 8.34E
Alabama *d.* U.S.A. **113** 32.50N 87.00W
Alabama *r.* U.S.A. **111** 31.08N 87.57W
Al 'Abbāsiyah Sudan **73** 14.27N 33.31E
Alaçati Turkey **35** 38.16N 26.23E
Ālādāgh, Kūh-e *mts.* Iran **65** 37.15N 57.30E
Alagoas *d.* Brazil **123** 9.30S 37.00W
Alagoinhas Brazil **123** 12.09S 38.21W
Alagón Spain **26** 41.46N 1.12W
Alakol, Ozero *l.* U.S.S.R. **52** 46.00N 81.40E
Alakurtti U.S.S.R. **44** 67.00N 30.23E
Al'Āl Syria **67** 32.48N 35.44E
Al 'Alamayn Egypt **64** 30.49N 28.57E
Al 'Amārah Iraq **65** 31.52N 47.50E
Al Āmirīyah Egypt **66** 31.01N 29.48E
Alamogordo U.S.A. **109** 32.54N105.57W
Alamos, Rio de los *r.* Mexico **111** 27.53N101.12W
Alamosa U.S.A. **108** 37.28N105.52W
Åland *is.* see Ahvenanmaa Finland **41**
Ålands Hav *sea* Finland **43** 59.50N 19.25E
Alanreed U.S.A. **111** 35.14N100.45W
Alanson U.S.A. **104** 45.27N 84.47W
Alanya Turkey **64** 36.32N 32.02E
Alaotra, Lac *l.* Madagascar **81** 17.30S 48.30E
Alapayevsk U.S.S.R. **44** 57.55N 61.42E
Al 'Aqabah Jordan **66** 29.32N 35.00E
Al 'Aramah *f.* Saudi Arabia **65** 25.30N 46.30E
Alarcón, Embalse de *resr.* Spain **27** 39.36N 2.10W
Al 'Arish Egypt **66** 31.08N 33.48E
Alaşehir Turkey **29** 38.22N 28.29E
Al 'Aşimah *d.* Jordan **67** 31.45N 36.05E
Alaska *d.* U.S.A. **98** 65.00N153.00W
Alaska, G. of U.S.A. **98** 58.45N145.00W
Alaska Pen. U.S.A. **98** 56.00N160.00W
Alaska Range *mts.* U.S.A. **98** 62.10N152.00W
Alassio Italy **30** 44.00N 8.10E
Al 'Atiqah Lebanon **66** 33.42N 35.27E
Alatri Italy **30** 41.43N 13.21E
Al 'Aṭrun Sudan **72** 18.11N 26.36E
Alatyr U.S.S.R. **44** 54.51N 46.35E
Alausi Ecuador **122** 2.00S 78.50W
Alava *d.* Spain **26** 42.55N 2.50W
Alavus Finland **40** 62.35N 23.37E
Alawoona Australia **92** 34.44S140.33E
Al 'Ayn *wells* Sudan **72** 16.36N 29.19E
Alayor Spain **25** 39.56N 4.08E
Al 'Ayyāṭ Egypt **66** 29.37N 31.15E
Alazani *r.* U.S.S.R. **65** 41.06N 46.40E
Alba Italy **30** 44.42N 8.02E
Albacete Spain **25** 38.59N 1.51W
Albacete *d.* Spain **25** 39.05N 1.45W
Al Bad' Saudi Arabia **66** 28.29N 35.02E
Al Badārī Egypt **64** 26.59N 31.25E
Alba de Tormes Spain **26** 40.49N 5.31W
Albaek Denmark **42** 57.36N 10.25E
Al Bahnasā Egypt **66** 28.32N 30.39E
Al Baḩr al Mayyit see Dead Sea Jordan **67**
Albaida Spain **25** 38.51N 0.31W
Alba-Iulia Romania **37** 46.04N 23.33E
Al Balqā' *d.* Jordan **67** 32.00N 35.40E
Alban France **20** 43.54N 2.28E
Albania Europe **34** 41.00N 20.00E
Albano Laziale Italy **30** 41.44N 12.39E
Albany Australia **89** 34.57S117.54E
Albany *r.* Canada **102** 52.10N 82.00W
Albany Ga. U.S.A. **113** 31.37N 84.10W
Albany Ky. U.S.A. **113** 36.42N 85.08W
Albany Minn. U.S.A. **110** 45.38N 94.34W
Albany N.Y. U.S.A. **115** 42.39N 73.45W
Albany Ohio U.S.A. **114** 39.14N 82.12W
Albany Oreg. U.S.A. **108** 44.38N123.06W
Al Bāriḩah Jordan **67** 32.34N 35.50E
Albarracín Spain **25** 40.25N 1.26W
Albarracín, Sierra de *mts.* Spain **25** 40.30N 1.40W
Al Başrah Iraq **65** 30.33N 47.50E
Al Bāṭinah *f.* Oman **65** 24.25N 56.50E
Albatross B. Australia **90** 12.45S141.43E
Al Batrūn Lebanon **66** 34.16N 35.40E
Al Bawīṭī Egypt **64** 28.21N 25.52E
Al Bayāḑ *f.* Saudi Arabia **71** 22.00N 47.00E
Al Bayḑā' Libya **75** 32.46N 21.43E
Albegna *r.* Italy **30** 42.30N 11.11E
Albemarle Sd. U.S.A. **107** 36.10N 76.00W
Albenga Italy **30** 44.03N 8.13E
Albens France **21** 45.47N 5.57E
Alberche *r.* Spain **27** 39.58N 4.46W
Alberga Australia **91** 27.12S135.28E
Alberga *r.* Australia **91** 27.12S135.28E
Albergaria-a-Velha Portugal **26** 40.42N 8.29W
Alberique Spain **25** 39.07N 0.31W
Albermarle U.S.A. **113** 35.21N 80.12W
Albermarle Sd. U.S.A. **113** 36.03N 76.12W
Alberni Canada **100** 49.20N124.50W
Alberobello Italy **33** 40.47N 17.15E
Albert Australia **93** 32.21S147.33E
Albert France **19** 50.00N 2.39E
Albert, L. Australia **92** 35.38S139.17E
Albert, L. Uganda / Zaïre **79** 1.45N 31.00E
Alberta *d.* Canada **100** 54.00N115.00W
Alberti Argentina **125** 35.01S 60.16W
Albertirsa Hungary **37** 47.15N 19.38E
Albert Kanaal *canal* Belgium **16** 51.00N 5.15E
Albert Lea U.S.A. **110** 43.39N 93.22W
Albert Nile *r.* Uganda **79** 3.30N 32.00E
Alberton Canada **103** 46.49N 64.04W
Albertville France **21** 45.41N 6.23E
Albi France **20** 43.56N 2.08E
Al Bidia Chad **73** 10.33N 20.13E
Albin U.S.A. **108** 41.26N104.08W
Albina Surinam **123** 5.30N 54.03W
Albino Italy **30** 45.46N 9.47E
Albion Mich. U.S.A. **112** 42.14N 84.45W
Albion Mont. U.S.A. **108** 45.11N104.15W
Albion Nebr. U.S.A. **110** 41.42N 98.00W
Albion N.Y. U.S.A. **114** 43.15N 78.12W
Albion Penn. U.S.A. **114** 41.53N 80.22W
Al Bi'r Saudi Arabia **66** 28.52N 36.15E
Al Bīrah Jordan **67** 31.54N 35.13E
Albo, Monte *mtn.* Italy **32** 40.29N 9.33E
Albocácer Spain **25** 40.21N 0.02E
Alborán, Isla de *i.* Spain **27** 35.58N 3.02W
Ålborg Denmark **42** 57.03N 9.56E
Ålborg Bugt *b.* Denmark **42** 56.55N 10.30E
Alborz, Reshteh-ye Kūhhā-ye *mts.* Iran **65** 36.00N 52.30E
Albufeira Portugal **27** 37.05N 8.15W
Albuñol Spain **27** 36.47N 3.12W
Albuquerque U.S.A. **109** 35.05N106.40W
Al Buraymī U.A.E. **65** 24.15N 55.45E
Alburg U.S.A. **105** 44.59N 73.18W
Al Burj Egypt **66** 31.35N 30.59E
Alburquerque Spain **27** 39.13N 7.00W
Albury Australia **93** 36.03S146.53E
Al Buṭanah *f.* Sudan **72** 14.50N 34.30E
Al Buwayḑah Jordan **67** 32.21N 36.03E
Alby Sweden **40** 62.30N 15.25E
Alcácer do Sal Portugal **27** 38.22N 8.30W
Alcains Portugal **27** 39.55N 7.27W
Alcalá de Chisvert Spain **25** 40.19N 0.13E
Alcalá de Guadaira Spain **27** 37.20N 5.50W
Alcalá de Henares Spain **26** 40.29N 3.22W
Alcalá la Real Spain **27** 37.28N 3.56W
Alcamo Italy **32** 37.59N 12.58E
Alcanadre *r.* Spain **25** 41.37N 0.12W
Alcanar Spain **25** 40.33N 0.29E
Alcañices Spain **26** 41.42N 6.21W
Alcañiz Spain **25** 41.03N 0.08W
Alcántara Spain **27** 39.43N 6.53W
Alcántara, Embalse de *resr.* Spain **27** 39.45N 6.25W
Alcantara L. Canada **101** 60.57N108.09W
Alcantarilla Spain **25** 37.58N 1.13W
Alcaraz Spain **26** 38.40N 2.29W
Alcaraz, Sierra de *mts.* Spain **27** 38.40N 2.30W
Alcarrache *r.* Portugal **27** 38.16N 7.24W
Alcaudete Spain **27** 37.36N 4.05W
Alcázar de San Juan Spain **27** 39.24N 3.12W
Alcira Spain **25** 39.09N 0.26W
Alcobaça Portugal **27** 39.33N 8.59W
Alcobendas Spain **26** 40.32N 3.38W
Alcolea del Pinar Spain **26** 41.02N 2.28W
Alconchel Portugal **27** 38.31N 7.04W
Alcova U.S.A. **108** 42.35N106.34W
Alcoy Spain **25** 38.42N 0.28W
Alcubierre Spain **25** 41.48N 0.27W
Alcubierre, Sierra de *mts.* Spain **25** 41.45N 0.21W
Alcudia Spain **25** 39.52N 3.07E
Alcudia, Bahía de *b.* Spain **25** 39.48N 3.13E
Alcudia, Sierra de la *mts.* Spain **27** 38.34N 4.30W
Aldabra Is. Seychelles **70** 9.00S 46.30E
Aldan U.S.S.R. **51** 58.44N125.22E
Aldan *r.* U.S.S.R. **51** 63.30N130.00E
Aldeburgh U.K. **13** 52.09N 1.35E
Aldeia Nova de Santo Bento Portugal **27** 37.55N 7.25W
Alder Creek *town* U.S.A. **115** 43.27N 75.17W
Alderney *i.* U.K. **13** 49.42N 2.11W
Aldershot U.K. **13** 51.15N 0.47W
Alderson Canada **101** 50.20N111.25W
Aldridge U.K. **13** 52.36N 1.55W
Aledo U.S.A. **110** 41.12N 90.45W
Aleg Mauritania **74** 17.03N 13.55W
Alegre Brazil **126** 20.44S 41.30W
Alegrete Brazil **125** 29.46S 55.46W
Aleksandrov Gay U.S.S.R. **45** 50.08N 48.34E
Aleksandrovsk Sakhalinskiy U.S.S.R. **51** 50.55N142.12E
Aleksinac Yugo. **34** 43.31N 21.42E
Alembe Gabon **78** 0.03N 10.57E
Além Paraíba Brazil **126** 21.49S 42.36W
Alençon France **18** 48.26N 0.05E
Alenuihaha Channel Hawaiian Is. **85** 20.26N156.00W
Aleppo see Ḩalab Syria **64**
Aléria France **21** 42.05N 9.30E
Alès France **21** 44.08N 4.05E
Alessandria Italy **30** 44.54N 8.37E
Alessano Italy **33** 39.53N 18.20E
Ålestrup Denmark **42** 56.42N 9.31E
Ålesund Norway **40** 62.28N 6.11E
Aleutian Basin Bering Sea **84** 57.00N179.00E
Aleutian Is. U.S.A. **48** 57.00N180.00
Aleutian Range *mts.* U.S.A. **98** 58.00N156.00W
Aleutian Trench Pacific Oc. **84** 50.00N176.00W
Alexander *r.* Israel **67** 32.24N 34.52E
Alexander U.S.A. **114** 42.54N 78.16W
Alexander Archipelago *is.* U.S.A. **100** 56.30N134.30W
Alexander Bay *town* R.S.A. **80** 28.36S 16.26E
Alexander I. Antarctica **128** 72.00S 70.00W
Alexandra Australia **93** 37.12S145.14E
Alexandra New Zealand **86** 45.14S169.26E
Alexandria B.C. Canada **100** 52.35N122.27W
Alexandria Ont. Canada **105** 45.19N 74.38W
Alexandria see Al Iskandarīyah Egypt **66**
Alexandria Romania **34** 43.58N 25.20E
Alexandria R.S.A. **80** 33.39S 26.24E
Alexandria La. U.S.A. **111** 31.18N 92.27W
Alexandria Minn. U.S.A. **110** 45.53N 95.22W
Alexandria Va. U.S.A. **114** 38.48N 77.03W
Alexandria Bay *town* U.S.A. **105** 44.20N 75.55W
Alexandrina, L. Australia **92** 35.26S139.10E
Alexandroúpolis Greece **34** 40.50N 25.52E
Alexis *r.* Canada **103** 52.32N 56.08W
Alexis Creek *town* Canada **100** 52.05N123.20W
Aleysk U.S.S.R. **50** 52.32N 82.45E
Alfambra Spain **25** 40.33N 1.02W
Al Fant Egypt **66** 28.46N 30.53E
Alfaro Spain **25** 42.11N 1.45W
Alfarrás Spain **25** 41.49N 0.35E
Al Fāshir Sudan **73** 13.38N 25.21E
Al Fashn Egypt **66** 28.49N 30.54E
Al Fāw Iraq **65** 29.57N 48.30E
Al Fayyūm Egypt **66** 29.19N 30.50E
Alfeld W. Germany **38** 51.59N 9.50E
Alfenas Brazil **126** 21.28S 45.48W
Al Fifi Sudan **73** 10.03N 25.01E
Alfiós *r.* Greece **35** 37.40N 21.33E
Alfonsine Italy **30** 44.30N 12.03E
Alford U.K. **14** 57.14N 2.42W
Alfred U.S.A. **114** 42.15N 77.47W
Al Fujayrah U.A.E. **65** 25.10N 56.20E
Al Furāt *r.* Asia **65** 31.00N 47.27E
Alga U.S.S.R. **50** 49.49N 57.16E
Ålgård Norway **42** 58.46N 5.51E
Al Gebir Sudan **73** 13.43N 29.49E
Algeciras Spain **27** 36.08N 5.30W
Algemesí Spain **25** 39.11N 0.26W
Algena Ethiopia **72** 16.20N 38.34E
Alger Algeria **75** 36.50N 3.00E
Alger U.S.A. **104** 44.08N 84.08W
Algeria Africa **74** 28.00N 2.00E
Al Ghawr *f.* Jordan **67** 32.00N 35.30E
Al Ghayl Saudi Arabia **65** 22.36N 46.19E
Alghero Italy **32** 40.34N 8.19E
Al Ghurdaqah Egypt **64** 27.14N 33.50E
Algiers see Alger Algeria **75**
Alginet Spain **25** 39.16N 0.28W
Algoa B. R.S.A. **80** 33.50S 26.00E
Algodor *r.* Spain **27** 39.55N 3.53W
Algoma U.S.A. **110** 44.36N 87.27W
Algoma Mills Canada **104** 46.10N 82.50W
Algoma Uplands Canada **104** 47.00N 83.35W
Algona U.S.A. **110** 43.04N 94.14W
Algonquin Park *town* Canada **104** 45.34N 78.36W
Algonquin Prov. Park Canada **104** 45.27N 78.26W
Algonquin Upland Canada **104** 45.40N 78.47W
Algorta Uruguay **125** 32.25S 57.23W
Al Ḩajar al Gharbī *mts.* Oman **65** 24.00N 56.30E
Al Ḩajar ash Sharqī *mts.* Oman **65** 22.45N 58.45E
Alhama Spain **25** 37.51N 1.25W
Al Ḩamād *des.* Saudi Arabia **64** 31.45N 39.00E
Alhama de Granada Spain **27** 37.00N 3.59W
Al Ḩamar Saudi Arabia **65** 22.26N 46.12E
Alhambra U.S.A. **109** 34.06N118.08W
Al Ḩamīdīyah Syria **66** 34.43N 35.56E
Al Ḩanākīyah Saudi Arabia **64** 24.53N 40.30E
Al Ḩarāk Syria **67** 32.44N 36.18E
Al Ḩariq Saudi Arabia **65** 23.37N 46.31E
Al Ḩārrah Syria **67** 33.03N 36.00E
Al Harūj al Aswad *hills* Libya **75** 27.00N 17.10E
Al Ḩasakah Syria **64** 36.29N 40.45E
Alhaurín el Grande Spain **27** 36.38N 4.41W
Al Ḩawāmidīyah Egypt **66** 29.54N 31.15E
Al Ḩayz Egypt **64** 28.02N 28.39E
Al Ḩijāz *f.* Saudi Arabia **64** 26.00N 37.30E
Al Ḩillah Iraq **65** 32.28N 44.29E
Al Ḩillah Saudi Arabia **65** 23.30N 46.51E
Al Hirmil Lebanon **66** 34.25N 36.23E
Al Ḩişn Jordan **67** 32.29N 35.53E
Al-Hoceima Morocco **74** 35.15N 3.55W
Al Ḩudaydah Yemen **72** 14.50N 42.58E
Al Hufūf Saudi Arabia **65** 25.20N 49.34E
Al Ḩumrah *des.* U.A.E. **65** 22.45N 55.10E
Al Ḩusaynīyah Egypt **66** 30.52N 31.55E
Al Ḩuwaymī S. Yemen **71** 14.05N 47.44E
Aliābād, Kūh-e *mtn.* Iran **65** 34.09N 50.48E
Aliaga Spain **25** 40.40N 0.42W
Aliákmon *r.* Greece **34** 40.30N 22.36E
Alicante Spain **25** 38.23N 0.29W
Alicante *d.* Spain **25** 38.30N 0.40W
Alice Canada **105** 45.44N 77.19W
Alice R.S.A. **80** 32.47S 26.49E
Alice U.S.A. **111** 27.45N 98.04W
Alice, Punta *c.* Italy **33** 39.24N 17.10E
Alice Arm Canada **100** 55.29N129.31W
Alice Springs *town* Australia **90** 23.42S133.52E
Alicudi, Isola *i.* Italy **33** 38.33N 14.21E
Al Ifranj Jordan **67** 31.11N 35.41E
Aligarh India **63** 27.53N 78.05E
Alīgūdarz Iran **65** 33.25N 49.38E
'Alījūq, Kūh-e *mtn.* Iran **65** 31.27N 51.43E
Alima *r.* Congo **78** 1.36S 16.35E
Alindao C.A.R. **73** 5.02N 21.13E
Alingsås Sweden **43** 57.56N 12.31E
Alīpur Pakistan **62** 29.23N 70.55E
Alīpur Duār India **63** 26.29N 89.44E
Alīpur Janūbī Pakistan **62** 30.13N 71.18E
Aliquippa U.S.A. **114** 40.37N 80.15W
Al 'Irq Libya **75** 29.05N 15.48E
Ali Sabieh Djibouti **73** 11.09N 42.42E
Aliseda Spain **27** 39.26N 6.41W
Al Iskandarīyah Egypt **66** 31.13N 29.55E
Al Ismā'īlīyah Egypt **66** 30.36N 32.15E
Al Istiwā'īyah *d.* Sudan **73** 5.00N 32.30E
Alistráti Greece **34** 41.04N 23.57E
Alivérion Greece **35** 38.24N 24.02E
Aliwal North R.S.A. **80** 30.41S 26.41E
Al Jabal al Akhḑar *d.* Libya **75** 32.00N 21.30E
Al Jafr Jordan **66** 30.16N 36.11E
Al Jāfūrah *des.* Saudi Arabia **65** 24.40N 50.20E
Al Jaghbūb Libya **72** 29.45N 24.31E
Al Jahrah Kuwait **65** 29.20N 47.41E
Al Jaladah *f.* Saudi Arabia **71** 18.30N 46.25E
Al Janūb *d.* Lebanon **67** 33.10N 35.22E
Al Jawārah Oman **60** 18.55N 57.17E
Al Jawb *f.* Saudi Arabia **65** 23.00N 50.00E
Al Jawf Libya **72** 24.12N 23.18E
Al Jawf Saudi Arabia **64** 29.49N 39.52E
Al Jawsh Libya **75** 32.00N 11.40E
Al Jazīrah *f.* Iraq **64** 35.00N 41.00E
Al Jazīrah *f.* Sudan **72** 14.25N 33.00E
Al Jibāb Syria **67** 33.06N 36.15E
Al Jifārah Saudi Arabia **65** 23.59N 45.11E
Al Jīzah Egypt **66** 30.01N 31.12E
Al Jīzah Jordan **67** 31.42N 35.57E
Al Jubayl Saudi Arabia **65** 27.59N 49.40E
Al Judayyidah Jordan **67** 31.15N 35.49E
Al Junaynah Sudan **73** 13.27N 22.27E
Aljustrel Portugal **26** 37.52N 8.10W
Al Karabah Sudan **72** 18.33N 33.42E
Al Karak Jordan **67** 31.11N 35.42E
Al Karak *d.* Jordan **67** 31.10N 36.00E
Al Kawah Sudan **73** 13.44N 32.30E
Al Khābūr *r.* Syria **64** 35.07N 40.30E
Al Khābūrah Oman **65** 23.58N 57.10E
Al Khalīl Jordan **67** 31.32N 35.06E
Al Khalīl *d.* Jordan **67** 31.29N 35.10E
Al Khamāsīn Saudi Arabia **71** 20.29N 44.49E
Al Khandaq Sudan **72** 18.36N 30.34E
Al Khānkah Egypt **66** 30.12N 31.21E
Al Khārijah Egypt **64** 25.26N 30.33E
Al Kharṭūm Sudan **72** 15.33N 32.35E
Al Kharṭūm *d.* Sudan **72** 15.45N 32.30E
Al Kharṭūm Baḩrī Sudan **72** 15.39N 32.34E
Al Khasfah *well* Oman **71** 19.45N 54.19E
Al Khawr Qatar **65** 25.39N 51.32E
Al Khirbah as Samrā' Jordan **67** 32.11N 36.10E
Al Khubar Saudi Arabia **65** 26.18N 50.06E
Al Khufayfīyah Saudi Arabia **65** 24.55N 44.42E
Al Khums Libya **75** 32.39N 14.16E
Al Khums *d.* Libya **75** 31.20N 14.10E
Al Khunn Saudi Arabia **65** 23.18N 49.15E
Al Khushnīyah Syria **67** 33.00N 35.48E
Al Kidn *des.* Saudi Arabia **65** 22.20N 54.20E
Al Kiswah Syria **66** 33.21N 36.14E
Alkmaar Neth. **16** 52.37N 4.44E
Al Kufrah Libya **72** 24.14N 23.15E
Al Kuntillah Egypt **66** 30.00N 34.41E
Al Kūt Iraq **65** 32.30N 45.51E
Al Kuwayt Kuwait **65** 29.20N 48.00E
Al Labwah Lebanon **66** 34.11N 36.21E
Al Lādhiqīyah Syria **66** 35.31N 35.47E
Al Lagowa Sudan **73** 11.24N 29.08E
Allāhābād India **63** 25.27N 81.51E
Allakaket U.S.A. **98** 66.30N152.45W
'Allān *r.* Syria **67** 32.45N 35.57E
Allanche France **20** 45.14N 2.56E
'Allāqī, Wādī al *r.* Egypt **64** 22.55N 33.02E
Allariz Spain **26** 42.11N 7.48W
Allauch France **21** 43.20N 5.29E
Ålleberg *hill* Sweden **43** 58.08N 13.36E
Allegany U.S.A. **114** 42.06N 78.30W
Allegany State Park U.S.A. **114** 42.04N 78.44W
Allegheny *r.* U.S.A. **114** 40.27N 80.00W
Allegheny Mts. U.S.A. **114** 38.30N 80.00W
Allegheny Resr. U.S.A. **114** 42.00N 78.56W
Allen, Lough Rep. of Ire. **15** 54.07N 8.04W
Allenby Bridge see Jisr al Ḩusayn Jordan **67**
Allenford Canada **104** 44.32N 81.10W
Allentown U.S.A. **115** 40.37N 75.30W
Alleppey India **60** 9.30N 76.22E
Aller *r.* W. Germany **38** 52.57N 9.11E
Allevard France **21** 45.24N 6.04E
Allgäu *f.* W. Germany **38** 47.40N 10.15E
Allgäuer Alpen *mts.* W. Germany / Austria **38** 47.26N 10.15E
Alliance Nebr. U.S.A. **110** 42.06N102.52W
Alliance Ohio U.S.A. **114** 40.55N 81.06W
Allier *d.* France **20** 46.25N 3.00E
Allier *r.* France **20** 46.58N 3.03E
Allinge Denmark **43** 55.16N 14.49E
Al Lisān *pen.* Jordan **67** 31.17N 35.28E
Alliston Canada **104** 44.09N 79.52W
Al Liṭānī *r.* Lebanon **66** 33.22N 35.14E
Al Līth Saudi Arabia **72** 20.09N 40.16E
Al Liwā' *f.* U.A.E. **71** 23.00N 54.00E
Alloa U.K. **14** 56.07N 3.49W
Allora Australia **91** 28.02S151.59E
Allos France **21** 44.14N 6.38E
Al Luḩayyah Yemen **72** 15.43N 42.42E
Alluitsup-Paa see Sydprøven Greenland **99**
Alma Canada **103** 48.32N 71.40W
Alma Ga. U.S.A. **113** 31.33N 82.29W
Alma Mich. U.S.A. **112** 43.23N 84.40W
Al Ma'āniyah *well* Iraq **64** 30.44N 43.00E
Alma-Ata U.S.S.R. **52** 43.19N 76.55E
Almada Portugal **27** 38.41N 9.09W
Almaden Australia **90** 17.20S144.41E
Almadén Spain **26** 38.46N 4.50W
Almadén de la Plata Spain **27** 37.52N 6.04W
Al Madīnah Saudi Arabia **64** 24.30N 39.35E
Al Madīnah al Fikrīyah Egypt **66** 27.56N 30.49E
Al Madwar Jordan **67** 32.17N 36.00E
Al Mafraq Jordan **67** 32.21N 36.12E
Al Maghrah *well* Egypt **64** 30.14N 28.56E
Almagor Israel **67** 32.55N 35.36E
Almagro Spain **26** 38.53N 3.43W

Al Maḩallah al Kubrá to Angara

Al Maḩallah al Kubrá Egypt 66 30.59N 31.12E
Al Maḩāriq Egypt 64 25.37N 30.39E
Alma Hill U.S.A. 114 42.03N 78.01W
Al Maḩmūdīyah Egypt 66 31.10N 30.30E
Al Majma'ah Saudi Arabia 65 25.52N 45.25E
Al Manāmah Bahrain 65 26.12N 50.36E
Almanor U.S.A. 108 40.15N121.08W
Almansa Spain 25 38.52N 1.05W
Al Manshāh Egypt 64 26.28N 31.48E
Almansor r. Portugal 27 38.56N 8.54W
Al Manşūrah Egypt 66 31.03N 31.23E
Almanza Spain 26 42.39N 5.02W
Al Manzil Jordan 66 31.03N 36.01E
Al Manzilah Egypt 66 31.10N 31.56E
Almanzor, Pico de mtn. Spain 26 40.15N 5.18W
Almanzora r. Spain 24 37.16N 1.49W
Almar r. Spain 26 40.54N 5.29W
Al Marj Libya 72 32.30N 20.50E
Al Maţarīyah Egypt 66 31.12N 32.02E
Al Matnah Sudan 72 13.47N 35.03E
Al Mawşil Iraq 64 36.21N 43.08E
Al Mayādīn Syria 64 35.01N 40.28E
Almazán Spain 26 41.29N 2.32W
Almazora Spain 25 39.57N 0.03W
Al Mazra'ah Jordan 67 31.16N 35.31E
Almeida Portugal 26 40.43N 6.54W
Almeirim Portugal 27 39.12N 8.38W
Almelo Neth. 16 52.21N 6.40E
Almenara, Sierra de mts. Spain 25 37.30N 1.40E
Almenar de Soria Spain 25 41.41N 2.12W
Almendra, Embalse de resr. Spain 26 41.15N 6.10W
Almendralejo Spain 27 38.41N 6.24W
Almería Spain 27 36.50N 2.27W
Almería d. Spain 27 37.05N 2.30W
Almería, Golfo di g. Spain 27 36.45N 2.30W
Älmhult Sweden 43 56.33N 14.08E
Al Midhnab Saudi Arabia 65 25.52N 44.15E
Al Miḩrāḑ des. Saudi Arabia 65 20.00N 52.30E
Al Minyā Egypt 66 28.06N 30.45E
Almiropótamos Greece 35 38.16N 24.11E
Almirós Greece 35 39.11N 22.46E
Almiroú, Kólpos g. Greece 35 35.23N 24.20E
Al Mismīyah Syria 66 33.08N 36.24E
Almodôvar Portugal 27 37.31N 8.36W
Almodóvar del Campo Spain 26 38.43N 4.10W
Almont U.S.A. 114 42.55N 83.03W
Almonte Canada 105 45.14N 76.12W
Almonte Spain 27 37.15N 6.31W
Almonte r. Spain 27 39.42N 6.20W
Almora India 63 29.37N 79.40E
Al Mudawwarah Jordan 66 29.20N 36.00E
Almudébar Spain 25 42.03N 0.35W
Al Muglad Sudan 73 11.02N 27.44E
Al Muḩarraq Bahrain 65 26.16N 50.38E
Al Mukallā S. Yemen 71 14.34N 49.09E
Al Mukhā Yemen 73 13.19N 43.15E
Almuñécar Spain 27 36.43N 3.41W
Al Muwaqqar site Jordan 67 31.39N 36.06E
Al Muwayh Saudi Arabia 64 22.41N 41.37E
Alnwick U.K. 12 55.25N 1.41W
Alofi Niue 84 19.03S169.55W
Alofi B. Niue 84 19.02S169.55W
Alónnisos Greece 35 39.08N 23.50E
Alónnisos i. Greece 35 39.08N 23.50E
Alonsa Canada 101 50.50N 99.00W
Alor i. Indonesia 59 8.20S124.30E
Álora Spain 27 36.48N 4.42W
Alor Setar Malaysia 58 6.06N100.23E
Alosno Spain 27 37.33N 7.07W
Alozero U.S.S.R. 44 65.02N 31.10E
Alpena U.S.A. 104 45.04N 83.26W
Alpes-de-Haute-Provence d. France 21 44.08N 6.10E
Alpes Maritimes d. France 21 44.00N 7.10E
Alpes Maritimes mts. France 17 44.07N 7.08E
Alpes Pennines mts. Switz. 39 46.08N 7.34E
Alpha Australia 90 23.39S146.38E
Alphen Neth. 16 52.08N 4.40E
Alpiarça Portugal 27 39.15N 8.35W
Alpine U.S.A. 111 30.22N103.40W
Alps mts. Europe 17 46.00N 7.30E
Al Qaḑārif Sudan 72 14.02N 35.24E
Al Qaḑimah Saudi Arabia 72 22.21N 39.09E
Al Qafā' des. U.A.E. 60 23.25N 53.50E
Al Qafā' des. U.A.E. 65 23.30N 53.30E
Al Qāhirah Egypt 66 30.03N 31.15E
Al Qā'iyah Saudi Arabia 64 24.18N 43.30E
Al Qā'iyah well Saudi Arabia 65 26.27N 45.35E
Al Qalībah Saudi Arabia 64 28.24N 37.42E
Al Qanāţir al Khayrīyah Egypt 66 30.12N 31.08E
Al Qanţarah Egypt 66 30.52N 32.20E
Al Qaryatayn Syria 66 34.13N 37.13E
Al Qaşabāt Libya 75 32.35N 14.03E
Al Qaşr Egypt 64 25.43N 28.54E
Al Qaşr Jordan 67 31.19N 35.45E
Al Qaşşāşīn Egypt 66 30.34N 31.56E
Al Qaţīf Saudi Arabia 65 26.31N 50.00E
Al Qaţrānah Jordan 67 31.15N 36.03E
Al Qaţrūn Libya 75 24.56N 14.38E
Al Qayşūmah Saudi Arabia 65 28.20N 46.07E
Al Qişfah Jordan 67 32.38N 35.52E
Al Quds d. Jordan 67 31.46N 35.25E
Al Qunayţirah Syria 67 33.08N 35.49E
Al Qunayţirah d. Syria 67 33.07N 35.50E
Al Qunfudhah Saudi Arabia 72 19.08N 41.05E
Al Qurnah Iraq 65 31.00N 47.26E
Al Quşaymah Egypt 66 30.40N 34.22E
Al Quşayr Egypt 64 26.06N 34.17E
Al Qūşīyah Egypt 64 27.26N 30.49E
Al Quţayfah Syria 66 33.44N 36.36E
Alroy Downs town Australia 90 19.18S136.04E
Als i. Denmark 42 54.59N 9.55E
Alsace d. France 19 48.25N 7.40E
Alsask Canada 101 51.23N109.59W
Alsasua Spain 25 42.54N 2.10W
Älsborg d. Sweden 41 58.00N 12.20E
Alsek Ranges mts. Canada 100 59.21N137.05W
Alsfeld W. Germany 38 50.45N 9.16E
Alsten i. Norway 40 65.55N 12.35E
Alsterbro Sweden 43 56.57N 15.55E
Alston U.K. 14 54.48N 2.26W
Alta Norway 40 70.00N 23.15E
Alta r. Norway 40 69.50N 23.30E
Altafjorden est. Norway 40 70.10N 23.00E
Alta Gracia Argentina 124 31.40S 64.26W
Altagracia de Orituco Venezuela 122 9.54N 66.24W
Altai mts. Mongolia 52 46.30N 93.30E
Altamaha r. U.S.A. 113 31.19N 81.17W
Altamira Brazil 123 3.12S 52.12W
Altamont N.Y. U.S.A. 115 42.42N 74.02W
Altamont Oreg. U.S.A. 108 42.12N121.44W
Altamura Italy 33 40.50N 16.33E
Altar, Desierto de des. Mexico 109 31.50N114.15W
Altavista U.S.A. 113 37.07N 79.18W
Altay China 52 47.48N 88.07E
Altay Mongolia 52 46.20N 97.00E
Altdorf Switz. 39 46.53N 8.39E
Altea Spain 25 38.38N 0.02W
Altenburg E. Germany 38 50.59N 12.27E
Altenkirchen W. Germany 16 50.41N 7.40E
Altentreptow E. Germany 38 53.42N 13.14E
Alter do Chão Portugal 27 39.12N 7.40W
Althofen Austria 31 46.54N 14.27E
Altiboullin, L. Australia 92 29.50S142.50E
Altiplanicie Mexicana mts. Mexico 111 29.00N105.00W
Altkirch France 19 47.37N 7.15E
Altmar U.S.A. 115 43.31N 76.00W
Altmark f. E. Germany 38 52.45N 11.15E
Altmühl r. W. Germany 39 48.55N 11.52E
Altnaharra U.K. 14 58.16N 4.26W
Alto Araguaia Brazil 123 17.19S 53.10W
Alto Molocue Mozambique 79 15.38S 37.42E
Altomünster W. Germany 39 48.28N 11.58E
Alton Canada 104 43.52N 80.04W
Alton U.K. 13 51.08N 0.59W
Alton U.S.A. 110 38.55N 90.10W
Altona Australia 88 27.34S120.00E
Altona W. Germany 38 53.32N 9.56E
Altoona U.S.A. 114 40.30N 78.24W
Altötting W. Germany 39 48.13N 12.40E
Altun Shan mts. China 52 38.10N 87.50E
Altus U.S.A. 111 34.38N 99.20W
Al Ubayyiḑ Sudan 73 13.11N 30.13E
Al Uḑayyah Sudan 73 12.03N 28.17E
Aluk Sudan 73 8.26N 27.32E
Al 'Ulá Saudi Arabia 64 26.39N 37.58E
'Alula Somali Rep. 71 11.58N 50.48E
Alunda Sweden 43 60.04N 18.05E
Al 'Uqaylah Libya 75 30.16N 19.12E
Al Uqşur Egypt 64 25.41N 32.24E
Al Urdunn r. Asia 67 31.47N 35.31E
Al 'Uwaynah well Saudi Arabia 65 26.46N 48.13E
Al 'Uwaynāt Libya 75 25.48N 10.33E
Al 'Uyūn Saudi Arabia 65 26.32N 43.41E
Alva U.S.A. 111 36.48N 98.40W
Alvaiázere Portugal 27 39.49N 8.23W
Älvängen Sweden 43 57.58N 12.07E
Alvarado Mexico 116 18.49N 95.46W
Älvdalen Sweden 41 61.14N 14.02E
Alverca Portugal 27 38.54N 9.02W
Alvesta Sweden 43 56.54N 14.33E
Älvho Sweden 41 61.30N 14.46E
Alvin U.S.A. 111 29.25N 95.15W
Alvinston Canada 104 42.49N 81.52W
Alvito Portugal 27 38.15N 8.00W
Älvkarleby Sweden 41 60.34N 17.27E
Älvsborg d. Sweden 43 57.50N 12.50E
Älvsbyn Sweden 40 65.39N 20.59E
Al Wajh Saudi Arabia 64 26.16N 36.28E
Al Wakrah Qatar 65 25.09N 51.36E
Alwar India 62 27.34N 76.36E
Al Wazz Sudan 72 15.01N 30.10E
Al Yamāmah Saudi Arabia 65 24.11N 47.21E
Al Yāmūn Jordan 67 32.29N 35.14E
Alyaty U.S.S.R. 65 39.59N 49.20E
Alytus U.S.S.R. 37 54.24N 24.03E
Alzada U.S.A. 108 45.01N104.26W
Alzette r. Lux. 16 49.52N 6.07E
Alzey W. Germany 39 49.45N 8.07E
Amadeus, L. Australia 88 24.50S130.45E
Amadi Sudan 73 5.31N 30.20E
Amadjuak Canada 99 64.00N 72.50W
Amadjuak L. Canada 99 65.00N 71.00W
Amagasaki Japan 57 34.43N135.25E
Amager i. Denmark 43 55.37N 12.37E
Åmål Sweden 43 59.03N 12.42E
Amalfi Italy 33 40.38N 14.36E
Amaliás Greece 35 37.49N 21.23E
Amalner India 62 21.03N 75.04E
Amami ō shima i. Japan 53 28.20N129.30E
Amamula Zaïre 79 0.17S 27.49E
Amanã, L. Brazil 122 2.35S 64.40W
Amānganj India 63 24.26N 80.02E
Amangeldy U.S.S.R. 50 50.12N 65.11E
Amantea Italy 33 39.08N 16.05E
Amapá Brazil 123 2.00N 50.50W
Amapá d. Brazil 123 2.00N 52.00W
Amarante Brazil 123 6.14S 42.51W
Amaranth Canada 101 50.36N 98.43W
Amareleja Portugal 27 38.12N 7.14W
Amares Portugal 26 41.38N 8.21W
Amarillo U.S.A. 111 35.13N101.49W
Amar Jadīd Sudan 72 14.28N 25.14E
Amarkantak India 63 22.40N 81.45E
Amaro, Monte mtn. Italy 31 42.05N 14.05E
Amarti Ethiopia 72 14.16N 41.10E
Amasya Turkey 64 40.37N 35.50E
Amatrice Italy 30 42.38N 13.17E
Amazon r. see Amazonas Brazil 123
Amazonas d. Brazil 122 4.50S 64.00W
Amazonas r. Brazil 123 2.00S 52.00W
Amazonas, Estuario do Rio f. Brazil 123 0.00 50.30W
Amazon Delta see Amazonas, Estuario do Rio Brazil 123
Amazya Israel 67 31.32N 34.55E
Amb Pakistan 62 34.19N 72.51E
Ambāla India 62 30.23N 76.46E
Ambalavao Madagascar 81 21.50S 46.56E
Ambam Cameroon 77 2.25N 11.16E
Ambarawa Indonesia 59 7.12S110.30E
Ambarchik U.S.S.R. 51 69.39N162.27E
Ambarnāth India 62 19.11N 73.10E
Ambarnyy U.S.S.R. 44 65.59N 33.53E
Ambato Ecuador 122 1.18S 78.36W
Ambato-Boeni Madagascar 81 16.28S 46.43E
Ambatofinandrahana Madagascar 81 20.33S 46.48E
Ambatolampy Madagascar 81 19.23S 47.25E
Ambatondrazaka Madagascar 81 17.50S 48.25E
Ámbelos, Ákra c. Greece 34 39.56N 23.55E
Amberg W. Germany 38 49.27N 11.52E
Ambergris Cay i. Belize 117 18.00N 87.58W
Ambérieu-en-Bugey France 21 45.57N 5.21E
Amberley Canada 104 44.02N 81.44W
Ambert France 20 45.33N 3.45E
Ambidédi Mali 76 14.35N 11.47W
Ambikāpur India 63 23.07N 83.12E
Ambilobe Madagascar 81 13.12S 49.04E
Amble U.K. 12 55.20N 1.34W
Ambleside U.K. 12 54.26N 2.58W
Ambodifototra Madagascar 81 16.59S 49.52E
Ambohidratrimo Madagascar 81 18.50S 47.26E
Ambohimahasoa Madagascar 81 21.07S 47.13E
Ambohimanga du Sud Madagascar 81 20.52S 47.36E
Amboise France 18 47.25N 0.59E
Ambon Indonesia 59 4.50S128.10E
Ambositra Madagascar 81 20.31S 47.15E
Ambovombe Madagascar 81 25.11S 46.05E
Amboy U.S.A. 109 34.33N115.44W
Ambre, Cap d' c. Madagascar 81 11.57S 49.17E
Ambridge U.S.A. 114 40.36N 80.14W
Ambrières France 18 48.24N 0.38W
Ambrim i. Vanuatu 84 16.15S168.10E
Ambriz Angola 78 7.54S 13.12E
Ambunten Indonesia 59 6.55S113.45E
Am Dam Chad 73 12.46N 20.29E
Amderma U.S.S.R. 50 69.44N 61.35E
Amdo China 63 32.22N 91.07E
Ameca Mexico 116 20.33N104.02W
Ameland i. Neth. 16 53.28N 5.48E
Amelia Italy 30 42.33N 12.25E
Amelia City U.S.A. 113 30.37N 81.27W
Americana Brazil 126 22.44S 47.19W
American Falls Resr. U.S.A. 108 43.00N113.00W
American Fork U.S.A. 108 40.23N111.48W
Americus U.S.A. 113 32.04N 84.14W
Amersfoort Neth. 16 52.10N 5.23E
Amery Australia 89 31.09S117.05E
Ames U.S.A. 110 42.02N 93.37W
Amesbury U.S.A. 115 42.51N 70.56W
Ameson Canada 102 49.50N 84.35W
Ametinho Angola 78 17.20S 17.20E
Amfíklia Greece 35 38.38N 22.35E
Amfilokhía Greece 35 38.51N 21.10E
Ámfissa Greece 35 38.32N 22.22E
Amga U.S.S.R. 51 60.51N131.59E
Amga r. U.S.S.R. 51 62.40N135.20E
Am Géréda Chad 73 12.52N 21.10E
Amgu U.S.S.R. 53 45.48N137.36E
Amguid Algeria 75 26.26N 5.22E
Amgun r. U.S.S.R. 51 53.10N139.47E
Amhara Plateau f. Ethiopia 73 11.00N 38.00E
Amherst Canada 103 45.49N 64.14W
Amherst Mass. U.S.A. 115 42.23N 72.31W
Amherstburg Canada 104 42.06N 83.06W
Amherst I. Canada 105 44.08N 76.45W
Amiata mtn. Italy 30 42.53N 11.37E
Amiens Australia 93 28.35S151.46E
Amiens France 19 49.54N 2.18E
Amíndaion Greece 34 40.42N 21.42E
Amīr Chāh well Pakistan 62 29.13N 62.28E
Amisk L. Canada 101 54.35N102.13W
Amistad Resr. U.S.A. 111 29.34N101.15W
Amite U.S.A. 111 30.44N 90.33W
Amla India 63 21.56N 78.07E
Amlekhganj Nepal 63 27.17N 85.00E
Åmli Norway 42 58.47N 8.30E
Amlwch U.K. 12 53.24N 4.21W
'Ammān Jordan 67 31.57N 35.56E
Ammanford U.K. 13 51.48N 4.00W
Ammassalik Greenland 99 65.40N 38.00W
Åmmeberg Sweden 43 58.52N 15.00E
Ammersee l. W. Germany 39 48.00N 11.08E
'Ammi'ad Israel 67 32.55N 35.32E
Ammókhostos Cyprus 66 35.07N 33.57E
Ammókhostou, Kólpos b. Cyprus 66 35.12N 34.05E
Amo r. India 63 25.58N 89.36E
Āmol Iran 65 36.26N 52.24E
Amorgós i. Greece 35 36.49N 25.54E
Amorgós town Greece 35 36.49N 25.54E
Amory U.S.A. 111 33.59N 88.29W
Amos Canada 102 48.35N 78.05W
Åmot Buskerud Norway 42 59.54N 9.54E
Åmot Telemark Norway 42 59.35N 8.00E
Ampala Honduras 117 13.16N 87.39W
Ampanihy Madagascar 81 24.42S 44.45E
Amparo Brazil 126 22.44S 46.44W
Amper r. W. Germany 39 48.10N 11.50E
Ampezzo Italy 30 46.25N 12.48E
Amphitheatre Australia 92 37.12S143.25E
Amposta Spain 25 40.43N 0.35E
'Amqa Israel 67 32.58N 35.10E
Amqui Canada 103 48.28N 67.26W
Amrāvati India 63 20.56N 77.45E
Amreli India 62 21.37N 71.14E
Amritsar India 62 31.38N 74.53E
Amroha India 63 28.55N 78.28E
Amrum i. W. Germany 38 54.39N 8.21E
Am Saterna Chad 73 12.26N 21.25E
Amsel Algeria 75 22.37N 5.26E
Amstelveen Neth. 16 52.18N 4.51E
Amsterdam Neth. 16 52.22N 4.54E
Amsterdam N.Y. U.S.A. 115 42.57N 74.11W
Amsterdam Ohio U.S.A. 114 40.28N 80.55W
Amsterdam, Île i. Indian Oc. 49 37.52S 77.32E
Am Timan Chad 73 11.02N 20.17E
Amu Darya r. U.S.S.R. 9 43.50N 59.00E
Amulet Canada 101 49.40N104.45W
Amundsen G. Canada 98 70.30N122.00W
Amundsen Sea Antarctica 128 72.00S120.00W
Amuntai Indonesia 58 2.24S115.14E
Amur r. U.S.S.R. 51 53.17N140.00E
'Amūr, Wādī r. Sudan 72 18.56N 33.34E
Amurrio Spain 26 43.04N 3.00W
Amurzet U.S.S.R. 53 47.50N131.05E
Amvrakikós Kólpos b. Greece 35 39.00N 21.00E
Anabar r. U.S.S.R. 51 72.40N113.30E
Ana Branch r. Australia 92 34.08S141.46E
'Anabtā Jordan 67 32.19N 35.07E
Anaco Venezuela 122 9.27N 64.28W
Anaconda U.S.A. 108 46.08N112.57W
Anadarko U.S.A. 111 35.04N 98.15W
Anadolu f. Turkey 64 38.00N 35.00E
Anadyr U.S.S.R. 51 64.40N177.32E
Anadyr r. U.S.S.R. 51 65.00N176.00E
Anadyrskiy Zaliv g. U.S.S.R. 51 64.30N177.50W
Anáfi i. Greece 35 36.21N 25.50E
Anagni Italy 30 41.44N 13.09E
Anaheim U.S.A. 109 33.51N117.57W
Analalava Madagascar 81 14.38S 47.45E
Anambas, Kepulauan is. Indonesia 58 3.00N106.10E
Anambra d. Nigeria 77 6.20N 7.25E
Anamoose U.S.A. 110 47.53N100.15W
Anamur Turkey 64 36.06N 32.49E
Anan Japan 57 33.55N134.39E
Ānand India 62 22.34N 72.56E
Anandpur India 63 21.16N 86.13E
Anantapur India 60 14.41N 77.36E
Anantnāg Jammu & Kashmir 62 33.44N 75.09E
Anápolis Brazil 123 16.19S 48.58W
Anapú r. Brazil 123 1.53S 50.53W
Anār Iran 65 30.54N 55.18E
Anārak Iran 65 33.20N 53.42E
Anār Darreh Afghan. 62 32.46N 61.39E
'Anātā Jordan 67 31.49N 35.16E
Anatolia f. see Anadolu Turkey 64
Anatone U.S.A. 108 46.08N117.09W
Añatuya Argentina 124 28.26S 62.48W
Ancenis France 18 47.22N 1.11W
Anchau Nigeria 77 11.00N 8.23E
Anchorage U.S.A. 98 61.10N150.00W
Anchuras Spain 27 39.29N 4.50W
Ancien Goubéré C.A.R. 73 5.51N 26.46E
Ancohuma mtn. Bolivia 124 16.05S 68.36W
Ancón Peru 122 11.50S 77.10W
Ancona Italy 31 43.38N 13.30E
Ancuabe Mozambique 79 13.00S 39.50E
Ancud Chile 125 41.05S 73.50W
Ancy-le-Franc France 19 47.46N 4.10E
Anda China 53 46.25N125.20E
Andalsnes Norway 40 62.33N 7.43E
Andalucía d. Spain 27 37.30N 4.30W
Andalusia U.S.A. 113 31.20N 86.30W
Andaman Is. India 56 12.00N 92.45E
Andaman Sea Indian Oc. 56 10.00N 95.00E
Andamooka Australia 92 30.27S137.12E
Andanga U.S.S.R. 44 59.11N 45.44E
Andara Namibia 80 18.04S 21.26E
Andelot France 19 48.15N 5.18E
Andenes Norway 40 69.18N 16.10E
Andenne Belgium 16 50.29N 5.04E
Anderlecht Belgium 16 50.51N 4.18E
Andermatt Switz. 39 46.38N 8.36E
Andernach W. Germany 39 50.26N 7.24E
Anderson r. Canada 98 69.45N129.00W
Anderson Ind. U.S.A. 112 40.05N 85.41W
Anderson S.C. U.S.A. 113 34.30N 82.39W
Anderstorp Sweden 43 57.17N 13.38E
Andes mts. S. America 125 32.40S 70.00W
Andevoranto Madagascar 81 18.57S 49.06E
Andfjorden est. Norway 40 68.55N 16.00E
Andhra Pradesh d. India 61 17.00N 79.00E
Andikíthira i. Greece 29 35.52N 23.18E
Andimákhia Greece 35 36.49N 27.04E
Andíparos i. Greece 35 37.00N 25.03E
Andirrion Greece 35 38.20N 21.46E
Andissa Greece 35 39.15N 26.00E
Andizhan U.S.S.R. 52 40.48N 72.23E
Andorra town Andorra 20 42.30N 1.31E
Andorra Europe 20 42.30N 1.32E
Andover U.K. 13 51.13N 1.29W
Andover N.J. U.S.A. 115 40.59N 74.45W
Andover N.Y. U.S.A. 114 42.09N 77.48W
Andover Ohio U.S.A. 114 41.36N 80.34W
Andöy i. Norway 40 69.05N 15.40E
Andrada Angola 78 7.41S 21.22E
Andrews N.C. U.S.A. 113 35.13N 83.49W
Andrews Tex. U.S.A. 111 32.19N102.33W
Andrews Pt. U.S.A. 115 42.42N 70.44W
Andreyevo-Ivanovka U.S.S.R. 37 47.28N 30.29E
Andria Italy 33 41.13N 16.18E
Andriba Madagascar 81 17.36S 46.55E
Andrijevica Yugo. 34 42.45N 19.48E
Andrítsaina Greece 35 37.29N 21.52E
Androka Madagascar 81 25.02S 44.05E
Ándros Greece 35 37.50N 24.57E
Ándros i. Greece 35 37.45N 24.42E
Andros I. Bahamas 113 24.25N 78.00W
Andros Town Bahamas 117 24.43N 77.47W
Andrushevka U.S.S.R. 37 50.00N 28.59E
Andújar Spain 26 38.03N 4.04W
Andulo Angola 78 11.28S 16.43E
Anduze France 20 44.03N 3.59E
Aneby Sweden 43 57.50N 14.48E
Anefis I-n-Darane Mali 76 17.57N 0.35E
Anegada i. B.V.Is. 117 18.46N 64.24W
Aného Togo 77 6.17N 1.40E
Aneityum i. Vanuatu 84 20.12S169.45E
Añelo Argentina 125 38.20S 68.45W
Aneto, Pico de mtn. Spain 25 42.38N 0.40E
Aney Niger 77 19.24N 12.56E
Angara r. U.S.S.R. 51 58.00N 93.00E

Armada to Aurich

Armada U.S.A. **114** 42.51N 82.53W
Armadale Australia **89** 32.10S115.57E
Armagh U.K. **15** 54.21N 6.41W
Armagh *d.* U.K. **15** 54.16N 6.35W
Armançon *r.* France **19** 47.57N 3.30E
Armavir U.S.S.R. **45** 44.59N 41.10E
Armenia Colombia **122** 4.32N 75.40W
Armeniş Romania **37** 45.12N 22.19E
Armenistís *i.* Greece **35** 37.36N 26.08E
Armentières France **19** 50.41N 2.53E
Armidale Australia **93** 30.32S151.40E
Armori India **63** 20.28N 79.59E
Armstrong Canada **100** 50.25N119.10W
Armstrong U.S.A. **111** 26.55N 97.47W
Ārmūr India **63** 18.48N 78.17E
Armyanskaya S.S.R. *d.* U.S.S.R. **65** 40.00N 45.00E
Arnaía Greece **34** 40.29N 23.35E
Arnaud *r.* Canada **99** 60.00N 69.45W
Arnay-le-Duc France **19** 47.08N 4.29E
Arnedo Spain **26** 42.13N 2.06W
Årnes Norway **42** 60.09N 11.28E
Arnett U.S.A. **111** 36.08N 99.46W
Arnhem Neth. **16** 52.00N 5.55E
Arnhem, C. Australia **90** 12.10S137.00E
Arnhem B. Australia **90** 12.20S136.12E
Arnhem Land *f.* Australia **90** 13.10S134.30E
Árnissa Greece **34** 40.47N 21.49E
Arno *r.* Italy **30** 43.41N 10.17E
Arno Bay *town* Australia **92** 33.54S136.34E
Arnon *r.* France **19** 47.12N 2.03E
Arnot Canada **101** 55.46N 96.41W
Årnotfors Sweden **43** 59.46N 12.22E
Arnprior Canada **105** 45.26N 76.21W
Arnsberg W. Germany **38** 51.24N 8.03E
Arnstadt E. Germany **38** 50.50N 10.57E
Arolsen W. Germany **38** 51.23N 9.01E
Aroma Sudan **72** 15.49N 36.08E
Aron *r.* France **19** 47.15N 2.02E
Arona Italy **30** 45.46N 8.34E
Arorangi Rarotonga Cook Is. **84** 21.13S159.49W
Arosa Switz. **39** 46.47N 9.41E
Arosa, Ría de *est.* Spain **26** 42.28N 8.57W
Arpajon France **19** 48.35N 2.15E
Arpino Italy **32** 41.40N 13.35E
Arra Ivory Coast **76** 6.42N 3.57W
Ar Rabbah Jordan **67** 31.16N 35.44E
Ar Rafid Syria **67** 32.57N 35.53E
Arrah India **63** 25.34N 84.40E
Ar Rahad Sudan **73** 12.43N 30.39E
Ar Ramādī Iraq **64** 33.27N 43.19E
Ar Ramthā Jordan **67** 32.34N 36.00E
Arran *i.* U.K. **14** 55.35N 5.14W
Ar Rank Sudan **73** 11.45N 32.48E
Ar Raqqah Syria **64** 35.57N 39.03E
Arras France **19** 50.17N 2.47E
Ar Rass Saudi Arabia **64** 25.54N 43.30E
Ar Rastān Syria **66** 34.55N 36.44E
Arrats *r.* France **20** 44.06N 0.52E
Arrecife Canary Is. **74** 28.57N 13.32W
Arrecifes Argentina **125** 34.05S 60.05W
Arrée, Monts d' *mts.* France **18** 48.26N 3.55W
Arrey U.S.A. **109** 32.51N107.19W
Ar Riyāḍ Saudi Arabia **65** 24.39N 46.44E
Arrochar U.K. **14** 56.12N 4.44W
Arromanches France **18** 49.20N 0.38W
Arronches Portugal **27** 39.07N 7.17W
Arros *r.* France **20** 43.40N 0.02W
Arroux *r.* France **19** 46.29N 3.58E
Arrow, Lough Rep.of Ire. **15** 54.03N 8.20W
Arrowsmith, Pt. Australia **90** 13.18S136.24E
Arrowtown New Zealand **86** 44.56S168.50E
Arroyo de la Luz Spain **27** 39.29N 6.35W
Arroyo Feliciano *r.* Argentina **125** 31.06S 59.53W
Arroyo Villimanca *r.* Argentina **125** 35.36S 59.05W
Ar Ru'at Sudan **73** 12.21N 32.17E
Ar Rub' al Khālī *des.* Saudi Arabia **60** 20.20N 52.30E
Ar Rubayqī Egypt **66** 30.10N 31.46E
Ar Rumaythah Iraq **65** 31.32N 45.12E
Ar Rummān Jordan **67** 32.10N 35.50E
Ar Ruṣayriṣ Sudan **73** 11.51N 34.23E
Ar Ruṭbah Iraq **64** 33.03N 40.18E
Ar Ruwayḍah Saudi Arabia **65** 23.46N 44.46E
Års Denmark **42** 56.48N 9.32E
Ars-en-Ré France **20** 46.12N 1.31W
Ársos Cyprus **66** 34.50N 32.46E
Árta Greece **35** 39.09N 20.59E
Artá Spain **25** 39.42N 3.21E
Artemón Greece **35** 36.59N 24.43E
Artemovsk U.S.S.R. **45** 48.35N 38.00E
Artenay France **19** 48.05N 1.53E
Artesia U.S.A. **109** 32.51N104.24W
Arthabaska Canada **105** 46.02N 71.55W
Arthal Jammu & Kashmir **62** 33.16N 76.11E
Arthington Liberia **76** 6.35N 10.45W
Arthur Canada **104** 43.50N 80.32W
Arthur's Pass New Zealand **86** 42.50S171.45E
Artigas Uruguay **125** 30.24S 56.28W
Artillery L. Canada **101** 63.09N107.52W
Artois *f.* France **16** 50.16N 2.50E
Artux China **52** 39.40N 75.49E
Artvin Turkey **64** 41.12N 41.48E
Aru, Kepulauan *is.* Indonesia **59** 6.00S134.30E
Arua Uganda **79** 3.02N 30.56E
Aruanã Brazil **123** 14.54S 51.05W
Aruba *i.* Neth. Ant. **117** 12.30N 70.00W
Arucas Canary Is. **127** 28.08N 15.32W
Arun *r.* U.K. **11** 50.48N 0.32W
Arunachal Pradesh *d.* India **61** 28.40N 94.60E
Arundel Canada **105** 45.58N 74.37W
Arusha Tanzania **79** 3.21S 36.40E
Arusha *d.* Tanzania **79** 4.00S 37.00E
Ārusī *d.* Ethiopia **73** 7.50N 39.50E
Aruwimi *r.* Zaïre **78** 1.20N 23.36E
Arvada Colo. U.S.A. **108** 39.50N105.05W
Arvada Wyo. U.S.A. **108** 44.39N105.05W
Arvagh Rep. of Ire. **15** 53.56N 7.35W
Arve *r.* France **21** 46.12N 6.08E
Arvi India **63** 20.59N 78.14E
Arvidsjaur Sweden **40** 65.35N 19.07E
Arvika Sweden **43** 59.39N 12.35E
Arwadin Ethiopia **72** 16.16N 38.46E
Arzachena Italy **32** 41.05N 9.22E
Arzamas U.S.S.R. **44** 55.24N 43.48E
Arzgir U.S.S.R. **45** 45.24N 44.04E
Arzignano Italy **32** 45.31N 11.20E
Arzúa Spain **26** 42.56N 8.09W
Ås Norway **42** 59.40N 10.48E
Asaba Nigeria **77** 6.12N 6.44E
Asadābād Afghan. **62** 34.52N 71.09E
Asahi dake *mtn.* Japan **57** 43.42N142.54E
Asahikawa Japan **57** 43.46N142.23E
Asansol India **63** 23.41N 86.59E
Åsarna Sweden **40** 62.40N 14.20E
Asarum Sweden **43** 56.12N 14.50E
Asayita Ethiopia **73** 11.33N 41.30E
Asbest U.S.S.R. **9** 57.05N 61.30E
Asbestos Canada **105** 45.46N 71.57W
Asbury Park U.S.A. **115** 40.13N 74.01W
Ascension *i.* Atlantic Oc. **127** 7.57S 14.22W
Aschaffenburg W. Germany **39** 49.59N 9.09E
Aschendorf W. Germany **38** 53.04N 7.22E
Aschersleben E. Germany **38** 51.45N 11.27E
Asciano Italy **30** 43.14N 11.33E
Ascoli Piceno Italy **31** 42.51N 13.34E
Ascoli Satriano Italy **33** 41.12N 15.34E
Ascona Switz. **39** 46.09N 8.46E
Aseb Ethiopia **73** 13.01N 42.47E
Åseda Sweden **43** 57.10N 15.20E
Asedjrad Algeria **75** 24.42N 1.40E
Asela Ethiopia **73** 7.59N 39.08E
Åsele Sweden **40** 64.10N 17.20E
Åsenbruk Sweden **43** 58.48N 12.25E
Asenovgrad Bulgaria **34** 42.01N 24.51E
Åseral Norway **42** 58.37N 7.25E
Asfeld France **19** 49.27N 4.05E
Asha Nigeria **77** 7.07N 3.43E
Ashanti *d.* Ghana **76** 6.30N 1.30W
Ashaway U.S.A. **115** 41.25N 71.47W
Ashbourne Rep. of Ire. **15** 53.31N 6.25W
Ashburn U.S.A. **113** 31.42N 83.41W
Ashburton *r.* Australia **88** 21.15S115.00E
Ashburton New Zealand **86** 43.54S171.46E
Ashby de la Zouch U.K. **13** 52.45N 1.29W
Ashcroft Canada **100** 50.40N121.20W
Ashdod Israel **67** 31.48N 34.38E
Asheboro U.S.A. **113** 35.42N 79.50W
Ashern Canada **101** 51.11N 98.21W
Asheville U.S.A. **113** 35.35N 82.35W
Ashewat Pakistan **62** 31.22N 68.32E
Ash Flat *town* U.S.A. **111** 36.12N 91.38W
Ashford Kent U.K. **13** 51.08N 0.53E
Ash Fork U.S.A. **109** 35.13N112.29W
Ashikaga Japan **57** 36.21N139.26E
Ashington U.K. **12** 55.11N 1.34W
Ashiya Japan **57** 34.43N135.17E
Ashizuri zaki *c.* Japan **57** 32.45N133.05E
Ashkhabad U.S.S.R. **65** 37.58N 58.24E
Ashland Ky. U.S.A. **114** 38.29N 82.39W
Ashland N.H. U.S.A. **105** 43.42N 71.38W
Ashland Ohio U.S.A. **114** 40.52N 82.19W
Ashland Oreg. U.S.A. **108** 42.12N122.42W
Ashland Wisc. U.S.A. **110** 46.35N 90.53W
Ashley Australia **93** 29.19S149.52E
Ashley U.S.A. **110** 38.20N 89.10W
Ashley Snow I. Antarctica **128** 72.30S 77.00W
Ashmūn Egypt **66** 30.18N 30.59E
Ashoknagar India **63** 24.34N 77.43E
Ashqelon Israel **67** 31.40N 34.35E
Ash Shabb *well* Egypt **72** 22.19N 29.46E
Ash Shāghūr Jordan **67** 31.50N 35.39E
Ash Shajarah Jordan **67** 32.39N 35.56E
Ash Shallūfah Egypt **66** 30.07N 32.34E
Ash Shāmah *des.* Saudi Arabia **64** 31.20N 38.00E
Ash Shamālīyah *d.* Sudan **72** 19.30N 31.30E
Ash Shāmīyah *des.* Iraq **65** 30.30N 45.30E
Ash Shāriqah U.A.E. **65** 25.20N 55.26E
Ash Sharmah Saudi Arabia **66** 28.01N 35.14E
Ash Shawbak Jordan **66** 30.33N 35.35E
Ash Shaykh Faḍl Egypt **66** 28.29N 30.50E
Ash Shaykh 'Ibādah Egypt **66** 27.48N 30.52E
Ash Shaykh Miskin Syria **67** 32.49N 36.09E
Ash Shiḥr S. Yemen **71** 14.45N 49.36E
Ash Shu'aybah Iraq **65** 30.30N 47.40E
Ash Shu'aybah Saudi Arabia **64** 27.53N 42.43E
Ash Shumlūl Saudi Arabia **65** 26.29N 47.20E
Ashta India **62** 23.01N 76.43E
Ashtabula U.S.A. **114** 41.52N 80.48W
Ashton R.S.A. **80** 33.49S 20.04E
Ashton U.S.A. **108** 44.04N111.27W
'Āsī *r.* Lebanon **66** 34.37N 36.30E
Asiago Italy **32** 45.52N 11.30E
Asilah Morocco **74** 35.32N 6.00W
Asinara *i.* Italy **32** 41.05N 8.18E
Asinara, Golfo dell' *g.* Italy **32** 41.00N 8.30E
'Asīr *f.* Saudi Arabia **71** 19.00N 42.00E
Asir, Ras *c.* Somali Rep. **71** 11.48N 51.22E
Aska India **63** 19.36N 84.39E
Askeaton Rep. of Ire. **15** 52.36N 9.00W
Asker Norway **42** 59.50N 10.26E
Askersund Sweden **43** 58.53N 14.54E
Askim Norway **42** 59.35N 11.10E
Askvoll Norway **41** 61.21N 5.04E
Āsmera Ethiopia **72** 15.20N 38.58E
Asnaes Denmark **42** 55.49N 11.31E
Åsnen *l.* Sweden **43** 56.38N 14.42E
Asola Italy **32** 45.13N 10.24E
Asosa Ethiopia **73** 10.03N 34.32E
Asoteriba, Jabal *mtn.* Sudan **72** 21.51N 36.30E
Aspe Spain **25** 38.21N 0.46W
Aspe, Gave d' *r.* France **20** 43.15N 0.29W
Aspen U.S.A. **108** 39.11N106.49W
Aspermont U.S.A. **111** 33.08N100.14W
Aspiring, Mt. New Zealand **86** 44.20S168.45E
Aspres-sur-Buëch France **21** 44.31N 5.45E
Asquith Canada **101** 52.08N107.13W
Assaba *d.* Mauritania **74** 16.40N 11.40W
As Sadd al 'Ālī *dam* Egypt **72** 23.59N 32.54E
Aş Şaff Egypt **66** 29.34N 31.17E
As Saffānīyah Saudi Arabia **65** 28.00N 48.48E
Aş Şāfīyah Sudan **72** 15.31N 30.07E
Aş Şa'īd *f.* Egypt **64** 25.30N 32.00E
Aş Şāliḥīyah Egypt **66** 30.47N 31.59E
As Sallūm Egypt **64** 31.31N 25.09E
As Salṭ Jordan **67** 32.03N 35.44E
As Salwa Saudi Arabia **65** 24.44N 50.50E
Assam *d.* India **61** 26.30N 93.00E
As Samāwah Iraq **65** 31.18N 45.18E
As Sāmirah *f.* Jordan **67** 32.15N 35.15E
As Samū' Jordan **67** 31.24N 35.04E
As Sanām *f.* Saudi Arabia **71** 22.00N 51.10E
Aş Şanamayn Syria **67** 33.05N 36.10E
Aş Şarafand Lebanon **66** 33.27N 35.18E
Aş Şarīḥ Jordan **67** 32.30N 35.54E
As Sarīrīyah Egypt **66** 28.20N 30.45E
Assebroek Belgium **16** 51.11N 3.16E
Assen Neth. **16** 53.00N 6.34E
Assens Denmark **42** 55.16N 9.55E
Asseria *site* Yugo. **31** 44.02N 15.39E
As Simākīyah Jordan **67** 31.18N 35.48E
As Sinbillāwayn Egypt **66** 30.53N 31.27E
Assiniboia Canada **101** 49.38N105.59W
Assiniboine *r.* Canada **101** 49.53N 97.08W
Assinica Prov. Park Canada **102** 50.24N 75.00W
Assis Brazil **126** 22.37S 50.25W
Assisi Italy **30** 43.04N 12.37E
As Sudd Sudan **73** 7.50N 30.00E
Aş Şufayyah Sudan **72** 15.30N 34.42E
As Sukhnah Jordan **67** 32.08N 36.04E
As Sulaymānīyah Iraq **65** 35.32N 45.27E
As Sulaymānīyah Saudi Arabia **65** 24.10N 47.20E
As Sulayyil Saudi Arabia **71** 20.27N 45.34E
As Sulṭān Libya **75** 31.07N 17.09E
As Sumayḥ Sudan **73** 9.49N 27.39E
Aş Şummān *f.* Saudi Arabia **65** 27.00N 47.00E
As Suwaydā' Syria **66** 32.43N 36.33E
As Suways Egypt **66** 29.59N 32.33E
Astaffort France **20** 44.04N 0.40E
Astakós Greece **35** 38.32N 21.05E
Asti Italy **30** 44.54N 8.12E
Astillero Spain **26** 43.24N 3.49W
Astipálaia Greece **35** 36.32N 26.22E
Astipálaia *i.* Greece **35** 36.35N 26.25E
Astorga Spain **26** 42.27N 6.03W
Astoria U.S.A. **108** 46.11N123.50W
Åstorp Sweden **43** 56.08N 12.57E
Astrakhan U.S.S.R. **45** 46.22N 48.00E
Åsträsk Sweden **40** 64.38N 20.00E
Astudillo Spain **26** 42.12N 4.18W
Asturias *d.* Spain **26** 43.30N 6.00W
Asunción Paraguay **126** 25.15S 57.40W
Åsunden *l.* Sweden **43** 57.45N 13.20E
'Āşūr, Tall *mtn.* Jordan **67** 31.59N 35.17E
Aswān Egypt **64** 24.05N 32.56E
Aswan High Dam *see* As Sadd al 'Ālī Egypt **64**
Asyūţ Egypt **64** 27.14N 31.07E
Atacama, Desierto *des.* S. America **124** 20.00S 69.00W
Atacama, Salar de *f.* Chile **124** 23.30S 68.46W
Atacama Desert *see* Atacama, Desierto S. America **124**
Atafu Pacific Oc. **84** 8.40S172.40W
Atakpamé Togo **77** 7.34N 1.14E
Atalándi Greece **35** 38.39N 22.58E
Atami Japan **57** 35.05N139.04E
Atapupu Indonesia **59** 9.00S124.51E
Atar Mauritania **74** 20.32N 13.08W
Atara U.S.S.R. **51** 63.10N129.10E
'Aṭārūt Jordan **67** 31.52N 35.13E
Atasu U.S.S.R. **50** 48.42N 71.38E
'Aṭbarah Sudan **72** 17.42N 33.59E
'Aṭbarah *r.* Sudan **72** 17.40N 33.58E
Atbasar U.S.S.R. **9** 51.49N 68.18E
Atchafalaya B. U.S.A. **111** 29.25N 91.20W
Atchison U.S.A. **110** 39.34N 95.07W
Ateca Spain **25** 41.20N 1.47W
Aterno *r.* Italy **31** 42.11N 13.51E
Ath Belgium **16** 50.38N 3.45E
Athabasca Canada **100** 54.45N113.20W
Athabasca *r.* Canada **101** 58.40N110.50W
Athabasca, L. Canada **101** 59.07N110.00W
Athea Rep. of Ire. **15** 52.28N 9.19W
Athenry Rep. of Ire. **15** 53.18N 8.45W
Athens Canada **105** 44.38N 75.57W
Athens *see* Athínai Greece **35**
Athens Ga. U.S.A. **113** 33.57N 83.24W
Athens Ohio U.S.A. **114** 39.20N 82.06W
Athens Penn. U.S.A. **115** 41.57N 76.31W
Athens Tenn. U.S.A. **113** 35.27N 84.38W
Athens Tex. U.S.A. **111** 32.12N 95.51W
Atherley Canada **104** 44.36N 79.22W
Athínai Greece **35** 38.00N 23.44E
Athlone Rep. of Ire. **15** 53.26N 7.57W
Athol U.S.A. **115** 42.36N 72.14W
Atholl, Forest of U.K. **14** 56.50N 3.55W
Áthos *mtn.* Greece **34** 40.09N 24.19E
Ath Thamad Egypt **66** 29.40N 34.18E
Ath Thanīyah Jordan **67** 31.10N 35.43E
Ati Chad **77** 13.11N 18.20E
Atico Peru **122** 16.12S 73.37W
Atienza Spain **26** 41.12N 2.52W
Atikonak L. Canada **103** 52.40N 64.30W
Atimaono Tahiti **85** 17.46S149.28W
Atkarsk U.S.S.R. **45** 51.55N 45.00E
Atkinson U.S.A. **113** 34.33N 78.12W
Atlanta Ga. U.S.A. **113** 33.45N 84.23W
Atlanta Mich. U.S.A. **104** 45.00N 84.09W
Atlanta Tex. U.S.A. **111** 33.07N 94.10W
Atlantic Iowa U.S.A. **110** 41.24N 95.01W
Atlantic-Antarctic Ridge *f.* Atlantic Oc. **127** 53.00S 0.00
Atlantic City U.S.A. **115** 39.22N 74.26W
Atlantic-Indian-Antarctic Basin *f.* Atl.Oc./Ind.Oc. **49** 59.00S 40.00E
Atlas Mts. Africa **22** 33.00N 2.00W
Atlas Saharien *mts.* Algeria **75** 34.00N 2.00E
Atlin Canada **100** 59.31N133.41W
Atlin L. Canada **100** 59.26N133.45W
'Atlit Israel **67** 32.41N 34.56E
'Atlit *site* Israel **67** 32.42N 34.56E
Atmore U.S.A. **111** 31.02N 87.29W
Atnarko Canada **100** 52.25N126.00W
Atnosen Norway **41** 61.44N 10.49E
Atoka U.S.A. **111** 34.23N 96.08W
Atouat *mtn.* Laos **56** 16.03N107.17E
Atouguia Portugal **27** 39.20N 9.20W
Atrå Norway **42** 59.59N 8.45E
Atrak *r. see* Atrek Iran **65**
Ätran *r.* Sweden **43** 56.53N 12.30E
Atrato *r.* Colombia **122** 8.15N 76.58W
Atrauli India **63** 28.02N 78.17E
Atrek *r.* Asia **65** 37.23N 54.00E
Atsugi Japan **57** 35.27N139.22E
Atsumi-hantō *pen.* Japan **57** 34.40N137.20E
Atsumi-wan *b.* Japan **57** 34.45N137.10E
Aṭ Ṭafīlah Jordan **66** 30.52N 35.36E
Aṭ Ṭā'if Saudi Arabia **72** 21.15N 40.21E
At Tall Syria **66** 33.36N 36.18E
Attapu Laos **58** 14.51N106.56E
Attar, Oued el *wadi* Algeria **75** 33.23N 5.12E
Attaviros *mtn.* Greece **35** 36.12N 27.52E
Attawapiskat *r.* Canada **102** 53.00N 82.30W
Attawapiskat L. Canada **102** 52.20N 88.00W
Aṭ Ṭayrīyah Egypt **66** 30.39N 30.46E
Aṭ Ṭayyibah Jordan **67** 31.57N 35.18E
Attendorn W. Germany **38** 51.07N 7.54E
Attersee *l.* Austria **39** 47.55N 13.33E
Attica N.Y. U.S.A. **114** 42.52N 78.17W
Attica Ohio U.S.A. **114** 41.04N 82.53W
Attigny France **19** 49.29N 4.35E
Attikamagen L. Canada **103** 55.00N 66.38W
'Attīl Jordan **67** 32.22N 35.04E
Attleboro U.S.A. **115** 41.56N 71.17W
Attleborough U.K. **13** 52.31N 1.01E
Attnang Austria **39** 48.01N 13.43E
Aṭ Ṭubayq *mts.* Saudi Arabia **64** 29.30N 37.15E
Aṭ Ṭunayb Jordan **67** 31.48N 35.56E
Aṭ Ṭūr Egypt **66** 28.14N 33.36E
Aṭ Ṭūr Jordan **67** 31.47N 35.15E
At Ṭuwayrifah *well* Saudi Arabia **71** 21.30N 49.35E
Atucha Argentina **125** 33.58S 59.17W
Atuel *r.* Argentina **125** 36.15S 66.55W
Atui, Uad *wadi* Mauritania **74** 20.03N 15.35W
Atui I. Cook Is. **85** 20.00S158.07W
Atuona Is. Marquises **85** 9.48S139.02W
Åtvidaberg Sweden **43** 58.12N 16.00E
Atwater U.S.A. **108** 37.21N120.36W
Atwood U.S.A. **110** 39.48N101.03W
Aubagne France **21** 43.17N 5.34E
Aube *d.* France **19** 48.15N 4.05E
Aube *r.* France **19** 48.34N 3.43E
Aubenton France **19** 49.50N 4.12E
Auberive France **19** 47.47N 5.03E
Aubigny-sur-Nère France **19** 47.29N 2.26E
Aubin France **20** 44.32N 2.14E
Aubinadong *r.* Canada **104** 46.51N 83.22W
Aubrac, Monts d' *mts.* France **20** 44.40N 3.00E
Auburn Ala. U.S.A. **113** 32.38N 85.38W
Auburn Calif. U.S.A. **108** 38.54N121.04W
Auburn Ind. U.S.A. **112** 41.22N 85.02W
Auburn Maine U.S.A. **112** 44.06N 70.14W
Auburn N.Y. U.S.A. **115** 42.56N 76.34W
Auburn Wash. U.S.A. **108** 47.18N122.13W
Aubusson France **20** 45.57N 2.11E
Auce U.S.S.R. **41** 56.28N 22.53E
Auch France **20** 43.39N 0.35E
Auchi Nigeria **77** 7.05N 6.16E
Auchterarder U.K. **14** 56.18N 3.43W
Auckland New Zealand **86** 36.55S174.45E
Auckland Is. Pacific Oc. **84** 50.35S166.00E
Aude *d.* France **20** 43.05N 2.30E
Aude *r.* France **20** 43.13N 3.14E
Auden Canada **102** 50.17N 87.54W
Audenge France **20** 44.41N 1.31W
Audierne France **18** 48.01N 4.32W
Audincourt France **19** 47.29N 6.50E
Audo Range *mts.* Ethiopia **73** 6.30N 41.30E
Audubon U.S.A. **110** 41.43N 94.55W
Aue E. Germany **38** 50.35N 12.42E
Augathella Australia **90** 25.48S146.35E
Augrabies Falls *f.* R.S.A. **80** 28.33S 20.27E
Au Gres U.S.A. **104** 44.03N 83.42W
Augsburg W. Germany **39** 48.23N 10.53E
Augusta Australia **89** 34.19S115.09E
Augusta Italy **33** 37.13N 15.13E
Augusta Ga. U.S.A. **113** 33.29N 82.00W
Augusta Ill. U.S.A. **110** 40.14N 90.56W
Augusta Kans. U.S.A. **111** 37.41N 96.58W
Augusta Maine U.S.A. **112** 44.19N 69.47W
Augusta, Golfo di *g.* Italy **33** 37.10N 15.20E
Augustín Codazzi Colombia **122** 10.01N 73.10W
Augustów Poland **37** 53.51N 22.59E
Augustus, Mt. Australia **88** 24.20S116.49E
Aulis *site* Greece **35** 38.27N 23.35E
Aulla Italy **30** 44.12N 9.58E
Aulnay France **20** 46.01N 0.21W
Aulne *r.* France **18** 48.17N 4.16W
Aulnoye-Aymeries France **19** 50.12N 3.50E
Ault France **18** 50.06N 1.27E
Ault U.S.A. **108** 40.35N104.44W
Aumale France **19** 49.46N 1.45E
Aumont-Aubrac France **20** 44.43N 3.17E
Auna Nigeria **77** 10.11N 4.46E
Auneau France **19** 48.27N 1.46E
Auning Denmark **42** 56.26N 10.23E
Aura Finland **41** 60.36N 22.34E
Auraiya India **63** 26.28N 79.31E
Aurangābād Bihār India **63** 24.45N 84.22E
Aurangābād Mahār India **62** 19.53N 75.20E
Auray France **18** 47.40N 2.59W
Aurdal Norway **41** 60.56N 9.24E
Aure Norway **40** 63.16N 8.34E
Aurich W. Germany **38** 53.28N 7.29E

Aurillac France **20** 44.56N 2.26E
Aurora Canada **104** 44.00N 79.28W
Aurora Colo. U.S.A. **108** 39.44N 104.52W
Aurora Ill. U.S.A. **110** 41.45N 88.20W
Aurora Mo. U.S.A. **111** 36.58N 93.43W
Aursunden *l.* Norway **40** 62.37N 11.40E
Aus Namibia **80** 26.41S 16.14E
Au Sable *r.* U.S.A. **104** 44.25N 83.20W
Au Sable Forks U.S.A. **105** 44.27N 73.41W
Aust-Agder *d.* Norway **42** 58.50N 7.50E
Austin Minn. U.S.A. **110** 43.40N 92.59W
Austin Nev. U.S.A. **108** 39.30N 117.04W
Austin Penn. U.S.A. **114** 41.38N 78.05W
Austin Tex. U.S.A. **111** 30.16N 97.45W
Austin, L. Australia **88** 27.40S 118.00E
Austral Downs *town* Australia **90** 20.28S 137.55E
Australia Austa. **87**
Australian Alps *mts.* Australia **93** 36.30S 148.30E
Australian Antarctic Territory Antarctica **128** 73.00S 90.00E
Australian Capital Territory *d.* Australia **93** 35.30S 149.00E
Austral Ridge Pacific Oc. **85** 24.00S 148.00W
Austria Europe **39** 47.20N 12.30E
Austvågöy *i.* Norway **40** 68.20N 14.40E
Authie *r.* France **19** 50.21N 1.38E
Autun France **19** 46.57N 4.18E
Auvergne *d.* France **20** 45.25N 2.30E
Auvézère *r.* France **20** 45.12N 0.51E
Aux Barques, Pointe *c.* U.S.A. **104** 44.04N 82.58W
Auxerre France **19** 47.48N 3.34E
Auxi-le-Château France **19** 50.14N 2.07E
Auxonne France **19** 47.12N 5.23E
Aux Sables *r.* Canada **104** 46.13N 82.04W
Auzances France **20** 46.02N 2.30E
Ava Burma **56** 21.49N 95.57E
Avaldsnes Norway **42** 59.21N 5.16E
Avallon France **19** 47.29N 3.54E
Avaloirs, Les *hills* France **18** 48.28N 0.07W
Avalon U.S.A. **115** 39.06N 74.43W
Avalon Pen. Canada **103** 47.00N 53.15W
Avanos Turkey **64** 38.44N 34.51E
Avaré Brazil **126** 23.06S 48.57W
Avarua Rarotonga Cook Is. **84** 21.12S 159.46W
Ávas Greece **34** 40.57N 25.56E
Avatele Niue **84** 19.06S 169.55W
Avatele B. Niue **84** 19.05S 169.56W
Avatiu Rarotonga Cook Is. **84** 21.12S 159.47W
Ave *r.* Portugal **26** 41.20N 8.45W
Aveiro Portugal **26** 40.38N 8.39W
Aveiro *d.* Portugal **26** 40.50N 8.35W
Aveiro, Ria de *est.* Portugal **26** 40.38N 8.44W
Avellaneda Argentina **125** 34.40S 58.20W
Avellino Italy **33** 40.54N 14.47E
Aversa Italy **33** 40.58N 14.12E
Avery U.S.A. **108** 47.15N 115.49W
Avesnes France **19** 50.07N 3.56E
Avesta Sweden **43** 60.09N 16.12E
Aveyron *d.* France **20** 44.15N 2.40E
Aveyron *r.* France **20** 44.05N 1.16E
Avezzano Italy **31** 42.02N 13.25E
Aviemore U.K. **14** 57.12N 3.50W
Avigliano Italy **33** 40.44N 15.44E
Avignon France **21** 43.57N 4.49E
Ávila Spain **26** 40.39N 4.42W
Ávila *d.* Spain **26** 40.35N 5.00W
Ávila, Sierra de *mts.* Spain **26** 40.35N 5.00W
Avilés Spain **26** 43.33N 5.55W
Avis U.S.A. **114** 41.11N 77.19W
Aviz Portugal **27** 39.03N 7.53W
Avlum Denmark **42** 56.16N 8.48E
Avoca *r.* Australia **92** 35.56S 143.44E
Avola Canada **100** 51.45N 119.19W
Avola Italy **33** 36.54N 15.09E
Avon *r.* Australia **89** 31.40S 116.07E
Avon *d.* U.K. **13** 51.35N 2.40W
Avon *r.* U.K. **11** 51.30N 2.43W
Avon *r.* Dorset U.K. **13** 50.43N 1.45W
Avon *r.* Glos. U.K. **13** 52.00N 2.10W
Avon U.S.A. **114** 42.55N 77.45W
Avon Downs *town* Australia **90** 20.05S 137.30E
Avonmouth U.K. **13** 51.30N 2.42W
Avon Park *town* U.S.A. **113** 27.36N 81.30W
Avranches France **18** 48.41N 1.22W
Avre *r.* France **19** 49.53N 2.20E
Awal Edo Ethiopia **73** 4.14N 40.39E
Awara Ethiopia **73** 5.30N 40.00E
Aware Ethiopia **71** 8.15N 44.10E
'Awartā Jordan **67** 32.10N 35.17E
Awasa, L. Ethiopia **73** 7.05N 38.25E
Āwash *r.* Ethiopia **73** 11.45N 41.05E
Awa shima *i.* Japan **57** 38.30N 139.20E
Awaso Ghana **76** 6.20N 2.22W
Awat China **52** 40.38N 80.22E
Awbārī Libya **75** 26.35N 12.46E
Awbārī *d.* Libya **75** 25.10N 12.45E
Awbārī, Şaḩrā' *des.* Libya **75** 27.30N 11.30E
Awdah, Hawr al *l.* Iraq **65** 31.36N 46.53E
Awe, Loch U.K. **14** 56.18N 5.24W
'Awjā', Wādī al Jordan **67** 31.56N 35.31E
Axarfjördhur *est.* Iceland **40** 66.10N 16.30W
Axat France **20** 42.48N 2.14E
Axel Heiberg I. Canada **99** 79.30N 90.00W
Axim Ghana **76** 4.53N 2.14W
Axiós *r.* Greece **34** 40.35N 22.50E
Ax-les-Thermes France **20** 42.43N 1.50E
Axminster U.K. **13** 50.47N 3.01W
Ayabaca Peru **122** 4.40S 79.53W
Ayachi, Ari n' *mtn.* Morocco **74** 32.29N 4.57W
Ayacucho Argentina **125** 37.10S 58.30W
Ayacucho Peru **122** 13.10S 74.15W
Ayaguz U.S.S.R. **52** 47.59N 80.27E
Ayamonte Spain **27** 37.13N 7.24W
Ayan U.S.S.R. **51** 56.29N 138.00E
'Aybāl, Jabal *mtn.* Jordan **67** 32.14N 35.16E
Aydin Turkey **64** 37.52N 27.50E
Ayelu *mtn.* Ethiopia **73** 10.04N 40.46E
Ayer U.S.A. **115** 42.34N 71.35W
Ayers Cliff *town* Canada **105** 45.10N 72.03W
Ayiá Greece **34** 39.43N 22.45E
Ayiá Ánna Greece **35** 38.52N 23.24E
Ayiá Marína Greece **35** 37.11N 26.48E
Ayía Paraskeví Greece **35** 39.14N 26.16E
Áyion Óros *f.* Greece **34** 40.15N 24.15E
Áyios Andréas Greece **35** 37.21N 22.45E
Áyios Evstrátios *i.* Greece **34** 39.34N 24.58E
Áyios Kírikos Greece **35** 37.37N 26.14E
Áyios Mattháios Greece **34** 39.30N 19.47E
Áyios Nikólaos Greece **35** 35.11N 25.42E
Aylássos Greece **35** 39.05N 26.23E
Aylen L. Canada **105** 45.37N 77.52W
Aylesbury U.K. **13** 51.48N 0.49W
Aylmer Canada **105** 45.23N 75.51W
Aylmer Canada **104** 42.47N 80.58W
Aylmer, L. Canada **105** 45.50N 71.22W
Aylmer L. Canada **98** 64.05N 108.30W
Aylsham U.K. **12** 52.48N 1.16E
'Ayn, Wādī al *r.* Oman **65** 22.18N 55.35E
'Ayn Dāllah *well* Egypt **64** 27.19N 27.20E
Ayod Sudan **73** 8.07N 31.26E
Ayom Sudan **73** 7.52N 28.23E
Ayon, Ostrov *i.* U.S.S.R. **51** 70.00N 169.00E
Ayora Spain **25** 39.04N 1.03W
Ayos Cameroon **77** 3.55N 12.30E
'Ayoûn el' Atroûs Mauritania **74** 16.40N 9.37W
Ayr Australia **90** 19.35S 147.24E
Ayr Canada **104** 43.17N 80.27W
Ayr U.K. **14** 55.28N 4.37W
Ayr *r.* U.K. **14** 55.28N 4.38W
Ayre, Pt. of U.K. **12** 54.25N 4.22W
Ayrolle, Etang de L' *l.* France **20** 43.05N 3.03E
Aysha Ethiopia **73** 10.46N 42.37E
Ayutthaya Thailand **56** 14.20N 100.40E
Ayvacik Turkey **34** 39.36N 26.23E
Ayvalik Turkey **29** 39.19N 26.42E
Azaila Spain **25** 41.17N 0.29W
Azambuja Portugal **27** 39.04N 8.52W
Azamgarh India **63** 26.04N 83.11E
Azao *mtn.* Algeria **75** 25.12N 8.08E
Azaouâd *des.* Mali **76** 18.00N 3.00W
Azaouak, Vallée de l' *f.* Mali **77** 16.00N 3.40E
Azare Nigeria **77** 11.40N 10.08E
Azay-le-Rideau France **18** 47.16N 0.28E
Azbine *mts. see* Aïr *mts.* Niger **77**
Azerbaydzhanskaya S.S.R. *d.* U.S.S.R. **65** 40.10N 47.50E
Azogues Ecuador **122** 2.35S 78.00W
Azopolye U.S.S.R. **44** 65.15N 45.18E
Azor Israel **67** 32.01N 34.48E
Azores *is. see* Açores, Arquipélago dos Atlantic Oc. **127**
Azoum *r.* Chad **73** 10.53N 20.15E
Azov, Sea of *see* Azovskoye More U.S.S.R. **45**
Azovskoye More *sea* U.S.S.R. **45** 46.00N 36.30E
Azpeitia Spain **26** 43.11N 2.16W
Azraq, Al Baḩr al *r.* Sudan **72** 15.38N 32.31E
Azrou Morocco **74** 33.27N 5.14W
Aztec U.S.A. **109** 32.48N 113.26W
Azua Dom. Rep. **117** 18.29N 70.44W
Azuaga Spain **26** 38.16N 5.41W
Azuer *r.* Spain **27** 39.08N 3.36W
Azuero, Península de *pen.* Panama **117** 7.30N 80.30W
Azul Argentina **125** 36.46S 59.50W
'Azūm, Wādī *r. see* Azoum Sudan **73**
Azurduy Bolivia **124** 19.59S 64.29W
Az Zāb al Kabīr *r.* Iraq **65** 35.37N 43.20E
Az Zāb aş Şaghīr *r.* Iraq **65** 35.15N 43.27E
Az Zabdānī Syria **66** 33.43N 36.05E
Az Ẕāhirīyah Jordan **67** 31.25N 34.58E
Az Ẕahrān Saudi Arabia **65** 26.18N 50.08E
Az Zaqāzīq Egypt **66** 30.36N 31.30E
Az Zarqā' Jordan **67** 32.05N 36.06E
Az Zarqā' *r.* Jordan **67** 32.08N 35.32E
Az Zāwiyah *d.* Libya **75** 32.40N 12.10E
Azzel Matti, Sebkha *f.* Algeria **74** 26.00N 0.55E
Az Zilfī Saudi Arabia **65** 26.15N 44.50E
Az Zrārīyah Lebanon **66** 33.21N 35.20E

B

Baan Baa Australia **93** 30.28S 149.58E
Baarle-Hertog Neth. **16** 51.26N 4.56E
Baba Burnu *c.* Turkey **34** 39.29N 26.02E
Babadag Romania **37** 44.54N 28.43E
Babahoyo Ecuador **122** 1.53S 79.31W
Babai Gaxun China **54** 40.30N 104.43E
Babakin Australia **89** 32.11S 117.58E
Babana Nigeria **77** 10.26N 3.51E
Babanka U.S.S.R. **37** 48.41N 30.30E
Babanūsah Sudan **73** 11.20N 27.48E
Babar, Kepulauan *is.* Indonesia **59** 8.00S 129.30E
Babayevo U.S.S.R. **44** 59.24N 35.50E
B'abdā Lebanon **66** 33.50N 35.31E
Babia Gora *mtn.* Czech./Poland **37** 49.38N 19.38E
Babīna India **63** 25.15N 78.28E
Babina Greda Yugo. **31** 45.07N 18.33E
Babine L. Canada **100** 54.48N 126.00W
Babo Indonesia **59** 2.33S 133.25E
Bābol Iran **65** 36.32N 52.42E
Baboua C.A.R. **77** 5.49N 14.51E
Babuyan Channel Phil. **55** 18.40N 121.30E
Babuyan Is. Phil. **59** 19.20N 121.30E
Babylon *ruins* Iraq **65** 32.33N 44.25E
Babylon U.S.A. **115** 40.42N 73.20W
Bacabal Maranhão Brazil **123** 4.15S 44.45W
Bacabal Para Brazil **123** 5.20S 56.45W
Bacău Romania **37** 46.32N 26.59E
Baccarat France **19** 48.27N 6.45E
Bacchus Marsh *town* Australia **92** 37.41S 144.27E
Bacharach W. Germany **39** 50.04N 7.46E
Bacheli India **61** 18.40N 81.16E
Bachelina U.S.S.R. **50** 57.45N 67.20E
Back *r.* Canada **99** 66.37N 96.00W
Bac Kan Vietnam **55** 22.06N 105.57E
Bačka Palanka Yugo. **31** 45.15N 19.24E
Bačka Topola Yugo. **31** 45.49N 19.38E
Backbone Mtn. U.S.A. **114** 39.18N 79.25W
Bäckefors Sweden **43** 58.48N 12.10E
Bački Petrovac Yugo. **31** 45.22N 19.35E
Backnang W. Germany **39** 48.56N 9.25E
Backstairs Passage *str.* Australia **92** 35.42S 138.05E
Bac Lieu Vietnam **56** 9.16N 105.45E
Bac Ninh Vietnam **56** 21.10N 106.04E
Bacolod Phil. **59** 10.38N 122.58E
Bac Phan *f.* Vietnam **56** 22.00N 105.00E
Bac Quang Vietnam **55** 22.30N 104.52E
Bácsalmás Hungary **31** 46.08N 19.20E
Bács-Kiskun *d.* Hungary **31** 46.30N 19.20E
Badagara India **60** 11.36N 75.35E
Badajós, Lago *l.* Brazil **122** 3.15S 62.47W
Badajoz Spain **27** 38.53N 6.58W
Badajoz *d.* Spain **27** 38.40N 6.10W
Badal Khān Goth Pakistan **62** 26.31N 67.06E
Badalona Spain **25** 41.27N 2.15E
Badanah Saudi Arabia **64** 30.59N 41.02E
Bad Ausee Austria wQ39 47.36N 13.47E
Bad Axe U.S.A. **112** 43.49N 82.59W
Bad Bergzabern W. Germany **39** 49.07N 8.00E
Bad Blankenburg E. Germany **38** 50.41N 11.16E
Bad Bramstedt W. Germany **38** 53.55N 9.53E
Baddo *r.* Pakistan **62** 28.15N 65.00E
Bad Doberan E. Germany **38** 54.06N 11.53E
Bad Dürrenberg E. Germany **38** 51.18N 12.04E
Badeggi Nigeria **77** 9.04N 6.09E
Bad Ems W. Germany **39** 50.20N 7.43E
Baden Austria **36** 48.01N 16.14E
Baden Ethiopia **72** 17.00N 38.00E
Baden Switz. **39** 47.29N 8.18E
Baden-Baden W. Germany **39** 48.46N 8.14E
Badenweiler W. Germany **39** 47.48N 7.40E
Baden-Württemberg *d.* W. Germany **39** 48.15N 9.00E
Bad Freienwalde E. Germany **38** 52.47N 14.01E
Badgastein Austria **39** 47.07N 13.08E
Bad Godesberg W. Germany **38** 50.41N 7.09E
Bad Hall Austria **39** 48.02N 14.13E
Bad Harzburg W. Germany **38** 51.53N 10.33E
Bad Hersfeld W. Germany **38** 50.52N 9.42E
Bad Homburg W. Germany **39** 50.13N 8.37E
Bad Honnef W. Germany **38** 50.39N 7.13E
Badīn Pakistan **62** 24.39N 68.50E
Bad Ischl Austria **39** 47.43N 13.37E
Badīyah Oman **71** 22.27N 58.48E
Bādiyat ash Shām *des.* Asia **64** 32.00N 39.00E
Bad Kissingen W. Germany **39** 50.12N 10.04E
Bad Kreuznach W. Germany **39** 49.52N 7.51E
Bad Langensalza E. Germany **38** 51.07N 10.40E
Bad Lauterberg W. Germany **38** 51.38N 10.28E
Bad Mergentheim W. Germany **39** 49.30N 9.46E
Bad Münstereifel W. Germany **38** 50.33N 6.46E
Bad Nauheim W. Germany **39** 50.22N 8.44E
Badnera India **63** 20.52N 77.44E
Bad Neuenahr-Ahrweiler W. Germany **38** 50.33N 7.08E
Bad Neustadt an der Saale W. Germany **39** 50.19N 10.13E
Bad Oeynhausen W. Germany **38** 52.12N 8.48E
Bad Oldesloe W. Germany **38** 53.48N 10.22E
Badong China **55** 31.02N 110.20E
Bad Orb W. Germany **39** 50.14N 9.20E
Badou Togo **76** 7.37N 0.37E
Badoumbé Mali **76** 13.42N 10.09W
Bad Pyrmont W. Germany **38** 51.59N 9.15E
Bad Ragaz Switz. **39** 47.00N 9.30E
Bad Reichenhall W. Germany **39** 47.43N 12.52E
Badrīnāth India **63** 30.44N 79.29E
Bad Salzuflen W. Germany **38** 52.05N 8.44E
Bad Salzungen E. Germany **38** 50.48N 10.13E
Bad Sankt Leonhard im Lavanttal Austria **31** 46.58N 14.48E
Bad Schwartau W. Germany **38** 53.55N 10.40E
Bad Segeberg W. Germany **38** 53.56N 10.17E
Bad Sülze E. Germany **38** 54.06N 12.38E
Bad Tölz W. Germany **39** 47.46N 11.34E
Bad Waldsee W. Germany **39** 47.55N 9.45E
Bad Wildungen W. Germany **38** 51.07N 9.07E
Bad Wörishofen W. Germany **39** 48.00N 10.36E
Baena Spain **27** 37.37N 4.19W
Baerami Australia **93** 32.23S 150.30E
Baeza Spain **27** 37.59N 3.28W
Bafa Gölü *l.* Turkey **35** 37.30N 27.29E
Bafang Cameroon **77** 5.11N 10.12E
Bafatá Guinea Bissau **76** 12.09N 14.38W
Baffin B. Canada **99** 74.00N 70.00W
Baffin I. Canada **99** 68.50N 70.00W
Bafia Cameroon **77** 4.39N 11.14E
Bafing *r.* Mali **76** 14.48N 12.10W
Bafoulabé Mali **76** 13.49N 10.50W
Bāfq Iran **65** 31.35N 55.21E
Bafra Turkey **64** 41.34N 35.56E
Bafut Cameroon **77** 6.06N 10.02E
Bafwasende Zaïre **79** 1.09N 27.12E
Bagaha India **63** 27.06N 84.05E
Bagamoyo Tanzania **79** 6.26S 38.55E
Bagarasi Turkey **35** 37.42N 27.33E
Bagasra India **62** 21.29N 70.57E
Bagawi Sudan **73** 12.19N 34.21E
Bagbele Zaïre **73** 4.21N 29.17E
Bagdarin U.S.S.R. **51** 54.28N 113.38E
Bagé Brazil **126** 31.22S 54.06W
Baggy Pt. U.K. **13** 51.08N 4.15W
Baghdād Iraq **65** 33.20N 44.26E
Bāgherhāt Bangla. **63** 22.40N 89.48E
Bagheria Italy **32** 38.05N 13.30E
Baghlān Afghan. **60** 36.11N 68.44E
Baghrān Khowleh Afghan. **62** 33.01N 64.58E
Bagnara Italy **33** 38.18N 15.49E
Bagnères-de-Bigorre France **20** 43.04N 0.09E
Bagnères-de-Luchon France **20** 42.47N 0.36E
Bagni di Lucca Italy **30** 44.01N 10.35E
Bagnols-sur-Cèze France **21** 44.10N 4.37E
Bagodar India **63** 24.05N 85.52E
Bagoé *r.* Mali **76** 12.34N 6.30W
Bagolino Italy **30** 45.49N 10.28E
Bagrationovsk U.S.S.R. **37** 54.26N 20.38E
Baguio Phil. **59** 16.25N 120.37E
Bagur, Cabo *c.* Spain **25** 41.57N 3.14E
Bāh India **63** 26.53N 78.36E
Bahamas C. America **113** 24.15N 76.00W
Bahāwalnagar Pakistan **62** 29.59N 73.16E
Bahāwalpur Pakistan **62** 29.24N 71.41E
Baheri India **63** 28.47N 79.30E
Bahi Tanzania **79** 5.59S 35.15E
Bahia *d.* Brazil **123** 12.30S 42.30W
Bahía, Islas de la *is.* Honduras **117** 16.10N 86.30W
Bahía Blanca Argentina **126** 38.45S 62.15W
Bahía de Caráquez Ecuador **122** 0.40S 80.25W
Bahía Kino Mexico **109** 28.50N 111.55W
Bahía Laura Argentina **125** 48.18S 66.30W
Bahía Negra Paraguay **126** 20.15S 58.12W
Bahir Dar Ethiopia **73** 11.35N 37.28E
Bahraich India **63** 27.35N 81.36E
Bahrain Asia **65** 26.00N 50.35E
Baḩr al Ghazāl *d.* Sudan **73** 8.00N 27.30E
Baḩr al Jabal *r.* Sudan **70** 9.30N 18.10E
Bahrāmābād Iran **60** 30.24N 56.00E
Bahrām Chāh Afghan. **62** 29.26N 64.03E
Bahr Aouk *r.* C.A.R. **77** 8.50N 18.50E
Bahr el Ghazal *r.* Chad **77** 12.26N 15.25E
Bahr Salamat *r.* Chad **77** 9.30N 18.10E
Bāhū Kalāt Iran **65** 25.42N 61.28E
Baia-Mare Romania **37** 47.40N 23.35E
Baião Brazil **123** 2.41S 49.41W
Baia Sprie Romania **37** 47.40N 23.42E
Baïbokoum Chad **77** 7.46N 15.43E
Baicheng China **54** 45.40N 122.52E
Baidoa Somali Rep. **79** 3.08N 43.34E
Baie Comeau Canada **103** 49.13N 68.10W
Baie des Ha Ha *town* Canada **103** 50.56N 58.58W
Baiersbronn W. Germany **39** 48.30N 8.22E
Baies, Lac des *l.* Canada **105** 47.18N 77.40W
Baie St. Paul *town* Canada **103** 47.27N 70.30W
Baigneux-les-Juifs France **19** 47.36N 4.38E
Baihar India **63** 22.06N 80.33E
Baijnāth India **63** 29.55N 79.37E
Baikunthapur India **63** 23.15N 82.33E
Bailén Spain **26** 38.06N 3.46W
Băileşti Romania **37** 44.02N 23.21E
Bailleul France **19** 50.44N 2.44E
Bailundo Angola **78** 12.13S 15.46E
Baimuru P.N.G. **59** 7.30S 144.49E
Bainang China **63** 29.10N 89.15E
Bainbridge U.S.A. **115** 42.18N 75.29W
Bainbridge U.S.A. **113** 30.54N 84.33W
Bain-de-Bretagne France **18** 47.50N 1.41W
Baing Indonesia **88** 10.15S 120.34E
Baingoin China **63** 31.45N 89.50E
Bains-les-Bains France **19** 48.00N 6.16E
Bāir Jordan **66** 30.46N 36.41E
Bā'ir, Wādī *r.* Jordan **66** 31.10N 36.55E
Baird Mts. U.S.A. **98** 67.35N 161.30W
Bairin Zuoqi China **54** 43.59N 119.11E
Bairnsdale Australia **93** 37.51S 147.38E
Bais France **18** 48.15N 0.22W
Baïse *r.* France **20** 44.07N 0.17E
Baisha China **55** 19.13N 109.26E
Baiyang Dian *l.* China **54** 38.55N 116.00E
Baiyin China **54** 36.40N 104.15E
Baja Hungary **31** 46.11N 18.57E
Baja California *pen.* Mexico **109** 28.40N 114.40W
Baja California Norte *d.* Mexico **109** 29.45N 115.30W
Baja California Sur *d.* Mexico **109** 26.00N 113.00W
Bajánsenye Hungary **31** 46.48N 16.22E
Bajina Bašta Yugo. **31** 43.58N 19.34E
Bajmok Yugo. **31** 45.58N 19.25E
Bakal U.S.S.R. **44** 54.58N 58.45E
Bakali *r.* Zaïre **78** 3.58S 17.10E
Bakel Senegal **76** 14.54N 12.26W
Baker Calif. U.S.A. **109** 35.16N 116.04W
Baker Mont. U.S.A. **108** 46.22N 104.17W
Baker Oreg. U.S.A. **108** 44.47N 117.50W
Baker, Mt. U.S.A. **108** 48.47N 121.49W
Baker I. U.S.A. **100** 55.20N 133.36W
Baker Lake *town* Canada **99** 64.20N 96.10W
Bakersfield U.S.A. **105** 44.48N 72.42W
Bakersfield U.S.A. **109** 35.23N 119.01W
Bâ Kêv Kampuchea **56** 13.42N 107.12E
Bako Ethiopia **73** 5.50N 36.40E
Bako Ivory Coast **76** 9.08N 7.40W
Bakony *mts.* Hungary **31** 47.00N 17.50E
Bakouma C.A.R. **73** 5.42N 22.47E
Baku U.S.S.R. **65** 40.22N 49.53E
Bala Canada **104** 45.01N 79.37W
Bal'ā Jordan **67** 32.20N 35.07E
Bala Senegal **76** 14.01N 13.08W
Bala U.K. **12** 52.54N 3.36W
Balabac *i.* Phil. **58** 7.57N 117.01E
Balabac Str. Malaysia / Phil. **58** 7.30N 117.00E
Ba'labakk Lebanon **66** 34.00N 36.12E
Balaclava Australia **92** 32.09S 141.25E
Balad Somali Rep. **71** 2.22N 45.25E
Bālāghāt India **63** 21.48N 80.11E
Bālāghāt Range *mts.* India **62** 19.00N 76.30E
Balaguer Spain **24** 41.50N 0.50E
Balaka Malaŵi **79** 15.00S 34.56E
Balaka Zaïre **78** 4.51S 19.57E
Balaklava Australia **92** 34.08S 138.24E
Balaklava U.S.S.R. **45** 44.31N 33.35E
Balakovo U.S.S.R. **44** 52.04N 47.46E

Bal'amā to Bāruni

Bal'amā Jordan **67** 32.14N 36.05E
Balama Mozambique **79** 13.19S 38.35E
Bālā Morghāb Afghan. **65** 35.34N 63.20E
Balāngīr India **63** 20.43N 83.29E
Balaquer Spain **25** 41.47N 0.49E
Balarāmpur India **63** 23.07N 86.13E
Balashov U.S.S.R. **45** 51.30N 43.10E
Balasore India **63** 21.30N 86.56E
Balassagyarmat Hungary **37** 48.05N 19.18E
Balāţ Egypt **64** 25.33N 29.16E
Balaton *l.* Hungary **31** 46.50N 17.45E
Balazote Spain **26** 38.53N 2.08W
Balboa Panama **117** 8.37N 79.33W
Balbriggan Rep. of Ire. **15** 53.36N 6.12W
Balcarce Argentina **125** 37.52S 58.15W
Balchik Bulgaria **37** 43.24N 28.10E
Balclutha New Zealand **86** 46.16S169.46E
Bald Eagle Mtn. U.S.A. **114** 41.00N 77.45W
Baldock L. Canada **101** 56.33N 97.57W
Baldwin Fla. U.S.A. **113** 30.18N 81.59W
Baldwin Mich. U.S.A. **112** 43.54N 85.50W
Baldwin Penn. U.S.A. **114** 40.23N 79.58W
Baldwinsville U.S.A. **115** 43.09N 76.20W
Baldy Mt. Canada **100** 51.28N120.02W
Balé Ethiopia **73** 6.30N 40.45E
Bâle *see* Basel Switz. **39**
Baleanoona Australia **92** 30.33S139.22E
Baleares *d.* Spain **25** 39.00N 2.10E
Baleares, Islas *is.* Spain **25** 39.20N 2.00E
Balearic Is. *see* Baleares, Islas Spain **25**
Baleine, Grande rivière de la *r.* Canada **102** 55.20N 77.40W
Baleine, Petite rivière de la *r.* Canada **102** 56.00N 76.45W
Balfate Honduras **117** 15.48N 86.25W
Balfour Downs *town* Australia **88** 22.57S120.46E
Balfouriyya Israel **67** 32.38N 35.18E
Bali India **62** 25.50N 74.05E
Bali *d.* Indonesia **59** 8.45S114.56E
Bali *i.* Indonesia **59** 8.20S115.07E
Bali, Laut *sea* Indonesia **59** 7.30S115.15E
Bali, Selat *str.* Indonesia **59** 8.21S114.30E
Balikesir Turkey **29** 39.38N 27.51E
Balīkh *r.* Syria **64** 35.58N 39.05E
Balikpapan Indonesia **58** 1.15S116.50E
Balingen W. Germany **39** 48.16N 8.51E
Bali Sea *see* Bali, Laut Indonesia **59**
Balkan Mts. *see* Stara Planina Bulgaria **34**
Balkhash U.S.S.R. **52** 46.51N 75.00E
Balkhash, Ozero *l.* U.S.S.R. **9** 46.40N 75.00E
Ballachulish U.K. **14** 56.40N 5.08W
Balladonia Australia **89** 32.27S123.51E
Ballālpur India **63** 19.50N 79.22E
Ballandean Australia **93** 28.39S151.50E
Ballantrae U.K. **14** 55.06N 5.01W
Ballarat Australia **92** 37.36S143.58E
Ballard, L. Australia **89** 29.27S120.55E
Ballater U.K. **14** 57.03N 3.03W
Ballenas, Bahía de *b.* Mexico **109** 26.45N113.25W
Ballenas, Canal de *str.* Mexico **109** 29.10N113.30W
Balleny Is. Antarctica **128** 66.30S163.00E
Balleroy France **18** 49.11N 0.50W
Ballia India **63** 25.45N 84.10E
Ballina Australia **93** 28.50S153.37E
Ballina Rep. of Ire. **15** 54.08N 9.10W
Ballinasloe Rep. of Ire. **15** 53.20N 8.15W
Ballingeary Rep. of Ire. **15** 51.50N 9.15W
Ballinger U.S.A. **111** 31.44N 99.57W
Ball's Pyramid *i.* Pacific Oc. **84** 31.45S159.15E
Ballybay Rep. of Ire. **15** 54.08N 6.56W
Ballycastle U.K. **15** 55.12N 6.15W
Ballyclare U.K. **15** 54.45N 6.00W
Ballyconnell Rep. of Ire. **15** 54.06N 7.37W
Ballydehob Rep. of Ire. **15** 51.34N 9.28W
Ballydonegan Rep. of Ire. **15** 51.38N 10.04W
Ballygar Rep. of Ire. **15** 53.32N 8.20W
Ballygawley U.K. **15** 54.28N 7.03W
Ballykelly U.K. **15** 55.03N 7.00W
Ballymena U.K. **15** 54.52N 6.17W
Ballymoney U.K. **15** 55.04N 6.31W
Ballyquintin Pt. U.K. **15** 54.40N 5.30W
Ballyragget Rep. of Ire. **15** 52.47N 7.21W
Ballyshannon Rep. of Ire. **15** 54.30N 8.11W
Ballyvaughan Rep.of Ire. **15** 53.06N 9.09W
Ballyvourney Rep. of Ire. **15** 51.57N 9.10W
Balmoral Australia **92** 37.17S141.50E
Balombo Angola **78** 12.20S 14.45E
Balonne *r.* Australia **93** 28.30S148.20E
Bālotra India **62** 25.50N 72.14E
Balpunga Australia **92** 33.44S141.50E
Balrāmpur India **63** 27.26N 82.11E
Balranald Australia **92** 34.37S143.37E
Balş Romania **37** 44.21N 24.06E
Balsam L. Canada **104** 44.35N 78.50W
Balsas *r.* Brazil **123** 9.00S 48.10W
Balsas *r.* Mexico **116** 18.10N102.05W
Bålsta Sweden **43** 59.35N 17.30E
Balta U.S.S.R. **37** 47.58N 29.39E
Baltanás Spain **26** 41.56N 4.15W
Baltasar Brum Uruguay **125** 30.44S 57.19W
Baltic Sea Europe **41** 57.00N 20.00E
Balţîm Egypt **66** 31.34N 31.05E
Baltimore Canada **104** 44.03N 78.08W
Baltimore U.S.A. **107** 39.18N 76.38W
Baltimore Md. U.S.A. **115** 39.17N 76.37W
Baltimore Ohio U.S.A. **114** 39.51N 82.36W
Baltiysk U.S.S.R. **43** 54.39N 19.55E
Baluchistān *d.* Pakistan **62** 28.30N 65.00E
Baluchistan *f.* Pakistan **60** 28.00N 66.00E
Bālurghāt India **63** 25.13N 88.46E
Balygychan U.S.S.R. **51** 63.55N154.12E
Balykshi U.S.S.R. **45** 47.04N 51.55E
Bām Iran **65** 29.07N 58.20E
Bama Nigeria **77** 11.35N 13.40E
Bamako Mali **76** 12.40N 7.59W
Bamako *d.* Mali **76** 12.40N 7.55W
Bamba Kenya **79** 3.33S 39.32E
Bamba Mali **76** 17.05N 1.23W
Bamba Zaïre **78** 5.45S 18.23E
Bambari C.A.R. **73** 5.45N 20.40E
Bamberg W. Germany **39** 49.53N 10.53E
Bambesa Zaïre **78** 3.27N 25.43E
Bambesi Ethiopia **73** 9.45N 34.40E
Bambili Zaïre **78** 3.34N 26.07E
Bambio C.A.R. **77** 3.55N 16.57E
Bambuí Brazil **126** 20.01S 45.59W
Bam Co *l.* China **63** 31.30N 91.10E
Bamenda Cameroon **77** 5.55N 10.09E
Bāmīān Afghan. **62** 34.50N 67.50E
Bamingui C.A.R. **73** 7.34N 20.11E
Bamingui Bangoran *d.* C.A.R. **73** 8.30N 20.30E
Bampton Devon U.K. **13** 51.00N 3.29W
Bampūr Iran **65** 27.13N 60.29E
Bampūr *r.* Iran **65** 27.18N 59.02E
Bāmra Hills India **63** 21.20N 84.30E
Baña, Punta de la *c.* Spain **25** 40.34N 0.38E
Banagher Rep. of Ire. **15** 53.12N 8.00W
Banalia Zaïre **78** 1.33N 25.23E
Banamba Mali **76** 13.29N 7.22W
Banana Australia **90** 24.30S150.08E
Banana Zaïre **78** 5.55S 12.27E
Bananal, Ilha do *f.* Brazil **123** 11.30S 50.15W
Ban Aranyaprathet Thailand **56** 13.43N102.31E
Banās *r.* India **62** 25.54N 76.45E
Banâs, Ra's *c.* Egypt **64** 23.54N 35.48E
Ban Ban Laos **56** 19.38N103.34E
Banbridge U.K. **15** 54.21N 6.17W
Ban Bua Chum Thailand **56** 15.15N101.15E
Banbury U.K. **13** 52.04N 1.21W
Banchory U.K. **14** 57.03N 2.30W
Bancroft Canada **105** 45.03N 77.51W
Band Afghan. **62** 33.17N 68.39E
Banda Gabon **78** 3.47S 11.04E
Banda Madhya P. India **63** 24.03N 78.57E
Bānda Uttar P. India **63** 25.29N 80.20E
Banda *i.* Indonesia **59** 4.30S129.55E
Banda, Laut *sea* Indonesia **59** 5.00S128.00E
Banda Aceh Indonesia **58** 5.35N 95.20E
Bānda Dāūd Shāh Pakistan **62** 33.16N 71.11E
Bandak *l.* Norway **42** 59.24N 8.15E
Bandama *r.* Ivory Coast **76** 5.10N 4.59W
Bandar 'Abbās Iran **65** 27.10N 56.15E
Bandar-e Anzalī Iran **65** 37.26N 49.29E
Bandar-e Deylam Iran **65** 30.05N 50.11E
Bandar-e Khomeyni Iran **65** 30.26N 49.03E
Bandar-e-Lengeh Iran **65** 26.34N 54.53E
Bandar-e Rīg Iran **65** 29.30N 50.40E
Bandar-e Torkeman Iran **65** 36.55N 54.05E
Bandar Seri Begawan Brunei **58** 4.56N114.58E
Banda Sea *see* Banda, Laut Indonesia **59**
Bandawe Malaŵi **79** 11.57S 34.11E
Bande Spain **26** 42.02N 7.58W
Bandeira *mtn.* Brazil **126** 20.25S 41.45W
Bāndhi Pakistan **62** 26.36N 68.18E
Bandiagara Mali **76** 14.12N 3.29W
Bāndikūi India **62** 27.03N 76.34E
Bandīpur Nepal **63** 27.56N 84.25E
Bandipura Jammu & Kashmir **62** 34.25N 74.39E
Bandirma Turkey **29** 40.22N 28.00E
Bandon Rep. of Ire. **15** 51.45N 8.45W
Bandon *r.* Rep. of Ire. **15** 51.43N 8.38W
Bandundu Zaïre **78** 3.20S 17.24E
Bandundu *d.* Zaïre **78** 4.00S 18.30E
Bandung Indonesia **59** 6.57S107.34E
Banes Cuba **117** 20.59N 75.24W
Banff Canada **100** 51.10N115.34W
Banff U.K. **14** 57.40N 2.31W
Banff Nat. Park Canada **100** 51.30N116.15W
Banfora U. Volta **76** 10.36N 4.45W
Bangalore India **60** 12.58N 77.35E
Bangassou C.A.R. **73** 4.50N 23.07E
Banggai, Kepulauan *is.* Indonesia **59** 1.30S123.10E
Banggi *i.* Malaysia **58** 7.17N117.12E
Banghāzī Libya **75** 32.07N 20.05E
Banghāzī *d.* Libya **75** 25.40N 21.00E
Bangil Indonesia **59** 7.34S112.47E
Bangka *i.* Indonesia **58** 2.20S106.10E
Bangkalan Indonesia **59** 7.05S112.44E
Bangkog Co *l.* China **63** 31.45N 89.30E
Bangkok *see* Krung Thep Thailand **56**
Bangladesh Asia **63** 24.30N 90.00E
Bangong Co *l.* China **61** 33.45N 79.15E
Bangor Rep. of Ire. **15** 54.09N 9.44W
Bangor U.K. **15** 54.40N 5.41W
Bangor U.K. **12** 53.13N 4.09W
Bangor Maine U.S.A. **112** 44.49N 68.47W
Bangor Penn. U.S.A. **115** 40.52N 75.13W
Bang Saphan Thailand **56** 11.14N 99.31E
Bangui C.A.R. **77** 4.23N 18.37E
Bangui Phil. **55** 18.33N120.45E
Banguru Zaïre **79** 0.30N 27.10E
Bangweulu, L. Zambia **79** 11.15S 29.45E
Banhâ Egypt **66** 30.28N 31.11E
Ban Hat Yai Thailand **56** 7.10N100.28E
Ban Houayxay Laos **56** 20.21N100.32E
Bani *r.* Mali **76** 14.30N 4.15W
Bani, Jbel *mtn.* Morocco **74** 30.00N 8.00W
Banikoara Benin **77** 11.21N 2.25E
Banī Mazār Egypt **66** 28.29N 30.48E
Banīnah Libya **75** 32.05N 20.16E
Banī Na'īm Jordan **67** 31.31N 35.10E
Banī Suwayf Egypt **66** 29.05N 31.05E
Banī Walīd Libya **75** 31.46N 13.59E
Bāniyās Syria **67** 33.15N 35.41E
Bāniyās Syria **66** 35.09N 35.58E
Banja Luka Yugo. **31** 44.46N 17.11E
Banjarmasin Indonesia **58** 3.22S114.36E
Banjul Gambia **76** 13.28N 16.39W
Bānka India **63** 24.53N 86.55E
Banka Banka Australia **90** 18.48S134.01E
Ban Kan Vietnam **56** 22.08N105.49E
Ban Kantang Thailand **56** 7.25N 99.35E
Bankasse Mali **76** 14.01N 3.29W
Bankeryd Sweden **43** 57.51N 14.07E
Banks Group *is.* Australia **92** 34.35S136.12E
Banks I. Australia **90** 10.12S142.16E
Banks I. B.C. Canada **100** 53.25N130.10W
Banks I. N.W.T. Canada **98** 73.00N122.00W
Banks Is. Vanuatu **84** 13.50S167.30E
Banks Pen. New Zealand **86** 43.45S173.10E
Banks Str. Australia **91** 40.37S148.07E
Bānkura India **63** 23.15N 87.04E
Ban-m'drack Vietnam **56** 12.45N108.50E
Bann *r.* U.K. **15** 55.10N 6.46W
Ban Na San Thailand **56** 8.53N 99.17E
Bannockburn Canada **105** 44.38N 77.33W
Bannockburn U.K. **14** 56.06N 3.55W
Bannockburn Zimbabwe **80** 20.16S 29.51E
Bannu Pakistan **62** 32.59N 70.36E
Bañolas Spain **25** 42.07N 2.46E
Banon France **21** 44.02N 5.38E
Baños de Cerrato Spain **26** 41.55N 4.28W
Ban Pak Phraek Thailand **56** 8.13N100.13E
Bānsda India **62** 20.45N 73.22E
Banská Bystrica Czech. **37** 48.44N 19.07E
Bansko Bulgaria **34** 41.52N 23.28E
Bānswāra India **62** 23.33N 74.27E
Banté Benin **77** 8.26N 1.54E
Bantry Rep. of Ire. **15** 51.41N 9.27W
Bantry B. Rep. of Ire. **15** 51.40N 9.40W
Bāntva India **62** 21.29N 70.05E
Banyak, Kepulauan *is.* Indonesia **58** 2.15N 97.10E
Banyo Cameroon **77** 6.47N 11.50E
Banyuwangi Indonesia **59** 8.12S114.22E
Banzare Coast *f.* Antarctica **128** 66.30S125.00E
Baode China **54** 39.00N111.05E
Baoding China **54** 38.50N115.26E
Bao Ha Vietnam **55** 22.10N104.22E
Baoji China **54** 34.20N107.17E
Baojing China **55** 28.43N109.37E
Bao-Loc Vietnam **56** 11.30N107.54E
Baoshan China **61** 25.07N 99.08E
Baotou China **54** 40.35N109.59E
Baoulé *r.* Mali **76** 13.47N 10.45W
Bāp India **62** 27.23N 72.21E
Bapaume France **19** 50.06N 2.51E
Bâqa el Gharbiyya Israel **67** 32.25N 35.03E
Baqên China **63** 31.56N 94.00E
Ba'qūbah Iraq **65** 33.45N 44.38E
Bar Albania **29** 42.05N 19.06E
Bar U.S.S.R. **37** 49.05N 27.40E
Bar Yugo. **31** 42.05N 19.05E
Bara Nigeria **77** 10.24N 10.43E
Barabinsk U.S.S.R. **9** 55.20N 78.18E
Baraboo U.S.A. **110** 43.28N 89.50W
Baracoa Cuba **117** 20.23N 74.31W
Baradero Argentina **125** 33.50S 59.30W
Baradine Australia **93** 30.56S149.05E
Baradine *r.* Australia **93** 30.17S148.27E
Baragoi Kenya **73** 1.47N 36.47E
Bārah Sudan **73** 13.42N 30.22E
Barahona Dom. Rep. **117** 18.13N 71.07W
Baraka Zaïre **79** 4.09S 29.05E
Barakī Barak Afghan. **62** 33.56N 68.55E
Bārākot India **63** 21.33N 85.01E
Bārāmūla Jammu & Kashmir **62** 34.12N 74.21E
Bārān India **62** 25.06N 76.31E
Baranagar India **63** 22.38N 88.22E
Baranoa Colombia **122** 10.50N 74.55W
Baranof I. U.S.A. **100** 57.00N135.00W
Baranovichi U.S.S.R. **44** 53.09N 26.00E
Baranya *d.* Hungary **31** 45.55N 18.20E
Baratta Australia **92** 32.01S139.10E
Barbacena Brazil **126** 21.13S 43.47W
Barbadillo del Mercado Spain **26** 42.02N 3.21W
Barbados Lesser Antilles **117** 13.20N 59.40W
Barbar Sudan **72** 18.01N 33.59E
Barbastro Spain **25** 42.02N 0.05E
Barbate *r.* Spain **27** 36.11N 5.55W
Barbate de Franco Spain **27** 36.12N 5.55W
Barberton R.S.A. **80** 25.46S 31.02E
Barberton U.S.A. **114** 41.01N 81.36W
Barbezieux France **20** 45.28N 0.09W
Barbil India **63** 22.06N 85.20E
Barbuda *i.* Leeward Is. **117** 17.41N 61.48W
Barcaldine Australia **90** 23.31S145.15E
Barcarrota Spain **27** 38.31N 6.51W
Barcellona Italy **33** 38.09N 15.13E
Barcelona Spain **25** 41.23N 2.11E
Barcelona *d.* Spain **25** 41.45N 2.00E
Barcelona Venezuela **122** 10.08N 64.43W
Barcelos Brazil **122** 0.59S 62.58W
Barcelos Portugal **26** 41.32N 8.37W
Barcoo *r.* Australia **90** 25.30S142.50E
Barcs Hungary **31** 45.58N 17.28E
Barcs Yugo. **29** 45.58N 17.28E
Bardai Chad **77** 21.21N 16.56E
Bardejov Czech. **37** 49.18N 21.16E
Bardera Somali Rep. **79** 2.18N 42.18E
Bardi Italy **30** 44.38N 9.44E
Bardīa Nepal **63** 28.18N 81.23E
Bardīyah Libya **72** 31.46N 25.06E
Bardnovichi U.S.S.R. **37** 53.09N 26.00E
Bardoc Australia **89** 30.20S121.17E
Bardoli India **62** 21.07N 73.07E
Bardonecchia Italy **30** 45.05N 6.42E
Bardsey *i.* U.K. **12** 52.45N 4.48W
Bardu Norway **40** 68.54N 18.20E
Bardufoss Norway **40** 69.00N 18.30E
Bareilly India **63** 28.21N 79.25E
Barellan Australia **93** 34.17S146.34E
Barengapāra India **63** 25.14N 90.14E
Barentsovo More *see* Barents Sea Arctic Oc. **44**
Barents Sea Arctic Oc. **44** 73.00N 40.00E
Barentu Ethiopia **72** 15.04N 37.37E
Barfleur France **18** 49.40N 1.15W
Barfleur, Pointe de *c.* France **18** 49.42N 1.16W
Barga China **63** 30.51N 81.20E
Bargal Somali Rep. **71** 11.18N 51.07E
Bargarh India **63** 21.20N 83.37E
Bargas Spain **27** 39.56N 4.02W
Barge Italy **30** 44.43N 7.20E
Barghanak Afghan. **62** 33.56N 62.26E
Barguzin U.S.S.R. **51** 53.40N109.35E
Barharwa India **63** 24.52N 87.47E
Barhi India **63** 24.18N 85.25E
Bāri Madhya P. India **63** 23.03N 78.05E
Bāri Rāj. India **63** 26.39N 77.36E
Bari Italy **33** 41.07N 16.52E
Baricho Kenya **79** 3.07S 39.47E
Barika Algeria **75** 35.25N 5.19E
Barīm *i.* S. Yemen **71** 12.40N 43.24E
Barinas Venezuela **122** 8.36N 70.15W
Baripāda India **63** 21.56N 86.43E
Bariri Brazil **126** 22.04S 48.41W
Bāris Egypt **64** 24.40N 30.36E
Bari Sādri India **62** 24.25N 74.28E
Barisāl Bangla. **63** 22.42N 90.22E
Barisan, Pegunungan *mts.* Indonesia **58** 3.30S102.30E
Barito *r.* Indonesia **58** 3.35S114.35E
Barjac France **21** 44.18N 4.21E
Barjols France **21** 43.33N 6.00E
Barjūj, Wādī Libya **75** 26.03N 12.50E
Barker U.S.A. **114** 43.20N 78.33W
Barker L. Australia **89** 31.45S120.05E
Bārkhān Pakistan **62** 29.54N 69.31E
Barking U.K. **13** 51.32N 0.05E
Bark L. Canada **104** 46.54N 82.28W
Barkley Sd. Canada **100** 48.53N125.20W
Barkly East R.S.A. **80** 30.58S 27.33E
Barkly Tableland *f.* Australia **90** 19.00S136.40E
Barkly West R.S.A. **80** 28.32S 24.29E
Bar-le-Duc France **19** 48.47N 5.10E
Barlee, L. Australia **89** 29.30S119.30E
Barlee Range *mts.* Australia **88** 23.40S116.00E
Barletta Italy **33** 41.19N 16.17E
Barlow L. Canada **101** 62.00N103.00W
Barmedman Australia **93** 34.08S147.25E
Barmer India **62** 25.45N 71.23E
Barmera Australia **92** 34.15S140.31E
Barm Fīrūz, Kūh-e *mtn.* Iran **65** 30.21N 52.00E
Barmouth U.K. **12** 52.44N 4.03W
Barnagar India **62** 23.03N 75.22E
Barnāla India **62** 30.22N 75.33E
Barnard Castle *town* U.K. **12** 54.33N 1.55W
Barnato Australia **93** 31.38S144.59E
Barnaul U.S.S.R. **9** 53.21N 83.15E
Barnegat U.S.A. **115** 39.45N 74.13W
Barnegat B. U.S.A. **115** 39.52N 74.07W
Barnegat Light U.S.A. **115** 39.46N 74.06W
Barnesboro U.S.A. **114** 40.40N 78.47W
Barnesville U.S.A. **114** 39.59N 81.11W
Barnet U.K. **13** 51.39N 0.11W
Barneveld Neth. **16** 52.10N 5.39E
Barneville France **18** 49.23N 1.45W
Barneys L. Australia **92** 33.16S144.13E
Barnsley U.K. **12** 53.33N 1.29W
Barnstable U.S.A. **115** 41.42N 70.18W
Barnstaple U.K. **13** 51.05N 4.03W
Baro *r.* Ethiopia **73** 8.26N 33.13E
Baro Nigeria **77** 8.37N 6.19E
Barpeta India **63** 26.19N 91.00E
Barqah *f.* Libya **72** 31.00N 23.00E
Barquisimeto Venezuela **122** 10.03N 69.18W
Barra Brazil **123** 11.06S 43.15W
Barra *i.* U.K. **14** 56.59N 7.28W
Barra, Sd. of U.K. **14** 57.04N 7.20W
Barraba Australia **93** 30.24S152.36E
Barra do Corda Brazil **123** 5.30S 45.15W
Barra do Piraí Brazil **126** 22.28S 43.49W
Barrafranca Italy **33** 37.23N 14.13E
Barra Head U.K. **10** 56.47N 7.36W
Barra Mansa Brazil **126** 22.35S 44.12W
Barranca Peru **122** 4.50S 76.40W
Barrancabermeja Colombia **122** 7.06N 73.54W
Barrancas Venezuela **122** 8.45N 62.13W
Barranco do Velho Portugal **27** 37.14N 7.56W
Barrancos Portugal **27** 38.08N 6.59W
Barranqueras Argentina **126** 27.30S 58.55W
Barranquilla Colombia **122** 11.10N 74.50W
Barraute Canada **102** 48.26N 77.39W
Barrax Spain **27** 39.03N 2.12W
Barre U.S.A. **105** 44.12N 72.30W
Barreiras Brazil **123** 12.09S 44.58W
Barreiro Portugal **27** 38.40N 9.04W
Barreiros Brazil **123** 8.49S 35.12W
Barrême France **21** 43.57N 6.22E
Barretos Brazil **126** 20.37S 48.38W
Barrhead Canada **100** 54.10N114.24W
Barrhead U.K. **14** 55.47N 4.24W
Barrie Canada **104** 44.24N 79.40W
Barrie I. Canada **104** 45.55N 82.40W
Barrington Tops *mts.* Australia **93** 32.30S151.28E
Barringun Australia **93** 29.01S145.43E
Barron U.S.A. **108** 48.44N120.43W
Barrow *r.* Rep. of Ire. **15** 52.17N 7.00W
Barrow U.S.A. **98** 71.16N156.50W
Barrow, Pt. U.S.A. **96** 71.22N156.30W
Barrow Creek *town* Australia **90** 21.32S133.53E
Barrow I. Australia **88** 21.40S115.27E
Barrow-in-Furness U.K. **12** 54.08N 3.15W
Barrow Range *mts.* Australia **88** 26.04S127.28E
Barry U.K. **13** 51.23N 3.19W
Barry's Bay *town* Canada **105** 45.30N 77.41W
Barryville U.S.A. **115** 41.29N 74.55W
Barsinghausen W. Germany **38** 52.18N 9.27E
Barstow U.S.A. **109** 34.54N117.01W
Bar-sur-Aube France **19** 48.14N 4.43E
Bar-sur-Seine France **19** 48.07N 4.22E
Barth E. Germany **38** 54.22N 12.43E
Bartica Guyana **122** 6.24N 58.38W
Bartin Turkey **64** 41.37N 32.20E
Bartlefrere *mt.* Australia **90** 17.23S145.49E
Bartlesville U.S.A. **111** 36.45N 95.59W
Bartlett L. Canada **100** 63.05N118.20W
Bartolomeu Dias Mozambique **81** 21.10S 35.09E
Barton U.S.A. **105** 44.45N 72.11W
Barton-upon-Humber U.K. **12** 53.41N 0.27W
Bartoszyce Poland **37** 54.16N 20.49E
Bartow U.S.A. **113** 27.54N 81.51W
Bāruni India **63** 25.29N 85.59E

Barwāh to Belyayevka

Barwāh India **62** 22.16N 76.03E
Barwāni India **62** 22.02N 74.54E
Barwa Sāgar India **63** 25.23N 78.44E
Barwon *r.* Australia **93** 30.00S148.05E
Barysh U.S.S.R. **44** 53.40N 47.09E
Basāl Pakistan **62** 33.33N 72.15E
Basankusu Zaïre **78** 1.12N 19.50E
Basavilbaso Argentina **125** 32.20S 58.52W
Basel Switz. **39** 47.33N 7.35E
Basella Spain **25** 42.01N 1.18E
Basento Italy **33** 40.21N 16.50E
Bashi Channel Taiwan/Phil. **55** 21.30N121.00E
Basilan Phil. **59** 6.40N121.59E
Basilan *i.* Phil. **59** 6.40N122.10E
Basildon U.K. **13** 51.34N 0.25E
Basilicata *d.* Italy **3** 40.30N 16.10E
Basin U.S.A. **108** 44.23N108.02W
Basingstoke U.K. **13** 51.15N 1.05W
Basin L. Canada **101** 52.38N105.18W
Baška Yugo. **31** 44.58N 14.46E
Baskatong, Rés. Canada **105** 46.48N 75.50W
Basmat India **62** 19.19N 77.10E
Bāsoda India **63** 23.51N 77.56E
Basoko Zaïre **73** 1.20N 23.30E
Basongo Zaïre **73** 4.23S 20.28E
Bas-Rhin *d.* France **19** 48.35N 7.40E
Bassano Canada **100** 50.48N112.20W
Bassano Italy **32** 45.46N 11.44E
Bassari Togo **76** 9.12N 0.18E
Bassein Burma **56** 16.46N 94.45E
Basse-Kotto *d.* C.A.R. **73** 5.00N 21.30E
Basse Normandie *d.* France **18** 49.00N 0.00
Basse Santa Su Gambia **76** 13.23N 14.15W
Basse-Terre Guadeloupe **117** 16.00N 61.43W
Bassett U.S.A. **110** 42.35N 99.32W
Basse-Yutz France **19** 49.21N 6.11E
Bass Is. U.S.A. **114** 41.42N 82.49W
Bass Str. Australia **91** 39.45S146.00E
Bassum W. Germany **38** 52.51N 8.43E
Båstad Sweden **43** 56.26N 12.51E
Bastak Iran **65** 27.15N 54.26E
Bastelica France **21** 42.00N 9.02E
Basti India **63** 26.48N 82.43E
Bastia France **21** 42.42N 9.27E
Bastogne Belgium **16** 50.00N 5.43E
Bastrop U.S.A. **111** 32.47N 91.55W
Basyûn Egypt **66** 30.57N 30.49E
Bas Zaïre *d.* Zaïre **78** 5.15S 14.00E
Bata Equat. Guinea **78** 1.51N 9.49E
Batabanó, Golfo de *g.* Cuba **117** 23.15N 82.30W
Batak Bulgaria **34** 41.57N 24.12E
Batak, Yazovir *l.* Bulgaria **34** 42.00N 24.11E
Batāla India **62** 31.48N 75.13E
Batalha Portugal **27** 39.39N 8.50W
Batang China **61** 30.02N 99.01E
Batangafo C.A.R. **77** 7.27N 18.11E
Batangas Phil. **59** 13.46N121.01E
Batan Is. Phil. **59** 20.50N121.55E
Bátaszék Hungary **31** 46.12N 18.44E
Batatais Brazil **126** 20.54S 47.37W
Batavia U.S.A. **114** 43.00N 78.11W
Bataysk U.S.S.R. **45** 47.09N 39.46E
Batchawana Canada **104** 46.54N 84.34W
Batchawana *r.* Canada **104** 46.55N 84.32W
Batchawana l. Canada **104** 46.45N 84.14W
Batchawana Mtn. Canada **104** 47.04N 84.24W
Batchelor Australia **90** 13.04S131.01E
Bătdâmbâng Kampuchea **56** 13.06N103.12E
Bateman's B. Australia **91** 35.55S150.09E
Batemans Bay *town* Australia **93** 35.55S150.09E
Batesville Ark. U.S.A. **111** 35.46N 91.39W
Batesville Miss. U.S.A. **111** 34.18N 90.00W
Bath Canada **105** 44.11N 76.47W
Bath Canada **103** 46.31N 67.37W
Bath U.K. **13** 51.22N 2.22W
Bath Maine U.S.A. **112** 43.55N 69.49W
Bath N.Y. U.S.A. **114** 42.20N 77.19W
Batha *d.* Chad **77** 14.30N 18.30E
Batha *r.* Chad **77** 12.47N 17.34E
Baṭḥā, Wādī al *r.* Oman **65** 20.01N 59.39E
Bathgate U.K. **14** 55.44N 3.38W
Bathurst Australia **93** 33.27S149.35E
Bathurst Canada **103** 47.36N 65.39W
Bathurst R.S.A. **80** 33.30S 26.48E
Bathurst, C. Canada **98** 70.30N128.00W
Bathurst I. Australia **88** 11.45S130.15E
Bathurst I. Canada **99** 76.00N100.00W
Bathurst Inlet *town* Canada **98** 66.48N108.00W
Batibla C.A.R. **73** 5.56N 21.09E
Batié U. Volta **76** 9.42N 2.53W
Batina Yugo. **31** 45.51N 18.51E
Batir Jordan **67** 31.16N 35.42E
Batiscan *r.* Canada **105** 46.31N 72.15W
Batley U.K. **12** 53.43N 1.38W
Batlow Australia **93** 35.32S148.10E
Batman Turkey **64** 37.52N 41.07E
Batna Algeria **75** 35.35N 6.11E
Baton Rouge U.S.A. **111** 30.23N 91.11W
Batopilas Mexico **109** 27.00N107.45W
Batouri Cameroon **77** 4.26N 14.27E
Bat Shelomo Israel **67** 32.36N 35.00E
Batson U.S.A. **111** 30.15N 94.37W
Batticaloa Sri Lanka **61** 7.43N 81.42E
Battle *r.* Canada **101** 52.43N108.15W
Battle U.K. **13** 50.55N 0.30E
Battle Creek *town* U.S.A. **112** 42.20N 85.11W
Battleford Canada **101** 52.45N108.15W
Battle Harbour Canada **103** 52.17N 55.35W
Batu *mtn.* Ethiopia **73** 6.55N 39.46E
Batu, Kepulauan *is.* Indonesia **58** 0.30S 98.20E
Batumi U.S.S.R. **64** 41.37N 41.36E
Batu Pahat Malaysia **58** 1.50N102.48E
Baturaja Indonesia **58** 4.10S104.10E
Baturité Brazil **123** 4.20S 38.53W
Bat Yam Israel **67** 32.01N 34.45E
Baubau Indonesia **59** 5.30S122.37E
Bauchi Nigeria **77** 10.16N 9.50E
Bauchi *d.* Nigeria **77** 10.40N 10.00E
Baud France **18** 47.52N 3.01W
Baudh India **63** 20.50N 84.19E
Baugé France **18** 47.33N 0.06W
Bauld, C. Canada **103** 51.38N 55.25W
Baume-les-Dames France **19** 47.21N 6.22E
Baunei Italy **32** 40.02N 9.40E
Bauru Brazil **126** 22.19S 49.07W
Baús Brazil **126** 18.19S 53.10W
Bauska U.S.S.R. **41** 56.24N 24.14E
Bautzen E. Germany **38** 51.11N 14.26E
Bavay France **16** 50.18N 3.48E
Båven *l.* Sweden **43** 59.01N 16.56E
Bawean *i.* Indonesia **59** 5.50S112.39E
Bawku Ghana **76** 11.05N 0.13W
Bayamo Cuba **117** 20.23N 76.39W
Bayamón Puerto Rico **117** 18.24N 66.10W
Bāyan, Band-e *mts.* Afghan. **62** 34.20N 65.00E
Bayāna India **62** 26.54N 77.17E
Bayan Har Shan *mts.* China **52** 34.00N 97.20E
Bayan Nur China **54** 38.14N103.56E
Bayard U.S.A. **114** 39.16N 79.22W
Bayburt Turkey **64** 40.15N 40.16E
Bay City Mich. U.S.A. **104** 43.36N 83.53W
Bay City Tex. U.S.A. **111** 28.59N 95.58W
Baydaratskaya Guba *b.* U.S.S.R. **50** 70.00N 66.00E
Bayerische Alpen *mts.* W. Germany **39** 47.38N 11.30E
Bayerischer Wald *mts.* W. Germany **39** 49.00N 12.50E
Bayern *d.* W. Germany **38** 49.06N 11.30E
Bayeux France **18** 49.17N 0.42W
Bayfield Canada **104** 43.33N 81.41W
Bayfield U.S.A. **110** 46.49N 90.49W
Baykal, Ozero *l.* U.S.S.R. **52** 53.30N100.00E
Baykit U.S.S.R. **51** 61.45N 96.22E
Bayo Spain **26** 43.09N 8.58W
Bayombong Phil. **59** 16.27N121.10E
Bayon France **19** 48.29N 6.19E
Bayona Spain **26** 42.07N 8.51W
Bayonne France **20** 43.29N 1.29W
Bayovar Peru **122** 5.50S 81.03W
Bay Port U.S.A. **104** 43.51N 83.23W
Bayramic Greece **34** 39.48N 26.37E
Bayreuth W. Germany **38** 49.57N 11.35E
Bayrischzell W. Germany **39** 47.40N 12.00E
Bayrūt Lebanon **66** 33.52N 35.30E
Bays, L. of Canada **104** 45.15N 79.04W
Bay Shore U.S.A. **115** 40.44N 73.15W
Baysville Canada **104** 45.09N 79.10W
Baytā al Fawqā Jordan **67** 32.09N 35.17E
Bayt Awlā Jordan **67** 31.36N 35.02E
Bayt Ḥānūn Egypt **67** 31.32N 34.32E
Baytik Shan *mts.* China **52** 45.15N 90.50E
Bayt Immar Jordan **67** 31.37N 35.06E
Bayt Jālā Jordan **67** 31.43N 35.11E
Bayt Lāhiyah Egypt **67** 31.33N 34.30E
Bayt Laḥm Jordan **67** 31.43N 35.12E
Baytown U.S.A. **111** 29.44N 94.58W
Bayt Rimā Jordan **67** 32.02N 35.06E
Baytūniyā Jordan **67** 31.53N 35.10E
Bay View New Zealand **86** 39.26S176.52E
Bay Village U.S.A. **114** 41.29N 81.55W
Baza Spain **27** 37.29N 2.46W
Baza, Sierra de *mts.* Spain **27** 37.20N 2.45W
Bazaliya U.S.S.R. **37** 49.42N 26.29E
Bazaruto, Ilha do *i.* Mozambique **81** 21.40S 35.28E
Bazas France **20** 44.26N 0.13W
Bazdār Pakistan **62** 26.21N 65.03E
Bazhong China **55** 31.51N106.42E
Bazièģe France **20** 43.27N 1.37E
Bazmān Iran **65** 27.48N 60.12E
Bazmān, Kūh-e *mtn.* Iran **65** 28.06N 60.00E
Beach U.S.A. **110** 46.55N103.52W
Beachburg Canada **105** 45.43N 76.53W
Beach Haven U.S.A. **115** 39.34N 74.14W
Beachport Australia **92** 37.29S140.01E
Beachwood U.S.A. **115** 39.56N 74.12W
Beachy Head U.K. **13** 50.43N 0.15E
Beacon U.S.A. **115** 41.30N 73.58W
Beagle Bay Mission Australia **88** 16.58S122.40E
Bealanana Madagascar **81** 14.33S 48.44E
Bear Brook State Park U.S.A. **115** 43.05N 71.26W
Beardstown U.S.A. **110** 40.01N 90.26W
Bear Island *town* Canada **104** 46.59N 80.05W
Bear L. U.S.A. **108** 42.00N111.20W
Bearskin Lake *town* Canada **102** 53.58N 91.02W
Beas *r.* India **62** 31.10N 75.00E
Beasain Spain **26** 43.03N 2.11W
Beas de Segura Spain **26** 38.15N 2.53W
Beatrice U.S.A. **110** 40.16N 96.44W
Beatrice, C. Australia **90** 14.15S136.59E
Beatton *r.* Canada **100** 56.15N120.45W
Beatton River *town* Canada **100** 57.26N121.20W
Beatty U.S.A. **108** 36.54N116.46W
Beattyville Canada **102** 48.53N 77.10W
Beaucaire France **21** 43.48N 4.38E
Beauce *d.* France **19** 48.22N 1.50E
Beauchêne Canada **104** 46.39N 78.55W
Beaufort Australia **92** 37.28S143.28E
Beaufort U.S.A. **113** 32.26N 80.40W
Beaufort Sea N. America **98** 72.00N141.00W
Beaufort West R.S.A. **80** 32.20S 22.34E
Beaugency France **19** 47.47N 1.38E
Beauharnois Canada **105** 45.19N 73.52W
Beaujolais, Monts du *mts.* France **21** 46.00N 4.30E
Beaulieu *r.* Canada **100** 62.03N113.11W
Beauly U.K. **14** 57.29N 4.29W
Beauly *r.* U.K. **14** 57.29N 4.25W
Beaumaris U.K. **12** 53.16N 4.07W
Beaumetz-lès-Loges France **19** 50.14N 2.39E
Beaumont Belgium **16** 50.14N 4.16E
Beaumont France **18** 49.40N 1.51W
Beaumont Miss. U.S.A. **111** 31.11N 88.55W
Beaumont Tex. U.S.A. **111** 30.05N 94.06W
Beaumont-le-Roger France **18** 49.05N 0.47E
Beaumont-sur-Sarthe France **18** 48.13N 0.08E
Beaune France **19** 47.02N 4.50E
Beaune-la-Rolande France **19** 48.04N 2.26E
Beaupréau France **18** 47.12N 1.00W
Beaurepaire France **21** 45.20N 5.03E
Beauséjour Canada **101** 50.04N 96.33W
Beauvais France **19** 49.26N 2.05E
Beauval Canada **101** 55.09N107.35W
Beauville France **20** 44.17N 0.52E
Beauvoir France **18** 46.55N 2.02W
Beauvoir-sur-Niort France **18** 46.11N 0.28W
Beaver *r.* N.W.T. Canada **100** 59.43N124.16W
Beaver *r.* Ont. Canada **102** 55.55N 87.50W
Beaver *r.* U.S.A. **114** 40.40N 80.18W
Beaver Alaska U.S.A. **98** 66.22N147.24W
Beaver Okla. U.S.A. **111** 36.49N100.31W
Beaver Penn. U.S.A. **114** 40.42N 80.18W
Beaver Dam *town* U.S.A. **110** 43.28N 88.50W
Beaver Falls *town* U.S.A. **114** 40.46N 80.19W
Beaverhill L. Alta. Canada **100** 53.27N112.32W
Beaverhill L. N.W.T. Canada **101** 63.02N104.22W
Beaver I. U.S.A. **112** 45.42N 85.28W
Beaverton Canada **104** 44.26N 79.09W
Beaverton U.S.A. **104** 43.53N 84.29W
Beāwar India **62** 26.06N 74.19E
Bebedouro Brazil **126** 20.54S 48.31W
Bebington U.K. **12** 53.23N 3.01W
Bécancour Canada **105** 46.20N 72.26W
Beccles U.K. **13** 52.27N 1.33E
Bečej Yugo. **31** 45.37N 20.03E
Béchar Algeria **74** 31.37N 2.13W
Bechater Tunisia **32** 37.18N 9.45E
Bechet Romania **34** 43.46N 23.58E
Beckley U.S.A. **113** 37.46N 81.12W
Beckum W. Germany **38** 51.45N 8.02E
Beclean Romania **37** 47.11N 24.10E
Bédarieux France **20** 43.37N 3.09E
Bedeso Ethiopia **73** 8.50N 40.45E
Bedford Canada **105** 45.07N 72.59W
Bedford U.K. **13** 52.08N 0.29W
Bedford U.S.A. **114** 40.01N 78.30W
Bedford, C. Australia **90** 15.14S145.21E
Bedford Levels *f.* U.K. **13** 52.35N 0.08W
Bedfordshire *d.* U.K. **13** 52.04N 0.28W
Bedi India **62** 22.30N 70.02E
Bedlington U.K. **12** 55.08N 1.34W
Bedourie Australia **90** 24.21S139.28E
Beech Grove U.S.A. **112** 39.42N 86.06W
Beechworth Australia **93** 36.23S146.42E
Beenleigh Australia **93** 27.43S153.09E
Be'eri Israel **67** 31.25N 34.29E
Be'er Menuha Israel **66** 30.19N 35.08E
Be'erotayim Israel **67** 32.19N 34.59E
Be'er Sheva' Israel **67** 31.15N 34.47E
Be'er Sheva', Nahal *wadi* Israel **67** 31.11N 34.35E
Beerta Neth. **16** 53.12N 7.07E
Be'er Toviyya Israel **67** 31.44N 34.44E
Beeskow E. Germany **38** 52.10N 14.14E
Beeston U.K. **12** 52.55N 1.11W
Beeville U.S.A. **111** 28.24N 97.45W
Befale Zaïre **78** 0.27N 21.01E
Befandriana Madagascar **81** 15.16S 48.32E
Befandriana Madagascar **81** 22.06S 43.54E
Beg, Lough U.K. **15** 54.47N 6.29W
Bega Australia **93** 36.41S149.50E
Begamganj India **63** 23.36N 78.20E
Begēmdir *d.* Ethiopia **73** 12.30N 37.30E
Bègles France **20** 44.47N 0.34W
Begna *r.* Norway **42** 60.10N 10.18E
Begusarai India **63** 25.25N 86.08E
Behara Madagascar **81** 25.00S 46.25E
Behbehān Iran **65** 30.35N 50.17E
Bei'an China **53** 48.17N126.33E
Beihai China **55** 21.29N109.09E
Bei Jiang *r.* China **55** 23.19N112.51E
Beijing China **54** 39.55N116.25E
Beijing *d.* China **54** 40.00N116.30E
Beijing Shi *d.* China **53** 40.15N116.30E
Beilen Neth. **16** 52.51N 6.31E
Beinn Dearg *mtn.* U.K. **14** 57.47N 4.55W
Beipa'a P.N.G. **90** 8.30S146.35E
Beipiao China **54** 41.47N120.40E
Beira *see* Sofala Mozambique **81**
Beirut *see* Bayrūt Lebanon **66**
Beitang China **54** 39.06N117.43E
Beitbridge Zimbabwe **80** 22.10S 30.01E
Beit Jann Israel **67** 32.58N 35.23E
Beiuș Romania **37** 46.40N 22.21E
Beja Portugal **27** 38.01N 7.52W
Beja *d.* Portugal **27** 37.50N 7.55W
Béja Tunisia **32** 36.44N 9.11E
Bejaïa Algeria **75** 36.45N 5.05E
Béjar Spain **26** 40.23N 5.46W
Bejestān Iran **65** 34.32N 58.08E
Bejhi *r.* Pakistan **62** 29.47N 67.58E
Bejoording Australia **89** 31.22S116.30E
Békés Hungary **37** 46.46N 21.08E
Békéscsaba Hungary **37** 46.41N 21.06E
Bekily Madagascar **81** 24.13S 45.19E
Bela India **63** 25.56N 81.59E
Bela Pakistan **62** 26.14N 66.19E
Bélabo Cameroon **77** 5.00N 13.20E
Bela Crkva Yugo. **37** 44.54N 21.26E
Bel Air U.S.A. **115** 39.32N 76.21W
Belalcázar Spain **26** 38.34N 5.10W
Belampalli India **63** 19.02N 79.30E
Belang Indonesia **59** 0.58N124.56E
Bela Palanka Yugo. **34** 43.13N 22.17E
Belau Pacific Oc. **59** 7.00N134.25E
Bela Vista Brazil **124** 22.05S 56.22W
Bela Vista Mozambique **81** 26.20S 32.41E
Belaya *r.* U.S.S.R. **50** 55.40N 52.30E
Belaya Glina U.S.S.R. **45** 46.04N 40.54E
Belaya Tserkov U.S.S.R. **37** 49.49N 30.10E
Belcher Is. Canada **102** 56.00N 79.00W
Belchite Spain **25** 41.18N 0.45W
Belcoo U.K. **15** 54.18N 7.53W
Belda India **63** 22.05N 87.21E
Belebey U.S.S.R. **44** 54.05N 54.07E
Beled Weyne Somali Rep. **71** 4.47N 45.12E
Belém Brazil **123** 1.27S 48.29W
Belem Mozambique **81** 14.11S 35.59E
Belén Uruguay **125** 30.47S 57.47W
Belen U.S.A. **109** 34.40N106.46W
Belén, Cuchilla de *mts.* Uruguay **125** 30.49S 56.28W
Belene Bulgaria **34** 43.39N 25.07E
Beles *r.* Ethiopia **71** 11.10N 35.10E
Belev U.S.S.R. **44** 53.50N 36.08E
Belfast U.K. **15** 54.36N 5.57W
Belfast Maine U.S.A. **112** 44.27N 69.01W
Belfast N.Y. U.S.A. **114** 42.21N 78.07W
Belfast Lough U.K. **15** 54.42N 5.45W
Belfield U.S.A. **110** 46.53N103.12W
Belfort France **17** 47.38N 6.52E
Belfry U.S.A. **108** 45.09N109.01W
Belgaum India **60** 15.54N 74.36E
Belgium Europe **16** 51.00N 4.30E
Belgodere France **21** 42.35N 9.01E
Belgorod U.S.S.R. **23** 50.38N 36.36E
Belgorod-Dnestrovskiy U.S.S.R. **37** 46.10N 30.19E
Belgrade *see* Beograd Yugo. **37**
Beli Nigeria **77** 7.53N 10.59E
Beli Drim *r.* Yugo. **34** 42.25N 20.34E
Beli Manastir Yugo. **31** 45.46N 18.36E
Belin France **20** 44.30N 0.47W
Belington U.S.A. **114** 39.01N 79.56W
Belitung *i.* Indonesia **58** 3.00S108.00E
Belize Belize **117** 17.29N 88.20W
Belize C. America **117** 17.00N 88.30W
Belka Australia **89** 31.45S118.09E
Bellac France **20** 46.07N 1.02E
Bella Coola Canada **100** 52.25N126.40W
Bellagio Italy **30** 45.59N 9.15E
Bellaire Ohio U.S.A. **114** 40.02N 80.45W
Bellaire Tex. U.S.A. **111** 29.44N 95.03W
Bellaria Italy **30** 44.09N 12.28E
Bellary India **60** 15.11N 76.54E
Bellata Australia **93** 29.55S149.50E
Bella Unión Uruguay **125** 30.15S 57.35W
Bella Vista Corrientes Argentina **124** 28.30S 59.00W
Bella Vista Tucuman Argentina **124** 27.02S 65.19W
Bellbrook Australia **93** 30.48S152.30E
Belle U.S.A. **114** 38.14N 81.32W
Belledonne, Chaîne de *mts.* France **21** 45.18N 6.08E
Bellefontaine U.S.A. **112** 40.22N 83.45W
Bellefonte U.S.A. **114** 40.55N 77.46W
Belle Fourche *r.* U.S.A. **110** 44.26N102.19W
Bellegarde France **21** 46.06N 5.49E
Belle Glade U.S.A. **113** 26.41N 80.41W
Belle Île France **17** 47.20N 3.10W
Belle Île *i.* France **18** 47.20N 3.10W
Belle Isle Canada **103** 51.55N 55.20W
Belle Isle, Str. of Canada **103** 51.35N 56.30W
Bellême France **18** 48.22N 0.34E
Belleoram Canada **103** 47.32N 55.28W
Belleterre Canada **104** 47.25N 78.41W
Belleville Canada **105** 44.10N 77.23W
Belleville Kans. U.S.A. **110** 39.49N 97.38W
Belleville-sur-Saône France **21** 46.06N 4.45E
Bellevue Canada **104** 46.42N 84.09W
Bellevue Canada **100** 49.35N114.22W
Bellevue Idaho U.S.A. **108** 43.28N114.16W
Bellevue Ohio U.S.A. **114** 41.17N 82.50W
Bellevue Penn. U.S.A. **114** 40.30N 80.03W
Bellevue Wash. U.S.A. **108** 47.37N122.12W
Bell Ewart Canada **104** 44.16N 79.33W
Belley France **21** 45.46N 5.41E
Belle Yella Liberia **76** 7.24N 10.09W
Bellin Canada **99** 60.01N 70.01W
Bellingen Australia **93** 30.28S152.43E
Bellingham U.K. **12** 55.09N 2.15W
Bellingham U.S.A. **108** 48.46N122.29W
Bellingshausen Sea Antarctica **128** 70.00S 88.00W
Bellinzona Switz. **39** 46.11N 9.02E
Bello Colombia **122** 6.20N 75.41W
Bellows Falls *town* U.S.A. **115** 43.08N 72.27W
Bellpat Pakistan **62** 28.59N 68.00E
Belluno Italy **30** 46.09N 12.13E
Bell Ville Argentina **125** 32.35S 62.41W
Bellville U.S.A. **114** 40.37N 82.31W
Bellwood U.S.A. **114** 40.36N 78.20W
Belmar U.S.A. **115** 40.11N 74.01W
Bélmez Spain **26** 38.16N 5.12W
Belmond U.S.A. **110** 42.51N 93.37W
Belmont U.S.A. **114** 42.13N 78.02W
Belmonte Portugal **26** 40.21N 7.21W
Belmonte Cuenca Spain **27** 39.34N 2.42W
Belmonte Oviedo Spain **26** 43.16N 6.13W
Belmopan Belize **117** 17.25N 88.46W
Belmullet Rep. of Ire. **15** 54.14N 10.00W
Belogradchik Bulgaria **34** 43.37N 22.40E
Belo Horizonte Brazil **126** 19.45S 43.54W
Beloit Kans. U.S.A. **110** 39.28N 98.06W
Beloit Wisc. U.S.A. **110** 42.31N 89.02W
Belo Jardim Brazil **123** 8.22S 36.22W
Belokorovichi U.S.S.R. **37** 51.04N 28.00E
Belomorsk U.S.S.R. **44** 64.34N 34.45E
Belonia India **63** 23.15N 91.27E
Belorado Spain **26** 42.25N 3.11W
Beloretsk U.S.S.R. **44** 53.59N 58.20E
Belorusskaya S.S.R. *d.* U.S.S.R. **37** 53.30N 28.00E
Beloye More *sea* U.S.S.R. **44** 65.30N 38.00E
Beloye Ozero *l.* U.S.S.R. **44** 60.12N 37.45E
Belozersk U.S.S.R. **44** 60.00N 37.49E
Belpasso Italy **33** 37.35N 14.59E
Belper U.K. **12** 53.02N 1.29W
Belpre U.S.A. **114** 39.17N 81.34W
Beltana Australia **92** 30.40S138.27E
Belterra Brazil **123** 2.38S 54.57W
Belton Australia **92** 32.12S138.45E
Belton U.S.A. **111** 31.04N 97.28W
Beltsy U.S.S.R. **37** 47.45N 27.59E
Belukha, Gora *mtn.* U.S.S.R. **52** 49.48N 86.40E
Belvedere Marittimo Italy **33** 39.37N 15.52E
Belvès France **20** 44.47N 1.00E
Belvidere U.S.A. **115** 40.49N 75.05W
Belvís de la Jara Spain **27** 39.45N 4.57W
Belyando *r.* Australia **90** 21.38S146.50E
Belyayevka U.S.S.R. **37** 46.30N 30.12E

Binéfar to **Bolus Head**

Binéfar Spain **25** 41.51N 0.18E
Binga Zimbabwe **80** 17.38S 27.19E
Binga, Mt. Zimbabwe **81** 19.47S 33.03E
Bingara Australia **93** 29.51S150.38E
Bingen W. Germany **39** 49.58N 7.55E
Bingerville Ivory Coast **76** 5.20N 3.53W
Bingham U.K. **12** 52.57N 0.57W
Bingham U.S.A. **112** 45.03N 69.53W
Binghamton U.S.A. **115** 42.08N 75.54W
Bingkor Malaysia **58** 5.26N116.15E
Bingöl Turkey **23** 38.54N 40.29E
Bingol Dağlari *mtn.* Turkey **64** 39.21N 41.22E
Binhai China **54** 34.00N119.55E
Binh Dinh Vietnam **56** 13.53N109.07E
Binjai Indonesia **58** 3.37N 98.25E
Binji Nigeria **77** 13.12N 4.55E
Binnaway Australia **93** 31.33S148.50E
Binscarth Canada **101** 50.37N101.16W
Bintan *i.* Indonesia **58** 1.10N104.30E
Bint Jubayl Lebanon **67** 33.07N 35.26E
Bintulu Malaysia **58** 3.12N113.01E
Bin Xian China **54** 35.02N108.04E
Binya Australia **93** 34.14S146.22E
Binyamina Israel **67** 32.31N 34.57E
Binyang China **55** 23.12N108.48E
Binzert Tunisia **32** 37.17N 9.52E
Biograd Yugo. **31** 43.56N 15.27E
Biq'at Bet Netofa *f.* Israel **67** 32.49N 35.19E
Bir India **62** 18.59N 75.46E
Bir, Ras *c.* Djibouti **71** 11.59N 43.25E
Bi'r Abū 'Uwayqīlah *well* Egypt **66** 30.50N 34.07E
Bi'r ad Dakhal *well* Egypt **66** 28.40N 32.24E
Birāk Libya **75** 27.32N 14.17E
Birak Sulaymān *site* Jordan **67** 31.41N 35.10E
Bi'r al Harash *well* Libya **75** 25.30N 22.06E
Bi'r al Jidy *well* Egypt **66** 30.13N 33.03E
Bi'r al Jufayr *well* Egypt **66** 30.49N 32.40E
Bi'r al 'Udayd *well* Egypt **66** 28.59N 34.05E
Birao C.A.R. **73** 10.17N 22.47E
Bi'r aş Şafrā' *well* Egypt **66** 28.46N 34.20E
Bi'r ath Thamadah *well* Egypt **66** 30.10N 33.28E
Birātnagar Nepal **63** 26.18N 87.17E
Bi'r Buerāt *well* Egypt **66** 28.59N 32.10E
Bi'r Bukhayt *well* Egypt **66** 29.13N 32.17E
Bîrca Romania **34** 43.59N 23.36E
Birch *r.* Canada **100** 58.30N112.15W
Birchip Australia **92** 35.59S142.59E
Birch L. N.W.T. Canada **100** 62.04N116.33W
Birch L. Ont. Canada **102** 51.24N 92.20W
Birch Mts. Canada **100** 57.30N112.30W
Bird Canada **101** 56.30N 94.13W
Birdsboro U.S.A. **115** 40.16N 75.48W
Birdsville Australia **90** 25.54S139.22E
Birdum Australia **88** 15.38S133.12E
Birecik Turkey **64** 37.03N 37.59E
Birganj Nepal **63** 27.01N 84.54E
Birhan *mtn.* Ethiopia **73** 11.00N 37.50E
Bi'r Hasanah *well* Egypt **66** 30.29N 33.47E
Bi'r Hooker *well* Egypt **66** 30.23N 30.20E
Birjand Iran **65** 32.54N 59.10E
Bi'r Jifjafah *well* Egypt **66** 30.28N 33.11E
Birk, Wādī *r.* Saudi Arabia **65** 24.08N 47.35E
Birkeland Norway **42** 58.20N 8.14E
Birkenfeld B.-Württ. W. Germany **39** 48.52N 8.38E
Birkenfeld Rhein.-Pfalz W. Germany **39** 49.39N 7.10E
Birkenhead U.K. **12** 53.24N 3.01W
Birkerød Denmark **43** 55.50N 12.26E
Birksgate Range *mts.* Australia **88** 27.10S129.45E
Bi'r Kusaybah *well* Egypt **66** 22.41N 29.55E
Bîrlad Romania **37** 46.14N 27.40E
Bi'r Lahfān *well* Egypt **66** 31.01N 33.52E
Birmingham U.K. **13** 52°30N 1.55W
Birmingham Ala. U.S.A. **113** 33.30N 86.55W
Birmingham Mich. U.S.A. **104** 42.33N 83.15W
Birmitrapur India **63** 22.24N 84.46E
Bir Mogreïn Mauritania **74** 25.14N 11.35W
Birni Benin **77** 9.59N 1.34E
Birnin Gwari Nigeria **77** 11.02N 6.47E
Birnin Kebbi Nigeria **77** 12.30N 4.11E
Birni N'Konni Niger **77** 13.49N 5.19E
Birobidzhan U.S.S.R. **53** 48.49N132.54E
Bir Ounâne *well* Mali **74** 21.02N 3.18W
Birr Rep. of Ire. **15** 53.06N 7.56W
Birrie *r.* Australia **93** 29.43S146.37E
Birsilpur India **62** 28.11N 72.15E
Birsk U.S.S.R. **44** 55.28N 55.31E
Bi'r Tābah *well* Egypt **66** 29.30N 34.53E
Bi'r Ţarfāwi *well* Egypt **72** 22.55N 28.53E
Birtle Canada **101** 50.32N101.02W
Bi'r Umm Sa'īd *well* Egypt **66** 29.40N 33.34E
Bi'r Umm 'Umayyid *well* Egypt **66** 27.53N 32.30E
Bi'r Ya'qūb *well* Jordan **67** 32.13N 35.17E
Biržai U.S.S.R. **44** 56.10N 24.48E
Bi'r Zalţan *well* Libya **75** 28.27N 19.46E
Bir Zreigat Mauritania **74** 22.27N 8.53W
Bisaccia Italy **33** 41.01N 15.22E
Bisalpur India **63** 28.18N 79.48E
Bisbee U.S.A. **109** 31.27N109.55W
Biscarosse France **20** 44.24N 1.10W
Biscarosse, Étang de *b.* France **20** 44.20N 1.10W
Biscay, B. of France **20** 44.00N 4.00W
Bisceglie Italy **33** 41.14N 16.31E
Bischheim France **19** 48.37N 7.45E
Bischofswerda E. Germany **38** 51.07N 14.10E
Biscotasi L. Canada **104** 47.19N 82.07W
Biscotasing Canada **104** 47.18N 82.08W
Bisha Ethiopia **72** 15.28N 37.34E
Bishnupur India **63** 23.05N 87.19E
Bishop Calif. U.S.A. **108** 37.22N118.24W
Bishop Tex. U.S.A. **111** 27.35N 97.48W
Bishop Auckland U.K. **12** 54.40N 1.40W
Bishop's Stortford U.K. **13** 51.53N 0.09E
Bisina, L. Uganda **79** 1.35N 34.08E
Biskra Algeria **75** 34.48N 5.40E
Bismarck U.S.A. **110** 46.48N100.47W
Bismarck Range *mts.* P.N.G. **59** 6.00S145.00E
Bismarck Sea Pacific Oc. **59** 4.00S146.30E
Bison U.S.A. **110** 45.31N102.28W
Bisotūn Iran **65** 34.22N 47.29E
Bispgården Sweden **40** 63.02N 16.40E
Bissau Guinea Bissau **76** 11.52N 15.39W
Bissett Canada **101** 51.02N 95.40W
Bissikrima Guinea **76** 10.50N 10.58W
Bistcho L. Canada **100** 59.45N118.50W
Bistreţ Romania **34** 43.54N 23.23E
Bistriţa Romania **37** 47.08N 24.30E
Bistriţa *r.* Romania **37** 46.30N 26.54E
Biswân India **63** 27.30N 81.00E
Bitam Gabon **78** 2.05N 11.30E
Bitburg W. Germany **39** 49.58N 6.31E
Bitche France **19** 49.03N 7.26E
Bitéa, Ouadi *wadi* Chad **73** 13.11N 20.10E
Bitlis Turkey **64** 38.23N 42.04E
Bitola Yugo. **34** 41.01N 21.20E
Bitonto Italy **33** 41.06N 16.42E
Bitter Creek *town* U.S.A. **108** 41.31N109.27W
Bitterfeld E. Germany **38** 51.37N 12.20E
Bitterfontein R.S.A. **80** 31.02S 18.14E
Bitterroot Range *mts.* U.S.A. **108** 47.06N115.10W
Bitti Italy **32** 40.29N 9.23E
Biu Nigeria **77** 10.36N 12.11E
Biumba Rwanda **79** 1.38S 30.02E
Biwa ko *l.* Japan **57** 35.10N136.00E
Biyalâ Egypt **66** 31.11N 31.13E
Biysk U.S.S.R. **9** 52.35N 85.16E
Bizerte *d.* Tunisia **32** 37.07N 9.45E
Bizerte *see* Binzert Tunisia **32**
Bizerte, Lac de *l.* Tunisia **32** 37.12N 9.52E
Bjärnum Sweden **43** 56.17N 13.42E
Bjelasica *mts.* Yugo. **31** 42.50N 19.40E
Bjelovar Yugo. **31** 45.54N 16.51E
Bjerringbro Denmark **42** 56.23N 9.40E
Björkelangen Norway **42** 59.53N 11.34E
Bjorli Norway **41** 62.16N 8.13E
Björna Sweden **40** 63.32N 18.36E
Björnafjorden *est.* Norway **42** 60.06N 5.22E
Bjuv Sweden **43** 56.05N 12.54E
Blace Yugo. **34** 43.18N 21.17E
Black *r.* Canada **104** 44.20N 79.20W
Black *r.* Ark. U.S.A. **111** 35.38N 91.19W
Black *r.* Mich. U.S.A. **104** 43.00N 82.25W
Black *r.* Mich. U.S.A. **104** 45.39N 84.29W
Black *r.* N.Y. U.S.A. **105** 44.01N 75.59W
Black *r.* Ohio U.S.A. **114** 41.28N 82.11W
Black *r. see* Dà Vietnam **56**
Blackall Australia **90** 24.25S145.28E
Blackburn U.K. **12** 53.44N 2.30W
Black Diamond Canada **100** 50.45N114.14W
Blackduck U.S.A. **110** 47.44N 94.33W
Blackfoot U.S.A. **108** 43.11N112.20W
Black Hills U.S.A. **110** 44.00N104.00W
Black L. Canada **101** 59.10N105.20W
Black L. U.S.A. **104** 45.28N 84.15W
Black L. U.S.A. **105** 44.31N 75.35W
Black Lake *town* Canada **105** 46.03N 71.21W
Black Mtn. U.K. **13** 51.52N 3.50W
Black Mts. U.K. **13** 51.52N 3.09W
Blackpool U.K. **12** 53.48N 3.03W
Black River *town* Jamaica **117** 18.02N 77.52W
Black River *town* Mich. U.S.A. **104** 44.47N 83.19W
Black River *town* N.Y. U.S.A. **105** 44.01N 75.48W
Black Rock *town* U.S.A. **108** 38.41N112.59W
Black Rock Desert U.S.A. **108** 41.10N119.00W
Black Sand Desert U.S.S.R. **65** 37.45N 60.00E
Black Sea Europe **37** 44.00N 30.00E
Blacksod B. Rep. of Ire. **15** 54.04N 10.00W
Blackstone U.S.A. **113** 37.05N 78.02W
Black Sugarloaf Mt. Australia **93** 31.24S151.34E
Blackville Australia **93** 31.34S150.10E
Blackville U.S.A. **113** 33.22N 81.17W
Black Volta *r.* Ghana / U. Volta **76** 8.14N 2.11W
Blackwater *r.* Waterford Rep. of Ire. **15** 51.58N 7.52W
Blackwater *r.* U.K. **11** 54.31N 6.36W
Blackwell U.S.A. **111** 36.48N 97.17W
Blackwood *r.* Australia **89** 34.15S115.10E
Blaenau Ffestiniog U.K. **12** 53.00N 3.57W
Blagaj Yugo. **31** 43.15N 17.50E
Blagoevgrad Bulgaria **34** 42.02N 23.05E
Blagoevgrad *d.* Bulgaria **34** 42.01N 23.05E
Blagoveshchensk U.S.S.R. **53** 50.19N127.30E
Blain France **18** 47.29N 1.46W
Blain U.S.A. **114** 40.20N 77.31W
Blair U.S.A. **110** 41.33N 96.08W
Blair Athol Australia **90** 22.42S147.33E
Blair Atholl U.K. **14** 56.46N 3.51W
Blairgowrie U.K. **14** 56.36N 3.21W
Blairmore Canada **100** 49.40N114.25W
Blairsville Ga. U.S.A. **113** 34.52N 83.52W
Blairsville Penn. U.S.A. **114** 40.26N 79.16W
Blakely U.S.A. **113** 31.22N 84.58W
Blakeslee U.S.A. **115** 41.06N 75.36W
Blanc, Cap *c.* Mauritania **76** 20.44N 17.05W
Blanc, Cap *c.* Tunisia **32** 37.20N 9.50E
Blanc, Mont *mtn.* France **21** 45.50N 6.52E
Blanca, Bahía *b.* Argentina **125** 39.20S 62.00W
Blanca, Sierra *mtn.* U.S.A. **109** 33.23N105.48W
Blanchard U.S.A. **108** 48.01N116.59W
Blanche, L. Australia **92** 29.15S139.40E
Blanchetown Australia **92** 34.21S139.38E
Blanchewater Australia **92** 29.32S139.28E
Blanco, C. Argentina **125** 47.12S 65.20W
Blanco, C. Costa Rica **117** 9.36N 85.06W
Blanco, C. U.S.A. **108** 42.50N124.34W
Bland *r.* Australia **93** 33.42S147.30E
Blandburg U.S.A. **114** 40.41N 78.25W
Blandford Forum U.K. **13** 50.52N 2.10W
Blanes Spain **25** 41.41N 2.48E
Blangy-sur-Bresle France **19** 49.56N 1.38E
Blankenberge Belgium **16** 51.18N 3.08E
Blankenburg E. Germany **38** 51.48N 10.58E
Blanquefort France **20** 44.53N 0.39W
Blansko Czech. **36** 49.22N 16.39E
Blantyre Malaŵi **79** 15.46S 35.00E
Blarney Rep. of Ire. **15** 51.56N 8.34W
Blatná Czech. **38** 49.26N 13.53E
Blatnica Bulgaria **37** 43.42N 28.31E
Blaubeuren W. Germany **39** 48.24N 9.47E
Blaufelden W. Germany **39** 49.18N 9.58E
Blavet *r.* France **18** 47.43N 3.18W
Blaye France **20** 45.08N 0.39W
Blayney Australia **93** 33.32S149.19E
Bled Yugo. **31** 46.22N 14.06E
Blednaya, Gora *mtn.* U.S.S.R. **50** 76.23N 65.08E
Bleiburg Austria **31** 46.35N 14.48E
Blekinge *d.* Sweden **43** 56.15N 15.15E
Blekinge *f.* Sweden **43** 56.20N 15.20E
Blenheim Canada **104** 42.20N 82.00W
Blenheim New Zealand **86** 41.32S173.58E
Bléone *r.* France **21** 44.03N 6.00E
Bléré France **18** 47.20N 1.00E
Blerick Neth. **16** 51.22N 6.08E
Bletchley U.K. **13** 51.59N 0.45W
Bletterans France **19** 46.45N 5.27E
Bleu, Lac *l.* Canada **104** 46.35N 78.20W
Blida Algeria **75** 36.30N 2.50E
Blidö *i.* Sweden **43** 59.37N 18.54E
Bligh Entrance Australia **90** 9.18S144.10E
Blind River *town* Canada **104** 46.10N 82.58W
Blinman Australia **92** 31.05S138.11E
Blitar Indonesia **59** 8.06S112.12E
Blitta Togo **77** 8.23N 1.06E
Block I. U.S.A. **115** 41.11N 71.35W
Bloemfontein R.S.A. **80** 29.07S 26.14E
Bloemhof R.S.A. **80** 27.37S 25.34E
Blois France **18** 47.35N 1.20E
Blönduós Iceland **40** 65.39N 20.18W
Bloods Creek *town* Australia **90** 26.28S135.17E
Bloody Foreland *c.* Rep. of Ire. **15** 55.09N 8.17W
Bloomfield Canada **105** 43.59N 77.14W
Bloomfield Iowa U.S.A. **110** 40.45N 92.25W
Bloomfield Nebr. U.S.A. **110** 42.36N 97.39W
Bloomfield N.J. U.S.A. **115** 40.48N 74.12W
Bloomingdale U.S.A. **105** 44.25N 74.06W
Bloomington Ill. U.S.A. **110** 40.29N 89.00W
Bloomington Ind. U.S.A. **112** 39.10N 86.31W
Bloomington Minn. U.S.A. **110** 44.50N 93.17W
Bloomsburg U.S.A. **115** 41.00N 76.27W
Blora Indonesia **59** 6.55S111.29E
Blossburg U.S.A. **114** 41.41N 77.04W
Blovice Czech. **38** 49.35N 13.33E
Bludenz Austria **39** 47.09N 9.49E
Blueberry *r.* Canada **100** 56.45N120.49W
Bluefield U.S.A. **113** 37.14N 81.17W
Bluefields Nicaragua **117** 12.00N 83.49W
Blue Hills of Couteau Canada **103** 47.59N 57.43W
Bluemont U.S.A. **114** 39.06N 77.51W
Blue Mountain Lake *town* U.S.A. **105** 43.53N 74.26W
Blue Mtn. U.S.A. **105** 44.47N 71.28W
Blue Mtn. U.S.A. **114** 40.15N 77.30W
Blue Mts. Australia **93** 33.30S150.15E
Blue Mts. U.S.A. **108** 45.30N118.15W
Blue Mud B. Australia **90** 13.26S135.56E
Blue Nile *r. see* Azraq, Al Baḩr al Sudan **72**
Bluenose L. Canada **98** 68.30N119.35W
Blue River *town* Canada **100** 52.05N119.09W
Blue Stack Mts. Rep. of Ire. **15** 54.44N 8.09W
Bluff New Zealand **86** 46.38S168.21E
Bluff U.S.A. **108** 37.17N109.33W
Bluff, C. Canada **103** 52.48N 55.53W
Bluff Knoll *mtn.* Australia **89** 34.25S118.15E
Blumberg W. Germany **39** 47.50N 8.31E
Blumenau Brazil **126** 26.55S 49.07W
Blunt U.S.A. **110** 44.31N 99.59W
Blyth Canada **104** 43.44N 81.26W
Blyth Northum. U.K. **12** 55.07N 1.29W
Blythe U.S.A. **109** 33.37N114.36W
Bö Nordland Norway **40** 68.38N 14.35E
Bö Telemark Norway **42** 59.25N 9.04E
Bo Sierra Leone **76** 7.58N 11.45W
Boa Esperança Brazil **126** 21.03S 45.37W
Bo'ai Henan China **54** 35.10N113.04E
Boane Mozambique **81** 26.02S 32.19E
Boa Vista Brazil **122** 2.51N 60.43W
Bobadah Australia **93** 32.18S146.42E
Bobadilla Spain **27** 37.02N 4.44W
Bobbili India **61** 18.34N 83.22E
Bobbio Italy **30** 44.46N 9.23E
Bobcaygeon Canada **104** 44.33N 78.33W
Böblingen W. Germany **39** 48.41N 9.01E
Bobo-Dioulasso U. Volta **76** 11.11N 4.18W
Bobonong Botswana **80** 21.59S 28.29E
Bóbr *r.* Poland **36** 52.04N 15.04E
Bobr U.S.S.R. **37** 54.19N 29.18E
Bobruysk U.S.S.R. **37** 53.08N 29.10E
Bôca do Acre Brazil **122** 8.45S 67.23W
Bocaranga C.A.R. **77** 7.01N 15.35E
Boca Raton U.S.A. **113** 26.22N 80.05W
Bochnia Poland **37** 49.58N 20.26E
Bocholt W. Germany **38** 51.50N 6.36E
Bochum R.S.A. **80** 23.12S 29.12E
Bochum W. Germany **38** 51.28N 7.13E
Bockum-Hövel W. Germany **38** 51.42N 7.46E
Bocognano France **21** 42.05N 9.03E
Boconó Venezuela **122** 9.17N 70.17W
Boda C.A.R. **77** 4.19N 17.26E
Böda Sweden **43** 57.15N 17.03E
Boda Glasbruk Sweden **43** 56.44N 15.40E
Bodalla Australia **93** 36.05S150.03E
Bodallin Australia **89** 31.22S118.52E
Bodélé Chad **75** 16.30N 16.30E
Bodélé *f.* Chad **77** 16.50N 17.10E
Boden Sweden **40** 65.50N 21.42E
Bodensee *l.* Europe **39** 47.35N 9.25E
Bode Sadu Nigeria **77** 8.57N 4.49E
Bodfish U.S.A. **109** 35.36N118.30W
Bodmin U.K. **13** 50.28N 4.44W
Bodmin Moor U.K. **13** 50.53N 4.35W
Bodo Canada **101** 52.11N110.04W
Bodö Norway **40** 67.18N 14.26E
Bodrum Turkey **35** 37.02N 27.26E
Boembé Congo **78** 2.59S 15.34E
Boende Zaïre **78** 0.15S 20.49E
Boën-sur-Lignon France **20** 45.44N 3.59E
Boeo, Capo *c.* Italy **32** 37.48N 12.26E
Boffa Guinea **76** 10.12N 14.02W
Bofors Sweden **43** 59.20N 14.32E
Bogale Burma **56** 16.17N 95.24E
Bogalusa U.S.A. **111** 30.47N 89.52W
Bogan *r.* Australia **93** 30.00S146.20E
Bogan Gate *town* Australia **93** 33.08S147.50E
Bogata U.S.A. **111** 33.28N 95.13W
Bogcang Zangbo *r.* China **63** 31.50N 87.25E
Bogen W. Germany **39** 48.55N 12.43E
Bogenfels Namibia **80** 27.26S 15.22E
Bogense Denmark **42** 55.34N 10.06E
Boggabilla Australia **93** 28.36S150.21E
Boggabri Australia **93** 30.42S150.02E
Boggeragh Mts. Rep. of Ire. **15** 52.03N 8.53W
Bogia P.N.G. **59** 4.16S145.00E
Bognes Norway **40** 68.15N 16.00E
Bognor Regis U.K. **13** 50.47N 0.40W
Bog of Allen *f.* Rep. of Ire. **15** 53.17N 7.00W
Bogol Manya Ethiopia **73** 4.32N 41.32E
Bogong, Mt. Australia **93** 36.45S147.21E
Bogor Indonesia **58** 6.34S106.45E
Bogor *mtn.* Indonesia **59** 6.34S106.45E
Bogotá Colombia **122** 4.38N 74.05W
Bogra Bangla. **63** 24.51N 89.22E
Bogué Mauritania **74** 16.35N 14.16W
Boguslav U.S.S.R. **37** 49.32N 30.52E
Bo Hai *b.* China **54** 38.30N119.30E
Bohain France **19** 49.59N 3.27E
Bohai Wan *b.* China **54** 38.30N117.55E
Bohemian Forest *see* Böhmerwald W. Germany / Czech. **39**
Bohinjska Bistrica Yugo. **31** 46.17N 13.57E
Böhmerwald *mts.* W. Germany / Czech. **39** 49.12N 12.55E
Bohol *i.* Phil. **59** 9.45N124.10E
Bohotleh Wein Somali Rep. **71** 8.16N 46.24E
Bohuslän *f.* Sweden **42** 58.15N 11.50E
Boiaçu Brazil **122** 0.27S 61.46W
Boiano Italy **33** 41.29N 14.29E
Boigu *i.* Australia **90** 9.16S142.12E
Boing Sudan **73** 9.58N 33.44E
Boiro Spain **26** 42.39N 8.54W
Bois, Lac des *l.* Canada **98** 66.40N125.15W
Bois Blanc I. U.S.A. **104** 45.45N 84.28W
Bois du Roi *mtn.* France **19** 47.00N 4.02E
Boise U.S.A. **108** 43.37N116.13W
Boise City U.S.A. **111** 36.44N102.31W
Bois-Guillaume France **18** 49.28N 1.08E
Boissevain Canada **101** 49.15N100.00W
Boizenburg E. Germany **38** 53.22N 10.43E
Bojador, Cabo *c.* W. Sahara **74** 26.08N 14.30W
Bojana *r.* Albania **31** 41.50N 19.25E
Bojeador, C. Phil. **55** 18.30N120.36E
Bojnūrd Iran **65** 37.28N 57.20E
Bojonegoro Indonesia **59** 7.06S111.50E
Bokani Nigeria **77** 9.27N 5.13E
Boké Guinea **76** 10.57N 14.13W
Bokhara *r.* Australia **93** 29.55S146.42E
Boknafjorden *est.* Norway **42** 59.10N 5.35E
Bokoro Chad **77** 12.17N 17.04E
Bokote Zaïre **78** 0.05S 20.08E
Bokpyin Burma **56** 11.16N 98.46E
Bokungu Zaïre **78** 0.44S 22.28E
Bol Chad **77** 13.27N 14.40E
Bol Yugo. **31** 43.16N 16.40E
Bolac, L. Australia **92** 37.45S142.55E
Bolafa Zaïre **78** 1.23N 22.06E
Bolama Guinea Bissau **76** 11.35N 15.30W
Bolān *r.* Pakistan **62** 29.05N 67.45E
Bolanda, Jabal *mtn.* Sudan **73** 7.44N 25.28E
Bolaños de Calatrava Spain **26** 38.54N 3.40W
Bolān Pass Pakistan **62** 29.45N 67.35E
Bolbec France **18** 49.34N 0.29E
Bole Ghana **76** 9.03N 2.23W
Bolesławiec Poland **36** 51.16N 15.34E
Bolgatanga Ghana **76** 10.42N 0.52W
Bolgrad U.S.S.R. **37** 45.42N 28.40E
Bolia Zaïre **78** 1.36S 18.23E
Bolívar Argentina **125** 36.14S 61.07W
Bolivar N.Y. U.S.A. **114** 42.04N 78.10W
Bolivar Tenn. U.S.A. **111** 35.16N 88.59W
Bolivia S. America **124** 17.00S 65.00W
Bollène France **21** 44.17N 4.45E
Bollnäs Sweden **41** 61.21N 16.25E
Bollon Australia **91** 28.02S147.28E
Bollstabruk Sweden **40** 62.59N 17.42E
Bollullos par del Condado Spain **27** 37.20N 6.32W
Bolmen *l.* Sweden **43** 56.55N 13.40E
Bolobo Zaïre **78** 2.10S 16.17E
Bologna Italy **30** 44.29N 11.20E
Bologoye U.S.S.R. **44** 57.58N 34.00E
Bolomba Zaïre **78** 0.30N 19.13E
Bolombo Zaïre **78** 3.59S 21.22E
Bolondo Equat. Guinea **78** 1.40N 9.38E
Bolongongo Angola **78** 8.28S 15.16E
Bolovens, Plateau des *f.* Laos **56** 15.10N106.30E
Bolsena Italy **30** 42.39N 11.59E
Bolsena, Lago di *l.* Italy **30** 42.36N 11.56E
Bolshaya Glushitsa U.S.S.R. **44** 52.28N 50.30E
Bolshaya Pyssa U.S.S.R. **44** 64.11N 48.44E
Bolsherechye U.S.S.R. **50** 56.07N 74.40E
Bol'shevik, Ostrov *i.* U.S.S.R. **51** 78.30N102.00E
Bolshezemelskaya Tundra *f.* U.S.S.R. **44** 67.00N 56.10E
Bolshoy Atlym U.S.S.R. **50** 62.17N 66.30E
Bol'shoy Balkhan, Khrebet *mts.* U.S.S.R. **65** 39.38N 54.30E
Bol'shoy Irgiz *r.* U.S.S.R. **44** 52.00N 47.20E
Bol'shoy Lyakhovskiy, Ostrov *i.* U.S.S.R. **51** 73.30N142.00E
Bol'shoy Onguren U.S.S.R. **51** 53.40N107.40E
Bolshoy Uzen *r.* U.S.S.R. **45** 49.00N 49.40E
Bolsover U.K. **12** 53.14N 1.18W
Boltaña Spain **25** 42.27N 0.04E
Bolton U.K. **12** 53.35N 2.26W
Bolton L. Canada **101** 54.16N 95.47W
Bolu Turkey **64** 40.45N 31.38E
Bolus Head Rep. of Ire. **15** 51.47N 10.20W

Bolvadin to Brescia

Bolvadin Turkey 64 38.43N 31.02E
Boly Hungary 31 45.58N 18.32E
Bolzano Italy 30 46.31N 11.22E
Boma Zaïre 78 5.50S 13.03E
Bomaderry Australia 93 34.21S150.34E
Bomadi Nigeria 77 5.13N 6.01E
Bombala Australia 93 36.55S149.16E
Bombarral Portugal 27 39.16N 9.09W
Bombay India 62 18.58N 72.50E
Bombo Uganda 71 0.35N 32.32E
Bomboma Zaïre 78 2.25N 18.54E
Bom Despacho Brazil 126 19.46S 45.15W
Bomi China 52 29.50N 95.45E
Bomi Hills Liberia 76 7.01N 10.38W
Bömitz E. Germany 38 53.08N 11.13E
Bömlafjorden est. Norway 42 59.39N 5.20E
Bömlo i. Norway 42 59.46N 5.12E
Bomokandi r. Zaïre 79 3.37N 26.09E
Bomongo Zaïre 78 1.30N 18.21E
Bomu r. see Mbomou Zaïre 73
Bon, Cap c. Tunisia 32 37.05N 11.03E
Bonaigarh India 63 21.50N 84.57E
Bonaire i. Neth. Antilles 122 12.15N 68.27W
Bonanza U.S.A. 108 40.01N109.11W
Bonaparte r. Canada 100 50.46N121.17W
Bonaparte Archipelago is. Australia 88 14.17S125.18E
Bonar-Bridge town U.K. 14 57.53N 4.21W
Bonarcado Italy 32 40.04N 8.38E
Bonavista Canada 103 48.39N 53.07W
Bonavista, C. Canada 103 48.42N 53.05W
Bonavista B. Canada 103 48.45N 53.20W
Bon Bon Australia 92 30.26S135.28E
Bondeno Italy 30 44.53N 11.25E
Bondo Zaïre 78 1.22S 23.53E
Bondo Zaïre 78 3.47N 23.45E
Bondoukou Ivory Coast 76 8.03N 2.15W
Bondowoso Indonesia 59 7.54S113.50E
Bone, Teluk b. Indonesia 59 4.00S120.50E
Bo'ness U.K. 14 56.01N 3.36W
Bonfield Canada 104 46.14N 79.10W
Bonga Ethiopia 73 7.17N 36.15E
Bongaigaon India 63 26.28N 90.34E
Bongak Sudan 73 7.27N 33.14E
Bongandanga Zaïre 78 1.28N 21.03E
Bongor Chad 77 10.18N 15.20E
Bongos, Massif des mts. C.A.R. 73 8.20N 21.35E
Bongouanou Ivory Coast 76 6.44N 4.10W
Bonham U.S.A. 111 33.35N 96.11W
Bonifacio France 21 41.23N 9.10E
Bonifacio, Str. of Italy 32 41.20N 9.15E
Bonin Is. Japan 84 27.00N142.10E
Bonn W. Germany 38 50.44N 7.05E
Bonnechere Canada 105 45.39N 77.35W
Bonnechère r. Canada 105 45.31N 76.33W
Bonners Ferry U.S.A. 108 48.41N116.18W
Bonnétable France 18 48.11N 0.26E
Bonneval France 18 48.11N 1.24E
Bonneville France 21 46.05N 6.25E
Bonneville Salt Flats f. U.S.A. 108 40.45N113.52W
Bonney, L. Australia 92 37.47S140.23E
Bonnie Rock town Australia 89 30.32S118.21E
Bonny Nigeria 77 4.25N 7.10E
Bonny, Bight of Africa 77 2.58N 7.00E
Bonnyville Canada 101 54.16N110.44W
Bonorva Italy 32 40.25N 8.45E
Bonshaw Australia 93 29.08S150.53E
Bontang Indonesia 58 0.05N117.31E
Bonthain Indonesia 58 5.32S119.58E
Bonthe Sierra Leone 76 7.32N 12.30W
Bonyhád Hungary 31 46.19N 18.32E
Bonython Range mts. Australia 88 23.51S129.00E
Boogah Australia 93 28.24S147.25E
Bookaloo Australia 92 31.56S137.21E
Boola Guinea 76 8.22N 8.41W
Boolaboolka, L. Australia 92 32.40S143.13E
Boolaloo Australia 88 22.30S115.51E
Booleroo Centre Australia 92 32.53S138.21E
Booligal Australia 93 33.54S144.54E
Boologooro Australia 88 24.21S114.02E
Boom Belgium 16 51.07N 4.21E
Boomrivier R.S.A. 80 29.34S 20.26E
Boonah Australia 93 28.00S152.36E
Boone U.S.A. 110 42.04N 93.53W
Booneville U.S.A. 111 34.39N 88.34W
Boonsboro U.S.A. 114 39.30N 77.39W
Boonville Mo. U.S.A. 110 38.58N 92.44W
Boonville N.Y. U.S.A. 115 43.29N 75.20W
Boorabbin Australia 89 31.14S120.21E
Boorindal Australia 93 30.23S146.11E
Booroorban Australia 93 34.56S144.46E
Boorowa Australia 93 34.26S148.48E
Boort Australia 92 36.08S143.46E
Boorthanna Australia 92 28.32S135.52E
Boothia, G. of Canada 99 70.00N 90.00W
Boothia Pen. Canada 99 70.30N 95.00W
Bootra Australia 92 30.00S143.00E
Booué Gabon 78 0.00 11.58E
Bopeechee Australia 92 29.36S137.23E
Boppard W. Germany 39 50.14N 7.35E
Boquilla, Presa de la l. Mexico 109 27.30N105.30W
Bor Czech. 38 49.43N 12.47E
Bor Sudan 73 6.12N 31.33E
Bor Yugo. 29 44.05N 22.07E
Bora Bora i. Îs. de la Société 85 16.30S151.45W
Borah Peak mtn. U.S.A. 108 44.08N113.38W
Borama Somali Rep. 71 9.58N 43.07E
Borås Sweden 43 57.43N 12.55E
Borāzjān Iran 65 29.14N 51.12E
Borba Brazil 122 4.24S 59.35W
Borba Portugal 27 38.48N 7.27W
Borda, C. Australia 92 35.45S136.34E
Bordeaux France 20 44.50N 0.34W
Borden Australia 89 34.05S118.16E
Borden I. Canada 98 78.30N111.00W
Borden Pen. Canada 99 73.00N 83.00W
Borders d. U.K. 14 55.30N 2.53W
Bordertown Australia 92 36.18S140.49E
Bordesholm W. Germany 38 54.11N 10.01E
Bordheyri Iceland 40 65.12N 21.06W
Bordighera Italy 30 43.46N 7.39E
Bordj Bou Arreridj Algeria 75 36.04N 4.46E
Bordj Flye Sainte Marie Algeria 74 27.17N 2.59W
Bordj Omar Driss Algeria 75 28.09N 6.49E
Bordö i. Faroe Is. 40 62.10N 7.13W
Bore Ethiopia 73 4.40N 37.40E
Boreda Ethiopia 73 6.32N 37.48E
Borensberg Sweden 43 58.34N 15.17E
Borgå Finland 41 60.24N 25.40E
Borga Sweden 40 64.49N 15.05E
Börgefjell mtn. Norway 40 65.20N 13.45E
Börgefjell Nat. Park Norway 40 65.00N 13.58E
Borger Neth. 16 52.57N 6.46E
Borger U.S.A. 111 35.39N101.24W
Borgholm Sweden 43 56.53N 16.39E
Borghorst W. Germany 16 52.08N 7.27E
Borgo Italy 30 46.03N 11.27E
Borgomanero Italy 30 45.42N 8.28E
Borgo San Dalmazzo Italy 30 44.20N 7.30E
Borgo San Lorenzo Italy 30 43.57N 11.23E
Borgosesia Italy 30 45.43N 8.16E
Borgo Val di Taro Italy 30 44.29N 9.46E
Borgund Norway 41 61.03N 7.49E
Borislav U.S.S.R. 37 49.18N 23.28E
Borisoglebsk U.S.S.R. 45 51.23N 42.02E
Borisov U.S.S.R. 37 54.09N 28.30E
Borispol U.S.S.R. 37 50.21N 30.59E
Borja Peru 122 4.20S 77.40W
Borja Spain 25 41.50N 1.32W
Borjas Blancas Spain 25 41.31N 0.52E
Borken W. Germany 38 51.51N 6.51E
Borkou-Ennedi-Tibesti d. Chad 75 18.15N 20.00E
Borkum W. Germany 38 53.35N 6.40E
Borkum i. W. Germany 38 53.35N 6.41E
Borlänge Sweden 41 60.29N 15.25E
Borley, C. Antarctica 128 66.15S 55.00E
Bormes-les-Mimosas France 21 43.09N 6.20E
Bormio Italy 30 46.28N 10.22E
Borna E. Germany 38 51.07N 12.30E
Borndiep g. Neth. 16 53.28N 5.35E
Borneo i. Asia 58 1.00N114.00E
Bornheim W. Germany 38 50.46N 6.59E
Bornholm i. Denmark 43 55.10N 15.00E
Borno d. Nigeria 77 12.20N 12.40E
Bornos, Embalse de resr. Spain 27 36.50N 5.42W
Bornu, Plain of f. Nigeria 77 12.30N 13.00E
Boro r. Sudan 73 8.52N 26.11E
Borodyanka U.S.S.R. 37 50.38N 29.59E
Boromo U. Volta 76 11.43N 2.53W
Borotou Ivory Coast 76 8.46N 7.30W
Boroughbridge U.K. 12 54.06N 1.23W
Borovan Bulgaria 34 43.27N 23.45E
Borovichi U.S.S.R. 44 58.22N 34.00E
Borrby Sweden 43 55.27N 14.10E
Borrika Australia 92 35.00S140.05E
Borroloola Australia 90 16.04S136.17E
Borşa Romania 37 47.39N 24.40E
Borşa Romania 37 46.56N 23.40E
Borsad India 62 22.25N 72.54E
Borth U.K. 13 52.29N 4.03W
Bort-les-Orgues France 20 45.24N 2.30E
Borūjerd Iran 65 33.54N 48.47E
Bory Tucholskie f. Poland 37 53.45N 17.30E
Borzhomi U.S.S.R. 45 41.49N 43.23E
Borzna U.S.S.R. 45 51.15N 32.25E
Borzya U.S.S.R. 51 50.24N116.35E
Bosa Italy 32 40.18N 8.30E
Bosanska Dubica Yugo. 31 45.11N 16.49E
Bosanska Gradiška Yugo. 31 45.09N 17.15E
Bosanska Krupa Yugo. 31 44.53N 16.10E
Bosanski Novi Yugo. 31 45.03N 16.23E
Bosanski Petrovac Yugo. 31 44.33N 16.22E
Bosanski Šamac Yugo. 31 45.03N 18.28E
Bosansko Grahovo Yugo. 31 44.11N 16.22E
Bosaso Somali Rep. 71 11.13N 49.08E
Boscastle U.K. 13 50.42N 4.42W
Bose China 55 23.58N106.32E
Boshan China 54 36.29N117.50E
Boshof R.S.A. 80 28.32S 25.12E
Bosilegrad Yugo. 34 42.29N 22.28E
Bosna r. Yugo. 31 45.04N 18.29E
Bosna i Hercegovina d. Yugo. 31 44.20N 18.00E
Bosnik Indonesia 59 1.09S136.14E
Bosobolo Zaïre 73 4.11N 19.54E
Bōsō-hantō pen. Japan 57 35.08N140.00E
Bosporus str. see Istanbul Boğazi Turkey 29
Bossangoa C.A.R. 77 6.27N 17.21E
Bossembélé C.A.R. 77 5.10N 17.44E
Bossier City U.S.A. 111 32.31N 93.43W
Bosso Niger 77 13.43N 13.19E
Bostān Pakistan 62 30.26N 67.02E
Bosten Hu l. China 52 42.00N 87.00E
Boston U.K. 12 52.59N 0.02W
Boston U.S.A. 115 42.21N 71.04W
Boston B. Australia 92 34.35S136.02E
Bosut r. Yugo. 31 44.57N 19.22E
Boswell U.S.A. 114 40.10N 79.02W
Botād India 62 22.10N 71.40E
Botany B. Australia 93 34.04S151.08E
Botev mtn. Bulgaria 34 42.43N 24.55E
Botevgrad Bulgaria 34 42.54N 23.47E
Bothnia, G. of Europe 40 63.30N 20.30E
Bothwell Canada 104 42.38N 81.52W
Boticas Portugal 26 41.41N 7.40W
Botletle r. Botswana 80 21.06S 24.47E
Botoşani Romania 37 47.44N 26.41E
Botou U. Volta 77 12.47N 2.02E
Botrange mtn. Belgium 16 50.30N 6.04E
Botro Ivory Coast 76 7.51N 5.19W
Botswana Africa 80 22.00S 24.15E
Bottrop W. Germany 38 51.31N 6.55E
Botucatu Brazil 126 22.52S 48.30W
Bouaflé Ivory Coast 76 7.01N 5.47W
Bouaké Ivory Coast 76 7.42N 5.00W
Bouar C.A.R. 77 5.58N 15.35E
Bou Arfa Morocco 74 32.30N 1.59W
Bouaye France 18 47.09N 1.42W
Bouca C.A.R. 77 6.30N 18.21E
Bouches-du-Rhône d. France 21 43.30N 5.00E
Bouchette Canada 105 46.11N 75.59W
Bouchoir France 19 49.45N 2.41E
Boudenib Morocco 74 31.57N 4.38W
Boufarik Algeria 75 36.36N 2.54E
Bougainville i. Pacific Oc. 84 6.00S155.00E
Bougouni Mali 76 11.25N 7.28W
Bouillon Belgium 16 49.48N 5.03E
Bouïra Algeria 75 36.23N 3.54E
Bou-Izakarn Morocco 74 29.09N 9.44W
Boulay-Moselle France 19 49.11N 6.30E
Boulder Australia 89 30.55S121.32E
Boulder U.S.A. 110 40.01N105.17W
Boulder City U.S.A. 109 35.59N114.50W
Boulia Australia 90 22.54S139.54E
Boulogne France 19 50.43N 1.37E
Boulogne r. France 18 46.50N 1.25W
Boulogne-Billancourt France 19 48.50N 2.15E
Boulogne-sur-Gesse France 20 43.18N 0.39E
Boultoum Niger 77 14.45N 10.25E
Boumba r. Cameroon 77 2.00N 15.10E
Boumdeit Mauritania 74 17.26N 9.50W
Boumo Chad 77 9.01N 16.24E
Bouna Ivory Coast 76 9.19N 2.53W
Boundary Peak mtn. U.S.A. 108 37.51N118.21W
Boundiali Ivory Coast 76 9.30N 6.31W
Bountiful U.S.A. 108 40.53N111.53W
Bounty Is. Pacific Oc. 84 48.00S178.30E
Bouraga well Mali 76 19.00N 3.36W
Bourail N. Cal. 84 21.34S165.30E
Bourbon-Lancy France 19 46.38N 3.46E
Bourbonne-les-Bains France 19 47.57N 5.45E
Bourem Mali 76 16.59N 0.20W
Bourg France 21 46.12N 5.13E
Bourganeuf France 20 45.57N 1.46E
Bourges France 19 47.05N 2.24E
Bourget Canada 105 45.26N 75.09W
Bourget, Lac du l. France 21 45.44N 5.52E
Bourg Madame France 20 42.26N 1.55E
Bourgneuf-en-Retz France 18 47.02N 1.57W
Bourgogne d. France 19 47.10N 4.20E
Bourgogne, Canal de France 19 47.58N 3.30E
Bourgoin France 21 45.36N 5.17E
Bourg-St. Andéol France 21 44.22N 4.39E
Bourg-St. Maurice France 21 45.37N 6.46E
Bourgueil France 18 47.17N 0.10E
Bourke Australia 93 30.09S145.59E
Bournemouth U.K. 13 50.43N 1.53W
Bou Saâda Algeria 75 35.12N 4.11E
Bou Salem Tunisia 32 36.36N 8.59E
Boussac France 20 46.21N 2.13E
Bousso Chad 77 10.32N 16.45E
Bouteldja Algeria 32 36.47N 8.13E
Boutilimit Mauritania 74 17.33N 14.42W
Boutonne r. France 20 45.53N 0.50W
Bouvard, C. Australia 89 32.40S115.34E
Bouvetöya i. Atlantic Oc. 127 54.26S 3.24E
Bovalino Marino Italy 33 38.09N 16.11E
Bovec Yugo. 31 46.20N 13.33E
Bovill U.S.A. 108 46.51N116.24W
Bovril Argentina 125 31.22S 59.25W
Bow r. Canada 100 51.10N115.00W
Bowelling Australia 89 33.25S116.27E
Bowen Australia 90 20.00S148.15E
Bowen, Mt. Australia 93 37.11S148.34E
Bowie Ariz. U.S.A. 109 32.19N109.29W
Bowie Tex. U.S.A. 111 33.34N 97.51W
Bow Island town Canada 101 49.52N111.22W
Bowling Green U.S.A. 113 37.00N 86.29W
Bowling Green, C. Australia 90 19.19S146.25E
Bowman U.S.A. 110 46.11N103.24W
Bowman I. Antarctica 128 65.00S104.00E
Bowmanville Canada 104 43.55N 78.41W
Bowral Australia 93 34.30S150.24E
Bowser Australia 93 36.19S146.23E
Boxholm Sweden 43 58.12N 15.03E
Bo Xian China 54 33.50N115.46E
Boxing China 54 37.08N118.05E
Box Tank Australia 92 32.13S142.17E
Boxtel Neth. 16 51.36N 5.20E
Boyabat Turkey 64 41.27N 34.45E
Boyang China 55 28.59N116.42E
Boyanup Australia 89 33.29S115.40E
Boyarka U.S.S.R. 37 50.20N 30.26E
Boyd r. Australia 93 29.51S152.25E
Boykétté C.A.R. 73 5.28N 20.50E
Boyle Rep. of Ire. 15 53.58N 8.19W
Boyne r. Rep. of Ire. 15 53.43N 6.17W
Boyoma Falls f. Zaïre 78 0.18N 25.32E
Boyup Brook Australia 89 33.50S116.22E
Bozburun Turkey 35 36.43N 28.08E
Bozcaada Turkey 34 39.49N 26.03E
Bozca Ada i. Turkey 34 39.49N 26.03E
Bozel France 21 45.27N 6.39E
Bozeman U.S.A. 108 45.41N111.02W
Bozen see Bolzano Italy 30
Bozoum C.A.R. 77 6.16N 16.22E
Bra Italy 30 44.42N 7.51E
Braås Sweden 43 57.04N 15.03E
Brabant d. Belgium 16 50.47N 4.30E
Brač i. Yugo. 29 43.20N 16.38E
Bracadale, Loch U.K. 14 57.22N 6.30W
Bracciano Italy 32 42.06N 12.10E
Bracciano, Lago di l. Italy 30 42.07N 12.14E
Bracebridge Canada 104 45.02N 79.19W
Bracieux France 19 47.33N 1.33E
Bräcke Sweden 40 62.44N 15.30E
Bracki Kanal str. Yugo. 31 43.24N 16.40E
Brad Romania 29 46.06N 22.48E
Bradano r. Italy 33 40.23N 16.51E
Bradenton U.S.A. 113 27.29N 82.33W
Bradford Canada 104 44.07N 79.34W
Bradford U.K. 12 53.47N 1.45W
Bradford N.H. U.S.A. 115 43.17N 71.59W
Bradford Penn. U.S.A. 114 41.58N 78.39W
Bradford Vt. U.S.A. 105 43.59N 72.09W
Bradley U.S.A. 111 33.06N 93.39W
Bradworthy U.K. 13 50.54N 4.22W
Brady U.S.A. 111 31.08N 99.20W
Braemar U.K. 14 57.01N 3.24W
Braga Portugal 26 41.33N 8.26W
Braga d. Portugal 26 41.30N 8.05W
Bragado Argentina 125 35.10S 60.30W
Bragança Brazil 123 1.03S 46.46W
Bragança Portugal 26 41.49N 6.45W
Bragança d. Portugal 26 41.30N 6.50W
Bragança Paulista Brazil 126 22.59S 46.32W
Bragin U.S.S.R. 37 51.49N 30.16E
Brāhmanbāria Bangla. 63 23.59N 91.07E
Brāhmani r. India 63 20.39N 86.46E
Brahmaputra r. Asia 63 23.50N 89.45E
Braidwood Australia 93 35.27S149.50E
Brăila Romania 37 45.18N 27.58E
Brainerd U.S.A. 107 46.20N 94.10W
Braintree U.K. 13 51.53N 0.32E
Brake W. Germany 38 53.19N 8.28E
Brakna d. Mauritania 74 17.00N 13.20W
Brålanda Sweden 43 58.34N 12.22E
Bramming Denmark 42 55.28N 8.42E
Brampton Canada 104 43.41N 79.46W
Brampton U.K. 12 54.56N 2.43W
Bramsche W. Germany 38 52.24N 7.58E
Brancaleone Marina Italy 33 37.58N 16.06E
Branco r. Brazil 122 1.00S 62.00W
Brandberg mtn. Namibia 80 21.08S 14.35E
Brandbu Norway 41 60.28N 10.30E
Brande Denmark 42 55.57N 9.07E
Brandenburg E. Germany 38 52.24N 12.32E
Brandenburg f. E. Germany 38 52.40N 13.00E
Brandfort R.S.A. 80 28.41S 26.27E
Brandon Canada 101 49.50N 99.57W
Brandon U.S.A. 105 43.48N 73.05W
Brandon Mtn. Rep. of Ire. 15 52.14N 10.15W
Brandon Pt. Rep. of Ire. 15 52.17N 10.11W
Braniewo Poland 37 54.24N 19.50E
Bransby Australia 92 28.40S142.00E
Branson U.S.A. 111 36.39N 93.13W
Brantas r. Indonesia 59 7.13S112.45E
Brantford Canada 104 43.08N 80.16W
Brantôme France 20 45.22N 0.39E
Branxholme Australia 92 37.51S141.49E
Bras d'Or L. Canada 103 45.52N 60.50W
Brasher Falls U.S.A. 105 44.48N 74.48W
Brasil, Planalto mts. Brazil 123 17.02S 50.00W
Brasiléia Brazil 122 11.00S 68.44W
Brasília Brazil 123 15.45S 47.57W
Braşov Romania 37 45.40N 25.35E
Brass Nigeria 77 4.20N 6.15E
Brasschaat Belgium 16 51.18N 4.28E
Bratislava Czech. 37 48.10N 17.10E
Bratsk U.S.S.R. 51 56.20N101.15E
Bratsk Vodokhranilishche resr. U.S.S.R. 51 54.40N103.00E
Bratslav U.S.S.R. 37 48.49N 28.51E
Brattleboro U.S.A. 115 42.51N 72.34W
Braunau Austria 39 48.15N 13.02E
Braunschweig W. Germany 38 52.16N 10.31E
Braunton U.K. 13 51.06N 4.09W
Brava Somali Rep. 79 1.02N 44.02E
Bråviken b. Sweden 43 58.38N 16.32E
Bravo del Norte, Rio r. see Rio Grande Mexico 111
Brawley U.S.A. 109 32.59N115.31W
Bray France 19 48.25N 3.14E
Bray Rep. of Ire. 15 53.12N 6.07W
Bray Head Kerry Rep. of Ire. 15 51.53N 10.26W
Brazeau r. Canada 100 52.55N115.15W
Brazil S. America 120 10.00S 52.00W
Brazilian Basin f. Atlantic Oc. 127 15.00S 25.00W
Brazilian Highlands see Brasil, Planalto Brazil 123
Brazos r. U.S.A. 111 28.53N 95.23W
Brazzaville Congo 78 4.14S 15.10E
Brčko Yugo. 31 44.53N 18.48E
Brda r. Poland 37 53.07N 18.08E
Breadalbane f. U.K. 14 56.30N 4.20W
Bream B. New Zealand 86 36.00S174.30E
Brebes Indonesia 59 6.54S109.00E
Brécey France 18 48.44N 1.10W
Brechin U.K. 14 56.44N 2.40W
Breckenridge U.S.A. 104 43.24N 84.29W
Breckenridge U.S.A. 111 32.45N 98.54W
Breckland f. U.K. 13 52.28N 0.40E
Břeclav Czech. 36 48.46N 16.53E
Brecon U.K. 13 51.57N 3.23W
Brecon Beacons mts. U.K. 13 51.53N 3.27W
Breda Neth. 16 51.35N 4.46E
Bredasdorp R.S.A. 80 34.31S 20.03E
Bredbo Australia 93 35.57S149.10E
Bredstedt W. Germany 38 54.37N 8.59E
Breezewood U.S.A. 114 40.01N 78.15W
Bregalnica r. Yugo. 34 41.50N 22.20E
Bregenz Austria 39 47.30N 9.46E
Bregovo Bulgaria 29 44.08N 22.39E
Bréhal France 18 48.54N 1.31W
Breidhafjördhur est. Iceland 40 65.15N 23.00W
Breim Norway 41 61.44N 6.25E
Breisach W. Germany 39 48.01N 7.40E
Brekstad Norway 40 63.42N 9.40E
Bremangerland i. Norway 41 61.51N 5.02E
Bremen U.S.A. 114 39.42N 82.26W
Bremen W. Germany 38 53.05N 8.49E
Bremen d. W. Germany 38 53.08N 8.46E
Bremerhaven W. Germany 38 53.33N 8.34E
Bremer Range mts. Australia 89 32.40S120.55E
Bremerton U.S.A. 108 47.34N122.38W
Bremervörde W. Germany 38 53.29N 9.08E
Brenda Australia 93 29.00S147.12E
Brenes Spain 27 37.33N 5.52W
Brenham U.S.A. 111 30.10N 96.24W
Brenner Pass Austria/Italy 39 47.00N 11.30E
Breno Italy 30 45.57N 10.18E
Brent Canada 104 46.02N 78.29W
Brenta r. Italy 32 45.11N 12.18E
Brentwood U.K. 13 51.38N 0.18E
Brescia Italy 30 45.33N 10.15E

Breskens to Burlington

Breskens Neth. **16** 51.24N 3.34E
Bresle r. France **19** 50.04N 1.22E
Bressanone Italy **30** 46.43N 11.39E
Bressay i. U.K. **14** 60.08N 1.05W
Bresse, Plaine de f. France **19** 46.20N 5.10E
Bressuire France **18** 46.51N 0.30W
Brest Bulgaria **34** 43.38N 24.35E
Brest France **18** 48.24N 4.29W
Brest U.S.S.R. **37** 52.08N 23.40E
Brestanica Yugo. **31** 45.59N 15.29E
Brest-Nantes Canal France **18** 48.13N 3.26W
Bretagne d. France **18** 48.15N 2.30W
Breteuil France **19** 49.38N 2.18E
Breteuil-sur-Iton France **18** 48.50N 0.55E
Breton, Pertuis str. France **20** 46.25N 1.20W
Breton Sd. U.S.A. **111** 29.30N 89.30W
Brett, C. New Zealand **86** 35.15S174.20E
Bretten W. Germany **39** 49.02N 8.42E
Breuil-Cervinia Italy **30** 45.56N 7.38E
Brevik Norway **42** 59.04N 9.42E
Brewarrina Australia **93** 29.57S147.54E
Brewer U.S.A. **112** 44.48N 68.46W
Brewster N.Y. U.S.A. **115** 41.24N 73.37W
Brewster Ohio U.S.A. **114** 40.43N 81.36W
Brewster, Kap c. Greenland **96** 70.00N 25.00W
Brewton U.S.A. **113** 31.07N 87.04W
Brežice Yugo. **31** 45.54N 15.36E
Březnice Czech. **38** 49.33N 13.57E
Breznik Bulgaria **34** 42.44N 22.50E
Brezovo Bulgaria **34** 42.20N 25.06E
Bria C.A.R. **73** 6.32N 21.59E
Briançon France **21** 44.54N 6.39E
Briare France **19** 47.38N 2.44E
Bribbaree Australia **93** 34.07S147.51E
Bribie I. Australia **91** 27.00S153.07E
Brichany U.S.S.R. **37** 48.20N 27.01E
Bricquebec France **18** 49.28N 1.38W
Bride U.K. **12** 54.23N 4.24W
Bridge r. Canada **100** 50.50N122.40W
Bridgen Canada **104** 42.47N 82.16W
Bridgend U.K. **13** 51.30N 3.35W
Bridgeport Calif. U.S.A. **108** 38.10N119.13W
Bridgeport Conn. U.S.A. **115** 41.11N 73.11W
Bridgeport Nebr. U.S.A. **110** 41.40N103.06W
Bridgeport Tex. U.S.A. **111** 33.13N 97.45W
Bridgeport W.Va. U.S.A. **114** 39.17N 80.15W
Bridger U.S.A. **108** 45.18N108.55W
Bridgeton U.S.A. **115** 39.26N 75.14W
Bridgetown Australia **89** 33.57S116.08E
Bridgetown Barbados **117** 13.06N 59.37W
Bridgetown Canada **103** 44.51N 65.18W
Bridgetown Rep. of Ire. **15** 52.14N 6.33W
Bridgeville U.S.A. **115** 38.45N 75.36W
Bridgewater Canada **103** 44.23N 64.31W
Bridgewater U.S.A. **114** 38.18N 78.59W
Bridgewater, C. Australia **92** 38.25S141.28E
Bridgnorth U.K. **13** 52.33N 2.25W
Bridgwater U.K. **13** 51.08N 3.00W
Bridlington U.K. **12** 54.06N 0.11W
Brie d. France **19** 48.40N 3.20E
Briec France **18** 48.06N 4.00W
Brienne-le-Château France **19** 48.24N 4.32E
Brienz Switz. **19** 46.46N 8.03E
Briey France **19** 49.15N 5.56E
Brig Switz. **19** 46.19N 8.00E
Brigantine U.S.A. **115** 39.24N 74.22W
Brigg U.K. **12** 53.33N 0.30W
Briggsdale U.S.A. **110** 40.38N104.20W
Brigham City U.S.A. **108** 41.31N112.01W
Bright Australia **93** 36.42S146.58E
Brighton Canada **105** 44.02N 77.44W
Brighton U.K. **13** 50.50N 0.09W
Brighton Colo. U.S.A. **108** 39.59N104.49W
Brighton Fla. U.S.A. **113** 27.13N 81.06W
Brighton Mich. U.S.A. **104** 42.32N 83.47W
Brighton Downs town Australia **90** 23.20S141.34E
Brignoles France **21** 43.24N 6.04E
Brihuega Spain **26** 40.48N 2.52W
Brikama Gambia **76** 13.15N 16.39W
Brilon W. Germany **38** 51.24N 8.34E
Brindisi Italy **33** 40.38N 17.56E
Brinje Yugo. **31** 45.00N 15.08E
Brinkley U.S.A. **111** 34.53N 91.12W
Brinkworth Australia **92** 33.42S138.24E
Brionne France **18** 49.12N 0.43E
Brioude France **20** 45.18N 3.23E
Briouze France **18** 48.42N 0.22W
Brisbane Australia **93** 27.30S153.00E
Brisighella Italy **30** 44.13N 11.46E
Bristol U.K. **13** 51.26N 2.35W
Bristol Conn. U.S.A. **115** 41.41N 72.57W
Bristol N.H. U.S.A. **115** 43.36N 71.45W
Bristol Penn. U.S.A. **115** 40.06N 74.52W
Bristol R.I. U.S.A. **115** 41.40N 71.16W
Bristol S.Dak. U.S.A. **110** 45.21N 97.45W
Bristol Tenn. U.S.A. **113** 36.33N 82.11W
Bristol Vt. U.S.A. **105** 44.08N 73.05W
Bristol B. U.S.A. **98** 58.00N158.50W
Bristol Channel U.K. **13** 51.17N 3.20W
British Antarctic Territory Antarctica **128** 70.00S 50.00W
British Columbia d. Canada **100** 55.00N125.00W
British Mts. Canada **98** 69.00N140.20W
British Virgin Is. C. America **117** 18.30N 64.30W
Britstown R.S.A. **80** 30.34S 23.30E
Britt Canada **104** 45.46N 80.35W
Britton U.S.A. **110** 45.48N 97.45W
Brive France **20** 45.10N 1.32E
Briviesca Spain **26** 42.33N 3.19W
Brixham U.K. **13** 50.24N 3.31W
Brno Czech. **36** 49.11N 16.39E
Broach India **62** 21.42N 72.58E
Broad Arrow Australia **89** 30.32S121.20E
Broad B. U.K. **14** 58.15N 6.15W
Broadback r. Canada **102** 51.20N 78.50W
Broadford Australia **93** 37.16S145.03E
Broadmere Australia **90** 25.30S149.30E
Broadsound Range mts. Australia **90** 22.30S149.30E
Broadus U.S.A. **108** 45.27N105.25W
Broadview Canada **101** 50.20N102.30W
Broadwater Australia **93** 28.59S 13.16E
Broadway U.K. **13** 52.02N 1.51W
Brochet Canada **101** 57.53N101.40W
Brochet, L. Canada **101** 58.36N101.35W
Brocken mtn. E. Germany **38** 51.50N 10.50E
Brockport U.S.A. **114** 43.13N 77.56W
Brockton U.S.A. **115** 42.05N 71.01W
Brockville Canada **105** 44.35N 75.41W
Brockway Mont. U.S.A. **108** 47.15N105.45W
Brockway Penn. U.S.A. **114** 41.15N 78.47W
Brocton U.S.A. **114** 42.23N 79.27W
Brod Hrvatska Yugo. **31** 45.10N 18.01E
Brod Makedonija Yugo. **34** 41.35N 21.17E
Brodeur Pen. Canada **99** 73.00N 88.00W
Brodick U.K. **14** 55.34N 5.09W
Brodnica Poland **37** 53.16N 19.23E
Brodribb River town Australia **93** 37.42S148.37E
Brody U.S.S.R. **37** 50.05N 25.08E
Broglie France **18** 49.01N 0.32E
Broken Arrow U.S.A. **111** 36.03N 95.48W
Broken B. Australia **93** 33.34S151.18E
Broken Bow U.S.A. **110** 41.24N 99.38W
Broken Hill town Australia **92** 31.57S141.30E
Bromley U.K. **13** 51.24N 0.02E
Bromley Plateau f. Atlantic Oc. **127** 30.00S 34.00W
Bromölla Sweden **43** 56.04N 14.28E
Bromsgrove U.K. **11** 52.20N 2.03W
Bron France **21** 45.44N 4.55E
Brönderslev Denmark **42** 57.16N 9.58E
Brong-Ahafo d. Ghana **76** 7.45N 1.30W
Brönnöysund Norway **40** 65.30N 12.10E
Bronte Canada **104** 43.23N 79.43W
Bronte Italy **33** 37.48N 14.50E
Brookes Inlet Australia **89** 34.55S116.25E
Brooke's Point town Phil. **58** 8.50N117.52E
Brookfield U.S.A. **110** 39.47N 93.04W
Brookhaven U.S.A. **111** 31.35N 90.26W
Brookings Oreg. U.S.A. **108** 42.03N124.17W
Brookings S.Dak. U.S.A. **110** 44.19N 96.48W
Brooklin Canada **104** 43.57N 78.57W
Brooklyn U.S.A. **104** 42.06N 84.15W
Brooklyn Center U.S.A. **110** 45.05N 93.20W
Brooks Canada **98** 50.35N111.53W
Brooks B. Canada **100** 50.15N127.55W
Brooks Range mts. U.S.A. **98** 68.50N152.00W
Brooksville U.S.A. **113** 28.34N 82.24W
Brookton Australia **89** 32.22S117.01E
Brookville U.S.A. **114** 41.09N 79.05W
Broom, Loch U.K. **14** 57.52N 5.07W
Broome Australia **88** 17.58S122.15E
Broome Hill town Australia **89** 33.50S117.35E
Broons France **18** 48.19N 2.16W
Brora U.K. **14** 58.01N 3.52W
Brora r. U.K. **14** 58.00N 3.51W
Brörup Denmark **42** 55.29N 9.01E
Brosna r. Rep.of Ire. **15** 53.13N 7.58W
Brossac France **20** 45.20N 0.03W
Brothers U.S.A. **108** 43.49N120.36W
Broto Spain **25** 42.36N 0.06W
Brou France **18** 48.13N 1.11E
Brough England U.K. **12** 54.32N 2.19W
Brough Scotland U.K. **14** 60.29N 1.12W
Broughton r. Australia **92** 33.21S137.46E
Broughton in Furness U.K. **12** 54.17N 3.12W
Brouwershaven Neth. **16** 51.44N 3.53E
Brovary U.S.S.R. **37** 50.30N 30.45E
Brovst Denmark **42** 57.06N 9.32E
Brown, Mt. Australia **92** 32.33S138.02E
Brown City U.S.A. **114** 43.13N 82.59W
Brownfield U.S.A. **111** 33.11N102.16W
Browning U.S.A. **108** 48.34N113.01W
Brownsburg Canada **105** 45.41N 74.25W
Brownsville Penn. U.S.A. **114** 40.01N 79.53W
Brownsville Tenn. U.S.A. **111** 35.36N 89.15W
Brownsville Tex. U.S.A. **111** 25.54N 97.30W
Brownville U.S.A. **105** 44.01N 75.59W
Brownwood U.S.A. **111** 31.43N 98.59W
Brozas Spain **27** 39.37N 6.46W
Bruay-en-Artois France **19** 50.29N 2.33E
Bruce Mines Canada **104** 46.18N 83.48W
Bruce Pen. Canada **104** 45.00N 81.20W
Bruce Rock town Australia **89** 31.52S118.09E
Bruche r. France **19** 48.31N 7.41E
Bruchsal W. Germany **39** 49.07N 8.35E
Bruck Austria **39** 47.17N 12.49E
Brückenau W. Germany **39** 50.18N 9.47E
Bruges see Brugge Belgium **16**
Brugg Switz. **19** 47.29N 8.12E
Brugge Belgium **16** 51.13N 3.14E
Brühl W. Germany **38** 50.48N 6.54E
Brûlé, Lac l. Canada **105** 46.57N 77.13W
Brûlé, Lac l. Canada **103** 52.17N 63.52W
Brumadinho Brazil **126** 20.09S 44.11W
Brumado Brazil **123** 14.13S 41.40W
Brumath France **19** 48.44N 7.43E
Brunei Asia **58** 4.56N114.58E
Brünen W. Germany **38** 51.43N 6.39E
Brunflo Sweden **40** 63.04N 14.50E
Brunico Italy **30** 46.48N 11.56E
Brunkeberg Norway **42** 59.26N 8.29E
Brunner New Zealand **86** 42.28S171.12E
Brunsbüttel W. Germany **38** 53.54N 9.05E
Brunssum Neth. **16** 50.57N 5.59E
Brunswick Ga. U.S.A. **113** 31.09N 81.30W
Brunswick Maine U.S.A. **112** 43.55N 69.58W
Brunswick Md. U.S.A. **114** 39.18N 77.37W
Brunswick B. Australia **88** 15.05S125.00E
Brunswick Junction Australia **89** 33.15S115.45E
Bruny I. Australia **91** 43.15S147.16E
Brushton U.S.A. **105** 44.51N 74.30W
Brusilovka U.S.S.R. **45** 50.39N 54.59E
Brussel see Bruxelles Belgium **16**
Brussels see Bruxelles Belgium **16**
Bruthen Australia **93** 37.44S147.49E
Bruton U.K. **13** 51.06N 2.28W
Bruxelles Belgium **16** 50.50N 4.23E
Bruyères France **19** 48.12N 6.43E
Bryagovo Bulgaria **34** 41.58N 25.08E
Bryan Ohio U.S.A. **112** 41.30N 84.34W
Bryan Tex. U.S.A. **111** 30.40N 96.22W
Bryan, Mt. Australia **92** 33.26S138.27E
Bryansk U.S.S.R. **44** 53.15N 34.09E
Bryne Norway **42** 58.44N 5.39E
Bryson Canada **105** 45.40N 76.36W
Bryson, Lac l. Canada **105** 46.27N 77.00W
Bryson City U.S.A. **113** 35.26N 83.27W
Brzeg Poland **37** 50.52N 17.27E
Bsharrī Lebanon **66** 34.15N 36.00E
Bua r. Malaŵi **79** 12.42S 34.15E
Bua Yai Thailand **56** 15.34N102.24E
Bu'ayrāt al Ḩasūn Libya **75** 31.24N 15.44E
Buba Guinea Bissau **76** 11.36N 14.55W
Būbiyān, Jazīrat i. Kuwait **71** 29.45N 48.15E
Bubye r. Zimbabwe **80** 22.18S 31.00E
Bucak Turkey **64** 37.28N 30.36E
Bucaramanga Colombia **122** 7.08N 73.10W
Buccino Italy **33** 40.37N 15.23E
Buchach U.S.S.R. **37** 49.09N 25.20E
Buchan Australia **93** 37.30S148.09E
Buchanan Liberia **76** 5.57N 10.02W
Buchanan, L. Australia **90** 21.28S145.52E
Buchanan L. U.S.A. **111** 30.48N 98.25W
Buchan Ness c. U.K. **14** 57.28N 1.47W
Buchans Canada **103** 48.49N 56.52W
Bucharest see Bucureşti Romania **37**
Buchen W. Germany **39** 49.32N 9.17E
Buchloe W. Germany **39** 48.02N 10.44E
Bucholz W. Germany **38** 53.20N 9.52E
Buchs Switz. **39** 47.10N 9.28E
Buchy France **18** 49.35N 1.22E
Buckambool Mt. Australia **93** 31.55S145.40E
Bückeburg W. Germany **38** 52.16N 9.02E
Buckeye Lake town U.S.A. **114** 39.56N 82.29W
Buckhannon U.S.A. **114** 38.59N 80.14W
Buckhaven and Methil U.K. **12** 56.11N 3.03W
Buckhorn Canada **104** 44.33N 78.20W
Buckhorn L. Canada **104** 44.28N 78.23W
Buckie U.K. **14** 57.40N 2.58W
Buckingham Canada **105** 45.35N 75.25W
Buckingham U.K. **13** 52.00N 0.59W
Buckingham B. Australia **90** 12.10S135.46E
Buckinghamshire d. U.K. **13** 51.50N 0.48W
Buckland Tableland f. Australia **90** 25.00S148.00E
Buckleboo Australia **92** 32.55S136.12E
Buckley U.S.A. **110** 40.35N 88.04W
Bucklin U.S.A. **111** 37.33N 99.38W
Buco Zau Angola **78** 4.46S 12.34E
Bucquoy France **19** 50.08N 2.42E
Bu Craa W. Sahara **74** 26.21N 12.57W
Buctouche Canada **103** 46.28N 64.43W
Bucureşti Romania **37** 44.25N 26.06E
Bucyrus U.S.A. **114** 40.48N 82.58W
Bud Norway **40** 62.54N 6.56E
Budapest Hungary **37** 47.30N 19.03E
Budaun India **63** 28.03N 79.07E
Budda Australia **92** 31.12S144.16E
Budd Coast f. Antarctica **128** 67.00S112.00E
Buddh Gaya India **63** 24.42N 84.59E
Buddusò Italy **32** 40.35N 9.16E
Bude U.K. **13** 50.49N 4.33W
Bude B. U.K. **13** 50.50N 4.40W
Budennovsk U.S.S.R. **45** 44.50N 44.10E
Büdingen W. Germany **39** 50.17N 9.07E
Budjala Zaïre **78** 2.38N 19.48E
Buea Cameroon **77** 4.09N 9.13E
Buenaventura Colombia **122** 3.54N 77.02W
Buenaventura Mexico **109** 29.51N107.29W
Buena Vista U.S.A. **113** 37.44N 79.22W
Buendia, Embalse de resr. Spain **26** 40.25N 2.43W
Buenos Aires Argentina **125** 34.40S 58.25W
Buenos Aires d. Argentina **125** 36.30S 59.00W
Buenos Aires, L. Argentina / Chile **125** 46.35S 72.00W
Buffalo Canada **101** 50.49N110.42W
Buffalo r. Canada **100** 60.55N115.00W
Buffalo Mo. U.S.A. **111** 37.39N 93.06W
Buffalo N.Y. U.S.A. **114** 42.54N 78.53W
Buffalo Okla. U.S.A. **111** 36.50N 99.38W
Buffalo S.Dak. U.S.A. **110** 45.35N103.33W
Buffalo W.Va. U.S.A. **114** 38.39N 81.57W
Buffalo Wyo. U.S.A. **108** 44.21N106.42W
Buffalo Head Hills Canada **100** 57.25N115.55W
Buffalo L. Canada **100** 60.10N115.30W
Buffalo Narrows town Canada **101** 55.51N108.30W
Bug r. Poland **37** 52.29N 21.11E
Buga Colombia **122** 3.53N 76.17W
Bugaldie Australia **93** 31.02S149.08E
Bugeat France **20** 45.35N 1.59E
Bugembe Uganda **79** 0.26N 33.16E
Bugene Tanzania **79** 1.34S 31.07E
Buggs Island L. U.S.A. **113** 36.35N 78.28W
Bugojno Yugo. **31** 44.03N 17.27E
Bugrino U.S.S.R. **44** 68.45N 49.15E
Bugt China **53** 48.45N121.58E
Bugulma U.S.S.R. **44** 54.32N 52.46E
Buguma Nigeria **77** 4.43N 6.53E
Buguruslan U.S.S.R. **44** 53.36N 52.30E
Buhera Zimbabwe **81** 19.21S 31.25E
Bühl W. Germany **39** 48.42N 8.08E
Buhuşi Romania **37** 46.43N 26.41E
Builth Wells U.K. **13** 52.09N 3.24W
Buinsk U.S.S.R. **44** 54.58N 48.15E
Buitenpost Neth. **16** 53.15N 6.09E
Bujalance Spain **27** 37.54N 4.22W
Bujaraloz Spain **25** 41.30N 0.09W
Buje Yugo. **31** 45.24N 13.40E
Buji P.N.G. **90** 9.07S142.26E
Bujumbura Burundi **79** 3.22S 29.21E
Bukama Zaïre **78** 9.16S 25.52E
Bukavu Zaïre **79** 2.30S 28.49E
Bukene Tanzania **79** 4.13S 32.52E
Bukhara U.S.S.R. **65** 39.47N 64.26E
Buki U.S.S.R. **37** 49.02N 30.29E
Bukima Tanzania **79** 1.48S 33.25E
Bukittinggi Indonesia **58** 0.18S100.20E
Bukoba Tanzania **79** 1.20S 31.49E
Bukovica f. Yugo. **31** 44.10N 15.40E
Bukrale Ethiopia **73** 4.30N 42.03E
Bukuru Nigeria **77** 9.48N 8.52E
Būl, Kūh-e mtn. Iran **65** 30.48N 52.45E
Bula Indonesia **59** 3.07S130.27E
Bülach Switz. **39** 47.31N 8.32E
Bulan Phil. **59** 12.40N123.53E
Bulandshahr India **63** 28.24N 77.51E
Bulawayo Zimbabwe **80** 20.10S 28.43E
Bulbjerg hill Denmark **42** 57.09N 9.02E
Buldāna India **62** 20.32N 76.11E
Buldern W. Germany **16** 51.52N 7.21E
Bulgan Mongolia **52** 48.34N103.12E
Bulgaria Europe **34** 42.35N 25.30E
Bulhar Somali Rep. **71** 10.23N 44.27E
Bullabulling Australia **89** 31.05S120.52E
Bullaque r. Spain **27** 38.59N 4.17W
Bullara Australia **88** 22.40S114.03E
Bullas Spain **25** 38.03N 1.40W
Bulle Switz. **39** 46.37N 7.04E
Buller r. New Zealand **86** 41.45S171.35E
Buller, Mt. Australia **93** 37.11S146.26E
Bullfinch Australia **89** 30.59S119.06E
Bulli Australia **93** 34.20S150.55E
Bull Mts. U.S.A. **108** 46.05N109.00W
Bulloo r. Australia **92** 28.43S142.27E
Bulloo Downs town Australia **92** 28.30S142.45E
Bull Run Mtn. U.S.A. **114** 38.52N 77.53W
Bull Shoals L. U.S.A. **111** 36.30N 92.50W
Bulo Burti Somali Rep. **71** 3.52N 45.40E
Bulolo P.N.G. **59** 7.13S146.35E
Bulong Australia **89** 30.44S121.48E
Bulsār India **62** 20.30N 72.56E
Bultfontein R.S.A. **80** 28.17S 26.09E
Bulu Indonesia **59** 4.34N126.45E
Bulu, Gunung mtn. Indonesia **58** 3.00N116.00E
Bulun U.S.S.R. **51** 70.50N127.20E
Bulunde Tanzania **79** 4.19S 32.57E
Bumba Bandundu Zaïre **78** 6.55S 19.16E
Bumba Equateur Zaïre **78** 2.15N 22.32E
Bumbuli Zaïre **78** 3.25S 20.30E
Buna Kenya **79** 2.49N 39.27E
Buna P.N.G. **90** 8.40S148.25E
Bunbury Australia **89** 33.20S115.34E
Buncrana Rep. of Ire. **15** 55.08N 7.27W
Bundaberg Australia **90** 24.50S152.21E
Bundaleer Australia **93** 28.39S146.31E
Bundarra Australia **93** 30.11S151.04E
Bunde Nschn. W. Germany **38** 53.11N 7.16E
Bünde Nschn. W. Germany **38** 52.12N 8.35E
Bundella Australia **93** 31.35S149.59E
Būndi India **62** 25.27N 75.39E
Bundoran Rep. of Ire. **15** 54.28N 8.17W
Būndu India **63** 23.11N 85.35E
Bungay U.K. **13** 52.27N 1.26E
Bungo Angola **78** 7.26S 15.23E
Bungo suidō str. Japan **57** 32.52N132.30E
Bungu Tanzania **79** 7.37S 39.07E
Bunguran i. Indonesia **58** 4.00N108.20E
Bunguran Selatan i. Indonesia **58** 3.00N108.50E
Buni Nigeria **77** 11.20N 11.59E
Bunia Zaïre **79** 1.30N 30.10E
Buninyong Australia **92** 37.41S143.58E
Bunker Hill town U.S.A. **114** 39.22N 78.04W
Bunkie U.S.A. **111** 30.57N 92.11W
Buñol Spain **25** 39.25N 0.47W
Bunyala Kenya **71** 0.07N 34.00E
Bunyan Australia **93** 36.11S149.09E
Buol Indonesia **59** 1.12N121.28E
Buqayq Saudi Arabia **65** 25.55N 49.40E
Bura Coast Kenya **79** 3.30S 38.19E
Bura Coast Kenya **79** 1.09S 39.55E
Burakin Australia **89** 30.30S117.08E
Buran Somali Rep. **71** 10.10N 48.48E
Burang China **63** 30.16N 81.11E
Burao Somali Rep. **71** 9.30N 45.30E
Buras U.S.A. **111** 29.21N 89.32W
Buraydah Saudi Arabia **65** 26.20N 43.58E
Burbach W. Germany **38** 50.45N 8.05E
Burcher Australia **93** 33.32S147.18E
Burdur Turkey **23** 37.44N 30.17E
Burdwān India **63** 23.15N 87.51E
Bure Ethiopia **73** 10.40N 37.04E
Büren W. Germany **38** 51.33N 8.33E
Burford Canada **104** 43.06N 80.26W
Burg E. Germany **38** 52.16N 11.51E
Burg W. Germany **38** 54.26N 11.12E
Burgas Bulgaria **29** 42.30N 27.29E
Bur Gavo Somali Rep. **73** 1.10S 41.50E
Burgdorf Switz. **39** 47.04N 7.37E
Burgenland d. Austria **36** 47.30N 16.20E
Burgeo Canada **103** 47.36N 57.34W
Burgess Hill U.K. **13** 50.57N 0.07W
Burghausen W. Germany **39** 48.09N 12.49E
Burglengenfeld W. Germany **39** 49.13N 12.03E
Burgos Spain **26** 42.21N 3.42W
Burgos d. Spain **26** 42.25N 3.40W
Burgstädt E. Germany **38** 50.55N 12.49E
Burgsteinfurt W. Germany **38** 52.08N 7.20E
Burgsvik Sweden **43** 57.03N 18.16E
Bur Hakkaba Somali Rep. **79** 2.43N 44.10E
Burhānpur India **62** 21.18N 76.14E
Buri Brazil **126** 23.46S 48.39W
Burias i. Phil. **59** 12.50N123.10E
Burica, Punta c. Panama **117** 8.05N 82.50W
Burin Pen. Canada **103** 47.00N 55.40W
Buriram Thailand **56** 14.59N103.08E
Burjasot Spain **25** 39.31N 0.25W
Burkburnett U.S.A. **111** 34.06N 98.34W
Burke r. Australia **90** 23.12S139.33E
Burketown Australia **90** 17.44S139.22E
Burk's Falls Canada **104** 45.37N 79.25W
Burleigh Falls Canada **104** 44.34N 78.11W
Burley U.S.A. **108** 42.32N113.48W
Burlington Canada **104** 43.19N 79.47W
Burlington Iowa U.S.A. **110** 40.49N 91.14W
Burlington Kans. U.S.A. **110** 38.12N 95.45W

Burlington to Canastota

Burlington N.C. U.S.A. 113 36.05N 79.27W
Burlington N.J. U.S.A. 115 40.04N 74.49W
Burlington Vt. U.S.A. 105 44.29N 73.13W
Burlington Wisc. U.S.A. 110 42.41N 88.17W
Burma Asia 56 21.45N 97.00E
Burngup Australia 89 33.00S118.39E
Burnham-on-Crouch U.K. 13 51.37N 0.50E
Burnham-on-Sea U.K. 13 51.15N 3.00W
Burnie Australia 91 41.03S145.55E
Burnley U.K. 12 53.47N 2.15W
Burns Australia 92 32.10S141.03E
Burns Oreg. U.S.A. 108 43.35N119.03W
Burns Wyo. U.S.A. 108 41.11N104.21W
Burnside r. Canada 98 66.51N108.04W
Burns Lake town Canada 100 54.20N125.45W
Burnsville U.S.A. 114 38.51N 80.40W
Burqā Jordan 67 32.18N 35.12E
Burqin Jordan 67 32.27N 35.16E
Burra Australia 92 33.40S138.57E
Burracoppin Australia 89 31.22S118.30E
Burrel Albania 34 41.36N 20.01E
Burren Junction Australia 93 30.08S148.59E
Burrewarra Pt. Australia 93 35.56S150.12E
Burriana Spain 25 39.53N 0.05W
Burrinjuck Australia 93 35.01S148.33E
Burrinjuck Resr. Australia 93 35.00S148.40E
Burro, Serranías del mts. Mexico 111 29.20N102.00W
Burrundie Australia 88 13.32S131.40E
Burry Port U.K. 13 51.41N 4.17W
Bursa Turkey 29 40.11N 29.04E
Būr Safājah Egypt 64 26.44N 33.56E
Būr Sa'īd Egypt 66 31.17N 32.18E
Būr Sūdān Sudan 72 19.39N 37.01E
Burta Australia 92 32.30S141.05E
Būr Tawfīq Egypt 66 29.57N 32.34E
Burt L. U.S.A. 104 45.27N 84.40W
Burton upon Trent U.K. 12 52.58N 1.39W
Burtundy Australia 92 33.45S142.22E
Buru i. Indonesia 59 3.30S126.30E
Burullus, Buḩayrat al l. Egypt 66 31.30N 30.45E
Burundi Africa 79 3.00S 30.00E
Bururi Burundi 79 3.58S 29.35E
Burutu Nigeria 77 5.20N 5.31E
Burwash Canada 104 46.19N 80.48W
Bury G.M. U.K. 12 53.36N 2.19W
Bury St. Edmunds U.K. 13 52.15N 0.42E
Burzil Jammu & Kashmir 62 34.52N 75.07E
Burzil Pass Jammu & Kashmir 62 34.54N 75.06E
Busalla Italy 30 44.34N 8.57E
Busambra, Rocca mtn. Italy 32 37.51N 13.24E
Busca Italy 30 44.31N 7.29E
Būsh Egypt 66 29.09N 31.07E
Būshehr Iran 65 28.57N 50.52E
Bushkill U.S.A. 115 41.06N 75.00W
Bushmanland f. R.S.A. 80 29.25S 19.40E
Busi Ethiopia 71 5.30N 44.30E
Busigny France 19 50.02N 3.28E
Businga Zaïre 78 3.16N 20.55E
Busira r. Zaïre 78 0.05N 18.18E
Buskerud Norway 41 60.20N 9.00E
Buskerud d. Norway 42 60.07N 9.45E
Buşrá al Ḩarīrī Syria 67 32.50N 36.20E
Buşrá ash Shām Syria 66 32.30N 36.29E
Busselton Australia 89 33.43S115.15E
Bussum Neth. 16 52.17N 5.10E
Bustard Head c. Australia 90 24.02S151.48E
Busto Arsizio Italy 30 45.37N 8.51E
Busu Djanoa Zaïre 78 1.42N 21.23E
Büsum W. Germany 38 54.08N 8.51E
Buta Zaïre 78 2.50N 24.50E
Butan Bulgaria 34 43.39N 23.45E
Butari Rwanda 79 2.38S 29.43E
Buţayḩah Syria 67 32.56N 35.53E
Bute Australia 92 33.24S138.01E
Bute i. U.K. 14 55.51N 5.07W
Bute, Sd. of U.K. 14 55.44N 5.10W
Butedale Canada 100 53.12N128.45W
Butera Italy 33 37.11N 14.11E
Buthroton site Albania 34 39.46N 20.00E
Butiaba Uganda 79 1.48N 31.15E
Butler Mo. U.S.A. 111 38.16N 94.20W
Butler N.J. U.S.A. 115 41.00N 74.21W
Butler Penn. U.S.A. 114 40.52N 79.54W
Butman U.S.A. 104 44.09N 84.34W
Butte Mont. U.S.A. 108 46.00N112.32W
Butte Nebr. U.S.A. 110 42.58N 98.51W
Butterworth Malaysia 58 5.24N100.22E
Buttevant Rep. of Ire. 15 52.14N 8.41W
Butt of Lewis c. U.K. 14 58.31N 6.15W
Butty Head Australia 89 33.52S121.35E
Butuan Phil. 59 8.56N125.31E
Butung i. Indonesia 59 5.00S122.50E
Butwal Nepal 63 27.42N 83.28E
Butzbach W. Germany 39 50.26N 8.40E
Bützow E. Germany 38 53.50N 11.59E
Buxtehude W. Germany 38 53.28N 9.41E
Buxton U.K. 12 53.16N 1.54W
Buxy France 19 46.43N 4.41E
Buy U.S.S.R. 44 58.23N 41.27E
Buyaga U.S.S.R. 51 59.42N126.59E
Buynaksk U.S.S.R. 45 42.48N 47.07E
Büyük Turkey 34 41.02N 26.35E
Büyük Menderes r. Turkey 35 37.28N 27.10E
Buzachi, Poluostrov pen. U.S.S.R. 45 45.00N 51.55E
Buzançais France 18 46.53N 1.25E
Buzancy France 19 49.25N 4.57E
Buzău Romania 37 45.10N 26.49E
Buzău r. Romania 37 45.24N 27.48E
Buzaymah Libya 75 24.55N 22.02E
Buzi r. Mozambique 81 19.52S 34.00E
Buzuluk U.S.S.R. 44 52.49N 52.19E
Buzzards B. U.S.A. 115 41.33N 70.47W
Bwasiaia P.N.G. 90 10.06S150.48E
Byala Bulgaria 34 43.28N 25.44E
Byala Slatina Bulgaria 34 43.26N 23.55E
Byam Martin I. Canada 98 75.15N104.00W
Bydgoszcz Poland 37 53.16N 17.33E
Byemoor Canada 100 52.00N112.17W
Byesville U.S.A. 114 39.58N 81.32W
Bygland Norway 42 58.50N 7.49E
Byglandsfjord town Norway 42 58.51N 7.48E
Byglandsfjorden l. Norway 42 58.48N 7.50E
Byhalia U.S.A. 111 34.52N 89.41W
Bykhov U.S.S.R. 37 53.30N 30.15E
Bykle Norway 42 59.21N 7.20E
Bylot I. Canada 99 73.00N 78.30W
Byng Inlet Canada 104 45.46N 80.33W
Byrd, Lac l. Canada 105 47.01N 76.56W
Byrd Land f. Antarctica 128 79.30S125.00W
Byrock Australia 93 30.40S146.25E
Byron, C. Australia 93 28.37S153.40E
Byron Bay town Australia 93 28.43S153.34E
Byrranga, Gory mts. U.S.S.R. 51 74.50N101.00E
Byske Sweden 40 64.57N 21.12E
Byske r. Sweden 40 64.57N 21.13E
Byten U.S.S.R. 37 52.50N 25.28E
Bytom Poland 37 50.22N 18.54E
Byxelkrok Sweden 43 57.20N 17.00E
Bzipi U.S.S.R. 45 43.15N 40.24E

C

Ca r. Vietnam 55 18.47N105.40E
Caballería, Cabo de c. Spain 25 40.05N 4.05E
Caballos Mesteños, Llano de los f. Mexico 111 28.15N104.00W
Cabanatuan Phil. 59 15.30N120.58E
Cabeza del Buey Spain 26 38.43N 5.13W
Cabimas Venezuela 122 10.26N 71.27W
Cabinda Angola 78 5.34S 12.12E
Cabinet Mts. U.S.A. 108 48.08N115.46W
Cabo Delgado d. Mozambique 79 12.30S 39.00E
Cabo Frio town Brazil 126 22.51S 42.03W
Cabonga, Résr. Canada 105 47.20N 76.35W
Cabool U.S.A. 111 37.07N 92.06W
Caboolture Australia 91 27.05S152.57E
Cabo Pantoja Peru 122 1.00S 75.10W
Cabora Bassa Dam Mozambique 79 15.36S 32.41E
Cabot, Mt. U.S.A. 105 44.31N 71.24W
Cabot Head c. Canada 104 45.14N 81.17W
Cabot Str. Canada 103 47.20N 59.30W
Cabra Spain 27 37.28N 4.27W
Cabras Italy 32 39.56N 8.32E
Cabrera i. Spain 25 39.09N 2.56E
Cabrera r. Spain 26 42.25N 6.49W
Cabrera, Sierra mts. Spain 26 42.10N 6.45W
Cabri Canada 101 50.37N108.28W
Cabriel r. Spain 25 39.14N 1.03W
Cabruta Venezuela 122 7.40N 66.16W
Čačak Yugo. 34 43.53N 20.21E
Caçapava Brazil 126 23.05S 45.40W
Caccamo Italy 32 37.56N 13.40E
Caccia, Capo c. Italy 32 40.34N 8.09E
Cáceres Brazil 123 16.05S 57.40W
Cáceres Spain 27 39.29N 6.22W
Cáceres d. Spain 27 39.40N 6.20W
Cacharí Argentina 125 36.23S 59.29W
Cache Bay town Canada 104 46.23N 80.00W
Cachimo r. Zaïre 78 7.02S 21.13E
Cachoeira Brazil 123 12.35S 38.59W
Cachoeira do Sul Brazil 126 30.03S 52.52W
Cachoeiro de Itapemirim Brazil 126 20.51S 41.07W
Cacín r. Spain 27 37.13N 4.00W
Cacine Guinea 76 11.08N 14.57W
Cacolo Angola 78 10.09S 19.15E
Caconda Angola 78 13.46S 15.06E
Cacuso Angola 78 9.26S 15.43E
Cadaqués Spain 25 42.17N 3.17E
Čadca Czech. 37 49.26N 18.48E
Cader Idris mtn. U.K. 13 52.40N 3.55W
Cadí, Sierra del mts. Spain 25 42.17N 1.42E
Cadibarrawirracanna, L. Australia 92 28.52S135.27E
Cadillac France 20 44.38N 0.19W
Cadillac U.S.A. 112 44.15N 85.23W
Cadiz Phil. 59 10.57N123.18E
Cádiz Spain 27 36.32N 6.18W
Cádiz d. Spain 27 36.40N 5.50W
Cadiz U.S.A. 114 40.16N 81.00W
Cádiz, Golfo de g. Spain 27 37.00N 7.00W
Cadomin Canada 100 53.02N117.20W
Cadoux Australia 89 30.47S117.05E
Caen France 18 49.11N 0.21W
Caernarfon U.K. 12 53.08N 4.17W
Caernarfon B. U.K. 12 53.05N 4.25W
Caerphilly U.K. 13 51.34N 3.13W
Caesarea see Horbat Qesari Israel 67
Caeté Brazil 126 19.54S 43.37W
Cafima Angola 78 16.34S 16.30E
Cafu Angola 78 16.30S 15.14E
Cagayan de Oro Phil. 59 8.29N124.40E
Cagli Italy 30 43.33N 12.39E
Cagliari Italy 32 39.13N 9.06E
Cagliari, Golfo di g. Italy 32 39.05N 9.10E
Cagnes France 21 43.40N 7.09E
Caguán r. Colombia 122 0.08S 74.18W
Caguas Puerto Rico 117 18.08N 66.00W
Cahama Angola 78 16.16S 14.23E
Caha Mts. Rep. of Ire. 15 51.44N 9.45W
Cahelli Italy 30 44.43N 8.17E
Caherciveen Rep. of Ire. 15 51.51N 10.14W
Cahir Rep. of Ire. 15 52.23N 7.56W
Cahore Pt. Rep. of Ire. 15 52.34N 6.12W
Cahors France 20 44.27N 1.26E
Cahuapanas Peru 122 5.15S 77.00W
Caia r. Portugal 27 38.50N 7.05W
Caianda Angola 78 11.02S 23.29E
Caibarién Cuba 117 22.31N 79.28W
Caicó Brazil 123 6.25S 37.04W
Caicos Is. C. America 97 21.30N 72.00W
Caicos Is. Turks & Caicos Is. 117 21.30N 72.00W
Caird Coast f. Antarctica 128 75.00S 20.00W
Cairngorms mts. U.K. 14 57.04N 3.30W
Cairns Australia 90 16.51S145.43E
Cairo see Al Qāhirah Egypt 66
Cairo Ill. U.S.A. 111 37.01N 89.09W
Cairo N.Y. U.S.A. 115 42.18N 74.00W
Cairo W.Va. U.S.A. 114 39.13N 81.09W
Cairo Montenotte Italy 30 44.24N 8.16E
Caiundo Angola 78 15.43S 17.30E
Caiwarro Australia 93 28.38S144.45E
Caizhai China 54 37.20N118.10E
Caizi Hu l. China 55 30.50N117.06E
Cajamarca Peru 122 7.09S 78.32W
Cajarc France 20 44.29N 1.50E
Cajàzeiras Brazil 123 6.52S 38.31W
Čajniče Yugo. 31 43.33N 19.04E
Cajuru Brazil 126 21.15S 47.18W
Čakovec Yugo. 31 46.23N 16.26E
Cala, Embalse de resr. Spain 27 37.45N 6.05W
Calabar Nigeria 77 4.56N 8.22E
Calabogie Canada 105 45.18N 76.43W
Calabozo Venezuela 122 8.58N 67.28W
Calabria d. Italy 33 39.25N 16.30E
Calacuccia France 21 42.20N 9.03E
Calafat Romania 34 43.58N 22.59E
Calafate Argentina 125 50.20S 72.16W
Calahorra Spain 26 42.18N 1.59W
Calais France 19 50.57N 1.50E
Calama Brazil 122 8.03S 62.53W
Calama Chile 121 22.30S 68.55W
Calamar Colombia 122 10.15N 74.55W
Calamian Group is. Phil. 59 12.00N120.05E
Cala Millor Spain 25 39.35N 3.22E
Calamocha Spain 25 40.55N 1.18W
Calañas Spain 27 37.39N 6.53W
Calanda Spain 25 40.56N 0.14W
Calangianus Italy 32 40.56N 9.12E
Calapan Phil. 59 13.23N121.10E
Călăraşi Romania 37 44.11N 27.21E
Calatafimi Italy 32 37.55N 12.52E
Calatayud Spain 25 41.21N 1.38W
Calatrava Equat. Guinea 78 1.09N 9.24E
Calau E. Germany 38 51.45N 13.56E
Calayan i. Phil. 55 19.20N121.25E
Calbayog Phil. 59 12.04N124.58E
Calbe E. Germany 38 51.54N 11.46E
Calcutta India 63 22.32N 88.22E
Caldaro Italy 30 46.25N 11.14E
Caldas Colombia 122 6.05N 75.36W
Caldas da Rainha Portugal 27 39.24N 9.08W
Caldas de Reyes Spain 26 42.36N 8.38W
Caldeirão, Serra do mts. Portugal 27 37.25N 8.10W
Caldera Chile 124 27.04S 70.50W
Caldwell Idaho U.S.A. 108 43.40N116.41W
Caldwell Ohio U.S.A. 114 39.45N 81.31W
Caledon r. R.S.A. 80 30.27S 26.12E
Caledon B. Australia 90 12.58S136.52E
Caledonia Canada 104 43.04N 79.56W
Caledonia U.S.A. 114 42.58N 77.51W
Caledonia Hills Canada 103 45.40N 65.00W
Calella Spain 25 41.37N 2.40E
Calexico Mexico 109 32.40N115.30W
Calf of Man i. U.K. 12 54.03N 4.49W
Calgary Canada 100 51.00N114.10W
Cali Colombia 122 3.24N 76.30W
Calicut India 60 11.15N 75.45E
Caliente U.S.A. 108 37.37N114.31W
California d. U.S.A. 108 37.29N119.58W
California, G. of see California, Golfo de Mexico 116
California, Golfo de g. Mexico 109 28.00N112.00W
Calingasta Argentina 124 31.15S 69.30W
Calingiri Australia 89 31.07S116.27E
Calitri Italy 33 40.54N 15.27E
Callabonna r. Australia 92 29.37S140.08E
Callabonna, L. Australia 92 29.47S140.07E
Callac France 18 48.25N 3.26W
Callander Canada 104 46.13N 79.23W
Callander U.K. 14 56.15N 4.13W
Callao Peru 124 12.05S 77.08W
Callicoon U.S.A. 115 41.46N 75.03W
Callosa de Ensarriá Spain 25 38.39N 0.07W
Callosa de Segura Spain 25 38.08N 0.52W
Caloocan Phil. 59 14.38N120.58E
Caltagirone Italy 33 37.14N 14.31E
Caltanissetta Italy 33 37.29N 14.04E
Caluire-et-Cuire France 21 45.48N 4.51E
Calulo Angola 78 10.05S 14.56E
Calumbo Angola 78 9.08S 13.24E
Calumet Canada 105 45.39N 74.41W
Calundau Angola 78 12.05S 19.10E
Calvados d. France 18 49.10N 0.30W
Calvert I. Canada 100 51.30N128.00W
Calverton U.S.A. 114 39.03N 76.56W
Calvi France 21 42.34N 8.45E
Calvinia R.S.A. 80 31.29S 19.44E
Calvo, Monte mtn. Italy 33 41.44N 15.46E
Calw W. Germany 39 48.43N 8.44E
Cam r. U.K. 13 52.34N 0.21E
Camabatela Angola 78 8.20S 15.29E
Camacupa Angola 78 12.01S 17.22E
Camagüey Cuba 117 21.25N 77.55W
Camagüey, Archipiélago de Cuba 117 22.30N 78.00W
Camaiore Italy 30 43.56N 10.18E
Camarat, Cap c. France 21 43.12N 6.41E
Camarès France 20 43.49N 2.53E
Camaret-sur-Mer France 18 48.16N 4.37W
Camargue d. France 21 43.20N 4.38E
Camariñas Spain 26 43.08N 9.12W
Camarón, C. Honduras 117 15.59N 85.00W
Camaronero, Laguna l. Mexico 109 23.00N106.07W
Camarones Argentina 125 44.45S 65.40W
Camas Spain 27 37.24N 6.02W
Camas U.S.A. 108 45.35N122.24W
Cambados Spain 26 42.30N 8.48W
Cambay India 62 22.18N 72.37E
Camberg W. Germany 39 50.18N 8.16E
Camberley U.K. 13 51.21N 0.45W
Camborne U.K. 13 50.12N 5.19W
Cambrai France 19 50.10N 3.14E
Cambria U.S.A. 109 35.34N121.05W
Cambrian Mts. U.K. 13 52.33N 3.33W
Cambridge Canada 114 43.22N 80.19W
Cambridge New Zealand 86 37.53S175.29E
Cambridge U.K. 13 52.13N 0.08E
Cambridge Idaho U.S.A. 108 44.34N116.41W
Cambridge Mass. U.S.A. 115 42.22N 71.06W
Cambridge Md. U.S.A. 115 38.34N 76.04W
Cambridge Minn. U.S.A. 110 45.31N 93.14W
Cambridge N.Y. U.S.A. 115 43.02N 73.23W
Cambridge Ohio U.S.A. 114 40.02N 81.35W
Cambridge Bay town Canada 98 69.09N105.00W
Cambridge G. Australia 88 15.00S128.05E
Cambridgeshire d. U.K. 13 52.15N 0.05E
Cambridge Springs town U.S.A. 114 41.48N 80.04W
Cambrils Spain 25 41.04N 1.03E
Camden U.K. 13 51.33N 0.10W
Camden Ark. U.S.A. 111 33.35N 92.50W
Camden N.J. U.S.A. 115 39.57N 75.07W
Camden N.Y. U.S.A. 115 43.20N 75.45W
Camden S.C. U.S.A. 113 34.16N 80.36W
Camden Haven b. Australia 93 31.40S152.49E
Cameia Nat. Park Angola 78 12.00S 21.30E
Camelford U.K. 13 50.37N 4.41W
Camerino Italy 30 43.08N 13.04E
Cameron Canada 104 44.27N 78.46W
Cameron Ariz. U.S.A. 109 35.51N111.25W
Cameron La. U.S.A. 111 29.48N 93.19W
Cameron Mo. U.S.A. 110 39.44N 94.14W
Cameron Tex. U.S.A. 111 30.51N 96.59W
Cameron W.Va. U.S.A. 114 39.50N 80.34W
Cameron Hills Canada 100 59.48N118.00W
Cameron Mts. New Zealand 86 45.50S167.00E
Cameroon Africa 77 6.00N 12.30E
Camerota Italy 33 40.02N 15.23E
Cameroun, Mont mtn. Cameroon 77 4.20N 9.05E
Cametá Brazil 123 2.12S 49.30W
Caminha Portugal 26 41.52N 8.50W
Camiri Bolivia 124 20.03S 63.31W
Camocim Brazil 123 2.55S 40.50W
Camooweal Australia 90 19.55S138.07E
Camopi Guiana 123 3.12N 52.15W
Campagna Italy 33 40.40N 15.08E
Campana Argentina 125 34.10S 58.57W
Campana, Isla i. Chile 125 48.25S 75.20W
Campanario Spain 26 38.52N 5.37W
Campania d. Italy 33 40.50N 14.50E
Campbell U.S.A. 114 41.05N 80.37W
Campbell, C. New Zealand 86 41.45S174.15E
Campbellford Canada 105 44.18N 77.48W
Campbell I. Pacific Oc. 84 52.30S169.02E
Campbellpore Pakistan 62 33.46N 72.22E
Campbell River town Canada 100 50.05N125.20W
Campbells Bay town Canada 105 45.44N 76.36W
Campbellsville U.S.A. 113 37.20N 85.21W
Campbellton Canada 103 48.00N 66.40W
Campbelltown Australia 93 34.04S150.49E
Campbeltown U.K. 14 55.25N 5.36W
Camp Borden Canada 104 44.18N 79.52W
Campeche Mexico 116 19.50N 90.30W
Campeche d. Mexico 116 19.00N 90.00W
Campeche, Bahía de b. Mexico 116 19.30N 94.00W
Campeche B. see Campeche, Bahía de Mexico 116
Camperdown Australia 92 38.15S143.14E
Cam Pha Vietnam 56 21.07N107.19E
Campiglia Marittima Italy 30 43.03N 10.37E
Campillo de Llerena Spain 26 38.30N 5.50W
Campillos Spain 27 37.03N 4.51W
Campina Grande Brazil 123 7.15S 35.50W
Campinas Brazil 126 22.54S 47.06W
Campo Cameroon 77 2.22N 9.50E
Campo r. Cameroon 78 2.21N 9.51E
Campo U.S.A. 111 37.06N102.35W
Campobasso Italy 33 41.34N 14.39E
Campobello di Mazara Italy 32 37.38N 12.45E
Campo Belo Brazil 126 20.52S 45.16W
Campo de Criptana Spain 27 39.24N 3.07W
Campo Gallo Argentina 124 26.35S 62.50W
Campo Grande Brazil 124 20.24S 54.35W
Campo Maior Brazil 123 4.50S 42.12W
Campo Maior Portugal 27 39.01N 7.04W
Campos Brazil 126 21.45S 41.18W
Campos Belos Brazil 123 13.09S 47.03W
Campos do Jordão Brazil 126 23.28S 46.10W
Campo Tures Italy 30 46.55N 11.57E
Campton U.S.A. 105 43.53N 71.38W
Camp Wood U.S.A. 111 29.40N100.01W
Cam Ranh Vietnam 56 11.54N109.14E
Camrose Canada 100 53.00N112.50W
Canaan Conn. U.S.A. 115 42.02N 73.20W
Canaan Vt. U.S.A. 105 45.00N 71.32W
Canada N. America 98 60.00N105.00W
Cañada de Gómez Argentina 124 32.49S 61.25W
Canadian U.S.A. 111 35.55N100.23W
Canadian r. U.S.A. 111 35.27N 95.03W
Canadian Shield f. Canada 96 50.00N 82.00W
Canajoharie U.S.A. 115 42.56N 74.38W
Çanakkale Turkey 34 40.09N 26.24E
Çanakkale Boğazi str. Turkey 34 40.15N 26.25E
Canal du Midi France 17 43.18N 2.00E
Canal Fulton U.S.A. 114 40.54N 81.36W
Canandaigua U.S.A. 114 42.54N 77.17W
Canandaigua L. U.S.A. 114 42.49N 77.16W
Cananea Mexico 109 30.57N110.18W
Canarias, Islas is. Atlantic Oc. 74 28.00N 15.00W
Canary Is. see Canarias, Islas Atlantic Oc. 74
Caneseraga U.S.A. 114 42.45N 77.50W
Canastota U.S.A. 115 43.10N 75.45W

Cauca to Chemainus

Cauca *r.* Colombia **122** 8.57N 74.30W
Caucasus Mts. *see* Kavkazskiy Khrebet U.S.S.R. **45**
Caudry France **19** 50.07N 3.25E
Caulonia Italy **33** 38.23N 16.25E
Caungula Angola **78** 8.26S 18.35E
Cauquenes Chile **125** 35.58S 72.21W
Caura *r.* Venezuela **122** 7.38N 64.53W
Caussade France **20** 44.10N 1.32E
Causse du Larzac *f.* France **20** 44.00N 3.15E
Causse Méjean *f.* France **20** 44.15N 3.30E
Cava Italy **33** 40.42N 14.42E
Cávado *r.* Portugal **26** 41.32N 8.48W
Cavaillon France **21** 43.50N 5.02E
Cavalaire-sur-Mer France **21** 43.10N 6.32E
Cavalese Italy **30** 46.17N 11.27E
Cavalier U.S.A. **110** 48.48N 97.37W
Cavally *r.* Ivory Coast **76** 4.25N 7.39W
Cavan Rep. of Ire. **15** 54.00N 7.22W
Cavan *d.* Rep. of Ire. **15** 53.58N 7.10W
Cavarzere Italy **30** 45.08N 12.05E
Caviana, Ilha *i.* Brazil **123** 0.02N 50.00W
Cavite Phil. **59** 14.30N120.54E
Cavtat Yugo. **31** 42.35N 18.13E
Cawndilla L. Australia **92** 32.30S142.18E
Caxambu Brazil **126** 21.59S 44.54W
Caxias Brazil **123** 4.53S 43.20W
Caxias do Sul Brazil **126** 29.14S 51.10W
Caxito Angola **78** 8.32S 13.38E
Cayambe Ecuador **122** 0.03N 78.08W
Cayenne Guiana **123** 4.55N 52.18W
Caylus France **20** 44.14N 1.46E
Cayman Brac *i.* Cayman Is. **117** 19.44N 79.48W
Cayman Is. C. America **117** 19.00N 81.00W
Cayman Trough Carib. Sea **127** 18.00N 8.00W
Cayuga Canada **104** 42.56N 79.51W
Cayuga L. U.S.A. **115** 42.55N 76.44W
Cazalla de la Sierra Spain **27** 37.56N 5.45W
Cazaux, Étang de *b.* France **20** 44.30N 1.10W
Cazenovia U.S.A. **115** 42.56N 75.51W
Cazères France **20** 43.13N 1.05E
Čazma Yugo. **31** 45.45N 16.37E
Cazombo Angola **78** 11.54S 22.56E
Cazorla Spain **27** 37.55N 3.00W
Cea *r.* Spain **26** 42.00N 5.36W
Ceara *d.* Brazil **123** 4.50S 39.00W
Ceba Canada **101** 53.07N102.14W
Ceballos Mexico **111** 26.32N104.09W
Cebollera, Sierra de *mts.* Spain **26** 41.55N 2.30W
Cebreros Spain **26** 40.27N 4.28W
Cebu Phil. **59** 10.17N123.56E
Cebu *i.* Phil. **59** 10.15N123.45E
Ceccano Italy **32** 41.34N 13.20E
Cecina Italy **30** 43.19N 10.31E
Cecita, Lago di *l.* Italy **33** 39.24N 16.30E
Cedar City U.S.A. **108** 37.41N113.04W
Cedar City U.S.A. **106** 37.40N113.04W
Cedar Falls *town* U.S.A. **110** 42.32N 92.27W
Cedar Grove U.S.A. **114** 38.13N 81.26W
Cedar Key U.S.A. **113** 29.08N 83.03W
Cedar L. Canada **104** 46.02N 78.30W
Cedar L. Canada **101** 53.20N100.00W
Cedar Rapids *town* U.S.A. **110** 41.59N 91.40W
Cedarville U.S.A. **115** 39.20N 75.12W
Cedeira Spain **26** 43.39N 8.03W
Cedillo, Embalse de *resr.* Spain / Portugal **27** 39.40N 7.25W
Cedrino *r.* Italy **32** 40.23N 9.44E
Cedrón *r.* Spain **27** 39.57N 3.51W
Cedros, Isla *i.* Mexico **109** 28.10N115.15W
Ceduna Australia **92** 32.07S133.42E
Ceepeecee Canada **100** 49.52N126.42W
Cefalù Italy **33** 38.02N 14.01E
Cega *r.* Spain **26** 41.33N 4.46W
Cegléd Hungary **37** 47.10N 19.48E
Ceglie Italy **33** 40.39N 17.31E
Cehegín Spain **25** 38.06N 1.48W
Cela Angola **78** 11.26S 15.05E
Celano Italy **31** 42.05N 13.33E
Celanova Spain **26** 42.09N 7.58W
Celaya Mexico **116** 20.32N100.48W
Celebes *i. see* Sulawesi Indonesia **59**
Celebes Sea Indonesia **59** 3.00N122.00E
Celina U.S.A. **112** 40.34N 84.35W
Celje Yugo. **31** 46.14N 15.16E
Celle W. Germany **38** 52.37N 10.05E
Celorico da Beira Portugal **26** 40.38N 7.23W
Cemaes Head U.K. **13** 52.08N 4.42W
Ceno Italy **30** 44.41N 10.05E
Centerburg U.S.A. **114** 40.18N 82.42W
Center Cross U.S.A. **113** 37.48N 76.48W
Centerville Iowa U.S.A. **110** 40.43N 92.52W
Centerville S.Dak. U.S.A. **110** 43.07N 96.58W
Centerville Tenn. U.S.A. **113** 35.45N 87.29W
Cento Italy **30** 44.43N 11.17E
Central *d.* Ghana **76** 5.30N 1.10W
Central *d.* Kenya **79** 0.30S 37.00E
Central *d.* U.K. **14** 56.10N 4.20W
Central *d.* Zambia **80** 14.30S 29.30E
Central, Cordillera *mts.* Bolivia **124** 18.30S 65.00W
Central, Cordillera *mts.* Colombia **120** 6.00N 75.00W
Central African Republic Africa **70** 7.00N 20.00E
Central Auckland *d.* New Zealand **86** 36.45S174.45E
Central Brāhui Range *mts.* Pakistan **62** 29.15N 67.15E
Central City Ky. U.S.A. **113** 37.17N 87.08W
Central City Nebr. U.S.A. **110** 41.07N 98.00W
Central I. Kenya **79** 3.30N 36.02E
Centralia Ill. U.S.A. **110** 38.32N 89.08W
Centralia Wash. U.S.A. **108** 46.43N122.58W
Central Makrān Range *mts.* Pakistan **62** 26.30N 65.00E
Central Siberian Plateau *see* Sredne Sibirskoye Ploskogor'ye U.S.S.R. **51**
Central Square U.S.A. **115** 43.17N 76.09W
Centre *d.* France **19** 47.40N 1.45E
Centre *d.* U. Volta **76** 13.30N 1.00W
Centre, Canal du France **19** 46.27N 4.07E
Centreville Ala. U.S.A. **113** 32.57N 87.08W
Centreville Md. U.S.A. **115** 39.03N 76.04W
Century Fla. U.S.A. **113** 30.59N 87.18W
Century W.Va. U.S.A. **114** 39.06N 80.11W
Cepu Indonesia **59** 7.07S111.35E
Ceram *i. see* Seram Indonesia **59**
Ceram Sea *see* Seram, Laut Pacific Oc. **59**
Cère *r.* France **20** 44.55N 1.53E
Ceres U.S.A. **108** 37.35N120.57W
Ceresole Reale Italy **30** 45.26N 7.15E
Céret France **20** 42.29N 2.45E
Cereté Colombia **122** 8.54N 75.51W
Cerignola Italy **33** 41.16N 15.54E
Cérilly France **20** 46.37N 2.49E
Cerisiers France **19** 48.08N 3.29E
Cerknica Yugo. **31** 45.48N 14.22E
Cernavodă Romania **37** 44.20N 28.02E
Cernay France **19** 47.49N 7.10E
Cerralvo, Isla *i.* Mexico **109** 24.17N109.52W
Cërrik Albania **34** 41.02N 19.57E
Cerritos Mexico **116** 22.26N100.17W
Cerro de Pasco Peru **122** 10.43S 76.15W
Cervaro *r.* Italy **33** 41.30N 15.52E
Cervati, Monte *mtn.* Italy **33** 40.17N 15.29E
Cervera Lérida Spain **25** 41.40N 1.17E
Cervera Logroño Spain **26** 42.01N 1.57W
Cervera de Pisuerga Spain **26** 42.52N 4.30W
Cervia Italy **30** 44.15N 12.22E
Cervialto, Monte *mtn.* Italy **33** 40.47N 15.08E
Cervignano del Friuli Italy **30** 45.49N 13.20E
Cervione France **21** 42.20N 9.31E
Cervo Spain **26** 43.40N 7.25W
Cesena Italy **30** 44.08N 12.15E
Cesenatico Italy **30** 44.12N 12.24E
Cēsis U.S.S.R. **44** 57.18N 25.18E
Česká Kamenice Czech. **38** 50.47N 14.26E
Česká Lípa Czech. **38** 50.42N 14.32E
České Budějovice Czech. **36** 49.00N 14.30E
Český Krumlov Czech. **39** 48.49N 14.19E
Çeşme Turkey **35** 38.18N 26.19E
Cessnock Australia **93** 32.51S151.21E
Cetinje Yugo. **31** 42.23N 18.55E
Ceuta Spain **27** 35.53N 5.19W
Ceva Italy **30** 44.23N 8.01E
Cévennes *mts.* France **21** 44.00N 3.30E
Ceyhan Turkey **64** 37.02N 35.48E
Ceyhan *r.* Turkey **64** 36.54N 34.58E
Cèze *r.* France **21** 44.06N 4.42E
Chabanais France **20** 45.52N 0.43E
Chablis France **19** 47.49N 3.48E
Chacabuco Argentina **125** 34.38S 60.29W
Chachani *mtn.* Peru **122** 16.12S 71.32W
Chachapoyas Peru **122** 6.13S 77.54W
Chāchro Pakistan **62** 25.07N 70.15E
Chaco *d.* Argentina **124** 26.30S 60.00W
Chad Africa **70** 16.00N 18.00E
Chad, L. Africa **77** 13.30N 14.00E
Chadron U.S.A. **110** 42.50N103.02W
Chafe Nigeria **77** 11.56N 6.55E
Chāgai Pakistan **62** 29.18N 64.42E
Chāgai Hills Pakistan **62** 29.10N 63.35E
Chagda U.S.S.R. **51** 58.44N130.38E
'Chaghcharān Afghan. **62** 34.32N 65.15E
Chagny France **19** 46.55N 4.45E
Chagos Archipelago *is.* Indian Oc. **49** 7.00S 72.00E
Chagrin Falls *town* U.S.A. **114** 41.26N 81.24W
Cha'gyüngoinba China **63** 31.10N 90.42E
Chahār Borjak Afghan. **62** 30.17N 62.03E
Chāh Bahār Iran **65** 25.17N 60.41E
Chāh Sandan *well* Pakistan **62** 28.59N 63.27E
Chaibāsā India **63** 22.34N 85.49E
Chaillé-les-Marais France **18** 46.24N 1.01W
Chainat Thailand **56** 15.10N100.10E
Chaiyaphum Thailand **56** 15.46N101.57E
Chajarí Argentina **125** 30.45S 57.59W
Chākāi India **63** 24.34N 86.24E
Chākdaha India **63** 23.05N 88.31E
Chake Chake Tanzania **79** 5.13S 39.46E
Chakhānsūr Afghan. **62** 31.10N 62.04E
Chakradharpur India **63** 22.42N 85.38E
Chakwāl Pakistan **62** 32.56N 72.52E
Chala Peru **122** 15.48S 74.20W
Chalais France **20** 45.16N 0.02E
Chaleur B. Canada **103** 48.00N 65.45W
Chalhuanca Peru **122** 14.20S 73.10W
Chālisgaon India **62** 20.28N 75.01E
Chalk River *town* Canada **105** 46.01N 77.27W
Challans France **18** 46.51N 1.53W
Challenger Depth Pacific Oc. **59** 11.19N142.15E
Challis U.S.A. **108** 44.30N114.14W
Chalonnes-sur-Loire France **18** 47.21N 0.46W
Châlons-sur-Marne France **19** 48.57N 4.22E
Chalon-sur-Saône France **19** 46.47N 4.51E
Chalosse *d.* France **20** 43.45N 0.30W
Châlus France **20** 45.39N 0.59E
Cham W. Germany **39** 49.13N 12.41E
Chama U.S.A. **108** 36.54N106.35W
Chama Zambia **79** 11.09S 33.10E
Chaman Pakistan **62** 30.55N 66.27E
Chamba India **62** 32.34N 76.08E
Chambal *r.* India **63** 26.29N 79.15E
Chamberlain U.S.A. **110** 43.49N 99.20W
Chambersburg U.S.A. **114** 39.56N 77.39W
Chambéry France **21** 45.34N 5.56E
Chambeshi Zambia **79** 10.57S 31.04E
Chambeshi *r.* Zambia **79** 11.15S 30.37E
Chambley-Bussières France **19** 49.03N 5.54E
Chambly Canada **105** 45.27N 73.17W
Chambly France **19** 49.10N 2.15E
Chambon-sur-Voueize France **20** 46.11N 2.25E
Chamburi Kalāt Pakistan **62** 26.09N 64.43E
Cha Messengue Angola **78** 11.04S 18.56E
Chamical Argentina **124** 30.22S 66.19W
Chamoli India **63** 30.24N 79.21E
Chamonix France **21** 45.55N 6.52E
Chāmpa India **63** 22.03N 82.39E
Champagne Canada **100** 60.47N136.29W
Champagne-Ardenne *d.* France **19** 49.00N 4.30E
Champagnole France **19** 46.45N 5.55E
Champaign U.S.A. **110** 40.07N 88.14W
Champdeniers France **18** 46.29N 0.24W
Champdoré, Lac *l.* Canada **103** 55.55N 65.50W
Champeix France **20** 45.36N 3.08E
Champéry Switz. **39** 46.10N 6.52E
Champlain Canada **105** 46.27N 72.21W
Champlain U.S.A. **105** 44.59N 73.27W
Champlain, L. U.S.A. **105** 44.45N 73.15W
Champlitte-et-le-Prélot France **19** 47.37N 5.31E
Champotón Mexico **116** 19.21N 90.43W
Chāmpua India **63** 22.05N 85.40E
Chamusca Portugal **27** 39.21N 8.29W
Chañaral Chile **124** 26.21S 70.37W
Chānasma India **62** 23.43N 72.07E
Chandausi India **63** 28.27N 78.46E
Chāndbāli India **63** 20.46N 86.49E
Chandeleur Is. U.S.A. **111** 29.48N 88.51W
Chandīgarh India **62** 30.44N 76.47E
Chandīgarh *d.* India **62** 30.45N 76.45E
Chāndil India **63** 22.58N 86.03E
Chandler Canada **103** 48.21N 64.41W
Chandler U.S.A. **111** 35.42N 96.53W
Chāndor Hills India **62** 20.30N 74.00E
Chandos L. Canada **105** 44.49N 78.00W
Chāndpur Bangla. **63** 23.13N 90.39E
Chāndpur Bangla. **61** 22.08N 91.55E
Chāndpur India **63** 29.09N 78.16E
Chandrapur India **63** 19.57N 79.18E
Chāndvad India **62** 20.20N 74.15E
Chānf Iran **65** 26.40N 60.31E
Chang, Ko *i.* Thailand **56** 12.04N102.23E
Changchun China **53** 43.51N125.15E
Changde China **55** 29.00N111.35E
Changfeng China **54** 32.27N117.09E
Changhua Jiang *r.* China **55** 19.20N108.38E
Chang Jiang *r.* China **55** 31.40N121.15E
Changjin N. Korea **53** 40.21N127.20E
Changle China **54** 36.42N118.49E
Changli China **54** 39.43N119.08E
Changling China **54** 44.16N123.58E
Changning China **55** 26.24N112.24E
Changping China **54** 40.12N116.12E
Changsha China **55** 28.09N112.59E
Changshan China **55** 28.57N118.31E
Changshan Qundao *is.* China **54** 39.20N123.00E
Changshou China **55** 29.50N107.02E
Changshu China **55** 31.48N120.52E
Changshun China **55** 25.59N106.25E
Changting China **55** 25.42N116.20E
Changyi China **54** 36.51N119.23E
Changzhi China **54** 36.10N113.00E
Changzhou China **55** 31.46N119.58E
Channel Is. U.K. **13** 49.28N 2.13W
Channel Is. U.S.A. **109** 34.00N120.00W
Channel-Port-aux-Basques *town* Canada **103** 47.35N 59.11W
Channing Mich. U.S.A. **112** 46.08N 88.06W
Channing Tex. U.S.A. **111** 35.41N102.20W
Chantada Spain **26** 42.37N 7.46W
Chanthaburi Thailand **56** 12.35N102.05E
Chantilly France **19** 49.12N 2.28E
Chanute U.S.A. **111** 37.41N 95.27W
Chao'an China **55** 23.40N116.32E
Chao Hu *l.* China **55** 31.32N117.30E
Chaonde Mozambique **81** 13.43S 40.31E
Chao Phraya *r.* Thailand **56** 13.34N100.35E
Chao Xian China **55** 31.36N117.52E
Chaoyang Guangdong China **55** 23.25N116.31E
Chaoyang Liaoning China **54** 41.35N120.20E
Chapada das Mangabeiras *mts.* Brazil **123** 10.00S 46.30W
Chapada Diamantina Brazil **126** 13.30S 42.30W
Chapala, Lago de *l.* Mexico **116** 20.00N103.00W
Chapayevo U.S.S.R. **45** 50.12N 51.09E
Chapayevsk U.S.S.R. **44** 52.58N 49.44E
Chapeau Canada **105** 45.54N 77.05W
Chapeau de Paille Canada **105** 47.10N 73.30W
Chapelle-d'Angillon France **19** 47.22N 2.26E
Chapicuy Uruguay **125** 31.39S 57.54W
Chapleau Canada **102** 47.50N 83.24W
Chāpra India **63** 25.46N 84.45E
Chaqui Bolivia **124** 19.36S 65.32W
Characot I. Antarctica **128** 70.00S 75.00W
Charay Mexico **109** 26.01N108.50W
Charcas Mexico **116** 23.08N101.07W
Chard U.K. **13** 50.52N 2.59W
Chardon U.S.A. **114** 41.35N 81.12W
Charduār India **63** 26.52N 92.46E
Chardzhou U.S.S.R. **65** 39.09N 63.34E
Charente *d.* France **20** 45.40N 0.10E
Charente *r.* France **20** 45.57N 1.05W
Charente-Maritime *d.* France **20** 45.30N 0.45W
Charenton-du-Cher France **19** 46.44N 2.38E
Chari *r.* Chad **77** 13.00N 14.30E
Chari-Baguirmi *d.* Chad **77** 12.20N 15.30E
Chārīkār Afghan. **62** 35.01N 69.11E
Charing U.K. **13** 51.12N 0.49E
Chariton U.S.A. **110** 41.01N 93.19W
Charleroi Belgium **16** 50.25N 4.27E
Charlesbourg Canada **105** 46.51N 71.16W
Charles City U.S.A. **110** 43.04N 92.40W
Charleston Miss. U.S.A. **111** 34.00N 90.04W
Charleston S.C. U.S.A. **113** 32.48N 79.58W
Charleston W.Va. U.S.A. **114** 38.21N 81.38W
Charlestown Rep. of Ire. **15** 53.57N 8.48W
Charlestown Ind. U.S.A. **112** 38.28N 85.40W
Charlestown N.H. U.S.A. **115** 43.14N 72.26W
Charles Town W.Va. U.S.A. **114** 39.17N 77.52W
Charlesville Zaïre **78** 5.27S 20.58E
Charleville Australia **90** 26.25S146.13E
Charleville-Mézières France **19** 49.46N 4.43E
Charlieu France **21** 46.10N 4.10E
Charlotte N.C. U.S.A. **113** 35.03N 80.50W
Charlotte Va. U.S.A. **113** 37.03N 78.44W
Charlottenberg Sweden **43** 59.53N 12.17E
Charlottesville U.S.A. **113** 38.02N 78.29W
Charlottetown Canada **103** 46.14N 63.08W
Charlton Australia **92** 36.18S143.27E
Charlton I. Canada **102** 52.00N 79.30W
Charly-sur-Marne France **19** 48.58N 3.17E
Charmes France **19** 48.22N 6.17E
Charny Canada **105** 46.43N 71.16W
Charolles France **19** 46.26N 4.17E
Charroux France **18** 46.09N 0.24E
Chārsadda Pakistan **62** 34.09N 71.44E
Charters Towers Australia **90** 20.05S146.16E
Chartres France **18** 48.27N 1.30E
Chascomas Argentina **125** 35.35S 58.00W
Chase City U.S.A. **113** 36.59N 78.30W
Châteaubriant France **18** 47.43N 1.23W
Château-Chinon France **19** 47.04N 3.56E
Château d'Oex Switz. **39** 46.28N 7.08E
Château-du-Loir France **18** 47.42N 0.25E
Châteaudun France **18** 48.05N 1.20E
Chateaugay U.S.A. **105** 44.56N 74.05W
Château Gontier France **18** 47.50N 0.42W
Châteauguay, Lac *l.* Canada **103** 56.27N 70.05W
Château Landon France **19** 48.09N 2.42E
Château-la-Vallière France **18** 47.33N 0.19E
Châteaulin France **18** 48.12N 4.05W
Châteaumeillant France **19** 46.34N 2.12E
Châteauneuf-de-Randon France **20** 44.39N 3.40E
Châteauneuf-en-Thymerais France **18** 48.35N 1.15E
Châteauneuf-sur-Charente France **20** 45.36N 0.03W
Châteauneuf-sur-Loire France **19** 47.52N 2.14E
Châteauneuf-sur-Sarthe France **18** 47.41N 0.30W
Château-Porcien France **19** 49.32N 4.15E
Château Renault France **18** 47.35N 0.55E
Châteauroux France **19** 46.49N 1.42E
Château-Salins France **19** 48.49N 6.30E
Château-Thierry France **19** 49.03N 3.24E
Châtelet Belgium **16** 50.24N 4.32E
Châtellerault France **18** 46.49N 0.33E
Châtel-sur-Moselle France **19** 48.18N 6.24E
Châtelus-Malvaleix France **20** 46.18N 2.01E
Chatham N.B. Canada **103** 47.02N 65.28W
Chatham Ont. Canada **104** 42.24N 82.11W
Chatham U.K. **13** 51.23N 0.32E
Chatham Alas. U.S.A. **100** 57.30N135.00W
Chatham Mass. U.S.A. **115** 41.41N 69.58W
Chatham N.Y. U.S.A. **115** 42.22N 73.36W
Chatham Is. Pacific Oc. **84** 44.00S176.35W
Chatham Rise Pacific Oc. **84** 43.30S178.00W
Chatham Str. U.S.A. **100** 57.30N134.45W
Châtillon-Coligny France **19** 47.50N 2.51E
Châtillon-en-Bazois France **19** 47.03N 3.49E
Châtillon-s-Seine France **17** 47.52N 4.35E
Châtillon-sur-Chalaronne France **21** 46.07N 4.58E
Châtillon-sur-Indre France **18** 46.59N 1.11E
Châtillon-sur-Seine France **19** 47.51N 4.33E
Chatra India **63** 24.13N 84.52E
Chatrapur India **63** 19.21N 84.59E
Chātsu India **62** 26.36N 75.57E
Chatsworth Canada **104** 44.27N 80.54W
Chattahoochee U.S.A. **113** 30.42N 84.51W
Chattahoochee *r.* U.S.A. **113** 30.52N 84.57W
Chattanooga U.S.A. **113** 35.02N 85.18W
Chatteris U.K. **13** 52.27N 0.03E
Chaudes-Aigues France **20** 44.51N 3.00E
Chauk Burma **56** 20.52N 94.50E
Chaulnes France **19** 49.49N 2.48E
Chaumont France **19** 48.07N 5.08E
Chaumont-en-Vexin France **19** 49.16N 1.53E
Chaungwabyin Burma **56** 13.41N 98.22E
Chauny France **19** 49.37N 3.13E
Chaupāran India **63** 24.23N 85.15E
Chau Phu Vietnam **56** 10.42N105.03E
Chaussin France **19** 46.58N 5.25E
Chausy U.S.S.R. **37** 53.49N 30.57E
Chautauqua L. U.S.A. **114** 42.12N 79.27W
Chauvigny France **18** 46.34N 0.39E
Chavanges France **19** 48.31N 4.34E
Chaves Brazil **123** 0.10S 49.55W
Chaves Portugal **26** 41.44N 7.28W
Chavuma Zambia **78** 13.04S 22.43E
Chawang Thailand **56** 8.25N 99.32E
Cheat *r.* U.S.A. **114** 39.06N 79.33W
Cheat Mtn. U.S.A. **114** 38.43N 79.51W
Cheb Czech. **39** 50.01N 12.25E
Cheboksary U.S.S.R. **44** 56.08N 47.12E
Cheboygan U.S.A. **104** 45.39N 84.29W
Chebsara U.S.S.R. **44** 59.14N 38.59E
Chebula Angola **78** 12.27S 23.49E
Chech, Erg *des.* Mali / Algeria **74** 24.30N 2.30W
Chechaouene Morocco **74** 35.10N 5.16W
Chechersk U.S.S.R. **37** 52.54N 30.54E
Checiny Poland **37** 50.48N 20.28E
Cheduba I. Burma **56** 18.50N 93.35E
Chef-Boutonne France **18** 46.07N 0.04W
Chegdomyn U.S.S.R. **51** 51.09N133.01E
Chegga *well* Mauritania **74** 25.30N 5.46W
Chegutu Zimbabwe **80** 18.09S 30.07E
Chehalis U.S.A. **108** 46.40N122.58W
Cheil, Ras el *c.* Somali Rep. **71** 7.45N 49.48E
Cheiron, Cime du *mtn.* France **21** 43.49N 6.58E
Cheju S. Korea **53** 33.31N126.29E
Cheju do *i.* S. Korea **53** 33.20N126.30E
Cheleken U.S.S.R. **65** 39.26N 53.11E
Chelforó Argentina **125** 39.04S 66.33W
Chelga Ethiopia **73** 12.30N 37.04E
Chelif, Oued *r.* Algeria **75** 36.15N 2.05E
Chelkar U.S.S.R. **50** 47.48N 59.39E
Chelles France **19** 48.53N 2.36E
Chełm Poland **37** 51.10N 23.28E
Chelmer *r.* U.K. **11** 51.43N 0.40E
Chelmsford Canada **104** 46.35N 81.12W
Chelmsford U.K. **13** 51.44N 0.28E
Chełmża Poland **37** 53.12N 18.37E
Chelsea Canada **105** 45.29N 75.48W
Chelsea U.S.A. **104** 42.19N 84.01W
Chelsea U.S.A. **105** 43.59N 72.27W
Cheltenham U.K. **13** 51.53N 2.07W
Chelva Spain **25** 39.45N 1.00W
Chelyabinsk U.S.S.R. **9** 55.12N 61.25E
Chelyuskin, Mys *c.* U.S.S.R. **51** 77.20N106.00E
Chemainus Canada **100** 48.55N123.48W

Chemba to Clamecy

Chemba Mozambique 79 17.11S 34.53E
Chemillé France 18 47.13N 0.44W
Chemult U.S.A. 108 43.13N121.47W
Chën, Gora mtn. U.S.S.R. 51 65.30N141.20E
Chenāb r. Pakistan 62 29.23N 71.02E
Chenachane Algeria 74 26.00N 4.15W
Chenango r. U.S.A. 115 42.05N 75.55W
Chénéville Canada 105 45.53N 75.03W
Cheney U.S.A. 108 47.29N117.34W
Chengchow see Zhengzhou China 54
Chengde China 54 41.00N117.52E
Chengdu China 55 30.41N104.05E
Chenggu China 54 33.10N107.22E
Chenghai China 55 23.31N116.43E
Chengkou China 55 31.58N108.48E
Chengmai China 55 19.44N109.59E
Cheng Xian China 54 33.42N105.36E
Chenoa U.S.A. 110 40.44N 88.43W
Chen Xian China 55 25.45N113.00E
Chepelare Bulgaria 34 41.44N 24.41E
Chepen Peru 122 7.15S 79.20W
Chepstow U.K. 13 51.38N 2.40W
Cher d. France 19 47.05N 2.30E
Cher r. France 18 47.21N 0.29E
Cherbourg France 18 49.39N 1.39W
Cherdyn U.S.S.R. 44 60.25N 55.22E
Cherelato Ethiopia 73 6.00N 38.10E
Cheremkhovo U.S.S.R. 51 53.08N103.01E
Cherepovets U.S.S.R. 44 59.05N 37.55E
Chergui, Chott ech f. Algeria 75 34.21N 0.30E
Cherikov U.S.S.R. 37 53.35N 31.23E
Cherkassy U.S.S.R. 45 49.27N 32.04E
Cherkessk U.S.S.R. 45 44.14N 42.05E
Cherkovitsa Bulgaria 34 43.41N 24.49E
Cherlak U.S.S.R. 50 54.10N 74.52E
Chernigov U.S.S.R. 37 51.30N 31.18E
Chernikovsk U.S.S.R. 44 54.51N 56.06E
Chernobyl U.S.S.R. 37 51.17N 30.15E
Chernovtsy U.S.S.R. 37 48.19N 25.52E
Chernyakhov U.S.S.R. 37 50.30N 28.38E
Chernyakhovsk U.S.S.R. 41 54.38N 21.49E
Cherokee Iowa U.S.A. 110 42.45N 95.33W
Cherokee Okla. U.S.A. 111 36.45N 98.21W
Cherquenco Chile 125 38.41S 72.00W
Cherrapunji India 63 25.18N 91.42E
Cherry Creek r. U.S.A. 110 44.36N101.30W
Cherry Creek town Nev. U.S.A. 108 39.54N113.53W
Cherry Creek town S.Dak. U.S.A. 110 44.36N101.26W
Cherry Valley town U.S.A. 115 42.48N 74.45W
Cherskogo, Khrebet mts. U.S.S.R. 51 65.50N143.00E
Chertkovo U.S.S.R. 45 49.22N 40.12E
Chertsey U.K. 13 51.23N 0.27W
Cherven-Bryag Bulgaria 34 43.17N 24.07E
Chervonograd U.S.S.R. 37 50.25N 24.10E
Cherwell r. U.K. 13 51.44N 1.15W
Chesaning U.S.A. 104 43.11N 84.07W
Chesapeake Ohio U.S.A. 114 38.26N 82.28W
Chesapeake Va. U.S.A. 113 36.43N 76.15W
Chesapeake W.Va. U.S.A. 114 38.12N 81.33W
Chesapeake B. U.S.A. 115 38.40N 76.25W
Chesapeake Beach town U.S.A. 115 38.41N 76.32W
Chesham U.K. 13 51.43N 0.38W
Cheshire d. U.K. 12 53.14N 2.30W
Chëshskaya Guba g. U.S.S.R. 44 67.20N 46.30E
Chesht-e Sharif Afghan. 62 34.21N 63.44E
Chesil Beach f. U.K. 13 50.37N 2.33W
Chesley Canada 104 44.17N 81.05W
Chester U.K. 12 53.12N 2.53W
Chester Mont. U.S.A. 108 48.31N110.58W
Chester Penn. U.S.A. 115 39.51N 75.21W
Chester Vt. U.S.A. 115 43.16N 72.36W
Chesterfield U.K. 12 53.14N 1.26W
Chesterfield, Îles is. N. Cal. 84 20.00S159.00E
Chesterfield Inlet town Canada 99 63.00N 91.00W
Chestertown Md. U.S.A. 115 39.13N 76.04W
Chestertown N.Y. U.S.A. 115 43.38N 73.49W
Chesterville Canada 105 45.06N 75.14W
Chestnut Ridge mtn. U.S.A. 114 40.09N 79.24W
Chesuncook L. U.S.A. 112 46.00N 69.20W
Chéticamp Canada 103 46.38N 61.01W
Chetumal Mexico 117 18.30N 88.17W
Chetumal B. Mexico 117 18.30N 88.00W
Chetwynd Canada 100 55.45N121.45W
Cheviot New Zealand 86 42.49S173.16E
Cheviot U.S.A. 112 39.10N 84.32W
Chew Bahir l. Ethiopia 73 4.40N 36.50E
Cheyenne r. U.S.A. 110 44.40N101.15W
Cheyenne Okla. U.S.A. 111 35.37N 99.40W
Cheyenne Wyo. U.S.A. 108 41.08N104.49W
Cheyne B. Australia 89 34.35S118.50E
Chhabra India 62 24.40N 76.50E
Chhātak Bangla. 63 25.02N 91.40E
Chhatarpur Bihār India 63 24.23N 84.11E
Chhatarpur Madhya P. India 63 24.54N 79.36E
Chhattisgarh f. India 63 21.00N 82.00E
Chhindwāra India 63 22.04N 78.56E
Chhota-Chhindwāra India 63 23.03N 79.29E
Chhota Udepur India 62 22.19N 74.01E
Chiali Taiwan 55 23.10N120.11E
Chiang Mai Thailand 56 18.48N 98.59E
Chiapas d. Mexico 116 16.30N 93.00W
Chiaramonte Gulfi Italy 33 37.01N 14.43E
Chiaravalle Centrale Italy 33 38.41N 16.25E
Chiari Italy 30 45.32N 9.56E
Chiavari Italy 30 44.19N 9.19E
Chiavenna Italy 30 46.19N 9.24E
Chiba Japan 57 35.36N140.07E
Chiba d. Japan 57 35.10N140.00E
Chibemba Angola 80 15.43S 14.07E
Chibia Angola 78 15.10S 13.32E
Chibougamau Canada 102 49.56N 74.24W
Chibougamau Lac l. Canada 102 49.50N 74.20W
Chibougamau Prov. Park Canada 103 49.25N 73.50W
Chibuk Nigeria 77 10.52N 12.50E
Chibuto Mozambique 81 24.41S 33.32E
Chicago U.S.A. 110 41.50N 87.45W
Chichagof I. U.S.A. 100 57.55N135.45W
Chichagof I. U.S.A. 98 57.55N135.45W
Chicheng China 54 40.52N115.50E
Chichester U.K. 13 50.50N 0.47W
Chichibu Japan 57 35.59N139.05E
Chickasha U.S.A. 111 35.02N 97.58W
Chiclana Spain 27 36.25N 6.08W
Chiclayo Peru 122 6.47S 79.47W
Chico r. Chubut Argentina 125 43.45S 66.10W
Chico r. Santa Cruz Argentina 125 50.03W 68.35W
Chico U.S.A. 108 39.44N121.50W
Chicomo Mozambique 81 24.33S 34.11E
Chicopee U.S.A. 115 42.10N 72.36W
Chicora U.S.A. 114 40.57N 79.45W
Chicoutimi-Jonquière Canada 103 48.26N 71.06W
Chicualacuala Mozambique 81 22.06S 31.42E
Chidambarum India 61 11.24N 79.42E
Chidembo Angola 78 14.34S 19.17E
Chidenguele Mozambique 81 24.54S 34.13E
Chidley, C. Canada 99 60.30N 65.00W
Chiemsee l. W. Germany 39 47.54N 12.29E
Chiengi Zambia 79 8.42S 29.07E
Chieri Italy 30 45.01N 7.49E
Chieti Italy 31 42.21N 14.10E
Chifeng China 54 42.13N118.56E
Chigasaki Japan 57 35.19N139.24E
Chignecto B. Canada 103 45.35N 64.45W
Chiguana Bolivia 124 21.05S 67.58W
Chigubo Mozambique 81 22.38S 33.18E
Chigu Co l. China 63 28.40N 91.50E
Chihuahua Mexico 109 28.38N106.05W
Chihuahua d. Mexico 109 28.40N106.00W
Chiili U.S.S.R. 50 44.10N 66.37E
Chikhli India 62 20.21N 76.15E
Chikumbi Zambia 79 15.14S 28.21E
Chikwawa Malaŵi 79 16.00S 34.54E
Chil r. Iran 65 25.12N 61.30E
Chilanga Zambia 80 15.33S 28.17E
Chilapa Mexico 116 17.38N 99.11W
Chilcoot U.S.A. 108 39.49N120.08W
Childers Australia 90 25.14S152.17E
Childress U.S.A. 111 34.25N100.13W
Chile S. America 124 32.30S 71.00W
Chile Basin Pacific Oc. 85 34.20S 80.00W
Chile Chico Chile 125 46.33S 71.44W
Chilka L. India 63 19.46N 85.20E
Chilko L. Canada 98 51.20N124.05W
Chillagoe Australia 90 17.09S144.32E
Chillán Chile 125 36.36S 72.07W
Chillicothe Mo. U.S.A. 110 39.48N 93.33W
Chillicothe Ohio U.S.A. 112 39.20N 82.59W
Chillingollah Australia 92 35.17S143.07E
Chilliwack Canada 100 49.10N122.00W
Chiloé, Isla de i. Chile 125 43.00S 73.00W
Chilonga Zambia 79 12.02S 31.17E
Chilpancingo Mexico 116 17.33N 99.30W
Chiltern Australia 93 36.11S146.36E
Chiltern Hills U.K. 13 51.40N 0.53W
Chilton U.S.A. 110 44.04N 88.10W
Chilumba Malaŵi 79 10.25S 34.18E
Chilwa, L. Malaŵi 79 15.15S 35.45E
Chimakela Angola 78 15.12S 16.58E
Chimanimani Zimbabwe 81 19.48S 32.52E
Chimay Belgium 16 50.03N 4.20E
Chimbas Argentina 124 31.28S 68.30W
Chimborazo mtn. Ecuador 122 1.29S 78.52W
Chimbote Peru 122 9.04S 78.34W
Chimishliya U.S.S.R. 37 46.30N 28.50E
Chimkent U.S.S.R. 52 42.16N 69.05E
Chimoio Mozambique 81 19.04S 33.29E
Chin d. Burma 56 22.00N 93.30E
China Asia 52 33.00N103.00E
China Lake town U.S.A. 109 35.46N117.39W
Chinandega Nicaragua 117 12.35N 87.10W
Chinati Peak U.S.A. 109 29.57N104.29W
Chincha Alta Peru 122 13.25S 76.07W
Chinchaga r. Canada 100 58.50N118.20W
Chinchón Spain 27 40.08N 3.25W
Chinchoua Gabon 78 0.00 9.48E
Chincilla de Monte Aragón Spain 25 38.55N 1.45W
Chincoteague U.S.A. 113 37.55N 75.23W
Chinde Mozambique 81 18.37S 36.24E
Chindio Mozambique 79 17.46S 35.23E
Chindwin r. Burma 56 21.30N 95.12E
Chinga Mozambique 79 15.14S 38.40E
Chingleput India 61 12.42N 79.59E
Chingola Zambia 79 12.29S 27.53E
Chingombe Zambia 79 14.25S 29.56E
Chingshui Taiwan 55 24.15N120.35E
Chin Hills Burma 56 22.30N 93.30E
Chinhoyi Zimbabwe 80 17.22S 30.10E
Chīni India 63 31.32N 78.15E
Chiniot Pakistan 62 31.43N 72.59E
Chinjan Pakistan 62 30.34N 67.58E
Chinko r. C.A.R. 73 4.50N 23.53E
Chinle U.S.A. 109 36.09N109.33W
Chinon France 18 47.10N 0.15E
Chinook U.S.A. 108 48.35N109.14W
Chino Valley town U.S.A. 109 34.45N112.27W
Chinsali Zambia 79 10.33S 32.05E
Chintheche Malaŵi 79 11.50S 34.13E
Chiny Belgium 16 49.45N 5.20E
Chiôco Mozambique 79 16.27S 32.49E
Chioggia Italy 30 45.13N 12.17E
Chipata Zambia 79 13.37S 32.40E
Chipera Mozambique 79 15.20S 32.35E
Chipie r. Canada 102 51.25N 83.20W
Chipinge Zimbabwe 81 20.12S 32.38E
Chippenham U.K. 13 51.27N 2.07W
Chippewa r. U.S.A. 104 43.35N 84.17W
Chippewa Falls town U.S.A. 110 44.56N 91.24W
Chipping Norton U.K. 13 51.56N 1.32W
Chiquian Peru 122 10.10S 77.00W
Chiquinquirá Colombia 122 5.37N 73.50W
Chir r. U.S.S.R. 45 48.34N 42.53E
Chirāwa India 62 28.15N 75.38E
Chirchik U.S.S.R. 9 41.28N 69.31E
Chiredzi Zimbabwe 81 21.03S 31.39E
Chiredzi r. Zimbabwe 81 21.10S 31.50E
Chiricahua Peak mtn. U.S.A. 109 31.52N109.20W
Chiriquí mtn. Panama 117 8.49N 82.38W
Chiriquí, Laguna de b. Panama 117 9.00N 82.00W
Chiromo Malaŵi 79 16.28S 35.10E
Chirpan Bulgaria 34 42.10N 25.19E
Chirripó mtn. Costa Rica 117 9.31N 83.30W
Chirundu Zimbabwe 80 16.04S 28.51E
Chisamba Zambia 80 14.58S 28.23E
Chishan Taiwan 55 22.53N120.29E
Chisholm U.S.A. 110 47.29N 92.53W
Chisholm Mills Canada 100 54.55N114.09W
Chishtiān Mandi Pakistan 62 29.48N 72.52E
Chishui China 55 28.29N105.38E
Chisone r. Italy 30 44.49N 7.25E
Chistopol U.S.S.R. 44 55.25N 50.38E
Chita U.S.S.R. 53 52.03N113.35E
Chitek L. Canada 101 52.25N 99.20W
Chitembo Angola 78 13.33S 16.47E
Chitipa Malaŵi 79 9.41S 33.19E
Chitorgarh India 62 24.53N 74.38E
Chitrakūt Dham India 63 25.11N 80.52E
Chitrāl Pakistan 60 35.52N 71.58E
Chitré Panama 97 7.58N 80.26W
Chittagong Bangla. 63 22.20N 91.50E
Chittenango U.S.A. 115 43.03N 75.52W
Chittoor India 61 13.13N 79.06E
Chiumbe r. Zaïre 78 6.37S 21.04E
Chiusi Italy 30 43.01N 11.57E
Chiuta, L. Malaŵi/Mozambique 79 14.45S 35.50E
Chiva Spain 25 39.28N 0.43W
Chivasso Italy 30 45.11N 7.53E
Chivhu Zimbabwe 80 19.01S 30.53E
Chivilcoy Argentina 125 34.52S 60.02W
Chiwanda Tanzania 79 11.21S 34.55E
Chobe r. Namibia/Botswana 80 17.48S 25.12E
Chobe Swamp f. Namibia 80 18.20S 23.40E
Chocolate Mts. U.S.A. 109 33.20N115.15W
Chocope Peru 122 7.47S 79.12W
Choele-Choel Argentina 125 39.15S 65.30W
Chōfu Japan 57 35.39N139.33E
Chohtan India 62 25.29N 71.04E
Choix Mexico 109 26.43N108.17W
Chojnice Poland 37 53.42N 17.32E
Chokai zan mtn. Japan 57 39.08N140.04E
Choke Mts. Ethiopia 73 11.00N 37.30E
Cholet France 18 47.04N 0.53W
Cholon Vietnam 56 10.40N106.30E
Choluteca Honduras 117 13.16N 87.11W
Choma Zambia 79 16.51S 27.04E
Chomu India 62 27.10N 75.44E
Chomutov Czech. 39 50.28N 13.26E
Chon Buri Thailand 56 13.20N101.02E
Chone Ecuador 122 0.44S 80.04W
Chong'an China 55 27.46N118.01E
Ch'ŏngjin N. Korea 53 41.55N129.50E
Ch'ŏngju S. Korea 53 36.39N127.31E
Chong Kal Kampuchea 56 13.57N103.35E
Chongming i. China 55 31.36N121.33E
Chongqing China 55 29.31N106.35E
Chongren China 55 27.44N116.02E
Chŏnju S. Korea 53 35.50N127.05E
Chonos, Archipelago de los is. Chile 125 45.00S 74.00W
Cho Oyu mtn. China/Nepal 63 28.06N 86.40E
Chopda India 62 21.15N 75.18E
Choptank r. U.S.A. 115 38.38N 76.13W
Chorges France 21 44.33N 6.17E
Chorley U.K. 12 53.39N 2.39W
Chortkov U.S.S.R. 37 49.01N 25.42E
Chorzów Poland 37 50.19N 18.56E
Chosica Peru 122 11.55S 76.38W
Chos Malal Argentina 125 37.20S 70.15W
Choszczno Poland 36 53.10N 15.26E
Choteau U.S.A. 108 47.49N112.11W
Chotila India 62 22.25N 71.11E
Choum Mauritania 74 21.10N 13.00W
Chowchilla U.S.A. 108 37.07N120.16W
Christchurch New Zealand 86 43.33S172.40E
Christchurch U.K. 13 50.44N 1.47W
Christian I. Canada 104 44.50N 80.13W
Christian Sd. U.S.A. 100 55.56N134.40W
Christiansfeld Denmark 42 55.21N 9.29E
Christianshåb Greenland 99 68.50N 51.00W
Christie B. Canada 101 62.32N111.10W
Christina r. Canada 101 56.40N111.03W
Christmas Creek town Australia 88 18.55S125.56E
Christmas I. Indian Oc. 58 10.30S105.40E
Christmas I. Kiribati 85 1.52N157.20W
Chrudim Czech. 36 49.57N 15.48E
Chu r. U.S.S.R. 52 42.30N 76.10E
Chuādānga Bangla. 63 23.38N 88.51E
Chubbuck U.S.A. 109 34.22N115.20W
Chūbu d. Japan 57 35.25N137.40E
Chubut d. Argentina 125 44.00S 68.00W
Chubut r. Argentina 125 43.18S 65.06W
Chu Chua Canada 100 51.22N120.10W
Chudleigh U.K. 13 50.35N 3.36W
Chudleigh Park town Australia 90 19.41S144.06E
Chudnov U.S.S.R. 37 50.05N 28.01E
Chudovo U.S.S.R. 44 59.10N 31.41E
Chudskoye, Ozero l. U.S.S.R. 44 58.30N 27.30E
Chūgoku d. Japan 57 35.00N133.00E
Chūgoku sanchi mts. Japan 57 35.30N133.00E
Chugwater U.S.A. 108 41.46N104.49W
Chuiquimula Guatemala 117 15.52N 89.50W
Chukai Malaysia 58 4.16N103.24E
Chukchi Sea Arctic Oc. 96 69.30N172.00W
Chukotskiy Poluostrov pen. U.S.S.R. 51 66.00N174.30W
Chukudukraal Botswana 80 22.30S 23.22E
Chula Vista U.S.A. 109 32.39N117.05W
Chulman U.S.S.R. 51 56.54N124.55E
Chulucanas Peru 122 5.08S 80.00W
Chulym U.S.S.R. 50 55.09N 80.59E
Chum U.S.S.R. 44 67.05N 63.15E
Chumbicha Argentina 124 28.50S 66.18W
Chumikan U.S.S.R. 51 54.40N135.15E
Chumphon Thailand 56 10.34N 99.15E
Chuna r. U.S.S.R. 51 58.00N 94.00E
Ch'unch'ŏn S. Korea 53 37.53N127.45E
Chungking see Chongqing China 55
Chunya Tanzania 79 8.31S 33.28E
Chuquicamata Chile 124 22.20S 68.56W
Chuquisaca d. Bolivia 124 21.00S 64.00W
Chur Switz. 39 46.51N 9.32E
Churchill Canada 101 58.46N 94.10W
Churchill r. Man. Canada 101 58.47N 94.12W
Churchill r. Nfld. Canada 103 53.20N 60.11W
Churchill, C. Canada 101 58.46N 93.12W
Churchill Falls f. Canada 103 53.35N 64.27W
Churchill L. Canada 101 55.55N108.20W
Churchill Peak mtn. Canada 100 58.10N125.10W
Church Stretton U.K. 13 52.32N 2.49W
Churia Range mts. Nepal 63 28.40N 81.30E
Churu India 62 28.18N 74.57E
Chusovoy U.S.S.R. 44 58.18N 57.50E
Chu Xian China 54 32.25N118.15E
Chuxiong China 61 25.03N101.33E
Chu Yang Sin mtn. Vietnam 56 12.25N108.25E
Ciamis Indonesia 59 7.20S108.21E
Cianjur Indonesia 59 6.50S107.09E
Cibatu Indonesia 59 7.10S107.59E
Ćićarija mts. Yugo. 31 45.30N 14.00E
Cidacos r. Spain 25 42.21N 1.38W
Ciechanów Poland 37 52.53N 20.38E
Ciego de Avila Cuba 117 21.51N 78.47W
Ciempozuelos Spain 26 40.10N 3.37W
Ciénaga Colombia 122 11.11N 74.15W
Cienfuegos Cuba 117 22.10N 80.27W
Cíes, Islas is. Spain 26 42.13N 8.54W
Cieszyn Poland 37 49.45N 18.38E
Cieza Spain 25 38.14N 1.25W
Cifuentes Spain 26 40.47N 2.37W
Cigüela r. Spain 27 39.08N 3.44W
Cijara, Embalse de resr. Spain 27 39.18N 4.52W
Cijulang Indonesia 59 7.44S108.30E
Cikampek Indonesia 59 6.21S107.25E
Cilacap Indonesia 59 7.44S109.00E
Ciledug Indonesia 59 6.56S108.43E
Cili China 55 29.24N111.04E
Cilleruelo de Bezana Spain 26 43.00N 3.51W
Cimanuk r. Indonesia 59 6.20S108.12E
Cimarron U.S.A. 111 37.48N100.21W
Cimarron r. U.S.A. 111 36.10N 96.17W
Cimone, Monte mtn. Italy 30 44.12N 10.42E
Cîmpina Romania 29 45.08N 25.44E
Cîmpulung Romania 29 45.16N 25.03E
Cinca r. Spain 25 41.26N 0.21E
Cincar Yugo. 31 43.54N 17.04E
Cincinnati U.S.A. 112 39.10N 84.30W
Ciney Belgium 16 50.17N 5.06E
Cingoli Italy 30 43.22N 13.13E
Cinto, Monte mtn. France 21 42.23N 8.56E
Cipolletti Argentina 125 38.56S 67.59W
Circeo, Parco Nazionale del Nat. Park Italy 32 41.17N 13.05E
Circle U.S.A. 108 47.25N105.35W
Circleville Ohio U.S.A. 112 39.36N 82.57W
Circleville Utah U.S.A. 108 38.10N112.16W
Cirebon Indonesia 59 6.46S108.33E
Cirencester U.K. 13 51.43N 1.59W
Cirey-sur-Vezouse France 19 48.35N 6.57E
Ciriè Italy 30 45.14N 7.36E
Cirò Marina Italy 33 39.22N 17.08E
Cisco U.S.A. 111 32.23N 98.59W
Cisterna di Latina Italy 32 41.35N 12.49E
Cistierna Spain 26 42.48N 5.07W
Citlaltepetl mtn. Mexico 97 19.00N 97.18W
Citra U.S.A. 113 29.24N 82.06W
Cittadella Italy 32 45.39N 11.47E
Città di Castello Italy 30 43.27N 12.14E
Cittanova Italy 33 38.21N 16.05E
Ciudad Acuña Mexico 111 29.18N100.55W
Ciudad Allende Mexico 111 28.20N100.51W
Ciudad Bolívar Venezuela 122 8.06N 63.36W
Ciudad Camargo Mexico 109 27.40N105.10W
Ciudad Delicias Mexico 97 28.13N105.28W
Ciudad de México Mexico 116 19.25N 99.10W
Ciudadela Spain 25 40.00N 3.50E
Ciudad Guayana Venezuela 122 8.22N 62.40W
Ciudad Guerrero Mexico 116 28.33N107.28W
Ciudad Guzmán Mexico 116 19.41N103.29W
Ciudad Ixtepec Mexico 116 16.32N 95.10W
Ciudad Jiménez Mexico 109 27.08N104.55W
Ciudad Juárez Mexico 109 31.44N106.29W
Ciudad Lerdo Mexico 111 25.32N103.32W
Ciudad Madero Mexico 116 22.19N 97.50W
Ciudad Mante Mexico 116 22.44N 98.57W
Ciudad Melchor Múzquiz Mexico 111 27.53N101.31W
Ciudad Mier Mexico 111 26.26N 99.09W
Ciudad Obregón Mexico 109 27.29N109.56W
Ciudad Ojeda Venezuela 122 10.05N 71.17W
Ciudad Piar Venezuela 122 7.27N 63.19W
Ciudad Real Spain 26 38.59N 3.56W
Ciudad Real d. Spain 27 38.50N 4.00W
Ciudad Rodrigo Spain 26 40.36N 6.32W
Ciudad Victoria Mexico 116 23.43N 99.10W
Ciurana r. Spain 25 41.08N 0.39E
Civita Castellana Italy 30 42.17N 12.25E
Civitanova Italy 31 43.18N 13.44E
Civitavecchia Italy 30 42.06N 11.48E
Civray France 18 46.09N 0.18E
Çivril Turkey 64 38.18N 29.43E
Ci Xian China 54 36.22N114.23E
Cizre Turkey 64 37.21N 42.11E
Clackline Australia 89 31.43S116.31E
Clacton on Sea U.K. 13 51.47N 1.10E
Clain r. France 18 46.47N 0.32E
Clairambault, Lac l. Canada 103 54.45N 69.22W
Claire, L. Canada 100 58.30N112.00W
Clairton U.S.A. 114 40.18N 79.53W
Clairvaux-les-Lacs France 19 46.34N 5.45E
Claise r. France 18 46.54N 0.45E
Clamecy France 19 47.27N 3.31E

Cunnamulla to Degerby

Cunnamulla Australia **93** 28.04S145.40E
Cuokkaraš'ša *mtn.* Norway **40** 69.57N 24.32E
Cuorgnè Italy **30** 45.23N 7.39E
Cupar U.K. **14** 56.19N 3.01W
Cupica, Golfo de *g.* Colombia **122** 6.35N 77.25W
Cuprija Yugo. **34** 43.56N 21.23E
Curaçao *i.* Neth. Antilles **122** 12.15N 69.00W
Curacautín Chile **125** 38.26S 71.53W
Curaco *r.* Argentina **125** 38.49S 65.01W
Curanilahue Chile **125** 37.28S 73.21W
Curaray *r.* Peru **122** 2.20S 74.05W
Curban Australia **93** 31.33S148.36E
Curdlawidny L. Australia **92** 30.16S136.20E
Cure *r.* France **19** 47.40N 3.41E
Curiapo Venezuela **122** 8.33N 61.05W
Curicó Chile **125** 34.59S 71.14W
Curitiba Brazil **126** 25.24S 49.16W
Curlewis Australia **93** 31.08S150.16E
Curnamona Australia **92** 31.40S139.35E
Currane, Lough Rep. of Ire. **15** 51.50N 10.07W
Currant U.S.A. **108** 38.44N115.30W
Curranyalpa Australia **93** 30.57S144.33E
Currie Australia **91** 39.56S143.52E
Currie U.S.A. **108** 40.17N114.44W
Curtin Australia **89** 30.50S122.05E
Curtis Spain **26** 43.07N 8.03W
Curtis U.S.A. **110** 40.38N100.31W
Curtis I. Australia **90** 23.38S151.09E
Curuá *r.* Brazil **123** 5.23S 54.22W
Čurug Yugo. **31** 45.29N 20.04E
Cururupu Brazil **123** 1.50S 44.52W
Curuzú Cuatiá Argentina **125** 29.50S 58.05W
Curvelo Brazil **126** 18.45S 44.27W
Curwensville U.S.A. **114** 40.58N 78.32W
Cushendall U.K. **15** 55.06N 6.05W
Cushing U.S.A. **111** 35.59N 96.46W
Cusna, Monte *mtn.* Italy **30** 44.17N 10.23E
Cutana Australia **92** 32.14S140.25E
Cut Bank U.S.A. **108** 48.38N112.20W
Cutro Italy **33** 39.02N 16.59E
Cuttaburra *r.* Australia **93** 29.18S145.00E
Cuttack India **63** 20.30N 85.50E
Cuxhaven W. Germany **38** 53.52N 8.42E
Cuyahoga Falls *town* U.S.A. **114** 41.08N 81.29W
Cuyuni *r.* Guyana **122** 6.24N 58.38W
Cuzco Peru **122** 13.32S 71.57W
Cuzna *r.* Spain **26** 38.04N 4.41W
Cwmbran U.K. **13** 51.39N 3.01W
Cyclades *is.* see Kikládhes Greece **35**
Cynthiana U.S.A. **112** 38.22N 84.18W
Cypress Hills Canada **101** 49.40N109.30W
Cyprus Asia **66** 35.00N 33.00E
Cyrenaica *f.* see Barqah Libya **72**
Czechoslovakia Europe **36** 49.30N 15.00E
Czeremcha Poland **37** 52.32N 23.15E
Czersk Poland **37** 53.48N 18.00E
Częstochowa Poland **37** 50.49N 19.07E

D

Dà *r.* Vietnam **56** 21.20N105.24E
Da'an China **54** 45.30N124.18E
Ḍab'ah Jordan **67** 31.36N 36.04E
Dabakala Ivory Coast **76** 8.19N 4.24W
Daba Shan *mts.* China **55** 32.00N109.00E
Dabat Ethiopia **73** 12.58N 37.48E
Dabbāgh, Jabal *mtn.* Saudi Arabia **66** 27.51N 35.43E
Dabhoi India **62** 22.11N 73.26E
Dabie Shan *mts.* China **55** 31.15N115.20E
Dabola Guinea **76** 10.48N 11.02W
Dabra India **63** 25.54N 78.20E
Dabu Jiangxi China **55** 26.47N116.04E
Dacca Bangla. **63** 23.43N 90.25E
Dachau W. Germany **39** 48.15N 11.26E
Dacre Canada **105** 45.22N 76.59W
Dadanawa Guyana **122** 2.30N 59.30W
Dade City U.S.A. **113** 28.23N 82.11W
Dādhar Pakistan **62** 29.28N 67.39E
Dādra & Nagar Haveli *d.* India **62** 20.05N 73.00E
Dādu Pakistan **62** 26.44N 67.47E
Dadu He *r.* China **61** 28.47N104.40E
Daet Phil. **59** 14.07N122.58E
Dagali Norway **41** 60.25N 8.27E
Dagana Senegal **76** 16.28N 15.35W
Daga Post Sudan **73** 9.12N 33.58E
Dagash Sudan **72** 19.22N 33.24E
Dagu China **54** 38.58N117.40E
Dagua P.N.G. **59** 3.25S143.20E
Daguan China **52** 27.44N103.53E
Dagupan Phil. **59** 16.02N120.21E
Dagzê China **63** 29.45N105.45E
Dagzê Co *l.* China **63** 31.45N 87.50E
Dahan-e Qowmghī Afghan. **62** 34.28N 66.31E
Da Hinggan Ling *mts.* China **53** 50.00N122.10E
Dahlak Archipelago *is.* Ethiopia **72** 15.45N 40.30E
Dahlak Kebir I. Ethiopia **72** 15.38N 40.11E
Dahlem W. Germany **39** 50.23N 6.33E
Dahlgren U.S.A. **114** 38.20N 77.03W
Dahme E. Germany **38** 51.52N 13.25E
Dahra Senegal **76** 15.21N 15.29W
Dahujiang China **55** 26.06N114.58E
Dahūk Iraq **64** 36.52N 43.00E
Dahy, Nafūd ad *f.* Saudi Arabia **71** 22.00N 45.25E
Ḍaḥyah, 'Urūq *f.* S. Yemen **71** 18.45N 51.15E
Dai Hai *l.* China **54** 40.31N112.43E
Dā'īl Syria **67** 32.45N 36.08E
Dailekh Nepal **63** 28.50N 81.43E
Daimiel Spain **27** 39.04N 3.37W
Daitō Japan **57** 34.42N135.38E
Daiyun Shan *mtn.* China **55** 25.41N118.11E
Dājal Pakistan **62** 29.33N 70.23E
Dajarra Australia **90** 21.42S139.31E
Dajing China **55** 28.25N121.10E
Dakar Senegal **76** 14.38N 17.27W
Dakhal, Wādī ad *r.* Egypt **66** 28.49N 32.45E
Dākhilah, Al Wāḥāt ad *oasis* Egypt **64** 25.30N 28.10E
Dakhla W. Sahara **74** 23.43N 15.57W
Dakhlet Nouadhibou *d.* Mauritania **74** 20.30N 16.00W
Dakhovskaya U.S.S.R. **23** 44.13N 40.13E
Dakingari Nigeria **77** 11.40N 4.06E
Dakota City U.S.A. **110** 42.25N 96.25W
Dakovica Yugo. **34** 42.22N 20.26E
Dakovo Yugo. **31** 45.19N 18.25E
Dal *r.* Sweden **41** 60.38N 17.27E
Dala Congo **78** 1.40N 16.39E
Dalaba Guinea **76** 10.47N 12.12W
Dalai Nur *l.* China **54** 43.27N116.25E
Dalandzadgad Mongolia **54** 43.30N104.18E
Dalane *f.* Norway **42** 58.35N 6.20E
Da Lat Vietnam **56** 11.56N108.25E
Dālbandin Pakistan **62** 28.53N 64.25E
Dalbeattie U.K. **14** 54.55N 3.49W
Dalbosjön *b.* Sweden **43** 58.45N 12.48E
Dalby Australia **91** 27.11S151.12E
Dalby Sweden **43** 55.40N 13.20E
Dale Hordaland Norway **41** 60.35N 5.49E
Dale Sogn og Fj. Norway **41** 61.22N 5.24E
Dalen Norway **42** 59.27N 8.00E
Dalgety Australia **93** 36.30S148.50E
Dalgonally Australia **90** 20.09S141.16E
Dalhart U.S.A. **111** 36.04N102.31W
Dalhousie Canada **103** 48.04N 66.23W
Dalhousie Jammu & Kashmir **62** 32.32N 75.59E
Dali China **52** 25.42N100.11E
Dalías Spain **27** 36.49N 2.52W
Dāliyat el Karmel Israel **67** 32.42N 35.03E
Dalj Yugo. **31** 45.29N 18.59E
Dalkeith U.K. **14** 55.54N 3.04W
Dallas Oreg. U.S.A. **108** 44.55N123.19W
Dallas Tex. U.S.A. **111** 32.47N 96.48W
Dallastown U.S.A. **115** 39.54N 76.39W
Dall I. U.S.A. **100** 55.00N133.00W
Dalli Rajhāra India **63** 20.35N 81.04E
Dalmacija *f.* Yugo. **31** 43.33N 16.40E
Dalmally U.K. **14** 56.25N 4.58W
Dalmas, Lac *l.* Canada **103** 53.27N 71.50W
Dalmellington U.K. **14** 55.19N 4.24W
Dalnerechensk U.S.S.R. **53** 45.55N133.45E
Daloa Ivory Coast **76** 6.56N 6.28W
Dalou Shan *mts.* China **55** 28.25N107.15E
Dalqū Sudan **72** 20.07N 30.35E
Dalrymple, Mt. Australia **90** 21.02S148.38E
Dalsingh Sarai India **63** 25.40N 85.50E
Dalsland *f.* Sweden **43** 59.00N 12.10E
Dalton Canada **102** 48.10N 84.00W
Dalton U.S.A. **113** 34.46N 84.59W
Daltonganj India **63** 24.02N 84.04E
Dalupiri *i.* Phil. **55** 19.05N121.13E
Dalveen Australia **93** 28.26S151.55E
Dalvik Iceland **40** 65.58N 18.28W
Dalwhinnie U.K. **14** 56.56N 4.15W
Daly *r.* Australia **88** 13.20S130.19E
Daly City U.S.A. **108** 37.42N122.29W
Daly Waters *town* Australia **90** 16.15S133.22E
Damā, Wādī *r.* Saudi Arabia **64** 27.04N 35.48E
Damān India **62** 20.25N 72.51E
Damān *d.* India **62** 20.10N 73.00E
Damanhûr Egypt **66** 31.03N 30.28E
Damar *i.* Indonesia **59** 7.10S128.30E
Damascus see Dimashq Syria **66**
Damaturu Nigeria **77** 11.49N 11.50E
Damāvand, Qolleh-ye *mtn.* Iran **65** 35.47N 52.04E
Damba Angola **78** 6.44S 15.17E
Damen *i.* China **55** 27.58N121.05E
Dāmghān Iran **65** 36.09N 54.22E
Damiaoshan China **55** 24.43N109.15E
Daming Shan *mts.* China **55** 23.23N108.30E
Dāmiyā Jordan **67** 32.06N 35.33E
Dammartin-en-Goële France **19** 49.03N 2.41E
Dāmodar *r.* India **63** 22.17N 88.05E
Damoh India **63** 23.50N 79.27E
Damongo Ghana **76** 9.06N 1.48W
Dampier Australia **88** 20.45S116.50E
Dampier, Selat *str.* Pacific Oc. **59** 0.30S130.50E
Dampier Land Australia **88** 17.20S123.00E
Damqawt S. Yemen **71** 16.34N 52.50E
Damxung China **63** 30.32N 91.06E
Dan Israel **67** 33.14N 35.39E
Dana Canada **101** 52.18N105.42W
Danakil *f.* Ethiopia **73** 13.00N 41.00E
Danané Ivory Coast **76** 7.21N 8.10W
Da Nang Vietnam **56** 16.04N108.13E
Dānāpur India **63** 25.38N 85.03E
Danba China **52** 30.57N101.55E
Danbury Conn. U.S.A. **115** 41.23N 73.27W
Danbury N.H. U.S.A. **115** 43.32N 71.54W
Dand Afghan. **62** 31.37N 65.41E
Dandaragan Australia **89** 30.40S115.42E
Dande *r.* Angola **78** 8.30S 13.23E
Dandeldhura Nepal **63** 29.17N 80.36E
Dandenong Australia **93** 37.59S145.14E
Dandong China **54** 40.10N124.25E
Danger Is. Cook Is. **84** 10.53S165.49W
Dangla Ethiopia **73** 11.18N 36.54E
Dangqên China **63** 31.41N 91.51E
Dangriga Belize **117** 16.58N 88.13W
Dangshan China **54** 34.25N116.24E
Dangyang China **55** 30.52N111.40E
Daniel U.S.A. **108** 42.52N110.04W
Daniell Australia **89** 32.37S121.30E
Daniel's Harbour Canada **103** 50.14N 57.35W
Danielson U.S.A. **115** 41.48N 71.53W
Danilov U.S.S.R. **44** 58.10N 40.12E
Daning China **54** 36.32N110.47E
Danisa Hills Kenya **79** 3.10N 39.37E
Danja Nigeria **77** 11.29N 7.30E
Danlí Honduras **117** 14.02N 86.30W
Dannenberg W. Germany **38** 53.06N 11.05E
Dannevirke New Zealand **86** 40.12S176.08E
Dannhauser R.S.A. **80** 28.00S 30.03E
Dansville U.S.A. **114** 42.34N 77.42W
Dantewāra India **63** 18.54N 81.21E
Danube *r.* Europe **31** 45.20N 29.40E
Danube, Mouths of the see Dunării, Delta Romania **37**
Danvers U.S.A. **115** 42.34N 70.56W
Danville Canada **105** 45.47N 72.01W
Danville Ill. U.S.A. **110** 40.09N 87.37W
Danville Ky. U.S.A. **113** 37.40N 84.49W
Danville Penn. U.S.A. **115** 40.57N 76.37W
Danville Va. U.S.A. **113** 36.34N 79.25W
Danville Vt. U.S.A. **105** 44.25N 72.09W
Dan Xian China **55** 19.30N109.35E
Danzig, G. of Poland **37** 54.45N 19.15E
Dão *r.* Portugal **26** 40.20N 8.11W
Daordeng China **54** 40.47N119.05E
Daosa India **62** 26.53N 76.20E
Daoukro Ivory Coast **76** 7.10N 3.58W
Daoulas France **18** 48.22N 4.15W
Dao Xian China **55** 25.32N111.35E
Daozhen China **55** 28.46N107.45E
Dapango Togo **76** 10.51N 0.15E
Dapingfang China **54** 41.25N120.07E
Da Qaidam China **52** 37.44N 95.08E
Daqinggou China **54** 41.22N114.13E
Daqing Shan *mts.* China **54** 41.00N111.00E
Daqqāq Sudan **73** 12.56N 26.58E
Daqq-e Patargān *f.* Iran **65** 33.30N 60.40E
Dar'ā Syria **67** 32.37N 36.06E
Dar'ā *d.* Syria **67** 32.50N 36.10E
Dārāb Iran **65** 28.45N 54.34E
Darāban Pakistan **62** 31.44N 70.20E
Darabani Romania **37** 48.11N 26.35E
Darakht-e Yaḥyā Afghan. **62** 31.50N 68.08E
Dārān Iran **65** 33.00N 50.27E
Darband, Kūh-e *mtn.* Iran **65** 31.33N 57.08E
Darbhanga India **63** 26.10N 85.54E
Darby Mont. U.S.A. **108** 46.01N114.11W
Darby Penn. U.S.A. **115** 39.54N 75.15W
D'Arcy Canada **100** 50.33N122.32W
Darda Yugo. **31** 45.37N 18.41E
Dardanelles see Çanakkale Boğazi Turkey **34**
Dareel Australia **93** 28.50S148.49E
Dar es Salaam Tanzania **79** 6.51S 39.18E
Dar es Salaam *d.* Tanzania **79** 6.45S 39.10E
Darfield New Zealand **86** 43.29S172.07E
Dārfūr *d.* Sudan **73** 13.20N 25.00E
Dargan Ata U.S.S.R. **50** 40.30N 62.10E
Dargaville New Zealand **86** 35.57S173.53E
Dargo Australia **93** 37.30S147.16E
Darhan Mongolia **52** 49.34N106.23E
Darie Hills Somali Rep. **71** 8.15N 47.25E
Darien U.S.A. **115** 41.05N 73.28W
Darién, Golfo del *g.* Colombia **122** 9.20N 77.30W
Darjeeling India **63** 27.02N 88.16E
Darkan Australia **89** 33.19S116.42E
Darke Peak *mtn.* Australia **92** 33.28S136.12E
Darling *r.* Australia **92** 34.05S141.57E
Darling Downs *f.* Australia **91** 28.00S149.45E
Darling Range *mts.* Australia **89** 32.00S116.30E
Darlington U.K. **12** 54.33N 1.33W
Darlington Point *town* Australia **93** 34.36S146.01E
Darłowe Poland **36** 54.26N 16.23E
Darmstadt W. Germany **39** 49.53N 8.40E
Darnah Libya **72** 32.45N 22.39E
Darnah *d.* Libya **72** 31.30N 23.30E
Darnétal France **18** 49.27N 1.09E
Darney France **19** 48.05N 6.03E
Darnick Australia **92** 32.55S143.39E
Darnley, C. Antarctica **128** 68.00S 69.00E
Daroca Spain **25** 41.07N 1.25W
Darreh Gaz Iran **65** 37.22N 59.08E
Dar Rounga *f.* C.A.R. **73** 9.25N 21.30E
Darsser Ort *c.* E. Germany **38** 54.29N 12.31E
Dartmoor Australia **92** 37.58S141.19E
Dartmoor Forest *hills* U.K. **13** 50.33N 3.55W
Dartmouth Canada **103** 44.40N 63.34W
Dartmouth U.K. **13** 50.21N 3.35W
Dartry Mts. Rep. of Ire. **15** 54.23N 8.25W
Dartuch, Cabo *c.* Spain **25** 39.56N 3.48E
Daru P.N.G. **90** 9.04S143.12E
Daruvar Yugo. **31** 45.36N 17.13E
Darvaza U.S.S.R. **50** 40.12N 58.24E
Darvel, Teluk *b.* Malaysia **58** 4.40N118.30E
Darwen U.K. **12** 53.42N 2.29W
Dārwha India **63** 20.19N 77.46E
Darwin Australia **90** 12.23S130.44E
Daryācheh-ye Bakhtegān *l.* Iran **65** 29.20N 54.05E
Daryācheh-ye Namak *l.* Iran **65** 34.45N 51.36E
Daryācheh-ye Rezā'īyeh *l.* Iran **65** 37.40N 45.28E
Daryācheh-ye Sīstān *f.* Iran **65** 31.00N 61.15E
Darya Khān Pakistan **62** 31.48N 71.06E
Daryāpur India **62** 20.56N 77.20E
Dasāda India **62** 23.19N 71.50E
Dasht *r.* Pakistan **62** 25.10N 61.40E
Dashte-e Mārgow *des.* Afghan. **62** 30.45N 63.00E
Dasht-e Kavīr *des.* Iran **65** 34.40N 55.00E
Dasht-e Lūt *des.* Iran **65** 31.30N 58.00E
Dashui Nur China **54** 42.45N116.47E
Daspalla India **63** 20.21N 84.51E
Dassa-Zoumé Benin **77** 7.50N 2.13E
Dassow E. Germany **38** 53.50N 10.59E
Dastgardān Iran **65** 34.19N 56.51E
Dastjerd Iran **65** 34.33N 50.15E
Datça Turkey **35** 36.46N 27.40E
Datia India **63** 25.40N 78.28E
Datong China **54** 40.10N113.15E
Datteln W. Germany **38** 51.40N 7.23E
Datu, Tanjung *c.* Malaysia **58** 2.00N109.30E
Datu Piang Phil. **59** 7.02N124.30E
Daua *r.* see Dawa Kenya **73**
Dāud Khel Pakistan **62** 32.53N 71.34E
Daudnagar India **63** 25.02N 84.24E
Daugavpils U.S.S.R. **44** 55.52N 26.31E
Daun W. Germany **39** 50.11N 6.50E
Dauphin Canada **101** 51.09N100.03W
Dauphiné, Alpes du *mts.* France **21** 44.35N 5.45E
Dauphin L. Canada **101** 51.17N 99.48W
Daura Nigeria **77** 13.05N 8.18E
Dāvangere India **60** 14.30N 75.52E
Davao Phil. **59** 7.05N125.38E
Davao G. Phil. **59** 6.30N126.00E
Daveluyville Canada **105** 46.12N 72.08W
Davenport U.S.A. **110** 41.32N 90.36W
Davenport Downs *town* Australia **90** 24.09S141.08E
Daventry U.K. **13** 52.16N 1.10W
Davenyns, L. Canada **105** 47.05N 73.45W
David Panama **117** 8.26N 82.26W
David-Gorodok U.S.S.R. **37** 52.04N 27.10E
Davis U.S.A. **108** 38.33N121.44W
Davis Creek *town* U.S.A. **108** 41.44N120.24W
Davison U.S.A. **104** 43.02N 83.31W
Davis Sea Antarctica **128** 66.00S 90.00E
Davis Str. N. America **99** 66.00N 58.00W
Davlekanovo U.S.S.R. **44** 54.12N 55.00E
Davos Switz. **39** 46.48N 9.50E
Davutlar Turkey **35** 37.43N 27.17E
Dawa China **54** 40.58N122.00E
Dawa *r.* Ethiopia **73** 4.11N 42.06E
Dawaxung China **63** 31.26N 85.06E
Dawlish U.K. **13** 50.34N 3.28W
Dawna Range *mts.* Burma **56** 17.00N 98.00E
Dawson Canada **98** 64.04N139.24W
Dawson U.S.A. **113** 31.47N 84.27W
Dawson Creek *town* Canada **100** 55.45N120.15W
Dawson Range *f.* Canada **98** 62.40N139.00W
Dawu China **52** 31.00N101.09E
Dax France **20** 43.43N 1.03W
Daxian China **55** 31.10N107.28E
Daxing China **54** 39.44N116.20E
Daylesford Australia **92** 37.22S144.12E
Dayman *r.* Uruguay **125** 31.25S 58.00W
Dayong Hunan China **55** 29.06N110.24E
Dayr Abū Sa'īd Jordan **67** 32.30N 35.41E
Dayr al Balaḥ Egypt **67** 31.25N 34.21E
Dayr al Ghuşūn Jordan **67** 32.21N 35.05E
Dayr az Zawr Syria **64** 35.20N 40.08E
Dayr Dibwān Jordan **67** 31.55N 35.16E
Dayr Sharaf Jordan **67** 32.15N 35.11E
Dayton N.Y. U.S.A. **114** 42.25N 78.58W
Dayton Ohio U.S.A. **112** 39.45N 84.10W
Dayton Penn. U.S.A. **114** 40.53N 79.16W
Dayton Tenn. U.S.A. **113** 35.30N 85.01W
Dayton Wash. U.S.A. **108** 46.19N117.59W
Daytona Beach *town* U.S.A. **113** 29.11N 81.01W
Dayu China **55** 25.24N114.22E
Da Yunhe *canal* China **54** 39.10N117.12E
Dazhu China **55** 30.50N107.12E
De Aar R.S.A. **80** 30.39S 24.01E
Dead Sea Jordan **67** 31.25N 35.30E
Deakin Australia **89** 30.46S128.58E
Deal U.K. **13** 51.13N 1.25E
De'an China **55** 29.20N115.46E
Deán Funes Argentina **124** 30.25S 64.20W
Dean Lake *town* Canada **104** 46.13N 83.09W
Dearborn U.S.A. **104** 42.18N 83.10W
Dease *r.* Canada **100** 59.54N128.30W
Dease Arm *b.* Canada **98** 66.52N119.37W
Dease L. Canada **100** 58.05N130.04W
Death Valley *f.* U.S.A. **109** 36.30N117.00W
Death Valley *town* U.S.A. **109** 36.18N116.25W
Death Valley Nat. Monument U.S.A. **108** 36.30N117.00W
Deauville France **18** 49.22N 0.04E
Debar Yugo. **34** 41.31N 20.30E
Debica Poland **37** 50.04N 21.24E
Deblin Poland **37** 51.35N 21.50E
Deborah, L. Australia **89** 30.45S119.07E
Debre Birhan Ethiopia **73** 9.40N 39.33E
Debrecen Hungary **37** 47.30N 21.37E
Debre Tabor Ethiopia **73** 11.50N 38.05E
Dečani Yugo. **34** 42.30N 20.10E
Decatur Ala. U.S.A. **113** 34.36N 87.00W
Decatur Ga. U.S.A. **113** 33.45N 84.17W
Decatur Ill. U.S.A. **110** 39.51N 89.32W
Decatur Ind. U.S.A. **112** 40.50N 84.57W
Decazeville France **20** 44.34N 2.15E
Deccan *f.* India **60** 18.30N 77.30E
Decelles, Lac *l.* Canada **102** 47.40N 78.10W
Dechu India **62** 26.47N 72.20E
Decimomannu Italy **32** 39.19N 8.58E
Děčín Czech. **38** 50.48N 14.13E
Decize France **19** 46.50N 3.27E
Deckerville U.S.A. **114** 43.32N 82.44W
De Cocksdorp Neth. **16** 53.12N 4.52E
Decorah U.S.A. **110** 43.18N 91.48W
Decs Hungary **31** 46.17N 18.46E
Deda Romania **37** 46.57N 24.53E
Dédi Ivory Coast **76** 8.34N 3.33W
Dediāpada India **62** 21.35N 73.40E
Dedza Malaŵi **79** 14.20S 34.24E
Dee *r.* D. and G. U.K. **14** 54.50N 4.05W
Dee *r.* Grampian U.K. **14** 57.07N 2.04W
Dee *r.* Wales U.K. **12** 53.13N 3.05W
Deep B. Canada **100** 61.15N116.35W
Deep Creek L. U.S.A. **114** 39.30N 79.19W
Deepdale Australia **88** 21.42S116.11E
Deep River *town* Canada **105** 46.06N 77.30W
Deep River *town* U.S.A. **115** 41.23N 72.26W
Deep Well Australia **90** 24.25S134.05E
Deerfield *r.* U.S.A. **115** 42.35N 72.35W
Deer Lake *town* Canada **103** 49.07N 57.35W
Deer Lodge U.S.A. **108** 46.24N112.44W
Deesa India **62** 24.15N 72.10E
Deeth U.S.A. **108** 41.04N115.18W
Defiance U.S.A. **112** 41.17N 84.21W
De Funiak Springs *town* U.S.A. **113** 30.41N 86.08W
Deganya Bet Israel **67** 32.42N 35.35E
Degeberga Sweden **43** 55.50N 14.05E
Degerby Finland **43** 60.02N 20.23E

Doda, Lac to **Dureji**

Doda, Lac *l.* Canada **102** 49.24N 75.14W
Dodecanese *is. see* Dhodhekánisos Greece **35**
Dodge City U.S.A. **111** 37.45N100.01W
Dodman Pt. U.K. **13** 50.13N 4.48W
Dodoma Tanzania **79** 6.10S 35.40E
Dodoma *d.* Tanzania **79** 6.00S 36.00E
Dodson U.S.A. **108** 48.24N108.15W
Doetinchem Neth. **16** 51.57N 6.17E
Dogai Coring *l.* China **61** 34.30N 89.00E
Doğanbey Turkey **35** 37.37N 27.11E
Dog Creek *town* Canada **100** 51.35N122.14W
Dogger Bank *f.* North Sea **11** 54.45N 2.00E
Doğubayazit Turkey **65** 39.32N 44.08E
Do'gyaling China **63** 31.58N 88.24E
Doha *see* Ad Dawḩah Qatar **65**
Dohad India **62** 22.50N 74.16E
Doheny Canada **105** 47.04N 72.36W
Dohhi India **63** 24.32N 84.54E
Doilungdêqên China **63** 30.06N 90.32E
Doiran, L. Greece / Yugo. **34** 41.13N 22.44E
Dokkum Neth. **16** 53.20N 6.00E
Dokri Pakistan **62** 27.23N 68.06E
Dolbeau Canada **103** 48.53N 72.14W
Dol-de-Bretagne France **18** 48.33N 1.45W
Dole France **19** 47.06N 5.30E
Dolgellau U.K. **13** 52.44N 3.53W
Dolina U.S.S.R. **37** 49.00N 23.59E
Dolinskaya U.S.S.R. **45** 48.06N 32.46E
Dolisie Congo **78** 4.09S 12.40E
Dollard *b.* W. Germany **38** 53.17N 7.10E
Dolni Dubnik Bulgaria **34** 43.24N 24.26E
Dolni Lom Bulgaria **34** 43.31N 22.47E
Dolny Kubín Czech. **37** 49.12N 19.17E
Dolo Somali Rep. **71** 4.13N 42.08E
Dolomiti *mts.* Italy **30** 46.15N 11.55E
Dolores Argentina **125** 36.19S 57.40W
Dolores Mexico **109** 28.53N108.27W
Dolores Spain **25** 38.08N 0.46W
Dolores Uruguay **125** 33.33S 58.13W
Dolores U.S.A. **108** 37.28N108.30W
Dolphin and Union Str. Canada **98** 69.20N118.00W
Doma Nigeria **77** 8.23N 8.21E
Domadare Somali Rep. **73** 1.48N 41.13E
Domažlice Czech. **38** 49.27N 12.56E
Dombås Norway **41** 62.05N 9.08E
Dombe Grande Angola **78** 13.00S 13.06E
Dombes *f.* France **21** 46.00N 5.03E
Dombey, C. Australia **92** 37.12S139.43E
Dombóvár Hungary **31** 46.23N 18.08E
Domburg Neth. **16** 51.35N 3.31E
Domfront France **18** 48.36N 0.39W
Dominica Windward Is. **117** 15.30N 61.30W
Dominican Republic C. America **117** 18.00N 70.00W
Dominion L. Canada **103** 52.40N 61.42W
Dommel *r.* Neth. **16** 51.44N 5.17E
Domo Ethiopia **71** 7.54N 46.52E
Domodossola Italy **30** 46.07N 8.17E
Dompierre-sur-Besbre France **20** 46.31N 3.41E
Domuyo *mtn.* Argentina **125** 36.37S 70.28W
Domvraína Greece **35** 38.15N 22.59E
Domžale Yugo. **31** 46.08N 14.36E
Don Mexico **109** 26.26N109.02W
Don *r.* U.K. **12** 53.41N 0.50W
Don *r.* Scotland U.K. **14** 57.10N 2.05W
Don *r.* U.S.S.R. **45** 47.06N 39.16E
Donaghadee U.K. **15** 54.39N 5.33W
Donald Australia **92** 36.25S143.04E
Donaldsonville U.S.A. **111** 30.06N 90.59W
Donau *r. see* Danube W. Germany **36**
Donaueschingen W. Germany **39** 47.57N 8.29E
Donauwörth W. Germany **39** 48.43N 10.46E
Don Benito Spain **27** 38.53N 5.51W
Doncaster U.K. **12** 53.31N 1.09W
Dondaicha India **62** 21.20N 74.34E
Dondo Angola **78** 9.40S 14.25E
Dondo Mozambique **81** 19.39S 34.39E
Donegal Rep. of Ire. **15** 54.39N 8.06W
Donegal *d.* Rep. of Ire. **15** 54.52N 8.00W
Donegal U.S.A. **114** 40.07N 79.23W
Donegal B. Rep. of Ire. **15** 54.32N 8.18W
Donegal Pt. Rep. of Ire. **15** 52.43N 9.38W
Donetsk U.S.S.R. **45** 48.00N 37.50E
Donga Nigeria **77** 7.45N 10.05E
Donga *r.* Nigeria **77** 8.20N 10.00E
Dongara Australia **89** 29.15S114.56E
Dongargarh India **63** 21.12N 80.44E
Dongbei Pingyuan *f.* China **54** 42.30N123.00E
Dongchuan China **52** 26.10N103.02E
Dongco China **63** 32.07N 84.35E
Dongfang China **55** 19.05N108.39E
Donggala Indonesia **58** 0.48S119.45E
Donggou China **54** 39.52N124.08E
Dongguang China **54** 37.53N116.32E
Donghai China **54** 34.35N118.49E
Donghai *i.* China **55** 21.02N110.25E
Dong Hoi Vietnam **56** 17.32N106.35E
Dong Jiang *r.* China **55** 23.00N113.33E
Dongkalang Indonesia **59** 0.12N120.07E
Dongling China **54** 41.44N123.32E
Dongou Congo **78** 2.05N 18.00E
Dongping Hu *l.* China **54** 35.55N116.15E
Dongqiao China **63** 31.57N 90.30E
Dongsheng China **54** 39.49N109.59E
Dongtai China **54** 32.42N120.26E
Dongting Hu *l.* China **55** 29.10N113.00E
Dongtou *i.* China **55** 27.50N121.08E
Dong Ujimqin Qi China **54** 45.33N116.50E
Dongxi China **55** 28.42N106.40E
Dongxing China **55** 21.33N107.58E
Donington U.K. **12** 52.55N 0.12W
Donja Stubica Yugo. **31** 45.59N 15.58E
Donji Vakuf Yugo. **31** 44.09N 17.25E
Dönna *i.* Norway **40** 66.05N 12.30E
Donnacona Canada **105** 46.40N 71.47W
Donnybrook Australia **89** 33.34S115.47E
Donnybrook R.S.A. **80** 29.55S 29.51E
Donora U.S.A. **114** 40.11N 79.52W
Doodlakine Australia **89** 31.41S117.23E
Doon, Loch U.K. **14** 55.15N 4.23W
Doondi Australia **93** 28.16S148.25E
Dor Israel **67** 32.37N 34.55E
Dora, L. Australia **88** 22.05S122.55E
Dora Baltea *r.* Italy **30** 45.11N 8.05E
Doran L. Canada **101** 61.13N108.06W
Dorchester U.K. **13** 50.52N 2.28W
Dorchester, C. Canada **99** 65.29N 77.30W
Dordogne *d.* France **20** 45.10N 0.45E
Dordogne *r.* France **20** 45.02N 0.35W
Dordrecht Neth. **16** 51.48N 4.40E
Dordrecht R.S.A. **80** 31.22S 27.02E
Dore, Mont *mtn.* France **20** 45.35N 2.48E
Doré L. Canada **101** 54.46N107.17W
Dorfen W. Germany **39** 48.17N 12.08E
Dorgali Italy **32** 40.17N 9.35E
Dori U. Volta **76** 14.03N 0.02W
Dorion Canada **105** 45.23N 74.03W
Dorking U.K. **13** 51.14N 0.20W
Dormagen W. Germany **38** 51.05N 6.50E
Dormans France **19** 49.04N 3.38E
Dornbirn Austria **39** 47.25N 9.44E
Dornie U.K. **14** 57.16N 5.31W
Dornoch U.K. **14** 57.52N 4.02W
Dornoch Firth *est.* U.K. **14** 57.50N 4.04W
Dornogovi *d.* Mongolia **54** 44.00N110.00E
Dornum W. Germany **38** 53.40N 7.28E
Doro Mali **76** 16.09N 0.51W
Dorohoi Romania **37** 47.57N 26.24E
Dörpen W. Germany **38** 52.57N 7.20E
Dorrigo Australia **93** 30.20S152.41E
Dorris U.S.A. **108** 41.58N121.55W
Dorset Canada **104** 45.14N 78.54W
Dorset *d.* U.K. **13** 50.48N 2.25W
Dorset U.S.A. **115** 43.15N 73.06W
Dorset, C. Canada **99** 64.10N 76.40W
Dorset Peak *mtn.* U.S.A. **115** 43.19N 73.02W
Dorsten W. Germany **38** 51.39N 6.58E
Dortmund W. Germany **38** 51.31N 7.28E
Dortmund-Ems Kanal W. Germany **38** 52.00N 7.36E
Dorval Canada **105** 45.27N 73.44W
Dos Bahías, C. Argentina **125** 44.55S 65.32W
Dos Hermanas Spain **27** 37.17N 5.55W
Dosquet Canada **105** 46.28N 71.33W
Dosse *r.* E. Germany **38** 53.13N 12.20E
Dosso Niger **77** 13.03N 3.10E
Dosso *d.* Niger **77** 13.00N 3.15E
Dossor U.S.S.R. **45** 47.31N 53.01E
Dothan U.S.A. **113** 31.12N 85.25W
Douai France **19** 50.22N 3.04E
Douako Guinea **76** 9.45N 10.08W
Douala Cameroon **77** 4.05N 9.43E
Douarnenez France **18** 48.06N 4.20W
Double Mer *g.* Canada **103** 54.05N 59.00W
Doubs *d.* France **19** 47.10N 6.25E
Doubs *r.* France **19** 46.54N 5.02E
Doubtful Island B. Australia **89** 34.15S119.30E
Doubtless B. New Zealand **86** 35.10S173.30E
Doudeville France **18** 49.43N 0.48E
Douentza Mali **76** 14.58N 2.48W
Douglas *r.* Australia **92** 28.35S136.50E
Douglas R.S.A. **80** 29.03S 23.45E
Douglas U.K. **12** 54.09N 4.29W
Douglas Ariz. U.S.A. **109** 31.21N109.33W
Douglas Ga. U.S.A. **113** 31.30N 82.54W
Douglas Mich. U.S.A. **112** 42.38N 86.13W
Douglas Wyo. U.S.A. **108** 42.45N105.24W
Douglas L. U.S.A. **104** 45.34N 84.39W
Douglas Pt. Canada **104** 44.20N 81.35W
Doulaincourt France **19** 48.19N 5.12E
Doulevant-le-Château France **19** 48.23N 4.55E
Doullens France **19** 50.09N 2.21E
Doumé Cameroon **77** 4.13N 13.30E
Douna Mali **76** 12.40N 6.00W
Dounreay U.K. **14** 58.35N 3.42W
Dourados Brazil **124** 22.09S 54.52W
Dourdan France **19** 48.32N 2.01E
Douro *r.* Portugal **26** 41.08N 8.40W
Douvres France **18** 49.17N 0.23W
Douze *r.* France **20** 43.54N 0.30W
Dove *r.* Derbys. U.K. **12** 52.50N 1.35W
Dover U.K. **13** 51.07N 1.19E
Dover Del. U.S.A. **115** 39.10N 75.32W
Dover N.H. U.S.A. **115** 43.12N 70.56W
Dover N.J. U.S.A. **115** 40.53N 74.34W
Dover Ohio U.S.A. **114** 40.32N 81.29W
Dover Tenn. U.S.A. **113** 36.30N 87.50W
Dover, Pt. Australia **89** 32.32S125.30E
Dover, Str. of U.K. **13** 51.00N 1.30E
Dovey *r.* U.K. **13** 52.33N 3.56W
Dovrefjell *mts.* Norway **41** 62.06N 9.25E
Dovsk U.S.S.R. **37** 53.07N 30.29E
Dowa Malawi **79** 13.40S 33.55E
Dowagiac U.S.A. **112** 41.58N 86.06W
Dowerin Australia **89** 31.15S117.00E
Dowlatābād Iran **65** 28.19N 56.40E
Dowlat Yār Afghan. **62** 34.33N 65.47E
Down *d.* U.K. **15** 54.20N 6.00W
Downey U.S.A. **108** 42.26N112.07W
Downham Market U.K. **13** 52.36N 0.22E
Downpatrick U.K. **15** 54.21N 5.43W
Downpatrick Head Rep. of Ire. **15** 54.20N 9.22W
Downton, Mt. Canada **100** 52.42N124.51W
Dowra Rep. of Ire. **15** 54.11N 8.02W
Doylestown U.S.A. **115** 40.19N 75.08W
Dozois, Résr. Canada **105** 47.30N 77.05W
Drâa, Hamada du *f.* Algeria **74** 29.00N 6.00W
Drâa, Oued *wadi* Morocco **74** 28.40N 11.06W
Drac *r.* France **21** 45.13N 5.41E
Drachten Neth. **16** 53.05N 6.06E
Dragaš Yugo. **34** 42.05N 20.35E
Drăgăşani Romania **37** 44.40N 24.16E
Dragoman, Pasul *pass* Bulgaria / Yugo. **29** 42.56N 22.52E
Dragonera, Isla *i.* Spain **25** 39.35N 2.19E
Dragon's Mouth *str.* Trinidad **122** 11.00N 61.35W
Dragovishtitsa Bulgaria **34** 42.22N 22.39E
Draguignan France **21** 43.32N 6.28E
Drake Australia **93** 28.55S152.24E
Drake U.S.A. **110** 47.55N100.23W
Drakensberge *mts.* R.S.A. / Lesotho **80** 30.00S 29.05E
Drake Passage *str.* Atlantic Oc. **127** 59.00S 65.00W
Dráma Greece **34** 41.09N 24.08E
Drammen Norway **42** 59.44N 10.15E
Drās Jammu & Kashmir **62** 34.27N 75.46E
Drau *r. see* Drava Austria **30**
Drava *r.* Yugo. **31** 45.33N 18.55E
Dravinja *r.* Yugo. **31** 46.22N 15.57E
Drayton Australia **91** 27.40S151.50E
Drayton Valley *town* Canada **100** 53.25N114.58W
Drenovets Bulgaria **34** 43.42N 22.59E
Drenthe *d.* Neth. **16** 52.52N 6.30E
Dresden E. Germany **38** 51.03N 13.44E
Dresden *d.* E. Germany **38** 51.03N 13.44E
Dresden U.S.A. **114** 40.07N 82.01W
Dreux France **18** 48.44N 1.22E
Driftwood Canada **102** 49.08N 81.23W
Driftwood U.S.A. **114** 41.20N 78.08W
Drin *r.* Albania **34** 41.37N 20.28E
Drina *r.* Yugo. **31** 44.53N 19.21E
Drniš Yugo. **31** 43.51N 16.09E
Dröbak Norway **42** 59.39N 10.39E
Drocourt Canada **104** 45.47N 80.22W
Drogheda Rep. of Ire. **15** 53.42N 6.23W
Drogobych U.S.S.R. **37** 49.10N 23.30E
Droitwich U.K. **13** 52.16N 2.10W
Drokiya U.S.S.R. **37** 48.07N 27.49E
Drôme *d.* France **21** 44.35N 5.10E
Drôme *r.* France **21** 44.46N 4.46E
Dromedary, C. Australia **93** 36.18S150.15E
Dronero Italy **30** 44.28N 7.22E
Dronfield U.K. **12** 53.18N 1.29W
Dronne *r.* France **20** 45.02N 0.09W
Dronninglund Denmark **42** 57.09N 10.18E
Dronning Maud Land *f.* Antarctica **128** 74.00S 10.00E
Drumbo Canada **104** 43.14N 80.33W
Drumheller Canada **100** 51.25N112.40W
Drum Hills Rep. of Ire. **15** 52.03N 7.42W
Drummond U.S.A. **104** 46.02N 83.42W
Drummond I. U.S.A. **104** 46.00N 83.40W
Drummond Range *mts.* Australia **90** 23.30S147.15E
Drummondville Canada **105** 45.53N 72.29W
Drummore U.K. **14** 54.41N 4.54W
Druskininkai U.S.S.R. **37** 53.48N 23.58E
Drut *r.* U.S.S.R. **37** 53.03N 30.42E
Drvar Yugo. **31** 44.22N 16.24E
Dryanovo Bulgaria **34** 42.58N 25.27E
Dry B. U.S.A. **100** 59.08N138.25W
Dryden Canada **102** 49.47N 92.50W
Dryden U.S.A. **115** 42.29N 76.18W
Drymen U.K. **14** 56.04N 4.27W
Drysdale *r.* Australia **88** 13.59S126.51E
Dschang Cameroon **77** 5.28N 10.02E
Dua *r.* Zaïre **78** 3.12N 20.55E
Du'an China **55** 24.01N108.06E
Ḑubā Saudi Arabia **64** 27.21N 35.40E
Dubai *see* Dubayy U.A.E. **65**
Dubawnt *r.* Canada **99** 62.50N102.00W
Dubawnt L. Canada **101** 63.04N101.42W
Dubayy U.A.E. **65** 25.13N 55.17E
Dubbo Australia **93** 32.16S148.41E
Dubica Yugo. **31** 45.11N 16.48E
Dublin Rep. of Ire. **15** 53.21N 6.18W
Dublin *d.* Rep. of Ire. **15** 53.20N 6.18W
Dublin U.S.A. **113** 32.31N 82.54W
Dublin B. Rep. of Ire. **15** 53.20N 6.09W
Dubno U.S.S.R. **37** 50.28N 25.40E
Dubois Idaho U.S.A. **108** 44.10N112.14W
Du Bois Penn. U.S.A. **114** 41.07N 78.46W
Dubovka U.S.S.R. **45** 49.04N 44.48E
Dubréka Guinea **76** 9.50N 13.32W
Dubrovitsa U.S.S.R. **37** 51.38N 26.40E
Dubrovnik Yugo. **31** 42.38N 18.07E
Dubuque U.S.A. **110** 42.30N 90.41W
Duchesne U.S.A. **108** 40.10N110.24W
Duchess Australia **90** 21.22S139.52E
Duchess Australia **87** 21.22S139.52E
Ducie I. Pacific Oc. **85** 24.40S124.48W
Du Couëdic, C. Australia **92** 36.00S136.10E
Duderstadt W. Germany **38** 51.31N 10.16E
Dudhnai India **63** 25.59N 90.44E
Dudinka U.S.S.R. **51** 69.27N 86.13E
Dudley U.K. **13** 52.30N 2.05W
Dudna *r.* India **62** 19.07N 76.54E
Dudo Somali Rep. **71** 9.20N 50.14E
Dudweiler W. Germany **39** 49.17N 7.02E
Duékoué Ivory Coast **76** 6.50N 7.22W
Duerna *r.* Spain **26** 42.19N 5.54W
Duero *r. see* Douro Spain **26**
Duff Creek *town* Australia **92** 28.28S135.51E
Dufftown U.K. **14** 57.27N 3.09W
Duga Poljana Yugo. **34** 43.15N 20.14E
Duga Resa Yugo. **31** 45.27N 15.30E
Dugi *i.* Yugo. **31** 44.00N 15.04E
Du Gué *r.* Canada **103** 57.20N 70.48W
Duifken Pt. Australia **90** 12.33S141.38E
Duisburg W. Germany **38** 51.25N 6.46E
Duitama Colombia **122** 5.50N 73.01W
Duiveland *i.* Neth. **16** 51.39N 4.00E
Dujuma Somali Rep. **79** 1.14N 42.37E
Dukat Albania **34** 40.16N 19.32E
Duk Fadiat Sudan **73** 7.45N 31.25E
Duk Faiwil Sudan **73** 7.30N 31.29E
Dukhān Qatar **65** 25.24N 50.47E
Duki Pakistan **62** 30.09N 68.34E
Dukou China **52** 26.33N101.44E
Dukye Dzong Bhutan **63** 27.20N 89.30E
Dulce *r.* Argentina **124** 30.40S 62.00W
Duleek Rep. of Ire. **15** 53.39N 6.24W
Dülmen W. Germany **38** 51.51N 7.16E
Dulovo Bulgaria **37** 43.49N 27.09E
Duluth U.S.A. **110** 46.47N 92.06W
Dūmā Syria **66** 33.33N 36.24E
Dumaguete Phil. **59** 9.20N123.18E
Dumai Indonesia **58** 1.41N101.27E
Dumaran *i.* Phil. **58** 10.33N119.50E
Dumaresq *r.* Australia **93** 28.40S150.28E
Dumaring Indonesia **58** 1.36N118.12E
Dumas Ark. U.S.A. **111** 33.53N 91.29W
Dumas Tex. U.S.A. **111** 35.52N101.58W
Dumbarton U.K. **14** 55.57N 4.35W
Dumbleyung Australia **89** 33.18S117.42E
Dumbrăveni Romania **37** 46.14N 24.35E
Dum-Dum India **63** 22.35N 88.24E
Dumfries U.K. **14** 55.04N 3.37W
Dumfries and Galloway *d.* U.K. **14** 55.05N 3.40W
Dumka India **63** 24.16N 87.15E
Dumoine *r.* Canada **105** 46.13N 77.50W
Dumoine, Lac *l.* Canada **105** 46.53N 77.54W
Dumont, Lac *l.* Canada **105** 46.04N 76.28W
Dumraon India **63** 25.33N 84.09E
Dumyāţ Egypt **66** 31.26N 31.48E
Duna *r. see* Danube Hungary **31**
Dunaföldvár Hungary **31** 46.48N 18.55E
Dunajec *r.* Poland **37** 50.15N 20.44E
Dunajská Streda Czech. **37** 48.01N 17.35E
Dunany Pt. Rep. of Ire. **15** 53.51N 6.15W
Dunărea *r. see* Danube Romania **37**
Dunării, Delta *f.* Romania **37** 45.05N 29.45E
Dunaújváros Hungary **31** 46.58N 18.57E
Dunav *r. see* Danube Bulgaria **37**
Dunav *r. see* Danube Yugo. **37**
Duna-völgyi-föcsatorno *r.* Hungary **31** 46.12N 18.56E
Dunbar U.K. **14** 56.00N 2.31W
Dunbar U.S.A. **114** 38.22N 81.45W
Dunblane U.K. **14** 56.12N 3.59W
Dunboyne Rep. of Ire. **15** 53.26N 6.30W
Duncan Canada **100** 48.45N123.40W
Duncan *r.* Canada **100** 50.11N116.57W
Duncan U.S.A. **111** 34.30N 97.57W
Duncan, C. Canada **102** 52.40N 80.48W
Duncan L. N.W.T. Canada **100** 62.51N113.58W
Duncan L. Que. Canada **102** 53.35N 77.55W
Duncannon U.S.A. **114** 40.23N 77.02W
Duncansby Head U.K. **14** 58.39N 3.01W
Dundalk Canada **104** 44.10N 80.24W
Dundalk Rep. of Ire. **15** 54.01N 6.25W
Dundalk U.S.A. **115** 39.15N 76.31W
Dundalk B. Rep. of Ire. **15** 53.55N 6.17W
Dundas Australia **89** 32.20S121.48E
Dundas Canada **104** 43.16N 79.58W
Dundas, L. Australia **89** 32.35S121.50E
Dundas I. Canada **100** 54.33N130.50W
Dundas Str. Australia **90** 11.20S131.35E
Dundee R.S.A. **80** 28.09S 30.14E
Dundee U.K. **14** 56.28N 3.00W
Dundee Mich. U.S.A. **104** 41.57N 83.40W
Dundee N.Y. U.S.A. **114** 42.31N 76.59W
Dundgovi *d.* Mongolia **54** 45.00N106.00E
Dundrum U.K. **15** 54.16N 5.51W
Dundrum B. U.K. **15** 54.12N 5.46W
Dunedin New Zealand **86** 45.52S170.30E
Dunedin U.S.A. **113** 28.02N 82.47W
Dunfermline U.K. **14** 56.04N 3.29W
Dungannon U.K. **15** 54.31N 6.47W
Dūngarpur India **62** 23.50N 73.43E
Dungarvan Rep. of Ire. **15** 52.06N 7.39W
Dungeness *c.* U.K. **13** 50.55N 0.58E
Dungiven U.K. **15** 54.56N 6.56W
Dungog Australia **93** 32.24S151.46E
Dungu Zaïre **79** 3.40N 28.40E
Dunhuang China **52** 40.00N 94.40E
Dunkeld Qld. Australia **91** 26.55S148.00E
Dunkeld Vic. Australia **92** 37.40S142.23E
Dunkeld U.K. **14** 56.34N 3.36W
Dunkerque France **16** 51.02N 2.23E
Dunkirk *see* Dunkerque France **36**
Dunkirk U.S.A. **114** 42.29N 79.20W
Dunkwa Central Ghana **76** 5.59N 1.45W
Dun Laoghaire Rep. of Ire. **15** 53.17N 6.09W
Dunlap U.S.A. **110** 41.51N 95.36W
Dunleer Rep. of Ire. **15** 53.49N 6.24W
Dun-le-Palestel France **20** 46.17N 1.48E
Dunmahon Rep. of Ire. **15** 52.09N 7.23W
Dunmore U.S.A. **115** 41.25N 75.38W
Dunnet Head U.K. **14** 58.40N 3.23W
Dunning U.S.A. **110** 41.50N100.06W
Dunnville Canada **104** 42.54N 79.36W
Dunoon U.K. **14** 55.57N 4.56W
Dunqulah Sudan **72** 19.10N 30.29E
Dunqunāb Sudan **72** 21.06N 37.05E
Duns U.K. **14** 55.47N 2.20W
Dunsborough Australia **89** 33.37S115.06E
Dunshaughlin Rep. of Ire. **15** 53.30N 6.34W
Dunstable U.K. **13** 51.53N 0.32W
Dunstan Mts. New Zealand **86** 44.45S169.45E
Dunster Canada **100** 53.08N119.50W
Dun-sur-Auron France **19** 46.53N 2.34E
Dun-sur-Meuse France **19** 49.23N 5.11E
Dunyāpur Pakistan **62** 29.48N 71.44E
Duolun China **54** 42.09N116.21E
Duong Dong Vietnam **56** 10.12N103.57E
Dupont U.S.A. **112** 38.53N 85.30W
Duque de Bragança Angola **78** 9.06S 16.11E
Duque de Caxias Brazil **126** 22.47S 43.18W
Duquesne U.S.A. **114** 40.21N 79.51W
Du Quoin U.S.A. **111** 38.01N 89.14W
Dūrā Jordan **67** 31.30N 35.02E
Duran U.S.A. **109** 34.28N105.24W
Durance *r.* France **21** 43.55N 4.44E
Durand U.S.A. **104** 42.55N 83.59W
Durango Mexico **116** 24.01N104.00W
Durango *d.* Mexico **111** 24.30N104.00W
Durango Spain **26** 43.10N 2.37W
Durango U.S.A. **108** 37.16N107.53W
Durant U.S.A. **111** 34.00N 96.23W
Duras France **20** 44.41N 0.11E
Duraton *r.* Spain **26** 41.37N 4.07W
Durazno Uruguay **125** 33.22S 56.31W
Durban R.S.A. **80** 29.50S 30.59E
Durbe U.S.S.R. **41** 56.35N 21.21E
Durbin U.S.A. **114** 38.33N 79.50W
Durdevac Yugo. **31** 46.03N 17.04E
Dureji Pakistan **62** 25.53N 67.18E

Düren to **Elo**

Düren W. Germany **38** 50.48N 6.28E
Durg India **63** 21.11N 81.17E
Durgāpur India **63** 23.29N 87.20E
Durham Canada **104** 44.10N 80.49W
Durham U.K. **12** 54.47N 1.34W
Durham *d.* U.K. **12** 54.42N 1.45W
Durham N.C. U.S.A. **113** 36.00N 78.54W
Durham N.H. U.S.A. **115** 43.08N 70.56W
Durham Sud Canada **105** 45.39N 72.19W
Durlston Head *c.* U.K. **13** 50.35N 1.58W
Durmitor *mtn.* Yugo. **31** 43.08N 19.01E
Durness U.K. **14** 58.33N 4.45W
Durrës Albania **34** 41.19N 19.26E
Durrow Rep. of Ire. **15** 52.51N 7.25W
Dursey Head Rep. of Ire. **15** 51.35N 10.15W
Durūz, Jabal ad *mtn.* Syria **66** 32.42N 36.42E
D'Urville I. New Zealand **86** 40.45S173.50E
Dushak U.S.S.R. **50** 37.13N 60.01E
Dushan China **55** 25.50N107.30E
Dushanbe U.S.S.R. **52** 38.38N 68.51E
Dushore U.S.A. **115** 41.31N 76.24W
Duskotna Bulgaria **29** 42.52N 27.10E
Düsseldorf W. Germany **38** 51.12N 6.47E
Dutch Creek *town* Canada **100** 50.18N115.58W
Dutlhe Botswana **80** 23.55S 23.47E
Dutton Canada **104** 42.39N 81.30W
Dutton, L. Australia **92** 31.49S137.08E
Duvno Yugo. **31** 43.43N 17.14E
Duxbury U.S.A. **115** 42.02N 70.40W
Duxun China **55** 23.57N117.37E
Duyun China **55** 26.12N107.29E
Dve Mogili Bulgaria **34** 43.36N 25.52E
Dvina *r.* U.S.S.R. **9** 57.03N 24.00E
Dvinskaya Guba *b.* U.S.S.R. **44** 64.40N 39.30E
Dwarda Australia **89** 32.45S116.23E
Dwārka India **62** 22.14N 68.58E
Dwellingup Australia **89** 32.42S116.04E
Dwight Canada **104** 45.21N 78.58W
Dyatlovichi U.S.S.R. **37** 52.08N 30.49E
Dyatlovo U.S.S.R. **37** 53.28N 25.28E
Dyer, C. Canada **99** 67.45N 61.45W
Dyer Bay *town* Canada **104** 45.10N 81.18W
Dyérem *r.* Cameroon **77** 6.36N 13.10E
Dyer Plateau Antarctica **128** 70.00S 65.00W
Dyersburg U.S.A. **111** 36.03N 89.23W
Dyfed *d.* U.K. **13** 52.00N 4.17W
Dykh Tau *mtn.* U.S.S.R. **45** 43.04N 43.10E
Dymer U.S.S.R. **37** 50.50N 30.20E
Dyulevo Bulgaria **29** 42.22N 27.10E
Dyultydag *mtn.* U.S.S.R. **65** 41.55N 46.52E
Dzamïn Üüd Mongolia **54** 43.50N111.53E
Dzerzhinsk B.S.S.R. U.S.S.R. **37** 53.40N 27.01E
Dzerzhinsk R.S.F.S.R. U.S.S.R. **44** 56.15N 43.30E
Dzhambul U.S.S.R. **52** 42.50N 71.25E
Dzhankoy U.S.S.R. **23** 45.42N 34.23E
Dzhardzhan U.S.S.R. **51** 68.49N124.08E
Dzhelinde U.S.S.R. **51** 70.09N114.00E
Dzhetygara U.S.S.R. **50** 52.14N 61.10E
Dzhezkazgan U.S.S.R. **50** 47.48N 67.24E
Dzhizak U.S.S.R. **50** 40.06N 67.45E
Dzhugdzhur, Khrebet *mts.* U.S.S.R. **51** 57.30N138.00E
Dzhurin U.S.S.R. **37** 48.40N 28.16E
Działdowo Poland **37** 53.15N 20.10E
Dzierżoniów Poland **36** 50.44N 16.39E
Dzodze Ghana **76** 6.14N 1.00E

E

Eabamet L. Canada **102** 51.30N 88.00W
Eads U.S.A. **110** 38.29N102.47W
Eagle *r.* Canada **103** 53.35N 57.25W
Eagle U.S.A. **110** 39.39N106.50W
Eagle Butte *town* U.S.A. **110** 45.00N101.14W
Eagle Grove U.S.A. **110** 42.40N 93.54W
Eagle L. U.S.A. **112** 46.17N 69.20W
Eagle Lake *town* Canada **104** 45.08N 78.29W
Eagle Lake *town* U.S.A. **112** 47.02N 68.36W
Eagle Pass *town* U.S.A. **111** 28.43N100.30W
Eagle River *town* U.S.A. **110** 45.55N 89.15W
Ealing U.K. **13** 51.31N 0.20W
Earlimart U.S.A. **109** 35.53N119.16W
Earlville U.S.A. **115** 42.44N 75.33W
Earn *r.* U.K. **14** 56.21N 3.18W
Earn, Loch U.K. **14** 56.23N 4.12W
Easingwold U.K. **12** 54.08N 1.11W
Easky Rep. of Ire. **15** 54.17N 8.58W
Easley U.S.A. **113** 34.50N 82.34W
East *r.* Canada **104** 45.20N 79.17W
East Anglian Heights *hills* U.K. **13** 52.03N 0.15E
East Angus Canada **105** 45.29N 71.40W
East Aurora U.S.A. **114** 42.46N 78.37W
East B. U.S.A. **111** 29.30N 94.35W
Eastbourne U.K. **13** 50.46N 0.18E
East Brady U.S.A. **114** 40.59N 79.37W
East Broughton Canada **105** 46.14N 71.05W
East C. New Zealand **86** 37.45S178.30E
East Caroline Basin Pacific Oc. **84** 3.00N147.00E
East China Sea Asia **53** 29.00N125.00E
East Coast *d.* New Zealand **86** 38.20S177.45E
East Dereham U.K. **11** 52.40N 0.57E
Easter I. *see* Pascua, Isla de Pacific Oc. **85**
Eastern *d.* Ghana **76** 6.20N 0.45W
Eastern *d.* Kenya **79** 0.00 38.00E
Eastern Desert *see* Sharqīyah, Aş Şaḩrā' ash Egypt **66**
Eastern Ghāts *mts.* India **61** 16.30N 80.30E
Eastern-Indian-Antarctic Basin *f.* Indian Oc. **49** 56.00S110.00E
Easterville Canada **101** 53.06N 99.53W
East Falkland *i.* Falkland Is. **125** 51.45W 58.50W
East Germany Europe **38** 52.30N 13.00E
East Grand Forks U.S.A. **110** 47.56N 96.55W
East Grinstead U.K. **13** 51.08N 0.01W
Easthampton Mass. U.S.A. **115** 42.16N 72.40W
East Hampton N.Y. U.S.A. **115** 40.58N 72.11W
East Hartford U.S.A. **115** 41.46N 72.39W
East Haven U.S.A. **115** 41.17N 72.52W
East Ilsley U.K. **13** 51.33N 1.15W
East Kilbride U.K. **14** 55.46N 4.09W
East Lansing U.S.A. **104** 42.44N 84.29W
Eastleigh U.K. **13** 50.58N 1.21W
East Liverpool U.S.A. **114** 40.38N 80.35W
East London R.S.A. **80** 33.00S 27.54E
Eastmain Canada **102** 52.15N 78.30W
Eastmain *r.* Canada **102** 52.15N 78.30W
Eastman Canada **105** 45.18N 72.19W
Easton Md. U.S.A. **115** 38.46N 76.04W
Easton Penn. U.S.A. **115** 40.42N 75.12W
Easton Wash. U.S.A. **108** 47.14N121.11W
East Pacific Ridge Pacific Oc. **85** 15.00S112.00W
East Palestine U.S.A. **114** 40.50N 80.33W
East Point *town* U.S.A. **113** 33.41N 84.29W
Eastport U.S.A. **115** 40.49N 72.44W
East Providence U.S.A. **115** 41.49N 71.23W
East Retford U.K. **12** 53.19N 0.55W
East Rochester U.S.A. **114** 43.07N 77.29W
East St. Louis U.S.A. **110** 38.34N 90.04W
East Springfield U.S.A. **114** 41.57N 80.28W
East Sussex *d.* U.K. **13** 50.56N 0.12E
East Sydenham *r.* Canada **104** 42.35N 82.23W
East Tawas U.S.A. **104** 44.17N 83.29W
Eaton U.S.A. **110** 40.32N104.42W
Eau Claire U.S.A. **110** 44.50N 91.30W
Eau-Claire, Lac à l' *l.* Canada **102** 56.10N 74.30W
Eauripik *i.* Caroline Is. **59** 6.42N143.04E
Eauripik-N. Guinea Rise Pacific Oc. **84** 2.00N141.00E
Eauze France **20** 43.52N 0.06E
Eban Nigeria **77** 9.41N 4.54E
Ebbw Vale U.K. **13** 51.47N 3.12W
Ebebiyin Equat. Guinea **78** 2.09N 11.20E
Ebeltoft Denmark **42** 56.12N 10.41E
Ebensburg U.S.A. **114** 40.29N 78.44W
Ebensee Austria **39** 47.48N 13.46E
Eberbach W. Germany **39** 49.28N 8.59E
Ebermannstadt W. Germany **38** 49.23N 11.13E
Ebern W. Germany **39** 50.05N 10.47E
Eberndorf Austria **31** 46.35N 14.38E
Ebersbach E. Germany **38** 51.00N 14.35E
Ebersberg W. Germany **39** 48.04N 11.59E
Eberstein Austria **31** 46.48N 14.34E
Eberswalde E. Germany **38** 52.50N 13.49E
Ebingen W. Germany **39** 48.13N 9.01E
Ebinur Hu *l.* China **52** 45.00N 83.00E
Ebola *r.* Zaïre **73** 3.20N 20.57E
Eboli Italy **33** 40.37N 15.04E
Ebolowa Cameroon **78** 2.56N 11.11E
Ebon *i.* Pacific Oc. **84** 4.38N168.43E
Ebony Namibia **80** 22.05S 15.15E
Ebro *r.* Spain **25** 40.43N 0.54E
Ebro, Delta del *f.* Spain **25** 40.43N 0.54E
Ebro, Embalse del *resr.* Spain **26** 43.00N 4.00W
Ecclefechan U.K. **12** 55.03N 3.18W
Eceabat Turkey **34** 40.11N 26.21E
Echeng China **55** 30.26N114.00E
Echo Bay *town* Canada **104** 46.29N 84.02W
Echternach Lux. **16** 49.49N 6.25E
Echuca Australia **93** 36.10S144.20E
Écija Spain **27** 37.32N 5.05W
Eckernförde W. Germany **38** 54.28N 9.50E
Écommoy France **18** 47.50N 0.16E
Ecuador S. America **122** 1.40S 79.00W
Écueillé France **18** 47.05N 1.21E
Ed Ethiopia **72** 13.52N 41.40E
Ed Sweden **42** 58.55N 11.55E
Edam Neth. **16** 52.30N 5.02E
Eday *i.* U.K. **10** 59.11N 2.47W
Eddrachillis B. U.K. **14** 58.17N 5.15W
Eddystone Pt. Australia **91** 40.58S148.12E
Ede Neth. **16** 52.03N 5.40E
Ede Nigeria **77** 7.45N 4.26E
Edea Cameroon **78** 3.47N 10.15E
Edehon L. Canada **101** 60.25N 97.15W
Eden Australia **93** 37.04S149.54E
Eden Canada **104** 42.47N 80.46W
Eden *r.* Cumbria U.K. **12** 54.57N 3.02W
Eden U.S.A. **108** 42.03N109.26W
Edenburg R.S.A. **80** 29.44S 25.55E
Edendale New Zealand **86** 46.19S168.47E
Edenderry Rep. of Ire. **15** 53.21N 7.05W
Edenhope Australia **92** 37.04S141.20E
Edenton U.S.A. **113** 36.04N 76.39W
Edeowie Australia **92** 31.28S138.29E
Eder *r.* W. Germany **38** 51.13N 9.27E
Ederny U.K. **15** 54.32N 7.40W
Edgartown U.S.A. **115** 41.23N 70.31W
Edgeley U.S.A. **110** 40.07N 98.43W
Edgeöya *i.* Arctic Oc. **128** 77.45N 22.30E
Edgeworthstown Rep. of Ire. **15** 53.42N 7.38W
Edgington Canada **104** 45.23N 79.47W
Édhessa Greece **34** 40.48N 22.05E
Ediacara Australia **92** 30.18S137.50E
Edina Liberia **76** 6.01N 10.10W
Edinboro U.S.A. **114** 41.52N 80.08W
Edinburgh U.K. **14** 55.57N 3.13W
Edirne Turkey **34** 41.40N 26.34E
Edithburgh Australia **92** 35.06S137.44E
Edjudina Australia **89** 29.48S122.23E
Edmond U.S.A. **111** 35.39N 97.29W
Edmonton Canada **100** 53.30N113.30W
Edmundston Canada **103** 47.22N 68.20W
Edna U.S.A. **111** 28.59N 96.39W
Edo *r.* Japan **57** 35.37N139.53E
Edolo Italy **30** 46.11N 10.20E
Edounga Gabon **78** 0.03S 13.43E
Edremit Turkey **29** 39.35N 27.02E
Edremit Körfezi *b.* Turkey **34** 39.30N 26.45E
Edsbruk Sweden **43** 58.02N 16.28E
Edson Canada **100** 53.35N116.26W
Edward, L. Uganda / Zaïre **79** 0.30S 29.30E
Edward's Creek *town* Australia **92** 28.15S135.49E
Edwards Plateau *f.* U.S.A. **111** 31.20N101.00W
Eeklo Belgium **16** 51.11N 3.34E
Eel *r.* U.S.A. **108** 40.40N124.20W
Efate *i.* Vanuatu **84** 17.40S168.25E
Eferding Austria **39** 48.18N 14.02E
Effingham U.S.A. **110** 39.07N 88.33W
Ega *r.* Spain **25** 42.19N 1.55W
Egadi, Isole *is.* Italy **32** 38.00N 12.10E
Egaña Argentina **125** 36.57S 59.06W
Eganville Canada **105** 45.32N 77.06W
Egbe Nigeria **77** 8.13N 5.31E
Egeland U.S.A. **110** 48.38N 99.10W
Eger Hungary **37** 47.54N 20.23E
Egersund Norway **42** 58.27N 6.00E
Egerton, Mt. Australia **88** 24.44S117.40E
Eggenfelden W. Germany **39** 48.25N 12.46E
Egg Harbor U.S.A. **115** 39.32N 74.39W
Égletons France **20** 45.24N 2.03E
Egmont, Mt. New Zealand **86** 39.20S174.05E
Eğridir Turkey **64** 37.52N 30.51E
Eğridir Gölü *l.* Turkey **64** 38.04N 30.55E
Egtved Denmark **42** 55.37N 9.18E
Egypt Africa **72** 26.00N 30.00E
Ehingen W. Germany **39** 48.17N 9.43E
Eiao *i.* Is. Marquises **85** 8.00S140.40W
Éibar Spain **26** 43.11N 2.28W
Eibiswald Austria **31** 46.41N 15.15E
Eichstätt W. Germany **38** 48.54N 11.12E
Eidsvåg Norway **40** 62.47N 8.03E
Eidsvold Australia **90** 25.23S151.08E
Eidsvoll Norway **42** 60.19N 11.14E
Eifel *f.* W. Germany **39** 50.10N 6.40E
Eigg *i.* U.K. **14** 56.53N 6.09W
Eighty Mile Beach *f.* Australia **88** 19.00S121.00E
Eil Somali Rep. **71** 8.00N 49.51E
Eil, Loch U.K. **14** 56.51N 5.12W
Eildon Resr. Australia **93** 37.10S146.00E
Eilenburg E. Germany **38** 51.27N 12.37E
Einasleigh Australia **90** 18.31S144.05E
Einbeck W. Germany **38** 51.49N 9.52E
Eindhoven Neth. **16** 51.26N 5.30E
Einsiedeln Switz. **39** 47.08N 8.45E
Eirunepé Brazil **122** 6.40S 69.52W
Eiseb *r.* Namibia **80** 20.26S 20.05E
Eisenach E. Germany **38** 50.59N 10.19E
Eisenberg E. Germany **38** 50.58N 11.53E
Eisenerz Austria **36** 47.33N 14.53E
Eisenhut *mtn.* Austria **36** 47.00N 13.45E
Eisenhüttenstadt E. Germany **38** 52.10N 14.39E
Eisfeld E. Germany **39** 50.26N 10.54E
Eišiškes U.S.S.R. **37** 54.09N 24.55E
Eisleben E. Germany **38** 51.31N 11.32E
Eitorf W. Germany **38** 50.46N 7.26E
Ejby Denmark **42** 55.26N 9.57E
Ejde Faroe Is. **10** 62.03N 7.06W
Ejea de los Caballeros Spain **25** 42.08N 1.08W
Ejin Qi China **52** 41.50N100.50E
Ejura Ghana **76** 7.24N 1.20W
Ekalaka U.S.A. **108** 45.53N104.33W
Eket Nigeria **77** 4.39N 7.56E
Eketahuna New Zealand **86** 40.39S175.44E
Ekhínos Greece **34** 41.17N 24.59E
Ekibastuz U.S.S.R. **50** 51.45N 75.22E
Ekimchan U.S.S.R. **51** 53.09N133.00E
Eksjö Sweden **43** 57.40N 14.57E
Ekträsk Sweden **40** 64.29N 19.50E
Ekuku Zaïre **78** 0.42S 21.38E
Ekwan *r.* Canada **102** 53.30N 84.00W
El Aaiún W. Sahara **74** 27.09N 13.12W
El Afwein Somali Rep. **71** 9.55N 47.14E
El Alia Tunisia **32** 37.10N 10.03E
Elands *r.* Trans. R.S.A. **80** 24.52S 29.20E
El Arahal Spain **27** 37.16N 5.33W
El Arco Mexico **109** 28.00N113.25W
El Arenal Spain **25** 39.30N 2.45E
El Asnam Algeria **75** 36.10N 1.20E
Elassón Greece **34** 39.54N 22.11E
Elat Israel **66** 29.33N 34.56E
Elâzig Turkey **64** 38.41N 39.14E
Elba *i.* Italy **30** 42.46N 10.17E
El Barco de Avilla Spain **26** 40.21N 5.31W
El Barco de Valdeorras Spain **26** 42.25N 6.59W
El Barril Mexico **109** 28.22N113.00W
Elbasan Albania **34** 41.09N 20.09E
Elbasan Berat *d.* Albania **34** 40.58N 20.00E
El Baúl Venezuela **122** 8.59N 68.16W
Elbe *r.* W. Germany **38** 53.50N 10.00E
Elbe-Havel-Kanal E. Germany **38** 52.23N 12.15E
Elbe-Lübeck-Kanal W. Germany **38** 53.50N 10.36E
El Beni *d.* Bolivia **124** 14.00S 65.30W
Elbert, Mt. U.S.A. **110** 39.07N106.27W
Elberton U.S.A. **113** 34.05N 82.54W
Elbeuf France **18** 49.17N 1.00E
Elbistan Turkey **64** 38.14N 37.11E
Elbląg Poland **37** 54.10N 19.25E
El Bonillo Spain **26** 38.57N 2.32W
Elbrus *mtn.* U.S.S.R. **45** 43.21N 42.29E
El Bur Somali Rep. **71** 4.40N 46.40E
Elburg Neth. **16** 52.27N 5.50E
El Burgo de Osma Spain **26** 41.35N 3.04W
Elburz Mts. *see* Alborz, Reshteh-ye Kūhhā-ye Iran **65**
El Cajon U.S.A. **109** 32.48N116.58W
El Callao Venezuela **122** 7.18N 61.48W
El Campo U.S.A. **111** 29.12N 96.16W
El Casco Mexico **111** 25.34N104.35W
El Cenajo, Embalse de *resr.* Spain **27** 38.25N 2.00W
El Centro U.S.A. **109** 32.48N115.34W
Elche Spain **25** 38.15N 0.42W
Elche de la Sierra Spain **25** 38.27N 2.03W
Elcho U.S.A. **110** 45.26N 89.11W
Elcho I. Australia **90** 11.55S135.45E
El Corral Mexico **111** 25.09N 97.58W
El Cozón Mexico **109** 31.18N112.29W
El Cuy Argentina **125** 39.57S 68.20W
Elda Spain **25** 38.29N 0.47W
El Dab Somali Rep. **71** 8.58N 46.38E
Elde *r.* E. Germany **36** 53.17N 12.40E
El Der Ethiopia **71** 5.08N 43.08E
Elder, L. Australia **92** 30.39S140.13E
El Dere Somali Rep. **71** 3.55N 47.10E
El Desemboque Mexico **109** 29.30N112.27W
El Djouf *des.* Mauritania **74** 20.30N 7.30W
Eldon U.S.A. **110** 38.21N 93.35W
Eldorado Canada **101** 59.35N108.30W
El Dorado Ark. U.S.A. **111** 33.13N 92.40W
El Dorado Kans. U.S.A. **111** 37.49N 96.52W
El Dorado Venezuela **122** 6.45N 61.37W
Eldoret Kenya **79** 0.31N 35.17E
Eldsdro Sweden **43** 59.53N 18.33E
Electra U.S.A. **111** 34.02N 98.55W
El Eglab *f.* Algeria **74** 26.30N 4.15W
Elei, Wādī Sudan **72** 22.04N 34.27E
Eleja U.S.S.R. **41** 56.26N 23.42E
Elektrostal U.S.S.R. **44** 55.46N 38.30E
Elena Bulgaria **34** 42.56N 25.53E
Elephant Butte Resr. U.S.A. **109** 33.19N107.10W
Elephant I. Atlantic Oc. **121** 61.00S 55.00W
El Eulma Algeria **75** 36.09N 5.41E
Eleuthera I. Bahamas **113** 25.15N 76.20W
Elevsís Greece **35** 38.02N 23.33E
Elevtheroúpolis Greece **34** 40.55N 24.16E
El Ferrol Spain **26** 43.29N 8.14W
Elgå Norway **41** 62.11N 11.07E
Elgenfield Canada **104** 43.10N 81.22W
Elgin Canada **105** 44.36N 76.13W
Elgin Canada **101** 49.26N100.15W
Elgin U.K. **14** 57.39N 3.20W
Elgin Ill. U.S.A. **110** 42.03N 88.19W
Elgin Nev. U.S.A. **108** 37.21N114.30W
Elgin Oreg. U.S.A. **108** 45.34N117.55W
Elgin Tex. U.S.A. **111** 30.21N 97.22W
El Golea Algeria **75** 30.34N 2.53E
Elgon, Mt. Kenya / Uganda **79** 1.07N 34.35E
El Grove Spain **26** 42.30N 8.52W
El Hamurre Somali Rep. **71** 7.11N 48.55E
El Haouaria Tunisia **32** 37.03N 11.02E
Elida U.S.A. **111** 33.57N103.39W
Elim Namibia **80** 17.47S 15.30E
Elin Pelin Bulgaria **34** 42.40N 23.38E
Elista U.S.S.R. **45** 46.18N 44.14E
Elizabeth Australia **92** 34.45S138.39E
Elizabeth N.J. U.S.A. **115** 40.40N 74.11W
Elizabeth W.Va. U.S.A. **114** 39.04N 81.24W
Elizabeth City U.S.A. **113** 36.18N 76.16W
Elizabethtown Ky. U.S.A. **113** 37.41N 85.51W
Elizabethtown N.Y. U.S.A. **105** 44.13N 73.36W
Elizabethtown Penn. U.S.A. **115** 40.09N 76.36W
El Jadida Morocco **74** 33.16N 8.30W
Elk *r.* Canada **100** 49.10N115.14W
Elk Poland **37** 53.50N 22.22E
Elk *r.* U.S.A. **114** 38.21N 81.38W
El Kairouan Tunisia **75** 35.41N 10.07E
El Kala Algeria **32** 36.50N 8.30E
El Kasserine Tunisia **75** 35.11N 8.48E
Elk City U.S.A. **111** 35.25N 99.25W
El Kef Tunisia **75** 36.11N 8.43E
El-Kelâa-des-Srarhna Morocco **74** 32.02N 7.23W
El Kere Ethiopia **73** 5.48N 42.10E
Elkhart Ind. U.S.A. **110** 41.52N 85.56W
Elkhart Kans. U.S.A. **111** 37.00N101.54W
El Khnâchîch *f.* Mali **76** 21.50N 3.45W
Elkhorn Canada **101** 49.58N101.14W
Elkhovo Bulgaria **34** 42.09N 26.35E
Elkins N.Mex. U.S.A. **109** 33.41N104.04W
Elkins W.Va. U.S.A. **114** 38.55N 79.51W
Elkland U.S.A. **114** 41.59N 77.21W
Elko U.S.A. **108** 40.50N115.46W
Elkton Md. U.S.A. **115** 39.36N 75.50W
Elkton Va. U.S.A. **114** 38.25N 78.38W
Elleker Australia **89** 34.55S117.40E
Ellen, Mt. U.S.A. **106** 38.06N110.50W
Ellenboro U.S.A. **114** 39.17N 81.04W
Ellenburg U.S.A. **105** 44.54N 73.51W
Ellendale Australia **88** 17.56S124.48E
Ellensburg U.S.A. **108** 47.00N120.32W
Ellenville U.S.A. **115** 41.43N 74.24W
Ellesmere I. Canada **99** 78.00N 82.00W
Ellesmere Port U.K. **12** 53.17N 2.55W
Ellicottville U.S.A. **114** 42.17N 78.40W
Elliot R.S.A. **80** 31.19S 27.49E
Elliot Lake *town* Canada **104** 46.23N 82.39W
Ellis U.S.A. **110** 38.56N 99.34W
Elliston Australia **92** 33.39S134.55E
Ellon U.K. **14** 57.22N 2.05W
Ellora India **62** 20.01N 75.10E
Ellwangen W. Germany **39** 48.57N 10.07E
Ellwood City U.S.A. **114** 40.50N 80.17W
Elm Switz. **39** 46.55N 9.11E
El Mahdia Tunisia **75** 35.30N 11.04E
Elmali Turkey **64** 36.43N 29.56E
El Maneadero Mexico **109** 31.45N116.35W
Elmer U.S.A. **115** 39.36N 75.10W
El Metlaoui Tunisia **75** 34.20N 8.24E
Elmhurst U.S.A. **110** 41.54N 87.56W
Elmina Ghana **76** 5.07N 1.21W
Elmira Canada **104** 43.36N 80.33W
Elmira U.S.A. **114** 42.06N 76.49W
El Molinillo Spain **27** 39.28N 4.13W
Elmore Australia **93** 36.30S144.40E
El Mreiti *well* Mauritania **74** 23.29N 7.52W
El Mreyyé *f.* Mauritania **74** 19.30N 7.00W
Elmshorn W. Germany **38** 53.45N 9.39E
Elmsta Sweden **43** 59.58N 18.45E
Elmvale Canada **104** 44.35N 79.52W
Elne France **20** 42.36N 2.58E
El Niybo Ethiopia **73** 4.32N 39.59E
Elo *d.* Ethiopia **73** 11.30N 40.00E

Eygurande to Floriano

Eygurande France 20 45.40N 2.26E
Eyjafjördhur est. Iceland 40 65.54N 18.15W
Eymet France 20 44.40N 0.24E
Eymoutiers France 20 45.44N 1.44E
Eyrarbakki Iceland 40 63.52N 21.09W
Eyre Australia 89 32.15S126.18E
Eyre r. Australia 90 26.40S139.00E
Eyre, L. Australia 92 28.30S137.25E
Eyre Pen. Australia 92 34.00S135.45E
Ezine Turkey 34 39.48N 26.12E

F

Faaone Tahiti 85 17.40S149.18W
Faberg Norway 41 61.10N 10.22E
Faborg Denmark 42 55.06N 10.15E
Fabre Canada 104 47.12N 79.23W
Fabriano Italy 30 43.20N 12.54E
Facatativá Colombia 122 4.48N 74.32W
Facundo Argentina 125 45.19S 69.59W
Fada Chad 72 17.14N 21.33E
Fada-N'Gourma U. Volta 76 12.03N 0.22E
Fadd Hungary 31 46.28N 18.50E
Faenza Italy 30 44.17N 11.53E
Fafa Mali 76 15.20N 0.43E
Fafe Portugal 26 41.27N 8.10W
Fafen r. Ethiopia 71 6.07N 44.20E
Fagamalo W. Samoa 84 13.24S172.22W
Făgăraş Romania 37 45.51N 24.58E
Fagernes Norway 41 60.59N 9.17E
Fagersta Sweden 43 60.00N 15.47E
Faguibine, Lac l. Mali 76 16.45N 3.54W
Fagus Egypt 66 30.44N 31.47E
Fā'id Egypt 66 30.19N 32.19E
Fairbanks U.S.A. 98 64.50N147.50W
Fairborn U.S.A. 112 39.48N 84.03W
Fairbury U.S.A. 110 40.08N 97.11W
Fairfax U.S.A. 111 36.34N 96.42W
Fairfield Ala. U.S.A. 113 33.29N 86.59W
Fairfield Calif. U.S.A. 108 38.15N122.03W
Fairfield Conn. U.S.A. 115 41.09N 73.15W
Fairfield Ill. U.S.A. 110 38.22N 88.23W
Fairfield Iowa U.S.A. 110 40.56N 91.57W
Fairgrove U.S.A. 104 43.31N 83.33W
Fairhaven Mass. U.S.A. 115 41.39N 70.54W
Fair Haven N.Y. U.S.A. 114 43.19N 76.42W
Fair Haven Vt. U.S.A. 115 43.36N 73.16W
Fair Head U.K. 15 55.13N 6.09W
Fair Isle U.K. 14 59.32N 1.38W
Fairlie New Zealand 86 44.06S170.50E
Fairmont Minn. U.S.A. 110 43.39N 94.28W
Fairmont W.Va. U.S.A. 114 39.29N 80.09W
Fairport U.S.A. 114 43.06N 77.27W
Fairport Harbor U.S.A. 114 41.45N 81.17W
Fairview Canada 100 56.05N118.25W
Fairview Mich. U.S.A. 104 44.44N 84.03W
Fairview Mont. U.S.A. 108 47.51N104.03W
Fairview Okla. U.S.A. 111 36.16N 98.29W
Fairview Penn. U.S.A. 114 42.03N 80.13W
Fairview Utah U.S.A. 108 39.38N111.26W
Fairweather, Mt. U.S.A. 100 59.00N137.30W
Faisalābād Pakistan 62 31.25N 73.05E
Faistós site Greece 35 35.01N 24.48E
Faith U.S.A. 110 45.02N102.02W
Faizābād India 63 26.47N 82.08E
Fajr, Wādī r. Saudi Arabia 64 30.00N 38.25E
Fakaofo Pacific Oc. 84 9.30S171.15W
Fakenham U.K. 12 52.50N 0.51E
Fakfak Indonesia 59 2.55S132.17E
Fakse Denmark 43 55.15N 12.08E
Fakse Bugte b. Denmark 43 55.10N 12.15E
Falaise France 18 48.54N 0.12W
Falakrón Óros mts. Greece 34 41.15N 23.58E
Falam Burma 56 22.58N 93.45E
Falcarragh Rep. of Ire. 15 55.08N 8.06W
Falconara Marittima Italy 30 43.37N 13.24E
Falconbridge Canada 104 46.35N 80.48W
Falcone, Capo del c. Italy 32 40.57N 8.12E
Falconer U.S.A. 114 42.07N 79.12W
Falcon Resr. U.S.A. 111 26.37N 99.11W
Falealupo W. Samoa 84 13.29S172.47W
Falémé r. Senegal 76 14.55N 12.00W
Faleshty U.S.S.R. 37 47.30N 27.45E
Falfurrias U.S.A. 111 27.14N 98.09W
Falkenberg E. Germany 38 51.35N 13.14E
Falkenberg Sweden 43 56.54N 12.28E
Falkenhagen E. Germany 38 53.12N 12.12E
Falkensee E. Germany 38 52.33N 13.04E
Falkenstein W. Germany 39 49.06N 12.30E
Falkirk U.K. 14 56.00N 3.48W
Falkland Is. Atlantic Oc. 125 51.45W 59.00W
Falkland Sd. str. Falkland Is. 125 51.45W 59.25W
Falköping Sweden 43 58.10N 13.31E
Fallbrook U.S.A. 109 33.23N117.15W
Fallon U.S.A. 108 46.50N105.07W
Fall River town U.S.A. 115 41.43N 71.08W
Falls City U.S.A. 110 40.03N 95.36W
Falmouth U.K. 13 50.09N 5.05W
Falmouth Mass. U.S.A. 115 41.34N 70.38W
Falmouth Va. U.S.A. 114 38.19N 77.28W
False B. R.S.A. 80 34.10S 18.40E
False C. U.S.A. 115 38.29N 74.59W
False Pt. India 63 20.22N 86.52E
Falset Spain 25 41.08N 0.49E
Falster i. Denmark 41 54.48N 11.58E
Fălticeni Romania 37 47.28N 26.18E
Falun Sweden 41 60.36N 15.38E
Famagusta see Ammókhostos Cyprus 66
Family L. Canada 101 51.54N 95.30W
Famoso U.S.A. 109 35.36N119.14W
Fanárion Greece 34 39.50N 21.47E
Fandriana Madagascar 81 20.14S 47.23E
Fangak Sudan 73 9.04N 30.53E
Fangcheng China 54 33.16N112.59E
Fangdou Shan mts. China 55 30.36N108.45E
Fang Xian China 55 32.04N110.47E
Fanjing Shan mtn. China 55 27.57N108.50E
Fannich, Loch U.K. 14 57.38N 5.00W
Fanö i. Denmark 42 55.25N 8.25E
Fano Italy 30 43.50N 13.00E
Fan Xian China 54 35.59N115.31E
Faradje Zaïre 79 3.45N 29.43E
Faradofay Madagascar 81 25.02S 47.00E
Farafangana Madagascar 81 22.49S 47.50E
Farāfirah, Wāḥāt al oasis Egypt 64 27.15N 28.10E
Farāh Afghan. 62 32.22N 62.07E
Farāh d. Afghan. 62 33.00N 62.00E
Farāh r. Afghan. 62 31.29N 61.24E
Faranah Guinea 76 10.01N 10.47W
Farasān, Jazā'ir is. Saudi Arabia 72 16.48N 41.54E
Faratsiho Madagascar 81 19.24S 46.57E
Faraulep is. Mariana Is. 59 8.36N144.33E
Fardes r. Spain 27 37.35N 3.00W
Fareara, Pt. Tahiti 85 17.52S149.39W
Fareham U.K. 13 50.52N 1.11W
Farewell, C. see Farvel, Kap Greenland 99
Farewell, C. New Zealand 86 40.30S172.35E
Färgelanda Sweden 42 58.34N 11.59E
Fargo U.S.A. 110 46.52N 96.48W
Fāri'ah r. Jordan 67 32.06N 35.31E
Faribault U.S.A. 110 44.18N 93.16W
Farīdpur Bangla. 63 23.36N 89.50E
Farim Guinea Bissau 76 12.30N 15.09W
Farina Australia 92 30.05S138.20E
Färjestaden Sweden 43 56.39N 16.27E
Farkwa Tanzania 79 5.26S 35.15E
Farley Canada 105 46.18N 76.00W
Farmerville U.S.A. 111 32.47N 92.24W
Farmington Mo. U.S.A. 111 37.47N 90.25W
Farmington N.H. U.S.A. 115 43.24N 71.04W
Farmington N.Mex. U.S.A. 108 36.44N108.12W
Farnborough Hants. U.K. 13 51.17N 0.46W
Farne Is. U.K. 12 55.38N 1.36W
Farnham Canada 105 45.17N 72.59W
Farnham U.K. 13 51.13N 0.49W
Faro Brazil 123 2.11S 56.44W
Faro Portugal 27 37.01N 7.56W
Faro d. Portugal 27 37.15N 8.10W
Faroe Bank f. Atlantic Oc. 10 61.00N 9.00W
Faroe Is. Europe 10 62.00N 7.00W
Fårön i. Sweden 43 57.56N 19.08E
Fårösund Sweden 43 57.52N 19.03E
Farrell U.S.A. 114 41.13N 80.30W
Farrukhābād India 63 27.24N 79.34E
Fársala Greece 35 39.18N 22.23E
Fārsī Afghan. 62 33.47N 63.15E
Farsö Denmark 42 56.47N 9.21E
Farsund Norway 42 58.05N 6.48E
Fartak, Ra's c. S. Yemen 71 15.38N 52.15E
Farvel, Kap c. Greenland 99 60.00N 44.20W
Farwell U.S.A. 111 34.23N103.02W
Fasā Iran 65 28.55N 53.38E
Fasano Italy 33 40.50N 17.22E
Fastov U.S.S.R. 37 50.08N 29.59E
Fatehābād India 62 29.31N 75.28E
Fatehjang Pakistan 62 33.34N 72.39E
Fatehpur Rāj. India 62 27.59N 74.57E
Fatehpur Uttar P. India 63 25.56N 80.48E
Fatehpur Pakistan 62 31.10N 71.13E
Fatehpur Sīkri India 63 27.06N 77.40E
Fatick Senegal 76 14.19N 16.27W
Fátima Portugal 27 39.37N 8.39W
Fatu Hiva i. Îs. Marquises 85 10.27S138.39W
Fatwā India 63 25.31N 85.19E
Faucilles, Monts mts. France 19 48.07N 6.16E
Faulkton U.S.A. 110 45.02N 99.08W
Faulquemont France 19 49.03N 6.36E
Făurei Romania 37 45.04N 27.15E
Fauske Norway 40 67.17N 15.25E
Favara Italy 32 37.19N 13.40E
Faverges France 21 45.45N 6.18E
Favignana i. Italy 32 37.56N 12.19E
Fawcett Canada 100 54.34N114.06W
Fawcett L. Canada 102 51.20N 91.46W
Fawn r. Canada 102 55.20N 88.20W
Faxaflói b. Iceland 40 64.30N 22.50W
Faxe r. Sweden 40 63.15N 17.15E
Fayence France 21 43.37N 6.41E
Fayette U.S.A. 113 33.42N 87.50W
Fayetteville Ark. U.S.A. 111 36.04N 94.10W
Fayetteville N.C. U.S.A. 113 35.03N 78.53W
Fayetteville N.Y. U.S.A. 115 43.02N 76.00W
Fayetteville Tenn. U.S.A. 113 35.08N 86.33W
Fayl-Billot France 19 47.47N 5.36E
Fāzilka India 62 30.24N 74.02E
Fāzilpur Pakistan 62 29.18N 70.27E
Fdérik Mauritania 74 22.30N 12.30W
Feale r. Rep. of Ire. 15 52.28N 9.37W
Fear, C. U.S.A. 113 33.50N 77.58W
Fécamp France 18 49.45N 0.22E
Federación Argentina 125 31.00S 57.55W
Federal Argentina 125 30.55S 58.45W
Federal Capital Territory d. Nigeria 77 8.50N 7.00E
Fedovo U.S.S.R. 44 62.22N 39.21E
Fedulki U.S.S.R. 44 65.00N 66.10E
Feeagh, Lough Rep. of Ire. 15 53.56N 9.35W
Fehmarn i. W. Germany 38 54.28N 11.08E
Fehmarn Belt str. W. Germany 38 54.33N 11.20E
Feia, Lagoa l. Brazil 126 22.00S 41.20W
Feijó Brazil 122 8.09S 70.21W
Feilding New Zealand 86 40.10S175.25E
Feira Zambia 79 15.30S 30.27E
Feira de Santana Brazil 123 12.17S 38.53W
Felanitx Spain 25 39.28N 3.08E
Feldbach Austria 31 46.57N 15.54E
Feldberg mtn. W. Germany 39 47.51N 8.02E
Feldkirch Austria 39 47.14N 9.36E
Feldkirchen in Kärnten Austria 39 46.43N 14.05E
Felixstowe U.K. 13 51.58N 1.20E
Fellbach W. Germany 39 48.48N 9.15E
Felletin France 20 45.53N 2.10E
Feltre Italy 30 46.01N 11.54E
Femunden l. Norway 41 62.12N 11.52E
Femundsenden Norway 41 61.55N 11.55E
Fenelon Falls Canada 104 44.32N 78.45W
Fenerwa Ethiopia 73 13.05N 38.58E
Fengcheng Jiangxi China 55 28.10N115.45E
Fengcheng Liaoning China 54 40.29N124.00E
Fengfeng China 54 36.35N114.28E
Fenggang China 55 27.58N107.47E
Fengjie China 55 31.02N109.31E
Fengnan China 54 39.30N117.58E
Fengpin Taiwan 55 23.36N121.31E
Fengrun China 54 39.51N118.08E
Fen He r. China 54 35.30N110.38E
Feni Bangla. 63 23.01N 91.20E
Feno, Capo di c. France 21 41.57N 8.36E
Fenoarivo Madagascar 81 18.26S 46.34E
Fenoarivo Atsinanana Madagascar 81 17.22S 49.25E
Fensfjorden est. Norway 41 60.51N 4.50E
Fenton U.S.A. 112 42.48N 83.42W
Fenwick U.S.A. 114 38.14N 80.35W
Fenyang China 54 37.10N111.40E
Feodosiya U.S.S.R. 45 45.03N 35.23E
Ferdows Iran 65 34.00N 58.10E
Fère-Champenoise France 19 48.45N 3.59E
Fère-en-Tardenois France 19 49.12N 3.31E
Ferentino Italy 32 41.42N 13.15E
Ferfer Somali Rep. 71 5.07N 45.07E
Fergana U.S.S.R. 52 40.23N 71.19E
Fergus Canada 104 43.42N 80.22W
Fergus Falls town U.S.A. 110 46.17N 96.04W
Ferguson U.S.A. 110 38.46N 90.19W
Fergusson I. P.N.G. 90 9.30S150.40E
Ferkéssédougou Ivory Coast 76 9.30N 5.10W
Ferlach Austria 31 46.31N 14.18E
Fermanagh d. U.K. 15 54.21N 7.40W
Fermo Italy 31 43.09N 13.43E
Fermoselle Spain 26 41.19N 6.23W
Fermoy Rep. of Ire. 15 52.08N 8.17W
Fernandina Beach town U.S.A. 113 30.40N 81.26W
Fernando de Noronha i Atlantic Oc. 127 3.50S 32.25W
Fernán-Núñez Spain 27 37.40N 4.43W
Fernlee Australia 93 28.12S147.05E
Férrai Greece 34 40.53N 26.10E
Ferrandina Italy 33 40.29N 16.28E
Ferrara Italy 30 44.50N 11.35E
Ferrato, Capo c. Italy 32 39.18N 9.38E
Ferreira do Alentejo Portugal 27 38.03N 8.07W
Ferreñafe Peru 122 6.42S 79.45W
Ferret, Cap c. France 20 44.37N 1.15W
Ferriday U.S.A. 111 31.38N 91.33W
Ferrières France 19 48.05N 2.47E
Fès Morocco 74 34.05N 4.57W
Feshi Zaïre 78 6.08S 18.12E
Festubert Canada 105 47.12N 72.40W
Festus U.S.A. 110 38.13N 90.24W
Feteşti Romania 37 44.23N 27.50E
Fethiye Turkey 64 36.37N 29.06E
Fetlar i. U.K. 14 60.37N 0.52W
Fetsund Norway 42 59.56N 11.10E
Feucht W. Germany 38 49.22N 11.13E
Feuchtwangen W. Germany 39 49.10N 10.20E
Feuilles, Rivière aux r. Canada 99 58.47N 70.06W
Feurs France 21 45.45N 4.14E
Fevik Norway 42 58.23N 8.42E
Fevzipaşa Turkey 64 37.07N 36.38E
Fianarantsoa Madagascar 81 21.26S 47.05E
Fiche Ethiopia 73 9.52N 38.46E
Fichtel Gebirge mts. W. Germany 38 50.00N 11.50E
Fidenza Italy 30 44.52N 10.03E
Field Canada 104 46.32N 80.03W
Fier Albania 34 40.43N 19.33E
Fiesch Switz. 39 46.20N 8.10E
Fife d. U.K. 14 56.10N 3.10W
Fife Ness c. U.K. 14 56.17N 2.36W
Figeac France 20 44.37N 2.02E
Figeholm Sweden 43 57.22N 16.33E
Figueira da Foz Portugal 26 40.09N 8.52W
Figueras Spain 25 42.16N 2.58E
Fihaonana Madagascar 81 18.36S 47.12E
Fiherenana r. Madagascar 81 23.19S 43.37E
Fiji Pacific Oc. 84 18.00S178.00E
Fik Ethiopia 73 8.10N 42.18E
Filabres, Sierra de los mts. Spain 27 37.13N 2.20W
Filabusi Zimbabwe 80 20.34S 29.20E
Filadelfia Italy 33 38.48N 16.18E
Fildegrand r. Canada 105 46.18N 77.51W
Filey U.K. 12 54.13N 0.18W
Fili site Greece 35 38.10N 23.40E
Filiaşi Romania 37 44.33N 23.31E
Filiátes Greece 34 39.38N 20.16E
Filiatrá Greece 35 37.09N 21.35E
Filicudi, Isola i. Italy 33 38.35N 14.34E
Filingué Niger 77 14.21N 3.22E
Filippoi site Greece 34 41.00N 24.16E
Filipstad Sweden 43 59.43N 14.10E
Fillmore Canada 101 49.50N103.25W
Fillmore Calif. U.S.A. 109 34.24N118.55W
Fillmore N.Y. U.S.A. 114 42.28N 78.07W
Fimi r. Zaïre 78 3.00S 17.00E
Finale Emilia Italy 30 44.50N 11.17E
Finale Ligure Italy 30 44.10N 8.20E
Finch Canada 105 45.11N 75.07W
Findhorn r. U.K. 14 57.38N 3.37W
Findlay U.S.A. 112 41.02N 83.40W
Findlay, Mt. Canada 100 50.04N116.10W
Finger Lakes U.S.A. 114 42.55N 76.44W
Finistère d. France 18 48.20N 4.00W
Finisterre, Cabo de c. Spain 26 42.53N 9.16W
Finke r. Australia 91 27.00S136.10E
Finland Europe 44 64.30N 27.00E
Finland, G. of Finland/U.S.S.R. 41 59.30N 24.00E
Finlay r. Canada 100 57.00N125.05W
Finley Australia 93 35.40S145.34E
Finmark Canada 102 48.36N 89.44W
Finn r. Rep. of Ire. 15 54.50N 7.30W
Finnmark d. Norway 40 70.10N 26.00E
Finschhafen P.N.G. 59 6.35S147.51E
Finse Norway 41 60.36N 7.30E
Finspång Sweden 43 58.43N 15.47E
Finsterwalde E. Germany 38 51.38N 13.42E
Fiora r. Italy 30 42.20N 11.34E
Fiorenzuola d'Arda Italy 30 44.56N 9.55E
Fiq Syria 67 32.47N 35.42E
Firat see Al Furāt Turkey 64
Firebag r. Canada 101 57.45N111.20W
Firedrake L. Canada 101 61.25N104.30W
Firenze Italy 30 43.46N 11.15E
Firenzuola Italy 30 44.07N 11.23E
Firminy France 21 45.23N 4.18E
Firozābād India 63 27.09N 78.25E
Firozpur India 62 30.55N 74.38E
Firozpur Jhirka India 62 27.48N 76.57E
Firth of Clyde est. U.K. 14 55.35N 4.53W
Firth of Forth est. U.K. 14 56.05N 3.00W
Firth of Lorn est. U.K. 14 56.20N 5.40W
Firth of Tay est. U.K. 14 56.24N 3.08W
Fīrūzābād Iran 65 28.50N 52.35E
Firyuza U.S.S.R. 50 37.55N 58.03E
Fish r. Namibia 80 28.07S 17.45E
Fisher U.S.A. 111 35.30N 90.58W
Fishers I. U.S.A. 115 41.16N 72.02W
Fisher Str. Canada 99 63.00N 84.00W
Fishguard U.K. 13 51.59N 4.59W
Fiskárdhon Greece 35 38.27N 20.35E
Fiskebäckskil Sweden 42 58.15N 11.27E
Fiskenaesset Greenland 99 63.05N 50.40W
Fiskivötn f. Iceland 40 64.50N 20.45W
Fismes France 19 49.18N 3.41E
Fitchburg U.S.A. 115 42.35N 71.48W
Fitu Ethiopia 73 5.05N 40.42E
Fitzgerald U.S.A. 113 31.43N 83.16W
Fitz Roy Argentina 125 47.00S 67.15W
Fitzroy r. Australia 88 17.31S123.35E
Fitzroy Crossing Australia 88 18.13S125.33E
Fitzwilliam I. Canada 104 45.30N 81.45W
Fiuggi Italy 32 41.48N 13.13E
Fiumicino Italy 32 41.46N 12.14E
Fivizzano Italy 30 44.14N 10.08E
Fizi Zaïre 79 4.18S 28.56E
Fjällåsen Sweden 40 67.29N 20.10E
Fjällbacka Sweden 42 58.36N 11.17E
Fjällsjo r. Sweden 40 63.27N 17.06E
Fjerritslev Denmark 42 57.05N 9.16E
Fjugesta Sweden 43 59.10N 14.52E
Flå Norway 41 60.25N 9.26E
Flagler U.S.A. 108 39.18N103.04W
Flagstaff U.S.A. 109 35.12N111.39W
Flagstaff B. St. Helena 127 15.55S 5.40W
Flåm Norway 41 60.50N 7.07E
Flamborough Head U.K. 12 54.06N 0.05W
Fläming f. E. Germany 38 52.00N 13.00E
Flaming Gorge Resr. U.S.A. 108 41.15N109.30W
Flandre f. Belgium 16 50.52N 3.00E
Flannan Is. U.K. 14 58.16N 7.40W
Flåren l. Sweden 43 57.02N 14.06E
Flåsjön l. Sweden 40 64.06N 15.51E
Flat r. Canada 100 61.51N126.00W
Flathead L. U.S.A. 108 47.52N114.08W
Flatonia U.S.A. 111 29.47N 97.06W
Flattery, C. Australia 90 14.58S145.21E
Flattery, C. U.S.A. 106 48.23N124.43W
Flatts Village Bermuda 127 32.19N 64.44W
Flaxton U.S.A. 110 48.54N102.24W
Fleetwood U.K. 12 53.55N 3.01W
Flekkefjord town Norway 42 58.17N 6.41E
Flemington U.S.A. 115 40.31N 74.52W
Flen Sweden 43 59.04N 16.35E
Flensburg W. Germany 38 54.47N 9.26E
Flers France 18 48.45N 0.34W
Flesherton Canada 104 44.16N 80.33W
Fletcher Pond resr. U.S.A. 104 44.58N 83.52W
Fleurance France 20 43.50N 0.40E
Fleur-de-Lys Canada 103 50.06N 56.08W
Flinders r. Australia 90 17.30S140.45E
Flinders B. Australia 89 34.23S115.19E
Flinders I. S.A. Australia 92 33.44S134.30E
Flinders I. Tas. Australia 91 40.00S148.00E
Flinders Range mts. Australia 92 31.25S138.45E
Flinders Reefs Australia 90 17.37S148.31E
Flin Flon Canada 101 54.46N101.53W
Flint U.K. 12 53.15N 3.07W
Flint U.S.A. 104 43.01N 83.41W
Flint r. Ga. U.S.A. 113 30.52N 84.38W
Flint r. Mich. U.S.A. 104 43.21N 84.03W
Flint I. Kiribati 85 11.26S151.48W
Flinton Australia 91 27.54S149.34E
Flisa Norway 41 60.34N 12.06E
Floby Sweden 43 58.08N 13.20E
Floda Sweden 43 57.48N 12.22E
Flora U.S.A. 110 38.40N 88.30W
Florac France 20 44.19N 3.36E
Florence see Firenze Italy 30
Florence Ala. U.S.A. 113 34.48N 87.40W
Florence Ariz. U.S.A. 109 33.02N111.23W
Florence Colo. U.S.A. 108 38.23N105.08W
Florence Oreg. U.S.A. 108 43.58N124.07W
Florence S.C. U.S.A. 113 34.12N 79.44W
Florence, L. Australia 92 28.52S138.08E
Florencia Colombia 122 1.37N 75.37W
Florennes Belgium 16 50.14N 4.35E
Florenville Belgium 16 49.42N 5.19E
Flores i. Indonesia 59 8.40S121.20E
Flores, Laut sea Indonesia 59 7.00S121.00E
Floreshty U.S.S.R. 37 47.52N 28.12E
Flores Sea see Flores, Laut Indonesia 59
Floriano Brazil 123 6.45S 43.00W

Florianópolis to Furneaux Group

Florianópolis Brazil 126 27.35S 48.34W
Florida Uruguay 125 34.06S 56.13W
Florida d. U.S.A. 113 28.00N 82.00W
Florida, Straits of U.S.A. 97 24.00N 81.00W
Florida, Str. of U.S.A. 113 24.00N 81.00W
Florida B. U.S.A. 113 25.00N 80.45W
Florida City U.S.A. 113 25.27N 80.30W
Florida Keys is. U.S.A. 113 24.45N 81.00W
Floridia Italy 33 37.04N 15.10E
Florina Australia 92 32.23S139.58E
Flórina Greece 34 40.47N 21.24E
Florö Norway 41 61.36N 5.00E
Fluessen l. Neth. 16 52.58N 5.23E
Flumen Spain 25 41.43N 0.09W
Flumendosa r. Italy 32 39.26N 9.38E
Fluminimaggiore Italy 32 39.26N 8.30E
Fluorite Canada 104 47.00N 81.50W
Flushing Mich. U.S.A. 104 43.04N 83.51W
Flushing Ohio U.S.A. 114 40.09N 81.04W
Fluvia Spain 25 42.12N 3.07E
Fly r. P.N.G. 90 8.22S142.23E
Foča Yugo. 31 43.31N 18.46E
Focşani Romania 37 45.40N 27.12E
Foggia Italy 33 41.27N 15.34E
Foggo Nigeria 77 11.21N 9.57E
Fogo Canada 103 49.43N 54.17W
Fogo I. Canada 103 49.40N 54.13W
Föhr i. W. Germany 38 54.43N 8.30E
Foia mtn. Portugal 27 37.19N 8.10W
Foins, Lac aux l. Canada 104 47.05N 78.11W
Foix France 20 42.58N 1.36E
Folda est. Nordland Norway 40 67.36N 14.50E
Folda est. N. Trönd. Norway 40 64.45N 11.20E
Folégandros i. Greece 35 36.38N 24.57E
Foley Botswana 80 21.34S 27.21E
Foleyet Canada 102 48.05N 82.26W
Folgares Angola 80 14.55S 15.03E
Folgares Angola 78 14.55S 15.03E
Folgefonna glacier Norway 41 60.00N 6.20E
Foligno Italy 30 42.57N 12.42E
Folkestone U.K. 13 51.05N 1.11E
Folkston U.S.A. 113 30.49N 82.02W
Follonica Italy 30 42.55N 10.45E
Follonica, Golfo di g. Italy 30 42.54N 10.43E
Folsom U.S.A. 108 38.41N121.15W
Fominskoye U.S.S.R. 44 59.45N 42.03E
Fond du Lac Canada 101 59.17N106.00W
Fond du Lac U.S.A. 110 43.48N 88.27W
Fondi Italy 32 41.21N 13.25E
Fonni Italy 32 40.07N 9.15E
Fonsagrada Spain 26 43.08N 7.04W
Fonseca, Golfo de g. Honduras 117 13.10N 87.30W
Fontaine France 21 45.11N 5.40E
Fontainebleau France 19 48.24N 2.42E
Fonte Boa Brazil 122 2.33S 65.59W
Fontenay France 18 46.28N 0.48W
Fonuafo'ou i. Tonga 85 18.47S173.58W
Fonyód Hungary 31 46.44N 17.33E
Foothills town Canada 100 53.04N116.47W
Forbach France 19 49.11N 6.54E
Forbes Australia 93 33.24S148.03E
Forbesganj India 63 26.18N 87.15E
Forcalquier France 21 43.58N 5.47E
Forchheim W. Germany 38 49.43N 11.04E
Ford City U.S.A. 114 40.46N 79.32W
Förde Norway 42 59.36N 5.29E
Ford's Bridge Australia 93 29.46S145.25E
Fordyce U.S.A. 111 33.49N 92.25W
Forécariah Guinea 76 9.28N 13.06W
Forel, Mt. Greenland 99 67.00N 37.00W
Foreland Pt. U.K. 13 51.15N 3.47W
Foremost Canada 101 49.29N111.25W
Forest Canada 104 43.06N 82.00W
Forest City U.S.A. 115 41.39N 75.28W
Forest of Bowland hills U.K. 12 53.57N 2.30W
Forest of Dean f. U.K. 13 51.48N 2.32W
Forez, Monts du mts. France 20 45.35N 3.48E
Forfar U.K. 14 56.38N 2.54W
Forked River town U.S.A. 115 39.51N 74.12W
Forksville U.S.A. 115 41.29N 76.36W
Forlì Italy 30 44.13N 12.03E
Forman U.S.A. 110 46.07N 97.38W
Formby Pt. U.K. 12 53.34N 3.07W
Formentera i. Spain 25 38.42N 1.28E
Formentor, Cabo de c. Spain 25 39.58N 3.12E
Formerie France 19 49.39N 1.44E
Formia Italy 32 41.15N 13.37E
Formiga Brazil 126 20.30S 45.27W
Formosa Argentina 124 26.06S 58.14W
Formosa d. Argentina 124 25.00S 60.00W
Formosa see Taiwan Asia 55
Formosa Brazil 123 15.30S 47.22W
Formosa, Serra mts. Brazil 123 12.00S 55.20W
Formosa Str. China / Taiwan 55 24.30N119.30E
Fornaes c. Denmark 42 56.27N 10.58E
Fornovo di Taro Italy 30 44.42N 10.06E
Forres U.K. 14 57.37N 3.38W
Forrest Australia 89 30.49S128.03E
Fors Sweden 43 60.13N 16.18E
Forsayth Australia 90 18.35S143.36E
Forserum Sweden 43 57.42N 14.28E
Forshaga Sweden 43 59.32N 13.28E
Forssa Finland 41 60.49N 23.38E
Forst E. Germany 38 51.44N 14.39E
Forsyth U.S.A. 108 46.16N106.41W
Fort Abbās Pakistan 62 29.12N 72.52E
Fort Adams U.S.A. 111 31.05N 91.33W
Fort Albany Canada 102 52.15N 81.35W
Fortaleza Brazil 123 3.45S 38.35W
Fort Atkinson U.S.A. 110 42.56N 88.50W
Fort Augustus U.K. 14 57.09N 4.41W
Fort Beaufort R.S.A. 80 32.46S 26.36E
Fort Benning U.S.A. 113 32.20N 84.58W
Fort Benton U.S.A. 108 47.49N110.40W
Fort Carnot Madagascar 81 21.53S 47.28E
Fort Chimo Canada 99 58.10N 68.15W
Fort Chipewyan Canada 101 58.42N111.08W
Fort Collins U.S.A. 108 40.35N105.05W
Fort Coulonge Canada 105 45.51N 76.44W
Fort Covington U.S.A. 105 44.59N 74.30W
Fort-de-France Martinique 117 14.36N 61.05W
Fort de Possel C.A.R. 77 5.03N 19.16E
Fort Dodge U.S.A. 110 42.30N 94.10W
Fort Drum U.S.A. 113 27.31N 80.49W
Forte dei Marmi Italy 30 43.57N 10.10E
Fort Erie Canada 104 42.54N 78.56W
Fortescue r. Australia 88 21.00S116.06E
Fortezza Italy 30 46.47N 11.37E
Fort Frances Canada 102 48.35N 93.25W
Fort Franklin Canada 98 65.11N123.45W
Fort Garland U.S.A. 108 37.26N105.26W
Fort George Canada 102 53.50N 79.00W
Fort Good Hope Canada 98 66.16N128.37W
Fort Grahame Canada 100 56.30N124.35W
Fort Grey Australia 92 29.04S141.13E
Forth r. U.K. 14 56.06N 3.48W
Fort Hancock U.S.A. 109 31.17N105.53W
Fort Hope Canada 102 51.32N 88.00W
Fortierville Canada 105 46.29N 72.02W
Fort Klamath U.S.A. 108 42.42N122.00W
Fort Lallemand Algeria 75 31.18N 6.20E
Fort Lauderdale U.S.A. 113 26.08N 80.08W
Fort Liard Canada 100 60.15N123.28W
Fort Lupton U.S.A. 108 40.05N104.49W
Fort Mackay Canada 101 57.12N111.41W
Fort Macleod Canada 100 49.45N113.30W
Fort MacMahon Algeria 75 29.46N 1.37E
Fort Madison U.S.A. 110 40.38N 91.27W
Fort Maguire Malaŵi 79 13.38S 34.59E
Fort McKenzie Canada 103 56.50N 68.59W
Fort McMurray Canada 101 56.45N111.27W
Fort McPherson Canada 98 67.29N134.50W
Fort Miribel Algeria 75 29.26N 3.00E
Fort Morgan U.S.A. 108 40.15N103.48W
Fort Myers U.S.A. 113 26.39N 81.51W
Fort Nelson Canada 100 58.49N122.39W
Fort Nelson r. Canada 100 59.30N124.00W
Fort Norman Canada 98 64.55N125.29W
Fort Peck Dam U.S.A. 108 47.52N106.38W
Fort Peck Resr. U.S.A. 108 47.45N106.50W
Fort Pierce U.S.A. 113 27.28N 80.20W
Fort Plain U.S.A. 115 42.56N 74.38W
Fort Portal Uganda 79 0.40N 30.17E
Fort Providence Canada 100 61.21N117.39W
Fort Qu'Appelle Canada 101 50.45N103.50W
Fort Randall U.S.A. 98 55.10N162.47W
Fort Reliance Canada 101 63.00N109.20W
Fort Resolution Canada 100 61.10N113.40W
Fortrose New Zealand 86 46.34S168.48E
Fortrose U.K. 14 57.34N 4.09W
Fort Rupert B.C. Canada 100 50.39N127.27W
Fort Rupert Que. Canada 102 51.29N 78.45W
Fort Saint Tunisia 75 30.19N 9.30E
Fort St. John Canada 100 56.15N120.51W
Fort Sandeman Pakistan 62 31.20N 69.27E
Fort Saskatchewan Canada 100 53.40N113.15W
Fort Scott U.S.A. 111 37.50N 94.42W
Fort Severn Canada 102 56.00N 87.40W
Fort Shevchenko U.S.S.R. 45 44.31N 50.15E
Fort Sibut C.A.R. 77 5.46N 19.06E
Fort Simpson Canada 100 61.46N121.15E
Fort Smith Canada 101 60.00N111.51W
Fort Smith U.S.A. 111 35.23N 94.25W
Fort Stockton U.S.A. 111 30.53N102.53W
Fort Sumner U.S.A. 109 34.28N104.15W
Fort Thomas U.S.A. 109 33.02N109.58W
Fortuna Calif. U.S.A. 108 40.36N124.09W
Fortuna N.Dak. U.S.A. 110 48.55N103.47W
Fortune B. Canada 103 47.25N 55.25W
Fort Valley U.S.A. 113 32.32N 83.56W
Fort Vermilion Canada 100 58.24N116.00W
Fort Wayne U.S.A. 112 41.05N 85.08W
Fort William U.K. 14 56.49N 5.07W
Fort Worth U.S.A. 111 32.45N 97.20W
Fort Yates U.S.A. 110 46.05N100.38W
Forty Mile town Canada 98 64.24N140.31W
Fort Yukon U.S.A. 98 66.35N145.20W
Foshan China 55 23.08N113.08E
Fossano Italy 30 44.33N 7.43E
Fossombrone Italy 30 43.41N 12.48E
Foster Australia 93 38.39S146.12E
Fostoria U.S.A. 112 41.10N 83.25W
Fouesnant France 18 47.54N 4.01W
Fougamou Gabon 78 1.10S 10.31E
Fougères France 18 48.21N 1.12W
Foula i. U.K. 14 60.08N 2.05W
Foulness I. U.K. 13 51.35N 0.55E
Foulwind, C. New Zealand 86 41.45S171.30E
Foumban Cameroon 77 5.43N 10.50E
Fountain U.S.A. 108 38.41N104.42W
Fourmies France 19 50.00N 4.03E
Foúrnoi i. Greece 35 37.34N 26.30E
Fours France 19 46.49N 3.43E
Fouta Djalon f. Guinea 76 11.30N 12.30W
Foveaux Str. New Zealand 86 46.40S168.00E
Fowey U.K. 13 50.20N 4.39W
Fowler U.S.A. 108 38.08N104.01W
Fowlers B. Australia 91 31.59S132.27E
Fowlerton U.S.A. 111 28.28N 98.48W
Fowlerville U.S.A. 104 42.40N 84.04W
Fox Creek town Canada 100 54.26N116.55W
Foxe Basin b. Canada 99 67.30N 79.00W
Foxe Channel Canada 99 65.00N 80.00W
Foxen l. Sweden 42 59.23N 11.52E
Foxe Pen. Canada 99 65.00N 76.00W
Fox Glacier town New Zealand 86 43.28S170.01E
Foxton New Zealand 86 40.27S175.18E
Fox Valley town Canada 101 50.29N109.28W
Foyle r. U.K. 15 55.00N 7.20W
Foyle, Lough U.K. 15 55.05N 7.10W
Foz do Cunene Angola 78 17.15S 11.48E
Foz do Iguaçu Brazil 126 25.33S 54.31W
Foz Giraldo Portugal 27 40.00N 7.43W
Fraga Spain 25 41.31N 0.21E
Franca Brazil 126 20.33S 47.27W
Francavilla Italy 33 40.31N 17.35E
Francavilla al Mare Italy 31 42.25N 14.17E
Francavilla Fontana Italy 29 40.31N 17.35E
France Europe 17 47.00N 2.00E
Frances Australia 92 36.41S140.59E
Frances r. Canada 100 60.16N129.10W
Frances L. Canada 100 61.23N129.30W
Frances Lake town Canada 100 61.15N129.12W
Francesville U.S.A. 112 40.59N 86.54W
Franceville Gabon 78 1.38S 13.31E
Franche-Comté d. France 19 47.10N 6.00E
Francia Uruguay 125 32.33S 56.37W
Francia, Peña de mtn. Spain 26 40.31N 6.10W
Francistown Botswana 80 21.12S 27.29E
Francofonte Italy 33 37.13N 14.53E
François L. Canada 100 54.00N125.40W
Franeker Neth. 16 53.13N 5.31E
Frangy France 21 46.01N 5.56E
Frankenberg E. Germany 38 50.54N 13.01E
Frankenberg-Eder W. Germany 38 51.03N 8.48E
Frankenmouth U.S.A. 104 43.19N 83.46W
Frankford Canada 105 44.12N 77.36W
Frankfort R.S.A. 80 27.15S 28.30E
Frankfort Kans. U.S.A. 110 39.42N 96.25W
Frankfort Ky. U.S.A. 112 38.11N 84.53W
Frankfort N.Y. U.S.A. 115 43.02N 75.04W
Frankfurt E. Germany 38 52.20N 14.33E
Frankfurt d. E. Germany 38 52.37N 14.00E
Frankfurt W. Germany 39 50.07N 8.40E
Fränkische Rezat r. W. Germany 39 49.11N 11.01E
Frankland r. Australia 89 34.58S116.49E
Franklin d. Canada 99 73.00N100.00W
Franklin Ky. U.S.A. 113 36.42N 86.35W
Franklin La. U.S.A. 111 29.48N 91.30W
Franklin Mass. U.S.A. 115 42.05N 71.24W
Franklin N.H. U.S.A. 115 43.27N 71.39W
Franklin Penn. U.S.A. 114 41.24N 79.50W
Franklin Tex. U.S.A. 111 31.02N 96.29W
Franklin W.Va. U.S.A. 114 38.39N 79.20W
Franklin B. Canada 98 70.00N126.30W
Franklin D. Roosevelt L. U.S.A. 108 48.20N118.10W
Franklin Harbour Australia 92 33.42S136.56E
Franklin I. Antarctica 128 76.10S168.30E
Franklinville U.S.A. 114 42.20N 78.28W
Frankston Australia 93 38.08S145.07E
Fransfontein Namibia 80 20.12S 15.01E
Frantsa Iosifa, Zemlya is. U.S.S.R. 50 81.00N 54.00E
Franz Canada 102 48.28N 84.25W
Franz Josef Land is. see Frantsa Iosifa, Zemlya U.S.S.R. 50
Frascati Italy 32 41.48N 12.41E
Fraser r. B.C. Canada 100 49.07N123.11W
Fraser r. Nfld. Canada 103 56.35N 61.55W
Fraser, I. Australia 90 25.15S153.10E
Fraser Basin f. Canada 100 54.29N124.00W
Fraserburg R.S.A. 80 31.55S 21.29E
Fraserburgh U.K. 14 57.42N 2.00W
Fraser Plateau f. Canada 100 52.52N124.00W
Frashër Albania 34 40.23N 20.26E
Fraustro Mexico 111 25.51N101.04W
Fray Bentos Uruguay 125 33.08S 58.18W
Fray Marcos Uruguay 125 34.11S 55.44W
Frazeysburg U.S.A. 114 40.07N 82.07W
Frechilla Spain 26 42.08N 4.50W
Frederica U.S.A. 115 39.01N 75.28W
Fredericia Denmark 42 55.35N 9.46E
Frederick Md. U.S.A. 114 39.23N 77.25W
Frederick Okla. U.S.A. 111 34.23N 99.01W
Frederick S.Dak. U.S.A. 110 45.50N 98.30W
Frederick Hills Australia 90 12.41S136.00E
Fredericksburg Tex. U.S.A. 111 30.17N 98.52W
Fredericksburg Va. U.S.A. 114 38.18N 77.29W
Frederick Sd. U.S.A. 100 57.00N133.00W
Fredericktown U.S.A. 114 40.29N 82.33W
Fredericton Canada 103 45.58N 66.39W
Frederikshåb Greenland 99 62.05N 49.30W
Frederikshavn Denmark 42 57.26N 10.32E
Frederikssund Denmark 43 55.50N 12.04E
Fredonia Kans. U.S.A. 111 37.32N 95.49W
Fredonia N.Y. U.S.A. 114 42.27N 79.20W
Fredrika Sweden 40 64.05N 18.24E
Fredriksberg Sweden 43 60.10N 14.22E
Fredrikstad Norway 42 59.13N 10.57E
Freehold U.S.A. 115 40.16N 74.17W
Freeland Mich. U.S.A. 104 43.32N 84.07W
Freeland Penn. U.S.A. 115 41.01N 75.47W
Freeling, Mt. Australia 90 22.35S133.06E
Freeling Heights mts. Australia 92 30.10S139.16E
Freels, C. Canada 103 49.15N 53.28W
Freelton Canada 104 43.22N 80.02W
Freeman U.S.A. 110 43.21N 97.26W
Freeport Bahamas 113 26.30N 78.45W
Freeport N.S. Canada 103 44.17N 66.19W
Freeport Ont. Canada 114 43.25N 80.25W
Freeport Ill. U.S.A. 110 42.17N 89.38W
Freeport N.Y. U.S.A. 115 40.39N 73.35W
Freeport Ohio U.S.A. 114 40.13N 81.16W
Freeport Penn. U.S.A. 114 40.40N 79.41W
Freeport Tex. U.S.A. 111 28.58N 95.22W
Freetown Sierra Leone 76 8.30N 13.17W
Fregenal de la Sierra Spain 26 38.10N 6.39W
Freiberg E. Germany 38 50.54N 13.20E
Freiburg see Fribourg Switz. 39
Freiburg W. Germany 39 47.59N 7.51E
Freilingen W. Germany 16 50.33N 7.50E
Freising W. Germany 39 48.23N 11.44E
Freistadt Austria 36 48.31N 14.31E
Freital E. Germany 38 51.00N 13.39E
Fréjus France 21 43.26N 6.44E
Fremantle Australia 89 32.07S115.44E
Fremont Calif. U.S.A. 108 37.34N122.01W
Fremont Nebr. U.S.A. 110 41.26N 96.30W
Fremont Ohio U.S.A. 112 41.21N 83.08W
French r. Canada 104 45.56N 80.54W
French Creek r. U.S.A. 114 41.25N 79.50W
Frenchglen U.S.A. 108 42.48N118.56W
French I. Australia 93 38.20S145.20E
Frenchman Butte town Canada 101 53.35N109.38W
French River town Canada 104 46.02N 80.35W
Frenda Algeria 75 35.04N 1.03E
Freren W. Germany 38 52.29N 7.32E
Fresco r. Brazil 123 7.10S 52.30W
Fresco Ivory Coast 76 5.03N 5.31W
Freshford Rep. of Ire. 15 52.44N 7.23W
Fresne-St. Mamès France 19 47.33N 5.52E
Fresnes-en-Woëvre France 19 49.08N 5.39E
Fresnillo Mexico 116 23.10N102.53W
Fresno U.S.A. 108 36.45N119.45W
Fresno, Portillo del pass Spain 26 42.38N 3.46W
Freu, Cabo del c. Spain 25 39.45N 3.27E
Freudenstadt W. Germany 39 48.28N 8.25E
Frewena Australia 90 19.25S135.25E
Frewsburg U.S.A. 114 42.03N 79.10W
Fria, C. Namibia 80 18.25S 12.01E
Frias Argentina 124 28.40S 65.10W
Fribourg Switz. 39 46.48N 7.09E
Friedberg Bayern W. Germany 39 48.21N 10.58E
Friedberg Hessen W. Germany 39 50.20N 8.45E
Friedland E. Germany 38 53.40N 13.33E
Friedrichshafen W. Germany 39 47.39N 9.28E
Friedrichsort W. Germany 38 54.24N 10.10E
Friedrichstadt W. Germany 38 54.22N 9.05E
Friendship U.S.A. 114 42.12N 78.08W
Friesach Austria 31 46.57N 14.24E
Friesland d. Neth. 16 53.05N 5.45E
Friesoythe W. Germany 38 53.01N 7.51E
Frio, Cabo c. Brazil 126 22.59S 42.00W
Frisian Is. Europe 8 53.30N 6.00E
Fritsla Sweden 43 57.33N 12.47E
Fritzlar W. Germany 38 51.08N 9.16E
Friuli-Venezia Giulia d. Italy 30 46.10N 13.00E
Frobisher B. Canada 99 63.00N 66.45W
Frobisher Bay town Canada 99 63.45N 68.30W
Frobisher L. Canada 101 56.25N108.20W
Frohavet est. Norway 40 63.55N 9.05E
Froid U.S.A. 108 48.20N104.30W
Frolovo U.S.S.R. 45 49.45N 43.40E
Frome r. Australia 92 29.49S138.40E
Frome U.K. 13 51.16N 2.17W
Frome, L. Australia 92 30.48S139.48E
Frome Downs town Australia 92 31.13S139.46E
Frontera Mexico 116 18.32N 92.38W
Frontignan France 20 43.27N 3.45E
Front Royal U.S.A. 114 38.55N 78.11W
Frosinone Italy 32 41.38N 13.19E
Frosinone Italy 28 41.36N 13.21E
Frostburg U.S.A. 114 39.39N 78.56W
Frövi Sweden 43 59.28N 15.22E
Fröya i. Norway 40 63.45N 8.45E
Fruges France 19 50.31N 2.08E
Frunze U.S.S.R. 52 42.53N 74.46E
Frunzovka U.S.S.R. 37 47.19N 29.44E
Frutigen Switz. 39 46.35N 7.39E
Frýdek-Místek Czech. 37 49.41N 18.22E
Fu'an China 55 27.04N119.37E
Fuchū Japan 57 35.40N139.29E
Fuchuan China 55 24.50N111.16E
Fuchun Jiang r. China 55 30.05N120.00E
Fuding China 55 27.18N120.12E
Fuefuki r. Japan 57 35.33N138.28E
Fuencaliente Spain 26 38.24N 4.18W
Fuencaliente mtn. Spain 26 38.24N 4.14W
Fuensalida Spain 27 40.03N 4.12W
Fuensanta, Embalse de la resr. Spain 26 38.23N 2.13W
Fuente de Cantos Spain 26 38.15N 6.18W
Fuente-obejuna Spain 26 38.16N 5.25W
Fuentesaúco Spain 26 41.14N 5.30W
Fuentes de Ebro Spain 25 41.31N 0.38W
Fuentes de Oñoro Spain 26 40.33N 6.52W
Fuerte r. Mexico 109 25.50N109.25W
Fuerteventura i. Canary Is. 74 28.20N 14.10W
Fuga i. Phil. 55 18.53N121.22E
Fuglö i. Faroe Is. 10 62.22N 6.15W
Fugou China 54 34.04N114.23E
Fugu China 54 39.02N111.03E
Fuji Japan 57 35.09N138.39E
Fuji r. Japan 57 35.07N138.38E
Fujian d. China 55 26.00N118.00E
Fu Jiang r. China 55 30.02N106.20E
Fujieda Japan 57 34.52N138.16E
Fujin China 53 47.15N131.59E
Fujinomiya Japan 57 35.12N138.38E
Fuji san mtn. Japan 57 35.22N138.44E
Fujisawa Japan 57 35.21N139.29E
Fuji-yoshida Japan 57 35.38N138.42E
Fukagawa Japan 57 43.43N142.03E
Fukui Japan 57 36.04N136.12E
Fukuoka Japan 57 33.39N130.21E
Fukuroi Japan 57 34.45N137.55E
Fukushima Japan 57 37.44N140.28E
Fukuyama Japan 57 34.29N133.21E
Fūlādī, Kūh-e mtn. Afghan. 62 34.38N 67.32E
Fulda W. Germany 38 50.33N 9.41E
Fulda r. W. Germany 38 51.25N 9.39E
Fuling China 55 29.40N107.20E
Fulton Mo. U.S.A. 110 38.52N 91.57W
Fulton N.Y. U.S.A. 115 43.19N 76.25W
Fumay France 19 49.59N 4.42E
Fumel France 20 44.29N 0.57E
Funabashi Japan 57 35.42N139.59E
Funafuti Tuvalu 84 8.31S179.13E
Funchal Madeira Is. 127 32.40N 16.55W
Fundão Portugal 27 40.08N 7.30W
Fundy, B. of Canada 103 45.00N 66.00W
Funing China 55 23.37N105.36E
Funiu Shan mts. China 54 33.40N112.20E
Funtua Nigeria 77 11.34N 7.18E
Funyan Goba Ethiopia 73 4.22N 37.58E
Fuping China 54 38.52N114.12E
Fuqing China 55 25.43N119.22E
Furakawa Japan 57 38.30N140.50E
Furancungo Mozambique 79 14.51S 33.38E
Furculeşti Romania 34 43.52N 25.09E
Fürg Iran 65 28.19N 55.10E
Furnas, Represa de resr. Brazil 126 20.45S 46.00W
Furneaux Group is. Australia 91 40.15S148.15E

George, L. to Gorki

George, L. Fla. U.S.A. 113 29.17N 81.36W
George, L. N.Y. U.S.A. 115 43.35N 73.35W
George B. Canada 103 45.50N 61.45W
George's Cove Canada 103 52.40N 55.50W
Georgetown Ascension 127 7.56S 14.25W
Georgetown Qld. Australia 90 18.18S143.33E
George Town Tas. Australia 91 41.04S146.48E
Georgetown Canada 103 46.11N 62.32W
Georgetown Cayman Is. 117 19.20N 81.23W
Georgetown Gambia 76 13.31N 14.50W
Georgetown Guyana 122 6.46N 58.10W
George Town Malaysia 58 5.30N100.16E
Georgetown Del. U.S.A. 115 38.42N 75.23W
Georgetown S.C. U.S.A. 113 33.23N 79.18W
Georgetown Tex. U.S.A. 111 30.38N 97.41W
George V Land f. Antarctica 128 69.00S145.00E
Georgia d. U.S.A. 113 32.50N 83.15W
Georgia, Str. of Canada 100 49.25N124.00W
Georgian B. Canada 104 45.15N 80.50W
Georgi Dimitrov Bulgaria 34 42.37N 23.04E
Georgina r. Australia 90 23.12S139.33E
Georgiu-Dezh U.S.S.R. 45 51.00N 39.30E
Georgiyevsk U.S.S.R. 45 44.10N 43.30E
Gera E. Germany 38 50.52N 12.04E
Gera d. E. Germany 38 50.48N 11.45E
Geraardsbergen Belgium 16 50.47N 3.53E
Geral de Goiás, Serra mts. Brazil 123 13.00S 45.40W
Geraldine New Zealand 86 44.05S171.15E
Geral do Paranã, Serra mts. Brazil 123 14.40S 47.30W
Geraldton Australia 89 28.49S114.36E
Geraldton Canada 102 49.44N 86.59W
Gerale Ethiopia 71 6.20N 42.32E
Gerar r. Israel 67 31.24N 34.26E
Gérardmer France 19 48.04N 6.53E
Gerede Turkey 64 40.48N 32.13E
Gereshk Afghan. 62 31.48N 64.34E
Gérgal Spain 27 37.07N 2.33W
Gering U.S.A. 110 41.50N103.40W
Gerlach U.S.A. 108 40.40N119.21W
Gerlachovka mtn. Czech. 8 49.10N 20.05E
Gerlachovsky mtn. Czech. 23 49.10N 20.05E
Germania U.S.A. 114 41.39N 77.40W
Germencik Turkey 35 37.51N 27.42E
Germersheim W. Germany 39 49.13N 8.22E
Germiston R.S.A. 80 26.14S 28.10E
Gerolstein W. Germany 39 50.13N 6.40E
Gerolzhofen W. Germany 39 49.54N 10.21E
Gerona Spain 25 41.59N 2.49E
Gerona d. Spain 25 42.05N 2.50E
Gerringong Australia 93 34.45S150.50E
Gers d. France 20 43.40N 0.30E
Gêrzê China 63 32.16N 84.12E
Gescher W. Germany 38 51.57N 6.59E
Geseke W. Germany 38 51.38N 8.31E
Getafe Spain 26 40.18N 3.43W
Gete r. Belgium 16 50.58N 5.07E
Gethsémani Canada 103 50.13N 60.40W
Getinge Sweden 43 56.49N 12.44E
Gettysburg Penn. U.S.A. 114 39.50N 77.14W
Gettysburg S.Dak. U.S.A. 110 45.01N 99.57W
Gevān Iran 65 26.03N 57.17E
Gevar'am Israel 67 31.35N 34.37E
Gevelsberg W. Germany 38 51.19N 7.20E
Gevgelija Yugo. 34 41.09N 22.30E
Gévora r. Spain 27 38.53N 6.57W
Gevulot Israel 67 31.12N 34.28E
Geyikli Turkey 34 39.50N 26.12E
Geysdorp R.S.A. 80 26.31S 25.17E
Geyser U.S.A. 108 47.16N110.30W
Geyve Turkey 64 40.32N 30.18E
Gezer Israel 67 31.52N 34.55E
Ghabāghib Syria 67 33.10N 36.13E
Ghābat al 'Arab Sudan 73 9.02N 29.29E
Ghadaf, Wādī al r. Jordan 66 31.46N 36.50E
Ghadāmis Libya 75 30.08N 9.30E
Ghaddūwah Libya 75 26.26N 14.18E
Ghāghra r. India 63 25.47N 84.37E
Ghana Africa 76 8.00N 1.00W
Ghanzi Botswana 80 21.42S 21.39E
Ghardaïa Algeria 75 32.29N 3.40E
Gharghoda India 63 22.10N 83.21E
Ghārib, Jabal mtn. Egypt 66 28.06N 32.54E
Ghārīyat ash Sharqīyah Syria 67 32.40N 36.16E
Gharo Pakistan 62 24.44N 67.35E
Gharyān Libya 75 32.10N 13.01E
Gharyān d. Libya 75 30.35N 12.00E
Ghāt Libya 75 24.58N 10.11E
Ghātsīla India 63 22.36N 86.29E
Ghazāl, Baḥr al r. Sudan 73 9.31N 30.25E
Ghāziābād India 63 28.40N 77.26E
Ghāzīpur India 63 25.35N 83.34E
Ghazlūna Pakistan 62 31.24N 67.49E
Ghaznī Afghan. 62 33.33N 68.26E
Ghaznī d. Afghan. 62 32.45N 68.30E
Ghaznī r. Afghan. 62 32.35N 67.58E
Ghazzah Egypt 67 31.30N 34.28E
Ghedi Italy 30 45.24N 10.16E
Gheorghe-Gheorghiu-Dej Romania 37 46.14N 26.44E
Gheorgheni Romania 37 46.43N 25.36E
Gherla Romania 37 47.02N 23.55E
Ghisonáccia France 21 42.00N 9.25E
Ghotki Pakistan 62 28.01N 69.19E
Ghowr d. Afghan. 62 34.00N 64.15E
Ghubaysh Sudan 73 12.09N 27.21E
Ghudāf, Wādī al r. Iraq 64 32.54N 43.33E
Ghūriān Afghan. 62 34.21N 61.30E
Gia Dinh Vietnam 56 10.54N106.43E
Giarre Italy 33 37.43N 15.11E
Gibb River town Australia 88 15.39S126.38E
Gibeon Namibia 80 25.09S 17.44E
Gibraleón Spain 27 37.23N 6.58W
Gibraltar Europe 27 36.09N 5.21W
Gibraltar, Str. of Africa/Europe 24 36.00N 5.25W
Gibraltar Pt. U.K. 12 53.05N 0.20E
Gibson Australia 89 33.39S121.48E
Gibson Desert Australia 88 24.30S123.00E
Giddings U.S.A. 111 30.11N 96.56W
Gide Ethiopia 73 9.40N 35.16E
Gien France 19 47.42N 2.38E
Giessen W. Germany 38 50.35N 8.40E
Gieten Neth. 16 53.01N 6.45E
Gifford r. Canada 99 70.21N 83.05W
Gifford U.S.A. 108 48.20N118.08W
Gifhorn W. Germany 38 52.29N 10.33E
Gifu Japan 57 35.25N136.45E
Gifu d. Japan 57 35.32N137.15E
Giganta, Sierra de la mts. Mexico 109 25.30N111.15W
Gigantes, Llanos de los f. Mexico 109 30.00N105.00W
Gigen Bulgaria 34 43.40N 24.28E
Gigha i. U.K. 14 55.41N 5.44W
Giglio i. Italy 30 42.21N 10.54E
Gijón Spain 26 43.32N 5.40W
Gila r. U.S.A. 109 32.43N114.33W
Gila Bend U.S.A. 109 32.57N112.43W
Gila Bend Mts. U.S.A. 109 33.10N113.10W
Gilardo Dam Canada 105 47.12N 73.48W
Gilat Israel 67 31.19N 34.40E
Gilbert r. Australia 90 16.35S141.15E
Gildford U.S.A. 108 48.34N110.18W
Gilé Mozambique 79 16.10S 38.17E
Gilgandra Australia 93 31.42S148.40E
Gil Gil r. Australia 93 29.10S148.50E
Gilgil Kenya 79 0.29S 36.19E
Gilgit Jammu & Kashmir 60 35.54N 74.20E
Gilgunnia Australia 93 32.25S146.04E
Giljeva Planina mts. Yugo. 31 43.15N 19.55E
Gill, Lough Rep. of Ire. 15 54.15N 8.14W
Gilleleje Denmark 43 56.07N 12.19E
Gilles, L. Australia 92 32.50S136.45E
Gillette U.S.A. 108 44.18N105.30W
Gillingham Kent U.K. 13 51.24N 0.33E
Gill Pt. c. St. Helena 127 15.59S 5.38W
Gilmour Canada 105 44.48N 77.37W
Gilo r. Ethiopia 73 8.10N 33.15E
Gimli Canada 101 50.39N 97.00W
Gimo Sweden 43 60.11N 18.11E
Gimone r. France 20 44.00N 1.06E
Gimont France 20 43.38N 0.53E
Gimzo Israel 67 31.56N 34.57E
Gingin Australia 89 31.21S115.42E
Ginir Ethiopia 73 7.07N 40.46E
Ginnosar Israel 67 32.51N 35.31E
Ginosa Italy 33 40.34N 16.46E
Ginzo de Limia Spain 26 42.03N 7.43W
Gioia del Colle Italy 33 40.48N 16.56E
Gioia Tauro Italy 33 38.26N 15.54E
Gióna mtn. Greece 35 38.38N 22.14E
Girard Ohio U.S.A. 114 41.10N 80.42W
Girard Penn. U.S.A. 114 42.00N 80.19W
Girardot Colombia 122 4.19N 74.47W
Girdle Ness U.K. 14 57.06N 2.02W
Giresun Turkey 64 40.55N 38.25E
Gīr Hills India 62 21.10N 71.00E
Giri r. Zaïre 78 0.30N 17.58E
Giridih India 63 24.11N 86.18E
Girilambone Australia 93 31.14S146.55E
Girna r. India 62 21.08N 75.19E
Giromagny France 19 47.45N 6.50E
Gironde d. France 20 44.45N 0.35W
Gironde r. France 20 45.35N 1.00W
Girvan U.K. 14 55.15N 4.51W
Girwa r. India 63 27.20N 81.25E
Gisborne New Zealand 86 38.41S178.02E
Gislaved Sweden 43 57.18N 13.32E
Gisors France 19 49.17N 1.47E
Gitega Burundi 79 3.25S 29.58E
Giugliano Italy 33 40.56N 14.12E
Giulianova Italy 31 42.45N 13.57E
Giurgiu Romania 34 43.53N 25.57E
Giv'atayim Israel 67 32.04N 34.49E
Giv'at Brenner Israel 67 31.52N 34.48E
Give Denmark 42 55.51N 9.15E
Givet France 17 50.08N 4.49E
Givors France 21 45.35N 4.46E
Givry France 19 46.47N 4.45E
Gīzāb Afghan. 62 33.23N 65.55E
Gizhiga U.S.S.R. 51 62.00N160.34E
Gizhiginskaya Guba g. U.S.S.R. 51 61.00N158.00E
Giżycko Poland 37 54.03N 21.47E
Gjerstad Norway 42 58.54N 9.00E
Gjirokastër Albania 34 40.05N 20.10E
Gjoa Haven town Canada 99 68.39N 96.08W
Gjövik Norway 41 60.48N 10.42E
Glace Bay town Canada 103 46.12N 59.57W
Glacier Nat. Park Canada 100 51.15N117.30W
Glacier Peak mtn. U.S.A. 108 48.07N121.06W
Gladewater U.S.A. 111 32.33N 94.56W
Gladmar Canada 101 49.12N104.31W
Gladstone Qld. Australia 90 23.52S151.16E
Gladstone S.A. Australia 92 33.17S138.22E
Gladstone Mich. U.S.A. 112 45.52N 87.02W
Gladstone N.J. U.S.A. 115 40.43N 74.40W
Gladwin U.S.A. 104 43.59N 84.29W
Glafsfjorden l. Sweden 43 59.34N 12.37E
Glåma r. Norway 42 59.12N 10.57E
Glamoč Yugo. 31 44.03N 16.51E
Glan l. Sweden 43 58.37N 15.58E
Glan r. W. Germany 16 49.46N 7.43E
Glanaman U.K. 13 51.49N 3.54W
Glandorf W. Germany 38 52.05N 7.59E
Glarner Alpen mts. Switz. 39 46.55N 9.00E
Glarus Switz. 39 47.02N 9.04E
Glasco Kans. U.S.A. 110 39.22N 97.50W
Glasco N.Y. U.S.A. 115 42.03N 73.57W
Glasgow U.K. 14 55.52N 4.15W
Glasgow Ky. U.S.A. 113 36.59N 85.56W
Glasgow Mont. U.S.A. 108 48.12N106.38W
Glassboro U.S.A. 115 39.42N 75.07W
Glastonbury U.K. 13 51.09N 2.42W
Glauchau E. Germany 38 50.49N 12.32E
Glazov U.S.S.R. 44 58.09N 52.42E
Gleisdorf Austria 31 47.06N 15.44E
Glen R.S.A. 80 28.57S 26.19E
Glen Affric f. U.K. 14 57.15N 5.03W
Glen Afton Canada 104 46.39N 80.17W
Glénans, Îles de is. France 18 47.43N 3.57W
Glenarm U.K. 15 54.57N 5.58W
Glenburnie Australia 92 37.49S140.56E
Glen Burnie U.S.A. 115 39.10N 76.37W
Glencoe Australia 92 37.41S140.05E
Glencoe Canada 104 42.45N 81.43W
Glen Coe f. U.K. 14 56.40N 5.03W
Glencoe U.S.A. 110 44.45N 94.10W
Glen Cove U.S.A. 115 40.52N 73.37W
Glendale Ariz. U.S.A. 109 33.32N112.11W
Glendale Calif. U.S.A. 109 34.10N118.17W
Glendale Oreg. U.S.A. 108 42.44N123.26W
Glen Davis Australia 93 33.07S150.22E
Glendive U.S.A. 108 47.06N104.43W
Glenelg Australia 92 34.59S138.31E
Glenelg r. Australia 92 38.03S141.00E
Glenfield U.S.A. 115 43.43N 75.24W
Glengarriff Rep. of Ire. 15 51.45N 9.33W
Glen Garry f. Highland U.K. 14 57.03N 5.04W
Glen Head Rep. of Ire. 15 54.44N 8.46W
Glen Ina Australia 92 31.45S143.33E
Glen Innes Australia 93 29.42S151.45E
Glen Lyon Australia 92 31.41S142.06E
Glen Lyon U.S.A. 115 41.10N 76.05W
Glen Mòr f. U.K. 14 57.15N 4.30W
Glenmora U.S.A. 111 30.59N 92.35W
Glen Moriston U.K. 14 57.09N 4.50W
Glennie U.S.A. 104 44.33N 83.44W
Glenns Ferry U.S.A. 108 42.57N115.18W
Glenrock U.S.A. 108 42.52N105.52W
Glenrothes U.K. 14 56.12N 3.10W
Glenroy Australia 88 17.23S126.01E
Glens Falls town U.S.A. 115 43.19N 73.39W
Glenshee f. U.K. 14 56.45N 3.25W
Glen Spean f. U.K. 14 56.53N 4.40W
Glenville U.S.A. 114 38.56N 80.50W
Glenwood Ark. U.S.A. 111 34.20N 93.33W
Glenwood Iowa U.S.A. 110 41.03N 95.45W
Glenwood Oreg. U.S.A. 108 45.39N123.16W
Glenwood Springs town U.S.A. 108 39.33N107.19W
Glífa Greece 35 38.57N 22.58E
Glimåkra Sweden 43 56.18N 14.08E
Glimmingehus Sweden 43 55.30N 14.13E
Glina Yugo. 31 45.20N 16.06E
Glina r. Yugo. 31 45.26N 16.07E
Glittertind mtn. Norway 41 61.39N 8.33E
Gliwice Poland 37 50.17N 18.40E
Globe U.S.A. 109 33.24N110.47W
Głogów Poland 36 51.40N 16.06E
Glotovo U.S.S.R. 44 63.25N 49.28E
Gloucester Australia 93 31.59S151.58E
Gloucester U.K. 13 51.52N 2.15W
Gloucester U.S.A. 115 42.41N 70.39W
Gloucester City U.S.A. 115 39.54N 75.07W
Gloucestershire d. U.K. 13 51.45N 2.00W
Glouster U.S.A. 114 39.30N 82.05W
Gloversville U.S.A. 115 43.03N 74.20W
Glubczyce Poland 37 50.13N 17.49E
Glücksburg W. Germany 38 54.50N 9.33E
Glückstadt W. Germany 38 53.47N 9.25E
Glusha U.S.S.R. 37 53.03N 28.55E
Glyngöre Denmark 42 56.46N 8.52E
Gmünd Austria 31 46.54N 13.32E
Gmunden Austria 39 47.55N 13.48E
Gnadenhutten U.S.A. 114 40.22N 81.26W
Gnarp Sweden 41 62.03N 17.16E
Gnesta Sweden 43 59.03N 17.18E
Gniewkowo Poland 37 52.24N 18.25E
Gniezno Poland 37 52.32N 17.32E
Gnjilane Yugo. 34 42.28N 21.58E
Gnoien E. Germany 38 53.58N 12.42E
Gnosjö Sweden 43 57.22N 13.44E
Gnowangerup Australia 89 33.57S117.58E
Gnuka Australia 89 31.08S117.24E
Goa d. India 60 15.30N 74.00E
Goageb Namibia 80 26.45S 17.18E
Goālpāra India 63 26.10N 90.37E
Goat Fell mtn. U.K. 14 55.37N 5.12W
Goba Ethiopia 73 7.02N 40.00E
Goba Mozambique 81 26.11S 32.08E
Gobabis Namibia 80 22.28S 18.58E
Gobi des. Asia 54 45.00N108.00E
Goch W. Germany 38 51.41N 6.10E
Gochas Namibia 80 24.50S 18.48E
Godalming U.K. 13 51.11N 0.37W
Godar Pakistan 62 28.10N 63.14E
Godāvari r. India 61 16.40N 82.15E
Godbout Canada 103 49.19N 67.37W
Goddard Creek r. Australia 89 31.10S124.30E
Goderich Canada 104 43.45N 81.43W
Goderville France 18 49.39N 0.22E
Godhavn Greenland 99 69.20N 53.30W
Godhra India 62 22.45N 73.38E
Godoy Cruz Argentina 125 32.55S 68.50W
Gods r. Canada 101 56.22N 92.51W
Gods L. Canada 101 54.45N 94.00W
Godthåb Greenland 99 64.10N 51.40W
Goéland, Lac au l. Canada 102 49.47N 76.41W
Goélands, Lac aux l. Canada 103 55.25N 64.20W
Goes Neth. 16 51.30N 3.54E
Goffstown U.S.A. 115 43.01N 71.36W
Gogama Canada 102 47.35N 81.35W
Gogeb r. Ethiopia 73 7.10N 37.27E
Gogeh Ethiopia 73 8.12N 38.27E
Göggingen W. Germany 39 48.20N 10.52E
Gogonou Benin 77 10.50N 2.50E
Gogra r. see Ghāghra India 63
Gogrial Sudan 73 8.32N 28.07E
Gohad India 63 26.26N 78.27E
Goiana Brazil 123 7.30S 35.00W
Goiânia Brazil 123 16.43S 49.18W
Goiás Brazil 123 15.57S 50.07W
Goiás d. Brazil 123 12.00S 48.00W
Goichran India 63 31.04N 78.07E
Góis Portugal 26 40.09N 8.07W
Goito Italy 32 45.15N 10.40E
Gojō Japan 57 34.21N135.42E
Gojra Pakistan 62 31.09N 72.41E
Gökçe Turkey 34 40.10N 25.57E
Gökçeada i. Turkey 34 40.10N 26.00E
Göksun Turkey 64 38.03N 36.30E
Gokteik Burma 61 22.26N 97.00E
Gokwe Zimbabwe 80 18.14S 28.54E
Gol Norway 41 60.42N 8.57E
Gola Gokaran Nath India 63 28.05N 80.28E
Golan Heights mts. Syria 67 32.55N 35.42E
Golconda U.S.A. 108 40.57N117.30W
Gold U.S.A. 114 41.52N 77.52W
Gołdap Poland 37 54.19N 22.19E
Gold Beach town U.S.A. 108 42.25N124.25W
Golden Canada 100 51.20N117.00W
Golden Rep. of Ire. 15 52.30N 7.59W
Golden U.S.A. 108 39.46N105.13W
Golden B. New Zealand 86 40.45S172.50E
Goldendale U.S.A. 108 45.49N120.50W
Golden Hinde mtn. Canada 100 49.40N125.44W
Golden L. Canada 105 45.35N 77.20W
Golden Lake town Canada 105 45.35N 77.16W
Golden Ridge town Australia 89 30.51S121.42E
Golden Vale f. Rep. of Ire. 15 52.30N 8.07W
Goldfield U.S.A. 108 37.42N117.14W
Goldfields Canada 101 59.28N108.31W
Goldpines Canada 102 50.45N 93.05W
Goldsand L. Canada 101 56.58N101.02W
Goldsboro U.S.A. 113 35.23N 78.00W
Goleniów Poland 36 53.36N 14.50E
Golets Skalisty mtn. U.S.S.R. 51 56.00N130.40E
Golfito Costa Rica 117 8.42N 83.10W
Golfo degli Aranci town Italy 32 41.00N 9.38E
Gol Gol Australia 92 34.10S142.17E
Goliad U.S.A. 111 28.40N 97.23W
Goljam Perelik mtn. Bulgaria 34 41.36N 24.34E
Golling Austria 39 47.36N 13.10E
Golmud China 52 36.22N 94.55E
Golo r. France 21 42.31N 9.32E
Golovanevsk U.S.S.R. 37 48.25N 30.30E
Golpāyegān Iran 65 33.23N 50.18E
Golspie U.K. 14 57.58N 3.58W
Goma Ethiopia 73 8.25N 36.53E
Goma Zaïre 79 1.37S 29.10E
Gomang Co l. China 63 31.10N 89.10E
Gombe Nigeria 77 10.17N 11.20E
Gombe r. Tanzania 79 4.43S 31.30E
Gomel U.S.S.R. 37 52.25N 31.00E
Gomera i. Canary Is. 74 28.08N 17.14W
Gómez Palacio Mexico 111 25.34N103.30W
Gomīshān Iran 65 37.04N 54.06E
Gompa Jammu & Kashmir 62 35.02N 77.20E
Gonaïves Haiti 117 19.29N 72.42W
Gonâve, Golfe de la g. Haiti 117 19.20N 73.00W
Gonâve, Île de la i. Haiti 117 18.50N 73.00W
Gonbad-e Kāvūs Iran 65 37.15N 55.11E
Gonda India 63 27.08N 81.56E
Gondal India 62 21.58N 70.48E
Gonder Ethiopia 73 12.39N 37.29E
Gondia India 63 21.27N 80.12E
Gondomar Portugal 26 41.09N 8.32W
Gondrecourt-le-Château France 19 48.31N 5.30E
Gonen Israel 67 33.08N 35.39E
Gongbo'gyamda China 63 29.56N 93.23E
Gonggar China 63 29.15N 90.50E
Gongga Shan mtn. China 52 29.30N101.30E
Gongola d. Nigeria 77 8.40N 11.30E
Gongola r. Nigeria 77 9.30N 12.06E
Gongolgon Australia 93 30.22S146.56E
Goñi Uruguay 125 33.31S 56.24W
Goniri Nigeria 77 11.30N 12.15E
Gonnesa Italy 32 39.15N 8.28E
Gonzaga Italy 30 44.57N 10.49E
Gonzales U.S.A. 111 29.30N 97.27W
Good Hope, C. of R.S.A. 80 34.21S 18.28E
Good Hope Mtn. Canada 100 51.09N124.10W
Gooding U.S.A. 108 42.56N114.43W
Goodland U.S.A. 110 39.21N101.43W
Goodooga Australia 93 29.08S147.30E
Goodsprings U.S.A. 109 35.50N115.26W
Goole U.K. 12 53.42N 0.52W
Goolgowi Australia 93 33.59S145.42E
Goolma Australia 93 32.21S149.20E
Gooloogong Australia 93 33.37S148.43E
Goolwa Australia 92 35.31S138.45E
Goomalling Australia 89 31.19S116.49E
Goombalie Australia 93 29.59S145.24E
Goondiwindi Australia 93 28.30S150.17E
Goongarrie Australia 89 30.03S121.09E
Goor Neth. 16 52.16N 6.33E
Goose r. Canada 103 53.18N 60.23W
Goose Bay town Canada 103 53.19N 60.24W
Goose L. U.S.A. 108 41.57N120.25W
Gopālganj Bangla. 63 23.01N 89.50E
Gopālganj India 63 26.28N 84.26E
Göppingen W. Germany 39 48.42N 9.40E
Gorakhpur India 63 26.45N 83.22E
Goras India 62 25.32N 76.56E
Goražde Yugo. 31 43.40N 18.56E
Gordon Australia 92 32.05S138.08E
Gordon r. Australia 89 34.12S117.00E
Gordon U.S.A. 110 42.48N102.12W
Gordon Downs town Australia 88 18.43S128.33E
Gordon L. Canada 100 63.05N113.11W
Gordonvale Australia 90 17.05S145.47E
Goré Chad 77 7.57N 16.31E
Gore Ethiopia 73 8.08N 35.33E
Gore New Zealand 86 46.06S168.58E
Gore Bay town Canada 104 45.55N 82.28W
Gore Mtn. U.S.A. 105 44.55N 71.48W
Gorgān Iran 65 36.50N 54.29E
Gorgān r. Iran 65 37.00N 54.00E
Gorgol d. Mauritania 74 15.45N 13.00W
Gori U.S.S.R. 65 41.59N 44.05E
Gorinchem Neth. 16 51.50N 4.59E
Gorizia Italy 31 45.57N 13.38E
Gorjani Yugo. 31 45.24N 18.21E
Gorki see Gor'kiy U.S.S.R. 44

Gor'kiy to Grote Nete

Gor'kiy U.S.S.R. 44 56.20N 44.00E
Gorkovskoye Vodokhraniiishche resr. U.S.S.R. 44 56.49N 43.00E
Görlitz E. Germany 38 51.09N 14.59E
Gorlovka U.S.S.R. 45 48.17N 38.05E
Gorna Oryakhovitsa Bulgaria 34 43.07N 25.40E
Gornja Radogna Yugo. 31 46.41N 16.00E
Gornji Grad Yugo. 31 46.18N 14.49E
Gornji Vakuf Yugo. 31 43.56N 17.35E
Gorno Altaysk U.S.S.R. 50 51.59N 85.56E
Gorno Filinskoye U.S.S.R. 50 60.06N 69.58E
Gornyatskiy U.S.S.R. 44 67.30N 64.03E
Gorochan mtn. Ethiopia 73 9.22N 37.04E
Gorodenka U.S.S.R. 37 48.40N 25.30E
Gorodishche B.S.S.R. U.S.S.R. 37 53.18N 26.00E
Gorodishche B.S.S.R. U.S.S.R. 37 53.45N 29.45E
Gorodnitsa U.S.S.R. 37 50.50N 27.19E
Gorodnya U.S.S.R. 37 51.54N 31.37E
Gorodok U.S.S.R. 37 49.48N 23.39E
Goroka P.N.G. 59 6.02S145.22E
Goroke Australia 92 36.43S141.30E
Gorokhov U.S.S.R. 37 50.30N 24.46E
Gorongosa r. Mozambique 81 20.29S 34.36E
Gorontalo Indonesia 59 0.33N123.05E
Gort Rep. of Ire. 15 53.04N 8.49W
Goryn r. U.S.S.R. 37 52.08N 27.17E
Gorzów Wielkopolski Poland 36 52.42N 15.12E
Gose Japan 57 34.27N135.44E
Gosford Australia 93 33.25S151.18E
Goslar W. Germany 38 51.54N 10.25E
Gospić Yugo. 31 44.33N 15.23E
Gosport U.K. 13 50.48N 1.08W
Gossi Mali 76 15.49N 1.17W
Gossinga Sudan 73 8.39N 25.59E
Gostivar Yugo. 34 41.47N 20.24E
Gostynin Poland 37 52.26N 19.29E
Göta r. Sweden 43 57.42N 11.52E
Göta Kanal Sweden 43 58.45N 14.05E
Göteborg Sweden 42 57.43N 11.58E
Göteborg och Bohus d. Sweden 42 58.30N 11.30E
Gotemba Japan 57 35.18N138.56E
Götene Sweden 43 58.32N 13.29E
Gotha E. Germany 38 50.57N 10.41E
Gothem Sweden 43 57.35N 18.43E
Gothenburg U.S.A. 110 40.56N100.09W
Gothèye Niger 77 13.51N 1.31E
Gotland d. Sweden 43 57.25N 18.25E
Gotland i. Sweden 43 57.30N 18.33E
Gotse Delchev Bulgaria 34 41.34N 23.44E
Gotska Sandön i. Sweden 43 58.23N 19.16E
Gōtsu Japan 57 35.00N132.14E
Göttingen W. Germany 38 51.32N 9.55E
Gottwaldov Czech. 37 49.13N 17.41E
Götzis Austria 39 47.20N 9.38E
Gouarec France 18 48.13N 3.11W
Gouda Neth. 16 52.01N 4.43E
Gough I. Atlantic Oc. 127 40.20S 10.00W
Gouin, Résr. Canada 102 48.38N 74.54W
Goulais River town Canada 104 46.43N 84.18W
Goulburn Australia 93 34.47S149.43E
Goulburn r. Australia 93 36.08S144.30E
Goulburn Is. Australia 90 11.33S133.26E
Gould Canada 105 45.35N 71.24W
Goulimime Morocco 74 28.56N 10.04W
Gouménissa Greece 34 40.56N 22.37E
Goundam Mali 76 17.27N 3.39W
Gourdon France 20 44.44N 1.23E
Gouré Niger 77 13.59N 10.15E
Gourin France 18 48.08N 3.36W
Gourma-Rharous Mali 76 16.58N 1.50W
Gournay France 17 49.29N 1.44E
Gouro Chad 75 19.33N 19.33E
Gourock Range mts. Australia 93 35.45S149.25E
Gouverneur U.S.A. 105 44.20N 75.28W
Governador Valadares Brazil 126 18.51S 42.00W
Govind Balabh Pant Sāgar resr. India 63 24.05N 82.50E
Govind Sāgar resr. India 62 31.20N 76.45E
Gowanda U.S.A. 114 42.28N 78.56W
Goward Canada 104 47.08N 79.49W
Gowd-e Zereh des. Afghan. 65 30.00N 62.00E
Gower pen. U.K. 13 51.37N 4.10W
Gowmal r. see Gumal Afghan. 62
Gowmal Kalay Afghan. 62 32.29N 68.55E
Goya Argentina 124 29.10S 59.20W
Goyder r. Australia 90 12.38S135.11E
Goz Béïda Chad 73 12.13N 21.25E
Gozo i. Malta 28 36.03N 14.16E
Graaff Reinet R.S.A. 80 32.15S 24.31E
Graben W. Germany 39 49.09N 8.29E
Grabow E. Germany 38 53.16N 11.34E
Gračac Yugo. 31 44.18N 15.51E
Gračanica Yugo. 31 44.42N 18.19E
Graçay France 19 47.08N 1.51E
Grace, L. Australia 89 33.18S118.15E
Gracefield Canada 105 46.06N 76.03W
Gracias à Dios, Cabo c. Honduras/Nicaragua 117 15.00N 83.10W
Gradačac Yugo. 31 44.53N 18.26E
Grado Italy 30 45.40N 13.23E
Grado Spain 26 43.23N 6.04W
Grafenau W. Germany 39 48.52N 13.25E
Gräfenhainichen E. Germany 38 51.44N 12.27E
Grafing W. Germany 39 48.02N 11.59E
Gråfjell mtn. Norway 42 60.16N 9.29E
Grafton Australia 93 29.40S152.56E
Grafton Canada 104 44.00N 78.01W
Grafton Mass. U.S.A. 115 42.12N 71.41W
Grafton N.Dak. U.S.A. 110 48.25N 97.25W
Grafton Ohio U.S.A. 114 41.16N 82.04W
Grafton Wisc. U.S.A. 110 43.20N 87.58W
Grafton W.Va. U.S.A. 114 39.20N 80.01W
Graham r. Canada 100 56.31N122.17W
Graham U.S.A. 111 33.06N 98.35W
Graham, Mt. U.S.A. 109 32.42N109.52W
Graham I. Canada 100 53.40N132.30W
Graham Land f. Antarctica 128 67.00S 60.00W
Grahamstown R.S.A. 80 33.18S 26.30E
Graiguenamanagh Rep. of Ire. 15 52.33N 6.57W
Grajaú r. Brazil 123 3.41S 44.48W
Gram Denmark 42 55.17N 9.04E
Gramada Bulgaria 34 43.49N 22.39E
Gramat France 20 44.47N 1.43E
Grammichele Italy 33 37.13N 14.38E
Grámmos, Óros mtn. Greece 34 40.23N 20.45E
Grampian d. U.K. 14 57.22N 2.35W
Grampian Mts. U.K. 14 56.55N 4.00W
Grampians mts. Australia 92 37.12S142.34E
Gramsh Albania 34 40.52N 20.12E
Granada Nicaragua 117 11.58N 85.59W
Granada Spain 27 37.13N 3.41W
Granada d. Spain 27 37.30N 3.00W
Granadella Spain 25 41.21N 0.40E
Granby Canada 105 45.24N 72.44W
Gran Canaria i. Canary Is. 74 28.00N 15.30W
Gran Chaco f. S. America 124 22.00S 60.00W
Grand r. Canada 104 42.51N 79.34W
Grand r. Ohio U.S.A. 114 41.46N 81.17W
Grand r. S.Dak. U.S.A. 110 45.40N100.32W
Grandas Spain 26 43.13N 6.52W
Grandas de Salime, Embalse de resr. Spain 26 43.10N 6.45W
Grand Bahama I. Bahamas 113 26.40N 78.20W
Grand Ballon mtn. France 19 47.55N 7.08E
Grand Bank town Canada 103 47.06N 55.47W
Grand Bassam Ivory Coast 76 5.14N 3.45W
Grand Bend Canada 104 43.15N 81.45W
Grand Blanc U.S.A. 104 42.56N 83.38W
Grand Canal China 54 34.00N118.25E
Grand Canal see Da Yunhe China 54
Grand Canyon f. U.S.A. 109 36.10N112.45W
Grand Canyon town U.S.A. 109 36.03N112.09W
Grand Canyon Nat. Park U.S.A. 109 36.15N112.58W
Grand Cayman i. Cayman Is. 117 19.20N 81.30W
Grand Centre Canada 101 54.25N110.13W
Grand Cess Liberia 76 4.40N 8.12W
Grand Couronne France 18 49.21N 1.00E
Grande r. Bolivia 124 15.10S 64.55W
Grande r. Bahia Brazil 123 11.05S 43.09W
Grande r. Minas Gerais Brazil 124 20.00S 51.00W
Grande r. Spain 25 39.07N 0.44W
Grande, Bahía b. Argentina 125 51.30S 67.30W
Grande, Ilha i. Brazil 126 23.07S 44.16W
Grande, Sierra mts. Mexico 109 29.35N104.55W
Grande Cascapédia Canada 103 48.19N 65.54W
Grande Comore i. Comoros 79 11.35S 43.20E
Grande do Gurupá, Ilha i. Brazil 123 1.00S 51.30W
Grande-Pointe, Lac l. Canada 102 53.52N 75.32W
Grande Prairie Canada 100 55.15N118.50W
Grand Erg de Bilma des. Niger 77 18.30N 14.00E
Grand Erg Occidental des. Algeria 74 30.10N 0.20E
Grand Erg Oriental f. Algeria 75 30.00N 7.00E
Grande Rivière town Canada 103 48.24N 64.30W
Grandes, Salinas f. Argentina 124 29.37S 64.56W
Grandes Bergeronnes Canada 103 48.15N 69.33W
Grande Vallée Canada 103 49.14N 65.08W
Grand Falls town N.B. Canada 103 46.55N 67.45W
Grand Falls town Nfld. Canada 103 48.56N 55.40W
Grand Forks Canada 100 49.00N118.30W
Grand Forks U.S.A. 110 47.55N 97.03W
Grand Fougeray France 18 47.44N 1.44W
Grand Gorge U.S.A. 115 42.22N 74.30W
Grand Hers r. France 20 43.47N 1.20E
Grand Island town U.S.A. 110 40.55N 98.21W
Grand Isle U.S.A. 105 44.44N 72.18W
Grand Junction U.S.A. 108 39.05N108.33W
Grand L. N.B. Canada 103 45.38N 67.38W
Grand L. Nfld. Canada 103 49.00N 57.25W
Grand L. U.S.A. 112 45.15N 67.50W
Grand Lahou Ivory Coast 76 5.09N 5.01W
Grand Lieu, Lac de l. France 18 47.06N 1.40W
Grand Manan I. Canada 103 44.40N 66.50W
Grand Marais U.S.A. 110 47.45N 90.20W
Grand' Mère Canada 105 46.37N 72.41W
Grandois Canada 103 51.07N 55.46W
Grândola Portugal 27 38.10N 8.34W
Grand Passage N. Cal. 84 18.45S163.10E
Grand Prairie town U.S.A. 111 32.45N 96.59W
Grand Rapids town Canada 101 53.08N 99.20W
Grand Rapids town Mich. U.S.A. 112 42.57N 85.40W
Grand Rapids town Minn. U.S.A. 110 47.14N 93.31W
Grand Récif de Cook reef N. Cal. 84 19.25S163.50E
Grand Remous Canada 105 46.37N 75.53W
Grandrieu France 20 44.47N 3.38E
Grand St. Bernard, Col du pass Italy/Switz. 30 45.52N 7.11E
Grand Teton mtn. U.S.A. 108 43.44N110.48W
Grand Teton Nat. Park U.S.A. 108 43.30N110.37W
Grand Traverse B. U.S.A. 112 45.02N 85.30W
Grand Valley Canada 104 43.54N 80.19W
Grand Valley town U.S.A. 108 39.27N108.03W
Grandville U.S.A. 112 42.54N 85.48W
Grañén Spain 25 41.56N 0.22W
Grangärde Sweden 43 60.16N 14.59E
Grangemouth U.K. 14 56.01N 3.44W
Granger U.S.A. 108 41.35N109.58W
Grängesberg Sweden 43 60.05N 14.59E
Grangeville U.S.A. 108 45.56N116.07W
Granite City U.S.A. 110 38.43N 90.04W
Granite Falls town U.S.A. 110 44.49N 95.31W
Granite Peak town Australia 88 25.38S121.21E
Granite Peak mtn. U.S.A. 106 45.10N109.50W
Granitola, Capo c. Italy 32 37.33N 12.40E
Granity New Zealand 86 41.38S171.51E
Granja Brazil 123 3.06S 40.50W
Gränna Sweden 43 58.01N 14.28E
Granollers Spain 25 41.37N 2.18E
Granön Sweden 40 64.15N 19.19E
Gran Paradiso mtn. Italy 30 45.32N 7.16E
Gran Sasso d'Italia mts. Italy 31 42.26N 13.35E
Gransee E. Germany 38 53.00N 13.09E
Grant Mich. U.S.A. 112 43.20N 85.49W
Grant Nebr. U.S.A. 110 40.50N101.56W
Grant City U.S.A. 110 40.29N 94.25W
Grantham U.K. 12 52.55N 0.39W
Grantown-on-Spey U.K. 14 57.20N 3.38W
Grant Range mts. U.S.A. 108 38.25N115.30W
Grants U.S.A. 109 35.09N107.52W
Grants Pass town U.S.A. 108 42.26N123.19W
Grantsville U.S.A. 114 38.55N 81.06W
Granville France 18 48.50N 1.36W
Granville N.Dak. U.S.A. 110 48.16N100.47W
Granville N.Y. U.S.A. 115 43.24N 73.16W
Granville L. Canada 101 56.18N100.30W
Gras, Lac de l. Canada 98 64.30N110.30W
Graskop R.S.A. 80 24.55S 30.50E
Grassano Italy 33 40.38N 16.18E
Grasse France 21 43.40N 6.55E
Grasset, L. Canada 102 49.55N 78.00W
Grass Lake town U.S.A. 104 42.15N 84.13W
Grass Patch Australia 89 33.14S121.43E
Grass Valley town Calif. U.S.A. 108 39.13N121.04W
Grass Valley town Oreg. U.S.A. 108 45.22N120.47W
Gråsten Denmark 42 54.55N 9.36E
Grates Pt. Canada 103 48.09N 52.57W
Grave Neth. 16 51.45N 5.45E
Grave, Pointe de c. France 20 45.34N 1.04W
Gravelbourg Canada 101 49.53N106.34W
Gravenhurst Canada 104 44.55N 79.22W
Gravesend Australia 93 29.35S150.20E
Gravesend U.K. 13 51.27N 0.24E
Gravina in Puglia Italy 33 40.49N 16.25E
Gray France 19 47.27N 5.35E
Grayling U.S.A. 104 44.40N 84.43W
Grays U.K. 13 51.29N 0.20E
Graz Austria 31 47.05N 15.27E
Grazalema Spain 27 36.46N 5.22W
Grdelica Yugo. 34 42.54N 22.04E
Great Abaco I. Bahamas 113 26.25N 77.10W
Great Artesian Basin f. Australia 90 26.30S143.02E
Great Australian Bight Australia 89 33.10S129.30E
Great B. U.S.A. 115 39.30N 74.23W
Great Bahama Bank f. Bahamas 113 23.15N 78.00W
Great Barrier I. New Zealand 86 36.15S175.30E
Great Barrier Reef f. Australia 90 16.30S146.30E
Great Barrington U.S.A. 115 42.12N 73.22W
Great Basin f. U.S.A. 108 40.35N116.00W
Great Bear L. Canada 98 66.00N120.00W
Great Bend town U.S.A. 110 38.22N 98.46W
Great Bitter L. see Murrah al Kubrá, Al Buḩayrah al Egypt 66
Great Blasket I. Rep. of Ire. 15 52.05N 10.32W
Great Cloche I. Canada 104 46.01N 81.54W
Great Coco i. Burma 56 14.06N 93.21E
Great Divide Basin f. U.S.A. 108 42.00N108.10W
Great Dividing Range mts. Australia 93 29.00S152.00E
Great Driffield U.K. 12 54.01N 0.26W
Great Duck I. Canada 104 45.40N 82.58W
Greater Antilles is. C. America 117 17.00N 70.00W
Greater London d. U.K. 13 51.31N 0.06W
Greater Manchester d. U.K. 12 53.30N 2.18W
Great Exuma i. Bahamas 117 23.00N 76.00W
Great Falls town U.S.A. 108 47.30N111.17W
Great Inagua I. Bahamas 117 21.00N 73.20W
Great Indian Desert see Thar Desert India/Pakistan 62
Great Karroo f. R.S.A. 80 32.40S 22.20E
Great Kei r. R.S.A. 80 32.39S 28.23E
Great L. Australia 91 41.50S146.43E
Great Malvern U.K. 13 52.07N 2.19W
Great Namaland f. Namibia 80 25.30S 17.20E
Great Nicobar i. India 56 7.00N 93.45E
Great North East Channel P.N.G./Australia 90 9.00S144.00E
Great Ouse r. U.K. 12 52.47N 0.23E
Great Pt. U.S.A. 115 41.23N 70.03W
Great Rift Valley f. Africa 70 8.00S 31.30E
Great Ruaha r. Tanzania 79 7.55S 37.52E
Great Sacandaga L. U.S.A. 115 43.08N 74.10W
Great Salt L. U.S.A. 108 41.10N112.30W
Great Salt Lake Desert U.S.A. 108 40.40N113.30W
Great Sand Hills Canada 101 50.35N109.05W
Great Sandy Desert Australia 88 20.30S123.35E
Great Sandy Desert Saudi Arabia 64 28.40N 41.30E
Great Sandy Desert see An Nafūd Saudi Arabia 71
Great Sea Reef Fiji 84 16.25S179.20E
Great Slave L. Canada 100 61.23N115.38W
Great Smoky Mountain Nat. Park U.S.A. 113 35.56N 82.48W
Great Sound b. Bermuda 127 32.18N 64.60W
Great Victoria Desert Australia 89 29.00S127.30E
Great Whernside mtn. U.K. 12 54.09N 1.59W
Great Yarmouth U.K. 13 52.40N 1.45E
Grebbestad Sweden 42 58.42N 11.15E
Gréboun, Mont mtn. Niger 75 20.01N 8.35E
Gredos, Sierra de mts. Spain 26 40.15N 5.20W
Greece Europe 34 40.00N 23.00E
Greeley U.S.A. 108 40.25N104.42W
Green r. U.S.A. 108 38.11N109.53W
Green B. U.S.A. 110 45.00N 87.30W
Green Bay town U.S.A. 110 44.30N 88.01W
Green Bluff f. Australia 93 30.10S153.14E
Greenbush Mich. U.S.A. 104 44.34N 83.19W
Greenbush Minn. U.S.A. 110 48.42N 96.11W
Greenbushes Australia 89 33.50S116.00E
Greencastle Ind. U.S.A. 112 39.39N 86.51W
Greencastle Penn. U.S.A. 114 39.47N 77.44W
Greene U.S.A. 115 42.20N 75.46W
Greene I. Canada 104 45.51N 83.08W
Greeneville U.S.A. 113 36.10N 82.50W
Greenfield Ill. U.S.A. 110 39.21N 90.21W
Greenfield Iowa U.S.A. 110 41.18N 94.28W
Greenfield Mass. U.S.A. 115 42.36N 72.36W
Greenfield Mo. U.S.A. 111 37.25N 93.51W
Greenhills Australia 89 31.58S117.01E
Greening Canada 102 48.08N 74.55W
Greenland N. America 99 68.00N 45.00W
Greenlaw U.K. 14 55.43N 2.28W
Greenly I. Australia 92 34.39S134.50E
Green Mts. U.S.A. 115 43.45N 72.45W
Greenock U.K. 14 55.57N 4.45W
Greenore Pt. Rep. of Ire. 15 52.14N 6.19W
Greenport U.S.A. 115 41.06N 72.22W
Green River town Utah U.S.A. 108 38.59N110.10W
Green River town Wyo. U.S.A. 108 41.32N109.28W
Greensboro N.C. U.S.A. 113 36.04N 79.47W
Greensboro Vt. U.S.A. 105 44.32N 72.17W
Greensburg Ind. U.S.A. 112 39.20N 85.29W
Greensburg Penn. U.S.A. 114 40.18N 79.33W
Greenville Canada 100 55.03N129.33W
Greenville Liberia 76 5.01N 9.03W
Greenville Ala. U.S.A. 113 31.50N 86.40W
Greenville Mich. U.S.A. 112 43.11N 85.13W
Greenville Miss. U.S.A. 111 33.25N 91.05W
Greenville Mo. U.S.A. 111 37.08N 90.27W
Greenville N.C. U.S.A. 113 35.36N 77.23W
Greenville N.H. U.S.A. 115 42.46N 71.49W
Greenville Penn. U.S.A. 114 41.24N 80.23W
Greenville S.C. U.S.A. 113 34.52N 82.25W
Greenville Tex. U.S.A. 111 33.08N 96.07W
Greenwich Conn U.S.A. 115 41.01N 73.38W
Greenwich N.Y. U.S.A. 115 43.05N 73.30W
Greenwich Ohio U.S.A. 114 41.02N 82.31W
Greenwood Miss. U.S.A. 111 33.31N 90.11W
Greenwood N.Y. U.S.A. 114 42.08N 77.39W
Greenwood S.C. U.S.A. 113 34.11N 82.10W
Gregory r. Australia 90 17.53S139.17E
Gregory U.S.A. 110 43.14N 99.26W
Gregory, L. S.A. Australia 92 28.55S139.00E
Gregory L. W.A. Australia 88 20.10S127.20E
Gregory Range mts. Australia 90 19.00S143.05E
Greifswald E. Germany 38 54.05N 13.23E
Greifswalder Bodden c. E. Germany 38 54.15N 13.35E
Greiz E. Germany 38 50.39N 12.12E
Gremikha U.S.S.R. 44 68.03N 39.38E
Grenå Denmark 42 56.25N 10.53E
Grenada C. America 122 12.07N 61.40W
Grenada i. Windward Is. 117 12.15N 61.45W
Grenade France 20 43.47N 1.10E
Grenchen Switz. 39 47.11N 7.24E
Grenen c. Denmark 42 57.45N 10.40E
Grenoble France 21 45.10N 5.43E
Grenville, C. Australia 90 12.00S143.13E
Gréoux-les-Bains France 21 43.45N 5.53E
Gresik Indonesia 59 7.12S112.38E
Gretna U.K. 14 55.00N 3.04W
Gretna U.S.A. 111 29.55N 90.03W
Greven W. Germany 38 52.05N 7.36E
Grevená Greece 34 40.04N 21.25E
Grevenbroich W. Germany 16 51.07N 6.33E
Grevesmühlen E. Germany 38 53.51N 11.10E
Grey r. New Zealand 86 42.28S171.13E
Grey, C. Australia 90 13.00S136.40E
Greybull U.S.A. 108 44.30N108.03W
Grey Is. Canada 103 50.50N 55.37W
Greylock, Mt. U.S.A. 115 42.38N 73.10W
Greymouth New Zealand 86 42.28S171.12E
Grey Range mts. Australia 91 27.00S143.35E
Greystones Rep. of Ire. 15 53.09N 6.04W
Greytown R.S.A. 80 29.04S 30.36E
Griesbach W. Germany 39 48.28N 13.11E
Griesheim W. Germany 39 49.50N 8.34E
Griffin U.S.A. 107 33.15N 84.17W
Griffith Australia 93 34.18S146.04E
Griffith Canada 105 45.14N 77.12W
Griffith I. Canada 104 44.51N 80.54W
Griggsville U.S.A. 110 39.42N 90.43W
Grignan France 21 44.25N 4.54E
Grignols France 20 44.23N 0.03W
Grigoriopol U.S.S.R. 37 47.08N 29.18E
Grim, C. Australia 91 40.45S144.45E
Grimari C.A.R. 73 5.44N 20.03E
Grimma E. Germany 38 51.14N 12.43E
Grimmen E. Germany 38 54.07N 13.02E
Grimsby Canada 104 43.12N 79.34W
Grimsby U.K. 12 53.35N 0.05W
Grimsel Pass Switz. 39 46.34N 8.21E
Grimstad Norway 42 58.20N 8.36E
Grimsvötn mtn. Iceland 40 64.30N 17.10W
Grindavik Iceland 40 63.50N 22.27W
Grindelwald Switz. 39 46.37N 8.02E
Grindsted Denmark 42 55.45N 8.56E
Grinnell U.S.A. 110 41.45N 92.43W
Grintavec mtn. Yugo. 31 46.21N 14.32E
Griqualand East f. R.S.A. 80 30.40S 29.10E
Griqualand West f. R.S.A. 80 28.50S 23.30E
Gris-Nez, Cap c. France 18 50.52N 1.35E
Grisslehamn Sweden 43 60.06N 18.50E
Griva U.S.S.R. 44 60.35N 50.58E
Grmeč mts. Yugo. 31 44.40N 16.15E
Grobina U.S.S.R. 41 56.33N 21.10E
Groblershoop R.S.A. 80 28.55S 20.59E
Grodno U.S.S.R. 37 53.40N 23.50E
Grodzisk Poland 36 52.14N 16.22E
Grodzyanka U.S.S.R. 37 53.30N 28.41E
Groenlo Neth. 16 52.02N 6.36E
Groix, Île de France 17 47.38N 3.26W
Groix, Île de i. France 18 47.38N 3.27W
Gronau W. Germany 38 52.13N 7.00E
Grong Norway 40 64.27N 12.19E
Groningen Neth. 16 53.13N 6.35E
Groningen d. Neth. 16 53.15N 6.45E
Groom U.S.A. 111 35.12N101.06W
Groot r. C.P. R.S.A. 80 33.58S 25.03E
Groote Eylandt i. Australia 90 14.00S136.40E
Grootfontein Namibia 80 19.32S 18.07E
Groot Karasberge mts. Namibia 80 27.20S 18.50E
Grootlaagte r. Botswana 80 20.58S 21.42E
Groot Swartberge mts. R.S.A. 80 33.20S 22.00E
Grossenbrode W. Germany 38 54.22N 11.05E
Grossenhain E. Germany 38 51.17N 13.31E
Grosser Arber mtn. W. Germany 39 49.07N 13.07E
Grosser Priel mtn. Austria 39 47.43N 14.04E
Grosseto Italy 30 42.46N 11.08E
Gross-Gerau W. Germany 39 49.55N 8.29E
Gross Glockner mtn. Austria 30 47.04N 12.42E
Grossräschen E. Germany 38 51.35N 14.00E
Gross Venediger mtn. Austria 30 47.06N 12.21E
Groswater B. Canada 103 54.20N 57.30W
Grote Nete r. Belgium 16 51.07N 4.20E

Groton to Halligen

Groton U.S.A. 115 42.35N 76.22W
Grottaglie Italy 33 40.32N 17.26E
Grottaminarda Italy 33 41.04N 15.02E
Grottammare Italy 31 42.59N 13.52E
Groundhog r. Canada 102 49.40N 82.06W
Grouse Creek town U.S.A. 108 41.22N113.53W
Grove City U.S.A. 114 41.10N 80.05W
Grover City U.S.A. 109 35.07N120.37W
Groves U.S.A. 111 29.57N 93.55W
Groveton N.H. U.S.A. 105 44.36N 71.31W
Groveton Tex. U.S.A. 111 31.03N 95.08W
Groznyy U.S.S.R. 45 43.21N 45.42E
Grubišno Polje Yugo. 31 45.42N 17.10E
Grudziądz Poland 37 53.29N 18.45E
Grumeti r. Tanzania 79 2.05S 33.45E
Grumo Appula Italy 33 41.01N 16.43E
Grums Sweden 43 59.21N 13.06E
Grünau Austria 39 47.51N 13.57E
Grünau Namibia 80 27.44S 18.18E
Grundarfjördhur town Iceland 40 64.55N 23.20W
Grundy U.S.A. 113 37.13N 82.08W
Grungedal Norway 42 59.44N 7.43E
Grünstadt W. Germany 39 49.34N 8.10E
Gruzinskaya S.S.R. d. U.S.S.R. 45 42.00N 43.30E
Gryazovets U.S.S.R. 44 58.52N 40.12E
Gryfice Poland 36 53.56N 15.12E
Grythyttan Sweden 43 59.42N 14.32E
Gstaad Switz. 39 46.28N 7.17E
Guachipas Argentina 124 25.31S 65.31W
Guacuí Brazil 126 20.44S 41.40W
Guadajoz r. Spain 27 37.50N 4.51W
Guadalajara Mexico 116 20.30N103.20W
Guadalajara Spain 26 40.38N 3.10W
Guadalajara d. Spain 26 40.50N 2.50W
Guadalamar r. Spain 26 38.05N 3.36W
Guadalaviar r. Spain 25 40.21N 1.08W
Guadalcanal i. Solomon Is. 84 9.32S160.12E
Guadalcanal Spain 26 38.06N 5.49W
Guadalén Spain 26 38.05N 3.32W
Guadalén, Embalse de resr. Spain 26 38.25N 3.15W
Guadalete r. Spain 27 36.35N 6.13W
Guadalmena r. Spain 26 38.19N 2.56W
Guadalmez r. Spain 26 38.46N 5.04W
Guadalope r. Spain 25 41.15N 0.03W
Guadalquivir r. Spain 27 36.47N 6.22W
Guadalupe Mexico 111 25.41N100.15W
Guadalupe, Isla de i. Mexico 109 29.00N118.16W
Guadalupe, Sierra de mts. Spain 27 39.35N 5.25W
Guadarrama r. Spain 27 39.53N 4.10W
Guadarrama, Puerto de pass Spain 26 40.43N 4.10W
Guadarrama, Sierra de mts. Spain 26 41.00N 3.50W
Guadazaón Spain 25 39.42N 1.36W
Guadeloupe C. America 120 16.20N 61.40W
Guadeloupe i. Leeward Is. 117 16.20N 61.40W
Guadiana r. Portugal 27 37.11N 7.24W
Guadiana Menor r. Spain 27 37.56N 3.15W
Guadiaro r. Spain 27 36.17N 5.17W
Guadix Spain 27 37.18N 3.08W
Guafo, Golfo de g. Chile 125 43.35S 74.15W
Guainía r. Colombia 122 2.01N 67.07W
Guaíra Falls see Sete Quedas, Salto das Brazil 124
Guajará Mirim Brazil 122 10.48S 65.22W
Guajira, Peninsula de la pen. Colombia 122 12.00N 72.00W
Gualdo Tadino Italy 30 43.14N 12.47E
Gualeguay Argentina 125 33.10S 59.20W
Gualeguay r. Argentina 125 33.18S 59.38W
Gualeguaychu Argentina 125 33.00S 58.30W
Guam i. Mariana Is. 84 13.30N144.40E
Guamal Colombia 122 9.10N 74.15W
Guanajuato Mexico 116 21.00N101.16W
Guanajuato d. Mexico 116 21.00N101.00W
Guanare Venezuela 122 9.04N 69.45W
Guanarito Venezuela 122 8.43N 69.12W
Guane Cuba 117 22.13N 84.07W
Guang'an China 55 30.30N106.35E
Guangchang China 55 26.50N116.16E
Guangdong d. China 55 23.00N113.00E
Guanghan China 55 30.59N104.15E
Guanghua China 54 32.26N111.41E
Guangji China 55 29.42N115.39E
Guangming Ding mtn. China 55 30.09N118.11E
Guangnan China 55 24.03N105.03E
Guangrao China 54 37.04N118.22E
Guangxi Zhuangzu d. China 55 23.30N109.00E
Guangyuan China 54 32.29N105.55E
Guangze China 55 27.27N117.23E
Guangzhou China 55 23.08N113.20E
Guanling China 55 25.57N105.38E
Guantánamo Cuba 117 20.09N 75.14W
Guan Xian Shandong China 54 36.29N115.25E
Guan Xian Sichuan China 61 30.59N103.40E
Guanyun China 54 34.17N119.15E
Guaporé r. Bolivia / Brazil 124 12.00S 65.15W
Guaqui Bolivia 124 16.35S 68.51W
Guara, Sierra de mts. Spain 25 42.20N 0.20W
Guarabira Brazil 123 6.46S 35.25W
Guarapuava Brazil 126 25.22S 51.28W
Guaratinguetá Brazil 126 22.49S 45.09W
Guarda Portugal 26 40.32N 7.16W
Guarda d. Portugal 26 40.40N 7.15W
Guardavalle Italy 33 38.30N 16.30E
Guardiagrele Italy 31 42.11N 14.13E
Guardo Spain 26 42.47N 4.50W
Guareim r. see Quarí Uruguay 125
Guareña Spain 27 38.51N 6.06W
Guareña r. Spain 26 41.29N 5.23W
Guasave Mexico 109 25.34N108.27W
Guasipati Venezuela 122 7.28N 61.54W
Guastalla Italy 30 44.55N 10.39E
Guatemala C. America 117 15.40N 90.00W
Guatemala town Guatemala 116 14.38N 90.22W
Guatemala Basin Pacific Oc. 85 12.00N 95.00W
Guatemala Trench Pacific Oc. 85 15.00N 93.00W
Guatire Venezuela 122 10.28N 66.32W
Guaviare r. Colombia 122 4.00N 67.35W
Guaxupé Brazil 126 21.17S 46.44W
Guayaquil Ecuador 122 2.13S 79.54W
Guayaquil, Golfo de g. Ecuador 122 3.00S 80.35W
Guaymallén Argentina 125 32.54S 68.47W
Guaymas Mexico 109 27.56N110.54W
Guayquiraró r. Argentina 125 30.25S 59.36W
Guba Zaïre 78 10.40S 26.26E
Gubakha U.S.S.R. 44 58.55N 57.30E
Gubbio Italy 30 43.21N 12.35E
Gubeikou China 54 40.41N117.09E
Gubin Poland 36 51.59N 14.42E
Gubio Nigeria 77 12.31N 12.44E
Guchab Namibia 80 19.40S 17.47E
Gucheng China 54 37.20N115.57E
Gúdar, Sierra de mts. Spain 25 40.30N 0.40W
Gudbrandsdalen f. Norway 41 61.30N 10.00E
Gudhjem Denmark 43 55.13N 14.59E
Gudvangen Norway 41 60.52N 6.50E
Guebwiller France 19 47.55N 7.12E
Guecho Spain 26 43.22N 3.00W
Guékédou Guinea 76 8.35N 10.11W
Guelma Algeria 75 36.28N 7.26E
Guelph Canada 104 43.33N 80.15W
Guelta Zemmur W. Sahara 74 25.15N 12.20W
Guéméné-sur-Scorff France 18 48.04N 3.12W
Guera d. Chad 77 11.22N 18.00E
Guerande France 18 47.20N 2.26W
Guérard, Lac l. Canada 103 56.20N 65.35W
Guéret France 20 46.10N 1.52E
Guernica Spain 26 43.19N 2.40W
Guernsey i. U.K. 13 49.27N 2.35W
Guerra Mozambique 79 13.05S 35.12E
Guerrero d. Mexico 116 18.00N100.00W
Guiana S. America 123 3.40N 53.00W
Guiana Highlands S. America 122 4.00N 59.00W
Guichen France 18 47.58N 1.48W
Guichón Uruguay 125 32.21S 57.12W
Guidimaka d. Mauritania 74 15.20N 12.00W
Guiding China 55 26.32N107.15E
Guidong China 55 26.12N114.00E
Guiers, Lac de l. Senegal 76 16.12N 15.50W
Gui Jiang r. China 55 23.25N111.20E
Guijuelo Spain 26 40.33N 5.40W
Guildford Australia 89 31.55S115.55E
Guildford U.K. 13 51.14N 0.35W
Guildhall U.S.A. 105 44.34N 71.34W
Guilherne Capelo Ihe Angola 78 5.11S 12.10E
Guilin China 55 25.20N110.10E
Guillaume-Delisle, Lac l. Canada 102 56.20N 75.50W
Guillaumes France 21 44.05N 6.51E
Guillestre France 21 44.40N 6.39E
Guilvinec France 18 47.47N 4.17W
Guimarães Brazil 123 2.08S 44.36W
Guimarães Portugal 26 41.27N 8.18W
Guimeng Ding mtn. China 54 35.34N117.50E
Guinan China 52 35.20N100.50E
Guinea Africa 76 10.30N 11.30W
Guinea, G. of Africa 77 3.00N 3.00E
Guinea Basin f. Atlantic Oc. 127 0.00 5.00W
Guinea Bissau Africa 76 11.30N 15.00W
Güines Cuba 117 22.50N 82.02W
Guînes France 19 50.52N 1.52E
Guingamp France 18 48.33N 3.11W
Guinguinéo Senegal 76 14.20N 15.57W
Guiping China 55 23.20N110.02E
Guipúzcoa d. Spain 26 43.00N 2.20W
Guir, Hammada du f. Morocco / Algeria 74 31.00N 3.20W
Güiria Venezuela 122 10.37N 62.21W
Guiscard France 19 49.39N 3.03E
Guise France 19 49.54N 3.38E
Guitiriz Spain 26 43.11N 7.54W
Guitres France 20 45.03N 0.11W
Guiuan Phil. 59 11.02N125.44E
Guixi China 55 28.12N117.10E
Gui Xian China 55 23.02N109.40E
Guiyang China 55 26.31N106.39E
Guizhou d. China 55 27.00N107.00E
Gujarat d. India 62 22.20N 70.30E
Gūjar Khān Pakistan 62 33.16N 73.19E
Gujrānwāla Pakistan 62 32.26N 74.33E
Gujrāt Pakistan 62 32.34N 74.05E
Gulang Gansu China 54 37.30N102.54E
Gulargambone Australia 93 31.21S148.32E
Gulbarga India 60 17.22N 76.47E
Gulch Ethiopia 72 14.43N 36.45E
Gulfport U.S.A. 111 30.22N 89.06W
Gulgong Australia 93 32.20S149.49E
Gulin China 55 28.07N105.51E
Gulistān Pakistan 62 30.36N 66.35E
Gullholmen Sweden 42 58.11N 11.24E
Gull Lake town Canada 101 50.08N108.27W
Gullspång Sweden 43 58.59N 14.06E
Güllük Turkey 35 37.14N 27.36E
Gulma Nigeria 77 12.41N 4.24E
Gülpinar Turkey 34 39.32N 26.10E
Gulshad U.S.S.R. 52 46.37N 74.22E
Gulu Uganda 79 2.46N 32.21E
Guluguba Australia 90 26.16S150.03E
Gulwe Tanzania 79 6.27S 36.27E
Gulyantsi Bulgaria 34 43.38N 24.42E
Gumal r. Pakistan 62 32.08N 69.50E
Gumel Nigeria 77 12.39N 9.23E
Gumla India 63 23.03N 84.33E
Gummersbach W. Germany 38 51.02N 7.34E
Gum Spring town U.S.A. 113 37.47N 77.54W
Gümüşhane Turkey 64 40.26N 39.26E
Guna India 62 24.39N 77.19E
Gunbar Australia 93 34.04S145.25E
Gundagai Australia 93 35.07S148.05E
Gundlupet India 60 11.48N 76.41E
Gungu Zaïre 78 5.43S 19.20E
Gunisao r. Canada 101 53.54N 97.58W
Gunisao L. Canada 101 53.33N 96.15W
Gunnebo Sweden 43 57.43N 16.32E
Gunnedah Australia 93 30.59S150.15E
Gunnison r. U.S.A. 108 39.03N108.35W
Gunnison Colo. U.S.A. 108 38.33N106.56W
Gunnison Utah U.S.A. 108 39.09N111.49W
Guntersville U.S.A. 113 34.20N 86.18W
Guntersville L. U.S.A. 113 34.45N 86.03W
Guntūr India 61 16.20N 80.27E
Gunungsitoli Indonesia 58 1.17N 97.37E
Gunupur India 63 19.05N 83.49E
Günz r. W. Germany 39 48.27N 10.16E
Günzburg W. Germany 39 48.27N 10.16E
Gunzenhausen W. Germany 39 49.07N 10.45E
Guochengyi China 54 36.14N104.52E
Gurais Jammu & Kashmir 62 34.38N 74.50E
Gura Portiței f. Romania 37 44.40N 29.00E
Gurban Obo China 54 43.05N112.27E
Gurdāspur Jammu & Kashmir 62 32.02N 75.31E
Gurgaon India 62 28.28N 77.02E
Gurgueia r. Brazil 123 6.45S 43.35W
Gūrha India 62 25.14N 71.45E
Gurk r. Austria 31 46.36N 14.31E
Gursköy i. Norway 40 62.16N 5.42E
Gurué Mozambique 81 15.30S 36.58E
Gürün Turkey 64 38.44N 37.15E
Gurupá Brazil 123 1.25S 51.39W
Gurupi r. Brazil 123 1.13S 46.06W
Guru Sikhar mtn. India 62 24.39N 72.46E
Guruwe Zimbabwe 80 16.42S 30.40E
Gurvan Sayhan Uul mts. Mongolia 54 43.45N103.30E
Guryev U.S.S.R. 45 47.08N 51.59E
Gusau Nigeria 77 12.12N 6.40E
Gusev U.S.S.R. 37 54.32N 22.12E
Gusong China 55 28.25N105.12E
Guspini Italy 32 39.32N 8.38E
Güssing Austria 31 47.04N 16.20E
Gustav Holm, Kap c. Greenland 99 67.00N 34.00W
Güstrow E. Germany 38 53.48N 12.10E
Gusum Sweden 43 58.16N 16.29E
Gütersloh W. Germany 38 51.54N 8.23E
Guthrie Ky. U.S.A. 113 36.40N 87.10W
Guthrie Okla. U.S.A. 111 35.53N 97.25W
Guvrin, Nahal wadi Israel 67 31.43N 34.42E
Guyana S. America 122 4.40N 59.00W
Guyang China 54 41.03N110.03E
Guymon U.S.A. 111 36.41N101.29W
Guyra Australia 93 30.14S151.40E
Guyuan Hebei China 54 41.40N115.41E
Guyuan Ningxia Huizu China 54 36.00N106.25E
Guzhen Anhui China 54 33.19N117.19E
Guzman, Laguna de l. Mexico 109 31.25N107.25W
Gwa Burma 61 17.36N 94.35E
Gwabegar Australia 93 30.34S149.00E
Gwadabawa Nigeria 77 13.23N 5.15E
Gwādar Pakistan 62 25.07N 62.19E
Gwagwada Nigeria 77 10.15N 7.15E
Gwai Zimbabwe 80 19.15S 27.42E
Gwai r. Zimbabwe 80 17.59S 26.55E
Gwalior India 63 26.13N 78.10E
Gwanda Zimbabwe 80 20.59S 29.00E
Gwane Zaïre 73 4.43N 25.50E
Gwasero Nigeria 77 9.30N 8.30E
Gweebarra B. Rep. of Ire. 15 54.52N 8.28W
Gwejam d. Ethiopia 73 11.10N 37.00E
Gwent d. U.K. 13 51.44N 3.00W
Gweru Zimbabwe 80 19.25S 29.50E
Gwydir r. Australia 93 29.35S148.45E
Gwynedd d. U.K. 12 53.00N 4.00W
Gy France 19 47.24N 5.49E
Gyaca China 63 29.05N 92.55E
Gyangrang China 63 30.47N 85.09E
Gyangzê China 63 28.57N 89.38E
Gyaring Co l. China 63 31.05N 88.00E
Gydanskiy Poluostrov pen. U.S.S.R. 50 70.00N 78.30E
Gyimda China 63 31.03N 97.18E
Gyirong China 63 29.00N 85.15E
Gympie Australia 90 26.11S152.40E
Gyōda Japan 57 36.08N139.28E
Gyöngyös Hungary 37 47.47N 19.56E
Györ Hungary 37 47.41N 17.40E
Gypsum Pt. Canada 100 61.53N114.35W
Gypsumville Canada 101 51.45N 98.35W
Gyueshovo Bulgaria 34 42.14N 22.28E

H

Haag W. Germany 39 48.10N 12.11E
Haan W. Germany 16 51.10N 7.02E
Ha'apai Group is. Tonga 85 19.50S174.30W
Haapajärvi Finland 40 63.45N 25.20E
Haapamäki Finland 40 62.15N 24.28E
Haapavesi Finland 40 64.08N 25.22E
Haapsalu U.S.S.R. 41 58.56N 23.33E
Haar W. Germany 39 48.06N 11.44E
Hā Arava r. Israel / Jordan 66 30.30N 35.10E
Haarlem Neth. 16 52.22N 4.38E
Haarlem R.S.A. 80 33.46S 23.28E
Hab r. Pakistan 62 24.53N 66.41E
Habahe China 52 47.53N 86.12E
Habarūt S. Yemen 60 17.18N 52.44E
Habaswein Kenya 79 1.06N 39.26E
Habay-la-Neuve Belgium 16 49.45N 5.38E
Habbān S. Yemen 71 14.21N 47.05E
Hab Chauki Pakistan 62 25.01N 66.53E
Habiganj Bangla. 63 24.23N 91.25E
Habikino Japan 57 34.33N135.37E
Habo Sweden 43 57.55N 14.04E
Hachinohe Japan 57 40.30N141.30E
Hachiōji Japan 57 35.39N139.20E
Hack, Mt. Australia 92 30.44S138.45E
Hadāli Pakistan 62 32.18N 72.12E
Hadano Japan 57 35.22N139.14E
Hadāribah, Ra's al c. Sudan 72 22.04N 36.54E
Hadarom d. Israel 67 31.15N 34.50E
Haḍbaram Oman 71 17.27N 55.15E
Hadd, Ra's al c. Oman 65 22.32N 59.49E
Haddington U.K. 14 55.57N 2.47W
Hadejia Nigeria 77 12.30N 10.03E
Hadejia r. Nigeria 77 12.47N 10.44E
Hadera Israel 67 32.26N 34.55E
Hadera r. Israel 67 32.27N 35.53E
Haderslev Denmark 42 55.15N 9.30E
Hadībоh S. Yemen 71 12.39N 54.02E
Hadjer Mornou mtn. Chad 72 17.12N 23.08E
Hadley N.Y. U.S.A. 115 43.19N 73.51W
Hadley Penn. U.S.A. 114 41.25N 80.14W
Ha Dong Vietnam 55 20.40N105.58E
Haḍramawt f. S. Yemen 71 16.30N 49.30E
Hadsten Denmark 42 56.20N 10.03E
Hadsund Denmark 42 56.43N 10.07E
Haedo, Cuchilla de mts. Uruguay 125 31.50S 56.10W
Haegeland Norway 42 58.15N 7.47E
Haeju N. Korea 53 38.04N125.40E
Haena Hawaiian Is. 85 22.14N159.34W
Hafar al Bāṭin Saudi Arabia 65 28.28N 46.00E
Ḥafīrah, Qā'al f. Jordan 67 31.06N 36.14E
Hāfizābād Pakistan 62 32.04N 73.41E
Hafnarfjördhur town Iceland 40 64.04N 21.58W
Haft Gel Iran 65 31.28N 49.35E
HaGalil f. Israel 67 32.54N 35.20E
Hagen W. Germany 38 51.22N 7.28E
Hagenow E. Germany 38 53.26N 11.11E
Hagerman U.S.A. 109 33.07N104.20W
Hagerstown U.S.A. 114 39.39N 77.43W
Hagersville Canada 104 42.58N 80.03W
Hagetmau France 20 43.40N 0.35W
Hagfors Sweden 43 60.02N 13.42E
Hagi Japan 57 34.25N131.22E
Ha Giang Vietnam 55 22.50N105.00E
Hagondange France 19 49.15N 6.10E
Hags Head Rep. of Ire. 15 52.56N 9.29W
Hague U.S.A. 115 43.45N 73.31W
Haguenau France 19 48.49N 7.47E
Hahn W. Germany 38 50.31N 7.53E
Hai'an Shan mts. China 55 23.00N115.30E
Haicheng China 54 40.52N122.48E
Hai Duong Vietnam 56 20.56N106.21E
Haifa see Hefa Israel 67
Haifa, B. of see Mifraz Hefa Israel 67
Haifeng China 55 22.58N115.20E
Haikang China 55 20.55N110.04E
Haikou China 55 20.03N110.27E
Ḥā'il Saudi Arabia 64 27.31N 41.45E
Hailākāndi India 63 24.41N 92.34E
Hailar China 53 49.15N119.41E
Haileybury Canada 104 47.27N 79.38W
Hailong China 54 42.39N125.49E
Hailsham U.K. 13 50.52N 0.17E
Hailun China 53 47.29N126.58E
Hailuoto i. Finland 40 65.02N 24.42E
Haimen China 55 28.41N121.30E
Hainan i. China 55 19.00N109.30E
Hainaut d. Belgium 16 50.30N 3.45E
Haines Alas. U.S.A. 100 59.11N135.23W
Haines Oreg. U.S.A. 108 44.55N117.56W
Haines Junction Canada 100 60.45N137.30W
Haining China 55 30.30N120.35E
Hai Phòng Vietnam 55 20.48N106.40E
Haiti C. America 117 19.00N 73.00W
Haiyang China 54 36.46N121.09E
Haiyuan China 54 36.35N105.40E
Hajar Banga Sudan 73 11.30N 23.00E
Hajdúböszörmény Hungary 37 47.41N 21.30E
Hajdúszoboszló Hungary 37 47.27N 21.24E
Hajiki saki c. Japan 57 38.25N138.32E
Hājīpur India 63 25.41N 85.13E
Hakkâri Turkey 65 37.36N 43.45E
Hakodate Japan 57 41.46N140.44E
Hakupu Niue 84 19.07S169.51W
Hala Pakistan 62 25.49N 68.25E
Halab Syria 64 36.14N 37.10E
Halabjah Iraq 65 35.10N 45.59E
Halā'ib Sudan 72 22.13N 36.38E
Hålaveden hills Sweden 43 58.05N 14.45E
Halbā Lebanon 66 34.34N 36.05E
Halberstadt E. Germany 38 51.54N 11.02E
Halden Norway 42 59.09N 11.23E
Haldensleben E. Germany 38 52.18N 11.26E
Haldia India 63 22.05N 88.03E
Haldwāni India 63 29.13N 79.31E
Hale U.S.A. 104 44.23N 83.48W
Haleyville U.S.A. 113 34.12N 87.38W
Half Assini Ghana 76 5.04N 2.53W
Halfmoon Bay town Canada 100 49.31N123.54W
Halhul Jordan 67 31.35N 35.07E
Haliburton Canada 104 45.03N 78.30W
Haliburton Highlands Canada 104 45.16N 78.19W
Halicarnassus site Turkey 35 37.03N 27.28E
Halifax Canada 103 44.39N 63.36W
Halifax U.K. 12 53.43N 1.51W
Halifax U.S.A. 113 36.46N 78.57W
Halifax B. Australia 90 18.50S146.30E
Halil r. Iran 60 27.35N 58.44E
Halin well Somali Rep. 71 9.08N 48.47E
Halkett, C. U.S.A. 98 71.00N152.00W
Halkirk U.K. 14 58.30N 3.30W
Halladale r. U.K. 14 58.34N 3.54W
Halland d. Sweden 43 56.48N 12.50E
Halland f. Sweden 43 57.00N 12.45E
Hallands Väderö i. Sweden 43 56.26N 12.33E
Hall B. Australia 92 34.00S135.03E
Halle Belgium 16 50.45N 4.14E
Halle E. Germany 38 51.29N 11.58E
Halle d. E. Germany 38 51.34N 11.45E
Hällefors Sweden 43 59.47N 14.30E
Hälleforsnäs Sweden 43 59.10N 16.30E
Hallein Austria 39 47.41N 13.06E
Halligen is. W. Germany 38 54.35N 8.35E

Hallingdal to Helgoländer Bucht

Hallingdal f. Norway 41 60.30N 9.00E
Hall Is. Pacific Oc. 84 8.37N152.00E
Hall Lake town Canada 99 68.40N 81.30W
Hällnäs Sweden 40 64.19N 19.38E
Hall Pen. Canada 99 63.30N 66.00W
Hallsberg Sweden 43 59.04N 15.07E
Hall's Creek town Australia 88 18.17S127.44E
Hallstahammar Sweden 43 59.37N 16.13E
Hallstatt Austria 39 47.33N 13.39E
Hallstavik Sweden 43 60.03N 18.36E
Hallstead U.S.A. 115 41.58N 75.45W
Hallton U.S.A. 114 41.26N 78.56W
Halmahera i. Indonesia 59 0.45N128.00E
Halmstad Sweden 43 56.39N 12.50E
Halsa Norway 40 63.03N 8.14E
Hälsingborg Sweden 43 56.03N 12.42E
Haltern W. Germany 38 51.46N 7.10E
Haltia Tunturi mtn. Finland 40 69.17N 21.21E
Haltwhistle U.K. 12 54.58N 2.27W
Ham France 19 49.45N 3.04E
Ham, Mt. Canada 105 45.47N 71.37W
Ḩamaḑ, Wādī al r. Saudi Arabia 64 25.49N 36.37E
Hamada f. see Drâa, Hamada du W. Sahara 74
Hamadān Iran 65 34.47N 48.33E
Ḩamādat Marzūq f. Libya 75 26.00N 12.30E
Ḩamāh Syria 66 35.09N 36.44E
Hamakita Japan 57 34.48N137.47E
Hamamatsu Japan 57 34.42N137.44E
Hamar Norway 41 60.48N 11.06E
Hamaröy Norway 40 68.05N 15.40E
Ḩamāţah, Jabal mtn. Egypt 64 24.11N 35.01E
Hamborn W. Germany 16 51.29N 6.46E
Hamburg R.S.A. 80 33.17S 27.27E
Hamburg N.J. U.S.A. 115 41.09N 74.35W
Hamburg N.Y. U.S.A. 114 42.43N 78.50W
Hamburg Penn. U.S.A. 115 40.34N 75.59W
Hamburg W. Germany 38 53.33N 9.59E
Hamburg d. W. Germany 38 53.35N 10.00E
Hamburgsund Sweden 42 58.33N 11.16E
Hamden U.S.A. 115 41.21N 72.56W
Häme d. Finland 41 61.20N 24.30E
Hämeenlinna Finland 41 61.00N 24.27E
Hamelin B. Australia 89 34.10S115.00E
Hameln W. Germany 38 52.06N 9.21E
HaMerkaz d. Israel 67 32.05N 34.55E
Hamer Koke Ethiopia 73 5.12N 36.45E
Hamersley Range mts. Australia 88 22.00S118.00E
Hamhŭng N. Korea 53 39.54N127.35E
Hami China 52 42.40N 93.30E
Hamidiye Turkey 34 41.09N 26.40E
Hamilton Australia 92 37.45S142.04E
Hamilton r. Australia 91 27.12S135.28E
Hamilton Bermuda 127 32.18N 64.48W
Hamilton Canada 104 43.15N 79.51W
Hamilton New Zealand 86 37.46S175.18E
Hamilton U.K. 14 55.46N 4.10W
Hamilton Mont. U.S.A. 108 46.15N114.09W
Hamilton N.Y. U.S.A. 115 42.50N 75.33W
Hamilton Ohio U.S.A. 112 39.23N 84.33W
Hamilton Tex. U.S.A. 111 31.42N 98.07W
Hamley Bridge town Australia 92 34.21S138.41E
Hamlin Tex. U.S.A. 111 32.53N100.08W
Hamlin W.Va. U.S.A. 114 38.17N 82.06W
Hamm W. Germany 38 51.41N 7.49E
Hammamet, Golfe de g. Tunisia 75 36.05N 10.40E
Hammam Lif Tunisia 32 36.44N 10.20E
Hammān, Wādī al Jordan 67 31.38N 36.00E
Ḩammār, Hawr al l. Iraq 65 30.50N 47.00E
Hammel Denmark 42 56.15N 9.52E
Hammelburg W. Germany 39 50.07N 9.53E
Hammerdal Sweden 40 63.35N 15.20E
Hammerfest Norway 40 70.40N 23.42E
Hammond Australia 92 32.33S138.20E
Hammond La. U.S.A. 111 30.30N 90.28W
Hammond N.Y. U.S.A. 105 44.27N 75.42W
Hammond B. U.S.A. 104 45.33N 84.00W
Hammondsport U.S.A. 114 42.25N 77.13W
Hammonton U.S.A. 115 39.38N 74.48W
Ham Nord Canada 105 45.54N 71.39W
Hamoir Belgium 16 50.25N 5.32E
Hamoyet, Jabal mtn. Sudan 72 17.33N 38.00E
Hampshire d. U.K. 13 51.03N 1.20W
Hampton N.H. U.S.A. 115 42.56N 70.50W
Hampton S.C. U.S.A. 113 32.52N 81.06W
Hampton Va. U.S.A. 113 37.02N 76.23W
Hampton Bays town U.S.A. 115 40.53N 72.31W
Hamra, Saguia el wadi W. Sahara 74 27.15N 13.21W
Ḩamrīn, Jabal mts. Iraq 65 34.40N 44.10E
Ham Sud Canada 105 45.46N 71.36W
Hāmūn-e Jaz Mūrīān l. Iran 60 27.20N 58.55E
Hana Hawaiian Is. 85 20.45N155.59W
Hanamaki Japan 57 39.23N141.07E
Hanang mtn. Tanzania 79 4.30S 35.21E
Hanau W. Germany 39 50.08N 8.55E
Hancheng China 54 35.29N110.30E
Hancock Md. U.S.A. 114 39.42N 78.13W
Hancock Mich. U.S.A. 112 47.08N 88.34W
Hancock N.Y. U.S.A. 115 41.57N 75.17W
Handa Japan 57 34.53N136.56E
Handan China 54 36.37N114.26E
Handen Sweden 43 59.10N 18.08E
Handeni Tanzania 79 5.25S 38.04E
Hando Somali Rep. 71 10.39N 51.08E
HaNegev des. Israel 66 30.42N 34.55E
Hanford U.S.A. 109 36.20N119.39W
Hanga Roa I. de Pascua 85 27.09S109.26W
Hanggin Houqi China 54 40.50N107.06E
Hanggin Qi China 54 39.56N108.54E
Hangö Finland 41 59.50N 22.57E
Hangu China 54 39.11N117.45E
Hangu Pakistan 62 33.32N 71.04E
Hangzhou China 55 30.14N120.08E
Hangzhou Wan b. China 55 30.25N121.00E
Hanita Israel 67 33.05N 35.10E
Hanjiang China 55 25.30N119.14E
Hankey R.S.A. 80 33.50S 24.52E
Hankinson U.S.A. 110 46.04N 96.55W
Hanksville U.S.A. 108 38.21N110.44W
Hānle Jammu & Kashmir 63 32.48N 79.00E
Hanmer Springs town New Zealand 86 42.31S172.50E
Hann, Mt. Australia 88 15.55S125.57E
Hanna Canada 101 51.38N111.54W
Hannaford U.S.A. 110 47.19N 98.11W
Hannah B. Canada 102 51.20N 80.00W
Hannibal Mo. U.S.A. 107 39.41N 91.25W
Hannibal Ohio U.S.A. 114 39.39N 80.51W
Hannover W. Germany 38 52.24N 9.44E
Hannut Belgium 16 50.40N 5.05E
Hanöbukten b. Sweden 43 55.47N 15.00E
Hà Nôi Vietnam 55 21.01N105.53E
Hanoi see Hà Nôi Vietnam 55
Hanover Canada 104 44.09N 81.02W
Hanover R.S.A. 80 31.04S 24.25E
Hanover Mass. U.S.A. 115 42.07N 70.49W
Hanover N.H. U.S.A. 115 43.42N 72.18W
Hanover Penn. U.S.A. 114 39.48N 76.59W
Hanover, Isla i. Chile 125 50.57S 74.40W
Han Pijesak Yugo. 31 44.04N 18.59E
Hānsdiha India 63 24.36N 87.05E
Hanshou China 55 28.55N111.58E
Han Shui r. China 55 30.32N114.20E
Hānsi Haryana India 62 29.06N 75.58E
Hansi Himachal P. India 63 32.27N 77.50E
Hanson, L. Australia 92 31.02S136.13E
Hanstholm Denmark 42 57.07N 8.38E
Hantengri Feng mtn. China 52 42.09N 80.12E
Han Ul China 54 45.10N119.48E
Hanyang China 55 30.42N113.50E
Hanyin China 54 32.53N108.37E
Hanzhong China 54 33.08N107.04E
Haouach, Ouadi wadi Chad 75 16.45N 19.35E
Haparanda Sweden 40 65.50N 24.10E
Happy Valley town Canada 103 53.16N 60.14W
Hapsu N. Korea 53 41.12N128.48E
Hāpur India 63 28.43N 77.47E
Ḩaql Saudi Arabia 66 29.14N 34.56E
Ḩaraḑ Saudi Arabia 65 24.12N 49.08E
Harardera Somali Rep. 71 4.32N 47.53E
Harare Zimbabwe 81 17.49S 31.04E
Har-Ayrag Mongolia 54 45.42N109.14E
Haraze Chad 73 9.55N 20.48E
Harbin China 53 45.45N126.41E
Harboör Denmark 42 56.37N 8.12E
Harbor Beach U.S.A. 104 43.51N 82.39W
Harborcreek U.S.A. 114 42.10N 79.57W
Harbour Deep town Canada 103 50.22N 56.27W
Harbour Grace town Canada 103 47.42N 53.13W
Harburg W. Germany 36 53.27N 9.58E
Hårby Denmark 42 55.13N 10.07E
Harda India 62 22.20N 77.06E
Hardangerfjorden est. Norway 41 60.10N 6.00E
Hardangerjökulen mtn. Norway 41 60.33N 7.26E
Hardanger Vidda f. Norway 42 60.15N 7.20E
Hardeeville U.S.A. 113 32.18N 81.05W
Hardenberg Neth. 16 52.36N 6.40E
Harderwijk Neth. 16 52.21N 5.37E
Harding R.S.A. 80 30.34S 29.52E
Hardman U.S.A. 108 45.10N119.40W
Hardoi India 63 27.25N 80.07E
Hardwār India 63 29.58N 78.10E
Hardwick U.S.A. 105 44.30N 72.22W
Hardwicke B. Australia 92 34.52S137.10E
Hardy U.S.A. 111 36.19N 91.29W
Hare B. Canada 103 51.18N 55.50W
Haren W. Germany 38 52.47N 7.14E
Hārer Ethiopia 73 9.20N 42.10E
Hārergē d. Ethiopia 73 8.00N 41.00E
Harfleur France 18 49.30N 0.12E
Hargeysa Somali Rep. 71 9.31N 44.02E
Har Hu l. China 52 38.20N 97.40E
Hari r. Indonesia 58 1.00S104.15E
Harima nada str. Japan 57 34.30N134.30E
Harīpur Pakistan 62 33.59N 72.56E
Ḩarīr r. Syria 67 32.45N 35.55E
Harīrūd r. Afghan. 60 35.42N 61.12E
Harlan U.S.A. 110 41.39N 95.19W
Harlech U.K. 12 52.52N 4.08W
Harlem U.S.A. 108 48.32N108.47W
Harlingen Neth. 16 53.10N 5.25E
Harlingen U.S.A. 111 26.11N 97.42W
Harlow U.K. 13 51.47N 0.08E
Harlowton U.S.A. 108 46.26N109.50W
Harman U.S.A. 114 38.55N 79.32W
Harnai Pakistan 62 30.06N 67.56E
Harnātānr India 63 27.19N 84.01E
Harney Basin f. U.S.A. 108 43.15N120.40W
Harney L. U.S.A. 108 43.14N119.07W
Härnösand Sweden 40 62.37N 17.55E
Har Nuur l. Mongolia 52 48.00N 93.25E
Haro Spain 26 42.35N 2.51W
Haroldswick U.K. 10 60.47N 0.50W
Harper Liberia 76 4.25N 7.43W
Harpers Ferry town U.S.A. 114 39.13N 77.45W
Harrai India 63 22.37N 79.13E
Harricana r. Canada 102 51.10N 79.45W
Harrigan, C. Canada 103 55.50N 60.21W
Harrington U.S.A. 115 38.56N 75.35W
Harrington Harbour Canada 103 50.31N 59.30W
Harris Canada 101 51.44N107.35W
Harris i. U.K. 14 57.50N 6.55W
Harris, L. Australia 91 31.08S135.14E
Harris, Sd. of U.K. 14 57.43N 7.05W
Harrisburg Ill. U.S.A. 111 37.44N 88.33W
Harrisburg Oreg. U.S.A. 108 44.16N123.10W
Harrisburg Penn. U.S.A. 114 40.16N 76.52W
Harrismith Australia 89 32.55S117.50E
Harrismith R.S.A. 80 28.15S 29.07E
Harrison Ark. U.S.A. 111 36.14N 93.07W
Harrison Nebr. U.S.A. 110 42.41N103.53W
Harrison, C. Canada 103 54.55N 57.55W
Harrisonburg U.S.A. 114 38.27N 78.54W
Harrison L. Canada 100 49.33N121.50W
Harrisonville U.S.A. 110 38.39N 94.21W
Harrisville U.S.A. 114 39.13N 81.03W
Harrisville Mich. U.S.A. 104 44.39N 83.17W
Harrisville N.Y. U.S.A. 105 44.09N 75.19W
Harrodsburg U.S.A. 113 37.46N 84.51W
Harrogate U.K. 12 53.59N 1.32W
Harrow Canada 104 42.02N 82.55W
Harrow U.K. 13 51.35N 0.21W
Harrowsmith Canada 105 44.24N 76.40W
Harstad Norway 40 68.48N 16.30E
Harsūd India 62 22.06N 76.44E
Hart, L. Australia 92 31.08S136.24E
Ḩartā Jordan 67 32.48N 36.34E
Hartford U.S.A. 115 41.46N 72.41W
Hartland Canada 103 46.18N 67.32W
Hartland U.K. 13 50.59N 4.29W
Hartland Pt. U.K. 13 51.01N 4.32W
Hartlepool U.K. 12 54.42N 1.11W
Hartley Bay town Canada 100 53.27N129.18W
Hartola Finland 41 61.35N 26.01E
Hartshorne U.S.A. 111 34.51N 95.33W
Hartsville U.S.A. 113 34.23N 80.05W
Hārūnābād Pakistan 62 29.37N 73.08E
Har Us Nuur l. Mongolia 52 48.10N 92.10E
Hārūt r. Afghan. 62 31.35N 61.18E
Harvey Australia 89 33.06S115.50E
Harvey Ill. U.S.A. 110 41.37N 87.39W
Harvey N.Dak. U.S.A. 110 47.47N 99.56W
Harwich U.K. 13 51.56N 1.18E
Haryana d. India 62 29.15N 76.30E
Harz mts. W. Germany/E. Germany 38 51.43N 10.40E
Ḩasā, Wādī al r. Jordan 66 31.01N 35.29E
Hasa Oasis see Aḩsā', Wāḩat al Saudi Arabia 65
Hasdo r. India 63 21.44N 82.44E
Hase r. W. Germany 38 52.41N 7.18E
Haselünne W. Germany 38 52.40N 7.29E
Hasenkamp Argentina 125 31.30S 59.50W
Hashābah Sudan 72 14.19N 32.19E
Ḩasharūd Iran 65 37.29N 47.05E
Hashefela f. Israel 67 31.40N 34.55E
Hashimoto Japan 57 34.19N135.37E
Haskell U.S.A. 111 33.10N 99.44W
Hasle Denmark 43 55.11N 14.43E
Haslemere U.K. 13 51.05N 0.41W
Haslev Denmark 42 55.20N 11.58E
Hasselt Belgium 16 50.56N 5.20E
Hassfurt W. Germany 39 50.02N 10.31E
Hassi bel Guebbour Algeria 75 28.30N 6.41E
Hassi er Rmel well Algeria 75 32.57N 3.11E
Hassi Messaoud Algeria 75 31.43N 6.03E
Hassi Tagsist well Algeria 74 25.20N 1.35E
Hässleholm Sweden 43 56.09N 13.46E
Hassloch W. Germany 39 49.22N 8.16E
Hastings Canada 105 44.18N 77.57W
Hastings New Zealand 86 39.39S176.52E
Hastings U.K. 13 50.51N 0.36E
Hastings Nebr. U.S.A. 110 40.35N 98.23W
Hastings Range mts. Australia 93 31.14S152.00E
Hatanbulag Mongolia 54 43.08N109.05E
Hatch U.S.A. 109 32.40N107.09W
Hatches Creek town Australia 90 20.56S135.12E
Hatfield Australia 92 33.53S143.47E
Hatfield U.K. 13 51.46N 0.13W
Hāthras India 63 27.36N 78.03E
Hātia I. Bangla. 63 22.40N 90.55E
Ha Tinh Vietnam 56 18.21N105.55E
Hatta India 63 24.07N 79.36E
Hattah Australia 92 34.52S142.23E
Hattem Neth. 16 52.29N 6.06E
Hatteras, C. U.S.A. 113 35.13N 75.32W
Hattiesburg U.S.A. 111 31.19N 89.16W
Hattingen W. Germany 16 51.24N 7.09E
Hatton U.S.A. 108 46.46N118.49W
Hatutu i. Is. Marquises 85 7.56S140.38W
Hatvan Hungary 37 47.40N 19.41E
Hauge Norway 42 58.18N 6.15E
Haugesund Norway 42 59.25N 5.18E
Haugsdorf Austria 36 48.42N 16.05E
Hauraki G. New Zealand 86 36.30S175.00E
Hausach W. Germany 39 48.17N 8.10E
Haut Atlas mts. Morocco 74 31.30N 7.00W
Haut-Bassins d. U. Volta 76 10.45N 3.45W
Haute-Corse d. France 21 42.30N 9.20E
Haute-Garonne d. France 20 43.25N 1.30E
Haute Kotto d. C.A.R. 73 7.15N 23.30E
Haute-Loire d. France 20 45.05N 3.50E
Haute-Marne d. France 19 48.05N 5.10E
Haute Maurice Prov. Park Canada 102 48.38N 74.30W
Haute-Normandie d. France 18 49.30N 1.00E
Haute-Pyrénées d. France 20 43.00N 0.10E
Hauterive Canada 103 49.11N 68.16W
Hautes-Alpes d. France 21 44.40N 6.30E
Haute-Saône d. France 19 47.40N 6.10E
Haute-Savoie d. France 21 46.00N 6.20E
Haute-Vienne d. France 20 45.50N 1.15E
Haut Mbomou d. C.A.R. 73 6.25N 26.10E
Hautmont France 19 50.15N 3.56E
Haut-Rhin d. France 19 47.53N 7.13E
Hauts Plateau f. Morocco/Algeria 74 34.00N 0.10W
Haut Zaïre d. Zaïre 79 2.00N 27.00E
Havana see La Habana Cuba 117
Havant U.K. 13 50.51N 0.59W
Havel r. E. Germany 38 52.53N 11.58E
Havelange Belgium 16 50.23N 5.14E
Havelberg E. Germany 38 52.50N 12.04E
Havelland f. E. Germany 38 52.30N 12.35E
Havelock Canada 105 44.26N 77.53W
Havelock New Zealand 86 41.17S173.46E
Haverfordwest U.K. 13 51.48N 4.59W
Haverhill U.K. 13 52.06N 0.27E
Haverhill U.S.A. 115 42.47N 71.05W
Havlíčkuv Brod Czech. 36 49.38N 15.35E
Havre U.S.A. 108 48.33N109.41W
Havre de Grace U.S.A. 115 39.33N 76.06W
Havre St. Pierre Canada 103 50.15N 63.36W
Hawaii d. U.S.A. 106 21.00N156.00W
Hawaii i. Hawaii U.S.A. 106 19.30N155.30W
Hawaiian Is. U.S.A. 106 21.00N157.00W
Hawdon, L. Australia 92 37.09S139.54E
Hawea, L. New Zealand 86 44.30S169.15E
Hawera New Zealand 86 39.35S174.19E
Hawick U.K. 14 55.25N 2.47W
Hawke, C. Australia 93 32.12S152.33E
Hawke B. New Zealand 86 39.18S177.15E
Hawker Australia 92 31.53S138.25E
Hawkers Gate Australia 92 29.46S141.00E
Hawke's Bay d. New Zealand 86 39.40S176.35E
Hawkesbury Canada 105 45.36N 74.37W
Hawks U.S.A. 104 45.16N 83.53W
Hawkwood Australia 90 25.46S150.48E
Hawley U.S.A. 115 41.28N 75.11W
Ḩawrān, Wādī r. Iraq 64 33.57N 42.35E
Ḩawsh 'Īsá Egypt 66 30.55N 30.17E
Hawthorne U.S.A. 108 38.32N118.38W
Hay Australia 93 34.31S144.31E
Hay r. Australia 90 25.00S138.00E
Hay r. Canada 100 60.49N115.52W
Haya r. Japan 57 35.30N138.26E
Hayange France 19 49.20N 6.03E
Haybān Sudan 73 11.13N 30.31E
Haydān, Wādī al Jordan 67 31.27N 35.36E
Hayden U.S.A. 109 33.00N110.47W
Hayes r. Canada 101 57.03N 92.09W
Hayesville U.S.A. 114 40.46N 82.16W
Hay-on-Wye U.K. 13 52.04N 3.09W
Hay River town Canada 100 60.51N115.44W
Hays U.S.A. 110 38.53N 99.20W
Hayward U.S.A. 110 46.02N 91.26W
Haywards Heath f. U.K. 13 51.00N 0.05E
HaZafon d. Israel 67 32.50N 35.20E
Hazārān, Kūh-e mtn. Iran 65 29.30N 57.18E
Hazard U.S.A. 113 37.14N 83.11W
Hazāribāgh India 63 23.59N 85.21E
Hazel Hurst U.S.A. 114 41.42N 78.35W
Hazelton Canada 100 55.20N127.42W
Hazelton U.S.A. 110 46.29N100.17W
Hazen U.S.A. 108 39.34N119.03W
Hazerim Israel 67 31.14N 34.43E
Hazlehurst Ga. U.S.A. 113 31.53N 82.34W
Hazlehurst Miss. U.S.A. 111 31.52N 90.24W
Hazleton U.S.A. 115 40.58N 75.59W
Hazor Israel 67 32.59N 35.33E
Hazor Ashdod Israel 67 31.46N 34.43E
Head Waters U.S.A. 114 38.20N 79.21W
Healdsburg U.S.A. 108 38.37N122.52W
Healesville Australia 93 37.40S145.31E
Healy U.S.A. 98 63.52N148.58W
Heanor U.K. 12 53.01N 1.20W
Heard I. Indian Oc. 49 53.07S 73.20E
Hearne L. Canada 100 62.20N113.10W
Hearst Canada 102 49.40N 83.41W
Heathcote Australia 93 36.54S144.42E
Hebei d. China 54 39.00N116.00E
Hebel Australia 93 28.55S147.49E
Heber Springs town U.S.A. 111 35.30N 92.02W
Hebi China 54 35.57N114.05E
Hebrides is. U.K. 8 57.45N 7.00W
Hebrides, Sea of the U.K. 10 57.00N 7.20W
Hebron Canada 99 58.05N 62.30W
Hebron see Al Khalīl Jordan 67
Hebron N.Dak. U.S.A. 110 46.54N102.03W
Hebron Nebr. U.S.A. 110 40.10N 97.35W
Heby Sweden 43 59.56N 16.53E
Hecate Str. Canada 100 53.00N131.00W
Hechi China 55 24.42N108.02E
Hechingen W. Germany 39 48.21N 8.58E
Hechtel Belgium 16 51.07N 5.22E
Hechuan China 55 30.05N106.14E
Hecla U.S.A. 110 45.53N 98.09W
Hede Sweden 41 62.25N 13.30E
Hedemora Sweden 43 60.17N 15.59E
Hedensted Denmark 42 55.46N 9.42E
Hedi Shuiku resr. China 55 21.50N110.19E
Hedley U.S.A. 111 34.52N100.39W
Hedmark d. Norway 41 61.20N 11.30E
Heemstede Neth. 16 52.21N 4.38E
Heerde Neth. 16 52.23N 6.02E
Heerenveen Neth. 16 52.57N 5.55E
Heerlen Neth. 16 50.53N 5.59E
Hefa Israel 67 32.49N 34.59E
Hefa d. Israel 67 32.50N 35.00E
Hefei China 55 31.50N117.16E
Hegang China 53 47.36N130.30E
Heide W. Germany 38 54.12N 9.06E
Heide f. W. Germany 38 52.50N 10.30E
Heidelberg C.P. R.S.A. 80 34.05S 20.58E
Heidelberg W. Germany 39 49.25N 8.43E
Heidenheim W. Germany 39 48.40N 10.08E
Heilbron R.S.A. 80 27.16S 27.57E
Heilbronn W. Germany 39 49.08N 9.13E
Heiligenblut Austria 39 47.02N 12.50E
Heiligenhafen W. Germany 38 54.22N 10.58E
Heiligenstadt E. Germany 38 51.23N 10.09E
Heilongjiang d. China 53 47.00N126.00E
Heiloo Neth. 16 52.37N 4.43E
Heinola Finland 41 61.13N 26.02E
Heinsberg W. Germany 38 51.03N 6.05E
Heishan China 54 41.40N122.03E
Heishui China 54 42.03N119.21E
Heishuisi China 54 36.01N108.56E
Hejaz f. see Al Ḩijāz Saudi Arabia 64
Hejian China 54 38.26N116.05E
Hejiang China 55 28.48N105.47E
Hekinan Japan 57 34.51N136.58E
Hekla, Mt. Iceland 40 64.00N 19.45W
Hekou Yaozu Zizhixian China 61 22.39N103.57E
Hekura jima i. Japan 57 37.52N136.56E
Helagsfjället mtn. Sweden 40 62.58N 12.25E
Helan China 54 38.35N106.16E
Helan Shan mts. China 54 38.40N106.00E
Helbra E. Germany 38 51.33N 11.29E
Helena U.S.A. 108 46.36N112.01W
Helen Reef i. Caroline Is. 59 2.43N131.46E
Helensburgh U.K. 14 56.01N 4.44W
Helensville New Zealand 86 36.40S174.27E
Helez Israel 67 31.35N 34.40E
Helgoland i. W. Germany 38 54.12N 7.53E
Helgoländer Bucht b. W. Germany 38 54.05N 8.15E

Hellendoorn to Hösbach

Hellendoorn Neth. 16 52.24N 6.29E
Hellenthal W. Germany 38 50.29N 6.26E
Hellesylt Norway 41 62.05N 6.54E
Hellevoetsluis Neth. 16 51.49N 4.08E
Hellín Spain 25 38.31N 1.41W
Hell-Ville Madagascar 81 13.25S 48.16E
Helmand d. Afghan. 62 31.15N 64.00E
Helmand r. Asia 62 31.12N 61.34E
Helmond Neth. 16 51.28N 5.40E
Helmsdale U.K. 14 58.07N 3.40W
Helmsdale r. U.K. 14 58.05N 3.39W
Helmstedt W. Germany 38 52.13N 11.00E
Helsingfors see Helsinki Finland 41
Helsingör Denmark 43 56.02N 12.37E
Helsinki Finland 41 60.08N 25.00E
Helston U.K. 13 50.07N 5.17W
Helvecia Argentina 125 31.06S 60.05W
Hemaruka Canada 101 51.48N111.10W
Hemau W. Germany 38 49.03N 11.47E
Hemel Hempstead U.K. 13 51.46N 0.28W
Hemingford U.S.A. 110 42.19N103.04W
Hemmingford Canada 105 45.03N 73.36W
Hempstead N.Y. U.S.A. 115 40.42N 73.37W
Hempstead Tex. U.S.A. 111 30.06N 96.05W
Hemse Sweden 43 57.14N 18.22E
Hemsedal Norway 41 60.52N 8.34E
Henan d. China 54 34.00N114.00E
Henares r. Spain 26 40.24N 3.30W
Henbury Australia 90 24.35S133.15E
Hendaye France 20 43.22N 1.46W
Henderson Ky. U.S.A. 113 37.50N 87.35W
Henderson N.C. U.S.A. 113 36.20N 78.26W
Henderson Nev. U.S.A. 109 36.02N114.59W
Henderson N.Y. U.S.A. 105 43.51N 76.11W
Henderson Tex. U.S.A. 111 32.09N 94.48W
Henderson I. Pacific Oc. 85 24.20S128.20W
Hendrik Verwoerd Dam R.S.A. 80 30.37S 25.29E
Hendrina R.S.A. 80 26.09S 29.42E
Hengelo Neth. 16 52.16N 6.46E
Hengshan Hunan China 55 27.14N112.52E
Hengshan Shaanxi China 54 37.57N109.11E
Hengshui China 54 37.40N115.48E
Heng Xian China 55 22.35N109.26E
Hengyang China 55 26.52N112.35E
Hénin-Beaumont France 19 50.25N 2.56E
Henlopen, C. U.S.A. 115 38.48N 75.05W
Hennebont France 18 47.48N 3.17W
Hennigsdorf E. Germany 38 52.38N 13.12E
Henniker U.S.A. 115 43.11N 71.49W
Henrietta Maria, C. Canada 102 55.00N 82.15W
Henryetta U.S.A. 111 35.27N 95.59W
Henryville Canada 105 45.08N 73.11W
Hentiesbaai Namibia 80 22.10S 14.19E
Henty Australia 93 35.30S147.03E
Henzada Burma 56 17.36N 95.26E
Heppenheim W. Germany 39 49.39N 8.38E
Heppner U.S.A. 108 45.21N119.33W
Hepu China 55 21.31N109.10E
Hepworth Canada 104 44.37N 81.09W
Heqing China 61 26.34N100.12E
Herāt Afghan. 62 34.20N 62.12E
Herāt d. Afghan. 62 34.10N 62.30E
Herault r. France 20 43.17N 3.26E
Herbignac France 18 47.27N 2.19W
Herborn W. Germany 38 50.40N 8.17E
Herceg-Novi Yugo. 31 42.27N 18.32E
Hereford U.K. 13 52.04N 2.43W
Hereford Md. U.S.A. 115 39.35N 76.40W
Hereford Tex. U.S.A. 111 34.49N102.24W
Hereford and Worcester d. U.K. 13 52.08N 2.30W
Herencia Spain 27 39.21N 3.22W
Herentals Belgium 16 51.12N 4.42E
Herford W. Germany 38 52.06N 8.40E
Herington U.S.A. 110 38.40N 96.57W
Herisau Switz. 39 47.23N 9.17E
Herleshausen W. Germany 38 51.00N 10.09E
Hermagor Austria 39 46.37N 13.22E
Hermanus R.S.A. 80 34.24S 19.16E
Hermidale Australia 93 31.33S146.44E
Hermiston U.S.A. 108 45.51N119.17W
Hermosillo Mexico 109 29.04N110.58W
Herndon U.S.A. 114 40.43N 76.50W
Herne W. Germany 38 51.32N 7.13E
Herne Bay town U.K. 13 51.23N 1.10E
Herning Denmark 42 56.08N 8.59E
Heron Bay town Canada 102 48.40N 86.25W
Herowābād Iran 65 37.36N 48.36E
Herrera del Duque Spain 27 39.10N 5.03W
Herrera de Pisuerga Spain 26 42.36N 4.20W
Herrljunga Sweden 43 58.05N 13.02E
Hershey U.S.A. 115 40.17N 76.39W
Herstal Belgium 16 50.14N 5.38E
Herten W. Germany 38 51.35N 7.07E
Hertford U.K. 13 51.48N 0.05W
Hertfordshire d. U.K. 13 51.51N 0.05W
Hervás Spain 26 40.16N 5.51W
Hervey B. Australia 90 25.00S153.00E
Herzberg E. Germany 38 51.41N 13.14E
Herzberg W. Germany 38 51.39N 10.20E
Herzliyya Israel 67 32.10N 34.50E
Hesbaye f. Belgium 16 50.32N 5.07E
Hesdin France 19 50.22N 2.02E
Hesel W. Germany 38 53.18N 7.35E
Heshui China 54 35.43N108.07E
Heshun China 54 37.19N113.34E
Hesselö i. Denmark 42 56.12N 11.43E
Hessen d. W. Germany 38 50.44N 9.00E
Hesso Australia 92 32.08S137.58E
Hetou China 55 21.05N109.44E
Hettinger U.S.A. 110 46.00N102.39W
Hettstedt E. Germany 38 51.38N 11.30E
Hetzerath W. Germany 39 49.52N 6.49E
Heuvelton U.S.A. 105 44.37N 75.25W
Hevron, Nahal wadi Israel 67 31.15N 34.50E
Hewett, C. Canada 99 70.20N 68.00W
Hexham U.K. 12 54.58N 2.06W
Hexi China 55 24.51N117.13E
He Xian China 55 24.25N111.31E
Hexigten Qi China 54 43.17N117.24E
Heyrieux France 21 45.38N 5.03E
Heysham U.K. 12 54.03N 2.53W
Heyuan China 55 23.42N114.48E
Heywood Australia 92 38.08S141.38E
Heywood U.K. 12 53.36N 2.13W
Heze China 54 35.12N115.15E
Hezhang China 55 27.08N104.43E
Hiawatha Kans. U.S.A. 110 39.51N 95.32W
Hiawatha Utah U.S.A. 108 39.29N111.01W
Hibbing U.S.A. 110 47.25N 92.55W
Hickman, Mt. Canada 100 57.11N131.10W
Hickory U.S.A. 113 35.44N 81.23W
Hicks Bay town New Zealand 86 37.35S178.18E
Hickson L. Canada 101 56.17N104.25W
Hicksville U.S.A. 115 40.46N 73.32W
Hidaka Sammyaku mts. Japan 57 42.50N143.00E
Hidalgo d. Mexico 116 20.50N 98.30W
Hidalgo Nuevo León Mexico 111 25.59N100.27W
Hidalgo Tamaulipas Mexico 116 24.15N 99.26W
Hidalgo del Parral Mexico 109 26.56N105.40W
Hieradhsvotn r. Iceland 40 65.45N 18.50W
Hierro i. Canary Is. 74 27.45N 18.00W
Higashimatsuyama Japan 57 36.02N139.24E
Higashimurayama Japan 57 35.46N139.29E
Higashiōsaka Japan 57 34.39N135.35E
Higgins U.S.A. 111 36.07N100.02W
Higgins L. U.S.A. 104 44.30N 84.45W
Higginsville Australia 89 31.46S121.43E
Highgate Canada 104 42.30N 81.49W
High Hill r. Canada 101 55.52N 94.42W
High Knob mtn. U.S.A. 114 39.08N 78.26W
Highland d. U.K. 14 57.42N 5.00W
Highland town U.S.A. 115 41.43N 73.58W
Highland Park town U.S.A. 114 42.24N 83.06W
High Level Canada 100 58.31N117.08W
Highmore U.S.A. 110 44.31N 99.27W
High Peak mtn. U.K. 12 53.22N 1.48W
High Point town U.S.A. 113 35.58N 80.00W
High Prairie Canada 100 55.30N116.30W
Highrock L. Man. Canada 101 55.45N100.30W
Highrock L. Sask. Canada 101 57.04N105.30W
High Willhays mtn. U.K. 13 50.41N 4.00W
High Wycombe U.K. 13 51.38N 0.46W
Hiiumaa i. U.S.S.R. 41 58.52N 22.40E
Híjar Spain 25 41.10N 0.27W
Ḩijāz, Jabal al mts. Saudi Arabia 72 19.45N 41.55E
Hikone Japan 57 35.15N136.15E
Hikurangi New Zealand 86 35.36S174.17E
Hikurangi mtn. New Zealand 86 37.50S178.10E
Hikutavake Niue 84 18.57S169.53W
Hildburghausen E. Germany 39 50.25N 10.44E
Hilden W. Germany 38 51.10N 6.56E
Hildesheim W. Germany 38 52.09N 9.57E
Hill City Kans. U.S.A. 110 39.22N 99.51W
Hill City Minn. U.S.A. 110 46.59N 93.44W
Hillegom Neth. 16 52.19N 4.35E
Hilleröd Denmark 43 55.56N 12.19E
Hill Island L. Canada 101 60.30N109.50W
Hillman U.S.A. 104 45.04N 83.54W
Hillsboro N.H. U.S.A. 115 43.07N 71.54W
Hillsboro Oreg. U.S.A. 108 45.31N122.59W
Hillsboro Tex. U.S.A. 111 32.01N 97.08W
Hillsdale U.S.A. 112 41.56N 84.37W
Hillsport Canada 102 49.27N 85.34W
Hillston Australia 93 33.30S145.33E
Hilo Hawaii U.S.A. 106 19.42N155.04W
Hilton U.S.A. 114 43.17N 77.48W
Hilton Beach Canada 104 46.16N 83.56W
Hilton Head I. U.S.A. 113 32.12N 80.45W
Hiltrup W. Germany 38 51.54N 7.38E
Hilversum Neth. 16 52.14N 5.12E
Himachal Pradesh d. India 62 32.05N 77.15E
Himalaya mts. Asia 63 29.00N 84.30E
Himanka Finland 40 64.04N 23.39E
Himarë Albania 34 40.08N 19.43E
Himatnagar India 62 23.36N 72.57E
Himeji Japan 57 34.50N134.40E
Himi Japan 57 36.51N136.59E
Himmerland f. Denmark 42 56.52N 9.30E
Ḩimş Syria 66 34.44N 36.43E
Hinchinbrook I. Australia 90 18.23S146.17E
Hinckley U.K. 13 52.33N 1.21W
Hinckley Resr. U.S.A. 115 43.20N 75.05W
Hindaun India 62 26.43N 77.01E
Hindmarsh, L. Australia 92 36.03S141.53E
Hindubāgh Pakistan 62 30.49N 67.45E
Hindu Kush mts. Asia 60 36.40N 70.00E
Hindupur India 60 13.49N 77.29E
Hines Creek town Canada 100 56.20N118.40W
Hinganghāt India 63 20.34N 78.50E
Hingol r. Pakistan 62 25.23N 65.28E
Hingoli India 62 19.43N 77.09E
Hinnöy i. Norway 40 68.35N 15.50E
Hinojosa Spain 26 38.30N 5.09W
Hinsdale Mont. U.S.A. 108 48.24N107.05W
Hinsdale N.H. U.S.A. 115 42.47N 72.29W
Hinterrhein r. Switz. 39 46.49N 9.25E
Hinton Canada 100 53.25N117.34W
Hipólito Mexico 111 25.41N101.26W
Hippolytushoef Neth. 16 52.57N 4.58E
Hirakata Japan 57 34.48N135.38E
Hīrākud India 63 21.31N 83.57E
Hīrākud resr. India 63 21.31N 83.52E
Hīrāpur India 63 24.22N 79.13E
Hiratsuka Japan 57 35.19N139.21E
Hirmand r. see Helmand Iran 62
Hirok Sāmi Pakistan 62 26.02N 63.25E
Hirosaki Japan 57 40.34N140.28E
Hiroshima Japan 57 34.30N132.27E
Hirson France 19 49.55N 4.05E
Hîrşova Romania 37 44.41N 27.57E
Hirtshals Denmark 42 57.35N 9.58E
Hisai Japan 57 34.40N136.28E
Hisār India 62 29.10N 75.43E
Ḩisbān Jordan 67 31.48N 35.48E
Ḩismá f. Saudi Arabia 66 28.45N 35.56E
Hispaniola i. C. America 117 19.00N 71.00W
Hisua India 63 24.50N 85.25E
Ḩisyah Syria 66 34.24N 36.45E
Hīt Iraq 64 33.38N 42.50E
Hitachi Japan 57 36.35N140.40E
Hitchin U.K. 13 51.57N 0.16W
Hitra i. Norway 40 63.37N 8.46E
Hiva Oa i. Is. Marquises 85 9.45S139.00W
Hixon Canada 100 53.27N122.36W
Hjälmaren l. Sweden 43 59.15N 15.45E
Hjalmar L. Canada 101 61.33N109.25W
Hjelmelandsvågen Norway 42 59.14N 6.11E
Hjo Sweden 43 58.18N 14.17E
Hjörring Denmark 42 57.28N 9.59E
Hlotse Lesotho 80 28.52S 28.02E
Ho Ghana 76 6.38N 0.38E
Hòa Bình Vietnam 55 20.40N105.17E
Hoare B. Canada 99 65.20N 62.30W
Hoarusib r. Namibia 80 19.04S 12.33E
Hobart Australia 91 42.54S147.18E
Hobart Ind. U.S.A. 112 41.32N 87.14W
Hobart Okla. U.S.A. 111 35.01N 99.06W
Hobbs U.S.A. 111 32.42N103.08W
Hoboken Belgium 16 51.11N 4.21E
Hoboken U.S.A. 115 40.45N 74.03W
Hobq Shamo des. China 54 40.00N109.00E
Hobro Denmark 42 56.38N 9.48E
Hoburgen c. Sweden 43 56.55N 18.07E
Hochgolling mtn. Austria 39 47.16N 13.45E
Ho Chi Minh City see Thành Pho Ho Chí Minh Vietnam 56
Höchstadt an der Aisch W. Germany 39 49.42N 10.44E
Hockenheim W. Germany 39 49.19N 8.33E
Hocking r. U.S.A. 114 39.12N 81.45W
Hockley U.S.A. 111 30.02N 95.51W
Hodal India 62 27.54N 77.22E
Hodgson Canada 101 51.13N 97.34W
Hod HaSharon Israel 67 32.15N 34.55E
Hodh ech Chargui d. Mauritania 76 19.00N 7.15W
Hodh el Gharbi d. Mauritania 76 16.30N 10.00W
Hodiyya Israel 67 31.41N 34.38E
Hódmezövásárhely Hungary 31 46.25N 20.20E
Hodna, Monts du mts. Algeria 75 35.50N 4.50E
Hoek van Holland Neth. 16 51.59N 4.08E
Hoeryŏng N. Korea 57 42.27N129.44E
Hof W. Germany 38 50.18N 11.55E
Hofgeismar W. Germany 38 51.30N 9.22E
Hofheim Bayern W. Germany 39 50.08N 10.31E
Hofheim Hessen W. Germany 39 50.07N 8.26E
Höfn Iceland 40 64.16N 15.10W
Hofors Sweden 41 60.33N 16.17E
Hofsjökull mtn. Iceland 40 64.50N 19.00W
Hofsos Iceland 40 65.53N 19.26W
Höganäs Sweden 43 56.12N 12.33E
Hogansburg U.S.A. 105 44.59N 74.40W
Hogeland U.S.A. 108 48.51N108.39W
Hogem Ranges f. Canada 100 55.40N126.00W
Högsby Sweden 43 57.10N 16.02E
Hohe Acht mtn. W. Germany 39 50.23N 7.00E
Hohenthurn Austria 39 46.33N 13.40E
Hoher Dachstein mtn. Austria 39 47.28N 13.35E
Hohhot China 54 40.42N111.38E
Hoh Tolgoin Sum China 54 44.27N112.41E
Hohultslätt Sweden 43 56.58N 15.39E
Hoi An Vietnam 56 15.54N108.19E
Hoima Uganda 79 1.25N 31.22E
Hojāi India 63 26.00N 92.51E
Höjer Denmark 42 54.58N 8.43E
Hökensås hills Sweden 43 58.11N 14.08E
Hokitika New Zealand 86 42.42S170.59E
Hokkaidō d. Japan 57 43.00N143.00E
Hokkaidō i. Japan 57 43.00N144.00E
Hokksund Norway 42 59.47N 9.59E
Hola Kenya 79 1.29S 40.02E
Holbaek Denmark 42 55.43N 11.43E
Holbrook Australia 93 35.46S147.20E
Holbrook U.S.A. 109 34.54N110.10W
Holdrege U.S.A. 110 40.26N 99.22W
Holguín Cuba 117 20.54N 76.15W
Höljes Sweden 41 60.54N 12.36E
Hollabrunn Austria 36 48.34N 16.05E
Holland Mich. U.S.A. 112 42.46N 86.06W
Holland N.Y. U.S.A. 114 42.38N 78.33W
Holland Centre Canada 104 44.24N 80.48W
Hollidaysburg U.S.A. 114 40.26N 78.23W
Holly Kans. U.S.A. 111 38.03N102.07W
Holly Mich. U.S.A. 104 42.48N 83.38W
Hollywood U.S.A. 113 26.01N 80.09W
Holman Island town Canada 98 70.43N117.43W
Holmavik Iceland 40 65.43N 21.39W
Holmenkollen Norway 42 59.58N 10.40E
Holmer, Lac l. Canada 103 54.10N 71.44W
Holmestrand Norway 42 59.29N 10.18E
Holmön i. Sweden 40 63.47N 20.53E
Holmsund Sweden 40 63.41N 20.20E
Holon Israel 67 32.01N 34.46E
Holroyd r. Australia 90 14.10S141.36E
Holstebro Denmark 42 56.21N 8.38E
Holstein Canada 104 44.03N 80.45W
Holsteinsborg Greenland 99 66.55N 53.30W
Holsworthy U.K. 13 50.48N 4.21W
Holt U.K. 12 52.55N 1.04E
Holten Neth. 16 52.18N 6.26E
Holwerd Neth. 16 53.22N 5.54E
Holy Cross U.S.A. 98 62.12N159.47W
Holyhead U.K. 12 53.18N 4.38W
Holyhead B. U.K. 12 53.22N 4.40W
Holy I. England U.K. 14 55.41N 1.47W
Holy I. Scotland U.K. 12 55.32N 5.04W
Holy I. Wales U.K. 12 53.15N 4.38W
Holyoke Colo. U.S.A. 110 40.35N102.18W
Holyoke Mass. U.S.A. 115 42.12N 72.37W
Holýšov Czech. 38 49.36N 13.05E
Holywood U.K. 15 54.38N 5.50W
Holzkirchen W. Germany 39 47.52N 11.42E
Holzminden W. Germany 38 51.50N 9.27E
Homberg W. Germany 38 51.02N 9.24E
Hombori Mali 76 15.20N 1.38W
Homburg W. Germany 39 49.19N 7.20E
Home B. Canada 99 69.00N 66.00W
Home Hill town Australia 90 19.40S147.25E
Homer Alas. U.S.A. 98 59.40N151.37W
Homer La. U.S.A. 111 32.48N 93.04W
Homer N.Y. U.S.A. 115 42.38N 76.11W
Homer Tunnel New Zealand 86 44.40S168.15E
Homestead U.S.A. 113 25.29N 80.29W
Hommersåk Norway 42 58.58N 5.42E
Homoine Mozambique 81 23.45S 35.09E
Homoljske Planina f. Yugo. 37 44.20N 21.45E
Honda Colombia 122 5.15N 74.50W
Hondeklipbaai R.S.A. 80 30.19S 17.12E
Hondo r. Mexico 117 18.33N 88.22W
Hondo U.S.A. 111 29.21N 99.09W
Honduras C. America 117 14.30N 87.00W
Honduras, G. of Carib. Sea 117 16.20N 87.30W
Honesdale U.S.A. 115 41.34N 75.16W
Honfleur France 18 49.25N 0.14E
Höng Denmark 42 55.31N 11.18E
Hong'an China 55 31.18N114.33E
Hòn Gay Vietnam 55 21.01N107.02E
Hong Hà r. Vietnam 55 20.15N106.36E
Honghu China 55 29.42N113.26E
Hong Hu l. China 55 29.50N113.15E
Hongjiang China 55 27.08N109.54E
Hongjian Nur l. China 54 39.09N109.56E
Hong Kong Asia 55 22.15N114.15E
Hongor Mongolia 54 45.45N112.56E
Hongshui He r. China 55 23.20N110.04E
Hongtong China 54 36.15N111.37E
Honguedo, Détroit d' str. Canada 103 49.25N 64.00W
Hongze China 54 33.18N118.51E
Hongze Hu l. China 54 33.15N118.40E
Honiton U.K. 13 50.48N 3.13W
Honjō Japan 57 39.23N140.03E
Honkajoki Finland 41 62.00N 22.15E
Hönö Sweden 42 57.42N 11.39E
Honokaa Hawaiian Is. 85 20.05N155.28W
Honokahua Hawaiian Is. 85 21.00N156.39W
Honolulu Hawaii U.S.A. 106 21.19N157.50W
Honshū i. Japan 57 36.00N138.00E
Hood, Mt. U.S.A. 108 45.23N121.41W
Hood Pt. Australia 89 34.23S119.34E
Hood Range mts. Australia 93 28.35S144.30E
Hoogeveen Neth. 16 52.44N 6.29E
Hoogezand Neth. 16 53.10N 6.47E
Hooghly r. India 63 21.55N 88.05E
Hoogstade Belgium 16 50.59N 2.42E
Hooker U.S.A. 111 36.52N101.13W
Hook Head Rep. of Ire. 15 52.07N 6.55W
Hoopa U.S.A. 108 41.03N123.40W
Hoopeston U.S.A. 110 40.28N 87.41W
Hoopstad R.S.A. 80 27.48S 25.52E
Höör Sweden 43 55.56N 13.32E
Hoorn Neth. 16 52.38N 5.03E
Hoosick Falls town U.S.A. 115 42.54N 73.21W
Hoover Dam U.S.A. 109 36.00N114.27W
Hope U.S.A. 111 33.40N 93.36W
Hope, L. Australia 89 32.40S120.10E
Hope, L. Australia 92 28.23S139.19E
Hope, Pt. U.S.A. 96 68.20N166.49W
Hopedale Canada 103 55.50N 60.10W
Hopefield R.S.A. 80 33.04S 18.19E
Hopetoun Vic. Australia 92 35.43S142.20E
Hopetoun W.A. Australia 89 33.57S120.05E
Hopetown R.S.A. 80 29.37S 24.04E
Hopkins r. Australia 92 38.25S142.00E
Hopkins, L. Australia 88 24.15S128.50E
Hopkinsville U.S.A. 113 36.50N 87.30W
Hopland U.S.A. 108 38.58N123.07W
Hoquiam U.S.A. 108 46.59N123.53W
Horaždovice Czech. 38 49.20N 13.43E
Horb W. Germany 39 48.26N 8.41E
Horbat Qesari site Israel 67 32.30N 34.53E
Hörby Sweden 43 55.51N 13.39E
Hordaland d. Norway 42 60.00N 6.00E
Horde W. Germany 16 51.29N 7.30E
Horgen Switz. 39 47.15N 8.36E
Hörh Uul mts. Mongolia 54 42.20N105.30E
Horinger China 54 40.23N111.53E
Horizonte Mexico 111 25.50N103.48W
Horlick Mts. Antarctica 128 86.00S102.00W
Hormuz, Str. of Asia 65 26.35N 56.20E
Horn Austria 36 48.40N 15.40E
Horn r. Canada 100 61.30N118.01W
Horn, C. see Hornos, Cabo de S. America 125
Hornavan l. Sweden 40 66.10N 17.30E
Horncastle U.K. 12 53.13N 0.08W
Horndal Sweden 43 60.18N 16.25E
Hornell U.S.A. 114 42.19N 77.40W
Hornell L. Canada 100 62.20N119.25W
Hornepayne Canada 102 49.14N 84.48W
Hornindal Norway 41 61.58N 6.31E
Horn Mts. Canada 100 62.15N119.15W
Hornos, Cabo de c. S. America 125 55.47S 67.00W
Hornsby Australia 93 33.11S151.06E
Hornsea U.K. 12 53.55N 0.10W
Hornslet Denmark 42 56.19N 10.20E
Hořovice Czech. 36 49.50N 13.54E
Horqin Zuoyi Houqi China 54 42.57N122.21E
Horqin Zuoyi Zhongqi China 54 44.08N123.18E
Horru China 63 30.30N 91.32E
Horse Creek town U.S.A. 108 41.25N105.11W
Horseheads U.S.A. 114 42.10N 76.50W
Horsens Denmark 42 55.52N 9.52E
Horsham Australia 92 36.45S142.15E
Horsham U.K. 13 51.04N 0.20W
Hörsholm Denmark 43 55.53N 12.30E
Horšovský Týn Czech. 38 49.32N 12.56E
Horta wadi Chad 72 17.15N 21.52E
Horten Norway 42 59.25N 10.30E
Horton r. Canada 98 70.00N127.00W
Horton L. Canada 98 67.30N122.28W
Horvot Mezada site Israel 67 31.19N 35.21E
Hosaina Ethiopia 73 7.38N 37.52E
Hösbach W. Germany 39 50.00N 9.12E

Hose, Pegunungan to Ille-et-Vilaine

Hose, Pegunungan *mts.* Malaysia **58** 1.30N114.10E
Hoshâb Pakistan **62** 26.01N 63.56E
Hoshangâbâd India **63** 22.45N 77.43E
Hoshiârpur India **62** 31.32N 75.54E
Hôsh 'Isa Egypt **66** 30.55N 30.17E
Hoskins P.N.G. **87** 5.30S150.27E
Hospital de Orbigo Spain **26** 42.28N 5.53W
Hospitalet Spain **25** 41.22N 2.08E
Hossegor France **20** 43.40N 1.27W
Hoste, Isla *i.* Chile **125** 55.10S 69.00W
Hotan China **52** 37.07N 79.57E
Hotazel R.S.A. **80** 27.16S 22.57E
Hotham *r.* Australia **89** 32.58S116.22E
Hotham, Mt. Australia **93** 36.58S147.11E
Hoting Sweden **40** 64.07N 16.10E
Hotin Gol China **54** 38.58N104.14E
Hot Springs *town* Ark. U.S.A. **111** 34.30N 93.02W
Hot Springs *town* S.Dak. U.S.A. **110** 43.26N103.29W
Hottah L. Canada **98** 65.04N118.29W
Houailou N. Cal. **84** 21.17S165.38E
Houdan France **19** 48.47N 1.36E
Houeillès France **20** 44.12N 0.02E
Houffalize Belgium **16** 50.08N 5.50E
Houghton L. U.S.A. **112** 44.16N 84.48W
Houghton-le-Spring U.K. **12** 54.51N 1.28W
Houlton U.S.A. **112** 46.08N 67.51W
Houma China **54** 35.36N111.21E
Houma U.S.A. **111** 29.36N 90.43W
Houndé U. Volta **76** 11.34N 3.31W
Hourn, Loch U.K. **14** 57.06N 5.33W
Housatonic *r.* U.S.A. **115** 41.10N 73.07W
Houston Mo. U.S.A. **111** 37.22N 91.58W
Houston Tex. U.S.A. **111** 29.46N 95.22W
Houtzdale U.S.A. **114** 40.49N 78.21W
Hova Sweden **43** 58.52N 14.13E
Hovd Mongolia **52** 46.40N 90.45E
Hove U.K. **13** 50.50N 0.10W
Hovlya U.S.S.R. **45** 49.19N 44.01E
Hövsgöl Mongolia **54** 43.36N109.40E
Hövsgöl Nuur *l.* Mongolia **52** 51.00N100.30E
Howa, Ouadi *see* Howar, Wâdî Chad **72**
Howar, Wâdî Sudan **72** 17.30N 27.08E
Howard Australia **90** 25.20S152.32E
Howard L. Canada **101** 62.15N105.57W
Howe, C. Australia **93** 37.30S149.59E
Howell Australia **93** 30.00S151.00E
Howell U.S.A. **104** 42.36N 83.55W
Howick Canada **105** 45.11N 73.51W
Howitt, Mt. Australia **93** 37.15S146.40E
Howrah India **63** 22.35N 88.20E
Howth Head Rep. of Ire. **15** 53.22N 6.03W
Höxter W. Germany **38** 51.46N 9.23E
Hoy *i.* U.K. **14** 58.51N 3.17W
Höyanger Norway **41** 61.13N 6.05E
Hoyerswerda E. Germany **38** 51.26N 14.14E
Hoyos Spain **27** 40.10N 6.43W
Hradec Králové Czech. **36** 50.13N 15.50E
Hron *r.* Czech. **37** 47.49N 18.45E
Hrubieszów Poland **37** 50.49N 23.55E
Hrvatska *d.* Yugo. **31** 45.35N 16.10E
Hsenwi Burma **56** 23.18N 97.58E
Hsipaw Burma **56** 22.42N 97.21E
Hsuphâng Burma **56** 20.18N 98.42E
Huab *r.* Namibia **80** 20.55S 13.28E
Huabei Pingyuan *f.* China **54** 35.00N115.30E
Huachi China **54** 36.32N108.14E
Huacho Peru **122** 11.05S 77.36W
Huachuca City U.S.A. **109** 31.34N110.21W
Huade China **54** 41.57N114.04E
Hua Hin Thailand **56** 12.34N 99.58E
Huahine *i.* Îs. de la Société **85** 16.45S151.00W
Huai'an Hebei China **54** 40.40N114.18E
Huai'an Jiangsu China **54** 33.29N119.15E
Huaibei China **54** 33.58N116.50E
Huai He *r.* China **54** 32.58N118.18E
Huaiji China **55** 23.58N112.10E
Huailai China **54** 40.25N115.27E
Huainan China **54** 32.39N117.01E
Huaining China **55** 30.21N116.42E
Huairen China **54** 39.50N113.07E
Huairou China **54** 40.20N116.37E
Huaiyang China **54** 33.47N114.59E
Huaiyuan China **54** 32.57N117.12E
Huajuápan Mexico **116** 17.50N 97.48W
Hualian Taiwan **55** 24.00N121.39E
Huallaga *r.* Peru **122** 5.02S 75.30W
Huamanrazo *mtn.* Peru **122** 12.54S 75.04W
Huambo Angola **78** 12.47S 15.44E
Huambo *d.* Angola **78** 12.30S 15.45E
Huanan China **53** 46.13N130.31E
Huancané Peru **122** 15.10S 69.44W
Huancapi Peru **122** 13.35S 74.05W
Huancavelica Peru **122** 12.45S 75.03W
Huancayo Peru **122** 12.05S 75.12W
Huangchuan China **55** 32.07N115.02E
Huanggang China **55** 30.33N114.59E
Huanggang Shan *mtn.* China **55** 27.50N117.47E
Huang Hai *b.* N. Korea **54** 39.30N123.40E
Huang He *r.* China **54** 38.00N118.40E
Huanghe Kou *est.* China **54** 37.54N118.48E
Huanghua China **54** 38.22N117.20E
Huangling China **54** 35.36N109.17E
Huangpi China **55** 30.52N114.22E
Huangping China **55** 26.54N107.53E
Huangshi China **55** 30.10N115.04E
Huang Xian China **54** 37.38N120.30E
Huangyan China **55** 28.42N121.25E
Huan Jiang *r.* China **54** 35.13N108.00E
Huanren China **54** 41.16N125.21E
Huanta Peru **122** 12.54S 74.13W
Huánuco Peru **122** 9.55S 76.11W
Huaráz Peru **122** 9.33S 77.31W
Huarmey Peru **122** 10.05S 78.05W
Huascaran *mtn.* Peru **122** 9.08S 77.36W
Huasco Chile **124** 28.28S 71.14W
Huatabampo Mexico **109** 26.50N109.38W
Huatong China **54** 40.03N121.56E
Hua Xian Guangdong China **55** 23.22N113.12E
Hua Xian Shaanxi China **54** 34.31N109.46E
Huayuan China **55** 28.37N109.28E
Hubbard L. U.S.A. **104** 44.49N 83.34W
Hubei *d.* China **55** 31.00N112.00E
Hubli India **60** 15.20N 75.14E
Hückelhoven W. Germany **38** 51.03N 6.13E
Hucknall U.K. **12** 53.03N 1.12W
Huddersfield U.K. **12** 53.38N 1.49W
Huddinge Sweden **43** 59.14N 17.59E
Hudiksvall Sweden **41** 61.44N 17.07E
Hudson *r.* U.S.A. **115** 40.42N 74.02W
Hudson Mich. U.S.A. **104** 41.51N 84.21W
Hudson N.Y. U.S.A. **115** 42.15N 73.47W
Hudson Wyo. U.S.A. **108** 42.54N108.35W
Hudson B. Canada **99** 58.00N 86.00W
Hudson Bay *town* Canada **101** 52.52N102.25W
Hudson Falls *town* U.S.A. **115** 43.18N 73.35W
Hudson Highlands U.S.A. **115** 41.24N 74.15W
Hudson Hope Canada **100** 56.03N121.59W
Hudson Mts. Antarctica **128** 76.00S 99.00W
Hudson Str. Canada **99** 62.00N 70.00W
Hue Vietnam **56** 16.28N107.40E
Huebra *r.* Spain **26** 41.02N 6.48W
Huedin Romania **37** 46.52N 23.02E
Huehuetenango Guatemala **116** 15.19N 91.26W
Huelgoat France **18** 48.22N 3.45W
Huelma Spain **27** 37.39N 3.27W
Huelva Spain **27** 37.16N 6.57W
Huelva *d.* Spain **27** 37.35N 7.10W
Huelva *r.* Spain **27** 37.27N 6.00W
Huércal-Overa Spain **25** 37.23N 1.57W
Huerva *r.* Spain **25** 41.39N 0.52W
Huesca Spain **25** 42.08N 0.25W
Huesca *d.* Spain **25** 42.20N 0.00
Huéscar Spain **27** 37.49N 2.32W
Huete Spain **26** 40.08N 2.41W
Hufrat an Nahâs Sudan **73** 9.45N 24.19E
Hugh *r.* Australia **90** 25.01S134.01E
Hughenden Australia **90** 20.51S144.12E
Hughes U.S.A. **98** 66.03N154.16W
Hugo U.S.A. **111** 34.01N 95.31W
Hugoton U.S.A. **111** 37.11N101.21W
Hugou China **54** 33.22N117.07E
Hui'an China **55** 25.02N118.48E
Huiarau Range *mts.* New Zealand **86** 38.20S177.15E
Huikou China **55** 29.49N116.15E
Huila *d.* Angola **78** 15.10S 15.30E
Huilai China **55** 23.03N116.17E
Huimin China **54** 37.30N117.29E
Huining China **54** 35.42N105.06E
Huisne *r.* France **18** 47.59N 0.11E
Huixtla Mexico **116** 15.09N 92.30W
Huizen Neth. **16** 52.18N 5.12E
Huizhou China **55** 23.05N114.29E
Hukuntsi Botswana **80** 24.02S 21.48E
Hulayfâ' Saudi Arabia **64** 26.00N 40.47E
Hulda Israel **67** 31.50N 34.53E
Hulín Czech. **37** 49.19N 17.28E
Hull Canada **105** 45.26N 75.43W
Hull I. Kiribati **84** 4.29S172.10W
Hüls W. Germany **38** 51.22N 6.30E
Hulst Neth. **16** 51.18N 4.01E
Hultsfred Sweden **43** 57.29N 15.50E
Hulun Nur *l.* China **53** 49.00N117.27E
Hulwân Egypt **66** 29.51N 31.20E
Humaitá Brazil **122** 7.31S 63.02W
Humansdorp R.S.A. **80** 34.02S 24.45E
Humaydah Sudan **72** 14.22N 22.31E
Humber *r.* U.K. **12** 53.40N 0.12W
Humberside *d.* U.K. **12** 53.48N 0.35W
Humble U.S.A. **111** 30.00N 95.16W
Humboldt Canada **101** 52.12N105.07W
Humboldt U.S.A. **111** 35.49N 88.55W
Humboldt *r.* U.S.A. **108** 40.02N118.31W
Hümedân Iran **65** 25.24N 59.39E
Humenné Czech. **37** 48.56N 21.55E
Hume Resr. Australia **93** 36.06S147.05E
Humphreys Peak *mtn.* U.S.A. **109** 35.20N111.40W
Humpty Doo Australia **88** 12.37S131.14E
Hün Libya **75** 29.07N 15.56E
Húnaflói *b.* Iceland **40** 65.45N 20.50W
Hunan *d.* China **55** 27.30N111.30E
Hundested Denmark **42** 55.58N 11.52E
Hundred U.S.A. **114** 39.41N 80.28W
Hundred Mile House *town* Canada **100** 51.38N121.18W
Hunedoara Romania **37** 45.45N 22.54E
Hünfeld W. Germany **38** 50.40N 9.46E
Hungary Europe **37** 47.30N 19.00E
Hungerford Australia **92** 29.00S144.26E
Hungerford U.K. **13** 51.25N 1.30W
Hungfou Hsü *i.* Taiwan **55** 22.03N121.33E
Hüngnam N. Korea **53** 39.49N127.40E
Hung Yen Vietnam **55** 20.38N106.05E
Huningue France **19** 47.36N 7.35E
Hunnebostrand Sweden **42** 58.27N 11.18E
Hunsberge *mts.* Namibia **80** 27.40S 17.12E
Hunse *r.* Neth. **16** 53.20N 6.18E
Hunsrück *mts.* W. Germany **39** 49.45N 7.00E
Hunstanton U.K. **12** 52.57N 0.30E
Hunte *r.* W. Germany **38** 53.14N 8.18E
Hunter *r.* Australia **93** 32.50S151.42E
Hunter I. Australia **91** 40.30S144.46E
Hunter I. Canada **100** 51.55N128.00W
Hunter Island Ridge Pacific Oc. **84** 21.30S175.00E
Hunter Range *mts.* Australia **93** 32.49S150.20E
Huntingdon Canada **105** 45.05N 74.10W
Huntingdon U.K. **13** 52.20N 0.11W
Huntingdon Penn. U.S.A. **114** 40.29N 78.01W
Huntington Ind. U.S.A. **112** 40.54N 85.30W
Huntington Mass. U.S.A. **115** 42.14N 72.53W
Huntington N.Y. U.S.A. **115** 40.51N 73.25W
Huntington Oreg. U.S.A. **108** 44.21N117.16W
Huntington Utah U.S.A. **108** 39.20N110.58W
Huntington W.Va. U.S.A. **114** 38.25N 82.26W
Huntington Beach *town* U.S.A. **109** 33.39N118.01W
Huntly New Zealand **86** 37.35S175.10E
Huntly U.K. **14** 57.27N 2.47W
Huntsville Canada **104** 45.20N 79.14W
Huntsville Ala. U.S.A. **113** 34.44N 86.35W
Huntsville Tex. U.S.A. **111** 30.43N 95.33W
Hunyani *r.* Mozambique **81** 15.41S 30.38E
Hunyuan China **54** 39.45N113.35E
Huon Pen. P.N.G. **59** 6.00S147.00E
Huonville Australia **91** 43.01S147.01E
Huoshan China **55** 31.24N116.20E
Huqoq Israel **67** 32.53N 35.29E
Hurd, C. Canada **104** 45.13N 81.44W
Hure Qi China **54** 42.44N121.44E
Huretin Sum China **54** 40.19N103.02E
Huriel France **20** 46.23N 2.29E
Hurlock U.S.A. **115** 38.38N 75.52W
Hurmâgai Pakistan **62** 28.18N 64.26E
Huron *r.* U.S.A. **104** 42.03N 83.14W
Huron Ohio U.S.A. **114** 41.24N 82.33W
Huron S.Dak. U.S.A. **110** 44.22N 98.13W
Huron, L. Canada/U.S.A. **114** 44.30N 82.15W
Hurso Ethiopia **73** 9.38N 41.38E
Hurup Denmark **42** 56.45N 8.25E
Húsavík Iceland **40** 66.03N 17.21W
Husevig Faroe Is. **10** 61.49N 6.41W
Huşi Romania **37** 46.40N 28.04E
Huskvarna Sweden **43** 57.48N 14.16E
Husum W. Germany **38** 54.28N 9.03E
Hutchinson R.S.A. **80** 31.30S 23.10E
Hutchinson U.S.A. **111** 38.05N 97.56W
Hüttental W. Germany **38** 50.54N 8.02E
Huttig U.S.A. **111** 33.02N 92.11W
Huttonsville U.S.A. **114** 38.43N 80.00W
Hutuo He *r.* China **54** 39.10N117.12E
Hut Yanchi *l.* China **54** 39.24N105.01E
Huwwârah Jordan **67** 32.09N 35.15E
Huy Belgium **16** 50.31N 5.14E
Hvar *i.* Yugo. **31** 43.09N 16.45E
Hvar *town* Yugo. **31** 43.10N 16.27E
Hvarski Kanal *str.* Yugo. **31** 43.20N 16.45E
Hvide Sande Denmark **42** 55.59N 8.08E
Hvita *r.* Iceland **40** 64.33N 21.45W
Hvittingfoss Norway **42** 59.29N 10.01E
Hwange Zimbabwe **80** 18.20S 26.29E
Hwang Ho *r. see* Huang He China **54**
Hyannis Mass. U.S.A. **115** 41.39N 70.17W
Hyannis Nebr. U.S.A. **110** 41.59N101.44W
Hyargas Nuur *l.* Mongolia **52** 49.30N 93.35E
Hydaburg U.S.A. **100** 55.15N132.50W
Hyde U.K. **12** 53.26N 2.06W
Hyden Australia **89** 32.27S118.53E
Hyde Park U.S.A. **105** 44.36N 72.37W
Hyde Park Corner *town* Canada **104** 43.00N 81.28W
Hyderâbâd India **61** 17.22N 78.26E
Hyderâbâd Pakistan **62** 25.22N 68.22E
Hydesville U.S.A. **108** 40.31N124.00W
Hydetown U.S.A. **114** 41.40N 79.44W
Hyères France **21** 43.07N 6.07E
Hyères, Îles d' *is.* France **21** 43.00N 6.20E
Hyland *r.* Canada **100** 59.50N128.10W
Hyland Post Canada **100** 57.40N128.10W
Hylestad Norway **42** 59.05N 7.32E
Hyllestad Norway **41** 61.10N 5.18E
Hyltebruk Sweden **43** 57.00N 13.14E
Hyndland, Mt. Australia **93** 30.09S152.25E
Hyndman U.S.A. **114** 39.49N 78.44W
Hyndman Peak U.S.A. **108** 43.50N114.10W
Hysham U.S.A. **108** 46.18N107.14W
Hythe Kent U.K. **13** 51.04N 1.05E
Hyvinkää Finland **41** 60.38N 24.52E

I

Iakoro Madagascar **81** 23.06S 46.40E
Ialomiţa *r.* Romania **37** 44.41N 27.52E
Iar Connacht *f.* Rep. of Ire. **15** 53.21N 9.22W
Iaşi Romania **37** 47.09N 27.38E
Íasmos Greece **34** 41.07N 25.12E
Iauaretê Brazil **122** 0.36N 69.12W
Iaupolo P.N.G. **90** 9.34S150.30E
Ibadan Nigeria **77** 7.23N 3.56E
Ibagué Colombia **122** 4.25N 75.20W
Ibar *r.* Yugo. **34** 43.15N 20.40E
Ibaraki Japan **57** 34.49N135.34E
Ibarra Ecuador **122** 0.23N 78.05W
Ibb Yemen **71** 13.58N 44.11E
Ibba Sudan **73** 4.48N 29.06E
Ibba *wadi* Sudan **73** 7.09N 28.41E
Ibbenbüren W. Germany **38** 52.16N 7.43E
Iberville Canada **105** 45.18N 73.14W
Ibi *r.* Japan **57** 35.03N136.42E
Ibi Nigeria **77** 8.11N 9.44E
Ibiapaba, Serra da *mts.* Brazil **123** 5.30S 41.00W
Ibicaraí Brazil **123** 14.52S 39.37W
Ibicuy Argentina **125** 33.45S 59.13W
Ibina *r.* Zaïre **79** 1.00N 28.40E
Ibitinga Brazil **126** 21.43S 48.47W
Ibiza *i.* Spain **25** 39.00N 1.25E
Ibiza *town* Spain **25** 38.54N 1.26E
Iblei, Monti *mts.* Italy **33** 37.07N 14.40E
Ibor *r.* Spain **27** 39.49N 5.33W
Ibotirama Brazil **123** 12.13S 43.12W
Ibrah, Wadi Sudan **73** 10.36N 25.05E
'Ibrî Oman **71** 23.14N 56.30E
Ibriktepe Turkey **34** 41.00N 26.30E
Ibshawây Egypt **66** 29.21N 30.40E
Ibta' Syria **67** 32.47N 36.09E
Ibusuki Japan **57** 31.16N130.39E
Içá *r.* Brazil **122** 3.07S 67.58W
Ica Peru **122** 14.02S 75.48W
Içana Brazil **122** 0.21N 67.19W
Içana *r.* Brazil **122** 0.00 67.10W
Iceland Europe **40** 64.45N 18.00W
Ichchâpuram India **63** 19.07N 84.42E
Ichihara Japan **57** 35.31N140.05E
Ichikawa Japan **57** 35.44N139.55E
Ichinomiya Japan **57** 35.18N136.48E
Icoraci Brazil **123** 1.16S 48.28W
Icy Str. U.S.A. **100** 58.20N135.30W
Idabel U.S.A. **111** 33.54N 94.50W
Ida Grove U.S.A. **110** 42.21N 95.28W
Idah Nigeria **77** 7.05N 6.45E
Idaho *d.* U.S.A. **108** 44.58N115.56W
Idaho Falls *town* U.S.A. **108** 43.30N112.02W
Idanha-a-Nova Portugal **27** 39.55N 7.14W
Idar India **62** 23.50N 73.00E
Idar-Oberstein W. Germany **39** 49.42N 7.19E
Iddan Somali Rep. **71** 6.03N 49.01E
Ideles Algeria **75** 23.49N 5.55E
Idfû Egypt **64** 24.58N 32.50E
Ídhi Óros *mtn.* Greece **35** 35.18N 24.43E
Ídhra *i.* Greece **35** 37.20N 23.32E
Ídhra *town* Greece **35** 37.20N 23.29E
Idiofa Zaïre **78** 4.58S 19.38E
Idmû Egypt **66** 28.09N 30.41E
Idnah Jordan **67** 31.34N 34.59E
Idre Sweden **41** 61.52N 12.43E
Idrija Yugo. **31** 46.00N 14.01E
Idstein W. Germany **39** 50.13N 8.16E
Ieper Belgium **16** 50.51N 2.53E
Ierápetra Greece **35** 35.00N 25.44E
Ierissós Greece **34** 40.24N 23.52E
Ierzu Italy **32** 39.48N 9.32E
Iesi Italy **30** 43.31N 13.14E
Iesolo Italy **30** 45.32N 12.38E
Ifakara Tanzania **79** 8.09S 36.41E
Ifalik *is.* Caroline Is. **59** 7.15N144.27E
Ifanadiana Madagascar **81** 21.19S 47.39E
Ife Oyo Nigeria **77** 7.33N 4.34E
Iferouâne Niger **77** 19.04N 8.24E
Iga *r.* Japan **57** 34.45N136.01E
Igal Hungary **37** 46.31N 17.55E
Igatpuri India **62** 19.42N 73.33E
Iggesund Sweden **41** 61.38N 17.04E
Iglesias Italy **32** 39.19N 8.32E
Igli Algeria **74** 30.27N 2.18W
Igloolik Island *town* Canada **99** 69.05N 81.25W
Ignace Canada **102** 49.30N 91.40W
Iğneada Burnu *c.* Turkey **29** 41.50N 28.05E
Igoumenítsa Greece **34** 39.30N 20.16E
Igra U.S.S.R. **44** 57.31N 53.09E
Iguaçu *r.* Brazil **126** 25.33S 54.35W
Iguala Mexico **116** 18.21N 99.31W
Igualada Spain **25** 41.35N 1.38E
Iguatu Brazil **123** 6.22S 39.20W
Iguéla Gabon **78** 1.57S 9.22E
Ihiala Nigeria **77** 5.51N 6.52E
Ihosy Madagascar **81** 22.24S 46.08E
Ihosy *r.* Madagascar **81** 21.58S 43.38E
Ii *r.* Finland **40** 65.19N 25.20E
Iida Japan **57** 35.31N137.50E
Iide yama *mtn.* Japan **57** 37.50N139.42E
Iisalmi Finland **40** 63.34N 27.11E
Ijebu Ode Nigeria **77** 6.47N 3.54E
Ijill, Kediet *mtn.* Mauritania **74** 22.38N 12.33W
IJmuiden Neth. **16** 52.28N 4.37E
IJssel *r.* Overijssel Neth. **16** 52.34N 5.50E
IJssel *r.* South Holland Neth. **16** 51.54N 4.32E
IJsselmeer *l.* Neth. **16** 52.45N 5.20E
Ijuí Brazil **126** 28.23S 53.55W
Ijzendijke Neth. **16** 51.19N 3.37E
Ijzer *r.* Belgium **16** 51.09N 2.44E
Ikaría *i.* Greece **35** 37.41N 26.20E
Ikdû Egypt **66** 31.18N 30.18E
Ikela Zaïre **78** 1.06S 23.04E
Ikelemba Congo **78** 1.15N 16.38E
Ikelemba *r.* Zaïre **78** 0.08N 18.19E
Ikerre Nigeria **77** 7.30N 5.14E
Ikhast Denmark **42** 56.09N 9.08E
Ikhtiman Bulgaria **34** 42.27N 23.48E
Iki shima *i.* Japan **57** 33.47N129.43E
Ikopa *r.* Madagascar **81** 16.29S 46.43E
Ila Nigeria **77** 8.01N 4.55E
Ilagan Phil. **59** 17.07N121.53E
Îlâm Iran **65** 33.27N 46.27E
Ilâm Nepal **63** 26.55N 87.56E
Ilan Taiwan **55** 24.45N121.44E
Ilangali Tanzania **79** 6.50S 35.06E
Ilanz Switz. **39** 46.46N 9.12E
Ilaro Nigeria **77** 6.53N 3.03E
Iława Poland **37** 53.37N 19.33E
Ilebo Zaïre **78** 4.20S 20.35E
Ilek *r.* U.S.S.R. **45** 51.30N 54.00E
Ileret Kenya **79** 4.22N 36.13E
Ilerh, Oued *wadi* Algeria **75** 20.59N 2.14E
Îles, Lac des *l.* Canada **105** 46.50N 77.10W
Ilesha Oyo Nigeria **77** 7.39N 4.45E
Ilford Canada **101** 56.04N 95.35W
Ilfracombe Australia **90** 23.30S144.30E
Ilfracombe U.K. **13** 51.13N 4.08W
Ilhabela Brazil **126** 23.47S 45.20W
Ilha Grande, Baía da *b.* Brazil **126** 23.09S 44.30W
Ilhavo Portugal **26** 40.36N 8.40W
Ilhéus Brazil **123** 14.50S 39.06W
Ili *r.* U.S.S.R. **52** 45.00N 74.20E
Ilia Romania **37** 45.56N 22.39E
Iliamna L. U.S.A. **98** 59.30N155.00W
Ilich U.S.S.R. **52** 40.50N 68.29E
Iligan Phil. **59** 8.12N124.13E
Ilintsy U.S.S.R. **37** 49.08N 29.11E
Ilion U.S.A. **115** 43.01N 75.02W
Ilirska Bistrica Yugo. **31** 45.34N 14.15E
Ilkley U.K. **12** 53.56N 1.49W
Illapel Chile **124** 31.38S 71.10W
Ille-et-Vilaine *d.* France **18** 48.10N 1.30W

Illéla to Izyum

Illéla Niger 77 14.30N 5.09E
Iller r. W. Germany 39 48.23N 9.58E
Illeret Kenya 73 4.19N 36.13E
Illertissen W. Germany 39 48.13N 10.06E
Illescas Spain 27 40.07N 3.50W
Illiers France 18 48.18N 1.15E
Illinois d. U.S.A. 110 40.30N 89.30W
Illinois r. U.S.A. 110 38.58N 90.27W
Illizi Algeria 75 26.29N 8.28E
Ilmajoki Finland 40 62.44N 22.34E
Ilmenau r. W. Germany 38 53.23N 10.10E
Ilminster U.K. 13 50.55N 2.56W
Ilo Peru 124 17.38S 71.20W
Iloilo Phil. 59 10.45N 122.33E
Ilorin Nigeria 77 8.32N 4.34E
Ilubabor d. Ethiopia 73 7.50N 34.55E
Imabari Japan 57 34.04N 132.59E
Imala Mozambique 79 14.39S 39.34E
Imandra U.S.S.R. 44 67.53N 33.30E
Imandra, Ozero l. U.S.S.R. 44 67.30N 32.45E
Imbābah Egypt 66 30.05N 31.12E
Imese Zaïre 78 2.07N 18.06E
Imī Ethiopia 73 6.28N 42.18E
Imlay City U.S.A. 104 43.02N 83.05W
Imlay City U.S.A. 114 43.02N 83.05W
Immenstadt W. Germany 38 47.33N 10.13E
Immingham U.K. 12 53.37N 0.12W
Immokalee U.S.A. 113 26.25N 81.26W
Imo d. Nigeria 77 5.30N 7.20E
Imola Italy 30 44.21N 11.42E
Imotski Yugo. 31 43.27N 17.13E
Imperatriz Brazil 123 5.32S 47.28W
Imperia Italy 30 43.53N 8.03E
Imperial Calif. U.S.A. 109 32.51N 115.34W
Imperial Nebr. U.S.A. 110 40.31N 101.39W
Imperial Dam U.S.A. 109 32.55N 114.30W
Imperial de Aragón, Canal Spain 25 41.37N 1.00W
Imperial Valley f. U.S.A. 109 32.50N 115.30W
Impfondo Congo 78 1.36N 17.58E
Imphāl India 61 24.47N 93.55E
Imroz i. see Gökçeada Turkey 34
Imst Austria 39 47.14N 10.44E
Ina Japan 57 35.50N 137.57E
Ina r. Japan 57 34.43N 135.28E
In Abbangarit well Niger 77 17.49N 6.15E
Inaccessible I. Tristan da Cunha 127 37.19S 12.44W
I-n-Amguel Algeria 75 23.40N 5.08E
Inangahua Junction New Zealand 86 41.53S 171.58E
Inanwatan Indonesia 59 2.08S 132.10E
Inarajan Guam 84 13.16N 144.45E
Inari l. Finland 40 69.00N 28.00E
Inari town Finland 40 68.54N 27.01E
Inazawa Japan 57 35.15N 136.47E
I-n-Belbel Algeria 74 27.54N 1.10E
Inca Spain 25 39.43N 2.54E
Incesu Turkey 64 38.39N 35.12E
Inchiri d. Mauritania 74 20.10N 15.00W
Inch'on S. Korea 53 37.30N 126.38E
Incudine, L' mtn. France 21 41.51N 9.12E
Indals r. Sweden 40 62.30N 17.20E
Indaw Burma 56 23.40N 94.46E
Independence Calif. U.S.A. 108 36.48N 118.12W
Independence Kans. U.S.A. 111 37.13N 95.42W
Independence Mo. U.S.A. 110 39.05N 94.24W
Inderagiri r. Indonesia 58 0.30S 103.08E
Inderborskiy U.S.S.R. 45 48.32N 51.44E
India Asia 61 23.00N 78.30E
Indian r. Canada 105 45.16N 76.14W
Indiana d. U.S.A. 112 40.00N 86.15W
Indiana town U.S.A. 114 40.37N 79.09W
Indian-Antarctic Ridge f. Indian Oc. 49 49.00S 125.00E
Indianapolis U.S.A. 112 39.45N 86.10W
Indian Cabins Canada 100 59.52N 117.02W
Indian Harbour Canada 103 54.25N 57.20W
Indian Head Canada 101 50.32N 103.40W
Indian L. Canada 104 47.08N 82.08W
Indian L. U.S.A. 115 43.47N 74.16W
Indian Lake town U.S.A. 105 43.47N 74.16W
Indian Ocean 49
Indianola U.S.A. 110 41.22N 93.34W
Indian River town U.S.A. 104 45.25N 84.37W
Indian River B. U.S.A. 115 38.36N 75.05W
Indiga U.S.S.R. 44 67.40N 49.00E
Indigirka r. U.S.S.R. 51 71.00N 148.45E
Indija Yugo. 31 45.03N 20.05E
Indio U.S.A. 109 33.43N 116.13W
Indonesia Asia 58 6.00S 118.00E
Indore India 62 22.43N 75.50E
Indramayu Indonesia 59 6.22S 108.20E
Indrāvati r. India 63 18.44N 80.16E
Indre d. France 19 46.45N 1.30E
Indre r. France 18 47.16N 0.19E
Indre-et-Loire d. France 18 47.15N 0.45E
Indus r. Pakistan 62 24.20N 67.47E
Inebolu Turkey 64 41.57N 33.45E
Inegöl Turkey 64 40.06N 29.31E
I-n-Eker Algeria 75 24.01N 5.05E
I-n-Ezzane well Algeria 75 23.29N 11.15E
Infiesto Spain 26 43.21N 5.22W
I-n-Gall Niger 77 16.47N 6.56E
Ingatestone U.K. 13 51.41N 0.22E
Ingelstad Sweden 43 56.45N 14.55E
Ingende Zaïre 78 0.17S 18.58E
Ingenika r. Canada 100 56.43N 125.07W
Ingersoll Canada 104 43.02N 80.53W
Inggen China 54 41.35N 104.47E
Ingham Australia 90 18.35S 146.12E
Ingleborough mtn. U.K. 12 54.10N 2.23W
Inglewood Australia 93 28.25S 151.02E
Inglewood Canada 104 43.47N 79.56W
Inglewood New Zealand 86 39.09S 174.12E
Inglewood U.S.A. 109 33.58N 118.21W
Ingolstadt W. Germany 39 48.46N 11.27E
Ingomar Australia 92 29.38S 134.48E
Ingraham U.S.A. 105 44.47N 73.30W
Ingulets U.S.S.R. 45 47.43N 33.16E
Ingwiller France 19 48.52N 7.29E
Inhambane Mozambique 81 23.51S 35.29E
Inhambane d. Mozambique 81 22.20S 34.00E
Inhaminga Mozambique 81 18.24S 35.00E
Inharrime Mozambique 81 24.29S 35.01E
Inhassoro Mozambique 81 21.32S 35.10E
Iniesta Spain 25 39.26N 1.45W
Inirida r. Colombia 122 3.59N 67.45W
Inishbofin i. Galway Rep. of Ire. 15 53.38N 10.14W
Inisheer i. Rep. of Ire. 15 53.04N 9.32W
Inishmaan i. Rep. of Ire. 15 53.06N 9.36W
Inishmore i. Rep. of Ire. 15 53.08N 9.43W
Inishowen Pen. Rep. of Ire. 15 55.08N 7.20W
Inishturk i. Rep. of Ire. 15 53.43N 10.08W
Injune Australia 90 25.51S 148.34E
Inklin Canada 100 58.56N 133.05W
Inklin r. Canada 100 58.50N 133.10W
Inkster U.S.A. 104 42.17N 83.17W
Inn r. Europe 39 48.35N 13.28E
Inner Hebrides is. U.K. 14 56.50N 6.45W
Inner Mongolia d. see Nei Monggol China 54
Inner Sd. U.K. 14 57.30N 5.55W
Innisfail Australia 90 17.32S 146.02E
Innisfail Canada 100 52.00N 113.57W
Innsbruck Austria 39 47.16N 11.24E
Innset Norway 40 68.41N 18.50E
Innviertel f. Austria 39 48.05N 13.08E
Inongo Zaïre 78 1.55S 18.20E
Inoucdjouac Canada 99 58.25N 78.18W
Inowrocław Poland 37 52.49N 18.12E
I-n-Salah Algeria 75 27.13N 2.28E
Insein Burma 56 16.54N 96.08E
In Tasik well Mali 77 18.03N 2.00E
Intepe Turkey 34 40.01N 26.19E
Interlaken Switz. 39 46.41N 7.51E
International Falls town U.S.A. 110 48.38N 93.26W
Intracoastal Waterway canal U.S.A. 111 28.45N 95.40W
Intute Mozambique 79 14.08S 39.55E
Inubō saki c. Japan 57 35.41N 140.52E
Inuvik Canada 98 68.16N 133.40W
Inuyama Japan 57 35.23N 136.56E
Inveraray U.K. 14 56.24N 5.05W
Inverbervie U.K. 14 56.51N 2.17W
Invercargill New Zealand 86 46.26S 168.21E
Inverell Australia 93 29.46S 151.10E
Invergordon U.K. 14 57.42N 4.10W
Inverhuron Canada 104 44.17N 81.34W
Inverness U.K. 14 57.27N 4.15W
Inverurie U.K. 14 57.17N 2.23W
Inverway Australia 88 17.49S 129.40E
Investigator Group is. Australia 92 33.45S 134.30E
Investigator Str. Australia 92 35.25S 137.10E
Invinheima r. Brazil 124 22.52S 53.20W
Inya U.S.S.R. 50 50.24N 86.47E
Inyangani mtn. Zimbabwe 81 18.18S 32.50E
Inyonga Tanzania 79 6.43S 32.02E
Inzia r. Zaïre 78 3.47S 17.57E
Ioánnina Greece 34 39.39N 20.57E
Iola U.S.A. 111 37.55N 95.24W
Iona i. U.K. 14 56.20N 6.25W
Iongo Angola 78 9.11S 17.45E
Ionia U.S.A. 112 42.58N 85.06W
Ionian Is. see Iónioi Nísoi Greece 35
Ionian Sea Med. Sea 35 38.30N 18.45E
Iónioi Nísoi is. Greece 35 38.40N 20.08E
Íos i. Greece 35 36.44N 25.16E
Íos town Greece 35 36.44N 25.16E
Iowa d. U.S.A. 110 42.00N 93.30W
Iowa r. U.S.A. 110 41.10N 91.02W
Iowa City U.S.A. 110 41.40N 91.32W
Iowa Falls town U.S.A. 110 42.31N 93.16W
Ipati Greece 35 38.52N 22.14E
Ipatovo U.S.S.R. 45 45.44N 42.56E
Ipeiros f. Greece 34 39.30N 20.30E
Ipiales Colombia 122 0.52N 77.38W
Ipiaú Brazil 123 14.07S 39.43W
Ipixuna Brazil 122 7.00S 71.30W
Ipoh Malaysia 58 4.36N 101.02E
Ippa r. U.S.S.R. 37 52.13N 29.08E
Ippy C.A.R. 73 6.15N 21.12E
Ipsala Turkey 34 40.55N 26.23E
Ipswich Australia 93 27.38S 152.40E
Ipswich U.K. 13 52.04N 1.09E
Ipu Brazil 123 4.23S 40.44W
Ipuh Indonesia 58 2.58S 101.28E
Iquique Chile 124 20.13S 70.10W
Iquitos Peru 122 3.51S 73.13W
Irago-suidō str. Japan 57 34.35N 137.00E
Iráklia i. Greece 35 36.50N 25.28E
Iráklion Greece 35 35.20N 25.09E
Iran Asia 65 32.00N 54.30E
Iran, Pegunungan mts. Indonesia / Malaysia 58 3.20N 115.00E
Īrānshahr Iran 65 27.14N 60.42E
Irapuato Mexico 116 20.40N 101.40W
Iraq Asia 64 33.00N 44.00E
Irauen, Wādī Libya 75 26.28N 12.00E
Irayel U.S.S.R. 44 64.23N 55.25E
Irazú mtn. Costa Rica 117 9.59N 83.52W
Irbid Jordan 67 32.33N 35.51E
Irbid d. Jordan 67 32.27N 35.51E
Irbīl Iraq 65 36.12N 44.01E
Irdning Austria 39 47.33N 14.01E
Irebu Zaïre 78 0.37S 17.45E
Iregua r. Spain 26 42.27N 2.24W
Ireland I. Bermuda 127 32.19N 64.51W
Irgiz U.S.S.R. 9 48.36N 61.14E
Irgiz r. U.S.S.R. 9 48.00N 62.30E
Irharhar, Oued wadi Algeria 75 23.45N 5.55E
Irian Jaya d. Indonesia 59 4.00S 138.00E
Iriba Chad 72 15.07N 22.15E
Irié Guinea 76 8.15N 9.10W
Iringa Tanzania 79 7.49S 35.39E
Iringa d. Tanzania 79 8.30S 35.00E
Iriomote jima i. Japan 53 24.30N 124.00E
Iriri r. Brazil 123 3.50S 52.40W
Irish Sea U.K. / Rep. of Ire. 15 53.30N 5.40W
Irkutsk U.S.S.R. 52 52.18N 104.15E
Iroise b. France 18 48.15N 4.55W
Iron Baron Australia 92 32.59S 137.09E
Iron Bridge town Canada 104 46.17N 83.14W
Iron Gate f. Romania / Yugo. 37 44.40N 22.30E
Iron Knob Australia 92 32.44S 137.08E
Iron Mountain town U.S.A. 112 45.51N 88.03W
Iron Mts. Rep. of Ire. 15 54.10N 7.56W
Iron River town U.S.A. 110 46.05N 88.38W
Irons U.S.A. 112 44.08N 85.55W
Ironton U.S.A. 114 38.31N 82.40W
Ironwood U.S.A. 112 46.25N 90.08W
Iroquois Canada 105 44.51N 75.19W
Iroquois Falls town Canada 102 48.40N 80.40W
Irosin Phil. 59 12.45N 124.02E
Irō-zaki c. Japan 57 34.36N 138.51E
Irpen U.S.S.R. 37 50.31N 30.29E
Irrapatana Australia 92 29.03S 136.28E
Irrawaddy d. Burma 56 17.00N 95.00E
Irrawaddy r. Burma 56 15.50N 95.00E
Irrawaddy Delta Burma 56 16.45N 95.00E
Irsha r. U.S.S.R. 37 50.45N 29.30E
Irsina Italy 33 40.45N 16.15E
Irthing r. U.K. 11 54.55N 2.50W
Irtysh r. U.S.S.R. 9 61.00N 69.00E
Iruma r. Japan 57 35.57N 139.30E
Irumu Zaïre 79 1.29N 29.48E
Irún Spain 26 43.20N 1.48W
Irurzun Spain 25 42.55N 1.50W
Irvine U.K. 14 55.37N 4.40W
Irvinestown U.K. 15 54.29N 7.40W
Irving U.S.A. 111 32.49N 96.56W
Irvona U.S.A. 114 40.46N 78.33W
Irwin, Pt. Australia 89 35.03S 116.20E
Is, Jabal mtn. Sudan 72 22.03N 35.28E
Isa Nigeria 77 13.14N 6.24E
Isaac r. Australia 90 22.52S 149.20E
Isaba Spain 25 42.52N 0.55W
Isabella, Cordillera mts. Nicaragua 117 13.30N 85.00W
Isábena r. Spain 25 42.11N 0.21E
Ísafjördhur town Iceland 40 66.05N 23.06W
Isaka Tanzania 79 3.52S 32.54E
Isaka Bandundu Zaïre 78 2.35S 18.48E
Isaka Equateur Zaïre 78 1.49S 20.50E
Īsa Khel Pakistan 62 32.41N 71.17E
Isakogorka U.S.S.R. 44 64.23N 40.31E
Isangi Zaïre 78 0.48N 24.03E
Isar r. W. Germany 39 48.49N 12.58E
Isbergues France 16 50.38N 2.24E
Ischia Italy 32 40.43N 13.57E
Ischia i. Italy 32 40.43N 13.54E
Ise Japan 57 34.29N 136.42E
Isefjord b. Denmark 42 55.52N 11.49E
Iseo, Lago d' l. Italy 30 45.43N 10.04E
Isère d. France 21 45.10N 5.50E
Isère r. France 21 44.59N 4.51E
Iserlohn W. Germany 38 51.22N 7.41E
Isernia Italy 33 41.36N 14.14E
Ise-wan b. Japan 57 34.45N 136.40E
Iseyin Nigeria 77 7.59N 3.36E
Isfahan see Eşfahān Iran 60
Ishikari r. Japan 57 43.15N 141.21E
Ishikari wan b. Japan 57 43.15N 141.20E
Ishim U.S.S.R. 50 56.10N 69.30E
Ishim r. U.S.S.R. 9 57.50N 71.00E
Ishinomaki Japan 57 38.25N 141.18E
Ishpeming U.S.A. 112 46.29N 87.40W
Ishurdi Bangla. 63 24.09N 89.03E
Isigny France 18 49.18N 1.06W
Isiolo Kenya 79 0.20N 37.36E
Isipingo Beach town R.S.A. 80 30.00S 30.57E
Isiro Zaïre 79 2.50N 27.40E
Iskâr r. Bulgaria 34 43.44N 24.27E
Iskenderun Turkey 64 36.37N 36.08E
Iskenderun Körfezi g. Turkey 64 36.40N 35.50E
Iskilip Turkey 64 40.45N 34.28E
Iskūr r. Bulgaria 34 43.35N 24.20E
Iskūr, Yazovir l. Bulgaria 34 42.27N 23.38E
Isla r. U.K. 14 56.32N 3.22W
Isla Cristina town Spain 27 37.12N 7.19W
Islāmābād Pakistan 62 33.40N 73.10E
Islāmkot Pakistan 62 24.42N 70.11E
Islāmpur Bihār India 63 25.09N 85.12E
Islāmpur W. Bengal India 63 26.16N 88.12E
Island L. Australia 92 31.30S 136.40E
Island L. Canada 101 53.47N 94.25W
Island Magee pen. U.K. 15 54.48N 5.44W
Island Pt. Australia 89 30.21S 115.01E
Islands, B. of Canada 103 49.10N 58.15W
Islands, B. of New Zealand 86 35.15S 174.15E
Islay i. U.K. 14 55.45N 6.20W
Isle r. France 20 44.55N 0.15W
Isle of Portland f. U.K. 13 50.32N 2.25W
Isle of Wight d. U.K. 13 50.40N 1.17W
Isleta U.S.A. 109 34.55N 106.42W
Ismael Cortinas Uruguay 125 33.58S 57.06W
Ismay U.S.A. 108 46.30N 104.48W
Isnā Egypt 64 25.16N 32.30E
Isny W. Germany 38 47.41N 10.02E
Isoka Zambia 79 10.06S 32.39E
Isola della Scala Italy 32 45.16N 11.00E
Isola del Liri town Italy 31 41.41N 13.34E
Isola di Capo Rizzuto town Italy 33 38.58N 17.06E
Isparta Turkey 64 37.46N 30.32E
Isperikh Bulgaria 34 43.43N 26.50E
Ispica Italy 33 36.46N 14.55E
Ispikān Pakistan 62 26.14N 62.12E
Israel Asia 67 32.00N 34.50E
Israelite B. Australia 89 33.40S 123.55E
Issia Ivory Coast 76 6.33N 6.33W
Issigeac France 20 44.44N 0.36E
Issoire France 20 45.33N 3.15E
Issoudun France 19 46.57N 2.00E
Is-sur-Tille France 19 47.31N 5.06E
Issyk Kul l. U.S.S.R. 52 43.30N 77.20E
Istanbul Turkey 29 41.02N 28.58E
Istanbul Bogazi str. Turkey 29 41.07N 29.04E
Isthmus of Kra Thailand 56 10.20N 99.10E
Istiaía Greece 35 38.57N 23.10E
Istok Yugo. 34 42.45N 20.24E
Istra pen. Yugo. 31 45.10N 13.55E
Itabaiana Brazil 123 7.20S 35.20W
Itabira Brazil 126 19.39S 43.14W
Itabirito Brazil 126 20.21S 43.45W
Itabuna Brazil 123 14.48S 39.18W
Itacajuna r. Brazil 123 5.20S 49.08W
Itacoatiara Brazil 122 3.06S 58.22W
Itagüí Colombia 122 6.10N 75.36W
Itaí Brazil 126 23.23S 49.05W
Itaim r. Brazil 123 6.43S 42.48W
Itaituba Brazil 123 4.17S 55.59W
Itajaí Brazil 126 26.50S 48.39W
Itajubá Brazil 126 22.24S 45.25W
Itaka Tanzania 79 8.51S 32.48E
Itálica site Spain 27 37.30N 6.05W
Italy Europe 28 43.00N 12.00E
Itami Japan 57 34.46N 135.25E
Itapecerica Brazil 126 20.28S 45.09W
Itapecuru Mirim Brazil 123 3.24S 44.20W
Itaperuna Brazil 126 21.14S 41.51W
Itapetinga Brazil 123 15.17S 40.16W
Itapetininga Brazil 126 23.36S 48.07W
Itapeva Brazil 126 23.59S 48.59W
Itapicuru r. Brazil 123 11.50S 37.30W
Itapira Brazil 126 22.24S 46.56W
Itaqui Brazil 126 29.07S 56.33W
Itārsi India 63 22.37N 77.45E
Itatiba Brazil 126 22.59S 46.51W
Itatinga Brazil 126 23.06S 48.36W
Itatuba Brazil 122 5.40S 63.20W
Itaúna Brazil 126 20.04S 44.14W
Itbayat i. Phil. 55 20.45N 121.50E
Itéa Greece 35 38.25N 22.25E
Ithaca U.S.A. 115 42.27N 76.30W
Itháki Greece 35 38.23N 20.42E
Itháki i. Greece 35 38.24N 20.42E
Itimbiri r. Zaïre 78 2.02N 22.47E
Itmurinkol, Ozero l. U.S.S.R. 45 49.30N 52.17E
Itō Japan 57 34.58N 139.05E
Itoko Zaïre 78 1.00S 21.45E
Iton r. France 18 49.09N 1.12E
Itsa Egypt 66 29.14N 30.47E
Ittel, Oued wadi Algeria 75 34.18N 6.02E
Ittiri Italy 32 40.36N 8.33E
Itu Brazil 126 23.17S 47.18W
Ituí r. Brazil 122 4.38S 70.19W
Ituiutaba Brazil 126 19.00S 49.25W
Ituri r. Zaïre 79 1.45N 27.06E
Iturup i. U.S.S.R. 53 44.00N 147.30E
Ituverava Brazil 126 20.22S 47.48W
Ituxi r. Brazil 122 7.20S 64.50W
Ityāy al Bārūd Egypt 66 30.53N 30.40E
Itzehoe W. Germany 38 53.55N 9.31E
Ivaí r. Brazil 126 23.20S 53.23W
Ivalo Finland 40 68.42N 27.30E
Ivalo r. Finland 40 68.43N 27.36E
Ivanec Yugo. 31 46.13N 16.08E
Ivangrad Yugo. 31 42.50N 19.52E
Ivanhoe Australia 92 32.56S 144.22E
Ivanhoe U.S.A. 110 44.28N 96.12W
Ivanić Grad Yugo. 31 45.42N 16.24E
Ivanjica Yugo. 34 43.35N 20.14E
Ivano-Frankovsk U.S.S.R. 37 48.55N 24.42E
Ivanovo B.S.S.R. U.S.S.R. 37 52.10N 25.13E
Ivanovo R.S.F.S.R. U.S.S.R. 44 57.00N 41.00E
Ivdel U.S.S.R. 44 60.45N 60.30E
Ivenets U.S.S.R. 37 53.50N 26.40E
Ivigtut Greenland 99 61.10N 48.00W
Ivindo Gabon 78 0.02S 12.13E
Iviza i. see Ibiza Spain 25
Ivohibe Madagascar 81 22.29S 45.52E
Ivory Coast Africa 76 8.00N 5.30W
Ivösjön l. Sweden 43 56.06N 14.27E
Ivrea Italy 30 45.28N 7.52E
Ivujivik Canada 99 62.24N 77.55W
Ivybridge U.K. 13 50.24N 3.56W
Ivydale U.S.A. 114 38.32N 81.03W
Iwaki Japan 57 36.58N 140.58E
Iwaki r. Japan 57 41.20N 140.00E
Iwakuni Japan 57 34.10N 132.09E
Iwata Japan 57 34.42N 137.48E
Iwo Nigeria 77 7.38N 4.11E
Ixiamas Bolivia 124 13.45S 68.09W
Iyo nada str. Japan 57 33.40N 132.20E
Izabal, Lago de l. Guatemala 117 15.30N 89.00W
Izberbash U.S.S.R. 45 42.31N 47.52E
Izhevsk U.S.S.R. 44 56.49N 53.11E
Izhma U.S.S.R. 44 65.03N 53.48E
Izhma r. U.S.S.R. 44 65.16N 53.18E
Izmail U.S.S.R. 37 45.20N 28.50E
Izmir Turkey 29 38.24N 27.09E
Izmir Körfezi g. Turkey 29 38.30N 26.45E
Izmit Turkey 64 40.48N 29.55E
Iznajar, Embalse de resr. Spain 27 37.15N 4.20W
Iznalloz Spain 27 37.23N 3.31W
Izozog, Bañados de f. Bolivia 124 18.30S 62.05W
Izozog Marshes f. see Izozog, Bañados de Bolivia 124
Izra' Syria 67 32.51N 36.15E
Izsák Hungary 31 46.48N 19.22E
Iztochni Rodopi mts. Bulgaria 34 41.44N 25.28E
Izu-hantō pen. Japan 57 34.53N 138.55E
Izuhara Japan 57 34.12N 129.17E
Izumi Japan 57 34.29N 135.26E
Izumi-ōtsu Japan 57 34.30N 135.24E
Izumi-sano Japan 57 34.25N 135.19E
Izumo Japan 57 35.33N 132.50E
Izumo r. Japan 57 34.38N 136.33E
Izyaslav U.S.S.R. 37 50.10N 26.46E
Izyum U.S.S.R. 45 49.12N 37.19E

Jaba to Jönköping

J

Jaba Ethiopia **73** 6.17N 35.12E
Jaba' Jordan **67** 32.19N 35.13E
Jabā Syria **67** 33.10N 35.56E
Jabal, Baḥr al *r.* Sudan **73** 9.30N 30.30E
Jabal al Awliyā' Sudan **72** 15.14N 32.30E
Jabal Dūd Sudan **73** 13.22N 33.09E
Jabalón *r.* Spain **26** 38.53N 4.05W
Jabalpur India **63** 23.10N 79.57E
Jabālyah Egypt **67** 31.32N 34.29E
Jabbān, Arḍ al *f.* Jordan **66** 32.08N 36.35E
Jabjabah, Wādī Egypt **72** 22.37N 33.17E
Jablah Syria **66** 35.22N 35.56E
Jablanac Yugo. **31** 44.42N 14.54E
Jablanica Yugo. **31** 43.39N 17.45E
Jablaničko Jezero *resr.* Yugo. **31** 43.40N 17.50E
Jablonec nad Nisou Czech. **36** 50.44N 15.10E
Jabori Pakistan **62** 34.36N 73.16E
Jaboticabal Brazil **126** 21.15S 48.17W
Jabrat Sa'īd *wells* Sudan **72** 16.06N 31.50E
Jaca Spain **25** 42.34N 0.33W
Jacareí Brazil **126** 23.17S 45.57W
Jackman U.S.A. **112** 45.38N 70.16W
Jacks Mtn. U.S.A. **114** 40.45N 77.30W
Jackson Ky. U.S.A. **113** 37.32N 83.24W
Jackson Mich. U.S.A. **104** 42.15N 84.24W
Jackson Miss. U.S.A. **111** 32.18N 90.12W
Jackson Mo. U.S.A. **111** 37.23N 89.40W
Jackson Ohio U.S.A. **114** 39.03N 82.39W
Jackson Tenn. U.S.A. **111** 35.37N 88.49W
Jackson Wyo. U.S.A. **108** 43.29N110.38W
Jackson Bay *town* Canada **100** 50.32N125.57W
Jacksonville Fla. U.S.A. **113** 30.20N 81.40W
Jacksonville Ill. U.S.A. **110** 39.44N 90.14W
Jacksonville N.C. U.S.A. **113** 34.45N 77.26W
Jacksonville Tex. U.S.A. **111** 31.58N 95.17W
Jacksonville Beach *town* U.S.A. **113** 30.18N 81.24W
Jacobābād Pakistan **62** 28.17N 68.26E
Jacobina Brazil **123** 11.13S 40.30W
Jacob Lake *town* U.S.A. **109** 36.41N112.14W
Jacob's Well *see* Bi'r Yaqūb Jordan **67**
Jacques Cartier, Détroit de *str.* Canada **103** 50.00N 63.30W
Jacques Cartier, Mt. Canada **103** 48.59N 65.57W
Jacuí *r.* Brazil **126** 29.56S 51.13W
Jacundá *r.* Brazil **123** 1.57S 50.26W
Jaddi, Râs *c.* Pakistan **62** 25.14N 63.31E
Jade W. Germany **38** 53.20N 8.14E
Jadebusen *b.* W. Germany **38** 53.30N 8.10E
Jadraque Spain **26** 40.55N 2.55W
Jādū Libya **75** 31.57N 12.01E
Jaén Peru **122** 5.21S 78.28W
Jaén Spain **27** 37.46N 3.47W
Jaén *d.* Spain **27** 37.55N 3.30W
Jaeren *f.* Norway **42** 58.40N 5.45E
Jāfarābād India **62** 20.52N 71.22E
Jaffa, C. Australia **92** 36.58S139.39E
Jaffna Sri Lanka **61** 9.38N 80.02E
Jaffrey U.S.A. **115** 42.50N 72.04W
Jagādhri India **62** 30.10N 77.18E
Jāgan Pakistan **62** 28.05N 68.30E
Jagatsingpur India **63** 20.16N 86.10E
Jagdalpur India **63** 19.04N 82.02E
Jaggang China **63** 32.52N 79.45E
Jagst *r.* W. Germany **39** 49.14N 9.11E
Jagtiāl India **63** 18.48N 78.56E
Jaguarão Brazil **126** 32.30S 53.25W
Jahānābād India **63** 25.13N 84.59E
Jahrom Iran **65** 28.30N 53.30E
Jailolo Indonesia **59** 1.05N127.29E
Jainti India **63** 26.42N 89.36E
Jaintiāpur Bangla. **63** 25.08N 92.07E
Jaipur India **62** 26.53N 75.50E
Jāis India **63** 26.15N 81.32E
Jaisalmer India **62** 26.55N 70.54E
Jājarkot Nepal **63** 28.42N 82.14E
Jajawijaya Mts. Asia **59** 4.20S139.10E
Jajce Yugo. **31** 44.21N 17.16E
Jajjha Pakistan **62** 28.45N 70.34E
Jājpur India **63** 20.51N 86.20E
Jakarta Indonesia **59** 6.08S106.45E
Jakarta *d.* Indonesia **59** 6.10S106.48E
Jakhāu India **62** 23.13N 68.43E
Jäkkvik Sweden **40** 66.23N 17.00E
Jakobstad *see* Pietarsaari Finland **40**
Jakupica *mts.* Yugo. **34** 41.45N 21.22E
Jal U.S.A. **111** 32.07N103.12W
Jalālābād Afghan. **62** 34.26N 70.28E
Jalālah al Baḥrīyah, Jabal *mts.* Egypt **66** 29.20N 32.12E
Jalālat al Qiblīyah, Jabal al *mts.* Egypt **66** 28.42N 32.23E
Jalālpur India **63** 26.19N 82.44E
Jalapa Mexico **116** 19.45N 96.48W
Jālaun India **63** 26.09N 79.21E
Jaldak Afghan. **62** 31.58N 66.44E
Jalesar India **63** 27.29N 78.19E
Jaleswar India **63** 21.49N 87.13E
Jālgaon Mahār. India **62** 21.01N 75.34E
Jālgaon Mahār. India **62** 21.03N 76.32E
Jalingo Nigeria **77** 8.54N 11.21E
Jalisco *d.* Mexico **116** 21.00N103.00W
Jallas *r.* Spain **26** 42.54N 9.08W
Jālna India **62** 19.50N 75.53E
Jalón *r.* Spain **25** 41.47N 1.04W
Jālor India **62** 25.21N 72.37E
Jalpaiguri India **63** 26.31N 88.44E
Jālū Libya **75** 29.02N 21.33E
Jaluit *i.* Pacific Oc. **84** 6.00N169.35E
Jalūlā Iraq **65** 34.16N 45.10E
Jamaari Nigeria **77** 11.44N 9.53E
Jamaica C. America **117** 18.00N 77.00W
Jamālpur Bangla. **63** 24.55N 89.56E
Jamālpur India **63** 25.18N 86.30E
Jamame Somali Rep. **79** 0.04N 42.46E
Jamanxim *r.* Brazil **123** 4.43S 56.18W
Jamberoo Australia **93** 34.40S150.44E
Jambes Belgium **16** 50.28N 4.52E
Jambi Indonesia **58** 1.36S103.39E
Jambi *d.* Indonesia **58** 2.00S102.30E
Jambusar India **62** 22.03N 72.48E
James *r.* S.Dak. U.S.A. **110** 42.55N 97.28W
James *r.* Va. U.S.A. **113** 36.57N 76.26W
James B. Canada **102** 53.30N 80.00W
James Bay Prov. Park Canada **102** 51.30N 79.00W
Jamestown Australia **92** 33.12S138.38E
Jamestown St. Helena **127** 15.56S 5.44W
Jamestown N.Dak. U.S.A. **110** 46.54N 98.42W
Jamestown N.Y. U.S.A. **114** 42.06N 79.14W
Jamestown Penn. U.S.A. **114** 41.29N 80.27W
Jamestown Tenn. U.S.A. **113** 36.24N 84.58W
Jamjodhpur India **62** 21.54N 70.01E
Jammerbught *b.* Denmark **42** 57.20N 9.30E
Jammu Jammu & Kashmir **62** 32.42N 74.52E
Jammu & Kashmir Asia **62** 34.45N 76.00E
Jāmnagar India **62** 22.28N 70.04E
Jamnotri India **63** 31.01N 78.27E
Jampang Kulon Indonesia **59** 7.18S106.33E
Jāmpur Pakistan **62** 28.45N 70.36E
Jamsah Egypt **66** 27.39N 33.35E
Jämsänkoski Finland **41** 61.55N 25.11E
Jamshedpur India **63** 22.48N 86.11E
Jämtland *d.* Sweden **40** 63.00N 14.30E
Jamūi India **63** 24.55N 86.13E
Jamuna *r.* Bangla. **63** 23.51N 89.45E
Jand Pakistan **62** 33.26N 72.01E
Janda, Laguna de la *l.* Spain **27** 36.15N 5.51W
Jandiāla India **62** 31.33N 75.02E
Jándula Spain **26** 38.03N 4.06W
Jándula, Embalse de *resr.* Spain **26** 38.30N 4.00W
Janesville U.S.A. **110** 42.42N 89.02W
Jangamo Mozambique **81** 24.06S 35.21E
Jangipur India **63** 24.28N 88.04E
Janin Jordan **67** 32.28N 35.18E
Janja Yugo. **31** 44.40N 19.15E
Janjevo Yugo. **34** 42.35N 21.19E
Janjina Yugo. **31** 42.56N 17.26E
Jan Kempdorp R.S.A. **80** 27.55S 24.48E
Jan Mayen *i.* Arctic Oc. **96** 68.00N 8.00W
Jánoshalma Hungary **31** 46.18N 19.20E
Januária Brazil **126** 15.28S 44.23W
Janzé France **18** 47.58N 1.30W
Jaora India **62** 23.38N 75.08E
Japan Asia **57** 36.00N138.00E
Japan, Sea of Asia **57** 40.00N135.00E
Japan Trench Pacific Oc. **84** 33.00N142.00E
Japla India **63** 24.33N 84.01E
Japurá *r.* Brazil **122** 3.00S 64.50W
Jaraicejo Spain **27** 39.40N 5.49W
Jaraiz de la Vera Spain **27** 40.04N 5.45W
Jarales U.S.A. **109** 34.37N106.46W
Jarama *r.* Spain **26** 40.02N 3.39W
Jarandilla Spain **27** 40.08N 5.39W
Jarānwāla Pakistan **62** 31.20N 73.26E
Jarash Jordan **67** 32.17N 35.54E
Jardee Australia **89** 34.18S116.04E
Jardines de la Reina *is.* Cuba **117** 20.30N 79.00W
Jardinópolis Brazil **126** 20.59S 47.48W
Jargeau France **19** 47.52N 2.07E
Jāria Jhānjail Bangla. **63** 25.02N 90.39E
Jaridih India **63** 23.38N 86.04E
Järna Sweden **43** 59.06N 17.34E
Jarnac France **20** 45.41N 0.10W
Jarocin Poland **37** 51.59N 17.31E
Jarosław Poland **37** 50.02N 22.42E
Jarrāhi *r.* Iran **65** 30.40N 48.23E
Jartai China **54** 39.45N105.46E
Jartai Yanchi *l.* China **54** 39.43N105.41E
Jarud Qi China **54** 44.30N120.35E
Järvenpää Finland **41** 60.28N 25.06E
Jarvis Canada **104** 42.53N 80.06W
Jarvis I. Pacific Oc. **84** 0.23S160.02W
Jasdan India **62** 22.02N 71.12E
Jāsk Iran **65** 25.40N 57.45E
Jasło Poland **37** 49.45N 21.29E
Jasper Canada **100** 52.55N118.05W
Jasper Ala. U.S.A. **113** 33.48N 87.18W
Jasper Fla. U.S.A. **113** 30.31N 82.58W
Jasper Tex. U.S.A. **111** 30.55N 94.01W
Jasper Nat. Park Canada **100** 52.50N118.08W
Jasra India **63** 25.17N 81.48E
Jastrebarsko Yugo. **31** 45.40N 15.39E
Jastrowie Poland **36** 53.26N 16.49E
Jászberény Hungary **37** 47.30N 19.55E
Jataí Brazil **126** 17.58S 51.45W
Jāti Pakistan **62** 24.21N 68.16E
Jatibarang Indonesia **59** 6.26S108.18E
Jatinegara Indonesia **59** 6.12S106.51E
Játiva Spain **25** 38.59N 0.31W
Jatni India **63** 20.10N 85.42E
Jatobá Brazil **123** 4.35S 49.33W
Jatt Israel **67** 32.24N 35.02E
Jaú Brazil **126** 22.11S 48.35W
Jauja Peru **122** 11.50S 75.15W
Jaunjelgava U.S.S.R. **44** 56.34N 25.02E
Jaunpur India **63** 25.44N 82.41E
Java *i. see* Jawa Indonesia **59**
Javalambre *mtn.* Spain **25** 40.06N 1.03W
Javari *r.* Peru **122** 4.30S 71.20W
Java Sea *see* Jawa, Laut Indonesia **58**
Java Trench *f.* Indonesia **58** 10.00S110.00E
Jávea Spain **25** 38.47N 0.10E
Jawa *i.* Indonesia **59** 7.25S110.00E
Jawa, Laut *sea* Indonesia **58** 5.00S111.00E
Jawa Barat *d.* Indonesia **59** 7.10S107.00E
Jawa Tengah *d.* Indonesia **59** 7.49S110.35E
Jawa Timur *d.* Indonesia **59** 8.42S113.10E
Jayah, Wādī al *see* Hā 'Arava Jordan/Israel **66**
Jayapura Indonesia **59** 2.28S140.38E
Jaynagar India **63** 26.32N 86.07E
Jay Peak *mtn.* U.S.A. **105** 44.55N 72.32W
Jazirah Doberai *f.* Indonesia **59** 1.10S132.30E
Jazzīn Lebanon **66** 33.32N 35.34E
Jean U.S.A. **109** 35.46N115.20W
Jeanerette U.S.A. **111** 29.55N 91.40W
Jean Marie River *town* Canada **98** 61.32N120.40W
Jebāl Bārez, Kūh-e *mts.* Iran **65** 28.40N 58.10E
Jebba Nigeria **77** 9.11N 4.49E
Jebri Pakistan **62** 27.18N 65.44E
Jedburgh U.K. **14** 55.29N 2.33W
Jedrzejów Poland **37** 50.39N 20.18E
Jefferson U.S.A. **114** 41.44N 80.46W
Jefferson, Mt. Nev. U.S.A. **108** 38.46N116.55W
Jefferson, Mt. Oreg. U.S.A. **108** 44.40N121.47W
Jefferson City U.S.A. **110** 38.34N 92.10W
Jeffersonville U.S.A. **112** 38.16N 85.45W
Jega Nigeria **77** 12.12N 4.23E
Jēkabpils U.S.S.R. **44** 56.28N 25.58E
Jelenia Góra Poland **36** 50.55N 15.45E
Jelgava U.S.S.R. **41** 56.39N 23.42E
Jelli Sudan **73** 5.22N 31.48E
Jelling Denmark **42** 55.45N 9.26E
Jember Indonesia **59** 8.07S113.45E
Jena E. Germany **38** 50.56N 11.35E
Jena U.S.A. **111** 31.41N 92.08W
Jenbach Austria **39** 47.24N 11.47E
Jendouba *d.* Tunisia **32** 36.45N 8.45E
Jennersdorf Austria **31** 46.57N 16.08E
Jenolan Caves *town* Australia **93** 33.53S150.03E
Jepara Indonesia **59** 6.32S110.40E
Jeparit Australia **92** 36.09S141.59E
Jeppo Finland **40** 63.24N 22.37E
Jequié Brazil **123** 13.52S 40.06W
Jequitinhonha *r.* Brazil **126** 16.46S 39.45W
Jerada Morocco **74** 34.17N 2.13W
Jerantut Malaysia **58** 3.56N102.22E
Jérémie Haiti **117** 18.40N 74.09W
Jerez Spain **27** 38.19N 6.46W
Jerez de la Frontera Spain **27** 36.41N 6.08W
Jericho *see* Arīḥā Jordan **67**
Jerilderie Australia **93** 35.23S145.41E
Jerome U.S.A. **108** 42.43N114.31W
Jersey *i.* U.K. **13** 49.13N 2.08W
Jersey City U.S.A. **115** 40.44N 74.02W
Jersey Shore U.S.A. **114** 41.12N 77.16W
Jerseyville U.S.A. **110** 39.07N 90.20W
Jerusalem *see* Yerushalayim Israel/Jordan **67**
Jervis B. Australia **93** 35.05S150.44E
Jesenice Czech. **39** 50.04N 13.29E
Jesenice Yugo. **31** 46.27N 14.04E
Jessen E. Germany **38** 51.47N 12.58E
Jessore Bangla. **63** 23.10N 89.13E
Jesup U.S.A. **113** 31.36N 81.54W
Jesús Carranza Mexico **116** 17.26N 95.02W
Jetmore U.S.A. **111** 38.03N 99.54W
Jetpur India **62** 21.44N 70.37E
Jever W. Germany **38** 53.34N 7.54E
Jevnaker Norway **42** 60.15N 10.28E
Jewett Ohio U.S.A. **114** 40.22N 81.00W
Jewett Tex. U.S.A. **111** 31.22N 96.09W
Jewett City U.S.A. **115** 41.36N 71.59W
Jeypore India **63** 18.51N 82.35E
Jezerce *mtn.* Albania **34** 42.26N 19.49E
Jeziorak, Jezioro *l.* Poland **37** 53.40N 19.04E
Jhābua India **62** 22.46N 74.36E
Jhajha India **63** 24.46N 86.22E
Jhal Pakistan **62** 28.17N 67.27E
Jhālakāti Bangla. **63** 22.39N 90.12E
Jhālawār India **62** 24.36N 76.09E
Jhal Jhao Pakistan **62** 26.18N 65.35E
Jhālod India **62** 23.06N 74.09E
Jhang Sadar Pakistan **62** 31.16N 72.20E
Jhānsi India **63** 25.26N 78.35E
Jharia India **63** 23.45N 86.24E
Jhārsuguda India **63** 21.51N 84.02E
Jhawāni Nepal **63** 27.35N 84.38E
Jhelum Pakistan **62** 32.56N 73.44E
Jhelum *r.* Pakistan **62** 31.12N 72.08E
Jhinkpāni India **63** 22.25N 85.47E
Jhok Rind Pakistan **62** 31.27N 70.26E
Jhūnjhunu India **62** 28.08N 75.24E
Jiaganj India **63** 24.14N 88.16E
Jialing Jiang *r.* China **55** 29.30N106.35E
Jiamusi China **53** 46.50N130.21E
Ji'an China **55** 27.03N115.00E
Jianchang China **54** 40.50N119.50E
Jiange China **54** 32.04N105.26E
Jiangling China **55** 30.20N112.14E
Jiangmen China **55** 22.31N113.08E
Jiangshan China **55** 28.43N118.39E
Jiangsu *d.* China **54** 33.00N119.30E
Jiangxi *d.* China **55** 27.00N115.30E
Jiangyou China **55** 31.47N104.45E
Jianhe China **55** 26.39N108.35E
Jian'ou China **55** 27.04N118.17E
Jianping China **54** 41.23N119.40E
Jianshi China **55** 30.42N109.20E
Jianyang Fujian China **55** 27.19N118.01E
Jianyang Sichuan China **55** 30.25N104.32E
Jiaochangba Sichuan China **54** 32.05N103.43E
Jiaohe China **53** 43.42N127.19E
Jiaolai He *r.* China **54** 43.48N123.00E
Jiaoling China **55** 24.40N116.10E
Jiaonan China **54** 35.53N119.58E
Jiao Xian China **54** 36.16N120.00E
Jiaozou China **54** 35.11N113.27E
Jiashan China **54** 32.49N118.01E
Jiawang China **54** 34.27N117.27E
Jiaxian China **54** 38.02N110.29E
Jiaxing China **55** 30.52N120.45E
Jiayi Taiwan **55** 23.30N120.24E
Jiazi China **55** 22.57N116.01E
Jiblava Czech. **23** 49.24N 15.36E
Jiddah Saudi Arabia **72** 21.30N 39.10E
Jiddat al Ḥarāsīs *f.* Oman **71** 19.45N 56.30E
Jiepai China **55** 31.11N113.42E
Jiexi China **55** 23.26N115.52E
Jiexiu China **54** 37.00N111.55E
Jieyang China **55** 23.29N116.19E
Jifnā Jordan **67** 31.58N 35.13E
Jihlava Czech. **36** 49.24N 15.35E
Jijel Algeria **75** 36.48N 5.46E
Jijiga Ethiopia **71** 9.22N 42.47E
Jijona Spain **25** 38.32N 0.30W
Jilib Somali Rep. **79** 0.28N 42.50E
Jilin China **53** 43.53N126.35E
Jilin *d.* China **53** 43.00N127.30E
Jiloca *r.* Spain **25** 41.21N 1.39W
Jilong Taiwan **55** 25.09N121.45E
Jima Ethiopia **73** 7.36N 36.50E
Jimbe Angola **78** 10.20S 16.40E
Jimena de la Frontera Spain **27** 36.26N 5.27W
Jiménez Mexico **97** 25.49N103.22W
Jiménez Mexico **116** 27.08N104.55W
Jimeta Nigeria **77** 9.19N 12.25E
Jimo China **54** 36.23N120.27E
Jinan China **54** 36.40N117.01E
Jind India **62** 29.19N 76.19E
Jing'an China **55** 28.52N115.22E
Jingbian China **54** 37.33N108.36E
Jingchuan China **54** 35.15N107.22E
Jingde China **55** 30.19N118.31E
Jingdezhen China **55** 29.14N117.14E
Jinggu Gansu China **54** 35.05N103.41E
Jinggu Yunnan China **61** 23.29N100.19E
Jinghai China **55** 23.02N116.31E
Jing He *r.* China **54** 34.26N109.00E
Jinghong China **52** 21.59N100.49E
Jingmen China **55** 31.02N112.06E
Jingning China **54** 35.30N105.45E
Jingou China **54** 41.37N120.33E
Jingtai China **54** 37.10N104.08E
Jingxi China **55** 23.03N106.36E
Jing Xian China **55** 26.35N109.41E
Jingyuan Gansu China **54** 36.40N104.40E
Jingyuan Ningxia Huizu China **54** 35.29N106.20E
Jinhua China **55** 29.05N119.40E
Jining Nei Monggol China **53** 40.56N113.00E
Jining Shantung China **54** 35.22N116.45E
Jinja Uganda **79** 0.27N 33.10E
Jinotepe Nicaragua **117** 11.50N 86.10W
Jinsha Jiang *r.* China **61** 26.30N101.40E
Jinshi China **55** 29.35N111.56E
Jintang China **55** 30.51N104.27E
Jinxi Fujian China **55** 26.12N117.34E
Jinxi Liaoning China **54** 40.48N120.46E
Jinxian China **55** 28.13N116.34E
Jin Xian Liaoning China **54** 39.06N121.49E
Jin Xian Liaoning China **54** 41.10N121.20E
Jinxiang China **54** 35.08N116.20E
Jinzhou China **54** 41.06N121.05E
Jipijapa Ecuador **122** 1.23S 80.35W
Jire Somali Rep. **71** 5.22N 48.05E
Jirjā Egypt **72** 26.20N 31.53E
Jishui China **55** 27.13N115.07E
Jisr al Ḥusayn Jordan **67** 31.52N 35.32E
Jitarning Australia **89** 32.48S117.57E
Jiu *r.* Romania **29** 43.44N 23.52E
Jiuding Shan *mtn.* China **55** 31.36N103.54E
Jiudongshan China **55** 23.44N117.32E
Jiujiang China **55** 29.39N116.02E
Jiulian Shan *mts.* China **55** 24.40N115.00E
Jiuling Shan *mts.* China **55** 28.40N114.45E
Jiulong Jiang *r.* China **55** 24.30N117.47E
Jiuzhou Jiang *r.* China **55** 21.25N109.58E
Jixi China **57** 45.17N130.59E
Ji Xian Henan China **54** 35.25N114.05E
Ji Xian Tianjin China **54** 40.03N117.24E
Jizān Saudi Arabia **72** 16.54N 42.32E
Jizl, Wādī al *r.* Saudi Arabia **64** 25.37N 38.20E
João Pessoa Brazil **123** 7.06S 34.53W
Jódar Spain **27** 37.50N 3.21W
Jodhpur India **62** 26.17N 73.02E
Jodiya India **62** 22.42N 70.18E
Jodoigne Belgium **16** 50.45N 4.52E
Joensuu Finland **44** 62.35N 29.46E
Jogdor China **54** 42.30N115.52E
Johannesburg R.S.A. **80** 26.11S 28.04E
Johannesburg U.S.A. **104** 44.59N 84.29W
Johi Pakistan **62** 26.41N 67.37E
John Day U.S.A. **108** 44.25N118.57W
John Day *r.* U.S.A. **108** 45.44N120.39W
John I. Canada **104** 46.09N 82.32W
John O'Groats U.K. **14** 58.39N 3.02W
Johnson U.S.A. **111** 37.34N101.45W
Johnsonburg U.S.A. **114** 41.29N 78.41W
Johnson City N.Y. U.S.A. **115** 42.07N 75.57W
Johnson City Tenn. U.S.A. **113** 36.20N 82.23W
Johnsons Crossing Canada **100** 60.29N133.18W
Johnstone Str. Canada **100** 50.28N126.00W
Johnston I. Pacific Oc. **84** 16.45N169.32W
Johnston Lakes, The Australia **89** 32.25S120.30E
Johnstown N.Y. U.S.A. **115** 43.00N 74.22W
Johnstown Ohio U.S.A. **114** 40.09N 82.41W
Johnstown Penn. U.S.A. **114** 40.20N 78.55W
Johor Baharu Malaysia **58** 1.29N103.40E
Joigny France **19** 47.59N 3.24E
Joinville Brazil **126** 26.20S 48.49W
Joinville France **19** 48.27N 5.08E
Jokkmokk Sweden **40** 66.37N 19.50E
Jökulsá á Brú *r.* Iceland **40** 65.33N 14.23W
Jökulsá á Fjöllum *r.* Iceland **40** 66.05N 16.32W
Jolfa Iran **65** 32.40N 51.39E
Joliet U.S.A. **110** 41.32N 88.05W
Joliette Canada **105** 46.01N 73.27W
Joliette Prov. Park Canada **105** 46.30N 74.00W
Jolo *i.* Phil. **59** 5.55N121.20E
Jolo *town* Phil. **59** 6.03N121.00E
Jombang Indonesia **59** 7.30S112.21E
Jombo *r.* Angola **78** 10.20S 16.37E
Jomda China **61** 31.30N 98.16E
Jonava U.S.S.R. **41** 55.05N 24.17E
Jonê China **54** 34.35N103.32E
Jonesboro Ark. U.S.A. **111** 35.50N 90.42W
Jonesboro La. U.S.A. **111** 32.15N 92.43W
Jones Sd. Canada **99** 76.00N 85.00W
Jönköping Sweden **43** 57.47N 14.11E

Jönköping to Kandos

Jönköping *d.* Sweden **43** 57.34N 14.40E
Jonzac France **20** 45.27N 0.26W
Joplin U.S.A. **111** 37.06N 94.31W
Jora India **63** 26.20N 77.49E
Jordan Asia **64** 31.00N 36.00E
Jordan *r. see* Al Urdunn Asia **67**
Jordan Mont. U.S.A. **108** 47.19N106.55W
Jordan N.Y. U.S.A. **105** 43.04N 76.30W
Jordan Valley *town* U.S.A. **108** 42.58N117.03W
Jorhāt India **61** 26.45N 94.13E
Jörn Sweden **40** 65.04N 20.02E
Jörpeland Norway **42** 59.01N 6.03E
Jos Nigeria **77** 9.54N 8.53E
José de San Martin Argentina **125** 44.04S 70.26W
José Enrique Rodó Uruguay **125** 33.41S 57.34W
Joseph, L. Canada **104** 45.14N 79.45W
Joseph, Lac *l.* Canada **103** 52.45N 65.15W
Joseph Bonaparte G. Australia **88** 14.00S128.30E
Joseph City U.S.A. **109** 34.57N110.20W
Joshimath India **63** 30.34N 79.34E
Jos Plateau *f.* Nigeria **77** 10.00N 9.00E
Josselin France **18** 47.57N 2.33W
Jotunheimen *mts.* Norway **41** 61.38N 8.18E
Joué-lès-Tours France **18** 47.21N 0.40E
Joure Neth. **16** 52.59N 5.49E
Joverega Botswana **80** 19.08S 24.15E
Jowai India **63** 25.27N 92.12E
Juan Aldama Mexico **111** 24.19N103.21W
Juan B. Arruabarrena Argentina **125** 30.25S 58.15W
Juan de Fuca, Str. of Canada / U.S.A. **100** 48.15N124.00W
Juan de Nova *i.* Madagascar **81** 17.03S 42.45E
Juan Fernández, Islas *is.* Chile **121** 34.20S 80.00W
Juárez Argentina **125** 37.40S 59.48W
Juárez Chihuahua Mexico **109** 30.20N108.03W
Juárez Coahuila Mexico **111** 27.37N100.44W
Juárez, Sierra de *mts.* Mexico **109** 32.00N115.45W
Juàzeiro Brazil **123** 9.25S 40.30W
Juàzeiro do Norte Brazil **123** 7.10S 39.18W
Juba *r.* Somali Rep. **79** 0.20S 42.40E
Jūbā Sudan **73** 4.51N 31.37E
Jūbāl, Maḍiq *str.* Egypt **66** 27.40N 33.55E
Jubal, Str. of *see* Jūbāl, Maḍiq Egypt **66**
Jubbātā al Khashab Syria **67** 33.13N 35.49E
Jubilee Downs *town* Australia **88** 18.22S125.17E
Juby, Cap *c.* Morocco **74** 27.58N 12.55W
Júcar *r.* Spain **25** 39.09N 0.14W
Juchitán Mexico **116** 16.27N 95.05W
Judaea *f.* Israel / Jordan **67** 31.10N 35.00E
Judenburg Austria **36** 47.10N 14.40E
Judith Basin *f.* U.S.A. **108** 47.10N109.58W
Juelsminde Denmark **42** 55.43N 10.01E
Jugon France **18** 48.25N 2.20W
Juillac France **20** 45.19N 1.19E
Juist W. Germany **38** 53.40N 6.59E
Juist *i.* W. Germany **38** 53.40N 7.00E
Juiz de Fora Brazil **126** 21.47S 43.23W
Jujuy *d.* Argentina **124** 23.00S 66.00W
Juklegga *mtn.* Norway **41** 61.03N 8.13E
Juliaca Peru **122** 15.29S 70.09W
Julia Creek *town* Australia **90** 20.39S141.45E
Juliana Kanaal *canal* Neth. **16** 51.00N 5.48E
Julian Alps *mts.* Yugo. **31** 46.20N 13.50E
Julianehåb Greenland **99** 60.45N 46.00W
Jülich W. Germany **38** 50.55N 6.21E
Jullundur India **62** 31.20N 75.35E
Jumbo Somali Rep. **79** 0.12S 42.38E
Jumbunna Australia **93** 38.30S145.38E
Jumet Belgium **16** 50.27N 4.27E
Jumilla Spain **25** 38.29N 1.17W
Jumla Nepal **63** 29.17N 82.13E
Jumna *r. see* Yamuna India **63**
Junāgadh India **62** 21.31N 70.28E
Junan China **54** 35.11N118.50E
Junction U.S.A. **111** 30.29N 99.46W
Junction B. Australia **90** 11.50S134.15E
Junction City Kans. U.S.A. **110** 39.02N 96.50W
Junction City Oreg. U.S.A. **108** 44.13N123.12W
Jundah Australia **90** 24.50S143.02E
Jundiaí Brazil **126** 23.10S 46.54W
Juneau U.S.A. **100** 58.26N134.30W
Junee Australia **93** 34.51S147.40E
Jungfrau *mtn.* Switz. **39** 46.32N 7.58E
Junggar Pendi *f.* Asia **52** 44.20N 86.30E
Junglinster Lux. **16** 49.41N 6.13E
Jungshāhi Pakistan **62** 24.51N 67.46E
Junín Argentina **125** 34.35S 60.58W
Junín de los Andes Argentina **125** 39.57S 71.05W
Juniville France **19** 49.24N 4.23E
Jūniyah Lebanon **66** 33.59N 35.38E
Junlian China **55** 28.08N104.29E
Junnah, Jabal *mts.* Egypt **66** 28.52N 34.15E
Junnar India **62** 19.12N 73.53E
Junsele Sweden **40** 63.40N 16.55E
Juntura U.S.A. **108** 43.46N118.05W
Jun Xian China **54** 32.40N111.18E
Jupiter *r.* Canada **103** 49.29N 63.32W
Jupiter U.S.A. **113** 26.57N 80.08W
Jur *r.* Sudan **73** 7.45N 28.00E
Jura *mts.* Europe **39** 46.48N 6.30E
Jura *d.* France **19** 46.50N 5.50E
Jura *i.* U.K. **14** 55.58N 5.55W
Jura, Sd. of U.K. **14** 56.00N 5.45W
Jurado Colombia **122** 7.07N 77.46W
Jura Krakowska *mts.* Poland **37** 50.30N 19.30E
Jurhen Ul Shan *mts.* China **63** 34.00N 91.00E
Jūrmala U.S.S.R. **41** 56.58N 23.42E
Juruá *r.* Brazil **122** 2.33S 65.50W
Juruena Brazil **124** 12.50S 58.58W
Juruena *r.* Brazil **123** 7.20S 57.30W
Juruti Brazil **123** 2.09S 56.04W
Jussey France **19** 47.49N 5.54E
Jutaí *r.* Brazil **122** 2.35S 67.00W
Jüterbog E. Germany **38** 51.59N 13.04E
Juticalpa Honduras **117** 14.45N 86.12W
Jutland *pen. see* Jylland Denmark **42**
Juye China **54** 35.23N116.06E
Jūyom Iran **65** 28.10N 53.52E
Južna *r.* Yugo. **34** 43.40N 21.22E
Jwayyā Lebanon **67** 33.14N 35.20E
Jyderup Denmark **42** 55.40N 11.26E
Jylland *pen.* Denmark **42** 56.12N 9.20E
Jyväskylä Finland **40** 62.14N 25.44E

K

K2 *mtn.* Asia **52** 35.53N 76.32E
Ka *r.* Nigeria **77** 11.35N 4.10E
Kaabong Uganda **79** 3.28N 34.08E
Kaapstad *see* Cape Town R.S.A. **80**
Kaba Guinea **76** 10.08N 11.49W
Kabaena *i.* Indonesia **59** 5.25S122.00E
Kabala Sierra Leone **76** 9.40N 11.36W
Kabale Uganda **79** 1.13S 30.00E
Kabalega Falls *f.* Uganda **79** 2.17N 31.46E
Kabalega Falls Nat. Park Uganda **79** 2.15N 31.45E
Kabalo Zaïre **79** 6.02S 27.00E
Kabambare Zaïre **79** 4.40S 27.41E
Kabanga Zambia **80** 17.36S 26.45E
Kabba Nigeria **77** 7.50N 6.07E
Kabberi Israel **67** 33.01N 35.09E
Kabia *i.* Indonesia **59** 6.07S120.28E
Kabinakagami *r.* Canada **112** 50.20N 84.20W
Kabinda Zaïre **78** 6.10S 24.29E
Kabīr Kūh *mts.* Iran **65** 33.00N 47.00E
Kabkābīyah Sudan **73** 13.39N 24.05E
Kabompo Zambia **78** 13.35S 24.10E
Kabompo *r.* Zambia **78** 14.17S 23.15E
Kabongo Zaïre **78** 7.22S 25.34E
Kabonzo Zaïre **79** 6.41S 27.49E
Kaboudia, Ra's *c.* Tunisia **75** 35.14N 11.10E
Kabūd Gonbad Iran **65** 37.02N 59.46E
Kābul Afghan. **62** 34.31N 69.12E
Kābul *d.* Afghan. **62** 34.45N 69.15E
Kabumbu Zaïre **78** 4.07S 26.17E
Kabunda Zaïre **79** 12.27S 29.15E
Kabundi Zaïre **79** 10.07S 27.13E
Kabwe Zambia **79** 14.27S 28.25E
Kačanik Yugo. **34** 42.13N 21.12E
Kāchā Kūh *mts.* Iran **65** 29.30N 61.20E
Kachin *d.* Burma **56** 26.00N 97.30E
Kachiry U.S.S.R. **9** 53.07N 76.08E
Kachisi Ethiopia **73** 9.39N 37.50E
Kadaň Czech. **39** 50.20N 13.15E
Kadaney *r.* Afghan. **62** 31.20N 65.47E
Kade Ghana **76** 6.08N 0.51W
Kadei *r.* C.A.R. **77** 3.28N 16.05E
Kadi India **62** 23.18N 72.20E
Kadina Australia **92** 33.58S137.14E
Kadioli Mali **76** 10.38N 5.45W
Kadoka U.S.A. **110** 43.50N101.31W
Kadoma Zimbabwe **80** 18.23S 29.52E
Kaduna Nigeria **77** 10.28N 7.25E
Kaduna *d.* Nigeria **77** 11.00N 7.35E
Kaduna *r.* Nigeria **77** 8.45N 5.45E
Kāduqlī Sudan **73** 11.01N 29.43E
Kadusam *mtn.* China **61** 28.30N 96.45E
Kadzherom U.S.S.R. **44** 64.42N 55.59E
Kaédi Mauritania **74** 16.09N 13.30W
Kaélé Cameroon **77** 10.05N 14.28E
Kaesŏng N. Korea **53** 37.59N126.30E
Kafanchan Nigeria **77** 9.38N 8.20E
Kaffrine Senegal **76** 14.08N 15.34W
Kafia Kingi Sudan **73** 9.16N 24.25E
Kafirévs, Ákra *c.* Greece **35** 38.10N 24.35E
Kafo *r.* Uganda **79** 1.40N 32.07E
Kafr ad Dawwār Egypt **66** 31.08N 30.08E
Kafr al Baṭṭīkh Egypt **66** 31.24N 31.44E
Kafr ash Shaykh Egypt **66** 31.07N 30.56E
Kafrayn, Wādī al Jordan **67** 31.50N 35.35E
Kafr az Zayyāt Egypt **66** 30.50N 30.49E
Kafr Kammā Israel **67** 32.43N 35.26E
Kafr Kannā Israel **67** 32.45N 35.20E
Kafr Mandā Israel **67** 32.49N 35.15E
Kafr Naffākh Syria **67** 33.04N 35.44E
Kafr Qaddūm Jordan **67** 32.13N 35.09E
Kafr Qūd Jordan **67** 32.27N 35.14E
Kafr Salīm Egypt **66** 31.09N 30.07E
Kafr Yāsīf Israel **67** 32.57N 35.10E
Kafta Ethiopia **72** 13.56N 37.13E
Kafue Zambia **79** 15.40S 28.13E
Kafue *r.* Zambia **79** 15.53S 28.55E
Kafue Dam Zambia **79** 15.40S 27.10E
Kafue Nat. Park Zambia **78** 15.30S 25.35E
Kafunzo Uganda **79** 1.05S 30.26E
Kaga Bandoro C.A.R. **77** 7.00N 19.10E
Kāgān Pakistan **62** 34.47N 73.32E
Kagan U.S.S.R. **50** 39.45N 64.32E
Kagarlyk U.S.S.R. **37** 49.50N 30.50E
Kagawong Canada **104** 45.54N 82.17W
Kagawong L. Canada **104** 45.49N 82.18W
Kagaznagar India **63** 19.18N 79.50E
Kagera *d.* Tanzania **79** 2.00S 31.20E
Kağizman Turkey **64** 40.08N 43.07E
Kagoshima Japan **57** 31.37N130.32E
Kagoshima wan *b.* Japan **57** 31.00N131.00E
Kagul U.S.S.R. **29** 45.54N 28.11E
Kahama Tanzania **79** 3.48S 32.38E
Kahayan *r.* Indonesia **58** 3.20S114.04E
Kahemba Zaïre **78** 7.20S 19.00E
Kahler Asten *mtn.* W. Germany **38** 51.11N 8.29E
Kahntah *r.* Canada **100** 58.15N120.55W
Kahnūj Iran **65** 27.55N 57.45E
Kahoolawe *i.* Hawaiian Is. **85** 20.33N156.37W
Kahraman Maraş Turkey **64** 37.34N 36.54E
Kai, Kepulauan *is.* Indonesia **59** 5.45S132.55E
Kaiama Nigeria **77** 9.37N 4.03E
Kaiapoi New Zealand **86** 43.23S172.39E
Kaiedin Sudan **73** 9.45N 32.11E
Kaifeng China **54** 34.46N114.22E
Kaikohe New Zealand **86** 35.25S173.49E
Kaikoura New Zealand **86** 42.24S173.41E
Kaikoura Range *mts.* New Zealand **86** 42.00S173.40E
Kailahun Sierra Leone **76** 8.21N 10.21W
Kaili China **55** 26.35N107.55E
Kailu China **54** 43.35N121.12E
Kailua Hawaiian Is. **85** 21.24N157.44W
Kaïmakchalán *mtn.* Greece **34** 40.55N 21.48E
Kaimana Indonesia **59** 3.39S133.44E
Kaimanawa Mts. New Zealand **86** 39.10S176.15E
Kainantu P.N.G. **59** 6.16S145.50E
Kainji Resr. Nigeria **77** 10.00N 4.35E
Kaintragarh India **63** 20.47N 84.40E
Kaipara Harbour New Zealand **86** 36.30S174.00E
Kaiserslautern W. Germany **39** 49.26N 7.46E
Kaitaia New Zealand **86** 35.08S173.18E
Kaithal India **62** 29.48N 76.23E
Kaitum *r.* Sweden **40** 67.30N 21.05E
Kaiwi Channel Hawaiian Is. **85** 21.15N157.30W
Kaiyuan China **54** 42.45N123.50E
Kaizuka Japan **57** 34.27N135.21E
Kajaani Finland **40** 64.14N 27.41E
Kajabbi Australia **90** 20.02S140.02E
Kajiado Kenya **79** 1.50S 36.48E
Kajo Kaji Sudan **73** 3.53N 31.40E
Kajuru Nigeria **77** 10.19N 7.40E
Kākā Sudan **73** 10.36N 32.11E
Kakamas R.S.A. **80** 28.44S 20.35E
Kakamega Kenya **79** 0.21N 34.47E
Kakamigahara Japan **57** 35.28N136.48E
Kākdwīp India **63** 21.53N 88.11E
Kakegawa Japan **57** 34.46N138.01E
Kakenge Zaïre **78** 4.51S 21.55E
Kakhovskoye Vodokhranilishche *resr.* U.S.S.R. **45** 47.33N 34.40E
Kākī Iran **65** 28.19N 51.34E
Kākināda India **61** 16.59N 82.20E
Kakisa *r.* Canada **100** 61.03N117.10W
Kakisa L. Canada **100** 60.55N117.40W
Kakonko Tanzania **79** 3.19S 30.54E
Kakuma Kenya **79** 3.38N 34.48E
Kakuto Uganda **79** 0.54S 31.26E
Kala *r.* Finland **40** 64.17N 23.55E
Kālābāgh Pakistan **62** 32.58N 71.34E
Kalabahi Indonesia **59** 8.13S124.31E
Kalabáka Greece **34** 39.42N 21.43E
Kalabity Australia **92** 31.53S140.18E
Kalabo Zambia **78** 14.58S 22.33E
Kalach-na-Donu U.S.S.R. **45** 48.43N 43.31E
Kaladan *r.* Burma **56** 20.09N 92.55E
Kaladar Canada **105** 44.39N 77.07W
Kalahari Desert Botswana **80** 23.30S 22.00E
Kalahari Gemsbok Nat. Park R.S.A. **80** 25.45S 20.25E
Kalajoki Finland **40** 64.15N 23.57E
Kalakan U.S.S.R. **51** 55.10N116.45E
Kalámai Greece **35** 37.04N 22.07E
Kalamariá Greece **34** 40.33N 22.55E
Kalamazoo U.S.A. **112** 42.17N 85.36W
Kalamb India **62** 18.56N 73.55E
Kalamera Tanzania **79** 2.07S 33.43E
Kalamurra, L. Australia **92** 28.00S138.00E
Kalannie Australia **89** 30.21S117.04E
Kalanshiyū, Sarīr *des.* Libya **75** 27.00N 21.30E
Kalarash U.S.S.R. **37** 47.18N 28.16E
Kalāt Pakistan **62** 29.02N 66.35E
Kalavárdha Greece **35** 36.20N 27.57E
Kalávrita Greece **35** 38.03N 22.08E
Kalb, Ra's al *c.* S. Yemen **71** 14.02N 48.41E
Kalchās Pakistan **62** 29.21N 69.42E
Kalecik Turkey **64** 40.06N 33.22E
Kalehe Zaïre **79** 2.05S 28.53E
Kalemie Zaïre **79** 5.57S 29.10E
Kalgan *r.* Australia **89** 34.55S117.58E
Kalgoorlie Australia **89** 30.49S121.29E
Kaliakra, Nos *c.* Bulgaria **29** 43.23N 28.29E
Kalianda Indonesia **58** 5.50S105.45E
Kalima Zaïre **78** 2.35S 26.34E
Kalimantan *d.* Indonesia **58** 1.00S113.00E
Kalimantan *f.* Indonesia **58** 0.05N112.30E
Kalimantan Barat *d.* Indonesia **58** 0.30N110.00E
Kalimantan Selatan *d.* Indonesia **58** 2.30S115.30E
Kalimantan Tengah *d.* Indonesia **58** 2.00S113.30E
Kalimantan Timur *d.* Indonesia **58** 2.20N116.30E
Kálimnos Greece **35** 36.57N 26.59E
Kálimnos *i.* Greece **35** 37.00N 27.00E
Kālimpong India **63** 27.04N 88.29E
Kalinin U.S.S.R. **44** 56.47N 35.57E
Kaliningrad U.S.S.R. **41** 54.43N 20.30E
Kalinkovichi U.S.S.R. **37** 52.10N 29.13E
Kalinovik Yugo. **31** 43.31N 18.26E
Kalinovka U.S.S.R. **37** 49.29N 28.30E
Kalisat Indonesia **59** 8.02S113.50E
Kāli Sindh *r.* India **62** 25.32N 76.17E
Kalispell U.S.A. **108** 48.12N114.19W
Kalisz Poland **37** 51.46N 18.02E
Kaliua Tanzania **79** 5.08S 31.50E
Kalix *r.* Sweden **40** 65.50N 23.11E
Kalkar W. Germany **38** 51.44N 6.17E
Kalkfontein Botswana **80** 22.08S 20.54E
Kalkrand Namibia **80** 24.05S 17.34E
Källandsö *i.* Sweden **43** 58.40N 13.09E
Kallinge Sweden **43** 56.14N 15.17E
Kallista Australia **91** 42.57S146.10E
Kallithea Greece **35** 37.05N 23.41E
Kallsjön *l.* Sweden **40** 63.35N 13.00E
Kalmar Sweden **43** 56.40N 16.22E
Kalmar *d.* Sweden **43** 57.15N 16.00E
Kalmarsund *str.* Sweden **43** 56.40N 16.25E
Kalmthout Belgium **16** 51.23N 4.28E
Kalmykovo U.S.S.R. **45** 49.02N 51.55E
Kālna India **63** 23.13N 88.22E
Kalničko Gorje *mts.* Yugo. **31** 46.10N 16.30E
Kalo P.N.G. **90** 10.05S147.45E
Kalocsa Hungary **31** 46.32N 18.59E
Kalofer Bulgaria **34** 42.37N 24.59E
Kaloko Zaïre **78** 6.47S 25.47E
Kālol Gujarat India **62** 22.36N 73.27E
Kālol Gujarat India **62** 23.15N 72.29E
Kalole Zaïre **79** 3.40S 27.22E
Kalomo Zambia **78** 16.55S 26.29E
Kalonje Zambia **79** 12.21S 31.06E
Kālpi India **63** 26.07N 79.44E
Kāl Qal 'eh Afghan. **62** 32.38N 62.32E
Kalsö *i.* Faroe Is. **10** 62.19N 6.42W
Kalsūbai *mtn.* India **62** 19.36N 73.43E
Kaltag U.S.A. **98** 64.20N158.44W
Kaluga U.S.S.R. **44** 54.31N 36.16E
Kālu Khuhar Pakistan **62** 25.08N 67.46E
Kalumburu Australia **88** 14.14S126.38E
Kalundborg Denmark **42** 55.41N 11.06E
Kalush U.S.S.R. **37** 49.02N 24.20E
Kalutara Sri Lanka **61** 6.35N 79.58E
Kalyān India **62** 19.15N 73.09E
Kama *r.* U.S.S.R. **44** 55.30N 52.00E
Kamaishi Japan **57** 39.16N141.53E
Kamakura Japan **57** 35.19N139.33E
Kamālia Pakistan **62** 30.44N 72.39E
Kaman Turkey **23** 39.22N 33.44E
Kamanashi *r.* Japan **57** 35.33N138.28E
Kamaniskeg L. Canada **105** 45.25N 77.42W
Kamanjab Namibia **80** 19.39S 14.50E
Kamarsuk Canada **103** 56.18N 61.38W
Kamba Nigeria **77** 11.52N 3.42E
Kamba Zaïre **78** 4.00S 22.22E
Kambalda Australia **89** 31.12S121.40E
Kambar Pakistan **62** 27.36N 68.00E
Kambarka U.S.S.R. **44** 56.18N 54.13E
Kambia Sierra Leone **76** 9.09N 12.53W
Kamchatka, Poluostrov *pen.* U.S.S.R. **51** 56.00N160.00E
Kameda Japan **57** 41.48N140.36E
Kamen *mtn.* U.S.S.R. **51** 68.40N 94.20E
Kamenets Podolskiy U.S.S.R. **37** 48.40N 26.36E
Kamenka R.S.F.S.R. U.S.S.R. **44** 53.10N 44.05E
Kamenka R.S.F.S.R. U.S.S.R. **44** 65.55N 44.02E
Kamenka Bugskaya U.S.S.R. **37** 50.07N 24.30E
Kamen Kashirskiy U.S.S.R. **37** 51.32N 24.59E
Kamen-na-Obi U.S.S.R. **50** 53.46N 81.18E
Kamenskoye U.S.S.R. **51** 62.31N165.15E
Kamensk-Shakhtinskiy U.S.S.R. **45** 48.20N 40.16E
Kamensk-Ural'skiy U.S.S.R. **50** 56.29N 61.49E
Kamenz E. Germany **38** 51.16N 14.06E
Kāmet *mtn.* India / China **63** 30.54N 79.37E
Kameyama Japan **57** 34.51N136.27E
Kamiah U.S.A. **108** 46.14N116.02W
Kamieskroon R.S.A. **80** 30.12S 17.53E
Kamilukuak L. Canada **101** 62.22N101.40W
Kamina Zaïre **78** 8.46S 24.58E
Kaminak L. Canada **101** 62.10N 95.00W
Kámiros *site* Greece **35** 36.19N 27.57E
Kamloops Canada **100** 50.40N120.20W
Kamloops Plateau *f.* Canada **100** 50.00N120.20W
Kamnik Yugo. **31** 46.13N 14.37E
Kamo *r.* Japan **57** 35.00N139.52E
Kāmoke Pakistan **62** 31.58N 74.13E
Kamp W. Germany **39** 50.14N 7.37E
Kampa Indonesia **58** 1.46S105.26E
Kampala Uganda **79** 0.19N 32.35E
Kampar *r.* Indonesia **58** 0.20N102.55E
Kampen Neth. **16** 52.33N 5.55E
Kampene Zaïre **78** 3.36S 26.40E
Kamphaeng Phet Thailand **56** 16.28N 99.31E
Kamp-Lintfort W. Germany **16** 51.34N 6.38E
Kamp 'O S. Korea **57** 35.48N129.29E
Kâmpóng Cham Kampuchea **56** 11.59N105.26E
Kâmpóng Chhnăng Kampuchea **56** 12.16N104.39E
Kâmpóng Saôm Kampuchea **58** 10.38N103.30E
Kâmpóng Thum Kampuchea **56** 12.42N104.52E
Kâmpôt Kampuchea **56** 10.37N104.11E
Kampti U. Volta **76** 10.07N 3.22W
Kampuchea Asia **56** 12.45N105.00E
Kamsack Canada **101** 51.34N101.54W
Kamskoye Vodokhranilishche *resr.* U.S.S.R. **44** 58.55N 56.20E
Kāmthi India **63** 21.14N 79.12E
Kamui misaki *c.* Japan **57** 43.30N140.15E
Kamyshin U.S.S.R. **45** 50.05N 45.24E
Kana *r.* Zimbabwe **80** 18.30S 26.50E
Kanaaupscow *r.* Canada **102** 53.40N 77.10W
Kanafis Sudan **73** 9.48N 25.40E
Kanagawa *d.* Japan **57** 35.25N139.10E
Kanairiktok *r.* Canada **103** 55.05N 60.20W
Kanākir Syria **67** 33.15N 36.05E
Kanália Greece **34** 39.30N 22.53E
Kananga Zaïre **78** 5.53S 22.26E
Kanash U.S.S.R. **44** 55.30N 47.27E
Kanastraion, Ákra *c.* Greece **34** 39.56N 23.47E
Kanaudi India **63** 23.36N 81.23E
Kanawha *r.* U.S.A. **114** 38.50N 82.08W
Kanazawa Japan **57** 36.35N136.40E
Kanchanaburi Thailand **56** 14.02N 99.28E
Kānchenjunga *mtn.* Nepal / India **63** 27.44N 88.11E
Kānchipuram India **61** 12.50N 79.44E
Kandāhu Pakistan **62** 27.33N 69.24E
Kandalaksha U.S.S.R. **44** 67.09N 32.31E
Kandalakshskaya Guba *g.* U.S.S.R. **44** 66.30N 34.00E
Kandangan Indonesia **58** 2.50S115.15E
Kandavu *i.* Fiji **84** 19.05S178.15E
Kandavu Passage Fiji **84** 18.45S178.00E
Kandel W. Germany **39** 49.05N 8.11E
Kandhkot Pakistan **62** 28.14N 69.11E
Kandi Benin **77** 11.05N 2.59E
Kāndi India **63** 23.57N 88.02E
Kandiāro Pakistan **62** 27.04N 68.13E
Kandira Turkey **64** 41.05N 30.08E
Kandla India **62** 23.00N 70.10E
Kandos Australia **93** 32.53S149.59E

Kandrāch to Kelvington

Kandrāch Pakistan 62 25.29N 65.29E
Kandreho Madagascar 81 17.29S 46.06E
Kandy Sri Lanka 61 7.18N 80.43E
Kane U.S.A. 114 41.40N 78.49W
Kanem *d.* Chad 77 15.10N 15.30E
Kanevka U.S.S.R. 44 67.08N 39.50E
Kang Botswana 80 23.43S 22.51E
Kangaba Mali 76 11.56N 8.25W
Kangān Iran 65 27.50N 52.07E
Kangar Malaysia 58 6.28N100.10E
Kangaroo I. Australia 92 35.50S137.06E
Kangding China 52 30.05N102.04E
Kangean, Kepulauan *is.* Indonesia 59 7.00S115.30E
Kangerlussuaq *see* Söndreströmfjord Greenland 99
Kangikajiip Agpalia *see* Brewster, K. Greenland 96
Kangle China 54 35.16N103.39E
Kangmar Xizang China 63 28.30N 89.45E
Kangmar Xizang China 63 30.45N 85.43E
Kango Gabon 78 0.15N 10.14E
Kangping China 54 42.45N123.20E
Kangrinboqê Feng *mtn.* China 63 31.05N 81.21E
Kangto *mtn.* China 63 27.54N 92.32E
Kanhar *r.* India 63 24.28N 83.08E
Kani Ivory Coast 76 8.34N 6.35W
Kaniama Zaïre 78 7.32S 24.11E
Kanin, Poluostrov *pen.* U.S.S.R. 44 68.00N 45.00E
Kaningo Kenya 79 0.52S 38.31E
Kanin Nos, Mys *c.* U.S.S.R. 44 68.38N 43.20E
Kaniva Australia 92 36.33S141.17E
Kanjiža Yugo. 31 46.04N 20.04E
Kankakee U.S.A. 110 41.08N 87.52W
Kankan Gabon 78 0.03S 12.14E
Kankan Guinea 76 10.22N 9.11W
Kānker India 63 20.17N 81.29E
Kankossa Mauritania 74 15.58N 11.31W
Kannack Vietnam 56 14.07N108.36E
Kannapolis U.S.A. 113 35.30N 80.36W
Kannauj India 63 27.04N 79.55E
Kannod India 62 22.40N 76.44E
Kano *r.* Japan 57 35.05N138.52E
Kano Nigeria 77 12.00N 8.31E
Kano *d.* Nigeria 77 12.00N 9.00E
Kanona Zambia 79 13.03S 30.37E
Kanowna Australia 89 30.36S121.36E
Kanoya Japan 57 31.22N130.50E
Kānpur India 63 26.28N 80.21E
Kansas *d.* U.S.A. 110 38.30N 99.00W
Kansas *r.* U.S.A. 110 39.07N 94.36W
Kansas City Kans. U.S.A. 110 39.07N 94.39W
Kansas City Mo. U.S.A. 110 39.05N 94.35W
Kansenia Zaïre 78 10.19S 26.02E
Kansk U.S.S.R. 51 56.11N 95.20E
Kansŏng S. Korea 53 38.20N128.28E
Kantābānji India 63 20.29N 82.55E
Kantché Niger 77 13.31N 8.30E
Kantemirovka U.S.S.R. 45 49.40N 39.52E
Kantō *d.* Japan 57 35.35N139.30E
Kantōheiya *f.* Japan 57 36.02N140.10E
Kantō-sanchi *mts.* Japan 57 36.00N138.35E
Kanye Botswana 80 24.58S 25.17E
Kanyu Botswana 80 20.05S 24.39E
Kao *i.* Tonga 85 19.40S175.01W
Kaohsiung Taiwan 48 22.36N120.17E
Kaoko Veld *f.* Namibia 80 18.30S 13.30E
Kaolack Senegal 76 14.09N 16.08W
Kaoma Zambia 78 14.55S 24.58E
Kapaa Hawaiian Is. 85 22.05N159.19W
Kapadvanj India 62 23.01N 73.04E
Kapanga Zaïre 78 8.22S 22.37E
Kapaonik *mts.* Yugo. 34 43.10N 21.00E
Kap Arkona *c.* E. Germany 38 54.41N 13.26E
Kapchagay U.S.S.R. 52 43.51N 77.14E
Kapenguria Kenya 79 1.13N 35.07E
Kapfenberg Austria 36 47.27N 15.18E
Kapiri Mposhi Zambia 79 13.59S 28.40E
Kapiskau Canada 102 52.20N 82.01W
Kapiskau *r.* Canada 102 52.20N 83.40W
Kapit Malaysia 58 2.01N112.56E
Kapiti I. New Zealand 86 40.50S174.50E
Kapoeta Sudan 73 4.47N 33.35E
Kapongolo Zaïre 79 7.51S 28.12E
Kapos *r.* Hungary 31 46.44N 18.30E
Kaposvár Hungary 31 46.22N 17.47E
Kappar Pakistan 62 25.19N 62.42E
Kappeln W. Germany 38 54.40N 9.56E
Kappelshamn Sweden 43 57.52N 18.50E
Kapps Namibia 80 22.22S 17.52E
Kapsabet Kenya 79 0.12N 35.05E
Kapsukas U.S.S.R. 41 54.33N 23.21E
Kaptai Bangla. 63 22.21N 92.17E
Kaptol Yugo. 31 45.26N 17.44E
Kapuas *r.* Indonesia 58 0.13S109.12E
Kapunda Australia 92 34.21S138.54E
Kapūrthala India 62 31.23N 75.23E
Kapuskasing Canada 102 49.25N 82.30W
Kaputar, Mt. Australia 93 30.20S150.10E
Kapuvár Hungary 37 47.36N 17.02E
Kara U.S.S.R. 50 69.12N 65.00E
Kara-Bogaz Gol, Zaliv *b.* U.S.S.R. 65 41.20N 53.40E
Karabük Turkey 64 41.12N 32.36E
Karabutak U.S.S.R. 50 49.55N 60.05E
Karāchi Pakistan 62 24.52N 67.03E
Karād India 60 17.17N 74.12E
Karaganda U.S.S.R. 9 49.53N 73.07E
Karaginskiy, Ostrov *i.* U.S.S.R. 51 59.00N165.00E
Karakas U.S.S.R. 52 48.20N 83.30E
Karakelong *i.* Indonesia 59 4.20N126.50E
Karakoram Pass Asia 61 35.53N 77.51E
Karakoram Range *mts.* Jammu & Kashmir 60 35.30N 76.30E
Karakoro *r.* Mauritania 74 14.43N 12.03W
Karaköse *see* Agri Turkey 45
Karakumskiy Kanal *canal* U.S.S.R. 65 37.30N 65.48E
Karakumy, Peski *f.* U.S.S.R. 65 37.45N 60.00E
Karakuwisa Namibia 80 18.56S 19.43E
Karaman Turkey 64 37.11N 33.13E
Karamay China 52 45.48N 84.30E
Karamea New Zealand 86 41.15S172.07E
Karamea Bight *b.* New Zealand 86 41.15S171.30E
Karamürsel Turkey 64 40.42N 29.37E
Karand Iran 65 34.16N 46.15E
Kāranja India 63 20.29N 77.29E
Karanjia India 63 21.47N 85.58E
Karasburg Namibia 80 28.00S 18.46E
Karasjok Norway 40 69.27N 25.30E
Karasuk U.S.S.R. 50 53.45N 78.01E
Karatau, Khrebet *mts.* U.S.S.R. 45 44.15N 52.10E
Karatobe U.S.S.R. 45 49.44N 53.30E
Karaton U.S.S.R. 45 46.26N 53.32E
Karauli India 62 26.30N 77.01E
Karawa Zaïre 78 3.12N 20.20E
Karawanken *mts.* Austria 31 46.30N 14.10E
Karazhal U.S.S.R. 50 48.00N 70.55E
Karbalā' Iraq 65 32.37N 44.03E
Karcag Hungary 37 47.19N 20.56E
Kardhámaina Greece 35 36.47N 27.09E
Kardhamíla Greece 35 36.53N 22.14E
Kardhámilia Greece 35 38.34N 26.05E
Kardhítsa Greece 35 39.21N 21.55E
Kärdla U.S.S.R. 41 59.00N 22.42E
Kareli India 63 22.55N 79.04E
Karema Tanzania 79 6.50S 30.25E
Karen *d.* Burma 56 17.30N 97.45E
Karen India 61 12.50N 92.55E
Karepino U.S.S.R. 44 61.05N 58.02E
Karesuando Finland 40 68.25N 22.30E
Kargasok U.S.S.R. 50 59.07N 80.58E
Kargi Kenya 79 2.31N 37.34E
Kargil Jammu & Kashmir 62 34.34N 76.06E
Kargopol U.S.S.R. 44 61.32N 38.59E
Kari Nigeria 77 11.17N 10.35E
Kariaí Greece 34 40.16N 24.15E
Kariba Zimbabwe 80 16.32S 28.50E
Kariba, L. Zimbabwe / Zambia 80 16.50S 28.00E
Kariba Dam Zimbabwe / Zambia 80 16.15S 28.55E
Karibib Namibia 80 21.56S 15.52E
Kārikāl India 61 10.58N 79.50E
Karimama Benin 77 12.02N 3.15E
Karimganj India 63 24.52N 92.20E
Karin Somali Rep. 71 10.51N 45.45E
Karis Finland 41 60.05N 23.40E
Karisimbi, Mt. Zaïre / Rwanda 79 1.31S 29.25E
Káristos Greece 35 38.01N 24.25E
Kariya Japan 57 34.59N136.59E
Kariyangwe Zimbabwe 80 17.57S 27.30E
Karkabet Ethiopia 72 16.13N 37.30E
Karkaralinsk U.S.S.R. 9 49.21N 75.27E
Karkar I. P.N.G. 59 4.40S146.00E
Karkas, Kūh-e *mtn.* Iran 65 33.25N 51.40E
Karkheh *r.* Iran 65 31.45N 47.52E
Karkinitskiy Zaliv *g.* U.S.S.R. 45 45.50N 32.45E
Karkur Israel 67 32.28N 35.00E
Karlino Poland 36 54.03N 15.51E
Karl-Marx-Stadt E. Germany 38 50.50N 12.55E
Karl-Marx-Stadt *d.* E. Germany 38 50.45N 13.00E
Karlobag Yugo. 31 44.32N 15.05E
Karlovac Yugo. 31 45.29N 15.34E
Karlovo Bulgaria 34 42.38N 24.48E
Karlovy Vary Czech. 39 50.11N 12.52E
Karlsborg Sweden 43 58.32N 14.31E
Karlshamn Sweden 43 56.10N 14.51E
Karlskoga Sweden 43 59.20N 14.31E
Karlskrona Sweden 43 56.10N 15.35E
Karlsruhe W. Germany 39 49.03N 8.24E
Karlstad Sweden 43 59.22N 13.30E
Karlstad U.S.A. 110 48.35N 96.31W
Karlstadt W. Germany 39 49.57N 9.45E
Karmah Sudan 72 19.38N 30.25E
Karmel, Har *mtn.* Israel 67 32.44N 35.02E
Karmi'el Israel 67 32.55N 35.18E
Karmöy *i.* Norway 42 59.15N 5.15E
Karnafuli Resr. Bangla. 61 22.40N 92.05E
Karnāl India 62 29.41N 76.59E
Karnāli *r.* Nepal 63 28.45N 81.16E
Karnaphuli Resr. Bangla. 63 22.30N 92.20E
Karnataka *d.* India 60 14.45N 76.00E
Karnes City U.S.A. 111 28.53N 97.54W
Karnobat Bulgaria 29 42.40N 27.00E
Kärnten *d.* Austria 39 46.50N 13.30E
Karoi Zimbabwe 80 16.51S 29.39E
Karokh Afghan. 62 34.28N 62.35E
Karonga Malaŵi 79 9.54S 33.55E
Karonie Australia 89 30.58S122.32E
Karoonda Australia 92 35.09S139.54E
Karor Pakistan 62 31.13N 70.57E
Karora Sudan 72 17.42N 38.22E
Káros *i.* Greece 35 36.54N 25.40E
Karos Dam R.S.A. 80 28.27S 21.39E
Karousádhes Greece 34 39.47N 19.45E
Karpach U.S.S.R. 37 48.00N 27.10E
Kárpathos Greece 35 35.40N 27.10E
Kárpathos *i.* Greece 35 35.40N 27.10E
Karpenísion Greece 35 38.55N 21.40E
Karpineny U.S.S.R. 37 46.46N 28.18E
Karpinsk U.S.S.R. 44 59.48N 59.59E
Karpogory U.S.S.R. 44 64.01N 44.30E
Karragullen Australia 89 32.05S116.03E
Karridale Australia 89 34.12S115.04E
Kars Turkey 64 40.35N 43.05E
Karsakpay U.S.S.R. 9 47.47N 66.43E
Kärsämäki Finland 40 63.58N 25.46E
Kārsava U.S.S.R. 44 56.45N 27.40E
Karskoye More *sea* U.S.S.R. 50 73.00N 65.00E
Karstädt E. Germany 38 53.09N 11.44E
Kartaly U.S.S.R. 50 53.06N 60.37E
Karufa Indonesia 59 3.50S133.27E
Kārūn *r.* Iran 65 30.25N 48.12E
Karunga Kenya 73 1.09S 36.49E
Karungi Sweden 40 66.03N 23.55E
Karungu Kenya 79 0.50S 34.09E
Karup Denmark 42 56.18N 9.10E
Karviná Czech. 37 49.50N 18.30E
Kasai *r.* Zaïre 78 3.10S 16.13E
Kasai Occidental *d.* Zaïre 78 5.00S 21.30E
Kasai Oriental *d.* Zaïre 78 5.00S 24.00E
Kasaji Zaïre 78 10.22S 23.27E
Kasama Zambia 79 10.10S 31.11E
Kasane Botswana 80 17.48S 25.09E
Kasanga Tanzania 79 8.27S 31.10E
Kāsaragod India 60 12.30N 75.00E
Kasba India 63 25.51N 87.33E
Kasba L. Canada 101 60.20N102.10W
Kasba-Tadla Morocco 22 32.34N 6.18W
Kåseberga Sweden 43 55.23N 14.04E
Kasempa Zambia 78 13.28S 25.48E
Kasese Uganda 79 0.07N 30.06E
Kāsganj India 63 27.49N 78.39E
Kāshān Iran 65 33.59N 51.31E
Kashi China 52 39.29N 76.02E
Kashin U.S.S.R. 44 57.22N 37.39E
Kashipur India 63 29.13N 78.57E
Kashiwa Japan 57 35.52N139.59E
Kāshmar Iran 65 35.12N 58.26E
Kashmor Pakistan 62 28.26N 69.35E
Kasia India 63 26.45N 83.55E
Kasimov U.S.S.R. 44 54.55N 41.25E
Kaskaskia *r.* U.S.A. 111 37.59N 89.56W
Kaskattama *r.* Canada 101 57.03N 90.07W
Kaskinen Finland 40 62.23N 21.13E
Kaskö *see* Kaskinen Finland 40
Kaslo Canada 100 49.55N117.00W
Kasongo Zaïre 78 4.32S 26.33E
Kasongo-Lunda Zaïre 78 6.30S 16.47E
Kásos *i.* Greece 35 35.22N 26.56E
Kassalā Sudan 72 15.28N 36.24E
Kassalā *d.* Sudan 72 17.30N 36.30E
Kassándra *pen.* Greece 34 40.00N 23.30E
Kassel W. Germany 38 51.19N 9.29E
Kastamonu Turkey 64 41.22N 33.47E
Kastanéai Greece 34 41.38N 26.28E
Kastl W. Germany 38 49.22N 11.42E
Kastoría Greece 34 40.30N 21.19E
Kastorías, Límni *l.* Greece 34 40.30N 21.20E
Kastrávion, Tekhnití Límni *l.* Greece 35 38.45N 21.20E
Kastrosikiá Greece 35 39.09N 20.36E
Kasugai Japan 57 35.14N136.58E
Kasukabe Japan 57 35.58N139.45E
Kasulu Tanzania 79 4.34S 30.06E
Kasumi Japan 57 35.38N134.38E
Kasungu Malaŵi 79 13.04S 33.29E
Kasūr Pakistan 62 31.07N 74.27E
Kataba Zambia 78 16.12S 25.05E
Katako Kombe Zaïre 78 3.27S 24.21E
Katákolon Greece 35 37.38N 21.19E
Katangi India 63 23.27N 79.47E
Katanning Australia 89 33.42S117.33E
Katanti Zaïre 79 2.19S 27.08E
Katarniān Ghāt India 63 28.20N 81.09E
Katchall *i.* India 61 7.57N 93.22E
Kateríni Greece 34 40.16N 22.30E
Katete Zambia 79 14.08S 31.50E
Katha Burma 56 24.11N 95.20E
Katherine Australia 90 14.29S132.20E
Kāthgodām India 63 29.16N 79.32E
Kathla India 62 32.00N 76.47E
Kathor India 62 21.18N 72.57E
Kathrabbā Jordan 67 31.08N 35.37E
Kathua Jammu & Kashmir 62 32.22N 75.31E
Kati Mali 76 12.41N 8.04W
Katihār India 63 25.32N 87.35E
Katima Rapids *f.* Zambia 78 17.15S 24.20E
Katiola Ivory Coast 76 8.10N 5.10W
Kātlang Pakistan 62 34.22N 72.05E
Katlanovo Yugo. 34 41.52N 21.40E
Kātmāndu Nepal 63 27.42N 85.20E
Káto Akhaia Greece 35 38.09N 21.32E
Kātol India 63 21.16N 78.35E
Katonah U.S.A. 115 41.16N 73.41W
Katonga *r.* Uganda 79 0.03N 30.15E
Katoomba Australia 93 33.42S150.23E
Katopa Zaïre 78 2.45S 25.06E
Káto Stavrós Greece 34 40.39N 23.43E
Katoúna Greece 35 38.47N 21.07E
Katowice Poland 37 50.15N 18.59E
Katrīnah, Jabal *mtn.* Egypt 66 28.30N 33.57E
Katrine, Loch U.K. 14 56.15N 4.30W
Katrineholm Sweden 43 59.00N 16.12E
Katsina Nigeria 77 13.00N 7.32E
Katsina Ala Nigeria 77 7.10N 9.30E
Katsina Ala *r.* Nigeria 77 7.50N 8.58E
Katsura *r.* Japan 57 34.53N135.42E
Katsuura Japan 57 35.08N140.18E
Kattaviá Greece 35 35.57N 27.46E
Kattegat *str.* Denmark / Sweden 42 57.25N 11.30E
Katthammarsvik Sweden 43 57.26N 18.50E
Katul, Jabal *mtn.* Sudan 72 14.16N 29.23E
Katumba Zaïre 78 7.45S 25.18E
Kātwa India 63 23.39N 88.08E
Katwijk aan Zee Neth. 16 52.13N 4.27E
Katzenbuckel *mtn.* W. Germany 39 49.28N 9.02E
Katzenfurt W. Germany 38 50.37N 8.21E
Kauai *i.* Hawaii U.S.A. 106 22.05N159.30W
Kaub W. Germany 39 50.05N 7.46E
Kaufbeuren W. Germany 39 47.53N 10.37E
Kauhajoki Finland 40 62.26N 22.11E
Kauhava Finland 40 63.06N 23.05E
Kaukauna U.S.A. 110 44.20N 88.16W
Kaukauveld *mts.* Namibia 80 20.00S 20.15E
Kauliranta Finland 40 66.26N 23.40E
Kaumba Zaïre 78 8.26S 24.40E
Kaunas U.S.S.R. 41 54.54N 23.54E
Kaura Namoda Nigeria 77 12.39N 6.38E
Kautokeino Norway 40 69.00N 23.02E
Kavadarci Yugo. 34 41.26N 22.03E
Kavajë Albania 34 41.11N 19.33E
Kavála Greece 34 40.56N 24.25E
Kāvali India 61 14.55N 80.01E
Kavarna Bulgaria 29 43.26N 28.22E
Kavimba Botswana 80 18.05S 24.34E
Kavkaz U.S.S.R. 45 45.20N 36.39E
Kavkazskiy Khrebet *mts.* U.S.S.R. 45 43.00N 44.00E
Kävlinge Sweden 43 55.48N 13.06E
Kaw Guiana 123 4.29N 52.02W
Kawachi-nagano Japan 57 34.25N135.32E
Kawagama L. Canada 104 45.18N 78.45W
Kawagoe Japan 57 35.55N139.29E
Kawaguchi Japan 57 35.48N139.43E
Kawambwa Zambia 79 9.47S 29.10E
Kawardha India 63 22.01N 81.15E
Kawartha L. Canada 104 44.40N 78.10W
Kawasaki Japan 57 35.32N139.43E
Kawerau New Zealand 86 38.05S176.42E
Kawhia New Zealand 86 38.04S174.49E
Kawm Sudan 73 13.31N 22.50E
Kawthaung Burma 56 10.09N 98.33E
Kaya U. Volta 76 13.04N 1.04W
Kayah *d.* Burma 56 19.15N 97.30E
Kayambi Zambia 79 9.26S 32.01E
Kayan *r.* Indonesia 58 2.47N117.46E
Kaycee U.S.A. 108 43.43N106.38W
Kayenta U.S.A. 108 36.44N110.17W
Kayes Congo 78 4.25S 11.41E
Kayes Mali 76 14.26N 11.28W
Kayes *d.* Mali 76 14.00N 10.55W
Kayonza Rwanda 73 1.53S 30.31E
Kayseri Turkey 64 38.42N 35.28E
Kaysville U.S.A. 108 41.02N111.56W
Kazabazua Canada 105 45.56N 76.01W
Kazachye U.S.S.R. 51 70.46N136.15E
Kazakhskaya S.S.R. *d.* U.S.S.R. 45 48.00N 52.30E
Kazakhskiy Zaliv *b.* U.S.S.R. 45 42.43N 52.30E
Kazan U.S.S.R. 44 55.45N 49.10E
Kazanlŭk Bulgaria 34 42.38N 25.35E
Kazatin U.S.S.R. 37 49.41N 28.49E
Kazaure Nigeria 77 12.40N 8.25E
Kazbek *mtn.* U.S.S.R. 45 42.42N 44.30E
Kāzerūn Iran 65 29.35N 51.39E
Kazhim U.S.S.R. 44 60.18N 51.34E
Kazima C.A.R. 73 5.16N 26.11E
Kazincbarcika Hungary 37 48.16N 20.37E
Kazo Japan 57 36.07N139.36E
Kazumba Zaïre 78 6.30S 22.02E
Kbal Dâmrei Kampuchea 56 14.03N105.20E
Kdyně Czech. 38 49.23N 13.02E
Kéa Greece 35 37.38N 24.21E
Kéa *i.* Greece 35 37.34N 24.22E
Kearney U.S.A. 110 40.42N 99.05W
Keban Turkey 64 38.48N 38.45E
Kebele Ethiopia 73 12.52N 40.40E
Kebili Tunisia 75 33.42N 8.58E
Kebnekaise *mtn.* Sweden 40 67.53N 18.33E
K'ebri Dehār Ethiopia 71 6.47N 44.17E
Kebumen Indonesia 59 7.40S109.41E
Kecel Hungary 31 46.32N 19.16E
Kech *r.* Pakistan 62 26.00N 62.44E
Kechika *r.* Canada 100 59.36N127.05W
Kecskemét Hungary 37 46.54N 19.42E
Kedada Ethiopia 73 5.20N 36.00E
Kedainiai U.S.S.R. 41 55.17N 24.00E
Kedgwick Canada 103 47.39N 67.21W
Kédhros Greece 35 39.13N 22.03E
Kediri Indonesia 59 7.45S112.01E
Kédougou Senegal 76 12.35N 12.09W
Keefers Canada 100 50.00N121.40W
Keele Peak *mtn.* Canada 98 63.15N129.50W
Keene Canada 104 44.15N 78.10W
Keene U.S.A. 115 42.56N 72.17W
Keepit Resr. Australia 93 30.52S150.30E
Keer-Weer, C. Australia 90 13.58S141.30E
Keeseville U.S.A. 105 44.30N 73.29W
Keetmanshoop Namibia 80 26.34S 18.07E
Keewatin Canada 102 49.46N 94.34W
Keewatin *d.* Canada 99 65.00N 90.00W
Kefa *d.* Ethiopia 73 7.00N 36.30E
Kefallinía *i.* Greece 35 38.15N 20.35E
Kefalos Greece 35 36.45N 27.00E
Kefar Ata Israel 67 32.48N 35.06E
Kefar 'Eqron Israel 67 31.51N 34.49E
Kefar Gil'adi Israel 67 33.15N 35.34E
Kefar Nahum *site* Israel 67 32.53N 35.34E
Kefar Sava Israel 67 32.11N 34.54E
Kefar Szold Israel 67 33.11N 35.39E
Kefar Tavor Israel 67 32.41N 35.25E
Kefar Vitkin Israel 67 32.23N 34.53E
Kefar Yona Israel 67 32.19N 34.56E
Kefar Zekharya Israel 67 31.42N 34.57E
Kefar Zetim Israel 67 32.49N 35.28E
Keffi Nigeria 77 8.52N 7.53E
Keflavík Iceland 40 64.01N 22.35W
Keg River *town* Canada 100 57.54N117.07W
Kehsi Mānsām Burma 56 21.56N 97.51E
Keighley U.K. 12 53.52N 1.54W
Keila U.S.S.R. 41 59.18N 24.29E
Keimoes R.S.A. 80 28.41S 20.58E
Keitele *l.* Finland 40 62.55N 26.00E
Keith Australia 92 36.06S140.22E
Keith U.K. 14 57.32N 2.57W
Keith Arm *b.* Canada 98 65.20N122.15W
Kekri India 62 25.58N 75.09E
Kelam Ethiopia 73 4.48N 36.06E
Kelang Malaysia 58 2.57N101.24E
Kelberg W. Germany 39 50.17N 6.55E
Kelheim W. Germany 39 48.55N 11.54E
Kelibia Tunisia 32 36.51N 11.06E
Kelkit *r.* Turkey 64 40.46N 36.32E
Kelle Congo 78 0.05S 14.33E
Keller U.S.A. 108 48.03N118.40W
Kellerberrin Australia 89 31.38S117.43E
Kellett, C. Canada 98 71.59N125.34W
Kelleys I. U.S.A. 114 41.36N 82.42W
Kelloselkä Finland 44 66.55N 28.50E
Kells Meath Rep. of Ire. 15 53.44N 6.53W
Kelme U.S.S.R. 41 55.38N 22.56E
Kélo Chad 77 9.21N 15.50E
Kelowna Canada 100 49.50N119.25W
Kelso U.K. 14 55.36N 2.26W
Kelso Calif. U.S.A. 109 35.01N115.39W
Kelso Wash. U.S.A. 108 46.09N122.54W
Keluang Malaysia 58 2.01N103.18E
Kelvedon U.K. 13 51.50N 0.43E
Kelvington Canada 101 52.10N103.30W

Kem to **Kipili**

Kem U.S.S.R. **44** 64.58N 34.39E
Kema Indonesia **59** 1.22N125.08E
Ke Macina Mali **76** 14.05N 5.20W
Kemah Turkey **64** 39.35N 39.02E
Kemaliye Turkey **64** 39.16N 38.29E
Kemano Canada **100** 53.35N128.00W
Kembolcha Ethiopia **73** 11.02N 39.43E
Kemerovo U.S.S.R. **50** 55.25N 86.10E
Kemi Finland **40** 65.49N 24.32E
Kemi *r.* Finland **40** 65.47N 24.30E
Kemijärvi Finland **40** 66.36N 27.24E
Kemmerer U.S.A. **108** 41.48N110.32W
Kemnath W. Germany **38** 49.52N 11.54E
Kempen *f.* Belgium **16** 51.05N 5.00E
Kemp Land *f.* Antarctica **128** 69.00S 57.00E
Kempsey Australia **93** 31.05S152.50E
Kempt, Lac *l.* Canada **105** 47.25N 74.22W
Kempten W. Germany **39** 47.43N 10.19E
Kemptville Canada **105** 45.01N 75.38W
Ken *r.* India **63** 25.46N 80.31E
Kenai U.S.A. **98** 60.33N151.15W
Kenai Pen. U.S.A. **96** 64.40N150.18W
Kenamuke Swamp Sudan **73** 5.55N 33.48E
Kenaston Canada **101** 51.30N106.18W
Kendai India **63** 22.45N 82.37E
Kendal Australia **93** 31.28S152.40E
Kendal Indonesia **59** 6.56S110.14E
Kendal U.K. **12** 54.19N 2.44W
Kendal U.K. **11** 54.19N 2.44W
Kendall U.S.A. **114** 43.20N 78.02W
Kendari Indonesia **59** 3.57S122.36E
Kendenup Australia **89** 34.28S117.35E
Kendrāpāra India **63** 20.30N 86.25E
Kendrick U.S.A. **108** 46.37N116.39W
Kenebri Australia **93** 30.45S149.02E
Kenema Sierra Leone **76** 7.57N 11.11W
Kenge Zaïre **78** 4.56S 17.04E
Kengeja Tanzania **79** 5.24S 39.45E
Keng Tung Burma **56** 21.16N 99.39E
Kenhardt R.S.A. **80** 29.21S 21.08E
Kenilworth U.K. **13** 52.22N 1.35W
Kenitra Morocco **74** 34.20N 6.34W
Kenli China **54** 37.35N118.34E
Kenmare Rep. of Ire. **15** 51.53N 9.36W
Kenmare U.S.A. **108** 48.40N102.05W
Kenmore U.S.A. **114** 42.58N 78.53W
Kennebec *r.* U.S.A. **112** 44.00N 69.50W
Kennebunk U.S.A. **115** 43.23N 70.33W
Kenner U.S.A. **111** 29.59N 90.15W
Kennet *r.* U.K. **13** 51.28N 0.57W
Kennett Square U.S.A. **115** 39.51N 75.43W
Kennewick U.S.A. **108** 46.12N119.07W
Kenogami *r.* Canada **102** 50.24N 84.20W
Keno Hill *town* Canada **98** 63.58N135.22W
Kenora Canada **102** 49.47N 94.29W
Kenosha U.S.A. **110** 42.35N 87.49W
Kenozero, Ozero *l.* U.S.S.R. **44** 62.20N 37.00E
Kent *d.* U.K. **13** 51.12N 0.40E
Kent Ohio U.S.A. **114** 41.09N 81.22W
Kent Tex. U.S.A. **109** 31.04N104.13W
Kent Wash. U.S.A. **108** 47.23N122.14W
Kentau U.S.S.R. **9** 43.28N 68.36E
Kentland U.S.A. **112** 40.46N 87.26W
Kenton U.S.A. **112** 40.38N 83.38W
Kent Pen. Canada **98** 68.30N107.00W
Kentucky *d.* U.S.A. **113** 37.30N 85.15W
Kentucky *r.* U.S.A. **113** 38.40N 85.09W
Kentucky L. U.S.A. **111** 36.25N 88.05W
Kentville Canada **103** 45.05N 64.30W
Kenya Africa **79** 1.00N 38.00E
Kenya, Mt. Kenya **79** 0.10S 37.19E
Keokuk U.S.A. **110** 40.24N 91.24W
Keonjhargarh India **63** 21.38N 85.35E
Kepi Indonesia **59** 6.32S139.19E
Kepno Poland **37** 51.17N 17.59E
Keppel B. Australia **90** 23.21S150.55E
Kerala *d.* India **60** 10.30N 76.30E
Kerang Australia **92** 35.42S143.59E
Keratéa Greece **35** 37.48N 23.59E
Kerch U.S.S.R. **45** 45.22N 36.27E
Kerchenskiy Proliv *str.* U.S.S.R. **45** 45.15N 36.35E
Kerema P.N.G. **59** 7.59S145.46E
Kerem Ben Zimra Israel **67** 33.02N 35.28E
Kerem Maharal Israel **67** 32.39N 34.59E
Keren Ethiopia **72** 15.46N 38.28E
Kerguelen, Îles de *is.* Indian Oc. **49** 49.15S 69.10E
Kerguelen Basin *f.* Indian Oc. **49** 35.00S 65.00E
Kerguelen-Gaussberg Ridge *f.* Indian Oc. **49** 55.00S 75.00E
Kericho Kenya **79** 0.22S 35.19E
Kerinci, Gunung *mtn.* Indonesia **58** 1.45S101.20E
Kerio *r.* Kenya **79** 3.00N 36.14E
Keríon Greece **35** 37.40N 20.48E
Kerkenna, Îles *is.* Tunisia **75** 34.44N 11.12E
Kerki R.S.F.S.R. U.S.S.R. **44** 63.40N 54.00E
Kerki Tk.S.S.R. U.S.S.R. **50** 37.53N 65.10E
Kerkinitis, Límni *l.* Greece **34** 41.10N 23.08E
Kérkira Greece **34** 39.36N 19.56E
Kérkira *i.* Greece **34** 39.40N 19.42E
Kerkrade Neth. **16** 50.52N 6.02E
Kermadec Is. Pacific Oc. **84** 30.00S178.30W
Kermadec Trench Pacific Oc. **84** 33.30S176.00W
Kermān Iran **65** 30.18N 57.05E
Kermānshāh Iran **65** 34.19N 47.04E
Kerme Körfezi *g.* Turkey **35** 36.50N 28.00E
Kermit U.S.A. **111** 31.51N103.06W
Kerouane Guinea **76** 9.16N 9.00W
Kerpen W. Germany **16** 50.52N 6.42E
Kerrobert Canada **101** 51.55N109.08W
Kerrville U.S.A. **111** 30.03N 99.08W
Kerry *d.* Rep. of Ire. **15** 52.07N 9.35W
Kerry Head Rep. of Ire. **15** 52.24N 9.56W
Kerteminde Denmark **42** 55.27N 10.40E
Kerulen *r.* Mongolia **53** 48.45N117.00E
Kesagami L. Canada **102** 50.23N 80.15W
Keşan Turkey **34** 40.51N 26.37E
Keshod India **62** 21.18N 70.15E
Keskal India **63** 20.03N 81.34E
Keski-Suomi *d.* Finland **40** 62.30N 25.30E
Keswick U.K. **12** 54.35N 3.09W
Keszthely Hungary **31** 46.46N 17.15E
Ketapang Jawa Indonesia **59** 6.56S113.14E
Ketapang Kalimantan Indonesia **58** 1.50S110.02E
Ketchikan U.S.A. **100** 55.25N131.40W
Ketchum U.S.A. **108** 43.41N114.22W
Kete Krachi Ghana **76** 7.50N 0.03W
Keti Bandar Pakistan **62** 24.08N 67.27E
Kętrzyn Poland **37** 54.06N 21.23E
Kettering U.K. **13** 52.24N 0.44W
Kettering U.S.A. **112** 39.41N 84.10W
Kettle *r.* Canada **101** 56.55N 89.25W
Kettle Falls *town* U.S.A. **108** 48.36N118.03W
Kettle Pt. Canada **104** 43.11N 82.01W
Keuka L. U.S.A. **114** 42.27N 77.10W
Keweenaw B. U.S.A. **112** 46.48N 88.26W
Keweenaw Pen. U.S.A. **112** 47.10N 88.30W
Key, Lough Rep. of Ire. **15** 54.00N 8.15W
Keyala Sudan **73** 4.27N 32.52E
Key Harbour Canada **104** 45.53N 80.44W
Keynsham U.K. **13** 51.25N 2.30W
Key West U.S.A. **113** 24.33N 81.48W
Kezhma U.S.S.R. **51** 58.58N101.08E
Kežmarok Czech. **37** 49.08N 20.25E
Khabab Syria **67** 33.01N 36.16E
Khabarovsk U.S.S.R. **53** 48.32N135.08E
Khairāgarh India **63** 21.25N 80.58E
Khairpur Punjab Pakistan **62** 29.35N 72.14E
Khairpur Sind Pakistan **62** 27.32N 68.46E
Khajrāho India **63** 24.50N 79.58E
Khalatse Jammu & Kashmir **62** 34.20N 76.49E
Khálki Greece **34** 39.36N 22.30E
Khálki *i.* Greece **35** 36.17N 27.35E
Khalkidhikí *f.* Greece **23** 40.25N 23.27E
Khalkís Greece **35** 38.28N 23.36E
Khalmer Yu U.S.S.R. **44** 67.58N 64.48E
Khālsar Jammu & Kashmir **63** 34.31N 77.41E
Khalturin U.S.S.R. **44** 58.38N 48.50E
Khalūf Oman **60** 20.31N 58.04E
Khambhāliya India **62** 22.12N 69.39E
Khambhāt, G. of India **62** 20.30N 71.45E
Khāmgaon India **62** 20.41N 76.34E
Khamkeut Laos **56** 18.14N104.44E
Khānaqīn Iraq **65** 34.22N 45.22E
Khān az Zabīb Jordan **67** 31.28N 36.06E
Khandela India **62** 27.36N 75.30E
Khandwa India **62** 21.50N 76.20E
Khāneh Khvodī Iran **65** 36.05N 56.04E
Khānewāl Pakistan **62** 30.18N 71.56E
Khāngarh Punjab Pakistan **62** 28.22N 71.43E
Khāngarh Punjab Pakistan **62** 29.55N 71.10E
Khanh Hung Vietnam **56** 9.36N105.55E
Khaniá Greece **35** 35.31N 24.02E
Khaníon, Kólpos *g.* Greece **35** 35.34N 23.48E
Khanka, Ozero *l.* U.S.S.R. **53** 45.00N132.30E
Khanna India **62** 30.42N 76.14E
Khannā, Qā' ** *f.* Jordan **67 32.04N 36.26E
Khānozai Pakistan **62** 30.37N 67.19E
Khānpur Pakistan **62** 28.39N 70.39E
Khanty-Mansiysk U.S.S.R. **50** 61.00N 69.00E
Khān Yūnus Egypt **67** 31.21N 34.18E
Khanzira, Ras *c.* Somali Rep. **71** 10.55N 45.47E
Khapalu Jammu & Kashmir **62** 35.10N 76.20E
Khapcheranga U.S.S.R. **53** 49.46N112.20E
Kharagpur India **63** 22.20N 87.20E
Khārān *r.* Iran **65** 27.37N 58.48E
Khārān Pakistan **62** 28.35N 65.25E
Kharbatā Jordan **67** 31.57N 35.04E
Khargon India **62** 21.49N 75.36E
Khāriān Pakistan **62** 32.49N 73.52E
Khariār Road *town* India **63** 20.54N 82.31E
Khārijah, Al Wāḥāt al *oasis* Egypt **64** 24.55N 30.35E
Kharkov U.S.S.R. **45** 50.00N 36.15E
Khār Kūh *mtn.* Iran **65** 31.37N 53.47E
Kharmanli Bulgaria **34** 41.56N 25.54E
Kharovsk U.S.S.R. **44** 59.67N 40.07E
Khartoum *see* Al Kharṭūm Sudan **72**
Kharutayuvam U.S.S.R. **44** 66.51N 59.31E
Khasavyurt U.S.S.R. **45** 43.16N 46.36E
Khāsh Afghan. **62** 31.31N 62.52E
Khāsh *r.* Afghan. **62** 31.11N 61.50E
Khāsh Iran **65** 28.14N 61.15E
Khāsh, Dasht-e *des.* Afghan. **62** 31.50N 62.30E
Khashgort U.S.S.R. **44** 65.25N 65.40E
Khashm al Qirbah Sudan **72** 14.58N 35.55E
Khaskovo Bulgaria **34** 41.56N 25.33E
Khaskovo *d.* Bulgaria **34** 41.57N 25.32E
Khatanga U.S.S.R. **51** 71.50N102.31E
Khatangskiy Zaliv *g.* U.S.S.R. **51** 75.00N112.10E
Khāvda India **62** 23.51N 69.43E
Khawr Barakah *r.* Sudan **72** 18.13N 37.35E
Khemisset Morocco **74** 33.50N 6.03W
Khemmarat Thailand **56** 16.00N105.10E
Khenchela Algeria **75** 35.26N 7.08E
Khenifra Morocco **74** 33.00N 5.40W
Khersān *r.* Iran **65** 31.29N 48.53E
Kherson U.S.S.R. **45** 46.39N 32.38E
Kherwāra India **62** 23.59N 73.35E
Khetia India **62** 21.40N 74.35E
Khewāri Pakistan **62** 26.36N 68.52E
Khiliomódhion Greece **35** 37.48N 22.51E
Khíos Greece **35** 38.22N 26.08E
Khíos *i.* Greece **35** 38.22N 26.00E
Khipro Pakistan **62** 25.50N 69.22E
Khirbat al Ghazālah Syria **67** 32.44N 36.12E
Khisfīn Syria **67** 32.51N 35.49E
Khiva U.S.S.R. **65** 41.25N 60.49E
Khmelnik U.S.S.R. **37** 49.36N 27.59E
Khmelnitskiy U.S.S.R. **37** 49.25N 26.49E
Khodorov U.S.S.R. **37** 49.20N 24.19E
Khogali Sudan **73** 6.08N 27.47E
Khok Kloi Thailand **56** 8.19N 98.18E
Kholm U.S.S.R. **44** 57.10N 31.11E
Kholmogory U.S.S.R. **44** 63.51N 41.46E
Khomas-Hochland *mts.* Namibia **80** 22.50S 16.25E
Khondmāl Hills India **63** 20.15N 84.00E
Khonu U.S.S.R. **51** 66.29N143.12E
Khoper *r.* U.S.S.R. **45** 49.35N 42.17E
Khóra Greece **35** 37.03N 21.42E
Khorāl India **62** 26.30N 71.14E
Khóra Sfakíon Greece **35** 35.12N 24.09E
Khorixas Namibia **80** 20.24S 14.58E
Khorog U.S.S.R. **52** 37.32N 71.32E
Khorramābād Iran **65** 33.29N 48.21E
Khorramshahr Iran **65** 30.26N 48.09E
Khotimsk U.S.S.R. **37** 53.24N 32.36E
Khotin U.S.S.R. **37** 48.30N 26.31E
Khouribga Morocco **74** 32.54N 6.57W
Khowai India **63** 24.06N 91.38E
Khowrnag, Kūh-e *mtn.* Iran **65** 32.10N 54.38E
Khowst Afghan. **62** 33.22N 69.57E
Khoyniki U.S.S.R. **37** 51.54N 30.00E
Khrisoúpolis Greece **34** 40.58N 24.42E
Khugīāni Afghan. **62** 31.33N 66.15E
Khūgīānī Šānī Afghan. **62** 31.31N 66.12E
Khūiāla India **62** 27.15N 70.25E
Khuis Botswana **80** 26.37S 21.45E
Khulga *r.* U.S.S.R. **44** 63.33N 61.53E
Khulna Bangla. **63** 22.48N 89.33E
Khumbur Khule Ghar *mtn.* Afghan. **62** 33.05N 69.00E
Khunti India **63** 23.05N 85.17E
Khurai India **63** 24.03N 78.19E
Khurda India **63** 20.11N 85.37E
Khurīyā Murīyā, Jazā'ir *is.* Oman **60** 17.30N 56.00E
Khurja India **63** 28.15N 77.51E
Khurli Pakistan **62** 28.59N 65.52E
Khurr, Wādī al *r.* Iraq **71** 31.02N 42.00E
Khurra Bārīk *r.* Iraq **64** 32.00N 44.15E
Khushāb Pakistan **62** 32.18N 72.21E
Khust U.S.S.R. **37** 48.11N 23.19E
Khuwayy Sudan **73** 13.05N 29.14E
Khuzdār Pakistan **62** 27.48N 66.37E
Khvājeh Ra'ūf Afghan. **62** 33.19N 64.43E
Khvor Iran **65** 33.47N 55.06E
Khvormuj Iran **65** 28.40N 51.20E
Khvoy Iran **65** 38.32N 45.02E
Khyber Pass Afghan./Pakistan **62** 34.06N 71.05E
Kiama Australia **93** 34.41S150.49E
Kiamika Canada **105** 46.25N 75.23W
Kiáton Greece **35** 38.01N 22.45E
Kibaek Denmark **42** 56.02N 8.51E
Kibali *r.* Zaïre **79** 3.37N 28.38E
Kibamba Zaïre **78** 4.53S 26.33E
Kibar India **63** 32.20N 78.01E
Kibenga Zaïre **78** 7.55S 17.35E
Kibombo Zaïre **78** 3.58S 25.57E
Kibondo Tanzania **79** 3.35S 30.41E
Kibre Mengist Ethiopia **73** 5.52N 39.00E
Kibungu Rwanda **79** 2.10S 30.31E
Kibwesa Tanzania **79** 6.30S 29.57E
Kibwezi Kenya **79** 2.28S 37.57E
Kičevo Yugo. **34** 41.34N 20.59E
Kichiga U.S.S.R. **51** 59.50N163.27E
Kicking Horse Pass Canada **100** 51.27N116.25W
Kidal Mali **77** 18.27N 1.25E
Kidderminster U.K. **13** 52.24N 2.13W
Kidete Morogoro Tanzania **79** 6.39S 36.42E
Kidsgrove U.K. **12** 53.06N 2.15W
Kiefersfelden Austria **39** 47.37N 12.11E
Kiel W. Germany **38** 54.20N 10.08E
Kiel Canal *see* Nord-Ostsee-Kanal W. Germany **38**
Kielce Poland **37** 50.52N 20.37E
Kieler Bucht *b.* W. Germany **38** 54.35N 10.35E
Kiev *see* Kiyev U.S.S.R. **37**
Kiffa Mauritania **74** 16.38N 11.28W
Kifisiá Greece **35** 38.04N 23.49E
Kifissós *r.* Greece **35** 38.30N 23.00E
Kigali Rwanda **79** 1.59S 30.05E
Kiglapait, C. Canada **103** 57.05N 61.05W
Kigoma Tanzania **79** 4.52S 29.36E
Kigoma *d.* Tanzania **79** 4.45S 30.00E
Kigosi *r.* Tanzania **79** 4.37S 31.29E
Kiiminkin *r.* Finland **40** 65.12N 25.18E
Kii sanchi *mts.* Japan **57** 34.00N135.20E
Kii suidō *str.* Japan **57** 34.00N135.00E
Kikinda Yugo. **37** 45.51N 20.30E
Kikládhes *is.* Greece **35** 37.30N 25.00E
Kikongo Zaïre **78** 4.16S 17.11E
Kikori P.N.G. **59** 7.25S144.13E
Kikori *r.* P.N.G. **59** 7.10S144.05E
Kikwissi, L. Canada **104** 47.00N 78.30W
Kikwit Zaïre **78** 5.02S 18.51E
Kil Sweden **43** 59.30N 13.19E
Kilafors Sweden **41** 61.14N 16.34E
Kila Kila P.N.G. **59** 9.31S147.10E
Kilchu N. Korea **53** 40.55N129.21E
Kilcoy Australia **91** 26.57S152.33E
Kilcullen Rep. of Ire. **15** 53.08N 6.46W
Kildare Rep. of Ire. **15** 53.10N 6.55W
Kildare *d.* Rep. of Ire. **15** 53.10N 6.50W
Kildonan Zimbabwe **80** 17.22S 30.33E
Kilfinan U.K. **14** 55.58N 5.18W
Kilgore U.S.A. **111** 32.23N 94.53W
Kilifi Kenya **79** 3.30S 39.50E
Kilimanjaro *d.* Tanzania **79** 3.45S 37.40E
Kilimanjaro *mtn.* Tanzania **79** 3.02S 37.20E
Kilindoni Tanzania **79** 7.55S 39.39E
Kilingi-Nõmme U.S.S.R. **41** 58.09N 24.58E
Kilis Turkey **64** 36.43N 37.07E
Kiliya U.S.S.R. **37** 45.30N 29.16E
Kilkee Rep. of Ire. **15** 52.41N 9.40W
Kilkenny Rep. of Ire. **15** 52.39N 7.16W
Kilkenny *d.* Rep. of Ire. **15** 52.35N 7.15W
Kilkieran B. Rep. of Ire. **15** 53.20N 9.42W
Kilkís Greece **34** 41.00N 22.53E
Killala B. Rep. of Ire. **15** 54.15N 9.10W
Killaloe Canada **105** 45.33N 77.25W
Killard Pt. U.K. **15** 54.19N 5.31W
Killarney Australia **93** 28.18S152.15E
Killarney Man. Canada **101** 49.12N 99.42W
Killarney Ont. Canada **104** 45.58N 81.31W
Killarney Rep. of Ire. **15** 52.04N 9.32W
Killarney Prov. Park Canada **104** 46.05N 81.30W
Killary Harbour *est.* Rep. of Ire. **15** 53.38N 9.56W
Killdeer U.S.A. **108** 47.22N102.45W
Killeen U.S.A. **111** 31.08N 97.44W
Killin U.K. **14** 56.29N 4.19W
Killíni Greece **35** 37.55N 21.09E
Killíni *mtn.* Greece **35** 37.57N 22.23E
Killorglin Rep. of Ire. **15** 52.07N 9.45W
Killybegs Rep. of Ire. **15** 54.38N 8.27W
Killyleagh U.K. **15** 54.24N 5.39W
Kilmarnock U.K. **14** 55.37N 4.30W
Kilmichael Pt. Rep. of Ire. **15** 52.44N 6.09W
Kilmore Australia **93** 37.18S144.58E
Kilninver U.K. **14** 56.21N 5.30W
Kilombero *r.* Tanzania **79** 8.30S 37.28E
Kilosa Tanzania **79** 6.49S 37.00E
Kilronan Rep. of Ire. **15** 53.08N 9.41W
Kilrush Rep. of Ire. **15** 52.39N 9.30W
Kilsyth U.K. **14** 55.59N 4.04W
Kilvo Sweden **40** 66.50N 21.04E
Kilwa Kivinje Tanzania **79** 8.45S 39.21E
Kilwa Masoko Tanzania **79** 8.55S 39.31E
Kimaān Indonesia **59** 7.54S138.51E
Kimba Australia **92** 33.09S136.25E
Kimball U.S.A. **110** 41.14N103.40W
Kimberley Canada **100** 49.40N115.59W
Kimberley R.S.A. **80** 28.44S 24.44E
Kimberley Plateau Australia **88** 17.20S127.20E
Kimch'aek N. Korea **57** 40.41N129.12E
Kími Greece **35** 38.38N 24.06E
Kimito *i.* Finland **41** 60.10N 22.30E
Kímolos *i.* Greece **35** 36.47N 24.35E
Kimparana Mali **76** 12.52N 4.59W
Kimry U.S.S.R. **44** 56.51N 37.20E
Kimsquit Canada **100** 52.45N126.57W
Kinabalu *mtn.* Malaysia **58** 6.10N116.40E
Kincaid Canada **101** 49.39N107.00W
Kincardine Canada **104** 44.11N 81.38W
Kindersley Canada **101** 51.27N109.10W
Kindia Guinea **76** 10.03N 12.49W
Kindu Zaïre **78** 3.00S 25.56E
Kinel U.S.S.R. **44** 53.17N 50.42E
Kineshma U.S.S.R. **44** 57.28N 42.08E
Kingaroy Australia **90** 26.33S151.50E
King City U.S.A. **109** 36.13N121.08W
Kingcome Inlet *town* Canada **100** 50.58N125.15W
King George Is. Canada **102** 57.20N 78.25W
King George Sd. Australia **89** 35.03S117.57E
King I. Australia **91** 39.50S144.00E
King I. Canada **100** 52.10N127.40W
Kingissepp U.S.S.R. **41** 58.12N 22.30E
King Leopold Ranges *mts* Australia **88** 17.00S125.30E
Kingman Ariz. U.S.A. **109** 35.12N114.04W
Kingman Kans. U.S.A. **111** 37.39N 98.07W
Kingman Reef Pacific Oc. **84** 6.24N162.22W
Kingoonya Australia **92** 30.54S135.18E
Kingri Pakistan **62** 30.27N 69.49E
Kings *r.* U.S.A. **109** 36.03N119.49W
Kingsbridge U.K. **13** 50.17N 3.46W
Kings Canyon Nat. Park U.S.A. **108** 36.48N118.30W
Kingsclere U.K. **13** 51.20N 1.14W
Kingscote Australia **92** 35.40S137.38E
King Sd. Australia **88** 17.00S123.30E
Kingsdown Kent U.K. **13** 51.21N 0.17E
Kingsley Dam U.S.A. **106** 41.15N101.30W
King's Lynn U.K. **12** 52.45N 0.25E
Kingsmill Group *is.* Kiribati **84** 1.00S175.00E
Kings Peaks *mts.* U.S.A. **108** 40.46N110.23W
Kingsport U.S.A. **113** 36.33N 82.34W
Kingston Australia **92** 36.50S139.50E
Kingston Canada **105** 44.14N 76.30W
Kingston Jamaica **117** 17.58N 76.48W
Kingston New Zealand **86** 45.20S168.43E
Kingston N.H. U.S.A. **115** 42.55N 71.02W
Kingston N.Y. U.S.A. **115** 41.56N 74.00W
Kingston Penn. U.S.A. **115** 41.16N 75.54W
Kingston W.Va. U.S.A. **113** 37.58N 81.19W
Kingston upon Hull U.K. **12** 53.45N 0.20W
Kingstown St. Vincent **117** 13.12N 61.14W
Kingstree U.S.A. **113** 33.40N 79.50W
Kingsville Canada **104** 42.02N 82.45W
Kingsville U.S.A. **111** 27.31N 97.52W
Kingswood Avon U.K. **13** 51.27N 2.29W
Kings Worthy U.K. **13** 51.06N 1.18W
Kington U.K. **13** 52.12N 3.02W
Kingurutik *r.* Canada **103** 56.49N 62.00W
Kingussie U.K. **14** 57.05N 4.04W
King William I. Canada **99** 69.00N 97.30W
King William's Town R.S.A. **80** 32.52S 27.23E
Kingwood U.S.A. **114** 39.28N 79.41W
Kinki *d.* Japan **57** 35.10N135.00E
Kinloch Rannoch U.K. **14** 56.42N 4.11W
Kinmount Canada **104** 44.47N 78.39W
Kinna Sweden **43** 57.30N 12.41E
Kinnairds Head U.K. **14** 57.42N 2.00W
Kinnegad Rep. of Ire. **15** 53.28N 7.08W
Kinnekulle *hill* Sweden **43** 58.35N 13.23E
Kinneret Israel **67** 32.44N 35.34E
Kinneret-Negev Conduit *canal* Israel **67** 32.52N 35.32E
Kino *r.* Japan **57** 34.13N135.09E
Kinross U.K. **14** 56.13N 3.27W
Kinsale Rep. of Ire. **15** 51.42N 8.32W
Kinshasa Zaïre **78** 4.18S 15.18E
Kinsley U.S.A. **111** 37.55N 99.25W
Kintyre *pen.* U.K. **14** 55.35N 5.35W
Kinuso Canada **100** 55.25N115.25W
Kinvara Rep. of Ire. **15** 53.08N 8.56W
Kinyeti *mtn.* Sudan **73** 3.57N 32.54E
Kinzia Zaïre **78** 3.36S 18.26E
Kiosk Canada **104** 46.06N 78.53W
Kiowa Kans. U.S.A. **111** 37.01N 98.29W
Kiowa Okla. U.S.A. **111** 34.43N 95.54W
Kiparissia Greece **35** 37.15N 21.40E
Kiparissiakós Kólpos *g.* Greece **35** 37.14N 21.40E
Kipawa Canada **104** 46.47N 79.00W
Kipawa, Lac *l.* Canada **104** 46.55N 79.00W
Kipawa Prov. Park Canada **104** 47.15N 78.15W
Kipengere Range *mts.* Tanzania **79** 9.15S 34.15E
Kipili Tanzania **79** 7.30S 30.39E

Kipini to **Koslan**

Kipini Kenya **79** 2.31S 40.32E
Kippure *mtn.* Rep. of Ire. **15** 53.11N 6.20W
Kipushi Zaïre **79** 11.46S 27.15E
Kirby U.S.A. **108** 43.49N108.10W
Kirbyville U.S.A. **111** 30.40N 93.54W
Kirchbach in Steiermark Austria **31** 46.54N 15.44E
Kircheim-Bolanden W. Germany **39** 49.40N 8.00E
Kircheimbolanden W. Germany **16** 49.39N 8.00E
Kirchheim W. Germany **39** 48.39N 9.27E
Kirchmöser E. Germany **38** 52.22N 12.25E
Kirensk U.S.S.R. **51** 57.45N108.00E
Kirgiziya Step *f.* U.S.S.R. **45** 50.00N 57.10E
Kirgizskaya S.S.R. *d.* U.S.S.R. **52** 41.30N 75.00E
Kirgiz Steppe *see* Kirgiziya Step U.S.S.R. **45**
Kiri Zaïre **78** 1.23S 19.00E
Kirikkale Turkey **64** 39.51N 33.32E
Kirillov U.S.S.R. **44** 59.53N 38.21E
Kirínia Cyprus **66** 35.20N 33.20E
Kirkby Lonsdale U.K. **12** 54.13N 2.36W
Kirkby Stephen U.K. **12** 54.27N 2.23W
Kirkcaldy U.K. **14** 56.07N 3.10W
Kirkcudbright U.K. **14** 54.50N 4.03W
Kirkenes Norway **40** 69.40N 30.03E
Kirkfield Canada **104** 44.33N 79.00W
Kirkland Ariz. U.S.A. **109** 34.26N112.43W
Kirkland Wash. U.S.A. **108** 47.41N122.12W
Kirkland Lake *town* Canada **102** 48.15N 80.00W
Kirklareli Turkey **29** 41.44N 27.12E
Kirkpatrick, Mt. Antarctica **128** 85.00S170.00E
Kirksville U.S.A. **110** 40.12N 92.35W
Kirkūk Iraq **65** 35.28N 44.26E
Kirkwall U.K. **14** 58.59N 2.58W
Kirkwood R.S.A. **80** 33.25S 25.24E
Kirkwood U.S.A. **110** 38.35N 90.24W
Kirn W. Germany **39** 49.47N 7.28E
Kirov R.S.F.S.R. U.S.S.R. **44** 58.38N 49.38E
Kirov R.S.F.S.R. U.S.S.R. **44** 53.59N 34.20E
Kirovabad U.S.S.R. **65** 40.39N 46.20E
Kirovakan U.S.S.R. **65** 40.49N 44.30E
Kirovo-Chepetsk U.S.S.R. **44** 58.40N 50.02E
Kirovograd U.S.S.R. **45** 48.31N 32.15E
Kirovsk U.S.S.R. **44** 67.37N 33.39E
Kirovskiy U.S.S.R. **57** 45.07N133.30E
Kirriemuir Canada **101** 51.56N110.20W
Kirriemuir U.K. **14** 56.41N 3.01W
Kirs U.S.S.R. **44** 59.21N 52.10E
Kirsanoy U.S.S.R. **45** 51.29N 52.30E
Kirşehir Turkey **23** 39.09N 34.08E
Kirşehir Turkey **64** 39.09N 34.08E
Kīrthar Range *mts.* Pakistan **62** 27.15N 67.00E
Kiruna Sweden **40** 67.51N 20.16E
Kiryu Japan **57** 36.26N139.18E
Kisa Sweden **43** 57.59N 15.37E
Kisaga Tanzania **79** 4.26S 34.26E
Kisangani Zaïre **78** 0.33N 25.14E
Kisantu Zaïre **78** 5.07S 15.05E
Kisaran Indonesia **58** 2.47N 99.29E
Kisarazu Japan **57** 35.23N139.55E
Kiselevsk U.S.S.R. **50** 54.01N 86.41E
Kishanganj India **63** 26.07N 87.56E
Kishangarh Rāj. India **62** 27.52N 70.34E
Kishangarh Rāj. India **62** 26.34N 74.52E
Kishinev U.S.S.R. **37** 47.00N 28.50E
Kishiwada Japan **57** 34.28N135.22E
Kishorganj Bangla. **63** 24.26N 90.46E
Kishtwār Jammu & Kashmir **62** 33.19N 75.46E
Kisii Kenya **79** 0.40S 34.44E
Kisiju Tanzania **79** 7.23S 39.20E
Kiskitto L. Canada **101** 54.16N 98.34W
Kiskörös Hungary **31** 46.38N 19.17E
Kiskunfélegyháza Hungary **31** 46.43N 19.52E
Kiskunhalas Hungary **31** 46.26N 19.30E
Kiskunmajsa Hungary **31** 46.30N 19.45E
Kislovodsk U.S.S.R. **45** 43.56N 42.44E
Kismayu Somali Rep. **79** 0.25S 42.31E
Kiso Japan **57** 35.02N136.45E
Kiso sammyaku *mts.* Japan **57** 35.42N137.50E
Kissamos Greece **35** 35.20N 23.38E
Kissidougou Guinea **76** 9.48N 10.08W
Kissimmee U.S.A. **113** 28.20N 81.24W
Kississing L. Canada **101** 55.10N101.20W
Kissū, Jabal *mtn.* Sudan **72** 21.35N 25.09E
Kistanje Yugo. **31** 43.59N 15.58E
Kistna *r. see* Krishna *r.* India **60**
Kisumu Kenya **79** 0.07S 34.47E
Kisvárda Hungary **37** 48.13N 22.05E
Kita Mali **76** 13.04N 9.29W
Kitab U.S.S.R. **50** 39.08N 66.51E
Kitabu Zaïre **78** 6.31S 26.40E
Kitakyūshū Japan **57** 33.50N130.50E
Kitale Kenya **79** 1.01N 35.01E
Kit Carson U.S.A. **110** 38.46N102.48W
Kitchener Australia **89** 31.01S124.20E
Kitchener Canada **104** 43.27N 80.29W
Kitchigama *r.* Canada **102** 51.12N 78.55W
Kitgum Uganda **79** 3.17N 32.54E
Kíthira Greece **35** 36.09N 23.00E
Kíthira *i.* Greece **35** 36.20N 22.58E
Kíthnos Greece **35** 37.26N 24.26E
Kíthnos *i.* Greece **35** 37.25N 24.28E
Kitimat Canada **100** 54.05N128.38W
Kitinen *r.* Finland **40** 67.20N 27.27E
Kítros Greece **34** 40.22N 22.34E
Kitsman U.S.S.R. **37** 48.30N 25.50E
Kittakittaooloo, L. Australia **92** 28.09S138.09E
Kittanning U.S.A. **114** 40.49N 79.32W
Kittery U.S.A. **115** 43.05N 70.45W
Kittilä Finland **40** 67.40N 24.54E
Kitui Kenya **79** 1.22S 38.01E
Kitunda Tanzania **79** 6.48S 33.17E
Kitwe Zambia **79** 12.50S 28.04E
Kitzbühel Austria **39** 47.27N 12.23E
Kitzingen W. Germany **39** 49.44N 10.09E
Kiumbi Zaïre **78** 5.31S 26.34E
Kiunga Kenya **79** 1.46S 41.30E
Kivijärvi *l.* Finland **40** 63.10N 25.09E
Kivik Sweden **43** 55.41N 14.15E
Kivotós Greece **34** 40.13N 21.26E
Kivu *d.* Zaïre **79** 3.00S 27.00E
Kivu, L. Rwanda / Zaïre **79** 2.00S 29.10E
Kiyev U.S.S.R. **37** 50.28N 30.29E
Kiyevskoye Vodokhranilishche *resr.* U.S.S.R. **37** 51.00N 30.25E
Kizel U.S.S.R. **44** 59.01N 57.42E
Kizema U.S.S.R. **44** 61.12N 44.52E
Kizil *r.* Turkey **64** 41.45N 35.57E
Kizlyar U.S.S.R. **45** 43.51N 46.43E
Kizlyarskiy Zaliv *b.* U.S.S.R. **45** 44.33N 47.00E
Kizu *r.* Japan **57** 34.53N135.42E
Kizyl-Arvat U.S.S.R. **65** 39.00N 56.23E
Kizyl Atrek Turkey **65** 37.37N 54.49E
Kladanj Yugo. **31** 44.13N 18.41E
Kladno Czech. **38** 50.08N 14.05E
Klagenfurt Austria **31** 46.38N 14.18E
Klaipeda U.S.S.R. **41** 55.43N 21.07E
Klakah Indonesia **59** 7.55S113.12E
Klaksvig Faroe Is. **10** 62.13N 6.34W
Klamath *r.* U.S.A. **108** 41.33N124.04W
Klamath Falls *town* U.S.A. **108** 42.14N121.47W
Klamath Mts. U.S.A. **108** 41.40N123.20W
Klamono Indonesia **59** 1.08S131.28E
Klar *r.* Sweden **43** 59.23N 13.32E
Klatovy Czech. **38** 49.24N 13.18E
Klawer R.S.A. **80** 31.48S 18.34E
Klawock U.S.A. **100** 55.33N133.06W
Kleena Kleene Canada **100** 51.58N124.50W
Kleinsee R.S.A. **80** 29.41S 17.04E
Klekovača *mtn.* Yugo. **31** 44.26N 16.31E
Klerksdorp R.S.A. **80** 26.51S 26.38E
Klevan U.S.S.R. **37** 50.44N 25.50E
Kleve W. Germany **38** 51.48N 6.09E
Klickitat U.S.A. **108** 45.49N121.09W
Klimovichi U.S.S.R. **37** 53.36N 31.58E
Klimpfjäll Sweden **40** 65.04N 14.52E
Klin U.S.S.R. **44** 56.20N 36.45E
Klinaklini *r.* Canada **100** 51.21N125.40W
Klingenthal E. Germany **39** 51.21N 12.28E
Klintehamn Sweden **43** 57.24N 18.12E
Klintsy U.S.S.R. **37** 52.45N 32.15E
Klipdale R.S.A. **80** 34.18S 19.58E
Klippan Sweden **43** 56.08N 13.06E
Klipplaat R.S.A. **80** 33.01S 24.19E
Klisura Bulgaria **34** 42.40N 24.28E
Klitmöller Denmark **42** 57.02N 8.31E
Kłobuck Poland **37** 50.55N 18.57E
Klock Canada **104** 46.18N 78.36W
Kłodzko Poland **36** 50.27N 16.39E
Klöfta Norway **42** 60.04N 11.09E
Klondike Canada **98** 64.02N139.24W
Klosters Switz. **39** 46.54N 9.53E
Kloten Switz. **39** 47.27N 8.35E
Klötze E. Germany **38** 52.38N 11.10E
Kluane Nat. Park Canada **100** 60.32N139.40W
Kluczbork Poland **37** 50.59N 18.13E
Klukwan U.S.A. **100** 59.25N135.55W
Klungkung Indonesia **59** 8.32S115.25E
Knäred Sweden **43** 56.32N 13.19E
Knaresborough U.K. **12** 54.01N 1.29W
Knezha Bulgaria **34** 43.30N 23.56E
Knić Yugo. **34** 43.55N 20.43E
Knight Inlet *f.* Canada **100** 50.45N125.40W
Knighton U.K. **13** 52.21N 3.02W
Knin Yugo. **31** 44.02N 16.12E
Knislinge Sweden **43** 56.11N 14.05E
Knivsta Sweden **43** 59.43N 17.48E
Knjaževac Yugo. **34** 43.35N 22.18E
Knobly Mtn. U.S.A. **114** 39.21N 79.32W
Knobs Mtn. U.S.A. **114** 41.12N 78.26W
Knockadoon Head Rep. of Ire. **15** 51.52N 7.52W
Knockalongy *mtn.* Rep. of Ire. **15** 54.12N 8.45W
Knockmealdown Mts. Rep. of Ire. **15** 52.15N 7.55W
Knokke Belgium **16** 51.21N 3.17E
Knolls U.S.A. **108** 40.44N113.18W
Knossos *site* Greece **35** 35.20N 25.10E
Knox U.S.A. **114** 41.14N 79.32W
Knox, C. Canada **100** 54.11N133.04W
Knox City U.S.A. **111** 33.25N 99.49W
Knoxville U.S.A. **113** 36.00N 83.57W
Knutsford U.K. **12** 53.18N 2.22W
Knyazhevo U.S.S.R. **44** 59.40N 43.51E
Knysna R.S.A. **80** 34.02S 23.03E
Koartac Canada **99** 61.05N 69.36W
Kobarid Yugo. **31** 46.15N 13.35E
Kobar Sink *f.* Ethiopia **72** 14.00N 40.30E
Kōbe Japan **57** 34.41N135.10E
København Denmark **43** 55.40N 12.35E
Koblenz W. Germany **39** 50.21N 7.35E
Kobowen Swamp Sudan **73** 5.38N 33.54E
Kobrin U.S.S.R. **37** 52.16N 24.22E
Kobroör *i.* Indonesia **59** 6.10S134.30E
Kočani Yugo. **34** 41.55N 22.25E
Koçarli Turkey **35** 37.45N 27.42E
Kočevje Yugo. **31** 45.38N 14.52E
Kocher *r.* W. Germany **39** 49.14N 9.12E
Kōchi Japan **57** 33.33N133.52E
Kochkoma U.S.S.R. **44** 64.03N 34.14E
Kochmes U.S.S.R. **44** 66.12N 60.48E
Kodaira Japan **57** 35.44N139.29E
Kodari Nepal **63** 27.56N 85.56E
Kodarma India **63** 24.28N 85.36E
Kodiak U.S.A. **98** 57.49N152.30W
Kodiak I. U.S.A. **98** 57.00N153.50W
Kodima U.S.S.R. **44** 62.24N 43.57E
Kodinār India **62** 20.47N 70.42E
Kodok Sudan **73** 9.53N 32.07E
Kodyma U.S.S.R. **37** 48.06N 29.04E
Koekelare Belgium **16** 51.08N 2.59E
Koekenaap R.S.A. **80** 31.30S 18.18E
Koersel Belgium **16** 51.04N 5.19E
Koës Namibia **80** 25.58S 19.07E
Koffiefontein R.S.A. **80** 29.24S 25.00E
Köflach Austria **31** 47.04N 15.05E
Koforidua Ghana **76** 6.01N 0.12W
Kōfu Japan **57** 35.39N138.35E
Koga Tanzania **79** 6.10S 32.21E
Kogaluk *r.* Canada **103** 56.12N 61.45W
Köge Denmark **43** 55.27N 12.11E
Köge Bugt *b.* Denmark **43** 55.30N 12.20E
Köge Bugt *b.* Greenland **99** 65.00N 40.30W
Kohak Pakistan **62** 25.44N 62.33E
Kohāt Pakistan **62** 33.35N 71.26E
Kohīma India **61** 25.40N 94.08E
Kohler Range *mts.* Antarctica **128** 77.00S110.00W
Kohtla-Järve U.S.S.R. **44** 59.28N 27.20E
Koidu Sierra Leone **76** 8.41N 10.55W
Koito *r.* Japan **57** 35.21N139.52E
Kojonup Australia **89** 33.50S117.05E
Kokand U.S.S.R. **52** 40.33N 70.55E
Kökar *i.* Finland **43** 59.56N 20.55E
Kokas Indonesia **59** 2.45S132.26E
Kokchetav U.S.S.R. **9** 53.18N 69.25E
Kokemäki Finland **41** 61.15N 22.21E
Kokka Sudan **72** 20.00N 30.35E
Kokkola Finland **40** 63.50N 23.07E
Koko Sokoto Nigeria **77** 11.27N 4.35E
Kokoda P.N.G. **90** 8.50S147.45E
Kokomo U.S.A. **112** 40.30N 86.09W
Kokonau Indonesia **59** 4.42S136.25E
Kokpekty U.S.S.R. **52** 48.45N 82.25E
Koksoak *r.* Canada **99** 58.30N 68.15W
Kokstad R.S.A. **80** 30.32S 29.25E
Kokuora U.S.S.R. **51** 71.33N144.50E
Kolāchi *r.* Pakistan **62** 26.25N 67.50E
Kolahun Liberia **76** 8.24N 10.02W
Kolaka Indonesia **59** 4.04S121.38E
Kolan Australia **90** 24.42S152.10E
Kola Pen. *see* Kolskiy Poluostrov U.S.S.R. **44**
Kolār India **61** 13.10N 78.10E
Kolāras India **63** 25.14N 77.36E
Kolari Finland **40** 67.20N 23.48E
Kolašin Yugo. **31** 42.49N 19.31E
Kolāyat India **62** 27.50N 72.57E
Kolbäck Sweden **43** 59.34N 16.15E
Kolbio Kenya **79** 1.11S 41.10E
Kolbotn Norway **42** 59.49N 10.48E
Kolda Senegal **76** 12.56N 14.55W
Kolding Denmark **42** 55.31N 9.29E
Kole H.Zaïre Zaïre **78** 2.07N 25.26E
Kole K.Oriental Zaïre **78** 3.28S 22.29E
Kolepom *i. see* Yos Sudarsa, Pulau Indonesia **59**
Kolguyev, Ostrov *i.* U.S.S.R. **44** 69.00N 49.00E
Kolhāpur India **60** 16.43N 74.15E
Kolia Ivory Coast **76** 9.46N 6.28W
Kolín Czech. **36** 50.02N 15.10E
Kolka U.S.S.R. **41** 57.45N 22.35E
Kolki U.S.S.R. **37** 51.09N 25.40E
Kolmården Sweden **43** 58.41N 16.45E
Köln W. Germany **38** 50.56N 6.59E
Kolno Poland **37** 53.25N 21.56E
Koło Poland **37** 52.12N 18.37E
Kołobrzeg Poland **36** 54.10N 15.35E
Kologriv U.S.S.R. **44** 58.49N 44.19E
Kolokani Mali **76** 13.35N 7.45W
Kololo Ethiopia **73** 7.29N 41.58E
Kolomna U.S.S.R. **44** 55.05N 38.45E
Kolomyya U.S.S.R. **37** 48.31N 25.00E
Kolondiéba Mali **76** 11.05N 6.54W
Kolosib India **63** 24.14N 92.42E
Kolpashevo U.S.S.R. **50** 58.21N 82.59E
Kolpino U.S.S.R. **44** 59.44N 30.39E
Kolskiy Poluostrov *pen.* U.S.S.R. **44** 67.00N 38.00E
Kolsva Sweden **43** 59.36N 15.50E
Kolubara *r.* Yugo. **31** 44.40N 20.15E
Koluszki Poland **37** 51.44N 19.49E
Kolvereid Norway **40** 64.53N 11.35E
Kolwezi Zaïre **78** 10.44S 25.28E
Kolyma *r.* U.S.S.R. **51** 68.50N161.00E
Kolymskiy, Khrebet *mts* U.S.S.R. **51** 63.00N160.00E
Kom *r.* Cameroon **78** 2.20N 10.38E
Kom Kenya **79** 1.06N 38.00E
Komadugu Gana *r.* Nigeria **77** 13.06N 12.23E
Komadugu Yobe *r.* Niger / Nigeria **77** 13.43N 13.19E
Komagane Japan **57** 35.43N137.55E
Komaga-take *mtn.* Japan **57** 35.47N137.48E
Komaki Japan **57** 35.17N136.55E
Komandorskiye Ostrova *is.* U.S.S.R. **84** 55.00N167.00E
Komárno Czech. **37** 47.45N 18.09E
Komarom Hungary **37** 47.44N 18.08E
Komatipoort R.S.A. **81** 25.25S 31.55E
Komatsu Japan **57** 36.24N136.27E
Komba Zaïre **78** 2.52N 24.03E
Komló Hungary **31** 46.12N 18.16E
Kommunarsk U.S.S.R. **23** 48.30N 38.47E
Kommunizma, Pik *mtn.* U.S.S.R. **52** 38.39N 72.01E
Komotiní Greece **34** 41.08N 25.25E
Komrat U.S.S.R. **37** 46.18N 28.40E
Komsberg *mtn.* R.S.A. **80** 32.40S 20.48E
Komsomolets, Ostrov *i.* U.S.S.R. **51** 80.20N 96.00E
Komsomolets, Zaliv *g.* U.S.S.R. **45** 45.17N 53.30E
Komsomolsk-na-Amure U.S.S.R. **51** 50.32N136.59E
Kōnan Japan **57** 35.20N136.53E
Konar *r.* Afghan. **62** 34.26N 70.32E
Konārak India **63** 19.54N 86.07E
Konar-e Khās Afghan. **62** 34.39N 70.54E
Konch India **63** 25.59N 79.09E
Kondagaon India **63** 19.36N 81.40E
Kondakovo U.S.S.R. **51** 69.38N152.00E
Kondinin Australia **89** 32.33S118.13E
Kondoa Tanzania **79** 4.54S 35.49E
Kondopoga U.S.S.R. **44** 62.12N 34.17E
Kondratyevo U.S.S.R. **51** 57.22N 98.15E
Kondut Australia **89** 30.44S117.06E
Koné N. Cal. **84** 21.04S164.52E
Konevo U.S.S.R. **9** 62.09N 39.22E
Kong Ivory Coast **76** 8.54N 4.36W
Kŏng *r.* Kampuchea **56** 13.32N105.57E
Kong Christian den IX Land *f.* Greenland **99** 68.20N 37.00W
Kong Christian den X Land *f.* Greenland **96** 73.00N 26.00W
Kong Frederik den VIII Land *f.* Greenland **96** 77.30N 25.00W
Kong Frederik den VI Kyst *f.* Greenland **99** 63.00N 44.00W
Kong Haakon VII Hav *sea* Antarctica **128** 65.00S 25.00E
Kongolo Zaïre **79** 5.20S 27.00E
Kongor Sudan **73** 7.10N 31.21E
Kongsberg Norway **42** 59.39N 9.39E
Kongsvinger Norway **43** 60.12N 12.00E
Kongur Shan *mtn.* China **52** 38.40N 75.30E
Kongwa Tanzania **79** 6.13S 36.28E
Königsmoor *f.* W. Germany **38** 53.15N 9.57E
Königs Wusterhausen E. Germany **38** 52.18N 13.37E
Konin Poland **37** 52.13N 18.16E
Kónitsa Greece **34** 40.02N 20.45E
Konjic Yugo. **31** 43.39N 17.57E
Könkämä *r.* Sweden / Finland **40** 68.29N 22.30E
Konkouré *r.* Guinea **76** 9.55N 13.45W
Konongo Ghana **76** 6.38N 1.12W
Konosha U.S.S.R. **44** 60.58N 40.08E
Kōnosu Japan **57** 36.03N139.31E
Konotop U.S.S.R. **45** 51.15N 33.14E
Końskie Poland **37** 51.12N 20.26E
Konstanz W. Germany **39** 47.40N 9.10E
Kontagora Nigeria **77** 10.24N 5.22E
Kontcha Cameroon **77** 7.59N 12.15E
Kontiomäki Finland **44** 64.21N 28.10E
Kontum Vietnam **56** 14.23N108.00E
Kontum, Plateau du *f.* Vietnam **56** 14.00N108.00E
Konya Turkey **64** 37.51N 32.30E
Konz W. Germany **39** 49.42N 6.34E
Konza Kenya **79** 1.45S 37.07E
Kookynie Australia **89** 29.20S121.29E
Koolatah Australia **90** 15.53S142.27E
Koolkootinnie L. Australia **92** 27.58S137.47E
Koolyanobbing Australia **89** 30.48S119.29E
Koondrook Australia **92** 35.39S144.11E
Koongawa Australia **92** 33.11S135.52E
Koonibba Australia **92** 31.58S133.29E
Koorawatha Australia **93** 34.02S148.33E
Koorda Australia **89** 30.50S117.51E
Kootenay L. Canada **100** 49.45N117.00W
Kootenay Nat. Park Canada **100** 51.00N116.00W
Kootjieskolk R.S.A. **80** 31.14S 20.18E
Kopāganj India **63** 26.01N 83.34E
Kopargaon India **62** 19.53N 74.29E
Kópavogur Iceland **40** 64.06N 21.53W
Koper Yugo. **31** 45.33N 13.44E
Kopervik Norway **42** 59.17N 5.18E
Kopet Dag, Khrebet *mts.* U.S.S.R. **65** 38.00N 58.00E
Kopeysk U.S.S.R. **9** 55.07N 61.37E
Köping Sweden **41** 59.31N 16.00E
Koplik Albania **34** 42.13N 19.26E
Koppány Hungary **31** 46.35N 18.26E
Kopparberg *d.* Sweden **41** 60.50N 15.00E
Koppom Sweden **43** 59.43N 12.09E
Koprivnica Yugo. **31** 46.10N 16.50E
Kopychintsy U.S.S.R. **37** 49.10N 25.58E
Kor *r.* Iran **65** 29.40N 53.17E
Koralpe *mts.* Austria **31** 46.40N 15.00E
Koraput India **63** 18.49N 82.43E
Koratla India **63** 18.49N 78.43E
Korba India **63** 22.21N 82.41E
Korbach W. Germany **38** 51.16N 8.52E
Korbous Tunisia **32** 36.49N 10.35E
Korçë Albania **34** 40.37N 20.50E
Korçë *d.* Albania **34** 40.40N 20.50E
Korčula Yugo. **31** 42.58N 17.08E
Korčula *i.* Yugo. **31** 42.57N 16.50E
Korčulanski Kanal *str.* Yugo. **31** 43.03N 16.40E
Kord Kūy Iran **65** 36.48N 54.07E
Korea Str. S. Korea / Japan **53** 35.00N129.20E
Korem Ethiopia **73** 12.30N 39.30E
Korets U.S.S.R. **37** 50.39N 27.10E
Korhogo Ivory Coast **76** 9.22N 5.31W
Korim Indonesia **59** 0.58S136.10E
Korinthiakós Kólpos *g.* Greece **35** 38.16N 22.30E
Kórinthos Greece **35** 37.56N 22.56E
Korinthou, Dhiórix *canal* Greece **35** 37.57N 22.56E
Kōriyama Japan **57** 37.23N140.22E
Korma U.S.S.R. **37** 53.08N 30.47E
Körmend Hungary **31** 47.01N 16.37E
Kornat *i.* Yugo. **31** 43.50N 15.16E
Korneshty U.S.S.R. **37** 47.21N 28.00E
Kornsjö Norway **42** 58.57N 11.39E
Koro *i.* Fiji **84** 17.22S179.25E
Koro Ivory Coast **76** 8.36N 7.28W
Koro Mali **76** 14.01N 2.58W
Korocha U.S.S.R. **45** 50.50N 37.13E
Korogwe Tanzania **79** 5.10S 38.35E
Koroit Australia **92** 38.17S142.26E
Korong Vale *town* Australia **92** 36.22S143.45E
Koróni Greece **35** 36.48N 21.56E
Koronia, Límni *l.* Greece **34** 40.41N 23.05E
Koropíon Greece **35** 37.54N 23.53E
Koror *i.* Belau **59** 7.30N134.30E
Koro Sea Fiji **84** 18.00S179.00E
Korosten U.S.S.R. **37** 51.00N 28.30E
Korostyshev U.S.S.R. **37** 50.19N 29.03E
Koro Toro Chad **77** 16.05N 18.30E
Korrat *i.* Yugo. **36** 43.48N 15.20E
Korsör Denmark **42** 55.20N 11.09E
Korsze Poland **37** 54.10N 21.09E
Kortrijk Belgium **16** 50.49N 3.17E
Koryakskiy Khrebet *mts.* U.S.S.R. **51** 62.20N171.00E
Koryazhma U.S.S.R. **44** 61.19N 47.12E
Kos Greece **35** 36.53N 27.18E
Kos *i.* Greece **35** 36.50N 27.10E
Kosa Ethiopia **73** 7.51N 36.51E
Kościan Poland **36** 52.06N 16.38E
Kościerzyna Poland **37** 54.08N 18.00E
Kosciusko U.S.A. **111** 32.58N 89.35W
Kosciusko, Mt. Australia **93** 36.28S148.17E
Kosha Sudan **72** 20.49N 30.32E
Koshikijima rettō *is.* Japan **57** 31.45N129.49E
Koshk-e Kohneh Afghan **65** 34.52N 62.29E
Košice Czech. **37** 48.44N 21.15E
Koski Finland **41** 60.39N 23.09E
Koslan U.S.S.R. **44** 63.29N 48.59E

Kosovska-Mitrovica to La Baleine

Kosovska-Mitrovica Yugo. 34 42.54N 20.52E
Kossanto Senegal 76 13.12N 11.56W
Kossovo U.S.S.R. 37 52.40N 25.18E
Kosta Sweden 43 56.51N 15.23E
Kostajnica Yugo. 31 45.14N 16.33E
Koster R.S.A. 80 25.51S 26.52E
Kostopol U.S.S.R. 37 50.51N 26.22E
Kostroma U.S.S.R. 44 57.46N 40.59E
Kostrzyn Poland 36 52.24N 17.11E
Kostyukovichi U.S.S.R. 37 53.20N 32.01E
Kosyu U.S.S.R. 44 65.36N 59.00E
Koszalin Poland 36 54.12N 16.09E
Kota Madhya P. India 63 22.18N 82.02E
Kota Rāj. India 62 25.11N 75.50E
Kota Baharu Malaysia 58 6.07N102.15E
Kota Belud Malaysia 58 6.00N116.00E
Kotabumi Indonesia 58 4.52S104.59E
Kot Addu Pakistan 62 30.28N 70.58E
Kota Kinabalu Malaysia 58 5.59N116.04E
Kotari mts. Yugo. 31 44.05N 15.17E
Kotelnich U.S.S.R. 44 58.20N 48.10E
Kotelnikovo U.S.S.R. 45 47.39N 43.08E
Kotel'nyy, Ostrov i. U.S.S.R. 51 75.30N141.00E
Köthen E. Germany 38 51.45N 11.58E
Kotka Finland 44 60.26N 26.55E
Kot Kapūra India 62 30.35N 74.49E
Kotlas U.S.S.R. 44 61.15N 46.28E
Kotli Jammu & Kashmir 62 33.31N 73.55E
Kotlik U.S.A. 98 63.02N163.33W
Kotor Yugo. 31 42.25N 18.46E
Kotoriba Yugo. 31 46.21N 16.49E
Kotor Varoš Yugo. 31 44.37N 17.23E
Kotovsk M.S.S.R. U.S.S.R. 37 46.50N 28.31E
Kotovsk Ukr.S.S.R. U.S.S.R. 37 47.42N 29.30E
Kot Pūtli India 62 27.43N 76.12E
Kotra India 62 24.22N 73.10E
Kotri Pakistan 62 25.22N 68.18E
Kotri Allāhrakhio Pakistan 62 24.24N 67.50E
Kötschach Austria 39 46.40N 13.00E
Kottagūdem India 61 17.32N 80.39E
Kotto r. C.A.R. 73 4.14N 22.02E
Kotuy r. U.S.S.R. 51 71.40N103.00E
Kotzebue U.S.A. 98 66.51N162.40W
Kotzebue Sd. U.S.A. 98 66.20N163.00W
Kötzting W. Germany 39 49.11N 12.52E
Kouango C.A.R. 73 4.58N 20.00E
Koudougou U. Volta 76 12.15N 2.21W
Kouibli Ivory Coast 76 7.09N 7.16W
Kouki C.A.R. 77 7.09N 17.13E
Koúklia Cyprus 66 34.42N 32.34E
Koula Moutou Gabon 78 1.12S 12.29E
Koulikoro Mali 76 12.55N 7.31W
Koumac N. Cal. 84 20.33S164.17E
Koumankou Mali 76 11.58N 6.06W
Koumbal C.A.R. 73 9.26N 22.39E
Koumbia Guinea 76 11.54N 13.40W
Koumbia U. Volta 76 11.18N 3.38W
Koumbisaleh site Mauritania 74 15.55N 8.05W
Koumongou Togo 76 10.10N 0.29E
Koumra Chad 77 8.56N 17.32E
Koupéla U. Volta 76 12.09N 0.22W
Kouroussa Guinea 76 10.40N 9.50W
Kousseri Chad 77 12.05N 14.56E
Koutiala Mali 76 12.20N 5.23W
Kouto Ivory Coast 76 9.53N 6.25W
Kouvola Finland 44 60.54N 26.45E
Kouyou r. Congo 78 0.40S 16.37E
Kovdor U.S.S.R. 44 67.33N 30.30E
Kovel U.S.S.R. 37 51.12N 24.48E
Kovpyta U.S.S.R. 37 51.22N 30.51E
Kovrov U.S.S.R. 44 56.23N 41.21E
Kovzha r. U.S.S.R. 44 61.05N 36.27E
Kowloon Hong Kong 55 22.19N114.12E
Kowt-e 'Ashrow Afghan. 62 34.27N 68.48E
Koyukuk r. U.S.A. 98 64.50N157.30W
Kozan Turkey 64 37.27N 35.47E
Kozáni Greece 34 40.19N 21.47E
Kozara mts. Yugo. 31 45.05N 16.50E
Kozarac Yugo. 31 44.58N 16.51E
Kozelets U.S.S.R. 37 50.54N 31.09E
Kozhim U.S.S.R. 44 65.45N 59.30E
Kozhposelok U.S.S.R. 44 63.10N 38.10E
Kpandu Ghana 76 7.02N 0.17E
Kpessi Togo 77 8.07N 1.17E
Krabi Thailand 56 8.08N 98.52E
Krâchéh Kampuchea 56 12.30N106.00E
Kragan Indonesia 59 6.40S111.33E
Kragerö Norway 42 58.52N 9.25E
Kragujevac Yugo. 29 44.01N 20.55E
Kraków Poland 37 50.03N 19.55E
Kraljevica Yugo. 31 45.16N 14.34E
Kraljevo Yugo. 34 43.43N 20.41E
Kralovice Czech. 38 49.59N 13.29E
Kralupy nad Vltavou Czech. 38 50.11N 14.18E
Kramatorsk U.S.S.R. 45 48.43N 37.33E
Kramer U.S.A. 110 48.20N100.42W
Kramfors Sweden 40 62.55N 17.50E
Kranídhion Greece 35 37.22N 23.10E
Kranj Yugo. 31 46.15N 14.21E
Kranskop R.S.A. 80 28.58S 30.52E
Krapina Yugo. 31 46.10N 15.52E
Krapkowice Poland 37 50.29N 17.56E
Krasavino U.S.S.R. 44 60.58N 46.25E
Krasilov U.S.S.R. 37 49.39N 26.59E
Kraskino U.S.S.R. 53 42.42N130.48E
Krasnaya Gora U.S.S.R. 37 53.00N 31.36E
Kraśnik Poland 37 50.56N 22.13E
Krasnodar U.S.S.R. 45 45.02N 39.00E
Krasnograd U.S.S.R. 45 49.22N 35.28E
Krasnokamsk U.S.S.R. 44 58.05N 55.49E
Krasnoperekopsk U.S.S.R. 45 45.56N 33.47E
Krasnoselkup U.S.S.R. 50 65.45N 82.31E
Krasnoturinsk U.S.S.R. 44 59.46N 60.10E
Krasnoufimsk U.S.S.R. 44 56.40N 57.49E
Krasnouralsk U.S.S.R. 50 58.25N 60.00E
Krasnovishersk U.S.S.R. 44 60.25N 57.02E
Krasnovodsk U.S.S.R. 65 40.01N 53.00E
Krasnovodskiy Poluostrov pen. U.S.S.R. 65 40.30N 53.10E
Krasnovodskiy Zaliv g. U.S.S.R. 65 39.50N 53.15E
Krasnoyarsk U.S.S.R. 51 56.05N 92.46E
Krasnyy Yar U.S.S.R. 45 46.32N 48.21E
Kratovo Yugo. 34 42.06N 22.10E
Krawang Indonesia 59 6.15S107.15E
Krefeld W. Germany 38 51.20N 6.34E
Kremastón, Tekhnití Límni l. Greece 35 38.52N 21.30E
Kremenchug U.S.S.R. 45 49.03N 33.25E
Kremenchugskoye Vodokhranilishche resr. U.S.S.R. 45 49.20N 32.30E
Kremenets U.S.S.R. 37 50.05N 25.48E
Kremmling U.S.A. 108 40.03N106.24W
Krems Austria 36 48.25N 15.36E
Krestovka U.S.S.R. 44 66.24N 52.31E
Kretinga U.S.S.R. 41 55.53N 21.13E
Kría Vrísi Greece 34 40.41N 22.18E
Kribi Cameroon 77 2.56N 9.56E
Krichev U.S.S.R. 37 53.40N 31.44E
Krichim Bulgaria 34 42.08N 24.32E
Kriens Switz. 39 47.02N 8.17E
Krimml Austria 39 47.13N 12.11E
Krionéri Greece 35 38.20N 21.35E
Krishna r. India 61 16.00N 81.00E
Krishnanagar India 63 23.24N 88.30E
Kristdala Sweden 43 57.24N 16.11E
Kristianopel Sweden 43 56.15N 16.02E
Kristiansand Norway 42 58.10N 8.00E
Kristianstad Sweden 43 56.02N 14.08E
Kristianstad d. Sweden 43 56.10N 13.40E
Kristiansund Norway 40 63.07N 7.45E
Kristiinankaupunki Finland 41 62.17N 21.23E
Kristinehamn Sweden 43 59.20N 14.07E
Kristinestad see Kristiinankaupunki Finland 41
Kristinovka U.S.S.R. 37 48.50N 29.58E
Kríti i. Greece 35 35.29N 24.42E
Kritikón Pélagos sea Greece 35 35.46N 23.54E
Kriva r. Yugo. 34 42.12N 22.18E
Krivaja r. Yugo. 31 44.27N 18.09E
Kriva Palanka Yugo. 34 42.12N 22.20E
Krivodol Bulgaria 34 43.23N 23.29E
Krivoy Rog U.S.S.R. 45 47.55N 33.24E
Križevci Yugo. 31 46.02N 16.33E
Krk i. Yugo. 31 45.05N 14.35E
Krnov Czech. 37 50.05N 17.41E
Kröderen l. Norway 42 60.15N 9.38E
Krokek Sweden 43 58.40N 16.24E
Kroken Norway 40 65.23N 14.15E
Krokom Sweden 40 63.20N 14.30E
Krokowa Poland 43 54.48N 18.11E
Kronach W. Germany 38 50.14N 11.20E
Króng Kaôh Kông Kampuchea 56 11.37N102.59E
Kronoberg d. Sweden 43 56.40N 14.35E
Kronprins Olav Kyst f. Antarctica 128 69.00S 42.00E
Kronshtadt U.S.S.R. 44 60.00N 29.40E
Kroonstad R.S.A. 80 27.38S 27.12E
Kropotkin U.S.S.R. 45 45.25N 40.35E
Kropperfjäll hill Sweden 43 58.40N 12.13E
Krosno Poland 37 49.42N 21.46E
Krotoszyn Poland 37 51.42N 17.26E
Kroya Indonesia 59 7.37S109.13E
Krško Yugo. 31 45.58N 15.29E
Kruger Nat. Park R.S.A. 81 24.10S 31.36E
Krugersdorp R.S.A. 80 26.06S 27.46E
Krujë Albania 34 41.30N 19.48E
Krumbach W. Germany 39 48.14N 10.22E
Krumovgrad Bulgaria 34 41.29N 25.38E
Krung Thep Thailand 56 13.44N100.30E
Krupki U.S.S.R. 37 54.19N 29.05E
Kruševac Yugo. 34 43.35N 21.20E
Kruševo Yugo. 34 41.23N 21.19E
Krušnéhory mts. see Erzgebirge Czech. 38
Krylbo Sweden 43 60.08N 16.13E
Krym pen. U.S.S.R. 45 45.30N 34.00E
Krymsk U.S.S.R. 45 44.56N 38.00E
Krzyz Poland 36 52.54N 16.01E
Ksar el Boukhari Algeria 75 35.53N 2.45E
Ksar-el-Kebir Morocco 74 35.01N 5.54W
Ksar Rhilane Tunisia 75 33.00N 9.38E
Ksel, Djebel mtn. Algeria 75 33.44N 1.10E
Kuala Dungun Malaysia 58 4.47N103.26E
Kualakapuas Indonesia 58 3.01S114.21E
Kuala Lipis Malaysia 58 4.11N102.00E
Kuala Lumpur Malaysia 58 3.08N101.42E
Kuala Trengganu Malaysia 58 5.10N103.10E
Kuancheng China 54 40.36N118.27E
Kuandang Indonesia 59 0.53N122.58E
Kuandian China 54 40.47N124.43E
Kuantan Malaysia 58 3.50N103.19E
Kuba U.S.S.R. 65 41.23N 48.33E
Kuban r. U.S.S.R. 45 45.20N 37.17E
Kubbum Sudan 73 11.47N 23.47E
Kubrat Bulgaria 34 43.49N 26.31E
Kuchaiburi India 63 22.16N 86.10E
Kuchāman India 62 27.09N 74.52E
Kuching Malaysia 58 1.32N110.20E
Kuchinoerabu jima i. Japan 57 30.30N130.20E
Küchnay Darvishān Afghan. 62 30.59N 64.11E
Küçükbahce Turkey 35 38.33N 26.24E
Kūd Jammu & Kashmir 62 33.05N 75.17E
Kudat Malaysia 58 6.45N116.47E
Kudus Indonesia 59 6.46S110.48E
Kufrinjah Jordan 67 32.18N 35.42E
Kufrinjah, Wādī Jordan 67 32.16N 35.33E
Kufstein Austria 39 47.35N 12.10E
Kūhpāyeh Iran 65 32.42N 52.25E
Kūhrān, Kūh-e mtn. Iran 65 26.46N 58.15E
Kuito Angola 78 12.25S 16.58E
Kuiu I. U.S.A. 100 56.40N134.00W
Kuivaniemi Finland 40 65.35N 25.11E
Kujū san mtn. Japan 57 33.08N131.10E
Kuke Botswana 80 23.19S 24.29E
Kukerin Australia 89 33.11S118.03E
Kukës Albania 34 42.05N 20.20E
Kukshi India 62 22.12N 74.45E
Kūl r. Iran 65 28.00N 55.45E
Kula Bulgaria 34 43.52N 22.36E
Kula Turkey 64 38.33N 28.38E
Kula Yugo. 31 45.36N 19.32E
Kulāchi Pakistan 62 31.56N 70.27E
Kulakshi U.S.S.R. 45 47.09N 55.22E
Kulal, Mt. Kenya 79 2.44N 36.56E
Kulaura Bangla. 63 24.30N 92.03E
Kuldīga U.S.S.R. 41 56.58N 21.59E
Kulen Vakuf Yugo. 31 44.34N 16.06E
Kulgera Australia 90 25.50S133.18E
Kulin Australia 89 32.40S118.10E
Kulja Australia 89 30.28S117.17E
Kulkyne r. Australia 93 30.16S144.12E
Kulmbach W. Germany 38 50.06N 11.27E
Kulpara Australia 92 34.07S137.59E
Kulsary U.S.S.R. 45 46.59N 54.02E
Kulu India 62 31.58N 77.07E
Kulu Turkey 45 39.06N 33.02E
Kulunda U.S.S.R. 50 52.34N 78.58E
Kulwin Australia 92 35.02S142.40E
Kulyab U.S.S.R. 52 37.55N 69.47E
Kuma r. U.S.S.R. 45 44.40N 46.55E
Kumagaya Japan 57 36.08N139.23E
Kumai Indonesia 58 2.45S111.44E
Kumamoto Japan 57 32.50N130.42E
Kumanovo Yugo. 34 42.08N 21.43E
Kumara New Zealand 86 42.38S171.11E
Kumarl Australia 89 32.47S121.33E
Kumasi Ghana 76 6.45N 1.35W
Kumba Cameroon 77 4.39N 9.26E
Kumbakonam India 61 10.59N 79.24E
Kum Dag U.S.S.R. 65 39.14N 54.33E
Kumdah Saudi Arabia 71 20.23N 45.05E
Kumertau U.S.S.R. 44 52.48N 55.46E
Kumi Uganda 79 1.26N 33.54E
Kumla Sweden 43 59.08N 15.08E
Kummerower See l. E. Germany 38 53.49N 12.52E
Kumon Range mts. Burma 56 26.30N 97.15E
Kunashir i. U.S.S.R. 53 44.25N146.00E
Kunchha Nepal 63 28.08N 84.22E
Kundam India 63 23.13N 80.21E
Kundelungu Mts. Zaïre 79 9.30S 27.50E
Kundiān Pakistan 62 32.27N 71.28E
Kundip Australia 89 33.44S120.11E
Kundla India 62 21.20N 71.18E
Kungälv Sweden 42 57.52N 11.58E
Kungsbacka Sweden 43 57.29N 12.04E
Kungshamn Sweden 42 58.22N 11.15E
Kungsör Sweden 43 59.25N 16.05E
Kungu Zaïre 78 2.47N 19.12E
Kungur U.S.S.R. 44 57.27N 56.50E
Kuningan Indonesia 59 7.02S108.30E
Kunkuri India 63 22.45N 83.57E
Kunlong Burma 56 23.25N 98.39E
Kunlun Shan mts. China 52 36.40N 88.00E
Kunming China 52 25.04N102.41E
Kunö i. Faroe Is. 10 62.20N 6.39W
Kunsan S. Korea 53 35.57N126.42E
Kunshan China 55 31.24N121.08E
Kunszentmárton Hungary 31 46.51N 20.18E
Kuntair Gambia 76 13.36N 16.20W
Kununoppin Australia 89 31.09S117.53E
Kununurra Australia 87 15.42S128.50E
Künzelsau W. Germany 39 49.16N 9.41E
Kuolayarvi U.S.S.R. 40 66.58N 29.12E
Kuopio Finland 44 62.51N 27.30E
Kupa r. Yugo. 31 45.28N 16.24E
Kupang Indonesia 59 10.13S123.38E
Küplü Turkey 34 41.07N 26.21E
Kupreanof I. U.S.A. 100 56.50N133.30W
Kupres Yugo. 31 44.00N 17.17E
Kupyansk U.S.S.R. 45 49.41N 37.37E
Kuqa China 52 41.43N 82.58E
Kura r. U.S.S.R. 65 39.18N 49.22E
Kurashiki Japan 57 34.36N133.43E
Kuraymah Sudan 72 18.33N 31.51E
Kurayyimah Jordan 67 32.16N 35.36E
Kurchum U.S.S.R. 52 48.35N 83.39E
Kurdistan f. Asia 65 37.00N 43.30E
Kurdufān d. Sudan 73 13.00N 29.00E
Kŭrdzhali Bulgaria 34 41.39N 25.22E
Kŭrdzhali d. Bulgaria 34 41.38N 25.21E
Kure Japan 57 34.20N132.40E
Kurgaldzhino U.S.S.R. 50 50.35N 70.03E
Kurgan U.S.S.R. 9 55.30N 65.20E
Kurigrām Bangla. 63 25.49N 89.39E
Kurikka Finland 40 62.37N 22.25E
Kuril Ridge Pacific Oc. 84 46.10N152.30E
Kurilskiye Ostrova is. U.S.S.R. 53 46.00N150.30E
Kuril Trench Pacific Oc. 84 46.00N155.00E
Kuring Kuru Namibia 80 17.36S 18.36E
Kurlovski U.S.S.R. 44 55.26N 40.40E
Kurmuk Sudan 73 10.33N 34.17E
Kurnalpi Australia 89 30.35S121.50E
Kurnool India 61 15.51N 78.01E
Kurow New Zealand 86 44.44S170.28E
Kurram Pakistan 62 30.06N 66.31E
Kurri Kurri Australia 93 32.49S151.29E
Kurseong India 63 26.53N 88.17E
Kursk U.S.S.R. 45 51.45N 36.14E
Kurškiy Zaliv b. U.S.S.R. 41 55.00N 21.00E
Kuršumlija Yugo. 34 43.09N 21.19E
Kūrtī Sudan 72 18.07N 31.33E
Kuru Finland 41 61.52N 23.44E
Kuru Sudan 73 7.43N 26.31E
Kuruman R.S.A. 80 27.28S 23.25E
Kuruman r. R.S.A. 80 26.53S 20.38E
Kurume Japan 57 33.20N130.29E
Kurur, Jabal mtn. Sudan 72 20.31N 31.32E
Kuşadasi Turkey 35 37.51N 27.15E
Kusadasi Körfezi b. Greece 35 37.50N 27.08E
Kusatsu Japan 57 35.02N135.57E
Kusel W. Germany 39 49.32N 7.24E
Kushālgarh India 62 23.10N 74.27E
Kushchevskaya U.S.S.R. 45 46.34N 39.39E
Kushida r. Japan 57 34.36N136.34E
Kushiro Japan 57 42.58N144.24E
Kushka U.S.S.R. 65 35.14N 62.15E
Kushtia Bangla. 63 23.55N 89.07E
Kusiyāra r. Bangla. 63 24.36N 91.44E
Kuskokwim B. U.S.A. 98 59.45N162.25W
Kuskokwim Mts. U.S.A. 98 62.50N156.00W
Kusma Nepal 63 28.13N 83.41E
Kussharo ko l. Japan 57 43.40N144.20E
Küssnacht Switz. 39 47.05N 8.27E
Kustanay U.S.S.R. 48 53.15N 63.40E
Küstenkanal W. Germany 38 53.08N 8.00E
Kūstī Sudan 73 13.10N 32.40E
Kütahya Turkey 64 39.25N 29.56E
Kutaisi U.S.S.R. 45 42.15N 42.44E
Kutch, G. of India 62 22.40N 69.30E
Kutina Yugo. 31 45.29N 16.46E
Kutiyāna India 62 21.38N 69.59E
Kutná Hora Czech. 36 49.57N 15.16E
Kutno Poland 37 52.15N 19.23E
Kutu Zaïre 78 2.42S 18.09E
Kutubdia I. Bangla. 63 21.50N 91.52E
Kutum Sudan 72 14.12N 24.40E
Kutztown U.S.A. 115 40.31N 75.47W
Kuusamo Finland 44 65.57N 29.15E
Kuwait Asia 65 29.20N 47.40E
Kuwait town see Al Kuwayt Kuwait 65
Kuwana Japan 57 35.04N136.42E
Kuybyshev U.S.S.R. 44 53.10N 50.15E
Kuybyshevskoye Vodokhranilishche resr. U.S.S.R. 44 55.00N 49.00E
Kuyeda U.S.S.R. 44 56.25N 55.33E
Kuzey Anadolu Dağlari mts. Turkey 64 40.32N 38.00E
Kuznetsk U.S.S.R. 44 53.08N 46.36E
Kuzomen U.S.S.R. 44 66.15N 36.51E
Kuzreka U.S.S.R. 44 66.35N 34.48E
Kvaenangen est. Norway 40 69.50N 21.30E
Kvarner g. Yugo. 31 45.00N 14.10E
Kvarnerić str. Yugo. 31 44.45N 14.35E
Kvenna r. Norway 42 60.01N 7.56E
Kvina r. Norway 42 58.17N 6.56E
Kwale Kenya 79 4.20S 39.25E
Kwamouth Zaïre 78 3.11S 16.16E
Kwangju S. Korea 53 35.07N126.52E
Kwango r. Zaïre 78 3.20S 17.23E
Kwara d. Nigeria 77 8.20N 5.35E
Kwatisore Indonesia 59 3.18S134.50E
Kwekwe Zimbabwe 80 18.59S 29.46E
Kwenge r. Zaïre 78 4.53S 18.47E
Kwethluk U.S.A. 98 60.49N161.27W
Kwidzyn Poland 37 53.45N 18.56E
Kwigillingok U.S.A. 98 59.51N163.08W
Kwiguk U.S.A. 98 62.45N164.28W
Kwilu r. Zaïre 78 3.18S 17.22E
Kwinana Australia 89 32.15S115.48E
Kwobrup Australia 89 33.36S117.55E
Kwoka mtn. Indonesia 59 1.30S132.30E
Kyabé Chad 77 9.28N 18.54E
Kyaiklat Burma 56 16.25N 95.42E
Kyaikto Burma 56 17.16N 97.01E
Kyaka Tanzania 79 1.16S 31.27E
Kyakhta U.S.S.R. 52 50.22N106.30E
Kyalite Australia 92 34.57S143.31E
Kyancutta Australia 92 33.08S135.34E
Kyaukpadaung Burma 56 20.50N 95.08E
Kyaukpyu Burma 56 19.20N 93.33E
Kybybolite Australia 92 36.54S140.58E
Kychema U.S.S.R. 44 65.32N 42.42E
Kyle of Lochalsh town U.K. 14 57.17N 5.43W
Kyll r. W. Germany 16 49.48N 6.42E
Kyllburg W. Germany 39 50.02N 6.35E
Kyluchevskaya mtn. U.S.S.R. 51 56.00N160.30E
Kynnefjäll hill Sweden 42 58.42N 11.41E
Kynuna Australia 90 21.35S141.55E
Kyoga, L. Uganda 79 1.30N 33.00E
Kyogle Australia 93 28.36S152.59E
Kyong Burma 56 20.49N 96.40E
Kyonpyaw Burma 56 17.18N 95.12E
Kyotera Uganda 79 0.40S 31.31E
Kyōto Japan 57 35.00N135.45E
Kyōto d. Japan 57 34.55N135.35E
Kyritz E. Germany 38 52.56N 12.23E
Kyrkheden Sweden 43 60.10N 13.29E
Kyrön r. Finland 40 63.14N 21.45E
Kyrta U.S.S.R. 44 64.02N 57.40E
Kyshtym U.S.S.R. 9 55.43N 60.32E
Kyūshū d. Japan 57 32.20N130.00E
Kyūshū i. Japan 57 32.00N130.00E
Kyushu Palau Ridge Pacific Oc. 84 15.00N135.00E
Kyūshū sanchi mts. Japan 57 32.20N131.20E
Kyustendil Bulgaria 34 42.25N 22.41E
Kyustendil d. Bulgaria 34 42.16N 22.40E
Kywong Australia 93 35.01S146.45E
Kyyjärvi Finland 40 63.02N 24.34E
Kyzyl U.S.S.R. 52 51.42N 94.28E
Kyzyl Kum, Peski f. U.S.S.R. 9 42.00N 64.30E
Kzyl Orda U.S.S.R. 9 44.52N 65.28E

L

La Alagaba Spain 27 37.28N 6.01W
La Albuera Spain 27 38.43N 6.49W
La Albufera l. Spain 25 39.20N 0.22W
La Almarcha Spain 27 39.41N 2.22W
La Almunia de Doña Godina Spain 25 41.29N 1.22W
La Asunción Venezuela 122 11.06N 63.53W
La Baleine r. Canada 99 58.00N 57.50W

La Banda to L'Arbresle

La Banda Argentina **124** 27.44S 64.15W
La Bañeza Spain **26** 42.18N 5.54W
Labao Indonesia **59** 8.12S122.49E
La Barca Mexico **116** 20.20N102.33W
La Barge U.S.A. **108** 42.16N110.12W
La Bassée France **19** 50.32N 2.48E
Labastide-Murat France **20** 44.39N 1.34E
La Baule France **18** 47.17N 2.24W
Labbezanga Mali **76** 14.57N 0.42E
Labe *r. see* Elbe Czech. **38**
Labé Guinea **76** 11.17N 12.11W
Labelle Canada **105** 46.16N 74.44W
La Belle U.S.A. **113** 26.43N 81.27W
Labelle Prov. Park Canada **105** 46.13N 75.19W
Laberge, L. Canada **100** 61.11N135.12W
Labin Yugo. **31** 45.05N 14.07E
Labinsk U.S.S.R. **45** 44.39N 40.44E
La Bisbal Spain **25** 41.57N 3.03E
La Blanquilla *i.* Venezuela **117** 11.53N 64.38W
Laboe W. Germany **38** 54.24N 10.15E
Labouheyre France **20** 44.13N 0.55W
Laboulaye Argentina **125** 34.05S 63.25W
Labrador *f.* Canada **103** 53.00N 62.00W
Labrador Basin *f.* Atlantic Oc. **127** 55.00N 45.00W
Labrador City Canada **103** 52.57N 66.54W
Labrador Sea Canada / Greenland **99** 57.00N 53.00W
Lábrea Brazil **122** 7.16S 64.47W
Labrède France **20** 44.41N 0.31W
Labrit France **20** 44.07N 0.33W
Labuan Indonesia **59** 6.25S105.49E
Labuan *i.* Malaysia **58** 5.20N115.15E
Labuha Indonesia **59** 0.37S127.29E
Labutta Burma **56** 16.09N 94.46E
Labyrinth, L. Australia **92** 30.43S135.07E
Laç Albania **34** 41.38N 19.40E
Lac *d.* Chad **77** 13.30N 14.35E
La Calera Chile **125** 32.47S 71.12W
La Campana Spain **27** 37.34N 5.26W
Lacanau France **20** 44.59N 1.05W
Lacanau, Étang de *b.* France **20** 44.58N 1.07W
La Cañiza Spain **26** 42.13N 8.16W
La Canourgue France **20** 44.26N 3.13E
La Capelle France **19** 49.58N 3.55E
Lacapelle-Marival France **20** 44.44N 1.54E
La Carlota Argentina **125** 33.25S 63.18W
La Carolina Spain **26** 38.15N 3.37W
Lacaune France **20** 43.43N 2.42E
Lacaune, Monts de *mts.* France **20** 43.43N 2.50E
Lac aux Sables *town* Canada **105** 46.52N 72.24W
Lacedonia Italy **33** 41.03N 15.25E
La Ceiba Honduras **117** 15.45N 86.45W
Lacepede B. Australia **92** 36.47S139.45E
Lac Gatineau *town* Canada **105** 46.34N 75.44W
Lac Giao Vietnam **56** 12.41N108.02E
Lacha, Ozero *l.* U.S.S.R. **44** 61.25N 39.00E
La Chaise-Dieu France **20** 45.19N 3.42E
La Chambre France **21** 45.22N 6.18E
La Charité France **19** 47.11N 3.01E
La Chartre France **18** 47.44N 0.35E
La Châtaigneraie France **18** 46.39N 0.44W
La Châtre France **19** 46.35N 1.59E
La Chaux-de-Fonds Switz. **39** 47.06N 6.50E
Lach Dera *r.* Somali Rep. **79** 0.01S 42.45E
Lachhmangarh India **62** 27.49N 75.02E
Lachine Canada **105** 45.26N 73.40W
Lachine U.S.A. **104** 45.26N 83.40W
Lachlan *r.* Australia **92** 34.21S143.58E
Lachute Canada **105** 45.38N 74.20W
La Ciotat France **21** 43.10N 5.36E
Lackan Resr. Rep. of Ire. **15** 53.09N 6.31W
Lackawanna U.S.A. **114** 42.49N 78.50W
Läckö Sweden **43** 58.41N 13.13E
Lac la Biche *town* Canada **101** 54.46N111.58W
Lac la Ronge Prov. Park Canada **101** 55.14N104.45W
La Clayette France **19** 46.18N 4.19E
La Cocha Argentina **124** 27.45S 65.35W
Lacolle Canada **105** 45.05N 73.22W
Lacombe Canada **100** 52.30N113.44W
La Concepción Venezuela **122** 10.25N 71.41W
La Concordia Mexico **116** 16.05N 92.38W
Laconia U.S.A. **115** 43.31N 71.29W
La Coruña Spain **26** 43.22N 8.23W
La Coruña *d.* Spain **26** 43.10N 8.30W
La Courtine le-Trucq France **20** 45.42N 2.16E
Lac Rémi *town* Canada **105** 46.01N 74.47W
La Crosse Kans. U.S.A. **110** 38.32N 99.18W
La Crosse Wisc. U.S.A. **110** 43.48N 91.15W
La Cruz Mexico **109** 27.50N105.11W
La Cruz Uruguay **125** 33.56S 56.15W
Lac St. Paul *town* Canada **105** 46.44N 75.18W
Ladākh Range *mts.* Jammu & Kashmir **63** 34.15N 78.00E
La Demanda, Sierra de *mts.* Spain **24** 42.10N 3.20W
Lādhi Greece **34** 41.28N 26.15E
Ladhón *r.* Greece **35** 37.40N 21.50E
Ladismith R.S.A. **80** 33.29S 21.15E
Ladispoli Italy **32** 41.56N 12.05E
Lādīz Iran **65** 28.57N 61.18E
Lādnun India **62** 27.39N 74.23E
Ladoga *l. see* Ladozhskoye Ozero U.S.S.R. **44**
La Dorada Colombia **122** 5.27N 74.40W
Ladozhskoye Ozero *l.* U.S.S.R. **44** 61.00N 32.00E
La Dura Mexico **109** 28.22N109.33W
Ladushkin U.S.S.R. **37** 54.30N 20.05E
Ladva Vetka U.S.S.R. **44** 61.16N 34.23E
Ladybrand R.S.A. **80** 29.11S 27.26E
Lady Evelyn L. Canada **104** 47.20N 80.10W
Ladysmith Canada **100** 49.58N123.49W
Ladysmith R.S.A. **80** 28.32S 29.47E
Ladysmith U.S.A. **110** 45.27N 91.07W
Lae P.N.G. **59** 6.45S146.30E
Lae Thailand **56** 19.25N101.00E
Laesö *i.* Denmark **42** 57.16N 11.01E
La Estrada Spain **26** 42.41N 8.29W
La Fayette Ga. U.S.A. **113** 34.42N 85.18W
Lafayette Ind. U.S.A. **112** 40.25N 86.54W
Lafayette La. U.S.A. **111** 30.14N 92.01W
Lafayette, Mt. U.S.A. **105** 44.10N 71.38W
La Fère France **19** 49.40N 3.22E
La Ferté-Bernard France **18** 48.11N 0.40E
La Ferté-Gaucher France **19** 48.47N 3.18E
La Ferté-Macé France **18** 48.36N 0.22W
La Ferté-St. Aubin France **19** 47.43N 1.56E
Lafia Nigeria **77** 8.35N 8.34E
Lafiagi Nigeria **77** 8.50N 5.23E
La Flèche France **18** 47.42N 0.05W
Lafollette U.S.A. **113** 36.23N 84.09W
Laforest Canada **104** 47.02N 81.13W
La Fregeneda Spain **26** 40.59N 6.52W
La Fuente de San Esteban Spain **26** 40.48N 6.15W
La Galite *i.* Tunisia **32** 37.32N 8.56E
La Galite, Canal de *str.* Tunisia **32** 37.20N 9.15E
La Gallega Spain **26** 41.54N 3.16W
Lagan Sweden **43** 56.55N 13.59E
Lagan *r.* Sweden **43** 56.33N 12.56E
Lagan *r.* U.K. **15** 54.37N 5.44W
La Garde, Lac *l.* Canada **104** 46.46N 78.14W
Lage Spain **26** 43.13N 9.00W
Lågen *r.* Akershus Norway **41** 60.10N 11.28E
Lågen *r.* Vestfold Norway **42** 59.03N 10.05E
Laghouat Algeria **75** 33.49N 2.55E
Lago Dilolo *town* Angola **78** 11.27S 22.03E
Lagonegro Italy **33** 40.07N 15.46E
Lagos Mexico **116** 21.21N101.55W
Lagos Nigeria **77** 6.27N 3.28E
Lagos *d.* Nigeria **77** 6.32N 3.30E
Lagos Portugal **27** 37.06N 8.40W
La Goulette Tunisia **32** 36.49N 10.18E
La Grand'Combe France **20** 44.13N 4.02E
La Grande *r.* Canada **102** 53.50N 79.00W
La Grande U.S.A. **108** 45.20N118.05W
La Grange Australia **88** 18.46S121.49E
La Grange U.S.A. **113** 33.02N 85.02W
La Grave France **21** 45.03N 6.18E
La Guaira Venezuela **122** 10.38N 66.55W
La Guardia Pontevedra Spain **26** 41.54N 8.51W
Laguardia Vascongadas Spain **26** 42.33N 2.35W
La Gudiña Spain **26** 42.04N 7.08W
La Guerche-de-Bretagne France **18** 47.56N 1.14W
La Guerche-sur-l'Aubois France **19** 46.57N 2.57E
Laguiole France **20** 44.41N 2.51E
Laguna Brazil **124** 28.29S 48.47W
Laguna Dam U.S.A. **109** 32.55N114.25W
Lagunas Chile **124** 20.59S 69.37W
Lagunas Peru **122** 5.10S 73.35W
Lagunillas Venezuela **122** 10.07N 71.16W
La Habana Cuba **117** 23.07N 82.25W
Lahad Datu Malaysia **58** 5.05N118.20E
La Hague, Cap de *c.* France **18** 49.44N 1.56W
La Harpe U.S.A. **110** 40.35N 90.57W
Lahat Indonesia **58** 3.46S103.32E
La Haye-du-Puits France **18** 49.18N 1.33W
Laḥij S. Yemen **71** 13.04N 44.53E
Lāhījān Iran **65** 37.12N 50.00E
Lahn *r.* W. Germany **16** 50.18N 7.36E
Lahnstein W. Germany **39** 50.18N 7.37E
Laholm Sweden **43** 56.31N 13.02E
Laholmsbukten *b.* Sweden **43** 56.35N 12.50E
Lahore Pakistan **62** 31.35N 74.18E
Lahr W. Germany **39** 48.20N 7.52E
Lahri Pakistan **62** 29.11N 68.13E
Lahti Finland **41** 60.58N 25.40E
Laï Chad **77** 9.22N 16.14E
Laiagam P.N.G. **59** 5.31S143.39E
Laibin China **55** 23.42N109.16E
Lai Chau Vietnam **56** 22.04N103.12E
L'Aigle *r.* Canada **105** 46.28N 76.01W
L'Aigle France **18** 48.45N 0.38E
Laignes France **19** 47.50N 4.22E
Laihia Finland **40** 62.58N 22.01E
Lainá Greece **34** 41.03N 26.19E
Laingsburg R.S.A. **80** 33.11S 20.49E
Laingsburg U.S.A. **104** 42.54N 84.21W
Lainio *r.* Sweden **40** 67.28N 22.50E
Lairg U.K. **14** 58.01N 4.25W
Laisamis Kenya **79** 1.38N 37.47E
Laissac France **20** 44.23N 2.49E
Laitila Finland **41** 60.53N 21.41E
Laiyuan China **54** 39.19N114.41E
Laizhou Wan *b.* China **54** 37.30N119.30E
La Jarrie France **20** 46.08N 1.00W
La Javie France **21** 44.10N 6.21E
Lajes Brazil **126** 27.48S 50.20W
La Junta U.S.A. **108** 37.59N103.33W
Lakaband Pakistan **62** 31.00N 69.30E
Lak Bor *r.* Kenya **73** 1.18N 40.40E
Lak Bor *r.* Somali Rep. **79** 0.32N 42.05E
Lake Biddy *town* Australia **89** 33.01S118.51E
Lake Brown *town* Australia **89** 30.57S118.19E
Lake Cargelligo *town* Australia **93** 33.19S146.23E
Lake Charles *town* U.S.A. **111** 30.13N 93.12W
Lake City U.S.A. **113** 30.12N 82.39W
Lake Clear *town* Canada **105** 45.27N 77.17W
Lake District *f.* U.K. **12** 54.30N 3.10W
Lakefield Canada **104** 44.26N 78.16W
Lake George *town* Colo. U.S.A. **108** 38.58N105.23W
Lake George *town* N.Y. U.S.A. **115** 43.26N 73.43W
Lake Grace *town* Australia **89** 33.06S118.28E
Lake Harbour *town* Canada **99** 62.50N 69.50W
Lake Hart *town* Australia **92** 31.16S136.21E
Lake King *town* Australia **89** 33.05S119.40E
Lakeland *town* U.S.A. **113** 28.02N 81.59W
Lake Mead Nat. Recreation Area U.S.A. **109** 36.00N114.30W
Lake Nash *town* Australia **90** 21.00S137.55E
Lake Orion *town* U.S.A. **114** 42.47N 83.14W
Lakepa Niue **84** 19.01S169.49W
Lake Placid *town* U.S.A. **112** 44.17N 73.59W
Lake River *town* Canada **102** 54.30N 82.30W
Lakes Entrance *town* Australia **93** 37.53S147.59E
Lakeshore U.S.A. **108** 37.15N119.12W
Lakeside Ohio U.S.A. **114** 41.32N 82.45W
Lakeside Utah U.S.A. **108** 41.13N112.54W
Lake Stewart *town* Australia **92** 29.22S140.12E
Lake Superior Prov. Park Canada **102** 47.30N 84.50W
Lake Varley *town* Australia **89** 32.46S119.27E
Lakeview U.S.A. **108** 42.11N120.21W
Lake Village U.S.A. **111** 33.20N 91.17W
Lakewood N.J. U.S.A. **115** 40.06N 74.13W
Lakewood N.Mex. U.S.A. **109** 32.39N104.39W
Lakewood N.Y. U.S.A. **114** 42.06N 79.20W
Lakewood Ohio U.S.A. **114** 41.29N 81.48W
Lākheri India **62** 25.40N 76.10E
Lakhimpur India **63** 27.57N 80.46E
Lakhish, Nahal *wadi* Israel **67** 31.37N 34.46E
Lakhnādon India **63** 22.36N 79.36E
Lakhpat India **62** 23.49N 68.47E
Lakonikós Kólpos *g.* Greece **35** 36.25N 22.37E
Lakota Ivory Coast **76** 5.50N 5.30W
Lakota U.S.A. **110** 48.02N 98.21W
Laksefjorden *est.* Norway **40** 70.58N 27.00E
Lakselv Norway **40** 70.03N 24.55E
Lakshadweep Is. Indian Oc. **60** 11.00N 72.00E
Lala India **63** 24.25N 92.40E
Lāla Mūsa Pakistan **62** 32.42N 73.58E
Lalaua Mozambique **79** 14.20S 38.30E
Lalbenque France **20** 44.20N 1.33E
Lālehzār, Kūh-e *mtn.* Iran **65** 29.26N 56.48E
Lālganj India **63** 25.52N 85.11E
Lalībela Ethiopia **73** 12.02N 39.02E
La Libertad El Salvador **117** 13.28N 89.20W
Lalín Spain **26** 42.39N 8.07W
Lalinde France **20** 44.51N 0.44E
La Línea Spain **27** 36.10N 5.19W
Lalitpur India **63** 24.41N 78.25E
Lalitpur Nepal **63** 27.41N 85.20E
Lālmanir Hāt Bangla. **63** 25.54N 89.27E
La Loche Canada **101** 56.29N109.27W
La Loche, Lac *l.* Canada **101** 56.25N109.30W
La Loupe France **18** 48.28N 1.01E
La Louvière Belgium **16** 50.29N 4.11E
Lālpur India **62** 22.12N 69.58E
Lālsot India **62** 26.34N 76.20E
La Maddalena Italy **32** 41.13N 9.24E
Lamar U.S.A. **110** 38.05N102.37W
Lamarche France **19** 48.04N 5.47E
La Marsa Tunisia **32** 36.53N 10.20E
Lamastre France **21** 44.59N 4.35E
Lamballe France **18** 48.28N 2.31W
Lambaréné Gabon **78** 0.40S 10.15E
Lambasa Fiji **84** 16.25S179.24E
Lambayeque Peru **122** 6.36S 79.50W
Lambay I. Rep. of Ire. **15** 53.29N 6.01W
Lambert's Bay *town* R.S.A. **80** 32.06S 18.16E
Lámbia Greece **35** 37.52N 21.53E
Lamé Chad **77** 9.14N 14.33E
Lame Nigeria **77** 10.27N 9.12E
Lamego Portugal **26** 41.06N 7.49W
Lameroo Australia **92** 35.20S140.33E
La Mesa Calif. U.S.A. **109** 32.46N117.01W
Lamesa Tex. U.S.A. **111** 32.44N101.57W
Lamía Greece **35** 38.54N 22.26E
La Minerve Canada **105** 46.15N 74.56W
Lammermuir Hills U.K. **14** 55.51N 2.40W
Lammhult Sweden **43** 57.10N 14.35E
Lamoille *r.* U.S.A. **105** 44.35N 73.10W
Lamongan Indonesia **59** 7.05S112.26E
Lamont U.S.A. **108** 42.12N107.28W
La Mothe-Achard France **18** 46.37N 1.40W
Lamotrek *i.* Caroline Is. **59** 7.28N146.23E
Lamotte-Beuvron France **19** 47.36N 2.01E
Lamotte-Beuvron France **17** 47.37N 2.01E
La Motte-Chalençon France **21** 44.29N 5.23E
La Motte du-Claire France **21** 44.21N 6.02E
La Moure U.S.A. **110** 46.21N 98.18W
Lampa Peru **122** 15.10S 70.30W
Lampasas U.S.A. **111** 31.04N 98.12W
Lampazos Mexico **111** 27.00N100.30W
Lampedusa *i.* Italy **28** 35.30N 12.35E
Lampertheim W. Germany **39** 49.35N 8.28E
Lampeter U.K. **13** 52.06N 4.06W
Lampinoú Greece **34** 39.22N 23.10E
Lampione *i.* Italy **28** 35.33N 12.18E
Lamu Kenya **79** 2.20S 40.54E
La Mure France **21** 44.54N 5.47E
Lana Italy **30** 46.37N 11.09E
Lanai *i.* Hawaiian Is. **85** 20.50N156.55W
Lanai City Hawaiian Is. **85** 20.50N156.55W
La Nao, Cabo de Spain **24** 38.42N 0.15E
Lanark U.K. **14** 55.41N 3.47W
La Nava de Ricomalillo Spain **27** 39.39N 4.59W
Lancang Jiang *r. see* Mekong China **56**
Lancashire *d.* U.K. **12** 53.53N 2.30W
Lancaster Canada **105** 45.08N 74.30W
Lancaster U.K. **12** 54.03N 2.48W
Lancaster Calif. U.S.A. **109** 34.42N118.08W
Lancaster N.H. U.S.A. **105** 44.29N 71.34W
Lancaster N.Y. U.S.A. **114** 42.54N 78.40W
Lancaster Ohio U.S.A. **114** 39.43N 82.36W
Lancaster Penn. U.S.A. **115** 40.02N 76.19W
Lancaster S.C. U.S.A. **113** 34.43N 80.47W
Lancaster Tex. U.S.A. **111** 32.36N 96.46W
Lancaster Sd. Canada **99** 74.00N 85.00W
Lancelin Australia **89** 31.01S115.19E
Lanchow *see* Lanzhou China **54**
Lanciano Italy **31** 42.14N 14.23E
Lancun China **54** 36.24N120.10E
Landau Bayern W. Germany **39** 48.40N 12.43E
Landau Rhein.-Pfalz. W. Germany **39** 49.12N 8.07E
Landay Afghan. **62** 30.31N 63.47E
Landeck Austria **39** 47.08N 10.34E
Landen Belgium **16** 50.46N 5.04E
Lander *r.* Australia **90** 20.25S132.00E
Lander U.S.A. **108** 42.50N108.44W
Landerneau France **18** 48.27N 4.15W
Landes *d.* France **20** 44.20N 1.00W
Landes *f.* France **20** 44.00N 1.00W
Landete Spain **25** 39.56N 1.25W
Landisville U.S.A. **115** 39.31N 74.55W
Landivisiau France **18** 48.31N 4.04W
Landor Australia **88** 25.06S116.50E
Landquart Switz. **39** 46.58N 9.33E
Landrecies France **19** 50.08N 3.42E
Landsberg W. Germany **39** 48.05N 10.55E
Landsbro Sweden **43** 57.22N 14.54E
Lands End *c.* Canada **96** 76.10N123.00W
Land's End *c.* U.K. **13** 50.03N 5.45W
Landshut W. Germany **39** 48.33N 12.09E
Landskrona Sweden **43** 55.52N 12.50E
Lanett U.S.A. **113** 32.52N 85.12W
Langå Denmark **42** 56.23N 9.55E
La'nga Co *l.* China **63** 30.45N 81.15E
Langadhás Greece **34** 40.45N 23.04E
Langádhia Greece **35** 37.41N 22.02E
Langanes *c.* Iceland **40** 66.30N 14.30W
Langao China **54** 33.22N109.04E
Långban Sweden **43** 59.51N 14.15E
Langdon U.S.A. **110** 48.46N 98.22W
Langeac France **20** 45.06N 3.30E
Langeais France **18** 47.20N 0.24E
L'Ange Gardien Canada **105** 46.55N 71.07W
Langeland *i.* Denmark **42** 55.00N 10.50E
Längelmävesi *l.* Finland **41** 61.32N 24.22E
Langen W. Germany **39** 49.59N 8.41E
Längenfeld Austria **39** 47.04N 10.58E
Langenhagen W. Germany **38** 52.27N 9.44E
Langenthal Switz. **39** 47.13N 7.47E
Langeoog *i.* W. Germany **38** 53.46N 7.32E
Langesund Norway **42** 59.00N 9.45E
Langholm U.K. **14** 55.09N 3.00W
Langjökull *ice cap* Iceland **40** 63.43N 20.03W
Langkawi *i.* Malaysia **58** 6.20N 99.30E
Langlade Canada **102** 48.14N 76.00W
Langnau Switz. **39** 46.57N 7.47E
Langogne France **20** 44.43N 3.51E
Langon France **20** 44.33N 0.15W
Langöy *i.* Norway **40** 68.45N 15.00E
Langres France **19** 47.52N 5.20E
Langres, Plateau de *f.* France **19** 47.41N 5.03E
Langsa Indonesia **58** 4.28N 97.59E
Langshan China **54** 41.02N107.27E
Lang Shan *mts.* China **54** 41.30N107.10E
Lang Son Vietnam **55** 21.49N106.45E
Langtry U.S.A. **111** 29.48N101.34W
Languedoc-Roussillon *d.* France **20** 43.50N 3.30E
Langxi China **55** 31.08N119.10E
Laniel Canada **104** 47.04N 79.18W
Lannemezan France **20** 43.08N 0.23E
Lannilis France **18** 48.34N 4.31W
Lannion France **18** 48.44N 3.28W
L'Annonciation Canada **105** 46.25N 74.52W
Lanoraie Canada **105** 45.58N 73.13W
Lansdale U.S.A. **115** 40.15N 75.17W
Lansdowne India **63** 29.50N 78.41E
L'Anse au Loup Canada **103** 51.34N 56.48W
Lansing U.S.A. **112** 42.44N 84.34W
Lanslebourg France **21** 45.17N 6.52E
Lantewa Nigeria **77** 12.15N 11.45E
Lanusei Italy **32** 39.52N 9.34E
Lanxi China **55** 29.17N119.31E
Lanzarote *i.* Canary Is. **74** 29.00N 13.40W
Lanzhou China **54** 36.01N103.46E
Lanzo Torinese Italy **30** 45.16N 7.28E
Laoag Phil. **59** 18.14N120.36E
Lào Cai Vietnam **56** 22.30N104.00E
Laochang China **55** 25.12N104.35E
Laoha He *r.* China **54** 43.30N120.42E
Laois *d.* Rep. of Ire. **15** 53.00N 7.20W
Laojun Shan *mtn.* China **54** 33.45N111.38E
Laon France **19** 49.34N 3.40E
Laona U.S.A. **102** 45.35N 88.40W
La Orotava Canary Is. **127** 28.26N 16.30W
La Oroya Peru **122** 11.36S 75.54W
Laos Asia **56** 18.30N104.00E
Lapage, L. Australia **89** 30.40S121.50E
Lapalisse France **20** 46.15N 3.38E
La Palma *i.* Canary Is. **74** 28.50N 18.00W
La Palma Spain **27** 37.23N 6.33W
La Pampa *d.* Argentina **125** 37.00S 66.00W
La Paragua Venezuela **122** 6.53N 63.22W
La Paz Entre Ríos Argentina **125** 30.45S 59.38W
La Paz Mendoza Argentina **125** 33.28S 67.34W
La Paz Bolivia **124** 16.30S 68.09W
La Paz *d.* Bolivia **124** 16.00S 68.10W
La Paz Mexico **109** 24.10N110.18W
La Paz, Bahía de *b.* Mexico **109** 24.15N110.30W
La Pedrera Colombia **122** 1.18S 69.43W
Lapeer U.S.A. **104** 43.03N 83.19W
La Peña, Sierra de *mts.* Spain **24** 42.30N 0.50W
La Perouse Str. U.S.S.R. **51** 45.50N142.30E
La Pine U.S.A. **108** 43.40N121.30W
Lapinjärvi Finland **41** 60.38N 26.13E
Lapland *f.* Sweden / Finland **40** 68.10N 24.10E
La Plata Argentina **125** 34.55S 57.57W
La Plata Md. U.S.A. **114** 38.32N 76.59W
La Plata Mo. U.S.A. **110** 40.02N 92.29W
La Plata, Río de *est.* Argentina / Uruguay **125** 35.15S 56.45W
Lapointe, Lac *l.* Canada **103** 53.32N 68.56W
Laporte U.S.A. **115** 41.25N 76.30W
Lappajärvi *l.* Finland **40** 63.08N 23.40E
Lappeenranta Finland **44** 61.04N 28.05E
Lappi *d.* Finland **40** 67.20N 26.00E
Laptevykh, More *sea* U.S.S.R. **51** 74.30N125.00E
Lapua Finland **40** 62.57N 23.00E
La Puebla Spain **25** 39.46N 3.01E
La Puebla de Cazalla Spain **27** 37.14N 5.19W
La Puebla de Montalbán Spain **27** 39.52N 4.21W
La Push U.S.A. **108** 47.55N124.38W
La Quiaca Argentina **124** 22.05S 65.36W
L'Aquila Italy **30** 42.22N 13.22E
Lār Iran **65** 27.37N 54.16E
Laracha Spain **26** 43.15N 8.35W
Larache Morocco **74** 35.12N 6.10W
Laragne-Montéglin France **21** 44.19N 5.49E
La Rambla Spain **27** 37.36N 4.44W
Laramie U.S.A. **108** 41.19N105.35W
Laramie Mts. U.S.A. **108** 42.00N105.40W
L'Arbresle France **21** 45.50N 4.37E

Lärbro to **Levice**

Lärbro Sweden **43** 57.47N 18.47E
Larche, Col de *pass* France **21** 44.25N 6.53E
Laredo Spain **26** 43.24N 3.25W
Laredo U.S.A. **111** 27.31N 99.30W
Laredo Sd. Canada **100** 52.30N128.53W
La Réole France **20** 44.35N 0.02E
Largeau Chad **77** 17.55N 19.07E
L'Argentière-la-Bessée France **21** 44.47N 6.33E
Largs U.K. **14** 55.48N 4.52W
Lariang Indonesia **58** 1.35S119.25E
Lárimna Greece **35** 38.34N 23.17E
Larino Italy **33** 41.48N 14.54E
La Rioja Argentina **124** 29.25S 66.50W
La Rioja *d.* Argentina **124** 29.00S 66.00W
La Rioja *d.* Spain **26** 42.25N 2.30W
Lárisa Greece **34** 39.38N 22.28E
Lark *r.* U.K. **13** 52.26N 0.20E
Lärkäna Pakistan **62** 27.33N 68.13E
Larkspur U.S.A. **108** 39.13N104.54W
Larnaca *see* Lárnax Cyprus **66**
Lárnax Cyprus **66** 34.54N 33.39E
Larne U.K. **15** 54.51N 5.49W
La Robla Spain **26** 42.48N 5.37W
La Roca de la Sierra Spain **27** 39.07N 6.41W
La Roche Belgium **16** 50.11N 5.35E
La Roche-Bernard France **18** 47.31N 2.18W
La Rochelle France **20** 46.10N 1.10W
La Roche-sur-Yon France **18** 46.40N 1.26W
La Roda Spain **27** 39.13N 2.09W
La Romana Dom. Rep. **117** 18.27N 68.57W
La Ronge Canada **101** 55.06N105.17W
La Ronge, Lac *l.* Canada **98** 55.07N105.15W
Laroquebrou France **20** 44.58N 2.11E
Larrimah Australia **90** 15.35S133.12E
Larvik Norway **42** 59.04N 10.00E
La Sagra *mtn.* Spain **27** 37.57N 2.34W
La Salle U.S.A. **110** 41.20N 89.06W
Las Animas U.S.A. **108** 38.04N103.13W
Las Anod Somali Rep. **71** 8.26N 47.24E
La Sarre Canada **102** 48.45N 79.15W
Las Cabezas de San Juan Spain **27** 36.59N 5.56W
Las Casitas, Cerro *mtn.* Mexico **109** 23.32N109.59W
L'Ascension Canada **105** 46.33N 74.50W
Las Cruces U.S.A. **109** 32.23N106.29W
Las Cuevas Mexico **111** 29.38N101.19W
Las Dawa'o Somali Rep. **71** 10.20N 49.03E
Las Dureh Somali Rep. **71** 10.10N 46.01E
La Seine, Baie de France **17** 49.40N 0.30W
La Serena Chile **124** 29.54S 71.16W
La Seyne France **21** 43.06N 5.53E
Las Flores Argentina **125** 36.02S 59.07W
Läsh-e Joveyn Afghan. **62** 31.43N 61.37E
Las Heras Argentina **125** 32.50S 68.50W
Lashio Burma **56** 22.58N 96.51E
Lashkar Gäh Afghan. **62** 31.30N 64.21E
Las Khoreh Somali Rep. **71** 11.10N 48.16E
Laško Yugo. **31** 46.09N 15.14E
Las Lomitas Argentina **124** 24.43S 60.35W
Las Marismas *f.* Spain **27** 37.05N 6.20W
La Solana Spain **26** 38.56N 3.14W
L'Asomption *r.* Canada **105** 45.43N 73.29W
Las Palmas de Gran Canaria Canary Is. **74** 28.08N 15.27W
Las Palomas Mexico **109** 31.44N107.37W
Las Perlas, Archipelago de Panama **117** 8.45N 79.30W
La Spezia Italy **30** 44.07N 9.50E
Las Piedras Uruguay **125** 34.44S 56.13W
Las Plumas Argentina **125** 43.40S 67.15W
Lassay France **18** 48.26N 0.30W
Lassen Peak *mtn.* U.S.A. **108** 40.29N121.31W
L'Assomption Canada **105** 45.50N 73.25W
Last Chance U.S.A. **108** 39.45N103.36W
Last Mountain L. Canada **101** 51.05N105.10W
Lastoursville Gabon **78** 0.50S 12.47E
Lastovo *i.* Yugo. **31** 42.45N 16.53E
Lastovski Kanal *str.* Yugo. **31** 42.50N 16.59E
Las Tres Virgenes, Volcán *mtn.* Mexico **109** 27.27N112.37W
Lastrup W. Germany **38** 52.48N 7.52E
La Suze France **18** 47.54N 0.02E
Las Vegas Nev. U.S.A. **109** 36.11N115.08W
Las Vegas N.Mex. U.S.A. **109** 35.36N105.13W
Latacunga Ecuador **122** 0.58S 78.36W
La Tagua Colombia **122** 0.03S 74.40W
Latakia *see* Al Lādhiqīyah Syria **66**
Latambar Pakistan **62** 33.07N 70.52E
Latchford Canada **104** 47.20N 79.48W
Late *i.* Tonga **85** 18.49S174.40W
Lätëhar India **63** 23.45N 84.30E
La Teste-de-Buch France **20** 44.38N 1.09W
Lathen W. Germany **38** 52.52N 7.19E
Läthi India **62** 21.43N 71.23E
Latina Italy **32** 41.28N 12.52E
Latisana Italy **32** 45.47N 13.00E
La Tortuga *i.* Venezuela **122** 11.00N 65.20W
La Tour-d'Auvergne France **20** 45.32N 2.41E
La Tour-du-Pin France **21** 45.34N 5.27E
La Tremblade France **20** 45.46N 1.08W
La Trimouille France **18** 46.28N 1.02E
Latrobe U.S.A. **114** 40.19N 79.23W
La Truite, Lac À *l.* Canada **104** 47.16N 78.17W
Latrūn Jordan **67** 31.50N 34.59E
La Tuque Canada **103** 47.27N 72.47W
Latviyskaya S.S.R. *d.* U.S.S.R. **41** 56.45N 23.00E
Lau Nigeria **77** 9.14N 11.15E
Lauchhammer E. Germany **38** 51.30N 13.47E
Lauenburg W. Germany **38** 53.22N 10.33E
Lauf an der Pegnitz W. Germany **38** 49.30N 11.17E
Laughlen, Mt. Australia **90** 23.23S134.23E
Lau Group *is.* Fiji **84** 19.00S178.30W
Launceston Australia **91** 41.25S147.07E
Launceston U.K. **13** 50.38N 4.21W
La Unión Chile **125** 40.15S 73.02W
La Unión Spain **25** 37.37N 0.52W
Laupheim W. Germany **39** 48.14N 9.52E
Laura Australia **92** 33.08S138.19E
La Urbana Venezuela **122** 7.08N 66.56W
Laureana di Borrello Italy **33** 38.30N 16.05E
Laurel Del. U.S.A. **115** 38.33N 75.34W
Laurel Miss. U.S.A. **111** 31.42N 89.08W
Laurel Mont. U.S.A. **108** 45.40N108.46W
Laurel Hill *mtn.* U.S.A. **114** 40.02N 79.17W
Laurel Ridge *mtn.* U.S.A. **114** 39.20N 79.53W
Laurelville U.S.A. **114** 39.28N 82.44W
Laurencekirk U.K. **14** 56.50N 2.29W
Laurens U.S.A. **113** 34.29N 82.01W
Laurentians *mts.* Canada **105** 45.43N 75.52W
Laurentides *mts.* Canada **105** 46.25N 73.28W
Laurentides Prov. Park Canada **103** 47.30N 71.30W
Lauria Italy **33** 40.02N 15.50E
Laurier Canada **105** 46.32N 71.38W
Laurière France **20** 46.05N 1.28E
Laurinburg U.S.A. **113** 34.46N 79.29W
Lauro, Monte *mtn.* Italy **33** 37.08N 14.47E
Lausanne Switz. **39** 46.31N 6.38E
Laut *i.* Indonesia **58** 3.45S116.20E
Lauta E. Germany **38** 51.27N 14.04E
Lautaro Chile **125** 38.31S 72.27W
Lauterbach W. Germany **38** 50.38N 9.24E
Lauterbrunnen Switz. **39** 46.36N 7.55E
Lauterecken W. Germany **39** 49.39N 7.35E
Lautoka Fiji **84** 17.37S177.27E
Lauzerte France **20** 44.15N 1.08E
Lauzon Canada **105** 46.50N 71.10W
Lauzun France **20** 44.38N 0.28E
Lavagh More *mtn.* Rep. of Ire. **15** 54.45N 8.07W
Lava Hot Springs *town* U.S.A. **108** 42.37N112.01W
Laval Canada **105** 45.35N 73.45W
Laval France **18** 48.04N 0.46W
Lávara Greece **34** 41.19N 26.22E
Lavardac France **20** 44.11N 0.18E
La Vecilla de Curueño Spain **26** 42.51N 5.24W
La Vega Dom. Rep. **117** 19.15N 70.33W
La Vela Venezuela **122** 11.27N 69.34W
Lavelanet France **20** 42.56N 1.51E
Lavello Italy **33** 41.03N 15.48E
La Verendrye Prov. Park Canada **105** 47.30N 77.30W
Laverlochère Canada **104** 47.26N 79.19W
Laverne U.S.A. **111** 36.43N 99.54W
Laverton Australia **89** 28.49S122.25E
Lavi Israel **67** 32.47N 35.26E
Lavia Finland **41** 61.36N 22.36E
Lavielle, L. Canada **104** 45.51N 78.14W
Lavigne Canada **104** 46.20N 80.05W
Lavik Norway **41** 61.06N 5.30E
La Voulte-sur-Rhône France **21** 44.48N 4.47E
Lavras Brazil **126** 21.15S 44.59W
Lávrion Greece **35** 37.44N 24.04E
Lawgi Australia **90** 24.34S150.39E
Lawra Ghana **76** 10.40N 2.49W
Lawrence New Zealand **86** 45.55S169.42E
Lawrence Kans. U.S.A. **110** 38.58N 95.14W
Lawrence Mass. U.S.A. **115** 42.42N 71.09W
Lawrenceburg U.S.A. **113** 35.16N 87.20W
Lawrenceville Canada **105** 45.25N 72.19W
Lawrenceville Penn. U.S.A. **114** 42.00N 77.08W
Lawton Okla. U.S.A. **111** 34.37N 98.25W
Lawton Penn. U.S.A. **115** 41.46N 76.05W
Lawz, Jabal al *mtn.* Saudi Arabia **66** 28.40N 35.20E
Laxå Sweden **43** 58.59N 14.37E
Lay *r.* France **18** 46.20N 1.18W
Laysan *i.* Hawaiian Is. **84** 25.46N171.44W
Laytonville U.S.A. **108** 39.41N123.29W
Lazio *d.* Italy **30** 42.05N 12.20E
Lead U.S.A. **110** 44.21N103.46W
Leader Canada **101** 50.53N109.31W
Leadhills U.K. **14** 55.25N 3.46W
Leamington Canada **104** 42.03N 82.36W
Leamington U.S.A. **108** 39.31N112.17W
Learmonth Australia **88** 22.13S114.04E
Leavenworth U.S.A. **110** 39.19N 94.55W
Lebak Phil. **59** 6.32N124.03E
Lebane Yugo. **34** 42.56N 21.44E
Lebango Congo **78** 0.24N 14.44E
Lebanon Asia **66** 34.00N 36.00E
Lebanon Ind. U.S.A. **112** 40.02N 87.28W
Lebanon Kans. U.S.A. **110** 39.49N 98.33W
Lebanon Ky. U.S.A. **113** 37.33N 85.15W
Lebanon Mo. U.S.A. **111** 37.41N 92.40W
Lebanon N.H. U.S.A. **115** 43.38N 72.15W
Lebanon Oreg. U.S.A. **108** 44.32N122.54W
Lebanon Penn. U.S.A. **115** 40.20N 76.25W
Lebanon Tenn. U.S.A. **113** 36.11N 86.19W
Lebec U.S.A. **109** 34.50N118.52W
Lebesby Norway **40** 70.34N 27.00E
Le Blanc France **18** 46.38N 1.04E
Lebork Poland **37** 54.33N 17.44E
Le Bourg-d'Oisans France **21** 45.03N 6.02E
Lebrija Spain **27** 36.55N 6.04W
Lebu Chile **125** 37.37S 73.39W
Le Bugue France **20** 44.55N 0.56E
Le Cannet France **21** 43.34N 7.01E
Le Cateau France **19** 50.06N 3.33E
Le Catelet France **19** 50.00N 3.15E
Lecce Italy **33** 40.23N 18.11E
Lecco Italy **30** 45.51N 9.23E
Lech *r.* W. Germany **39** 48.44N 10.56E
Lechang China **55** 25.08N113.20E
Le Château d'Oléron France **20** 45.53N 1.11W
Le Châtelet France **19** 46.39N 2.17E
Le Chesne France **19** 49.31N 4.46E
Le Cheylard France **21** 44.54N 4.25E
Lechiguanas, Islas de las *is.* Argentina **125** 33.26S 59.42W
Lechtaler Alpen *mts.* Austria **39** 47.15N 10.33E
Le Conquet France **18** 48.22N 4.46W
L'Écorce, Lac de *l.* Canada **105** 47.05N 76.24W
Le Creusot France **19** 46.48N 4.26E
Le Croisic France **18** 47.18N 2.31W
Lectoure France **20** 43.56N 0.38E
Lectoure France **17** 43.56N 0.38E
Ledbury U.K. **13** 52.03N 2.25W
Ledesma Spain **26** 41.05N 6.00W
Le Donjon France **20** 46.21N 3.48E
Le Dorat France **20** 46.13N 1.05E
Leduc Canada **100** 53.20N113.30W
Lee *r.* Rep. of Ire. **15** 51.53N 8.25W
Lee U.S.A. **115** 42.19N 73.15W
Leechburg U.S.A. **114** 40.38N 79.36W
Leech L. U.S.A. **110** 47.09N 94.23W
Leedey U.S.A. **111** 35.52N 99.21W
Leeds Canada **105** 46.16N 71.22W
Leeds U.K. **12** 53.48N 1.34W
Leeds U.S.A. **113** 33.32N 86.31W
Leek U.K. **12** 53.07N 2.02W
Leer W. Germany **38** 53.14N 7.26E
Leesburg Fla. U.S.A. **113** 28.49N 81.54W
Leesburg Va. U.S.A. **114** 39.07N 77.34W
Leeton Australia **93** 34.33S146.24E
Leeuwarden Neth. **16** 53.12N 5.48E
Leeuwin, C. Australia **89** 34.22S115.08E
Leeward Is. C. America **117** 18.00N 61.00W
Lefroy, L. Australia **89** 31.15S121.40E
Legazpi Phil. **59** 13.10N123.45E
Legget U.S.A. **108** 39.52N123.34W
Leghorn *see* Livorno Italy **30**
Legion Mine Zimbabwe **80** 21.23S 28.33E
Legionowo Poland **37** 52.25N 20.56E
Legnago Italy **32** 45.11N 11.18E
Legnano Italy **30** 45.36N 8.54E
Legnica Poland **36** 51.12N 16.10E
Le Grand-Lucé France **18** 47.52N 0.28E
Le Grand-Quevilly France **18** 49.25N 1.02E
Le Grau-du-Roi France **21** 43.32N 4.08E
Leh Jammu & Kashmir **63** 34.10N 77.35E
Le Havre France **18** 49.30N 0.08E
Lehighton U.S.A. **115** 40.49N 75.45W
Lehrte W. Germany **38** 52.22N 9.59E
Lehututu Botswana **80** 23.54S 21.52E
Leiah Pakistan **62** 30.58N 70.56E
Leibnitz Austria **31** 46.48N 15.32E
Leicester U.K. **13** 52.39N 1.09W
Leicestershire *d.* U.K. **13** 52.29N 1.10W
Leichardt *r.* Australia **90** 17.35S139.48E
Leiden Neth. **16** 52.10N 4.30E
Leie *r.* Belgium **16** 51.03N 3.44E
Leifeng China **55** 25.35N118.17E
Leigh *r.* Australia **92** 29.49S138.10E
Leigh Creek *town* Australia **92** 30.31S138.25E
Leighton Buzzard U.K. **13** 51.55N 0.39W
Leikanger Norway **41** 61.10N 6.52E
Leine W. Germany **38** 52.41N 9.36E
Leipzig E. Germany **38** 51.19N 12.20E
Leipzig *d.* E. Germany **38** 51.20N 12.45E
Leiria Portugal **27** 39.45N 8.48W
Leiria *d.* Portugal **27** 39.50N 8.50W
Leirvik Norway **42** 59.45N 5.30E
Lei Shui *r.* China **55** 26.57N112.33E
Leithbridge Canada **100** 49.40N112.45W
Leitrim *d.* Rep. of Ire. **15** 54.08N 8.00W
Leiyang China **55** 26.30N112.42E
Leizhou Bandao *pen.* China **55** 21.00N110.00E
Lek *r.* Neth. **16** 51.55N 4.29E
Lekhainá Greece **35** 37.56N 21.17E
Leksvik Norway **40** 63.40N 10.40E
Leland U.S.A. **111** 33.24N 90.54W
Leland Lakes Canada **101** 60.00N110.59W
Lelång *l.* Sweden **43** 59.08N 12.10E
Lelchitsy U.S.S.R. **37** 51.48N 28.20E
Leleque Argentina **125** 42.24S 71.04W
Leling China **54** 37.45N117.13E
Le Lion-d'Angers France **18** 47.38N 0.43W
Le Locle Switz. **39** 47.03N 6.45E
Le Lude France **18** 47.39N 0.09E
Lelystad Neth. **16** 52.32N 5.29E
Le Madonie Italy **33** 37.55N 14.00E
Léman, Lac *l.* Switz. **39** 46.25N 6.30E
Le Mans France **18** 48.00N 0.12E
Le Mars U.S.A. **110** 42.47N 96.10W
Le Mayet-de-Montagne France **20** 46.05N 3.40E
Leme Brazil **126** 22.10S 47.23W
Le Merlerault France **18** 48.42N 0.18E
Lemesós Cyprus **66** 34.40N 33.03E
Lemgo W. Germany **38** 52.02N 8.54E
Lemhi Range *mts.* U.S.A. **108** 44.30N113.25W
Lemland *i.* Finland **43** 60.03N 20.10E
Lemmer Neth. **16** 52.50N 5.43E
Lemmon U.S.A. **110** 45.56N102.10W
Le Monastier France **20** 44.56N 4.00E
Le Montet France **20** 46.25N 3.03E
Lemsid W. Sahara **74** 26.32N 13.49W
Lemvig Denmark **42** 56.32N 8.18E
Lena U.S.A. **111** 31.47N 92.48W
Lena *r.* U.S.S.R. **51** 72.00N127.10E
Lenakel Vanuatu **84** 19.32S169.16E
Lenart Yugo. **31** 46.35N 15.50E
Lencloître France **18** 46.49N 0.20E
Lendery U.S.S.R. **44** 63.24N 31.04E
Lendinara Italy **32** 45.05N 11.36E
Lengerich W. Germany **38** 52.11N 7.50E
Lengoue *r.* Congo **78** 1.15S 16.42E
Lenhovda Sweden **43** 57.00N 15.17E
Lenina, Kanal *canal* U.S.S.R. **45** 43.46N 45.00E
Lenina, Pik *mtn.* U.S.S.R. **52** 40.14N 69.40E
Leninabad U.S.S.R. **52** 40.14N 69.40E
Leninakan U.S.S.R. **45** 40.47N 43.49E
Leningrad U.S.S.R. **44** 59.55N 30.25E
Leninogorsk U.S.S.R. **50** 50.23N 83.32E
Leninsk U.S.S.R. **45** 48.42N 45.14E
Leninsk Kuznetskiy U.S.S.R. **50** 54.44N 86.13E
Lenk Switz. **39** 46.28N 7.27E
Lenkoran U.S.S.R. **65** 38.45N 48.50E
Lenmalu Indonesia **59** 1.58S130.00E
Lenne *r.* W. Germany **38** 51.25N 7.30E
Lennonville Australia **88** 27.58S117.50E
Lennoxville Canada **105** 45.22N 71.51W
Lenoir U.S.A. **113** 35.56N 81.31W
Lenora Czech. **38** 48.56N 13.48E
Lenora U.S.A. **110** 39.38N100.03W
Lenore L. Canada **101** 52.30N105.00W
Lenox U.S.A. **115** 42.22N 73.17W
Lens France **19** 50.26N 2.50E
Lenti Hungary **31** 46.37N 16.33E
Lentini Italy **33** 37.17N 15.00E
Lenvik Norway **40** 69.22N 18.10E
Léo U. Volta **76** 11.05N 2.06W
Leoben Austria **36** 47.23N 15.06E
Leominster U.K. **13** 52.15N 2.43W
Leominster U.S.A. **115** 42.32N 71.45W
Léon France **20** 43.53N 1.18W
León Mexico **116** 21.10N101.42W
León *d.* Mexico **111** 25.00N100.20W
León Nicaragua **117** 12.24N 86.52W
León Spain **26** 42.36N 5.34W
León *d.* Spain **26** 42.40N 6.00W
Leon U.S.A. **110** 40.44N 93.45W
León, Montes de *mts.* Spain **26** 42.30N 6.15W
Leonardtown U.S.A. **115** 38.17N 76.38W
Leonardville Namibia **80** 23.21S 18.47E
Leonárison Cyprus **66** 35.28N 34.08E
Leonberg W. Germany **39** 48.48N 9.01E
Leondári Greece **35** 39.11N 22.08E
Leonforte Italy **33** 37.39N 14.24E
Leongatha Australia **93** 38.29S145.57E
Leonídhion Greece **35** 37.10N 22.52E
Leonora Australia **89** 28.54S121.20E
Leopoldina Brazil **126** 21.30S 42.38W
Leopoldsburg Belgium **16** 51.08N 5.13E
Leovo U.S.S.R. **37** 46.29N 28.12E
Le Palais France **18** 47.21N 3.09W
Lepe Spain **27** 37.15N 7.12W
Lepel U.S.S.R. **44** 54.48N 28.40E
Le Pellerin France **18** 47.12N 1.45W
Leping China **55** 28.58N117.08E
L'Epiphanie Canada **105** 45.51N 73.30W
Le Pont-de-Beauvoisin France **21** 45.32N 5.40E
Lepontine, Alpi *mts.* Switz. **39** 46.20N 8.37E
Le Puy France **20** 45.02N 3.53E
Lequeitio Spain **26** 43.22N 2.30W
Le Quesnoy France **19** 50.15N 3.38E
Lerbäck Sweden **43** 58.56N 15.02E
Lercara Friddi Italy **32** 37.45N 13.36E
Léré Chad **77** 9.41N 14.17E
Lerici Italy **30** 44.04N 9.55E
Lérida Spain **25** 41.37N 0.37E
Lérida *d.* Spain **25** 42.00N 1.10E
Lerma Spain **26** 42.02N 3.45W
Le Rochefoucauld France **20** 45.45N 0.23E
Léros Greece **35** 37.10N 26.50E
Leross Canada **101** 51.17N103.53W
Le Roy Kans. U.S.A. **111** 38.05N 95.38W
Le Roy Mich. U.S.A. **112** 44.03N 85.29W
Le Roy N.Y. U.S.A. **114** 42.59N 77.59W
Lerwick U.K. **14** 60.09N 1.09W
Les Aix-d'Angillon France **19** 47.12N 2.34E
Les Andelys France **18** 49.15N 1.25E
Les Cayes Haiti **117** 18.15N 73.46W
Leschenault, C. Australia **89** 31.50S115.23E
Les Échelles France **21** 45.26N 5.45E
Les Ecrins *mtn.* France **21** 44.50N 6.20E
Les Essarts France **18** 46.46N 1.14W
Lesh Albania **34** 41.46N 19.39E
Leshan China **55** 29.30N103.45E
Les Herbiers France **18** 46.52N 1.01W
Leshukonskoye U.S.S.R. **44** 64.55N 45.50E
Lesina, Lago di *l.* Italy **31** 41.53N 15.26E
Lesjaskog Norway **41** 62.15N 8.22E
Lesjöfors Sweden **43** 59.59N 14.11E
Leskovac Yugo. **34** 42.59N 21.57E
Leslie Ark. U.S.A. **111** 35.50N 92.34W
Leslie Mich. U.S.A. **104** 42.27N 84.26W
Leśnica Yugo. **31** 44.39N 19.19E
Lesotho Africa **80** 29.00S 28.00E
Lesozavodsk U.S.S.R. **53** 45.30N133.29E
Les Pieux France **18** 49.31N 1.48W
Les Riceys France **19** 47.59N 4.22E
Les Sables d'Olonne France **18** 46.30N 1.47W
Lessay France **18** 49.13N 1.32W
Lessebo Sweden **43** 56.45N 15.16E
Lesser Antilles *is.* C. America **117** 13.00N 65.00W
Lesser Slave L. Canada **100** 55.30N115.25W
Lesser Sunda Is. *see* Nusa Tenggara Indonesia **58**
Lessines Belgium **16** 50.43N 3.50E
Lesti *r.* Finland **40** 64.04N 23.38E
Le Sueur U.S.A. **110** 44.27N 93.54W
Les Vans France **21** 44.24N 4.08E
Lésvos *i.* Greece **35** 39.10N 25.50E
Leszno Poland **36** 51.51N 16.35E
Letchworth U.K. **13** 51.58N 0.13W
Letchworth State Park U.S.A. **114** 42.42N 77.56W
Letenye Hungary **31** 46.26N 16.43E
Lethbridge Canada **98** 49.43N112.48W
Lethem Guyana **122** 3.18N 59.46W
Le Thillot France **19** 47.53N 6.46E
Leti, Kepulauan *is.* Indonesia **59** 8.20S128.00E
Letiahau *r.* Botswana **80** 21.16S 24.00E
Leticia Colombia **122** 4.09S 69.57W
Leting China **54** 39.26N118.56E
Letchatchee U.S.A. **113** 32.08N 86.30W
Le Trayas France **21** 43.28N 6.55E
Le Tréport France **18** 50.04N 1.22E
Lette Australia **92** 34.22S143.15E
Letterkenny Rep. of Ire. **15** 54.56N 7.45W
Leucate, Étang de *b.* France **20** 42.51N 3.00E
Leuk Switz. **39** 46.19N 7.38E
Leuser *mtn.* Indonesia **58** 3.50N 97.10E
Leutkirch W. Germany **39** 47.49N 10.01E
Leuven Belgium **16** 50.53N 4.45E
Leuze Hainaut Belgium **16** 50.36N 3.37E
Leuze Namur Belgium **16** 50.34N 4.53E
Levack Canada **104** 46.38N 81.23W
Levádhia Greece **35** 38.27N 22.54E
Levanger Norway **40** 63.45N 11.19E
Levanto Italy **30** 44.10N 9.38E
Levanzo, Isola di *i.* Italy **32** 38.00N 12.20E
Levelland U.S.A. **111** 33.35N102.23W
Lévêque, C. Australia **88** 16.25S123.00E
Le Verdon France **20** 45.33N 1.04W
Leverkusen W. Germany **38** 51.03N 6.59E
Levice Czech. **37** 48.13N 18.37E

Levier to Lodhrān

Levier France 19 46.57N 6.08E
Levin New Zealand 86 40.37S175.18E
Lévis Canada 105 46.48N 71.11W
Levittown U.S.A. 115 40.41N 73.31W
Lévka Cyprus 66 35.06N 32.51E
Lévka Óri mtn. Greece 35 35.18N 24.01E
Lévkás Greece 35 38.48N 20.43E
Levkás i. Greece 35 38.39N 20.27E
Levkimni Greece 34 39.25N 20.04E
Levkosía Cyprus 66 35.11N 33.23E
Levroux France 19 46.59N 1.37E
Levski Bulgaria 34 43.21N 25.10E
Lewes U.K. 13 50.53N 0.02E
Lewes U.S.A. 115 38.47N 75.08W
Lewis i. U.K. 14 58.10N 6.40W
Lewisburg U.S.A. 114 40.58N 76.53W
Lewis Pass f. New Zealand 86 42.30S172.15E
Lewisporte Canada 103 49.15N 55.04W
Lewis Range mts. U.S.A. 108 48.30N113.15W
Lewiston Idaho U.S.A. 108 46.25N117.01W
Lewiston Maine U.S.A. 112 44.06N 70.13W
Lewiston Mich. U.S.A. 104 44.53N 84.18W
Lewistown Mont. U.S.A. 108 47.04N109.26W
Lewistown Penn. U.S.A. 114 40.36N 77.31W
Lexington Ky. U.S.A. 113 38.03N 84.30W
Lexington Mich. U.S.A. 114 43.16N 82.32W
Lexington Miss. U.S.A. 111 33.07N 90.03W
Lexington Nebr. U.S.A. 110 40.47N 99.45W
Lexington Oreg. U.S.A. 108 45.27N119.41W
Leyburn U.K. 12 54.19N 1.50W
Leydsdorp R.S.A. 80 23.59S 30.32E
Leyre r. France 20 44.39N 1.01W
Leyte i. Phil. 59 10.40N124.50E
Lezignan France 20 43.12N 2.46E
Lhari China 63 30.47N 93.24E
Lhasa China 63 29.39N 91.06E
Lhasa He r. China 63 29.21N 90.45E
Lhazê China 63 29.10N 87.45E
Lhazhong China 63 32.02N 86.34E
Lhokseumawe Indonesia 58 5.09N 97.09E
Lhozhag China 63 28.23N 90.49E
Lhuntsi Dzong Bhutan 63 27.39N 91.09E
Lhünzê China 63 28.26N 92.27E
Lhünzhub China 63 30.00N 91.12E
Lhut r. Somali Rep. 71 10.25N 51.05E
Li Thailand 56 17.50N 98.55E
Liancheng China 55 25.47N116.48E
Liangcheng China 54 40.31N112.29E
Liangdang China 54 33.59N106.23E
Lianjiang Fujian China 55 26.10N119.33E
Lianjiang Guangdong China 55 21.33N110.19E
Lianshan China 55 24.37N112.02E
Lianshui China 54 33.46N119.18E
Lian Xian China 55 24.52N112.27E
Lianyungang China 54 34.36N119.10E
Liaocheng China 54 36.25N115.58E
Liaodong Bandao pen. China 54 40.00N122.20E
Liaodong Wan b. China 54 40.00N121.00E
Liao He r. China 54 40.40N122.20E
Liaoning d. China 54 42.00N122.00E
Liaoyang China 54 41.17N123.13E
Liaoyuan China 54 42.50N125.08E
Liapádhes Greece 34 39.40N 19.44E
Liard r. Canada 100 61.51N121.18W
Liāri Pakistan 62 25.41N 66.29E
Liart France 19 49.46N 4.20E
Libby U.S.A. 108 48.23N115.33W
Libenge Zaïre 78 3.39N 18.39E
Liberal U.S.A. 111 37.02N100.55W
Liberdade Brazil 126 22.01S 44.22W
Liberec Czech. 36 50.48N 15.05E
Liberia Africa 76 6.30N 9.30W
Liberia Costa Rica 117 10.39N 85.28W
Liberty N.Y. U.S.A. 115 41.48N 74.45W
Liberty Tex. U.S.A. 111 30.03N 94.47W
Lībīyah, Aş Şaḩrā' al des. Africa 64 24.00N 25.30E
Libo China 55 25.25N107.53E
Libourne France 20 44.55N 0.14W
Libramont Belgium 16 49.56N 5.22E
Librazhd Albania 34 41.12N 20.22E
Libreville Gabon 78 0.25N 9.30E
Libya Africa 75 26.30N 17.00E
Libyan Desert see Lībīyah, Aş Şaḩrā' al Africa 64
Libyan Plateau see Aḑ Ḑiffah Africa 64
Licantén Chile 125 34.59S 72.00W
Licata Italy 32 37.05N 13.56E
Lich W. Germany 38 50.33N 8.50E
Lichfield U.K. 13 52.40N 1.50W
Lichinga Mozambique 79 13.09S 35.17E
Lichtenburg R.S.A. 80 26.08S 26.09E
Lichtenfels W. Germany 38 50.09N 11.04E
Lichtenvoorde Neth. 16 51.59N 6.32E
Lichuan Hubei China 55 30.18N108.51E
Lichuan Jiangxi China 55 27.22N116.59E
Lickdale U.S.A. 115 40.28N 76.31W
Lickershamn Sweden 43 57.50N 18.31E
Licko Polje f. Yugo. 31 44.35N 15.25E
Lida U.S.A. 108 37.29N117.29W
Lida U.S.S.R. 37 53.50N 25.19E
Lidan r. Sweden 43 58.31N 13.09E
Lidhorikion Greece 35 38.28N 22.12E
Lidingö Sweden 43 59.22N 18.08E
Lidköping Sweden 43 58.30N 13.10E
Liechtenstein Europe 39 47.09N 9.32E
Liège Belgium 16 50.38N 5.35E
Liège d. Belgium 16 50.32N 5.35E
Lien-Huong Vietnam 56 11.13N108.48E
Lienz Austria 30 46.50N 12.47E
Liepāja U.S.S.R. 41 56.31N 21.01E
Lier Belgium 16 51.08N 4.35E
Lierneux Belgium 16 50.18N 5.50E
Liestal Switz. 39 47.29N 7.44E
Lieşti Romania 37 45.38N 27.32E
Lietariegos, Puerto de pass Spain 26 43.00N 6.25W
Liévin France 19 50.25N 2.46E
Liévre, Rivière du r. Canada 105 45.31N 75.26W
Liffey r. Rep. of Ire. 15 53.21N 6.14W
Liffré France 18 48.13N 1.30W
Lifjell mtn. Norway 42 59.30N 8.52E
Lifou, Île i. N. Cal. 84 20.53S167.13E
Lignières France 19 46.45N 2.11E
Ligny-en-Barrois France 19 48.41N 5.20E
Ligoúrion Greece 35 37.37N 23.02E
Ligueil France 18 47.03N 0.49E
Liguria d. Italy 30 44.30N 8.50E
Ligurian Sea Med. Sea 30 43.40N 9.00E
Lihou Reef and Cays Australia 90 17.25S151.40E
Lihue Hawaiian Is. 85 21.59N159.23W
Lihula U.S.S.R. 41 58.41N 23.50E
Lijiang China 61 26.50N100.15E
Lijin China 54 37.29N118.16E
Likasi Zaïre 78 10.58S 26.50E
Likati Zaïre 78 3.21N 23.53E
Liknes Norway 42 58.19N 6.59E
Likona r. Congo 78 0.11N 16.25E
Likouala r. Congo 78 0.51S 17.17E
Liku Niue 84 19.03S169.48W
L'Île Bouchard France 18 47.07N 0.25E
L'Île Rousse France 21 42.38N 8.56E
Lilla Edet Sweden 43 58.08N 12.08E
Lille France 19 50.38N 3.04E
Lille Baelt str. Denmark 42 55.20N 9.45E
Lillebonne France 18 49.31N 0.33E
Lillehammer Norway 41 61.08N 10.30E
Lillers France 19 50.34N 2.29E
Lillesand Norway 42 58.15N 8.24E
Lilleström Norway 42 59.57N 11.05E
Lillhärdal Sweden 41 61.51N 14.04E
Lillo Spain 27 39.43N 3.18W
Lillooet Canada 100 50.42N121.56W
Lillooet r. Canada 100 49.15N121.57W
Lilongwe Malaŵi 79 13.58S 33.49E
Liloy Phil. 59 8.08N122.40E
Lilydale Australia 92 32.58S139.59E
Lim r. Yugo. 31 43.45N 19.13E
Lima Peru 122 12.06S 77.03W
Lima r. Portugal 26 41.41N 8.50W
Lima Sweden 41 60.56N 13.26E
Lima Mont. U.S.A. 108 44.38N112.36W
Lima Ohio U.S.A. 112 40.43N 84.06W
Limassol see Lemesós Cyprus 66
Limavady U.K. 15 55.03N 6.57W
Limay r. Argentina 125 39.02S 68.07W
Limbang Malaysia 58 4.50N115.00E
Limbara, Monte mtn. Italy 32 40.51N 9.11E
Limbdi India 62 22.34N 71.48E
Limbe Cameroon 77 4.01N 9.12E
Limbourg Belgium 16 50.36N 5.57E
Limburg d. Belgium 16 50.36N 5.57E
Limburg d. Neth. 16 51.15N 5.45E
Limburg an der Lahn W. Germany 39 50.23N 8.04E
Limeira Brazil 126 22.34S 47.25W
Limerick Rep. of Ire. 15 52.40N 8.37W
Limerick d. Rep. of Ire. 15 52.40N 8.37W
Limfjorden str. Denmark 42 56.55N 9.10E
Liminka Finland 40 64.49N 25.24E
Limmared Sweden 43 57.32N 13.21E
Limmen Bight Australia 90 14.45S135.40E
Límni Greece 35 38.43N 23.18E
Límnos i. Greece 34 39.54N 25.21E
Limoges France 20 45.50N 1.16E
Limogne France 20 44.24N 1.46E
Limón Costa Rica 117 10.00N 83.01W
Limon U.S.A. 108 39.16N103.41W
Limone Piemonte Italy 30 44.12N 7.34E
Limousin d. France 20 45.45N 1.30E
Limousin, Plateaux du f. France 20 45.30N 1.15E
Limoux France 20 43.04N 2.14E
Limpopo r. Mozambique 81 25.14S 33.33E
Linah Saudi Arabia 65 28.48N 43.45E
Linakhamari U.S.S.R. 44 69.39N 31.21E
Linares Chile 125 35.51S 71.36W
Linares Mexico 111 24.52N 99.34W
Linares Spain 26 38.05N 3.38W
Linariá Greece 35 38.50N 24.32E
Lincang China 52 24.00N100.10E
Lincheng China 54 37.26N114.34E
Lincoln Argentina 125 34.55S 61.30W
Lincoln New Zealand 86 43.38S172.29E
Lincoln U.K. 12 53.14N 0.32W
Lincoln Ill. U.S.A. 110 40.10N 89.21W
Lincoln Mich. U.S.A. 104 44.41N 83.25W
Lincoln Nebr. U.S.A. 110 40.48N 96.42W
Lincoln N.H. U.S.A. 105 44.03N 71.40W
Lincoln City U.S.A. 108 44.59N124.00W
Lincoln Gap town Australia 92 32.45S137.18E
Lincoln Park town U.S.A. 114 42.14N 83.09W
Lincoln Sea Greenland 128 82.00N 55.00W
Lincolnshire d. U.K. 12 53.14N 0.32W
Lincoln Wolds hills U.K. 12 53.22N 0.08W
Lindau W. Germany 39 47.33N 9.41E
Linden Ala. U.S.A. 111 32.18N 87.47W
Linden Penn. U.S.A. 114 41.14N 77.08W
Lindenhurst U.S.A. 115 40.41N 73.22W
Linderödsåsen hills Sweden 43 55.44N 13.06E
Lindesberg Sweden 43 59.35N 15.15E
Lindesnes c. Norway 42 58.00N 7.02E
Líndhos Greece 35 36.06N 28.04E
Líndhos site Greece 35 36.06N 28.05E
Lindi Tanzania 79 10.00S 39.41E
Lindi r. Zaïre 78 0.30N 25.06E
Lindome Sweden 43 57.34N 12.05E
Lindsay Canada 104 44.21N 78.44W
Lindsay U.S.A. 109 36.12N119.05W
Line Is. Pacific Oc. 85 3.00S155.00W
Linesville U.S.A. 114 41.39N 80.26W
Linfen China 54 36.07N111.34E
Lingao China 55 19.54N109.40E
Lingayen Phil. 59 16.02N120.14E
Lingbo Sweden 41 61.03N 16.41E
Lingchuan China 55 25.25N110.20E
Lingen W. Germany 38 52.31N 7.19E
Lingga i. Indonesia 58 0.20S104.30E
Lingling China 55 26.12N111.30E
Lingshan China 55 22.17N109.27E
Lingshui China 55 18.31N110.00E
Linguère Senegal 76 15.22N 15.11W
Linhai China 55 28.49N121.08E
Linhe China 54 40.50N107.30E
Linköping Sweden 43 58.25N 15.37E
Linnhe, Loch U.K. 14 56.35N 5.25W
Linosa i. Italy 28 35.52N 12.50E
Linquan China 54 33.03N115.17E
Linru China 54 34.12N112.45E
Lins Brazil 126 21.40S 49.44W
Linshui China 55 30.18N106.55E
Lintan China 54 34.33N103.40E
Lintao China 54 35.20N104.00E
Linthal Switz. 39 46.55N 9.00E
Linton Canada 105 47.16N 72.15W
Linton Ind. U.S.A. 112 39.01N 87.10W
Linton N.Dak. U.S.A. 110 46.16N100.14W
Lintong China 54 34.24N109.13E
Lintorf W. Germany 38 51.20N 6.49E
Linwood U.S.A. 104 43.44N 83.59W
Linxe France 20 43.56N 1.10W
Linxi China 54 43.31N118.02E
Linxia China 54 35.30N103.10E
Lin Xian China 54 37.57N110.57E
Linyi Shandong China 54 35.08N118.20E
Linyi Shanxi China 54 35.12N110.45E
Linz Austria 39 48.18N 14.18E
Linz W. Germany 38 50.34N 7.17E
Linzgau f. W. Germany 39 47.50N 9.20E
Lion, Golfe du g. France 20 43.00N 4.00E
Lions, G. of see Lion, Golfe du France 20
Lion's Head town Canada 104 44.59N 81.15W
Liouesso Congo 78 1.12N 15.47E
Lipari, Isola i. Italy 33 38.30N 14.57E
Lipéité Congo 78 3.09N 17.22E
Lipetsk U.S.S.R. 44 52.37N 39.36E
Liphook U.K. 13 51.05N 0.49W
Liping China 55 26.16N109.08E
Lipkany U.S.S.R. 37 48.18N 26.48E
Lipova Romania 37 46.05N 21.40E
Lipovets U.S.S.R. 37 49.11N 29.01E
Lippe r. W. Germany 38 51.39N 6.38E
Lippstadt W. Germany 38 51.40N 8.19E
Lipsoí i. Greece 35 37.19N 26.50E
Liptovský Mikuláš Czech. 37 49.06N 19.37E
Lipu China 55 24.28N110.12E
Lira Uganda 79 2.15N 32.55E
Liranga Congo 78 0.43S 17.32E
Liri r. Italy 32 41.25N 13.52E
Liria Spain 25 39.38N 0.36W
Liria Sudan 73 4.38N 32.05E
Lisala Zaïre 78 2.13N 21.37E
Lisboa Portugal 27 38.43N 9.08W
Lisboa d. Portugal 27 39.05N 9.00W
Lisbon see Lisboa Portugal 27
Lisbon N.Dak. U.S.A. 110 46.27N 97.41W
Lisbon Ohio U.S.A. 114 40.47N 80.46W
Lisburn U.K. 15 54.30N 6.03W
Lisburne, C. U.S.A. 98 69.00N165.50W
Liscannor B. Rep. of Ire. 15 52.55N 9.24W
Liscia r. Italy 32 41.05N 9.17E
Lishi China 54 37.30N111.07E
Lishui China 55 28.28N119.59E
Lisianski i. Hawaiian Is. 84 26.04N173.58W
Lisichansk U.S.S.R. 45 48.53N 38.25E
Lisieux France 18 49.09N 0.14E
Liskeard U.K. 13 50.27N 4.29W
L'Isle Jourdain H.-Gar. France 20 43.37N 1.05E
L'Isle Jourdain Poit.-Char. France 18 46.14N 0.41E
L'Isle-sur-le-Doubs France 19 47.27N 6.35E
Lismore N.S.W. Australia 93 28.48S153.17E
Lismore Vic. Australia 92 37.58S143.22E
Lismore Rep. of Ire. 15 52.08N 7.57W
Liss U.K. 13 51.03N 0.53W
Lisse Neth. 16 52.18N 4.33E
Lista f. Norway 42 58.07N 6.40E
Lištica Yugo. 31 43.23N 17.36E
Listowel Canada 104 43.44N 80.57W
Listowel Rep. of Ire. 15 52.27N 9.30W
Litang China 55 23.09N109.09E
Litang Qu r. China 61 28.09N101.30E
Litchfield Conn. U.S.A. 115 41.45N 73.11W
Litchfield Ill. U.S.A. 110 39.11N 89.40W
Litchfield Minn. U.S.A. 110 45.08N 94.31W
Litchfield Nebr. U.S.A. 110 41.09N 99.09W
Lithgow Australia 93 33.30S150.09E
Líthinon, Ákra c. Greece 35 34.55N 24.44E
Lititz U.S.A. 115 40.09N 76.18W
Litókhoron Greece 34 40.06N 22.30E
Litoměřice Czech. 38 50.35N 14.09E
Litovskaya S.S.R. d. U.S.S.R. 37 54.30N 24.00E
Little Andaman i. India 56 10.40N 92.24E
Little Bahama Bank f. Bahamas 113 26.40N 78.00W
Little Belt Mts. U.S.A. 108 46.45N110.35W
Little Cayman i. Cayman Is. 117 19.40N 80.00W
Little Coco i. Burma 56 13.59N 93.12E
Little Colorado r. U.S.A. 109 36.11N111.48W
Little Current r. Canada 102 50.00N 84.35W
Little Current town Canada 104 45.58N 81.56W
Little Falls town Minn. U.S.A. 110 45.59N 94.21W
Little Falls town N.Y. U.S.A. 115 43.03N 74.52W
Littlefield U.S.A. 111 33.55N102.20W
Little Grand Rapids town Canada 101 52.05N 95.29W
Littlehampton U.K. 13 50.48N 0.32W
Little Inagua i. Bahamas 117 21.30N 73.00W
Little Kanawha r. U.S.A. 114 39.16N 81.34W
Little Karroo f. R.S.A. 80 33.40S 21.40E
Little Lake town U.S.A. 109 35.58N117.53W
Little Mecatina r. Canada 103 50.28N 59.35W
Little Missouri r. U.S.A. 110 47.30N102.25W
Little Nicobar i. India 61 7.20N 93.40E
Little Ouse r. U.K. 13 52.34N 0.20E
Little Quill L. Canada 101 51.55N104.05W
Little Rann of Kutch f. India 62 23.25N 71.30E
Little Rock town U.S.A. 111 34.44N 92.15W
Little Smoky r. Canada 100 55.42N117.38W
Littlestown U.S.A. 114 39.45N 77.05W
Littleton Colo. U.S.A. 108 39.37N105.01W
Littleton N.H. U.S.A. 105 44.18N 71.46W
Little Topar Australia 92 31.44S142.14E
Little Valley town U.S.A. 114 42.15N 78.48W
Little White r. Canada 104 46.21N 83.20W
Litvínov Czech. 38 50.37N 13.36E
Liuba China 54 33.37N106.55E
Liucheng China 55 24.39N109.14E
Liuchong He r. China 55 26.50N106.04E
Liuli Tanzania 79 11.07S 34.34E
Liulin China 54 37.26N110.52E
Liuzhou China 55 24.19N109.12E
Livadherón Greece 34 40.02N 21.57E
Livanátai Greece 35 38.42N 23.03E
Livanjsko Polje f. Yugo. 31 44.00N 16.40E
Livarot France 18 49.01N 0.09E
Lively Canada 104 46.26N 81.09W
Live Oak U.S.A. 113 30.19N 82.59W
Livermore, Mt. U.S.A. 109 30.39N104.11W
Liverpool Australia 93 33.57S150.52E
Liverpool Canada 103 44.02N 64.43W
Liverpool U.K. 12 53.25N 3.00W
Liverpool U.S.A. 115 43.06N 76.13W
Liverpool, C. Canada 99 73.38N 78.06W
Liverpool B. U.K. 12 53.30N 3.10W
Liverpool Plains f. Australia 93 31.20S150.00E
Liverpool Range mts. Australia 93 31.45S150.45E
Livigno Italy 30 46.32N 10.04E
Livingston U.K. 14 55.54N 3.31W
Livingston Mont. U.S.A. 108 45.40N110.34W
Livingston Tex. U.S.A. 111 30.43N 94.56W
Livingstone see Maramba Zambia 80
Livingstonia Malaŵi 79 10.35S 34.10E
Livno Yugo. 31 43.50N 17.01E
Livo r. Finland 40 65.24N 26.48E
Livonia Mich. U.S.A. 104 42.25N 83.23W
Livonia N.Y. U.S.A. 114 42.49N 77.40W
Livorno Italy 30 43.33N 10.18E
Liwale Tanzania 79 9.47S 38.00E
Liwan Sudan 73 4.55N 35.41E
Li Xian Gansu China 54 34.11N105.02E
Li Xian Hunan China 55 29.38N111.45E
Lixoúrion Greece 35 38.14N 20.24E
Liyujiang China 55 25.59N113.12E
Lizard U.K. 13 49.58N 5.12W
Lizard Pt. U.K. 13 49.57N 5.15W
Lizemores U.S.A. 114 38.20N 81.12W
Ljan Norway 42 59.51N 10.48E
Ljubija Yugo. 31 44.56N 16.37E
Ljubinje Yugo. 31 42.57N 18.05E
Ljubljana Yugo. 31 46.03N 14.31E
Ljubovija Yugo. 31 44.11N 19.22E
Ljubški Yugo. 31 43.12N 17.33E
Ljugarn Sweden 43 57.19N 18.42E
Ljungan r. Sweden 41 62.19N 17.23E
Ljungby Sweden 43 56.50N 13.56E
Ljungbyholm Sweden 43 56.38N 16.10E
Ljungdalen Sweden 40 62.54N 12.45E
Ljungsbro Sweden 43 58.31N 15.30E
Ljusdal Sweden 41 61.50N 16.05E
Ljusnan r. Sweden 41 61.12N 17.08E
Ljusne Sweden 41 61.13N 17.08E
Ljusterö i. Sweden 43 59.31N 18.37E
Ljutomer Yugo. 31 46.31N 16.12E
Llandeilo U.K. 13 51.54N 4.00W
Llandovery U.K. 13 51.59N 3.49W
Llandrindod Wells U.K. 13 52.15N 3.23W
Llandudno U.K. 12 53.19N 3.49W
Llanelli U.K. 13 51.41N 4.11W
Llanes Spain 26 43.25N 4.45W
Llangadfan U.K. 13 52.41N 3.28W
Llangollen U.K. 12 52.58N 3.10W
Llanidloes U.K. 13 52.28N 3.31W
Llanos f. S. America 122 7.30N 70.00W
Llansá Spain 25 42.22N 3.09E
Llanwrtyd Wells U.K. 13 52.06N 3.39W
Llentrisca, Cabo de c. Spain 25 38.51N 1.14E
Llerena Spain 26 38.14N 6.01W
Llobregat r. Spain 25 41.19N 2.09E
Lloret de Mar Spain 25 41.42N 2.53E
Lloydminster Canada 101 53.17N110.00W
Lluchmayor Spain 25 39.29N 2.54E
Loange r. Zaïre 78 4.18S 20.05E
Lobatse Botswana 80 25.12S 25.39E
Löbau E. Germany 38 51.05N 14.40E
Lobaye r. C.A.R. 77 3.40N 18.35E
Lobería Argentina 125 38.08S 58.48W
Lobito Angola 78 12.20S 13.34E
Lobonäs Sweden 41 61.33N 15.20E
Lobos Argentina 125 35.10S 59.05W
Lobstick L. Canada 103 54.00N 64.50W
Locarno Switz. 39 46.10N 8.48E
Lochboisdale town U.K. 14 57.09N 7.19W
Lochem Neth. 16 52.10N 6.25E
Loches France 18 47.08N 1.00E
Lochgilphead U.K. 14 56.02N 5.26W
Lochinver U.K. 14 58.09N 5.15W
Lochmaddy town U.K. 14 57.36N 7.10W
Lochnagar mtn. U.K. 14 56.57N 3.15W
Lochranza U.K. 14 55.42N 5.18W
Loch Raven Resr. U.S.A. 115 39.27N 76.36W
Lochy, Loch U.K. 14 56.58N 4.55W
Lock Australia 92 33.34S135.46E
Lockeport Canada 103 43.42N 65.07W
Lockerbie U.K. 14 55.07N 3.21W
Lockhart Australia 93 35.16S146.42E
Lockhart U.S.A. 111 29.53N 97.41W
Lockhart, L. Australia 89 33.27S119.00E
Lock Haven U.S.A. 114 41.08N 77.27W
Löcknitz E. Germany 38 53.27N 14.12E
Lockport U.S.A. 114 43.10N 78.42W
Loc Ninh Vietnam 56 11.51N106.35E
Locri Italy 33 38.14N 16.16E
Lod Israel 67 31.57N 34.54E
Lodalskåpa mtn. Norway 41 61.47N 7.13E
Loddon r. Australia 92 35.40S143.59E
Lodève France 20 43.43N 3.19E
Lodeynoye Pole U.S.S.R. 44 60.43N 33.30E
Lodge Grass U.S.A. 108 45.19N107.22W
Lodhrān Pakistan 62 29.32N 71.38E

Lodi Italy 30 45.19N 9.30E
Lodi Calif. U.S.A. 108 38.08N121.16W
Lodi Ohio U.S.A. 114 41.03N 82.01W
Lodja Zaïre 78 3.29S 23.33E
Lodosa Spain 25 42.25N 2.05W
Lodwar Kenya 79 3.06N 35.38E
Łódź Poland 37 51.49N 19.28E
Loei Thailand 56 17.32N101.34E
Lofer Austria 39 47.35N 12.41E
Lofoten is. Norway 8 68.15N 13.50E
Lofoten Vesterålen is. Norway 40 68.15N 13.50E
Log U.S.S.R. 45 49.28N 43.51E
Loga Niger 77 13.40N 3.15E
Logan Australia 93 27.48S153.04E
Logan N.Mex. U.S.A. 109 35.22N103.25W
Logan Ohio U.S.A. 114 39.32N 82.25W
Logan Utah U.S.A. 108 41.44N111.50W
Logan, Mt. Canada 100 60.34N140.24W
Logansport U.S.A. 112 40.45N 86.25W
Loganton U.S.A. 114 41.02N 77.18W
Loge r. Angola 78 7.52S 13.08E
Logone r. Cameroon/Chad 77 12.10N 15.00E
Logone Occidental d. Chad 77 8.40N 15.50E
Logone Oriental d. Chad 77 8.10N 16.00E
Logoysk U.S.S.R. 37 54.08N 27.42E
Logroño Spain 25 42.28N 2.27W
Logrosán Spain 27 39.20N 5.29W
Løgstør Denmark 42 56.58N 9.15E
Løgumkloster Denmark 42 55.03N 8.57E
Lohārdaga India 63 23.26N 84.41E
Lohāru India 62 28.27N 75.49E
Lohja Finland 41 60.15N 24.05E
Lohjanjärvi l. Finland 41 60.15N 23.55E
Lohne W. Germany 38 52.42N 8.12E
Lohr W. Germany 39 50.00N 9.34E
Loikaw Burma 56 19.40N 97.17E
Loimaa Finland 41 60.51N 23.03E
Loir r. France 18 47.33N 0.32W
Loire d. France 21 45.30N 4.00E
Loire r. France 18 47.16N 2.11W
Loire-Atlantique d. France 18 47.20N 1.35W
Loiret d. France 19 47.55N 2.20E
Loir-et-Cher d. France 18 47.30N 1.30E
Loja Ecuador 122 3.59S 79.16W
Loja Spain 27 37.10N 4.09W
Loka Sudan 73 4.16N 31.01E
Loka Zaïre 78 0.20N 17.57E
Löken Norway 42 59.48N 11.29E
Loken tekojärvi resr. Finland 40 67.55N 27.40E
Lokeren Belgium 16 51.06N 3.59E
Loket Czech. 39 50.09N 12.43E
Lokichar Kenya 79 2.23N 35.39E
Lokitaung Kenya 79 4.15N 35.45E
Lokka Finland 40 67.49N 27.44E
Løkken Denmark 42 57.22N 9.43E
Løkken Norway 40 63.06N 9.43E
Loknya U.S.S.R. 44 56.49N 30.00E
Lokoja Nigeria 77 7.49N 6.44E
Lokolo r. Zaïre 78 0.45S 19.36E
Lokoro r. Zaïre 78 1.40S 18.29E
Lol r. Sudan 73 9.11N 29.12E
Lolland i. Denmark 41 54.46N 11.30E
Lom Bulgaria 34 43.49N 23.14E
Lom Norway 41 61.50N 8.33E
Loma U.S.A. 108 47.57N110.30W
Lomami r. Zaïre 78 0.45N 24.10E
Lomas de Zamora Argentina 125 34.46S 58.24W
Lombardia d. Italy 30 45.45N 9.00E
Lombok i. Indonesia 58 8.30S116.20E
Lombok, Selat str. Indonesia 59 8.38S115.40E
Lomé Togo 77 6.10N 1.21E
Lomela Zaïre 78 2.15S 23.15E
Lomela r. Zaïre 78 0.14S 20.45E
Lomié Cameroon 77 3.09N 13.35E
Lomme France 19 50.39N 2.59E
Lommel Belgium 16 51.15N 5.18E
Lomond Canada 100 50.21N112.39W
Lomond, Loch U.K. 14 56.07N 4.36W
Lompoc U.S.A. 109 34.38N120.27W
Łomża Poland 37 53.11N 22.04E
Lonaconing U.S.A. 114 39.34N 78.59W
Londinières France 18 49.50N 1.24E
London Canada 104 42.59N 81.14W
London Kiribati 85 1.58N157.28W
London U.K. 13 51.32N 0.06W
Londonderry U.K. 15 55.00N 7.21W
Londonderry d. U.K. 15 55.00N 7.00W
Londonderry, C. Australia 88 13.58S126.55E
Londonderry, Isla i. Chile 125 55.03S 70.40W
Londrina Brazil 124 23.30S 51.13W
Lonely I. Canada 104 45.34N 81.29W
Lone Pine U.S.A. 109 36.36N118.04W
Long, L. Canada 105 47.05N 74.06W
Longa r. Angola 78 16.15S 19.07E
Longá Greece 35 36.53N 21.55E
Longa, Proliv str. U.S.S.R. 51 70.00N178.00E
Long'an China 55 23.11N107.41E
Longarone Italy 30 46.16N 12.18E
Long Beach town Calif. U.S.A. 109 33.46N118.11W
Long Beach town N.Y. U.S.A. 115 40.35N 73.41W
Long Branch U.S.A. 115 40.18N 74.00W
Long Broad Sd. Australia 90 22.20S149.50E
Longchamps Belgium 16 50.05N 5.42E
Longchang China 55 29.18N105.20E
Longchuan China 55 24.12N115.25E
Long Creek town U.S.A. 108 44.43N119.06W
Long Eaton U.K. 12 52.54N 1.16W
Longeau France 19 47.46N 5.18E
Longford Rep. of Ire. 15 53.44N 7.48W
Longford d. Rep. of Ire. 15 53.42N 7.45W
Longhua Hebei China 54 41.17N117.37E
Long I. Bahamas 117 23.00N 75.00W
Long I. Canada 102 54.55N 79.30W
Long I. U.S.A. 115 40.50N 73.00W
Longido Tanzania 79 2.43S 36.41E
Longiram Indonesia 58 0.05S115.45E
Long Island Sd. U.S.A. 115 41.05N 72.58W
Long Jiang r. China 55 24.12N109.30E
Long L. Canada 102 49.30N 86.50W
Long L. U.S.A. 105 44.04N 74.20W
Longlac town Canada 102 49.45N 86.25W
Long Lake town U.S.A. 105 43.58N 74.25W
Longli China 55 26.29N107.59E
Longlin China 55 24.43N105.26E
Longmeadow U.S.A. 115 42.03N 72.34W
Longmont U.S.A. 108 40.10N105.06W
Longnan China 55 24.54N114.47E
Longnawan Indonesia 58 1.54N114.53E
Longniddry U.K. 14 55.58N 2.53W
Long Point B. Canada 104 42.40N 80.14W
Long Pt. Canada 104 42.33N 80.04W
Longquan China 55 28.05N119.07E
Long Range Mts. Nfld. Canada 103 48.00N 58.30W
Long Range Mts. Nfld. Canada 103 50.00N 57.00W
Longreach Australia 90 23.26S144.15E
Long Sault Canada 105 45.00N 74.55W
Longsheng China 55 25.59N110.01E
Longs Peak U.S.A. 108 40.15N105.37W
Longtown U.K. 12 55.01N 2.58W
Longué France 18 47.23N 0.06W
Longueuil Canada 105 45.32N 73.30W
Longuyon France 19 49.26N 5.36E
Longview Tex. U.S.A. 111 32.30N 94.44W
Longview Wash. U.S.A. 108 46.08N122.57W
Longwood St. Helena 127 15.57S 5.42W
Longwy France 19 49.31N 5.46E
Longxi China 54 34.59N104.45E
Long Xian China 54 34.52N106.50E
Long Xuyen Vietnam 56 10.23N105.23E
Longyan China 55 25.10N117.02E
Longzhou China 55 22.24N106.50E
Lonigo Italy 32 45.23N 11.23E
Löningen W. Germany 38 52.44N 7.46E
Lonja r. Yugo. 31 45.30N 16.40E
Lönsboda Sweden 43 56.24N 14.19E
Lönsdal Norway 40 66.46N 15.26E
Lonsdale, L. Australia 92 37.05S142.15E
Lons-le-Saunier France 19 46.40N 5.33E
Looc Phil. 59 12.20N122.05E
Looe U.K. 13 50.51N 4.26W
Lookout, C. U.S.A. 113 34.35N 76.32W
Loolmalassin mtn. Tanzania 79 3.00S 35.45E
Loongana Australia 89 30.57S127.02E
Loon Lake Mts. U.S.A. 105 44.35N 74.08W
Loop Head Rep. of Ire. 15 52.33N 9.56W
Lopari Zaïre 73 1.15N 19.59E
Lopari r. Zaïre 78 1.20N 20.22E
Lop Buri Thailand 56 14.49N100.37E
Lopez, C. Gabon 78 0.36S 8.40E
Lopi Congo 78 2.57N 16.47E
Lop Nur l. China 52 40.30N 90.30E
Lopphavet est. Norway 40 70.30N 20.00E
Lopydino U.S.S.R. 44 61.10N 52.02E
Lora, Hāmūn-i- l. Pakistan 62 29.20N 64.50E
Lora del Río Spain 27 37.39N 5.32W
Lorain U.S.A. 114 41.28N 82.10W
Loralai Pakistan 62 30.22N 68.36E
Lorca Spain 25 37.40N 1.42W
Lord Howe I. Pacific Oc. 84 31.28S159.09E
Lord Howe Rise Pacific Oc. 84 29.00S162.30E
Lordsburg U.S.A. 109 32.21N108.43W
Lorena Brazil 126 22.44S 45.07W
Lorengau P.N.G. 59 2.01S147.15E
Lorenzo Geyres Uruguay 125 32.05S 57.55W
Loreto Brazil 123 7.05S 45.09W
Loreto Italy 31 43.26N 13.36E
Loreto Mexico 109 26.01N111.21W
Loretteville Canada 105 46.51N 71.21W
Lorian Swamp Kenya 79 0.35N 39.40E
Lorient France 18 47.45N 3.22W
Loriol France 21 44.45N 4.49E
Lormes France 19 47.17N 3.49E
Lorne Australia 92 38.34S144.01E
Lörrach W. Germany 39 47.37N 7.40E
Lorraine d. France 19 49.00N 6.00E
Lorrainville Canada 104 47.20N 79.21W
Lorris France 19 47.53N 2.31E
Lorsch W. Germany 39 49.39N 8.34E
Lorup W. Germany 38 52.55N 7.38E
Los Alamos Mexico 111 28.40N103.30W
Los Alamos U.S.A. 109 35.53N106.19W
Los Andes Chile 125 32.50S 70.37W
Los Angeles Chile 125 37.28S 72.21W
Los Angeles U.S.A. 106 34.00N118.17W
Los Bajíos Mexico 109 28.31N108.25W
Los Banos U.S.A. 108 37.04N120.51W
Los Blancos Argentina 124 23.40S 62.35W
Los Blancos Spain 25 37.38N 0.49W
Los Canarreos, Archipiélago de Cuba 117 21.40N 82.30W
Los Herreras Mexico 111 25.55N 99.24W
Lošinj i. Yugo. 31 44.36N 14.24E
Losinovka U.S.S.R. 37 50.50N 31.57E
Los Llanos de Aridane Canary Is. 127 28.39N 17.54W
Los Lunas U.S.A. 109 34.48N106.44W
Los Mochis Mexico 116 25.45N108.57W
Los Navalmorales Spain 27 39.43N 4.38W
Los Olivos U.S.A. 109 34.40N120.06W
Los Palacios y Villafranca Spain 27 37.10N 5.56W
Los Roques is. Venezuela 122 12.00N 67.00W
Los Santos de Maimona Spain 27 38.27N 6.23W
Lossiemouth U.K. 14 57.43N 3.18W
Lost r. U.S.A. 114 39.05N 78.36W
Lost Cabin U.S.A. 108 43.19N107.36W
Lost City U.S.A. 114 38.55N 78.51W
Los Teques Venezuela 122 10.25N 67.01W
Lost River town U.S.A. 114 38.57N 78.50W
Los Vilos Chile 124 31.55S 71.31W
Los Yébenes Spain 27 39.34N 3.53W
Lot d. France 20 44.35N 1.40E
Lot r. France 20 44.18N 0.20E
Lota Chile 125 37.05S 73.10W
Lot-et-Garonne d. France 20 44.20N 0.20E
Lothian d. U.K. 14 55.50N 3.00W
Lotoi r. Zaïre 78 1.30S 18.30E
Lotsani r. Botswana 80 22.42S 28.11E
Lötschberg Tunnel Switz. 38 46.25N 7.53E
Lotuke mtn. Sudan 73 4.07N 33.48E
Louang Namtha Laos 56 20.57N101.25E
Louangphrabang Laos 56 19.53N102.10E
Loudéac France 18 48.10N 2.45W
Loudima Congo 78 4.06S 13.05E
Loudonville U.S.A. 114 40.38N 82.14W
Loudun France 18 47.01N 0.05E
Loué France 18 48.00N 0.09W
Loue r. France 19 47.04N 6.10E
Louga Senegal 76 15.37N 16.13W
Loughborough U.K. 12 52.47N 1.11W
Loughrea Rep. of Ire. 15 53.12N 8.35W
Loughros More B. Rep. of Ire. 15 54.48N 8.32W
Louhans France 19 46.38N 5.13E
Louisburgh Rep. of Ire. 15 53.46N 9.49W
Louiseville Canada 105 46.14N 72.56W
Louisiade Archipelago is. P.N.G. 90 11.00S153.00E
Louisiana d. U.S.A. 111 30.60N 92.30W
Louis Trichardt R.S.A. 80 23.03S 29.54E
Louisville Ky. U.S.A. 112 38.13N 85.48W
Louisville Miss. U.S.A. 111 33.07N 89.03W
Louisville Ohio U.S.A. 114 40.50N 81.16W
Louis XIV, Pointe c. Canada 102 54.35N 79.50W
Loukhi U.S.S.R. 44 66.05N 33.04E
Loukouo Congo 78 3.38S 14.39E
Loulé Portugal 27 37.08N 8.00W
Loum Cameroon 77 4.46N 9.45E
Louny Czech. 39 50.19N 13.46E
Lourches France 19 50.19N 3.21E
Lourdes France 20 43.06N 0.03W
Loures Portugal 27 38.50N 9.10W
Lourinhã Portugal 27 39.14N 9.19W
Lourosa Portugal 26 40.19N 7.56W
Lousã Portugal 27 40.07N 8.15W
Louth Australia 93 30.34S145.09E
Louth d. Rep. of Ire. 15 53.55N 6.30W
Louth U.K. 12 53.23N 0.00
Loutra Greece 35 37.51N 21.06E
Loutrá Aidhipsoú Greece 35 38.54N 23.02E
Louviers France 18 49.13N 1.10E
Louvigné-du-Désert France 18 48.29N 1.08W
Lövånger Sweden 40 64.22N 21.18E
Lovat r. U.S.S.R. 44 58.06N 31.37E
Lovech Bulgaria 34 43.08N 24.43E
Lovech d. Bulgaria 34 43.08N 24.45E
Loveland U.S.A. 108 40.24N105.05W
Lovell U.S.A. 108 44.50N108.24W
Lovelock U.S.A. 108 40.11N118.28W
Love Point town U.S.A. 115 39.02N 76.18W
Lovere Italy 30 45.49N 10.04E
Lovington U.S.A. 111 32.57N103.21W
Lovoi r. Zaïre 79 8.14S 26.40E
Lovosice Czech. 38 50.31N 14.03E
Lovozero U.S.S.R. 44 68.01N 35.08E
Lovrin Romania 37 45.58N 20.48E
Lovua r. Zaïre 78 6.08S 20.35E
Low Canada 105 45.48N 75.57W
Lowa Zaïre 78 1.24S 25.51E
Lowa r. Kivu Zaïre 78 1.25S 25.55E
Lowell U.S.A. 115 42.39N 71.18W
Löwenberg E. Germany 38 52.54N 13.08E
Lower Arrow L. Canada 100 49.40N118.05W
Lower California pen. see Baja California Mexico 116
Lower Egypt see Mişr Baḩrī Egypt 66
Lower Hutt New Zealand 86 41.13S174.55E
Lower Lough Erne U.K. 15 54.28N 7.48W
Lower Pen. f. U.S.A. 104 44.34N 84.28W
Lower Post Canada 100 59.55N128.30W
Lower Red L. U.S.A. 110 48.00N 94.50W
Lowestoft U.K. 13 52.29N 1.44E
Lowgar d. Afghan. 62 34.10N 69.20E
Łowicz Poland 37 52.06N 19.55E
Lowrah r. see Pishīn Lora Afghan. 62
Lowville U.S.A. 105 43.47N 75.29W
Loxton Australia 92 34.38S140.38E
Loyalsock r. U.S.A. 114 41.14N 76.56W
Loyalty Is. see Loyauté, Îles N. Cal. 84
Loyauté, Îles is. N. Cal. 84 21.00S167.00E
Loyoro Uganda 79 3.22N 34.16E
Lozère d. France 20 44.30N 3.30E
Loznica Yugo. 31 44.32N 19.13E
Lozoyuela Spain 26 40.55N 3.37W
Lua r. Zaïre 78 2.45N 18.28E
Luabo Mozambique 81 18.30S 36.10E
Luachimo Angola 78 7.25S 20.43E
Lualaba r. Zaïre 78 0.18N 25.32E
Luama r. Zaïre 79 4.45S 26.55E
Luampa Zambia 78 15.04S 24.20E
Lu'an China 55 31.47N116.30E
Luancheng Guang. Zhuang.China 55 22.48N108.55E
Luancheng Hebei China 54 37.53N114.39E
Luanda Angola 78 8.50S 13.20E
Luanda d. Angola 78 9.00S 13.30E
Luando Game Res. Angola 78 11.00S 17.45E
Luanginga r. Zambia 78 15.11S 23.05E
Luangwa r. Central Zambia 79 15.32S 30.28E
Luan He r. China 54 39.25N119.10E
Luanping China 54 40.55N117.17E
Luanshya Zambia 79 13.09S 28.24E
Luan Xian China 54 39.45N118.44E
Luao Angola 78 10.41S 22.09E
Luapula r. Zambia 79 9.25S 28.36E
Luarca Spain 26 43.32N 6.32W
Lubalo Angola 78 9.13S 19.21E
Lubango Angola 78 14.52S 13.30E
Lubao Zaïre 78 5.19S 25.43E
Lübben E. Germany 38 51.56N 13.53E
Lübbenau E. Germany 38 51.52N 13.57E
Lubbock U.S.A. 111 33.35N101.51W
Lubeck Australia 92 36.47S142.38E
Lübeck W. Germany 38 53.52N 10.40E
Lübecker Bucht b. E. Germany 38 54.10N 11.20E
Lubefu r. Zaïre 78 4.05S 23.00E
Lubenka U.S.S.R. 45 50.22N 54.13E
Lubersac France 20 45.27N 1.24E
Lubia Angola 78 11.01S 17.06E
Lubika Zaïre 79 7.50S 29.12E
Lubilash r. Zaïre 78 4.59S 23.25E
Lubin Poland 36 51.24N 16.13E
Lublin Poland 37 51.18N 22.31E
Lubliniec Poland 37 50.40N 18.41E
Lubny U.S.S.R. 45 50.01N 33.00E
Lübtheen E. Germany 38 53.18N 11.04E
Lubudi Zaïre 78 9.57S 25.59E
Lubudi r. K.Occidental Zaïre 78 4.00S 21.23E
Lubudi r. Shaba Zaïre 78 9.13S 25.40E
Lubumbashi Zaïre 79 11.44S 27.29E
Lubutu Zaïre 78 0.48S 26.19E
Lübz E. Germany 38 53.27N 12.01E
Lucas González Argentina 125 32.25S 59.33W
Lucca Italy 30 43.50N 10.29E
Luce B. U.K. 14 54.45N 4.47W
Lucena Phil. 59 13.56N121.37E
Lucena Spain 27 37.24N 4.29W
Lucena del Cid Spain 25 40.08N 0.17W
Lucenay-l'Évêque France 19 47.05N 4.15E
Luc-en-Diois France 21 44.37N 5.27E
Lučenec Czech. 37 48.20N 19.40E
Lucera Italy 33 41.30N 15.20E
Lucerne U.S.A. 108 48.12N120.36W
Lucero Mexico 109 30.49N106.30W
Luchena r. Spain 25 37.44N 1.50W
Lüchow W. Germany 38 52.58N 11.10E
Lucin U.S.A. 108 41.22N113.55W
Lucindale Australia 92 36.59S140.25E
Lucira Angola 78 13.51S 12.31E
Luckau E. Germany 38 51.51N 13.43E
Luckeesarai India 63 25.11N 86.05E
Luckenwalde E. Germany 38 52.05N 13.10E
Lucknow Canada 104 43.57N 81.31W
Lucknow India 63 26.51N 80.55E
Luçon France 18 46.27N 1.10W
Lucy Creek town Australia 90 22.25S136.20E
Lüda China 54 38.49N121.48E
Luda Kamchiya r. Bulgaria 34 42.50N 27.00E
Ludbreg Yugo. 31 46.15N 16.37E
Lüdenscheid W. Germany 38 51.13N 7.38E
Lüderitz Namibia 80 26.37S 15.09E
Ludgate Canada 104 45.54N 80.32W
Ludhiāna India 62 30.55N 75.51E
Lüdinghausen W. Germany 16 51.46N 7.27E
Ludington U.S.A. 112 43.58N 86.27W
Ludlow U.K. 13 52.23N 2.42W
Ludlow Penn. U.S.A. 114 41.44N 78.57W
Ludlow Vt. U.S.A. 115 43.24N 72.42W
Ludogorie mts. Bulgaria 37 43.45N 27.00E
Luduş Romania 37 46.29N 24.05E
Ludvika Sweden 43 60.09N 15.11E
Ludwigsburg W. Germany 39 48.53N 9.11E
Ludwigsfelde E. Germany 38 52.17N 13.16E
Ludwigshafen W. Germany 39 49.29N 8.26E
Ludwigslust E. Germany 38 53.19N 11.30E
Luebo Zaïre 78 5.16S 21.27E
Luena Angola 78 11.46S 19.55E
Luena r. Angola 78 12.30S 22.37E
Luena Zaïre 78 9.27S 25.47E
Luena Zambia 79 10.40S 30.21E
Luena r. Western Zambia 78 14.47S 23.05E
Luengue r. Angola 78 16.58S 21.15E
Luenha r. Mozambique 81 16.29S 33.40E
Lüeyang China 54 33.20N106.03E
Lufeng China 55 23.01N115.35E
Lufira r. Zaïre 78 8.15S 26.30E
Lufkin U.S.A. 107 31.21N 94.47W
Luga U.S.S.R. 44 58.42N 29.49E
Lugano Switz. 39 46.01N 8.58E
Lugano, Lago di l. Switz./Italy 39 46.00N 9.00E
Luganville Vanuatu 84 15.32S167.08E
Lugela Mozambique 81 16.25S 36.42E
Lugenda r. Mozambique 79 11.23S 38.30E
Lugh Ganane Somali Rep. 79 3.56N 42.32E
Luginy U.S.S.R. 37 51.05N 28.21E
Lugnaquilla Mtn. Rep. of Ire. 15 52.58N 6.28W
Lugo Italy 30 44.25N 11.54E
Lugo Spain 26 43.02N 7.34W
Lugo d. Spain 26 42.55N 7.30W
Lugoj Romania 37 45.42N 21.56E
Luiana Angola 78 17.08S 22.59E
Luiana r. Angola 78 17.28S 23.02E
Luilaka r. Zaïre 78 0.15S 19.00E
Luilu r. Zaïre 78 6.22S 23.53E
Luino Italy 30 46.00N 8.44E
Luiro r. Finland 40 67.18N 27.28E
Luisa Zaïre 78 7.15S 22.27E
Lujiang China 55 31.14N117.17E
Lukala Zaïre 78 5.23S 13.02E
Lukanga Swamp f. Zambia 79 14.15S 27.30E
Lukenie r. Zaïre 78 2.43S 18.12E
Lukka Sudan 72 14.33N 23.42E
Lukovit Bulgaria 34 43.12N 24.10E
Łuków Poland 37 51.56N 22.23E
Lukoyanov U.S.S.R. 44 55.03N 44.29E
Lukuga r. Zaïre 79 5.37S 26.58E
Lukula r. Zaïre 78 4.15S 17.59E
Lukulu Zambia 78 14.35S 23.25E
Lukumbule Tanzania 79 11.34S 37.24E
Lule r. Sweden 40 65.35N 22.03E
Luleå Sweden 40 65.34N 22.10E
Lüleburgaz Turkey 29 41.25N 27.23E
Lüliang Shan mts. China 54 37.00N111.20E
Lulonga r. Zaïre 78 0.42N 18.26E
Lulu r. Zaïre 78 1.18N 23.42E
Lulua r. Zaïre 78 5.03S 21.07E
Lumai Angola 78 13.13S 21.13E
Lumajangdong Co l. China 63 34.02N 81.40E
Lumbala Angola 78 14.02S 21.35E
Lumbala Angola 78 12.37S 22.33E
Lumberton Miss. U.S.A. 111 31.00N 89.27W
Lumberton N.Mex. U.S.A. 108 36.55N106.56W
Lumbrales Spain 26 40.56N 6.43W
Lumbres France 19 50.42N 2.08E
Lumsden New Zealand 86 45.44S168.26E
Lūnāvāda India 62 23.08N 73.37E
Lund Sweden 43 55.42N 13.11E

M

Marchant Hill to Maysah, Tall al

Marchant Hill Australia 92 32.16S138.49E
Marche Belgium 16 50.13N 5.21E
Marche d. Italy 30 43.35N 13.00E
Marchena Spain 27 37.20N 5.24W
Mar Chiquita l. Argentina 124 30.42S 62.36W
Marcigny France 19 46.17N 4.02E
Marcos Paz Argentina 125 34.49S 58.51W
Marcounda C.A.R. 77 7.37N 16.59E
Marcq-en-Baroeul France 16 50.40N 3.01E
Marcus Hook U.S.A. 115 39.49N 75.25W
Marcus I. Pacific Oc. 84 24.18N153.58E
Marcy, Mt. U.S.A. 105 44.07N 73.56W
Mardān Pakistan 62 34.12N 72.02E
Mar del Plata Argentina 125 38.00S 57.32W
Marden U.K. 13 51.11N 0.30E
Mardie Australia 88 21.14S115.57E
Mardin Turkey 64 37.19N 40.43E
Maré, Île i. N. Cal. 84 21.30S168.00E
Maree, Loch U.K. 14 57.41N 5.28W
Mareeba Australia 90 17.00S145.26E
Mareg Somali Rep. 71 3.47N 47.18E
Marennes France 20 45.50N 1.06W
Marettimo i. Italy 32 37.58N 12.04E
Mareuil-sur-Belle France 20 45.28N 0.28E
Marfa U.S.A. 111 30.18N104.01W
Margai Caka l. China 61 35.11N 86.57E
Margaret r. Australia 92 29.26S137.00E
Margaret Bay town Canada 100 51.20N127.20W
Margaret L. Canada 100 58.56N115.25W
Margaret River town W. Aust. Australia 89 33.57S115.04E
Margaret River town W. Aust. Australia 88 18.38S126.52E
Margarita, Isla de i. Venezuela 122 11.00N 64.00W
Margarítion Greece 34 39.22N 20.26E
Margate R.S.A. 80 30.51S 30.22E
Margate U.K. 13 51.23N 1.24E
Margeride, Monts de la mts. France 20 44.50N 3.30E
Margherita di Savoia Italy 33 41.23N 16.09E
Mārgow, Dasht-e des. Afghan. 62 30.45N 63.10E
Maria Elena Chile 124 22.21S 69.40W
Maria Gail Austria 39 46.36N 13.52E
Mariager Denmark 42 56.39N 10.00E
María Grande Argentina 125 31.40S 59.55W
Maria I. Australia 90 14.52S135.40E
Mariana Brazil 126 20.23S 43.23W
Mariana Is. Pacific Oc. 84 15.00N145.00E
Marianao Cuba 117 23.03N 82.29W
Mariana Ridge Pacific Oc. 84 17.00N146.00E
Mariana Trench Pacific Oc. 84 16.00N148.00E
Marianna Ark. U.S.A. 111 34.46N 90.46W
Marianna Fla. U.S.A. 113 30.45N 85.15W
Mariannelund Sweden 43 57.37N 15.34E
Mariánské Lázně Czech. 39 49.59N 12.43E
Marias r. U.S.A. 108 47.56N110.30W
Maribo Denmark 41 54.46N 11.31E
Maribor Yugo. 31 46.33N 15.39E
Marico r. R.S.A. 80 24.12S 26.57E
Maricopa U.S.A. 109 35.03N119.24W
Maricourt Canada 99 61.30N 72.00W
Marīdī Sudan 73 4.55N 29.28E
Marīdī r. Sudan 73 6.55N 29.00E
Marié r. Brazil 122 0.27S 66.26W
Marieburg Belgium 16 50.07N 4.30E
Mariefred Sweden 43 59.18N 17.15E
Marie-Galante i. Guadeloupe 117 15.54N 61.11W
Mariehamn see Maarianhamina Finland 43
Mariemberg Neth. 16 52.32N 6.35E
Mariental Namibia 80 24.38S 17.58E
Marienville U.S.A. 114 41.28N 79.07W
Mariestad Sweden 43 58.43N 13.51E
Marietta Ga. U.S.A. 113 33.57N 84.34W
Marietta Ohio U.S.A. 114 39.25N 81.27W
Marieville Canada 105 45.26N 73.10W
Mariga r. Nigeria 77 9.37N 5.55E
Marignane France 21 43.25N 5.13E
Marília Brazil 126 22.13S 50.20W
Marín Spain 26 42.23N 8.42W
Marina di Gioiosa Ionica Italy 33 38.18N 16.20E
Marina di Ravenna Italy 30 44.29N 12.17E
Marine City U.S.A. 114 42.43N 82.30W
Marineland U.S.A. 113 29.39N 81.13W
Marinette U.S.A. 110 45.06N 87.38W
Maringá Brazil 126 23.36S 52.02W
Maringa Zaïre 73 1.14N 20.00E
Maringa r. Zaïre 78 1.13N 19.50E
Maringue Mozambique 81 17.55S 34.24E
Marinha Grande Portugal 27 39.45N 8.56W
Marion Canada 104 47.00N 84.10W
Marion Ill. U.S.A. 111 37.44N 88.56W
Marion Ind. U.S.A. 112 40.33N 85.40W
Marion Iowa U.S.A. 110 42.02N 91.36W
Marion Ohio U.S.A. 112 40.35N 83.08W
Marion S.C. U.S.A. 113 34.11N 79.23W
Marion Va. U.S.A. 113 36.51N 81.30W
Marion, L. U.S.A. 113 33.30N 80.25W
Marion Reef Australia 90 19.10S152.17E
Mariposa U.S.A. 108 37.29N119.58W
Mariscal Estigarribia Paraguay 126 22.03S 60.35W
Maritimes, Alpes mts. France 21 44.15N 7.10E
Maritsa Bulgaria 34 42.02N 25.50E
Maritsa r. Bulgaria 34 42.15N 24.00E
Maritsa r. Turkey 29 41.00N 26.15E
Mārkā Jordan 67 31.59N 35.59E
Marka Somali Rep. 79 1.42N 44.47E
Markaryd Sweden 43 56.26N 13.36E
Markdale Canada 104 44.19N 80.39W
Marked Tree U.S.A. 111 35.32N 90.25W
Marken i. Neth. 16 52.28N 5.03E
Markerwaard f. Neth. 16 52.30N 5.15E
Market Drayton U.K. 12 52.55N 2.30W
Market Harborough U.K. 13 52.29N 0.55W
Market Rasen U.K. 12 53.24N 0.20W
Market Weighton U.K. 12 53.52N 0.04W
Markha r. U.S.S.R. 51 63.37N119.00E
Markham Canada 104 43.52N 79.16W
Markham, Mt. Antarctica 128 83.00S164.00E
Markoupolon Greece 35 37.53N 23.57E
Marks U.S.S.R. 45 51.43N 46.45E
Markstay Canada 104 46.29N 80.33W
Marktheidenfeld W. Germany 39 49.50N 9.36E
Marktoberdorf W. Germany 39 47.47N 10.37E
Marktredwitz W. Germany 39 50.00N 12.06E
Marl W. Germany 38 51.38N 7.05E
Marlboro U.S.A. 115 42.21N 71.33W
Marlborough Australia 90 22.51S149.50E
Marlborough U.K. 13 51.26N 1.44W
Marlborough U.S.A. 105 42.21N 71.33W
Marle France 19 49.44N 3.46E
Marlette U.S.A. 114 43.20N 83.05W
Marlin U.S.A. 111 31.18N 96.53W
Marlo Australia 93 37.50S148.35E
Marmande France 20 44.30N 0.10E
Marmara i. Turkey 29 40.38N 27.37E
Marmara, Sea of see Marmara Denizi Turkey 29
Marmara Denizi sea Turkey 29 40.45N 28.15E
Marmaris Turkey 35 36.50N 28.14E
Marmarth U.S.A. 110 46.18N103.54W
Marmet U.S.A. 114 38.15N 81.04W
Marmion L. Canada 102 48.55N 91.25W
Marmolada mtn. Italy 30 46.26N 11.51E
Marmora Canada 105 44.29N 77.41W
Marnay France 19 47.17N 5.46E
Marne d. France 19 48.55N 4.10E
Marne r. France 19 48.49N 2.24E
Marne W. Germany 38 53.57N 9.00E
Marne à la Saône, Canal de la France 19 49.44N 4.36E
Marne au Rhin, Canal de la France 19 48.35N 7.47E
Marnoo Australia 92 36.40S142.55E
Maroantsetra Madagascar 81 15.26S 49.44E
Marobi Pakistan 62 32.36N 69.52E
Marolambo Madagascar 81 20.02S 48.07E
Maromme France 18 49.28N 1.02E
Marondera Zimbabwe 81 18.11S 31.31E
Maroni r. Guiana 123 5.30N 54.00W
Maronne r. France 20 45.07N 1.57E
Maros r. Hungary 31 46.15N 20.13E
Maroua Cameroon 77 10.35N 14.20E
Marovoay Madagascar 81 16.06S 46.39E
Marquard R.S.A. 80 28.39S 27.25E
Marquesas Is. see Marquises, Îles Pacific Oc. 85
Marquette U.S.A. 112 46.33N 87.23W
Marquina-Jemein Spain 26 43.16N 2.30W
Marquise France 19 50.49N 1.42E
Marquises, Îles is. Pacific Oc. 85 9.00S139.30W
Marra Australia 92 31.11S144.03E
Marra r. Australia 93 30.05S147.05E
Marracuene Mozambique 81 25.44S 32.41E
Marradi Italy 30 44.04N 11.37E
Marradong Australia 89 32.45S116.27E
Marrah, Jabal mtn. Sudan 73 13.10N 24.22E
Marrakech Morocco 74 31.49N 8.00W
Marree Australia 92 29.40S138.04E
Marromeu Mozambique 81 18.20S 35.56E
Marrupa Mozambique 79 13.10S 37.30E
Marsá al Burayqah Libya 72 30.25N 19.35E
Marsabit Kenya 79 2.20N 37.59E
Marsala Italy 32 37.48N 12.26E
Marsá Maṭrūḥ Egypt 64 31.21N 27.14E
Marsciano Italy 30 42.54N 12.20E
Marsden Australia 93 33.46S147.35E
Marseille France 21 43.18N 5.24E
Marseille-en-Beauvaisis France 19 49.35N 1.57E
Marsfjället mtn. Sweden 40 65.05N 15.28E
Marshall Liberia 76 6.10N 10.23W
Marshall Ark. U.S.A. 111 35.55N 92.38W
Marshall Minn. U.S.A. 110 44.27N 95.47W
Marshall Mo. U.S.A. 110 39.07N 93.12W
Marshall Tex. U.S.A. 111 32.33N 94.23W
Marshall Va. U.S.A. 114 38.52N 77.52W
Marshall Is. Pacific Oc. 84 10.00N172.00E
Marshalltown U.S.A. 110 42.03N 92.55W
Marshyhope Creek r. U.S.A. 115 38.32N 75.45W
Märsta Sweden 43 59.37N 17.51E
Marstrand Sweden 42 57.53N 11.35E
Martaban Burma 56 16.32N 97.35E
Martaban, G. of Burma 56 15.10N 96.30E
Martapura Indonesia 58 3.22S114.56E
Marte Nigeria 77 12.23N 13.46E
Martelange Belgium 16 49.50N 5.44E
Marten River town Canada 104 46.42N 79.41W
Martés, Sierra mts. Spain 25 39.20N 1.10W
Marthaguy r. Australia 93 30.16S147.35E
Martha's Vineyard i. U.S.A. 115 41.25N 70.40W
Martigny Switz. 39 46.06N 7.04E
Martigues France 21 43.24N 5.03E
Martin Czech. 37 49.05N 18.55E
Martin r. Spain 25 41.18N 0.19W
Martin U.S.A. 110 43.10N101.44W
Martina Franca Italy 33 40.42N 17.21E
Martinique i. Windward Is. 117 14.40N 61.00W
Martin L. U.S.A. 113 32.50N 85.55W
Martin Pt. U.S.A. 98 70.10N143.50W
Martinsburg Penn. U.S.A. 114 40.19N 78.20W
Martinsburg W.Va. U.S.A. 114 39.27N 77.58W
Martins Ferry town U.S.A. 114 40.06N 80.44W
Martinsville Ind. U.S.A. 112 39.25N 86.25W
Martinsville Va. U.S.A. 113 36.43N 79.53W
Martin Vaz is. Atlantic Oc. 127 20.30S 28.51W
Marton New Zealand 86 40.04S175.25E
Martos Spain 27 37.43N 3.58W
Martre, Lac la l. Canada 100 63.15N116.55W
Martti Finland 40 67.28N 28.28E
Marudi Malaysia 58 4.15N114.19E
Ma'rūf Afghan. 62 31.34N 67.03E
Marula Zimbabwe 80 20.26S 28.06E
Marum Neth. 16 53.06N 6.16E
Marvejols France 20 44.33N 3.18E
Marvel Loch town Australia 89 31.31S119.30E
Marviken Sweden 43 58.34N 16.51E
Mārwār India 62 25.44N 73.36E
Mary U.S.S.R. 50 37.42N 61.54E
Maryborough Qld. Australia 90 25.32S152.36E
Maryborough Vic. Australia 92 37.05S143.47E
Marydale R.S.A. 80 29.24S 22.06E
Mary Frances L. Canada 101 63.19N106.13W
Mary Kathleen Australia 90 20.49S140.00E
Maryland d. U.S.A. 114 39.00N 76.45W
Maryland Beach town U.S.A. 115 38.26N 74.59W
Maryport U.K. 12 54.43N 3.30W
Mary's Harbour Canada 103 52.18N 55.51W
Marystown Canada 103 47.11N 55.10W
Marysvale U.S.A. 108 38.27N112.11W
Marysville Calif. U.S.A. 108 39.09N121.35W
Marysville Kans. U.S.A. 110 39.51N 96.39W
Marysville Mich. U.S.A. 114 42.54N 82.29W
Marysville Penn. U.S.A. 114 40.20N 76.56W
Maryvale Australia 93 28.04S152.12E
Maryville Mo. U.S.A. 110 40.21N 94.52W
Maryville Tenn. U.S.A. 113 35.45N 83.59W
Marzūq Libya 75 25.55N 13.55E
Marzūq, Ṣaḥrā' des. Libya 75 24.30N 13.00E
Mas'adah Syria 67 33.14N 35.45E
Masāhim, Kūh-e mtn. Iran 65 30.26N 55.08E
Masai Steppe f. Tanzania 79 4.30S 37.00E
Masaka Uganda 79 0.20S 31.46E
Masan S. Korea 53 35.10N128.35E
Masasi Tanzania 79 10.43S 38.48E
Masba Nigeria 77 10.35N 13.01E
Masbate i. Phil. 59 12.00N123.30E
Mascara Algeria 74 35.24N 0.08E
Mascarene Basin f. Indian Oc. 49 17.00S 55.00E
Mascarene Is. Indian Oc. 49 21.00S 56.00E
Mascarene Ridge f. Indian Oc. 49 10.00S 60.00E
Maseru Lesotho 80 29.18S 27.28E
Mashhad Iran 65 36.16N 59.34E
Mashkai r. Pakistan 62 26.02N 65.19E
Māshkel r. Pakistan 62 28.02N 63.25E
Māshkel, Hāmūn-i- l. Pakistan 62 28.15N 63.00E
Mashki Chāh Pakistan 62 29.01N 62.27E
Mashonaland f. Zimbabwe 81 18.20S 32.00E
Mashūray Afghan. 62 32.12N 68.21E
Masi Norway 40 69.26N 23.40E
Masīlah, Wādī al f. S.Yemen 71 15.10N 51.08E
Masi-Manimba Zaïre 78 4.47S 17.54E
Masindi Uganda 79 1.41N 31.45E
Maṣīrah i. Oman 60 20.30N 58.50E
Maṣīrah, Khalīj b. Oman 71 20.10N 58.10E
Masjed Soleymān Iran 65 31.59N 49.18E
Mask, Lough Rep. of Ire. 15 53.38N 9.22W
Maskinongé Canada 105 46.35N 73.30W
Masoala, Cap, c. Madagascar 81 15.59S 50.13E
Mason Mich. U.S.A. 104 42.35N 84.26W
Mason Tex. U.S.A. 111 30.45N 99.14W
Mason W.Va. U.S.A. 114 39.00N 82.02W
Mason City U.S.A. 110 43.09N 93.12W
Masontown U.S.A. 114 39.51N 79.54W
Maspalomas Canary Is. 127 27.42N 15.34W
Masqaṭ Oman 65 23.36N 58.37E
Massa Italy 30 44.01N 10.09E
Massachusetts d. U.S.A. 115 42.15N 71.50W
Massachusetts B. U.S.A. 115 42.20N 70.50W
Massafra Italy 33 40.35N 17.07E
Massakory Chad 77 13.02N 15.43E
Massa Marittima Italy 30 43.03N 10.53E
Massangena Mozambique 81 21.31S 33.03E
Massangulo Mozambique 81 13.54S 35.24E
Massarosa Italy 30 43.52N 10.20E
Massena U.S.A. 105 44.56N 74.54W
Massenya Chad 77 11.21N 16.09E
Masset Canada 100 54.00N132.09W
Masseube France 20 43.26N 0.35E
Massey Canada 104 46.12N 82.05W
Massiac France 20 45.15N 3.12E
Massif Central mts. France 20 45.00N 3.10E
Massillon U.S.A. 114 40.48N 81.32W
Massinga Mozambique 81 23.20S 35.25E
Massingir Mozambique 81 23.49S 32.04E
Masterton New Zealand 86 40.57S175.39E
Mastic Beach town U.S.A. 115 40.45N 72.50W
Mastigouche Prov. Park Canada 105 46.39N 73.24W
Mastung Pakistan 62 29.48N 66.51E
Mastūrah Saudi Arabia 64 23.06N 38.50E
Masuda Japan 57 34.40N131.51E
Masvingo Zimbabwe 80 20.10S 30.49E
Maṣyāf Syria 66 35.03N 36.21E
Mat r. Albania 34 41.40N 20.00E
Matabeleland f. Zimbabwe 80 19.50S 28.15E
Matabuena Spain 26 41.06N 3.48W
Matachel r. Spain 26 38.50N 6.17W
Matachewan Canada 102 47.56N 80.39W
Matadi Zaïre 78 5.50S 13.36E
Matagami Canada 102 49.45N 77.34W
Matagami, L. Canada 102 49.50N 77.40W
Matagorda B. U.S.A. 111 28.35N 96.20W
Matakana Australia 93 32.59S145.53E
Matakana I. New Zealand 86 37.35S176.15E
Matala Angola 78 14.45S 15.02E
Matam Senegal 74 15.40N 13.15W
Matamata New Zealand 86 37.49S175.46E
Matameye Niger 77 13.26N 8.28E
Matamoros Coahuila Mexico 111 25.32N103.15W
Matamoros Tamaulipas Mexico 111 25.53N 97.30W
Ma'ṭan Bishrah well Libya 72 22.58N 22.39E
Matandu r. Tanzania 79 8.44S 39.22E
Matane Canada 103 48.51N 67.32W
Matang China 55 29.30N113.08E
Matankari Niger 77 13.47N 4.00E
Matanzas Cuba 117 23.04N 81.35W
Mataram Indonesia 59 8.36S116.07E
Matarani Peru 124 16.58S 72.07W
Mataranka Australia 88 14.56S133.07E
Mataró Spain 25 41.32N 2.27E
Matarraña r. Spain 25 41.14N 0.22E
Matatiele R.S.A. 80 30.19S 28.48E
Matatula, C. Samoa 84 14.15S170.35W
Mataura r. New Zealand 86 46.34S168.45E
Matautu W. Samoa 84 13.57S171.56W
Matavera Rarotonga Cook Is. 84 21.13S159.44W
Matawai New Zealand 86 38.21S177.32E
Matawin r. Canada 105 46.50N 72.45W
Matawin, Résr. Canada 103 46.45N 73.50W
Maṭāy Egypt 66 28.25N 30.46E
Matehuala Mexico 116 23.40N100.40W
Mateke Hills Zimbabwe 80 21.48S 31.00E
Matelica Italy 30 43.15N 13.00E
Matera Italy 33 40.40N 16.37E
Matetsi Zimbabwe 80 18.17S 25.57E
Mateur Tunisia 32 37.03N 9.40E
Matfors Sweden 41 62.21N 17.02E
Matha France 20 45.52N 0.19W
Mathews Peak mtn. Kenya 79 1.18N 37.20E
Mathis U.S.A. 111 28.06N 97.50W
Mathoura Australia 93 35.49S144.54E
Mathura India 63 27.30N 77.41E
Mati Phil. 59 6.55N126.15E
Matias Barbosa Brazil 126 21.52S 43.21W
Matignon France 18 48.36N 2.18W
Matinenda L. Canada 104 46.22N 82.57W
Matipó Brazil 126 20.16S 42.17W
Mātli Pakistan 62 25.02N 68.39E
Matlock U.K. 12 53.09N 1.32W
Matochkin Shar U.S.S.R. 50 73.15N 56.35E
Mato Grosso d. Brazil 124 13.00S 55.00W
Mato Grosso town Brazil 124 15.05S 59.57W
Mato Grosso, Planalto do f. Brazil 124 16.00S 54.00W
Mato Grosso do Sul d. Brazil 124 20.00S 54.30W
Matope Malaŵi 79 15.20S 34.57E
Matopo Hills Zimbabwe 80 20.45S 28.30E
Matosinhos Portugal 26 41.11N 8.42W
Maṭraḥ Oman 65 23.37N 58.33E
Matrei in Osttirol Austria 39 47.00N 12.32E
Matsena Nigeria 77 13.13N 10.04E
Matsiatra r. Madagascar 81 21.25S 45.33E
Matsubara Japan 57 34.34N135.33E
Matsudo Japan 57 35.47N139.54E
Matsue Japan 57 35.29N133.00E
Matsumae Japan 57 41.26N140.07E
Matsumoto Japan 57 36.18N137.58E
Matsusaka Japan 57 34.34N136.32E
Matsuyama Japan 57 33.50N132.47E
Mattagami r. Canada 102 50.43N 81.29W
Mattawa Canada 104 46.19N 78.42W
Mattawamkeag U.S.A. 112 45.31N 68.21W
Mattawin Canada 105 46.55N 72.55W
Matterhorn mtn. Switz./Italy 39 45.59N 7.43E
Matterhorn mtn. U.S.A. 108 41.49N115.23W
Matthews Ridge town Guyana 122 7.30N 60.10W
Matthew Town Bahamas 117 20.57N 73.40W
Mattice Canada 102 49.39N 83.20W
Mattighofen Austria 39 48.06N 13.09E
Mattmar Sweden 40 63.19N 13.45E
Mattoon U.S.A. 110 39.29N 88.21W
Matua Indonesia 58 2.58S110.52E
Maturín Venezuela 122 9.45N 63.10W
Maua Mozambique 81 13.53S 37.10E
Mau Aimma India 63 25.42N 81.55E
Maubeuge France 19 50.17N 3.58E
Maudaha India 63 25.41N 80.07E
Maude Australia 92 34.27S144.21E
Maués Brazil 123 3.24S 57.42W
Mauganj India 63 24.41N 81.53E
Maui i. Hawaii U.S.A. 106 20.45N156.15W
Mauléon France 18 46.56N 0.45W
Mauléon-Licharre France 20 43.14N 0.54W
Maulvi Bāzār Bangla. 63 24.29N 91.42E
Maumee U.S.A. 112 41.34N 83.41W
Maumee r. U.S.A. 112 41.40N 83.35W
Maumere Indonesia 59 8.35S122.13E
Maun Botswana 80 19.52S 23.40E
Maunaloa Hawaiian Is. 85 21.08N157.13W
Mauna Loa mtn. Hawaiian Is. 85 19.29N155.36W
Maunath Bhanjan India 63 25.57N 83.33E
Mau Rānīpur India 63 25.15N 79.08E
Maure-de-Bretagne France 18 47.54N 1.59W
Maures mts. France 21 43.16N 6.23E
Mauriac France 20 45.13N 2.20E
Maurice, L. Australia 91 29.28S130.58E
Maurice Nat. Park Canada 105 46.42N 73.00W
Mauritania Africa 74 20.00N 10.00W
Mauritius Indian Oc. 49 20.10S 58.00E
Mauritius Basin f. Indian Oc. 49 26.00S 55.00E
Mauron France 18 48.05N 2.18W
Maurs France 20 44.43N 2.11E
Mauston U.S.A. 110 43.48N 90.05W
Mauvezin France 20 43.44N 0.55E
Mavinga Angola 78 15.47S 20.21E
Mavqi'im Israel 67 31.37N 34.35E
Mavuradonha Mts. Zimbabwe 81 16.30S 31.20E
Mawjib, Wādī al Jordan 67 31.28N 35.34E
Mawlaik Burma 56 23.50N 94.30E
Maxcanú Mexico 116 20.35N 89.59W
Maxville Canada 105 45.17N 74.51W
May, C. U.S.A. 115 38.56N 74.55W
Maya Spain 26 43.12N 1.29W
Mayaguana I. Bahamas 117 22.30N 73.00W
Mayagüez Puerto Rico 117 18.13N 67.09W
Mayāmey Iran 65 36.27N 55.40E
Maya Mts. Belize 117 16.30N 89.00W
Maybole U.K. 14 55.21N 4.41W
Maych'ew Ethiopia 71 13.02N 39.34E
Mayen W. Germany 39 50.19N 7.13E
Mayenne France 18 48.18N 0.37W
Mayenne d. France 18 48.05N 0.40W
Mayenne r. France 18 47.30N 0.33W
Mayerthorpe Canada 100 53.57N115.08W
Mayfield U.S.A. 111 36.44N 88.38W
Maykop U.S.S.R. 45 44.37N 40.48E
Maymyo Burma 56 22.05N 96.28E
Maynooth Canada 105 45.13N 77.57W
Maynooth Rep. of Ire. 15 53.23N 6.37W
Mayo r. Mexico 109 26.45N109.47W
Mayo d. Rep. of Ire. 15 53.47N 9.07W
Mayo, Plains of f. Rep. of Ire. 15 53.46N 9.05W
Mayo Daga Nigeria 77 6.59N 11.25E
Mayo Landing Canada 98 63.45N135.45W
Mayor I. New Zealand 86 37.15S176.15E
Mayotte, Île i. Comoros 79 12.50S 45.10E
May Pen Jamaica 117 17.58N 77.14W
Maysah, Tall al mtn. Jordan 67 31.08N 35.40E

Mays Landing to Mezzolombardo

Mays Landing U.S.A. **115** 39.27N 74.44W
Maysville U.S.A. **112** 38.38N 83.46W
Maythalūn Jordan **67** 32.21N 35.16E
Mayumba Gabon **78** 3.23S 10.38E
Mayville Mich. U.S.A. **104** 43.20N 83.21W
Mayville N.Dak. U.S.A. **110** 47.30N 97.19W
Mayville N.Y. U.S.A. **114** 42.15N 79.30W
Mazabuka Zambia **79** 15.50S 27.47E
Mazagão Brazil **123** 0.07S 51.17W
Mazamba Mozambique **81** 18.32S 34.50E
Mazamet France **20** 43.30N 2.24E
Mazán Peru **122** 3.15S 73.00W
Mazara del Vallo Italy **32** 37.39N 12.36E
Mazarredo Argentina **125** 47.00S 66.45W
Mazarrón Spain **25** 37.36N 1.19W
Mazarrón, Golfo de *g.* Spain **25** 37.30N 1.18W
Mazatenango Guatemala **116** 14.31N 91.30W
Mazatlán Mexico **109** 23.13N106.25W
Mażeikiai U.S.S.R. **41** 56.19N 22.20E
Mazinaw L. Canada **105** 44.55N 77.12W
Mazirbe U.S.S.R. **41** 57.41N 22.21E
Mazoe *r.* Mozambique **81** 16.32S 33.25E
Mazowe Zimbabwe **81** 17.30S 30.58E
Mazu Liedao *is.* China **53** 26.12N120.00E
Mazunga Zimbabwe **80** 21.45S 29.52E
Mazurski, Pojezierze *lakes* Poland **37** 53.50N 21.00E
Mbabane Swaziland **80** 26.19S 31.08E
Mbagne Mauritania **74** 16.06N 14.47W
M'Baiki C.A.R. **77** 3.53N 18.01E
Mbala C.A.R. **73** 7.48N 20.51E
Mbala Zambia **79** 8.50S 31.24E
Mbale Uganda **79** 1.04N 34.12E
Mbalmayo Cameroon **77** 3.35N 11.31E
Mbamba Bay *town* Tanzania **79** 11.18S 34.50E
Mbandaka Zaïre **78** 0.03N 18.21E
Mbanza Congo Angola **78** 6.18S 14.16E
Mbarara Uganda **79** 0.36S 30.40E
Mbari *r.* C.A.R. **73** 4.34N 22.43E
Mbeya Tanzania **79** 8.54S 33.29E
Mbeya *d.* Tanzania **79** 8.30S 32.30E
Mbinda Congo **78** 2.11S 12.55E
Mbogo Tanzania **79** 7.26S 33.26E
Mbomou *d.* C.A.R. **73** 5.10N 23.00E
Mbomou *r.* C.A.R. **73** 4.08N 22.26E
Mboro Sudan **73** 6.18N 28.45E
M'Bour Senegal **76** 14.22N 16.54W
Mbout Mauritania **74** 16.02N 12.35W
M'bridge *r.* Angola **78** 7.12S 12.55E
Mbua Fiji **84** 16.48S178.37E
Mbuji Mayi Zaïre **78** 6.08S 23.39E
Mbulamuti Uganda **79** 0.50N 33.05E
Mbura Tanzania **79** 11.14S 35.25E
Mbutha Fiji **84** 16.39S179.50E
Mbuzi Zambia **79** 12.20S 32.17E
McAlester U.S.A. **111** 34.56N 95.46W
McAlister, Mt. Australia **93** 34.27S149.45E
McAllen U.S.A. **111** 26.12N 98.15W
McArthur *r.* Australia **90** 15.54S136.40E
McArthur U.S.A. **114** 39.15N 82.29W
McArthurs Mills Canada **105** 45.06N 77.38W
McBride Canada **100** 53.20N120.10W
McCamey U.S.A. **111** 31.08N102.13W
McClintock Canada **101** 57.50N 94.10W
McClintock Channel Canada **99** 71.20N102.00W
McClure U.S.A. **114** 40.42N 77.19W
McClure Str. Canada **98** 74.30N116.00W
McComb U.S.A. **111** 31.14N 90.27W
McConaughy, L. U.S.A. **110** 41.15N102.00W
McConnel Creek *town* Canada **100** 56.53N126.30W
McConnellsburg U.S.A. **114** 39.57N 78.01W
McConnelsville U.S.A. **114** 39.39N 81.51W
McCook U.S.A. **110** 40.12N100.38W
McDermitt U.S.A. **108** 41.59N117.36W
McDouall Peak Australia **92** 29.51S134.55E
McGrath U.S.A. **98** 62.58N155.40W
McGregor U.S.A. **110** 46.36N 93.19W
McHenry U.S.A. **110** 42.21N 88.16W
Mchinja Tanzania **79** 9.44S 39.45E
Mchinji Malaŵi **79** 13.48S 32.55E
McIlwraith Range *mts.* Australia **90** 14.00S143.10E
McKeesport U.S.A. **114** 40.21N 79.52W
McKees Rocks *town* U.S.A. **114** 40.28N 80.10W
Mckellar Canada **104** 45.30N 79.55W
McKenzie U.S.A. **111** 36.08N 88.31W
McKerrow Canada **104** 46.18N 81.44W
McKinley, Mt. U.S.A. **98** 63.00N151.00W
McKinney U.S.A. **111** 33.12N 96.37W
McKittrick U.S.A. **109** 35.18N119.37W
McLaughlin U.S.A. **110** 45.49N100.49W
McLennan Canada **100** 55.42N116.50W
McLeod *r.* Canada **100** 54.08N115.42W
McLeod, L. Australia **88** 24.10S113.35E
McLeod B. Canada **101** 62.53N110.00W
Mcleod Lake *town* Canada **100** 54.58N123.00W
M'Clintock Canada **100** 60.35N134.25W
McMinnville Oreg. U.S.A. **108** 45.13N123.12W
McMinnville Tenn. U.S.A. **113** 35.40N 85.49W
McNary U.S.A. **109** 34.04N109.51W
McPherson U.S.A. **110** 38.22N 97.40W
Mdatsane R.S.A. **80** 32.54S 27.24E
Mead, L. U.S.A. **109** 36.05N114.25W
Meade U.S.A. **111** 37.17N100.20W
Meadow Lake *town* Canada **101** 54.07N108.20W
Meadville U.S.A. **114** 41.38N 80.09W
Meaford Canada **104** 44.36N 80.35W
Mealhada Portugal **26** 40.22N 8.27W
Meander River *town* Canada **100** 59.02N117.42W
Mearim *r.* Brazil **123** 3.20S 44.20W
Meath *d.* Rep. of Ire. **15** 53.32N 6.40W
Meaux France **19** 48.57N 2.52E
Mécatina, Cap *c.* Canada **103** 50.45N 59.01W
Mecca *see* Makkah Saudi Arabia **72**
Mecca U.S.A. **109** 33.35N116.03W
Mechanicsville U.S.A. **114** 38.26N 76.44W
Mechanicville U.S.A. **115** 42.54N 73.42W
Mechelen Belgium **16** 51.01N 4.28E
Mecheria Algeria **74** 33.33N 0.17W
Mecidiye Turkey **34** 40.38N 26.32E
Mecklenburg *f.* E. Germany **38** 53.33N 12.15E
Mecklenburger Bucht *b.* E. Germany **38** 54.20N 11.50E
Mecklenburgische Seenplatte *f.* E. Germany **38** 53.15N 13.00E
Meconta Mozambique **79** 15.00S 39.50E
Mecsek *mts.* Hungary **31** 46.15N 18.05E
Mecufi Mozambique **79** 13.20S 40.32E
Meda Portugal **26** 40.58N 7.16W
Medan Indonesia **58** 3.35N 98.39E
Mede Italy **30** 45.06N 8.44E
Médéa Algeria **75** 36.15N 2.48E
Mededsiz *mtn.* Turkey **64** 37.33N 34.38E
Medegue Gabon **78** 0.37N 10.08E
Medellín Colombia **122** 6.15N 75.36W
Medemblik Neth. **16** 52.48N 5.06E
Médenine Tunisia **75** 33.21N 10.30E
Mederdra Mauritania **76** 17.02N 15.41W
Medevi Sweden **43** 58.40N 14.57E
Medford Mass. U.S.A. **115** 42.25N 71.07W
Medford Oreg. U.S.A. **108** 42.19N122.52W
Medford Wisc. U.S.A. **110** 45.09N 90.20W
Medgidia Romania **37** 44.15N 28.16E
Medi Sudan **73** 5.04N 30.44E
Media U.S.A. **115** 39.54N 75.23W
Mediaş Romania **37** 46.10N 24.21E
Medicina Italy **30** 44.28N 11.38E
Medicine Bow Mts. U.S.A. **108** 41.10N106.10W
Medicine Bow Peak *mtn.* U.S.A. **108** 41.21N106.19W
Medicine Hat Canada **101** 50.03N110.40W
Medicine Lake *town* U.S.A. **108** 48.30N104.30W
Medicine Lodge U.S.A. **111** 37.17N 98.35W
Medina *see* Al Madīnah Saudi Arabia **64**
Medina N.Dak. U.S.A. **110** 46.54N 99.18W
Medina N.Y. U.S.A. **114** 43.13N 78.23W
Medina Ohio U.S.A. **114** 41.08N 81.52W
Medinaceli Spain **26** 41.10N 2.26W
Medina del Campo Spain **26** 41.18N 4.55W
Medina de Ríoseco Spain **26** 41.53N 5.02W
Medina-Sidonia Spain **27** 36.27N 5.55W
Mediterranean Sea 23 36.00N 16.00E
Medjerda, Monts de la *mts.* Tunisia **32** 36.40N 8.40E
Medjerda, Oued *r.* Tunisia **32** 37.07N 10.13E
Medjez el Bab Tunisia **32** 36.39N 9.37E
Medoc *d.* France **20** 45.20N 1.00W
Mêdog China **52** 29.19N 95.19E
Medstead Canada **101** 53.19N108.02W
Medveda Yugo. **34** 42.50N 21.32E
Medveditsa *r.* U.S.S.R. **45** 49.35N 42.45E
Medvezhyegorsk U.S.S.R. **44** 62.56N 34.28E
Medvin U.S.S.R. **37** 49.25N 30.48E
Medway *r.* U.K. **13** 51.24N 0.31E
Medzhibozh U.S.S.R. **37** 49.29N 27.28E
Meeberrie Australia **88** 26.58S115.51E
Meekatharra Australia **88** 26.35S118.30E
Meeker U.S.A. **108** 40.02N107.55W
Meer Belgium **16** 51.27N 4.46E
Meerane E. Germany **38** 50.51N 12.28E
Meerhusener Moor *f.* W. Germany **38** 53.35N 7.30E
Meersburg W. Germany **39** 47.41N 9.16E
Meerut India **63** 28.59N 77.42E
Mefallesim Israel **67** 31.30N 34.34E
Mega Ethiopia **73** 4.07N 38.16E
Megalon Khorion Greece **35** 36.27N 27.24E
Megalópolis Greece **35** 37.24N 22.08E
Mégara Greece **35** 38.00N 23.20E
Megasini *mtn.* India **63** 21.38N 86.21E
Meghalaya *d.* India **63** 25.30N 91.00E
Meghna *r.* Bangla. **63** 22.50N 90.50E
Mégiscane *r.* Canada **102** 48.36N 76.00W
Mehadia Romania **37** 44.55N 22.22E
Mehar Pakistan **62** 27.11N 67.49E
Mehekar India **62** 20.09N 76.34E
Mehidpur India **62** 23.49N 75.40E
Mehndāwal India **63** 26.59N 83.07E
Mehsāna India **62** 23.36N 72.24E
Mehtar Lām Afghan. **62** 34.39N 70.10E
Mehun-sur-Yèvre France **19** 47.09N 2.13E
Meiktila Burma **56** 20.53N 95.50E
Meiningen E. Germany **38** 50.34N 10.25E
Meira, Sierra de *mts.* Spain **26** 43.15N 7.15W
Meiringen Switz. **39** 46.43N 8.12E
Me'ir Shefeya Israel **67** 32.35N 34.57E
Meishan China **55** 30.02N103.50E
Meissen E. Germany **38** 51.10N 13.28E
Mei Xian China **55** 24.20N116.15E
Meiyino Sudan **73** 6.12N 34.40E
Mekatina Canada **104** 47.05N 84.07W
Mekdela Ethiopia **73** 11.28N 39.23E
Mekele Ethiopia **73** 13.33N 39.30E
Mekerrhane, Sebkha *f.* Algeria **74** 26.22N 1.20E
Mekhtar Pakistan **62** 30.28N 69.22E
Mekinac, L. Canada **105** 47.05N 73.39W
Meknès Morocco **74** 33.53N 5.37W
Mekong *r.* Asia **56** 10.00N106.40E
Mekong Delta Vietnam **56** 10.00N105.40E
Mekongga *mtn.* Indonesia **59** 3.39S121.15E
Mékôngk *r. see* Mekong Kampuchea **56**
Mékrou *r.* Benin **77** 12.20N 2.47E
Melaka Malaysia **58** 2.11N102.16E
Melanesia *is.* Pacific Oc. **84** 5.00N165.00E
Melbourne Australia **93** 37.45S144.58E
Melbourne U.S.A. **113** 28.04N 80.38W
Meldorf W. Germany **38** 54.05N 9.05E
Meldrum Bay *town* Canada **104** 45.56N 83.07W
Mélé C.A.R. **73** 9.46N 21.33E
Melegnano Italy **30** 45.21N 9.19E
Meleuz U.S.S.R. **44** 52.58N 55.56E
Mélèzes, Rivière aux *r.* Canada **103** 57.40N 69.29W
Melfi Chad **77** 11.04N 18.03E
Melfi Italy **33** 40.59N 15.40E
Melfort Canada **101** 52.52N104.36W
Melgaço Portugal **26** 42.07N 8.16W
Melilla Morocco **74** 35.17N 2.57W
Melilla Spain **24** 35.17N 2.57W
Melilot Israel **67** 31.23N 34.36E
Melipilla Chile **125** 33.42S 71.13W
Melito di Porto Salvo Italy **33** 37.56N 15.47E
Melitopol U.S.S.R. **45** 46.51N 35.22E
Melk Austria **36** 48.14N 15.20E
Melle France **18** 46.13N 0.09W
Mellen U.S.A. **110** 46.20N 90.40W
Mellerud Sweden **43** 58.42N 12.28E
Mellid Spain **26** 42.55N 8.00W
Mellit Sudan **72** 14.08N 25.33E
Melmore Pt. Rep. of Ire. **15** 55.15N 7.49W
Melnik Bulgaria **34** 41.58N 23.25E
Mělník Czech. **36** 50.20N 14.29E
Melo Uruguay **126** 32.22S 54.10W
Melrhir, Chott *f.* Algeria **75** 34.20N 6.20E
Melrose U.K. **14** 55.36N 2.43W
Melrose Mont. U.S.A. **108** 45.37N112.41W
Melrose N.Mex U.S.A. **109** 34.26N103.38W
Melstone U.S.A. **108** 46.36N107.52W
Melsungen W. Germany **38** 51.08N 9.32E
Meltaus Finland **40** 66.54N 25.22E
Melton Mowbray U.K. **12** 52.46N 0.53W
Melun France **19** 48.32N 2.40E
Melvich U.K. **14** 58.33N 3.55W
Melville Canada **101** 50.55N102.48W
Melville, C. Australia **90** 14.11S144.30E
Melville, L. Canada **103** 53.45N 59.30W
Melville B. Australia **90** 12.10S136.32E
Melville Hills Canada **98** 69.20N122.00W
Melville I. Australia **90** 11.30S131.00E
Melville I. Canada **98** 75.30N110.00W
Melville Pen. Canada **99** 68.00N 84.00W
Melvin, Lough Rep. of Ire./U.K. **15** 54.26N 8.12W
Mélykút Hungary **31** 46.13N 19.24E
Melzo Italy **30** 45.30N 9.25E
Mêmar Co *l.* China **63** 34.10N 82.15E
Memba Mozambique **81** 14.16S 40.30E
Memboro Indonesia **58** 9.22S119.32E
Memmingen W. Germany **39** 47.59N 10.11E
Memphis *ruins* Egypt **66** 29.52N 31.12E
Memphis Mich. U.S.A. **114** 42.54N 82.46W
Memphis Tenn. U.S.A. **111** 35.08N 90.03W
Memphremagog, L. Canada **105** 45.05N 72.15W
Mena U.S.A. **111** 34.35N 94.15W
Mena U.S.S.R. **37** 51.30N 32.15E
Menai Str. U.K. **12** 53.17N 4.20W
Ménaka Mali **75** 15.55N 2.24E
Mènam Khong *r. see* Mekong Laos **56**
Menarandra *r.* Madagascar **81** 25.17S 44.30E
Menard U.S.A. **111** 30.55N 99.47W
Menawashei Sudan **73** 12.40N 24.59E
Mendawai *r.* Indonesia **58** 3.17S113.20E
Mende France **20** 44.30N 3.30E
Mendebo Mts. Ethiopia **73** 7.00N 39.30E
Mendi P.N.G. **59** 6.13S143.39E
Mendip Hills U.K. **13** 51.15N 2.40W
Mendocino, C. U.S.A. **108** 40.25N124.25W
Mendoza Argentina **125** 32.54S 68.50W
Mendoza *d.* Argentina **125** 34.30S 68.00W
Mendung Indonesia **58** 0.31N103.12E
Ménéac France **18** 48.09N 2.28W
Mene Grande Venezuela **122** 9.51N 70.57W
Menemen Turkey **64** 38.34N 27.03E
Menen Belgium **16** 50.48N 3.07E
Menfi Italy **32** 37.36N 12.59E
Mengcheng China **54** 33.16N116.33E
Mengzi China **61** 23.20N103.21E
Menihek Lakes Canada **103** 54.00N 66.35W
Menindee Australia **92** 32.23S142.30E
Menindee L. Australia **92** 32.21S142.20E
Menominee U.S.A. **110** 45.07N 87.37W
Menomonie U.S.A. **110** 44.53N 91.55W
Menongue Angola **78** 14.40S 17.41E
Menor, Mar *b.* Spain **25** 37.43N 0.48W
Menorca *i.* Spain **25** 40.00N 4.00E
Mens France **21** 44.49N 5.45E
Mentawai, Kepulauan *is.* Indonesia **58** 2.50S 99.00E
Mentekab Malaysia **58** 3.29N102.21E
Mentok Indonesia **58** 2.04S105.12E
Menton France **21** 43.47N 7.30E
Mentor U.S.A. **114** 41.40N 81.20W
Menyapa, Gunung *mtn.* Indonesia **58** 1.00N116.20E
Menzel Bourguiba Tunisia **32** 37.10N 9.48E
Menzel Bou Zelfa Tunisia **32** 36.41N 10.36E
Menzel Djemil Tunisia **32** 37.14N 9.55E
Menzel Temime Tunisia **32** 36.47N 10.59E
Menzies Australia **89** 29.41S121.02E
Menzies, Mt. Antarctica **128** 71.50S 61.00E
Me'ona Israel **67** 33.01N 35.16E
Meppel Neth. **16** 52.42N 6.12E
Meppen W. Germany **38** 52.41N 7.17E
Mer France **18** 47.42N 1.30E
Merambéllou, Kólpos *g.* Greece **35** 35.14N 25.47E
Merano Italy **30** 46.40N 11.09E
Merauke Indonesia **90** 8.30S140.22E
Merbein Australia **92** 34.11S142.04E
Mercato Saraceno Italy **30** 43.57N 12.12E
Merced U.S.A. **108** 37.18N120.29W
Mercedes Buenos Aires Argentina **125** 34.40S 59.25W
Mercedes Corrientes Argentina **124** 29.15S 58.05W
Mercedes San Luis Argentina **125** 33.40S 65.30W
Mercedes Uruguay **125** 33.16S 58.01W
Mercer U.S.A. **114** 41.14N 80.15W
Mercy, C. Canada **99** 65.00N 63.30W
Mere U.K. **13** 51.05N 2.16W
Meredith Australia **92** 37.50S144.05E
Meredith, L. U.S.A. **111** 35.36N101.42W
Merefa U.S.S.R. **45** 49.49N 36.05E
Mereke C.A.R. **73** 7.34N 23.09E
Mergenevo U.S.S.R. **45** 49.59N 51.19E
Mergui Burma **56** 12.26N 98.38E
Mergui Archipelago *is.* Burma **56** 11.15N 98.00E
Meribah Australia **92** 34.42S140.53E
Meriç *r.* Turkey **34** 40.52N 26.12E
Mérida Mexico **117** 20.59N 89.39W
Mérida Spain **27** 38.55N 6.20W
Mérida Venezuela **122** 8.24N 71.08W
Mérida, Cordillera de *mts.* Venezuela **122** 8.30N 71.00W
Meriden U.S.A. **115** 41.32N 72.48W
Meridian U.S.A. **111** 32.22N 88.42W
Mérignac France **20** 44.50N 0.42W
Merikarvia Finland **41** 61.51N 21.30E
Merino Australia **92** 37.45S141.35E
Merir *i.* Caroline Is. **59** 4.19N132.18E
Merirumã Brazil **123** 1.15N 54.50W
Merizo Guam **84** 13.16N144.40E
Merkendorf W. Germany **39** 49.12N 10.42E
Merksem Belgium **16** 51.14N 4.25E
Merlin Canada **104** 42.14N 82.14W
Merlo Argentina **125** 34.40S 58.45W
Merne Merna Australia **92** 31.45S138.21E
Meron, Har *mtn.* Israel **67** 33.00N 35.25E
Merredin Australia **89** 31.29S118.16E
Merrick *mtn.* U.K. **14** 55.08N 4.29W
Merrickville Canada **105** 44.55N 75.50W
Merrill Oreg. U.S.A. **108** 42.01N121.36W
Merrill Wisc. U.S.A. **110** 45.11N 89.41W
Merriman U.S.A. **110** 42.55N101.42W
Merritt Canada **100** 50.10N120.45W
Merriwa Australia **93** 32.08S150.20E
Merrygoen Australia **93** 31.51S149.16E
Mersa Fatma Ethiopia **72** 14.55N 40.20E
Mersch Lux. **16** 49.44N 6.05E
Mersea I. U.K. **13** 51.47N 0.58E
Merseburg E. Germany **38** 51.21N 11.59E
Mersey *r.* U.K. **12** 53.22N 2.37W
Merseyside *d.* U.K. **12** 53.28N 3.00W
Mersin Turkey **64** 36.47N 34.37E
Mersing Malaysia **58** 2.25N103.50E
Merta India **62** 26.39N 74.02E
Merta Road *town* India **62** 26.43N 73.55E
Merthyr Tydfil U.K. **13** 51.45N 3.23W
Mértola Portugal **27** 37.38N 7.40W
Merton U.K. **13** 51.25N 0.12W
Mertzon U.S.A. **111** 31.16N100.49W
Méru France **19** 49.14N 2.08E
Meru *mtn.* Tanzania **79** 3.15S 36.44E
Méry France **19** 48.30N 3.53E
Merzifon Turkey **64** 40.52N 35.28E
Merzig W. Germany **39** 49.27N 6.36E
Mesa *r.* Spain **25** 41.15N 1.48W
Mesa U.S.A. **109** 33.25N111.50W
Mesagne Italy **33** 40.33N 17.49E
Mesarás, Kólpos *g.* Greece **35** 34.58N 24.36E
Meschede W. Germany **38** 51.20N 8.17E
Mesewa Ethiopia **72** 15.36N 39.29E
Mesewa Channel Ethiopia **72** 15.30N 40.00E
Meshoppen U.S.A. **115** 41.34N 76.03W
Meslay-du-Maine France **18** 47.57N 0.33W
Mesocco Switz. **39** 46.23N 9.14E
Mesolóngion Greece **35** 38.21N 21.17E
Mesopotamia *f.* Iraq **65** 33.30N 44.30E
Messalo *r.* Mozambique **79** 11.38S 40.27E
Messina Italy **33** 38.11N 15.33E
Messina R.S.A. **80** 22.20S 30.03E
Messina, Stretto di *str.* Italy **33** 38.10N 15.35E
Messines Canada **105** 46.14N 76.01W
Messíni Greece **35** 37.03N 22.00E
Messíni *site* Greece **35** 37.11N 21.57E
Messiniakós, Kólpos *g.* Greece **35** 36.58N 22.00E
Messkirch W. Germany **39** 47.59N 9.07E
Mesta *r. see* Néstos Bulgaria **34**
Mestá Greece **35** 38.16N 25.53E
Mestre Italy **30** 45.29N 12.15E
Meta *r.* Venezuela **122** 6.10N 67.30W
Metagama Canada **104** 47.05N 81.57W
Metallifere, Colline *mts.* Italy **30** 43.15N 11.00E
Metán Argentina **124** 25.30S 65.00W
Metangula Mozambique **79** 12.41S 34.51E
Metapontum *site* Italy **33** 40.24N 16.49E
Metéora *site* Greece **34** 39.46N 21.36E
Methóni Greece **35** 36.50N 21.43E
Methuen U.S.A. **115** 42.44N 71.11W
Metkovets Bulgaria **34** 43.37N 23.10E
Metković Yugo. **31** 43.03N 17.39E
Metlakatla U.S.A. **100** 55.09N131.35W
Metlika Yugo. **31** 45.39N 15.19E
Métsovon Greece **34** 39.46N 21.11E
Metulla Israel **67** 33.16N 35.35E
Metz France **19** 49.08N 6.10E
Metzingen W. Germany **39** 48.32N 9.17E
Meu *r.* France **18** 48.02N 1.47W
Meulaboh Indonesia **58** 4.10N 96.09E
Meulan France **19** 49.01N 1.54E
Meurthe *r.* France **19** 48.47N 6.09E
Meurthe-et-Moselle *d.* France **19** 48.35N 6.10E
Meuse *r. see* Maas Belgium **16**
Meuse *d.* France **19** 49.00N 5.30E
Meuselwitz E. Germany **38** 51.02N 12.17E
Mexia U.S.A. **111** 31.41N 96.29W
Mexicali Mexico **109** 32.40N115.29W
Mexico C. America **116** 20.00N100.00W
México *d.* Mexico **116** 19.45N 99.30W
Mexico Mo. U.S.A. **110** 39.10N 91.53W
Mexico N.Y. U.S.A. **115** 43.28N 76.14W
Mexico, G. of N. America **116** 25.00N 90.00W
Mexico B. U.S.A. **115** 43.31N 76.17W
Mexico City *see* Ciudad de México Mexico **116**
Meximieux France **21** 45.54N 5.12E
Meydān Kalay Afghan. **62** 32.25N 66.44E
Meydān Khvolah Afghan. **62** 33.36N 69.51E
Meyenburg E. Germany **38** 53.18N 12.14E
Meyersdale U.S.A. **114** 39.45N 79.05W
Meymac France **20** 45.32N 2.09E
Meymaneh Afghan. **60** 35.54N 64.43E
Meyrueis France **20** 44.10N 3.26E
Mezdra Bulgaria **34** 43.12N 23.35E
Mèze France **20** 43.25N 3.36E
Mézel France **21** 43.59N 6.12E
Mezen U.S.S.R. **44** 65.50N 44.20E
Mezen *r.* U.S.S.R. **44** 65.50N 44.18E
Mézenc, Mont *mtn.* France **21** 44.55N 4.11E
Mezenskaya Guba *g.* U.S.S.R. **44** 66.30N 44.00E
Mezer Israel **67** 32.26N 35.03E
Mézières-en-Brenne France **18** 46.49N 1.13E
Mézin France **20** 44.03N 0.16E
Mezökövesd Hungary **37** 47.50N 20.34E
Mezzolombardo Italy **30** 46.13N 11.05E

M'goun, Irhil to Mogil-Mogil

M'goun, Irhil *mtn.* Morocco **22** 31.31N 6.25W
Mhow India **62** 22.33N 75.46E
Miahuatlán Mexico **116** 16.20N 96.36W
Miajadas Spain **27** 39.09N 5.54W
Miājlar India **62** 26.15N 70.23E
Miami Fla. U.S.A. **113** 25.45N 80.15W
Miami Okla. U.S.A. **111** 36.53N 94.53W
Miami Tex. U.S.A. **111** 35.42N100.38W
Miami Beach *town* U.S.A. **113** 25.47N 80.07W
Miāndow Āb Iran **65** 36.57N 46.06E
Miandrivazo Madagascar **81** 19.31S 45.28E
Miāneh Iran **65** 37.23N 47.45E
Miang, Phukao *mtn.* Thailand **56** 16.55N101.00E
Miāni India **62** 21.51N 69.23E
Miāni Hōr *b.* Pakistan **62** 25.34N 66.19E
Miānwāli Pakistan **62** 32.35N 71.33E
Mianyang Hubei China **55** 30.25N113.30E
Mianyang Sichuan China **55** 31.26N104.45E
Miao'er Shan *mtn.* China **55** 25.50N110.22E
Miaoli Taiwan **55** 24.34N120.48E
Miarinarivo Madagascar **81** 18.57S 46.55E
Miass U.S.S.R. **50** 55.00N 60.00E
Mibu *r.* Japan **57** 35.49N137.57E
Mica R.S.A. **80** 24.09S 30.49E
Micang Shan *mts.* China **54** 32.40N107.28E
Michael, L. Canada **103** 54.32N 58.15W
Michalovce Czech. **37** 48.45N 21.55E
Michelson, Mt. U.S.A. **98** 69.19N144.17W
Michigan *d.* U.S.A. **112** 44.00N 85.00W
Michigan, L. U.S.A. **112** 44.00N 87.00W
Michigan Center U.S.A. **104** 42.14N 84.20W
Michigan City U.S.A. **112** 41.43N 86.54W
Michikamau L. Canada **103** 54.00N 64.00W
Michipicoten Canada **102** 47.59N 84.55W
Michipicoten I. Canada **102** 47.40N 85.50W
Michoacán *d.* Mexico **116** 19.20N101.00W
Michurin Bulgaria **29** 42.09N 27.51E
Michurinsk U.S.S.R. **44** 52.54N 40.30E
Micronesia *is.* Pacific Oc. **84** 8.00N160.00E
Midale Canada **101** 49.22N103.27W
Mid Atlantic Ridge *f.* Atlantic Oc. **127** 20.00N 45.00W
Middelburg Neth. **16** 51.30N 3.36E
Middelburg C.P. R.S.A. **80** 31.29S 25.00E
Middelburg Trans. R.S.A. **80** 25.45S 29.27E
Middelfart Denmark **42** 55.30N 9.45E
Middelharnis Neth. **16** 51.46N 4.09E
Middenmeer Neth. **16** 52.51N 4.59E
Middleboro Canada **101** 49.01N 95.21W
Middleboro U.S.A. **115** 41.49N 70.55W
Middleburg N.Y. U.S.A. **115** 42.36N 74.20W
Middleburg Va. U.S.A. **114** 38.58N 77.44W
Middlebury U.S.A. **105** 44.01N 73.10W
Middlefield U.S.A. **114** 41.28N 81.05W
Middle I. Australia **89** 34.07S123.12E
Middle Loup *r.* U.S.A. **110** 41.17N 98.23W
Middleport N.Y. U.S.A. **114** 43.13N 78.29W
Middleport Ohio U.S.A. **114** 39.00N 82.03W
Middlesboro U.S.A. **113** 36.37N 83.43W
Middlesbrough U.K. **12** 54.34N 1.13W
Middleton Canada **103** 44.57N 65.04W
Middleton Reef Pacific Oc. **84** 29.28S159.06E
Middletown Conn. U.S.A. **115** 41.33N 72.39W
Middletown Del. U.S.A. **115** 39.25N 75.47W
Middletown Ind. U.S.A. **112** 39.31N 84.13W
Middletown N.Y. U.S.A. **115** 41.27N 74.25W
Middletown Penn. U.S.A. **114** 40.12N 76.44W
Middletown R.I. U.S.A. **115** 41.32N 71.17W
Mid Glamorgan *d.* U.K. **13** 51.38N 3.25W
Midi, Canal du France **20** 43.26N 1.58E
Midi de Bigorre, Pic du *mtn.* France **20** 42.56N 0.08E
Mid-Indian Basin *f.* Indian Oc. **49** 15.00S 80.00E
Mid-Indian Ridge *f.* Indian Oc. **49** 30.00S 75.00E
Midi-Pyrénées *d.* France **20** 44.10N 2.00E
Midland Canada **104** 44.45N 79.53W
Midland U.S.A. **104** 43.37N 84.14W
Midland Tex. U.S.A. **111** 32.00N102.05W
Midland Junction Australia **89** 31.54S115.57E
Midleton Rep. of Ire. **15** 51.55N 8.10W
Midnapore India **63** 22.26N 87.20E
Midongy-Sud Madagascar **81** 23.35S 47.01E
Midou *r.* France **20** 43.54N 0.30W
Midway Is. Hawaiian Is. **84** 28.15N177.25W
Midwest U.S.A. **108** 43.25N106.16W
Midwest City U.S.A. **111** 35.27N 97.24W
Midyan *f.* Saudi Arabia **66** 27.50N 35.30E
Midye Turkey **29** 41.37N 28.07E
Midžor *mtn.* Bulgaria **34** 43.24N 22.40E
Mie *d.* Japan **57** 34.42N136.08E
Miechów Poland **37** 50.23N 20.01E
Miedzychód Poland **36** 52.36N 15.55E
Miélan France **20** 43.26N 0.19E
Mielec Poland **37** 50.18N 21.25E
Mien *l.* Sweden **43** 56.25N 14.51E
Mienga Angola **78** 17.16S 19.50E
Mieres Spain **26** 43.15N 5.46W
Miesbach W. Germany **39** 47.47N 11.50E
Mifflin U.S.A. **114** 40.34N 77.24W
Mifraz Hefa *b.* Israel **67** 32.52N 35.03E
Migang Shan *mtn.* China **54** 35.32N106.13E
Migdal Israel **67** 32.50N 35.30E
Migdal Ha'Emeq Israel **67** 32.41N 35.15E
Miguel Hidalgo, Presa *resr.* Mexico **109** 26.41N108.19W
Migyaunglaung Burma **56** 14.40N 98.09E
Mijares *r.* Spain **25** 39.55N 0.01W
Mijet *i.* Yugo. **31** 42.45N 17.30E
Mikhaylov U.S.S.R. **44** 54.14N 39.00E
Mikhaylovgrad Bulgaria **34** 43.27N 23.16E
Mikhaylovgrad *d.* Bulgaria **34** 43.25N 23.11E
Mikhaylovka U.S.S.R. **45** 50.05N 43.15E
Miki Japan **57** 34.48N134.59E
Mikínai Greece **35** 37.43N 22.46E
Mikindani Tanzania **79** 10.16S 40.05E
Mikkeli Finland **44** 61.44N 27.15E
Mikkwa *r.* Canada **100** 58.25N114.46W
Mikonos Greece **35** 37.30N 25.25E
Míkonos *i.* Greece **35** 37.29N 25.25E
Mikre Bulgaria **34** 43.02N 24.31E
Mikumi Tanzania **79** 7.22S 37.00E
Mikun U.S.S.R. **44** 62.20N 50.01E
Mikuni sammyaku *mts.* Japan **57** 37.00N139.20E
Milagro Ecuador **122** 2.11S 79.36W
Milan *see* Milano Italy **30**
Milan Mich. U.S.A. **104** 42.05N 83.40W
Milan Mo. U.S.A. **110** 40.12N 93.07W
Milange Mozambique **79** 16.09S 35.44E
Milano Italy **30** 45.28N 9.12E
Milâs Turkey **35** 37.19N 27.47E
Milazzo Italy **33** 38.14N 15.15E
Milbank U.S.A. **110** 45.14N 96.38W
Milbanke Sd. Canada **100** 52.18N128.33W
Mildenhall U.K. **13** 52.20N 0.30E
Mildmay Canada **104** 44.03N 81.07W
Mildura Australia **92** 34.14S142.13E
Miléai Greece **35** 39.20N 23.09E
Miles Australia **90** 26.40S150.11E
Miles City U.S.A. **108** 46.25N105.51W
Miletto, Monte *mtn.* Italy **33** 41.27N 14.22E
Miletus *site* Turkey **35** 37.30N 27.18E
Milevsko Czech. **39** 49.27N 14.22E
Milford Conn. U.S.A. **115** 41.13N 73.04W
Milford Del. U.S.A. **115** 38.55N 75.25W
Milford Mass. U.S.A. **115** 42.08N 71.32W
Milford Mich. U.S.A. **104** 42.35N 83.36W
Milford N.H. U.S.A. **115** 42.50N 71.39W
Milford N.Y. U.S.A. **115** 42.35N 74.57W
Milford Penn. U.S.A. **115** 41.19N 74.48W
Milford Utah U.S.A. **108** 38.24N113.01W
Milford Haven *town* U.K. **13** 51.43N 5.02W
Milford Sound *town* New Zealand **86** 44.41S167.56E
Milgarra Australia **90** 18.10S140.55E
Miliana Algeria **75** 27.21N 2.28E
Miling Australia **89** 30.27S116.20E
Milk *r.* U.S.A. **108** 48.05N106.15W
Millau France **20** 44.06N 3.05E
Millbrook Canada **104** 44.09N 78.27W
Millbrook U.S.A. **115** 41.47N 73.42W
Mille Lacs, Lac des *l.* Canada **102** 48.45N 90.35W
Mille Lacs L. U.S.A. **110** 46.10N 93.45W
Miller *r.* Australia **92** 30.05S136.07E
Millerovo U.S.S.R. **45** 48.55N 40.25E
Millers *r.* U.S.A. **115** 42.35N 72.30W
Millersburg Mich. U.S.A. **104** 45.20N 84.04W
Millersburg Ohio U.S.A. **114** 40.33N 81.55W
Millersburg Penn. U.S.A. **114** 40.33N 76.58W
Millerton U.S.A. **115** 41.57N 73.31W
Miller Pt. U.K. **14** 55.01N 5.07W
Millicent Australia **92** 37.36S140.22E
Millie Australia **93** 29.49S149.34E
Millington U.S.A. **115** 39.16N 75.50W
Millinocket U.S.A. **112** 45.39N 68.43W
Millom U.K. **12** 54.13N 3.16W
Mills L. Canada **100** 61.30N118.10W
Millstatt Austria **31** 46.48N 13.35E
Millville U.S.A. **115** 39.24N 75.02W
Milne Inlet *town* Canada **99** 72.30N 80.59W
Milnet Canada **104** 46.49N 80.59W
Milo *r.* Guinea **76** 11.05N 9.05W
Milos Greece **35** 36.45N 24.27E
Mílos *i.* Greece **35** 36.41N 24.15E
Milparinka Australia **92** 29.45S141.55E
Milroy U.S.A. **114** 40.43N 77.35W
Miltenberg W. Germany **39** 49.42N 9.15E
Milton Australia **93** 35.19S150.24E
Milton Canada **104** 43.31N 79.53W
Milton Del. U.S.A. **115** 38.47N 75.19W
Milton Mass. U.S.A. **115** 42.15N 71.05W
Milton N.H. U.S.A. **115** 43.23N 70.59W
Milton Penn. U.S.A. **114** 41.01N 76.51W
Milton Vt. U.S.A. **105** 44.38N 73.07W
Milton W.Va. U.S.A. **114** 38.26N 82.08W
Milton Keynes U.K. **13** 52.03N 0.42W
Miltou Chad **77** 10.10N 17.30E
Miluo China **55** 28.50N113.06E
Milverton Canada **104** 43.34N 80.55W
Milwaukee U.S.A. **110** 43.02N 87.55W
Milwaukie U.S.A. **108** 45.27N122.38W
Milyatino U.S.S.R. **44** 54.30N 34.20E
Mim Ghana **76** 6.55N 2.34W
Miminiska L. Canada **102** 51.32N 88.33W
Mimizan France **20** 44.12N 1.14W
Mina U.S.A. **108** 38.24N118.07W
Mīnā 'al Aḥmadī Kuwait **60** 29.04N 48.08E
Mīnāb Iran **65** 27.07N 57.05E
Mīnā Baranis Egypt **72** 23.55N 35.28E
Minaki Canada **102** 50.00N 94.48W
Minamata Japan **57** 32.13N130.24E
Minas Uruguay **125** 34.23S 55.14W
Minas Basin *b.* Canada **103** 45.20N 64.00W
Minas Channel *str.* Canada **103** 45.15N 64.45W
Minas de Corrales Uruguay **125** 31.35S 55.28W
Minas de Riotinto Spain **27** 37.42N 6.22W
Minas Gerais *d.* Brazil **126** 18.00S 45.00W
Minatitlán Mexico **116** 17.59N 94.32W
Minbu Burma **56** 20.09N 94.52E
Mindanao *i.* Phil. **59** 7.30N125.00E
Mindanao Sea Phil. **59** 9.10N124.25E
Mindanao Trench Pacific Oc. **84** 9.00N127.00E
Mindarie Australia **92** 34.51S140.12E
Mindemoya Canada **104** 45.44N 82.10W
Minden Canada **104** 44.55N 78.43W
Minden U.S.A. **111** 32.37N 93.17W
Minden W. Germany **38** 52.17N 8.55E
Minden City U.S.A. **104** 43.40N 82.47W
Minderoo Australia **88** 21.59S115.04E
Mindif Cameroon **77** 10.25N 14.23E
Mindiptana Indonesia **59** 5.45S140.22E
Mindona L. Australia **92** 33.09S142.09E
Mindoro *i.* Phil. **59** 13.00N121.00E
Mindoro Str. Pacific Oc. **59** 12.30N120.10E
Mindra *mtn.* Romania **37** 45.20N 23.32E
Minehead U.K. **13** 51.12N 3.29W
Mineola U.S.A. **111** 32.40N 95.29W
Minerva Australia **90** 24.00S148.05E
Minerva U.S.A. **114** 40.44N 81.06W
Minervino Murge Italy **33** 41.05N 16.05E
Mingan Canada **103** 50.18N 64.02W
Mingary Australia **92** 32.09S140.46E
Mingela Australia **90** 19.53S146.40E
Mingenew Australia **89** 29.11S115.26E
Mingin Burma **56** 22.52N 94.39E
Mingin Range *mts.* Burma **56** 24.00N 95.45E
Minglanilla Spain **25** 39.32N 1.36W
Mingorría Spain **26** 40.45N 4.40W
Minhe China **54** 36.12N102.59E
Minho *r. see* Miño Portugal **26**
Minićevo Yugo. **34** 43.42N 22.18E
Minidoka U.S.A. **108** 42.46N113.30W
Minigwal, L. Australia **89** 29.35S123.12E
Min Jiang *r.* China **55** 26.06N119.15E
Minna Nigeria **77** 9.39N 6.32E
Minneapolis Kans. U.S.A. **110** 39.08N 97.42W
Minneapolis Minn. U.S.A. **110** 44.59N 93.13W
Minnedosa Canada **101** 50.14N 99.51W
Minnesota *d.* U.S.A. **110** 46.00N 94.00W
Minnesota *r.* U.S.A. **110** 44.54N 93.10W
Minnesota Lake *town* U.S.A. **110** 43.51N 93.50W
Minnipa Australia **92** 32.51S135.09E
Minnitaki L. Canada **102** 50.00N 91.50W
Miño *r.* Spain **26** 41.52N 8.51W
Minobu-sanchi *mts.* Japan **57** 35.05N138.15E
Mino-kamo Japan **57** 35.26N137.01E
Mino-mikawa-kōgen *mts.* Japan **57** 35.16N137.10E
Minorca *i. see* Menorca Spain **25**
Minot U.S.A. **110** 48.16N101.19W
Minqin China **54** 38.42N103.11E
Minsen W. Germany **38** 53.42N 7.58E
Min Shan *mts.* China **54** 32.40N104.40E
Minsk U.S.S.R. **37** 53.51N 27.30E
Minta Cameroon **77** 4.37N 12.47E
Minto, L. Canada **99** 51.00N 73.37W
Minto, Lac *l.* Canada **102** 57.15N 74.50W
Minturno Italy **32** 41.15N 13.45E
Minūf Egypt **66** 30.28N 30.56E
Min Xian China **54** 34.26N104.02E
Minyā al Qamḩ Egypt **66** 30.31N 31.21E
Minyar U.S.S.R. **44** 55.06N 57.29E
Mio U.S.A. **104** 44.39N 84.08W
Mionica Yugo. **31** 44.15N 20.05E
Miquelon Canada **102** 49.25N 76.32W
Mira Italy **30** 45.26N 12.08E
Mira Portugal **26** 40.26N 8.44W
Mira *r.* Portugal **27** 37.43N 8.47W
Mīrābād Afghan. **62** 30.25N 61.50E
Miracema Brazil **126** 21.22S 42.09W
Mīreh, Wādī al *r.* Iraq **64** 32.27N 41.21E
Miraj India **60** 16.51N 74.42E
Miramas France **21** 43.35N 5.00E
Mirambeau France **20** 45.23N 0.34W
Miramichi B. Canada **103** 47.08N 65.08W
Mīram Shāh Pakistan **62** 33.01N 70.04E
Mīrān Pakistan **62** 31.24N 70.43E
Miranda de Ebro Spain **26** 42.41N 2.57W
Miranda do Douro Portugal **26** 41.30N 6.16W
Mirande France **20** 43.31N 0.25E
Mirandela Portugal **26** 41.29N 7.11W
Mirando City U.S.A. **111** 27.26N 99.00W
Mirandola Italy **30** 44.53N 11.04E
Miravete, Puerto de *pass* Spain **27** 39.43N 5.43W
Mīr Bachcheh Kūt Afghan. **62** 34.45N 69.08E
Mirbāţ Oman **60** 17.00N 54.45E
Mirebeau-sur-Bèze France **19** 47.24N 5.19E
Mirecourt France **19** 48.18N 6.08E
Miri Malaysia **58** 4.28N114.00E
Mirim, L. Brazil **126** 33.10S 53.30W
Mírina Greece **34** 39.52N 25.04E
Mironovka U.S.S.R. **37** 49.40N 30.59E
Miroşi Romania **37** 44.25N 24.58E
Mirow E. Germany **38** 53.16N 12.49E
Mīrpur Jammu & Kashmir **62** 33.15N 73.55E
Mīrpur Batoro Pakistan **62** 24.44N 68.16E
Mīrpur Khās Pakistan **60** 25.33N 69.05E
Mīrpur Sakro Pakistan **62** 24.33N 67.37E
Mirtóön Pélagos *sea* Greece **35** 36.51N 23.18E
Miryeny U.S.S.R. **37** 47.00N 29.06E
Mirzāpur India **63** 25.09N 82.35E
Mi saki *c.* Japan **57** 40.09N141.52E
Misawa Japan **57** 40.41N141.24E
Miscou I. Canada **103** 47.57N 64.33W
Mishawaka U.S.A. **112** 41.38N 86.10W
Mishima Japan **57** 35.07N138.55E
Mishkino U.S.S.R. **44** 55.34N 56.00E
Mishmar Ayyalon Israel **67** 31.52N 34.57E
Mishmar Ha'Emeq Israel **67** 32.36N 35.09E
Mishmar HaNegev Israel **67** 31.21N 34.43E
Mishmar Hayarden Israel **67** 33.00N 35.36E
Mishomis Canada **105** 47.11N 75.40W
Misilmeri Italy **32** 38.01N 13.27E
Misima I. P.N.G. **90** 10.40S152.45E
Misiones *d.* Argentina **124** 27.00S 54.40W
Miskī Sudan **72** 14.51N 24.13E
Miskolc Hungary **37** 48.07N 20.47E
Mismār Sudan **72** 18.13N 35.38E
Misoöl *i.* Indonesia **59** 1.50S130.10E
Miṣr al Jadīdah Egypt **66** 30.06N 31.20E
Miṣrātah Libya **75** 32.23N 15.06E
Miṣrātah *d.* Libya **75** 30.30N 17.00E
Miṣr Baḩrī *f.* Egypt **66** 30.30N 31.00E
Missinaibi *r.* Canada **102** 50.44N 81.29W
Mission U.S.A. **110** 43.18N100.40W
Mississagi *r.* Canada **104** 46.10N 83.01W
Mississagi Prov. Park Canada **104** 46.35N 82.30W
Mississauga Canada **104** 43.35N 79.37W
Mississippi *r.* Canada **105** 45.26N 76.16W
Mississippi *d.* U.S.A. **111** 32.40N 90.00W
Mississippi *r.* U.S.A. **111** 29.00N 89.15W
Mississippi Delta U.S.A. **111** 29.10N 89.15W
Mississippi L. Canada **105** 45.05N 76.12W
Mississippi Sd. U.S.A. **111** 30.15N 88.40W
Missoula U.S.A. **108** 46.52N114.01W
Missouri *d.* U.S.A. **110** 38.30N 92.00W
Missouri *r.* U.S.A. **110** 38.50N 90.08W
Missouri Valley *town* U.S.A. **110** 41.33N 95.53W
Mistake Creek *town* Australia **88** 17.06S129.04E
Mistassini Canada **103** 48.54N 72.13W
Mistassini *r.* Canada **103** 48.53N 72.14W
Mistassini, Lac *l.* Canada **103** 51.15N 73.10W
Mistassini Prov. Park Canada **103** 51.30N 73.20W
Mistastin Canada **103** 55.55N 63.30W
Misterbianco Italy **33** 37.31N 15.01E
Mistinibi, L. Canada **103** 55.55N 64.10W
Mistretta Italy **33** 37.56N 14.22E
Mitchell Australia **90** 26.29S147.58E
Mitchell *r.* N.S.W. Australia **93** 29.40S152.18E
Mitchell *r.* Qld. Australia **90** 15.12S141.35E
Mitchell *r.* Vic. Australia **93** 37.53S147.41E
Mitchell Canada **104** 43.28N 81.12W
Mitchell Oreg. U.S.A. **108** 44.34N120.09W
Mitchell S.Dak. U.S.A. **110** 43.40N 98.00W
Mitchell, Mt. U.S.A. **113** 35.47N 82.16W
Mitchell River *town* Australia **90** 15.28S141.44E
Mitchells Bay *town* Canada **104** 42.28N 82.26W
Mitchelstown Rep. of Ire. **15** 52.16N 8.17W
Mīt Ghamr Egypt **66** 30.43N 31.16E
Mithapur India **62** 22.25N 69.00E
Mithi Pakistan **62** 24.44N 69.48E
Mitilíni Greece **35** 39.00N 26.20E
Mitla, Mamarr *pass* Egypt **66** 30.00N 32.53E
Mitla Pass *see* Mitla, Mamarr Egypt **66**
Mito Japan **57** 36.30N140.29E
Mitri Prespa, Límni *l.* Greece **34** 40.55N 21.00E
Mitsinjo Madagascar **81** 16.01S 45.52E
Mittagong Australia **93** 34.27S150.25E
Mittelandkanal W. Germany **38** 52.23N 8.00E
Mittenwald W. Germany **39** 47.27N 11.15E
Mittersill Austria **39** 47.16N 12.29E
Mittweida E. Germany **38** 50.59N 12.59E
Mitú Colombia **122** 1.08N 70.03W
Mitumba, Monts *mts.* Zaïre **79** 3.00S 28.30E
Mitwaba Zaïre **79** 8.32S 27.20E
Mitzic Gabon **78** 0.48N 11.30E
Miura Japan **57** 35.08N139.37E
Mivtahim Israel **67** 31.14N 34.23E
Miya *r.* Japan **57** 34.32N136.44E
Miyako Japan **57** 39.40N141.59E
Miyako jima *i.* Japan **53** 24.45N125.25E
Miyakonojō Japan **57** 31.43N131.02E
Miyazaki Japan **57** 31.58N131.50E
Mizdah Libya **75** 31.26N 12.59E
Mizen Head Rep. of Ire. **15** 51.27N 9.50W
Mizil Romania **37** 45.00N 26.26E
Mizoch U.S.S.R. **37** 50.30N 25.50E
Mizoram *d.* India **61** 23.40N 92.40E
Mizpa Israel **67** 32.47N 35.31E
Mizpe Ramon Israel **66** 30.36N 34.48E
Mizra' Israel **67** 32.39N 35.17E
Mizukaidō Japan **57** 36.01N139.59E
Mizunami Japan **57** 35.22N137.15E
Mizusawa Japan **57** 39.08N141.08E
Mjölby Sweden **43** 58.19N 15.08E
Mjöndalen Norway **42** 59.45N 10.01E
Mjörn *l.* Sweden **43** 57.54N 12.25E
Mjøsa *l.* Norway **41** 60.40N 11.00E
Mkata Tanga Tanzania **79** 5.47S 38.18E
Mkushi Zambia **79** 13.40S 29.26E
Mkuze R.S.A. **81** 27.10S 32.00E
Mkwaja Tanzania **79** 5.46S 38.51E
Mkwiti Tanzania **79** 10.27S 39.18E
Mladá Boleslav Czech. **36** 50.26N 14.55E
Mława Poland **37** 53.06N 20.23E
Mljet *i.* Yugo. **29** 42.45N 17.30E
Mljetski Kanal *str.* Yugo. **31** 42.48N 17.35E
Mneni Zimbabwe **80** 20.38S 30.03E
Moab U.S.A. **108** 38.35N109.33W
Moama Australia **93** 36.05S144.50E
Moamba Mozambique **81** 25.35S 32.13E
Moanda Gabon **78** 1.25S 13.18E
Moapa U.S.A. **109** 36.40N114.39W
Moatize Mozambique **81** 16.10S 33.40E
Moba Zaïre **79** 7.03S 29.42E
Mobara Japan **57** 35.25N140.18E
Mobaye C.A.R. **73** 4.19N 21.11E
Moberly U.S.A. **110** 39.25N 92.26W
Mobert Canada **102** 48.41N 85.40W
Mobile U.S.A. **111** 30.42N 88.05W
Mobile B. U.S.A. **111** 30.25N 88.00W
Mobridge U.S.A. **110** 45.32N100.26W
Moçambique *town* Mozambique **79** 15.00S 40.47E
Moçâmedes Angola **78** 15.10S 12.10E
Moçâmedes *d.* Angola **80** 15.30S 12.30E
Mochudi Botswana **80** 24.26S 26.07E
Mocimboa da Praia Mozambique **79** 11.19S 40.19E
Mocimboa do Ruvuma Mozambique **79** 11.05S 39.15E
Möckeln *l.* Sweden **43** 56.40N 14.10E
Moclips U.S.A. **108** 47.14N124.13W
Mococa Brazil **126** 21.28S 47.00W
Moctezuma Mexico **109** 30.10N106.28W
Mocuba Mozambique **79** 16.52S 37.02E
Močurica *r.* Bulgaria **34** 42.31N 26.32E
Modane France **21** 45.12N 6.40E
Modāsa India **62** 23.28N 73.18E
Modder *r.* R.S.A. **80** 29.03S 23.56E
Modena Italy **30** 44.40N 10.54E
Modena U.S.A. **108** 37.48N113.57W
Modesto U.S.A. **108** 37.39N121.00W
Modica Italy **33** 36.51N 14.47E
Modjamboli Zaïre **78** 2.28N 22.06E
Modriča Yugo. **31** 44.57N 18.18E
Moe Australia **93** 38.10S146.15E
Moebase Mozambique **81** 17.04S 38.41E
Moelv Norway **41** 60.56N 10.42E
Moffat U.K. **14** 55.20N 3.27W
Moga India **62** 30.48N 75.10E
Mogadisho Somali Rep. **79** 2.02N 45.21E
Mogadouro Portugal **26** 41.20N 6.39W
Mogaung Burma **56** 25.15N 96.54E
Mogi das Cruzes Brazil **126** 23.33S 46.14W
Mogi-Guaçu Brazil **126** 20.55S 48.06W
Mogilev U.S.S.R. **37** 53.54N 30.20E
Mogilev Podolskiy U.S.S.R. **37** 48.29N 27.49E
Mogil-Mogil Australia **93** 29.21S148.44E

Mogilno to Mosel

Mogilno Poland **37** 52.40N 17.58E
Mogi-Mirim Brazil **126** 22.29S 46.55W
Mogincual Mozambique **79** 15.33S 40.29E
Mogliano Veneto Italy **30** 45.33N 12.14E
Mogok Burma **56** 23.00N 96.30E
Mogollon Rim *f.* U.S.A. **109** 32.30N111.00W
Moguer Spain **27** 37.16N 6.50W
Mogumber Australia **89** 31.01S116.02E
Mohács Hungary **31** 45.59N 18.42E
Mohameru, Gunung *mtn.* Indonesia **59** 8.04S112.53E
Mohammedia Morocco **74** 33.44N 7.24W
Mohana India **63** 25.54N 77.45E
Mohawk *r.* U.S.A. **115** 42.47N 73.42W
Mohawk Ariz. U.S.A. **109** 32.41N113.47W
Mohawk N.Y. U.S.A. **115** 43.00N 75.00W
Moheda Sweden **43** 57.00N 14.34E
Mohéli *i.* Comoros **79** 12.22S 43.45E
Mohon France **19** 49.45N 4.44E
Mohoro Tanzania **79** 8.09S 39.07E
Mohoru Kenya **79** 1.01S 34.07E
Moi Norway **42** 58.28N 6.32E
Moincêr China **63** 31.10N 80.52E
Moindi Gabon **78** 3.24S 11.43E
Mointy U.S.S.R. **9** 47.10N 73.18E
Moira *r.* Canada **105** 44.09N 77.23W
Moira U.S.A. **105** 44.50N 74.34W
Mo-i-Rana Norway **40** 66.19N 14.10E
Mõisaküla U.S.S.R. **41** 58.06N 25.11E
Moisdon France **18** 47.37N 1.22W
Moisie *r.* Canada **103** 50.13N 66.02W
Moissac France **20** 44.06N 1.05E
Moïssala Chad **77** 8.20N 17.40E
Moita Portugal **27** 38.39N 8.59W
Mojácar Spain **27** 37.09N 1.50W
Mojave U.S.A. **109** 35.03N118.10W
Mojave Desert U.S.A. **109** 35.00N117.00W
Mojokerto Indonesia **59** 7.25S112.31E
Mokameh India **63** 25.24N 85.55E
Mokau New Zealand **86** 38.41S174.37E
Mokmer Indonesia **59** 1.13S136.13E
Mokpo S. Korea **53** 34.50N126.25E
Mokra Gora *mts.* Yugo. **34** 42.50N 20.30E
Mokren Bulgaria **34** 42.45N 26.39E
Mol Belgium **16** 51.11N 5.09E
Mola di Bari Italy **33** 41.04N 17.05E
Moláoi Greece **35** 36.48N 22.52E
Molat *i.* Yugo. **31** 44.15N 14.49E
Molchanovo U.S.S.R. **50** 57.39N 83.45E
Mold U.K. **12** 53.10N 3.08W
Moldavskaya S.S.R. *d.* U.S.S.R. **37** 47.30N 28.30E
Molde Norway **40** 62.44N 7.08E
Molepolole Botswana **80** 24.26S 25.34E
Molfetta Italy **33** 41.12N 16.36E
Molihong Shan *mtn.* China **54** 42.11N124.43E
Molina de Aragón Spain **25** 40.51N 1.53W
Molina de Segura Spain **25** 38.04N 1.12W
Moline U.S.A. **110** 41.30N 90.30W
Molinella Italy **30** 44.37N 11.40E
Molino Lacy Mexico **109** 30.05N114.24W
Molins de Rey Spain **25** 41.25N 2.01E
Moliro Zaïre **79** 8.11S 30.29E
Molise *d.* Italy **33** 41.40N 14.30E
Molkom Sweden **43** 59.36N 13.43E
Mölle Sweden **43** 56.17N 12.29E
Mollendo Peru **124** 17.02S 72.01W
Mölln W. Germany **38** 53.37N 10.41E
Mollösund Sweden **42** 58.04N 11.28E
Mölndal Sweden **43** 57.39N 12.01E
Molodechno U.S.S.R. **37** 54.16N 26.50E
Molokai *i.* Hawaii U.S.A. **106** 21.20N157.00W
Molong Australia **93** 33.08S148.53E
Molopo *r.* R.S.A. **80** 28.30S 20.22E
Mólos Greece **35** 38.47N 22.37E
Moloundou Cameroon **78** 2.55N 12.01E
Molsheim France **19** 48.32N 7.29E
Molson L. Canada **101** 54.12N 96.45W
Molt U.S.A. **110** 46.22N102.20W
Molteno R.S.A. **80** 31.23S 26.21E
Moluccas *is.* Indonesia **59** 4.00S128.00E
Molucca Sea *see* Maluku, Laut Pacific Oc. **59**
Moma Mozambique **79** 16.40S 39.10E
Mombasa Kenya **79** 4.04S 39.40E
Mombuey Spain **26** 42.02N 6.20W
Momchilgrad Bulgaria **34** 41.32N 25.25E
Momi Zaïre **79** 1.42S 27.03E
Mommark Denmark **36** 54.55N 10.03E
Mompós Colombia **122** 9.15N 74.29W
Mon *d.* Burma **56** 16.45N 97.25E
Møn *i.* Denmark **43** 55.00N 12.20E
Mona *i.* Puerto Rico **117** 18.06N 67.54W
Monaco Europe **21** 43.40N 7.25E
Monadhliath Mts. U.K. **14** 57.09N 4.08W
Monaghan Rep. of Ire. **15** 54.15N 6.58W
Monaghan *d.* Rep. of Ire. **15** 54.10N 7.00W
Monahans U.S.A. **111** 31.36N102.54W
Monarch Mt. Canada **100** 51.55N125.57W
Monastir Tunisia **75** 35.35N 10.50E
Mon Cai Vietnam **55** 21.36N107.55E
Moncalieri Italy **30** 45.00N 7.40E
Moncão Portugal **26** 42.05N 8.29W
Moncayo, Sierra del *mts.* Spain **25** 41.48N 1.50W
Monchegorsk U.S.S.R. **44** 67.55N 33.01E
Mönchen Gladbach W. Germany **38** 51.12N 6.28E
Monchique Portugal **27** 37.19N 8.33W
Monclova Mexico **111** 26.54N101.25W
Moncontour France **18** 48.21N 2.39W
Moncton Canada **103** 46.06N 64.47W
Mondego *r.* Portugal **26** 40.09N 8.52W
Mondego, Cabo *c.* Portugal **26** 40.11N 8.55W
Mondo Tanzania **79** 5.00S 35.54E
Mondoñedo Spain **26** 43.26N 7.22W
Mondoubleau France **18** 47.59N 0.54E
Mondovì Italy **30** 44.23N 7.49E
Mondragone Italy **32** 41.07N 13.53E
Mondrain I. Australia **89** 34.08S122.15E
Monemvasía Greece **35** 36.41N 23.03E
Monessen U.S.A. **114** 40.09N 79.53W
Monesterio Spain **26** 38.05N 6.16W
Monet Canada **102** 48.10N 75.40W
Monett U.S.A. **111** 36.55N 93.55W
Monfalcone Italy **31** 45.49N 13.32E
Monflanquin France **20** 44.32N 0.46E
Monforte Portugal **27** 39.03N 7.26W
Monforte Spain **26** 42.31N 7.33W
Monga Zaïre **73** 4.12N 22.49E
Mongala *r.* Zaïre **78** 1.58N 19.55E
Mongalla Sudan **73** 5.12N 31.46E
Mong Cai Vietnam **55** 21.36N107.55E
Monger, L. Australia **89** 29.15S117.05E
Monghyr India **63** 25.23N 86.28E
Mongo Chad **77** 12.14N 18.45E
Mongolia Asia **52** 46.30N104.00E
Mongororo Chad **73** 12.01N 22.28E
Mongu Zambia **78** 15.10S 23.09E
Monheim W. Germany **39** 48.50N 10.51E
Monifieth U.K. **14** 56.29N 2.50W
Monistrol-sur-Loire France **21** 45.17N 4.10E
Monitor Range *mts.* U.S.A. **108** 38.45N116.30W
Monkoto Zaïre **73** 1.38S 20.39E
Monmouth U.K. **13** 51.48N 2.43W
Monmouth Ill. U.S.A. **110** 40.54N 90.39W
Monmouth Oreg. U.S.A. **108** 44.51N123.14W
Monocacy *r.* U.S.A. **114** 39.13N 77.27W
Mono L. U.S.A. **108** 38.00N119.00W
Monomoy Pt. U.S.A. **115** 41.33N 70.02W
Monongahela *r.* U.S.A. **114** 40.27N 80.00W
Monopoli Italy **33** 40.57N 17.19E
Monor Hungary **37** 47.21N 19.27E
Monóvar Spain **25** 38.25N 0.47W
Monreal Spain **25** 42.42N 1.30W
Monreal del Campo Spain **25** 40.47N 1.21W
Monreale Italy **32** 38.05N 13.17E
Monroe La. U.S.A. **111** 32.33N 92.07W
Monroe Mich. U.S.A. **104** 41.55N 83.24W
Monroe N.C. U.S.A. **113** 35.00N 80.35W
Monroe N.Y. U.S.A. **115** 41.20N 74.11W
Monroe Wisc. U.S.A. **110** 42.36N 89.38W
Monroe City U.S.A. **110** 39.39N 91.44W
Monroeville U.S.A. **113** 31.32N 87.21W
Monrovia Liberia **76** 6.20N 10.46W
Mons Belgium **16** 50.27N 3.57E
Monselice Italy **32** 45.14N 11.45E
Mönsterås Sweden **43** 57.02N 16.26E
Montabaur W. Germany **39** 50.26N 7.50E
Montagnana Italy **32** 45.14N 11.28E
Montague Canada **103** 46.10N 62.39W
Montaigu France **18** 46.59N 1.19W
Montaigut-en-Combraille France **20** 46.11N 2.38E
Montalbán Spain **25** 40.50N 0.48W
Montalbano di Elicona Italy **33** 38.02N 15.02E
Montalbano Ionico Italy **33** 40.17N 16.34E
Montalcino Italy **30** 43.03N 11.29E
Montalegre Portugal **26** 41.49N 7.48W
Montalto *mtn.* Italy **33** 38.10N 15.55E
Montalto di Castro Italy **30** 42.21N 11.37E
Montalto Uffugo Italy **33** 39.25N 16.09E
Montana Switz. **39** 46.18N 7.29E
Montana *d.* U.S.A. **108** 47.14N109.26W
Montánchez Spain **27** 39.13N 6.09W
Montargil Portugal **27** 39.05N 8.10W
Montargis France **19** 48.00N 2.45E
Montauban France **20** 44.01N 1.21E
Montauk U.S.A. **115** 41.03N 71.57W
Montbard France **19** 47.37N 4.20E
Montbarrey France **19** 47.01N 5.39E
Montbéliard France **19** 47.31N 6.48E
Montblanch Spain **25** 41.22N 1.10E
Montbrison France **21** 45.36N 4.03E
Montbron France **20** 45.40N 0.30E
Montceau-les-Mines France **19** 46.40N 4.22E
Mont Cenis, Col du *pass* France **21** 45.15N 6.54E
Montcerf Canada **105** 46.32N 76.02W
Montchannin France **19** 46.45N 4.27E
Montcornet France **19** 49.41N 4.01E
Mont de Marsan *town* France **20** 43.53N 0.30W
Montdidier France **19** 49.39N 2.34E
Monte Alegre *town* Brazil **123** 2.01S 54.04W
Monte Azul *town* Brazil **126** 15.53S 42.53W
Montebello Canada **105** 45.39N 74.56W
Montebello Iónico Italy **33** 37.59N 15.45E
Monte Carlo Monaco **21** 43.44N 7.25E
Monte Caseros Argentina **125** 30.15S 57.38W
Montecatini Terme Italy **30** 43.53N 10.46E
Montecollina Australia **92** 29.22S139.56E
Montecristo *i.* Italy **30** 42.20N 10.19E
Montefalco Italy **30** 42.54N 12.39E
Montefrío Spain **27** 37.19N 4.01W
Montego Bay *town* Jamaica **117** 18.27N 77.56W
Montejicar Spain **27** 37.34N 3.30W
Montélimar France **21** 44.34N 4.45E
Montellano Spain **27** 37.00N 5.34W
Montemor-o-Novo Portugal **27** 38.39N 8.13W
Montemor-o-Velho Portugal **26** 40.10N 8.41W
Montemura *mtn.* Portugal **26** 40.59N 7.59W
Montendre France **20** 45.17N 0.24W
Montenegro *see* Crna Gora Yugo. **31**
Montenero di Bisaccia Italy **33** 41.57N 14.47E
Montepuez Mozambique **81** 13.09S 39.33E
Montepulciano Italy **30** 43.05N 11.47E
Montereau France **19** 48.23N 2.57E
Monterey Calif. U.S.A. **108** 36.37N121.55W
Monterey Va. U.S.A. **114** 38.25N 79.35W
Monterey B. U.S.A. **108** 36.45N121.55W
Montería Colombia **122** 8.45N 75.54W
Montero Bolivia **124** 17.20S 63.15W
Monteros Argentina **124** 27.10S 65.30W
Monterotondo Italy **30** 42.03N 12.37E
Monterrey Mexico **111** 25.40N100.19W
Montesano Italy **33** 40.16N 15.43E
Monte Sant 'Angelo Italy **33** 41.42N 15.59E
Monte Santu, Capo di *c.* Italy **32** 40.05N 9.44E
Montesarchio Italy **33** 41.04N 14.38E
Montes Claros Brazil **126** 16.45S 43.52W
Montevarchi Italy **30** 43.31N 11.34E
Montevideo Uruguay **125** 34.53S 56.11W
Montevideo U.S.A. **110** 44.57N 95.43W
Montezuma U.S.A. **111** 37.36N100.26W
Montfaucon France **21** 45.10N 4.18E
Montfort-sur-Meu France **18** 48.08N 1.58W
Montgomery U.K. **13** 52.34N 3.09W
Montgomery Ala. U.S.A. **113** 32.22N 86.20W
Montgomery Penn. U.S.A. **114** 41.10N 76.52W
Montguyon France **20** 45.13N 0.11W
Monthey Switz. **39** 46.15N 6.57E
Monthois France **19** 49.19N 4.43E
Monticello Ark. U.S.A. **111** 33.38N 91.47W
Monticello Miss. U.S.A. **111** 31.33N 90.07W
Monticello N.Y. U.S.A. **115** 41.39N 74.42W
Monticello Utah U.S.A. **108** 37.52N109.21W
Montichiari Italy **32** 45.25N 10.23E
Montiel, Campo de *f.* Spain **26** 38.46N 2.45W
Montignac France **20** 45.04N 1.10E
Montigny-le-Roi France **19** 48.00N 5.30E
Montijo Portugal **27** 38.42N 8.58W
Montijo Spain **27** 38.55N 6.37W
Montijo Dam Spain **24** 38.52N 6.20W
Montilla Spain **27** 37.35N 4.38W
Montivilliers France **18** 49.33N 0.12E
Mont Joli *town* Canada **103** 48.35N 68.14W
Mont Laurier *town* Canada **105** 46.33N 75.30W
Mont Louis *town* Canada **103** 49.15N 65.46W
Mont-Louis France **20** 42.31N 2.07E
Montluçon France **20** 46.21N 2.36E
Montmagny Canada **103** 46.59N 70.33W
Montmédy France **19** 49.31N 5.22E
Montmirail France **19** 48.52N 3.32E
Montmoreau St. Cybard France **20** 45.24N 0.08E
Montmorillon France **18** 46.26N 0.52E
Montmort France **19** 48.55N 3.49E
Monto Australia **90** 24.52S151.07E
Montorio al Vomano Italy **31** 42.35N 13.38E
Montoro Spain **26** 38.01N 4.23W
Montour Falls *town* U.S.A. **114** 42.21N 76.51W
Montoursville U.S.A. **114** 41.15N 76.55W
Montpelier Idaho U.S.A. **108** 42.20N111.20W
Montpelier Vt. U.S.A. **105** 44.16N 72.35W
Montpellier France **20** 43.36N 3.53E
Montpon-sur-l'Isle France **20** 45.00N 0.10E
Montreal Canada **105** 45.31N 73.34W
Montreal *r.* Canada **104** 47.14N 84.39W
Montreal L. Canada **101** 54.20N105.40W
Montreal Lake *town* Canada **101** 54.03N105.46W
Montréal-Nord Canada **105** 45.36N 73.38W
Montreal River *town* Canada **104** 46.41N 79.50W
Montrejeau France **20** 43.05N 0.33E
Montrésor France **18** 47.09N 1.12E
Montreuil France **19** 50.28N 1.46E
Montreuil-Bellay France **18** 47.08N 0.09W
Montreux Switz. **39** 46.26N 6.55E
Montrevel France **21** 46.20N 5.08E
Montrichard France **18** 47.21N 1.11E
Montrose U.K. **14** 56.43N 2.29W
Montrose Colo. U.S.A. **108** 38.29N107.53W
Montrose Penn. U.S.A. **115** 41.50N 75.56W
Montsant, Sierra de *mts.* Spain **25** 41.15N 0.55E
Montserrat *i.* Leeward Is. **117** 16.45N 62.14W
Mont Tremblant Prov. Park Canada **105** 46.42N 74.20W
Montuenga Spain **26** 41.03N 4.37W
Montville U.S.A. **115** 41.27N 72.08W
Monument Valley *f.* U.S.A. **108** 36.50N110.20W
Monveda Zaïre **78** 2.57N 21.27E
Monywa Burma **56** 22.05N 95.15E
Monza Italy **30** 45.35N 9.16E
Monze Zambia **79** 16.16S 27.28E
Monzón Spain **25** 41.55N 0.12E
Moolawatana Australia **92** 29.55S139.43E
Mooloogool Australia **88** 26.06S119.05E
Moomin *r.* Australia **93** 29.35S148.45E
Moonbi Range *mts.* Australia **93** 31.00S151.10E
Moonie Australia **91** 27.40S150.19E
Moonie *r.* Australia **91** 29.30S148.40E
Moonta Australia **92** 34.04S137.37E
Moora Australia **89** 30.40S116.01E
Mooraberree Australia **90** 25.12S140.57E
Moorarie Australia **88** 25.56S117.35E
Moorcroft U.S.A. **108** 44.16N104.57W
Moore *r.* Australia **89** 31.22S115.29E
Moore, L. Australia **89** 29.30S117.30E
Mooréa *i.* Îs. de la Société **85** 17.32S149.50W
Moorefield U.S.A. **114** 39.04N 78.58W
Moorefield *r.* U.S.A. **114** 39.04N 78.58W
Moorfoot Hills U.K. **14** 55.43N 3.03W
Moorhead U.S.A. **110** 46.53N 96.45W
Moor Lake *town* Canada **105** 46.09N 77.42W
Moorlands Australia **92** 35.20S139.40E
Moornanyah L. Australia **92** 33.02S143.58E
Mooroopna Australia **93** 36.24S145.22E
Moosburg W. Germany **39** 48.29N 11.57E
Moose Creek *town* Canada **105** 45.15N 74.58W
Moosehead L. U.S.A. **112** 45.40N 69.40W
Moose Jaw Canada **101** 50.23N105.32W
Moose Lake *town* U.S.A. **110** 46.26N 92.45W
Moosomin Canada **101** 50.07N101.40W
Moosonee Canada **102** 51.17N 80.39W
Mootwingee Australia **92** 31.52S141.14E
Mopanzhang China **54** 33.07N117.22E
Mopêia Velha Mozambique **81** 17.58S 35.40E
Mopti Mali **76** 14.29N 4.10W
Mopti *d.* Mali **74** 15.30N 3.40W
Moqor Afghan. **62** 32.55N 67.40E
Moquegua Peru **124** 17.20S 70.55W
Mora Cameroon **77** 11.02N 14.07E
Mora Portugal **27** 38.56N 8.10W
Mora Spain **27** 39.41N 3.46W
Mora Sweden **41** 61.00N 14.33E
Mora U.S.A. **110** 45.53N 93.18W
Morādābād India **63** 28.50N 78.47E
Mora de Rubielos Spain **25** 40.15N 0.45W
Morafenobe Madagascar **81** 17.49S 44.45E
Mórahalom Hungary **31** 46.13N 19.54E
Moralana Australia **92** 31.42S138.12E
Moral de Calatrava Spain **26** 38.50N 3.35W
Moramanga Madagascar **81** 18.56S 48.12E
Moran U.S.A. **104** 46.00N 84.50W
Morar, Loch U.K. **14** 56.56N 4.00W
Morasverdes Spain **26** 40.36N 6.16W
Moratalla Spain **25** 38.12N 1.53W
Morava *r.* Czech. **37** 48.10N 16.59E
Morava *r.* Yugo. **37** 44.43N 21.02E
Moravia U.S.A. **115** 42.43N 76.25W
Moravské Budějovice Czech. **36** 49.03N 15.49E
Morawhanna Guyana **122** 8.17N 59.44W
Moray Firth *est.* U.K. **14** 57.35N 5.15W
Morbach W. Germany **39** 49.48N 7.07E
Morbegno Italy **30** 46.08N 9.34E
Morbihan *d.* France **18** 47.55N 2.50W
Mörbylånga Sweden **43** 56.31N 16.23E
Morcenx France **20** 44.02N 0.55W
Morden Australia **92** 30.30S142.23E
Morden Canada **101** 49.11N 98.05W
Mordialloc Australia **93** 38.00S145.05E
Mordovo U.S.S.R. **45** 52.06N 40.45E
Moreau *r.* U.S.A. **110** 45.18N100.43W
Morecambe U.K. **12** 54.03N 2.52W
Morecambe B. U.K. **12** 54.05N 3.00W
Moree Australia **93** 29.29S149.53E
Morée France **18** 47.54N 1.14E
Morehead U.S.A. **113** 38.11N 83.27W
Morehead City U.S.A. **113** 34.43N 76.44W
Morelia Mexico **116** 19.40N101.11W
Morella Spain **25** 40.37N 0.06W
Morelos *d.* Mexico **116** 18.40N 99.00W
Morena India **63** 26.30N 78.09E
Morena, Sierra *mts.* Spain **27** 38.20N 4.25W
Morenci U.S.A. **109** 33.05N109.22W
Moreno Mexico **109** 28.29N110.41W
Möre og Romsdal *d.* Norway **40** 63.00N 9.00E
Moresby I. Canada **100** 52.30N131.40W
Moreton I. Australia **91** 27.10S153.25E
Morez France **19** 46.31N 6.02E
Mórfou Cyprus **66** 35.12N 33.00E
Mórfou, Kólpos *b.* Cyprus **66** 35.15N 32.50E
Morgan Australia **92** 34.02S139.40E
Morgan U.S.A. **111** 32.01N 97.37W
Morgan City U.S.A. **111** 29.42N 91.12W
Morganfield U.S.A. **113** 37.41N 87.55W
Morgantown U.S.A. **114** 39.38N 79.57W
Morghāb *r.* Afghan. **60** 36.50N 63.00E
Morgongåva Sweden **43** 59.56N 16.57E
Moriki Nigeria **77** 12.55N 6.30E
Moringen W. Germany **38** 51.42N 9.52E
Morin Heights Canada **105** 45.54N 74.21W
Morioka Japan **57** 39.43N141.10E
Morisset Australia **93** 33.06S151.29E
Moriyama Japan **57** 35.04N135.59E
Morkalla Australia **92** 34.22S141.10E
Morlaix France **18** 48.35N 3.50W
Mörlunda Sweden **43** 57.19N 15.51E
Mormanno Italy **33** 39.53N 16.00E
Mormon Range *mts.* U.S.A. **108** 37.08N114.20W
Mornington Australia **93** 38.12S145.05E
Mornington I. Australia **90** 16.33S139.24E
Mornington Mission Australia **90** 16.40S139.10E
Morobe P.N.G. **59** 7.45S147.35E
Morocco Africa **74** 32.30N 5.00W
Moro G. Phil. **59** 6.30N123.20E
Morogoro Tanzania **79** 6.47S 37.40E
Morogoro *d.* Tanzania **79** 8.30S 37.00E
Moroleón Mexico **116** 20.08N101.12W
Morombe Madagascar **81** 21.45S 43.22E
Morón Argentina **125** 34.39S 58.37W
Morón Cuba **117** 22.08N 78.39W
Mörön Mongolia **52** 49.36N100.08E
Morón Spain **27** 37.08N 5.27W
Morondava Madagascar **81** 20.17S 44.17E
Morón de Almazán Spain **25** 41.25N 2.25W
Moroni Comoros **79** 11.40S 43.19E
Morotai *i.* Indonesia **59** 2.10N128.30E
Moroto Uganda **79** 2.32N 34.41E
Moroto, Mt. Uganda **79** 2.30N 34.46E
Morpeth U.K. **12** 55.10N 1.40W
Morrilton U.S.A. **111** 35.09N 92.45W
Morrinsville New Zealand **86** 37.39S175.32E
Morris Minn. U.S.A. **110** 45.35N 95.55W
Morris Penn. U.S.A. **114** 41.36N 77.18W
Morrisburg Canada **105** 44.54N 75.11W
Morristown Ariz. U.S.A. **109** 33.51N112.37W
Morristown N.J. U.S.A. **115** 40.48N 74.29W
Morristown N.Y. U.S.A. **105** 44.35N 75.39W
Morristown S.Dak. U.S.A. **110** 45.56N101.43W
Morristown Tenn. U.S.A. **113** 36.13N 83.18W
Morrisville N.Y. U.S.A. **115** 42.54N 75.39W
Morrisville Vt. U.S.A. **105** 44.34N 72.44W
Mörrum Sweden **43** 56.11N 14.45E
Morrumbene Mozambique **81** 23.41S 35.25E
Mörrumsån *r.* Sweden **43** 56.09N 14.44E
Mors *i.* Denmark **42** 56.50N 8.45E
Morsbach W. Germany **38** 50.52N 7.43E
Morsi India **63** 21.21N 78.00E
Mortagne France **18** 48.31N 0.33E
Mortagne *r.* France **19** 48.33N 6.27E
Mortagne-sur-Sèvre France **18** 47.00N 0.57W
Mortain France **18** 48.39N 0.56W
Mortara Italy **30** 45.15N 8.44E
Morteau France **19** 47.04N 6.37E
Mortes *r.* Brazil **126** 21.09S 45.06W
Mortes *r. see* Manso *r.* Brazil **124**
Mortlake *town* Australia **92** 38.05S142.48E
Morundah Australia **93** 34.56S146.18E
Moruya Australia **93** 35.56S150.06E
Morvan, Monts du *mts.* France **19** 47.05N 4.00E
Morven Australia **90** 26.25S147.05E
Morvern *f.* U.K. **14** 56.37N 5.45W
Morvi India **62** 22.49N 70.50E
Morwell Australia **93** 38.14S146.25E
Morzhovets *i.* U.S.S.R. **44** 66.45N 42.30E
Mosbach W. Germany **39** 49.21N 9.08E
Mosby Norway **42** 58.14N 7.54E
Moscow U.S.A. **108** 46.44N117.00W
Moscow *see* Moskva U.S.S.R. **44**
Mosel *r.* W. Germany **39** 50.22N 7.36E

Moselle to Mutoray

Moselle d. France 19 49.00N 6.30E
Moselle r. see Mosel France 19
Moses Lake town U.S.A. 108 47.08N119.17W
Mosgiel New Zealand 86 45.53S170.22E
Moshi Tanzania 79 3.20S 37.21E
Mosjöen Norway 40 65.50N 13.10E
Moskenes Norway 40 67.55N 13.00E
Moskenesöy i. Norway 40 67.55N 13.00E
Moskva U.S.S.R. 44 55.45N 37.42E
Moskva r. U.S.S.R. 44 55.08N 38.50E
Mosquera Colombia 122 2.30N 78.29W
Mosquero U.S.A. 109 35.47N103.58W
Mosquitia Plain Honduras 117 15.00N 84.00W
Mosquito Creek Resr. U.S.A. 114 41.10N 80.45W
Mosquitos, Costa de f. Nicaragua 117 13.00N 84.00W
Mosquitos, Golfo de los g. Panama 117 9.00N 81.00W
Moss Norway 42 59.26N 10.42E
Mossaka Congo 78 1.20S 16.44E
Mossburn New Zealand 86 45.41S168.15E
Mosselbaai R.S.A. 80 34.11S 22.08E
Mossendjo Congo 78 2.52S 12.46E
Mossgiel Australia 93 33.18S144.05E
Mossman Australia 90 16.28S145.22E
Mossoró Brazil 123 5.10S 37.18W
Mossuril Mozambique 81 14.58S 40.42E
Most Czech. 38 50.32N 13.39E
Mostaganem Algeria 74 35.56N 0.05E
Mostar Yugo. 31 43.20N 17.49E
Mösting, Kap c. Greenland 99 64.00N 41.00W
Mostiska U.S.S.R. 37 49.48N 23.05E
Mosul see Al Mawşil Iraq 64
Mösvatnet l. Norway 42 59.52N 8.05E
Mota del Cuervo Spain 27 39.30N 2.52W
Mota del Marqués Spain 26 41.38N 5.10W
Motagua r. Guatemala 117 15.56N 87.45W
Motala Sweden 43 58.33N 15.03E
Moth India 63 25.43N 78.57E
Motherwell U.K. 14 55.48N 4.00W
Motihāri India 63 26.39N 84.55E
Motilla del Palancar Spain 25 39.34N 1.53W
Motloutse r. Botswana 80 22.15S 29.00E
Motol U.S.S.R. 37 52.25N 25.05E
Motou China 54 32.17N120.35E
Motril Spain 27 36.45N 3.31W
Mott U.S.A. 108 46.22N102.20W
Mottola Italy 33 40.38N 17.03E
Motueka New Zealand 86 41.08S173.01E
Motu Iti i. Îs. de la Société 85 16.15S151.50W
Motutapu Niue 84 19.02S169.52W
Mouali Congo 78 0.10N 15.33E
Mouchalagane r. Canada 103 53.32N 69.00W
Moúdhros Greece 34 39.52N 25.16E
Moudjéria Mauritania 74 17.53N 12.20W
Moudon Switz. 39 46.40N 6.48E
Mouila Gabon 78 1.50S 11.02E
Mouka C.A.R. 73 7.16N 21.52E
Moulamein Australia 92 35.03S144.05E
Moulhoulé Djibouti 73 12.36N 43.12E
Moulins France 20 46.34N 3.20E
Moulins-la-Marche France 18 48.39N 0.29E
Moulmein Burma 56 16.55N 97.49E
Moulouya, Oued r. Morocco 74 35.05N 2.25W
Moultrie U.S.A. 113 31.11N 83.47W
Moultrie, L. U.S.A. 113 33.20N 80.05W
Mound City U.S.A. 110 40.07N 95.14W
Moundou Chad 77 8.36N 16.02E
Moundsville U.S.A. 114 39.55N 80.44W
Moundville U.S.A. 111 32.59N 87.38W
Mountain Ash U.K. 13 51.42N 3.22W
Mountain City U.S.A. 108 41.50N115.58W
Mountain Grove Canada 105 44.44N 76.51W
Mountain Home Ark. U.S.A. 111 36.20N 92.23W
Mountain Home Idaho U.S.A. 108 43.08N115.41W
Mountain Nile r. see Jabal, Baḩr al Sudan 73
Mountain Village U.S.A. 98 62.05N163.44W
Mount Airy town U.S.A. 114 39.23N 77.09W
Mount Barker town S.A. Australia 92 35.06S138.52E
Mount Barker town W.A. Australia 89 34.36S117.37E
Mount Bellew town Rep. of Ire. 15 53.28N 8.30W
Mount Brown town Australia 92 29.45S141.52E
Mount Brydges town Canada 104 42.54N 81.29W
Mount Carmel town Ill. U.S.A. 110 38.25N 87.46W
Mount Carmel town Penn. U.S.A. 115 40.48N 76.25W
Mount Clemens town U.S.A. 114 42.36N 82.53W
Mount Darwin town Zimbabwe 81 16.46S 31.36E
Mount Douglas town Australia 90 21.31S146.50E
Mount Drysdale town Australia 93 31.11S145.51E
Mount Eba town Australia 92 30.12S135.33E
Mount Fletcher town R.S.A. 80 30.41S 28.30E
Mount Forest town Canada 104 43.59N 80.44W
Mount Gambier town Australia 92 37.51S140.50E
Mount Gilead town U.S.A. 114 40.33N 82.50W
Mount Goldsworthy town Australia 88 20.20S119.31E
Mount Hagen town P.N.G. 59 5.54S144.13E
Mount Holly town U.S.A. 115 39.59N 74.47W
Mount Holly Springs town U.S.A. 114 40.07N 77.11W
Mount Hope town N.S.W. Australia 93 32.49S145.48E
Mount Hope town S.A. Australia 92 34.07S135.23E
Mount Isa town Australia 90 20.50S139.29E
Mount Ive town Australia 92 32.24S136.10E
Mount Lebanon town U.S.A. 114 40.23N 80.03W
Mount Lofty Range mts. Australia 92 34.40S139.03E
Mount Magnet town Australia 89 28.06S117.50E
Mountmellick Rep. of Ire. 15 53.08N 7.21W
Mount Morgan town Australia 90 23.39S150.23E
Mount Morris town Mich. U.S.A. 104 43.07N 83.42W
Mount Morris town N.Y. U.S.A. 114 42.44N 77.53W
Mount Morris town Penn. U.S.A. 114 39.44N 80.02W
Mount Murchison town Australia 92 31.23S143.42E
Mount Newman town Australia 88 23.20S119.40E
Mount Nicholas town Australia 88 22.54S120.27E
Mount Pleasant town Canada 104 43.05N 80.19W
Mount Pleasant town Mich. U.S.A. 112 43.36N 84.46W
Mount Pleasant town S.C. U.S.A. 113 32.48N 79.54W
Mount Pleasant town Tex. U.S.A. 111 33.09N 94.58W
Mount Robson town Canada 100 52.56N119.15W
Mount Savage town U.S.A. 114 39.42N 78.53W
Mount's B. U.K. 13 50.05N 5.25W
Mount Sterling town U.S.A. 113 38.03N 83.56W
Mount Sturgeon town Australia 90 20.08S144.00E
Mount Swan town Australia 90 22.31S135.00E
Mount Union town U.S.A. 114 40.23N 77.53W
Mount Upton town U.S.A. 115 42.26N 75.23W
Mount Vernon town Australia 88 24.09S118.10E
Mount Vernon town Ill. U.S.A. 110 38.19N 88.52W
Mount Vernon town N.Y. U.S.A. 115 40.54N 73.50W
Mount Vernon town Ohio U.S.A. 114 40.23N 82.29W
Mount Vernon town Wash. U.S.A. 108 48.25N122.20W
Mount Willoughby Australia 92 27.58S134.08E
Moura Brazil 122 1.27S 61.38W
Moura Chad 72 13.47N 21.13E
Moura Portugal 27 38.08N 7.27W
Mourdi, Dépression de f. Chad 72 18.10N 23.00E
Mourdiah Mali 76 14.35N 7.25W
Mourne r. U.K. 11 54.50N 7.29W
Mourne Mts. U.K. 15 54.10N 6.02W
Mouscron Belgium 16 50.46N 3.10E
Moussoro Chad 77 13.41N 16.31E
Mouth of Seneca U.S.A. 114 38.52N 79.21W
Moutier Switz. 39 47.17N 7.23E
Moûtiers France 21 45.29N 6.32E
Mouzákion Greece 34 39.26N 21.40E
Moxico Angola 78 11.50S 20.05E
Moxico d. Angola 78 13.00S 21.00E
Moy r. Rep. of Ire. 15 54.10N 9.09W
Moyale Kenya 79 3.31N 39.04E
Moyamba Sierra Leone 76 8.04N 12.03W
Moyen Atlas mts. Morocco 74 33.30N 5.00W
Moyen-Chari d. Chad 77 9.20N 17.35E
Moyeni Lesotho 80 30.24S 27.41E
Moyeuvre-Grande France 19 49.15N 6.02E
Moyie Canada 100 49.17N115.50W
Moyobamba Peru 122 6.04S 76.56W
Moyowosi r. Tanzania 79 4.59S 30.58E
Moza Israel 67 31.47N 35.09E
Mozambique Africa 81 17.30S 35.45E
Mozambique Channel Indian Oc. 81 16.00S 42.30E
Mozdok U.S.S.R. 45 43.45N 44.43E
Mozyr U.S.S.R. 37 52.02N 29.10E
Mpala Zaïre 79 6.45S 29.31E
M'Pama r. Congo 78 0.59S 15.40E
Mpanda Tanzania 79 6.21S 31.01E
Mpésoba Mali 76 12.31N 5.39W
Mphoengs Zimbabwe 80 21.10S 27.51E
Mpika Zambia 79 11.52S 31.30E
Mponela Malaŵi 79 13.32S 33.43E
Mporokoso Zambia 79 9.22S 30.06E
M'Pouya Congo 78 2.38S 16.08E
Mpunde mtn. Tanzania 79 6.12S 33.48E
Mpwapwa Tanzania 79 6.23S 36.38E
M'qoun, Irhil mtn. Morocco 74 31.31N 6.25W
Mrhila, Djebel mtn. Tunisia 75 35.25N 9.14E
Mrkonjić Grad Yugo. 31 44.25N 17.05E
Mrkopalj Yugo. 31 45.19N 14.51E
Msaken Tunisia 22 35.42N 10.33E
Mseleni R.S.A. 81 27.21S 32.33E
Msingu Tanzania 79 4.52S 39.08E
Msta r. U.S.S.R. 44 58.28N 31.20E
Mtakuja Tanzania 79 7.21S 30.37E
Mtama Tanzania 79 10.20S 39.19E
Mtito Andei Kenya 79 2.32S 38.10E
Mtsensk U.S.S.R. 44 53.18N 36.35E
Mtwara Tanzania 79 10.17S 40.11E
Mtwara d. Tanzania 79 10.00S 38.30E
Mu r. Japan 57 42.30N142.20E
Muaná Brazil 123 1.32S 49.13W
Muangangia Angola 78 13.33S 18.04E
Muang Chiang Rai Thailand 56 19.56N 99.51E
Muang Khammouan Laos 56 17.22N104.50E
Muang Khon Kaen Thailand 56 16.25N102.52E
Muang Lampang Thailand 56 18.16N 99.30E
Muang Lamphun Thailand 56 18.36N 99.02E
Muang Nakhon Phanom Thailand 56 17.22N104.45E
Muang Nakhon Sawan Thailand 56 15.42N100.04E
Muang Nan Thailand 56 18.47N100.50E
Muang Ngoy Laos 56 20.43N102.41E
Muang Pak Lay Laos 56 18.12N101.25E
Muang Phaya Thailand 56 19.10N 99.55E
Muang Phetchabun Thailand 56 16.25N101.08E
Muang Phichit Thailand 56 16.29N100.21E
Muang Phitsanulok Thailand 56 16.45N100.18E
Muang Phrae Thailand 56 18.07N100.09E
Muang Sakon Nakhon Thailand 56 17.10N104.08E
Muang Sing Laos 56 21.11N101.09E
Muang Soum Laos 56 18.46N102.36E
Muang Ubon Thailand 56 15.15N104.50E
Muar Malaysia 58 2.01N102.35E
Muara Brunei 58 5.01N115.01E
Muara Indonesia 58 0.32S101.20E
Muarakaman Indonesia 58 0.02S116.45E
Muaratewe Indonesia 58 0.57S114.53E
Muāri, Rās c. Pakistan 62 24.49N 66.40E
Mubende Uganda 79 0.30N 31.24E
Mubi Nigeria 77 10.16N 13.17E
Mucanona Angola 78 8.13S 16.39E
Muchea Australia 89 31.36S115.57E
Mücheln E. Germany 38 51.18N 11.48E
Muchinga Mts. Zambia 79 12.15S 31.00E
Muck i. U.K. 14 56.50N 6.14W
Mucojo Mozambique 79 12.05S 40.26E
Mudanjiang China 53 44.36N129.42E
Mudaysīsāt, Jabal al mtn. Jordan 67 31.39N 36.14E
Mudgee Australia 93 32.37S149.36E
Mudon Burma 56 16.15N 97.44E
Mudyuga U.S.S.R. 44 63.45N 39.29E
Muèda Mozambique 79 11.40S 39.31E
Muene Quibau Angola 78 11.27S 19.14E
Mufulira Zambia 79 12.30S 28.12E
Mufu Shan mts. China 55 29.30N114.45E
Muganskaya Step f. U.S.S.R. 65 39.40N 48.30E
Mughr Syria 67 33.05N 35.43E
Mughshin, Wādī Oman 71 19.44N 55.15E
Mugi Japan 57 33.40N134.25E
Mugía Spain 26 43.06N 9.10W
Muğla Turkey 29 37.12N 28.22E
Muhamdi India 63 27.57N 80.13E
Muḩammad, Ra's c. Egypt 66 27.42N 34.13E
Mühlacker W. Germany 39 48.57N 8.50E
Mühldorf W. Germany 39 48.15N 12.32E
Mühlhausen E. Germany 38 51.12N 10.27E
Mühlig Hofmann fjella mts. Antarctica 128 72.30S 5.00E
Muhola Finland 40 63.20N 25.05E
Muhos Finland 40 64.48N 25.59E
Muhu i. U.S.S.R. 41 58.32N 23.20E
Muhuru Kenya 73 1.01S 34.07E
Muhu Väin str. U.S.S.R. 41 58.45N 23.30E
Mui Ca Mau c. Vietnam 56 8.30N104.35E
Muine Bheag town Rep. of Ire. 15 52.42N 6.58W
Muir, L. Australia 89 34.30S116.30E
Mukachevo U.S.S.R. 37 48.26N 22.45E
Mukah Malaysia 58 2.56N112.02E
Mukallik, Wādī al Jordan 67 31.46N 35.29E
Mukandwara India 62 24.49N 75.59E
Mukawa P.N.G. 90 9.48S150.00E
Mukāwir site Jordan 67 31.34N 35.38E
Mukeriān India 62 31.57N 75.37E
Mukinbudin Australia 89 30.52S118.08E
Muko r. Japan 57 34.41N135.23E
Mukoba Zaïre 78 6.50S 20.50E
Mukongo Zaïre 78 6.32S 23.30E
Muktsar India 62 30.28N 74.31E
Mukwela Zambia 78 17.00S 26.40E
Mūl India 63 20.04N 79.40E
Mula r. India 62 19.35N 74.50E
Mūla r. Pakistan 62 27.57N 67.37E
Mula Spain 25 38.03N 1.30W
Mulanje Mts. Malaŵi 79 15.57S 35.33E
Mulchén Chile 125 37.43S 72.14W
Mulde r. E. Germany 38 51.10N 12.48E
Mulgathing Australia 92 30.15S134.00E
Mulgrave Canada 103 45.37N 61.23W
Mulgrave I. Australia 90 10.07S142.08E
Mulhacén mtn. Spain 27 37.03N 3.19W
Mülheim N.-Westfalen W. Germany 38 51.24N 6.54E
Mülheim N.-Westfalen W. Germany 38 50.58N 7.00E
Mulhouse France 19 47.45N 7.20E
Mull i. U.K. 14 56.28N 5.56W
Mull, Sd. of str. U.K. 14 56.32N 5.55W
Mullaghanattin mtn. Rep. of Ire. 15 51.56N 9.51W
Mullaghareirk Mts. Rep. of Ire. 15 52.19N 9.06W
Mullaghmore mtn. U.K. 15 54.51N 6.51W
Mullaley Australia 93 31.06S149.55E
Mullen U.S.A. 110 42.03N101.01W
Mullengudgery Australia 93 31.40S147.23E
Mullens U.S.A. 113 37.35N 81.25W
Mullet Pen. Rep. of Ire. 15 54.12N 10.04W
Mullett L. U.S.A. 104 45.30N 84.30W
Mullewa Australia 89 28.33S115.31E
Müllheim W. Germany 39 47.48N 7.38E
Mullingar Rep. of Ire. 15 53.31N 7.21W
Mullion Creek town Australia 93 33.09S149.09E
Mull of Galloway c. U.K. 14 54.39N 4.52W
Mull of Kintyre c. U.K. 14 55.17N 5.45W
Mullovka U.S.S.R. 44 54.12N 49.26E
Mullsjö Sweden 43 57.55N 13.53E
Mullumbimby Australia 93 28.32S153.30E
Mulobezi Zambia 80 16.49S 25.09E
Muloorina Australia 92 29.10S137.51E
Muloowurtina Australia 92 30.06S140.04E
Multai India 63 21.46N 78.15E
Multān Pakistan 62 30.11N 71.29E
Multyfarnham Rep. of Ire. 15 53.37N 7.25W
Mulyungarie Australia 92 31.30S140.45E
Mumbwa Zambia 79 14.57S 27.01E
Mumcular Turkey 35 37.05N 27.40E
Mun r. Thailand 56 15.15N104.50E
Mun, Jabal mtn. Sudan 72 14.08N 22.42E
Muna i. Indonesia 59 5.00S122.30E
Munābāo India 62 25.45N 70.17E
Munan Pass China/Vietnam 55 22.06N106.46E
Münchberg W. Germany 38 50.11N 11.47E
München W. Germany 39 48.08N 11.34E
Muncho Lake town Canada 100 59.00N125.50W
Muncie U.S.A. 112 40.11N 85.23W
Mundaring Weir Australia 89 31.59S116.13E
Münden W. Germany 38 51.25N 9.39E
Mundiwindi Australia 88 23.50S120.07E
Mundo r. Spain 25 38.19N 1.40W
Mundra India 62 22.51N 69.44E
Munera Spain 27 39.02N 2.28W
Mungallala r. Australia 91 28.53S147.05E
Mungari Mozambique 81 17.12S 33.31E
Mungbere Zaïre 79 2.40N 28.25E
Mungeli India 63 22.04N 81.41E
Mungerannie Australia 92 28.00S138.36E
Mungindi Australia 93 28.58S148.56E
Munhango Angola 78 12.10S 18.36E
Munich see München W. Germany 39
Muniesa Spain 25 41.02N 0.48W
Muniz Freire Brazil 126 20.25S 41.23W
Munkedal Sweden 42 58.29N 11.41E
Munkfors Sweden 43 59.50N 13.32E
Munning r. Australia 93 31.50S152.30E
Münsingen Switz. 39 46.53N 7.34E
Münsingen W. Germany 39 48.25N 9.29E
Munster France 19 48.03N 7.08E
Munster Nschn. W. Germany 38 52.59N 10.05E
Münster N.-Westfalen W. Germany 38 51.57N 7.37E
Muntadgin Australia 89 31.41S118.32E
Munuscong L. U.S.A. 104 46.10N 84.08W
Muong Hinh Vietnam 55 19.49N105.03E
Muonio Finland 40 67.57N 23.42E
Muonio r. Finland/Sweden 40 67.10N 23.40E
Mupa Angola 80 16.07S 15.45E
Mupa r. Mozambique 81 19.07S 35.50E
Muping China 54 37.23N121.35E
Muqaddam, Wādī Sudan 72 18.04N 31.30E
Mur r. see Mura Austria 31
Mura r. Yugo. 31 46.18N 16.53E
Murallón mtn. Argentina/Chile 125 49.48S 73.25W
Muranga Kenya 79 0.43S 37.10E
Murashi U.S.S.R. 44 59.20N 48.59E
Murat France 20 45.07N 2.52E
Murau Austria 39 47.07N 14.10E
Muravera Italy 32 39.25N 9.35E
Murça Portugal 26 41.24N 7.27W
Murchison r. Australia 88 27.30S114.10E
Murchison New Zealand 86 41.48S172.20E
Murcia Spain 25 37.59N 1.07W
Murcia d. Spain 25 37.55N 1.40W
Mur-de-Barrez France 20 44.51N 2.39E
Murdo U.S.A. 110 43.53N100.43W
Mureş r. Romania 37 46.16N 20.10E
Muret France 20 43.28N 1.21E
Murewa Zimbabwe 81 17.40S 31.47E
Murfreesboro U.S.A. 113 35.50N 86.25W
Murg r. W. Germany 39 48.55N 8.10E
Murgha Faqīrzai Pakistan 62 31.03N 67.48E
Murgha Kibzai Pakistan 62 30.44N 69.25E
Murgon Australia 90 26.15S151.57E
Murguía Spain 26 42.57N 2.49W
Muri Cook Is. 84 21.14S159.43W
Muriaé Brazil 126 21.08S 42.33W
Murias de Paredes Spain 26 42.51N 6.11W
Müritzsee l. E. Germany 38 53.25N 12.43E
Murjek Sweden 40 66.29N 20.50E
Murliganj India 63 25.54N 86.59E
Murmansk U.S.S.R. 44 68.59N 33.08E
Murnau W. Germany 39 47.40N 11.12E
Murnei Sudan 73 12.57N 22.52E
Muro, Capo di c. France 21 41.44N 8.40E
Muro Lucano Italy 33 40.45N 15.30E
Murom U.S.S.R. 44 55.04N 42.04E
Muroran Japan 57 42.21N140.59E
Muros Spain 26 42.47N 9.02W
Muros y Noya, Ría de est. Spain 26 42.45N 9.00W
Murrah al Kubrá, Al Buḩayrah al l. Egypt 66 30.20N 32.20E
Murra Murra Australia 93 28.18S146.48E
Murray r.S.A. Australia 92 35.23S139.20E
Murray r.W.A. Australia 89 32.35S115.46E
Murray r. Canada 100 56.11N120.45W
Murray Ky. U.S.A. 111 36.37N 88.19W
Murray Utah U.S.A. 108 40.40N111.53W
Murray, L. P.N.G. 59 7.00S141.30E
Murray, L. U.S.A. 113 34.04N 81.23W
Murray Bridge town Australia 92 35.10S139.17E
Murrayville Australia 92 35.16S141.14E
Murree Pakistan 62 33.54N 73.24E
Murrhardt W. Germany 39 48.59N 9.34E
Murringo Australia 93 34.19S148.36E
Murrumbidgee r. Australia 92 34.38S143.10E
Murrumburrah Australia 93 34.33S148.21E
Murrurundi Australia 93 31.47S150.51E
Murshidābād India 63 24.11N 88.16E
Murska Sobota Yugo. 31 46.40N 16.10E
Murtee Australia 92 31.05S143.35E
Murten Switz. 39 46.56N 7.07E
Murtoa Australia 92 36.40S142.31E
Murtosa Portugal 26 40.44N 8.38W
Murud mtn. Malaysia 58 3.45N115.30E
Murwāra India 63 23.51N 80.24E
Murwillumbah Australia 93 28.20S153.24E
Muryo, Gunung mtn. Indonesia 59 6.39S110.51E
Muş Turkey 64 38.45N 41.30E
Mūsá, Jabal mtn. Egypt 66 28.31N 33.59E
Musadi Zaïre 78 2.31S 22.50E
Mūsa Khel Pakistan 62 32.38N 71.44E
Mūsa Khel Bāzār Pakistan 62 30.52N 69.49E
Musala mtn. Bulgaria 34 42.13N 23.37E
Musan N. Korea 57 42.14N129.13E
Mūsā Qal 'eh Afghan. 62 32.05N 64.51E
Mūsā Qal 'eh r. Afghan. 62 32.22N 64.46E
Musay'id Qatar 65 24.47N 51.36E
Mūsāzai Pakistan 62 30.23N 66.32E
Muscat see Masqaţ Oman 65
Muscatine U.S.A. 110 41.25N 91.03W
Müsgebi Turkey 35 37.02N 27.21E
Musgrave Australia 90 14.47S143.30E
Musgrave Ranges mts. Australia 88 26.10S131.50E
Mushāsh, Wādī al Jordan 67 31.35N 35.22E
Mushie Zaïre 78 2.59S 16.55E
Mushima Zambia 80 14.13S 25.05E
Mushin Nigeria 77 6.33N 3.22E
Musi r. Indonesia 58 2.20S104.57E
Muskegon U.S.A. 112 43.13N 86.15W
Muskegon r. U.S.A. 112 43.13N 86.16W
Muskegon Heights town U.S.A. 112 43.03N 86.16W
Muskingum r. U.S.A. 114 40.03N 81.59W
Muskö i. Sweden 43 59.00N 18.06E
Muskogee U.S.A. 111 35.45N 95.22W
Muskoka, L. Canada 104 45.00N 79.25W
Muskwa r. Alta. Canada 100 56.16N114.06W
Muskwa r. B.C. Canada 100 58.47N122.48W
Musoma Tanzania 79 1.31S 33.48E
Mussari Angola 80 13.07S 17.56E
Musselburgh U.K. 14 55.57N 3.04W
Musselkanaal Neth. 16 52.57N 7.01E
Musselshell r. U.S.A. 108 47.21N107.58W
Mussende Angola 78 10.33S 16.02E
Musserra Angola 78 7.31S 13.02E
Mussidan France 20 45.02N 0.22E
Mussomeli Italy 32 37.35N 13.46E
Mustahil Ethiopia 71 5.12N 44.17E
Mustāng Nepal 63 29.11N 83.57E
Mustjala U.S.S.R. 41 58.28N 22.14E
Muswellbrook Australia 93 32.17S150.55E
Mūţ Egypt 72 25.29N 28.59E
Mut Turkey 64 36.38N 33.27E
Mutala Mozambique 81 15.54S 37.51E
Mutalau Niue 84 18.58S169.50W
Mutanda Zambia 78 12.23S 26.16E
Mutare Zimbabwe 81 18.59S 32.40E
Mutbīn Syria 67 33.09N 36.15E
Mutoko Zimbabwe 81 17.23S 32.13E
Mutooroo Australia 92 32.30S140.58E
Mutoray U.S.S.R. 51 61.20N100.32E

Mutshatsha to **Nawākot**

Mutshatsha Zaïre **78** 10.39S 24.27E
Mutsu Japan **57** 41.17N141.10E
Mutsu wan *b.* Japan **57** 41.10N141.05E
Mutton Bay *town* Canada **103** 50.47N 59.02W
Muwale Tanzania **79** 6.22S 33.46E
Muxima Angola **78** 9.33S 13.58E
Muya U.S.S.R. **51** 56.28N115.50E
Muyinga Burundi **79** 2.48S 30.21E
Muynak U.S.S.R. **50** 43.46N 59.00E
Muzaffarābād Jammu & Kashmir **62** 34.22N 73.28E
Muzaffargarh Pakistan **62** 30.04N 71.12E
Muzaffarnagar India **63** 29.28N 77.41E
Muzaffarpur India **63** 26.07N 85.24E
Muzhi U.S.S.R. **44** 65.25N 64.40E
Muzillac France **18** 47.33N 2.29W
Muzoka Zambia **80** 16.43S 27.18E
Muztag *mtn.* China **52** 36.25N 87.25E
Mvadhi Gabon **78** 1.13N 13.10E
Mvolo Sudan **73** 6.03N 29.56E
Mvomero Tanzania **79** 6.18S 37.26E
Mvuma Zimbabwe **80** 19.16S 30.30E
Mwanza Tanzania **79** 2.30S 32.54E
Mwanza *d.* Tanzania **79** 3.00S 32.30E
Mwanza Zaïre **78** 7.51S 26.43E
Mwaya Mbeya Tanzania **79** 9.33S 33.56E
Mweka Zaïre **78** 4.51S 21.34E
Mwene Ditu Zaïre **78** 7.04S 23.27E
Mwenezi *r.* Mozambique **81** 22.42S 31.45E
Mwenezi Zimbabwe **80** 21.22S 30.45E
Mweru, L. Zaïre / Zambia **79** 9.00S 28.40E
Mwingi Kenya **79** 1.00S 38.04E
Mwinilunga Zambia **78** 11.44S 24.24E
Mya, Oued *wadi* Algeria **75** 31.40N 5.15E
Myanaung Burma **61** 18.25N 95.10E
Myaungmya Burma **56** 16.33N 94.55E
Myingyan Burma **56** 21.22N 95.28E
Myinkyado Burma **56** 20.56N 96.42E
Myinmu Burma **56** 21.58N 95.43E
Myitkyinā Burma **56** 25.24N 97.25E
Mymensingh Bangla. **63** 24.45N 90.24E
Myrdal Norway **41** 60.44N 7.08E
Myrdalsjökull *ice cap* Iceland **40** 63.40N 19.06W
Myrtle Beach *town* U.S.A. **113** 33.42N 78.54W
Myrtle Creek *town* U.S.A. **108** 43.01N123.17W
Myrtleford Australia **93** 36.35S146.44E
Myrtle Point *town* U.S.A. **108** 43.04N124.08W
Mysen Norway **42** 59.33N 11.20E
Myślenice Poland **37** 49.51N 19.56E
Mysore India **60** 12.18N 76.37E
Mystic U.S.A. **115** 41.21N 71.58W
My Tho Vietnam **56** 10.27N106.20E
Mytishchi U.S.S.R. **44** 55.54N 37.47E
Mziha Tanzania **79** 5.53S 37.48E
Mzimba Malaŵi **79** 12.00S 33.39E

N

Naab *r.* W. Germany **39** 49.01N 12.02E
Naalehu Hawaiian Is. **85** 19.04N155.35W
Na'ām *r.* Sudan **73** 6.48N 29.57E
Na'an Israel **67** 31.53N 34.51E
Naantali Finland **41** 60.27N 22.02E
Naas Rep. of Ire. **15** 53.13N 6.41W
Näätamö *r.* Norway **40** 69.40N 29.30E
Nabā, Jabal *mtn.* Jordan **67** 31.46N 35.45E
Nababeep R.S.A. **80** 29.36S 17.44E
Nabadwip India **63** 23.25N 88.22E
Nabari *r.* Japan **57** 34.45N136.01E
Naberezhnyye Chelny U.S.S.R. **44** 55.42N 52.20E
Nabeul Tunisia **75** 36.28N 10.44E
Nabeul *d.* Tunisia **32** 36.45N 10.45E
Nābha India **62** 30.22N 76.09E
Nabingora Uganda **79** 0.31N 31.11E
Nabi Shu'ayb, Jabal an *mtn.* Yemen **71** 15.17N 43.59E
Naboomspruit R.S.A. **80** 24.31S 28.24E
Nabq Egypt **66** 28.04N 34.26E
Nābulus Jordan **67** 32.13N 35.16E
Nābulus *d.* Jordan **67** 32.15N 35.17E
Nacala Mozambique **81** 14.34S 40.41E
Nacchio Ethiopia **73** 7.30N 40.15E
Nachikapau L. Canada **103** 56.44N 68.00W
Nachingwea Tanzania **79** 10.21S 38.46E
Nāchna India **62** 27.30N 71.43E
Nacka Sweden **43** 59.18N 18.10E
Nackara Australia **92** 32.51S139.13E
Naco Mexico **109** 31.20N109.56W
Nacogdoches U.S.A. **111** 31.36N 94.39W
Nadela Spain **26** 42.58N 7.30W
Nadiād India **62** 22.42N 72.52E
Nador Morocco **74** 35.12N 2.55W
Nadūshan Iran **65** 32.03N 53.33E
Nadvoitsy U.S.S.R. **44** 63.56N 34.20E
Nadvornaya U.S.S.R. **37** 48.37N 24.30E
Nadym U.S.S.R. **50** 65.25N 72.40E
Naenwa India **62** 25.46N 75.51E
Naerbö Norway **42** 58.40N 5.39E
Naeröy Norway **40** 64.48N 11.17E
Naestved Denmark **42** 55.14N 11.46E
Nafada Nigeria **77** 11.08N 11.20E
Nafishah Egypt **66** 30.34N 32.15E
Naft-e Safīd Iran **65** 31.38N 49.20E
Nāg Pakistan **62** 27.24N 65.08E
Naga Phil. **59** 13.36N123.12E
Nāgāland *d.* India **61** 26.10N 94.30E
Nagambie Australia **93** 36.48S145.12E
Nagano Japan **57** 36.39N138.10E
Nagano *d.* Japan **57** 35.33N137.50E
Nagaoka Japan **57** 37.30N138.50E
Nāgappattinam India **61** 10.45N 79.50E
Nagara *r.* Japan **57** 35.01N136.43E
Nagar Pārkar Pakistan **62** 24.22N 70.45E
Nagarzê China **63** 28.58N 90.24E
Nagasaki Japan **57** 32.45N129.52E
Nāgaur India **62** 27.12N 73.44E
Nāgāvali *r.* India **63** 18.13N 83.56E
Nāgda India **62** 23.27N 75.25E
Nagele Neth. **16** 52.39N 5.43E
Nāgercoil India **60** 8.11N 77.30E
Nagichot Sudan **73** 4.16N 33.34E
Nagina India **63** 29.27N 78.27E
Nagles Mts. Rep. of Ire. **15** 52.06N 8.26W
Nagold W. Germany **39** 48.33N 8.43E
Nagorskoye U.S.S.R. **44** 58.18N 50.50E
Nagoya Japan **57** 35.10N136.55E
Nāgpur India **63** 21.09N 79.06E
Nagqên China **61** 32.15N 96.13E
Nagqu China **63** 31.30N 92.00E
Nagyatád Hungary **31** 46.14N 17.22E
Nagybajom Hungary **31** 46.23N 17.31E
Nagykanizsa Hungary **31** 46.27N 16.59E
Naha Japan **53** 26.10N127.40E
Nahalal Israel **67** 32.41N 35.12E
Nāhan India **63** 30.33N 77.18E
Nahanni Butte *town* Canada **100** 61.02N123.20W
Nahanni Butte *town* Canada **98** 61.03N123.31W
Nahariyya Israel **67** 33.01N 35.05E
Nahāvand Iran **65** 34.13N 48.23E
Nahe *r.* W. Germany **39** 49.58N 7.57E
Nahf Israel **67** 32.56N 35.19E
Nahunta U.S.A. **113** 31.12N 82.00W
Nai Ga Burma **56** 27.48N 97.30E
Naila W. Germany **38** 50.19N 11.42E
Naiman Qi China **54** 42.53N120.40E
Nain Canada **103** 57.00N 61.40W
Nā'īn Iran **65** 32.52N 53.05E
Naini Tāl India **63** 29.23N 79.27E
Nainpur India **63** 22.26N 80.07E
Nairn Canada **104** 46.21N 81.36W
Nairn U.K. **14** 57.35N 3.52W
Nairobi Kenya **79** 1.17S 36.50E
Naita, Mt. Ethiopia **73** 5.31N 35.18E
Naivasha Kenya **79** 0.44S 36.26E
Najac France **20** 44.17N 2.00E
Najd *f.* Saudi Arabia **64** 25.00N 45.00E
Nájera Spain **26** 42.25N 2.44W
Naj 'Hammādī Egypt **66** 26.04N 32.13E
Najrān *see* Abā as Su'ūd Saudi Arabia **71**
Nāka Khārari Pakistan **62** 25.15N 66.44E
Nakaminato Japan **57** 36.21N140.36E
Nakano shima *i.* Japan **57** 29.55N129.55E
Nakape Sudan **73** 5.47N 28.38E
Nakatsu Japan **57** 33.37N131.11E
Nakatsugawa Japan **57** 35.29N137.30E
Nakfa Ethiopia **72** 16.43N 38.32E
Nakhichevan U.S.S.R. **65** 39.12N 45.24E
Nakhodka U.S.S.R. **53** 42.53N132.54E
Nakhola India **63** 26.07N 92.11E
Nakhon Pathom Thailand **56** 13.50N100.01E
Nakhon Ratchasima Thailand **56** 14.58N102.06E
Nakhon Si Thammarat Thailand **56** 8.24N 99.58E
Nakhtarana India **62** 23.20N 69.15E
Nakina Canada **102** 50.10N 86.40W
Nakło Poland **37** 53.08N 17.35E
Naknek U.S.A. **98** 58.45N157.00W
Nakop Namibia **80** 28.05S 19.57E
Nakskov Denmark **41** 54.50N 11.09E
Näkten *l.* Sweden **40** 65.50N 14.35E
Nakuru Kenya **79** 0.16S 36.04E
Nāl *r.* Pakistan **62** 26.02N 65.19E
Nalbāri India **63** 26.26N 91.30E
Nalchik U.S.S.R. **45** 43.31N 43.38E
Nalón *r.* Spain **26** 43.32N 6.04W
Nālūt Libya **75** 31.52N 10.59E
Namacurra Mozambique **79** 17.35S 37.00E
Namakī *r.* Iran **65** 31.02N 55.20E
Namanga Kenya **79** 2.33S 36.48E
Namangan U.S.S.R. **52** 40.59N 71.41E
Namanyere Tanzania **79** 7.34S 31.00E
Namapa Mozambique **81** 13.48S 39.44E
Namaponda Mozambique **81** 15.51S 39.52E
Namari Senegal **74** 15.05N 13.39W
Namarroi Mozambique **81** 15.58S 36.55E
Namatele Tanzania **79** 10.01S 38.26E
Namba Angola **78** 11.32S 15.33E
Nambala Zambia **80** 15.07S 27.02E
Nambour Australia **91** 26.40S152.52E
Nambucca Heads *town* Australia **93** 30.38S152.59E
Namco China **63** 30.53N 91.06E
Nam Co *l.* China **63** 30.45N 90.30E
Nam Dinh Vietnam **55** 20.21N106.09E
Namecala Mozambique **81** 12.50S 39.38E
Nametil Mozambique **81** 15.41S 39.30E
Namib Desert Namibia **80** 23.00S 15.20E
Namibia Africa **80** 21.30S 16.45E
Namīn Iran **65** 38.25N 48.30E
Namlea Indonesia **59** 3.15S127.07E
Namling China **63** 29.40N 89.03E
Namoi *r.* Australia **93** 30.14S148.28E
Namonuito *i.* Pacific Oc. **84** 8.46N150.02E
Namous, Oued *wadi* Algeria **74** 30.28N 0.14W
Nampa Canada **100** 56.02N117.07W
Nampa U.S.A. **108** 43.44N116.34W
Nam Phan *f.* Vietnam **56** 10.40N106.00E
Nam Phong Thailand **56** 16.45N102.52E
Namp'o N. Korea **53** 38.40N125.30E
Nampula Mozambique **81** 15.09S 39.14E
Nampula *d.* Mozambique **81** 15.00S 39.00E
Namsen *r.* Norway **40** 64.27N 12.19E
Namsos Norway **40** 64.28N 11.30E
Namtu Burma **56** 23.04N 97.26E
Namu Canada **100** 51.52N127.41W
Namuchabawashan *mtn.* China **61** 29.30N 95.10E
Namungua Mozambique **79** 13.11S 40.30E
Namur Belgium **16** 50.28N 4.52E
Namur *d.* Belgium **16** 50.20N 4.45E
Namur Canada **105** 45.54N 74.56W
Namutoni Namibia **80** 18.48S 16.58E
Namwala Zambia **78** 15.44S 26.25E
Nana Candundo Angola **78** 11.28S 23.01E
Nanaimo Canada **100** 49.10N124.00W
Nanam N. Korea **57** 41.43N129.41E
Nanango Australia **91** 26.42S151.58E
Nanao Japan **57** 37.03N136.58E
Nanchang China **55** 28.37N115.57E
Nancheng China **55** 27.35N116.33E
Nanchong China **55** 30.53N106.05E
Nanchuan China **55** 29.12N107.30E
Nancy France **19** 48.41N 6.12E
Nanda Devi *mtn.* India **63** 30.23N 79.59E
Nandan China **55** 24.59N107.32E
Nānded India **62** 19.09N 77.20E
Nandewar Range *mts.* Australia **93** 30.20S150.45E
Nāndgaon India **62** 20.19N 74.39E
Nandi Fiji **84** 17.48S177.25E
Nandu Jiang *r.* China **55** 20.04N110.20E
Nandurbār India **62** 21.22N 74.15E
Nandyāl India **61** 15.29N 78.29E
Nanfeng China **55** 27.10N116.24E
Nanga Eboko Cameroon **77** 4.41N 12.21E
Nānga Parbat *mtn.* Jammu & Kashmir **60** 35.10N 74.35E
Nangapinoh Indonesia **58** 0.20S111.44E
Nangola Mali **76** 12.41N 6.35W
Nangqên China **52** 32.15N 96.13E
Nangrūl Pīr India **62** 20.19N 77.21E
Nang Xian China **63** 29.03N 93.12E
Nanhui China **55** 31.03N121.46E
Nanjiang China **54** 32.21N106.50E
Nanjing China **55** 32.02N118.52E
Nanking *see* Nanjing China **55**
Nanling China **55** 30.56N118.19E
Nan Ling *mts.* China **55** 25.10N110.00E
Nannine Australia **88** 26.53S118.20E
Nanning China **55** 22.48N108.18E
Nannup Australia **89** 33.57S115.42E
Nanortalik Greenland **99** 60.09N 45.15W
Nānpāra India **63** 27.52N 81.30E
Nanpi China **54** 38.02N116.42E
Nanping Fujian China **55** 26.38N118.10E
Nanpu Xi *r.* China **55** 26.38N118.10E
Nanri *i.* China **55** 25.13N119.30E
Nansa *r.* Spain **26** 43.23N 4.29W
Nansei shotō *is.* Japan **53** 26.30N125.00E
Nansei-Shotō Trench Pacific Oc. **84** 25.00N129.00E
Nanshan *is.* S. China Sea **58** 10.30N116.00E
Nant France **20** 44.01N 3.18E
Nantes France **18** 47.13N 1.33W
Nanteuil-le-Haudouin France **19** 49.08N 2.48E
Nanticoke U.S.A. **115** 41.12N 76.00W
Nanton Canada **100** 50.21N113.46W
Nantong China **54** 32.02N120.55E
Nantou Taiwan **55** 23.54N120.41E
Nantua France **21** 46.09N 5.37E
Nantucket U.S.A. **115** 41.17N 70.06W
Nantucket I. U.S.A. **115** 41.16N 70.03W
Nantucket Sd. U.S.A. **115** 41.30N 70.15W
Nantwich U.K. **12** 53.05N 2.31W
Nanumea *i.* Tuvalu **84** 5.40S176.10E
Nanwan Shuiku *resr.* China **55** 32.05N113.55E
Nanxi China **55** 28.52N104.59E
Nan Xian China **55** 29.22N112.25E
Nanxiong China **55** 25.10N114.16E
Nanyang China **54** 33.07N112.30E
Nanyō Japan **57** 38.03N140.10E
Nanzhang China **55** 31.47N111.42E
Nao, Cabo de la *c.* Spain **25** 38.44N 0.14E
Naococane, Lac *l.* Canada **103** 52.50N 70.40W
Naogaon Bangla. **63** 24.47N 88.56E
Naokot Pakistan **62** 24.51N 69.27E
Náousa Greece **34** 40.37N 22.05E
Napa U.S.A. **108** 38.18N122.17W
Napadogan Canada **103** 46.24N 67.01W
Napanee Canada **105** 44.15N 76.57W
Napè Laos **56** 18.18N105.07E
Napier New Zealand **86** 39.29S176.58E
Napierville Canada **105** 45.11N 73.25W
Naples Italy **70** 40.50N 14.14E
Naples *see* Napoli Italy **33**
Naples Fla. U.S.A. **113** 26.09N 81.48W
Naples N.Y. U.S.A. **114** 42.37N 77.25W
Napo China **55** 23.23N105.48E
Napo *r.* Peru **122** 3.30S 73.10W
Napoleon U.S.A. **112** 41.24N 84.09W
Napoli Italy **33** 40.51N 14.17E
Napoli, Golfo di *g.* Italy **33** 40.45N 14.15E
Naqb Ishtar Jordan **66** 30.00N 35.30E
Nār, Wādī an Jordan **67** 31.40N 35.27E
Nara Japan **57** 34.41N135.50E
Nara *d.* Japan **57** 34.27N135.55E
Nara Mali **74** 15.13N 7.20W
Nāra Pakistan **62** 24.07N 69.07E
Naracoorte Australia **92** 36.58S140.46E
Naradhan Australia **93** 33.39S146.20E
Naraini India **63** 25.11N 80.29E
Naran Mongolia **54** 45.20N113.41E
Narathiwat Thailand **56** 6.25N101.48E
Nara Visa U.S.A. **111** 35.37N103.06W
Nārāyanganj Bangla. **63** 23.37N 90.30E
Narbada *r. see* Narmada India **62**
Narbonne France **20** 43.11N 3.00E
Narcea Spain **26** 43.28N 6.06W
Nardò Italy **33** 40.11N 18.02E
Narembeen Australia **89** 32.04S118.23E
Nares Str. Canada **99** 78.30N 75.00W
Naretha Australia **89** 31.01S124.50E
Nāri *r.* Pakistan **62** 29.10N 67.50E
Naria U.S.A. **63** 23.18N 90.25E
Narita Japan **57** 35.47N140.19E
Närke *f.* Sweden **43** 59.03N 14.55E
Narmada *r.* India **62** 21.40N 73.00E
Nārnaul India **62** 28.03N 76.06E
Narni Italy **30** 42.31N 12.31E
Naro Italy **32** 37.17N 13.48E
Nāro, Koh-i- *mtn.* Pakistan **62** 29.15N 63.30E
Narodichi U.S.S.R. **37** 51.11N 29.01E
Narodnaya *mtn.* U.S.S.R. **44** 65.00N 61.00E
Narok Kenya **79** 1.04S 35.54E
Narón Spain **26** 43.32N 8.10W
Narooma Australia **93** 36.15S150.06E
Narrabri Australia **93** 30.20S149.49E
Narrabri West Australia **93** 30.22S149.47E
Narran *r.* Australia **93** 29.45S147.20E
Narrandera Australia **93** 34.36S146.34E
Narran L. Australia **93** 29.40S147.25E
Narrogin Australia **89** 32.58S117.10E
Narromine Australia **93** 32.17S148.20E
Narsimhapur India **63** 22.57N 79.12E
Narsingdi Bangla. **63** 23.55N 90.43E
Narsinghgarh India **62** 23.42N 77.06E
Narubis Namibia **80** 26.56S 18.36E
Narva U.S.S.R. **44** 59.22N 28.17E
Narvik Norway **40** 68.26N 17.25E
Narwāna India **62** 29.37N 76.07E
Naryan Mar U.S.S.R. **44** 67.37N 53.02E
Naryilco Australia **92** 28.41S141.50E
Naryn U.S.S.R. **50** 41.24N 76.00E
Nasa *mtn.* Norway **40** 66.29N 15.23E
Nasarawa Nigeria **77** 8.35N 7.44E
Nasbinals France **20** 44.40N 3.03E
Naseby New Zealand **86** 45.01S170.09E
Nashua Iowa U.S.A. **110** 42.57N 92.32W
Nashua Mont. U.S.A. **108** 48.08N106.22W
Nashua N.H. U.S.A. **115** 42.46N 71.27W
Nashville U.S.A. **113** 36.10N 86.50W
Naşīb Syria **67** 32.33N 36.11E
Našice Yugo. **31** 45.29N 18.06E
Näsijärvi *l.* Finland **41** 61.37N 23.42E
Nāsik India **62** 19.59N 73.48E
Nāşir Sudan **73** 8.36N 33.04E
Nāşir, Buḩayrat *l.* Egypt **72** 22.40N 32.00E
Nasīrābād India **62** 26.18N 74.44E
Nasirābād Pakistan **62** 28.23N 68.24E
Naskaupi *r.* Canada **103** 53.45N 60.50W
Naşr Egypt **66** 30.36N 30.23E
Nass *r.* Canada **100** 55.00N129.50W
Nassau Bahamas **113** 25.05N 77.21W
Nassau I. Cook Is. **84** 11.33S165.25W
Nasser, L. *see* Nāşir, Buḩayrat Egypt **72**
Nassereith Austria **39** 47.19N 10.50E
Nassian Ivory Coast **76** 8.33N 3.18W
Nässjö Sweden **43** 57.39N 14.41E
Nastapoca *r.* Canada **102** 56.55N 76.33W
Nastapoka Is. Canada **102** 57.00N 77.00W
Nata Botswana **80** 20.12S 26.12E
Natal Brazil **123** 5.46S 35.15W
Natal Indonesia **58** 0.35N 99.07E
Natal *d.* R.S.A. **80** 28.30S 30.30E
Natal Basin *f.* Indian Oc. **49** 35.00S 39.00E
Natanes Plateau *f.* U.S.A. **109** 33.35N110.15W
Naţanz Iran **65** 33.30N 51.57E
Natashquan Canada **103** 50.11N 61.49W
Natashquan *r.* Canada **103** 50.06N 61.49W
Natchez U.S.A. **111** 31.34N 91.23W
Natchitoches U.S.A. **111** 31.46N 93.05W
Nāthdwāra India **62** 24.56N 73.49E
National City U.S.A. **109** 32.40N117.06W
Natitingou Benin **77** 10.17N 1.19E
Natl Jordan **67** 31.39N 35.52E
Natoma U.S.A. **110** 39.11N 99.01W
Natron, L. Tanzania **79** 2.18S 36.05E
Naţrūn, Wādī an *f.* Egypt **66** 30.25N 30.18E
Naturaliste, C. Australia **89** 33.32S115.01E
Naturaliste Channel Australia **88** 25.25S113.00E
Naubinway U.S.A. **112** 46.05N 85.27W
Naucelle France **20** 44.12N 2.20E
Nauders Austria **39** 46.53N 10.30E
Nauen E. Germany **38** 52.36N 12.52E
Naugatuck U.S.A. **115** 41.30N 73.04W
Naumburg E. Germany **38** 51.09N 11.48E
Nā'ūr Jordan **67** 31.53N 35.50E
Nauroz Kalāt Pakistan **62** 28.47N 65.38E
Nauru Pacific Oc. **84** 0.32S166.55E
Naushahro Fīroz Pakistan **62** 26.50N 68.07E
Naustdal Norway **41** 61.31N 5.43E
Nauta Peru **122** 4.30S 73.40W
Nautanwa India **63** 27.26N 83.25E
Nautla Mexico **116** 20.13N 96.47W
Nava Mexico **111** 28.25N100.46W
Nava *r.* Zaïre **79** 1.45N 27.06E
Nava del Rey Spain **26** 41.20N 5.05W
Navahermosa Spain **27** 39.38N 4.28W
Navalcarnero Spain **26** 40.18N 4.00W
Navalmoral de la Mata Spain **27** 39.54N 5.32W
Navalvillar de Pela Spain **27** 39.06N 5.28W
Navan Rep. of Ire. **15** 53.39N 6.42W
Navāpur India **62** 21.15N 73.55E
Navarra *d.* Spain **25** 42.45N 1.30W
Navarre Australia **92** 36.54S143.09E
Navarre U.S.A. **114** 40.43N 81.32W
Navarro Argentina **125** 35.00S 59.10W
Navasota U.S.A. **111** 30.23N 96.05W
Naver *r.* U.K. **14** 58.32N 4.14W
Navia Spain **26** 43.32N 6.43W
Navia *r.* Spain **26** 43.33N 6.44W
Navlya U.S.S.R. **44** 52.51N 34.30E
Navoi U.S.S.R. **9** 40.04N 65.20E
Navojoa Mexico **109** 27.06N109.26W
Návpaktos Greece **35** 38.23N 21.50E
Návplion Greece **35** 37.34N 22.48E
Navrongo Ghana **76** 10.51N 1.03W
Navsāri India **62** 20.57N 72.59E
Nawá Syria **67** 32.53N 36.03E
Nawābganj Bangla. **63** 24.36N 88.17E
Nawābganj India **63** 26.56N 81.13E
Nawābshāh Pakistan **62** 26.15N 68.25E
Nawāda India **63** 24.53N 85.33E
Nāwah Afghan. **62** 32.19N 67.53E
Nawākot Nepal **63** 27.55N 85.10E

Nida to **Nouzonville**

Nida *r.* Poland **37** 50.18N 20.52E
Nido, Sierra de *mts.* Mexico **109** 29.30N107.00W
Nidzica Poland **37** 53.22N 20.26E
Niebüll W. Germany **38** 54.48N 8.50E
Niederbronn-les-Bains France **19** 48.57N 7.38E
Niederösterreich *d.* Austria **36** 48.20N 15.50E
Niedersachsen *d.* W. Germany **38** 52.53N 9.30E
Niekerkshoop R.S.A. **80** 29.19S 22.48E
Niéllé Ivory Coast **76** 10.05N 5.28W
Nienburg W. Germany **38** 52.38N 9.13E
Niéré Chad **72** 14.30N 21.09E
Niers *r.* Neth. **16** 51.43N 5.56E
Niesky E. Germany **38** 51.17N 14.49E
Nieuw Nickerie Surinam **123** 5.57N 56.59W
Nieuwpoort Belgium **16** 51.08N 2.45E
Nièvre *d.* France **19** 47.05N 3.30E
Nifi Ya'qūb Jordan **67** 31.50N 35.14E
Nigde Turkey **64** 37.58N 34.42E
Niger Africa **70** 17.00N 10.00E
Niger *d.* Nigeria **77** 9.50N 6.00E
Niger *r.* Nigeria **77** 4.15N 6.05E
Niger Delta Nigeria **77** 4.00N 6.10E
Nigeria Africa **77** 9.00N 9.00E
Nightcaps New Zealand **86** 45.58S168.02E
Nightingale I. Tristan da Cunha **127** 37.28S 12.32W
Nigrita Greece **34** 40.55N 23.30E
Nihing *r.* Pakistan **62** 26.00N 62.44E
Nihoa *i.* Hawaiian Is. **84** 23.03N161.55W
Niigata Japan **57** 37.58N139.02E
Niihama Japan **57** 33.57N133.15E
Niihau *i.* Hawaiian Is. **85** 21.55N160.10W
Niiza Japan **57** 35.48N139.34E
Níjar Spain **27** 36.58N 2.11W
Nijmegen Neth. **16** 51.50N 5.52E
Nikel U.S.S.R. **40** 69.20N 30.00E
Nikiniki Indonesia **88** 9.49S124.29E
Nikki Benin **77** 9.55N 3.18E
Nikolayev U.S.S.R. **45** 46.57N 32.00E
Nikolayevskiy U.S.S.R. **45** 50.05N 45.32E
Nikolayevsk-na-Amure U.S.S.R. **51** 53.20N140.44E
Nikolsk U.S.S.R. **44** 59.33N 45.30E
Nikopol Bulgaria **34** 43.43N 24.54E
Nikopol U.S.S.R. **45** 47.34N 34.25E
Niksar Turkey **64** 40.35N 36.59E
Nīkshahr Iran **65** 26.14N 60.15E
Nikšić Yugo. **31** 42.46N 18.56E
Nīl, An *r.* Egypt **66** 31.30N 30.25E
Nila *i.* Indonesia **59** 6.45S129.30E
Nile *r. see* Nīl, An Egypt **66**
Nile Delta Egypt **66** 31.00N 31.00E
Niles Mich. U.S.A. **112** 41.51N 86.15W
Niles Ohio U.S.A. **114** 41.11N 80.45W
Nilgaut, Lac *l.* Canada **105** 46.36N 77.15W
Nilgiri India **63** 21.28N 86.46E
Nilgiri Hills India **60** 11.30N 77.30E
Nimach India **62** 24.28N 74.52E
Nimai *r.* Burma **56** 25.44N 97.30E
Nimba, Mt. Guinea **76** 7.35N 8.28W
Nimbin Australia **93** 28.35S153.12E
Nîmes France **21** 43.50N 4.21E
Nimfaíon, Ákra *c.* Greece **34** 40.05N 24.20E
Nim Ka Thāna India **62** 27.44N 75.48E
Nimrūz *d.* Afghan. **62** 30.40N 62.15E
Nimule Sudan **73** 3.36N 32.03E
Nindigully Australia **93** 28.20S148.47E
Ninety-East Ridge *f.* Indian Oc. **49** 21.00S 89.00E
Ninety Mile Beach *f.* Australia **93** 38.07S147.30E
Ninety Mile Beach *f.* New Zealand **86** 34.45S173.00E
Nineveh *ruins* Iraq **64** 36.24N 43.08E
Ningan China **57** 44.22N129.25E
Ningbo China **55** 29.56N121.32E
Ningde China **55** 26.41N119.32E
Ningdu China **55** 26.29N115.46E
Ninggang China **55** 26.45N113.58E
Ningguo China **55** 30.38N118.58E
Ningming China **55** 22.04N107.02E
Ningnan China **52** 27.03N102.46E
Ningqiang China **54** 32.49N106.13E
Ningwu China **54** 38.59N112.12E
Ningxia Huizu *d.* China **54** 39.00N105.00E
Ning Xian China **54** 35.27N107.50E
Ningxiang China **55** 28.15N112.33E
Ninh Binh Vietnam **56** 20.14N106.00E
Niningarra Australia **88** 20.35S119.58E
Ninove Belgium **16** 50.50N 4.02E
Niobrara U.S.A. **110** 42.45N 98.02W
Niobrara *r.* U.S.A. **110** 42.45N 98.00W
Nioki Zaïre **78** 2.43S 17.41E
Nioro Mali **74** 15.12N 9.35W
Nioro du Rip Senegal **76** 13.40N 15.50W
Niort France **18** 46.19N 0.27W
Niout *well* Mauritania **74** 16.03N 6.52W
Nipāni India **60** 16.24N 74.23E
Nipigon Canada **102** 49.00N 88.17W
Nipigon, L. Canada **102** 49.50N 88.30W
Nipigon B. Canada **102** 48.55N 88.00W
Nipissing Canada **104** 46.06N 79.30W
Nipissing *r.* Canada **104** 46.00N 78.30W
Nipissing, L. Canada **104** 46.17N 80.00W
Niquelândia Brazil **126** 14.27S 48.27W
Nirasaki Japan **57** 35.42N138.27E
Nirim Israel **67** 31.20N 34.24E
Nirmal India **63** 19.06N 78.21E
Nirmali India **63** 26.19N 86.35E
Nirwāno Pakistan **62** 26.22N 62.43E
Nir Yisra'el Israel **67** 31.41N 34.38E
Niš Yugo. **34** 43.19N 21.58E
Nisa Portugal **27** 39.31N 7.39W
Nisava *r.* Yugo. **34** 43.20N 22.10E
Niscemi Italy **33** 37.08N 14.24E
Nishi China **55** 29.54N110.38E
Nishinomiya Japan **57** 34.43N135.20E
Nisiros *i.* Greece **35** 36.35N 27.10E
Niška Banja Yugo. **34** 43.17N 22.02E
Niskibi *r.* Canada **102** 56.28N 88.10W
Nisko Poland **37** 50.35N 22.07E
Nissan *r.* Sweden **43** 56.40N 12.51E
Nissedal Norway **42** 59.15N 8.30E
Nisser *l.* Norway **42** 59.10N 8.30E
Nissum Bredning *b.* Denmark **42** 56.38N 8.22E
Nissum Fjord *est.* Denmark **42** 56.21N 8.14E
Niţā' Saudi Arabia **65** 27.13N 48.25E
Nitchequon Canada **103** 53.12N 70.47W
Niterói Brazil **126** 22.54S 43.06W
Nith *r.* Canada **104** 43.12N 80.22W
Nith *r.* U.K. **14** 55.00N 3.35W
Nitra Czech. **37** 48.20N 18.05E
Nitro Canada **104** 46.51N 81.42W
Nitro U.S.A. **114** 38.25N 81.50W
Nittedal Norway **42** 60.04N 10.53E
Niue *i.* Cook Is. **84** 19.02S169.52W
Niut, Gunung *mtn.* Indonesia **58** 1.00N110.00E
Nivala Finland **40** 63.55N 24.58E
Nivelles Belgium **16** 50.36N 4.20E
Nixon U.S.A. **111** 29.16N 97.46W
Nizāmābād India **61** 18.40N 78.05E
Nizgān *r.* Afghan. **62** 33.05N 63.20E
Nizhneangarsk U.S.S.R. **51** 55.48N109.35E
Nizhne Kolymsk U.S.S.R. **51** 68.34N160.58E
Nizhneudinsk U.S.S.R. **51** 54.55N 99.00E
Nizhnevartovsk U.S.S.R. **50** 60.57N 76.40E
Nizhniy Tagil U.S.S.R. **44** 58.00N 60.00E
Nizhnyaya Tunguska *r.* U.S.S.R. **51** 65.50N 88.00E
Nizhnyaya Tura U.S.S.R. **44** 58.40N 59.48E
Nizke Tatry *mts.* Czech. **37** 48.54N 19.40E
Nizza Monferrato Italy **30** 44.46N 8.21E
Nizzanim Israel **67** 31.43N 34.38E
Njombe Tanzania **79** 9.20S 34.47E
Njombe *r.* Tanzania **79** 7.02S 35.55E
Njoro Tanzania **79** 5.16S 36.30E
Nkalagu Nigeria **77** 6.28N 7.46E
Nkawkaw Ghana **76** 6.35N 0.47W
Nkayi Zimbabwe **80** 19.00S 28.54E
Nkhata Bay *town* Malaŵi **79** 11.37S 34.20E
Nkhotakota Malaŵi **79** 12.55S 34.19E
Nkongsamba Cameroon **77** 4.59N 9.53E
Nkungwe Mt. Tanzania **79** 6.15S 29.54E
Noākhāli Bangla. **63** 22.51N 91.06E
Noatak U.S.A. **98** 67.34N162.59W
Nobel Canada **104** 45.25N 80.06W
Nobeoka Japan **57** 32.36N131.40E
Noboribetsu Japan **57** 42.27N141.11E
Noce *r.* Italy **30** 46.09N 11.04E
Nocera Italy **33** 40.44N 14.39E
Noci Italy **33** 40.48N 17.08E
Noelville Canada **104** 46.09N 80.26W
Nogal *r.* Somali Rep. **71** 7.58N 49.52E
Nogales Mexico **109** 31.20N110.56W
Nogara Italy **32** 45.11N 11.04E
Nogaro France **20** 43.46N 0.02W
Nogayskiye Step *f.* U.S.S.R. **45** 44.25N 45.30E
Nogent-le-Rotrou France **18** 48.19N 0.50E
Nogent-sur-Seine France **19** 48.29N 3.30E
Nogoyá Argentina **125** 32.22S 59.49W
Noguera Pallarese *r.* Spain **25** 42.15N 0.54E
Noguera Ribagorzana *r.* Spain **25** 41.40N 0.43E
Nohar India **62** 29.11N 74.46E
Nohta India **63** 23.40N 79.34E
Noire *r.* Que. Canada **105** 45.55N 76.56W
Noire *r.* Que. Canada **105** 46.35N 72.58W
Noire, Montagne *mtn.* France **18** 48.11N 3.40W
Noire, Montagne *mts.* France **20** 43.26N 2.12E
Noirétable France **20** 45.49N 3.46E
Noirmoutier France **18** 47.00N 2.14W
Noirmoutier, Île de *i.* France **18** 47.00N 2.15W
Nojima-zaki *c.* Japan **57** 34.56N139.53E
Nokha India **62** 27.35N 73.29E
Nokia Finland **41** 61.28N 23.30E
Nok Kundi Pakistan **62** 28.46N 62.46E
Nokomis Canada **101** 51.30N105.00W
Nokou Chad **77** 14.35N 14.47E
Nola C.A.R. **77** 3.28N 16.08E
Nola Italy **33** 40.55N 14.33E
Nolinsk U.S.S.R. **44** 57.38N 49.52E
Noman L. Canada **101** 62.15N108.55W
Noma Omuramba *r.* Botswana **80** 19.14S 22.15E
Nombre de Dios Mexico **109** 28.41N106.05W
Nome U.S.A. **98** 64.30N165.30W
Nomgon Mongolia **54** 42.50N105.13E
Nominingue Canada **105** 46.24N 75.02W
Nomuka Group *is.* Tonga **85** 20.15S174.46W
Nonancourt France **18** 48.46N 1.12E
Nonburg U.S.S.R. **44** 65.32N 50.37E
Nong Khai Thailand **56** 17.50N102.46E
Nongoma R.S.A. **81** 27.58S 31.35E
Nongpoh India **63** 25.54N 91.53E
Nongstoin India **63** 25.31N 91.16E
Nonning Australia **92** 32.30S136.30E
Nonthaburi Thailand **56** 13.48N100.11E
Nontron France **20** 45.32N 0.40E
Noojee Australia **93** 37.57S146.00E
Noonan U.S.A. **110** 48.54N103.01W
Noongaar Australia **89** 31.21S118.55E
Noonkanbah Australia **88** 18.30S124.50E
Noord Beveland *f.* Neth. **16** 51.35N 3.45E
Noord Brabant *d.* Neth. **16** 51.37N 5.00E
Noord Holland *d.* Neth. **16** 52.37N 4.50E
Noordoost-Polder *f.* Neth. **16** 52.45N 5.45E
Noordwijk Neth. **16** 52.16N 4.29E
Noorvik U.S.A. **98** 66.50N161.14W
Nootka I. Canada **100** 49.32N126.42W
Noqui Angola **78** 5.51S 13.25E
Nora Sweden **43** 59.31N 15.02E
Noranda Canada **102** 48.20N 79.00W
Norberg Sweden **43** 60.04N 15.56E
Norcia Italy **30** 42.48N 13.05E
Nord *d.* France **19** 50.20N 3.40E
Nordaustlandet *i.* Arctic Oc. **128** 79.55N 23.00E
Nordborg Denmark **42** 55.03N 9.45E
Norddeich W. Germany **38** 53.37N 7.10E
Nordegg Canada **100** 52.29N116.05W
Norden W. Germany **38** 53.36N 7.12E
Nordenham W. Germany **38** 53.29N 8.28E
Norderney W. Germany **38** 53.42N 7.08E
Norderney *i.* W. Germany **38** 53.42N 7.10E
Norderstedt W. Germany **38** 53.43N 9.59E
Nordfjord *est.* Norway **41** 61.54N 5.12E
Nordfjordeid Norway **41** 61.54N 6.00E
Nordfold Norway **40** 67.48N 15.20E
Nordfriesische Inseln *is.* W. Germany **38** 54.35N 8.30E
Nordhausen E. Germany **38** 51.30N 10.47E
Nordhorn W. Germany **38** 52.27N 7.05E
Nordkapp *c.* Norway **40** 71.11N 25.48E
Nordkinnhalvöya *pen.* Norway **40** 70.55N 27.45E
Nordland *d.* Norway **40** 66.50N 14.50E
Nördlingen W. Germany **39** 48.51N 10.30E
Nord-Ostsee-Kanal W. Germany **38** 54.10N 9.25E
Nordreisa Norway **40** 69.46N 21.00E
Nordrhein-Westfalen *d.* W. Germany **38** 52.04N 7.20E
Nordstrand *i.* W. Germany **38** 54.30N 8.53E
Nord Tröndelag *d.* Norway **40** 64.20N 12.00E
Nordvik U.S.S.R. **51** 73.40N110.50E
Nore Norway **42** 60.10N 9.01E
Nore *r.* Rep. of Ire. **15** 52.25N 6.58W
Norfolk *d.* U.K. **13** 52.39N 1.00E
Norfolk Conn. U.S.A. **115** 41.59N 73.12W
Norfolk Nebr. U.S.A. **110** 42.02N 97.25W
Norfolk Va. U.S.A. **113** 36.54N 76.18W
Norfolk Broads *f.* U.K. **12** 52.43N 1.35E
Norfolk I. Pacific Oc. **84** 29.02S167.57E
Norfolk Island Ridge Pacific Oc. **84** 29.00S167.00E
Norheimsund Norway **41** 60.22N 6.08E
Norilsk U.S.S.R. **51** 69.21N 88.02E
Norland Canada **104** 44.43N 78.49W
Normal U.S.A. **110** 40.31N 89.00W
Norman *r.* Australia **90** 17.28S140.49E
Norman U.S.A. **111** 35.13N 97.26W
Normanby *r.* Australia **90** 14.25S144.08E
Normanby New Zealand **86** 39.32S174.16E
Normanby I. P.N.G. **90** 10.05S151.05E
Normandie, Collines de *hills* France **18** 48.55N 0.45W
Normanton Australia **90** 17.40S141.05E
Norman Wells Canada **98** 65.19N126.46W
Nornalup Australia **89** 34.58S116.49E
Ñorquinco Argentina **125** 41.50S 70.55W
Norrahammar Sweden **43** 57.42N 14.06E
Norra Kvarken *str.* Sweden / Finland **40** 63.36N 20.43E
Norra Storfjället *mtn.* Sweden **40** 65.52N 15.18E
Norrbotten *d.* Sweden **40** 67.00N 19.50E
Nörresundby Denmark **42** 57.04N 9.55E
Norris L. U.S.A. **113** 36.18N 83.58W
Norristown U.S.A. **115** 40.07N 75.21W
Norrköping Sweden **43** 58.36N 16.11E
Norrsundet Sweden **41** 60.56N 17.08E
Norrtälje Sweden **43** 59.46N 18.42E
Norseman Australia **89** 32.15S121.47E
Norsjå *l.* Norway **42** 59.18N 9.20E
Norsk U.S.S.R. **51** 52.22N129.57E
Norte *d.* W. Sahara **74** 26.50N 11.15W
Norte, C. Brazil **123** 1.40N 49.55W
Norte, Cabo *c.* I. de Pascua **85** 27.03S109.24W
Norte, Punta *c.* Argentina **125** 36.17S 56.46W
Norte Interior *d.* Portugal **26** 41.30N 7.00W
Norte Litoral *d.* Portugal **26** 41.00N 8.25W
North, C. Canada **103** 47.01N 60.28W
North Adams U.S.A. **115** 42.42N 73.07W
Northallerton U.K. **12** 54.20N 1.26W
Northam Australia **89** 31.41S116.40E
North America **96**
Northampton Australia **89** 28.21S114.37E
Northampton U.K. **13** 52.14N 0.54W
Northampton Mass. U.S.A. **115** 42.19N 72.38W
Northampton Penn. U.S.A. **115** 40.41N 75.30W
Northamptonshire *d.* U.K. **13** 52.18N 0.55W
North Augusta Canada **105** 44.44N 75.45W
North Battleford Canada **101** 52.47N108.17W
North Bay *town* Canada **104** 46.19N 79.28W
North Bend Penn. U.S.A. **114** 41.21N 77.42W
North Berwick U.K. **14** 56.04N 2.43W
North Bourke Australia **93** 30.01S145.59E
North Bradley U.S.A. **114** 43.44N 84.31W
North C. Antarctica **128** 71.00S166.00E
North C. New Zealand **86** 34.28S173.00E
North Canadian *r.* U.S.A. **111** 35.17N 95.31W
North Caribou L. Canada **102** 52.50N 90.50W
North Carolina *d.* U.S.A. **113** 35.30N 80.00W
North Channel *str.* Canada **104** 46.02N 82.50W
North Channel U.K. **15** 55.15N 5.52W
North Chicago U.S.A. **110** 42.20N 87.51W
North China Plain *f. see* Huabei Pingyuan China **54**
Northcliffe Australia **89** 34.36S116.04E
North Creek *town* U.S.A. **115** 43.42N 73.59W
North Dakota *d.* U.S.A. **110** 47.00N100.00W
North Dorset Downs *hills* U.K. **13** 50.46N 2.25W
North Downs *hills* U.K. **13** 51.18N 0.40E
North East U.S.A. **114** 42.13N 79.50W
North Eastern *d.* Kenya **79** 1.00N 40.00E
North Eastern Atlantic Basin *f.* Atlantic Oc. **127** 45.00N 17.00W
North East Pt. Kiribati **85** 1.57N157.16W
Northeim W. Germany **38** 51.42N 10.00E
Northern *d.* Ghana **76** 9.00N 1.30W
Northern Indian L. Canada **101** 57.20N 97.20W
Northern Ireland *d.* U.K. **15** 54.40N 6.45W
Northern Territory *d.* Australia **90** 20.00S133.00E
North Esk *r.* U.K. **14** 56.45N 2.25W
Northfield U.S.A. **105** 44.09N 72.40W
North Fiji Basin Pacific Oc. **84** 17.00S173.00E
North Foreland *c.* U.K. **13** 51.23N 1.26E
North French *r.* Canada **102** 51.04N 80.46W
North Frisian Is. *see* Nordfriesische Inseln W. Germany **36**
North Gower Canada **105** 45.08N 75.43W
North Head *c.* Canada **103** 53.42N 56.24W
North Henik L. Canada **101** 61.45N 97.40W
North Horr Kenya **79** 3.19N 37.00E
North I. Kenya **73** 4.04N 36.03E
North I. New Zealand **86** 39.00S175.00E
Northiam U.K. **13** 50.59N 0.39E
North Knife *r.* Canada **101** 58.53N 94.45W
North Korea Asia **53** 40.00N128.00E
Northland *d.* New Zealand **86** 35.25S174.00E
North Las Vegas U.S.A. **109** 36.12N115.07W
North Little Rock U.S.A. **111** 34.46N 92.14W
North Loup *r.* U.S.A. **110** 41.17N 98.23W
North Mankato U.S.A. **110** 44.15N 94.06W
North Nahanni *r.* Canada **100** 62.15N123.20W
North Ogden U.S.A. **108** 41.18N112.00W
North Olmsted U.S.A. **114** 41.25N 81.56W
Northome U.S.A. **110** 47.52N 94.17W
North Platte U.S.A. **110** 41.08N100.46W
North Platte *r.* U.S.A. **110** 41.15N100.45W
Northport U.S.A. **113** 33.14N 87.33W
North Powder U.S.A. **108** 45.13N117.55W
North Pt. Canada **103** 47.05N 64.00W
North Pt. U.S.A. **104** 45.02N 83.16W
North Rona *i.* U.K. **10** 59.09N 5.43W
North Ronaldsay *i.* U.K. **14** 59.23N 2.26W
North Saskatchewan *r.* Canada **101** 53.15N105.06W
North Sea Europe **36** 54.00N 4.00E
North Seal *r.* Canada **101** 58.50N 98.10W
North Sporades *see* Vorίai Sporádhes Greece **35**
North Stratford U.S.A. **105** 44.46N 71.36W
North Sydney Canada **103** 46.13N 60.15W
North Syracuse U.S.A. **115** 43.08N 76.08W
North Taranaki Bight *b.* New Zealand **86** 38.45S174.15E
North Tawton U.K. **13** 50.48N 3.55W
North Thames *r.* Canada **104** 42.59N 81.16W
North Thompson *r.* Canada **100** 50.40N120.20W
North Tonawanda U.S.A. **114** 43.02N 78.53W
North Troy U.S.A. **105** 45.00N 72.24W
North Twin I. Canada **102** 53.20N 80.00W
North Uist *i.* U.K. **14** 57.35N 7.20W
Northumberland *d.* U.K. **12** 55.12N 2.00W
Northumberland U.S.A. **114** 40.49N 76.39W
Northumberland, C. Australia **92** 38.04S140.40E
Northumberland Is. Australia **90** 21.40S150.00E
Northumberland Str. Canada **103** 46.00N 63.30W
Northville U.S.A. **115** 43.13N 74.11W
North Wabasca L. Canada **100** 56.00N113.55W
North Walsham U.K. **12** 52.49N 1.22E
Northway U.S.A. **98** 62.58N142.00W
North West C. Australia **88** 21.48S114.10E
North West Chile Ridge Pacific Oc. **85** 42.00S 90.00W
North West Christmas Island Ridge Pacific Oc. **85** 6.30N159.00W
North Western *d.* Zambia **80** 13.00S 25.00E
North Western Atlantic Basin *f.* Atlantic Oc. **127** 33.00N 55.00W
Northwest Frontier *d.* Pakistan **62** 33.45N 71.00E
North West Highlands U.K. **14** 57.30N 5.15W
Northwest Providence Channel Bahamas **113** 26.10N 78.20W
North West Pt. Kiribati **85** 2.02N157.29W
North West River *town* Canada **103** 53.32N 60.09W
Northwest Territories *d.* Canada **99** 66.00N 95.00W
Northwich U.K. **12** 53.16N 2.30W
Northwood Iowa U.S.A. **110** 43.27N 93.13W
Northwood N.Dak. U.S.A. **110** 47.44N 97.34W
North Woodstock U.S.A. **105** 44.02N 71.41W
North York Moors *hills* U.K. **12** 54.21N 0.50W
North Yorkshire *d.* U.K. **12** 54.14N 1.14W
Norton Kans. U.S.A. **110** 39.50N 99.53W
Norton W.Va. U.S.A. **114** 38.58N 79.55W
Norton Sound *b.* U.S.A. **98** 63.50N164.00W
Nortorf W. Germany **38** 54.10N 9.50E
Nort-sur-Erdre France **18** 47.26N 1.30W
Norwalk Conn. U.S.A. **115** 41.07N 73.27W
Norwalk Ohio U.S.A. **114** 41.15N 82.37W
Norway Europe **40** 65.00N 13.00E
Norway House *town* Canada **101** 53.59N 97.50W
Norwegian Dependency Antarctica **128** 77.00S 10.00E
Norwegian Sea Europe **128** 65.00N 5.00E
Norwich Canada **104** 42.59N 80.36W
Norwich U.K. **13** 52.38N 1.17E
Norwich Conn. U.S.A. **115** 41.32N 72.05W
Norwich N.Y. U.S.A. **115** 42.32N 75.31W
Norwood Canada **105** 44.23N 77.59W
Norwood Mass. U.S.A. **115** 42.11N 71.12W
Norwood N.Y. U.S.A. **105** 44.45N 75.00W
Norwood Ohio U.S.A. **112** 39.12N 84.21W
Nosbonsing, L. Canada **104** 46.12N 79.13W
Noshiro Japan **57** 40.12N140.02E
Noshul U.S.S.R. **44** 60.04N 49.30E
Nosovka U.S.S.R. **37** 50.55N 31.37E
Noşratābād Iran **65** 29.54N 59.58E
Nossebro Sweden **43** 58.11N 12.43E
Noss Head U.K. **14** 58.28N 3.03W
Nosy Be *i.* Madagascar **81** 13.20S 48.15E
Nosy Boraha *i.* Madagascar **81** 16.50S 49.55E
Nosy Varika Madagascar **81** 20.35S 48.32E
Noteć *r.* Poland **36** 52.44N 15.26E
Notera Israel **67** 33.06N 35.38E
Noto Italy **33** 36.53N 15.05E
Noto, Golfo di *g.* Italy **33** 36.50N 15.15E
Notodden Norway **42** 59.34N 9.17E
Notre Dame, Monts *mts.* Canada **103** 48.00N 69.00W
Notre Dame B. Canada **103** 49.45N 55.15W
Notre Dame de la Salette Canada **105** 45.46N 75.35W
Notre Dame du Lac *town* Canada **104** 46.19N 80.10W
Notre Dame du Laus Canada **105** 46.05N 75.37W
Nottawasaga *r.* Canada **104** 44.32N 80.01W
Nottawasaga B. Canada **104** 44.40N 80.30W
Nottaway *r.* Canada **102** 51.25N 78.50W
Nottingham U.K. **12** 52.57N 1.10W
Nottinghamshire *d.* U.K. **12** 53.10N 1.00W
Notwani *r.* Botswana **80** 23.46S 26.57E
Nouadhibou Mauritania **74** 20.54N 17.01W
Nouakchott Mauritania **74** 18.09N 15.58W
Nouméa New Caledonia **84** 22.16S166.27E
Nouna U. Volta **76** 12.44N 3.54W
Noupoort R.S.A. **80** 31.11S 24.56E
Nouveau, Lac *l.* Canada **103** 51.59N 68.58W
Nouveau-Comptoir Canada **102** 53.02N 78.55W
Nouvelle Anvers Zaïre **78** 1.38N 19.10E
Nouvelle Calédonie *is.* Pacific Oc. **84** 21.30S165.30E
Nouzonville France **19** 49.49N 4.45E

Nova Caipemba to Okučani

Nova Caipemba Angola **78** 7.25S 14.36E
Nova Chaves Angola **78** 10.31S 21.20E
Novafeltria Bagnodi Romagna Italy **30** 43.53N 12.17E
Nova Friburgo Brazil **126** 22.16S 42.32W
Nova Gaia Angola **78** 10.09S 17.35E
Nova Gradiška Yugo. **31** 45.16N 17.23E
Nova Iguaçu Brazil **126** 22.45S 43.27W
Nova Lamego Guinea Bissau **76** 12.19N 14.11W
Nova Lima Brazil **126** 19.59S 43.51W
Novara Italy **30** 45.28N 8.38E
Nova Scotia *d.* Canada **103** 45.00N 63.30W
Nova Sofala Mozambique **81** 20.09S 34.24E
Novato U.S.A. **108** 38.06N122.34W
Nova Varoš Yugo. **31** 43.28N 19.48E
Novaya Ladoga U.S.S.R. **44** 60.09N 32.15E
Novaya Lyalya U.S.S.R. **50** 59.02N 60.38E
Novaya Sibir, Ostrov *i.* U.S.S.R. **51** 75.20N148.00E
Novaya Ushitsa U.S.S.R. **37** 48.50N 27.12E
Novaya Zemlya *i.* U.S.S.R. **50** 74.00N 56.00E
Nova Zagora Bulgaria **34** 42.29N 26.01E
Novelda Spain **25** 38.23N 0.46W
Nové Zámky Czech. **37** 47.59N 18.11E
Novgorod U.S.S.R. **44** 58.30N 31.20E
Novgorod Severskiy U.S.S.R. **44** 52.00N 33.15E
Novi Bečej Yugo. **31** 45.36N 20.08E
Novi di Modena Italy **30** 44.54N 10.54E
Novigrad Yugo. **31** 45.19N 13.34E
Novi Liqure Italy **30** 44.46N 8.47E
Novi Pazar Yugo. **34** 43.08N 20.31E
Novi Sad Yugo. **31** 45.15N 19.50E
Novi Vinodolski Yugo. **31** 45.08N 14.48E
Novoanninskiy U.S.S.R. **45** 50.32N 42.42E
Novo Arkhangel'sk U.S.S.R. **37** 48.34N 30.50E
Novocherkassk U.S.S.R. **45** 47.25N 40.05E
Novofedorovka U.S.S.R. **45** 47.04N 35.18E
Novograd Volynskiy U.S.S.R. **37** 50.34N 27.32E
Novogrudok U.S.S.R. **37** 53.35N 25.50E
Novo Hamburgo Brazil **126** 29.37S 51.07W
Novokazalinsk U.S.S.R. **9** 45.48N 62.06E
Novokuznetsk U.S.S.R. **48** 53.45N 87.12E
Novo Mesto Yugo. **31** 45.48N 15.10E
Novomoskovsk R.S.F.S.R. U.S.S.R. **44** 54.06N 38.15E
Novomoskovsk Ukr.S.S.R. U.S.S.R. **45** 48.38N 35.15E
Novorossiysk U.S.S.R. **45** 44.44N 37.46E
Novoshakhtinsk U.S.S.R. **45** 47.46N 39.55E
Novosibirsk U.S.S.R. **9** 55.04N 83.05E
Novosibirskiye Ostrova *is.* U.S.S.R. **51** 76.00N144.00E
Novouzensk U.S.S.R. **45** 50.29N 48.08E
Novo-Vyatsk U.S.S.R. **44** 58.30N 49.40E
Novozybkov U.S.S.R. **37** 52.31N 31.58E
Novska Yugo. **31** 45.21N 16.59E
Nový Bor Czech. **38** 50.40N 14.33E
Nový Jičín Czech. **37** 49.36N 18.00E
Novyy Bykhov U.S.S.R. **37** 53.20N 30.21E
Novyy Port U.S.S.R. **50** 67.38N 72.33E
Nowa Ruda Poland **36** 50.34N 16.30E
Nowa Sól Poland **36** 51.49N 15.41E
Nowendoc Australia **93** 31.35S151.45E
Nowgong Assam India **63** 26.21N 92.40E
Nowgong Madhya P. India **63** 25.04N 79.27E
Nowingi Australia **92** 34.36S142.15E
Nowra Australia **93** 35.54S150.36E
Nowrangapur India **63** 19.14N 82.33E
Nowshera Pakistan **62** 34.01N 71.59E
Nowy Dwór Mazowiecki Poland **37** 52.26N 20.43E
Nowy Korczyn Poland **37** 50.19N 20.48E
Nowy Sącz Poland **37** 49.39N 20.40E
Nowy Targ Poland **37** 49.29N 20.02E
Nowy Tomśyl Poland **36** 52.20N 16.07E
Now Zād Afghan. **62** 32.24N 64.28E
Noxon U.S.A. **108** 48.01N115.47W
Noya Spain **26** 42.47N 8.53W
Noya *r.* Spain **25** 41.28N 1.56E
Noyant France **18** 47.31N 0.08E
Noyes I. U.S.A. **100** 55.30N133.40W
Noyon France **19** 49.35N 3.00E
Nozay France **18** 47.34N 1.38W
Nsanje Malaŵi **79** 16.55S 35.12E
Nsawam Ghana **76** 5.49N 0.20W
Nsok Equat. Guinea **78** 1.10N 11.19E
Nsombo Zambia **79** 10.50S 29.56E
Nsukka Nigeria **77** 6.51N 7.29E
Nuatja Togo **77** 6.59N 1.11E
Nubian Desert Sudan **72** 20.30N 34.00E
Nueces *r.* U.S.A. **111** 27.50N 97.30W
Nueces Plains *f.* U.S.A. **111** 28.30N 99.15W
Nueltin L. Canada **101** 60.30N 99.30W
Nueva Casas Grandes Mexico **109** 30.25N107.55W
Nueva Gerona Cuba **117** 21.53N 82.49W
Nueva Helvecia Uruguay **125** 34.19S 57.13W
Nueva Palmira Uruguay **125** 33.53S 58.25W
Nueva Rosita Mexico **111** 27.57N101.13W
Nueve de Julio Argentina **125** 35.30S 60.50W
Nuevitas Cuba **117** 21.34N 77.18W
Nuevo *d.* Mexico **111** 26.00N100.00W
Nuevo, Golfo *g.* Argentina **125** 42.42S 64.35W
Nuevo Berlin Uruguay **125** 32.59S 58.03W
Nuevo Laredo Mexico **111** 27.30N 99.31W
Nuevo León *d.* Mexico **116** 26.00N 99.00W
Nuevo Rocafuerte Ecuador **122** 0.56S 75.24W
Nūh, Rās *c.* Pakistan **62** 25.05N 62.24E
Nui *i.* Tuvalu **84** 7.12S177.10E
Nuits-St. Georges France **19** 47.08N 4.57E
Nu Jiang *r. see* Salween *r.* China **61**
Nukha U.S.S.R. **65** 41.12N 47.10E
Nukhaylah Sudan **72** 19.03N 26.19E
Nuku'alofa Tonga **85** 21.07S175.12W
Nuku Hiva *i.* Is. Marquises **85** 8.56S140.00W
Nukunonu Pacific Oc. **84** 9.10S171.55W
Nulato U.S.A. **98** 64.43N158.06W
Nules Spain **25** 39.51N 0.09W
Nullagine Australia **88** 21.56S120.06E
Nullarbor Australia **89** 31.26S130.55E
Nullarbor Plain *f.* Australia **89** 31.30S128.00E
Numalla, L. Australia **92** 28.45S144.21E
Numan Nigeria **77** 9.30N 12.01E
Numancia *site* Spain **25** 41.48N 2.25W
Numazu Japan **57** 35.06N138.52E
Numedal *f.* Norway **42** 60.06N 9.06E
Numurkah Australia **93** 36.05S145.26E
Nunavik *c.* Greenland **99** 71.55N 55.00W
Nunda U.S.A. **114** 42.35N 77.57W
Nundle Australia **93** 31.28S151.08E
Nuneaton U.K. **13** 52.32N 1.29W
Nungo Mozambique **81** 13.25S 37.45E
Nunivak I. U.S.A. **98** 60.00N166.30W
Nunkun *mtn.* Jammu & Kashmir **62** 33.59N 76.01E
Nunthurungie Australia **92** 30.55S142.29E
Nuoro Italy **32** 40.19N 9.20E
Nuqūb S. Yemen **71** 14.59N 45.48E
Nurallao Italy **32** 39.46N 9.05E
Nürburg W. Germany **39** 50.21N 6.57E
Nürnberg W. Germany **38** 49.27N 11.04E
Nurri Italy **32** 39.42N 9.14E
Nurri, Mt. Australia **93** 31.44S146.04E
Nürtingen W. Germany **39** 48.38N 9.20E
Nusa Tenggara *is.* Indonesia **58** 8.30S118.00E
Nusa Tenggara Barat *d.* Indonesia **58** 8.50S117.30E
Nusa Tenggara Timur *d.* Indonesia **59** 9.30S122.00E
Nusaybin Turkey **64** 37.05N 41.11E
Nushki Pakistan **62** 29.33N 66.01E
Nutak Canada **103** 57.39N 61.50W
Nutter Fort U.S.A. **114** 39.20N 80.19W
Nuuk *see* Godthåb Greenland **99**
Nuwākot Nepal **63** 28.08N 83.53E
Nuwaybi'al Muzayyinah Egypt **66** 28.58N 34.38E
Nuweveldberge *mts.* R.S.A. **80** 32.15S 21.50E
Nuyts, Pt. Australia **89** 35.02S116.32E
Nuyts Archipelago *is.* Australia **91** 32.35S133.17E
Nxaunxau Botswana **80** 18.19S 21.04E
Nyaake Liberia **76** 4.52N 7.37W
Nyabing Australia **89** 33.32S118.09E
Nyahua Tanzania **79** 5.25S 33.16E
Nyahururu Falls *town* Kenya **79** 0.04N 36.22E
Nyainqêntanglha Feng *mtn.* China **63** 30.27N 90.33E
Nyainqêntanglha Shan *mts.* China **63** 30.00N 90.00E
Nyainrong China **63** 32.02N 92.15E
Nyakanazi Tanzania **79** 3.05S 31.16E
Nyaksimvol U.S.S.R. **44** 62.30N 60.52E
Nyala Sudan **73** 12.03N 24.53E
Nyalam China **63** 28.12N 85.58E
Nyamandhlovu Zimbabwe **80** 19.50S 28.15E
Nyamapanda Zimbabwe **81** 16.59S 32.50E
Nyamlell Sudan **73** 9.07N 26.58E
Nyamtukusa Tanzania **79** 3.03S 32.44E
Nyandoma U.S.S.R. **44** 61.33N 40.05E
Nyanga *r.* Gabon **78** 3.00S 10.17E
Nyang Qu *r.* China **63** 29.19N 88.52E
Nyanza *d.* Kenya **79** 0.30S 34.30E
Nyanza Rwanda **79** 2.20S 29.42E
Nyashabozh U.S.S.R. **44** 65.28N 53.42E
Nyaunglebin Burma **56** 17.57N 96.44E
Nyaungu Burma **56** 21.12N 94.55E
Nyborg Denmark **42** 55.19N 10.48E
Nybro Sweden **43** 56.45N 15.54E
Nyda U.S.S.R. **50** 66.35N 72.58E
Nyêmo China **63** 29.25N 90.15E
Nyeri Kenya **79** 0.22S 36.56E
Nyerol Sudan **73** 8.41N 32.02E
Nyhammar Sweden **43** 60.17N 14.58E
Nyika Plateau *f.* Malaŵi **79** 10.25S 33.50E
Nyima China **63** 31.50N 87.48E
Nyimba Zambia **79** 14.33S 30.49E
Nyíregyháza Hungary **37** 47.59N 21.43E
Nyköbing Falster Denmark **41** 54.46N 11.53E
Nyköbing Jylland Denmark **42** 56.48N 8.52E
Nyköbing Sjaelland Denmark **42** 55.55N 11.41E
Nyköping Sweden **43** 58.45N 17.00E
Nykroppa Sweden **43** 59.38N 14.18E
Nylstroom R.S.A. **80** 24.42S 28.24E
Nymagee Australia **93** 32.05S146.20E
Nymboida Australia **93** 29.57S152.32E
Nymboida *r.* Australia **93** 29.39S152.30E
Nymburk Czech. **36** 50.11N 15.03E
Nynäshamn Sweden **43** 58.54N 17.57E
Nyngan Australia **93** 31.34S147.14E
Nyoma Jammu & Kashmir **63** 33.11N 78.38E
Nyon Switz. **39** 46.23N 6.14E
Nyong *r.* Cameroon **77** 3.15N 9.55E
Nyons France **21** 44.22N 5.08E
Nýřany Czech. **38** 49.43N 13.13E
Nýrsko Czech. **38** 49.18N 13.09E
Nysa Poland **37** 50.29N 17.20E
Nysa Kłodzka *r.* Poland **37** 50.49N 17.50E
Nyssa U.S.A. **108** 43.53N117.00W
Nyuksenitsa U.S.S.R. **44** 60.24N 44.08E
Nyunzu Zaïre **79** 5.55S 28.00E
Nyurba U.S.S.R. **51** 63.18N118.28E
Nyuri India **63** 27.42N 92.13E
Nzega Tanzania **79** 4.13S 33.09E
N'zérékoré Guinea **76** 7.49N 8.48W
Nzeto Angola **78** 7.13S 12.56E

O

Oahe Resr. U.S.A. **110** 45.30N100.25W
Oahu *i.* Hawaiian Is. **85** 21.30N158.00W
Oakbank Australia **92** 33.07S140.33E
Oakdale U.S.A. **111** 30.49N 92.40W
Oakesdale U.S.A. **108** 47.08N117.15W
Oakey Australia **91** 27.26S151.43E
Oak Harbour U.S.A. **108** 48.18N122.39W
Oak Hill *town* Fla. U.S.A. **113** 28.52N 80.52W
Oak Hill *town* Ohio U.S.A. **114** 38.54N 82.34W
Oakland Calif. U.S.A. **108** 37.47N122.13W
Oakland Md. U.S.A. **114** 39.25N 79.24W
Oakland Oreg. U.S.A. **108** 43.25N123.18W
Oaklands Australia **93** 35.25S146.15E
Oakley U.S.A. **108** 42.15N113.53W
Oak Ridge *f.* Canada **104** 44.01N 79.19W
Oakridge U.S.A. **108** 43.45N122.28W
Oak Ridge *town* U.S.A. **113** 36.02N 84.12W
Oakvale Australia **92** 33.01S140.41E
Oakville Canada **104** 43.27N 79.41W
Oamaru New Zealand **86** 45.07S170.58E
Oates Land *f.* Antarctica **128** 70.00S155.00E
Oaxaca Mexico **116** 17.05N 96.41W
Oaxaca *d.* Mexico **116** 17.30N 97.00W
Ob *r.* U.S.S.R. **44** 66.50N 69.00E
Oba Canada **102** 49.04N 84.07W
Oba *i.* Vanuatu **84** 15.25S167.50E
Oban U.K. **14** 56.26N 5.28W
Obbia Somali Rep. **71** 5.20N 48.30E
Oberá Argentina **124** 27.30S 55.07W
Oberammergau W. Germany **39** 47.35N 11.04E
Oberdrauburg Austria **39** 46.45N 12.58E
Obergurgl Austria **39** 46.52N 11.01E
Oberhausen W. Germany **38** 51.28N 6.50E
Oberkirch W. Germany **39** 48.31N 8.05E
Oberlin Kans. U.S.A. **110** 39.49N100.32W
Oberlin Ohio U.S.A. **114** 41.18N 82.13W
Obernai France **19** 48.28N 7.29E
Oberösterreich *d.* Austria **39** 48.05N 13.40E
Oberpfälzer Wald *mts.* W. Germany **39** 49.35N 12.15E
Oberursel W. Germany **39** 50.11N 8.35E
Obervellach Austria **39** 46.56N 13.12E
Obi *i.* Indonesia **59** 1.45S127.30E
Obidos Brazil **123** 1.55S 55.31W
Obihiro Japan **57** 42.55N143.00E
Obing W. Germany **39** 48.00N 12.24E
Obitsu *r.* Japan **57** 35.24N139.54E
Obnova Bulgaria **34** 43.26N 24.59E
Obo C.A.R. **73** 5.24N 26.30E
Obock Djibouti **73** 11.59N 43.16E
Obodovka U.S.S.R. **37** 48.28N 29.10E
Oboyan U.S.S.R. **45** 51.13N 36.17E
Obozerskiy U.S.S.R. **44** 63.28N 40.29E
Obregón, Presa *resr.* Mexico **109** 28.00N109.50W
Obrenovac Yugo. **31** 44.39N 20.12E
Obrovac Yugo. **31** 44.12N 15.41E
Obruk Platosu *f.* Turkey **64** 38.00N 33.30E
Obskaya Guba *g.* U.S.S.R. **50** 68.30N 74.00E
Ōbu Japan **57** 35.00N136.58E
Obuasi Ghana **76** 6.15N 1.36W
Obudu Nigeria **77** 6.42N 9.07E
Ocala U.S.A. **113** 29.11N 82.09W
Ocaña Colombia **122** 8.16N 73.21W
Ocaña Spain **27** 39.56N 3.31W
Occidental, Cordillera *mts.* Colombia **122** 5.00N 76.15W
Occidental, Cordillera *mts.* S. America **124** 17.00S 69.00W
Ocean City Md. U.S.A. **115** 38.20N 75.05W
Ocean City N.J. U.S.A. **115** 39.16N 74.36W
Ocean Falls *town* Canada **100** 52.25N127.40W
Ocean I. Kiribati **84** 0.52S169.35E
Oceanside Calif. U.S.A. **109** 33.12N117.23W
Oceanside N.Y. U.S.A. **115** 40.38N 73.38W
Ochamchire U.S.S.R. **45** 42.44N 41.30E
Ochil Hills U.K. **14** 56.16N 3.25W
Ochsenfurt W. Germany **39** 49.40N 10.03E
Ockelbo Sweden **41** 60.53N 16.43E
Öckerö Sweden **42** 57.43N 11.39E
Ocmulgee *r.* U.S.A. **113** 31.58N 82.32W
Oconee *r.* U.S.A. **113** 31.58N 82.32W
Oconto U.S.A. **110** 44.55N 87.52W
Ocotal Nicaragua **117** 13.37N 86.31W
Ocotlán Mexico **116** 20.21N102.42W
Ocreza, Ribeira da *r.* Portugal **27** 39.32N 7.50W
Octeville France **18** 49.37N 1.39W
Ocua Mozambique **81** 13.40S 39.46E
Oda Ghana **76** 5.55N 0.56W
Oda, Jabal *mtn.* Sudan **72** 20.21N 36.39E
Ódádhahraun *mts.* Iceland **40** 65.00N 17.30W
Ōdate Japan **57** 40.16N140.34E
Odawara Japan **57** 35.15N139.10E
Odda Norway **42** 60.04N 6.33E
Odder Denmark **42** 55.58N 10.10E
Oddur Somali Rep. **71** 4.10N 43.53E
Ödeborg Sweden **43** 58.30N 12.01E
Odeleite *r.* Portugal **27** 37.21N 7.27W
Odemira Portugal **27** 37.36N 8.38W
Ödemiş Turkey **29** 38.12N 28.00E
Odense Denmark **42** 55.24N 10.23E
Odenwald *mts.* W. Germany **39** 49.35N 9.05E
Oder *r. see* Odra E. Germany **36**
Oderberg E. Germany **38** 52.52N 14.02E
Oderhaff *b.* E. Germany **38** 53.46N 14.14E
Oder-Havel-Kanal E. Germany **38** 52.51N 13.30E
Oder-Spree-Kanal E. Germany **38** 52.16N 14.30E
Oderzo Italy **32** 45.47N 12.29E
Ödeshög Sweden **43** 58.14N 14.39E
Odessa N.Y. U.S.A. **114** 42.20N 76.48W
Odessa Tex. U.S.A. **111** 31.51N102.22W
Odessa U.S.S.R. **37** 46.30N 30.46E
Odiel *r.* Spain **27** 37.10N 6.55W
Odienné Ivory Coast **76** 9.36N 7.32W
Odorhei Romania **37** 46.18N 25.18E
Odra *r.* Poland **36** 53.30N 14.36E
Odžaci Yugo. **31** 45.30N 19.16E
Odžak Yugo. **31** 45.03N 18.18E
Odzi *r.* Zimbabwe **81** 19.46S 32.22E
Oebisfelde E. Germany **38** 52.25N 10.59E
Oegstgeest Neth. **16** 52.12N 4.31E
Oeiras Brazil **123** 7.00S 42.07W
Oelde W. Germany **38** 51.59N 8.08E
Oelrichs U.S.A. **110** 43.10N103.13W
Oelsnitz E. Germany **39** 50.24N 12.10E
Oelwein U.S.A. **110** 42.41N 91.55W
Oeno I. Pacific Oc. **85** 23.55S130.45W
Oenpelli Australia **90** 12.20S133.04E
Oettingen in Bayern W. Germany **39** 48.57N 10.36E
Oetz Austria **39** 47.12N 10.54E
Ofanto *r.* Italy **33** 41.22N 16.13E
Ofaqim Israel **67** 31.19N 34.37E
Offa Nigeria **77** 8.09N 4.44E
Offaly *d.* Rep. of Ire. **15** 53.15N 7.30W
Offenbach W. Germany **39** 50.08N 8.47E
Offenburg W. Germany **39** 48.28N 7.57E
Offerdal Sweden **40** 63.28N 14.03E
Offida Italy **31** 42.56N 13.41E
Offranville France **18** 49.52N 1.03E
Ofir Portugal **26** 41.31N 8.47W
Ofotfjorden *est.* Norway **40** 68.25N 17.00E
Ofu *i.* Samoa **84** 14.11S169.40W
Ōfunato Japan **57** 39.04N141.43E
Oga Japan **57** 39.53N139.51E
Ōgaki Japan **57** 35.21N136.37E
Ogallala U.S.A. **110** 41.08N101.43W
Ogbomosho Nigeria **77** 8.05N 4.11E
Ogden Iowa U.S.A. **110** 42.02N 94.02W
Ogden Utah U.S.A. **108** 41.14N111.58W
Ogdensburg U.S.A. **105** 44.42N 75.29W
Ogeechee *r.* U.S.A. **113** 31.51N 81.06W
Ogilvie Mts. Canada **98** 65.00N139.30W
Oginskiy, Kanal *canal* U.S.S.R. **37** 52.25N 25.55E
Oglio *r.* Italy **30** 45.02N 10.39E
Ognon *r.* France **19** 47.20N 5.29E
Ogoja Nigeria **77** 6.40N 8.45E
Ogoki Canada **102** 51.35N 86.00W
Ogoki *r.* Canada **102** 51.35N 86.00W
Ogoki Resr. Canada **102** 51.00N 88.15W
Ogooué *r.* Gabon **78** 1.00S 9.05E
Ogosta *r.* Bulgaria **34** 43.35N 23.35E
Ogr Sudan **73** 12.02N 27.06E
Ograżden *mts.* Yugo. **34** 41.30N 22.50E
Ogulin Yugo. **31** 45.16N 15.14E
Ogun *d.* Nigeria **77** 6.50N 3.20E
Ogunquit U.S.A. **115** 43.15N 70.36W
Ohai New Zealand **86** 45.56S167.57E
Ohanet Algeria **75** 28.40N 8.50E
Ohey Belgium **16** 50.26N 5.06E
O'Higgins, Cabo *c.* I. de Pascua **85** 27.05S109.15W
O'Higgins, L. Chile **125** 48.03S 73.10W
Ohio *d.* U.S.A. **112** 40.15N 82.45W
Ohio *r.* U.S.A. **112** 36.59N 89.08W
Ōhito Japan **57** 34.59N138.56E
Ohne W. Germany **38** 52.42N 8.12E
Ohře *r.* Czech. **39** 50.32N 14.08E
Ohrid Yugo. **34** 41.07N 20.47E
Ohrid, L. Albania / Yugo. **34** 41.08N 20.52E
Öhringen W. Germany **39** 49.12N 9.29E
Ōi *r.* Japan **57** 34.45N138.18E
Oil City U.S.A. **114** 41.26N 79.42W
Oise *d.* France **19** 49.30N 2.30E
Oise *r.* France **19** 49.00N 2.04E
Oisterwijk Neth. **16** 51.34N 5.10E
Oita Japan **57** 33.15N131.40E
Ojai U.S.A. **109** 34.27N119.15W
Ojika zan *pen.* Japan **57** 38.20N141.32E
Ojocaliente Mexico **116** 22.35N102.18W
Ojo de Agua Argentina **124** 29.30S 63.44W
Ojos del Salado *mtn.* Argentina / Chile **124** 27.05S 68.05W
Oka Canada **105** 45.29N 74.06W
Oka Nigeria **77** 7.28N 5.48E
Oka *r.* U.S.S.R. **44** 56.09N 43.00E
Okaba Indonesia **59** 8.06S139.46E
Okahandja Namibia **80** 21.58S 16.44E
Okanagan L. Canada **100** 50.00N119.30W
Okanogan U.S.A. **108** 48.39N120.41W
Okanogan *r.* U.S.A. **108** 48.22N119.35W
Okaputa Namibia **80** 20.08S 16.58E
Okāra Pakistan **62** 30.49N 73.27E
Okarito New Zealand **86** 43.14S.170.07
Okaukuejo Namibia **80** 19.12S 15.56E
Okavango *r.* Botswana **80** 18.30S 22.04E
Okavango Basin *f.* Botswana **80** 19.30S 22.30E
Okayama Japan **57** 34.40N133.54E
Okeechobee U.S.A. **113** 27.14N 80.50W
Okeechobee, L. U.S.A. **113** 26.55N 80.45W
Okefenokee Swamp *f.* U.S.A. **113** 30.42N 82.20W
Okehampton U.K. **13** 50.44N 4.01W
Okere *r.* Uganda **79** 1.37N 33.53E
Okha U.S.S.R. **51** 53.35N142.50E
Okhaldhunga Nepal **63** 27.19N 86.31E
Okhansk U.S.S.R. **44** 57.42N 55.20E
Okhotsk U.S.S.R. **51** 59.20N143.15E
Okhotsk, Sea of *see* Okhotskoye More U.S.S.R. **51**
Okhotskiy Perevoz U.S.S.R. **51** 61.55N135.40E
Okhotskoye More *sea* U.S.S.R. **51** 55.00N150.00E
Okiep R.S.A. **80** 29.36S 17.49E
Oki guntō *is.* Japan **57** 36.10N133.10E
Okinawa jima *i.* Japan **53** 26.30N128.00E
Okino Torishima *i.* Pacific Oc. **59** 20.24N136.02E
Okipoko *r.* Namibia **80** 18.40S 16.03E
Okitipupa Nigeria **77** 6.31N 4.50E
Oklahoma *d.* U.S.A. **111** 35.20N 98.00W
Oklahoma City U.S.A. **111** 35.28N 97.32W
Okmulgee U.S.A. **111** 35.37N 95.58W
Oknitsa U.S.S.R. **37** 48.22N 27.30E
Oko, Wādī Sudan **72** 21.15N 35.56E
Okola Cameroon **77** 4.03N 11.23E
Okolona U.S.A. **111** 34.00N 88.45W
Okondja Gabon **78** 0.03S 13.45E
Okoyo Congo **78** 1.28S 15.00E
Oksböl Denmark **42** 55.38N 8.17E
Oksskolten *mtn.* Norway **40** 65.59N 14.15E
Oktyabr'sk U.S.S.R. **45** 49.30N 57.22E
Oktyabrskiy B.S.S.R. U.S.S.R. **37** 52.35N 28.45E
Oktyabrskiy R.S.F.S.R. U.S.S.R. **44** 54.30N 53.30E
Oktyabr'skoy Revolyutsii, Ostrov *i.* U.S.S.R. **51** 79.30N 96.00E
Okučani Yugo. **31** 45.16N 17.12E

Okuru to Otsego, L.

Okuru New Zealand **86** 43.56S168.55E
Okushiri tō *i.* Japan **57** 42.00N139.50E
Okuta Nigeria **77** 9.13N 3.12E
Ola U.S.A. **111** 35.02N 93.13W
Ólafsvík Iceland **40** 64.53N 23.44W
Olancha U.S.A. **109** 36.17N118.01W
Öland *i.* Sweden **43** 56.45N 16.38E
Olary Australia **92** 32.18S140.19E
Olascoaga Argentina **125** 35.14S 60.37W
Olavarría Argentina **125** 36.57S 60.20W
Oława Poland **37** 50.57N 17.17E
Olbia Italy **32** 40.55N 9.29E
Old Crow Canada **98** 67.34N139.43W
Oldenburg *f.* W. Germany **38** 53.06N 8.25E
Oldenburg Nschn. W. Germany **38** 53.08N 8.13E
Oldenburg Sch.-Hol. W. Germany **38** 54.17N 10.52E
Oldenzaal Neth. **16** 52.19N 6.55E
Old Forge N.Y. U.S.A. **115** 43.43N 74.58W
Old Forge Penn. U.S.A. **115** 41.22N 75.44W
Old Fort *r.* Canada **101** 58.30N110.30W
Old Gumbiro Tanzania **79** 10.00S 35.24E
Oldham U.K. **12** 53.33N 2.08W
Old Head of Kinsale *c.* Rep. of Ire. **15** 51.37N 8.33W
Oldman *r.* Canada **101** 49.56N111.42W
Olds Canada **100** 51.50N114.10W
Old Saybrook U.S.A. **115** 41.18N 72.23W
Old Town U.S.A. **112** 44.56N 68.39W
Olean U.S.A. **114** 42.05N 78.26W
Olecko Poland **37** 54.03N 22.30E
Olekma *r.* U.S.S.R. **51** 60.20N120.30E
Olekminsk U.S.S.R. **51** 60.25N120.00E
Olema U.S.S.R. **44** 64.25N 40.15E
Ölen Norway **42** 59.36N 5.48E
Olenëk U.S.S.R. **51** 68.38N112.15E
Olenëk *r.* U.S.S.R. **51** 73.00N120.00E
Olenëkskiy Zaliv *g.* U.S.S.R. **51** 74.00N120.00E
Oléron, Île d' *i.* France **20** 45.56N 1.15W
Oleśnica Poland **37** 51.13N 17.23E
Olevsk U.S.S.R. **37** 51.12N 27.35E
Olga U.S.S.R. **53** 43.46N135.14E
Olga L. Canada **102** 49.44N 77.18W
Ölgiy Mongolia **52** 48.54N 90.00E
Ølgod Denmark **42** 55.49N 8.37E
Olgopol U.S.S.R. **37** 48.10N 29.30E
Olhão Portugal **27** 37.02N 8.50W
Olib *i.* Yugo. **31** 44.22N 14.48E
Oliena Italy **32** 40.16N 9.24E
Olifants *r.* Namibia **80** 25.28S 19.23E
Olifants *r.* C.P. R.S.A. **80** 31.42S 18.10E
Olifants *r.* Trans. R.S.A. **80** 24.08S 32.39E
Olimbia *site* Greece **35** 37.38N 21.41E
Ólimbos *mtn.* Cyprus **66** 34.55N 32.52E
Ólimbos Greece **35** 35.44N 27.11E
Ólimbos *mtn.* Greece **34** 40.05N 22.21E
Olinda Brazil **123** 8.00S 34.51W
Olite Spain **25** 42.29N 1.39W
Oliva Argentina **124** 32.05S 63.35W
Oliva Spain **25** 38.55N 0.07W
Oliva de la Frontera Spain **27** 38.16N 6.55W
Olivares Spain **27** 39.46N 2.20W
Oliveira Brazil **126** 20.39S 44.47W
Olivenza Spain **27** 38.41N 7.06W
Olmedillo de Roa Spain **26** 41.47N 3.56W
Olmedo Spain **26** 41.23N 4.41W
Olney U.K. **13** 52.09N 0.42W
Olney U.S.A. **110** 38.45N 88.05W
Olofström Sweden **43** 56.16N 14.30E
Olomouc Czech. **37** 49.36N 17.16E
Olonets U.S.S.R. **44** 61.00N 32.59E
Oloron France **20** 43.12N 0.36W
Oloron, Gave d' *r.* France **20** 43.33N 1.05W
Olosega *i.* Samoa **84** 14.12S169.38W
Olot Spain **25** 42.11N 2.29E
Olovyannaya U.S.S.R. **53** 50.58N115.35E
Olshammar Sweden **43** 58.45N 14.48E
Olsztyn Poland **37** 53.48N 20.29E
Olsztynek Poland **37** 53.36N 20.17E
Olt *r.* Romania **34** 43.43N 24.51E
Olten Switz. **39** 47.21N 7.54E
Oltenița Romania **37** 44.05N 26.31E
Olteț *r.* Romania **37** 44.13N 24.28E
Olvera Spain **27** 36.56N 5.16W
Olympia U.S.A. **108** 47.03N122.53W
Olympic Mts. U.S.A. **108** 47.50N123.45W
Olympic Nat. Park U.S.A. **108** 47.48N123.30W
Olympus *mtn. see* Ólimbos Greece **34**
Olympus, Mt. U.S.A. **108** 47.48N123.43W
Oma China **63** 32.30N 83.14E
Omae-zaki *c.* Japan **57** 34.36N138.14E
Omagh U.K. **15** 54.36N 7.20W
Omaha U.S.A. **110** 41.16N 95.57W
Oman Asia **60** 22.30N 57.30E
Oman, G. of Asia **65** 25.00N 58.00E
Omarama New Zealand **86** 44.29S169.58E
Omaruru Namibia **80** 21.25S 15.57E
Omate Peru **124** 16.40S 70.58W
Omberg *hill* Sweden **43** 58.20N 14.39E
Omboué Gabon **78** 1.38S 9.20E
Ombrone *r.* Italy **30** 42.39N 11.00E
Ombu China **63** 31.20N 86.34E
Omdurman *see* Umm Durmān Sudan **72**
Omegna Italy **30** 45.53N 8.24E
'Omer Israel **67** 31.17N 34.51E
Omer U.S.A. **104** 44.03N 83.50W
Ometepec Mexico **116** 16.41N 98.25W
Om Hajer Ethiopia **72** 14.24N 36.46E
Ōmi-hachiman Japan **57** 35.08N136.06E
Omineca *r.* Canada **100** 56.05N124.30W
Omišalj Yugo. **31** 45.13N 14.34E
Omitara Namibia **80** 22.18S 18.01E
Ōmiya Japan **57** 35.54N139.38E
Ommen Neth. **16** 52.32N 6.25E
Ömnögovi *d.* Mongolia **54** 43.00N105.00E
Omo *r.* Ethiopia **73** 4.51N 36.55E
Omolon *r.* U.S.S.R. **51** 68.50N158.30E
Omomee Canada **104** 44.19N 78.31W
Omono *r.* Japan **57** 39.44N140.05E
Ompah Canada **105** 45.00N 76.49W
Omsk U.S.S.R. **9** 55.00N 73.22E
Omulew *r.* Poland **37** 53.05N 21.32E
Omuramba Omatako *r.* Namibia **80** 18.19S 19.52E
Omurtag Bulgaria **34** 43.08N 26.26E
Ōmuta Japan **57** 33.02N130.26E
Oña Spain **26** 42.43N 3.25W
Onaga U.S.A. **110** 39.29N 96.10W
Onai Angola **80** 16.43S 17.33E
Onancock U.S.A. **113** 37.43N 75.46W
Onaping L. Canada **104** 46.57N 81.30W
Onaway U.S.A. **104** 45.21N 84.14W
Oncocua Angola **80** 16.40S 13.25E
Onda Spain **25** 39.58N 0.15W
Ondangua Namibia **80** 17.59S 16.02E
Ondo *d.* Nigeria **77** 7.10N 5.20E
Onega U.S.S.R. **44** 63.57N 38.11E
Onega *r.* U.S.S.R. **44** 63.59N 38.11E
Oneida U.S.A. **115** 43.06N 75.39W
Oneida L. U.S.A. **115** 43.13N 76.00W
O'Neill U.S.A. **110** 42.27N 98.39W
Oneonta U.S.A. **115** 42.27N 75.04W
Onezhskaya Guba *b.* U.S.S.R. **44** 63.55N 37.30E
Onezhskoye Ozero *l.* U.S.S.R. **44** 62.00N 35.30E
Ongerup Australia **89** 33.58S118.29E
Ongiyn Gol *r.* Mongolia **54** 43.40N103.45E
Ongniud Qi China **54** 43.00N118.43E
Ongole India **61** 15.31N 80.04E
Onilahy *r.* Madagascar **81** 23.34S 43.45E
Onitsha Nigeria **77** 6.10N 6.47E
Ons, Isla de *i.* Spain **26** 42.23N 8.56W
Onslow Australia **88** 21.41S115.12E
Onslow B. U.S.A. **113** 34.20N 77.20W
Onstwedde Neth. **16** 53.04N 7.02E
Ontake san *mtn.* Japan **57** 35.55N137.29E
Ontario *d.* Canada **102** 51.00N 88.00W
Ontario Calif. U.S.A. **109** 34.04N117.39W
Ontario Oreg. U.S.A. **108** 44.02N116.58W
Ontario, L. Canada / U.S.A. **114** 43.45N 78.00W
Onteniente Spain **25** 38.49N 0.37W
Ontonagon U.S.A. **112** 46.52N 89.18W
Oodnadatta Australia **91** 27.30S135.27E
Ooldea Australia **91** 30.27S131.50E
Oostelijk-Flevoland *f.* Neth. **16** 52.30N 5.40E
Oostende Belgium **16** 51.13N 2.55E
Oosterhout Neth. **16** 51.38N 4.50E
Oosterschelde *est.* Neth. **16** 51.35N 3.57E
Oosthuizen Neth. **16** 52.33N 5.00E
Oostmalle Belgium **16** 51.18N 4.45E
Oost Vlaanderen *d.* Belgium **16** 51.00N 3.45E
Oost Vlieland Neth. **16** 53.18N 5.04E
Ootsa L. Canada **100** 53.50N126.20W
Opaka Bulgaria **34** 43.28N 26.10E
Opal Mexico **111** 24.18N102.22W
Opala U.S.S.R. **51** 51.58N156.30E
Opala Zaïre **78** 0.42S 24.15E
Oparino U.S.S.R. **44** 59.53N 48.10E
Opasatika Canada **102** 49.30N 82.50W
Opasatika *r.* Canada **102** 50.24N 82.26W
Opasquia Canada **102** 53.16N 93.34W
Opatija Yugo. **31** 45.21N 14.19E
Opava Czech. **37** 49.56N 17.54E
Opelousas U.S.A. **111** 30.32N 92.05W
Opeongo L. Canada **104** 45.42N 78.23W
Opheim U.S.A. **108** 48.51N106.24W
Opinaca *r.* Canada **102** 52.20N 78.00W
Opinnagau *r.* Canada **102** 54.12N 82.21W
Opiscotéo, Lac *l.* Canada **103** 53.10N 68.10W
Opochka U.S.S.R. **44** 56.41N 28.42E
Opole Poland **37** 50.40N 17.56E
Oporto *see* Porto Portugal **26**
Opotiki New Zealand **86** 38.00S177.18E
Opp U.S.A. **113** 31.16N 86.18W
Oppdal Norway **40** 62.36N 9.41E
Oppido Mamertina Italy **33** 38.16N 16.00E
Oppland *d.* Norway **41** 61.30N 9.00E
Opportunity U.S.A. **108** 47.39N117.15W
Opthalmia Range *mts.* Australia **88** 23.25S120.00E
Opunake New Zealand **86** 39.27S173.51E
Ora Italy **30** 46.21N 11.18E
Ora Banda Australia **89** 30.27S121.04E
Oradea Romania **37** 47.03N 21.55E
Öraefajökull *mtn.* Iceland **40** 64.02N 16.39W
Orahovica Yugo. **31** 45.31N 17.53E
Orai India **63** 25.59N 79.28E
Oran Algeria **74** 35.42N 0.38W
Orán Argentina **124** 23.07S 64.16W
Orange Australia **93** 33.19S149.10E
Orange France **21** 44.08N 4.48E
Orange *r.* R.S.A. **80** 28.38S 16.38E
Orange Mass. U.S.A. **115** 42.35N 72.19W
Orange N.J. U.S.A. **115** 40.46N 74.14W
Orange Tex. U.S.A. **111** 30.01N 93.44W
Orange, C. Brazil **123** 4.25N 51.32W
Orangeburg U.S.A. **113** 33.28N 80.53W
Orange Free State *d.* R.S.A. **80** 28.00S 28.00E
Orangevale U.S.A. **108** 38.41N121.13W
Orangeville Canada **104** 43.55N 80.06W
Oranienburg E. Germany **38** 52.45N 13.14E
Oranjefontein R.S.A. **80** 23.27S 27.40E
Oranjemond Namibia **80** 28.35S 16.26E
Or 'Aqiva Israel **67** 32.30N 34.55E
Orarak Sudan **73** 6.15N 32.23E
Oras Phil. **59** 12.09N125.22E
Orbe Switz. **39** 46.43N 6.32E
Orbetello Italy **30** 42.27N 11.13E
Orbieu *r.* France **20** 43.14N 2.54E
Orbigo *r.* Spain **26** 41.58N 5.40W
Orbisonia U.S.A. **114** 40.15N 77.54W
Orbost Australia **93** 37.42S148.30E
Örbyhus Sweden **41** 60.14N 17.42E
Orcera Spain **26** 38.19N 2.39W
Orchies France **19** 50.28N 3.14E
Orchila *i.* Venezuela **117** 11.52N 66.10W
Ord *r.* Australia **88** 15.30S128.30E
Ordenes Spain **26** 43.04N 8.24W
Ordu Turkey **64** 41.00N 37.52E
Orduña Spain **26** 42.58N 2.58W
Ordzhonikidze U.S.S.R. **45** 43.02N 44.43E
Örebro Sweden **43** 59.17N 15.13E
Örebro *d.* Sweden **43** 59.30N 15.00E
Oregon *d.* U.S.A. **108** 43.49N120.36W
Oregon City U.S.A. **108** 45.21N122.36W
Öregrund Sweden **41** 60.20N 18.26E
Orekhovo-Zuyevo U.S.S.R. **44** 55.47N 39.00E
Orel U.S.S.R. **44** 52.58N 36.04E
Orellana, Embalse de *resr.* Spain **27** 39.00N 5.25W
Orem U.S.A. **108** 40.19N111.42W
Orenburg U.S.S.R. **44** 51.50N 55.00E
Orense Spain **26** 42.20N 7.51W
Orense *d.* Spain **26** 42.15N 7.40W
Oressa *r.* U.S.S.R. **37** 52.33N 28.45E
Orestiás Greece **34** 41.30N 26.31E
Orfanoú, Kólpos *g.* Greece **34** 40.33N 24.00E
Orford U.S.A. **105** 43.54N 72.10W
Orford, Mt. Canada **105** 45.18N 72.08W
Orfordness *c.* Australia **90** 11.22S142.50E
Orford Ness *c.* U.K. **13** 52.05N 1.36E
Orgaz Spain **27** 39.39N 3.54W
Orgelet France **19** 46.31N 5.37E
Orgeyev U.S.S.R. **37** 47.24N 28.50E
Orgūn Afghan. **62** 32.55N 69.10E
Orick U.S.A. **108** 41.17N124.04W
Orient Australia **92** 28.10S142.50E
Oriental, Cordillera *mts.* Bolivia **124** 17.00S 65.00W
Oriental, Cordillera *mts.* Colombia **122** 5.00N 74.30W
Origny France **19** 49.54N 3.30E
Orihuela Spain **25** 38.05N 0.57W
Orillia Canada **104** 44.37N 79.25W
Orimattila Finland **41** 60.48N 25.45E
Orinduik Guyana **122** 4.42N 60.01W
Orinoco *r.* Venezuela **122** 9.00N 61.30W
Orinoco, Delta del *f.* Venezuela **122** 9.00N 61.00W
Orissa *d.* India **63** 20.20N 84.00E
Oristano Italy **32** 39.54N 8.35E
Oristano, Golfo di *g.* Italy **32** 39.50N 8.30E
Orizaba Mexico **116** 18.51N 97.08W
Örje Norway **42** 59.29N 11.39E
Orjen *mtn.* Yugo. **31** 42.30N 18.38E
Orjiva Spain **27** 36.53N 3.24W
Orkanger Norway **40** 63.17N 9.52E
Orkney Is. *d.* U.K. **14** 59.00N 3.00W
Orlândia Brazil **126** 20.55S 47.54W
Orlando U.S.A. **113** 28.33N 81.21W
Orléans Canada **105** 45.28N 75.31W
Orléans France **19** 47.55N 1.54E
Orleans Mass. U.S.A. **115** 41.47N 70.00W
Orleans N.H. U.S.A. **105** 44.49N 72.12W
Orléans, Canal d' France **19** 47.54N 1.55E
Ormāra Pakistan **62** 25.12N 64.38E
Ormāra, Rās *c.* Pakistan **62** 25.09N 64.35E
Ormilia Greece **34** 40.16N 23.33E
Ormoc Phil. **59** 11.00N124.37E
Ormond New Zealand **86** 38.35S177.58E
Ormož Yugo. **31** 46.25N 16.09E
Ormskirk U.K. **12** 53.35N 2.53W
Ormstown Canada **105** 45.08N 74.00W
Ornans France **19** 47.06N 6.09E
Orne *d.* France **18** 48.40N 0.05E
Orne *r.* France **18** 49.17N 0.11W
Ornö *i.* Sweden **43** 59.04N 18.24E
Örnsköldsvik Sweden **40** 63.17N 18.50E
Orobie, Alpi *mts.* Italy **30** 46.03N 10.00E
Orocué Colombia **122** 4.48N 71.20W
Orodara U. Volta **76** 11.00N 4.54W
Orogrande U.S.A. **109** 32.23N106.28W
Orohena *mtn.* Tahiti **85** 17.37S149.28W
Oromocto Canada **103** 45.51N 66.29W
Oron Israel **66** 30.55N 35.01E
Oron Nigeria **77** 4.49N 8.15E
Orono Canada **104** 43.59N 78.37W
Orono U.S.A. **112** 44.53N 68.40W
Orosei Italy **32** 40.23N 9.42E
Orosei, Golfo di *g.* Italy **32** 40.10N 9.50E
Orosháza Hungary **37** 46.34N 20.40E
Orote Pen. Guam **84** 13.26N144.38E
Orotukan U.S.S.R. **51** 62.16N151.43E
Oroville Calif. U.S.A. **108** 39.31N121.33W
Oroville Wash. U.S.A. **108** 48.56N119.26W
Orrefors Sweden **43** 56.50N 15.45E
Orroroo Australia **92** 32.46S138.39E
Orrville U.S.A. **114** 40.50N 81.46W
Orsa Sweden **41** 61.07N 14.37E
Orsha U.S.S.R. **44** 54.30N 30.23E
Orsières Switz. **39** 46.02N 7.09E
Orsk U.S.S.R. **44** 51.13N 58.35E
Orşova Romania **37** 44.42N 22.22E
Ortaklar Turkey **35** 37.53N 27.30E
Orta Nova Italy **33** 41.19N 15.42E
Ortegal, Cabo *c.* Spain **26** 43.45N 7.53W
Orthez France **20** 43.29N 0.46W
Ortigueira Spain **26** 43.41N 7.51W
Ortigueira, Ría de *est.* Spain **26** 43.45N 7.50W
Ortisei Italy **30** 46.34N 11.40E
Ortona Italy **31** 42.21N 14.24E
Ortonville U.S.A. **110** 45.18N 96.28W
Oruro Bolivia **124** 17.59S 67.09W
Oruro *d.* Bolivia **124** 18.00S 72.30W
Orust *i.* Sweden **42** 58.10N 11.38E
Orūzgān Afghan. **62** 32.56N 66.38E
Orūzgān *d.* Afghan. **62** 33.30N 66.00E
Orvieto Italy **30** 42.43N 12.07E
Orwell U.S.A. **114** 41.32N 80.52W
Oryakhovo Bulgaria **34** 43.40N 23.57E
Or Yehuda Israel **67** 32.01N 34.51E
Orzinuovi Italy **30** 45.24N 9.55E
Os Norway **40** 62.31N 11.11E
Osa, Península de *pen.* Costa Rica **117** 8.20N 83.30W
Osage *r.* U.S.A. **107** 38.35N 91.57W
Osage Iowa U.S.A. **110** 43.17N 92.49W
Osage Wyo. U.S.A. **108** 43.59N104.25W
Ōsaka Japan **57** 34.40N135.30E
Ōsaka *d.* Japan **57** 34.24N135.25E
Ōsaka-wan *b.* Japan **57** 34.30N135.18E
Osborne U.S.A. **110** 39.26N 98.42W
Osby Sweden **43** 56.22N 13.59E
Osceola Iowa U.S.A. **110** 41.02N 93.46W
Osceola Mo. U.S.A. **111** 38.03N 93.42W
Osceola Mills U.S.A. **114** 40.51N 78.16W
Oschatz E. Germany **38** 51.18N 13.07E
Oschersleben E. Germany **38** 52.01N 11.13E
Oscoda U.S.A. **104** 44.26N 83.20W
Osečina Yugo. **31** 44.23N 19.36E
Osen Norway **40** 64.18N 10.32E
Osh U.S.S.R. **50** 40.37N 72.49E
Oshawa Canada **104** 43.54N 78.51W
Ō shima *i.* Hokkaido Japan **57** 41.40N139.40E
Ō shima *i.* Tosan Japan **57** 34.43N139.24E
Oshkosh Nebr. U.S.A. **110** 41.24N102.21W
Oshmyany U.S.S.R. **37** 54.22N 25.52E
Oshnovīyeh Iran **65** 37.03N 45.05E
Oshogbo Nigeria **77** 7.50N 4.35E
Oshtorān, Kūh *mtn.* Iran **65** 33.18N 49.15E
Oshvor U.S.S.R. **44** 66.59N 62.59E
Oshwe Zaïre **78** 3.27S 19.32E
Osiān India **62** 26.43N 72.55E
Osijek Yugo. **31** 45.33N 18.41E
Osilo Italy **32** 40.44N 8.39E
Osimo Italy **31** 43.29N 13.29E
Osipovichi U.S.S.R. **37** 53.19N 28.36E
Oskaloosa U.S.A. **110** 41.18N 92.39W
Oskarshamn Sweden **43** 57.16N 16.26E
Oskarström Sweden **43** 56.48N 12.58E
Oskol *r.* U.S.S.R. **45** 49.08N 37.10E
Oslo Norway **42** 59.55N 10.45E
Oslofjorden *est.* Norway **42** 59.20N 10.35E
Osmancık Turkey **64** 40.58N 34.50E
Osmaniye Turkey **64** 37.04N 36.15E
Ösmo Sweden **43** 58.59N 17.54E
Osnabrück W. Germany **38** 52.16N 8.02E
Osogovska Planina *mts.* Yugo. **34** 42.08N 22.18E
Osorno Chile **125** 40.35S 73.14W
Osorno Spain **26** 42.24N 4.22W
Osöyra Norway **42** 60.11N 5.28E
Osprey Reef Australia **90** 13.55S146.38E
Oss Neth. **16** 51.46N 5.31E
Ossa *mtn.* Greece **34** 39.47N 22.42E
Ossa, Mt. Australia **91** 41.52S146.04E
Ossabaw I. U.S.A. **113** 31.47N 81.06W
Osse *r.* France **20** 44.07N 0.17E
Osse *r.* Nigeria **77** 5.55N 5.15E
Ossineke U.S.A. **104** 44.54N 83.27W
Ossining U.S.A. **115** 41.10N 73.52W
Ossokmanuan L. Canada **103** 53.25N 65.00W
Ostaboningue, L. Canada **104** 47.09N 78.53W
Ostashkov U.S.S.R. **44** 57.09N 33.10E
Ost-Berlin *d.* E. Germany **38** 52.30N 13.25E
Oste *r.* W. Germany **38** 53.33N 9.10E
Ostend *see* Oostende Belgium **16**
Oster U.S.S.R. **37** 50.55N 30.53E
Oster *r.* U.S.S.R. **37** 53.47N 31.46E
Osterburg E. Germany **38** 52.47N 11.44E
Österbybruk Sweden **43** 60.12N 17.54E
Österbymo Sweden **43** 57.50N 15.16E
Österdal *r.* Sweden **41** 61.03N 14.30E
Österdalen *f.* Norway **41** 61.15N 11.10E
Östergötland *d.* Sweden **43** 58.20N 16.00E
Östergötland *f.* Sweden **43** 58.17N 15.40E
Osterholz-Scharmbeck W. Germany **38** 53.14N 8.47E
Osterö *i.* Faroe Is. **10** 62.16N 6.54W
Osterode W. Germany **38** 51.43N 10.14E
Osteröy *i.* Norway **41** 60.33N 5.35E
Östersund Sweden **40** 63.10N 14.40E
Östervåla Sweden **43** 60.11N 17.11E
Osterwieck E. Germany **38** 51.58N 10.42E
Östfold *d.* Norway **42** 59.20N 11.25E
Ostfriesische Inseln *is.* W. Germany **38** 53.44N 7.25E
Östhammar Sweden **41** 60.16N 18.22E
Ostia Italy **32** 41.44N 12.14E
Östmark Sweden **43** 60.17N 12.45E
Ostrava Czech. **37** 49.50N 18.15E
Ostróda Poland **37** 53.43N 19.59E
Ostrog U.S.S.R. **37** 50.20N 26.29E
Ostrołeka Poland **37** 53.06N 21.34E
Ostrov Czech. **39** 50.17N 12.57E
Ostrov U.S.S.R. **44** 57.22N 28.22E
Ostrowiec-Świetokrzyski Poland **37** 50.57N 21.23E
Ostrów Mazowiecka Poland **37** 52.50N 21.51E
Ostrów Wielkopolski Poland **37** 51.39N 17.49E
Ostuni Italy **33** 40.44N 17.35E
Osum *r.* Albania **34** 40.40N 20.10E
Osüm *r.* Bulgaria **29** 43.41N 24.51E
Ōsumi kaikyō *str.* Japan **57** 31.30N131.00E
Ōsumi shotō *is.* Japan **53** 30.30N131.00E
Osuna Spain **27** 37.14N 5.07W
Oswego U.S.A. **115** 43.27N 76.31W
Oswestry U.K. **12** 52.52N 3.03W
Otago *d.* New Zealand **86** 45.10S169.20E
Otago Pen. New Zealand **86** 45.48S170.45E
Otaki New Zealand **86** 40.45S175.08E
Otaru Japan **57** 43.14N140.59E
Otavalo Ecuador **122** 0.14N 78.16W
Otavi Namibia **80** 19.37S 17.21E
Ōtawara Japan **57** 36.52N140.02E
Otelec Romania **37** 45.36N 20.50E
Otematata New Zealand **86** 44.37S170.11E
Othonoí *i.* Greece **33** 39.50N 19.26E
Óthris, Óros *mtn.* Greece **35** 39.04N 22.42E
Oti *r.* Ghana **76** 8.43N 0.10E
Otira New Zealand **86** 42.51S171.33E
Otish, Monts *mts.* Canada **103** 52.22N 70.30W
Otisville U.S.A. **115** 41.28N 74.32W
Otiwarongo Namibia **80** 20.30S 16.39E
Otjiwero Namibia **80** 17.59S 13.22E
Otju Namibia **80** 18.15S 13.18E
Otočac Yugo. **31** 44.52N 15.14E
Otog Qi China **54** 39.05N107.59E
Otosquen Canada **101** 53.17N102.01W
Otra *r.* Norway **42** 58.09N 8.00E
Otradnyy U.S.S.R. **44** 53.26N 51.30E
Otranto Italy **33** 40.09N 18.30E
Otranto, Str. of Med. Sea **33** 40.00N 19.00E
Otrokovice Czech. **37** 49.13N 17.31E
Otsego U.S.A. **112** 42.26N 85.42W
Otsego L. U.S.A. **115** 42.45N 74.52W

Otsego Lake to Paraná

Otsego Lake *town* U.S.A. 104 44.55N 84.41W
Ōtsu Japan 57 35.02N135.52E
Ōtsuki Japan 57 35.36N138.57E
Otta Norway 41 61.46N 9.32E
Ottawa Canada 105 45.25N 75.42W
Ottawa *r.* Canada 105 45.20N 73.58W
Ottawa Ill. U.S.A. 110 41.21N 88.51W
Ottawa Kans. U.S.A. 110 38.37N 95.16W
Ottawa Is. Canada 99 59.50N 80.00W
Ottenby Sweden 43 56.14N 16.25E
Otter *r.* U.K. 13 50.38N 3.19W
Otterbäcken Sweden 43 58.57N 14.02E
Otterburn U.K. 12 55.14N 2.10W
Otter Creek *r.* U.S.A. 105 44.13N 73.17W
Otter L. Canada 101 55.35N104.39W
Otter Lake *town* Canada 105 45.51N 76.26W
Otterndorf W. Germany 38 53.48N 8.53E
Otteröy *i.* Norway 40 62.45N 6.50E
Otterup Denmark 42 55.31N 10.24E
Ottosdal R.S.A. 80 26.48S 26.00E
Ottumwa U.S.A. 110 41.01N 92.25W
Oturkpo Nigeria 77 7.13N 8.10E
Otway, C. Australia 92 38.51S143.34E
Ötztaler Alpen *mts.* Austria/Italy 30 46.52N 10.50E
Ou *r.* Laos 56 20.03N102.19E
Ouachita *r.* U.S.A. 111 31.38N 91.49W
Ouachita, L. U.S.A. 111 34.40N 93.25W
Ouachita Mts. U.S.A. 111 34.40N 94.25W
Ouada, Djebel *mtn.* C.A.R. 73 8.56N 23.26E
Ouadane Mauritania 74 20.56N 11.37W
Ouadda C.A.R. 73 8.04N 22.24E
Ouaddaï *d.* Chad 73 13.00N 21.00E
Ouagadougou U. Volta 76 12.20N 1.40W
Ouahigouya U. Volta 76 13.31N 2.21W
Ouaka *d.* C.A.R. 73 6.00N 21.00E
Oualâta Mauritania 74 17.18N 7.02W
Ouallam Niger 77 14.23N 2.09E
Ouallene Algeria 74 24.35N 1.17E
Ouanda Djallé C.A.R. 73 8.54N 22.48E
Ouarane *f.* Mauritania 74 21.00N 9.30W
Ouararda, Passe de *pass* Mauritania 74 21.01N 13.03W
Ouareau *r.* Canada 105 45.56N 73.25W
Ouargla Algeria 75 31.57N 5.20E
Ouarra *r.* C.A.R. 73 5.05N 24.26E
Ouarzazate Morocco 74 30.57N 6.50W
Ouassouas *well* Mali 74 16.01N 1.26E
Ouche *r.* France 19 47.06N 5.16E
Ouddorp Neth. 16 51.49N 3.57E
Oudenaarde Belgium 16 50.50N 3.37E
Oudenbosch Neth. 16 51.35N 4.30E
Oude Rijn *r.* Neth. 16 52.14N 4.26E
Oudon *r.* France 18 47.47N 1.02W
Oudtshoorn R.S.A. 80 33.35S 22.11E
Oued Zarga Tunisia 32 36.40N 9.25E
Oued-Zem Morocco 74 32.55N 6.30W
Ouellé Ivory Coast 76 7.26N 4.01W
Ouenza Algeria 75 35.57N 8.07E
Ouessant, Île d' *i.* France 18 48.28N 5.05W
Ouesso Congo 78 1.38N 16.03E
Ouezzane Morocco 74 34.52N 5.35W
Oughter, Lough Rep. of Ire. 15 54.01N 7.28W
Ouham *r.* Chad 77 9.15N 18.13E
Ouimet Canada 102 48.43N 88.35W
Ouistreham France 18 49.17N 0.15W
Oujda Morocco 74 34.41N 1.45W
Oulu Finland 40 65.01N 25.28E
Oulu *d.* Finland 40 65.00N 27.00E
Oulu *r.* Finland 40 65.01N 25.25E
Oulujärvi *l.* Finland 40 64.20N 27.15E
Oum Chalouba Chad 75 15.48N 20.46E
Oumé Ivory Coast 76 6.25N 5.23W
Oum er Rbia, Oued *r.* Morocco 74 33.19N 8.21W
Oumm ed Droûs Guebli, Sebkhet *f.* Mauritania 74 24.03N 11.45W
Oumm ed Droûs Telli, Sebkhet *f.* Mauritania 74 24.20N 11.30W
Ounas *r.* Finland 40 66.30N 25.45E
Oundle U.K. 13 52.28N 0.28W
Ounianga Kébir Chad 75 19.04N 20.29E
Our *r.* Lux. 16 49.53N 6.16E
Ouray U.S.A. 108 40.06N109.40W
Ourcq *r.* France 19 49.01N 3.01E
Ouri Chad 75 21.34N 19.13E
Ourinhos Brazil 126 23.00S 49.54W
Ourique Portugal 26 37.39N 8.13W
Ouro Fino Brazil 126 22.16S 46.25W
Ouro Prêto Brazil 126 20.54S 43.30W
Ourthe *r.* Belgium 16 50.38N 5.36E
Ouse *r.* Humber. U.K. 12 53.41N 0.42W
Oust *r.* France 18 47.39N 2.06W
Outardes, Rivière aux *r.* Canada 103 49.04N 68.25W
Outer Hebrides *is.* U.K. 14 57.40N 7.35W
Outjo Namibia 80 20.07S 16.10E
Outlook U.S.A. 108 48.53N104.47W
Ouvèze *r.* France 21 43.59N 4.51E
Ouyen Australia 92 35.06S142.22E
Ouzouer-le-Marché France 19 47.55N 1.32E
Ouzzal, Oued I-n- *wadi* Algeria 75 20.54N 2.28E
Ovalle Chile 124 30.36S 71.12W
Ovamboland *f.* Namibia 80 17.45S 16.00E
Ovar Portugal 26 40.52N 8.38W
Ovens *r.* Australia 93 36.20S146.18E
Overath W. Germany 16 50.56N 7.18E
Overflakkee *i.* Neth. 16 51.45N 4.08E
Overijssel *d.* Neth. 16 52.25N 6.30E
Överkalix Sweden 40 66.21N 22.56E
Overland Park *town* U.S.A. 110 38.59N 94.40W
Overton U.S.A. 109 36.33N114.27W
Övertorneå Sweden 40 66.23N 23.40E
Överum Sweden 43 57.59N 16.19E
Ovid Mich. U.S.A. 104 43.01N 84.22W
Ovid N.Y. U.S.A. 114 42.41N 76.49W
Ovidiopol U.S.S.R. 37 46.18N 30.28E
Oviedo Spain 26 43.22N 5.50W
Oviedo *d.* Spain 26 43.20N 6.10W
Ovinishche U.S.S.R. 44 58.20N 37.00E
Övörhangay *d.* Mongolia 54 45.00N103.00E
Ovruch U.S.S.R. 37 51.20N 28.50E
Owaka New Zealand 86 46.27S169.40E
Owando Congo 78 0.30S 15.48E
Owase Japan 57 34.04N136.12E
Owatonna U.S.A. 110 44.06N 93.10W
Owbeh Afghan. 62 34.22N 63.10E
Owego U.S.A. 115 42.06N 76.16W
Owel, Lough Rep. of Ire. 15 53.34N 7.24W
Owen Channel Canada 104 45.31N 81.48W
Owen Falls Dam Uganda 79 0.30N 33.07E
Owensboro U.S.A. 113 37.46N 87.07W
Owen Sd. *b.* Canada 104 44.40N 80.55W
Owens L. U.S.A. 109 36.25N117.56W
Owen Sound *town* Canada 104 44.34N 80.56W
Owen Stanley Range *mts.* P.N.G. 90 9.30S148.00E
Owerri Nigeria 77 5.29N 7.02E
Owl *r.* Canada 101 57.51N 92.44W
Owo Nigeria 77 7.10N 5.39E
Owosso U.S.A. 104 43.00N 84.10W
Owyhee *r.* U.S.A. 108 43.46N117.02W
Oxelösund Sweden 43 58.40N 17.06E
Oxford U.K. 13 51.45N 1.15W
Oxford Md. U.S.A. 115 38.42N 76.10W
Oxford Mich. U.S.A. 104 42.49N 83.18W
Oxford Penn. U.S.A. 115 39.47N 75.59W
Oxfordshire *d.* U.K. 13 51.46N 1.10W
Oxley Australia 92 34.11S144.10E
Oxnard U.S.A. 109 34.12N119.11W
Oxtongue Lake *town* Canada 104 45.22N 78.55W
Oyapock *r.* Guiana 123 4.10N 51.40W
Oyem Gabon 78 1.34N 11.31E
Oyen Canada 101 51.22N110.28W
Öyer Norway 41 61.12N 10.22E
Öyeren *l.* Norway 42 59.48N 11.14E
Oykel *r.* U.K. 14 57.53N 4.21W
Oymyakon U.S.S.R. 51 63.30N142.44E
Oyo Nigeria 77 7.50N 3.55E
Oyo *d.* Nigeria 77 8.10N 3.40E
Oyonnax France 21 46.15N 5.40E
Ozamiz Phil. 59 8.09N123.59E
Ozarichi U.S.S.R. 37 52.28N 29.12E
Ozark Ala. U.S.A. 113 31.27N 85.40W
Ozark Ark. U.S.A. 111 35.29N 93.50W
Ozark Mo. U.S.A. 111 37.01N 93.12W
Ozark Plateau U.S.A. 111 37.00N 93.00W
Ózd Hungary 37 48.14N 20.18E
Ozernoye U.S.S.R. 44 51.45N 51.29E
Ozersk U.S.S.R. 37 54.26N 22.00E
Ozieri Italy 32 40.35N 9.00E
Ozinki U.S.S.R. 45 51.11N 49.43E
Ozona U.S.A. 111 30.43N101.12W

P

Paamiut *see* Frederikshåb Greenland 99
Pa-an Burma 56 16.51N 97.37E
Paarl R.S.A. 80 33.44S 18.58E
Pabianice Poland 37 51.40N 19.22E
Pābna Bangla. 63 24.00N 89.15E
Pacaraima, Sierra *mts.* Venezuela 122 4.00N 62.30W
Pacasmayo Peru 122 7.27S 79.33W
Pachino Italy 33 36.42N 15.06E
Pachmarhi India 63 22.28N 78.26E
Pāchora India 62 20.40N 75.21E
Pachuca Mexico 116 20.10N 98.44W
Pacific-Antarctic Basin Pacific Oc. 85 58.00S 98.00W
Pacific-Antarctic Ridge Pacific Oc. 85 57.00S145.00W
Pacific Ocean 85
Pacitan Indonesia 59 8.12S111.05E
Packwood U.S.A. 108 46.36N121.40W
Pacy-sur-Eure France 18 49.01N 1.23E
Padam Jammu & Kashmir 62 33.28N 76.53E
Padampur India 63 20.59N 83.04E
Padang Indonesia 58 0.55S100.21E
Padangpanjang Indonesia 58 0.30S100.26E
Padangsidempuan Indonesia 58 1.20N 99.11E
Padany U.S.S.R. 44 63.12N 33.20E
Padauari *r.* Brazil 122 0.15S 64.05W
Paden City U.S.A. 114 39.36N 80.56W
Paderborn W. Germany 38 51.43N 8.45E
Padilla Bolivia 124 19.19S 64.20W
Padlei Canada 101 62.10N 97.05W
Padloping Island *town* Canada 99 67.00N 62.50W
Padova Italy 32 45.25N 11.53E
Pādra India 62 22.14N 73.05E
Padrauna India 63 26.55N 83.59E
Padre I. U.S.A. 111 27.00N 97.15W
Padrón Spain 26 42.44N 8.40W
Padstow U.K. 13 50.33N 4.57W
Padthaway Australia 92 36.37S140.28E
Padua *see* Padova Italy 32
Paducah U.S.A. 111 37.05N 88.36W
Paeroa New Zealand 86 37.23S175.41E
Paestum *site* Italy 33 40.25N 15.00E
Pafúri Mozambique 81 22.27S 31.21E
Pag Yugo. 31 44.27N 15.04E
Pag *i.* Yugo. 31 44.30N 15.00E
Pagadian Phil. 59 7.50N123.30E
Pagai Selatan *i.* Indonesia 58 3.00S100.18E
Pagai Utara *i.* Indonesia 58 2.42S100.05E
Pagan Burma 56 21.07N 94.53E
Pagasitikós Kólpos *b.* Greece 35 39.15N 23.12E
Page U.S.A. 106 36.57N111.27W
Pager *r.* Uganda 79 3.05N 32.28E
Paget Canada 104 46.18N 80.48W
Paghmān Afghan. 62 34.36N 68.57E
Pago Pago Samoa 84 14.16S170.42W
Pagosa Springs *town* U.S.A. 108 37.16N107.01W
Pagri China 63 27.45N 89.10E
Paguchi L. Canada 102 49.38N 91.40W
Pagwa River *town* Canada 102 50.02N 85.14W
Pahala Hawaii U.S.A. 106 19.12N155.28W
Pahiatua New Zealand 86 40.26S175.49E
Pahlavī Dezh Iran 65 35.51N 46.02E
Paible U.K. 14 57.35N 7.27W
Paide U.S.S.R. 41 58.54N 25.33E
Paihia New Zealand 86 35.16S174.05E
Päijänne *l.* Finland 41 61.35N 25.30E
Paikü Co *l.* China 63 28.48N 85.36E
Paimboeuf France 18 47.17N 2.02W
Paimpol France 18 48.46N 3.03W
Painan Indonesia 58 1.21S100.34E
Painesville U.S.A. 114 41.43N 81.15W
Pains Brazil 126 20.23S 45.38W
Paintsville U.S.A. 113 37.49N 82.48W
Paisley Canada 104 44.18N 81.16W
Paisley U.K. 14 55.50N 4.26W
Paiton Indonesia 59 7.42S113.30E
Pajala Sweden 40 67.11N 23.22E
Pajares, Puerto de *pass* Spain 26 43.00N 5.46W
Pajule Uganda 79 2.58N 32.53E
Pakanbaru Indonesia 58 0.33N101.20E
Pakaraima Mts. Guyana 122 5.00N 60.00W
Pakaur India 63 24.38N 87.51E
Pakenham Canada 105 45.20N 76.17W
Paki Nigeria 77 11.33N 8.08E
Pakistan Asia 62 29.00N 67.00E
Pakokku Burma 56 21.20N 95.10E
Pākpattan Pakistan 62 30.21N 73.24E
Paks Hungary 31 46.39N 18.53E
Paktīā *d.* Afghan. 62 33.25N 69.30E
Pakwach Uganda 79 2.27N 31.18E
Pakxé Laos 56 15.07N105.47E
Pala Chad 77 9.25N 15.05E
Palagonia Italy 33 37.19N 14.45E
Palaiá Epídhavros Greece 35 37.38N 23.09E
Palaia Kórinthos *site* Greece 35 37.54N 22.56E
Palaiá Psará Greece 35 38.46N 25.36E
Palaiokhóra Greece 35 35.14N 23.41E
Pálairos Greece 35 38.45N 20.51E
Palaiseau France 19 48.43N 2.15E
Palamás Greece 34 39.26N 22.04E
Palamós Spain 25 41.51N 3.08E
Palana U.S.S.R. 51 59.05N159.59E
Palangkaraya Indonesia 58 2.16S113.56E
Palanguinos Spain 24 42.27N 5.31W
Pālanpur India 62 24.10N 72.26E
Palanquinos Spain 26 42.27N 5.30W
Palapye Botswana 80 22.33S 27.07E
Palas del Rey Spain 26 42.52N 7.52W
Palatka U.S.A. 113 29.38N 81.40W
Palaw Burma 56 12.58N 98.39E
Palawan *i.* Phil. 58 9.30N118.30E
Palazzolo Acreide Italy 33 37.03N 14.54E
Palazzo San Gervasio Italy 33 40.56N 16.00E
Paldiski U.S.S.R. 41 59.20N 24.06E
Paleleh Indonesia 59 1.04N121.57E
Palembang Indonesia 58 2.59S104.50E
Palena Italy 33 41.59N 14.08E
Palencia Spain 26 42.01N 4.32W
Palencia *d.* Spain 26 42.30N 4.40W
Palenque Mexico 116 17.32N 91.59W
Palermo Italy 32 38.07N 13.21E
Palermo, Golfo di *g.* Italy 32 38.10N 13.30E
Palestine U.S.A. 111 31.46N 95.38W
Palestrina Italy 32 41.50N 12.53E
Paletwa Burma 56 21.25N 92.49E
Pāli India 62 25.46N 73.20E
Palimé Togo 76 6.55N 0.38E
Palinges France 19 46.33N 4.13E
Palisades Resr. U.S.A. 108 43.15N111.05W
Palit, Kep-i- *c.* Albania 34 41.24N 19.24E
Pālitāna India 62 21.31N 71.50E
Palizada Mexico 116 18.15N 92.05W
Palk Str. India/Sri Lanka 61 10.00N 79.40E
Pallinup *r.* Australia 89 34.29S118.54E
Palliser, C. New Zealand 86 41.35S175.15E
Pallu India 62 28.56N 74.13E
Palma Mozambique 79 10.48S 40.25E
Palma Spain 25 39.34N 2.39E
Palma, Bahía de *b.* Spain 25 39.27N 2.35E
Palma del Río Spain 27 37.42N 5.17W
Palma di Montechiaro Italy 32 37.11N 13.46E
Palmahim Israel 67 31.56N 34.42E
Palmanova Italy 30 45.54N 13.19E
Palmares Brazil 123 8.41S 35.36W
Palmas, C. Liberia 76 4.30N 7.55W
Palmas, Golfo di *g.* Italy 32 39.00N 8.30E
Palm Beach *town* U.S.A. 113 26.41N 80.02W
Palmeira dos Indios Brazil 123 9.25S 36.38W
Palmeirinhas, Punta das Angola 78 9.09S 12.58E
Palmer *r.* Australia 88 24.46S133.25E
Palmer U.S.A. 98 61.36N149.07W
Palmer Land Antarctica 128 74.00S 61.00W
Palmerston Canada 104 43.50N 80.51W
Palmerston New Zealand 86 45.29S170.43E
Palmerston, C. Australia 90 21.32S149.29E
Palmerston Atoll Cook Is. 84 18.04S163.10W
Palmerston North New Zealand 86 40.20S175.39E
Palmerton U.S.A. 115 40.48N 75.37W
Palmetto U.S.A. 113 27.31N 82.32W
Palmi Italy 33 38.21N 15.51E
Palmira Colombia 122 3.33N 76.17W
Palm Is. Australia 90 18.48S146.37E
Palms U.S.A. 114 43.37N 82.46W
Palm Springs *town* U.S.A. 109 33.50N116.33W
Palmyra I. Pacific Oc. 84 5.52N162.05W
Palmyras Pt. India 63 20.46N 87.02E
Paloh Indonesia 58 1.46N109.17E
Paloich Sudan 73 10.28N 32.32E
Palojoensuu Finland 40 68.17N 23.05E
Palomani *mtn.* Bolivia 124 14.38S 69.14W
Palopo Indonesia 59 3.01S120.12E
Palos, Cabo de *c.* Spain 25 37.38N 0.41W
Pålsboda Sweden 43 59.04N 15.20E
Palu Turkey 64 38.43N 39.56E
Palwal India 62 28.09N 77.20E
Pama U. Volta 76 11.15N 0.44E
Pamanukan Indonesia 59 6.16S107.46E
Pamekasan Indonesia 59 7.11S113.30E
Pameungpeuk Indonesia 59 7.39S107.40E
Pamiers France 20 43.07N 1.36E
Pamir *mts.* U.S.S.R. 52 37.50N 73.30E
Pamlico Sd. U.S.A. 113 35.20N 75.55W
Pampa U.S.A. 111 35.32N100.58W
Pampas *f.* Argentina 125 34.00S 64.00W
Pamplona Colombia 122 7.24N 72.38W
Pamplona Spain 25 42.49N 1.38W
Pana U.S.A. 110 39.23N 89.05W
Panaca U.S.A. 108 37.47N114.23W
Panache, L. Canada 104 46.15N 81.20W
Panagyurishte Bulgaria 34 42.39N 24.15E
Panaji India 60 15.29N 73.50E
Panama C. America 117 9.00N 80.00W
Panamá *town* Panama 117 8.57N 79.30W
Panama Sri Lanka 61 6.46N 81.47E
Panamá, Golfo de *g.* Panama 117 8.30N 79.00W
Panama City U.S.A. 113 30.10N 85.41W
Panamint Range *mts.* U.S.A. 109 36.30N117.20W
Panarea, Isola *i.* Italy 33 38.38N 15.05E
Panaro *r.* Italy 30 44.55N 11.25E
Panay *i.* Phil. 59 11.10N122.30E
Panayía Greece 34 39.56N 25.20E
Pandan Phil. 59 11.45N122.10E
Pandaria India 63 22.14N 81.25E
Pandeglang Indonesia 59 6.19S106.05E
Pāndharkawada India 63 20.01N 78.32E
Pāndhurna India 63 21.36N 78.31E
Pando *d.* Bolivia 124 11.20S 67.40W
Pando Uruguay 125 34.43S 55.57W
Panevežys U.S.S.R. 41 55.44N 24.21E
Panfilov U.S.S.R. 52 44.10N 80.01E
Panga Zaïre 78 1.51N 26.25E
Pangaíon Óros *mts.* Greece 34 40.50N 24.00E
Pangandaran Indonesia 59 7.41S108.40E
Pangani Tanga Tanzania 79 5.21S 39.00E
Pangi Zaïre 78 3.10S 26.38E
Pangkalpinang Indonesia 58 2.05S106.09E
Pang Long Burma 61 23.11N 98.45E
Pangnirtung Canada 99 66.05N 65.45W
Panīpat India 62 29.23N 76.58E
Panjāb Afghan. 62 34.22N 67.01E
Panjgūr Pakistan 62 26.58N 64.06E
Panjpāi Pakistan 62 29.55N 66.30E
Pankshin Nigeria 77 9.22N 9.25E
Panna India 63 24.43N 80.12E
Páno Lévkara Cyprus 66 34.55N 33.10E
Páno Plátres Cyprus 66 34.53N 32.52E
Pánormos Greece 35 37.38N 25.02E
Panshan China 54 41.10N122.01E
Pantano del Esla *l.* Spain 24 41.40N 5.50W
Pantelleria Italy 32 36.49N 11.57E
Pantelleria *i.* Italy 32 36.47N 12.00E
Pánuco Mexico 116 22.03N 98.10W
Panvel India 62 18.59N 73.06E
Pan Xian China 55 25.46N104.39E
Panyu China 55 23.00N113.30E
Paola Italy 33 39.22N 16.03E
Paola U.S.A. 110 38.35N 94.53W
Paoua C.A.R. 77 7.09N 16.20E
Paôy Pêt Thailand 56 13.41N102.34E
Papa Hawaiian Is. 85 19.12N155.53W
Pápa Hungary 37 47.19N 17.28E
Papa Stour *i.* U.K. 10 60.20N 1.42W
Papa Westray *i.* U.K. 10 59.22N 2.54W
Papeete Tahiti 85 17.32S149.34W
Papenburg W. Germany 38 53.05N 7.23E
Papenoo Tahiti 85 17.30S149.25W
Papetoai Îs. de la Société 85 17.29S149.52W
Paphos *see* Néa Páfos Cyprus 66
Papigochic *r.* Mexico 109 29.09N109.40W
Papillion U.S.A. 110 41.09N 96.04W
Papineau, Lac *l.* Canada 105 45.48N 74.46W
Papineau Prov. Park Canada 105 45.55N 75.20W
Papineauville Canada 105 45.37N 75.01W
Papua, G. of P.N.G. 90 8.30S145.00E
Papua New Guinea Austa. 87 6.00S144.00E
Papun Burma 56 18.05N 97.26E
Para *d.* Brazil 123 4.00S 53.00W
Paracatu Brazil 126 17.14S 46.52W
Paracatu *r.* Brazil 126 16.30S 45.10W
Paracel Is. S. China Sea 58 16.20N112.00E
Parachilna Australia 92 31.09S138.24E
Pārachinār Pakistan 62 33.54N 70.06E
Paraćin Yugo. 34 43.52N 21.24E
Pará de Minas Brazil 126 19.53S 44.35W
Paradip India 63 20.15N 86.35E
Paradise *r.* Canada 103 53.23N 57.18W
Paradise Calif. U.S.A. 108 39.46N121.37W
Paradise Nev. U.S.A. 109 36.09N115.10W
Paragonah U.S.A. 108 37.53N112.46W
Paragould U.S.A. 111 36.03N 90.29W
Paragua *r.* Venezuela 122 6.55N 62.55W
Paraguaçu *r.* Brazil 123 12.35S 38.59W
Paraguaná, Península de *pen.* Venezuela 122 11.50N 69.59W
Paraguarí Paraguay 126 25.36S 57.06W
Paraguay *r.* Argentina 126 27.30S 58.50W
Paraguay S. America 126 23.00S 57.00W
Paraíba *d.* Brazil 123 7.30S 36.30W
Paraíba *r.* Brazil 126 21.45S 41.10W
Paraibuna Brazil 126 23.29S 45.32W
Paraisópolis Brazil 126 22.33S 45.48W
Parakou Benin 77 9.23N 2.40E
Parálion Astrous Greece 35 37.25N 22.45E
Paramagudi India 61 9.33N 78.36E
Paramaribo Surinam 123 5.52N 55.14W
Paramithiá Greece 34 39.30N 20.35E
Paramonga Peru 122 10.42S 77.50W
Paraná Argentina 125 31.45S 60.30W

Paraná to **Pestovo**

Paraná *r.* Argentina **125** 34.00S 58.30W
Paranã Brazil **123** 12.33S 47.48W
Paranã *d.* Brazil **126** 24.30S 52.00W
Paranã *r.* Brazil **123** 12.30S 48.10W
Paranaguá Brazil **126** 25.32S 48.36W
Paranaíba Brazil **126** 19.44S 51.12W
Paranaíba *r.* Brazil **126** 20.00S 51.00W
Paranapanema *r.* Brazil **126** 22.30S 53.03W
Paranapiacaba, Serra *mts.* Brazil **126** 24.30S 49.15W
Paranavaí Brazil **126** 23.02S 52.36W
Paranéstion Greece **34** 41.16N 24.32E
Parangaba Brazil **123** 3.45S 38.33W
Paraparaumu New Zealand **86** 40.55S175.00E
Paratoo Australia **92** 32.46S139.40E
Paray-le-Monial France **19** 46.27N 4.07E
Pārbati *r.* India **62** 25.51N 76.36E
Pārbatipur Bangla. **63** 25.39N 88.55E
Parbhani India **62** 19.16N 76.47E
Parchim E. Germany **38** 53.25N 11.51E
Parczew Poland **37** 51.39N 22.54E
Pardes Hanna Israel **67** 32.28N 34.58E
Pārdi India **62** 20.31N 72.57E
Pardo *r.* Bahia Brazil **126** 15.40S 39.38W
Pardo *r.* Mato GrossoBrazil **126** 21.56S 52.07W
Pardo *r.* São PauloBrazil **126** 20.10S 48.36W
Pardubice Czech. **36** 50.03N 15.45E
Parecis, Serra dos *mts.* Brazil **122** 13.30S 58.30W
Paredes de Nava Spain **26** 42.09N 4.41W
Pareloup, Lac de *l.* France **20** 44.15N 2.45E
Parent Canada **102** 47.55N 74.35W
Parent, Lac *l.* Canada **102** 48.40N 77.03W
Parentis-en-Born France **20** 44.21N 1.05W
Parepare Indonesia **58** 4.03S119.40E
Párga Greece **35** 39.17N 20.23E
Pargas Finland **41** 60.18N 22.18E
Paria, Golfo de *g.* Venezuela **122** 10.30S 62.00W
Paria, Península de *pen.* Venezuela **122** 10.45N 62.30W
Pariaguán Venezuela **122** 8.51N 64.43W
Pariaman Indonesia **58** 0.36S100.09E
Parichi U.S.S.R. **37** 52.48N 29.25E
Parigi Indonesia **59** 0.49S120.10E
Parika Guyana **122** 6.51N 58.25W
Parima, Sierra *mts.* Venezuela **122** 2.30N 64.00W
Parinari Peru **122** 4.35S 74.25W
Paringa Australia **92** 34.10S140.49E
Parintins Brazil **123** 2.36S 56.44W
Paris Canada **104** 43.12N 80.23W
Paris France **19** 48.52N 2.20E
Paris Kiribati **85** 1.56N157.29W
Paris Ill. U.S.A. **110** 39.35N 87.41W
Paris Ky. U.S.A. **112** 38.13N 84.15W
Paris Tenn. U.S.A. **111** 36.19N 88.20W
Paris Tex. U.S.A. **111** 33.40N 95.33W
Parish U.S.A. **115** 43.24N 76.08W
Parisienne *d.* France **19** 48.30N 2.30E
Parisienne, Île *i.* Canada **104** 46.40N 84.44W
Parkano Finland **41** 62.01N 23.01E
Parkbeg Canada **101** 50.28N106.18W
Parker Ariz. U.S.A. **109** 34.09N114.17W
Parker Penn. U.S.A. **114** 41.06N 79.41W
Parker, C. Canada **99** 75.04N 79.40W
Parker Dam U.S.A. **109** 34.18N114.10W
Parkersburg U.S.A. **114** 39.17N 81.32W
Parkes Australia **93** 33.10S148.13E
Park Falls *town* U.S.A. **110** 45.56N 90.32W
Park Forest *town* U.S.A. **110** 41.35N 87.41W
Parkhill Canada **104** 43.09N 81.41W
Parkland U.S.A. **108** 47.09N122.26W
Park Range *mts.* U.S.A. **108** 40.00N106.30W
Parkton U.S.A. **115** 39.38N 76.40W
Parlākimidi India **63** 18.46N 84.05E
Parma Italy **30** 44.48N 10.20E
Parma U.S.A. **114** 41.22N 81.43W
Parnaguá Brazil **123** 10.17S 44.39W
Parnaíba Brazil **123** 2.58S 41.46W
Parnaíba *r.* Brazil **123** 2.58S 41.47W
Parnassós *mtn.* Greece **35** 38.17N 21.30E
Parndana Australia **92** 35.44S137.14E
Párnis *mtn.* Greece **35** 38.11N 23.42E
Párnon Óros *mts.* Greece **35** 37.18N 22.35E
Pärnu U.S.S.R. **41** 58.24N 24.32E
Pärnu *r.* U.S.S.R. **41** 58.23N 24.29E
Pārola India **62** 20.53N 75.07E
Paroo *r.* Australia **92** 31.30S143.34E
Páros Greece **35** 37.04N 25.08E
Páros *i.* Greece **35** 37.08N 25.12E
Parral Chile **125** 36.09S 71.50W
Parramatta Australia **93** 33.50S150.57E
Parras Mexico **111** 25.30N102.11W
Parras, Sierra de *mts.* Mexico **111** 25.20N102.10W
Parrett *r.* U.K. **13** 51.10N 3.00W
Parry Canada **101** 49.47N104.41W
Parry, C. Greenland **99** 76.50N 71.00W
Parry I. Canada **104** 45.18N 80.10W
Parry Is. Canada **99** 76.00N102.00W
Parry Sound *town* Canada **104** 45.21N 80.02W
Parsad India **62** 24.11N 73.42E
Parseta *r.* Poland **36** 54.12N 15.33E
Parsnip *r.* Canada **100** 55.10N123.02W
Parsons Kans. U.S.A. **111** 37.20N 95.16W
Parsons W.Va. U.S.A. **114** 39.06N 79.41W
Partanna Italy **32** 37.43N 12.53E
Parthenay France **18** 46.39N 0.15W
Partille Sweden **43** 57.44N 12.07E
Partinico Italy **32** 38.03N 13.07E
Partry Mts. Rep. of Ire. **15** 53.40N 9.30W
Paru *r.* Brazil **123** 1.33S 52.38W
Pārvatīpuram India **63** 18.47N 83.26E
Paryang China **63** 30.04N 83.28E
Parys R.S.A. **80** 26.54S 27.26E
Pasadena Calif. U.S.A. **109** 34.09N118.09W
Pasadena Tex. U.S.A. **111** 29.42N 95.13W
Pasaje Ecuador **122** 3.23S 79.50W
Pasawng Burma **56** 18.52N 97.18E
Pascagoula U.S.A. **111** 30.23N 88.31W
Paşcani Romania **37** 47.15N 26.44E
Pasco U.S.A. **108** 46.14N119.06W
Pascoag U.S.A. **115** 41.57N 71.42W
Pascua, Isla de *i.* Pacific Oc. **85** 27.08S109.23W
Pas-de-Calais *d.* France **19** 50.30N 2.20E
Pasewalk E. Germany **38** 53.30N 14.00E
Pasfield L. Canada **101** 58.25N105.20W
Pasinler Turkey **64** 39.59N 41.41E
Pasir Puteh Malaysia **58** 5.50N102.24E
Påskallavik Sweden **43** 57.10N 16.27E
Pasley, C. Australia **89** 33.55S123.30E
Pašman *i.* Yugo. **31** 43.58N 15.21E
Pasmore *r.* Australia **92** 31.07S139.48E
Pasni Pakistan **62** 25.16N 63.28E
Paso de Bermejo *f.* Argentina **121** 32.50S 70.00W
Paso de los Libres *town* Argentina **125** 29.45S 57.05W
Paso de los Toros *town* Uruguay **125** 32.49S 56.31W
Paso Robles U.S.A. **109** 35.38N120.41W
Paso Socompa *f.* Chile **121** 24.27S 68.18W
Paspébiac Canada **103** 48.01N 65.20W
Pasquia Hills Canada **101** 53.13N102.37W
Pasrūr Pakistan **62** 32.16N 74.40E
Passaic U.S.A. **115** 40.51N 74.08W
Passau W. Germany **39** 48.35N 13.28E
Passero, C. Italy **28** 36.40N 15.08E
Passero, Capo *c.* Italy **33** 36.40N 15.09E
Passo Fundo Brazil **126** 28.16S 52.20W
Passos Brazil **126** 20.45S 46.38W
Pastaza *r.* Peru **122** 4.50S 76.25W
Pasto Colombia **122** 1.12N 77.17W
Pastrana Spain **26** 40.25N 2.55W
Pasuquin Phil. **55** 18.25N120.37E
Pasuruan Indonesia **59** 7.38S112.54E
Patagonia *f.* Argentina **125** 42.20S 67.00W
Pātan India **62** 23.50N 72.07E
Patchogue U.S.A. **115** 40.46N 73.00W
Patea New Zealand **86** 39.46S174.29E
Pategi Nigeria **77** 8.44N 5.47E
Pate I. Kenya **79** 2.08S 41.02E
Paterna Spain **25** 39.30N 0.26W
Paternion Austria **39** 46.43N 13.38E
Paternò Italy **33** 37.34N 14.54E
Paterson U.S.A. **115** 40.55N 74.10W
Pathānkot India **62** 32.17N 75.39E
Pathfinder Resr. U.S.A. **108** 42.30N106.50W
Pathiong Sudan **73** 6.46N 30.54E
Pati Indonesia **59** 6.45S111.00E
Patía *r.* Colombia **122** 1.54N 78.30W
Patiāla India **62** 30.19N 76.23E
Pati Pt. Guam **84** 13.36N144.57E
Patkai Hills Burma **56** 26.30N 95.30E
Pátmos *i.* Greece **35** 37.20N 26.33E
Patna India **63** 25.36N 85.07E
Patnāgarh India **63** 20.43N 83.09E
Patos Brazil **123** 6.55S 37.15W
Patos, Lagoa dos *l.* Brazil **126** 31.00S 51.10W
Patos de Minas Brazil **126** 18.35S 46.32W
Patquía Argentina **124** 30.02S 66.55W
Pátrai Greece **35** 38.15N 21.44E
Patraïkós Kólpos *g.* Greece **35** 38.14N 21.15E
Patrasuy U.S.S.R. **44** 63.35N 61.50E
Patrickswell Rep. of Ire. **15** 52.36N 8.43W
Pattada Italy **32** 40.35N 9.07E
Pattani Thailand **56** 6.51N101.16E
Patterson Creek *r.* U.S.A. **114** 39.34N 78.23W
Patti Italy **33** 38.09N 14.58E
Patti, Golfo di *g.* Italy **33** 38.12N 15.05E
Pattoki Pakistan **62** 31.01N 73.51E
Patton U.S.A. **114** 40.38N 78.39W
Patuākhāli Bangla. **63** 22.21N 90.21E
Patuca *r.* Honduras **117** 15.50N 84.18W
Pātūr India **62** 20.27N 76.56E
Patuxent *r.* U.S.A. **115** 38.18N 76.25W
Pau France **20** 43.18N 0.22W
Pau, Gave de *r.* France **20** 43.33N 1.12W
Pauillac France **20** 45.12N 0.44W
Paúl do Mar Madeira Is. **127** 32.45N 17.14W
Paulhan France **20** 43.32N 3.27E
Paulina U.S.A. **108** 44.09N119.58W
Paulistana Brazil **123** 8.09S 41.09W
Paulo Afonso Brazil **123** 9.25S 38.15W
Paulsboro U.S.A. **115** 39.50N 75.15W
Pauls Valley *town* U.S.A. **111** 34.44N 97.13W
Paungde Burma **56** 18.30N 95.30E
Pauni India **63** 20.47N 79.38E
Pauri Madhya P. India **62** 25.32N 77.21E
Pauri Uttar P. India **63** 30.09N 78.47E
Pavia Italy **30** 45.10N 9.10E
Pavilly France **18** 49.34N 0.58E
Pavlikeni Bulgaria **34** 43.14N 25.20E
Pavlodar U.S.S.R. **9** 52.21N 76.59E
Pavlograd U.S.S.R. **45** 48.34N 35.50E
Pavlovo U.S.S.R. **44** 55.58N 43.05E
Pavlovsk U.S.S.R. **45** 50.28N 40.07E
Pavlovskaya U.S.S.R. **45** 46.18N 39.48E
Pavullo nel Frignano Italy **30** 44.20N 10.50E
Pawnee U.S.A. **111** 36.20N 96.48W
Pawtucket U.S.A. **115** 41.53N 71.23W
Paxoí *i.* Greece **35** 39.14N 20.12E
Paxton U.S.A. **110** 41.07N101.21W
Payerne Switz. **39** 46.49N 6.56E
Payette U.S.A. **108** 44.05N116.56W
Payne, L. Canada **99** 59.25N 74.00W
Paynes Find Australia **89** 29.15S117.41E
Paysandú Uruguay **125** 32.19S 58.05W
Pays de Caux *f.* France **18** 49.40N 0.40E
Pays de la Loire *d.* France **18** 47.30N 1.00W
Pazardzhik Bulgaria **34** 42.12N 24.20E
Pazardzhik *d.* Bulgaria **34** 42.10N 24.20E
Pazin Yugo. **31** 45.14N 13.56E
Pčinja *r.* Yugo. **34** 42.00N 21.45E
Peace *r.* Canada **100** 59.00N111.25W
Peace River *town* Canada **100** 56.15N117.18W
Peach Springs *town* U.S.A. **109** 35.32N113.25W
Peacock Hills Canada **98** 66.05N110.45W
Peak, The *mtn.* Ascension **127** 7.57S 14.21W
Peake *r.* Australia **92** 28.05S136.07E
Peak Hill *town* N.S.W. Australia **93** 32.47S148.13E
Peak Hill *town* W.A. Australia **88** 25.40S118.41E
Peak Range *mts.* Australia **90** 23.18S148.30E
Peale, Mt. U.S.A. **108** 38.26N109.14W
Pearl *r.* U.S.A. **111** 30.11N 89.32W
Pearland U.S.A. **111** 29.34N 95.17W
Pearsall U.S.A. **111** 28.53N 99.06W
Peary Land *f.* Greenland **96** 83.00N 35.00W
Pebane Mozambique **81** 17.14S 38.10E
Pebas Peru **122** 3.17S 71.55W
Peć Yugo. **34** 42.40N 20.17E
Pechenga U.S.S.R. **40** 69.28N 31.04E
Pechora U.S.S.R. **44** 65.14N 57.18E
Pechora *r.* U.S.S.R. **44** 68.10N 54.00E
Pechorskaya Guba *g.* U.S.S.R. **44** 69.00N 56.00E
Pechorskoye More *sea* U.S.S.R. **44** 69.00N 55.00E
Pecoraro, Monte *mtn.* Italy **33** 38.32N 16.20E
Pecos U.S.A. **111** 31.25N103.30W
Pecos *r.* U.S.A. **111** 29.42N101.22W
Pécs Hungary **31** 46.05N 18.13E
Pécs *d.* Hungary **31** 46.05N 18.10E
Peddie R.S.A. **80** 33.12S 27.07E
Pedras Salgadas Portugal **26** 41.32N 7.36W
Pedregulho Brazil **126** 20.15S 47.29W
Pedreiras Brazil **123** 4.32S 44.40W
Pedrinhas Brazil **123** 11.12S 37.41W
Pedro Afonso Brazil **123** 8.59S 48.11W
Pedro de Valdivia Chile **124** 22.36S 69.40W
Pedrógão Grande Portugal **27** 39.55N 8.09W
Pedro Juan Caballero Paraguay **126** 22.30S 55.44W
Pedro Muñoz Spain **27** 39.24N 2.58W
Peduyim Israel **67** 31.20N 34.37E
Peebinga Australia **92** 34.55S140.57E
Peebles U.K. **14** 55.39N 3.12W
Peebles U.S.A. **112** 38.57N 83.14W
Peekskill U.S.A. **115** 41.17N 73.55W
Peel *r.* Canada **98** 68.13N135.00W
Peel U.K. **12** 54.14N 4.42W
Peel Inlet Australia **89** 32.35S115.44E
Peel Pt. Canada **98** 73.22N114.35W
Peene *r.* E. Germany **38** 54.09N 13.46E
Peera Peera Poolanna L. Australia **90** 26.43S137.42E
Peerless L. Canada **100** 56.37N114.35W
Peery L. Australia **92** 30.44S143.34E
Pegasus B. New Zealand **86** 43.15S173.00E
Pegin Albania **34** 41.04N 19.44E
Pegnitz W. Germany **38** 49.45N 11.33E
Pegnitz *r.* W. Germany **38** 49.29N 11.00E
Pego Spain **25** 38.51N 0.07W
Pegu Burma **56** 17.20N 96.36E
Pegu *d.* Burma **56** 17.30N 96.30E
Pegunungan Van Rees *mts.* Indonesia **59** 2.35S138.15E
Pegu Yoma *mts.* Burma **56** 18.30N 96.00E
Pehčevo Yugo. **34** 41.41N 23.03E
Pehuajó Argentina **125** 35.50S 61.50W
Peikang Taiwan **55** 23.35N120.19E
Peine W. Germany **38** 52.19N 10.13E
Peissenberg W. Germany **39** 47.48N 11.04E
Peixe Brazil **123** 12.03S 48.32W
Pei Xian China **54** 34.44N116.55E
Pekalongan Indonesia **59** 6.54S109.37E
Pekin U.S.A. **110** 40.34N 89.40W
Peking *see* Beijing China **54**
Pelabuanratu Indonesia **59** 7.00S106.32E
Pelat, Mont *mtn.* France **21** 44.16N 6.42E
Peleaga *mtn.* Romania **37** 45.22N 22.54E
Pelee, Pt. Canada **114** 41.54N 82.30W
Pelee I. Canada **114** 41.46N 82.39W
Peleng *i.* Indonesia **59** 1.30S123.10E
Peleniya U.S.S.R. **37** 47.58N 27.48E
Pelican U.S.A. **100** 57.55N136.10W
Pelister *mtn.* Yugo. **34** 41.00N 21.12E
Pelješac, Poluotok *pen.* Yugo. **31** 42.58N 17.20E
Pelkum W. Germany **38** 51.39N 7.45E
Pélla *site* Greece **34** 40.45N 22.33E
Pelleg i Drinit *b.* Albania **34** 41.45N 19.28E
Pellegrino, Cozzo *mtn.* Italy **33** 39.45N 16.03E
Pello Finland **40** 66.47N 24.00E
Pellston U.S.A. **104** 45.33N 84.47W
Pellworm *i.* W. Germany **38** 54.31N 8.38E
Pelly *r.* Canada **98** 62.50N137.35W
Pelly Bay *town* Canada **99** 68.38N 89.45W
Pelly L. Canada **99** 65.59N101.12W
Peloncillo Mts. U.S.A. **109** 32.16N109.00W
Peloponnisos *f.* Greece **35** 37.30N 22.00E
Peloritani, Monti *mts.* Italy **33** 38.00N 15.25E
Pelotas Brazil **126** 31.45S 52.20W
Pelvoux, Massif du *f.* France **21** 44.55N 6.20E
Pemalang Indonesia **59** 6.53S109.21E
Pematangsiantar Indonesia **58** 2.59N 99.01E
Pemba Mozambique **81** 13.02S 40.30E
Pemba Zambia **79** 16.33S 27.20E
Pemba I. Tanzania **79** 5.10S 39.45E
Pemberton Australia **89** 34.28S116.01E
Pemberton Canada **100** 50.20N122.48W
Pembina *r.* Canada **100** 54.45N114.15W
Pembroke Canada **105** 45.49N 77.07W
Pembroke U.K. **13** 51.41N 4.57W
Pembroke U.S.A. **113** 32.09N 81.39W
Peña, Sierra de la *mts.* Spain **25** 42.30N 0.50W
Penacook U.S.A. **115** 43.17N 71.37W
Penafiel Portugal **26** 41.12N 8.17W
Peñafiel Spain **26** 41.36N 4.07W
Peñagolosa *mtn.* Spain **25** 40.13N 0.21W
Peñalara *mtn.* Spain **26** 40.51N 3.57W
Peñaranda de Bracamonte Spain **26** 40.54N 5.12W
Pen Argyl U.S.A. **115** 40.52N 75.16W
Peñarroya *mtn.* Spain **25** 40.24N 0.40W
Peñarroya-Pueblonuevo Spain **26** 38.18N 5.16W
Penarth U.K. **13** 51.26N 3.11W
Peñas, Cabo de *c.* Spain **26** 43.39N 5.51W
Penas, Golfo de *g.* Chile **125** 47.20S 75.00W
Pendálofon Greece **34** 40.14N 21.12E
Pende *r.* Chad **77** 7.30N 16.20E
Pendembu Eastern Sierra Leone **76** 8.09N 10.42W
Pendine U.K. **13** 51.44N 4.33W
Pendleton U.S.A. **108** 45.40N118.47W
Penedo Brazil **123** 10.16S 36.33W
Penedono Portugal **26** 40.59N 7.24W
Penela Portugal **27** 40.02N 8.23W
Penetanguishene Canada **104** 44.47N 79.55W
Penfield U.S.A. **114** 41.13N 78.34W
Penganga *r.* India **63** 19.53N 79.09E
Penge Zaïre **78** 5.31S 24.37E
Penghu Liedao *is.* Taiwan **55** 23.35N119.32E
Pengshui China **55** 29.17N108.13E
Peniche Portugal **27** 39.21N 9.23W
Penicuik U.K. **14** 55.49N 3.13W
Peninsular Malaysia *d.* Malaysia **58** 5.00N102.00E
Peñíscola Spain **25** 40.21N 0.25E
Penmarc'h, Pointe de *c.* France **18** 47.48N 4.22W
Penne Italy **31** 42.27N 13.55E
Penne-d'Agenais France **20** 44.23N 0.49E
Penneshaw Australia **92** 35.42S137.55E
Pennsauken U.S.A. **115** 39.58N 75.04W
Pennsboro U.S.A. **114** 39.17N 80.58W
Penns Grove U.S.A. **115** 39.43N 75.28W
Pennsylvania *d.* U.S.A. **114** 40.45N 77.30W
Penn Yan U.S.A. **114** 42.40N 77.03W
Penny Highland *mtn.* Canada **99** 67.10N 66.50W
Penobscot *r.* U.S.A. **112** 44.30N 68.50W
Penola Australia **92** 37.23S140.21E
Penong Australia **89** 31.55S133.01E
Penonomé Panama **117** 8.30N 80.20W
Penrhyn Atoll Cook Is. **85** 9.00S158.00W
Penrith Australia **93** 33.47S150.44E
Penrith U.K. **12** 54.40N 2.45W
Penryn U.K. **13** 50.10N 5.07W
Pensacola U.S.A. **113** 30.26N 87.12W
Pensacola Mts. Antarctica **128** 84.00S 45.00W
Penshurst Australia **92** 37.52S142.20E
Pentecost I. Vanuatu **84** 15.42S168.10E
Penticton Canada **100** 49.30N119.30W
Pentland Australia **90** 20.32S145.24E
Pentland Firth *str.* U.K. **14** 58.40N 3.00W
Pentland Hills U.K. **14** 55.50N 3.20W
Penylan L. Canada **101** 61.50N106.20W
Penza U.S.S.R. **44** 53.11N 45.00E
Penzance U.K. **13** 50.07N 5.32W
Penzberg W. Germany **39** 47.45N 11.23E
Penzhinskaya Guba *g.* U.S.S.R. **51** 61.00N163.00E
Peoria Ariz. U.S.A. **109** 33.35N112.14W
Peoria Ill. U.S.A. **110** 40.43N 89.38W
Pepacton Resr. U.S.A. **115** 42.06N 74.54W
Peper Sudan **73** 7.04N 33.00E
Pepperell U.S.A. **115** 42.40N 71.35W
Perabumulih Indonesia **58** 3.29S104.14E
Perales de Alfambra Spain **25** 40.38N 1.00W
Perche, Collines du *hills* France **18** 48.25N 0.40E
Percival Lakes Australia **88** 21.25S125.00E
Perdido, Monte *mtn.* Spain **25** 42.40N 0.05E
Pereira Colombia **122** 4.47N 75.46W
Perekop U.S.S.R. **45** 46.10N 33.42E
Perené *r.* Peru **124** 11.02S 74.19W
Perevolotskiy U.S.S.R. **44** 51.10N 54.15E
Pereyaslav-Khmelnitskiy U.S.S.R. **37** 50.05N 31.28E
Pergamino Argentina **125** 33.53S 60.35W
Pergine Valsugana Italy **30** 46.04N 11.14E
Pergola Italy **30** 43.34N 12.50E
Perham U.S.A. **110** 46.36N 95.34W
Péribonca *r.* Canada **103** 48.45N 72.05W
Pericos Mexico **109** 25.03N107.42W
Périers France **18** 49.11N 1.25W
Périgueux France **20** 45.11N 0.43E
Perija, Sierra de *mts.* Venezuela **122** 10.30N 72.30W
Perleberg E. Germany **38** 53.04N 11.51E
Perm U.S.S.R. **44** 58.01N 56.10E
Përmet Albania **34** 40.15N 20.21E
Pernambuco *d.* Brazil **123** 8.00S 39.00W
Pernatty L. Australia **92** 31.31S137.14E
Pernik Bulgaria **34** 42.36N 23.03E
Pernik *d.* Bulgaria **34** 42.36N 23.02E
Perniö Finland **41** 60.12N 23.08E
Péronne France **19** 49.56N 2.56E
Perosa Argentina Italy **30** 44.58N 7.10E
Pérouse, Bahía la *b.* I. de Pascua **85** 27.04S109.20W
Perpignan France **20** 42.41N 2.53E
Perranporth U.K. **13** 50.21N 5.09W
Perro, Punta del *c.* Spain **27** 36.45N 6.26W
Perros-Guirec France **18** 48.49N 3.27W
Perry Fla. U.S.A. **113** 30.08N 83.36W
Perry Iowa U.S.A. **110** 41.50N 94.06W
Perry Mich. U.S.A. **104** 42.50N 84.13W
Perry Okla. U.S.A. **111** 36.17N 97.17W
Perryton U.S.A. **111** 36.24N100.48W
Perryville U.S.A. **111** 37.43N 89.52W
Persberg Sweden **43** 59.45N 14.15E
Persepolis *ruins* Iran **65** 29.55N 53.00E
Perth Australia **89** 31.58S115.49E
Perth Canada **105** 44.54N 76.15W
Perth U.K. **14** 56.24N 3.28W
Perth Amboy U.S.A. **115** 40.31N 74.16W
Pertuis France **21** 43.41N 5.30E
Peru S. America **122** 10.00S 75.00W
Peru Ill. U.S.A. **110** 41.19N 89.11W
Peru Basin Pacific Oc. **85** 19.00S 96.00W
Peru-Chile Trench Pacific Oc. **121** 23.00S 71.30W
Perugia Italy **30** 43.08N 12.22E
Perušić Yugo. **31** 44.39N 15.23E
Péruwelz Belgium **16** 50.32N 3.36E
Pervomaysk U.S.S.R. **37** 48.03N 30.50E
Pervouralsk U.S.S.R. **44** 56.59N 59.58E
Pesaro Italy **30** 43.54N 12.55E
Pescara Italy **31** 42.28N 14.13E
Pescara *r.* Italy **31** 42.28N 14.13E
Pescia Italy **30** 43.54N 10.41E
Peshāwar Pakistan **62** 34.01N 71.33E
Peshīn Jān Afghan. **62** 33.25N 61.28E
Peshkopi Albania **34** 41.41N 20.25E
Peshtera Bulgaria **34** 42.02N 24.18E
Pesmes France **19** 47.17N 5.34E
Peso da Régua Portugal **26** 41.10N 7.47W
Pesqueira Brazil **123** 8.24S 36.38W
Pesqueria *r.* Mexico **111** 25.55N 99.28W
Pessac France **20** 44.48N 0.38W
Peşteana Jiu Romania **37** 44.50N 23.15E
Pestovo U.S.S.R. **44** 58.32N 35.42E

Petah Tiqwa to Pofadder

Petah Tiqwa Israel **67** 32.05N 34.53E
Petalídhion Greece **35** 36.57N 21.55E
Petalión, Kólpos *g.* Greece **35** 37.59N 24.02E
Petaluma U.S.A. **108** 38.14N122.39W
Pétange Lux. **16** 49.32N 5.56E
Petare Venezuela **122** 10.31N 66.50W
Petatlán Mexico **116** 17.31N101.16W
Petauke Zambia **79** 14.16S 31.21E
Petawawa Canada **105** 45.54N 77.17W
Petawawa *r.* Canada **105** 45.55N 77.15W
Peterborough S.A. Australia **92** 33.00S138.51E
Peterborough Vic. Australia **92** 38.36S142.55E
Peterborough Canada **104** 44.18N 78.19W
Peterborough U.K. **13** 52.35N 0.14W
Peterborough U.S.A. **115** 42.53N 71.57W
Peterhead U.K. **14** 57.30N 1.46W
Peterlee U.K. **12** 54.45N 1.18W
Petermann Ranges *mts.* Australia **88** 25.00S129.46E
Peter Pond L. Canada **101** 55.55N108.44W
Petersburg Alas. U.S.A. **100** 56.49N132.58W
Petersburg Va. U.S.A. **113** 37.14N 77.24W
Petersburg W.Va. U.S.A. **114** 39.00N 79.09W
Petersfield U.K. **13** 51.00N 0.56W
Petilia Policastro Italy **33** 39.07N 16.47E
Petitot *r.* Canada **100** 60.14N123.29W
Petit St. Bernard, Col du *pass* France / Italy **30** 45.40N 6.53E
Petitsikapau L. Canada **103** 54.45N 66.25W
Petlād India **62** 22.30N 72.45E
Petoskey U.S.A. **112** 45.22N 84.59W
Petra *ruins* Jordan **66** 30.19N 35.26E
Petre, Pt. Canada **105** 43.50N 77.09W
Petrich Bulgaria **34** 41.24N 23.13E
Petrikov U.S.S.R. **37** 52.09N 28.30E
Petrinja Yugo. **31** 45.26N 16.17E
Petrodvorets U.S.S.R. **44** 59.50N 29.57E
Petrolia Canada **104** 42.52N 82.09W
Petrolina Brazil **123** 9.22S 40.30W
Petropavlovsk U.S.S.R. **9** 54.53N 69.13E
Petropavlovsk Kamchatskiy U.S.S.R. **51** 53.03N158.43E
Petrópolis Brazil **126** 22.30S 43.06W
Petroşani Romania **37** 45.25N 23.22E
Petrovaradin Yugo. **31** 45.16N 19.55E
Petrovsk U.S.S.R. **44** 52.20N 45.24E
Petrovsk Zabaykal'skiy U.S.S.R. **51** 51.20N108.55E
Petrozavodsk U.S.S.R. **44** 61.46N 34.19E
Petrus Steyn R.S.A. **80** 27.38S 28.08E
Peuerbach Austria **39** 48.21N 13.56E
Peureulak Indonesia **58** 4.48N 97.45E
Pevek U.S.S.R. **51** 69.41N170.19E
Peyruis France **21** 44.02N 5.56E
Pézenas France **20** 43.27N 3.25E
Pezinok Czech. **37** 48.18N 17.17E
Pezmog U.S.S.R. **44** 61.50N 51.45E
Pezu Pakistan **62** 32.19N 70.44E
Pfaffenhofen W. Germany **39** 48.31N 11.30E
Pfalzel W. Germany **39** 49.47N 6.41E
Pfarrkirchen W. Germany **39** 48.27N 12.56E
Pforzheim W. Germany **39** 48.54N 8.42E
Pfronten W. Germany **38** 47.34N 10.33E
Pfunds Austria **39** 46.58N 10.33E
Pfungstadt W. Germany **39** 49.48N 8.36E
Phagwāra India **62** 31.13N 75.47E
Phalodi India **62** 27.08N 72.22E
Phalsbourg France **19** 48.46N 7.16E
Phangan, Ko *i.* Thailand **58** 9.50N100.00E
Phangnga Thailand **56** 8.29N 98.31E
Phan Rang Vietnam **56** 11.34N109.00E
Phan Thiet Vietnam **56** 11.00N108.06E
Pharenda India **63** 27.06N 83.17E
Phariāro Pakistan **62** 27.12N 68.59E
Phat Diem Vietnam **55** 20.06N106.07E
Phatthalung Thailand **56** 7.38N100.04E
Phelps U.S.A. **114** 42.57N 77.03W
Phelps L. Canada **101** 59.15N103.15W
Phenix City U.S.A. **113** 32.28N 85.01W
Phet Buri Thailand **56** 13.00N 99.58E
Philadelphia Miss. U.S.A. **111** 32.46N 89.07W
Philadelphia N.Y. U.S.A. **105** 44.09N 75.43W
Philadelphia Penn. U.S.A. **115** 39.57N 75.07W
Philippeville Belgium **16** 50.12N 4.32E
Philippi U.S.A. **114** 39.09N 80.02W
Philippines Asia **59** 13.00N123.00E
Philippine Sea Pacific Oc. **84** 18.00N135.00E
Philippine Trench Pacific Oc. **59** 8.45N127.20E
Philipsburg Canada **105** 45.02N 73.05W
Philipsburg U.S.A. **114** 40.45N 78.14W
Philip Smith Mts. U.S.A. **96** 68.30N147.00W
Philipstown R.S.A. **80** 30.25S 24.26E
Phillip U.S.A. **110** 44.02N101.40W
Phillip Edward I. Canada **104** 45.58N 81.17W
Phillip I. Australia **93** 38.29S145.14E
Phillips *r.* Australia **89** 33.55S120.01E
Phillips Maine U.S.A. **112** 44.49N 70.21W
Phillips Wisc. U.S.A. **110** 45.41N 90.24W
Phillipsburg Kans. U.S.A. **110** 39.45N 99.19W
Phillipsburg N.J. U.S.A. **115** 40.42N 75.12W
Phillipson, L. Australia **92** 29.28S134.28E
Philo U.S.A. **114** 39.52N 81.55W
Phnom Penh *see* Phnum Pénh Kampuchea **56**
Phnum Pénh Kampuchea **56** 11.35N104.55E
Phoenicia U.S.A. **115** 42.05N 74.19W
Phoenix Ariz. U.S.A. **109** 33.27N112.05W
Phoenix N.Y. U.S.A. **115** 43.14N 76.18W
Phoenix I. Kiribati **84** 3.43S170.43W
Phoenix Is. Kiribati **84** 4.00S172.00W
Phoenixville Conn. U.S.A. **115** 41.51N 72.03W
Phoenixville Penn. U.S.A. **115** 40.08N 75.31W
Phon Thailand **56** 15.50N102.35E
Phôngsali Laos **56** 21.40N102.11E
Phou Loi *mtn.* Laos **56** 20.16N103.18E
Phu Huu Vietnam **55** 19.00N105.35E
Phukao Miang *mtn.* Thailand **61** 16.50N101.00E
Phuket Thailand **56** 7.55N 98.23E
Phuket, Ko *i.* Thailand **56** 8.10N 98.20E
Phu Ly Vietnam **55** 20.30N105.58E
Phumi Chuuk Vietnam **56** 10.50N104.28E
Phumi Sâmraông Kampuchea **56** 14.12N103.31E
Phu Quoc *i.* Kampuchea **56** 10.20N104.00E
Phu Tho Vietnam **56** 21.23N105.13E
Phu Vinh Vietnam **56** 9.57N106.20E
Piacá Brazil **123** 7.42S 47.18W
Piacenza Italy **30** 45.01N 9.40E
Pian *r.* Australia **93** 30.03S148.18E
Piana France **21** 42.14N 8.38E
Pianella Italy **31** 42.24N 14.02E
Piangil Australia **92** 35.04S143.20E
Pianoro Italy **30** 44.22N 11.20E
Pianosa *i.* Italy **30** 42.36N 10.04E
Piatra-Neamţ Romania **37** 46.56N 26.22E
Piauí *d.* Brazil **123** 7.45S 42.30W
Piauí *r.* Brazil **123** 6.14S 42.51W
Piave *r.* Italy **30** 45.32N 12.44E
Piawaning Australia **89** 30.51S116.22E
Piazza Armerina Italy **33** 37.23N 14.22E
Pibor *r.* Sudan **73** 8.26N 33.13E
Pibor Post Sudan **73** 6.48N 33.08E
Pic *r.* Canada **102** 48.38N 86.25W
Picardie *d.* France **19** 49.42N 2.40E
Pickens U.S.A. **114** 38.39N 80.13W
Pickerel *r.* Canada **104** 45.55N 80.50W
Pickerel River *town* Canada **104** 46.01N 80.45W
Pickering U.K. **12** 54.15N 0.46W
Pickford U.S.A. **104** 46.10N 84.22W
Pickle Crow Canada **102** 51.30N 90.04W
Pickwick L. *resr.* U.S.A. **111** 34.55N 88.10W
Picola Australia **93** 35.59S145.06E
Picos Brazil **123** 7.05S 41.28W
Picos Ancares, Sierra de *mts.* Spain **26** 42.51N 6.52W
Picquigny France **19** 49.57N 2.09E
Picton Australia **93** 34.12S150.35E
Picton Canada **105** 44.00N 77.08W
Picton New Zealand **86** 41.17S174.02E
Picún Leufú Argentina **125** 39.30S 69.15W
Pidálion, Akrotírion *c.* Cyprus **66** 34.56N 34.05E
Pidarak Pakistan **62** 25.51N 63.14E
Piedecuesta Colombia **122** 6.59N 73.03W
Piedicroce France **21** 42.23N 9.23E
Piedimonte Matese Italy **33** 41.21N 14.22E
Piedmont U.S.A. **113** 33.55N 85.39W
Piedrabuena Spain **27** 39.02N 4.10W
Piedrafita, Puerto de *pass* Spain **26** 42.40N 7.01W
Piedrahita Spain **26** 40.28N 5.19W
Piedras *r.* Peru **122** 12.30S 69.10W
Piedras, Punta *c.* Argentina **125** 35.25S 57.07W
Piedras Negras Mexico **111** 28.40N100.32W
Piedra Sola Uruguay **125** 32.04S 56.21W
Pielavesi Finland **40** 63.14N 26.45E
Pielinen *l.* Finland **44** 63.20N 29.50E
Piemonte *d.* Italy **30** 44.55N 8.00E
Pienza Italy **30** 43.04N 11.41E
Pierce U.S.A. **108** 46.29N115.48W
Pierr-Buffière France **20** 45.42N 1.21E
Pierre U.S.A. **110** 44.22N100.21W
Pierreville Canada **105** 46.04N 72.49W
Piesseville Australia **89** 33.11S117.12E
Piešťany Czech. **37** 48.36N 17.50E
Pietarsaari Finland **40** 63.40N 22.42E
Pietermaritzburg R.S.A. **80** 29.36S 30.23E
Pietersburg R.S.A. **80** 23.54S 29.27E
Pietrasanta Italy **30** 43.57N 10.14E
Piet Retief R.S.A. **80** 27.00S 30.49E
Pietrosu *mtn.* Romania **37** 47.36N 24.38E
Pietrosul *mtn.* Romania **37** 47.08N 25.11E
Pieve di Cadore Italy **30** 46.26N 12.22E
Pigailoe *i.* Caroline Is. **59** 8.08N146.40E
Pigeon U.S.A. **104** 43.50N 83.16W
Pigeon L. Canada **104** 44.30N 78.30W
Pigna Italy **30** 43.56N 7.40E
Pihtipudas Finland **40** 63.23N 25.34E
Pikalevo U.S.S.R. **44** 59.35N 34.07E
Pikangikum Canada **102** 51.49N 94.00W
Pikes Peak *mtn.* U.S.A. **108** 38.51N105.03W
Pikesville U.S.A. **114** 39.25N 77.25W
Piketberg R.S.A. **80** 32.54S 18.43E
Piketon U.S.A. **112** 39.03N 83.01W
Pikeville U.S.A. **113** 37.29N 82.33W
Pila Argentina **125** 36.00S 58.10W
Piła Poland **36** 53.09N 16.44E
Pilar Paraguay **126** 26.52S 58.23W
Pilar do Sul Brazil **126** 23.48S 47.45W
Pilcomayo *r.* Argentina / Paraguay **124** 25.15S 57.43W
Pīlībhīt India **63** 28.38N 79.48E
Pilica *r.* Poland **37** 51.52N 21.17E
Pilliga Australia **93** 30.23S148.55E
Pílos Greece **35** 36.55N 21.43E
Pilot Point *town* U.S.A. **111** 33.24N 96.58W
Pilsum W. Germany **38** 53.29N 7.04E
Pimba Australia **92** 31.18S136.47E
Pimenta Bueno Brazil **122** 11.40S 61.14W
Pina Spain **25** 41.29N 0.32W
Pinang, Pulau *i.* Malaysia **58** 5.30N100.10E
Pinar Turkey **35** 37.02N 27.57E
Pinarbaşi Turkey **64** 38.43N 36.23E
Pinar del Río Cuba **117** 22.24N 83.42W
Pincher Creek *town* Canada **100** 49.30N113.57W
Pinconning U.S.A. **104** 43.51N 83.59W
Píndhos Óros *mts.* Greece **34** 39.49N 21.14E
Pindiga Nigeria **77** 9.58N 10.53E
Pindi Gheb Pakistan **62** 33.14N 72.16E
Pindus Mts. *see* Píndhos Óros Greece **34**
Pindwāra India **62** 24.48N 73.04E
Pine *r.* Canada **100** 56.08N120.41W
Pine *r.* U.S.A. **104** 43.35N 84.08W
Pine, C. Canada **103** 46.37N 53.30W
Pine Bluff *town* U.S.A. **111** 34.13N 92.01W
Pine Bluffs *town* U.S.A. **108** 41.11N104.04W
Pine City U.S.A. **110** 45.50N 92.59W
Pine Creek *town* Australia **88** 13.51S131.50E
Pine Creek *r.* U.S.A. **114** 41.10N 77.16W
Pinega U.S.S.R. **44** 64.42N 43.28E
Pinega *r.* U.S.S.R. **44** 63.51N 41.48E
Pine Grove U.S.A. **115** 40.33N 76.23W
Pinehouse L. Canada **101** 55.32N106.35W
Pine Is. U.S.A. **113** 26.35N 82.06W
Pine Point *town* Canada **100** 60.50N114.28W
Pine River *town* Canada **101** 51.45N100.40W
Pine River *town* U.S.A. **110** 46.43N 94.24W
Pinerolo Italy **30** 44.53N 7.21E
Pinetown R.S.A. **80** 29.49S 30.52E
Pineville U.S.A. **111** 31.19N 92.26W
Piney France **19** 48.22N 4.20E
Ping *r.* Thailand **56** 15.47N100.05E
Pingaring Australia **89** 34.45S118.34E
Pingba China **55** 26.25N106.15E
Pingdingshan Henan China **54** 33.38N113.30E
Pingdingshan Liaoning China **54** 41.28N124.45E
Pingdong Taiwan **55** 22.44N120.30E
Pingelap *i.* Pacific Oc. **84** 6.15N160.40E
Pingelly Australia **89** 32.34S117.04E
Pingle China **55** 24.38N110.38E
Pingliang China **54** 35.21N107.12E
Pingluo China **54** 38.56N106.34E
Pingnan China **55** 23.33N110.23E
Pingrup Australia **89** 33.33S118.30E
Pingtan *i.* China **55** 25.36N119.48E
Pingwu China **54** 32.25N104.36E
Pingxiang Guang. Zhuang.China **55** 22.07N106.42E
Pingxiang Jiangxi China **55** 27.36N113.48E
Pingyang China **55** 27.40N120.33E
Pingyao China **54** 37.12N112.08E
Pingyi China **54** 35.30N117.36E
Pingyuan China **55** 24.34N115.54E
Pinhal Brazil **126** 22.10S 46.46W
Pinhal Novo Portugal **27** 38.38N 8.55W
Pinhel Portugal **26** 40.46N 7.04W
Pini *i.* Indonesia **58** 0.10N 98.30E
Piniós *r.* Greece **34** 39.54N 22.45E
Pinjarra Australia **89** 32.37S115.53E
Pinnaroo Australia **92** 35.18S140.54E
Pinneberg W. Germany **38** 53.40N 9.47E
Pinos, Isla de *i.* Cuba **117** 21.40N 82.40W
Pinos-Puente Spain **27** 37.15N 3.45W
Pinrang Indonesia **58** 3.48S119.41E
Pins, Île des *i.* N. Cal. **84** 22.37S167.30E
Pins, Pointe aux *c.* Canada **104** 42.15N 81.51W
Pinsk U.S.S.R. **37** 52.08N 26.01E
Pinto Argentina **124** 29.09S 62.38W
Pinto Butte *mtn.* Canada **101** 49.22N107.25W
Pinyug U.S.S.R. **44** 60.10N 47.43E
Pinzgau *f.* Austria **39** 47.09N 12.30E
Piombino Italy **30** 42.55N 10.32E
Piorini, L. Brazil **122** 3.34S 63.15W
Piotrków Trybunalski Poland **37** 51.25N 19.42E
Piove di Sacco Italy **30** 45.18N 12.02E
Pipār India **62** 26.23N 73.32E
Piparia India **63** 22.45N 78.21E
Pipestone *r.* Ont. Canada **102** 52.48N 89.35W
Pipestone *r.* Sask. Canada **101** 58.40N105.45W
Pipestone U.S.A. **110** 43.58N 96.10W
Pipinas Argentina **125** 35.30S 57.19W
Piplān Pakistan **62** 32.17N 71.21E
Pipmouacane, Résr. Canada **103** 49.35N 70.30W
Piqua U.S.A. **112** 40.08N 84.14W
Piracicaba Brazil **126** 22.45S 47.40W
Piracicaba *r.* Brazil **126** 22.35S 48.14W
Piracuruca Brazil **123** 3.56S 41.42W
Piraeus *see* Piraiévs Greece **35**
Piraiévs Greece **35** 37.57N 23.38E
Piram I. India **62** 21.36N 72.41E
Piran Yugo. **31** 45.32N 13.34E
Pirassununga Brazil **126** 21.59S 47.25W
Pirdop Bulgaria **34** 42.42N 24.11E
Pírgos Greece **35** 37.41N 21.28E
Pírgos Greece **35** 36.38N 22.22E
Pirin Planina *mts.* Bulgaria **34** 41.40N 23.30E
Pirmasens W. Germany **39** 49.12N 7.36E
Pirna E. Germany **38** 50.58N 13.56E
Pirojpur Bangla. **63** 22.34N 89.59E
Pirón *r.* Spain **26** 41.23N 4.31W
Pirot Yugo. **34** 43.09N 22.39E
Pīr Panjāl Range *mts.* Jammu & Kashmir **62** 33.50N 74.30E
Piryatin U.S.S.R. **45** 50.14N 32.31E
Pisa Italy **30** 43.43N 10.23E
Pisciotta Italy **33** 40.07N 15.12E
Pisco Peru **122** 13.46S 76.12W
Piseco L. U.S.A. **115** 43.24N 74.33W
Písek Czech. **39** 49.19N 14.10E
Pishan China **52** 37.30N 78.20E
Pishin Pakistan **62** 30.35N 67.00E
Pishin Lora *r.* Pakistan **62** 29.09N 64.55E
Pissos France **20** 44.19N 0.47W
Pisticci Italy **33** 40.23N 16.34E
Pistoia Italy **30** 43.55N 10.54E
Pisuerga *r.* Spain **26** 41.33N 4.52W
Pisz Poland **37** 53.38N 21.49E
Pita Guinea **76** 11.05N 12.15W
Pitalito Colombia **122** 1.51N 76.01W
Pitarpunga, L. Australia **92** 34.23S143.32E
Pitcairn I. Pacific Oc. **85** 25.04S130.06W
Pite *r.* Sweden **40** 65.14N 21.32E
Piteå Sweden **40** 65.20N 21.30E
Piteşti Romania **37** 44.52N 24.51E
Pithāpuram India **61** 17.07N 82.16E
Píthion Greece **34** 41.24N 26.40E
Pithiviers France **19** 48.10N 2.15E
Pithoragarh India **63** 29.35N 80.13E
Piti Guam **84** 13.28N144.41E
Pitigliano Italy **30** 42.38N 11.40E
Pitlochry U.K. **14** 56.43N 3.45W
Pitomača Yugo. **31** 45.59N 17.14E
Pitt I. Canada **100** 53.35N129.45W
Pittsburg Kans. U.S.A. **111** 37.25N 94.42W
Pittsburg N.H. U.S.A. **105** 45.03N 71.21W
Pittsburg Tex. U.S.A. **111** 32.60N 94.58W
Pittsburgh U.S.A. **114** 40.26N 80.00W
Pittsfield U.S.A. **115** 42.27N 73.15W
Pittston U.S.A. **115** 41.19N 75.47W
Pittsville U.S.A. **115** 38.24N 75.52W
Pittville U.S.A. **108** 41.03N121.20W
Piūí Brazil **126** 20.28S 45.58W
Piura Peru **122** 5.15S 80.38W
Piuthān Nepal **63** 28.06N 82.54E
Piva *r.* Yugo. **31** 43.21N 18.51E
Pizzo Italy **33** 38.44N 16.10E
Placentia Canada **103** 47.15N 53.58W
Placentia B. Canada **103** 47.15N 54.30W
Plaćkovica *mts.* Yugo. **34** 41.45N 22.30E
Plain Dealing U.S.A. **111** 32.54N 93.42W
Plainfield Conn. U.S.A. **115** 41.41N 71.55W
Plainfield N.J. U.S.A. **115** 40.37N 74.26W
Plains U.S.A. **108** 47.27N114.53W
Plainview U.S.A. **111** 34.11N101.43W
Plakenska Planina *mts.* Yugo. **34** 41.10N 21.10E
Plampang Indonesia **58** 8.48S117.48E
Planá Czech. **39** 49.52N 12.44E
Plana, Isla *i.* Spain **25** 38.10N 0.28W
Plana Cays *is.* Bahamas **117** 21.31N 72.14W
Plantagenet Canada **105** 45.32N 75.00W
Plasencia Spain **27** 40.02N 6.05W
Plaški Yugo. **31** 45.05N 15.22E
Plassen Norway **41** 61.08N 12.31E
Plaster Rock *town* Canada **103** 46.54N 67.24W
Plasy Czech. **39** 49.56N 13.24E
Platani *r.* Italy **32** 37.23N 13.16E
Plate, R. *est. see* La Plata, Río de Argentina / Uruguay **125**
Plateau *d.* Nigeria **77** 8.50N 9.00E
Platí Greece **34** 40.38N 22.31E
Platí, Ákra *c.* Greece **34** 40.27N 24.00E
Platikambos Greece **34** 39.37N 22.32E
Platinum U.S.A. **98** 59.00N161.50W
Plato Colombia **122** 9.54N 74.46W
Platte *r.* U.S.A. **110** 41.04N 95.53W
Platteville U.S.A. **110** 42.44N 90.29W
Plattling W. Germany **39** 48.47N 12.54E
Plattsburgh U.S.A. **105** 44.42N 73.28W
Plau E. Germany **38** 53.27N 12.16E
Plauen E. Germany **38** 50.30N 12.08E
Plauer See *l.* E. Germany **38** 53.30N 12.20E
Plav Yugo. **34** 42.38N 19.57E
Plavsk U.S.S.R. **44** 53.40N 37.20E
Playa de Castilla *f.* Spain **27** 37.05N 6.35W
Pleasant City U.S.A. **114** 39.54N 81.34W
Pleasantville U.S.A. **115** 39.23N 74.32W
Pleasonton U.S.A. **111** 28.58N 98.29W
Pléaux France **20** 45.08N 2.14E
Pleiku Vietnam **56** 13.57N108.01E
Pleisse *r.* E. Germany **38** 51.20N 12.22E
Pléneuf France **18** 48.36N 2.33W
Plenty, B. of New Zealand **86** 37.40S176.50E
Plentywood U.S.A. **108** 48.47N104.34W
Plesetsk U.S.S.R. **44** 62.42N 40.21E
Pleshchenitsy U.S.S.R. **37** 54.24N 27.52E
Plessisville Canada **105** 46.14N 71.47W
Pleszew Poland **37** 51.54N 17.48E
Pleternica Yugo. **31** 45.17N 17.48E
Plétipi, Lac *l.* Canada **103** 51.44N 70.06W
Pleven Bulgaria **34** 43.25N 24.37E
Pleven *d.* Bulgaria **34** 43.25N 24.40E
Plješevica Yugo. **31** 44.30N 15.45E
Pljevlja Yugo. **34** 43.21N 19.21E
Ploče Yugo. **31** 43.04N 17.26E
Płock Poland **37** 52.33N 19.43E
Plöckenpass Austria / Italy **30** 46.36N 12.58E
Pločno Yugo. **31** 43.35N 17.34E
Ploërmel France **18** 47.56N 2.24W
Ploieşti Romania **37** 44.57N 26.02E
Plomárion Greece **35** 38.59N 26.22E
Plomb du Cantal *mtn.* France **20** 45.03N 2.46E
Plombières France **19** 47.58N 6.29E
Plön W. Germany **38** 54.09N 10.25E
Plonge, Lac la *l.* Canada **101** 55.05N107.15W
Płońsk Poland **37** 52.38N 20.23E
Plouay France **18** 47.55N 3.20W
Ploudalmézeau France **18** 48.32N 4.39W
Plouescat France **18** 48.40N 4.10W
Plouguenast France **18** 48.17N 2.43W
Plouha France **18** 48.41N 2.56W
Plovdiv Bulgaria **34** 42.09N 24.45E
Plovdiv *d.* Bulgaria **34** 42.08N 24.44E
Plum I. U.S.A. **115** 41.11N 72.12W
Plumtree Zimbabwe **80** 20.30S 27.50E
Plunkett Canada **101** 51.56N105.29W
Plymouth U.K. **13** 50.23N 4.09W
Plymouth Ind. U.S.A. **112** 41.20N 86.19W
Plymouth Mass. U.S.A. **115** 41.58N 70.41W
Plymouth N.H. U.S.A. **105** 43.45N 71.41W
Plymouth Ohio U.S.A. **114** 40.59N 82.40W
Plymouth Penn. U.S.A. **115** 41.14N 75.58W
Plymouth Vt. U.S.A. **115** 43.32N 72.45W
Plymouth Wisc. U.S.A. **110** 43.44N 87.58W
Plzeň Czech. **38** 49.45N 13.23E
Po *r.* Italy **30** 44.57N 12.04E
Pô U. Volta **76** 11.11N 1.10W
Pobé Benin **77** 7.00N 2.56E
Pobeda, Gora *mtn.* U.S.S.R. **51** 65.20N145.50E
Pobla de Segur Spain **25** 42.15N 0.58E
Pocahontas Canada **100** 53.15N118.00W
Pocahontas Ark. U.S.A. **111** 36.16N 90.58W
Pocahontas Iowa U.S.A. **110** 42.44N 94.40W
Pocatello U.S.A. **108** 42.52N112.27W
Pocklington U.K. **12** 53.56N 0.48W
Pocono Mts. U.S.A. **115** 41.10N 75.20W
Poços de Caldas Brazil **126** 21.48S 46.33W
Podĕbrady Czech. **36** 50.08N 15.07E
Podensac France **20** 44.39N 0.22W
Podgaytsy U.S.S.R. **37** 49.19N 25.10E
Podkamennaya Tunguska U.S.S.R. **51** 61.45N 90.13E
Podkamennaya Tunguska *r.* U.S.S.R. **51** 61.40N 90.00E
Podolsk U.S.S.R. **44** 55.23N 37.32E
Podor Senegal **76** 16.35N 15.02W
Podporozhye U.S.S.R. **44** 60.55N 34.02E
Podravska Slatina Yugo. **31** 45.42N 17.42E
Podujevó Yugo. **34** 42.54N 21.10E
Poel *i.* E. Germany **38** 54.00N 11.26E
Pofadder R.S.A. **80** 29.08S 19.22E

Poggibonsi to **Prachatice**

Poggibonsi Italy **30** 43.28N 11.09E
Pogoniani Greece **34** 40.00N 20.25E
Pogradec Albania **34** 40.57N 20.48E
Pogrebishche U.S.S.R. **37** 49.30N 29.15E
Poh Indonesia **59** 1.00S122.50E
P'ohang S. Korea **53** 36.00N129.26E
Pohorje Yugo. **31** 46.30N 15.20E
Poiana Mare Romania **34** 43.57N 23.05E
Poinsett, C. Antarctica **128** 65.35S113.00E
Point Arena *f.* U.S.A. **108** 38.55N123.41W
Pointe-à-Pitre Guadeloupe **117** 16.14N 61.32W
Pointe-au-Baril *town* Canada **104** 45.35N 80.30W
Pointe-au-Baril Station *town* Canada **104** 45.36N 80.23W
Pointe aux Anglais *town* Canada **103** 49.34N 67.10W
Pointe-aux-Trembles *town* Canada **105** 45.39N 73.30W
Pointe-Claire Canada **105** 45.26N 73.50W
Point Edward *town* Canada **104** 43.00N 82.24W
Pointe Noire *town* Congo **78** 4.46S 11.53E
Point Hope *town* U.S.A. **98** 68.21N166.41W
Point Lookout *town* Australia **93** 30.33S152.20E
Point Marion *town* U.S.A. **114** 39.44N 79.53W
Point of Rocks *town* U.S.A. **114** 39.17N 77.32W
Point Pelee Nat. Park Canada **104** 41.57N 82.30W
Point Pleasant *town* N.J. U.S.A. **115** 40.05N 74.04W
Point Pleasant *town* W.Va. U.S.A. **114** 38.52N 82.08W
Poisson Blanc, Lac *l.* Canada **105** 46.00N 75.45W
Poissy France **19** 48.56N 2.03E
Poitiers France **18** 46.35N 0.20E
Poitou-Charentes *d.* France **20** 46.00N 0.00
Poix France **19** 49.47N 1.59E
Poix-Terron France **19** 49.39N 4.39E
Pokaran India **62** 26.55N 71.55E
Pokataroo Australia **93** 29.37S148.44E
Pokhara Nepal **63** 28.12N 83.59E
Poko Zaïre **78** 3.08N 26.51E
Pokoinu Rarotonga Cook Is. **84** 21.12S159.50W
Polacca U.S.A. **109** 35.50N110.23W
Pola de Laviana Spain **26** 43.15N 5.34W
Pola de Lena Spain **26** 43.10N 5.49W
Pola de Siero Spain **26** 43.23N 5.40W
Polān Iran **65** 25.29N 61.15E
Poland Europe **37** 52.30N 19.00E
Polatli Turkey **64** 39.34N 32.08E
Polch W. Germany **39** 50.18N 7.18E
Polda Australia **92** 33.30S135.10E
Pole Zaïre **78** 2.51S 23.12E
Polesye *f.* U.S.S.R. **37** 52.15N 28.00E
Poli Cameroon **77** 8.30N 13.15E
Políaigos *i.* Greece **35** 36.45N 24.38E
Policastro, Golfo di *g.* Italy **33** 40.00N 15.30E
Poligny France **19** 46.50N 5.43E
Polikastron Greece **34** 41.00N 22.34E
Polikhnitos Greece **35** 39.04N 26.10E
Pólis Cyprus **66** 35.02N 32.26E
Polistena Italy **33** 38.25N 16.05E
Políyiros Greece **34** 40.23N 23.27E
Polk U.S.A. **114** 41.22N 79.56W
Polla Italy **33** 40.30N 15.30E
Pollino, Monte *mtn.* Italy **33** 39.55N 16.11E
Pollock Reef Australia **89** 34.28S123.40E
Polnovat U.S.S.R. **50** 63.47N 65.54E
Polonnoye U.S.S.R. **37** 50.10N 27.30E
Polotsk U.S.S.R. **44** 55.30N 28.43E
Polperro U.K. **13** 50.19N 4.31W
Polski Trŭmbesh Bulgaria **34** 43.20N 25.38E
Polson U.S.A. **108** 47.41N114.09W
Poltava U.S.S.R. **45** 49.35N 34.35E
Polunochnoye U.S.S.R. **44** 60.52N 60.28E
Polyarnyy U.S.S.R. **44** 69.14N 33.30E
Polynesia *is.* Pacific Oc. **84** 4.00S165.00W
Pomarkku Finland **41** 61.42N 22.00E
Pombal Brazil **123** 6.45S 37.45W
Pombal Portugal **27** 39.55N 8.38W
Pomene Mozambique **81** 22.53S 35.33E
Pomeranian Bay E. Germany / Poland **38** 54.06N 14.25E
Pomeroy Ohio U.S.A. **114** 39.02N 82.02W
Pomeroy Wash. U.S.A. **108** 46.28N117.36W
Pomona Namibia **80** 27.09S 15.18E
Pomona U.S.A. **109** 34.04N117.45W
Pompano Beach *town* U.S.A. **113** 26.14N 80.07W
Pompei *site* Italy **33** 40.45N 14.30E
Pompey's Pillar *town* U.S.A. **108** 45.59N107.56W
Ponape *i.* Pacific Oc. **84** 6.55N158.15E
Ponca City U.S.A. **111** 36.42N 97.05W
Ponce Puerto Rico **117** 18.00N 66.40W
Pondicherry India **61** 11.59N 79.50E
Pond Inlet *str.* Canada **99** 72.30N 75.00W
Ponds, I. of Canada **103** 53.24N 55.55W
Ponferrada Spain **26** 42.33N 6.35W
Pongani P.N.G. **90** 9.05S148.35E
Pongo *r.* Sudan **73** 8.52N 27.40E
Pongola *r.* Mozambique **81** 26.13S 32.38E
Ponnāni India **60** 10.46N 75.54E
Ponnyadaung Range *mts.* Burma **56** 22.30N 94.20E
Ponoka Canada **100** 52.42N113.40W
Ponorogo Indonesia **59** 7.51S111.30E
Ponoy U.S.S.R. **44** 67.02N 41.03E
Ponoy *r.* U.S.S.R. **44** 67.00N 41.10E
Pons France **20** 45.35N 0.33W
Pons Spain **25** 41.55N 1.12E
Ponsul *r.* Portugal **27** 39.40N 7.31W
Ponta Grossa Brazil **126** 25.00S 50.09W
Pont-à-Mousson France **19** 48.54N 6.04E
Pontão Portugal **27** 39.55N 8.22W
Ponta Porā Brazil **126** 22.27S 55.39W
Pontarlier France **19** 46.54N 6.22E
Pontassieve Italy **30** 43.46N 11.26E
Pont-Audemer France **18** 49.21N 0.31E
Pontaumur France **20** 45.52N 2.40E
Pont-Aven France **18** 47.51N 3.45W
Pontax *r.* Canada **102** 51.30N 78.48W
Pont Canavese Italy **30** 45.25N 7.36E
Pontchartrain, L. U.S.A. **111** 30.10N 90.10W
Pontchâteau France **18** 47.26N 2.05W
Pont-Croix France **18** 48.02N 4.29W
Pont d'Ain France **21** 46.03N 5.20E
Pont-de-Salars France **20** 44.17N 2.44E
Pont de Suert Spain **25** 42.24N 0.45E
Pont-de-Vaux France **21** 46.26N 4.56E
Pontecorvo Italy **32** 41.27N 13.40E
Ponte da Barca Portugal **26** 41.48N 8.25W
Pontedera Italy **30** 43.40N 10.38E
Ponte de Sor Portugal **27** 39.15N 8.01W
Ponte do Lima Portugal **26** 41.46N 8.35W
Pontefract U.K. **12** 53.42N 1.19W
Ponteix Canada **101** 49.49N107.30W
Ponte Nova Brazil **126** 20.25S 42.54W
Pontevedra Spain **26** 42.26N 8.38W
Pontevedra *d.* Spain **26** 42.35N 8.35W
Pontevedra, Ría de *est.* Spain **26** 42.22N 8.45W
Pontgibaud France **20** 45.50N 2.51E
Pontiac Ill. U.S.A. **110** 40.54N 88.36W
Pontiac Mich. U.S.A. **104** 42.37N 83.18W
Pontiac Prov. Park Canada **105** 46.36N 76.32W
Pontianak Indonesia **58** 0.05S109.16E
Pontivy France **18** 48.04N 2.59W
Pont-l'Abbé France **18** 47.52N 4.13W
Pont l'Évêque France **18** 49.18N 0.11E
Pontoise France **19** 49.03N 2.06E
Pontorson France **18** 48.33N 1.31W
Pontremoli Italy **30** 44.22N 9.53E
Pontresina Switz. **39** 46.28N 9.53E
Pontrilas U.K. **13** 51.56N 2.53W
Pont Rouge Canada **105** 46.45N 71.42W
Pont-sur-Yonne France **19** 48.17N 3.12E
Pontypool Canada **104** 44.06N 78.38W
Pontypool U.K. **13** 51.42N 3.01W
Pontypridd U.K. **13** 51.36N 3.21W
Ponziane, Isole *is.* Italy **32** 40.55N 12.57E
Poochera Australia **92** 32.42S134.52E
Poole U.K. **13** 50.42N 2.02W
Pooncarie Australia **92** 33.23S142.34E
Poopelloe, L. Australia **92** 31.39S144.00E
Poopó, Lago de *l.* Bolivia **124** 19.00S 67.00W
Popayán Colombia **122** 2.27N 76.32W
Poperinge Belgium **16** 50.51N 2.44E
Popes Creek *town* U.S.A. **114** 38.09N 76.58W
Popilta Australia **92** 33.15S141.49E
Popilta L. Australia **92** 33.09S141.45E
Popintsi Bulgaria **34** 42.25N 24.17E
Poplar *r.* Canada **101** 53.00N 97.18W
Poplar U.S.A. **108** 48.07N105.12W
Poplar Bluff *town* U.S.A. **111** 36.45N 90.24W
Poplarville U.S.A. **111** 30.51N 89.32W
Popocatépetl *mtn.* Mexico **116** 19.02N 98.38W
Popokabaka Zaïre **78** 5.41S 16.40E
Popoli Italy **31** 42.10N 13.50E
Popondetta P.N.G. **90** 8.45S148.15E
Popovo Bulgaria **34** 43.21N 26.18E
Poppi Italy **30** 43.43N 11.46E
Poprad Czech. **37** 49.03N 20.18E
Popricani Romania **37** 47.18N 27.31E
Porāli *r.* Pakistan **62** 25.30N 66.25E
Porbandar India **62** 21.38N 69.36E
Por Chaman Afghan. **62** 33.08N 63.51E
Porcher I. Canada **100** 54.00N130.30W
Porcuna Spain **27** 37.52N 4.11W
Porcupine *r.* U.S.A. **98** 66.25N145.20W
Porcupine Hills Canada **101** 52.30N101.45W
Pordenone Italy **32** 45.57N 12.39E
Pordim Bulgaria **34** 43.23N 24.51E
Poreč Yugo. **31** 45.13N 13.37E
Pori Finland **41** 61.29N 21.47E
Porirua New Zealand **86** 41.08S174.50E
Porjus Sweden **40** 66.57N 19.50E
Porkhov U.S.S.R. **44** 57.43N 29.31E
Porkkala Finland **41** 59.59N 24.26E
Porlamar Venezuela **122** 11.01N 63.54W
Porma *r.* Spain **26** 42.29N 5.28W
Pornic France **18** 47.07N 2.06W
Porog U.S.S.R. **44** 63.50N 38.32E
Poronaysk U.S.S.R. **51** 49.13N142.55E
Póros Greece **35** 37.30N 23.30E
Porosozero U.S.S.R. **44** 62.45N 32.48E
Porrentruy Switz. **39** 47.25N 7.05E
Porretta Terme Italy **30** 44.09N 10.59E
Porsangen *est.* Norway **40** 70.58N 25.30E
Porsangerhalvöya *pen.* Norway **40** 70.50N 25.00E
Porsgrunn Norway **42** 59.09N 9.40E
Porsuk *r.* Turkey **64** 39.41N 31.56E
Portachuela Bolivia **124** 17.21S 63.24W
Port Adelaide Australia **92** 34.52S138.30E
Portadown U.K. **15** 54.25N 6.27W
Portaferry U.K. **15** 54.23N 5.33W
Portage Penn. U.S.A. **114** 40.23N 78.41W
Portage Wisc. U.S.A. **110** 43.33N 89.28W
Portage du Fort Canada **105** 45.36N 76.38W
Portage la Prairie *town* Canada **101** 49.57N 98.25W
Port Alberni Canada **100** 49.14N124.48W
Port Albert Australia **93** 38.09S146.40E
Portalegre Portugal **27** 39.17N 7.26W
Portalegre *d.* Portugal **27** 39.10N 7.40W
Portales U.S.A. **111** 34.11N103.20W
Port Alfred R.S.A. **80** 33.36S 26.52E
Port Alice Canada **100** 50.25N127.25W
Port Allegany U.S.A. **114** 41.49N 78.17W
Port Angeles U.S.A. **108** 48.07N123.27W
Port Antonio Jamaica **117** 18.10N 76.27W
Port Arthur Australia **91** 43.08S147.50E
Port Arthur U.S.A. **111** 29.55N 93.55W
Port Augusta Australia **92** 32.30S137.46E
Port au Port Canada **103** 48.33N 58.45W
Port-au-Prince Haiti **117** 18.33N 72.20W
Port Austin U.S.A. **104** 44.03N 83.01W
Port Bergé Madagascar **81** 15.33S 47.40E
Port Blair India **56** 11.40N 92.40E
Port Bolster Canada **104** 44.20N 79.10W
Port Bou Spain **25** 42.25N 3.09E
Port Bouet Ivory Coast **76** 5.14N 3.58W
Port Bradshaw *b.* Australia **90** 12.30S136.42E
Port Broughton Australia **92** 33.36S137.56E
Port Burwell Canada **104** 42.39N 80.49W
Port Campbell Australia **92** 38.37S143.04E
Port Canning India **63** 22.18N 88.40E
Port Carling Canada **104** 45.07N 79.35W
Port Cartier Canada **103** 50.01N 66.53W
Port Chalmers New Zealand **86** 45.49S170.37E
Port Chester U.S.A. **115** 41.00N 73.40W
Port Clinton U.S.A. **114** 41.31N 82.56W
Port Colborne Canada **104** 42.53N 79.14W
Port Coquitlam Canada **100** 49.20N122.45W
Port Credit Canada **104** 43.33N 79.35W
Port Curtis Australia **90** 23.50S151.13E
Port Dalhousie Canada **104** 43.12N 79.16W
Port-de-Paix Haiti **117** 19.57N 72.50W
Port Dover Canada **104** 42.47N 80.12W
Port Edward R.S.A. **80** 31.03S 30.13E
Portel Portugal **27** 38.18N 7.42W
Portela Brazil **126** 21.38S 41.59W
Port Elgin Canada **104** 44.26N 81.24W
Port Elizabeth R.S.A. **80** 33.57S 25.34E
Port Ellen U.K. **14** 55.38N 6.12W
Port-en-Bessin France **18** 49.21N 0.45W
Port Erin U.K. **12** 54.05N 4.45W
Porter Landing Canada **100** 58.46N130.05W
Porterville R.S.A. **80** 33.01S 19.00E
Porterville U.S.A. **109** 36.04N119.01W
Porte-Vecchio France **22** 41.35N 9.16E
Port Fairy Australia **92** 38.23S142.17E
Port Gentil Gabon **78** 0.40S 8.46E
Port Germein Australia **92** 33.01S138.00E
Port Gibson U.S.A. **111** 31.58N 90.58W
Portglenone U.K. **15** 54.52N 6.30W
Port Harcourt Nigeria **77** 4.43N 7.05E
Port Harrison *see* Inoucdjouac Canada **99**
Port Hawkesbury Canada **103** 45.37N 61.21W
Porthcawl U.K. **13** 51.28N 3.42W
Port Hedland Australia **88** 20.24S118.36E
Port Henry U.S.A. **105** 44.03N 73.28W
Porthill U.S.A. **108** 49.00N116.30W
Porthmadog U.K. **12** 52.55N 4.08W
Port Hope Canada **104** 43.57N 78.18W
Port Hope U.S.A. **104** 43.57N 82.43W
Port Huron U.S.A. **114** 42.58N 82.27W
Portimão Portugal **27** 37.08N 8.32W
Port Isaac B. U.K. **13** 50.36N 4.50W
Portiţei, Gura *f.* Romania **29** 44.40N 29.00E
Port Jefferson U.S.A. **115** 40.57N 73.04W
Port Jervis U.S.A. **115** 41.22N 74.41W
Port Keats Australia **88** 14.15S129.35E
Port Kenny Australia **92** 33.09S134.42E
Portland N.S.W. Australia **93** 33.20S150.00E
Portland Vic. Australia **92** 38.21S141.38E
Portland Canada **105** 44.41N 76.13W
Portland Maine U.S.A. **112** 43.39N 70.17W
Portland Oreg. U.S.A. **108** 45.33N122.36W
Portland Tex. U.S.A. **111** 27.53N 97.20W
Portland Pt. Ascension **127** 7.58S 14.26W
Port-La-Nouvelle France **20** 43.01N 3.03E
Port Laoise Rep. of Ire. **15** 53.03N 7.20W
Port Lavaca U.S.A. **111** 28.37N 96.38W
Port Lincoln Australia **92** 34.43S135.49E
Port Loko Sierra Leone **76** 8.50N 12.50W
Port Loring Canada **104** 45.56N 79.58W
Port Louis France **18** 47.43N 3.21W
Port Luck Canada **104** 46.20N 83.52W
Port MacDonnell Australia **92** 38.03S140.46E
Port Macquarie Australia **93** 31.28S152.25E
Port Maitland N.S. Canada **103** 43.59N 66.09W
Port Maitland Ont. Canada **104** 42.52N 79.34W
Portmarnock Rep. of Ire. **15** 53.25N 6.09W
Port Menier Canada **103** 49.49N 64.20W
Port Moresby P.N.G. **90** 9.30S147.07E
Port Musgrave *b.* Australia **90** 11.59S142.00E
Portnaguiran U.K. **14** 58.15N 6.10W
Port Neill Australia **92** 34.07S136.20E
Port Nelson Canada **101** 57.03N 92.36W
Portneuf Canada **105** 46.42N 71.53W
Portneuf Prov. Park Canada **105** 47.12N 72.05W
Port Nolloth R.S.A. **80** 29.16S 16.54E
Port Norris U.S.A. **115** 39.15N 75.02W
Port-Nouveau Québec Canada **99** 58.35N 65.59W
Porto Portugal **26** 41.11N 8.36W
Porto *d.* Portugal **26** 41.15N 8.15W
Pôrto Alegre Brazil **126** 30.03S 51.10W
Porto Alexandre Angola **78** 15.55S 11.51E
Porto Amboim Angola **78** 10.45S 13.43E
Pôrto de Mós Portugal **27** 39.36N 8.39W
Pôrto de Moz Brazil **123** 1.45S 52.13W
Porto Empedocle Italy **32** 37.17N 13.32E
Porto Esperança Brazil **126** 19.36S 57.24W
Porto Farina Tunisia **32** 37.10N 10.12E
Pôrto Feliz Brazil **126** 23.11S 47.32W
Portoferraio Italy **30** 42.49N 10.19E
Port of Ness U.K. **14** 58.30N 6.13W
Pôrto Franco Brazil **123** 6.21S 47.25W
Port of Spain Trinidad **117** 10.38N 61.31W
Porto Grande Brazil **123** 0.42N 51.24W
Portogruaro Italy **32** 45.47N 12.50E
Pórto Lágo Greece **34** 41.01N 25.06E
Pörtom Finland **40** 62.42N 21.37E
Portomaggiore Italy **30** 44.42N 11.48E
Pôrto Mendes Brazil **126** 24.30S 54.20W
Porto Moniz Madeira Is. **127** 32.52N 17.12W
Pôrto Murtinho Brazil **126** 21.42S 57.52W
Porton U.K. **13** 51.08N 1.44W
Pôrto Nacional Brazil **123** 10.42S 48.25W
Porto-Novo Benin **77** 6.30N 2.47E
Port Ontario U.S.A. **115** 43.32N 76.11W
Porto Recanati Italy **31** 43.26N 13.40E
Porto San Giorgio Italy **31** 43.11N 13.48E
Porto Santo *i.* Madeira Is. **74** 33.04N 16.20W
Porto Santo Stefano Italy **30** 42.26N 11.07E
Porto Tolle Italy **30** 44.56N 12.22E
Porto Torres Italy **32** 40.50N 8.23E
Pôrto Valter Brazil **122** 8.15S 72.45W
Porto-Vecchio France **21** 41.35N 9.16E
Pôrto Velho Brazil **122** 8.45S 63.54W
Portoviejo Ecuador **122** 1.07S 80.28W
Portpatrick U.K. **14** 54.51N 5.07W
Port Perry Canada **104** 44.06N 78.57W
Port Phillip B. Australia **93** 38.05S144.50E
Port Pirie Australia **92** 33.11S138.01E
Port Radium Canada **98** 66.05N118.02W
Portree U.K. **14** 57.24N 6.12W
Port Renfrew Canada **100** 48.30N124.20W
Port Rowan Canada **104** 42.37N 80.28W
Portrush U.K. **15** 55.12N 6.40W
Port Said *see* Būr Sa'īd Egypt **66**
Port-Sainte-Marie France **20** 44.15N 0.24E
Port St. Joe U.S.A. **113** 29.49N 85.19W
Port St. Louis France **21** 43.23N 4.48E
Port Sanilac U.S.A. **114** 43.26N 82.33W
Port Saunders Canada **103** 50.39N 57.18W
Port Severn Canada **104** 44.47N 79.42W
Port Shepstone R.S.A. **80** 30.44S 30.27E
Port Simpson Canada **100** 54.32N130.25W
Portsmouth U.K. **13** 50.48N 1.06W
Portsmouth N.H. U.S.A. **115** 43.04N 70.46W
Portsmouth Ohio U.S.A. **112** 38.45N 82.59W
Portsmouth Va. U.S.A. **113** 36.50N 76.20W
Portsoy U.K. **14** 57.41N 2.41W
Port Stanley Canada **104** 42.40N 81.13W
Portstewart U.K. **15** 55.11N 6.43W
Port Sudan *see* Būr Sūdān Sudan **72**
Port Talbot U.K. **13** 51.35N 3.48W
Porttipahdan tekojärvi *resr.* Finland **40** 68.08N 26.40E
Port Townsend U.S.A. **108** 48.07N122.46W
Portugal Europe **24** 39.30N 8.05W
Portugalete Spain **26** 43.19N 3.01W
Portumna Rep. of Ire. **11** 53.06N 8.14W
Port Vendres France **20** 42.31N 3.07E
Port Victoria Australia **92** 34.30S137.30E
Portville U.S.A. **114** 42.02N 78.20W
Port Wakefield Australia **92** 34.12S138.11E
Porvenir Chile **125** 53.18S 70.22W
Porz W. Germany **38** 50.53N 7.03E
Porzuna Spain **27** 39.09N 4.09W
Posada Italy **32** 40.38N 9.43E
Posada *r.* Italy **32** 40.39N 9.45E
Posadas Argentina **124** 27.25S 55.48W
Posavina *f.* Yugo. **31** 45.20N 17.00E
Poschiavo Switz. **39** 46.18N 10.04E
Posen U.S.A. **104** 45.16N 83.42W
Posets, Pico de *mtn.* Spain **25** 42.39N 0.25E
Posht *r.* Iran **65** 29.09N 58.09E
Positano Italy **33** 40.38N 14.29E
Poso Indonesia **59** 1.23S120.45E
Posse Brazil **126** 14.05S 46.22W
Possidhonia *site* Greece **35** 37.40N 24.00E
Pössneck E. Germany **38** 50.42N 11.37E
Post U.S.A. **111** 33.12N101.23W
Postavy U.S.S.R. **44** 55.07N 26.50E
Poste-de-la-Baleine *town* Canada **102** 55.20N 77.40W
Poste Maurice Cortier Algeria **74** 22.18N 1.05E
Poste Weygand Algeria **74** 24.29N 0.40E
Postmasburg R.S.A. **80** 28.19S 23.03E
Postojna Yugo. **31** 45.47N 14.13E
Postoli U.S.S.R. **37** 52.30N 28.00E
Potamós Greece **35** 36.38N 22.59E
Potchefstroom R.S.A. **80** 26.42S 27.05E
Poteau U.S.A. **111** 35.03N 94.37W
Potelu, Lacul *l.* Romania **34** 43.44N 24.20E
Potenza Italy **33** 40.38N 15.49E
Potes Spain **26** 43.09N 4.37W
Potgietersrus R.S.A. **80** 24.11S 29.00E
Poti *r.* Brazil **123** 5.01S 42.48W
Poti U.S.S.R. **45** 42.11N 41.41E
Potiskum Nigeria **77** 11.40N 11.03E
Potomac *r.* U.S.A. **114** 38.00N 76.18W
Potomac, North Branch *r.* U.S.A. **114** 39.15N 79.21W
Potomac, South Branch *r.* U.S.A. **114** 39.04N 78.59W
Potosí Bolivia **124** 19.35S 65.45W
Potosí *d.* Bolivia **124** 21.00S 67.00W
Potosi Cerro *mtn.* Mexico **111** 24.50N100.15W
Pototan Phil. **59** 10.54N122.38E
Potsdam E. Germany **38** 52.24N 13.04E
Potsdam *d.* E. Germany **38** 52.40N 12.50E
Potsdam U.S.A. **105** 44.40N 74.59W
Pottstown U.S.A. **115** 40.15N 75.38W
Pottsville U.S.A. **115** 40.41N 76.12W
Pouancé France **18** 47.44N 1.11W
Poughkeepsie U.S.A. **115** 41.42N 73.56W
Poultney U.S.A. **115** 43.31N 73.14W
Pouso Alegre Brazil **126** 22.13S 45.49W
Pouté Senegal **74** 15.42N 14.10W
Poûthisăt Kampuchea **56** 12.27N103.50E
Pouzauges France **18** 46.47N 0.50W
Povenets U.S.S.R. **44** 62.52N 34.05E
Póvoa de Varzim Portugal **26** 41.23N 8.46W
Povorino U.S.S.R. **45** 51.12N 42.15E
Powassan Canada **104** 46.05N 79.22W
Powder *r.* U.S.A. **108** 46.44N105.26W
Powder River *town* U.S.A. **108** 43.03N106.58W
Powell U.S.A. **108** 44.45N108.46W
Powell, L. U.S.A. **108** 37.25N110.45W
Powell Creek *town* Australia **88** 18.05S133.40E
Powell River *town* Canada **100** 49.22N124.31W
Powers U.S.A. **102** 45.42N 87.31W
Powers Lake *town* U.S.A. **110** 48.34N102.39W
Powhatan Point *town* U.S.A. **114** 39.52N 80.49W
Pownal U.S.A. **115** 42.46N 73.14W
Powys *d.* U.K. **13** 52.26N 3.26W
Poyang Hu *l.* China **55** 29.10N116.20E
Požarevac Yugo. **37** 44.38N 21.12E
Poza Rica Mexico **97** 20.34N 97.26W
Poza Rica de Hidalgo Mexico **116** 20.34N 97.26W
Požega Yugo. **34** 43.50N 20.02E
Poznań Poland **36** 52.25N 16.53E
Pozo Alcón Spain **27** 37.42N 2.56W
Pozoblanco Spain **26** 38.22N 4.51W
Pozo-Cañada Spain **25** 38.48N 1.45W
Pozuela de Alarcón Spain **26** 40.26N 3.49W
Pozzallo Italy **33** 36.43N 14.52E
Pozzuoli Italy **33** 40.49N 14.07E
Prachatice Czech. **38** 49.01N 14.00E

Qila Saifullāh to Rauch

Qila Saifullāh Pakistan **62** 30.43N 68.21E
Qilian Shan *mts.* China **52** 38.30N 99.20E
Qimantag *mts.* China **52** 37.45N 89.40E
Qimen China **55** 29.50N117.38E
Qinā Egypt **64** 26.10N 32.43E
Qinā, Wādī *r.* Egypt **64** 26.07N 32.42E
Qingdao China **54** 36.02N120.25E
Qinghai *d.* China **63** 34.20N 91.00E
Qinghai Hu *l.* China **52** 36.40N100.00E
Qingjian China **54** 37.02N110.06E
Qingjiang China **55** 28.01N115.30E
Qing Jiang Shuiku *resr.* China **55** 30.00N112.12E
Qinglong Guizhou China **55** 25.47N105.12E
Qinglong Hebei China **54** 40.24N118.53E
Qingshui Jiang *r.* China **55** 28.08N110.06E
Qing Xian China **54** 38.35N116.48E
Qingxu China **54** 37.36N112.21E
Qingyang China **54** 36.03N107.52E
Qingyuan Guangdong China **55** 23.42N113.00E
Qingyuan Jilin China **54** 42.05N125.01E
Qingyuan Zhejiang China **55** 27.37N119.03E
Qing Zang Gaoyuan *f.* China **63** 33.40N 86.00E
Qing Zang Gaoyuan *see* Tibetan Plateau China **52**
Qinhuangdao China **54** 39.52N119.42E
Qin Ling *mts.* China **54** 33.30N109.00E
Qin Xian China **54** 36.45N112.41E
Qinyang China **54** 35.06N112.57E
Qinzhou China **55** 21.58N108.34E
Qionghai China **55** 19.12N110.31E
Qiongshan China **55** 19.59N110.30E
Qiongzhou Haixia *str.* China **55** 20.09N110.20E
Qipanshan China **54** 42.05N117.37E
Qiqihar China **53** 47.23N124.00E
Qira China **52** 37.02N 80.53E
Qiryat Bialik Israel **67** 32.50N 35.05E
Qiryat Gat Israel **67** 31.37N 34.47E
Qiryat Motzkin Israel **67** 32.50N 35.04E
Qiryat Shemona Israel **67** 33.13N 35.35E
Qiryat Tiv'on Israel **67** 32.43N 35.08E
Qiryat Yam Israel **67** 32.51N 35.04E
Qishn S. Yemen **60** 15.25N 51.40E
Qishon *r.* Israel **67** 32.49N 35.02E
Qiuxizhen China **55** 29.54N104.40E
Qi Xian Henan China **54** 34.30N114.50E
Qi Xian Henan China **54** 35.35N114.08E
Qom Iran **65** 34.40N 50.57E
Qonggyai China **63** 29.03N 91.41E
Qornet'es Sauda *mtn.* Lebanon **66** 34.17N 36.04E
Qoṭūr Iran **65** 38.28N 44.25E
Quabbin Resr. U.S.A. **115** 42.22N 72.18W
Quadeville Canada **105** 45.18N 77.24W
Quairading Australia **89** 32.00S117.22E
Quakenbrück W. Germany **38** 52.40N 7.57E
Quakertown U.S.A. **115** 40.26N 75.21W
Qu'ali China **55** 29.46N117.15E
Quambatook Australia **92** 35.52S143.36E
Quambone Australia **93** 30.54S147.55E
Quang Ngai Vietnam **56** 15.09N108.50E
Quang Tri Vietnam **56** 16.44N107.10E
Quang Yen Vietnam **56** 20.56N106.49E
Quan Long Vietnam **56** 9.11N105.09E
Quannan China **55** 24.45N114.32E
Quantico U.S.A. **114** 38.31N 77.17W
Quanzhou Fujian China **55** 24.57N118.36E
Quanzhou Guang. Zhuang.China **55** 26.00N111.00E
Qu'Appelle *r.* Canada **101** 50.33N101.20W
Quaraí Brazil **125** 30.23S 56.27W
Quaraí *r.* Brazil **125** 30.12S 57.36W
Quarryville U.S.A. **115** 39.54N 76.10W
Quartu Sant'Elena Italy **32** 39.14N 9.11E
Quartzsite U.S.A. **109** 33.40N114.13W
Quatsino Sd. Canada **100** 50.42N127.58W
Qūchān Iran **65** 37.04N 58.29E
Queanbeyan Australia **93** 35.24S149.17E
Québec Canada **105** 46.50N 71.20W
Québec *d.* Canada **103** 51.20N 68.45W
Quebracho Uruguay **125** 31.57S 57.53W
Quedlinburg E. Germany **38** 51.48N 11.09E
Queen Anne U.S.A. **115** 38.55N 75.57W
Queen Charlotte Canada **100** 53.18N132.04W
Queen Charlotte Is. Canada **100** 53.00N132.00W
Queen Charlotte Sd. Canada **100** 51.30N129.30W
Queen Charlotte Str. Canada **100** 51.00N128.00W
Queen Elizabeth Is. Canada **99** 78.30N 99.00W
Queen Maud G. Canada **99** 68.30N 99.00W
Queen Maud Range *mts.* Antarctica **128** 86.20S165.00W
Queens Channel Australia **88** 14.46S129.24E
Queenscliff Australia **93** 38.17S144.42E
Queensland *d.* Australia **90** 23.30S144.00E
Queenstown Australia **91** 42.07S145.33E
Queenstown New Zealand **86** 45.03S168.41E
Queenstown R.S.A. **80** 31.52S 26.51E
Queenstown U.S.A. **115** 38.59N 76.09W
Queguay Grande *r.* Uruguay **125** 32.09S 58.09W
Queimadas Brazil **123** 10.58S 39.38W
Quela Angola **78** 9.18S 17.05E
Quelimane Mozambique **79** 17.53S 36.57E
Quemado U.S.A. **109** 34.20N108.30W
Quemoy *i.* China **55** 24.30N118.20E
Quentico Prov. Park Canada **102** 48.20N 91.30W
Quequén Argentina **125** 38.34S 58.42W
Querétaro Mexico **116** 20.38N100.23W
Querétaro *d.* Mexico **116** 21.03N100.00W
Querobabi Mexico **109** 30.03N111.01W
Quesada Spain **27** 37.51N 3.04W
Queshan China **54** 32.48N114.01E
Quesnel Canada **100** 53.05N122.30W
Quesnel *r.* Canada **100** 52.58N122.29W
Questembert France **18** 47.40N 2.27W
Quetta Pakistan **62** 30.12N 67.00E
Quettehou France **18** 49.36N 1.18W
Quevedo Ecuador **122** 0.59S 79.27W
Quezaltenango Guatemala **116** 14.50N 91.30W
Quezon City Phil. **59** 14.39N121.01E
Quibala Angola **78** 10.48S 14.56E
Quibaxi Angola **78** 8.34S 14.37E
Quibdo Colombia **122** 5.40N 76.38W
Quiberon France **18** 47.29N 3.07W
Quibocolo Angola **78** 6.20S 15.05E
Quicama Nat. Park Angola **78** 9.40S 13.30E
Quiet L. Canada **100** 61.05N133.05W
Quilán, C. Chile **125** 43.16S 74.27W
Quilengues Angola **78** 14.09S 14.04E
Quillabamba Peru **122** 12.50S 72.50W
Quillacollo Bolivia **124** 17.26S 66.17W
Quillan France **20** 42.52N 2.11E
Quillota Chile **125** 32.53S 71.16W
Quilon India **60** 8.53N 76.38E
Quilpie Australia **90** 26.37S144.15E
Quilpué Chile **125** 33.03S 71.27W
Quimbele Angola **78** 6.29S 16.25E
Quimilí Argentina **124** 27.35S 62.25W
Quimper France **18** 48.00N 4.06W
Quimperlé France **18** 47.52N 3.33W
Quincy Ill. U.S.A. **110** 39.56N 91.23W
Quincy Mass. U.S.A. **115** 42.15N 71.01W
Quincy Wash. U.S.A. **108** 47.14N119.51W
Qui Nhon Vietnam **56** 13.47N109.11E
Quintanar de la Orden Spain **27** 39.34N 3.03W
Quintana Roo *d.* Mexico **117** 19.00N 88.00W
Quinte, B. of Canada **105** 44.07N 77.15W
Quinter U.S.A. **110** 39.04N100.14W
Quintin France **18** 48.24N 2.55W
Quinto Spain **25** 41.25N 0.29W
Quinzau Angola **78** 6.51S 12.46E
Quionga Mozambique **79** 10.37S 40.31E
Quipar *r.* Spain **25** 38.14N 1.36W
Quirigua *ruins* Guatemala **117** 15.20N 89.25W
Quirimbo Angola **78** 10.41S 14.16E
Quiroga Spain **26** 42.29N 7.16W
Quiros, C. Vanuatu **84** 14.55S167.01E
Quissanga Mozambique **79** 12.24S 40.33E
Quissico Mozambique **81** 24.42S 34.44E
Quitapa Angola **78** 10.10S 18.16E
Quiterajo Mozambique **79** 11.46S 40.25E
Quito Ecuador **122** 0.14S 78.30W
Qu Jiang *r.* China **55** 30.02N106.20E
Qumigxung China **63** 30.53N 86.38E
Qumrān *site* Jordan **67** 31.44N 35.27E
Quorn Australia **92** 32.20S138.02E
Qurayyah, Wādī *r.* Egypt **66** 30.26N 34.01E
Qurdūd Sudan **73** 10.17N 29.56E
Quṣrah Jordan **67** 32.05N 35.20E
Qū' Wishām *f.* Oman **71** 18.55N 55.55E
Quxian China **55** 30.50N106.54E
Qu Xian China **55** 28.59N118.56E
Quyon Canada **105** 45.31N 76.14W
Qüzü China **63** 29.21N 90.39E

R

Raab *r. see* Rába Austria **31**
Raahe Finland **40** 64.41N 24.29E
Raalte Neth. **16** 52.22N 6.17E
Ra'anana Israel **67** 32.11N 34.53E
Raasay *i.* U.K. **14** 57.25N 6.05W
Rab Yugo. **31** 44.46N 14.46E
Rab *i.* Yugo. **31** 44.45N 14.45E
Rába *r.* Hungary **31** 47.42N 17.38E
Raba Indonesia **58** 8.27S118.45E
Rabaçal *r.* Portugal **26** 41.30N 7.12W
Rábade Spain **26** 43.07N 7.37W
Rabak Sudan **73** 13.09N 32.44E
Rabang China **63** 33.03N 80.29E
Rabat Morocco **74** 34.02N 6.51W
Rabbit L. Canada **104** 47.00N 79.37W
Rabbitskin *r.* Canada **100** 61.47N120.42W
Rābor Iran **65** 29.18N 56.56E
Rabyānah Libya **72** 24.14N 21.59E
Rabyānah, Ṣaḥrā' *f.* Libya **75** 24.30N 21.00E
Racconigi Italy **30** 44.46N 7.46E
Raccoon Creek U.S.A. **114** 40.02N 82.24W
Race, C. Canada **103** 46.40N 53.10W
Race Pt. U.S.A. **115** 42.04N 70.14W
Rach Gia Vietnam **56** 10.02N105.05E
Racibórz Poland **37** 50.06N 18.13E
Racine U.S.A. **110** 42.42N 87.50W
Raco U.S.A. **104** 46.24N 84.31W
Rădăuţi Romania **37** 47.51N 25.55E
Råde Norway **42** 59.21N 10.51E
Radeberg E. Germany **38** 51.13N 13.43E
Radebeul E. Germany **38** 51.06N 13.40E
Radeče Yugo. **31** 46.04N 15.11E
Radekhov U.S.S.R. **37** 50.18N 24.35E
Radford U.S.A. **113** 37.07N 80.34W
Rādhanpur India **62** 23.50N 71.36E
Radium Hill *town* Australia **92** 32.30S140.32E
Radium Hot Springs *town* Canada **100** 50.48N116.12W
Radnevo Bulgaria **34** 42.18N 25.56E
Radnice Czech. **38** 49.51N 13.37E
Radom Poland **37** 51.26N 21.10E
Radomir Bulgaria **34** 42.37N 23.04E
Radomsko Poland **37** 51.05N 19.25E
Radomyshl U.S.S.R. **37** 50.30N 29.14E
Radotin Czech. **38** 50.00N 14.22E
Radoviš Yugo. **34** 41.38N 22.28E
Radovljica Yugo. **31** 46.21N 14.11E
Radöy *i.* Norway **41** 60.38N 5.05E
Radstadt Austria **39** 47.23N 13.27E
Radstock U.K. **13** 51.17N 2.25W
Radstock, C. Australia **92** 33.11S134.21E
Radville Canada **101** 49.27N104.17W
Raḍwá, Jabal *mtn.* Saudi Arabia **64** 24.36N 38.18E
Rae Canada **100** 62.50N116.03W
Rāe Bareli India **63** 26.13N 81.14E
Raeren W. Germany **38** 50.41N 6.07E
Raeside, L. Australia **89** 29.30S122.00E
Rafaela Argentina **124** 31.16S 61.44W
Rafaḥ Egypt **67** 31.18N 34.15E
Rafaï C.A.R. **73** 4.58N 23.56E
Raffadali Italy **32** 37.24N 13.33E
Raffili Mission Sudan **73** 6.53N 27.58E
Rafḥā Saudi Arabia **64** 29.38N 43.30E
Rafsanjān Iran **65** 30.24N 56.00E
Raga Sudan **73** 8.28N 25.41E
Ragged, Mt. Australia **89** 33.27S123.27E
Ragunda Sweden **40** 63.06N 16.23E
Ragusa Italy **33** 36.55N 14.44E
Raha Indonesia **59** 4.50S122.43E
Raḥá, Ḥarrat ar *f.* Saudi Arabia **66** 28.00N 36.35E
Rahad *r.* Sudan **72** 14.28N 33.31E
Rahad al Bardī Sudan **73** 11.18N 23.53E
Rahīm Ki Bāzār Pakistan **62** 24.19N 69.09E
Rahīmyār Khān Pakistan **62** 28.25N 70.18E
Raiatea *i.* Îs. de la Société **85** 16.50S151.25W
Rāichūr India **60** 16.15N 77.20E
Raiganj India **63** 25.37N 88.07E
Raigarh India **63** 21.54N 83.24E
Rainbow Australia **92** 35.56S142.01E
Rainelle U.S.A. **113** 37.58N 80.47W
Rainier, Mt. U.S.A. **108** 46.52N121.46W
Rainy L. Canada/U.S.A. **102** 48.42N 93.10W
Rainy River *town* Canada **102** 48.43N 94.29W
Raipur India **63** 21.14N 81.38E
Raipur Uplands *mts.* India **63** 20.45N 82.30E
Rairākhol India **63** 21.03N 84.23E
Ra's Saudi Arabia **64** 23.35N 38.36E
Raisen India **63** 23.20N 77.48E
Raisin *r.* U.S.A. **104** 41.53N 83.20W
Raivavae *i.* Pacific Oc. **85** 23.52S147.40W
Rājahmundry India **61** 17.01N 81.52E
Rajāj Sudan **73** 10.55N 24.43E
Rajang *r.* Malaysia **58** 2.10N112.45E
Rājanpur Pakistan **62** 29.06N 70.19E
Rājapālaiyam India **60** 9.26N 77.36E
Rājasthān *d.* India **62** 26.15N 74.00E
Rājasthān Canal India **62** 31.10N 75.00E
Rājbāri Bangla. **63** 23.46N 89.39E
Rāj Gāngpur India **63** 22.11N 84.36E
Rājgarh Madhya P. India **62** 23.56N 76.58E
Rājgarh Rāj. India **62** 27.14N 76.38E
Rājgarh Rāj. India **62** 28.38N 75.23E
Rājkot India **62** 22.18N 70.47E
Rāj-Nāndgaon India **63** 21.06N 81.02E
Rājpīpla India **62** 21.47N 73.34E
Rājpur India **62** 21.56N 75.08E
Rājshāhi Bangla. **63** 24.22N 88.36E
Rājula India **62** 21.01N 71.34E
Rakahanga Atoll Cook Is. **84** 10.03S161.06W
Rakaia New Zealand **86** 43.45S172.01E
Rakaia *r.* New Zealand **86** 43.52S172.13E
Raka Zangbo *r.* China **63** 29.24N 87.58E
Rakhni Pakistan **62** 30.03N 69.55E
Rakhov U.S.S.R. **37** 48.02N 24.10E
Rakhshān *r.* Pakistan **62** 27.10N 63.25E
Rākin Jordan **67** 31.14N 35.42E
Rakitnoye U.S.S.R. **37** 51.18N 27.10E
Rakkestad Norway **42** 59.26N 11.21E
Rakops Botswana **80** 21.00S 24.32E
Rakov U.S.S.R. **37** 53.58N 26.59E
Rakovník Czech. **39** 50.05N 13.43E
Rakovski Bulgaria **34** 42.18N 24.58E
Rakulka U.S.S.R. **44** 62.19N 46.52E
Råkvåg Norway **40** 63.47N 10.10E
Rakvere U.S.S.R. **44** 59.22N 26.28E
Raleigh U.S.A. **113** 35.46N 78.39W
Raleigh B. U.S.A. **113** 35.47N 76.09W
Ralik Chain *is.* Pacific Oc. **84** 8.00N168.00E
Ram *r.* Canada **100** 62.01N123.41W
Rama Israel **67** 32.56N 35.22E
Rama Nicaragua **117** 12.09N 84.15W
Ramacca Italy **33** 37.23N 14.42E
Rāmah Saudi Arabia **65** 25.33N 47.08E
Ramales de la Victoria Spain **26** 43.15N 3.27W
Rām Allāh Jordan **67** 31.55N 35.12E
Ramallo Argentina **125** 33.28S 60.02W
Rāmānuj Ganj India **63** 23.48N 83.42E
Ramat Dawid Israel **67** 32.40N 35.12E
Ramat Gan Israel **67** 32.05N 34.48E
Ramat HaSharon Israel **67** 32.09N 34.50E
Ramat HaShofet Israel **67** 32.37N 35.06E
Ramat Yishay Israel **67** 32.42N 35.10E
Ramat Yohanan Israel **67** 32.47N 35.07E
Rambau, Lac *l.* Canada **103** 53.40N 70.10W
Rambervillers France **19** 48.21N 6.38E
Rambla del Judio *r.* Spain **25** 38.15N 1.27W
Rambouillet France **19** 48.39N 1.50E
Rām Dās India **62** 31.58N 74.55E
Rame Head U.K. **13** 50.18N 4.13W
Ramelton Rep. of Ire. **15** 55.02N 7.40W
Rāmgarh Bangla. **63** 22.59N 91.43E
Rāmgarh Bihār India **63** 23.38N 85.31E
Rāmgarh Rāj. India **62** 27.15N 75.11E
Rāmgarh Rāj. India **62** 27.22N 70.30E
Rāmhormoz Iran **65** 31.14N 49.37E
Ramillies Belgium **16** 50.39N 4.56E
Ramingstein Austria **39** 47.04N 13.50E
Ramis *r.* Ethiopia **73** 7.59N 41.34E
Ramla Israel **67** 31.56N 34.52E
Ramlo *mtn.* Ethiopia **73** 13.20N 41.45E
Rāmnagar India **63** 25.17N 83.02E
Ramnäs Sweden **43** 59.46N 16.12E
Ramona Calif. U.S.A. **109** 33.08N116.52W
Ramona Okla. U.S.A. **111** 36.32N 95.55W
Ramore Canada **102** 48.30N 80.25W
Ramos Arizpe Mexico **111** 25.33N100.58W
Ramot Naftali Israel **67** 33.06N 35.33E
Rāmpur Himachal P. India **63** 31.27N 77.38E
Rāmpur Uttar P. India **63** 28.49N 79.02E
Rampura India **62** 24.28N 75.26E
Ramree I. Burma **56** 19.06N 93.48E
Rāmsar Iran **65** 36.54N 50.41E
Ramsey England U.K. **13** 52.27N 0.06W
Ramsey I.o.M. U.K. **12** 54.19N 4.23W
Ramsey L. Canada **104** 47.15N 82.16W
Ramsgate U.K. **13** 51.20N 1.25E
Rāmshīr Iran **65** 30.54N 49.24E
Ramsjö Sweden **41** 62.11N 15.39E
Rāmtek India **63** 21.24N 79.20E
Ramu *r.* P.N.G. **59** 4.00S144.40E
Ramusio, Lac *l.* Canada **103** 55.04N 63.40W
Ranau Malaysia **58** 5.58N116.41E
Rancagua Chile **125** 34.10S 70.45W
Rance *r.* France **18** 48.31N 1.59W
Rancheria *r.* Canada **100** 60.13N129.07W
Rānchī India **63** 23.21N 85.20E
Rand Australia **93** 35.34S146.35E
Randalstown U.K. **15** 54.45N 6.20W
Randan France **20** 46.01N 3.21E
Randazzo Italy **33** 37.53N 14.57E
Rānder India **62** 21.14N 72.47E
Randers Denmark **42** 56.28N 10.03E
Randolph Kans. U.S.A. **110** 39.27N 96.44W
Randolph N.Y. U.S.A. **114** 42.10N 78.59W
Randolph Vt. U.S.A. **105** 43.55N 72.40W
Randsburg U.S.A. **109** 35.22N117.39W
Randsfjorden *l.* Norway **41** 60.25N 10.24E
Råne *r.* Sweden **40** 65.52N 22.19E
Råneå Sweden **40** 65.52N 22.18E
Rāner India **62** 28.53N 73.17E
Rangdong China **54** 32.51N112.18E
Rangely U.S.A. **108** 40.05N108.48W
Rangemore Australia **92** 35.19S144.22E
Ranger U.S.A. **113** 38.07N 82.10W
Ranger L. Canada **104** 46.54N 83.35W
Ranger Lake *town* Canada **104** 46.52N 83.36W
Rangia India **63** 26.28N 91.38E
Rangiora New Zealand **86** 43.18S172.38E
Rangiroa *i.* Pacific Oc. **85** 15.00S147.40W
Rangitaiki *r.* New Zealand **86** 37.55S176.50E
Rangkasbitung Indonesia **59** 6.21S106.12E
Rangoon Burma **56** 16.47N 96.10E
Rangpur Bangla. **63** 25.45N 89.15E
Rānīganj India **63** 23.37N 87.08E
Rānīkhet India **63** 29.39N 79.25E
Rāniwāra India **62** 24.45N 72.13E
Rankin Inlet *town* Canada **99** 62.52N 92.00W
Rankins Springs *town* Australia **93** 33.52S146.18E
Rannoch, Loch U.K. **14** 56.41N 4.20W
Rann of Kutch *f.* India **62** 23.50N 69.50E
Ranohira Madagascar **81** 22.29S 45.24E
Rano Kao *mtn.* I. de Pascua **85** 27.11S109.27W
Ranong Thailand **56** 9.59N 98.40E
Ransäter Sweden **43** 59.46N 13.26E
Rantauparapat Indonesia **58** 2.05N 99.46E
Rantekombola *mtn.* Indonesia **58** 3.30S119.58E
Råö Sweden **42** 57.24N 11.56E
Rao Co *mtn.* Laos **56** 18.10N105.25E
Raoping China **55** 23.45N117.05E
Raoul *i.* Pacific Oc. **84** 29.15S177.55W
Rapa *i.* Pacific Oc. **85** 27.35S144.20W
Rapallo Italy **30** 44.21N 9.14E
Rāpar India **62** 23.34N 70.38E
Rapidan *r.* U.S.A. **114** 38.22N 77.37W
Rapid Bay *town* Australia **92** 35.33S138.09E
Rapid City U.S.A. **110** 44.05N103.14W
Rapides des Joachims *town* Canada **105** 46.13N 77.43W
Rappahannock *r.* U.S.A. **114** 37.34N 76.18W
Rapperswil Switz. **39** 47.14N 8.50E
Rapsáni Greece **34** 39.54N 22.33E
Raquette *r.* U.S.A. **105** 45.00N 74.42W
Raquette L. U.S.A. **105** 43.52N 74.38W
Raquette Lake *town* U.S.A. **105** 43.49N 74.41W
Rarotonga *i.* Cook Is. **84** 21.14S159.46W
Ra's al Ḥadd *c.* Oman **60** 22.32N 59.49E
Ra's al Khaymah U.A.E. **65** 25.48N 55.56E
Ra's al Unūf Libya **75** 30.31N 18.34E
Ra's an Nabq *town* Egypt **66** 29.36N 34.51E
Ra's an Naqb *town* Jordan **66** 30.30N 35.29E
Ras Dashen *mtn.* Ethiopia **73** 13.20N 38.10E
Ras Djebel Tunisia **32** 37.13N 10.09E
Râs Ghârib Egypt **66** 28.22N 33.04E
Rashād Sudan **73** 11.51N 31.04E
Rashid Egypt **66** 31.25N 30.25E
Rashid Qal 'eh Afghan. **62** 31.31N 67.31E
Rasht Iran **65** 37.18N 49.38E
Rasina *r.* Yugo. **34** 43.38N 21.21E
Raška Yugo. **34** 43.17N 20.37E
Rās Koh *mtn.* Pakistan **62** 28.50N 65.12E
Rason, L. Australia **89** 28.46S124.20E
Rasra India **63** 25.51N 83.51E
Rastatt W. Germany **39** 48.51N 8.12E
Rastede W. Germany **38** 53.15N 8.11E
Rasu, Monte *mtn.* Italy **32** 40.25N 9.00E
Ratak Chain *is.* Pacific Oc. **84** 8.00N172.00E
Ratangarh India **62** 28.05N 74.36E
Rat Buri Thailand **56** 13.30N 99.50E
Rāth India **63** 25.35N 79.34E
Rathcormack Rep. of Ire. **15** 52.05N 8.18W
Rathdrum Rep. of Ire. **15** 52.56N 6.15W
Rathenow E. Germany **38** 52.36N 12.20E
Rathlin I. U.K. **15** 55.17N 6.15W
Rath Luirc Rep. of Ire. **15** 52.21N 8.41W
Rathmullen Rep. of Ire. **15** 55.06N 7.32W
Ratlām India **62** 23.19N 75.04E
Ratnāgiri India **60** 16.59N 73.18E
Ratno U.S.S.R. **37** 51.40N 24.32E
Ratodero Pakistan **62** 27.48N 68.18E
Raton U.S.A. **108** 36.54N104.24W
Rats, Rivière aux *r.* Canada **105** 47.12N 72.52W
Rattlesnake Range *mts.* U.S.A. **108** 42.45N107.10W
Rattray Head U.K. **14** 57.37N 1.50W
Rättvik Sweden **41** 60.53N 15.06E
Ratzeburg W. Germany **38** 53.42N 10.46E
Ratzeburger See *l.* W. Germany **38** 53.45N 10.47E
Rauch Argentina **125** 36.47S 59.05W

Raufoss to **Rivoli**

Raufoss Norway **41** 60.43N 10.37E
Raul Soares Brazil **126** 20.04S 42.27W
Rauma Finland **41** 61.08N 21.30E
Rauma *r.* Norway **40** 62.32N 7.43E
Raung, Gunung *mtn.* Indonesia **59** 8.07S114.03E
Raurkela India **63** 22.13N 84.53E
Rautas Sweden **40** 68.00N 19.55E
Ravalgaon India **62** 20.38N 74.25E
Ravanusa Italy **32** 37.16N 13.58E
Rāvar Iran **65** 31.14N 56.51E
Rava-Russkaya U.S.S.R. **37** 50.15N 23.36E
Ravena U.S.A. **115** 42.29N 73.49W
Ravenna Italy **30** 44.25N 12.12E
Ravenna U.S.A. **114** 41.09N 81.15W
Ravensburg W. Germany **39** 47.47N 9.37E
Ravenshoe Australia **90** 17.37S145.29E
Ravensthorpe Australia **89** 33.35S120.02E
Ravenswood Australia **90** 20.05S146.52E
Ravenswood U.S.A. **114** 38.57N 81.46W
Rāver India **62** 21.15N 76.05E
Ravi *r.* Pakistan **60** 30.30N 72.13E
Ravna Gora Yugo. **31** 45.23N 14.57E
Rāwalpindi Pakistan **62** 33.36N 73.04E
Rawāndūz Iraq **65** 36.38N 44.32E
Rawdon Canada **105** 46.03N 73.44W
Rawene New Zealand **86** 35.24S173.30E
Rawicz Poland **36** 51.37N 16.52E
Rawlinna Australia **89** 31.00S125.21E
Rawlins U.S.A. **108** 41.47N107.14W
Rawson Argentina **125** 34.40S 60.02W
Raxaul India **63** 26.59N 84.51E
Ray U.S.A. **110** 48.21N103.10W
Ray, C. Canada **103** 47.40N 59.18W
Raya *mtn.* Indonesia **58** 0.45S112.45E
Rāyagada India **63** 19.10N 83.25E
Rāyen Iran **65** 29.34N 57.26E
Raymond Canada **100** 49.30N112.35W
Raymond U.S.A. **108** 46.41N123.44W
Raymond Terrace Australia **93** 32.47S151.45E
Raymondville U.S.A. **111** 26.29N 97.47W
Rayong Thailand **56** 12.43N101.20E
Raz, Pointe du *c.* France **18** 48.02N 4.44W
Razan Iran **65** 35.22N 49.02E
Razanj Yugo. **34** 43.40N 21.31E
Razdelnaya U.S.S.R. **37** 46.50N 30.02E
Razgrad Bulgaria **34** 43.33N 26.34E
Razgrad *d.* Bulgaria **34** 43.32N 26.31E
Razlog Bulgaria **34** 41.53N 23.28E
Ré, Île de *i.* France **20** 46.10N 1.26W
Reading U.K. **13** 51.27N 0.57W
Reading U.S.A. **115** 40.20N 75.56W
Readsboro U.S.A. **115** 42.46N 72.57W
Realicó Argentina **125** 35.02S 64.14W
Réalmont France **20** 43.47N 2.12E
Reay Forest *f.* U.K. **14** 58.17N 4.48W
Rebi Indonesia **59** 6.24S134.07E
Rebiana Sand Sea *see* Rabyānah, Ṣaḥrā'. Libya **75**
Reboly U.S.S.R. **44** 63.50N 30.49E
Rebun jima *i.* Japan **57** 45.25N141.04E
Recalde Argentina **125** 36.39S 61.05W
Recanati Italy **31** 43.24N 13.32E
Rechāh Lām Afghan. **62** 34.58N 70.51E
Recherche, Archipelago of the *is.* Australia **89** 34.05S122.45E
Rechitsa U.S.S.R. **37** 52.21N 30.24E
Recife Brazil **123** 8.06S 34.53W
Recklinghausen W. Germany **38** 51.36N 7.13E
Recknitz *r.* E. Germany **38** 54.14N 12.28E
Reconquista Argentina **124** 29.08S 59.38W
Recreo Argentina **124** 29.20S 65.04W
Red *r.* Canada **101** 50.20N 96.50W
Red *r.* U.S.A. **111** 31.00N 91.40W
Red *r. see* Hong Hà Vietnam **55**
Red Bank U.S.A. **115** 40.21N 74.03W
Red Basin *f. see* Sichuan Pendi China **55**
Red Bay *town* Canada **103** 51.44N 56.45W
Red Bluff U.S.A. **108** 40.11N122.15W
Redcar U.K. **12** 54.37N 1.04W
Red Cliffs *town* Australia **92** 34.22S142.13E
Red Cloud U.S.A. **110** 40.04N 98.31W
Red Deer Canada **100** 52.20N113.50W
Red Deer *r.* Canada **101** 50.56N109.54W
Redding U.S.A. **108** 40.35N122.24W
Redditch U.K. **13** 52.18N 1.57W
Rede *r.* U.K. **12** 55.08N 2.13W
Redfield U.S.A. **110** 44.53N 98.31W
Red Hill *town* Australia **92** 33.34S138.12E
Red Hook U.S.A. **115** 41.55N 73.53W
Red Indian L. Canada **103** 48.40N 56.50W
Red L. U.S.A. **107** 48.00N 95.00W
Red Lake *town* Canada **102** 51.03N 93.49W
Redlands U.S.A. **109** 34.03N117.11W
Red Lion U.S.A. **115** 39.54N 76.36W
Red Lodge U.S.A. **108** 45.11N109.15W
Redmond U.S.A. **108** 44.17N121.11W
Rednitz *r.* W. Germany **38** 49.28N 10.59E
Red Oak U.S.A. **110** 41.01N 95.14W
Redon France **18** 47.39N 2.05W
Redondela Spain **26** 42.17N 8.36W
Redondo Portugal **27** 38.39N 7.33W
Redondo Beach *town* U.S.A. **109** 33.51N118.23W
Red Rock Canada **100** 53.39N122.41W
Redrock U.S.A. **109** 32.35N111.19W
Redruth U.K. **13** 50.14N 5.14W
Red Sea Africa / Asia **71** 20.00N 39.00E
Redstone Canada **100** 52.13N123.50W
Red Volta *r.* Ghana **76** 10.32N 0.31W
Redwater Alta. Canada **100** 53.55N113.06W
Redwater Ont. Canada **104** 46.54N 79.34W
Red Wing U.S.A. **110** 44.33N 92.31W
Redwood City U.S.A. **108** 37.29N122.13W
Ree, Lough Rep. of Ire. **15** 53.31N 7.58W
Reed City U.S.A. **112** 43.54N 85.31W
Reeder U.S.A. **110** 46.06N102.57W
Reedsport U.S.A. **108** 43.42N124.06W
Reedy U.S.A. **114** 38.54N 81.26W
Reefton New Zealand **86** 42.07S171.52E
Reese *r.* U.S.A. **108** 40.39N116.54W
Reftele Sweden **43** 57.11N 13.35E
Refuge Cove *town* Canada **100** 50.07N124.50W
Refugio U.S.A. **111** 28.18N 97.17W
Rega *r.* Poland **36** 54.10N 15.18E
Regavim Israel **67** 32.32N 35.02E
Regen W. Germany **39** 48.59N 13.07E
Regen *r.* W. Germany **39** 49.01N 12.06E
Regensburg W. Germany **39** 49.01N 12.06E
Reggane Algeria **74** 26.42N 0.10E
Reggello Italy **30** 43.41N 11.32E
Reggio Calabria Italy **33** 38.07N 15.39E
Reggio Emilia-Romagnaltaly **30** 44.43N 10.36E
Reghin Romania **37** 46.47N 24.42E
Regina Canada **101** 50.25N104.39W
Regiwar Pakistan **62** 25.57N 65.44E
Regnéville France **18** 49.01N 1.33W
Reguengos de Monsaraz Portugal **27** 38.25N 7.32W
Rehau W. Germany **39** 50.15N 12.02E
Rehoboth Namibia **80** 23.19S 17.10E
Rehoboth B. U.S.A. **115** 38.40N 75.06W
Rehoboth Beach *town* U.S.A. **115** 38.43N 75.05W
Rehovot Israel **67** 31.54N 34.46E
Reichenbach E. Germany **38** 50.37N 12.18E
Reidsville U.S.A. **113** 36.21N 79.40W
Reigate U.K. **13** 51.14N 0.13W
Reims France **19** 49.15N 4.02E
Reinach Switz. **39** 47.30N 7.35E
Reindeer L. Canada **101** 57.15N102.40W
Reinosa Spain **26** 43.00N 4.08W
Reisterstown U.S.A. **114** 39.28N 76.50W
Rejmyra Sweden **43** 58.50N 15.55E
Rekovac Yugo. **34** 43.51N 21.03E
Relizane Algeria **75** 35.45N 0.33E
Remanso Brazil **123** 9.41S 42.04W
Remarkable, Mt. Australia **92** 32.48S138.10E
Rembang Indonesia **59** 6.45S111.22E
Remeshk Iran **65** 26.52N 58.46E
Remich Lux. **16** 49.34N 6.23E
Remington U.S.A. **114** 38.32N 77.49W
Remiremont France **19** 48.01N 6.35E
Remo Ethiopia **73** 6.50N 41.15E
Remoulins France **21** 43.56N 4.34E
Remscheid W. Germany **38** 51.11N 7.11E
Remsen U.S.A. **115** 43.19N 75.11W
Rena Norway **41** 61.08N 11.22E
Rende Italy **33** 39.19N 16.11E
Rendina Greece **35** 39.04N 21.58E
Rendsburg W. Germany **38** 54.18N 9.40E
Renfrew Canada **105** 45.28N 76.41W
Rengat Indonesia **58** 0.26S102.35E
Rengo Chile **125** 34.25S 70.52W
Renheji China **55** 31.56N115.07E
Reni India **62** 28.41N 75.02E
Reni U.S.S.R. **37** 45.28N 28.17E
Renkum Neth. **16** 51.59N 5.46E
Renmark Australia **92** 34.10S140.45E
Rennell Sd. Canada **100** 53.23N132.35W
Renner Springs *town* Australia **90** 18.20S133.48E
Rennes France **18** 48.05N 1.41W
Reno *r.* Italy **30** 44.37N 12.17E
Reno U.S.A. **108** 39.31N119.48W
Renovo U.S.A. **114** 41.20N 77.38W
Rensselaer U.S.A. **115** 42.39N 73.44W
Rentería Spain **26** 43.19N 1.54W
Renton U.S.A. **108** 47.30N122.11W
Ren Xian China **54** 37.07N114.41E
Réo U. Volta **76** 12.20N 2.27W
Repki U.S.S.R. **37** 51.47N 31.06E
Republic Penn. U.S.A. **114** 39.56N 79.55W
Republic Wash. U.S.A. **108** 48.39N118.44W
Republican *r.* U.S.A. **110** 39.03N 96.48W
Republic of Ireland Europe **15** 53.00N 8.00W
Republic of South Africa Africa **80** 28.30S 24.50E
Repulse B. Australia **90** 20.36S148.43E
Repulse Bay *town* Canada **99** 66.35N 86.20W
Requa U.S.A. **108** 41.34N124.05W
Requena Peru **122** 5.05S 73.52W
Requena Spain **25** 39.29N 1.06W
Réquista France **20** 44.02N 2.31E
Resadiye Karimadasi *pen.* Turkey **35** 36.45N 27.40E
Reschenpass Italy / Austria **39** 46.50N 10.30E
Resen Yugo. **34** 41.05N 21.00E
Reserve Canada **101** 52.28N102.39W
Resistencia Argentina **124** 27.28S 59.00W
Reşiţa Romania **37** 45.17N 21.53E
Resolute Canada **99** 74.40N 95.00W
Resolution I. Canada **99** 61.30N 65.00W
Resolution I. New Zealand **86** 45.40S166.30E
Restigouche *r.* Canada **103** 48.04N 66.20W
Restoule Canada **104** 46.03N 79.47W
Rethel France **19** 49.31N 4.22E
Réthimnon Greece **35** 35.22N 24.29E
Réunion *i.* Indian Oc. **49** 22.00S 55.00E
Reus Spain **25** 41.09N 1.07E
Reusel Neth. **16** 51.21N 5.09E
Reuterstadt Stavenhagen E. Germany **38** 53.40N 12.54E
Reutlingen W. Germany **39** 48.29N 9.11E
Reutte Austria **39** 47.29N 10.43E
Revda U.S.S.R. **44** 56.49N 59.58E
Revelstoke Canada **100** 51.00N118.00W
Revigny-sur-Ornain France **19** 48.50N 4.59E
Revilla del Campo Spain **26** 42.13N 3.32W
Revilla Gigedo, Islas de *is.* Mexico **116** 19.00N111.00W
Revillagigedo I. U.S.A. **100** 55.50N131.20W
Revin France **19** 49.56N 4.38E
Revue *r.* Mozambique **81** 19.58S 34.40E
Rewa India **63** 24.32N 81.18E
Rewāri India **62** 28.11N 76.37E
Rexburg U.S.A. **108** 43.49N111.47W
Rexford U.S.A. **108** 48.53N115.13W
Rey Iran **65** 35.35N 51.27E
Reykjavik Iceland **40** 64.09N 21.58W
Reynoldsville U.S.A. **114** 41.06N 78.53W
Reynosa Mexico **111** 26.07N 98.18W
Rezā'īyeh Iran **65** 37.32N 45.02E
Rezé France **18** 47.12N 1.34W
Rēzekne U.S.S.R. **44** 56.30N 27.22E
Rhaetian Alps *mts.* Switz. **39** 46.45N 9.55E
Rhayader U.K. **13** 52.19N 3.30W
Rheda-Wiedenbrück Schloss W. Germany **38** 51.51N 8.17E
Rheden Neth. **16** 52.01N 6.02E
Rhein *r.* Europe **16** 51.53N 6.03E
Rheinbach W. Germany **38** 50.37N 6.57E
Rheine W. Germany **38** 52.17N 7.26E
Rheinfelden W. Germany **39** 47.33N 7.47E
Rheinland-Pfalz *d.* W. Germany **39** 49.50N 7.30E
Rheinsberg E. Germany **38** 53.06N 12.53E
Rhenen Neth. **16** 51.58N 5.34E
Rheydt W. Germany **38** 51.10N 6.25E
Rhine *see* Rhein Europe **16**
Rhinebeck U.S.A. **115** 41.56N 73.55W
Rhinelander U.S.A. **110** 45.39N 89.23W
Rhino Camp *town* Uganda **79** 2.58N 31.20E
Rhir, Cap *c.* Morocco **74** 30.38N 9.55W
Rho Italy **30** 45.32N 9.02E
Rhode Island *d.* U.S.A. **115** 41.40N 71.30W
Rhode Island Sd. U.S.A. **115** 41.25N 71.15W
Rhodes *i. see* Ródhos Greece **35**
Rhodope Mts. *see* Rhodopi Planina Bulgaria **34**
Rhodopi Planina *mts.* Bulgaria **34** 41.40N 24.20E
Rhondda U.K. **13** 51.39N 3.30W
Rhône *d.* France **21** 45.54N 4.35E
Rhône *r.* France **21** 43.20N 4.50E
Rhône-Alpes *d.* France **21** 45.20N 5.45E
Rhône au Rhin, Canal du France **19** 47.06N 5.19E
Rhosneigr U.K. **12** 53.14N 4.31W
Rhue *r.* France **20** 45.23N 2.29E
Rhum *i.* U.K. **14** 57.00N 6.20W
Rhyl U.K. **12** 53.19N 3.29W
Riachão Brazil **123** 7.22S 46.37W
Riāng India **63** 27.32N 92.56E
Riaño Spain **26** 42.58N 5.01W
Riánsares *r.* Spain **27** 39.32N 3.18W
Riāsi Jammu & Kashmir **62** 33.05N 74.50E
Riau *d.* Indonesia **58** 0.00 102.35E
Riau, Kepulauan *is.* Indonesia **58** 0.50N104.00E
Riaza Spain **26** 41.17N 3.28W
Riaza *r.* Spain **26** 41.42N 3.55W
Ribadeo Spain **26** 43.33N 7.02W
Ribadesella Spain **26** 43.28N 5.04W
Ribarroja, Embalse de *resr.* Spain **25** 41.12N 0.20E
Ribauè Mozambique **79** 14.57S 38.27E
Ribble *r.* U.K. **12** 53.45N 2.44W
Ribe Denmark **42** 55.21N 8.46E
Ribeauvillé France **19** 48.12N 7.19E
Ribécourt France **19** 49.31N 2.55E
Ribeirão Prêto Brazil **126** 21.09S 47.48W
Ribera Italy **32** 37.30N 13.16E
Ribérac France **20** 45.14N 0.22E
Riberalta Bolivia **124** 10.59S 66.06W
Ribnica Yugo. **31** 45.44N 14.44E
Ribnitz-Damgarten E. Germany **38** 54.15N 12.28E
Ribstone Creek *r.* Canada **101** 52.51N110.05W
Riccia Italy **33** 41.29N 14.50E
Riccione Italy **30** 43.59N 12.39E
Rice U.S.A. **109** 34.06N114.50W
Rice L. Canada **104** 44.08N 78.13W
Rice Lake *town* U.S.A. **110** 45.30N 91.43W
Rich, C. Canada **104** 44.43N 80.38W
Richard's Bay *town* R.S.A. **81** 28.47S 32.06E
Richardson *r.* Canada **101** 58.30N111.30W
Richardson U.S.A. **111** 32.57N 96.44W
Richelieu *r.* Canada **105** 46.03N 73.07W
Richelieu France **18** 47.01N 0.19E
Richfield Idaho U.S.A. **108** 43.03N114.09W
Richfield Utah U.S.A. **108** 38.46N112.05W
Richfield Springs U.S.A. **115** 42.51N 74.59W
Richford U.S.A. **105** 45.00N 72.40W
Rich Hill *town* U.S.A. **111** 38.06N 94.22W
Richibucto Canada **103** 46.41N 64.52W
Richland U.S.A. **108** 46.17N119.18W
Richmond N.S.W. Australia **93** 33.36S150.46E
Richmond Qld. Australia **90** 20.44S143.08E
Richmond Ont. Canada **105** 45.11N 75.50W
Richmond Que. Canada **105** 45.40N 72.09W
Richmond New Zealand **86** 41.20S173.10E
Richmond C.P. R.S.A. **80** 31.24S 23.56E
Richmond U.K. **12** 54.24N 1.43W
Richmond Ind. U.S.A. **112** 39.50N 84.51W
Richmond Utah U.S.A. **108** 41.55N111.48W
Richmond Va. U.S.A. **113** 37.34N 77.27W
Richmond Dale U.S.A. **114** 39.13N 82.54W
Richmond Hill Canada **104** 43.52N 79.27W
Richmond Range *mts.* Australia **93** 29.00S152.48E
Richwood U.S.A. **114** 38.14N 80.32W
Ricobayo, Embalse de *resr.* Spain **26** 41.30N 5.55W
Ridderkerk Neth. **16** 51.53N 4.39E
Rideau *r.* Canada **105** 45.27N 75.42W
Rideau Hills Canada **105** 44.37N 77.00W
Rideau Lakes Canada **105** 44.45N 76.17W
Ridgetown Canada **104** 42.26N 81.54W
Ridgway U.S.A. **114** 41.26N 78.44W
Riding Mtn. Canada **101** 50.37N 99.50W
Riding Mtn. Nat. Park Canada **101** 50.55N100.25W
Ried Austria **39** 48.13N 13.30E
Riemst Belgium **16** 50.49N 5.38E
Riesa E. Germany **38** 51.18N 13.17E
Riesi Italy **33** 37.17N 14.05E
Rieti Italy **30** 42.24N 12.51E
Rifle U.S.A. **108** 39.32N107.47W
Rift Valley *d.* Kenya **79** 1.00N 36.00E
Riga U.S.S.R. **41** 56.53N 24.08E
Riga, G. of *see* Rīgas Jūras Līcis U.S.S.R. **41**
Rīgān Iran **65** 28.40N 58.58E
Rīgas Jūras Līcis *g.* U.S.S.R. **41** 57.30N 23.35E
Rīgestān *f.* Afghan. **62** 30.35N 65.00E
Riggins U.S.A. **108** 45.25N116.19W
Rīg Matī Iran **65** 27.40N 58.11E
Rigo P.N.G. **90** 9.50S147.35E
Rigolet Canada **103** 54.20N 58.35W
Riihimäki Finland **41** 60.45N 24.46E
Riiser-Larsenhalvöya *pen.* Antarctica **128** 68.00S 35.00E
Riječki Zaljev *b.* Yugo. **31** 45.15N 14.25E
Rijeka Yugo. **31** 45.20N 14.27E
Rijssen Neth. **16** 52.19N 6.31E
Rijswijk Neth. **16** 52.03N 4.22E
Rila Planina *mts.* Bulgaria **34** 42.10N 23.30E
Riley U.S.A. **108** 43.31N119.28W
Rimah, Wādī ar *r.* Saudi Arabia **64** 26.10N 44.00E
Rimavská Sobota Czech. **37** 48.23N 20.02E
Rimbo Sweden **43** 59.45N 18.22E
Rimersburg U.S.A. **114** 41.02N 79.30W
Rimforsa Sweden **43** 58.08N 15.40E
Rimini Italy **30** 44.04N 12.34E
Rîmnicu-Sărat Romania **37** 45.24N 27.06E
Rîmnicu-Vîlcea Romania **37** 45.06N 24.22E
Rimouski Canada **103** 48.27N 68.32W
Rinbung China **63** 29.16N 89.54E
Rinconada Argentina **124** 22.26S 66.10W
Rindal Norway **40** 63.04N 9.13E
Ringe Denmark **42** 55.14N 10.29E
Ringebu Norway **41** 61.31N 10.10E
Ringerike Norway **42** 60.10N 10.18E
Ringim Nigeria **77** 12.09N 9.08E
Ringköbing Denmark **42** 56.05N 8.15E
Ringköbing Fjord *est.* Denmark **42** 56.00N 8.15E
Ringling U.S.A. **108** 46.16N110.49W
Ringsted Denmark **42** 55.27N 11.49E
Rīngus India **62** 27.21N 75.34E
Ringvassöy *i.* Norway **40** 69.55N 19.10E
Ringwood Australia **93** 37.51S145.13E
Ringwood U.K. **13** 50.50N 1.48W
Rintein W. Germany **38** 52.11N 9.04E
Riobamba Ecuador **122** 1.44S 78.40W
Rio Branco Brazil **122** 9.59S 67.49W
Rio Bueno Chile **125** 40.20S 72.55W
Rio Casca Brazil **126** 20.13S 42.38W
Rio Claro Brazil **126** 22.19S 47.35W
Río Cuarto Argentina **125** 33.08S 64.20W
Rio de Janeiro Brazil **126** 22.53S 43.17W
Rio de Janeiro *d.* Brazil **126** 22.00S 42.30W
Río Gallegos Argentina **125** 51.37S 69.10W
Rio Grande *town* Argentina **125** 53.50S 67.40W
Rio Grande *town* Brazil **126** 32.03S 52.08W
Rio Grande *r.* Mexico / U.S.A. **111** 25.57N 97.09W
Rio Grande *r.* Nicaragua **117** 12.48N 83.30W
Rio Grande City U.S.A. **111** 26.23N 98.49W
Rio Grande do Norte *d.* Brazil **123** 6.00S 36.30W
Rio Grande do Sul *d.* Brazil **126** 30.15S 53.30W
Riohacha Colombia **122** 11.34N 72.58W
Rio Largo Brazil **123** 9.28S 35.50W
Riom France **20** 45.54N 3.07E
Río Negro *d.* Argentina **125** 40.00S 67.00W
Rio Negro Brazil **126** 26.06S 49.48W
Río Negro, Embalse del *resr.* Uruguay **125** 32.45S 56.00W
Rionero in Vulture Italy **33** 40.56N 15.41E
Rio Novo Brazil **126** 21.15S 43.09W
Riópar Spain **26** 38.30N 2.27W
Rio Piracicaba Brazil **126** 19.54S 43.10W
Rio Pomba Brazil **126** 21.15S 43.12W
Rio Prêto Brazil **126** 22.06S 43.52W
Riosucio Colombia **122** 7.27N 77.07W
Rio Tercero Argentina **124** 32.10S 64.05W
Rio Verde *town* Brazil **124** 17.50S 50.55W
Rioz France **19** 47.25N 6.04E
Ripatransone Italy **31** 43.00N 13.46E
Ripley Canada **104** 44.04N 81.34W
Ripley N.Y. U.S.A. **114** 42.16N 79.43W
Ripley W.Va. U.S.A. **114** 38.49N 81.43W
Ripoll Spain **25** 42.12N 2.12E
Ripon Canada **105** 45.47N 75.06W
Ripon U.K. **12** 54.08N 1.31W
Riposto Italy **33** 37.45N 15.12E
Riripora Brazil **126** 17.20S 45.02W
Risbäck Sweden **40** 64.42N 15.32E
Riscle France **20** 43.40N 0.05W
Rishā, Wādī ar *r.* Saudi Arabia **65** 25.40N 44.08E
Rishikesh India **63** 30.07N 78.42E
Rishiri tō *i.* Japan **57** 45.11N141.15E
Rishon LeZiyyon Israel **67** 31.57N 34.48E
Rishpon Israel **67** 32.12N 34.49E
Risle *r.* France **18** 49.26N 0.23E
Risnjak *mtn.* Yugo. **31** 45.26N 14.37E
Rison U.S.A. **111** 33.58N 92.11W
Risör Norway **42** 58.43N 9.14E
Rissani Morocco **74** 31.23N 4.09W
Riti Nigeria **77** 7.57N 9.41E
Ritidian Pt. Guam **84** 13.39N144.51E
Rittman U.S.A. **114** 40.58N 81.47W
Ritzville U.S.A. **108** 47.08N118.23W
Riva Italy **30** 45.53N 10.50E
Rivadavia Argentina **124** 24.11S 62.53W
Rivarolo Canavese Italy **30** 45.19N 7.43E
Rivas Nicaragua **117** 11.26N 85.50W
Rive-de-Gier France **21** 45.32N 4.37E
Rivera Uruguay **125** 30.54S 55.31W
River Cess *town* Liberia **76** 5.28N 9.32W
Rivergaro Italy **30** 44.55N 9.36E
Riverhead U.S.A. **115** 40.55N 72.40W
Riverina *f.* Australia **93** 34.30S145.20E
Rivers Canada **101** 50.02N100.12W
Rivers *d.* Nigeria **77** 4.45N 6.35E
Riversdale R.S.A. **80** 34.05S 21.15E
Riverside U.S.A. **109** 33.59N117.22W
Rivers Inlet *town* Canada **100** 51.40N127.20W
Riverton Australia **92** 34.08S138.24E
Riverton Canada **101** 50.59N 96.59W
Riverton New Zealand **86** 46.21S168.01E
Riverton U.S.A. **108** 43.02N108.23W
River Valley *town* Canada **104** 46.35N 80.10W
Rivesaltes France **20** 42.46N 2.52E
Rivesville U.S.A. **114** 39.32N 80.07W
Riviera di Levante *f.* Italy **30** 44.00N 9.40E
Riviera di Ponente *f.* Italy **30** 43.40N 8.00E
Rivière à Pierre *town* Canada **105** 46.59N 72.11W
Rivière aux Rats *town* Canada **105** 47.13N 72.54W
Rivière-du-Loup *town* Canada **103** 47.50N 69.32W
Rivière Pentecôte *town* Canada **103** 49.47N 67.10W
Rivoli Italy **30** 45.04N 7.31E

Riyadh to Rüsselsheim

Riyadh *see* Ar Riyāḍ Saudi Arabia **65**
Rize Turkey **64** 41.03N 40.31E
Rizhao China **54** 35.26N119.27E
Rizokárpason Cyprus **66** 35.35N 34.24E
Rizzuto, Capo *c.* Italy **33** 38.54N 17.06E
Rjukan Norway **42** 59.52N 8.34E
Roa Norway **42** 60.17N 10.37E
Roa Spain **26** 41.42N 3.55W
Roag, Loch U.K. **14** 58.14N 6.50W
Roanne France **21** 46.02N 4.04E
Roanoke *r.* U.S.A. **113** 35.56N 76.43W
Roanoke Ala. U.S.A. **113** 33.09N 85.24W
Roanoke Va. U.S.A. **113** 37.15N 79.58W
Roanoke Rapids *town* U.S.A. **113** 36.28N 77.40W
Roaring Branch U.S.A. **114** 41.34N 76.57W
Roaring Spring U.S.A. **114** 40.20N 78.24W
Roaring Springs U.S.A. **111** 33.54N100.52W
Robāţ Iran **65** 30.04N 54.49E
Robe Australia **92** 37.11S139.45E
Robe, Mt. Australia **92** 31.39S141.16E
Röbel E. Germany **38** 53.23N 12.35E
Roberts, Mt. Australia **93** 28.12S152.21E
Robertsdale U.S.A. **114** 40.11N 78.07W
Robertsganj India **63** 24.42N 83.04E
Robertson R.S.A. **80** 33.48S 19.52E
Robertsport Liberia **76** 6.45N 11.22W
Robertstown Australia **92** 33.59S139.03E
Roberval Canada **103** 48.31N 72.13W
Robin Hood's Bay *town* U.K. **12** 54.26N 0.31W
Robinson *r.* Australia **90** 16.03S137.16E
Robinson Ranges *mts.* Australia **88** 25.45S119.00E
Robinvale Australia **92** 34.37S142.50E
Robleda Spain **26** 40.23N 6.36W
Robledo Spain **26** 38.46N 2.26W
Roblin Man. Canada **101** 51.17N101.28W
Roblin Ont. Canada **105** 44.21N 77.01W
Roboré Bolivia **124** 18.20S 59.45W
Robson, Mt. Canada **100** 53.10N119.10W
Rocas *i.* Atlantic Oc. **127** 3.50S 33.50W
Roccadaspide Italy **33** 40.26N 15.12E
Roccastrada Italy **30** 43.00N 11.10E
Roccella Italy **29** 38.19N 16.24E
Rocciamelone *mtn.* Italy **30** 45.12N 7.05E
Rocella Italy **33** 38.20N 16.24E
Rocha Uruguay **126** 34.30S 54.22W
Rocha da Gale, Barragem *dam* Portugal **24** 37.42N 7.35W
Rochdale U.K. **12** 53.36N 2.10W
Rochechouart France **20** 45.50N 0.50E
Rochefort Belgium **16** 50.10N 5.13E
Rochefort France **20** 45.57N 0.58W
Rochefort-Montagne France **20** 45.41N 2.48E
Rochelle U.S.A. **110** 41.55N 89.05W
Rocher River *town* Canada **100** 61.23N112.44W
Rochester Australia **93** 36.22S144.42E
Rochester Kent U.K. **13** 51.22N 0.30E
Rochester Minn. U.S.A. **110** 44.01N 92.27W
Rochester N.H. U.S.A. **115** 43.18N 70.59W
Rochester N.Y. U.S.A. **114** 43.10N 77.36W
Rochester Penn. U.S.A. **114** 40.43N 80.17W
Rochfort Bridge Rep. of Ire. **15** 53.25N 7.19W
Rochlitz E. Germany **38** 51.03N 12.47E
Rock *r.* Canada **100** 60.07N127.07W
Rock U.S.A. **112** 46.03N 87.10W
Rockall *i.* U.K. **10** 57.39N 13.44W
Rockall Bank *f.* Atlantic Oc. **10** 57.30N 14.00W
Rock Creek *town* U.S.A. **114** 41.40N 80.52W
Rockdale U.S.A. **114** 39.21N 76.46W
Rockefeller Plateau Antarctica **128** 80.00S140.00W
Rockford U.S.A. **110** 42.17N 89.06W
Rock Hall U.S.A. **115** 39.08N 76.14W
Rockhampton Australia **90** 23.22S150.32E
Rock Hill *town* U.S.A. **113** 34.55N 81.01W
Rockingham Australia **89** 32.16S115.21E
Rockingham U.S.A. **113** 34.56N 79.47W
Rock Island *town* Canada **105** 45.01N 72.06W
Rock Island *town* U.S.A. **110** 41.30N 90.34W
Rockland Canada **105** 45.32N 75.19W
Rockland Idaho U.S.A. **108** 42.34N112.53W
Rockland Maine U.S.A. **112** 44.06N 69.06W
Rockland Mich. U.S.A. **112** 46.44N 89.12W
Rocklands Resr. Australia **92** 37.13S141.52E
Rockport Canada **105** 44.22N 75.58W
Rockport U.S.A. **108** 39.45N123.47W
Rock Rapids *town* U.S.A. **110** 43.26N 96.10W
Rock Sound *town* Bahamas **117** 24.54N 76.11W
Rocksprings Tex. U.S.A. **111** 30.01N100.13W
Rock Springs Wyo. U.S.A. **108** 41.35N109.13W
Rockville U.S.A. **114** 39.05N 77.09W
Rockwood Mich. U.S.A. **104** 42.10N 83.15W
Rockwood Penn. U.S.A. **114** 39.54N 79.09W
Rockwood Tenn. U.S.A. **113** 35.52N 84.40W
Rocky Ford U.S.A. **106** 38.03N103.44W
Rocky Gully *town* Australia **89** 34.31S117.01E
Rocky Island L. Canada **104** 46.56N 83.04W
Rocky Mount *town* U.S.A. **113** 35.56N 77.48W
Rocky Mountain Foothills *f.* Canada **100** 57.17N123.21W
Rocky Mountain Nat. Park U.S.A. **108** 40.19N105.42W
Rocky Mountain Trench *f.* Canada **100** 56.45N124.47W
Rocky Mts. N. America **108** 43.21N109.50W
Rocky Pt. Australia **89** 33.30S124.01E
Rocky Pt. Namibia **80** 19.00S 12.29E
Rocky River *town* U.S.A. **114** 41.30N 81.40W
Rocroi France **19** 49.55N 4.31E
Rod Pakistan **62** 28.06N 63.12E
Rodalben W. Germany **39** 49.14N 7.38E
Rodalquilar Spain **27** 37.40N 2.08W
Rödberg Norway **42** 60.16N 8.58E
Rödby Denmark **41** 54.42N 11.24E
Roddickton Canada **103** 50.52N 56.08W
Rödekro Denmark **42** 55.04N 9.21E
Rodel U.K. **14** 57.44N 6.58W
Rodeo Mexico **111** 25.11N104.34W
Rodewisch E. Germany **39** 50.32N 12.24E
Rodez France **20** 44.21N 2.35E
Ródhos *i.* Greece **35** 36.10N 28.00E
Ródhos *town* Greece **35** 36.26N 28.13E
Rodi Garganico Italy **31** 41.55N 15.53E
Roding W. Germany **39** 49.12N 12.32E
Rodney Canada **104** 42.34N 81.41W
Rodonit, Kep-i- *c.* Albania **34** 41.32N 19.30E
Rodrigues *i.* Indian Oc. **49** 19.42S 63.25E
Roe, L. Australia **89** 30.40S122.10E
Roebourne Australia **88** 20.48S117.10E
Roebuck B. Australia **88** 19.04S122.17E
Roermond Neth. **16** 51.12N 6.00E
Roeselare Belgium **16** 50.57N 3.06E
Rogachev U.S.S.R. **37** 53.05N 30.02E
Rogaland *d.* Norway **42** 59.10N 6.25E
Rogaška Slatina Yugo. **31** 46.14N 15.38E
Rogatica Yugo. **31** 43.48N 19.00E
Rogers, Mt. U.S.A. **113** 36.35N 81.32W
Rogers City U.S.A. **104** 45.25N 83.49W
Rogerson U.S.A. **108** 42.14N114.47W
Roggan *r.* Canada **102** 54.24N 78.05W
Roggan L. Canada **102** 54.10N 77.58W
Roggan River *town* Canada **102** 54.24N 78.05W
Roggeveen, Cabo *c.* I. de Pascua **85** 27.06S109.16W
Roggiano Gravina Italy **33** 39.37N 16.09E
Rogliano France **21** 42.57N 9.25E
Rogliano Italy **33** 39.11N 16.20E
Rogue *r.* U.S.A. **108** 42.26N124.25W
Rohri Pakistan **62** 27.41N 68.54E
Rohtak India **62** 28.54N 76.34E
Rojas Argentina **125** 34.15S 60.44W
Rokan *r.* Indonesia **58** 2.00N101.00E
Rokel *r.* Sierra Leone **76** 8.36N 12.55W
Rokycany Czech. **38** 49.45N 13.36E
Rola Co *l.* China **61** 35.26N 88.24E
Röldal Norway **42** 59.49N 6.48E
Roldskov *f.* Denmark **42** 56.46N 9.50E
Rolette U.S.A. **110** 48.40N 99.51W
Rolla Mo. U.S.A. **111** 37.57N 91.46W
Rolla N.Dak. U.S.A. **110** 48.52N 99.37W
Rolle Switz. **39** 46.28N 6.20E
Rolleston Australia **90** 24.25S148.35E
Rolleville Bahamas **117** 23.41N 76.00W
Rolvsöya *i.* Norway **40** 70.58N 24.00E
Roma Australia **90** 26.35S148.47E
Roma Italy **32** 41.54N 12.29E
Roma Sweden **43** 57.32N 18.28E
Romain, C. U.S.A. **113** 33.00N 79.22W
Romaine *r.* Canada **103** 50.18N 63.47W
Roman Romania **37** 46.55N 26.56E
Romanche *r.* France **21** 45.05N 5.43E
Romang *i.* Indonesia **59** 7.45S127.20E
Romania Europe **37** 46.30N 24.00E
Romano, C. U.S.A. **113** 25.50N 81.41W
Romans France **21** 45.03N 5.03E
Romanshorn Switz. **39** 47.34N 9.22E
Rome *see* Roma Italy **32**
Rome Ga. U.S.A. **113** 34.01N 85.02W
Rome N.Y. U.S.A. **115** 43.13N 75.27W
Romeleåsen *f.* Sweden **43** 55.34N 13.33E
Romeo U.S.A. **114** 42.48N 83.01W
Romilly France **19** 48.31N 3.43E
Romney Marsh *f.* U.K. **13** 51.03N 0.55E
Römö *i.* Denmark **42** 55.08N 8.31E
Romont Switz. **39** 46.42N 6.55E
Romorantin France **19** 47.22N 1.45E
Rona *i.* U.K. **14** 57.33N 5.58W
Ronan U.S.A. **108** 47.32N114.06W
Ronas Hill U.K. **10** 60.32N 1.26W
Roncesvalles Spain **25** 43.01N 1.19W
Ronchamp France **19** 47.42N 6.39E
Ronda Spain **27** 36.44N 5.10W
Ronda, Serranía de *mts.* Spain **27** 36.44N 5.05W
Rondane *mtn.* Norway **41** 61.55N 9.45E
Rönde Denmark **42** 56.18N 10.29E
Rondônia *d.* Brazil **122** 12.10S 62.30W
Rondonópolis Brazil **123** 16.29S 54.37W
Rondout Resr. U.S.A. **115** 41.50N 74.29W
Ronehamn Sweden **43** 57.10N 18.29E
Rongcheng China **54** 37.09N122.23E
Ronge, Lac la *l.* Canada **101** 55.07N104.45W
Rongjiang China **55** 25.56N108.31E
Rongxar China **63** 28.14N 87.44E
Rong Xian China **55** 29.28N104.32E
Roniu *mtn.* Tahiti **85** 17.49S149.12W
Rönne Denmark **43** 55.06N 14.42E
Ronneby Sweden **43** 56.12N 15.18E
Ronse Belgium **16** 50.45N 3.36E
Ronuro *r.* Brazil **123** 11.56S 53.33W
Roof Butte *mtn.* U.S.A. **109** 36.28N109.05W
Roorkee India **63** 29.52N 77.53E
Roosendaal Neth. **16** 51.32N 4.28E
Roosevelt *r.* Brazil **122** 7.35S 60.20W
Roosevelt U.S.A. **108** 40.18N109.59W
Roosevelt I. Antarctica **128** 79.00S161.00W
Root *r.* Canada **100** 62.50N123.40W
Ropcha U.S.S.R. **44** 62.50N 51.55E
Roper *r.* Australia **90** 14.40S135.30E
Roper Valley *town* Australia **90** 14.56S134.00E
Roquefort France **20** 44.02N 0.19W
Roquemaure France **21** 44.03N 4.47E
Roque Pérez Argentina **125** 35.23S 59.22W
Roraima *d.* Brazil **122** 2.00N 62.00W
Roraima, Mt. Guyana **122** 5.14N 60.44W
Rörholtfjorden *l.* Norway **42** 59.01N 9.15E
Rorketon Canada **101** 51.26N 99.32W
Röros Norway **40** 62.35N 11.23E
Rorschach Switz. **39** 47.29N 9.30E
Rosa, Cap *c.* Algeria **32** 36.58N 8.15E
Rosa, Monte *mtn.* Italy / Switz. **39** 45.57N 7.53E
Rosamond U.S.A. **109** 34.52N118.10W
Rosans France **21** 44.23N 5.28E
Rosario Argentina **125** 32.57S 60.40W
Rosário Brazil **123** 3.00S 44.15W
Rosario Mexico **109** 23.00N105.52W
Rosario Uruguay **125** 34.19S 57.21W
Rosario de la Frontera Argentina **124** 25.50S 64.55W
Rosario del Tala Argentina **125** 32.20S 59.10W
Rosário do Sul Brazil **126** 30.15S 54.55W
Rosarito Mexico **109** 28.38N114.04W
Rosarito, Embalse de *resr.* Spain **27** 40.05N 5.15W
Rosarno Italy **33** 38.29N 15.59E
Rosas Spain **25** 42.19N 3.10E
Rosas, Golfo de *g.* Spain **25** 42.10N 3.15E
Roscoe N.Y. U.S.A. **115** 41.56N 74.55W
Roscoe S.Dak. U.S.A. **110** 45.27N 99.20W
Roscoff France **18** 48.44N 4.00W
Roscommon Rep. of Ire. **15** 53.38N 8.13W
Roscommon *d.* Rep. of Ire. **15** 53.38N 8.11W
Roscommon U.S.A. **104** 44.30N 84.35W
Roscrea Rep. of Ire. **15** 52.57N 7.49W
Roseau *r.* Canada **101** 49.10N 97.20W
Roseau Dominica **117** 15.18N 61.23W
Roseau U.S.A. **110** 48.51N 95.46W
Rose Blanche Canada **103** 47.37N 58.43W
Rosebud Australia **93** 38.21S144.54E
Rosebud *r.* Canada **100** 51.25N112.37W
Roseburg U.S.A. **108** 43.13N123.20W
Rose City U.S.A. **104** 44.25N 84.07W
Rose Harbour Canada **100** 52.15N131.10W
Rosenberg U.S.A. **111** 29.33N 95.48W
Rosendal Norway **42** 59.59N 6.01E
Rosenheim W. Germany **39** 47.51N 12.07E
Roseto degli Abruzzi Italy **31** 42.41N 14.00E
Rosetown Canada **101** 51.33N108.00W
Rosetta R.S.A. **80** 29.18S 29.58E
Roseville Calif. U.S.A. **108** 38.45N121.17W
Roseville Mich. U.S.A. **114** 42.30N 82.56W
Roshage *c.* Denmark **42** 57.08N 8.37E
Rosh Ha'Ayin Israel **67** 32.06N 34.57E
Rosh Pinna Israel **67** 32.58N 35.32E
Rosières France **19** 49.49N 2.43E
Rosignano Marittimo Italy **30** 43.24N 10.28E
Roșiori-de-Vede Romania **37** 44.07N 25.00E
Rositsa Bulgaria **37** 43.57N 27.57E
Roska *r.* U.S.S.R. **37** 49.27N 29.45E
Roskilde Denmark **43** 55.39N 12.05E
Roslagen *f.* Sweden **43** 59.40N 18.30E
Roslags-Näsby Sweden **43** 59.26N 18.04E
Roslavl U.S.S.R. **44** 53.55N 32.53E
Roslev Denmark **42** 56.42N 8.59E
Rosporden France **18** 47.58N 3.50W
Ross New Zealand **86** 42.54S170.49E
Rossano Italy **33** 39.35N 16.39E
Ross Dependency Antarctica **128** 75.00S170.00W
Rosseau, L. Canada **104** 45.10N 79.35W
Rossignol, L. Canada **103** 44.10N 65.10W
Rossing Namibia **80** 22.31S 14.52E
Rossiter U.S.A. **114** 40.53N 78.56W
Rossiyskaya S.F.S.R. *d.* U.S.S.R. **50** 62.00N 80.00E
Rosslare Rep. of Ire. **15** 52.17N 6.23W
Rosslau E. Germany **38** 51.53N 12.14E
Rossmore Canada **105** 44.06N 77.23W
Rosso Mauritania **74** 16.30N 15.49W
Rosso, Cap *c.* France **21** 42.14N 8.33E
Ross-on-Wye U.K. **13** 51.55N 2.36W
Rossosh U.S.S.R. **45** 50.12N 39.35E
Ross River *town* Canada **100** 62.30N131.30W
Rössvatnet *l.* Norway **40** 65.45N 14.00E
Rosta Norway **40** 68.59N 19.40E
Rosthern Canada **101** 52.40N106.17W
Rostock E. Germany **38** 54.05N 12.07E
Rostock *d.* E. Germany **38** 54.05N 12.07E
Rostov R.S.F.S.R. U.S.S.R. **45** 47.15N 39.45E
Rostov R.S.F.S.R. U.S.S.R. **44** 57.11N 39.23E
Roswell Ga. U.S.A. **113** 34.02N 84.21W
Roswell N.Mex. U.S.A. **109** 33.24N104.32W
Rota Spain **27** 36.37N 6.21W
Rotem Belgium **16** 51.04N 5.44E
Rotenburg Hessen W. Germany **38** 51.00N 9.45E
Rotenburg Nschn. W. Germany **38** 53.06N 9.24E
Roth W. Germany **38** 49.14N 11.04E
Rothaargebirge *mts.* W. Germany **38** 51.05N 8.15E
Rothbury U.K. **12** 55.19N 1.54W
Rothenburg ob der Tober W. Germany **39** 49.23N 10.10E
Rother *r.* U.K. **11** 50.56N 0.46E
Rotherham U.K. **12** 53.26N 1.21W
Rothes U.K. **14** 57.31N 3.13W
Rothesay Canada **103** 45.23N 66.00W
Rothesay U.K. **14** 55.50N 5.03W
Roti *i.* Indonesia **88** 10.30S123.10E
Roto Australia **93** 33.04S145.27E
Rotondella Italy **33** 40.10N 16.32E
Rotondo, Monte *mtn.* France **21** 42.13N 9.03E
Rotorua New Zealand **86** 38.07S176.17E
Rotorua, L. New Zealand **86** 38.00S176.00E
Rottenburg W. Germany **39** 48.28N 8.56E
Rottenburg an der Laaber W. Germany **39** 48.42N 12.02E
Rotterdam Neth. **16** 51.55N 4.29E
Rottnest I. Australia **89** 32.01S115.28E
Rottweil W. Germany **39** 48.10N 8.37E
Roubaix France **16** 50.42N 3.10E
Roudnice Czech. **38** 50.22N 14.16E
Rouen France **18** 49.26N 1.05E
Rouge *r.* Canada **105** 45.39N 74.41W
Rougé France **18** 47.47N 1.27W
Rougemont France **19** 47.29N 6.21E
Rouillac France **20** 45.47N 0.04W
Rouku P.N.G. **90** 8.40S141.35E
Round I. U.S.A. **104** 45.51N 84.37W
Round L. Canada **105** 45.38N 77.32W
Round Mt. Australia **93** 30.26S152.15E
Round Pond *l.* Canada **103** 48.10N 56.00W
Roundup U.S.A. **108** 46.27N108.33W
Rousay *i.* U.K. **14** 59.10N 3.02W
Roussillon *f.* France **20** 42.30N 2.30E
Rouyn Canada **102** 48.20N 79.00W
Rovaniemi Finland **40** 66.30N 25.40E
Rovato Italy **30** 45.34N 10.00E
Rovereto Italy **32** 45.53N 11.02E
Roverud Norway **43** 60.15N 12.03E
Rovigo Italy **32** 45.04N 11.47E
Rovinj Yugo. **31** 45.05N 13.38E
Rovno U.S.S.R. **37** 50.39N 26.10E
Rowanton Canada **105** 46.24N 77.46W
Rowena Australia **93** 29.49S148.54E
Rowlesburg U.S.A. **114** 39.21N 79.40W
Rowley Shoals *f.* Australia **88** 17.30S119.00E
Roxboro U.S.A. **113** 36.24N 79.00W
Roxburgh New Zealand **86** 45.33S169.19E
Roxbury U.S.A. **115** 42.17N 74.34W
Roxen *l.* Sweden **43** 58.30N 15.41E
Roxton Canada **105** 45.29N 72.36W
Roy U.S.A. **109** 35.57N104.12W
Royale, Isle *i.* U.S.A. **112** 48.00N 89.00W
Royal L. Canada **101** 56.00N103.15W
Royal Leamington Spa U.K. **13** 52.18N 1.32W
Royal Oak U.S.A. **104** 42.30N 83.08W
Royalton U.S.A. **114** 41.18N 81.45W
Royal Tunbridge Wells U.K. **13** 51.07N 0.16E
Royan France **20** 45.37N 1.01W
Roye France **19** 49.42N 2.48E
Royston Herts. U.K. **13** 52.03N 0.01W
Rožaj Yugo. **34** 42.50N 20.15E
Rozhishche U.S.S.R. **37** 50.58N 25.15E
Rožňava Czech. **37** 48.40N 20.32E
Roztoky Czech. **38** 50.09N 14.22E
Rrëshen Albania **34** 41.47N 19.54E
Rrogozhinë Albania **34** 41.04N 19.19E
Rtishchevo U.S.S.R. **44** 52.16N 43.45E
Ruahine Range *mts.* New Zealand **86** 40.00S176.00E
Ruapehu *mtn.* New Zealand **86** 39.20S175.30E
Ruapuke I. New Zealand **86** 46.45S168.30E
Rub 'al Khali *des. see* Ar Rub 'al Khālī Saudi Arabia **60**
Rubbestadneset Norway **42** 59.49N 5.17E
Rubi *r.* Zaïre **78** 2.50N 24.06E
Rubino Ivory Coast **76** 6.04N 4.18W
Rubio Colombia **122** 7.42N 72.23W
Rubryn U.S.S.R. **37** 51.52N 27.30E
Rubtsovsk U.S.S.R. **50** 51.29N 81.10E
Ruby Mts. U.S.A. **108** 40.25N115.35W
Rūdān *r.* Iran **65** 27.02N 56.53E
Rudauli India **63** 26.45N 81.45E
Rūdbār Afghan. **62** 30.09N 62.36E
Rüdersdorf E. Germany **38** 52.29N 13.47E
Rudewa Tanzania **79** 6.40S 37.08E
Rudki U.S.S.R. **37** 49.40N 23.28E
Rudköbing Denmark **42** 54.56N 10.43E
Rudnaya Pristan U.S.S.R. **53** 44.18N135.51E
Rudnichnyy U.S.S.R. **44** 59.10N 52.28E
Rudnik Poland **37** 50.28N 22.15E
Rudnyy U.S.S.R. **50** 53.00N 63.05E
Rudo Yugo. **31** 43.37N 19.22E
Rudolstadt E. Germany **38** 50.43N 11.20E
Rudozem Bulgaria **34** 41.29N 24.51E
Rudrón *r.* Spain **26** 42.44N 3.25W
Rudyard U.S.A. **104** 46.14N 84.36W
Rue France **19** 50.16N 1.40E
Ruel Canada **104** 47.16N 81.29W
Ruen *mtn.* Bulgaria **34** 42.10N 22.31E
Rufā'ah Sudan **72** 14.46N 33.22E
Ruffec France **20** 46.02N 0.42E
Ruffieux France **21** 45.51N 5.50E
Rufiji *r.* Tanzania **79** 8.02S 39.19E
Rufino Argentina **125** 34.16S 62.45W
Rufisque Senegal **76** 14.43N 17.16W
Rufunsa Zambia **79** 15.02S 29.35E
Rugao China **54** 32.25N120.40E
Rugby U.K. **13** 52.23N 1.16W
Rugby U.S.A. **110** 48.22N100.00W
Rügen *i.* E. Germany **38** 54.25N 13.24E
Ruhpolding W. Germany **39** 47.45N 12.38E
Ruhr *f.* W. Germany **38** 51.21N 7.26E
Ruhr *r.* W. Germany **38** 51.27N 6.44E
Rui'an China **55** 26.50N120.40E
Ruijin China **55** 25.49N116.00E
Ruinen Neth. **16** 52.47N 6.21E
Rukwa *d.* Tanzania **79** 7.05S 31.25E
Rukwa, L. Tanzania **79** 8.00S 32.20E
Ruma Yugo. **31** 45.00N 19.49E
Rumaysh Lebanon **67** 33.05N 35.22E
Rumbek Sudan **73** 6.48N 29.41E
Rum Cay *i.* Bahamas **117** 23.41N 74.53W
Rumford U.S.A. **112** 44.33N 70.33W
Rum Jungle Australia **88** 13.01S131.00E
Rummāna Israel **67** 32.47N 35.18E
Rummānah Egypt **66** 31.01N 32.40E
Rumney U.S.A. **105** 43.58N 71.49W
Rumoi Japan **57** 43.56N141.39E
Runcorn U.K. **12** 53.20N 2.44W
Rundvik Sweden **40** 63.30N 19.24E
Rungāni Pakistan **62** 26.38N 65.43E
Rungwa *r.* Tanzania **79** 7.38S 31.55E
Rungwa Singida Tanzania **79** 6.57S 33.35E
Rungwe Mt. Tanzania **79** 9.10S 33.40E
Runka Nigeria **77** 12.28N 7.20E
Ruoqiang China **52** 39.00N 88.00E
Ruo Shui *r.* China **52** 41.15N101.03E
Rūpar India **62** 30.58N 76.32E
Rupert *r.* Canada **102** 51.30N 78.45W
Rupununi *r.* Guyana **122** 4.00N 58.30W
Ruqqad *r.* Syria **67** 32.44N 35.46E
Rur *r.* Neth. **16** 51.12N 5.58E
Rurutu *i.* Pacific Oc. **85** 22.25S151.20W
Rusape Zimbabwe **81** 18.30S 32.08E
Ruşayriş, Khazzān ar *resr.* Sudan **73** 11.40N 34.20E
Ruse Bulgaria **34** 43.48N 25.59E
Ruse *d.* Bulgaria **34** 43.50N 25.57E
Rusera India **63** 25.45N 86.02E
Rushan China **54** 36.54N121.30E
Rushden U.K. **13** 52.17N 0.37W
Rush Springs *town* U.S.A. **111** 34.47N 97.58W
Rushworth Australia **93** 36.38S145.02E
Rusken *l.* Sweden **43** 57.17N 14.20E
Russell Canada **105** 45.17N 75.17W
Russell U.S.A. **105** 44.26N 75.11W
Russellkonda India **63** 19.56N 84.35E
Russell L. Man. Canada **101** 56.15N101.30W
Russell L. N.W.T. Canada **100** 63.05N115.44W
Russell Pt. Canada **98** 73.30N115.00W
Russell Range *mts.* Australia **89** 33.15S123.30E
Russellville U.S.A. **111** 35.17N 93.08W
Rüsselsheim W. Germany **39** 50.00N 8.25E

Russkaya Polyana to St. Mary's, C.

Russkaya Polyana U.S.S.R. **50** 53.48N 73.54E
Rustavi U.S.S.R. **45** 41.34N 45.03E
Rustenburg R.S.A. **80** 25.39S 27.13E
Ruston U.S.A. **111** 32.32N 92.38W
Rutana Burundi **79** 3.58S 30.00E
Rütenbrock W. Germany **38** 52.50N 7.10E
Ruteng Indonesia **59** 8.35S 120.28E
Rutenga Zimbabwe **80** 21.15S 30.46E
Ruth U.S.A. **108** 39.17N 114.59W
Rutherglen Canada **104** 46.16N 79.04W
Ruthin U.K. **12** 53.07N 3.18W
Rutland U.S.A. **115** 43.36N 72.59W
Rutledge *r.* Canada **101** 61.04N 112.00W
Rutledge L. Canada **101** 61.33N 110.47W
Rutog China **63** 33.27N 79.43E
Rutshuru Zaïre **79** 1.10S 29.26E
Rutter Canada **104** 46.06N 80.40W
Ruvu Coast Tanzania **79** 6.50S 38.42E
Ruvuma *r.* Mozambique / Tanzania **79** 10.30S 40.30E
Ruvuma *d.* Tanzania **79** 10.45S 36.15E
Ruwaybah *wells* Sudan **72** 15.39N 28.45E
Ruwayfi, Jabal ar *mtn.* Jordan **67** 31.12N 36.00E
Ruwenzori Range *mts.* Uganda / Zaïre **79** 0.30N 30.00E
Ruyigi Burundi **79** 3.26S 30.14E
Ruzayevka U.S.S.R. **44** 54.04N 44.55E
Ruzitgort U.S.S.R. **44** 62.51N 64.52E
Ružomberok Czech. **37** 49.06N 19.18E
Rwanda Africa **79** 2.00S 30.00E
Ryan, Loch U.K. **14** 54.56N 5.02W
Ryasna U.S.S.R. **37** 54.00N 31.14E
Ryazan U.S.S.R. **44** 54.37N 39.43E
Ryazhsk U.S.S.R. **44** 53.40N 40.07E
Rybachiy, Poluostrov *pen.* U.S.S.R. **44** 69.45N 32.30E
Rybachye U.S.S.R. **52** 46.27N 81.30E
Rybinsk U.S.S.R. **44** 58.01N 38.52E
Rybinskoye Vodokhranilishche *resr.* U.S.S.R. **44** 58.30N 38.25E
Rybnik Poland **37** 50.06N 18.32E
Rybnitsa U.S.S.R. **37** 47.42N 29.00E
Ryd Sweden **43** 56.28N 14.41E
Rydaholm Sweden **43** 56.59N 14.16E
Rye U.K. **13** 50.57N 0.46E
Rye *r.* U.K. **12** 54.10N 0.44W
Ryfylke *f.* Norway **42** 59.30N 5.30E
Rygnestad Norway **42** 59.16N 7.29E
Ryki Poland **37** 51.39N 21.56E
Rylstone Australia **93** 32.48S 149.58E
Ryōtsu Japan **57** 38.05N 138.26E
Ryūgasaki Japan **57** 35.54N 140.11E
Ryukyu Is. *see* Nansei shotō Japan **53**
Rzeszów Poland **37** 50.04N 22.00E
Rzhev U.S.S.R. **44** 56.15N 34.18E

S

Saa Cameroon **77** 4.24N 11.25E
Sa'ad Israel **67** 31.28N 34.32E
Saale *r.* E. Germany **38** 51.57N 11.55E
Saales France **19** 48.21N 7.07E
Saalfeld E. Germany **38** 50.39N 11.22E
Saanich Canada **100** 48.28N 123.22W
Saar *r.* W. Germany **39** 49.42N 6.34E
Saarbrücken W. Germany **39** 49.14N 6.59E
Saarburg W. Germany **39** 49.36N 6.33E
Saaremaa *i.* U.S.S.R. **41** 58.25N 22.30E
Saarijärvi Finland **40** 62.43N 25.16E
Saariselkä *mts.* Finland **40** 68.15N 28.30E
Saarland *d.* W. Germany **39** 49.25N 6.45E
Saarlouis W. Germany **39** 49.21N 6.45E
Saba *i.* Leeward Is. **117** 17.42N 63.26W
Šabac Yugo. **31** 44.45N 19.42E
Sabadell Spain **25** 41.33N 2.06E
Sabah *d.* Malaysia **58** 5.30N 117.00E
Sabalān, Kūhhā-ye *mts.* Iran **65** 38.15N 47.50E
Sabana, Archipiélago de Cuba **117** 23.30N 80.00W
Sabanalarga Colombia **122** 10.38N 75.00W
Sabasṭiyah Jordan **67** 32.17N 35.12E
Sab'atayn, Ramlat as *f.* Yemen / S. Yemen **71** 15.30N 46.10E
Sabatini, Monti *mts.* Italy **30** 42.10N 12.15E
Sabaudia Italy **32** 41.18N 13.01E
Sabbioneta Italy **32** 45.00N 10.39E
Sabhā Libya **75** 27.02N 14.26E
Sabhā *d.* Libya **75** 27.02N 15.30E
Sabi *r.* Zimbabwe **81** 21.16S 32.20E
Sabiñánigo Spain **25** 42.31N 0.22W
Sabinas Mexico **111** 27.51N 101.07W
Sabinas Hidalgo Mexico **111** 26.30N 100.10W
Sabine *r.* U.S.A. **111** 30.00N 93.45W
Sabine L. U.S.A. **111** 29.50N 93.50W
Sabini, Monti *mts.* Italy **30** 42.13N 12.50E
Sabkhat al Bardawīl *l.* Egypt **66** 31.10N 33.15E
Sablayan Phil. **59** 12.50N 120.50E
Sable, C. Canada **103** 43.25N 65.35W
Sable, C. U.S.A. **113** 25.05N 65.50W
Sable I. Canada **103** 43.55N 59.50W
Sablé-sur-Sarthe France **18** 47.50N 0.20W
Sabon Birni Nigeria **77** 13.37N 6.15E
Sabongidda Nigeria **77** 6.54N 5.56E
Sabor *r.* Portugal **26** 41.10N 7.07W
Sabres France **20** 44.09N 0.44W
Sabrina Coast *f.* Antarctica **128** 67.00S 120.00E
Sabugal Portugal **26** 40.21N 7.05W
Ṣabyā Saudi Arabia **72** 17.09N 42.37E
Sabzevār Iran **65** 36.13N 57.38E
Sacaca Bolivia **124** 18.05S 66.25W
Sacajawea *mtn.* U.S.A. **108** 45.15N 117.17W
Sacandica Angola **78** 5.58S 15.56E
Sac City U.S.A. **110** 42.25N 95.00W
Sacedón Spain **26** 40.29N 2.43W
Sachigo *r.* Canada **102** 55.00N 89.00W
Sachigo L. Canada **102** 53.50N 92.00W
Sachsen *f.* E. Germany **38** 52.20N 11.20E
Sachsenburg Austria **39** 46.50N 13.21E
Sackets Harbor U.S.A. **105** 43.57N 76.07W
Säckingen W. Germany **39** 47.43N 7.56E
Sackville Canada **103** 45.54N 64.22W
Saco U.S.A. **115** 43.29N 70.28W
Sacramento Brazil **126** 19.51S 26.47W
Sacramento U.S.A. **108** 38.35N 121.30W
Sacramento *r.* U.S.A. **108** 38.03N 121.56W
Sacramento Mts. U.S.A. **109** 33.10N 105.50W
Sacramento Valley *f.* U.S.A. **108** 39.15N 122.00W
Sada Spain **26** 43.21N 8.15W
Sádaba Spain **25** 42.17N 1.16W
Sadani Tanzania **79** 6.00S 38.40E
Sadda Pakistan **62** 33.42N 70.20E
Sa Dec Vietnam **56** 10.19N 105.45E
Sādiqābād Pakistan **62** 28.18N 70.08E
Sadiya India **61** 27.49N 95.38E
Sado *i.* Japan **57** 38.00N 138.20E
Sado *r.* Portugal **27** 38.29N 8.55W
Sādri India **62** 25.11N 73.26E
Sadulgarh India **62** 29.35N 74.19E
Saeby Denmark **42** 57.20N 10.32E
Saegertown U.S.A. **114** 41.43N 80.09W
Ṣafājah *des.* Saudi Arabia **64** 26.30N 39.30E
Ṣafānīyah Egypt **66** 28.49N 30.48E
Ṣafarābād Iran **65** 38.59N 47.25E
Säffle Sweden **43** 59.08N 12.56E
Saffron Walden U.K. **13** 52.02N 0.15E
Safi Morocco **74** 32.20N 9.17W
Safīd *r.* Iran **65** 37.23N 50.11E
Safonovo R.S.F.S.R. U.S.S.R. **44** 55.08N 33.16E
Safonovo R.S.F.S.R. U.S.S.R. **44** 65.40N 48.10E
Saga China **63** 29.30N 85.09E
Saga Japan **57** 33.08N 130.30E
Sagaing Burma **56** 22.00N 96.00E
Sagaing *d.* Burma **56** 24.00N 95.00E
Sagala Mali **76** 14.09N 6.38W
Sagami *r.* Japan **57** 35.14N 139.23E
Sagamihara Japan **57** 35.32N 139.23E
Sagami-nada *b.* Japan **57** 34.55N 139.30E
Sagamore Mass. U.S.A. **115** 41.45N 70.33W
Sagamore Penn. U.S.A. **114** 40.47N 79.14W
Sāgar India **63** 23.50N 78.43E
Sagara Japan **57** 34.41N 138.12E
Sage U.S.A. **108** 41.49N 110.59W
Sag Harbor U.S.A. **115** 41.00N 72.18W
Saginaw U.S.A. **104** 43.25N 83.58W
Saginaw *r.* U.S.A. **104** 43.39N 83.51W
Saginaw B. U.S.A. **104** 43.50N 83.40W
Sagiz U.S.S.R. **45** 47.31N 54.55E
Saglouc Canada **99** 62.10N 75.40W
Sagres Portugal **27** 37.00N 8.56W
Saguache U.S.A. **108** 38.05N 106.08W
Sagua la Grande Cuba **117** 22.55N 80.05W
Saguenay *r.* Canada **103** 48.10N 69.43W
Sagunto Spain **25** 39.41N 0.16W
Sāgwāra India **62** 23.41N 74.01E
Sa'gya China **63** 28.55N 88.03E
Saḥāb Jordan **67** 31.53N 36.00E
Sahaba Sudan **72** 18.55N 30.28E
Sahagún Spain **26** 42.22N 5.02W
Saḥam Jordan **67** 32.42N 35.47E
Saḥam al Jawlān Syria **67** 32.46N 35.56E
Sahand, Kūh-e *mtn.* Iran **65** 37.37N 46.27E
Sahara *des.* Africa **75** 22.30N 3.00E
Sahāranpur India **63** 29.58N 77.33E
Saharsa India **63** 25.53N 86.36E
Sahaswān India **63** 28.05N 78.45E
Sahbā, Wādī as *r.* Saudi Arabia **65** 23.48N 49.50E
Sāhibganj India **63** 25.15N 87.39E
Sāhīwāl Punjab Pakistan **62** 31.58N 72.20E
Sāhīwāl Punjab Pakistan **62** 30.40N 73.06E
Sahtaneh *r.* Canada **100** 59.02N 122.28W
Sahuarita U.S.A. **109** 31.57N 110.58W
Sahwat al Qamḥ Syria **67** 32.36N 36.23E
Saibai *i.* Australia **90** 9.24S 142.40E
Sa'īdābād Iran **65** 29.28N 55.43E
Saidpur Bangla. **63** 25.47N 88.54E
Saidu Pakistan **62** 34.45N 72.21E
Saillans France **21** 44.42N 5.11E
Saimaa *l.* Finland **44** 61.20N 28.00E
Saimbeyli Turkey **64** 38.07N 36.08E
Saindak Pakistan **62** 29.17N 61.34E
St. Abb's Head U.K. **14** 55.54N 2.07W
St. Afrique France **20** 43.57N 2.53E
St. Agapit Canada **105** 46.34N 71.27W
St. Agathe des Monts Canada **105** 46.03N 74.17W
St. Agrève France **21** 45.01N 4.24E
St. Alban's Canada **103** 47.52N 55.51W
St. Albans U.K. **13** 51.46N 0.21W
St. Albans Vt. U.S.A. **105** 44.49N 73.05W
St. Albans W.Va. U.S.A. **114** 38.23N 81.49W
St. Albert Canada **100** 53.37N 113.40W
St. Alexis des Monts Canada **105** 46.28N 73.08W
St. Amand France **19** 50.26N 3.26E
St. Amand-Mont-Rond France **19** 46.44N 2.30E
St. Ambroix France **21** 44.15N 4.11E
St. Amour France **19** 46.26N 5.21E
St. André, Cap *c.* Madagascar **81** 16.11S 44.27E
St. André-les-Alpes France **21** 43.58N 6.30E
St. Andrews U.K. **14** 56.20N 2.48W
St. Andries Belgium **16** 51.12N 3.10E
St. Anicet Canada **105** 45.07N 74.20W
St. Ann's Bay *town* Jamaica **117** 18.26N 77.12W
St. Anthony Canada **103** 51.22N 55.35W
St. Anthony U.S.A. **106** 43.59N 111.40W
St. Antoine Canada **105** 46.39N 71.34W
St. Antonin France **20** 44.09N 1.45E
St. Arnaud Australia **92** 36.40S 143.20E
St. Astier France **20** 45.09N 0.32E
St. Auban France **21** 43.51N 6.44E
St. Augustin *r.* Canada **103** 51.14N 58.41W
St. Augustine U.S.A. **113** 29.54N 81.19W
St. Augustin Saguenay Canada **103** 51.14N 58.39W
St. Aulaye France **20** 45.12N 0.08E
St. Austell U.K. **13** 50.20N 4.48W
St. Avold France **19** 49.06N 6.42E
St. Barthélemy Canada **105** 46.12N 73.08W
St. Barthélemy *i.* Leeward Is. **117** 17.55N 62.50W
St. Basile de Portneuf Canada **105** 46.45N 71.49W
St. Béat France **20** 42.55N 0.42E
St. Bees Head U.K. **12** 54.31N 3.39W
St. Benoît-du-Sault France **18** 46.27N 1.23E
St. Boniface Canada **101** 49.55N 97.06W
St. Bonnet-de-Joux France **19** 46.29N 4.27E
St. Boswells U.K. **14** 55.35N 2.40W
St. Brides B. U.K. **13** 51.48N 5.03W
St. Brieuc France **18** 48.31N 2.47W
St. Bruno de Guigues Canada **104** 47.27N 79.26W
St. Calais France **18** 47.55N 0.45E
St. Casimir Canada **105** 46.40N 72.08W
St. Catharines Canada **104** 43.10N 79.15W
St. Catherine's Pt. U.K. **13** 50.34N 1.18W
St. Céré France **20** 44.52N 1.53E
St. Chamond France **21** 45.28N 4.30E
St. Charles Mich. U.S.A. **104** 43.18N 84.09W
St. Charles Mo. U.S.A. **110** 38.47N 90.29W
St. Chély d'Apcher France **20** 44.48N 3.17E
St. Ciers-sur-Gironde France **20** 45.18N 0.37W
St. Clair *r.* Canada **104** 42.37N 82.31W
St. Clair U.S.A. **114** 42.49N 82.30W
St. Clair, L. Canada **104** 42.25N 82.41W
St. Clair Shores *town* U.S.A. **114** 42.30N 82.54W
St. Clairsville U.S.A. **114** 40.05N 80.54W
St. Claud France **20** 45.53N 0.23E
St. Claude Canada **105** 45.40N 72.00W
St. Claude France **19** 46.23N 5.52E
St. Cloud U.S.A. **110** 45.33N 94.10W
St. Croix *i.* U.S.V.Is. **117** 17.45N 64.35W
St. Cyprien France **20** 44.52N 1.02E
St. Cyrille de Wendover Canada **105** 45.56N 72.26W
St. David's U.K. **13** 51.54N 5.16W
St. David's I. Bermuda **127** 32.23N 64.42W
St. Denis France **19** 48.56N 2.22E
St. Dié France **19** 48.17N 6.57E
St. Dizier France **19** 48.38N 4.57E
St. Donat Canada **105** 46.19N 74.13W
Sainte-Agathe-des-Monts Canada **102** 46.03N 74.17W
Sainte Anne, Rivière *r.* Canada **105** 46.52N 71.49W
Sainte Anne de Beaupré Canada **105** 47.02N 70.56W
Sainte Anne de la Pérade Canada **105** 46.35N 72.12W
Sainte-Anne-des-Monts Canada **103** 49.07N 66.29W
Sainte Anne du Lac Canada **105** 46.52N 75.21W
Sainte Croix Canada **105** 46.38N 71.44W
Sainte-Croix Switz. **39** 46.49N 6.31E
Sainte Emelie Canada **105** 46.19N 73.39W
Sainte Famille d'Aumond Canada **105** 46.27N 75.52W
Sainte Foy la Grande France **20** 44.50N 0.13E
Sainte Hermine France **18** 46.33N 1.04W
St. Elias, Mt. U.S.A. **100** 60.18N 140.55W
St. Elias Mts. Canada **100** 60.30N 139.30W
St. Éloi Canada **103** 48.02N 69.13W
Sainte-Lucia France **21** 41.42N 9.22E
Sainte Lucie Canada **105** 46.07N 74.13W
Sainte Marguerite Canada **105** 46.03N 74.05W
Sainte Marguerite *r.* Canada **103** 50.10N 66.40W
Sainte Marie, Cap *c.* Madagascar **81** 25.36S 45.08E
Sainte-Marie-aux-Mines France **19** 48.15N 7.11E
Sainte-Mathieu, Pointe de *c.* France **18** 48.20N 4.46W
Sainte Maure de Touraine France **18** 47.07N 0.37E
Sainte-Maxime France **21** 43.18N 6.38E
Sainte Menehould France **19** 49.05N 4.54E
Sainte Mère-Église France **18** 49.24N 1.19W
St. Enimie France **20** 44.22N 3.26E
Saintes France **20** 45.44N 0.38W
Saintes-Maries-de-la-Mer France **21** 43.27N 4.26E
St. Espirit Canada **105** 45.56N 73.40W
Sainte Thècle Canada **105** 46.49N 72.31W
Sainte-Thérèse-de-Blainville Canada **105** 45.38N 73.51W
St. Étienne France **21** 45.26N 4.24E
St. Fargeau France **19** 47.38N 3.04E
St. Faustin Canada **105** 46.07N 74.30W
St. Félix Canada **105** 46.10N 73.26W
Saintfield U.K. **15** 54.28N 5.50W
St. Fintan's Canada **103** 48.10N 58.50W
St. Florent France **21** 42.41N 9.18E
St. Florentin France **19** 48.00N 3.44E
St. Florent-sur-Cher France **19** 46.59N 2.15E
St. Flour France **20** 45.02N 3.05E
St. Francis U.S.A. **110** 39.47N 101.47W
St. Francisville U.S.A. **111** 30.47N 91.23W
St. Francois *r.* Canada **105** 46.07N 72.55W
St. François, Lac *l.* Canada **105** 45.55N 71.10W
St. Gabriel Canada **105** 46.17N 73.23W
St. Gallen Switz. **39** 47.25N 9.23E
St. Gaudens France **20** 43.07N 0.44E
St. Gaultier France **18** 46.38N 1.25E
St. Genis-de-Saintonge France **20** 45.29N 0.34W
St. George Australia **91** 28.03S 148.30E
St. George Bermuda **127** 32.24N 64.42W
St. George N.B. Canada **103** 45.11N 66.57W
St. George Ont. Canada **104** 43.15N 80.15W
St. George U.S.A. **108** 37.06N 113.35W
St. George, C. U.S.A. **113** 29.35N 85.04W
St. George Head Australia **93** 35.11S 150.40E
St. Georges Belgium **16** 50.37N 5.20E
St. Georges Canada **105** 46.37N 72.40W
St. George's Grenada **117** 12.04N 61.44W
St. Georges Guiana **123** 3.54N 51.48W
St. George's B. Canada **103** 48.20N 59.00W
St. George's Channel Rep. of Ire. / U.K. **15** 51.30N 6.20W
St. George's I. Bermuda **127** 32.24N 64.42W
St. Germain France **19** 48.54N 2.05E
St. Germain de Grantham Canada **105** 45.50N 72.34W
St. Germain-du-Bois France **19** 46.45N 5.15E
St. Germain-Lembron France **20** 45.28N 3.14E
St. Germain-l'Herm France **20** 45.28N 3.33E
St. Gervais d'Auvergne France **20** 46.02N 2.49E
St. Géry France **20** 44.29N 1.35E
St. Gheorghe's Mouth *est.* Romania **29** 44.51N 29.37E
St. Gilles-Croix-de-Vie France **18** 46.42N 1.57W
St. Girons France **20** 42.59N 1.09E
St. Gotthard Pass Switz. **17** 46.30N 8.55E
St. Govan's Head U.K. **13** 51.36N 4.55W
St. Grégoire Canada **105** 46.16N 72.30W
St. Guénolé France **18** 47.49N 4.20W
St. Guillaume d'Upton Canada **105** 45.53N 72.46W
St. Helena *i.* Atlantic Oc. **127** 15.58S 5.43W
St. Helena B. R.S.A. **80** 32.35S 18.05E
St. Helens U.K. **12** 53.28N 2.43W
St. Helens U.S.A. **108** 45.52N 122.48W
St. Helens, Mt. U.S.A. **108** 46.12N 122.11W
St. Helier U.K. **13** 49.12N 2.07W
St. Hilaire-du-Harcouët France **18** 48.35N 1.06W
St. Hippolyte France **19** 47.19N 6.49E
St. Hubert Belgium **16** 50.02N 5.22E
St. Hyacinthe Canada **105** 45.37N 72.57W
St. Ignace U.S.A. **104** 45.52N 84.43W
St. Ignace du Lac Canada **105** 46.43N 73.49W
St. Ives U.K. **13** 50.13N 5.29W
St. Jacobs Canada **104** 43.32N 80.33W
St. Jacques Canada **105** 45.57N 73.34W
St. Jean Canada **105** 45.19N 73.16W
St. Jean *r.* Canada **103** 50.17N 64.20W
St. Jean France **21** 45.17N 6.21E
St. Jean, Lac *l.* Canada **103** 48.35N 72.00W
St. Jean-d'Angély France **20** 45.57N 0.31W
St. Jean-de-Bournay France **21** 45.29N 5.08E
St. Jean-de-Losne France **19** 47.06N 5.15E
St. Jean-de-Luz France **20** 43.23N 1.40W
St. Jean de Matha Canada **105** 46.14N 73.33W
St. Jean-de-Monts France **18** 46.48N 2.03W
St. Jean-du-Gard France **20** 44.06N 3.53E
St. Jean Pied-de-Port France **20** 43.10N 1.14W
St. Jérôme Canada **105** 45.47N 74.00W
St. John Canada **103** 45.16N 66.03W
St. John *r.* Canada **103** 45.16N 66.04W
St. John U.S.A. **111** 38.00N 98.46W
St. John, C. Canada **103** 50.00N 55.32W
St. John B. Canada **103** 50.40N 57.08W
St. John's Antigua **117** 17.07N 61.51W
St. John's Canada **103** 47.34N 52.43W
St. Johns U.S.A. **109** 34.30N 109.22W
St. Johns *r.* U.S.A. **113** 30.24N 81.24W
St. Johnsbury U.S.A. **105** 44.25N 72.01W
St. John's Pt. U.K. **15** 54.14N 5.39W
St. Joseph La. U.S.A. **111** 31.55N 91.14W
St. Joseph Mich. U.S.A. **112** 42.05N 86.30W
St. Joseph Mo. U.S.A. **110** 39.46N 94.51W
St. Joseph, L. Canada **102** 51.05N 90.35W
St. Joseph I. Canada **104** 46.13N 83.57W
St. Jovite Canada **105** 46.07N 74.36W
St. Jude Canada **105** 45.46N 72.59W
St. Julien-en-Born France **20** 44.04N 1.14W
St. Julien-en-Genevois France **21** 46.08N 6.05E
St. Junien France **20** 45.53N 0.54E
St. Just-en-Chaussée France **19** 49.30N 2.26E
St. Just-en-Chevalet France **20** 45.55N 3.50E
St. Kilda *i.* U.K. **10** 57.55N 8.20W
St. Kitts-Nevis Leeward Is. **117** 17.20N 62.45W
St. Lambert Canada **105** 45.30N 73.30W
St. Laurent Man. Canada **101** 50.24N 97.56W
St. Laurent Que. Canada **105** 45.30N 73.40W
St. Laurent du Maroni Guiana **123** 5.30N 54.02W
St. Laurent-et-Benon France **20** 45.09N 0.49W
St. Lawrence *r.* Canada **105** 44.15N 76.10W
St. Lawrence, G. of Canada **103** 48.00N 62.00W
St. Lawrence I. U.S.A. **98** 63.00N 170.00W
St. Léonard d'Aston Canada **105** 46.06N 72.22W
St. Lewis Sd. Canada **103** 52.20N 55.40W
St. Lin Canada **105** 45.51N 73.45W
St. Lô France **18** 49.07N 1.05W
St. Louis Senegal **76** 16.01N 16.30W
St. Louis U.S.A. **110** 38.38N 90.11W
St. Louis Park *town* U.S.A. **110** 44.56N 93.22W
St. Loup-sur-Semouse France **19** 47.53N 6.16E
St. Lucia Windward Is. **117** 14.05N 61.00W
St. Lucia, L. R.S.A. **81** 28.05S 32.26E
St. Magnus B. U.K. **10** 60.25N 1.35W
St. Maixent France **18** 46.25N 0.12W
St. Malo Canada **105** 45.12N 71.30W
St. Malo France **18** 48.39N 2.01W
St. Malo, Golfe de *g.* France **18** 48.45N 2.00W
St. Mamert France **21** 43.53N 4.12E
St.-Marc Haiti **117** 19.08N 72.41W
St. Marc des Carrières Canada **105** 46.41N 72.03W
St. Marcellin France **21** 45.09N 5.19E
St. Margaret's Hope U.K. **14** 58.49N 2.57W
St. Maries U.S.A. **108** 47.19N 116.35W
St. Martin *i.* Leeward Is. **117** 18.05N 63.05W
St. Martin U.K. **13** 49.27N 2.34W
St. Martin, L. Canada **101** 51.37N 98.29W
St. Martin B. U.S.A. **104** 45.57N 84.35W
St. Martin-de-Londres France **20** 43.47N 3.44E
St. Martin d'Hères France **21** 45.10N 5.46E
St. Martin's *i.* U.K. **13** 49.57N 6.16W
St. Mary U.K. **13** 49.14N 2.10W
St. Mary *r.* U.S.A. **104** 46.30N 84.36W
St. Marys Australia **91** 41.33S 148.12E
St. Mary's Canada **104** 43.16N 81.08W
St. Mary's *r.* Canada **103** 45.02N 61.54W
St. Mary's *i.* U.K. **13** 49.55N 6.16W
St. Marys Penn. U.S.A. **114** 41.26N 78.34W
St. Marys W.Va. U.S.A. **114** 39.23N 81.12W
St. Mary's, C. Canada **103** 46.49N 54.12W

St. Mary's B. to **Sangonera**

St. Mary's B. Canada **103** 46.50N 53.47W
St. Mathieu France **20** 45.42N 0.46E
St. Matthew I. U.S.A. **98** 60.30N172.45W
St. Maur France **19** 48.48N 2.30E
St. Maurice *r.* Canada **105** 46.21N 72.31W
St. Maurice Prov. Park Canada **105** 46.52N 73.10W
St. Méen-le-Grand France **18** 48.11N 2.12W
St. Michel des Saints Canada **105** 46.41N 73.55W
St. Mihiel France **19** 48.54N 5.33E
St. Moritz Switz. **39** 46.30N 9.50E
St. Nazaire France **18** 47.17N 2.12W
St. Neots U.K. **13** 52.14N 0.16W
St. Niklaas Belgium **16** 51.10N 4.09E
St. Omer France **19** 50.45N 2.15E
St. Pacôme Canada **103** 47.24N 69.57W
St. Pascal Canada **103** 47.32N 69.48W
St. Patrick, Lac *l.* Canada **105** 46.21N 77.18W
St. Paul *r.* Canada **103** 51.26N 57.40W
St. Paul A.H.Prov. France **21** 44.31N 6.45E
St. Paul Pyr.Or. France **20** 42.49N 2.29E
St. Paul Ark. U.S.A. **111** 35.50N 93.48W
St. Paul Minn. U.S.A. **110** 45.00N 93.10W
St. Paul Nebr. U.S.A. **110** 41.13N 98.27W
St. Paul, Île *i.* Indian Oc. **49** 38.43S 77.29E
St. Paul de Chester Canada **105** 45.57N 71.49W
St. Paul du Nord Canada **103** 48.27N 69.15W
St. Paulien France **20** 45.08N 3.49E
St. Paulin Canada **105** 46.25N 73.01W
St. Paul Rocks *is.* Atlantic Oc. **127** 1.00N 29.23W
St. Peter U.S.A. **110** 44.17N 93.57W
St. Peter Port U.K. **13** 49.27N 2.32W
St. Petersburg U.S.A. **113** 27.45N 82.40W
St. Pierre Ch.Mar. France **20** 45.59N 1.14W
St. Pierre S.Mar. France **18** 49.48N 0.29E
St. Pierre, Lac *l.* Canada **105** 46.12N 72.52W
St. Pierre and Miquelon *is.* N. America **103** 46.55N 56.10W
St. Pierre-Église France **18** 49.40N 1.24W
St. Pierre le Moûtier France **19** 46.48N 3.07E
St. Pierreville France **21** 44.49N 4.29E
St. Pol-de-Leon France **18** 48.41N 3.59W
St. Pol-sur-Ternoise France **19** 50.23N 2.20E
St. Pölten Austria **36** 48.13N 15.37E
St. Polycarpe Canada **105** 45.18N 74.18W
St. Pons France **20** 43.29N 2.46E
St. Pourçain France **20** 46.19N 3.17E
St. Priest France **21** 45.42N 4.57E
St. Quentin France **19** 49.51N 3.17E
St. Raphaël France **21** 43.25N 6.46E
St. Raymond Canada **105** 46.54N 71.50W
St. Regis Falls U.S.A. **105** 44.40N 74.33W
St. Rémy France **21** 43.47N 4.50E
St. Renan France **18** 48.26N 4.37W
St. Roch de Mekinac Canada **105** 46.48N 72.44W
St. Savin France **18** 46.34N 0.52E
St. Savinien France **20** 45.53N 0.50W
St. Seine-l'Abbaye France **19** 47.26N 4.47E
St. Siméon Canada **103** 47.55N 69.58W
St. Stephen Canada **103** 45.12N 67.17W
St. Sulpice les Feuilles France **20** 46.19N 1.22E
St. Symphorien France **20** 44.26N 0.30W
St. Thomas Canada **104** 42.47N 81.12W
St. Thomas *i.* U.S.V.Is. **117** 18.22N 64.57W
St. Tite Canada **105** 46.44N 72.34W
St. Tropez France **21** 43.16N 6.38E
St. Truiden Belgium **16** 50.49N 5.11E
St. Ubald Canada **105** 46.45N 72.16W
St. Valéry France **18** 49.52N 0.44E
St. Valéry-sur-Somme France **19** 50.11N 1.38E
St. Vallier France **21** 45.10N 4.49E
St. Vallier-de-Thiey France **21** 43.42N 6.51E
St. Varent France **18** 46.53N 0.14W
St. Vincent, Cap *c.* Madagascar **81** 21.57S 43.16E
St. Vincent, G. Australia **92** 35.00S138.05E
St. Vincent and the Grenadines Windward Is. **117** 13.00N 61.15W
St. Vincent-de-Tyrosse France **20** 43.40N 1.18W
St. Vith Belgium **16** 50.15N 6.08E
St. Vivien-de-Médoc France **20** 45.26N 1.02W
St. Wendel W. Germany **39** 49.28N 7.10E
St. Yrieix France **20** 45.31N 1.12E
St. Zénon Canada **105** 46.33N 73.49W
Sairs, L. Canada **104** 46.51N 78.12W
Saitama *d.* Japan **57** 35.55N139.00E
Sajama *mtn.* Bolivia **124** 18.06S 69.00W
Saka Kenya **79** 0.09S 39.18E
Sakai Japan **57** 34.35N135.28E
Sakākah Saudi Arabia **64** 29.59N 40.12E
Sakakawea, L. *see* Garrison Resr. U.S.A. **110**
Sakami *r.* Canada **102** 53.40N 76.40W
Sakami, Lac *l.* Canada **102** 53.10N 77.00W
Sakâne, Erg i-n *f.* Mali **74** 21.00N 1.00W
Sakania Zaïre **79** 12.44S 28.34E
Sakarya *r.* Turkey **64** 41.08N 30.36E
Sakata Japan **57** 38.55N139.51E
Sakété Benin **77** 6.45N 2.45E
Sakhalin *i.* U.S.S.R. **53** 50.00N143.00E
Sākhar Afghan. **62** 32.57N 65.32E
Sakhi Sarwar Pakistan **62** 29.59N 70.18E
Sakhnin Israel **67** 32.52N 35.17E
Sākib Jordan **67** 32.17N 35.49E
Sākoli India **63** 21.05N 79.59E
Sakrand Pakistan **62** 26.08N 68.16E
Sakri India **62** 21.02N 74.40E
Sakrivier R.S.A. **80** 30.53S 20.24E
Sakti India **63** 22.02N 82.58E
Sakuma Japan **57** 35.05N137.48E
Sal *r.* U.S.S.R. **45** 47.33N 40.40E
Sala Ethiopia **72** 16.58N 37.27E
Sala Sweden **43** 59.55N 16.36E
Salaca *r.* U.S.S.R. **41** 57.45N 24.21E
Salacgriva U.S.S.R. **41** 57.45N 24.21E
Sala Consilina Italy **33** 40.24N 15.36E
Salado *r.* Buenos Aires Argentina **125** 35.44S 57.22W
Salado *r.* Santa Fé Argentina **125** 31.40S 60.41W
Salado *r.* La Pampa Argentina **125** 36.15S 66.55W
Salado *r.* Mexico **111** 26.50N 99.17W
Salaga Ghana **76** 8.36N 0.32W
Salailua W. Samoa **84** 13.42S172.35W
Salālah Oman **60** 17.00N 54.04E
Salālah Sudan **72** 21.19N 36.13E
Salamanca Spain **26** 40.58N 5.39W
Salamanca *d.* Spain **26** 40.45N 6.00W
Salamanca U.S.A. **114** 42.09N 78.43W
Salamat *d.* Chad **73** 11.00N 20.40E
Salāmbek Pakistan **62** 28.18N 65.09E
Salamina Colombia **122** 5.24N 75.31W
Salamís *i.* Greece **35** 37.54N 23.26E
Salamís *town* Greece **35** 37.59N 23.28E
Salām Khān Afghan. **62** 31.47N 66.45E
Salani W. Samoa **84** 14.02S171.35W
Salar de Uyuni *l.* Bolivia **121** 20.30S 67.45W
Salas de los Infantes Spain **26** 42.01N 3.17W
Salatiga Indonesia **59** 7.15S110.34E
Salāya India **62** 22.19N 69.35E
Sala y Gomez *i.* Pacific Oc. **85** 26.28S105.28W
Salbris France **19** 47.26N 2.03E
Salcia Romania **34** 43.57N 24.56E
Salcombe U.K. **13** 50.14N 3.47W
Saldaña Spain **26** 42.31N 4.44W
Saldanha R.S.A. **80** 33.00S 17.56E
Saldanha B. R.S.A. **80** 33.05S 17.50E
Saldus U.S.S.R. **41** 56.40N 22.30E
Sale Australia **93** 38.06S147.06E
Salé Morocco **74** 34.04N 6.50W
Salekhard U.S.S.R. **44** 66.33N 66.35E
Salelologa W. Samoa **84** 13.43S172.13W
Salem India **61** 11.38N 78.08E
Salem Ind. U.S.A. **112** 38.38N 86.06W
Salem Mass. U.S.A. **115** 42.31N 70.55W
Salem Mo. U.S.A. **111** 37.39N 91.32W
Salem N.H. U.S.A. **115** 42.47N 71.12W
Salem N.J. U.S.A. **115** 39.34N 75.28W
Salem N.Y. U.S.A. **115** 43.10N 73.20W
Salem Ohio U.S.A. **114** 40.54N 80.52W
Salem Oreg. U.S.A. **108** 44.57N123.01W
Salem Va. U.S.A. **113** 37.17N 80.04W
Salem W.Va. U.S.A. **114** 39.17N 80.34W
Salemi Italy **32** 37.49N 12.49E
Sälen Sweden **41** 61.10N 13.16E
Salerno Italy **33** 40.41N 14.47E
Salerno, Golfo di *g.* Italy **33** 40.32N 14.42E
Salers France **20** 45.08N 2.30E
Salfit Jordan **67** 32.05N 35.11E
Salford U.K. **12** 53.30N 2.17W
Salgótarján Hungary **37** 48.07N 19.48E
Salgueiro Brazil **123** 8.04S 39.05W
Sali Yugo. **31** 43.56N 15.10E
Salies-de-Béarn France **20** 43.29N 0.55W
Salignac Eyvignes France **20** 44.59N 1.19E
Salima Malaŵi **79** 13.45S 34.29E
Salim's Tanzania **79** 10.37S 36.33E
Salina U.S.A. **110** 38.50N 97.37W
Salina, Isola *i.* Italy **33** 38.34N 14.51E
Salina Cruz Mexico **116** 16.11N 95.12W
Salinas Ecuador **122** 2.13S 80.58W
Salinas U.S.A. **108** 36.40N121.38W
Salinas *r.* U.S.A. **106** 36.45N121.48W
Salinas, Cabo de *c.* Spain **25** 39.16N 3.03E
Saline U.S.A. **104** 42.10N 83.47W
Saline *r.* U.S.A. **110** 38.51N 97.30W
Salineville U.S.A. **114** 40.37N 80.51W
Salinópolis Brazil **123** 0.37S 47.20W
Salins France **19** 46.57N 5.53E
Salisbury U.K. **13** 51.04N 1.48W
Salisbury Md. U.S.A. **115** 38.22N 75.36W
Salisbury N.C. U.S.A. **113** 35.20N 80.30W
Salisbury Plain *f.* U.K. **13** 51.15N 1.55W
Salisbury Sd. U.S.A. **100** 57.30N135.56W
Şalkhad Syria **66** 32.29N 36.42E
Sallanches France **21** 45.56N 6.38E
Salles-Curan France **20** 44.11N 2.47E
Salling *f.* Denmark **42** 56.40N 9.00E
Sallisaw U.S.A. **111** 35.28N 94.47W
Sallyāna Nepal **63** 28.22N 82.12E
Salmās Iran **65** 38.13N 44.50E
Salmi U.S.S.R. **44** 61.19N 31.46E
Salmon *r.* Canada **100** 54.03N122.40W
Salmon U.S.A. **108** 45.11N113.55W
Salmon *r.* U.S.A. **108** 45.51N116.46W
Salmon Gums Australia **89** 32.59S121.39E
Salmon River Mts. U.S.A. **108** 44.45N115.30W
Salo Finland **41** 60.23N 23.08E
Salò Italy **30** 45.36N 10.31E
Salobreña Spain **27** 36.44N 3.35W
Salome U.S.A. **109** 33.47N113.37W
Salon France **21** 43.38N 5.06E
Salonga *r.* Zaïre **78** 0.09S 19.52E
Salonika *see* Thessaloniki Greece **34**
Salonta Romania **37** 46.48N 21.40E
Salor *r.* Spain **27** 39.39N 7.03W
Salsk U.S.S.R. **45** 46.30N 41.33E
Salso *r.* Italy **32** 37.05N 13.57E
Salsomaggiore Terme Italy **30** 44.49N 9.59E
Salt *r.* U.S.A. **109** 33.23N112.18W
Salta Argentina **124** 24.47S 65.24W
Salta *d.* Argentina **124** 25.00S 65.00W
Saltdal Norway **40** 67.06N 15.25E
Saltee Is. Rep. of Ire. **15** 52.08N 6.36W
Saltfjorden *est.* Norway **40** 67.15N 14.10E
Saltfleet U.K. **12** 53.25N 0.11E
Salt Fork *r.* U.S.A. **107** 36.41N 97.05W
Saltillo Mexico **111** 25.25N101.00W
Salt Lake City U.S.A. **108** 40.46N111.53W
Salto Argentina **125** 34.17S 60.15W
Salto Brazil **126** 23.10S 47.16W
Salto *r.* Italy **30** 42.23N 12.54E
Salto Uruguay **125** 31.23S 57.58W
Salto da Divisa Brazil **123** 16.04S 40.00W
Salton Sea *l.* U.S.A. **109** 33.19N115.50W
Salūmbar India **62** 24.08N 74.03E
Saluzzo Italy **30** 44.39N 7.29E
Salvador Brazil **123** 12.58S 38.29W
Salvador Canada **101** 52.12N109.32W
Salvaterra de Magos Portugal **27** 39.01N 8.48W
Salversville U.S.A. **113** 37.43N 83.06W
Salviac France **20** 44.41N 1.16E
Salween *r.* Burma / China **56** 16.32N 97.35E
Salyany U.S.S.R. **65** 39.36N 48.59E
Salzach *r.* Austria **39** 48.12N 12.56E
Salzbrunn Namibia **80** 24.23S 18.00E
Salzburg Austria **39** 47.48N 13.02E
Salzburg *d.* Austria **39** 47.15N 13.00E
Salzgitter W. Germany **38** 52.02N 10.22E
Salzkammergut *f.* Austria **39** 47.38N 13.30E
Salzwedel E. Germany **38** 52.51N 11.09E
Sam India **62** 26.50N 70.31E
Sama Spain **26** 43.18N 5.41W
Samalambo Angola **78** 14.16S 17.53E
Samālūt Egypt **66** 28.18N 30.43E
Samaná Dom. Rep. **117** 19.14N 69.20W
Samana Cay *i.* Bahamas **117** 23.05N 73.45W
Samanga Tanzania **79** 8.24S 39.18E
Samannūd Egypt **66** 30.58N 31.14E
Samar Jordan **67** 32.41N 35.47E
Samar *i.* Phil. **59** 11.45N125.15E
Samara *r.* U.S.S.R. **44** 53.17N 50.42E
Samarai P.N.G. **90** 10.37S150.40E
Samaria *see* As Sāmirah Jordan **67**
Samarinda Indonesia **58** 0.30S117.09E
Samarkand U.S.S.R. **9** 39.40N 66.57E
Sāmarrā Iraq **65** 34.13N 43.52E
Samāstipur India **63** 25.51N 85.47E
Samawāri Pakistan **62** 28.34N 66.46E
Samba Zaïre **78** 0.14N 21.19E
Sambalpur India **63** 21.27N 83.58E
Sambao *r.* Madagascar **81** 16.40S 44.26E
Sambava Madagascar **81** 14.16S 50.10E
Sambāza Pakistan **62** 31.46N 69.20E
Sambhal India **63** 28.35N 78.33E
Sāmbhar India **62** 26.55N 75.12E
Sāmbhar L. India **62** 26.58N 75.05E
Sambor U.S.S.R. **37** 49.31N 23.10E
Samborombón, Bahía *b.* Argentina **125** 36.00S 57.00W
Sambre *r.* Belgium **16** 50.29N 4.52E
Samburu Kenya **79** 3.46S 39.17E
Samch'ŏk S. Korea **53** 37.30N129.10E
Samdari India **62** 25.49N 72.35E
Same Tanzania **79** 4.10S 37.43E
Samnū Libya **75** 27.16N 14.54E
Samoa *is.* Pacific Oc. **84** 14.20S170.00W
Samoa Is. Pacific Oc. **84** 14.00S171.00W
Samobor Yugo. **36** 45.48N 15.43E
Samokov Bulgaria **34** 42.20N 23.33E
Samorogouan U. Volta **76** 11.21N 4.57W
Sámos *i.* Greece **35** 37.45N 26.50E
Sámos *town* Greece **35** 37.45N 27.00E
Samothráki *i.* Greece **34** 40.30N 25.32E
Samothráki *town* Greece **34** 40.28N 25.31E
Sampang Indonesia **59** 7.13S113.15E
Sampit Indonesia **58** 2.34S112.59E
Sampson U.S.A. **114** 42.44N 76.54W
Sam Rayburn Resr. U.S.A. **111** 31.27N 94.37W
Samsang China **63** 30.22N 82.57E
Samsö Denmark **42** 55.52N 10.37E
Sam Son Vietnam **55** 19.44N105.53E
Samsun Turkey **64** 41.17N 36.22E
Samtredia U.S.S.R. **45** 42.10N 42.22E
Samui, Ko *i.* Thailand **56** 9.30N100.00E
Samur *r.* U.S.S.R. **45** 42.00N 48.20E
Samut Prakan Thailand **56** 13.32N100.35E
Samut Sakhon Thailand **56** 13.31N100.13E
San *r.* Kampuchea **56** 13.32N105.57E
San Mali **76** 13.21N 4.57W
San *r.* Poland **37** 50.25N 22.20E
Şan'ā' Yemen **71** 15.23N 44.14E
Sana *see* Şan'ā' Yemen **71**
Sana *r.* Yugo. **31** 45.03N 16.23E
Sanaba U. Volta **76** 12.25N 3.47W
Sanaga *r.* Cameroon **77** 3.35N 9.40E
San Ambrosio *i.* Chile **121** 26.28S 79.53W
Sānand India **62** 22.59N 72.23E
Sanandaj Iran **65** 35.18N 47.01E
San Andreas U.S.A. **108** 38.12N120.41W
San Andrés, Isla de *i.* Colombia **117** 12.33N 81.42W
San Andrés Tuxtla Mexico **116** 18.27N 95.13W
San Angelo U.S.A. **111** 31.28N100.26W
San Antonio Chile **125** 33.35S 71.38W
San Antonio N.Mex. U.S.A. **109** 33.55N106.52W
San Antonio Tex. U.S.A. **111** 29.28N 98.31W
San Antonio, C. Cuba **117** 21.50N 84.57W
San Antonio, Cabo *c.* Argentina **125** 36.40S 56.42W
San Antonio, Punta *c.* Mexico **109** 29.45N115.41W
San Antonio, Sierra de *mts.* Mexico **109** 30.00N110.10W
San Antonio Abad Spain **25** 38.59N 1.18E
San Antonio de Areco Argentina **125** 34.16S 59.30W
San Antonio Oeste Argentina **125** 40.44S 64.57W
San Augustine U.S.A. **111** 31.32N 94.07W
Sanāwad India **62** 22.11N 76.04E
San Bartolomeo Italy **33** 41.24N 15.01E
San Baudilio Spain **25** 41.21N 2.03E
San Benedetto Italy **31** 42.57N 13.53E
San Benedetto Po Italy **32** 45.02N 10.55E
San Benito Guatemala **117** 16.55N 89.54W
San Benito U.S.A. **111** 26.08N 97.38W
San Bernardino U.S.A. **109** 34.06N117.17W
San Bernardo Chile **125** 33.36S 70.43W
San Blas, C. U.S.A. **113** 29.40N 85.22W
San Bonifacio Italy **32** 45.24N 11.16E
Sanbornville U.S.A. **115** 43.30N 70.57W
San Candido Italy **30** 46.44N 12.17E
San Carlos Chile **125** 36.25S 71.58W
San Carlos Mexico **111** 29.01N100.51W
San Carlos Nicaragua **117** 11.07N 84.47W
San Carlos Phil. **59** 15.59N120.22E
San Carlos Venezuela **122** 1.55N 67.04W
San Carlos Venezuela **122** 9.39N 68.35W
San Carlos de Bariloche Argentina **125** 41.08S 71.15W
San Carlos de la Rápita Spain **25** 40.37N 0.36E
San Carlos del Zulia Venezuela **122** 9.01N 71.55W
San Cataldo Italy **32** 37.29N 14.00E
Sancergues France **19** 47.09N 2.55E
Sancerre France **19** 47.20N 2.51E
Sancerrois, Collines du *hills* France **19** 47.25N 2.45E
Sancha He *r.* China **55** 26.50N106.04E
San Clemente Spain **27** 39.24N 2.26W
San Clemente U.S.A. **109** 33.26N117.37W
San Clemente *i.* U.S.A. **109** 32.54N118.29W
Sancoins France **19** 46.50N 2.55E
San Cristóbal Argentina **124** 30.20S 61.41W
San Cristóbal Dom. Rep. **117** 18.27N 70.07W
San Cristóbal Venezuela **122** 7.46N 72.15W
Sancti Spíritus Cuba **117** 21.55N 79.28W
Sand Norway **42** 59.29N 6.15E
Sanda *i.* U.K. **14** 55.17N 5.34W
Sandakan Malaysia **58** 5.52N118.04E
Sandanski Bulgaria **34** 41.34N 23.17E
Sandaré Mali **76** 14.40N 10.15W
Sandared Sweden **43** 57.43N 12.47E
Sanday *i.* U.K. **14** 59.15N 2.33W
Sandbach U.K. **12** 53.09N 2.23W
Sandefjord Norway **42** 59.08N 10.14E
Sanders U.S.A. **109** 35.13N109.20W
Sanderson U.S.A. **111** 30.09N102.24W
Sandersville U.S.A. **113** 32.59N 82.49W
Sandgate Australia **93** 27.18S153.00E
Sandgirt L. Canada **103** 53.50N 65.10W
Sandhammaren *c.* Denmark **43** 55.23N 14.12E
Sandhornöy *i.* Norway **40** 67.05N 14.10E
Sāndi India **63** 27.18N 79.57E
Sandia Peru **122** 14.14S 69.25W
San Diego U.S.A. **109** 32.43N117.09W
San Diego, C. Argentina **125** 54.38S 65.05W
Sandīla India **63** 27.05N 80.31E
Sand Lake *town* Canada **102** 47.45N 84.30W
Sandnes Norway **42** 58.51N 5.44E
Sandness U.K. **14** 60.18N 1.38W
Sandö *i.* Faroe Is. **10** 61.50N 6.45W
Sandoa Zaïre **78** 9.41S 22.56E
Sandomierz Poland **37** 50.41N 21.45E
San Donà di Piave Italy **32** 45.38N 12.34E
Sandover *r.* Australia **90** 21.43S136.32E
Sandoway Burma **56** 18.28N 94.20E
Sandown U.K. **13** 50.39N 1.09W
Sandpoint *town* U.S.A. **108** 48.17N116.34W
Sandringham U.K. **12** 52.50N 0.30E
Sandstone Australia **89** 27.59S119.17E
Sandu Shuizu Zizhixian China **55** 25.59N107.52E
Sandusky Mich. U.S.A. **114** 43.25N 82.50W
Sandusky Ohio U.S.A. **114** 41.27N 82.42W
Sandveld *f.* Namibia **80** 21.25S 20.00E
Sandvika Norway **42** 59.54N 10.31E
Sandviken Sweden **41** 60.37N 16.46E
Sandwich B. Canada **103** 53.35N 57.15W
Sandwip I. Bangla. **63** 22.29N 91.26E
Sandy U.S.A. **108** 40.35N111.53W
Sandy B. St. Helena **127** 16.02S 5.42W
Sandy Bight *b.* Australia **89** 33.53S123.25E
Sandy C. Australia **90** 24.42S153.17E
Sandy Creek *town* U.S.A. **115** 43.39N 76.05W
Sandy Desert Pakistan **62** 28.00N 65.00E
Sandy Hook *f.* U.S.A. **115** 40.27N 74.00W
Sandy L. Nfld. Canada **103** 49.16N 57.00W
Sandy L. Ont. Canada **102** 53.00N 93.00W
Sandy Lake *town* Ont. Canada **102** 53.00N 93.00W
Sandy Lake *town* Sask. Canada **101** 57.00N107.15W
San Enrique Argentina **125** 35.47S 60.22W
San Esteban, Isla *i.* Mexico **109** 28.41N112.35W
San Esteban de Gormaz Spain **26** 41.35N 3.12W
San Felipe Chile **125** 32.45S 70.44W
San Felipe Colombia **122** 1.55N 67.06W
San Felipe Mexico **109** 31.00N114.52W
San Felipe Venezuela **122** 10.25N 68.40W
San Felíu de Guixols Spain **25** 41.47N 3.02E
San Félix *i.* Chile **121** 26.23S 80.05W
San Fernando Argentina **125** 34.26S 58.34W
San Fernando Chile **125** 34.35S 71.00W
San Fernando *r.* Mexico **111** 24.55N 97.40W
San Fernando Phil. **59** 16.39N120.19E
San Fernando Spain **27** 36.28N 6.12W
San Fernando Trinidad **122** 10.16N 61.28W
San Fernando de Apure Venezuela **122** 7.35N 67.15W
San Fernando de Atabapo Venezuela **122** 4.03N 67.45W
Sanford *r.* Australia **88** 27.22S115.53E
Sanford Fla. U.S.A. **113** 28.49N 81.17W
Sanford Maine U.S.A. **115** 43.26N 70.46W
Sanford N.C. U.S.A. **113** 35.29N 79.10W
San Francisco Argentina **124** 31.29S 62.06W
San Francisco Mexico **109** 30.50N112.40W
San Francisco U.S.A. **108** 37.48N122.24W
San Francisco *r.* U.S.A. **109** 32.59N109.22W
San Francisco, C. Ecuador **122** 0.50N 80.05W
San Francisco del Oro Mexico **109** 26.52N105.51W
San Francisco de Macorís Dom. Rep. **117** 19.19N 70.15W
San Fratelo Italy **33** 38.01N 14.36E
Sanga Angola **78** 11.09S 15.21E
Sanga-Tolon U.S.S.R. **51** 61.44N149.30E
San Gavino Monreale Italy **32** 39.33N 8.48E
Sang-e Māsheh Afghan. **62** 33.08N 67.27E
Sangerhausen E. Germany **38** 51.28N 11.17E
Sanggan He *r.* China **54** 40.23N115.18E
Sangha *r.* Congo **78** 1.10S 16.47E
Sanghar Pakistan **62** 26.02N 68.57E
Sangihe *i.* Indonesia **59** 3.30N125.30E
Sangihe, Kepulauan *is.* Indonesia **59** 2.45N125.20E
San Gil Colombia **122** 6.35N 73.08W
San Gimignano Italy **30** 43.28N 11.02E
San Giovanni in Fiore Italy **33** 39.16N 16.42E
San Giovanni in Persiceto Italy **30** 44.38N 11.11E
San Giovanni Rotondo Italy **31** 41.42N 15.44E
San Giovanni Valdarno Italy **30** 43.34N 11.32E
Sangkulirang Indonesia **58** 1.00N117.58E
Sāngli India **60** 16.55N 74.37E
Sangmélima Cameroon **77** 2.55N 12.01E
Sangonera *r.* Spain **25** 37.59N 1.04W

San Gottardo, Passo del to Sátão

San Gottardo, Passo del *pass* Switz. **39** 46.33N 8.34E
Sangre de Cristo Mts. U.S.A. **108** 37.30N105.15W
San Gregorio Uruguay **125** 32.37S 55.40W
Sangri China **63** 29.18N 92.05E
Sangro *r.* Italy **31** 42.14N 14.32E
Sangrūr India **62** 30.14N 75.51E
Sangsues, Lac aux *l.* Canada **105** 46.29N 77.57W
Sangüesa Spain **25** 42.35N 1.17W
Sangzhi China **55** 29.24N110.09E
Sanhala Ivory Coast **76** 10.01N 6.48W
San Ignacio Bolivia **124** 16.23S 60.59W
San Ignacio Mexico **109** 27.27N112.51W
San Ignacio Paraguay **124** 26.52S 57.03W
San Ignacio, Laguna *l.* Mexico **109** 26.50N113.11W
San Ildefonso o La Granja Spain **26** 40.54N 4.00W
San Isidro Argentina **125** 34.29S 58.31W
Sanīyah, Hawr as *l.* Iraq **65** 31.52N 46.50E
San Javier Argentina **125** 30.40S 59.55W
San Javier Bolivia **124** 16.22S 62.38W
San Javier Chile **125** 35.35S 71.45W
Sanjāwi Pakistan **62** 30.17N 68.21E
Sanjō Japan **57** 37.37N138.57E
San Joaquin *r.* U.S.A. **108** 38.03N121.50W
San Jorge, Bahía de *b.* Mexico **109** 31.08N113.15W
San Jorge, Golfo *g.* Argentina **125** 46.00S 66.00W
San Jorge, Golfo de *g.* Spain **25** 40.53N 1.00E
San José Costa Rica **117** 9.59N 84.04W
San José Guatemala **116** 13.58N 90.50W
San José Mexico **109** 27.32N110.09W
San Jose U.S.A. **108** 37.20N121.53W
San José, Isla *i.* Mexico **109** 25.00N110.38W
San José de Chiquitos Bolivia **124** 17.53S 60.45W
San José de Feliciano Argentina **125** 30.25S 58.45W
San José de Guanipa Venezuela **122** 8.54N 64.09W
San José del Cabo *town* Mexico **109** 23.03N109.41W
San José del Guaviare Colombia **122** 2.35N 72.38W
San José de Mayo Uruguay **125** 34.20S 56.42W
San José de Ocuné Colombia **122** 4.15N 70.20W
San Juan Argentina **124** 31.30S 68.30W
San Juan *d.* Argentina **124** 31.00S 68.30W
San Juan *r.* Costa Rica **117** 10.50N 83.40W
San Juan Dom. Rep. **117** 18.40N 71.05W
San Juan Peru **124** 15.20S 75.09W
San Juan Phil. **59** 8.25N126.22E
San Juan Puerto Rico **117** 18.29N 66.08W
San Juan *r.* U.S.A. **108** 37.18N110.28W
San Juan, C. Argentina **125** 54.45S 63.50W
San Juan, Embalse de *resr.* Spain **26** 40.25N 4.25W
San Juan Bautista Spain **25** 39.05N 1.30E
San Juan de Guadalupe Mexico **111** 24.38N102.44W
San Juan del Norte Nicaragua **117** 10.58N 83.40W
San Juan de los Morros Venezuela **122** 9.53N 67.23W
San Juan del Río Durango Mexico **111** 24.47N104.27W
San Juan del Río Querétaro Mexico **116** 20.23N100.00W
San Juan Mts. U.S.A. **108** 37.35N107.10W
San Julián Argentina **121** 49.19S 67.40W
San Justo Argentina **125** 30.47S 60.35W
Sankh *r.* India **63** 22.15N 84.48E
Sankheda India **62** 22.10N 73.35E
Sānkra India **63** 20.18N 82.03E
Sankt Anton Austria **39** 47.08N 10.16E
Sankt Gilgen Austria **39** 47.46N 13.22E
Sankt Ingbert W. Germany **39** 49.17N 7.06E
Sankt Johann im Pongau Austria **39** 47.21N 13.12E
Sankt Johann in Tirol Austria **39** 47.31N 12.26E
Sankt Niklaus Switz. **39** 46.11N 7.48E
Sankt Paul Austria **31** 46.42N 14.52E
Sankt Peter W. Germany **38** 54.18N 8.38E
Sankt Veit an der Glan Austria **31** 46.46N 14.21E
Sankt Wolfgang Austria **39** 47.44N 13.27E
Sankuru *r.* Zaïre **78** 4.20S 20.27E
San Lázaro, Cabo *c.* Mexico **109** 24.50N112.18W
San Lázaro, Sierra de *mts.* Mexico **109** 23.20N110.00W
San Leonardo Spain **26** 41.51N 3.05W
San Leonardo in Passiria Italy **30** 46.49N 11.15E
San Lorenzo Argentina **125** 32.45S 60.44W
San Lorenzo *mtn.* Chile **125** 47.37S 72.19W
San Lorenzo Ecuador **122** 1.17N 78.50W
San Lorenzo *r.* Mexico **109** 24.15N107.25W
San Lorenzo de El Escorial Spain **26** 40.35N 4.09W
San Lorenzo de la Parrilla Spain **27** 39.51N 2.22W
Sanlúcar de Barrameda Spain **27** 36.47N 6.21W
Sanlúcar la Mayor Spain **27** 37.23N 6.12W
San Lucas Bolivia **124** 20.06S 65.07W
San Lucas, Cabo *c.* Mexico **109** 22.50N109.55W
San Luis Argentina **125** 33.20S 66.20W
San Luis *d.* Argentina **125** 34.00S 66.00W
San Luis Cuba **117** 20.13N 75.50W
San Luis Obispo U.S.A. **109** 35.17N120.40W
San Luis Potosí Mexico **116** 22.10N101.00W
San Luis Potosí *d.* Mexico **116** 23.00N100.00W
San Luis Rio Colorado Mexico **109** 32.29N114.48W
San Luis Valley *f.* U.S.A. **108** 37.25N106.00W
Sanluri Italy **32** 39.33N 8.54E
San Marco Spain **26** 43.13N 8.17W
San Marcos U.S.A. **111** 29.53N 97.57W
San Marino Europe **30** 43.56N 12.25E
San Marino *town* San Marino **30** 43.55N 12.28E
San Martin *r.* Bolivia **124** 12.25S 64.25W
San Martin de Valdeiglesias Spain **26** 40.21N 4.24W
San Mateo Spain **25** 40.28N 0.11E
San Mateo U.S.A. **108** 37.35N122.19W
San Matías Bolivia **122** 16.22S 58.24W
San Matías, Golfo *g.* Argentina **125** 41.30S 64.00W
Sanmenxia China **54** 35.45N111.22E
Sanmenxia Shuiku *resr.* China **54** 34.38N111.05E
San Miguel *r.* Bolivia **122** 13.52S 63.56W
San Miguel *r.* Bolivia **124** 12.25S 64.25W
San Miguel El Salvador **117** 13.28N 88.10W
San Miguel del Monte Argentina **125** 35.25S 58.49W
San Miguel de Tucumán Argentina **124** 26.49S 65.13W
San Miguelito Panama **117** 9.02N 79.30W
Sanming China **55** 26.25N117.35E
San Miniato Italy **30** 43.41N 10.51E
Sannār Sudan **73** 13.33N 33.38E
Sannicandro Italy **31** 41.50N 15.34E
San Nicolas Argentina **125** 33.20S 60.13W
Sanniquellie Liberia **76** 7.24N 8.45W
Sanok Poland **37** 49.35N 22.10E
San Pablo Phil. **59** 13.58N121.10E
San Pedro Buenos Aires Argentina **125** 33.40S 59.41W
San Pedro Jujuy Argentina **124** 24.14S 64.50W
San Pedro Dom. Rep. **117** 18.30N 69.18W
San Pedro Ivory Coast **76** 4.45N 6.37W
San Pedro Sonora Mexico **109** 27.00N109.53W
San Pedro Paraguay **126** 24.08S 57.08W
San Pedro, Punta *c.* Costa Rica **117** 8.38N 83.45W
San Pedro, Sierra de *mts.* Spain **27** 39.20N 6.40W
San Pedro de las Colonais Mexico **111** 25.45N102.59W
San Pedro Mártir, Sierra *mts.* Mexico **109** 30.45N115.30W
San Pedro Sula Honduras **117** 15.26N 88.01W
San Pellegrino Terme Italy **30** 45.50N 9.40E
San Pietro *i.* Italy **28** 39.09N 8.16E
Sanquhar U.K. **14** 55.22N 3.56W
San Quintín Mexico **109** 30.28N115.58W
San Rafael U.S.A. **108** 37.59N122.31W
San Raphael Argentina **125** 34.40S 68.21W
San Remo Italy **30** 43.49N 7.46E
San Roque Spain **27** 36.13N 5.24W
San Salvador Argentina **125** 31.37S 58.30W
San Salvador *i.* Bahamas **117** 24.00N 74.32W
San Salvador El Salvador **117** 13.40N 89.10W
San Salvador de Jujuy Argentina **124** 24.10S 65.20W
San Sebastián Argentina **125** 53.15S 68.30W
San Sebastián Spain **26** 43.19N 1.59W
Sansepolcro Italy **30** 43.34N 12.08E
San Severino Marche Italy **30** 43.13N 13.10E
San Severo Italy **31** 41.41N 15.23E
Sanshui China **55** 23.09N112.52E
San Simon U.S.A. **109** 32.16N109.14W
Sanski Most Yugo. **31** 44.46N 16.40E
Santa *r.* Peru **122** 9.00S 78.35W
Santa Amalia Spain **26** 39.01N 6.01W
Santa Ana Argentina **124** 27.20S 65.35W
Santa Ana Bolivia **124** 13.45S 65.35W
Santa Ana El Salvador **117** 14.00N 89.31W
Santa Ana Mexico **109** 30.33N111.07W
Santa Ana U.S.A. **109** 33.44N117.54W
Santa Bárbara Mexico **109** 26.48N105.49W
Santa Barbara U.S.A. **109** 34.25N119.42W
Santa Catalina de Armara Spain **26** 43.02N 8.49W
Santa Catarina *d.* Brazil **126** 27.00S 52.00W
Santa Catarina Mexico **111** 25.41N100.28W
Santa Cesarea Terme Italy **33** 40.02N 18.29E
Santa Clara Cuba **117** 22.25N 79.58W
Santa Clara Calif. U.S.A. **108** 37.21N121.57W
Santa Clara Utah U.S.A. **108** 37.08N113.39W
Santa Clotilde Peru **122** 2.25S 73.35W
Santa Coloma de Farnés Spain **25** 41.52N 2.40E
Santa Comba Dão Portugal **26** 40.24N 8.08W
Santa Cruz *d.* Argentina **125** 48.00S 69.30W
Santa Cruz *r.* Argentina **125** 50.03S 68.35W
Santa Cruz Bolivia **124** 17.45S 63.14W
Santa Cruz *d.* Bolivia **124** 17.45S 62.00W
Santa Cruz Madeira Is. **127** 32.41N 16.48W
Santa Cruz Spain **70** 28.29N 16.26W
Santa Cruz U.S.A. **108** 36.58N122.08W
Santa Cruz *i.* U.S.A. **109** 34.01N119.45W
Santa Cruz de la Zarza Spain **27** 39.58N 3.10W
Santa Cruz de Mudela Spain **26** 38.38N 3.28W
Santa Cruz de Tenerife Canary Is. **74** 28.28N 16.15W
Santa Cruz Is. Solomon Is. **84** 10.30S166.00E
Santa Domingo Mexico **109** 25.32N112.02W
Santa Elena Argentina **125** 31.00S 59.50W
Santa Elena U.S.A. **111** 26.46N 98.30W
Santa Elena, C. Costa Rica **117** 10.54N 85.56W
Santa Eufemia Spain **26** 38.36N 4.52W
Santa Eugenia Spain **26** 42.33N 9.00W
Santa Eulalia Spain **25** 40.34N 1.19W
Santa Eulalia del Río Spain **25** 38.59N 1.31E
Santa Fé Argentina **125** 31.40S 60.40W
Santa Fé *d.* Argentina **124** 30.00S 61.00W
Santa Fe Spain **27** 37.11N 3.43W
Santa Fe U.S.A. **109** 35.42N106.57W
Santa Filomena Brazil **123** 9.07S 45.56W
Sant'Agata di Militello Italy **33** 38.04N 14.38E
Santai China **55** 31.10N105.02E
Santa Inés, Isla *i.* Chile **125** 53.40S 73.00W
Santa Isabel Argentina **125** 36.15S 66.55W
Santa Isabel do Morro Brazil **123** 11.36S 50.37W
Sāntalpur India **62** 23.45N 71.10E
Santa Lucía Uruguay **125** 34.27S 56.24W
Santa Lucía *r.* Uruguay **125** 34.48S 56.22W
Santa Lucia Range *mts.* U.S.A. **109** 36.00N121.20W
Santa Luzia Portugal **26** 37.44N 8.24W
Santa Margarita, Isla de *i.* Mexico **109** 24.25N111.50W
Santa Margarita, Sierra de *mts.* Mexico **109** 30.00N110.00W
Santa Margherita Ligure Italy **30** 44.20N 9.12E
Santa María Brazil **126** 29.40S 53.47W
Santa Maria U.S.A. **109** 34.57N120.26W
Santa Maria, Cabo de *c.* Portugal **27** 36.58N 7.54W
Santa María, Laguna de *l.* Mexico **109** 31.07N107.17W
Santa Maria Capua Vetere Italy **33** 41.05N 14.15E
Santa Maria di Leuca, Capo *c.* Italy **33** 39.47N 18.22E
Santa María la Real de Nieva Spain **26** 41.04N 4.24W
Santa Maria Madalena Brazil **126** 21.58S 42.02W
Santa-Maria-Siché France **30** 41.52N 8.59E
Santa Marinella Italy **30** 42.02N 11.51E
Santa Marta Colombia **122** 11.18N 74.10W
Santa Marta, Sierra Nevada de *mts.* Colombia **122** 11.20N 73.00W
Santa Monica U.S.A. **109** 34.01N118.30W
Santana Madeira Is. **127** 32.48N 16.54W
Santana do Livramento Brazil **125** 30.53S 55.31W
Santander Colombia **122** 3.00N 76.25W
Santander Spain **26** 43.28N 3.48W
Santander *d.* Spain **26** 43.15N 4.00W
Sant'Angelo dei Lombardi Italy **33** 40.56N 15.11E
Santanoni Pk. U.S.A. **105** 44.08N 74.11W
Sant'Antioco Italy **32** 39.02N 8.30E
Sant'Antioco, Isola di *i.* Italy **32** 39.00N 8.25E
Santañy Spain **25** 39.22N 3.07E
Santa Pola, Cabo de *c.* Spain **25** 38.12N 0.31W
Sant'Arcangelo Italy **33** 40.15N 16.17E
Santarém Brazil **123** 2.26S 54.41W
Santarém Portugal **27** 39.14N 8.41W
Santarem *d.* Portugal **27** 39.10N 8.40W
Santa Rosa Argentina **125** 36.00S 64.40W
Santa Rosa Bolivia **122** 10.36S 67.25W
Santa Rosa Brazil **126** 27.52S 54.29W
Santa Rosa Honduras **117** 14.47N 88.46W
Santa Rosa *i.* U.S.A. **109** 33.58N120.06W
Santa Rosa Calif. U.S.A. **108** 38.26N122.34W
Santa Rosa N.Mex. U.S.A. **109** 34.57N104.41W
Santa Rosa, Mt. Guam **84** 13.32N144.55E
Santa Rosa de Cabal Colombia **122** 4.52N 75.37W
Santa Rosalía Mexico **109** 27.19N112.17W
Santa Rosa Range *mts.* U.S.A. **108** 41.00N117.40W
Santa Teresa Mexico **111** 25.19N 97.50W
Santa Teresa, Embalse de *resr.* Spain **26** 40.40N 5.37W
Santa Teresa Gallura Italy **32** 41.15N 9.12E
Santa Vitória do Palmar Brazil **126** 33.31S 53.21W
San Telmo Mexico **109** 31.00N116.06W
Sant'Eufemia, Golfo di *g.* Italy **33** 38.50N 16.00E
Santhià Italy **30** 45.22N 8.10E
Santiago Chile **125** 33.27S 70.40W
Santiago Dom. Rep. **117** 19.30N 70.42W
Santiago Panama **117** 8.08N 80.59W
Santiago *r.* Peru **122** 4.30S 77.48W
Santiago de Compostela Spain **26** 42.53N 8.33W
Santiago de Cuba Cuba **117** 20.00N 75.49W
Santiago del Estero Argentina **124** 27.50S 64.15W
Santiago del Estero *d.* Argentina **124** 27.40S 63.30W
Santiago do Cacém Portugal **27** 38.01N 8.42W
Santiago Vázquez Uruguay **125** 34.48S 56.21W
Sāntipur India **63** 23.15N 88.26E
Säntis *mtn.* Switz. **39** 47.15N 9.21E
Santisteban del Puerto Spain **26** 38.15N 3.12W
Santo Amaro Brazil **123** 12.35S 38.41W
Santo André Brazil **126** 23.39S 46.29W
Santo Angelo Brazil **126** 28.18S 54.16W
Santo Antônio do Içá Brazil **122** 3.05S 67.57W
Santo Domingo Dom. Rep. **117** 18.30N 69.57W
Santo Domingo de la Calzada Spain **26** 42.26N 2.57W
Santo Domingo Pueblo U.S.A. **109** 35.31N106.22W
Santolea, Embalse de *resr.* Spain **25** 40.47N 0.19W
Santoña Spain **26** 43.27N 3.27W
Santos Brazil **126** 23.56S 46.22W
Santos Dumont Brazil **126** 21.30S 43.34W
Santo Tirso Portugal **26** 41.21N 8.28W
Santo Tomás Peru **122** 14.34S 72.30W
Santo Tomé Argentina **124** 28.31S 56.03W
Santpoort Neth. **16** 52.27N 4.38E
Şānūr Jordan **67** 32.21N 35.15E
San Valentin, Cerro *mtn.* Chile **125** 46.40S 73.25W
San Vicente El Salvador **117** 13.38N 88.42W
San Vicente de Alcántara Spain **27** 39.21N 7.08W
San Vicente de Baracaldo Spain **26** 43.18N 2.59W
San Vicente de la Barquera Spain **26** 43.23N 4.24W
San Vincenzo Italy **30** 43.06N 10.32E
San Vito Italy **32** 39.27N 9.32E
San Vito, Capo *c.* Italy **32** 38.11N 12.43E
San Vito al Tagliamento Italy **32** 45.54N 12.52E
San Vito dei Normanni Italy **33** 40.39N 17.42E
Sanyuan China **54** 34.30N108.52E
Sanza Pombo Angola **78** 7.20S 16.12E
São Borja Brazil **126** 28.35S 56.01W
São Bras de Alportel Portugal **27** 37.08N 7.58W
São Caetano do Sul Brazil **126** 23.36S 46.34W
São Carlos Brazil **126** 22.01S 47.54W
São Domingos Guinea Bissau **76** 12.22N 16.08W
São Francisco *r.* Brazil **123** 10.20S 36.20W
São Francisco do Sol Brazil **126** 26.17S 48.39W
São Gabriel Brazil **126** 30.20S 54.19W
São Gonçalo do Sapucaí Brazil **126** 21.54S 45.35W
Sao Hill *town* Tanzania **79** 8.21S 35.10E
São João da Boa Vista Brazil **126** 21.59S 46.45W
São João da Madeira Portugal **26** 40.54N 8.30W
São João del Rei Brazil **126** 21.08S 44.15W
São João do Piauí Brazil **123** 8.21S 42.15W
São Joaquim da Barra Brazil **126** 20.36S 47.51W
São José do Calçado Brazil **126** 21.01S 41.37W
São José do Rio Prêto Brazil **126** 20.50S 49.20W
São José dos Campos Brazil **126** 23.07S 45.52W
São Leopoldo Brazil **126** 29.46S 51.09W
São Lourenço Brazil **126** 22.08S 45.05W
São Luís Brazil **123** 2.34S 44.16W
São Manuel Brazil **126** 22.40S 48.35W
São Manuel *r.* see Teles Pires Brazil **123**
São Miguel d'Oeste Brazil **126** 26.45S 53.34W
Saona *i.* Dom. Rep. **117** 18.09N 68.42W
Saône *r.* France **21** 45.44N 4.50E
Saône-et-Loire *d.* France **19** 46.42N 4.45E
Saoner India **63** 21.23N 78.54E
São Nicolau Angola **78** 14.19S 12.23E
São Paulo Brazil **126** 23.33S 46.39W
São Paulo *d.* Brazil **126** 22.05S 48.00W
São Paulo de Olivença Brazil **122** 3.34S 68.55W
São Pedro do Sul Portugal **26** 40.45N 8.04W
São Roque Brazil **126** 23.31S 47.09W
São Roque, Cabo de *c.* Brazil **121** 5.00S 35.00W
São Sebastião Brazil **126** 23.48S 45.26W
São Sebastião, Ilha de *i.* Brazil **126** 23.53S 45.17W
São Sebastião do Paraíso Brazil **126** 20.54S 46.59W
São Tiago Brazil **126** 20.54S 44.30W
São Tomé & Príncipe Africa **70** 0.19N 6.05E
Saoura, Oued *wadi* Algeria **74** 28.48N 0.50W
São Vicente Brazil **126** 23.57S 46.23W
São Vicente, Cabo de *c.* Portugal **27** 37.01N 8.59W
São Vicente de Minas Brazil **126** 21.40S 44.26W
Sápai Greece **34** 41.02N 25.41E
Sapé Brazil **123** 7.06S 35.13W
Sapele Nigeria **77** 5.53N 5.41E
Sapelo I. U.S.A. **113** 31.28N 81.15W
Sapporo Japan **57** 43.05N141.21E
Sapri Italy **33** 40.04N 15.38E
Sapt Kosi *r.* Nepal **63** 26.30N 86.55E
Sapu Angola **78** 12.28S 19.26E
Sapulpa U.S.A. **111** 36.00N 96.06W
Saqin Sum China **54** 42.06N111.03E
Saqqārah Egypt **66** 29.51N 31.13E
Saqqez Iran **65** 36.14N 46.15E
Sarāb Iran **65** 37.56N 47.35E
Sarābiyūm Egypt **66** 30.23N 32.17E
Sara Buri Thailand **56** 14.30N100.59E
Sarāi Naurang Pakistan **62** 32.50N 70.47E
Sarajevo Yugo. **31** 43.52N 18.26E
Saranac L. U.S.A. **105** 44.20N 74.10W
Saranac Lake *town* U.S.A. **105** 44.20N 74.08W
Sarandë Albania **34** 39.52N 20.00E
Sarandí del Yi Uruguay **125** 33.21S 55.38W
Sarandí Grande Uruguay **125** 33.44S 56.20W
Sārangarh India **63** 21.36N 83.05E
Sārangpur India **62** 23.34N 76.28E
Saranpaul U.S.S.R. **44** 64.15N 60.58E
Saransk U.S.S.R. **44** 54.12N 45.10E
Sarapul U.S.S.R. **44** 56.30N 53.49E
Sarar Plain Somali Rep. **71** 9.35N 46.15E
Sarasota U.S.A. **113** 27.20N 82.32W
Sarata U.S.S.R. **37** 46.00N 29.40E
Saratoga U.S.A. **108** 37.16N122.02W
Saratoga Springs U.S.A. **115** 43.05N 73.47W
Saratov U.S.S.R. **45** 51.30N 45.55E
Saravan Laos **56** 15.43N106.24E
Sarawak *d.* Malaysia **58** 2.00N113.00E
Sarayakpinar Turkey **34** 41.46N 26.29E
Saraychik U.S.S.R. **45** 47.29N 51.42E
Sarbāz Iran **65** 26.39N 61.20E
Sárbogárd Hungary **31** 46.53N 18.38E
Sarcelles France **19** 49.00N 2.23E
Sardār Chāh Pakistan **62** 27.58N 64.50E
Sardārpur India **62** 22.39N 74.59E
Sardārshahr India **62** 28.26N 74.29E
Sardegna *d.* Italy **32** 40.15N 9.00E
Sardegna *i.* Italy **32** 40.00N 9.00E
Sardinia *i. see* Sardegna Italy **32**
Sarek *mtn.* Sweden **40** 67.25N 17.46E
Sareks Nat. Park Sweden **40** 67.15N 17.30E
Sargasso Sea Atlantic Oc. **127** 28.00N 60.00W
Sargodha Pakistan **60** 32.01N 72.40E
Sarh Chad **77** 9.08N 18.22E
Sarhro, Jbel *mts.* Morocco **74** 31.00N 5.55W
Sarī Iran **65** 36.33N 53.06E
Saría *i.* Greece **35** 35.50N 27.15E
Sarikamiş Turkey **64** 40.19N 42.35E
Sarikei Malaysia **58** 2.07N111.31E
Sarina Australia **90** 21.26S149.13E
Sariñena Spain **25** 41.48N 0.10W
Sarita U.S.A. **111** 37.13N 97.47W
Sark *i.* U.K. **13** 49.26N 2.22W
Sarlat France **20** 44.53N 1.13E
Sărmasu Romania **37** 46.46N 24.11E
Sármellék Hungary **31** 46.44N 17.10E
Sarmi Indonesia **59** 1.51S138.45E
Sarmiento Argentina **125** 45.35S 69.05W
Särna Sweden **41** 61.41N 13.08E
Sarnen Switz. **39** 46.54N 8.15E
Sarnia Canada **104** 42.58N 82.23W
Sarno Italy **33** 40.49N 14.37E
Sarny U.S.S.R. **37** 51.21N 26.31E
Saronikós Kólpos *g.* Greece **35** 37.54N 23.12E
Saronno Italy **30** 45.38N 9.02E
Saros Körfezi *g.* Turkey **34** 40.30N 26.20E
Sárospatak Hungary **37** 48.19N 21.34E
Šar Planina *mts.* Yugo. **34** 42.10N 21.00E
Sarpsborg Norway **42** 59.17N 11.07E
Sarralbe France **19** 49.00N 7.01E
Sarre *r. see* Saar France **19**
Sarrebourg France **19** 48.44N 7.03E
Sarreguemines France **19** 49.06N 7.03E
Sarre-Union France **19** 48.56N 7.05E
Sarria Spain **26** 42.47N 7.24W
Sarro Mali **76** 13.40N 5.05W
Sartène France **21** 41.36N 8.59E
Sarthe *d.* France **18** 48.00N 0.05E
Sarthe *r.* France **18** 47.30N 0.32W
Sartilly France **18** 48.45N 1.27W
Sartynya U.S.S.R. **50** 63.22N 63.11E
Şarūr Oman **65** 23.25N 58.10E
Sárvár Hungary **36** 47.15N 16.57E
Sárvíz *r.* Hungary **31** 46.24N 18.41E
Saryshagan U.S.S.R. **52** 46.08N 73.32E
Sarzana Italy **30** 44.07N 9.58E
Sarzeau France **18** 47.32N 2.46W
Sasa Israel **67** 33.02N 35.24E
Sasabeneh Ethiopia **71** 7.55N 43.39E
Sasarām India **63** 24.57N 84.02E
Sasebo Japan **57** 33.10N129.42E
Saseginaga, L. Canada **104** 47.06N 78.35W
Saser *mtn.* Jammu & Kashmir **63** 34.50N 77.50E
Saskatchewan *d.* Canada **101** 55.00N106.00W
Saskatchewan *r.* Canada **101** 53.12N 99.16W
Saskatoon Canada **101** 52.07N106.38W
Sasovo U.S.S.R. **44** 54.21N 41.58E
Sassandra Ivory Coast **76** 4.58N 6.08W
Sassandra *r.* Ivory Coast **76** 5.00N 6.04W
Sassari Italy **32** 40.44N 8.33E
Sassnitz E. Germany **38** 54.31N 13.38E
Sassoferrato Italy **30** 43.26N 12.51E
Sasso Marconi Italy **30** 44.24N 11.15E
Sassuolo Italy **30** 44.33N 10.47E
Sastown Liberia **76** 4.44N 8.01W
Sasyk, Ozero *l.* U.S.S.R. **37** 45.38N 29.38E
Satadougou Mali **76** 12.30N 11.30W
Satāna India **62** 20.35N 74.12E
Satanta U.S.A. **111** 37.26N100.59W
Sátão Portugal **26** 40.44N 7.44W

Sātāra to **Setúbal**

Sātāra India 60 17.43N 74.05E
Satīt *r.* Sudan 72 14.20N 35.50E
Satkānia Bangla. 63 22.04N 92.03E
Satna India 63 24.35N 80.50E
Sátoraljaújhely Hungary 37 48.24N 21.39E
Sātpura Range *mts.* India 62 21.30N 76.00E
Satu Mare Romania 37 47.48N 22.52E
Satun Thailand 56 6.38N 100.05E
Sauce Argentina 125 30.05S 58.45W
Sauda Norway 42 59.39N 6.20E
Saudi Arabia Asia 64 26.00N 44.00E
Sauerland *f.* W. Germany 38 51.23N 8.20E
Saugeen *r.* Canada 104 44.30N 81.22W
Saujon France 20 45.40N 0.56W
Sauk Centre U.S.A. 110 45.44N 94.57W
Saulgau W. Germany 39 48.01N 9.30E
Saulieu France 19 47.16N 4.14E
Sault-de-Vaucluse France 21 44.05N 5.25E
Sault Sainte Marie Canada 104 46.31N 84.20W
Sault Sainte Marie U.S.A. 104 46.30N 84.21W
Saumarez Reef Australia 90 21.50S 153.40E
Saumlaki Indonesia 90 7.59S 131.22E
Saumur France 18 47.16N 0.05W
Saurimo Angola 78 9.38S 20.20E
Sausar India 63 21.42N 78.52E
Sauveterre-de-Béarn France 20 43.29N 0.56W
Sauveterre-en-Guyenne France 20 44.42N 0.05W
Sava Italy 33 40.24N 17.34E
Sava *r.* Yugo. 31 44.50N 20.26E
Savage U.S.A. 108 47.27N 104.21W
Savai'i *i.* W. Samoa 84 13.36S 172.27W
Savalou Benin 77 7.55N 1.59E
Savanna U.S.A. 110 42.06N 90.07W
Savannah *r.* U.S.A. 113 32.02N 80.53W
Savannah Ga. U.S.A. 113 32.04N 81.05W
Savannah Tenn. U.S.A. 111 35.14N 88.14W
Savannakhét Laos 56 16.34N 104.48E
Savant L. Canada 102 50.48N 90.20W
Savant Lake *town* Canada 102 50.20N 90.40W
Savé Benin 77 8.04N 2.37E
Save *r.* France 20 43.47N 1.17E
Save *r.* Mozambique 81 20.59S 35.02E
Sāveh Iran 65 35.00N 50.25E
Savelugu Ghana 76 9.39N 0.48W
Savenay France 18 47.22N 1.57W
Saverdun France 20 43.14N 1.35E
Saverne France 19 48.44N 7.22E
Savigliano Italy 30 44.38N 7.40E
Savigny-sur-Braye France 18 47.53N 0.49E
Šavnik Yugo. 31 42.57N 19.05E
Savoie *d.* France 21 45.30N 6.25E
Savona Italy 30 44.17N 8.30E
Savonlinna Finland 44 61.52N 28.51E
Savoonga U.S.A. 98 63.42N 170.27W
Sävsjö Sweden 43 57.25N 14.40E
Savu Sea *see* Sawu, Laut Pacific Oc. 59
Sawai Mādhopur India 62 25.59N 76.22E
Sawākin Sudan 72 19.07N 37.20E
Sawatch Range *mts.* U.S.A. 110 39.10N 106.25W
Sawbridgeworth U.K. 13 51.50N 0.09W
Sawdā', Jabal as *hills* Libya 75 28.40N 15.00E
Sawdā', Qurnat as *mtn.* Lebanon 66 34.17N 36.04E
Sawdirī Sudan 72 14.25N 29.05E
Sawfajjin, Wādī Libya 75 31.54N 15.07E
Sawhāj Egypt 64 26.33N 31.42E
Şawqirah, Ghubbat *b.* Oman 71 18.35N 57.00E
Sawston U.K. 13 52.07N 0.11E
Sawtooth Mts. U.S.A. 108 44.03N 114.35W
Sawu *i.* Indonesia 59 10.30S 121.50E
Sawu, Laut *sea* Pacific Oc. 59 9.30S 122.30E
Saxmundham U.K. 13 52.13N 1.29E
Saxon Switz. 39 46.09N 7.11E
Saxton U.S.A. 114 40.13N 78.15W
Say Mali 76 13.08N 2.22E
Say Niger 77 13.08N 2.22E
Sayda Japan 57 35.51N 139.24E
Şaydā Lebanon 66 33.32N 35.22E
Sayers Lake *town* Australia 92 32.46S 143.20E
Saylūn *site* Jordan 67 32.03N 35.17E
Saynshand Mongolia 54 44.58N 110.12E
Sayre U.S.A. 115 41.59N 76.32W
Sayula Mexico 116 19.52N 103.36W
Sayville U.S.A. 115 40.44N 73.05W
Sazliyka *r.* Bulgaria 34 42.15N 25.50E
Sázava *r.* Czech. 36 49.53N 14.21E
Sbaa Algeria 74 28.13N 0.10W
Scaër France 18 48.02N 3.42W
Scafell Pike *mtn.* U.K. 12 54.27N 3.12W
Scalea Italy 33 39.49N 15.48E
Scalloway U.K. 14 60.08N 1.17W
Scammon Bay *town* U.S.A. 98 61.50N 165.35W
Scansano Italy 30 42.41N 11.20E
Scapa Flow *str.* U.K. 14 58.53N 3.05W
Scarborough Canada 104 43.44N 79.16W
Scarborough Tobago 122 11.11N 60.45W
Scarborough U.K. 12 54.17N 0.24W
Sceale Bay *town* Australia 92 33.00S 134.15E
Scenic U.S.A. 108 43.46N 102.32W
Schaalsee *l.* W. Germany / E. Germany 38 53.35N 10.57E
Schaerbeek Belgium 16 50.54N 4.20E
Schaffhausen Switz. 39 47.42N 8.38E
Schagen Neth. 16 52.47N 4.47E
Schärding Austria 39 48.27N 13.26E
Schefferville Canada 99 54.50N 67.00W
Scheinfeld W. Germany 39 49.40N 10.27E
Schelde *r.* Belgium 16 51.13N 4.25E
Schell Creek Range *mts.* U.S.A. 108 39.10N 114.40W
Schenectady U.S.A. 115 42.47N 73.53W
Schesslitz W. Germany 38 49.59N 11.01E
Scheveningen Neth. 16 52.07N 4.16E
Schiedam Neth. 16 51.55N 4.25E
Schiermonnikoog *i.* Neth. 16 53.28N 6.15E
Schiltigheim France 19 48.36N 7.45E
Schio Italy 32 45.43N 11.21E
Schkeuditz E. Germany 38 51.24N 12.13E
Schladming Austria 39 47.23N 13.41E
Schleiden W. Germany 38 50.31N 6.28E
Schleswig W. Germany 38 54.31N 9.33E
Schleswig-Holstein *d.* W. Germany 38 54.39N 9.30E
Schleusingen E. Germany 39 50.31N 10.45E
Schlitz W. Germany 38 50.40N 9.33E
Schlüchtern W. Germany 39 50.20N 9.31E
Schmalkalden E. Germany 38 50.43N 10.26E
Schmidmühlen W. Germany 38 49.16N 11.56E
Schmölln E. Germany 38 50.53N 12.20E
Schmutter *r.* W. Germany 39 48.43N 10.47E
Schneeberg *mtn.* W. Germany 38 50.03N 11.51E
Schneverdingen W. Germany 38 53.07N 9.47E
Schoharie U.S.A. 115 42.40N 74.19W
Schoharie Creek *r.* U.S.A. 115 42.57N 74.18W
Schönebeck E. Germany 38 52.01N 11.45E
Schongau W. Germany 39 47.49N 10.54E
Schopfheim W. Germany 39 47.39N 7.49E
Schorndorf W. Germany 39 48.48N 9.31E
Schouten, Kepulauan *is.* Indonesia 59 0.45S 135.50E
Schouwen *i.* Neth. 16 51.42N 3.45E
Schramberg W. Germany 39 48.13N 8.23E
Schreiber Canada 102 48.45N 87.20W
Schrobenhausen W. Germany 39 48.33N 11.17E
Schroon Lake *town* U.S.A. 105 43.47N 73.46W
Schuler Canada 101 50.22N 110.05W
Schuykill *r.* U.S.A. 115 39.53N 75.12W
Schuylerville U.S.A. 115 43.06N 73.35W
Schuylkill Haven U.S.A. 115 40.38N 76.12W
Schwabach W. Germany 38 49.20N 11.01E
Schwaben *f.* W. Germany 39 48.10N 10.50E
Schwäbische Alb *mts.* W. Germany 39 48.30N 9.38E
Schwäbisch Gmünd W. Germany 39 48.48N 9.47E
Schwäbisch Hall W. Germany 39 49.07N 9.44E
Schwabmünchen W. Germany 39 48.11N 10.45E
Schwandorf W. Germany 39 49.20N 12.08E
Schwaner, Pegunungan *mts.* Indonesia 58 0.45S 113.20E
Schwarze Elster *r.* E. Germany 38 51.49N 12.51E
Schwarzenburg Switz. 39 46.49N 7.21E
Schwarzrand *mts.* Namibia 80 25.40S 16.53E
Schwarzwald *f.* W. Germany 36 48.00N 7.45E
Schwaz Austria 39 47.20N 11.42E
Schwedt E. Germany 38 53.03N 14.17E
Schweich W. Germany 39 49.49N 6.45E
Schweinfurt W. Germany 39 50.03N 10.14E
Schweitzingen W. Germany 39 49.23N 8.34E
Schwelm W. Germany 38 51.17N 7.17E
Schwenningen W. Germany 39 48.04N 8.32E
Schwerin E. Germany 38 53.38N 11.25E
Schwerin *d.* E. Germany 38 53.28N 11.35E
Schweriner See *l.* E. Germany 38 53.45N 11.28E
Schwyz Switz. 39 47.02N 8.40E
Schyan Canada 105 46.10N 77.00W
Sciacca Italy 32 37.30N 13.06E
Scicli Italy 33 36.47N 14.43E
Scilla Italy 33 38.15N 15.44E
Scilly, Isles of U.K. 13 49.55N 6.20W
Šćit *mtn.* Yugo. 31 44.02N 17.47E
Scituate U.S.A. 115 42.12N 70.44W
Scobey U.S.A. 108 48.47N 105.25W
Scone Australia 93 32.01S 150.53E
Scordia Italy 33 37.18N 14.51E
Scorno, Punta di *c.* Italy 32 41.07N 8.19E
Scotia Calif. U.S.A. 108 40.26N 123.31W
Scotia N.Y. U.S.A. 115 42.47N 73.59W
Scotia Ridge *f.* Atlantic Oc. 127 60.00S 35.00W
Scotia Sea Atlantic Oc. 127 57.00S 45.00W
Scotland U.K. 14 55.30N 4.00W
Scotsbluff U.S.A. 110 41.52N 103.40W
Scotstown Canada 105 45.32N 71.17W
Scott *r.* Australia 92 30.41S 137.50E
Scott Canada 105 46.30N 71.04W
Scottburgh R.S.A. 80 30.17S 30.45E
Scott City U.S.A. 110 38.29N 100.54W
Scottdale U.S.A. 114 40.06N 79.35W
Scott Is. Canada 100 50.48N 128.40W
Scott L. Canada 101 59.55N 106.18W
Scott Reef Australia 88 14.00S 121.50E
Scottsbluff U.S.A. 108 41.52N 103.40W
Scottsboro U.S.A. 111 34.40N 86.02W
Scottsdale Australia 91 41.09S 147.31E
Scottsdale U.S.A. 109 33.30N 111.56W
Scottsville U.S.A. 111 36.45N 86.11W
Scranton U.S.A. 115 41.24N 75.40W
Scugog, L. Canada 104 44.10N 78.51W
Scunthorpe U.K. 12 53.35N 0.38W
Scuol Switz. 39 46.48N 10.18E
Scutari, L. Yugo. / Albania 34 42.17N 19.17E
Seabrook, L. Australia 89 30.56S 119.40E
Seaford U.S.A. 115 38.39N 75.37W
Seaforth Canada 104 43.33N 81.24W
Seagroves U.S.A. 111 32.57N 102.34W
Seahouses U.K. 12 55.35N 1.38W
Sea Isle City U.S.A. 115 39.09N 74.42W
Seal *r.* Canada 101 59.04N 94.48W
Sea Lake *town* Australia 92 35.31S 142.54E
Seal Bight Canada 103 52.27N 55.40W
Searchlight U.S.A. 109 35.28N 114.55W
Seascale U.K. 12 54.24N 3.29W
Seaside Calif. U.S.A. 108 36.37N 121.50W
Seaside Oreg. U.S.A. 108 46.02N 123.55W
Seaton U.K. 13 50.43N 3.05W
Seattle U.S.A. 108 47.36N 122.20W
Seaview Range *mts.* Australia 90 18.56S 146.00E
Sebastian U.S.A. 113 27.50N 80.29W
Sebastián Vizcaíno, Bahía *b.* Mexico 109 28.00N 114.30W
Sebba U. Volta 76 13.27N 0.33E
Sebeş Romania 37 45.58N 23.34E
Sebewaing U.S.A. 104 43.44N 83.27W
Sebidiro P.N.G. 59 9.00S 142.15E
Sebinkarahisar Turkey 64 40.19N 38.25E
Sebnitz E. Germany 38 50.58N 14.16E
Sebou, Oued *r.* Morocco 74 34.15N 6.40W
Sebring U.S.A. 113 27.30N 81.28W
Sechura, Desierto de *des.* Peru 122 6.00S 80.30W
Seclin France 16 50.34N 3.01E
Sêda *r.* Portugal 27 38.55N 8.01W
Sedalia U.S.A. 110 38.42N 93.14W
Sedan Australia 92 34.34S 139.19E
Sedan France 19 49.42N 4.57E
Sedan U.S.A. 111 37.08N 96.11W
Sedano Spain 26 42.43N 3.45W
Seddon New Zealand 86 41.40S 174.04E
Séderon France 21 44.12N 5.32E
Sederot Israel 67 31.31N 34.35E
Sedgewick Canada 101 52.46N 111.41W
Sédhiou Senegal 76 12.44N 15.30W
Sedini Italy 32 40.50N 8.49E
Sedom Israel 66 31.04N 35.23E
Sedot Yam Israel 67 32.29N 34.53E
Seefeld Austria 39 47.20N 11.11E
Seehausen E. Germany 38 52.53N 11.45E
Seeheim Namibia 80 26.50S 17.45E
Seeleys Bay *town* Canada 105 44.29N 76.14W
Seelow E. Germany 38 52.32N 14.23E
Sées France 18 48.36N 0.10E
Seesen W. Germany 38 51.53N 10.10E
Seevetal W. Germany 38 53.26N 9.58E
Sefrou Morocco 74 33.50N 4.50W
Segbwema Sierra Leone 76 8.00N 11.00W
Segesta *site* Italy 32 37.56N 12.50E
Seggueur, Oued es *wadi* Algeria 75 31.44N 2.18E
Segni Italy 30 41.41N 13.01E
Ségou Mali 76 13.28N 6.18W
Ségou *d.* Mali 76 13.55N 6.20W
Segovia Spain 26 40.57N 4.07W
Segovia *d.* Spain 26 41.10N 4.00W
Segozero, Ozero *l.* U.S.S.R. 44 63.15N 33.40E
Segré France 18 47.41N 0.53W
Segre *r.* Spain 25 41.40N 0.43E
Séguédine Niger 77 20.12N 12.59E
Séguéla Ivory Coast 76 7.58N 6.44W
Seguin U.S.A. 111 29.34N 97.58W
Segura Portugal 27 39.50N 6.59W
Segura *r.* Spain 25 38.06N 0.38W
Segura, Sierra de *mts.* Spain 27 38.15N 2.30W
Sehore India 62 23.12N 77.05E
Sehwān Pakistan 62 26.26N 67.52E
Seia Portugal 26 40.25N 7.42W
Seiches-sur-le-Loir France 18 47.35N 0.22W
Seiland *i.* Norway 40 70.25N 23.10E
Seilhac France 20 45.22N 1.42E
Seille *r.* France 19 49.07N 6.11E
Seinäjoki Finland 40 62.47N 22.50E
Seine *r.* France 18 49.26N 0.26E
Seine, Baie de la *b.* France 18 49.25N 0.15E
Seine-et-Marne *d.* France 19 48.30N 3.00E
Seine-Maritime *d.* France 18 49.45N 1.00E
Seixal Portugal 27 38.38N 9.06W
Sejerö *i.* Denmark 42 55.53N 11.09E
Sekaju Indonesia 58 2.58S 103.58E
Seki Japan 57 35.29N 136.55E
Sekoma Botswana 80 24.41S 23.50E
Sekondi-Takoradi Ghana 76 4.57N 1.44W
Sekota Ethiopia 73 12.38N 39.03E
Seküheh Iran 65 30.45N 61.29E
Selaru *i.* Indonesia 90 8.09S 131.00E
Selatan, Tanjung *c.* Indonesia 58 4.20S 114.45E
Selb W. Germany 39 50.10N 12.08E
Selbu Norway 40 63.14N 11.03E
Selby U.K. 12 53.47N 1.05W
Selby U.S.A. 110 45.31N 100.02W
Selbyville U.S.A. 115 38.28N 75.13W
Seldovia U.S.A. 98 59.27N 151.43W
Sele *r.* Italy 33 40.27N 14.58E
Selenga *r.* U.S.S.R. 52 52.20N 106.20E
Selenge Mörön *r. see* Selenga Mongolia 52
Selenicë Albania 34 40.33N 19.39E
Sélestat France 19 48.16N 7.27E
Seligman U.S.A. 109 35.20N 112.53W
Selimiye Turkey 35 37.24N 27.40E
Selinoús Greece 35 37.35N 21.37E
Selinsgrove U.S.A. 114 40.48N 76.52W
Selinunte *site* Italy 32 37.35N 12.50E
Seljord Norway 42 59.29N 8.37E
Selkirk Man. Canada 101 50.09N 96.52W
Selkirk Ont. Canada 104 42.49N 79.56W
Selkirk U.K. 14 55.33N 2.51W
Selkirk Mts. Canada 100 50.02N 116.20W
Selles-sur-Cher France 19 47.16N 1.33E
Sells U.S.A. 109 31.55N 111.53W
Selma Ala. U.S.A. 111 32.25N 87.01W
Selma Calif. U.S.A. 109 36.34N 119.37W
Selmer U.S.A. 111 35.11N 88.36W
Selseleh ye Safid Küh *mts.* Afghan 65 34.30N 63.30E
Selsey Bill *c.* U.K. 13 50.44N 0.47W
Selty U.S.S.R. 44 57.19N 52.12E
Sélune *r.* France 18 48.35N 1.15W
Selva Argentina 126 29.50S 62.02W
Selvas *f.* Brazil 122 6.00S 65.00W
Selwyn Australia 90 21.32S 140.30E
Selwyn L. Canada 101 60.00N 104.30W
Selwyn Mts. Canada 98 63.00N 130.00W
Selwyn Range *mts.* Australia 90 21.35S 140.35E
Seman *r.* Albania 34 40.45N 19.50E
Semara W. Sahara 74 26.44N 14.41W
Semarang Indonesia 59 6.58S 110.29E
Sembabule Uganda 79 0.08S 31.27E
Seminoe Resr. U.S.A. 108 42.00N 106.50W
Seminole U.S.A. 111 32.43N 102.39W
Semiozernoye U.S.S.R. 50 52.22N 64.06E
Semipalatinsk U.S.S.R. 9 50.26N 80.16E
Semīrom Iran 65 31.31N 52.10E
Semiyarka U.S.S.R. 50 50.52N 78.23E
Semliki *r.* Zaïre 79 1.12N 30.27E
Semmering Pass Austria 36 47.40N 16.00E
Semnān Iran 65 35.31N 53.24E
Semois *r.* France 16 49.53N 4.45E
Semporna Malaysia 58 4.27N 118.36E
Semu *r.* Tanzania 79 3.57S 34.20E
Semur-en-Auxois France 19 47.29N 4.20E
Senador Pompeu Brazil 123 5.30S 39.25W
Senaja Malaysia 58 6.49N 117.02E
Sena Madureira Brazil 122 9.04S 68.40W
Senanga Zambia 78 15.52S 23.19E
Senatobia U.S.A. 111 34.39N 89.58W
Sendai Kyushu Japan 57 31.49N 130.18E
Sendai Tofuku Japan 57 38.20N 140.50E
Sendenhorst W. Germany 38 51.50N 7.49E
Sendhwa India 62 21.41N 75.06E
Sendurjana India 63 21.32N 78.17E
Seneca Oreg. U.S.A. 108 44.08N 118.58W
Seneca S.C. U.S.A. 113 34.41N 82.59W
Seneca Falls *town* U.S.A. 114 42.55N 76.48W
Seneca L. U.S.A. 114 42.40N 76.57W
Senegal Africa 76 14.30N 14.30W
Sénégal *r.* Senegal / Mauritania 76 16.00N 16.28W
Senekal R.S.A. 80 28.18S 27.37E
Senetosa, Punta di *c.* France 21 41.33N 8.47E
Senftenberg E. Germany 38 51.31N 14.00E
Senhor do Bonfim Brazil 123 10.28S 40.11W
Senica Czech. 37 48.41N 17.22E
Senigallia Italy 30 43.43N 13.13E
Senise Italy 33 40.09N 16.18E
Senj Yugo. 31 44.59N 14.54E
Senja *i.* Norway 40 69.15N 17.20E
Senlis France 19 49.12N 2.35E
Senmonoron Vietnam 56 12.27N 107.12E
Sennan Japan 57 34.22N 135.17E
Sennen U.K. 13 50.04N 5.42W
Sennestadt W. Germany 38 51.57N 8.31E
Senneterre Canada 102 48.25N 77.15W
Sennori Italy 32 40.48N 8.34E
Sens France 19 48.12N 3.17E
Senta Yugo. 31 45.56N 20.04E
Sentinel U.S.A. 109 32.53N 113.12W
Šentjur Yugo. 31 46.13N 15.24E
Seo de Urgel Spain 25 42.22N 1.23E
Seonāth *r.* India 63 21.44N 82.28E
Seoni India 63 22.05N 79.32E
Seoni Mālwa India 62 22.27N 77.28E
Seorināräyan India 63 21.44N 82.35E
Seoul *see* Sŏul S. Korea 53
Sepik *r.* P.N.G. 59 3.54S 144.30E
Sepopa Botswana 80 18.45S 22.11E
Sept Îles *town* Canada 103 50.12N 66.23W
Sepúlveda Spain 26 41.18N 3.45W
Sequeros Spain 26 40.31N 6.01W
Seraing Belgium 16 50.37N 5.33E
Seram *i.* Indonesia 59 3.10S 129.30E
Seram, Laut *sea* Pacific Oc. 59 2.50S 128.00E
Serang Indonesia 59 6.07S 106.09E
Serbia *d. see* Srbija Yugo. 31
Serdo Ethiopia 73 11.59N 41.30E
Seremban Malaysia 58 2.42N 101.54E
Serengeti Nat. Park Tanzania 79 2.30S 35.00E
Serengeti Plain *f.* Tanzania 79 3.00S 35.00E
Serenje Zambia 79 13.12S 30.50E
Serenli Somali Rep. 73 2.28N 42.08E
Sergach U.S.S.R. 44 55.32N 45.27E
Sergipe *d.* Brazil 123 11.00S 37.00W
Sergiyevsk U.S.S.R. 44 53.56N 50.01E
Seria Brunei 58 4.39N 114.23E
Serian Malaysia 58 1.10N 110.35E
Sericho Kenya 73 1.05N 39.05E
Sérifos Greece 35 37.09N 24.31E
Sérifos *i.* Greece 35 37.11N 24.31E
Sérigny *r.* Canada 103 55.59N 68.43W
Serkout, Djebel *mtn.* Algeria 75 23.40N 6.48E
Serle, Mt Australia 92 30.34S 138.55E
Sermata *i.* Indonesia 59 8.30S 129.00E
Serodino Argentina 125 32.37S 60.57W
Serov U.S.S.R. 44 59.42N 60.32E
Serowe Botswana 80 22.22S 26.42E
Serpa Portugal 27 37.56N 7.36W
Serpeddi, Punta *mtn.* Italy 32 39.22N 9.18E
Serpentine *r.* Australia 89 32.33S 115.46E
Serpent's Mouth *str.* Venezuela 122 9.50N 61.00W
Serpis *r.* Spain 25 38.59N 0.09W
Serpukhov U.S.S.R. 44 54.53N 37.25E
Serra do Navio Brazil 123 0.59N 52.03W
Sérrai Greece 34 41.05N 23.32E
Serramanna Italy 32 39.25N 8.54E
Serra San Bruno Italy 33 38.35N 16.20E
Serrat, Cap *c.* Tunisia 32 37.14N 9.13E
Serra Talhada Brazil 123 8.01S 38.17W
Serravalle Scrivia Italy 30 44.43N 8.51E
Serre *r.* France 16 49.40N 3.22E
Serres France 21 44.26N 5.43E
Serri Italy 32 39.41N 9.09E
Serrières France 21 45.19N 4.45E
Serrinha Brazil 123 11.38S 38.56W
Sersale Italy 33 39.01N 16.44E
Sertã Portugal 27 39.48N 8.06W
Seru Ethiopia 73 7.50N 40.28E
Serui Indonesia 59 1.53S 136.15E
Serule Botswana 80 21.54S 27.17E
Sérvia Greece 34 40.09N 21.58E
Serviceton Australia 92 36.22S 141.02E
Şes, Munţii *mts.* Romania 37 47.05N 22.30E
Seseganaga L. Canada 102 50.00N 90.10W
Sese Is. Uganda 79 0.20S 32.30E
Sesepe Indonesia 59 1.30S 127.59E
Sesheke Zambia 78 17.14S 24.22E
Sesia *r.* Italy 30 45.05N 8.37E
Sesimbra Portugal 24 38.26N 9.06W
Sessa Aurunca Italy 32 41.14N 13.56E
Sestao Spain 26 43.18N 3.00W
Sestri Levante Italy 30 44.16N 9.24E
Setana Japan 57 42.26N 139.51E
Sète France 20 43.24N 3.41E
Sete Lagoas Brazil 126 19.29S 44.15W
Sete Quedas, Salto das *f.* Brazil 126 24.00S 54.10W
Setesdal *f.* Norway 42 59.25N 7.25E
Sétif Algeria 22 36.10N 5.26E
Seto Japan 57 35.14N 137.06E
Settat Morocco 74 33.04N 7.37W
Setté Cama Gabon 78 2.32S 9.46E
Settimo Torinese Italy 30 45.09N 7.46E
Settle U.K. 12 54.05N 2.18W
Settlement of Edinburgh Tristan da Cunha 127 37.03S 12.18W
Setúbal Portugal 27 38.32N 8.54W
Setúbal *d.* Portugal 27 38.15N 8.35W

Setúbal, Baía de to Sierra Leone

Setúbal, Baía de b. Portugal 27 38.20N 9.00W
Seugne r. France 20 45.41N 0.34W
Seui Italy 32 39.50N 9.20E
Seul, Lac l. Canada 102 50.20N 92.30W
Seurre France 19 47.00N 5.09E
Sevagram India 63 20.45N 78.30E
Sevan, Ozero l. U.S.S.R. 65 40.22N 45.20E
Sevastopol' U.S.S.R. 45 44.36N 33.31E
Sevenoaks U.K. 13 51.16N 0.12E
Seven Sisters Peaks mts. Canada 100 54.56N128.10W
Sévérac France 20 44.19N 3.04E
Severn r. Australia 93 29.08S150.50E
Severn r. Canada 102 56.00N 87.38W
Severn r. U.K. 13 51.50N 2.21W
Severnaya Zemlya is. U.S.S.R. 51 80.00N 96.00E
Severn Falls Canada 104 44.51N 79.38W
Severnyy U.S.S.R. 44 69.55N 49.01E
Severnyy Donets r. U.S.S.R. 45 49.08N 37.28E
Severnyy Dvina r. U.S.S.R. 44 57.03N 24.00E
Severočeský d. Czech. 39 50.26N 13.45E
Severodvinsk U.S.S.R. 44 64.35N 39.50E
Severomorsk U.S.S.R. 44 69.05N 33.30E
Severskiy Donets r. U.S.S.R. 23 47.35N 40.55E
Sevier r. U.S.A. 108 39.04N113.06W
Sevier L. U.S.A. 108 38.55N113.09W
Sevilla Spain 27 37.23N 5.59W
Sevilla d. Spain 27 37.35N 6.00W
Sevlievo Bulgaria 34 43.01N 25.06E
Sèvre-Nantaise r. France 18 47.08N 1.26W
Sèvre Niortaise r. France 20 46.20N 1.09W
Sevrey Mongolia 54 43.33N102.13E
Sewa r. Sierra Leone 76 7.15N 12.08W
Seward U.S.A. 98 60.05N149.34W
Seward Nebr. U.S.A. 110 40.55N 97.06W
Seward Penn. U.S.A. 114 40.25N 79.01W
Seward Pen. U.S.A. 98 65.00N164.10W
Seychelles Indian Oc. 49 5.00S 55.00E
Seydhisfjördhur town Iceland 40 65.16N 14.02W
Seym r. U.S.S.R. 45 51.30N 32.30E
Seymour Australia 93 37.01S145.10E
Seymour U.S.A. 111 33.35N 99.16W
Seyne France 21 44.21N 6.21E
Seyssel France 21 45.57N 5.49E
Sežana Yugo. 31 45.42N 13.52E
Sézanne France 19 48.43N 3.43E
Sezimbra Portugal 27 38.26N 9.06W
Sezze Italy 32 41.30N 13.03E
Sfax Tunisia 22 34.45N 10.43E
Sfintu-Gheorghe Romania 37 45.52N 25.50E
Sforströmmen str. Denmark 42 54.58N 11.55E
'sGravenhage Neth. 16 52.05N 4.16E
Shaanxi d. China 54 35.00N108.30E
Shaba d. Zaïre 79 8.00S 27.00E
Shabunda Zaïre 79 2.42S 27.20E
Shache China 52 38.27N 77.16E
Shafter U.S.A. 109 35.30N119.16W
Shaftesbury U.K. 13 51.00N 2.12W
Shagamu r. Canada 102 55.50N 86.48W
Shāhābād India 63 27.39N 79.57E
Shāhāda India 62 21.28N 74.18E
Shahbā' Syria 66 32.51N 36.37E
Shāhbandar Pakistan 62 24.10N 67.54E
Shāhbāz Kalāt Pakistan 62 26.42N 63.58E
Shahdād Iran 65 30.27N 57.44E
Shāhdādkot Pakistan 62 27.51N 67.54E
Shāhdādpur Pakistan 62 25.56N 68.37E
Shahdol India 63 23.17N 81.21E
Shāhganj India 63 26.03N 82.41E
Shāhgarh India 62 27.07N 69.54E
Shaḥḥāt Libya 72 32.50N 21.52E
Shāh Jahān, Kūh-e mts. Iran 65 37.00N 58.00E
Shāhjahānpur India 63 27.53N 79.55E
Shāh Jūy Afghan. 62 32.31N 67.25E
Shāh Kot Pakistan 62 31.34N 73.29E
Shāh Kūh mtn. Iran 65 31.38N 59.16E
Shāhpur Pakistan 62 28.43N 68.25E
Shāhpura India 62 25.35N 75.00E
Shāhpur Chākar Pakistan 62 26.09N 68.39E
Shahrak Afghan. 62 34.06N 64.18E
Shahr-e Bābak Iran 65 30.08N 55.04E
Shahrestān Afghan. 62 34.22N 66.47E
Shahrezā Iran 65 32.00N 51.52E
Shahr Kord Iran 65 32.40N 50.52E
Sha'ib Abā al Qūr wadi Saudi Arabia 64 31.02N 42.00E
Shaikhpura India 63 25.09N 85.51E
Shājāpur India 62 23.26N 76.16E
Shakawe Botswana 80 18.22S 21.50E
Shaker Heights town U.S.A. 114 41.29N 81.36W
Shakhty U.S.S.R. 23 47.43N 40.16E
Shakhunya U.S.S.R. 44 57.41N 46.46E
Shaki Nigeria 77 8.41N 3.24E
Shakshūk Egypt 66 29.28N 30.42E
Shala, L. Ethiopia 73 7.25N 38.30E
Shalingzi China 54 40.42N114.55E
Shallotte U.S.A. 113 33.58N 78.25W
Shalwa Israel 67 31.34N 34.46E
Shām, Jabal ash mtn. Oman 65 23.14N 57.17E
Shāmat al Akbād des. Saudi Arabia 64 28.15N 43.05E
Shamir Israel 67 33.10N 35.39E
Shāmli India 62 29.27N 77.19E
Shamo, L. Ethiopia 73 5.49N 37.35E
Shamokin U.S.A. 115 40.47N 76.34W
Shamrock U.S.A. 111 35.13N100.15W
Shamva Zimbabwe 79 17.20S 31.38E
Shan d. Burma 56 22.00N 98.00E
Shandī Sudan 72 16.42N 33.26E
Shandong d. China 54 36.00N119.00E
Shandong Bandao pen. China 54 37.00N121.30E
Shangcheng China 55 31.48N115.24E
Shangdu China 54 41.33N113.31E
Shanggao China 55 28.15N114.55E
Shanghai China 55 31.18N121.50E
Shanghai d. China 55 31.00N121.30E
Shanglin China 55 23.26N108.36E
Shangqiu China 54 34.21N115.40E
Shangrao China 55 28.24N117.56E
Shangshui China 54 33.31N114.39E
Shang Xian China 54 33.49N109.56E
Shangyi China 54 41.06N114.00E
Shangyou Shuiku resr. China 55 25.52N114.21E
Shangyu China 55 30.01N120.52E
Shanhaiguan China 54 39.58N119.45E
Shannon r. Rep. of Ire. 15 52.39N 8.43W
Shannon, Mouth of the est. Rep. of Ire. 15 52.29N 9.57W
Shan Plateau Burma 56 18.50N 98.00E
Shanshan China 52 42.52N 90.10E
Shantarskiy Ostrova is. U.S.S.R. 51 55.00N138.00E
Shantou China 55 23.22N116.39E
Shanwa Tanzania 79 3.09S 33.48E
Shanxi d. China 54 37.00N112.00E
Shanyin China 54 39.30N112.50E
Shaoguan China 55 24.53N113.31E
Shaoxing China 55 30.01N120.40E
Shaoyang China 55 27.10N111.14E
Shap U.K. 12 54.32N 2.40W
Shapinsay i. U.K. 14 59.03N 2.51W
Shapur ruins Iran 65 29.42N 51.30E
Shaqrā Lebanon 67 33.12N 35.28E
Shaqrā' Saudi Arabia 65 25.17N 45.14E
Shaqrā' S. Yemen 71 13.21N 45.42E
Shaqrā' Syria 67 32.54N 36.14E
Sharan Jogizai Pakistan 62 31.02N 68.33E
Sharbot Lake town Canada 105 44.46N 76.41W
Shark B. Australia 88 25.30S113.30E
Sharlyk U.S.S.R. 44 52.58N 54.46E
Sharm ash Shaykh Egypt 66 27.51N 34.16E
Sharon U.S.A. 114 41.14N 80.31W
Sharon Springs town U.S.A. 110 38.54N101.45W
Sharqī, Al Jabal ash mts. Lebanon 66 34.00N 36.25E
Sharqiyah, Aş Şaḥrā' ash des. Egypt 66 27.40N 32.00E
Sharya U.S.S.R. 44 58.22N 45.50E
Shashi r. Botswana / Zimbabwe 80 22.10S 29.15E
Shashi China 55 30.18N112.20E
Shasta, Mt. U.S.A. 108 41.20N122.20W
Shatt al Arab r. Iraq 65 30.00N 48.30E
Shaunavon Canada 101 49.40N108.25W
Shawanaga Canada 104 45.32N 80.24W
Shawangunk Mts. U.S.A. 115 41.35N 74.30W
Shawano U.S.A. 102 44.46N 88.38W
Shawbridge Canada 105 45.52N 74.05W
Shaw I. Australia 90 20.29S149.05E
Shawinigan Canada 105 46.33N 72.45W
Shawinigan Sud Canada 105 46.30N 72.45W
Shawnee Ohio U.S.A. 114 39.36N 82.13W
Shawnee Okla. U.S.A. 111 35.20N 96.55W
Shawville Canada 105 45.36N 76.29W
Sha Xi r. China 55 26.38N118.10E
Sha Xian China 55 26.27N117.42E
Shayang China 55 30.42N112.29E
Shaykh, Jabal ash mtn. Lebanon 66 33.24N 35.52E
Shaykh 'Uthmān S. Yemen 71 12.52N 44.59E
Shchara r. U.S.S.R. 37 53.27N 24.45E
Shchelyayur U.S.S.R. 44 65.16N 53.17E
Shchors U.S.S.R. 37 51.50N 31.59E
Shebele r. see Shebelle Ethiopia 71
Shebelle r. Somali Rep. 79 0.30N 43.10E
Sheboygan U.S.A. 110 43.46N 87.36W
Shebshi Mts. Nigeria 77 8.30N 11.45E
Shediac Canada 103 46.13N 64.32W
Sheeffry Hills Rep. of Ire. 15 53.41N 9.42W
Sheelin, Lough Rep. of Ire. 15 53.48N 7.20W
Sheep Range mts. U.S.A. 109 36.45N115.05W
Sheet Harbour Canada 103 44.55N 62.32W
Shefar'am Israel 67 32.48N 35.10E
Sheffield U.K. 12 53.23N 1.28W
Sheffield Ala. U.S.A. 113 34.46N 87.40W
Sheffield Penn. U.S.A. 114 41.42N 79.02W
Sheffield Tex. U.S.A. 111 30.41N101.49W
Shefford U.K. 13 52.02N 0.20W
Shegaon India 62 20.47N 76.41E
Sheguiandah Canada 104 45.53N 81.57W
Shekatika Bay town Canada 103 51.17N 58.20W
Shēkhābād Afghan. 62 34.05N 68.45E
Shek Hasan Ethiopia 73 12.09N 35.54E
Shekhūpura Pakistan 62 31.42N 73.59E
Sheki U.S.S.R. 45 41.12N 47.10E
Sheksna r. U.S.S.R. 44 60.00N 37.49E
Shelburne N.S. Canada 103 43.46N 65.19W
Shelburne Ont. Canada 104 44.04N 80.12W
Shelburne U.S.A. 105 44.22N 73.15W
Shelburne B. Australia 90 11.49S143.00E
Shelby Mich. U.S.A. 112 43.36N 86.22W
Shelby Mont. U.S.A. 108 48.30N111.51W
Shelby Ohio U.S.A. 114 40.53N 82.40W
Shelbyville Ind. U.S.A. 112 39.31N 85.46W
Shelbyville Tenn. U.S.A. 113 35.29N 86.30W
Sheldon Iowa U.S.A. 110 43.11N 95.51W
Sheldon N.Dak. U.S.A. 110 46.35N 97.30W
Sheldrake Canada 103 50.20N 64.51W
Shelikof Str. U.S.A. 98 58.00N153.45W
Shelley U.S.A. 108 43.23N112.07W
Shellharbour Australia 93 34.35S150.52E
Shell Lake town Canada 101 53.18N107.07W
Shelton U.S.A. 108 47.13N123.06W
Shenandoah r. U.S.A. 114 38.56N 78.12W
Shenandoah Iowa U.S.A. 110 40.46N 95.22W
Shenandoah Penn. U.S.A. 115 40.49N 76.12W
Shenandoah Va. U.S.A. 114 38.29N 78.37W
Shenandoah, North Fork r. U.S.A. 114 38.57N 78.12W
Shenandoah, South Fork r. U.S.A. 114 38.57N 78.12W
Shenandoah Mts. U.S.A. 114 38.55N 78.56W
Shenandoah Nat. Park U.S.A. 114 38.48N 78.12W
Shenandoah Tower mtn. U.S.A. 114 38.30N 79.09W
Shenandoah Valley f. U.S.A. 114 38.42N 78.48W
Shenchi China 54 39.08N112.10E
Shëngjin Albania 34 41.50N 19.35E
Shengze China 55 30.53N120.40E
Shenkursk U.S.S.R. 44 62.05N 42.58E
Shenmu China 54 38.54N110.24E
Shennongjia China 55 31.44N110.44E
Shen Xian China 54 36.15N115.40E
Shenyang China 54 41.48N123.27E
Shenzhen China 55 22.32N114.08E
Sheo India 62 26.11N 71.15E
Sheoganj India 62 25.09N 73.04E
Sheopur India 62 25.40N 76.42E
Shepetovka U.S.S.R. 37 50.12N 27.01E
Shepherd Is. Vanuatu 84 16.55S168.36E
Shepparton Australia 93 36.25S145.26E
Sheppey, Isle of U.K. 13 51.24N 0.50E
Sherada Ethiopia 73 7.21N 36.32E
Sherborne U.K. 13 50.56N 2.31W
Sherbro I. Sierra Leone 76 7.30N 12.50W
Sherbrooke Canada 105 45.24N 71.54W
Sherburne U.S.A. 115 42.41N 75.30W
Sheridan U.S.A. 108 44.48N106.58W
Sheringa Australia 92 33.51S135.15E
Sheringham U.K. 12 52.56N 1.11E
Sherkin I. Rep. of Ire. 15 51.28N 9.25W
Sherman N.Y. U.S.A. 114 42.10N 79.36W
Sherman Tex. U.S.A. 111 33.38N 96.36W
Sherman Mills U.S.A. 112 45.52N 68.23W
Sherridon Canada 101 55.07N101.05W
'sHertogenbosch Neth. 16 51.42N 5.19E
Shesh Gāv Afghan. 62 33.45N 68.33E
Shetland Is. d. U.K. 14 60.20N 1.15W
Shetpe U.S.S.R. 45 44.09N 52.06E
Shetrunji r. India 62 21.20N 72.05E
Shevchenko U.S.S.R. 45 43.37N 51.11E
Shewa d. Ethiopia 73 8.40N 38.00E
Shewa Gimira Ethiopia 73 7.00N 35.50E
Sheyang China 54 33.47N120.19E
Sheyenne r. U.S.A. 110 47.05N 96.50W
Shiawassee r. U.S.A. 104 43.06N 84.10W
Shibām S. Yemen 71 15.56N 48.38E
Shibecha Japan 57 43.17N144.36E
Shibīn al Kawm Egypt 66 30.33N 31.00E
Shibīn al Qanāṭir Egypt 66 30.19N 31.19E
Shibogama L. Canada 102 53.35N 88.10W
Shickshinny U.S.A. 115 41.09N 76.09W
Shidao China 54 36.52N122.26E
Shiel, Loch U.K. 14 56.48N 5.33W
Shiga d. Japan 57 34.55N136.00E
Shigaib Sudan 72 15.01N 23.36E
Shihpao Shan mts. China 55 30.00N112.00E
Shijak Albania 34 41.21N 19.33E
Shijiazhuang China 54 38.03N114.26E
Shijiu Hu l. China 55 31.20N118.48E
Shikārpur Pakistan 62 27.57N 68.38E
Shikohābād India 63 27.06N 78.36E
Shikoku d. Japan 57 33.30N133.00E
Shikoku i. Japan 57 33.30N133.00E
Shikoku sanchi mts. Japan 57 34.00N134.00E
Shikotsu ko l. Japan 57 43.50N141.26E
Shilabo Ethiopia 71 6.05N 44.48E
Shilka U.S.S.R. 53 51.55N116.01E
Shilka r. U.S.S.R. 53 53.20N121.10E
Shillington U.S.A. 115 40.18N 75.58W
Shillo r. Israel 67 32.07N 34.53E
Shillong India 63 25.34N 91.53E
Shiloh see Saylūn Jordan 67
Shilong China 55 23.02N113.50E
Shima Japan 57 34.13N136.51E
Shimada Japan 57 34.49N138.11E
Shima-hantō pen. Japan 57 34.25N136.45E
Shimizu Japan 57 35.01N138.29E
Shimoda Japan 57 34.40N138.57E
Shimoga India 60 13.56N 75.31E
Shimo jima i. Japan 57 32.10N130.30E
Shimo Koshiki jima i. Japan 57 31.50N130.00E
Shimonoseki Japan 57 34.02N130.58E
Shimpek U.S.S.R. 52 44.50N 74.10E
Shin, Loch U.K. 14 58.06N 4.32W
Shinano r. Japan 57 37.58N139.02E
Shindand Afghan. 62 33.18N 62.08E
Shinglehouse U.S.A. 114 41.58N 78.12W
Shingleton U.S.A. 112 46.21N 86.28W
Shingū Japan 57 33.44N135.59E
Shinkay Afghan. 62 31.57N 67.26E
Shin Naray Afghan. 62 31.19N 66.43E
Shinnston U.S.A. 114 39.24N 80.18W
Shinshār Syria 66 34.36N 36.45E
Shinshiro Japan 57 34.54N137.30E
Shinyanga Tanzania 79 3.40S 33.20E
Shinyanga d. Tanzania 79 3.30S 33.00E
Shiono zaki c. Japan 57 33.28N135.47E
Ship Bottom U.S.A. 115 39.39N 74.11W
Shipka Pass Bulgaria 34 42.46N 25.33E
Shippegan Canada 103 47.45N 64.42W
Shippensburg U.S.A. 114 40.03N 77.31W
Shiprock U.S.A. 108 36.47N108.41W
Shipston on Stour U.K. 13 52.04N 1.38W
Shiqian China 55 27.20N108.10E
Shiqiao China 55 31.19N111.59E
Shiqizhen China 55 22.22N113.21E
Shiqma r. Israel 67 31.36N 34.30E
Shiquan China 54 33.03N108.17E
Shiquan He r. China 63 32.30N 79.40E
Shirakawa Japan 57 37.10N140.15E
Shirakskaya Step f. U.S.S.R. 65 41.40N 46.20E
Shirane san mtn. Japan 57 35.40N138.15E
Shīrāz Iran 65 29.36N 52.33E
Shirbīn Egypt 66 31.13N 31.31E
Shire r. Mozambique 79 17.46S 35.20E
Shiriya saki c. Japan 57 41.24N141.30E
Shīr Kūh mtn. Iran 65 31.38N 54.07E
Shiroishi Japan 57 38.00N140.37E
Shirpur India 62 21.21N 74.53E
Shīrvān Iran 65 37.24N 57.55E
Shivpuri India 63 25.26N 77.39E
Shiwan Dashan mts. China 55 21.48N107.50E
Shiyan Hubei China 54 32.38N110.47E
Shizuishan China 54 39.14N106.47E
Shizuoka Japan 57 34.58N138.23E
Shizuoka d. Japan 57 35.00N138.00E
Shklov U.S.S.R. 37 54.16N 30.16E
Shkodër Albania 34 42.05N 19.30E
Shkodër d. Albania 34 42.10N 19.40E
Shkumbin r. Albania 34 41.01N 19.26E
Shoal C. Australia 89 33.51S121.10E
Sholāpur India 60 17.43N 75.56E
Shomera Israel 67 33.05N 35.17E
Shonai r. Japan 57 35.04N136.50E
Shoshone Calif. U.S.A. 109 35.58N116.17W
Shoshone Idaho U.S.A. 108 42.57N114.25W
Shoshone Mts. U.S.A. 108 39.25N117.15W
Shoshoni U.S.A. 108 43.14N108.07W
Shostka U.S.S.R. 44 51.53N 33.30E
Shou Xian China 54 32.30N116.35E
Shouyang China 54 37.55N113.10E
Show Low U.S.A. 109 34.15N110.02W
Shpola U.S.S.R. 37 49.00N 31.25E
Shreve U.S.A. 114 40.41N 82.01W
Shreveport U.S.A 111 32.30N 93.45W
Shrewsbury U.K. 13 52.42N 2.45W
Shropshire d. U.K. 13 52.35N 2.40W
Shuangliao China 54 43.28N123.27E
Shuangyashan China 53 46.37N131.22E
Shu'ayb, Wādī Jordan 67 31.54N 35.38E
Shubenacadie Canada 103 45.05N 63.25W
Shubrā al Khaymah Egypt 66 30.06N 31.15E
Shuicheng China 55 26.36N104.51E
Shujāābād Pakistan 62 29.53N 71.18E
Shujālpur India 62 23.24N 76.43E
Shuksan U.S.A. 108 48.55N121.43W
Shule China 52 39.25N 76.06E
Shumagin Is. U.S.A. 98 55.00N160.00W
Shumerlya U.S.S.R. 44 55.30N 46.25E
Shumikha U.S.S.R. 50 55.15N 63.14E
Shumyachi U.S.S.R. 37 53.52N 32.25E
Shūnat Nimrīn Jordan 67 31.54N 35.37E
Shunayn, Sabkhat f. Libya 72 30.10N 21.00E
Shunchang China 55 26.48N117.47E
Shunde China 55 22.40N113.20E
Shuo Xian China 54 39.19N112.25E
Shur r. Iran 65 34.05N 60.22E
Shūr r. Kermān Iran 65 31.14N 55.29E
Shūr r. Khorāsān Iran 65 34.11N 60.07E
Shūrāb Iran 65 28.09N 60.18E
Shūrāb r. Iran 65 31.30N 55.18E
Shurugwi Zimbabwe 80 19.40S 30.00E
Shūshtar Iran 65 32.04N 48.53E
Shuswap L. Canada 100 50.55N119.03W
Shuttleton Australia 93 32.08S146.08E
Shuwak Sudan 72 14.23N 35.52E
Shuya U.S.S.R. 44 56.49N 41.23E
Shwebo Burma 56 22.35N 95.42E
Shyok Jammu & Kashmir 63 34.11N 78.08E
Siāhān Range mts. Pakistan 62 27.30N 64.30E
Siālkot Pakistan 62 32.30N 74.31E
Sian see Xi'an China 54
Siargao i. Phil. 59 9.55N126.05E
Siari Jammu & Kashmir 62 34.56N 76.44E
Siasconset U.S.A. 115 41.16N 69.58W
Siátista Greece 34 40.15N 21.33E
Siau i. Indonesia 59 2.42N125.24E
Siauliai U.S.S.R. 41 55.56N 23.19E
Sibasa R.S.A. 80 22.56S 30.28E
Šibenik Yugo. 31 43.44N 15.54E
Siberut i. Indonesia 58 1.30S 99.00E
Sibi Pakistan 62 29.33N 67.53E
Sibiti Congo 78 3.40S 13.24E
Sibiti r. Tanzania 79 3.47S 34.45E
Sibiu Romania 29 45.47N 24.09E
Sibley U.S.A. 110 43.25N 95.43W
Sibolga Indonesia 58 1.42N 98.48E
Sibu Malaysia 58 2.18N111.49E
Sicasica Bolivia 124 17.22S 67.45W
Siccus r. Australia 92 31.26S139.30E
Sichuan d. China 52 30.30N103.00E
Sichuan Pendi f. China 55 31.00N106.00E
Sicié, Cap c. France 21 43.03N 5.51E
Sicilia d. Italy 33 37.45N 14.00E
Sicilia i. Italy 33 37.30N 14.00E
Sicily i. Italy 70 37.30N 14.00E
Sicily i. see Sicilia Italy 33
Sicuani Peru 122 14.21S 71.13W
Šid Yugo. 31 45.08N 19.13E
Sidamo d. Ethiopia 73 4.30N 39.00E
Sidaouet Niger 77 18.34N 8.03E
Siderno Italy 33 38.16N 16.18E
Sidheros, Ákra c. Greece 35 35.19N 26.19E
Sidhi India 63 24.25N 81.53E
Sidhirókastron Greece 34 41.14N 23.22E
Sidhpur India 62 23.55N 72.23E
Sīdī Barrānī Egypt 64 31.38N 25.58E
Sidi bel Abbès Algeria 74 35.12N 0.38W
Sidi Daoud Tunisia 32 37.01N 10.55E
Sidi Ifni Morocco 74 29.24N 10.12W
Sidi-Kacem Morocco 74 34.15N 5.39W
Sīdī Sālim Egypt 66 31.16N 30.47E
Sidi Smaïl Morocco 74 32.49N 8.30W
Sidlaw Hills U.K. 14 56.31N 3.10W
Sidley, Mt. Antarctica 128 77.30S125.00W
Sidmouth U.K. 13 50.40N 3.13W
Sidney Canada 100 48.39N123.24W
Sidney Mont. U.S.A. 108 47.43N104.09W
Sidney Nebr. U.S.A. 110 41.09N102.59W
Sidney N.Y. U.S.A. 115 42.19N 75.24W
Sidney Ohio U.S.A. 112 40.16N 84.10W
Sidon see Şaydā Lebanon 66
Sidra, G. of see Surt, Khalīj Libya 75
Siedlce Poland 37 52.10N 22.18E
Sieg r. W. Germany 16 50.49N 7.11E
Siegburg W. Germany 38 50.47N 7.12E
Siegen W. Germany 38 50.52N 8.02E
Siemiatycze Poland 37 52.26N 22.53E
Siĕmréab Kampuchea 56 13.21N103.50E
Siena Italy 30 43.19N 11.21E
Sieradz Poland 37 51.36N 18.45E
Sierck-les-Bains France 19 49.26N 6.21E
Sierpc Poland 37 52.52N 19.41E
Sierra Blanca town U.S.A. 109 31.11N105.12W
Sierra Colorada Argentina 125 40.35S 67.50W
Sierra de Outes town Spain 26 42.51N 8.54W
Sierra Leone Africa 76 9.00N 12.00W

Sierra Mojada to Södermanland

Sierra Mojada *town* Mexico **111** 27.17N103.42W
Sierra Nevada *mts.* U.S.A. **108** 37.45N119.30W
Sierre Switz. **39** 46.18N 7.32E
Sifani Ethiopia **73** 12.20N 40.24E
Sifnos *i.* Greece **35** 36.59N 24.40E
Sig Algeria **74** 35.32N 0.11W
Sig U.S.S.R. **44** 65.31N 34.16E
Sigean France **20** 43.02N 2.59E
Sighetul Marmaţiei Romania **37** 47.56N 23.54E
Sighişoara Romania **37** 46.13N 24.49E
Sigli Indonesia **58** 5.23N 95.57E
Siglufjördhur Iceland **40** 66.12N 18.55W
Sigmaringen W. Germany **39** 48.05N 9.13E
Signy France **19** 49.42N 4.25E
Sigtuna Sweden **43** 59.37N 17.43E
Sigüenza Spain **26** 41.04N 2.38W
Sigües Spain **25** 42.38N 1.00W
Siguiri Guinea **76** 11.28N 9.07W
Sihor India **62** 21.42N 71.58E
Sihorā India **63** 23.29N 80.07E
Siika *r.* Finland **40** 64.50N 24.44E
Si'īr Jordan **67** 31.35N 35.09E
Siirt Turkey **64** 37.56N 41.56E
Sikanni Chief *r.* Canada **100** 58.20N121.50W
Sīkar India **62** 27.37N 75.09E
Sikasso Mali **76** 11.18N 5.38W
Sikasso *d.* Mali **76** 11.20N 6.05W
Sikeston U.S.A. **111** 36.53N 89.35W
Sikhote Alin *mts.* U.S.S.R. **53** 44.00N135.00E
Sikiá Greece **34** 40.02N 23.56E
Síkinos *i.* Greece **35** 36.39N 25.06E
Sikión *site* Greece **35** 37.59N 22.44E
Sikkim *d.* India **63** 27.30N 88.30E
Sil *r.* Spain **26** 42.27N 7.43W
Silandro Italy **30** 46.38N 10.46E
Silba Yugo. **31** 44.23N 14.42E
Silba *i.* Yugo. **31** 44.23N 14.42E
Silchar India **61** 24.49N 92.47E
Silcox Canada **101** 57.12N 94.10W
Silet Algeria **75** 22.39N 4.35E
Silgarhi-Doti Nepal **63** 29.16N 80.58E
Silghāt India **63** 26.37N 92.56E
Silifke Turkey **64** 36.22N 33.57E
Siliguri India **63** 26.42N 88.26E
Silil Somali Rep. **71** 10.59N 43.31E
Siling Co *l.* China **63** 31.45N 88.50E
Silistra Bulgaria **29** 44.07N 27.17E
Šiljak *mtn.* Yugo. **34** 43.45N 21.50E
Siljan *l.* Sweden **41** 60.50N 14.45E
Silkeborg Denmark **42** 56.10N 9.34E
Sillé-le-Guillaume France **18** 48.12N 0.08W
Sillian Austria **39** 46.45N 12.25E
Sillian Italy **30** 46.45N 12.25E
Sillon de Talbert *c.* France **18** 48.53N 3.05W
Silloth U.K. **12** 54.53N 3.25W
Silogui Indonesia **58** 1.10S 98.46E
Silsbee U.S.A **111** 30.21N 94.11W
Silvassa India **62** 20.17N 73.00E
Silver Bow U.S.A. **108** 46.00N112.40W
Silver City U.S.A. **109** 32.46N108.17W
Silver Creek *town* U.S.A. **114** 42.33N 79.10W
Silverdalen Sweden **43** 57.32N 15.44E
Silver Lake *town* U.S.A. **108** 43.08N120.56W
Silver Spring *town* U.S.A. **114** 39.02N 77.03W
Silverstone U.K. **13** 52.05N 1.03W
Silverthrone Mtn. Canada **100** 51.31N126.06W
Silverton Australia **92** 31.53S141.13E
Silverton U.S.A. **108** 45.01N122.47W
Silves Portugal **27** 37.11N 8.26W
Silvi Italy **31** 42.34N 14.05E
Simanggang Malaysia **58** 1.10N111.32E
Simàrd, Lac *l.* Canada **102** 47.40N 78.40W
Simav *r.* Turkey **29** 40.24N 28.31E
Simba Kenya **79** 2.10S 37.37E
Simba Zaïre **78** 0.36N 22.55E
Simbach W. Germany **39** 48.34N 12.45E
Simcoe Canada **104** 42.50N 80.18W
Simcoe, L. Canada **104** 44.20N 79.20W
Simdega India **63** 22.37N 84.31E
Simenga U.S.S.R. **51** 62.42N108.25E
Simeria Romania **29** 45.51N 23.01E
Simeto *r.* Italy **33** 37.24N 15.06E
Simeulue *i.* Indonesia **58** 2.30N 96.00E
Simferopol' U.S.S.R. **45** 44.57N 34.05E
Sími Greece **35** 36.35N 27.50E
Sími *i.* Greece **35** 36.35N 27.50E
Simikot Nepal **63** 29.58N 81.51E
Simitli Bulgaria **34** 41.52N 23.07E
Simiyu *r.* Tanzania **79** 2.32S 33.25E
Simla India **62** 31.06N 77.09E
Simleul Silvaniei Romania **37** 47.14N 22.48E
Simmern W. Germany **39** 49.59N 7.31E
Simo *r.* Finland **40** 65.37N 25.03E
Simojärvo *l.* Finland **40** 66.06N 27.03E
Simon, Lac *l.* Canada **105** 45.58N 75.05W
Simonstown R.S.A. **80** 34.12S 18.26E
Simoom Sound *town* Canada **98** 50.45N126.45W
Simplon Pass Switz. **39** 46.15N 8.02E
Simplon Tunnel Switz. **39** 46.15N 8.10E
Simpson Desert Australia **90** 25.00S136.50E
Simrishamn Sweden **43** 55.33N 14.20E
Simuco Mozambique **79** 14.00S 40.35E
Sinā', Shibh Jazīrat *pen.* Egypt **66** 29.00N 34.00E
Sinadogo Somali Rep. **71** 5.22N 46.22E
Sinai *see* Sinā', Shibh Jazīrat Egypt **66**
Sinaloa *d.* Mexico **109** 25.00N107.30W
Sinaloa *r.* Mexico **109** 25.18N108.30W
Sinalunga Italy **30** 43.12N 11.44E
Sinan China **55** 27.51N108.24E
Sināwin Libya **75** 31.02N 10.36E
Sincelejo Colombia **122** 9.17N 75.23W
Sinclair U.S.A. **108** 41.47N107.07W
Sinclair Mills Canada **100** 54.05N121.40W
Sind *r.* India **63** 26.26N 79.13E
Sind *d.* Pakistan **62** 26.45N 69.00E
Sindal Denmark **42** 57.28N 10.13E
Sindara Gabon **78** 1.07S 10.41E
Sindari India **62** 25.35N 71.55E
Sindelfingen W. Germany **39** 48.42N 9.00E
Sindhūli Gārhi Nepal **63** 27.16N 85.58E
Sindri India **63** 23.45N 86.42E
Sines Portugal **26** 37.57N 8.52W
Sines, Cabo de *c.* Portugal **26** 37.57N 8.53W
Sinfāis Portugal **26** 41.04N 8.05W
Sinfra Ivory Coast **76** 6.35N 5.56W
Singālila *mtn.* India **63** 27.13N 88.01E
Singapore Asia **58** 1.20N103.45E
Singapore *town* Singapore **58** 1.20N103.45E
Singaraja Indonesia **59** 8.06S115.07E
Singatoka Fiji **84** 18.08S177.30E
Sing Buri Thailand **56** 14.56N100.21E
Singida Tanzania **79** 4.45S 34.42E
Singida *d.* Tanzania **79** 6.00S 34.30E
Singing India **61** 28.53N 94.47E
Singitikós Kólpos *g.* Greece **34** 40.06N 24.00E
Singkaling Hkāmti Burma **61** 26.00N 95.42E
Singkang Indonesia **59** 4.09S120.02E
Singkawang Indonesia **58** 0.57N108.57E
Singkep *i.* Indonesia **58** 0.30S104.20E
Singleton Australia **93** 32.33S151.11E
Singoli India **62** 25.00N 75.25E
Singosan N. Korea **53** 38.50N127.27E
Siniscola Italy **32** 40.34N 9.41E
Sinj Yugo. **31** 43.42N 16.38E
Sinjah Sudan **73** 13.09N 33.56E
Sinjajevina *mts.* Yugo. **31** 43.00N 19.15E
Sinjil Jordan **67** 32.02N 35.16E
Sinkāt Sudan **72** 18.50N 36.50E
Sinnai Italy **32** 39.18N 9.12E
Sinnar India **62** 19.51N 74.00E
Sinnemahoning *r.* U.S.A. **114** 41.19N 78.06W
Sinnes Norway **42** 58.56N 6.50E
Sinni *r.* Italy **33** 40.09N 16.42E
Sînnicolau Mare Romania **29** 46.05N 20.38E
Sinnūris Egypt **66** 29.25N 30.52E
Sinop Turkey **64** 42.02N 35.09E
Sinsheim W. Germany **39** 49.16N 8.53E
Sintang Indonesia **58** 0.03N111.31E
Sint Eustatius *i.* Leeward Is. **117** 17.33N 63.00W
Sint Maarten *i. see* St. Martin Leeward Is. **117**
Sinton U.S.A. **111** 29.41N 95.58W
Sintra Portugal **27** 38.48N 9.23W
Sinŭiju N. Korea **53** 40.04N124.25E
Sinyavka U.S.S.R. **37** 52.58N 26.30E
Sinyukha *r.* U.S.S.R. **37** 48.03N 30.51E
Sió *r.* Hungary **31** 46.20N 18.55E
Siocon Phil. **59** 7.42N122.08E
Siófok Hungary **31** 46.54N 18.04E
Sion Switz. **39** 46.14N 7.21E
Sioux City U.S.A. **110** 42.30N 96.23W
Sioux Falls *town* U.S.A. **110** 43.32N 96.44W
Sioux Lookout *town* Canada **102** 50.06N 91.55W
Siphaqeni R.S.A. **80** 31.05S 29.29E
Siping Hubei China **55** 31.58N111.10E
Siping Jilin China **54** 43.10N124.24E
Sipiwesk L. Canada **101** 55.05N 97.35W
Sipura *i.* Indonesia **58** 2.10S 99.40E
Sira Norway **42** 58.25N 6.38E
Sira *r.* Norway **42** 58.17N 6.24E
Siracusa Italy **33** 37.04N 15.17E
Sirājganj Bangla. **63** 24.27N 89.43E
Sirakoro Mali **76** 12.41N 9.14W
Sirasso Ivory Coast **76** 9.16N 6.06W
Sirdalsvatn *l.* Norway **42** 58.33N 6.41E
Sire Ethiopia **73** 9.00N 36.55E
Sir Edward Pellew Group *is.* Australia **90** 15.40S136.48E
Siret *r.* Romania **29** 45.28N 27.56E
Sirevåg Norway **42** 58.30N 5.47E
Sirha Nepal **63** 26.39N 86.12E
Sirḩān, Wādī as *f.* Saudi Arabia **64** 31.00N 37.30E
Sir James MacBrien, Mt. Canada **100** 62.07N127.41W
Sirohi India **62** 24.53N 72.52E
Sironj India **63** 24.06N 77.42E
Síros *i.* Greece **35** 37.26N 24.54E
Sirrah, Wādī as *r.* Saudi Arabia **65** 23.10N 44.22E
Sirsa India **62** 29.32N 75.02E
Sir Wilfrid, Mt. Canada **105** 46.41N 75.35W
Sisak Yugo. **31** 45.29N 16.23E
Sisaket Thailand **56** 15.08N104.18E
Sishen R.S.A. **80** 27.46S 22.59E
Sisimiut *see* Holsteinsborg Greenland **99**
Sisipuk L. Canada **101** 55.45N101.50W
Sisŏphŏn Kampuchea **56** 13.37N102.58E
Sissach Switz. **39** 47.28N 7.49E
Sisseton U.S.A. **110** 45.40N 97.03W
Sissonne France **19** 49.34N 3.54E
Sistema Central *mts.* Spain **26** 41.00N 3.30W
Sistema Ibérico *mts.* Spain **26** 41.00N 2.25W
Sistemas Béticos *mts.* Spain **27** 37.20N 3.00W
Sisteron France **21** 44.12N 5.56E
Sītāmarhi India **63** 26.36N 85.29E
Sītāpur India **63** 27.34N 80.41E
Sithonia *pen.* Greece **34** 40.00N 23.45E
Sitia Greece **35** 35.13N 26.06E
Sitka U.S.A. **100** 57.05N135.20W
Sitnica *r.* Yugo. **34** 42.45N 21.01E
Sittang *r.* Burma **56** 17.25N 96.50E
Sittard Neth. **16** 51.00N 5.52E
Sittensen W. Germany **38** 53.17N 9.30E
Sittwe Burma **56** 20.09N 92.50E
Situbondo Indonesia **59** 7.40S114.01E
Siuruan *r.* Finland **40** 65.20N 25.55E
Sīvan *r.* Iran **65** 29.50N 52.47E
Sivas Turkey **64** 39.44N 37.01E
Sivomaskinskiy U.S.S.R. **44** 66.45N 62.44E
Sivrihisar Turkey **64** 39.29N 31.32E
Sīwah Egypt **64** 29.12N 25.31E
Sīwah, Wāḩat *oasis* Egypt **64** 29.10N 25.40E
Siwalik Range *mts.* India **63** 31.15N 77.45E
Siwān India **63** 26.13N 84.22E
Siwa Oasis *see* Sīwah, Wāḩat Egypt **64**
Sixmilecross U.K. **15** 54.34N 7.08W
Siya U.S.S.R. **44** 63.38N 41.40E
Sizun France **18** 48.24N 4.05W
Sjaelland *i.* Denmark **42** 55.30N 11.45E
Sjaellands Odde *c.* Denmark **42** 55.58N 11.22E
Sjenica Yugo. **31** 43.16N 20.00E
Sjeništa *mtn.* Yugo. **31** 43.42N 18.37E
Sjöbo Sweden **43** 55.38N 13.42E
Sjötorp Sweden **43** 58.50N 13.59E
Skaelskör Denmark **42** 55.15N 11.19E
Skaerbaek Denmark **42** 55.09N 8.46E
Skagafjördhur *est.* Iceland **40** 65.55N 19.35W
Skagen Denmark **42** 57.44N 10.36E
Skagern *l.* Sweden **43** 58.59N 14.17E
Skagerrak *str.* Norway/Denmark **42** 58.00N 9.30E
Skagway U.S.A. **100** 59.23N135.20W
Skaill U.K. **14** 58.56N 2.43W
Skála Greece **35** 36.51N 22.40E
Skála Oropoú Greece **35** 38.20N 23.46E
Skala Podolskaya U.S.S.R. **37** 48.51N 26.11E
Skalat U.S.S.R. **37** 49.20N 25.59E
Skälderviken *b.* Sweden **43** 56.18N 12.38E
Skanderborg Denmark **42** 56.02N 9.56E
Skåne *f.* Sweden **43** 55.59N 13.30E
Skaneateles U.S.A. **115** 42.57N 76.26W
Skånevik Norway **42** 59.44N 5.59E
Skanör Falsterbo Sweden **43** 55.25N 12.52E
Skara Sweden **43** 58.22N 13.25E
Skaraborg *d.* Sweden **43** 58.20N 13.30E
Skärhamn Sweden **42** 58.00N 11.33E
Skarnes Norway **42** 60.15N 11.41E
Skarżysko-Kamienna Poland **37** 51.08N 20.53E
Skead Canada **104** 46.40N 80.45W
Skeena *r.* Canada **100** 54.09N130.02W
Skeena Mts. Canada **100** 57.00N128.30W
Skegness U.K. **12** 53.09N 0.20E
Skeleton L. Canada **104** 45.15N 79.27W
Skellefte *r.* Sweden **40** 64.42N 21.06E
Skellefteå Sweden **40** 64.46N 20.57E
Skelleftehamn Sweden **40** 64.41N 21.14E
Skelmersdale U.K. **12** 53.34N 2.49W
Skene Sweden **43** 57.29N 12.38E
Skerries Rep. of Ire. **15** 53.35N 6.07W
Skhíza *i.* Greece **35** 36.43N 21.46E
Ski Norway **42** 59.43N 10.50E
Skiáthos Greece **35** 39.10N 23.29E
Skiathos *i.* Greece **35** 39.12N 23.30E
Skiddaw *mtn.* U.K. **12** 54.40N 3.09W
Skidel U.S.S.R. **37** 53.37N 24.19E
Skien Norway **42** 59.12N 9.36E
Skierniewice Poland **37** 51.58N 20.08E
Skikda Algeria **75** 36.53N 6.54E
Skillingaryd Sweden **43** 57.26N 14.05E
Skinners Eddy U.S.A. **115** 41.37N 76.08W
Skinnskatteberg Sweden **43** 59.50N 15.41E
Skipness U.K. **14** 56.45N 5.22W
Skipton U.K. **12** 53.57N 2.01W
Skíros Greece **35** 38.55N 24.34E
Skíros *i.* Greece **35** 38.53N 24.32E
Skive Denmark **42** 56.34N 9.02E
Skjálfanda Fljót *r.* Iceland **40** 65.55N 17.30W
Skjálfandi *est.* Iceland **40** 66.08N 17.38W
Skjern Denmark **42** 55.57N 8.30E
Skjönsta Norway **40** 67.12N 15.45E
Škofja Loka Yugo. **31** 46.10N 14.18E
Skoghall Sweden **43** 59.19N 13.26E
Skole U.S.S.R. **37** 49.00N 23.30E
Skópelos Greece **35** 39.09N 26.47E
Skópelos Greece **35** 39.07N 23.43E
Skópelos *i.* Greece **35** 39.10N 23.40E
Skopje Yugo. **34** 42.01N 21.32E
Skörping Denmark **42** 56.50N 9.53E
Skotfoss Norway **42** 59.12N 9.30E
Skotterud Norway **43** 59.59N 12.07E
Skövde Sweden **43** 58.24N 13.50E
Skovorodino U.S.S.R. **51** 54.00N123.53E
Skradin Yugo. **31** 43.49N 15.56E
Skreia Norway **41** 60.39N 10.56E
Skruv Sweden **43** 56.41N 15.22E
Skudeneshavn Norway **42** 59.09N 5.17E
Skull Rep. of Ire. **15** 51.32N 9.33W
Skultorp Sweden **43** 58.21N 13.49E
Skultuna Sweden **43** 59.43N 16.25E
Skuodas U.S.S.R. **41** 56.16N 21.32E
Skurup Sweden **43** 55.28N 13.30E
Skutskär Sweden **41** 60.38N 17.25E
Skvira U.S.S.R. **37** 49.42N 29.40E
Skye *i.* U.K. **14** 57.20N 6.15W
Slagelse Denmark **42** 55.24N 11.22E
Stalowa Wola Poland **37** 50.40N 22.05E
Slamet *mtn.* Indonesia **59** 7.14S109.10E
Slaney *r.* Rep. of Ire. **15** 52.21N 6.30W
Slano Yugo. **31** 42.47N 17.54E
Slantsy U.S.S.R. **44** 59.09N 28.09E
Slaný Czech. **38** 50.11N 14.04E
Slatina Romania **29** 44.26N 24.23E
Slatina Yugo. **34** 43.04N 20.58E
Slaton U.S.A. **111** 33.26N101.39W
Slave *r.* Canada **100** 61.18N113.39W
Slavgorod B.S.S.R. U.S.S.R. **37** 53.25N 31.00E
Slavgorod R.S.F.S.R. U.S.S.R. **9** 53.01N 78.37E
Slavonski Požega Yugo. **31** 45.20N 17.41E
Slavuta U.S.S.R. **37** 50.20N 26.58E
Slavyansk U.S.S.R. **45** 48.51N 37.36E
Sławno Poland **36** 54.22N 16.40E
Sleaford U.K. **12** 53.00N 0.22W
Sleaford B. Australia **92** 35.00S136.50E
Sleat, Sd. of *str.* U.K. **14** 57.05N 5.48W
Sledge U.S.A. **111** 34.26N 90.13W
Sledmere U.K. **12** 54.04N 0.35W
Sleeper Is. Canada **102** 56.50N 80.30W
Sleetmute U.S.A. **98** 61.40N157.11W
Slide Mtn. U.S.A. **115** 42.00N 74.23W
Sliedrecht Neth. **16** 51.48N 4.46E
Slieve Aughty Mts. Rep. of Ire. **15** 53.05N 8.31W
Slieve Bloom Mts. Rep. of Ire. **15** 53.03N 7.35W
Slieve Callan *mtn.* Rep. of Ire. **15** 52.51N 9.18W
Slieve Donard *mtn.* U.K. **15** 54.11N 5.56W
Slieve Gamph *mts.* Rep. of Ire. **15** 54.06N 8.52W
Slievekimalta *mtn.* Rep. of Ire. **15** 52.45N 8.17W
Slieve Mish *mts.* Rep. of Ire. **15** 52.48N 9.48W
Slieve Miskish *mts.* Rep. of Ire. **15** 51.41N 9.56W
Slievenamon *mtn.* Rep. of Ire. **15** 52.25N 7.34W
Slieve Snaght *mtn.* Donegal Rep. of Ire. **15** 55.12N 7.20W
Sligo Rep. of Ire. **15** 54.17N 8.28W
Sligo *d.* Rep. of Ire. **15** 54.10N 8.35W
Sligo U.S.A. **114** 41.07N 79.29W
Sligo B. Rep. of Ire. **15** 54.18N 8.40W
Slippery Rock *town* U.S.A. **114** 41.04N 80.03W
Slite Sweden **43** 57.43N 18.48E
Sliven Bulgaria **34** 42.42N 26.19E
Sliven *d.* Bulgaria **34** 42.42N 26.19E
Slivnitsa Bulgaria **34** 42.50N 23.00E
Sloan U.S.A. **110** 42.14N 96.14W
Slobodka U.S.S.R. **37** 47.56N 29.18E
Slobodskoy U.S.S.R. **44** 58.42N 50.10E
Slobozia Romania **34** 43.52N 25.55E
Slonim U.S.S.R. **37** 53.05N 25.21E
Slough U.K. **13** 51.30N 0.35W
Slovechna *r.* U.S.S.R. **37** 51.41N 29.41E
Slovechno U.S.S.R. **37** 51.23N 28.20E
Slovenija *d.* Yugo. **31** 46.00N 15.00E
Slovenjgradec Yugo. **31** 46.31N 15.05E
Slovenska Bistrica Yugo. **31** 46.23N 15.34E
Słubice Poland **36** 52.20N 14.32E
Sluch *r.* U.S.S.R. **37** 52.08N 27.31E
Sluis Neth. **16** 51.18N 3.23E
Slunj Yugo. **31** 45.07N 15.35E
Słupsk Poland **37** 54.28N 17.01E
Slurry R.S.A. **80** 25.48S 25.49E
Slutsk U.S.S.R. **37** 53.02N 27.31E
Slyne Head Rep. of Ire. **15** 53.25N 10.12W
Slyudyanka U.S.S.R. **52** 51.40N103.40E
Småland *f.* Sweden **43** 57.20N 15.00E
Smålandsfarvandet *str.* Denmark **42** 55.05N 11.20E
Smålandsstenar Sweden **43** 57.10N 13.24E
Smeaton Canada **101** 53.30N104.49W
Smederevo Yugo. **29** 44.40N 20.56E
Smela U.S.S.R. **45** 49.15N 31.54E
Smethport U.S.A. **114** 41.49N 78.27W
Smilde Neth. **16** 52.58N 6.28E
Smilovichi U.S.S.R. **37** 53.45N 28.00E
Smith Canada **100** 55.10N114.00W
Smith Arm *b.* Canada **98** 66.15N124.00W
Smithers Canada **100** 54.45N127.10W
Smithfield R.S.A. **80** 30.11S 26.31E
Smiths Falls *town* Canada **105** 44.54N 76.01W
Smithton Australia **91** 40.52S145.07E
Smithtown Australia **93** 31.03S152.53E
Smithville U.S.A. **114** 39.04N 81.06W
Smoke Hole U.S.A. **114** 38.52N 79.18W
Smoky *r.* Canada **100** 56.10N117.21W
Smoky Bay *town* Australia **92** 32.22S133.56E
Smoky C. Australia **93** 30.55S153.05E
Smoky Hill *r.* U.S.A. **110** 39.03N 96.48W
Smöla *i.* Norway **40** 63.20N 8.00E
Smolensk U.S.S.R. **44** 54.49N 32.04E
Smolevichi U.S.S.R. **37** 54.00N 28.01E
Smólikas *mtn.* Greece **34** 40.06N 20.52E
Smolyan Bulgaria **34** 41.36N 24.38E
Smolyan *d.* Bulgaria **34** 41.34N 24.42E
Smorgon U.S.S.R. **37** 54.28N 26.20E
Smygehuk *c.* Sweden **43** 55.21N 13.23E
Smyrna U.S.A. **115** 39.18N 75.36W
Snaefell *mtn.* Iceland **40** 64.48N 15.34W
Snaefell *mtn.* U.K. **12** 54.16N 4.28W
Snake *r.* Idaho U.S.A. **106** 43.50N117.05W
Snake *r.* Wash. U.S.A. **108** 46.12N119.02W
Snake Range *mts.* U.S.A. **108** 39.00N114.15W
Snake River *town* U.S.A. **108** 44.10N110.40W
Snake River Plain *f.* U.S.A. **108** 43.00N113.00W
Snåsa Norway **40** 64.15N 12.23E
Snåsavatn *l.* Norway **40** 64.05N 12.00E
Snedsted Denmark **42** 56.54N 8.32E
Sneek Neth. **16** 53.03N 5.40E
Sneem Rep. of Ire. **15** 51.50N 9.54W
Sneeuwberg *mtn.* R.S.A. **80** 32.30S 19.09E
Sněžnik *mtn.* Yugo. **31** 45.35N 14.27E
Śniardwy, Jezioro *l.* Poland **37** 53.46N 21.44E
Snina Czech. **37** 48.59N 22.07E
Snizort, Loch U.K. **14** 57.35N 6.30W
Snöhetta *mtn.* Norway **41** 62.20N 9.17E
Snov *r.* U.S.S.R. **37** 51.45N 31.45E
Snowbird L. Canada **101** 60.45N103.00W
Snowdon *mtn.* U.K. **12** 53.05N 4.05W
Snowdrift Canada **101** 62.24N110.44W
Snowdrift *r.* Canada **101** 62.24N110.44W
Snowflake U.S.A. **109** 34.30N110.05W
Snow Hill *town* U.S.A. **113** 38.11N 75.23W
Snowtown Australia **92** 33.47S138.13E
Snowy *r.* Australia **93** 37.49S148.30E
Snowy Mts. Australia **93** 36.30S148.20E
Snyatyn U.S.S.R. **37** 48.30N 25.50E
Snyder U.S.A. **111** 32.44N100.05W
Soacha Colombia **122** 4.35N 74.13W
Soalala Madagascar **81** 16.06S 45.20E
Soanierana-Ivongo Madagascar **81** 16.55S 49.35E
Soasiu Indonesia **59** 0.40N127.25E
Soavinandriana Madagascar **81** 19.09S 46.45E
Sob *r.* U.S.S.R. **37** 48.42N 29.17E
Sobat *r.* Sudan **73** 9.30N 31.30E
Sobernheim W. Germany **39** 49.47N 7.38E
Soboko C.A.R. **73** 6.49N 24.50E
Sobrado Portugal **26** 41.02N 8.16W
Sobral Brazil **123** 3.45S 40.20W
Sochi U.S.S.R. **45** 43.35N 39.46E
Société, Îles de la *is.* Pacific Oc. **85** 17.00S150.00W
Society Is. *see* Société, Îles de la Pacific Oc. **85**
Socorro Colombia **122** 6.30N 73.16W
Socorro U.S.A. **109** 34.04N106.54W
Socorro, Isla *i.* Mexico **116** 18.45N110.58W
Socotra *i. see* Suquṭrá S. Yemen **71**
Socuéllamos Spain **27** 39.17N 2.48W
Sodankylä Finland **40** 67.29N 26.32E
Söderhamn Sweden **41** 61.18N 17.03E
Söderköping Sweden **43** 58.29N 16.18E
Södermanland *d.* Sweden **43** 59.12N 16.49E
Södermanland *f.* Sweden **43** 58.56N 16.50E

Srnetica to Sundsvall

Srnetica Yugo. **31** 44.26N 16.40E
Staaten *r.* Australia **90** 16.24S141.17E
Stade W. Germany **38** 53.36N 9.28E
Stadskanaal Neth. **16** 53.02N 6.55E
Stadt Allendorf W. Germany **38** 50.50N 9.01E
Stadthagen W. Germany **38** 52.19N 9.13E
Stadtkyll W. Germany **39** 50.21N 6.32E
Stadtlohn W. Germany **38** 51.59N 6.55E
Stadtoldendorf W. Germany **38** 51.53N 9.37E
Staffa *i.* U.K. **14** 56.26N 6.21W
Staffelstein W. Germany **38** 50.06N 11.00E
Stafford U.K. **12** 52.49N 2.09W
Stafford U.S.A. **114** 38.09N 76.51W
Staffordshire *d.* U.K. **12** 52.40N 1.57W
Staines U.K. **13** 51.26N 0.31W
Stainforth U.K. **12** 53.37N 1.01W
Stainz Austria **31** 46.54N 15.16E
Stakhanov U.S.S.R. **45** 48.34N 38.40E
Stalać Yugo. **34** 43.43N 21.28E
Stalin Albania **34** 40.48N 19.54E
Stalina Kanal *canal* U.S.S.R. **44** 64.33N 34.48E
Ställdalen Sweden **43** 59.56N 14.56E
Stamford U.K. **13** 52.39N 0.28W
Stamford Conn. U.S.A. **115** 41.03N 73.32W
Stamford N.Y. U.S.A. **115** 42.25N 74.37W
Stamford Tex. U.S.A. **111** 32.57N 99.48W
Stanardsville U.S.A. **114** 38.18N 78.26W
Stanberry U.S.A. **110** 40.13N 94.35W
Standerton R.S.A. **80** 26.57S 29.14E
Standish U.S.A. **104** 43.59N 83.57W
Stanger R.S.A. **80** 29.20S 31.17E
Stanke Dimitrov Bulgaria **34** 42.27N 23.09E
Stanley Canada **98** 55.45N104.55W
Stanley Falkland Is. **125** 51.42W 57.51W
Stanley U.K. **12** 54.53N 1.42W
Stanley Idaho U.S.A. **108** 44.13N114.35W
Stanley Wisc. U.S.A. **110** 44.58N 90.56W
Stanley Mission Canada **101** 55.27N104.33W
Stanovoy Khrebet *mts.* U.S.S.R. **51** 56.00N125.40E
Stanthorpe Australia **93** 28.37S151.52E
Stanton U.S.A. **111** 32.08N101.48W
Stapleton U.S.A. **110** 41.29N100.31W
Starachowice Poland **37** 51.03N 21.04E
Stara Dorogi U.S.S.R. **37** 53.02N 28.18E
Stara Pazova Yugo. **31** 44.59N 20.10E
Stara Planina *mts.* Bulgaria **34** 43.15N 25.00E
Staraya Russa U.S.S.R. **44** 58.00N 31.22E
Staraya Sinyava U.S.S.R. **37** 49.38N 27.39E
Stara Zagora Bulgaria **34** 42.26N 25.39E
Stara Zagora *d.* Bulgaria **34** 42.25N 25.37E
Starbuck I. Kiribati **85** 5.37S155.55W
Stargard Szczecinski Poland **36** 53.21N 15.01E
Stari Bar Yugo. **31** 42.06N 19.08E
Stari Grad Yugo. **31** 43.11N 16.36E
Staritsa U.S.S.R. **44** 56.29N 34.59E
Starke U.S.A. **113** 29.55N 82.06W
Starkville U.S.A. **111** 33.28N 88.48W
Starnberg W. Germany **39** 48.00N 11.20E
Starnberger See *l.* W. Germany **39** 47.55N 11.18E
Starobin U.S.S.R. **37** 52.40N 27.29E
Starogard Gdański Poland **37** 53.59N 18.33E
Starokonstantinov U.S.S.R. **37** 49.48N 27.10E
Start Pt. U.K. **13** 50.13N 3.38W
Staryy Oskol U.S.S.R. **45** 51.20N 37.50E
Stassfurt E. Germany **38** 51.51N 11.34E
State College U.S.A. **114** 40.48N 77.52W
Staten I. *see* Estados, Isla de los Argentina **125**
Statesville U.S.A. **113** 35.46N 80.54W
Staunton U.S.A. **113** 38.09N 79.04W
Stavanger Norway **42** 58.58N 5.45E
Stavelot Belgium **16** 50.23N 5.54E
Staveren Neth. **16** 52.53N 5.21E
Stavern Norway **42** 59.00N 10.02E
Stavropol' U.S.S.R. **45** 45.03N 41.59E
Stavropolskaya Vozvyshennost *mts.* U.S.S.R. **45** 45.00N 42.30E
Stavrós Greece **34** 39.18N 22.15E
Stavroúpolis Greece **34** 41.12N 24.45E
Stawell Australia **92** 37.06S142.52E
Stawiski Poland **37** 53.23N 22.09E
Stayner Canada **104** 44.25N 80.05W
Stayton U.S.A. **108** 44.48N122.48W
Steamboat Springs *town* U.S.A. **108** 40.29N106.50W
Steele U.S.A. **110** 46.51N 99.55W
Steelpoort R.S.A. **80** 24.44S 30.13E
Steelton U.S.A. **114** 40.14N 76.49W
Steenbergen Neth. **16** 51.36N 4.19E
Steenvoorde France **19** 50.48N 2.35E
Steenwijk Neth. **16** 52.47N 6.07E
Steep Rock Lake *town* Canada **102** 48.50N 91.38W
Stege Denmark **43** 54.59N 12.18E
Stegeborg Sweden **43** 58.26N 16.35E
Steiermark *d.* Austria **36** 47.10N 15.10E
Steilloopbrug R.S.A. **80** 23.26S 28.37E
Steinach Austria **39** 47.05N 11.28E
Steinbach Canada **101** 49.32N 96.41W
Steinhuder Meer *l.* W. Germany **38** 52.28N 9.19E
Steinkjer Norway **40** 64.00N 11.30E
Steinkopf R.S.A. **80** 29.16S 17.41E
Stella R.S.A. **80** 26.32S 24.51E
Stellarton Canada **103** 45.34N 62.40W
Stellenbosch R.S.A. **80** 33.56S 18.51E
Stelvio, Passo dello *pass* Italy **30** 46.32N 10.27E
Stenay France **19** 49.29N 5.11E
Stendal E. Germany **38** 52.36N 11.51E
Stenstorp Sweden **43** 58.16N 13.43E
Stenstrup Denmark **42** 56.59N 9.52E
Stenträsk Sweden **40** 66.21N 19.50E
Stepan U.S.S.R. **37** 51.09N 26.18E
Stepanakert U.S.S.R. **65** 39.48N 46.45E
Stephens City U.S.A. **114** 39.05N 78.13W
Stephens Passage *str.* U.S.A. **100** 57.50N133.50W
Stephenville Canada **103** 48.33N 58.35W
Stephenville U.S.A. **111** 32.13N 98.12W
Stepnyak U.S.S.R. **50** 52.52N 70.49E
Steps Pt. *c.* Samoa **84** 14.22S170.45W
Sterkstroom R.S.A. **80** 31.32S 26.31E
Sterling Colo. U.S.A. **108** 40.37N103.13W
Sterling Ill. U.S.A. **110** 41.48N 89.43W
Sterling Mich. U.S.A. **104** 44.02N 84.02W
Sterling Run U.S.A. **114** 41.25N 78.12W
Sterlitamak U.S.S.R. **44** 53.40N 55.59E
Šternberk Czech. **37** 49.44N 17.18E
Stettler Canada **100** 52.19N112.40W
Steuben U.S.A. **112** 46.12N 86.27W
Steubenville U.S.A. **114** 40.22N 80.37W
Stevenage U.K. **13** 51.54N 0.11W
Stevenson L. Canada **101** 53.56N 96.09W
Stevens Point *town* U.S.A. **110** 44.32N 89.33W
Stevenston U.K. **14** 55.39N 4.45W
Stewart Canada **100** 55.56N130.01W
Stewart I. New Zealand **86** 47.00S168.00E
Stewart River *town* Canada **98** 63.19N139.26W
Stewartstown U.S.A. **105** 45.01N 71.30W
Steynsburg R.S.A. **80** 31.17S 25.48E
Steyr Austria **36** 48.04N 14.25E
Stigliano Italy **33** 40.24N 16.14E
Stigtomta Sweden **43** 58.48N 16.47E
Stikine *r.* Canada / U.S.A. **100** 56.40N132.30W
Stikine Mts. Canada **98** 59.00N129.00W
Stikine Plateau *f.* Canada **100** 58.45N130.00W
Stiklestad Norway **40** 63.48N 11.22E
Stilbaai R.S.A. **80** 34.22S 21.22E
Stilís Greece **35** 38.55N 22.36E
Stillwater U.S.A. **111** 36.07N 97.04W
Stillwater Range *mts.* U.S.A. **108** 39.50N118.15W
Stillwater Resr. U.S.A. **105** 43.57N 74.58W
Stilo, Punta *c.* Italy **33** 38.28N 16.36E
Stilton U.K. **13** 52.29N 0.17W
Stimson Canada **102** 48.58N 80.36W
Stinchar *r.* U.K. **14** 55.06N 5.00W
Stînisoara, Munţii *mts.* Romania **37** 47.10N 26.00E
Štip Yugo. **34** 41.42N 22.10E
Stira Greece **35** 38.09N 24.14E
Stirling Canada **105** 44.18N 77.33W
Stirling U.K. **14** 56.07N 3.57W
Stirling Range *mts.* Australia **89** 34.23S117.50E
Stjernöya *i.* Norway **40** 70.17N 22.40E
Stjördalshalsen Norway **40** 63.29N 10.51E
Stobi *site* Yugo. **34** 41.34N 21.58E
Stockach W. Germany **39** 47.51N 9.00E
Stockaryd Sweden **43** 57.18N 14.35E
Stockbridge U.K. **13** 51.07N 1.30W
Stockbridge U.S.A. **104** 42.27N 84.11W
Stockdale U.S.A. **111** 29.14N 97.58W
Stockerau Austria **36** 48.23N 16.13E
Stockett U.S.A. **108** 47.21N111.10W
Stockholm Sweden **43** 59.20N 18.03E
Stockholm *d.* Sweden **43** 59.20N 18.03E
Stockinbingal Australia **93** 34.03S147.53E
Stockport U.K. **12** 53.25N 2.11W
Stocksbridge U.K. **12** 53.30N 1.36W
Stockton Australia **93** 32.55S151.47E
Stockton Calif. U.S.A. **108** 37.57N121.17W
Stockton Kans. U.S.A. **110** 39.26N 99.16W
Stockton-on-Tees U.K. **12** 54.34N 1.20W
Stoeng Tréng Kampuchea **56** 13.31N105.59E
Stoffberg R.S.A. **80** 25.25S 29.49E
Stogovo *mts.* Yugo. **34** 41.31N 20.38E
Stoke-on-Trent U.K. **12** 53.01N 2.11W
Stokes Bay *town* Canada **104** 45.00N 81.23W
Stokhod *r.* U.S.S.R. **37** 51.52N 25.38E
Stokksund Norway **40** 64.03N 10.05E
Stolac Yugo. **31** 43.05N 17.58E
Stolberg W. Germany **38** 50.46N 6.13E
Stolbtsy U.S.S.R. **37** 53.30N 26.44E
Stolin U.S.S.R. **37** 51.52N 26.51E
Ston Yugo. **31** 42.50N 17.42E
Stone Staffs. U.K. **12** 52.55N 2.10W
Stoneboro U.S.A. **114** 41.20N 80.07W
Stonecliffe Canada **105** 46.12N 77.54W
Stone Harbor U.S.A. **115** 39.03N 74.45W
Stonehaven U.K. **14** 56.58N 2.13W
Stony I. Canada **103** 53.00N 55.48W
Stony L. Canada **104** 44.33N 78.05W
Stony Pt. *c.* U.S.A. **105** 43.52N 76.15W
Stony Rapids *town* Canada **101** 59.16N105.50W
Stooping *r.* Canada **102** 52.08N 82.00W
Storå *r.* Denmark **42** 56.19N 8.19E
Stora Gla *l.* Sweden **43** 59.30N 12.30E
Stora Le *l.* Sweden **42** 59.05N 11.53E
Stora Lulevatten *l.* Sweden **40** 67.10N 19.16E
Stora Möja Sweden **43** 59.26N 18.55E
Stora Sjöfallets Nat. Park Sweden **40** 67.44N 18.16E
Storavan *l.* Sweden **40** 65.40N 18.15E
Storby Finland **41** 60.13N 19.34E
Stord *i.* Norway **42** 59.53N 5.25E
Store Baelt *str.* Denmark **42** 55.30N 11.00E
Store Heddinge Denmark **43** 55.19N 12.25E
Stor Elvdal Norway **41** 61.32N 11.02E
Stören Norway **40** 63.03N 10.18E
Storfors Sweden **43** 59.32N 14.16E
Storlien Sweden **40** 63.20N 12.05E
Storm Lake *town* U.S.A. **110** 42.39N 95.10W
Stornoway U.K. **14** 58.12N 6.23W
Storozhevsk U.S.S.R. **44** 62.00N 52.20E
Storozhinets U.S.S.R. **37** 48.11N 25.40E
Storsjön *l.* Sweden **40** 63.10N 14.20E
Storuman Sweden **40** 65.06N 17.06E
Storuman *l.* Sweden **40** 65.10N 16.40E
Storvreta Sweden **43** 59.58N 17.42E
Stouffville Canada **104** 43.59N 79.15W
Stoughton U.S.A. **110** 42.55N 89.13W
Stour *r.* Dorset U.K. **13** 50.43N 1.47W
Stour *r.* Kent U.K. **13** 51.19N 1.22E
Stour *r.* Suffolk U.K. **13** 51.56N 1.03E
Stourport-on-Severn U.K. **13** 52.21N 2.16W
Stowmarket U.K. **13** 52.11N 1.00E
Stow on the Wold U.K. **13** 51.55N 1.42W
Strabane U.K. **15** 54.50N 7.30W
Stradbally Laois Rep. of Ire. **15** 53.01N 7.09W
Stradbroke I. Australia **91** 27.38S153.45E
Stradella Italy **30** 45.05N 9.18E
Straelen W. Germany **38** 51.27N 6.16E
Strahan Australia **91** 42.08S145.21E
Strakonice Czech. **38** 49.16N 13.55E
Stralsund E. Germany **38** 54.19N 13.05E
Strand R.S.A. **80** 34.07S 18.50E
Stranda Norway **40** 62.19N 6.58E
Strangford Lough U.K. **15** 54.28N 5.35W
Strangways Springs *town* Australia **92** 29.08S136.35E
Stranraer U.K. **14** 54.54N 5.02W
Strasbourg France **19** 48.35N 7.45E
Strasburg E. Germany **38** 53.30N 13.44E
Strasburg N.Dak. U.S.A. **110** 46.08N100.10W
Strasburg Ohio U.S.A. **114** 40.36N 81.32W
Stråssa Sweden **43** 59.45N 15.13E
Strasswalchen Austria **39** 47.59N 13.15E
Stratford Australia **93** 37.57S147.05E
Stratford Canada **104** 43.22N 80.57W
Stratford New Zealand **86** 39.20S174.18E
Stratford Conn. U.S.A. **115** 41.14N 73.07W
Stratford N.H. U.S.A. **105** 44.40N 71.34W
Stratford Tex. U.S.A. **111** 36.20N102.04W
Stratford-upon-Avon U.K. **13** 52.12N 1.42W
Strathalbyn Australia **92** 35.16S138.54E
Strathclyde *d.* U.K. **14** 55.45N 4.45W
Strathcona Prov. Park Canada **100** 49.38N125.40W
Strathmore *f.* Tayside U.K. **14** 56.44N 2.45W
Strathroy Canada **104** 42.57N 81.38W
Strathspey *f.* U.K. **14** 57.25N 3.25W
Stratton U.S.A. **110** 39.18N102.36W
Stratton Mtn. U.S.A. **115** 43.05N 72.56W
Straubing W. Germany **39** 48.53N 12.34E
Straumnes *c.* Iceland **40** 66.30N 23.05W
Strausberg E. Germany **38** 52.35N 13.53E
Strawn U.S.A. **111** 32.33N 98.30W
Streaky B. Australia **92** 32.36S134.08E
Streaky Bay *town* Australia **92** 32.48S134.13E
Streator U.S.A. **110** 41.07N 88.53W
Street U.K. **13** 51.07N 2.43W
Streeter U.S.A. **110** 46.39N 99.21W
Streetsville Canada **104** 43.35N 79.42W
Stresa Italy **30** 45.53N 8.32E
Stretton Australia **89** 32.30S117.42E
Striberg Sweden **43** 59.33N 14.56E
Strimon *r.* Greece **34** 40.47N 23.51E
Stromboli *i.* Italy **33** 38.48N 15.13E
Stromeferry U.K. **14** 57.21N 5.34W
Stromness U.K. **14** 58.57N 3.18W
Strömö *i.* Faroe Is. **10** 62.08N 7.00W
Strömsbruk Sweden **41** 61.53N 17.19E
Strömstad Sweden **42** 58.56N 11.10E
Strömsund Sweden **40** 63.51N 15.35E
Strömsvattudal *f.* Sweden **40** 64.15N 15.00E
Strongfield Canada **101** 51.20N106.36W
Strongoli Italy **33** 39.15N 17.03E
Stronsay *i.* U.K. **14** 59.07N 2.36W
Stroud U.K. **13** 51.44N 2.12W
Stroud Road *town* Australia **93** 32.18S151.58E
Stroudsburg U.S.A. **115** 40.59N 75.12W
Struan Australia **92** 37.08S140.49E
Struer Denmark **42** 56.29N 8.37E
Struga Yugo. **34** 41.11N 20.40E
Struma *see* Strimon Bulgaria **34**
Strumica Yugo. **34** 41.28N 22.41E
Struthers U.S.A. **114** 41.04N 80.38W
Stryama *r.* Bulgaria **34** 42.40N 24.28E
Strydenburg R.S.A. **80** 29.56S 23.39E
Stryker U.S.A. **108** 48.40N114.44W
Stryy U.S.S.R. **37** 49.16N 23.51E
Strzelecki Creek *r.* Australia **92** 29.37S139.59E
Strzelno Poland **37** 52.38N 18.11E
Stuart Fla. U.S.A. **113** 27.12N 80.16W
Stuart Nebr. U.S.A. **110** 42.36N 99.08W
Stuart Creek *town* Australia **92** 29.43S137.01E
Stuart L. Canada **100** 54.30N124.30W
Stuart Range *mts.* Australia **92** 29.10S134.56E
Stuart Town Australia **93** 32.51S149.08E
Stubbeköbing Denmark **43** 54.53N 12.03E
Studenica Yugo. **34** 43.21N 20.35E
Studen Kladenets, Yazovir *l.* Bulgaria **34** 41.37N 25.29E
Studsvik Sweden **43** 58.46N 17.23E
Stupart *r.* Canada **101** 56.00N 93.22W
Sturgeon *r.* Canada **104** 46.19N 79.58W
Sturgeon Bay *town* U.S.A. **110** 44.50N 87.23W
Sturgeon Falls *town* Canada **104** 46.22N 79.55W
Sturgeon L. Ont. Canada **104** 44.28N 78.42W
Sturgeon L. Ont. Canada **102** 50.00N 90.40W
Sturgis U.S.A. **110** 44.25N103.31W
Sturminster Newton U.K. **13** 50.56N 2.18W
Sturt B. Australia **92** 35.24S137.32E
Sturt Creek *r.* Australia **88** 20.08S127.24E
Sturt Desert Australia **92** 28.30S141.12E
Sturt Plain *f.* Australia **90** 17.00S132.48E
Stutterheim R.S.A. **80** 32.32S 27.25E
Stuttgart W. Germany **39** 48.46N 9.11E
Stviga *r.* U.S.S.R. **37** 52.04N 27.54E
Stykkishólmur Iceland **40** 65.06N 22.48W
Styr *r.* U.S.S.R. **37** 52.07N 26.35E
Suao Taiwan **55** 24.36N121.51E
Subarnarekha *r.* India **63** 21.34N 87.24E
Subay', 'Urūq *f.* Saudi Arabia **72** 22.15N 43.05E
Subei Guangai Zongqu *canal* China **54** 34.06N120.19E
Subiaco Italy **30** 41.55N 13.06E
Subotica Yugo. **31** 46.06N 19.39E
Suceava Romania **37** 47.39N 26.19E
Suchan U.S.S.R. **57** 43.03N133.05E
Suck *r.* Rep. of Ire. **15** 53.16N 8.04W
Suckling, Mt. P.N.G. **90** 9.45S148.55E
Sucre Bolivia **124** 19.02S 65.17W
Sucuriu *r.* Brazil **126** 20.44S 51.40W
Sudalsvatnet *l.* Norway **42** 59.35N 6.45E
Sudan Africa **72** 14.30N 29.00E
Sudan U.S.A. **111** 34.04N102.32W
Sudbury Canada **104** 46.30N 81.00W
Sudbury U.K. **13** 52.03N 0.45E
Sude *r.* E. Germany **38** 53.22N 10.45E
Sudety *mts.* Czech. / Poland **36** 50.30N 16.30E
Sudirman, Pegunungan *mts.* Indonesia **59** 3.50S136.30E
Sudzukhe U.S.S.R. **57** 42.50N133.43E
Sueca Spain **25** 39.12N 0.19W
Suez *see* As Suways Egypt **66**
Suez, G. of *see* Suways, Khalīj as Egypt **66**
Suez Canal *see* Suways, Qanāt as Egypt **66**
Sūf Jordan **67** 32.19N 35.50E
Şufaynah Saudi Arabia **64** 23.09N 40.32E
Suffolk *d.* U.K. **13** 52.16N 1.00E
Suffolk U.S.A. **113** 36.44N 76.37W
Sugargrove U.S.A. **114** 41.59N 79.21W
Sugar I. U.S.A. **104** 46.25N 84.12W
Sugarloaf Pt. Australia **93** 32.25S152.30E
Suhaia, Lacul *l.* Romania **34** 43.45N 25.15E
Şuḩār Oman **65** 24.23N 56.43E
Sühbaatar *d.* Mongolia **54** 45.30N114.00E
Suhl E. Germany **38** 50.37N 10.41E
Suhl *d.* E. Germany **38** 50.33N 10.35E
Suhopolje Yugo. **31** 45.48N 17.30E
Sūi Pakistan **62** 28.37N 69.19E
Suibin China **53** 47.19N131.49E
Suichang China **55** 28.36N119.16E
Suichuan China **55** 26.24N114.31E
Suide China **54** 37.35N110.08E
Suihua China **53** 46.39N126.59E
Suileng China **53** 47.15N127.05E
Suining Jiangsu China **54** 33.54N117.56E
Suining Sichuan China **55** 30.31N105.32E
Suipacha Argentina **125** 34.47S 59.40W
Suippes France **19** 49.08N 4.32E
Suir *r.* Rep. of Ire. **15** 52.17N 7.00W
Suita Japan **57** 34.45N135.32E
Sui Xian Henan China **54** 34.25N115.04E
Sui Xian Hubei China **55** 31.45N113.30E
Suiyang Guizhou China **55** 27.57N107.11E
Suizhong China **54** 40.25N120.25E
Suj China **54** 42.02N107.58E
Sūjāngarh India **62** 27.42N 74.28E
Sujāwal Pakistan **62** 24.36N 68.05E
Sukabumi Indonesia **59** 6.55S106.50E
Sukadana Indonesia **58** 1.15S110.00E
Sukaraja Indonesia **58** 2.23S110.35E
Sukhinichi U.S.S.R. **44** 54.07N 35.21E
Sukhona *r.* U.S.S.R. **44** 61.30N 46.28E
Sukhumi U.S.S.R. **45** 43.01N 41.01E
Sukkertoppen Greenland **99** 65.40N 53.00W
Sukkur Pakistan **62** 27.42N 68.52E
Sukoharjo Indonesia **59** 7.40S110.50E
Sukumo Japan **57** 32.56N132.44E
Sul *d.* Portugal **27** 38.50N 8.05W
Sula *i.* Norway **41** 61.08N 4.55E
Sula, Kepulauan *is.* Indonesia **59** 1.50S125.10E
Sulaimān Range *mts.* Pakistan **62** 30.00N 69.50E
Sulak *r.* U.S.S.R. **45** 43.18N 47.35E
Sulawesi *i.* Indonesia **59** 2.00S120.30E
Sulawesi Selatan *d.* Indonesia **59** 3.45S120.30E
Sulawesi Utara *d.* Indonesia **59** 1.45S120.30E
Sulechów Poland **36** 52.06N 15.37E
Sulejów Poland **37** 51.22N 19.53E
Sulina Romania **29** 45.08N 29.40E
Sulingen W. Germany **38** 52.41N 8.47E
Sulitjelma Norway **40** 67.10N 16.05E
Sullana Peru **122** 4.52S 80.39W
Sullivan U.S.A. **110** 38.13N 91.10W
Sully France **19** 47.46N 2.22E
Sulmona Italy **31** 42.03N 13.55E
Sulphur U.S.A. **111** 34.31N 96.58W
Sultan Canada **102** 47.36N 82.47W
Sultan Hamud Kenya **79** 2.02S 37.20E
Sultānpur India **63** 26.16N 82.04E
Sulu Archipelago Phil. **59** 5.30N121.00E
Sulūq Libya **75** 31.40N 20.15E
Sulu Sea Pacific Oc. **59** 8.00N120.00E
Sulzbach-Rosenburg W. Germany **38** 49.30N 11.45E
Sumatera *i.* Indonesia **58** 2.00S102.00E
Sumatera Barat *d.* Indonesia **58** 1.00S100.00E
Sumatera Selatan *d.* Indonesia **58** 3.00S104.00E
Sumatera Utara *d.* Indonesia **58** 2.00N 99.00E
Sumatra *see* Sumatera Indonesia **58**
Sumatra U.S.A. **108** 46.38N107.31W
Sumba *i.* Indonesia **58** 9.30S119.55E
Sumbar *r.* U.S.S.R. **65** 38.00N 55.20E
Sumbawa *i.* Indonesia **58** 8.45S117.50E
Sumbawanga Tanzania **79** 7.58S 31.36E
Sumbilla Spain **25** 43.10N 1.40W
Sumburgh Head U.K. **14** 59.51N 1.16W
Sumedang Indonesia **59** 6.54S107.55E
Sümeg Hungary **31** 46.59N 17.17E
Šumen Bulgaria **29** 43.15N 26.55E
Sumenep Indonesia **59** 7.01S113.51E
Sumgait U.S.S.R. **65** 40.35N 49.38E
Summerland Canada **100** 49.32N119.41W
Summerside Canada **103** 46.24N 63.47W
Summersville U.S.A. **114** 38.17N 80.51W
Summerville Ga. U.S.A. **113** 34.29N 85.21W
Summerville S.C. U.S.A. **113** 33.02N 80.11W
Šumperk Czech. **36** 49.58N 16.58E
Sumprabum Burma **56** 26.33N 97.34E
Sumuşţā al Waqf Egypt **66** 28.55N 30.51E
Sumy U.S.S.R. **45** 50.55N 34.49E
Sunagawa Japan **57** 43.30N141.55E
Sunām India **62** 30.08N 75.48E
Sunāmganj Bangla. **63** 25.04N 91.24E
Sunart, Loch U.K. **14** 56.43N 5.45W
Sunburst U.S.A. **108** 48.53N111.55W
Sunbury Australia **93** 37.36S144.45E
Sunbury Ohio U.S.A. **114** 40.14N 82.52W
Sunbury Penn. U.S.A. **114** 40.52N 76.47W
Sunda, Selat *str.* Indonesia **58** 6.00S105.50E
Sundance U.S.A. **108** 44.24N104.23W
Sundarbans *f.* India / Bangla. **63** 21.45N 89.00E
Sundargarh India **63** 22.07N 84.02E
Sundays *r.* R.S.A. **80** 33.43S 25.50E
Sundbyberg Sweden **43** 59.22N 17.58E
Sunde Norway **42** 59.50N 5.43E
Sunderland Canada **104** 44.16N 79.04W
Sunderland U.K. **12** 54.55N 1.22W
Sundridge Canada **104** 45.46N 79.24W
Sundsvall Sweden **41** 62.23N 17.18E

Sungai Kolok to Taneytown

Sungai Kolok Thailand 56 6.02N101.58E
Sungaipakning Indonesia 58 1.19N102.00E
Sungaipenuh Indonesia 58 2.00S101.28E
Sungguminasa Indonesia 58 5.14S119.27E
Sungurlu Turkey 64 40.10N 34.23E
Sunjikāy Sudan 73 12.20N 29.46E
Sunne Sweden 43 59.50N 13.09E
Sunnersta Sweden 43 59.48N 17.39E
Sunnyside U.S.A. 108 46.20N120.00W
Suntar U.S.S.R. 51 62.10N117.35E
Suntsar Pakistan 62 25.31N 62.00E
Sun Valley *town* U.S.A. 106 43.42N114.21W
Sunwu China 53 49.40N127.10E
Sunyani Ghana 76 7.22N 2.18W
Suō nada *str.* Japan 57 33.45N131.30E
Suoyarvi U.S.S.R. 44 62.02N 32.20E
Supaul India 63 26.07N 86.36E
Superior Mont. U.S.A. 108 47.12N114.53W
Superior Wisc. U.S.A. 110 46.42N 92.05W
Superior Wyo. U.S.A. 108 41.46N108.58W
Superior, L. Canada / U.S.A. 112 48.00N 88.00W
Supetar Yugo. 31 43.23N 16.33E
Suphan Buri Thailand 56 14.14N100.07E
Suphan Buri *r.* Thailand 56 13.34N100.15E
Süphan Dagi *mtn.* Turkey 45 38.55N 42.55E
Süphan Daglari *mtn.* Turkey 64 38.55N 42.55E
Suqian China 54 33.59N118.25E
Suquṭrá *i.* S. Yemen 71 12.30N 54.00E
Şūr Lebanon 67 33.16N 35.12E
Şūr Oman 65 22.23N 59.32E
Sur *d.* W. Sahara 74 23.40N 14.15W
Sur, Cabo *c.* I. de Pascua 85 27.12S109.26W
Sur, Punta *c.* Argentina 125 36.53S 56.41W
Sura U.S.S.R. 44 53.52N 45.45E
Sūrāb Pakistan 62 28.29N 66.16E
Surabaya Indonesia 59 7.14S112.45E
Surakarta Indonesia 59 7.32S110.50E
Şūrān Syria 66 35.18N 36.44E
Surany Czech. 37 48.06N 18.14E
Surat India 62 21.12N 72.50E
Sūratgarh India 62 29.18N 73.54E
Surat Thani Thailand 56 9.09N 99.23E
Surazh U.S.S.R. 37 53.00N 32.22E
Surdulica Yugo. 34 42.41N 22.10E
Sûre *r.* Lux. 16 49.43N 6.31E
Sureau, Lac *l.* Canada 103 53.10N 70.50W
Surendranagar India 62 22.42N 71.41E
Surfer's Paradise Australia 93 27.58S153.26E
Surgères France 20 46.07N 0.45W
Surgut U.S.S.R. 9 61.13N 73.20E
Sūri India 63 23.55N 87.32E
Şūrīf Jordan 67 31.39N 35.04E
Surigao Phil. 59 9.47N125.29E
Surin Thailand 56 14.58N103.33E
Surinam S. America 123 4.00N 56.00W
Suriname *r.* Surinam 123 5.52N 55.14W
Surkole Ethiopia 73 10.25N 34.38E
Surrey *d.* U.K. 13 51.16N 0.30W
Sursee Switz. 39 47.10N 8.06E
Surt Libya 75 31.13N 16.35E
Surt, Khalīj *g.* Libya 75 31.45N 17.50E
Surtanāhu Pakistan 62 26.22N 70.00E
Surte Sweden 43 57.49N 12.01E
Surtsey *i.* Iceland 40 63.18N 20.30W
Surud Ad *mtn.* Somali Rep. 71 10.41N 47.18E
Suruga-wan *b.* Japan 57 34.45N138.30E
Susa Italy 30 45.08N 7.03E
Susak *i.* Yugo. 31 44.31N 14.18E
Susanino U.S.S.R. 51 52.46N140.09E
Susanville U.S.A. 108 40.25N120.39W
Sušice Czech. 38 49.14N 13.32E
Susquehanna U.S.A. 115 41.57N 75.36W
Susquehanna *r.* U.S.A. 115 39.33N 76.05W
Susquehanna, West Branch *r.* U.S.A. 114 40.53N 76.47W
Sussex N.J. U.S.A. 115 41.13N 74.36W
Sussex Wyo. U.S.A. 108 43.42N106.19W
Sutak Jammu & Kashmir 63 33.12N 77.28E
Sutherland R.S.A. 80 32.23S 20.38E
Sutherlin U.S.A. 108 43.25N123.19W
Sutlej *r.* Pakistan 62 29.23N 71.02E
Sutton Canada 104 44.18N 79.22W
Sutton *r.* Canada 102 55.22N 83.48W
Sutton England U.K. 13 51.22N 0.12W
Sutton Nebr. U.S.A. 110 40.36N 97.52W
Sutton W. Va. U.S.A. 114 38.40N 80.43W
Sutton in Ashfield U.K. 12 53.08N 1.16W
Suva Fiji 84 18.08S178.25E
Suva Planina *mts.* Yugo. 34 43.10N 22.05E
Suva Reka Yugo. 34 42.21N 20.50E
Suwałki Poland 37 54.07N 22.56E
Suwanee *r.* U.S.A. 113 29.18N 83.09W
Şuwaylih Jordan 67 32.02N 35.50E
Suwaymah Jordan 67 31.47N 35.36E
Suways, Khalīj as *g.* Egypt 66 28.48N 33.00E
Suways, Qanāt as *canal* Egypt 66 30.40N 32.20E
Suwon S. Korea 53 37.16N126.59E
Suzhou China 55 31.22N120.45E
Suzu Japan 57 37.25N137.17E
Suzuka Japan 57 34.51N136.35E
Suzuka *r.* Japan 57 34.54N136.39E
Suzuka-sammyaku *mts.* Japan 57 35.00N136.20E
Suzu misaki *c.* Japan 57 37.30N137.21E
Suzzara Italy 32 45.00N 10.45E
Svalyava U.S.S.R. 37 48.33N 23.00E
Svaneke Denmark 43 55.08N 15.09E
Svanskog Sweden 43 59.11N 12.33E
Svanvik Norway 40 69.25N 30.00E
Svappavaara Sweden 40 67.39N 21.04E
Svarhofthalvöya Norway 40 70.35N 26.00E
Svartå Sweden 43 59.08N 14.31E
Svartån *r.* Sweden 43 59.37N 16.33E
Svartisen *mtn.* Norway 40 66.40N 13.56E
Svatovo U.S.S.R. 45 49.24N 38.11E
Svay Riêng Kampuchea 56 11.05N105.48E
Svedala Sweden 43 55.30N 13.14E
Sveg Sweden 41 62.02N 14.21E
Svelgen Norway 41 61.47N 5.15E
Svelvik Norway 42 59.37N 10.24E
Svendborg Denmark 42 55.03N 10.37E
Svenljunga Sweden 43 57.30N 13.07E
Svenstrup Denmark 42 56.59N 9.52E
Sverdlovsk U.S.S.R. 44 56.52N 60.35E
Sveti Nikole Yugo. 34 41.51N 21.56E
Svetlograd U.S.S.R. 45 45.25N 42.58E
Svetogorsk U.S.S.R. 44 61.07N 28.50E
Svetozarevo Yugo. 34 43.58N 21.16E
Svilengrad Bulgaria 34 41.49N 26.12E
Svindal Norway 42 58.30N 7.28E
Svinesund Sweden 42 59.06N 11.16E
Svinninge Denmark 42 55.43N 11.28E
Svinö *i.* Faroe Is. 10 62.17N 6.18W
Svir *r.* U.S.S.R. 44 60.09N 32.15E
Svishtov Bulgaria 34 43.36N 25.23E
Svisloch U.S.S.R. 37 53.28N 29.00E
Svitavy Czech. 36 49.45N 16.27E
Svobodnyy U.S.S.R. 53 51.24N128.05E
Svoge Bulgaria 34 42.58N 23.21E
Svolvaer Norway 40 68.15N 14.40E
Swaffham U.K. 13 52.38N 0.42E
Swain Reefs Australia 90 21.40S152.15E
Swains I. Samoa 84 11.03S171.06W
Swakop *r.* Namibia 80 22.38S 14.32E
Swakopmund Namibia 80 22.40S 14.34E
Swale *r.* U.K. 12 54.05N 1.20W
Swan *r.* Australia 89 32.03S115.45E
Swanage U.K. 13 50.36N 1.59W
Swan Hill *town* Australia 92 35.23S143.37E
Swan Hills Canada 100 54.42N115.24W
Swan L. Canada 101 52.30N100.45W
Swan River *town* Canada 101 52.10N101.17W
Swansea Australia 91 42.08S148.00E
Swansea U.K. 13 51.37N 3.57W
Swanton U.S.A. 105 44.55N 73.07W
Swan Vale *town* Australia 93 29.43S151.25E
Swastika Canada 102 48.07N 80.06W
Swaziland Africa 80 26.30S 32.00E
Sweden Europe 40 63.00N 16.00E
Swedru Ghana 76 5.31N 0.42W
Sweetwater U.S.A. 111 32.28N100.25W
Swidnica Poland 36 50.51N 16.29E
Swiebodzin Poland 36 52.15N 15.32E
Świetokrzyskie, Góry *mts.* Poland 37 51.00N 20.30E
Swift Current *town* Canada 101 50.17N107.50W
Swilly, Lough Rep. of Ire. 15 55.10N 7.32W
Swindon U.K. 13 51.33N 1.47W
Świnoujście Poland 36 53.55N 14.18E
Switzerland Europe 39 46.45N 8.30E
Swords Rep. of Ire. 11 53.27N 6.15W
Syderö *i.* Faroe Is. 10 61.30N 6.50W
Sydney Australia 93 33.55S151.10E
Sydney Canada 103 46.09N 60.11W
Sydney Mines *town* Canada 103 46.14N 60.14W
Sydpröven Greenland 99 60.30N 45.35W
Syke W. Germany 38 52.54N 8.49E
Syktyvkar U.S.S.R. 44 61.42N 50.45E
Sylacauga U.S.A. 113 33.10N 86.15W
Sylhet Bangla. 63 24.54N 91.52E
Sylt *i.* W. Germany 38 54.54N 8.20E
Sylte Norway 40 62.31N 7.07E
Sylvan Lake *town* Canada 100 52.20N114.10W
Syracuse *see* Siracusa Italy 33
Syracuse Kans. U.S.A. 111 37.59N101.45W
Syracuse N.Y. U.S.A. 115 43.03N 76.09W
Syr Darya *r.* U.S.S.R. 9 46.00N 61.21E
Syria Asia 64 35.00N 38.00E
Syriam Burma 58 16.45N 96.17E
Syrian Desert *see* Bādiyat ash Shām Asia 64
Syzran U.S.S.R. 44 53.10N 48.29E
Szarvas Hungary 37 46.52N 20.34E
Szczecin Poland 36 53.25N 14.32E
Szczecinek Poland 36 53.42N 16.41E
Szczytno Poland 37 53.34N 21.00E
Szécsény Hungary 37 48.06N 19.31E
Szeged Hungary 31 46.15N 20.09E
Székesfehérvár Hungary 37 47.12N 18.25E
Szekszárd Hungary 31 46.21N 18.42E
Szentes Hungary 31 46.39N 20.16E
Szentgotthárd Hungary 31 46.57N 16.18E
Szolnok Hungary 37 47.10N 20.12E
Szombathely Hungary 36 47.12N 16.38E
Sztutowo Poland 37 54.20N 19.15E

T

Tabagne Ivory Coast 76 7.59N 3.04W
Ţābah Saudi Arabia 64 27.02N 42.10E
Tábara Spain 26 41.49N 5.57W
Tabarka Tunisia 32 36.57N 8.45E
Ţabas Khorāsān Iran 65 32.48N 60.14E
Ţabas Khorāsān Iran 65 33.36N 56.55E
Tabasco *d.* Mexico 116 18.30N 93.00W
Tābask, Kūh-e *mtn.* Iran 65 29.51N 51.52E
Tabelbala Algeria 74 29.24N 3.15W
Taber Canada 100 49.47N112.08W
Tabernes de Valldigna Spain 25 39.04N 0.16W
Tabili Zaïre 79 0.04N 28.01E
Table B. R.S.A. 80 33.52S 18.26E
Tábor Czech. 36 49.25N 14.41E
Tabora Tanzania 79 5.02S 32.50E
Tabora *d.* Tanzania 79 5.30S 32.50E
Tabou Ivory Coast 76 4.28N 7.20W
Tabrīz Iran 65 38.05N 46.18E
Tabuaço Portugal 26 41.07N 7.34W
Tabūk Saudi Arabia 66 28.23N 36.36E
Tabulam Australia 93 28.50S152.35E
Ţabūt S. Yemen 71 15.57N 52.09E
Tachia Taiwan 55 24.21N120.37E
Tachikawa Japan 57 35.42N139.25E
Tachov Czech. 38 49.48N 12.38E
Tacloban Phil. 59 11.15N124.59E
Tacna Peru 124 18.01S 70.15W
Tacoma U.S.A. 108 47.15N122.27W
Taconic Mts. U.S.A. 115 42.36N 73.14W
Taconic State Park U.S.A. 115 42.05N 73.34W
Tacora *mtn.* Chile 124 17.40S 69.45W
Tacuarembó Uruguay 125 31.44S 55.59W
Tademaït, Plateau du *f.* Algeria 75 28.30N 2.15E
Tadjetaret, Oued Algeria 75 21.00N 7.30E
Tadjmout Algeria 75 25.30N 3.42E
Tadjoura, Golfe de *g.* Djibouti 71 11.42N 43.00E
Tadmor New Zealand 86 41.26S172.47E
Tadoule L. Canada 101 58.36N 98.20W
Tadoussac Canada 103 48.09N 69.43W
Tadzhikskaya S.S.R. *d.* U.S.S.R. 52 39.00N 70.30E
Taegu S. Korea 53 35.52N128.36E
Taejin S. Korea 57 36.34N129.24E
Taejŏn S. Korea 53 36.20N127.26E
Tafalla Spain 25 42.31N 1.40W
Ţafas Syria 67 32.44N 36.04E
Tafassasset, Oued *wadi* Niger 75 22.00N 9.55E
Tafassasset, Ténéré du *des.* Niger 77 21.00N 11.00E
Taffanel, Lac *l.* Canada 103 53.22N 70.56W
Tafí Viejo Argentina 124 26.45S 65.15W
Tafraout Morocco 74 29.40N 8.58W
Taftān, Kūh-e *mtn.* Iran 65 28.38N 61.08E
Taga W. Samoa 84 13.47S172.30W
Taganrog U.S.S.R. 45 47.14N 38.55E
Taganrogskiy Zaliv *g.* U.S.S.R. 45 47.00N 38.30E
Tagant *d.* Mauritania 74 18.30N 10.30W
Tagant *f.* Mauritania 74 18.20N 11.00W
Tagaytay City Phil. 59 14.07N120.58E
Tagbilaran Phil. 59 9.38N123.53E
Tagish Canada 100 60.19N134.16W
Tagliacozzo Italy 30 42.04N 13.14E
Tagliamento *r.* Italy 30 45.38N 13.06E
Taglio di Po Italy 30 45.00N 12.12E
Tagounit Morocco 74 29.58N 5.36W
Tagula I. P.N.G. 90 11.30S153.30E
Tagum Phil. 59 7.33N125.53E
Tagus *r.* *see* Tejo Portugal / Spain 27
Tahaa *i.* Îs. de la Société 85 16.38S151.30W
Tahara Japan 57 34.40N137.16E
Tahat *mtn.* Algeria 75 23.18N 5.32E
Tahe China 53 52.35N124.48E
Tahiti *i.* Îs. de la Société 85 17.37S149.27W
Tahiti, Archipel de *is.* Îs. de la Société 85 17.00S149.35W
Tahlequah U.S.A. 111 35.55N 94.58W
Tahoe, L. U.S.A. 108 39.07N120.03W
Tahoua Niger 77 14.57N 5.16E
Tahoua *d.* Niger 77 15.38N 4.50E
Ţahţā Egypt 64 26.46N 31.30E
Tahuna Indonesia 59 3.37N125.29E
Taï Ivory Coast 76 5.52N 7.28W
Tai'an China 54 36.16N117.13E
Taiarapu, Presqu'île de *pen.* Tahiti 85 17.47S149.14W
Taibai China 54 36.08N108.41E
Taibai Shan *mtn.* China 54 33.55N107.45E
Taibus Qi China 54 41.55N115.23E
Taidong Taiwan 55 22.49N121.10E
Taigu China 54 37.23N112.34E
Taihang Shan *mts.* China 54 36.00N113.35E
Taihape New Zealand 86 39.40S175.48E
Taihe Anhui China 54 33.10N115.36E
Taihe Jiangxi China 55 26.48 114.56E
Tai Hu *l.* China 55 31.15N120.10E
Tailai China 53 46.23N123.24E
Tain U.K. 14 57.48N 4.04W
Tainan Taiwan 55 23.01N120.12E
Tainaron, Ákra *c.* Greece 35 36.22N 22.30E
Tai-o-haé Îs. Marquises 85 8.55S140.04W
Taipei Taiwan 55 25.05N121.30E
Taiping Anhui China 55 30.18N118.06E
Taiping Malaysia 58 4.54N100.42E
Taishan China 55 22.10N112.57E
Taito, Península de *pen.* Chile 125 46.30S 74.25W
Taitze He *r.* China 54 41.07N122.43E
Taivalkoski Finland 40 65.34N 28.15E
Taiwan Asia 55 24.00N121.00E
Taiyetos Óros *mts.* Greece 35 37.16N 22.12E
Taiyuan China 54 37.48N112.33E
Taiyue Shan *mts.* China 54 36.40N112.00E
Taizhong Taiwan 55 24.11N120.40E
Taizhou China 54 32.22N119.58E
Ta'izz Yemen 71 13.35N 44.02E
Tajarḥī Libya 75 24.21N 14.28E
Tajimi Japan 57 35.19N137.08E
Tajitos Mexico 109 30.58N112.18W
Tajo *r.* *see* Tejo Spain 27
Tajrish Iran 65 35.48N 51.20E
Tajuna *r.* Spain 24 40.10N 3.35W
Tak Thailand 56 16.51N 99.08E
Takachu Botswana 80 22.37S 21.58E
Takada Japan 57 37.06N138.15E
Takaka New Zealand 86 40.51S172.48E
Takalar Indonesia 58 5.29S119.26E
Takamatsu Japan 57 34.28N134.05E
Takaoka Japan 57 36.47N137.00E
Takapuna New Zealand 86 36.48S174.47E
Takarazuka Japan 57 34.49N135.21E
Takasaki Japan 57 36.20N139.00E
Takatsuki Japan 57 34.51N135.37E
Takayama Japan 57 36.08N137.15E
Takern *l.* Sweden 43 58.21N 14.48E
Tākestān Iran 65 36.02N 49.40E
Takêv Kampuchea 56 11.00N104.46E
Takhādīd *well* Iraq 65 29.59N 44.30E
Takla L. Canada 100 55.15N125.45W
Taklimakan Shamo *des.* China 52 38.10N 82.00E
Taku *r.* Canada / U.S.A. 100 58.30N133.50W
Talā Egypt 66 30.41N 30.56E
Tala Uruguay 125 34.21S 55.46W
Talagang Pakistan 62 32.55N 72.25E
Talagante Chile 125 33.40S 70.56W
Talāja India 62 21.21N 72.03E
Tālāla India 62 21.02N 70.32E
Talangbetutu Indonesia 58 2.48S104.42E
Talara Peru 122 4.38S 81.18W
Talarrubias Spain 27 39.02N 5.14W
Talasskiy Alatau *mts.* U.S.S.R. 52 42.20N 73.20E
Talata Mafara Nigeria 77 12.37N 6.05E
Talaud, Kepulauan *is.* Indonesia 59 4.20N126.50E
Talavera de la Reina Spain 27 39.57N 4.50W
Talawdī Sudan 73 10.38N 30.23E
Talbragar *r.* Australia 93 32.12S148.37E
Talca Chile 125 35.26S 71.40W
Talcahuano Chile 125 36.43S 73.07W
Tālcher India 63 20.57N 85.13E
Taldom U.S.S.R. 44 56.49N 37.30E
Taldy Kurgan U.S.S.R. 52 45.02N 78.23E
Taleh *well* Somali Rep. 71 9.12N 48.23E
Talia Australia 92 33.16S134.53E
Taliabu *i.* Indonesia 59 1.50S124.55E
Tali Post Sudan 73 5.54N 30.47E
Talkeetna U.S.A. 98 62.20N150.09W
Ţalkhā Egypt 66 31.04N 31.22E
Tallahassee U.S.A. 113 30.26N 84.19W
Tallangatta Australia 93 36.14S147.19E
Tallard France 21 44.28N 6.03E
Tallinn U.S.S.R. 41 59.22N 24.48E
Tall Kalakh Syria 66 34.40N 36.18E
Tall Kūshik Syria 64 36.48N 42.04E
Tall Salḥab Syria 66 35.15N 36.22E
Tallulah U.S.A. 111 32.25N 91.11W
Ţallūzā Jordan 67 32.16N 35.18E
Talmont France 18 46.28N 1.37W
Talnoye U.S.S.R. 37 48.55N 30.40E
Taloda India 62 21.34N 74.13E
Talofofo Guam 84 13.21N144.45E
Talsi U.S.S.R. 41 57.15N 22.36E
Taltal Chile 124 25.24S 70.29W
Talvik Norway 40 70.05N 22.52E
Talwood Australia 93 28.29S149.25E
Talyawalka *r.* Australia 92 31.49S143.25E
Tama *r.* Japan 57 35.32N139.47E
Tamala Australia 88 26.42S113.47E
Tamale Ghana 76 9.26N 0.49W
Tamanar Morocco 74 31.00N 9.35W
Tamanrasset Algeria 75 22.47N 5.31E
Tamanrasset, Oued *wadi* Algeria 74 21.24N 1.00E
Tamanthi Burma 56 25.19N 95.18E
Tamaqua U.S.A. 115 40.48N 75.58W
Tamar *r.* U.K. 13 50.28N 4.13W
Tamarite de Litera Spain 25 41.52N 0.26E
Tamási Hungary 31 46.38N 18.18E
Tamaské Niger 77 14.55N 5.55E
Tamaulipas *d.* Mexico 111 24.30N 98.50W
Tamazunchale Mexico 116 21.16N 98.47W
Tambacounda Senegal 76 13.45N 13.40W
Tambara Mozambique 79 16.42S 34.17E
Tambellup Australia 89 34.03S117.36E
Tambo Australia 90 24.53S146.15E
Tambo *r.* Australia 93 37.51S147.48E
Tambohorano Madagascar 81 17.30S 43.58E
Tambor Mexico 109 25.08N105.27W
Tambov U.S.S.R. 44 52.44N 41.28E
Tambre *r.* Spain 26 42.49N 8.53W
Tambura Sudan 73 5.36N 27.28E
Tamchaket Mauritania 74 17.25N 10.40W
Tâmega *r.* Portugal 26 41.05N 8.21W
Tamil Nadu *d.* India 61 11.15N 79.00E
Ţāmiyah Egypt 66 29.29N 30.58E
Tamkuhi India 63 26.41N 84.11E
Tam Ky Vietnam 56 15.34N108.29E
Tammisaari Finland 41 59.58N 23.26E
Ţammūn Jordan 67 32.17N 35.23E
Tämnaren *l.* Sweden 43 60.10N 17.20E
Tampa U.S.A. 113 27.58N 82.38W
Tampa B. U.S.A. 113 27.45N 82.35W
Tampere Finland 41 61.30N 23.45E
Tampico Mexico 116 22.18N 97.52W
Tamra Israel 67 32.51N 35.12E
Tamra Israel 67 32.38N 35.24E
Tamri Morocco 74 30.43N 9.43W
Tamsagbulag Mongolia 53 47.10N117.21E
Tamworth Australia 93 31.07S150.57E
Tamworth Canada 105 44.29N 77.00W
Tamworth U.K. 13 52.38N 1.42W
Tana *r.* Kenya 79 2.32S 40.32E
Tana Norway 40 70.26N 28.14E
Tana *r.* Norway 40 69.45N 28.15E
Tana *i.* Vanuatu 84 19.30S169.20E
Tana, L. Ethiopia 73 12.00N 37.20E
Tanacross U.S.A. 98 63.12N143.30W
Tanafjorden Norway 40 70.54N 28.40E
Tanahgrogot Indonesia 58 1.55S116.12E
Tanahmerah Indonesia 59 6.08S140.18E
Tanakpur India 63 29.05N 80.07E
Tanami Australia 88 19.59S129.43E
Tanana U.S.A. 98 65.11N152.10W
Tanana *r.* U.S.A. 98 65.09N151.55W
Tanaro *r.* Italy 30 45.01N 8.47E
Tanch 'On N. Korea 57 40.27N128.54E
Tānda India 63 26.33N 82.39E
Tanda Ivory Coast 76 7.48N 3.10W
Tandaltī Sudan 73 13.01N 31.50E
Tăndărei Romania 37 44.38N 27.40E
Tandil Argentina 125 37.18S 59.10W
Tandjilé *d.* Chad 77 9.45N 16.28E
Tando Ādam Pakistan 62 25.46N 68.40E
Tando Allāhyār Pakistan 62 25.28N 68.43E
Tando Bāgo Pakistan 62 24.47N 68.58E
Tando Muhammad Khan Pakistan 62 25.08N 68.32E
Tandou L. Australia 92 32.38S142.05E
Tandula Tank *resr.* India 63 20.40N 81.12E
Tanega shima *i.* Japan 57 30.32N131.00E
Taneytown U.S.A. 114 39.40N 77.10W

Tanezrouft to Tete

Tanezrouft des. Algeria 74 22.25N 0.30E
Tanga Tanzania 79 5.07S 39.05E
Tanga d. Tanzania 79 5.20S 38.30E
Tangalla Sri Lanka 61 6.02N 80.47E
Tanganyika, L. Africa 79 6.00S 29.30E
Tanger Morocco 74 35.48N 5.45W
Tangerhütte E. Germany 38 52.26N 11.48E
Tangermünde E. Germany 38 52.32N 11.58E
Tanggo China 63 31.37N 93.18E
Tanggu China 54 39.01N117.43E
Tanggula Shan mts. China 63 33.00N 90.00E
Tanggula Shankou pass China 63 32.45N 92.24E
Tanggulashanqu China 63 34.10N 92.23E
Tanghe China 54 32.41N112.49E
Tāngi India 63 19.57N 85.30E
Tangi Pakistan 62 34.18N 71.40E
Tangier see Tanger Morocco 74
Tangmarg Jammu & Kashmir 62 34.02N 74.26E
Tangra Yumco l. China 63 31.00N 86.15E
Tangshan China 54 39.32N118.08E
Tangtse Jammu & Kashmir 63 34.02N 78.11E
Tanguiéta Benin 77 10.37N 1.18E
Tanimbar, Kepulauan is. Indonesia 59 7.50S131.30E
Taninges France 21 46.07N 6.36E
Tanishpa mtn. Pakistan 62 31.10N 68.24E
Tanjay Phil. 59 9.31N123.10E
Tanjung Indonesia 58 2.10S115.25E
Tanjungbalai Indonesia 58 2.59N 99.46E
Tanjungkarang Indonesia 58 5.28S105.16E
Tanjungpandan Indonesia 58 2.44S107.36E
Tanjungredeb Indonesia 58 2.09N117.29E
Tānk Pakistan 62 32.13N 70.23E
Tankapirtti Finland 40 68.16N 27.20E
Tännäs Sweden 41 62.27N 12.40E
Tannersville U.S.A. 115 42.12N 74.08W
Tannin Canada 102 49.40N 91.00W
Tannis Bugt b. Denmark 42 57.40N 10.15E
Tannu Ola mts. U.S.S.R. 51 51.00N 93.30E
Tannūrah, Ra's c. Saudi Arabia 71 26.39N 50.10E
Tano r. Ghana 76 5.07N 2.54W
Tanout Niger 77 14.55N 8.49E
Ţanţā Egypt 66 30.48N 31.00E
Tanumshede Sweden 42 58.44N 11.19E
Tanzania Africa 79 5.00S 35.00E
Tao'an China 54 45.20N122.48E
Taole China 54 38.50N106.40E
Taormina Italy 33 37.52N 15.17E
Taoudenni Mali 76 22.45N 4.00W
Tapachula Mexico 116 14.54N 92.15W
Tapajós r. Brazil 123 2.25S 54.40W
Tapaktuan Indonesia 58 3.30N 97.10E
Tapalquén Argentina 125 36.20S 60.02W
Tapanahoni r. Surinam 123 4.20N 54.25W
Tapanlieh Taiwan 55 21.58N120.47E
Tapanui New Zealand 86 45.57S169.16E
Tapauá r. Brazil 122 5.40S 64.20W
Tapeta Liberia 76 6.25N 8.47W
Tapirapecó, Serra mts. Venezuela/Brazil 122 1.00N 64.30W
Tāplejung Nepal 63 27.21N 87.40E
Tapolca Hungary 31 46.53N 17.27E
Tāpti r. India 62 21.05N 72.40E
Tapurucuara Brazil 122 0.24S 65.02W
Taquari r. Brazil 126 19.00S 57.27W
Taquaritinga Brazil 126 21.23S 48.33W
Tar r. U.S.A. 113 35.33N 77.05W
Tara Canada 104 44.28N 81.09W
Tara U.S.S.R. 9 56.55N 74.24E
Tara r. U.S.S.R. 50 56.30N 74.40E
Tara r. Yugo. 31 43.21N 18.51E
Tarabine, Oued Ti-n- wadi Algeria 75 21.16N 7.24E
Tarabuco Bolivia 124 19.10S 64.57W
Ţarābulus Lebanon 66 34.27N 35.50E
Ţarābulus d. Libya 75 32.40N 13.15E
Ţarābulus f. Libya 75 31.00N 13.30E
Ţarābulus town Libya 75 32.58N 13.12E
Tarago Australia 93 35.05S149.10E
Tarakan Indonesia 58 3.20N117.38E
Taranaki d. New Zealand 86 39.00S174.30E
Tarancón Spain 27 40.01N 3.01W
Taranto Italy 33 40.28N 17.15E
Taranto, Golfo di g. Italy 33 40.00N 17.10E
Tarapacá Colombia 122 2.52S 69.44W
Tarapoto Peru 122 6.31S 76.23W
Tarare France 21 45.54N 4.26E
Tarascon Ariège France 20 42.51N 1.36E
Tarascon Vaucluse France 21 43.48N 4.40E
Tarashcha U.S.S.R. 37 49.35N 30.20E
Tarasovo U.S.S.R. 44 66.14N 46.43E
Tarauacá Brazil 122 8.10S 70.46W
Tarauacá r. Brazil 122 6.42S 69.48W
Taravao, Isthme de Tahiti 85 17.43S149.19W
Taravo r. France 21 41.42N 8.49E
Tarawa i. Kiribati 84 1.25N173.00E
Tarawera New Zealand 86 39.02S176.36E
Tarazona Spain 25 41.54N 1.44W
Tarazona de la Mancha Spain 25 39.15N 1.55W
Tarbagatay, Khrebet mts. U.S.S.R. 52 47.00N 83.00E
Tarbat Ness c. U.K. 14 57.52N 3.46W
Tarbert Rep. of Ire. 15 52.34N 9.24W
Tarbert Strath. U.K. 14 55.51N 5.25W
Tarbert W. Isles U.K. 14 57.54N 6.49W
Tarbes France 20 43.14N 0.05E
Tarcento Italy 30 46.13N 13.13E
Tarcoola N.S.W. Australia 92 33.31S142.40E
Tarcoola S.A. Australia 92 30.41S134.33E
Tarcoon Australia 93 30.19S146.43E
Tarcutta Australia 93 35.17S147.45E
Tardajos Spain 26 42.21N 3.49W
Taree Australia 93 31.54S152.26E
Tarella Australia 92 30.55S143.06E
Tärendö Sweden 40 67.10N 22.38E
Tarentum U.S.A. 114 40.36N 79.45W
Ţarfā, Wādī aţ r. Egypt 66 28.36N 30.50E
Tarfaya Morocco 74 27.58N 12.55W
Targon France 20 44.44N 0.16W
Tarhjicht Morocco 74 29.05N 9.24W
Tarifa Spain 27 36.01N 5.36W
Tarifa, Punta de c. Spain 27 36.00N 5.37W
Tarija Bolivia 124 21.31S 64.45W
Tarija d. Bolivia 124 21.40S 64.20W
Tarīm S. Yemen 71 16.03N 49.00E
Tarim He r. China 52 41.00N 83.30E
Tarīn Kowt Afghan. 62 32.52N 65.38E
Taritatu r. Indonesia 59 2.54S138.27E
Tarka La mtn. Bhutan 63 27.05N 89.40E
Tarkwa Ghana 76 5.16N 1.59W
Tarlac Phil. 59 15.29N120.35E
Tarm Denmark 42 55.55N 8.32E
Tarma Peru 122 11.28S 75.41W
Tarn d. France 20 43.50N 2.00E
Tarn r. France 20 44.05N 1.06E
Tärnaby Sweden 40 65.43N 15.16E
Tarnak r. Afghan. 62 31.26N 65.31E
Tarn-et-Garonne d. France 20 44.05N 1.20E
Tarnica mtn. Poland 37 49.05N 22.44E
Tarnobrzeg Poland 37 50.35N 21.41E
Tarnów Poland 37 50.01N 20.59E
Tärnsjö Sweden 43 60.09N 16.56E
Taro r. Italy 30 45.00N 10.15E
Taroom Australia 90 25.39S149.49E
Tarouca Portugal 26 41.00N 7.40W
Taroudant Morocco 74 30.31N 8.55W
Tarpon Springs town U.S.A. 113 28.08N 82.45W
Tarquinia Italy 30 42.15N 11.45E
Tarqūmiyah Jordan 67 31.35N 35.01E
Tarragona Spain 25 41.07N 1.15E
Tarragona d. Spain 25 41.10N 0.40E
Tarran Hills Australia 93 32.27S146.27E
Tarrasa Spain 25 41.34N 2.01E
Tárrega Spain 25 41.39N 1.09E
Tarrytown U.S.A. 115 41.05N 73.52W
Tarso Ahon mtn. Chad 77 20.23N 18.18E
Tarso Ouri mtn. Chad 77 21.25N 18.56E
Tarsus Turkey 64 36.52N 34.52E
Tartagal Argentina 124 22.32S 63.50W
Tartas France 20 43.50N 0.48W
Tartu U.S.S.R. 44 58.20N 26.44E
Ţarţūs Syria 66 34.55N 35.52E
Tarutino U.S.S.R. 37 46.09N 29.04E
Tarutung Indonesia 58 2.01N 98.54E
Tarvisio Italy 31 46.30N 13.35E
Tashan China 54 40.51N120.56E
Tashauz U.S.S.R. 9 41.49N 59.58E
Tashi Gang Dzong Bhutan 63 27.19N 91.34E
Tashkent U.S.S.R. 9 41.16N 69.13E
Tasiilaq see Ammassalik Greenland 99
Tasikmalaya Indonesia 59 7.20S108.16E
Tasīl Syria 67 32.50N 35.58E
Tåsinge i. Denmark 42 55.00N 10.36E
Tåsjön Sweden 40 64.15N 15.47E
Tasman B. New Zealand 86 41.00S173.15E
Tasmania d. Australia 91 42.00S147.00E
Tasman Mts. New Zealand 86 41.00S172.40E
Tasman Pen. Australia 91 43.08S147.51E
Tasman Sea Pacific Oc. 84 38.00S162.00E
Tassili-n-Ajjer f. Algeria 75 26.05N 7.00E
Tassili oua-n-Ahaggar f. Algeria 75 20.30N 5.00E
Tataa, Pt. Tahiti 85 17.33S149.36W
Tatabánya Hungary 37 47.34N 18.26E
Tatarsk U.S.S.R. 50 55.14N 76.00E
Tatarskiy Proliv g. U.S.S.R. 51 47.40N141.00E
Tateyama Japan 57 34.59N139.52E
Tathlina L. Canada 100 60.32N117.32W
Tathra Australia 93 36.44S149.58E
Tatinnai L. Canada 101 60.55N 97.40W
Tatnam, C. Canada 101 57.16N 91.00W
Tatong Australia 93 36.46S146.03E
Tatta Pakistan 62 24.45N 67.55E
Tatvan Turkey 64 38.31N 42.15E
Tau Norway 42 59.04N 5.54E
Tau i. Samoa 84 14.15S169.30W
Taubaté Brazil 126 23.00S 45.36W
Tauber r. W. Germany 39 49.46N 9.31E
Tauberbischofsheim W. Germany 39 49.37N 9.40E
Taulihawa Nepal 63 27.32N 83.05E
Taumarunui New Zealand 86 38.53S175.16E
Taumaturgo Brazil 122 8.57S 72.48W
Taung R.S.A. 80 27.32S 24.46E
Taungdwingyi Burma 56 20.00N 95.30E
Taung-gyi Burma 56 20.49N 97.01E
Taungup Burma 56 18.51N 94.14E
Taunoa Tahiti 85 17.45S149.21W
Taunsa Pakistan 62 30.42N 70.39E
Taunton U.K. 13 51.01N 3.07W
Taunton U.S.A. 115 41.54N 71.06W
Taunus mts. W. Germany 36 50.07N 7.48E
Taupo New Zealand 86 38.42S176.06E
Taupo, L. New Zealand 86 38.45S175.30E
Taurage U.S.S.R. 41 55.15N 22.17E
Tauranga New Zealand 86 37.42S176.11E
Taureau, Résr. Canada 105 46.46N 73.50W
Taurianova Italy 33 38.21N 16.01E
Taurus Mts. see Toros Dağlari Turkey 64
Tauste Spain 25 41.55N 1.15W
Tautira Tahiti 85 17.45S149.10W
Tavani Canada 101 62.10N 93.30W
Tavda U.S.S.R. 50 58.04N 65.12E
Tavda r. U.S.S.R. 50 57.40N 67.00E
Taveta Kenya 79 3.23S 37.42E
Taveuni i. Fiji 84 16.56S179.58W
Tavira Portugal 27 37.07N 7.39W
Tavistock Canada 104 43.19N 80.50W
Tavistock U.K. 13 50.33N 4.09W
Tavor, Har mtn. Israel 67 32.41N 35.23E
Távora r. Portugal 26 41.08N 7.35W
Tavoy Burma 56 14.02N 98.12E
Taw r. U.K. 13 51.05N 4.05W
Tawas City U.S.A. 104 44.16N 83.31W
Tawau Malaysia 58 4.16N117.54E
Tawitawi i. Phil. 59 5.10N120.05E
Ţawkar Sudan 72 18.26N 37.44E
Tawu Taiwan 55 22.22N120.54E
Tāwurghā', Sabkhat f. Libya 22 31.10N 15.15E
Tay r. U.K. 14 56.21N 3.18W
Tay, L. Australia 89 33.00S120.52E
Tay, Loch U.K. 14 56.32N 4.08W
Tayabamba Peru 122 8.15S 77.15W
Tayan Indonesia 58 0.02S110.05E
Tayegle Somali Rep. 71 4.02N 44.36E
Taylor Tex. U.S.A. 111 30.34N 97.25W
Taylor, Mt. U.S.A. 109 35.14N107.37W
Taylors Island town U.S.A. 115 38.28N 76.18W
Taymā' Saudi Arabia 64 27.37N 38.30E
Taymyr, Ozero l. U.S.S.R. 51 74.20N101.00E
Taymyr, Poluostrov pen. U.S.S.R. 51 75.30N 99.00E
Tay Ninh Vietnam 56 11.21N106.02E
Tayport U.K. 14 56.27N 2.53W
Tayshet U.S.S.R. 51 55.56N 98.01E
Tayside d. U.K. 14 56.35N 3.28W
Taytay Phil. 58 10.47N119.32E
Taz r. U.S.S.R. 50 67.30N 78.50E
Taza Morocco 74 34.16N 4.01W
Tazawa ko l. Japan 57 39.43N140.40E
Tazenakht Morocco 74 30.35N 7.12W
Tazin L. Canada 101 59.40N109.00W
Tāzirbū Libya 72 25.45N 21.00E
Tazovskiy U.S.S.R. 50 67.28N 78.43E
Tbilisi U.S.S.R. 65 41.43N 44.48E
Tchad, Lac see Chad, L. Africa 77
Tchamba Togo 77 9.05N 1.27E
Tchibanga Gabon 78 2.52S 11.07E
Tchien Liberia 76 6.00N 8.10W
Tchigaï, Plateau du f. Niger/Chad 77 21.30N 14.50E
Tcholliré Cameroon 77 8.25N 14.10E
Tczew Poland 37 54.06N 18.47E
Te Anau New Zealand 86 45.25S167.43E
Te Anau, L. New Zealand 86 45.10S167.15E
Teaneck U.S.A. 115 40.53N 74.01W
Teano Italy 33 41.15N 14.04E
Teapa Mexico 116 17.33N 92.57W
Te Araroa New Zealand 86 37.38S178.25E
Tea Tree Australia 90 22.11S133.17E
Teba Spain 27 36.58N 4.56W
Tébessa Algeria 75 35.22N 8.08E
Tebingtinggi Indonesia 58 3.20N 99.08E
Tebingtinggi Indonesia 58 3.37S103.09E
Téboursa Tunisia 32 36.49N 9.51E
Teboursouk, Monts de mts. Tunisia 32 36.45N 9.20E
Tebulos Mta mtn. U.S.S.R. 45 42.34N 45.17E
Tech r. France 20 42.36N 3.03E
Techiman Ghana 76 7.36N 1.55W
Tecuci Romania 37 45.49N 27.27E
Tecumseh U.S.A. 104 42.00N 83.57W
Tedesa Ethiopia 73 5.07N 37.45E
Tees r. U.K. 12 54.35N 1.11W
Tefé Brazil 122 3.24S 64.45W
Tefé r. Brazil 122 3.35S 64.47W
Tegal Indonesia 59 6.52S109.07E
Tegelen Neth. 16 51.20N 6.08E
Tegernsee W. Germany 39 47.43N 11.45E
Tegina Nigeria 77 10.06N 6.11E
Tego Australia 93 28.48S146.47E
Tegouma well Niger 77 15.33N 9.19E
Tegucigalpa Honduras 117 14.05N 87.14W
Teguidda I-n-Tessoum Niger 77 17.21N 6.32E
Tehamiyam Sudan 72 18.20N 36.32E
Tehata Bangla. 63 23.43N 88.32E
Téhini Ivory Coast 76 9.39N 3.32W
Tehkummah Canada 104 45.39N 81.59W
Tehrān Iran 65 35.40N 51.26E
Tehri India 63 30.23N 78.29E
Tehuacán Mexico 116 18.30N 97.26W
Tehuantepec Mexico 116 16.21N 95.13W
Tehuantepec, Golfo de g. Mexico 116 16.00N 95.00W
Tehuantepec, Istmo de f. Mexico 116 17.00N 94.30W
Teifi r. U.K. 13 52.05N 4.41W
Teignmouth U.K. 13 50.33N 3.30W
Teixeiras Brazil 126 20.37S 42.52W
Tejakula Indonesia 59 8.09S115.19E
Tejo r. Portugal 27 38.40N 9.24W
Te Kaha New Zealand 86 37.44S177.52E
Tekamah U.S.A. 110 41.47N 96.13W
Tekapo, L. New Zealand 86 43.35S170.30E
Tekax Mexico 117 20.12N 89.17W
Teke Burnu c. Turkey 34 40.02N 26.10E
Tekezē r. see Satīt Ethiopia 72
Tekirdag Turkey 29 40.59N 27.30E
Tekkali India 63 18.37N 84.14E
Tekouiat, Oued wadi Algeria 75 22.20N 2.30E
Tekro well Chad 72 19.30N 20.58E
Te Kuiti New Zealand 86 38.20S175.10E
Tel r. India 63 20.50N 83.54E
Tela Honduras 117 15.56N 87.25W
Tel 'Adashim Israel 67 32.39N 35.18E
Tel Arshaf site Israel 67 32.12N 34.48E
Tel Ashqelon site Israel 67 31.39N 34.32E
Telavåg Norway 42 60.16N 4.49E
Telavi U.S.S.R. 65 41.56N 45.30E
Tel Aviv d. Israel 67 32.05N 34.48E
Tel Aviv-Yafo Israel 67 32.05N 34.46E
Tele r. Zaïre 78 2.48N 24.00E
Telegraph Creek town Canada 100 57.55N131.10W
Telemark d. Norway 42 59.40N 8.45E
Teleneshty U.S.S.R. 37 47.35N 28.17E
Teles Pires r. Brazil 123 7.20S 57.30W
Telford U.K. 13 52.42N 2.30W
Telfs Austria 39 47.18N 11.04E
Telgte W. Germany 38 51.59N 7.47E
Tel Hazor site Israel 67 33.01N 35.34E
Telichie Australia 92 31.43S139.54E
Télimélé Guinea 76 10.54N 13.02W
Tel Lakhish site Israel 67 31.34N 34.51E
Tell Atlas mts. Algeria 75 36.00N 1.00E
Tell City U.S.A. 113 37.56N 86.46W
Teller U.S.A. 98 65.16N166.22N
Tel Mediggo site Israel 67 32.35N 35.11E
Tel Mond Israel 67 32.15N 34.56E
Telok Anson Malaysia 58 4.00N101.00E
Telpos-Iz mtn. U.S.S.R. 44 63.56N 59.02E
Telsen Argentina 125 42.25S 67.00W
Telšiai U.S.S.R. 41 55.59N 22.15E
Telti Italy 32 40.52N 9.21E
Teltow E. Germany 38 52.23N 13.16E
Telukbetung Indonesia 58 5.28S105.16E
Tema Ghana 76 5.41N 0.01W
Temagami, L. Canada 104 47.00N 80.05W
Te Manga mtn. RarotongaCook Is. 84 21.13S159.45W
Temaverachi, Sierra mts. Mexico 109 29.30N109.30W
Tembleque Spain 27 39.42N 3.30W
Tembo Aluma Angola 78 7.42S 17.15E
Teme r. U.K. 13 52.10N 2.13W
Temerin Yugo. 31 45.24N 19.53E
Temir U.S.S.R. 45 49.09N 57.06E
Temirtau U.S.S.R. 9 50.05N 72.55E
Témiscaming Canada 104 46.43N 79.06W
Témiscaming Canada 102 46.44N 79.05W
Temora Australia 93 34.27S147.35E
Tempe U.S.A. 109 33.25N111.56W
Tempino Indonesia 58 1.55S103.23E
Tempio Italy 32 40.54N 9.07E
Temple U.S.A. 111 31.06N 97.21W
Temple B. Australia 90 12.10S143.04E
Templemore Rep. of Ire. 15 52.48N 7.51W
Templin E. Germany 38 53.07N 13.30E
Temuco Chile 125 38.44S 72.36W
Tenabo Mexico 116 20.03N 90.14W
Tenaha U.S.A. 111 31.57N 94.15W
Tenasserim Burma 56 12.05N 99.00E
Tenasserim d. Burma 56 13.00N 99.00E
Tenby U.K. 13 51.40N 4.42W
Tenby Bay town Canada 104 46.06N 83.56W
Tendaho Ethiopia 73 11.48N 40.52E
Tende France 21 44.05N 7.36E
Ten Degree Channel Indian Oc. 56 10.00N 93.00E
Tendrara Morocco 74 33.04N 1.59W
Tenenkou Mali 76 14.25N 4.58W
Tenerife i. Canary Is. 74 28.10N 16.30W
Ténès Algeria 75 36.31N 1.18E
Teng r. Burma 56 19.50N 97.40E
Tengchong China 61 25.02N 98.28E
Tengger Shamo des. China 54 39.00N104.10E
Tengiz, Ozero l. U.S.S.R. 9 50.30N 69.00E
Teng Xian China 54 35.08N117.20E
Tenke Zaïre 78 10.34S 26.07E
Tenkodogo U. Volta 76 11.47N 0.19W
Tenna r. Italy 31 43.14N 13.47E
Tennant Creek town Australia 90 19.31S134.15E
Tennessee d. U.S.A. 113 35.50N 85.30W
Tennessee r. U.S.A. 113 37.04N 88.33W
Tenosique Mexico 116 17.29N 91.26W
Tenryū Japan 57 34.52N137.49E
Tenryū r. Japan 57 34.39N137.47E
Tensift, Oued r. Morocco 74 32.02N 9.22W
Tenterfield Australia 93 29.01S152.04E
Teófilo Otoni Brazil 126 17.52S 41.31W
Tepa Indonesia 59 7.52S129.31E
Tepa Pt. Niue 84 19.07S169.56W
Tepelenë Albania 34 40.18N 20.01E
Tepic Mexico 116 21.30N104.51W
Teplice Czech. 38 50.39N 13.48E
Ter r. Spain 25 42.01N 3.12E
Téra Niger 76 14.01N 0.45E
Tera r. Portugal 27 38.55N 8.04W
Tera r. Spain 26 41.54N 5.44W
Teramo Italy 31 42.39N 13.42E
Tercan Turkey 64 39.47N 40.23E
Terebovlya U.S.S.R. 37 49.18N 25.44E
Terekhova U.S.S.R. 37 52.13N 31.28E
Teresina Brazil 123 5.09S 42.46W
Teresópolis Brazil 126 22.26S 42.59W
Terevaka mtn. I. de Pascua 85 27.05S109.23W
Tergnier France 19 49.39N 3.18E
Terhazza Mali 76 23.45N 4.59W
Termez U.S.S.R. 50 37.15N 67.15E
Termination I. Australia 89 34.25S121.53E
Termini Italy 28 37.59N 13.42E
Termini Imerese Italy 32 37.59N 13.42E
Termini Imerese, Golfo di g. Italy 32 38.05N 13.50E
Términos, Laguna de b. Mexico 116 18.30N 91.30W
Termoli Italy 33 41.58N 14.59E
Ternate Indonesia 59 0.48N127.23E
Terneuzen Neth. 16 51.20N 3.50E
Terney U.S.S.R. 57 45.05N136.36E
Terni Italy 30 42.34N 12.37E
Ternopol U.S.S.R. 37 49.35N 25.39E
Terra Alta U.S.A. 114 39.25N 79.35W
Terra Bella U.S.A. 109 35.58N119.03W
Terrace Canada 100 54.31N128.35W
Terracina Italy 32 41.17N 13.15E
Terralba Italy 32 39.43N 8.38E
Terrasson-la-Villedieu France 20 45.08N 1.18E
Terre Adélie f. Antarctica 128 80.00S140.00E
Terrebonne Canada 105 45.42N 73.38W
Terre Haute U.S.A. 112 39.27N 87.24W
Terrenceville Canada 103 47.42N 54.43W
Terry U.S.A. 108 46.47N105.19W
Terschelling i. Neth. 16 53.25N 5.25E
Teruel Spain 25 40.21N 1.06W
Teruel d. Spain 25 40.40N 1.00W
Tervola Finland 40 66.05N 24.48E
Teryaweynya Australia 92 32.18S143.29E
Tešanj Yugo. 31 44.37N 18.00E
Tesaret, Oued wadi Algeria 75 25.32N 2.52E
Teshio Japan 57 44.53N141.44E
Teshio r. Japan 57 44.53N141.44E
Teslić Yugo. 31 44.37N 17.51E
Teslin Canada 100 60.10N132.43W
Teslin r. Canada 100 61.34N134.54W
Teslin L. Canada 100 60.15N132.57W
Tessalit Mali 76 20.12N 1.00E
Tessaoua Niger 77 13.46N 7.55E
Tessy-sur-Vire France 18 48.58N 1.04W
Test r. U.K. 13 50.55N 1.29W
Testa, Capo c. Italy 32 41.14N 9.09E
Têt r. France 20 42.44N 3.02E
Tetachuck L. Canada 100 53.18N125.55W
Tete Mozambique 81 16.10S 33.30E
Tete d. Mozambique 79 15.30S 33.00E

Teterev to Toledo

Teterev *r.* U.S.S.R. **37** 51.03N 30.30E
Teterow E. Germany **38** 53.46N 12.34E
Teteven Bulgaria **34** 42.58N 24.17E
Tethul *r.* Canada **100** 60.35N 112.12W
Tetiaora *i.* Îs. de la Société **85** 17.05S 149.32W
Tetica de Bacares *mtn.* Spain **27** 37.16N 2.26W
Tetiyev U.S.S.R. **37** 49.22N 29.40E
Tétouan Morocco **74** 35.34N 5.23W
Tetovo Yugo. **34** 42.01N 21.02E
Tetuan *see* Tétouan Morocco **74**
Tetyukhe U.S.S.R. **57** 44.31N 135.31E
Teulada Italy **32** 38.58N 8.46E
Teulada, Capo *c.* Italy **32** 38.52N 8.39E
Teun *i.* Indonesia **59** 6.59S 129.08E
Teutoburger Wald W. Germany **38** 52.10N 8.15E
Teuva Finland **40** 62.29N 21.44E
Tevere *r.* Italy **30** 41.44N 12.14E
Teverya Israel **67** 32.48N 35.32E
Teviot *r.* U.K. **14** 55.36N 2.27W
Teviotdale *f.* U.K. **12** 55.26N 2.46W
Teviothead U.K. **14** 55.20N 2.56W
Tewkesbury U.K. **13** 51.59N 2.09W
Tewksburg U.S.A. **115** 42.37N 71.14W
Texarkana Ark. U.S.A. **111** 33.26N 94.02W
Texarkana Tex. U.S.A. **111** 33.26N 94.03W
Texarkana, L. U.S.A. **111** 33.16N 94.14W
Texas Australia **93** 28.50S 151.09E
Texas *d.* U.S.A. **111** 31.30N 100.00W
Texas *town* U.S.A. **115** 43.30N 76.16W
Texas City U.S.A. **111** 29.23N 94.54W
Texel *i.* Neth. **16** 53.05N 4.47E
Texoma, L. U.S.A. **111** 33.55N 96.37W
Texon U.S.A. **111** 31.13N 101.43W
Teyea *site* Greece **35** 37.29N 22.24E
Teyvareh Afghan. **62** 33.21N 64.25E
Tezpur India **63** 26.38N 92.48E
Tha-anne *r.* Canada **101** 60.31N 94.37W
Thabana Ntlenyana *mtn.* Lesotho **80** 29.28S 29.17E
Thabazimbi R.S.A. **80** 24.36S 27.23E
Thādiq Saudi Arabia **65** 25.18N 45.52E
Thai Binh Vietnam **55** 20.30N 106.26E
Thailand Asia **56** 17.00N 101.30E
Thailand, G. of Asia **56** 11.00N 101.00E
Thai Nguyen Vietnam **55** 21.46N 105.52E
Thak Pakistan **62** 30.32N 70.13E
Thal Pakistan **62** 33.22N 70.33E
Thal Desert Pakistan **62** 31.30N 71.40E
Thale Luang *l.* Thailand **56** 7.40N 100.20E
Thallon Australia **93** 28.39S 148.49E
Thalwil Switz. **39** 47.17N 8.34E
Thamarīt Oman **60** 17.39N 54.02E
Thames *r.* Canada **104** 42.19N 82.28W
Thames New Zealand **86** 37.08S 175.35E
Thames *r.* U.K. **13** 51.30N 0.05E
Thamesford Canada **104** 43.04N 81.00W
Thamesville Canada **104** 42.33N 81.59W
Thāna India **62** 19.12N 72.58E
Thāna Pakistan **62** 28.55N 63.45E
Thane Australia **93** 28.08S 151.39E
Thanh Hóa Vietnam **55** 19.47N 105.49E
Thành Pho Ho Chí Minh Vietnam **56** 10.46N 106.43E
Thanjāvūr India **61** 10.46N 79.09E
Thann France **19** 47.49N 7.05E
Thāno Bula Khān Pakistan **62** 25.22N 67.50E
Tharād India **62** 24.24N 71.38E
Thar Desert Pakistan / India **62** 28.00N 72.00E
Thargomindah Australia **91** 27.59S 143.45E
Tharrawaddy Burma **56** 17.37N 95.48E
Tharthār, Wādī ath *r.* Iraq **64** 34.18N 43.07E
Thásos Greece **34** 40.47N 24.42E
Thásos *i.* Greece **34** 40.41N 24.47E
Thatcher U.S.A. **109** 32.51N 109.56W
Thaton Burma **56** 16.50N 97.21E
Thau, Bassin de *b.* France **20** 43.23N 3.36E
Thaungdut Burma **56** 24.26N 94.45E
Thayer U.S.A. **111** 36.31N 91.33W
Thayetmyo Burma **56** 19.20N 95.10E
Thazi Burma **56** 20.51N 96.05E
Theano Pt. Canada **104** 47.11N 84.43W
Thebes *ruins* Egypt **64** 25.41N 32.40E
The Bight *town* Bahamas **117** 24.19N 75.24W
The Cherokees, L. O' U.S.A. **111** 36.45N 94.50W
The Cheviot *mtn.* U.K. **12** 55.29N 2.10W
The Cheviot Hills U.K. **12** 55.22N 2.24W
The Coorong *g.* Australia **92** 36.00S 139.30E
The Dalles *town* U.S.A. **108** 45.36N 121.10W
Thedford Canada **104** 43.09N 81.51W
Thedford U.S.A. **110** 41.59N 100.35W
The Everglades *f.* U.S.A. **113** 26.00N 80.40W
The Fens *f.* U.K. **13** 55.10N 4.13W
The Granites *town* Australia **88** 20.35S 130.21E
The Gulf Asia **65** 27.00N 50.00E
The Hague *see* 'sGravenhage Neth. **16**
Thekulthili L. Canada **101** 61.03N 110.00W
The Little Minch *str.* U.K. **14** 57.40N 6.45W
Thelon *r.* Canada **99** 64.23N 96.15W
The Machers *f.* U.K. **14** 54.45N 4.28W
The Minch *str.* U.K. **14** 58.10N 5.50W
The Needles *c.* U.K. **13** 50.39N 1.35W
Thénezay France **18** 46.43N 0.02W
Theodore Australia **90** 24.57S 150.05E
Theodore Roosevelt L. U.S.A. **109** 33.30N 110.57W
Theog India **62** 31.07N 77.21E
Theólogos Greece **34** 40.39N 24.41E
The Pas Canada **101** 53.50N 101.15W
The Pennines *hills* U.K. **12** 55.40N 2.20W
Thérain *r.* France **19** 49.15N 2.27E
Theresa U.S.A. **105** 44.13N 75.48W
The Rhinns *f.* U.K. **14** 54.50N 5.02W
Thermaïkós Kólpos *g.* Greece **34** 40.23N 22.47E
Thermopolis U.S.A. **108** 43.39N 108.13W
Thermopylae Pass Greece **35** 38.48N 22.33E
The Rock *town* Australia **93** 35.16S 147.07E
The Salt L. Australia **92** 30.05S 142.10E
The Snares *is.* New Zealand **84** 48.00S 166.30E
The Solent *str.* U.K. **13** 50.45N 1.20W
The Sound *str.* Denmark / Sweden **43** 55.30N 12.40E
Thesprotikón Greece **35** 39.15N 20.47E
Thessalía *f.* Greece **34** 39.30N 22.00E
Thessalon Canada **104** 46.15N 83.34W
Thessaloníki Greece **34** 40.38N 22.56E
Thetford U.K. **13** 52.25N 0.44E
Thetford Mines *town* Canada **105** 46.05N 71.18W
The Twins *town* Australia **92** 30.00S 135.16E
The Wash *b.* U.K. **12** 52.55N 0.15E
The Weald *f.* U.K. **13** 51.05N 0.20E
Thibodaux U.S.A. **111** 29.48N 90.49W
Thicket Portage Canada **101** 55.19N 97.42W
Thief River Falls *town* U.S.A. **110** 48.07N 96.10W
Thiene Italy **32** 45.42N 11.29E
Thiers France **20** 45.51N 3.34E
Thiès Senegal **76** 14.50N 16.55W
Thiesi Italy **32** 40.31N 8.43E
Thika Kenya **79** 1.04S 37.04E
Thimbu Bhutan **63** 27.28N 89.39E
Thingvallavatn *l.* Iceland **40** 64.10N 21.10W
Thionville France **19** 49.22N 6.10E
Thíra *i.* Greece **35** 36.24N 25.29E
Thíra *town* Greece **35** 36.24N 25.27E
Thirsk U.K. **12** 54.15N 1.20W
Thisted Denmark **42** 56.57N 8.42E
Thistilfjördhur *b.* Iceland **40** 66.11N 15.20W
Thistle I. Australia **92** 35.00S 136.09E
Thívai Greece **35** 38.21N 23.19E
Thiviers France **20** 45.25N 0.56E
Thjórsá *r.* Iceland **40** 63.53N 20.38W
Thoa *r.* Canada **101** 60.31N 109.47W
Thoen Thailand **56** 17.41N 99.14E
Tholen *i.* Neth. **16** 51.34N 4.07E
Thomas U.S.A. **114** 39.09N 79.30W
Thomaston U.S.A. **113** 32.55N 84.20W
Thomasville Ala. U.S.A. **111** 31.55N 87.51W
Thomasville Fla. U.S.A. **113** 30.50N 83.59W
Thompson Canada **101** 55.45N 97.52W
Thompson Utah U.S.A. **108** 38.58N 109.43W
Thompson Landing Canada **101** 62.56N 110.40W
Thompsonville U.S.A. **112** 44.32N 85.57W
Thomson *r.* Australia **90** 25.11S 142.53E
Thonburi Thailand **56** 13.43N 100.27E
Thonon-les-Bains France **21** 46.22N 6.29E
Thórisvatn *l.* Iceland **40** 64.15N 18.50W
Thornbury Canada **104** 44.34N 80.26W
Thornton U.S.A. **114** 39.22N 79.56W
Thorshavn Faroe Is. **10** 62.02N 6.47W
Thorshöfn Iceland **40** 66.12N 15.17W
Thouars France **18** 46.59N 0.13W
Thousand Is. Canada **105** 44.15N 76.12W
Thowa *r.* Kenya **73** 1.33S 40.03E
Thrace *f.* Greece **34** 41.10N 25.30E
Thrakikón Pélagos *f.* Greece **34** 40.15N 24.28E
Thrapston U.K. **13** 52.24N 0.32W
Three Forks U.S.A. **108** 45.54N 111.33W
Three Hills *town* Canada **100** 51.43N 113.15W
Three Kings Is. New Zealand **84** 34.09S 172.09E
Three Rivers *town* Australia **88** 25.07S 119.09E
Three Rivers *town* U.S.A. **111** 28.28N 98.11W
Three Sisters Mt. U.S.A. **108** 44.10N 121.46W
Thueyts France **21** 44.41N 4.13E
Thuin Belgium **16** 50.21N 4.20E
Thul Pakistan **62** 28.14N 68.46E
Thule Greenland **99** 77.30N 69.29W
Thun Switz. **39** 46.45N 7.37E
Thunder B. U.S.A. **104** 44.58N 83.24W
Thunder Bay *town* Canada **102** 48.25N 89.14W
Thunder Bay *r.* U.S.A. **104** 45.04N 83.25W
Thunder Hills Canada **101** 54.30N 106.00W
Thunersee *l.* Switz. **39** 46.40N 7.45E
Thung Song Thailand **56** 8.10N 99.41E
Thunkar Bhutan **63** 27.55N 91.00E
Thüringen *f.* E. Germany **38** 50.57N 11.30E
Thüringer Wald *mts.* E. Germany **38** 50.40N 10.52E
Thurles Rep. of Ire. **15** 52.41N 7.50W
Thurloo Downs *town* Australia **92** 29.18S 143.30E
Thurmont U.S.A. **114** 39.37N 77.25W
Thursday I. Australia **84** 10.35S 142.13E
Thurso U.K. **14** 58.35N 3.32W
Thurso *r.* U.K. **10** 58.35N 3.32W
Thury-Harcourt France **18** 48.59N 0.29W
Thusis Switz. **39** 46.42N 9.26E
Thy *f.* Denmark **42** 57.00N 8.30E
Thyborön Denmark **42** 56.42N 8.13E
Thysville Zaïre **78** 5.15S 14.52E
Tia Australia **93** 31.15S 151.40E
Tiandong China **55** 23.36N 107.08E
Tian'e China **55** 25.00N 107.10E
Tian Head Canada **100** 53.47N 133.06W
Tianjin China **54** 39.07N 117.08E
Tianjin *d.* China **54** 39.30N 117.20E
Tianjun China **52** 37.16N 98.52E
Tianlin China **55** 24.18N 106.13E
Tianmen China **55** 30.40N 113.25E
Tian Shan *mts.* Asia **52** 42.00N 80.30E
Tianshui China **54** 34.25N 105.58E
Tiantai China **55** 29.09N 121.02E
Tianyang China **55** 23.45N 106.54E
Tiarei Tahiti **85** 17.32S 149.20W
Tiaret Algeria **75** 35.28N 1.21E
Tiavea W. Samoa **84** 13.57S 171.28W
Tibasti, Sarīr *des.* Libya **75** 24.00N 17.00E
Tibati Cameroon **77** 6.25N 12.33E
Tiber *r.* *see* Tevere Italy **30**
Tiberias *see* Teverya Israel **67**
Tiberias, L. *see* Yam Kinneret Israel **67**
Tibesti *mts.* Chad **77** 21.00N 17.30E
Tibet *d.* *see* Xizang China **63**
Tibetan Plateau *see* Qing Zang Gaoyuans China **63**
Tibooburra Australia **92** 29.28S 142.04E
Tibro Sweden **43** 58.26N 14.10E
Tiburón, Isla Mexico **109** 29.00N 112.20W
Tichborne Canada **105** 44.40N 76.41W
Tichît Mauritania **74** 18.28N 9.30W
Tichla W. Sahara **74** 21.35N 14.58W
Ticino *r.* Italy **30** 45.09N 9.14E
Ticonderoga U.S.A. **105** 43.51N 73.26W
Tidaholm Sweden **43** 58.11N 13.57E
Tidikelt *f.* Algeria **75** 27.00N 1.30E
Tidioute U.S.A. **114** 41.41N 79.24W
Tidirhine, Jbel *mtn.* Morocco **74** 34.50N 4.30W
Tidjikdja Mauritania **74** 18.29N 11.31W
Tiel Neth. **16** 51.53N 5.26E
Tieling China **54** 42.13N 123.48E
Tielt Belgium **16** 51.00N 3.20E
Tienen Belgium **16** 50.49N 4.56E
Tiénigbé Ivory Coast **76** 8.11N 5.43W
Tientsin *see* Tianjin China **54**
Tierga Spain **25** 41.37N 1.36W
Tierp Sweden **41** 60.20N 17.30E
Tierra Amarilla U.S.A. **108** 36.42N 106.33W
Tierra Blanca Mexico **116** 18.28N 96.12W
Tierra del Fuego *d.* Argentina **125** 54.30S 67.00W
Tierra del Fuego *i.* Argentina / Chile **125** 54.00S 69.00W
Tietar *r.* Spain **27** 39.50N 6.01W
Tietê Brazil **126** 23.04S 47.41W
Tifi Ethiopia **73** 6.15N 37.00E
Tifrah Israel **67** 31.20N 34.40E
Tifton U.S.A. **113** 31.27N 83.31W
Tiger U.S.A. **108** 48.42N 117.24W
Tiger Hills Canada **101** 49.25N 99.30W
Tigil U.S.S.R. **51** 57.49N 158.40E
Tiglit Morocco **74** 28.31N 10.15W
Tignère Cameroon **77** 7.23N 12.37E
Tignish Canada **103** 46.57N 64.02W
Tigrē *d.* Ethiopia **72** 14.10N 39.35E
Tigre *r.* Venezuela **122** 9.20N 62.30W
Tigris *r.* *see* Dijlah Asia **65**
Tīh, Jabal at *f.* Egypt **66** 28.50N 34.00E
Tihāmah *f.* Saudi Arabia **72** 19.00N 41.00E
Tijesno Yugo. **31** 43.48N 15.39E
Tijuana Mexico **109** 32.32N 117.01W
Tikamgarh India **63** 24.44N 78.50E
Tikaré U. Volta **76** 13.16N 1.44W
Tikhoretsk U.S.S.R. **45** 45.52N 40.07E
Tikhvin U.S.S.R. **44** 59.35N 33.29E
Tikitiki New Zealand **86** 37.47S 178.25E
Tiksha U.S.S.R. **44** 64.04N 32.35E
Tiksi U.S.S.R. **51** 71.40N 128.45E
Tilburg Neth. **16** 51.34N 5.05E
Tilbury Canada **104** 42.16N 82.26W
Tilbury U.K. **13** 51.28N 0.23E
Tilemsi, Vallée du *f.* Mali **76** 16.15N 0.02E
Tilghman U.S.A. **115** 38.42N 76.20W
Tilhar India **63** 27.59N 79.44E
Till *r.* Northum. U.K. **12** 55.41N 2.12W
Tillabéri Niger **77** 14.28N 1.27E
Tillamook U.S.A. **108** 45.27N 123.51W
Tillsonburg Canada **104** 42.51N 80.44W
Tílos *i.* Greece **35** 36.25N 27.25E
Tilpa Australia **92** 30.57S 144.24E
Tilton U.S.A. **115** 43.27N 71.35W
Timagami Canada **104** 47.05N 79.50W
Timanskiy Kryazh *mts.* U.S.S.R. **44** 66.00N 49.00E
Timaru New Zealand **86** 44.23S 171.41E
Timashevsk U.S.S.R. **45** 45.38N 38.56E
Timbákion Greece **35** 35.04N 24.45E
Timbédra Mauritania **74** 16.17N 8.16W
Timboon Australia **92** 38.32S 143.02E
Timbuktu *see* Tombouctou Mali **76**
Timfi Óros *mtn.* Greece **34** 39.59N 20.45E
Timimoun Algeria **74** 29.15N 0.15E
Timimoun, Sebkha de *f.* Algeria **74** 29.10N 0.05E
Timiris, Cap *c.* Mauritania **76** 19.23N 16.32W
Timiş *r.* Yugo. / Romania **37** 44.49N 20.28E
Timiskaming, L. Canada **104** 47.35N 79.35W
Timişoara Romania **37** 45.47N 21.15E
Timişul *r.* Yugo. **29** 44.49N 20.28E
Timmernabben Sweden **43** 56.58N 16.26E
Timmins Canada **102** 48.28N 81.25W
Timok *r.* Yugo. **34** 44.10N 22.40E
Timor *i.* Indonesia **88** 9.30S 125.00E
Timor Sea Austa. **88** 11.00S 127.00E
Timor Timur *d.* Indonesia **59** 9.00S 125.00E
Timpahute Range *mts.* U.S.A. **108** 37.38N 115.34W
Tinahely Rep. of Ire. **15** 52.48N 6.19W
Tindouf Algeria **74** 27.42N 8.09W
Tindouf, Sebkha de *f.* Algeria **74** 27.45N 7.30W
Tineo Spain **26** 43.20N 6.25W
Tingha Australia **93** 29.58S 151.16E
Tinglev Denmark **42** 54.56N 9.15E
Tingo María Peru **122** 9.09S 75.56W
Tingping China **55** 26.10N 110.17E
Tingréla Ivory Coast **76** 10.26N 6.20W
Tingri China **63** 28.30N 86.34E
Tingsryd Sweden **43** 56.32N 14.59E
Tingstäde Sweden **43** 57.44N 18.36E
Tinguipaya Bolivia **124** 19.11S 65.51W
Tinkisso *r.* Guinea **76** 11.25N 9.05W
Tinnenburra Australia **93** 28.40S 145.30E
Tinnoset Norway **42** 59.43N 9.02E
Tínos *i.* Greece **35** 37.38N 25.10E
Tínos *town* Greece **35** 37.32N 25.10E
Tinsukia India **61** 27.30N 95.22E
Tintinara Australia **92** 35.52S 140.04E
Tinto *r.* Spain **27** 37.10N 6.54W
Tioga U.S.A. **114** 41.55N 77.08W
Tioman, Pulau *i.* Malaysia **58** 2.45N 104.10E
Tionaga Canada **102** 48.05N 82.00W
Tione di Trento Italy **30** 46.02N 10.43E
Tionesta U.S.A. **114** 41.30N 79.27W
Tionesta Creek *r.* U.S.A. **114** 41.28N 79.22W
Tioughnioga *r.* U.S.A. **115** 42.14N 75.51W
Tipperary Rep. of Ire. **15** 52.29N 8.10W
Tipperary *d.* Rep. of Ire. **15** 52.37N 7.55W
Tirān, Jazīrat Saudi Arabia **66** 27.56N 34.34E
Tiranë Albania **34** 41.20N 19.50E
Tiranë Durrës *d.* Albania **34** 41.19N 19.26E
Tirano Italy **30** 46.13N 10.11E
Tiraspol U.S.S.R. **37** 46.50N 29.38E
Tirat Karmel Israel **67** 32.46N 34.58E
Tirat Yehuda Israel **67** 32.01N 34.57E
Tirat Zevi Israel **67** 32.25N 35.32E
Tirebolu Turkey **64** 41.02N 38.49E
Tiree *i.* U.K. **14** 56.30N 6.50W
Tîrgovişte Romania **37** 44.56N 25.27E
Tîrgu-Jiu Romania **37** 45.03N 23.17E
Tîrgu-Lăpuş Romania **37** 47.27N 23.52E
Tîrgu Mureş Romania **37** 46.33N 24.34E
Tîrgu-Neamţ Romania **37** 47.12N 26.22E
Tîrgu-Ocna Romania **37** 46.15N 26.37E
Tîrgu-Secuiesc Romania **37** 46.00N 26.08E
Tirins *site* Greece **35** 37.36N 22.48E
Tiris Zemmour *d.* Mauritania **74** 24.00N 9.00W
Tírnavos Greece **34** 39.45N 22.17E
Tirodi India **63** 21.41N 79.42E
Tirol *d.* Austria **39** 47.10N 11.00E
Tirón *r.* Spain **26** 41.23N 4.31W
Tir Pol Afghan. **65** 34.38N 61.19E
Tirschenreuth W. Germany **39** 49.53N 12.21E
Tirso *r.* Italy **32** 39.52N 8.33E
Tiruchchirāppalli India **61** 10.50N 78.43E
Tirunelveli India **60** 8.45N 77.43E
Tirupati India **61** 13.39N 79.25E
Tiruppur India **60** 11.05N 77.20E
Tisa *r.* Yugo. **31** 45.09N 20.16E
Tis'ah Egypt **66** 30.02N 32.35E
Tisdale Canada **101** 52.51N 104.04W
Tisnaren *l.* Sweden **43** 58.57N 15.57E
Tisza *r.* *see* Tisa Hungary **31**
Tit Algeria **75** 22.58N 5.11E
Titel Yugo. **31** 45.12N 20.18E
Titicaca, L. Bolivia / Peru **124** 16.00S 69.00W
Titikaveka Rarotonga Cook Is. **84** 21.16S 159.45W
Titiwa Nigeria **77** 12.14N 12.53E
Titlagarh India **63** 20.18N 83.09E
Titograd Yugo. **31** 42.26N 19.14E
Titova Korenica Yugo. **31** 44.45N 15.43E
Titovo Užice Yugo. **31** 43.51N 19.51E
Titov Veles Yugo. **34** 41.46N 21.47E
Titov Vrh *mtn.* Yugo. **34** 42.00N 20.51E
Titran Norway **40** 63.42N 8.22E
Tittabawassee *r.* U.S.A. **104** 43.23N 83.59W
Tittmoning W. Germany **39** 48.04N 12.46E
Titule Zaïre **78** 3.17N 25.32E
Titusville Fla. U.S.A. **113** 28.37N 80.50W
Titusville Penn. U.S.A. **114** 41.38N 79.41W
Tiuni India **63** 30.57N 77.51E
Tivaouane Senegal **76** 14.57N 16.49W
Tiveden *hills* Sweden **43** 58.45N 14.40E
Tiverton U.K. **13** 50.54N 3.30W
Tiverton U.S.A. **115** 41.38N 71.12W
Tivoli Italy **32** 41.58N 12.48E
Tiyo Ethiopia **72** 14.40N 40.15E
Tizimín Mexico **117** 21.10N 88.09W
Tizi Ouzou Algeria **75** 36.44N 4.05E
Tiznit Morocco **74** 29.43N 9.44W
Tjeuke Meer *l.* Neth. **16** 52.55N 5.51E
Tjöme *i.* Norway **42** 59.07N 10.24E
Tjörn *i.* Sweden **42** 58.00N 11.38E
Tlaxcala *d.* Mexico **116** 19.45N 98.20W
Tlemcen Algeria **74** 34.52N 1.19W
Tmassah Libya **75** 26.22N 15.48E
Tni Haïa *well* Algeria **74** 24.15N 2.45W
Toab U.K. **14** 59.53N 1.16W
Toamasina Madagascar **81** 18.10S 49.23E
Toano Italy **30** 44.23N 10.34E
Toanoano Tahiti **85** 17.52S 149.12W
Toba Japan **57** 34.29N 136.51E
Toba, Danau *l.* Indonesia **58** 2.45S 98.50E
Toba Kākar Range *mts.* Pakistan **62** 31.15N 68.00E
Tobar U.S.A. **108** 40.53N 114.54W
Tobarra Spain **25** 38.35N 1.41W
Toba Tek Singh Pakistan **62** 30.58N 72.29E
Tobelo Indonesia **59** 1.45N 127.59E
Tobermory Canada **104** 45.15N 81.39W
Tobermory U.K. **14** 56.37N 6.04W
Tobi *i.* Caroline Is. **59** 3.01N 131.10E
Tobin L. Canada **101** 53.40N 103.35W
Tobi shima *i.* Japan **57** 39.12N 139.32E
Toboali Indonesia **58** 3.00S 106.30E
Tobol *r.* U.S.S.R. **9** 58.15N 68.12E
Tobolsk U.S.S.R. **9** 58.15N 68.12E
Tobruk *see* Ţubruq Libya **72**
Tobseda U.S.S.R. **44** 68.34N 52.16E
Tocantinópolis Brazil **123** 6.20S 47.25W
Tocantins *r.* Brazil **123** 1.50S 49.15W
Toccoa U.S.A. **113** 34.34N 83.21W
Töcksfors Sweden **42** 59.30N 11.50E
Tocopilla Chile **124** 22.05S 70.12W
Tocorpuri *mtn.* Bolivia / Chile **124** 22.26S 67.53W
Tocumwal Australia **93** 35.51S 145.34E
Tocuyo *r.* Venezuela **122** 11.03N 68.23W
Todenyang Kenya **79** 4.34N 35.52E
Todi Italy **30** 42.47N 12.24E
Todos Santos Mexico **109** 23.27N 110.13W
Todtnau W. Germany **39** 47.50N 7.56E
Tofte Norway **42** 59.33N 10.34E
Tofua *i.* Tonga **85** 19.45S 175.05W
Togian, Kepulauan *is.* Indonesia **59** 0.20S 122.00E
Togo Africa **76** 8.00N 1.00E
Tohen Somali Rep. **71** 11.42N 51.17E
Tōhuku *d.* Japan **57** 35.00N 137.00E
Toi Niue **84** 18.58S 169.52W
Toijala Finland **41** 61.10N 23.52E
Tojg Afghan. **62** 32.04N 61.48E
Tokaj Hungary **37** 48.08N 21.27E
Tokala *mtn.* Indonesia **59** 1.36S 121.41E
Tokara kaikyō *str.* Japan **57** 30.10N 130.10E
Tokat Turkey **64** 40.20N 36.35E
Tokelau Is. Pacific Oc. **84** 9.00S 171.45W
Toki Japan **57** 35.21N 137.11E
Toki *r.* Japan **57** 35.12N 136.52E
Tokmak U.S.S.R. **52** 42.49N 75.15E
Tokoname Japan **57** 34.53N 136.51E
Tokoroa New Zealand **86** 38.13S 175.53E
Tokuno shima *i.* Japan **53** 27.40N 129.00E
Tokushima Japan **57** 34.03N 134.34E
Tokuyama Japan **57** 34.04N 131.48E
Tōkyō Japan **57** 35.42N 139.46E
Tōkyō-wan *b.* Japan **57** 35.25N 139.45E
Tolaga Bay *town* New Zealand **86** 38.22S 178.18E
Tolbukhin Bulgaria **29** 43.34N 27.52E
Toledo Spain **27** 39.52N 4.01W

Toledo to Trumansburg

Toledo d. Spain 27 39.45N 4.10W
Toledo U.S.A. 112 41.40N 83.35W
Toledo, Montes de mts. Spain 27 39.33N 4.20W
Toledo Bend Resr. U.S.A. 111 31.46N 93.25W
Tolentino Italy 30 43.12N 13.17E
Toliary Madagascar 81 23.21S 43.40E
Tolland U.S.A. 115 41.52N 72.22W
Tollarp Sweden 43 55.56N 13.59E
Tollense r. E. Germany 38 53.54N 13.02E
Tolmezzo Italy 30 46.24N 13.01E
Tolmin Yugo. 31 46.11N 13.44E
Tolna Hungary 31 46.26N 18.46E
Tolna d. Hungary 31 46.35N 18.30E
Tolo, Teluk g. Indonesia 59 2.00S122.30E
Tolosa Spain 26 43.08N 2.04W
Tolstyy-Les U.S.S.R. 37 51.24N 29.48E
Tolti Jammu & Kashmir 62 35.02N 76.06E
Toluca Mexico 116 19.20N 99.40W
Toluca mtn. Mexico 116 19.10N 99.40W
Tol'yatti U.S.S.R. 44 53.32N 49.24E
Tomah U.S.A. 110 43.59N 90.30W
Tomakomai Japan 57 42.39N141.33E
Tomar Portugal 27 39.36N 8.25W
Tomás Gomensoro Uruguay 125 30.26S 57.26W
Tomaszów Lubelski Poland 37 50.28N 23.25E
Tomaszów Mazowiecki Poland 37 51.32N 20.01E
Tombe Sudan 73 5.49N 31.41E
Tombigbee r. U.S.A. 111 31.04N 87.58W
Tombos Brazil 126 20.53S 42.03W
Tombouctou Mali 76 16.49N 2.59W
Tomé Chile 125 36.37S 72.57W
Tomelilla Sweden 43 55.33N 13.57E
Tomelloso Spain 27 39.10N 3.01W
Tomiko Canada 104 46.32N 79.49W
Tomingley Australia 93 32.06S148.15E
Tomini Indonesia 59 0.31N120.30E
Tomini, Teluk g. Indonesia 59 0.30S120.45E
Tominian Mali 76 13.17N 4.35W
Tomintoul U.K. 14 57.15N 3.24W
Tomkinson Ranges mts. Australia 88 26.11S129.05E
Tom Price Australia 88 22.49S117.51E
Tomra China 63 30.52N 87.30E
Tomra Norway 40 62.34N 6.55E
Tomsk U.S.S.R. 50 56.30N 85.05E
Toms River town U.S.A. 115 39.57N 74.07W
Tomtabacken hill Sweden 43 57.30N 14.28E
Tonalá Mexico 116 16.08N 93.41W
Tonalea U.S.A. 109 36.20N110.58W
Tonasket U.S.A. 108 48.42N119.26W
Tonawanda U.S.A. 114 43.01N 78.53W
Tonbridge U.K. 13 51.12N 0.16E
Tondano Indonesia 59 1.19N124.56E
Tönder Denmark 42 54.56N 8.54E
Tondibi Mali 76 16.39N 0.14W
Tondoro Namibia 80 17.45S 18.50E
Tone r. Japan 57 35.44N140.51E
Tonekābon Iran 65 36.49N 50.54E
Tonga Pacific Oc. 85 20.00S175.00W
Tonga Sudan 73 9.28N 31.03E
Tongaat R.S.A. 80 29.34S 31.07E
Tong'an China 55 24.44N118.09E
Tongatapu i. Tonga 85 21.10S175.10W
Tongatapu Group is. Tonga 85 21.10S175.10W
Tonga Trench f. Pacific Oc. 84 20.00S173.00W
Tongchuan China 54 35.05N109.10E
Tongeren Belgium 16 50.47N 5.28E
Tongguan Hunan China 55 28.27N112.48E
Tongguan Shaanxi China 54 34.32N110.26E
Tonghai China 61 24.07N102.45E
Tonghua China 53 41.40N126.52E
Tongking, G. of China / Vietnam 56 20.00N108.00E
Tongliao China 54 43.40N122.20E
Tongling China 55 30.55N117.42E
Tonglu China 55 29.49N119.40E
Tongnae S. Korea 57 35.12N129.05E
Tongo Australia 92 30.30S143.47E
Tongoa i. Vanuatu 84 16.54S168.34E
Tongobory Madagascar 81 23.32S 44.20E
Tongoy Chile 124 30.15S 71.30W
Tongren China 55 27.41N109.08E
Tongsa Dzong Bhutan 63 27.31N 90.30E
Tongtianheyan China 63 33.50N 92.19E
Tongue U.K. 14 58.28N 4.25W
Tongue r. U.S.A. 108 46.24N105.25W
Tongwei China 54 35.18N105.10E
Tong Xian China 54 39.52N116.45E
Tongxin China 54 36.59N105.50E
Tongyu China 54 44.48N123.06E
Tongzi China 55 28.08N106.49E
Tonj Sudan 73 7.17N 28.45E
Tonk India 62 26.10N 75.47E
Tônlé Sap l. Kampuchea 56 12.50N104.15E
Tonnay-Boutonne France 20 45.58N 0.42W
Tonneins France 20 44.23N 0.19E
Tonnerre France 19 47.51N 3.58E
Tönning W. Germany 38 54.19N 8.56E
Tonopah U.S.A. 108 38.04N117.14W
Tonota Botswana 80 21.28S 27.24E
Tons r. India 63 25.17N 82.04E
Tönsberg Norway 42 59.17N 10.25E
Tonstad Norway 42 58.40N 6.43E
Tonto Basin town U.S.A. 109 33.55N111.18W
Toobeah Australia 93 28.22S149.50E
Toodyay Australia 89 31.35S116.26E
Tooele U.S.A. 108 40.32N112.18W
Tooligie Australia 92 33.51S135.41E
Toolondo Australia 92 36.55S142.00E
Toowoomba Australia 91 27.35S151.54E
Topeka U.S.A. 110 39.03N 95.41W
Topko mtn. U.S.S.R. 51 57.20N138.10E
Topley Canada 100 54.32N126.05W
Toplica r. Yugo. 34 43.15N 21.30E
Topliţa Romania 37 46.55N 25.21E
Topock U.S.A. 109 34.44N114.27W
Topolovgrad Bulgaria 34 42.05N 26.20E
Topozero, Ozero l. U.S.S.R. 44 65.45N 32.00E
Toppenish U.S.A. 108 46.23N120.19W
Tora-Khem U.S.S.R. 51 52.31N 96.13E
Tor B. Australia 89 35.00S117.40E
Torbat-e Ḩeydarīyeh Iran 65 35.16N 59.13E
Torbat-e Jām Iran 65 35.15N 60.37E
Torbay town U.K. 13 50.27N 3.31W
Tördal Norway 42 59.16N 8.49E
Tordera r. Spain 25 41.39N 2.47E
Tordesillas Spain 26 41.30N 5.00W
Tordino Italy 31 42.44N 13.59E
Töre Sweden 40 65.54N 22.39E
Töreboda Sweden 43 58.43N 14.08E
Torekov Sweden 43 56.26N 12.37E
Toreno Spain 26 42.42N 6.30W
Torgau E. Germany 38 51.34N 13.00E
Torhamn Sweden 43 56.05N 15.50E
Torhout Belgium 16 51.04N 3.06E
Tori Ethiopia 73 7.53N 33.40E
Toride Japan 57 35.53N140.04E
Torington Australia 93 29.20S151.40E
Torino Italy 30 45.03N 7.40E
Torio r. Spain 26 42.35N 5.34W
Torit Sudan 73 4.24N 32.34E
Tormes r. Spain 26 41.18N 6.29W
Torne r. Sweden 8 67.13N 23.30E
Torne r. see Tornio Sweden 40
Torneträsk Sweden 40 68.15N 19.30E
Torneträsk l. Sweden 40 68.20N 19.10E
Tornio Finland 40 65.52N 24.10E
Tornio r. Finland 40 65.53N 24.07E
Tornquist Argentina 125 38.06S 62.14W
Toro Spain 26 41.31N 5.24W
Toronaíos Kólpos g. Greece 34 40.05N 23.30E
Toronto Canada 104 43.39N 79.23W
Toropets U.S.S.R. 44 56.30N 31.40E
Tororo Uganda 79 0.42N 34.13E
Toros Daglari mts. Turkey 64 37.15N 34.15E
Torquemada Spain 26 42.02N 4.19W
Torrance U.S.A. 109 33.50N118.19W
Torrão Portugal 27 38.18N 8.13W
Torre Annunziata Italy 33 40.45N 14.27E
Torre Baja Spain 25 40.07N 1.15W
Torreblanca Spain 25 40.13N 0.12E
Torrecilla mtn. Spain 27 36.41N 4.59W
Torrecilla en Cameros Spain 26 42.16N 2.37W
Torre del Campo Spain 27 37.46N 3.53W
Torre de Moncorvo Portugal 26 41.10N 7.03W
Torredonjimeno Spain 27 37.46N 3.57W
Torrejón, Embalse de resr. Spain 27 39.50N 5.50W
Torrejoncillo Spain 27 39.54N 6.28W
Torrejón de Ardoz Spain 26 40.27N 3.29W
Torrelaguna Spain 26 40.50N 3.32W
Torrelavega Spain 26 43.21N 4.03W
Torremaggiore Italy 33 41.41N 15.17E
Torremolinos Spain 27 36.37N 4.30W
Torrens r. Australia 90 22.22S145.09E
Torrens, L. Australia 92 31.00S137.50E
Torrens Creek town Australia 90 20.50S145.00E
Torrente Spain 25 39.26N 0.28W
Torreón Mexico 111 25.33N103.26W
Torre Pellice Italy 30 44.49N 7.13E
Torreperogil Spain 26 38.02N 3.17W
Torres Novas Portugal 27 39.29N 8.32W
Torres Str. Australia 90 10.30S142.20E
Torres Vedras Portugal 27 39.06N 9.16W
Torrevieja Spain 25 37.59N 0.41W
Torrey U.S.A. 108 38.18N111.25W
Torridge r. U.K. 13 51.01N 4.12W
Torridon U.K. 14 57.23N 5.31W
Torridon, Loch U.K. 14 57.35N 5.45W
Torriglia Italy 30 44.31N 9.10E
Torrijos Spain 27 39.59N 4.17W
Torrington Conn. U.S.A. 115 41.48N 73.08W
Torrington Wyo. U.S.A. 108 42.04N104.11W
Torrox Spain 27 36.46N 3.58W
Torsås Sweden 43 56.24N 16.00E
Torsby Sweden 43 60.08N 13.00E
Torsö i. Sweden 43 58.48N 13.50E
Tortola i. B.V.Is. 117 18.28N 64.40W
Tortoli Italy 32 39.55N 9.39E
Tortona Italy 30 44.54N 8.52E
Tortorici Italy 33 38.02N 14.39E
Tortosa Spain 25 40.48N 0.31E
Tortosa, Cabo de c. Spain 25 40.43N 0.55E
Tortue, Île de la i. Cuba 117 20.05N 72.57W
Toruń Poland 37 53.01N 18.35E
Torup Sweden 43 56.58N 13.05E
Tory Hill town Canada 104 44.58N 78.18W
Tory I. Rep. of Ire. 15 55.16N 8.13W
Tory Sd. Rep. of Ire. 15 55.14N 8.15W
Torzhok U.S.S.R. 44 57.02N 34.51E
Tosas, Puerto de pass Spain 25 42.19N 2.01E
Tosa wan b. Japan 57 33.10N133.40E
Toscana d. Italy 30 43.35N 11.00E
Tosen Norway 40 65.16N 12.50E
Tosno U.S.S.R. 44 59.38N 30.46E
Tostado Argentina 124 29.15S 61.45W
Totak l. Norway 42 59.42N 7.57E
Totana Spain 25 37.46N 1.30W
Tôtes France 18 49.41N 1.03E
Totma U.S.S.R. 44 59.59N 42.44E
Totora Bolivia 124 17.42S 65.09W
Tottenham Australia 93 32.14S147.24E
Tottenham Canada 104 44.01N 79.49W
Tottori Japan 57 35.32N134.12E
Touba Ivory Coast 76 8.22N 7.42W
Toubkal mtn. Morocco 74 31.03N 7.57W
Toucy France 19 47.44N 3.18E
Tougan U. Volta 76 13.05N 3.04W
Touggourt Algeria 75 33.06N 6.04E
Tougué Guinea 76 11.25N 11.50W
Toul France 19 48.41N 5.54E
Toulnustouc r. Canada 103 49.35N 68.25W
Toulon France 21 43.07N 5.56E
Toulon-sur-Arroux France 19 46.42N 4.08E
Toulouse France 20 43.36N 1.26E
Toummo Niger 75 22.45N 14.08E
Tounassine, Hamada des. Algeria 74 28.36N 5.00W
Toungoo Burma 56 18.57N 96.26E
Touques r. France 18 49.22N 0.06E
Tourassine well Mauritania 74 24.40N 11.20W
Tourcoing France 19 50.43N 3.09E
Tourinan, Cabo c. Spain 26 43.03N 9.18W
Tournai Belgium 16 50.36N 3.23E
Tournon France 21 45.04N 4.50E
Tournus France 19 46.34N 4.54E
Tours France 18 47.23N 0.41E
Toury France 19 48.12N 1.56E
Toustain Algeria 32 36.40N 8.15E
Touwsrivier town R.S.A. 80 33.20S 20.02E
Toužim Czech. 39 50.04N 13.00E
Tovdals r. Norway 42 58.13N 8.08E
Towada ko l. Japan 57 40.28N140.55E
Towamba Australia 93 37.09S149.43E
Towanda U.S.A. 115 41.46N 76.27W
Towcester U.K. 13 52.07N 0.56W
Tower U.S.A. 110 47.47N 92.19W
Towerhill r. Australia 90 22.29S144.39E
Towner U.S.A. 110 48.21N100.25W
Townsend, Mt. Australia 93 36.24S148.15E
Townshend, C. Australia 90 22.10S150.30E
Townshend I. Australia 90 22.15S150.30E
Townsville Australia 90 19.13S146.48E
Towrzī Afghan. 62 30.11N 65.59E
Towson U.S.A. 115 39.24N 76.36W
Towyn U.K. 13 52.37N 4.08W
Toyah U.S.A. 111 31.19N103.47W
Toyama Japan 57 36.42N137.14E
Toyama wan b. Japan 57 36.50N137.10E
Toyo r. Japan 57 34.47N137.20E
Toyohashi Japan 57 34.46N137.23E
Toyokawa Japan 57 34.49N137.24E
Toyota Japan 57 35.05N137.09E
Tozeur Tunisia 75 33.55N 8.08E
Traben-Trarbach W. Germany 39 49.57N 7.06E
Trabzon Turkey 64 41.00N 39.43E
Tracadie Canada 103 47.31N 64.54W
Tracy Canada 105 46.01N 73.09W
Tracy U.S.A. 110 44.14N 95.37W
Trade Town Liberia 76 5.43N 9.56W
Trafalgar, Cabo c. Spain 27 36.11N 6.02W
Tragacete Spain 25 40.21N 1.51W
Traid Spain 25 40.40N 1.49W
Traiguén Chile 125 38.15S 72.41W
Trail Canada 100 49.05N117.40W
Trajanova Vrata pass Bulgaria 34 42.18N 23.58E
Trakt U.S.S.R. 44 62.40N 51.26E
Tralee Rep. of Ire. 15 52.16N 9.42W
Tralee B. Rep. of Ire. 15 52.18N 9.55W
Tranås Sweden 43 58.03N 14.59E
Tranco, Embalse del resr. Spain 26 38.10N 2.45W
Trancoso Portugal 26 40.47N 7.21W
Tranebjerg Denmark 42 50.50N 10.36E
Trang Thailand 56 7.35N 99.35E
Trangan i. Indonesia 59 6.30S134.15E
Trangie Australia 93 32.03S148.01E
Trani Italy 33 41.17N 16.26E
Tranoroa Madagascar 81 24.42S 45.04E
Tranqueras Uruguay 125 31.12S 55.45W
Transkei f. R.S.A. 80 32.12S 28.20E
Transvaal d. R.S.A. 80 24.30S 29.30E
Transylvanian Alps see Carpaţii Meridionalimts. Romania 29
Trapani Italy 32 38.01N 12.31E
Traralgon Australia 93 38.12S146.32E
Traryd Sweden 43 56.35N 13.45E
Trarza d. Mauritania 74 18.00N 14.50W
Trarza f. Mauritania 74 18.00N 15.00W
Trasacco Italy 31 41.57N 13.32E
Trasimeno, Lago l. Italy 30 43.08N 12.06E
Träslövsläge Sweden 43 57.04N 12.16E
Trat Thailand 56 12.14N102.33E
Traun Austria 39 48.13N 14.14E
Traunsee l. Austria 39 47.51N 13.48E
Traunstein W. Germany 39 47.52N 12.38E
Trave r. W. Germany 38 53.54N 10.50E
Travellers L. Australia 92 33.18S142.00E
Travers, Mt. New Zealand 86 42.05S172.45E
Traverse City U.S.A. 112 44.46N 85.38W
Travnik Yugo. 31 44.14N 17.40E
Trayning Australia 89 31.09S117.46E
Trbovlje Yugo. 31 46.10N 15.03E
Trebbia r. Italy 30 45.04N 9.41E
Trebel r. E. Germany 38 53.55N 13.01E
Třebíč Czech. 36 49.13N 15.55E
Trebinje Yugo. 31 42.43N 18.20E
Trebisacce Italy 33 39.52N 16.32E
Trebišov Czech. 37 48.40N 21.47E
Třeboň Czech. 36 49.01N 14.50E
Trecate Italy 30 45.26N 8.44E
Tredegar U.K. 13 51.47N 3.16W
Treene r. W. Germany 38 54.22N 9.05E
Tregaron U.K. 13 52.14N 3.56W
Tregosse Islets and Reefs Australia 90 17.41S150.43E
Tréguier France 18 48.47N 3.14W
Treinta-y-Tres Uruguay 126 33.16S 54.17W
Treis W. Germany 39 50.10N 7.17E
Trélazé France 18 47.27N 0.28W
Trelew Argentina 125 43.15S 65.20W
Trelleborg Sweden 43 55.22N 13.10E
Trélon France 19 50.04N 4.06E
Tremadog B. U.K. 12 52.52N 4.14W
Tremblant, Mont Canada 105 46.16N 74.35W
Tremont U.S.A. 115 40.38N 76.23W
Tremp Spain 25 42.10N 0.54E
Trena Ethiopia 73 10.45N 40.38E
Trenčín Czech. 37 48.54N 18.04E
Trenggalek Indonesia 59 8.01S111.38E
Trenque Lauquen Argentina 125 35.56S 62.43W
Trent r. Canada 105 44.06N 77.34W
Trent r. U.K. 12 53.41N 0.41W
Trente-et un Milles, Lac des l. Canada 105 46.12N 75.49W
Trentino-Alto Adige d. Italy 30 46.35N 11.20E
Trento Italy 30 46.04N 11.08E
Trenton Canada 105 44.06N 77.35W
Trenton Mich. U.S.A. 104 42.09N 83.11W
Trenton Mo. U.S.A. 110 40.05N 93.37W
Trenton Nebr. U.S.A. 110 40.11N101.01W
Trenton N.J. U.S.A. 115 40.13N 74.45W
Trepassey Canada 99 46.44N 53.22W
Trepuzzi Italy 33 40.24N 18.05E
Tres Árboles Uruguay 125 32.24S 56.43W
Tres Arroyos Argentina 125 38.26S 60.17W
Três Corações Brazil 126 21.44S 45.15W
Três Lagoas Brazil 126 20.46S 51.43W
Três Marias, Reprêsa resr. Brazil 126 18.15S 45.15W
Três Pontas Brazil 126 21.23S 45.29W
Três Rios Brazil 126 22.07S 43.12W
Treuchtlingen W. Germany 39 48.57N 10.54E
Treuenbrietzen E. Germany 38 52.06N 12.52E
Treviglio Italy 30 45.31N 9.35E
Treviño Spain 26 42.44N 2.45W
Treviso Italy 32 45.40N 12.15E
Trévoux France 21 45.56N 4.46E
Trgovište Yugo. 34 42.21N 22.05E
Triánda Greece 35 36.25N 28.10E
Triberg W. Germany 39 48.08N 8.13E
Tribsees E. Germany 38 54.05N 12.45E
Tribulation, C. Australia 90 16.03S145.30E
Tribune U.S.A. 110 38.28N101.45W
Tricarico Italy 33 40.37N 16.09E
Tricase Italy 33 39.56N 18.22E
Trida Australia 93 33.00S145.01E
Trier W. Germany 39 49.45N 6.38E
Trieste Italy 31 45.40N 13.46E
Trieux r. France 18 48.47N 3.07W
Triglav mtn. Yugo. 31 46.23N 13.50E
Trigno r. Italy 33 42.04N 14.48E
Trigueros Spain 27 37.23N 6.50W
Trikala Greece 34 39.34N 21.46E
Trikhonis, Limni l. Greece 35 38.34N 21.28E
Trikomon Cyprus 66 35.17N 33.53E
Triman Pakistan 62 29.38N 69.05E
Trincomalee Sri Lanka 61 8.34N 81.13E
Trinidad Bolivia 124 14.47S 64.47W
Trinidad Colombia 122 5.25N 71.40W
Trinidad Cuba 117 21.48N 80.00W
Trinidad Uruguay 125 33.32S 56.54W
Trinidad U.S.A. 108 37.10N104.31W
Trinidad & Tobago S. America 117 10.30N 61.20W
Trinity r. U.S.A. 111 29.55N 94.45W
Trinity B. Australia 90 16.56S145.50E
Trinity B. Canada 103 48.00N 53.40W
Trinity Range mts. U.S.A. 108 40.13N119.12W
Trinkitat Sudan 72 18.41N 37.43E
Trino Italy 30 45.12N 8.18E
Tripoli see Ţarābulus Lebanon 66
Tripoli see Ţarābulus Libya 75
Tripolis Greece 35 37.31N 22.21E
Tripolitania f. see Ţarābulus Libya 75
Tripp U.S.A. 110 43.13N 97.58W
Tripura d. India 63 23.50N 92.00E
Tristan da Cunha i. Atlantic Oc. 127 37.50S 12.30W
Triste Spain 25 42.23N 0.43W
Trivandrum India 60 8.41N 76.57E
Trivento Italy 33 41.47N 14.33E
Trnava Czech. 37 48.23N 17.35E
Troarn France 18 49.11N 0.11W
Trobriand Is. P.N.G. 90 8.35S151.05E
Trogir Yugo. 31 43.31N 16.15E
Troglav mtn. Yugo. 31 43.57N 16.36E
Troia Italy 33 41.22N 15.18E
Troina Italy 33 37.47N 14.37E
Troisdorf W. Germany 38 50.49N 7.08E
Trois Rivières town Canada 105 46.21N 72.33W
Troitsk U.S.S.R. 9 54.08N 61.33E
Troitsko-Pechorsk U.S.S.R. 44 62.40N 56.08E
Troitskoye R.S.F.S.R. U.S.S.R. 44 52.18N 56.26E
Troitskoye UKr.S.S.R. U.S.S.R. 37 47.38N 30.19E
Trölladyngja mtn. Iceland 40 64.54N 17.16W
Trollhättan Sweden 43 58.16N 12.18E
Trollheimen mts. Norway 40 62.50N 9.15E
Tromelin i. Indian Oc. 49 15.52S 54.25E
Troms d. Norway 40 69.20N 19.30E
Tromsö Norway 40 69.42N 19.00E
Trondheim Norway 40 63.36N 10.23E
Trondheimsfjorden est. Norway 40 63.40N 10.30E
Troödos mts. Cyprus 66 34.57N 32.50E
Troon U.K. 14 55.33N 4.40W
Tropea Italy 33 38.41N 15.54E
Tropic U.S.A. 108 37.37N112.05W
Tropoja Albania 34 42.23N 20.10E
Trosa Sweden 43 58.54N 17.33E
Trosh U.S.S.R. 44 66.24N 56.08E
Trostan mtn. N. Ireland 15 55.03N 6.10W
Trostyanets U.S.S.R. 37 48.35N 29.10E
Trout r. Canada 100 61.19N119.51W
Trout Creek town Canada 104 45.59N 79.22W
Trout L. N.W.T. Canada 100 60.35N121.10W
Trout L. Ont. Canada 102 51.13N 93.20W
Trout River town Canada 103 49.29N 58.08W
Trout Run U.S.A. 114 41.23N 77.03W
Trouville France 18 49.22N 0.05E
Trowbridge U.K. 13 51.18N 2.12W
Troy site Turkey 34 39.57N 26.15E
Troy Ala. U.S.A. 113 31.49N 86.00W
Troy Mo. U.S.A. 110 38.59N 90.59W
Troy Mont. U.S.A. 108 48.28N115.53W
Troy N.H. U.S.A. 115 42.50N 72.11W
Troy N.Y. U.S.A. 115 42.43N 73.40W
Troy Ohio U.S.A. 112 40.02N 84.12W
Troy Penn. U.S.A. 114 41.47N 76.47W
Troyan Bulgaria 34 42.51N 24.43E
Troyes France 19 48.18N 4.05E
Troy Peak mtn. U.S.A. 108 38.19N115.30W
Trpanj Yugo. 31 43.00N 17.17E
Trstenik Yugo. 34 43.37N 21.00E
Truchas Peak mtn. U.S.A. 109 35.58N105.39W
Truckee U.S.A. 108 39.20N120.11W
Trujillo Honduras 117 15.55N 86.00W
Trujillo Peru 122 8.06S 79.00W
Trujillo Spain 27 39.28N 5.53W
Trujillo Venezuela 122 9.20N 70.37W
Trumansburg U.S.A. 105 42.33N 76.40W

Trumansburg to Umm el Faḩm

Trumansburg U.S.A. 115 42.33N 76.40W
Trûn Bulgaria 34 42.51N 22.38E
Trundle Australia 93 32.54S147.35E
Trung-Luong Vietnam 56 13.55N109.15E
Trunmore B. Canada 103 53.48N 57.10W
Truro Australia 92 34.23S139.09E
Truro Canada 103 45.22N 63.16W
Truro U.K. 13 50.17N 5.02W
Truslove Australia 89 33.19S121.40E
Trûstenik Bulgaria 34 43.31N 24.28E
Trustrup Denmark 42 56.21N 10.47E
Trust Territory of the Pacific Is. Pacific Oc. 84 10.00N155.00E
Truth or Consequences U.S.A. 109 33.08N107.15W
Truyère r. France 20 44.39N 2.34E
Tryavna Bulgaria 34 42.54N 25.25E
Trysil Norway 41 61.19N 12.16E
Trysil r. Norway 41 61.03N 12.30E
Trzemeszno Poland 37 52.35N 17.50E
Tržič Yugo. 31 46.22N 14.19E
Tsamandás Greece 34 39.46N 20.21E
Tsaratanana Madagascar 81 16.47S 47.39E
Tsaratanana, Massif de mts. Madagascar 81 14.00S 49.00E
Tsaritsáni Greece 34 39.53N 22.14E
Tsau Botswana 80 20.10S 22.29E
Tsavo Nat. Park Kenya 79 2.45S 38.45E
Tselinograd U.S.S.R. 9 51.10N 71.28E
Tsenovo Bulgaria 34 43.32N 25.39E
Tses Namibia 80 25.58S 18.08E
Tsévié Togo 77 6.28N 1.15E
Tshabong Botswana 80 26.03S 22.25E
Tshane Botswana 80 24.02S 21.54E
Tshela Zaïre 78 4.57S 12.57E
Tshesebe Botswana 80 20.45S 27.31E
Tshikapa Zaïre 78 6.28S 20.48E
Tshofa Zaïre 78 5.13S 25.20E
Tshopo r. Zaïre 78 0.30N 25.07E
Tshuapa r. Zaïre 78 0.14S 20.45E
Tsihombé Madagascar 81 25.18S 45.29E
Tsimlyansk U.S.S.R. 45 47.40N 42.06E
Tsimlyanskoye Vodokhranilishche resr. U.S.S.R. 45 48.00N 43.00E
Tsinan see Jinan China 54
Tsinga mtn. Greece 34 41.23N 24.44E
Tsingtao see Qingdao China 54
Tsiribihina Madagascar 81 19.42S 44.31E
Tsiroanomandidy Madagascar 81 18.46S 46.02E
Tsivilsk U.S.S.R. 44 55.50N 47.28E
Tsivory Madagascar 81 24.04S 46.05E
Tskhinvali U.S.S.R. 45 42.14N 43.58E
Tsna r. U.S.S.R. 37 52.10N 27.03E
Tsna r. R.S.F.S.R. U.S.S.R. 44 54.45N 41.54E
Tsobis Namibia 80 19.27S 17.30E
Tso Moriri l. Jammu & Kashmir 63 32.54N 78.20E
Tsu Japan 57 34.43N136.31E
Tsuchiura Japan 57 36.05N140.12E
Tsudakhar U.S.S.R. 45 42.20N 47.11E
Tsugaru kaikyō str. Japan 57 41.30N140.50E
Tsumeb Namibia 80 19.12S 17.43E
Tsuru Japan 57 35.30N138.56E
Tsuruga Japan 57 35.40N136.05E
Tsuruoka Japan 57 38.44N139.50E
Tsushima Japan 57 35.10N136.43E
Tsushima i. Japan 57 34.30N129.20E
Tsuyama Japan 57 35.04N134.01E
Tua r. Portugal 26 41.13N 7.26W
Tuam Rep. of Ire. 15 53.32N 8.52W
Tuamotu, Îles is. Pacific Oc. 85 17.00S142.00W
Tuapa Niue 84 18.59S169.54W
Tuapse U.S.S.R. 45 44.06N 39.05E
Tuatapere New Zealand 86 46.08S167.41E
Tubac U.S.A. 109 31.37N111.03W
Tuba City U.S.A. 109 36.08N111.14W
Tuban Indonesia 59 6.55S112.01E
Tubarão Brazil 126 28.30S 49.01W
Ţūbās Jordan 67 32.19N 35.22E
Ţubayq, Jabal aţ mts. Saudi Arabia 66 29.30N 37.15E
Tubbercurry Rep. of Ire. 15 54.03N 8.45W
Tübingen W. Germany 39 48.31N 9.02E
Ţubjah, Wādī r. Saudi Arabia 64 25.35N 38.22E
Ţubruq Libya 72 32.06N 23.58E
Tubuai i. Pacific Oc. 85 23.23S149.27W
Tubuai Is. Pacific Oc. 85 23.00S150.00W
Tucacas Venezuela 122 10.48N 68.19W
Tuchola Poland 37 53.35N 17.50E
Tuckerton U.S.A. 115 39.36N 74.20W
Tucson U.S.A. 109 32.13N110.58W
Tucumán d. Argentina 124 26.30S 65.20W
Tucumcari U.S.A. 109 35.10N103.44W
Tucupita Venezuela 122 9.02N 62.04W
Tucuruí Brazil 123 3.42S 49.44W
Tudela Spain 25 42.05N 1.36W
Tudela de Duero Spain 26 41.35N 4.35W
Tudmur Syria 64 34.36N 38.15E
Tuela r. Portugal 26 41.30N 7.12W
Tuen Australia 93 28.33S145.38E
Tufi P.N.G. 90 9.05S149.20E
Tugela R.S.A. 80 29.10S 31.25E
Tug Hill mtn. U.S.A. 115 43.45N 75.39W
Tuguegarao Phil. 59 17.36N121.44E
Tugur U.S.S.R. 51 53.44N136.45E
Tuineje Canary Is. 127 28.18N 14.03W
Tukangbesi, Kepulauan is. Indonesia 59 5.30S124.00E
Tukayyid well Iraq 65 29.47N 45.36E
Ţūkh Egypt 66 30.21N 31.12E
Tūkrah Libya 75 32.32N 20.34E
Tuktoyaktuk Canada 98 69.27N133.00W
Tukums U.S.S.R. 41 57.00N 23.10E
Tukuyu Tanzania 79 9.20S 33.37E
Tula Mexico 116 23.00N 99.43W
Tula U.S.S.R. 44 54.11N 37.38E
Tūlāk Afghan. 62 33.58N 63.44E
Tulare U.S.A. 109 36.13N119.21W
Tulare L. resr. U.S.A. 109 36.03N119.49W
Tularosa U.S.A. 109 33.04N106.01W
Tulcan Ecuador 122 0.50N 77.48W
Tulcea Romania 29 45.10N 28.50E
Tulchin U.S.S.R. 37 48.40N 28.49E
Tulemalu L. Canada 101 62.58N 99.25W
Tuli Indonesia 59 1.25S122.23E
Tuli Zimbabwe 80 21.50S 29.15E
Tuli r. Zimbabwe 80 21.49S 29.00E
Tulia U.S.A. 111 34.32N101.46W
Ţūlkarm Jordan 67 32.19N 35.02E
Tullahoma U.S.A. 113 35.21N 86.12W
Tullamore Australia 93 32.39S147.39E
Tullamore Rep. of Ire. 15 53.17N 7.31W
Tulle France 20 45.16N 1.46E
Tullins France 21 45.18N 5.29E
Tullow Rep. of Ire. 15 52.49N 6.45W
Tully Australia 90 17.55S145.59E
Tully U.S.A. 115 42.48N 76.07W
Tuloma r. U.S.S.R. 44 68.56N 33.00E
Tulsa U.S.A. 111 36.09N 95.58W
Tulsequah Canada 100 58.39N133.35W
Tuluá Colombia 122 4.05N 76.12W
Tulumbasy U.S.S.R. 44 57.27N 57.40E
Tulun U.S.S.R. 51 54.32N100.35E
Tulungagung Indonesia 59 8.03S111.54E
Tulu Welel mtn. Ethiopia 73 8.53N 34.47E
Tum Indonesia 59 3.28S130.21E
Tumaco Colombia 122 1.51N 78.46W
Tumba Sweden 43 59.12N 17.49E
Tumba, L. Zaïre 78 0.45S 18.00E
Tumbarumba Australia 93 35.49S148.01E
Tumbes Peru 122 3.37S 80.27W
Tumby Bay town Australia 92 34.20S136.05E
Tumd Youqi China 54 40.33N110.30E
Tumd Zuoqi China 54 40.42N111.08E
Tumeremo Venezuela 122 7.18N 61.30W
Tummel, Loch U.K. 14 56.43N 3.55W
Tump Pakistan 62 26.07N 62.22E
Tumsar India 63 21.23N 79.44E
Tumuc Humac Mts. S. America 123 2.20N 54.50W
Tumut Australia 93 35.20S148.14E
Tunari mtn. Bolivia 124 17.18S 66.22W
Tūnat al Jabal Egypt 66 27.46N 30.44E
Tunceli Turkey 64 39.07N 39.34E
Tundubai well Sudan 72 18.31N 28.33E
Tunduma Tanzania 79 9.19S 32.47E
Tunduru Tanzania 79 11.08S 37.21E
Tundzha r. Bulgaria 34 42.00N 26.35E
Tungabhadra r. India 60 16.00N 78.15E
Tungaru Sudan 73 10.14N 30.42E
Tungchiang Taiwan 55 22.28N120.26E
Tungsten Canada 100 62.00N128.15W
Tungsten U.S.A. 108 40.48N118.08W
Tunica U.S.A. 111 34.41N 90.23W
Tunis Tunisia 32 36.48N 10.11E
Tunis, Golfe de g. Tunisia 32 37.00N 10.30E
Tunisia Africa 75 34.00N 9.00E
Tunja Colombia 122 5.33N 73.23W
Tunkhannock U.S.A. 115 41.32N 75.57W
Tunnsjöen l. Norway 40 64.45N 13.25E
Tunungayualok I. Canada 103 56.05N 61.05W
Tunuyán r. Argentina 125 33.33S 67.30W
Tunxi China 55 29.41N118.22E
Tuoy-Khaya U.S.S.R. 51 62.33N111.25E
Tupã Brazil 126 21.57S 50.28W
Tupelo U.S.A. 111 34.16N 88.43W
Tupinambaranas, Ilha f. Brazil 123 3.00S 58.00W
Tupiza Bolivia 124 21.27S 65.43W
Tupper Lake town U.S.A. 105 44.13N 74.29W
Tuquan China 54 45.22N121.41E
Túquerres Colombia 122 1.06N 77.37W
Tura India 63 25.31N 90.13E
Tura Tanzania 79 5.30S 33.50E
Tura U.S.S.R. 51 64.05N100.00E
Turabah Saudi Arabia 72 21.13N 41.39E
Turangi New Zealand 86 38.59S175.48E
Turano r. Italy 30 42.26N 12.47E
Turbaco Colombia 122 10.20N 75.25W
Turbanovo U.S.S.R. 44 60.05N 50.46E
Turbat Pakistan 62 25.59N 63.04E
Turbine Canada 104 46.22N 81.31W
Turbo Colombia 122 8.06N 76.44W
Turda Romania 37 46.34N 23.47E
Turek Poland 37 52.02N 18.30E
Turgay U.S.S.R. 9 49.38N 63.25E
Turgeon r. Canada 102 50.00N 78.54W
Tŭrgovishte Bulgaria 34 43.17N 26.38E
Tŭrgovishte d. Bulgaria 34 43.15N 26.34E
Turgutlu Turkey 29 38.30N 27.43E
Turhal Turkey 64 40.23N 36.05E
Türi U.S.S.R. 41 58.48N 25.26E
Turia r. Spain 25 39.27N 0.19W
Turiaçu Brazil 123 1.41S 45.21W
Turiaçu r. Brazil 123 1.36S 45.19W
Turin Canada 100 49.59N112.35W
Turin see Torino Italy 30
Turka U.S.S.R. 37 49.10N 23.02E
Turkana, L. Kenya 79 4.00N 36.00E
Turkestan f. Asia 65 40.00N 56.00E
Turkestan U.S.S.R. 52 43.17N 68.16E
Turkey Asia 64 39.00N 35.00E
Turkey U.S.A. 111 34.23N100.54W
Turkey Creek town Australia 88 17.04S128.15E
Turkmenskaya S.S.R. d. U.S.S.R. 9 40.00N 60.00E
Turks Is. Turks & Caicos Is. 117 21.30N 71.10W
Turku Finland 41 60.27N 22.17E
Turku-Pori d. Finland 41 61.00N 22.35E
Turkwel r. Kenya 79 3.08N 35.39E
Turnagain r. Canada 100 59.06N127.35W
Turnberry Canada 101 53.25N101.45W
Turneffe Is. Belize 117 17.30N 87.45W
Turner U.S.A. 108 48.51N108.24W
Turnhout Belgium 16 51.19N 4.57E
Turnovo d. Bulgaria 34 43.04N 25.39E
Turnu Măgurele Romania 34 43.45N 24.53E
Turnu Roşu, Pasul pass Romania 29 45.37N 24.17E
Turnu-Severin Romania 29 44.37N 22.39E
Turon r. Australia 93 33.03S149.33E
Turon U.S.A. 111 37.48N 98.26W
Turopolje f. Yugo. 31 45.40N 16.00E
Turov U.S.S.R. 37 52.04N 27.40E
Turpan China 52 42.55N 89.06E
Turpan Pendi f. China 52 43.40N 89.00E
Turquino mtn. Cuba 117 20.05N 76.50W
Turret Range mts. Australia 92 29.43S136.42E
Turriff U.K. 14 57.32N 2.28W
Turtkul U.S.S.R. 65 41.30N 61.00E
Turtle Lake town N.Dak. U.S.A. 110 47.31N100.53W
Turtle Lake town Wisc. U.S.A. 110 45.23N 92.09W
Turtle Mtn. Canada/U.S.A. 101 49.05N 99.45W
Turukhansk U.S.S.R. 51 65.21N 88.05E
Turya r. U.S.S.R. 37 51.48N 24.52E
Tuscaloosa U.S.A. 113 33.12N 87.33W
Tuscarawas r. U.S.A. 114 40.17N 81.52W
Tuscarora U.S.A. 108 41.19N116.14W
Tuscarora Mts. U.S.A. 114 40.10N 77.45W
Tuscola Ill. U.S.A. 110 39.48N 88.17W
Tuscola Tex. U.S.A. 111 32.12N 99.48W
Tuticorin India 61 8.48N 78.10E
Tutin Yugo. 34 43.00N 20.20E
Tutóia Brazil 123 2.45S 42.16W
Tutrakan Bulgaria 29 44.02N 26.40E
Tuttle U.S.A. 110 47.09N100.00W
Tuttlingen W. Germany 39 47.59N 8.49E
Tutuala Indonesia 59 8.24S127.15E
Tutubu Tanzania 79 5.28S 32.43E
Tutuila i. Samoa 84 14.18S170.42W
Ţuţūn Egypt 66 29.09N 30.46E
Tutzing W. Germany 39 47.54N 11.17E
Tuul Gol r. Mongolia 52 48.53N104.35E
Tuvalu Pacific Oc. 84 8.00S178.00E
Tuwayq, Jabal mts. Saudi Arabia 71 23.30N 46.20E
Tuxpan Mexico 116 21.00N 97.23W
Tuxtla Gutiérrez Mexico 116 16.45N 93.09W
Tūy Spain 26 42.03N 8.38W
Tuyen Quang Vietnam 55 21.48N105.21E
Tuz Gölü l. Turkey 64 38.45N 33.24E
Ţūz Khurmātū Iraq 65 34.53N 44.38E
Tuzla Yugo. 31 44.32N 18.41E
Tvaerå Faroe Is. 10 61.34N 6.48W
Tvedestrand Norway 42 58.37N 8.55E
Tveitsund Norway 42 59.01N 8.32E
Tvŭrditsa Bulgaria 34 42.42N 25.52E
Tweed Canada 105 44.29N 77.19W
Tweed r. U.K. 14 55.46N 2.00W
Tweedsmuir Prov. Park Canada 100 52.55N126.20W
Twentynine Palms U.S.A. 109 34.08N116.03W
Twin Bridges town U.S.A. 108 45.33N112.20W
Twin Falls town U.S.A. 108 42.34N114.28W
Twining U.S.A. 104 44.07N 83.48W
Twins Creek r. Australia 92 29.10S139.27E
Twin Valley town U.S.A. 110 47.16N 96.16W
Twizel New Zealand 86 44.15S170.06E
Twofold B. Australia 93 37.06S149.55E
Two Harbors town U.S.A. 110 47.02N 91.40W
Twyford Hants. U.K. 13 51.01N 1.19W
Tygart r. U.S.A. 114 38.30N 80.03W
Tyler Minn. U.S.A. 110 44.17N 96.08W
Tyler Tex. U.S.A. 111 32.21N 95.18W
Tylösand Sweden 43 56.39N 12.44E
Tylöskog hills Sweden 43 58.45N 15.20E
Tyndinskiy U.S.S.R. 51 55.11N124.34E
Tyne r. U.K. 12 55.00N 1.25W
Tyne and Wear d. U.K. 12 54.57N 1.35W
Tynemouth U.K. 12 55.01N 1.24W
Tynset Norway 41 62.17N 10.47E
Tyre see Şūr Lebanon 67
Tyrifjorden l. Norway 42 60.02N 10.08E
Tyringe Sweden 43 56.10N 13.35E
Tyron U.S.A. 113 35.13N 82.14W
Tyrone d. U.K. 15 54.35N 7.15W
Tyrone U.S.A. 114 40.40N 78.14W
Tyrrel Canada 101 54.35N 99.10W
Tyrrell r. Australia 92 35.28S142.55E
Tyrrell, L. Australia 92 35.22S142.50E
Tyrrhenian Sea Med. Sea 32 40.00N 12.00E
Tysnesöy i. Norway 42 60.00N 5.35E
Tyssedal Norway 42 60.07N 6.34E
Tyumen U.S.S.R. 9 57.11N 65.29E
Tywi r. U.K. 13 51.46N 4.22W
Tzaneen R.S.A. 80 23.49S 30.10E

U

Ua Huka i. Îs. Marquises 85 8.55S139.32W
Uanda Australia 90 21.34S144.54E
Ua Pu i. Îs. Marquises 85 9.25S140.00W
Uatumã r. Brazil 123 2.30S 57.40W
Uaupés Brazil 122 0.07S 67.05W
Uaupés r. Brazil 122 0.00S 67.10W
Ubá Brazil 126 21.08S 42.59W
Ubangi r. Congo/Zaïre 78 0.25S 17.40E
Ubatuba Brazil 126 23.26S 45.05W
Ubauro Pakistan 62 28.10N 69.44E
Ubayyiḑ, Wādī al r. Iraq 64 32.04N 42.17E
Ube Japan 57 34.00N131.16E
Ubeda Spain 26 38.01N 3.22W
Uberaba Brazil 126 19.47S 47.57W
Uberlândia Brazil 126 18.57S 48.17W
Überlingen W. Germany 39 47.46N 9.10E
Ubombo R.S.A. 81 27.35S 32.05E
Ubort r. U.S.S.R. 37 52.06N 28.28E
Ubrique Spain 27 36.41N 5.27W
Ubundu Zaïre 78 0.24S 25.28E
Ucayali r. Peru 122 4.40S 73.20W
Uch Pakistan 62 29.14N 71.03E
Uchiura wan b. Japan 57 42.20N140.40E
Uckermark f. E. Germany 38 52.11N 13.50E
Udaipur India 62 24.35N 73.41E
Udalguri India 63 26.46N 92.08E
Udaquiola Argentina 125 36.35S 58.30W
Udaypur Nepal 63 26.54N 86.32E
Udbina Yugo. 31 44.32N 15.46E
Uddeholm Sweden 43 60.01N 13.37E
Uddevalla Sweden 42 58.21N 11.55E
Uddjaur l. Sweden 40 65.55N 17.49E
Udhampur Jammu & Kashmir 62 32.56N 75.08E
Udine Italy 30 46.03N 13.14E
Udipi India 60 13.21N 74.45E
údolni nádrž Lipno l. Czech. 39 48.43N 14.04E
Udon Thani Thailand 56 17.25N102.45E
Ueckermünde E. Germany 38 53.44N 14.03E
Uele r. Zaïre 73 4.09N 22.26E
Uelzen W. Germany 38 52.58N 10.33E
Ueno Japan 57 34.45N136.08E
Uere r. Zaïre 73 3.42N 25.24E
Uetersen W. Germany 38 53.41N 9.39E
Ufa U.S.S.R. 44 54.45N 55.58E
Ufa r. U.S.S.R. 44 54.45N 56.00E
Uffculme U.K. 13 50.45N 3.19W
Uffenheim W. Germany 39 49.32N 10.14E
Ugab r. Namibia 80 21.12S 13.37E
Ugalla r. Tanzania 79 5.43S 31.10E
Uganda Africa 79 2.00N 33.00E
Ugep Nigeria 77 5.48N 8.05E
Ughelli Nigeria 77 5.33N 6.00E
Ugijar Spain 27 36.57N 3.03W
Ugine France 21 45.45N 6.25E
Uglegorsk U.S.S.R. 51 49.01N142.04E
Ugljan i. Yugo. 31 44.05N 15.10E
Uglovka U.S.S.R. 44 58.13N 33.30E
Ugoma mtn. Zaïre 79 4.00S 28.45E
Ugra r. U.S.S.R. 44 54.30N 36.10E
Ugŭrchin Bulgaria 34 43.06N 24.26E
Uherske Hradiště Czech. 37 49.05N 17.28E
Uhrichsville U.S.A. 114 40.24N 81.20W
Uig U.K. 14 57.35N 6.22W
Uíge Angola 78 7.40S 15.09E
Uíge d. Angola 78 7.00S 15.30E
Uil U.S.S.R. 45 49.08N 54.43E
Uil r. U.S.S.R. 45 48.33N 52.25E
Uinta Mts. U.S.A. 108 40.45N110.05W
Uitenhage R.S.A. 80 33.46S 25.23E
Uithuizen Neth. 16 53.24N 6.41E
Uivlleq see Nanortalik Greenland 99
Ujhāni India 63 28.01N 79.01E
Uji r. Japan 57 34.53N135.48E
Ujiji Tanzania 79 4.55S 29.39E
Ujjain India 62 23.11N 75.46E
Ujpest Hungary 37 47.33N 19.05E
Ujście Poland 36 53.04N 16.43E
Ujung Pandang Indonesia 58 5.09S119.28E
Uka U.S.S.R. 51 57.50N162.02E
Ukerewe I. Tanzania 79 2.00S 33.00E
Ukhta U.S.S.R. 44 63.33N 53.44E
Ukiah U.S.A. 108 39.09N123.13W
Ukmerge U.S.S.R. 44 55.14N 24.49E
Ukrainskaya S.S.R. d. U.S.S.R. 37 49.45N 27.00E
Ukrina r. Yugo. 31 45.05N 17.56E
Ukwi Botswana 80 23.22S 20.30E
Ulaanbaatar Mongolia 52 47.54N106.52E
Ulaangom Mongolia 52 49.59N 92.00E
Ulamba Zaïre 78 9.07S 23.40E
Ulan Bator see Ulaanbaatar Mongolia 52
Ulansuhai Nur l. China 54 40.56N108.49E
Ulan-Ude U.S.S.R. 52 51.55N107.40E
Ulan Ul Hu l. China 61 34.45N 90.25E
Ulcinj Yugo. 31 41.55N 19.11E
Ulefoss Norway 42 59.17N 9.16E
Ulenia, L. Australia 92 29.57S142.24E
Ulfborg Denmark 42 56.16N 8.20E
Ulhāsnagar India 62 19.13N 73.07E
Uliastay Mongolia 52 47.42N 96.52E
Ulindi r. Zaïre 78 1.38S 25.55E
Ulla r. Spain 26 42.40N 8.43W
Ulladulla Australia 93 35.21S150.25E
Ullånger Sweden 40 62.58N 18.16E
Ullapool U.K. 14 57.54N 5.10W
Ullswater l. U.K. 12 54.34N 2.52W
Ulm W. Germany 39 48.24N 10.00E
Ulongwé Mozambique 79 14.34S 34.21E
Ulricehamn Sweden 43 57.47N 13.25E
Ulsan S. Korea 57 35.34N129.19E
Ulsberg Norway 40 62.45N 9.59E
Ulster U.S.A. 115 41.51N 76.30W
Ultima Australia 92 35.30S143.20E
Ulu Sudan 73 10.43N 33.29E
Ulúa r. Honduras 117 15.50N 87.38W
Uluguru Mts. Tanzania 79 7.05S 37.40E
Ulverston U.K. 12 54.13N 3.07W
Ulverstone Australia 91 41.09S146.10E
Ul'yanovsk U.S.S.R. 44 54.19N 48.22E
Ulysses U.S.A. 111 37.35N101.22W
Ulzë Albania 34 41.41N 19.54E
Umag Yugo. 31 45.25N 13.32E
Umaisha Nigeria 77 8.01N 7.12E
Umala Bolivia 124 17.21S 68.00W
Uman U.S.S.R. 37 48.45N 30.10E
Umaria India 63 23.32N 80.50E
Umarkot Pakistan 62 25.22N 69.44E
Umbertide Italy 30 43.18N 12.20E
Umbria d. Italy 30 43.05N 12.30E
Ume r. Sweden 40 63.47N 20.16E
Ume r. Zimbabwe 80 17.00S 28.22E
Umeå Sweden 40 63.45N 20.20E
Umfors Sweden 40 65.56N 15.00E
Umfuli r. Zimbabwe 80 17.32S 29.23E
Umiat U.S.A. 98 69.25N152.20W
Umm-al-Qaywayn U.A.E. 65 25.32N 55.34E
Umm Badr Sudan 72 14.14N 27.57E
Umm Bel Sudan 73 13.32N 28.04E
Umm Durmān Sudan 72 15.37N 32.59E
Umm el Faḩm Israel 67 32.31N 35.09E

Umm Kuwaykah to Varginha

Umm Kuwaykah Sudan **73** 12.49N 31.52E
Umm Lajj Saudi Arabia **64** 25.03N 37.17E
Umm Qays Jordan **67** 32.39N 35.41E
Umm Qurayn Sudan **73** 9.58N 28.55E
Umm Ruwābah Sudan **73** 12.54N 31.13E
Umm Shalīl Sudan **73** 10.51N 23.42E
Umm Shanqah Sudan **73** 13.14N 27.14E
Umniati Zimbabwe **80** 18.41S 29.45E
Umniati *r.* Zimbabwe **80** 17.32S 29.23E
Umrer India **63** 20.51N 79.20E
Umreth India **62** 22.42N 73.07E
Umtata R.S.A. **80** 31.35S 28.47E
Umuahia Nigeria **77** 5.31N 7.26E
Umvukwe Range *mts.* Zimbabwe **80** 17.10S 30.45E
Umzimkulu R.S.A. **80** 30.15S 29.56E
Umzimvubu R.S.A. **80** 31.37S 29.32E
Una India **62** 20.49N 71.02E
Una *r.* Yugo. **31** 45.16N 16.55E
Unac *r.* Yugo. **31** 44.30N 16.09E
Unadilla *r.* U.S.A. **115** 42.20N 75.19W
Unalakleet U.S.A. **98** 63.53N 160.47W
'Unayzah Jordan **66** 30.29N 35.48E
'Unayzah Saudi Arabia **65** 26.05N 43.57E
'Unayzah, Jabal *mtn.* Iraq **64** 32.15N 39.19E
Uncia Bolivia **124** 18.27S 66.37W
Uncompahgre Peak U.S.A. **108** 38.04N 107.28W
Uncompahgre Plateau *f.* U.S.A. **108** 38.30N 108.25W
Unden *l.* Sweden **43** 58.47N 14.26E
Underberg R.S.A. **80** 29.46S 29.26E
Underbool Australia **92** 35.10S 141.50E
Undu, C. Fiji **84** 16.08S 179.57W
Unecha U.S.S.R. **37** 52.52N 32.42E
Ungarie Australia **93** 33.38S 147.00E
Ungava, Péninsule d' *pen.* Canada **99** 60.00N 74.00W
Ungava B. Canada **99** 59.00N 67.30W
Unggi N. Korea **53** 42.19N 130.24E
União Brazil **123** 4.35S 42.52W
União da Vitória Brazil **126** 26.13S 51.05W
Unije *i.* Yugo. **31** 44.38N 14.15E
Unimak I. U.S.A. **98** 54.50N 164.00W
Unini Peru **122** 10.41S 73.59W
Union Miss U.S.A. **111** 32.34N 89.14W
Union S.C. U.S.A. **113** 34.42N 81.37W
Union City Penn. U.S.A. **114** 41.54N 79.51W
Union City Tenn. U.S.A. **111** 36.26N 89.03W
Uniondale R.S.A. **80** 33.39S 23.07E
Union Gap U.S.A. **108** 46.34N 120.34W
Union of Soviet Socialist Republics Europe / Asia **37** 50.00N 28.00E
Union Springs *town* U.S.A. **113** 32.08N 85.44W
Uniontown U.S.A. **114** 39.54N 79.44W
Unionville U.S.A. **110** 40.29N 93.01W
United Arab Emirates Asia **65** 24.00N 54.00E
United Kingdom Europe **11** 55.00N 2.00W
United States of America N. America **106** 39.00N 100.00W
Unity Canada **101** 52.27N 109.10W
Universales, Montes *mts.* Spain **25** 40.20N 1.30W
University Park *town* U.S.A. **109** 32.17N 106.45W
Unjha India **62** 23.48N 72.24E
Unna W. Germany **38** 51.32N 7.41E
Unnão India **63** 26.32N 80.30E
Unst *i.* U.K. **14** 60.45N 0.55W
Unstrut *r.* E. Germany **38** 51.10N 11.48E
Ünye Turkey **64** 41.09N 37.15E
Upata Venezuela **122** 8.02N 62.25W
Upemba, L. Zaïre **78** 8.35S 26.28E
Upemba Nat. Park Zaïre **78** 9.00S 26.30E
Upernavik Greenland **99** 72.50N 56.00W
Upington R.S.A. **80** 28.26S 21.12E
Upleta India **62** 21.44N 70.17E
Upolu *i.* W. Samoa **84** 13.55S 171.45W
Upolu Pt. Hawaiian Is. **85** 20.16N 155.51W
Upper *d.* Ghana **76** 10.30N 1.40W
Upper Arrow L. Canada **100** 50.30N 117.50W
Upper Egypt *see* Aş Şa'īd Egypt **64**
Upper Hutt New Zealand **86** 41.07S 175.04E
Upper Klamath L. U.S.A. **108** 42.23N 122.55W
Upper Laberge Canada **100** 60.54N 135.12W
Upper Lough Erne N. Ireland **15** 54.13N 7.32W
Upper Pen. *f.* U.S.A. **104** 46.12N 84.32W
Upper Red L. U.S.A. **110** 48.05N 94.50W
Upper Tean U.K. **12** 52.57N 1.59W
Upper Volta Africa **76** 12.30N 2.00W
Upper Yarra Dam Australia **93** 37.43S 145.56E
Uppland *f.* Sweden **43** 59.59N 17.48E
Upplands-Väsby Sweden **43** 59.31N 17.54E
Uppsala Sweden **43** 59.52N 17.38E
Uppsala *d.* Sweden **41** 60.10N 17.50E
Upshi Jammu & Kashmir **63** 33.50N 77.49E
Upton Canada **105** 45.39N 72.41W
Upton U.S.A. **108** 44.06N 104.38W
Uqlat aş Şuqūr Saudi Arabia **64** 25.50N 42.12E
Ur *ruins* Iraq **65** 30.55N 46.07E
Uracoa Venezuela **122** 9.03N 62.27W
Uraga-suido *str.* Japan **57** 35.10N 139.42E
Urahoro Japan **57** 42.48N 143.39E
Urakawa Japan **57** 42.09N 142.47E
Ural *r.* U.S.S.R. **45** 47.00N 52.00E
Uralla Australia **93** 30.40S 151.31E
Ural Mts. *see* Uralskiy Khrebet U.S.S.R. **44**
Ural'sk U.S.S.R. **45** 51.19N 51.20E
Uralskiy Khrebet *mts.* U.S.S.R. **44** 60.00N 59.00E
Urana Australia **93** 35.21S 146.19E
Urana, L. Australia **93** 35.21S 146.19E
Urandangi Australia **90** 21.36S 138.18E
Uranium City Canada **101** 59.28N 108.40W
Uraricoera *r.* Brazil **122** 3.10N 60.30W
Urawa Japan **57** 35.51N 139.39E
Uray U.S.S.R. **50** 60.11N 65.00E
Urbana U.S.A. **110** 40.07N 88.12W
Urbania Italy **30** 43.40N 12.31E
Urbino Italy **30** 43.43N 12.38E
Urcos Peru **122** 13.40S 71.38W
Urda U.S.S.R. **45** 48.44N 47.30E
Urdzhar U.S.S.R. **50** 47.06N 81.33E
Ure *r.* U.K. **12** 54.05N 1.20W
Urechye U.S.S.R. **37** 52.59N 27.50E
Uren U.S.S.R. **44** 57.30N 45.50E
Urengoy U.S.S.R. **50** 65.59N 78.30E
Ures Mexico **116** 29.26N 110.24W
Urfa Turkey **64** 37.08N 38.45E
Ürgüp Turkey **64** 38.39N 34.55E
Uribia Colombia **122** 11.43N 72.16W
Urim Israel **67** 31.18N 34.31E
Urimbin Australia **92** 28.15S 143.46E
Urisino Australia **92** 29.44S 143.49E
Urjala Finland **41** 61.05N 23.32E
Urk Neth. **16** 52.40N 5.36E
Urlingford Rep. of Ire. **15** 52.44N 7.35W
Urmia, L. *see* Daryācheh-ye Rezā'īyeh Iran **65**
Urnograč Yugo. **36** 45.10N 15.57E
Uroševac Yugo. **34** 42.22N 21.09E
Ursus Poland **37** 52.12N 20.53E
Uruaçu Brazil **123** 14.30S 49.10W
Uruapan Mexico **116** 19.26N 102.04W
Urubamba Peru **122** 13.20S 72.07W
Urubamba *r.* Peru **122** 10.43S 73.55W
Urucará Brazil **123** 2.32S 57.45W
Uruçui Brazil **123** 7.14S 44.33W
Uruguaiana Brazil **125** 29.45S 57.05W
Uruguay *r.* Argentina / Uruguay **125** 34.00S 58.30W
Uruguay S. America **126** 33.15S 56.00W
Ürümqi China **52** 43.43N 87.38E
Urun P.N.G. **90** 8.36S 147.15E
Urunga Australia **93** 30.30S 152.28E
Urup *r.* U.S.S.R. **45** 44.59N 41.12E
Uryu ko *l.* Japan **57** 44.22N 142.15E
Urzhum U.S.S.R. **44** 57.08N 50.00E
Urziceni Romania **29** 44.43N 26.38E
Usa *r.* U.S.S.R. **44** 65.58N 56.35E
Uşak Turkey **64** 38.42N 29.25E
Usakos Namibia **80** 22.02S 15.35E
Usambara Mts. Tanzania **79** 4.45S 38.25E
Ušće Yugo. **34** 43.28N 20.37E
Usedom *i.* E. Germany **38** 54.00N 14.00E
Ushant *i.* *see* Ouessant, Île d' France **18**
Ush-Tobe U.S.S.R. **52** 45.15N 77.59E
Ushuaia Argentina **125** 54.47S 68.20W
Ushumun U.S.S.R. **51** 52.48N 126.27E
Usisya Malaŵi **79** 11.10S 34.12E
Usk *r.* U.K. **13** 51.34N 2.59W
Uskedal Norway **42** 59.56N 5.52E
Üsküdar Turkey **29** 41.00N 29.03E
Uslar W. Germany **38** 51.39N 9.38E
Usman U.S.S.R. **45** 52.02N 39.43E
Usovo U.S.S.R. **37** 51.20N 28.01E
Uspenskiy U.S.S.R. **50** 48.41N 72.43E
Ussel France **20** 45.33N 2.18E
Ussuriysk U.S.S.R. **53** 43.48N 131.59E
Ustaoset Norway **41** 60.30N 8.04E
Ustaritz France **20** 43.24N 1.27W
Ustica *i.* Italy **32** 38.42N 13.10E
Ust'-Ilga U.S.S.R. **51** 54.59N 105.00E
Ústí nad Labem Czech. **38** 50.40N 14.02E
Ust Ishim U.S.S.R. **50** 57.45N 71.05E
Ustka Poland **36** 54.35N 16.50E
Ust'kamchatsk U.S.S.R. **51** 56.14N 162.28E
Ust-Kamenogorsk U.S.S.R. **50** 50.00N 82.40E
Ust Kulom U.S.S.R. **44** 61.34N 53.40E
Ust Kut U.S.S.R. **51** 56.40N 105.50E
Ust Lyzha U.S.S.R. **44** 65.45N 56.38E
Ust'Maya U.S.S.R. **51** 60.25N 134.28E
Ust Nem U.S.S.R. **44** 61.38N 54.50E
Ust Olenëk U.S.S.R. **51** 72.59N 120.00E
Ust-Omchug U.S.S.R. **51** 61.08N 149.38E
Ust Port U.S.S.R. **50** 69.44N 84.23E
Ust Tapsuy U.S.S.R. **44** 62.25N 61.42E
Ust'Tsilma U.S.S.R. **44** 65.28N 53.09E
Ust-Tungir U.S.S.R. **51** 55.25N 120.15E
Ust Ura U.S.S.R. **44** 63.06N 44.41E
Ust Vaga U.S.S.R. **44** 62.42N 42.45E
Ust Vym U.S.S.R. **44** 62.15N 50.25E
Ustyurt, Plato *f.* U.S.S.R. **45** 43.30N 55.00E
Usu China **52** 44.27N 84.37E
Usumacinta *r.* Mexico **116** 18.22N 92.40W
U.S. Virgin Is. C. America **117** 18.30N 65.00W
Ut U.S.S.R. **37** 52.18N 31.10E
Utah *d.* U.S.A. **108** 39.37N 112.28W
Utah L. U.S.A. **108** 40.13N 111.49W
'Uta Vava'u Tonga **85** 18.35S 174.00W
'Utaybah, Buḩayrat al *l.* Syria **66** 33.31N 36.37E
Utembo *r.* Angola **78** 17.03S 22.00E
Utengule Tanzania **79** 8.55S 35.43E
Utersum W. Germany **38** 54.43N 8.24E
Utete Tanzania **79** 8.00S 38.49E
Uthal Pakistan **62** 25.48N 66.37E
Utiariti Brazil **122** 13.02S 58.17W
Utica Kans. U.S.A. **110** 38.39N 100.10W
Utica Mich. U.S.A. **114** 42.38N 83.02W
Utica N.Y. U.S.A. **115** 43.05N 75.14W
Utica Ohio U.S.A. **114** 40.14N 82.27W
Utiel Spain **25** 39.34N 1.12W
Utikuma L. Canada **100** 55.50N 115.30W
Utique Tunisia **32** 37.03N 10.03E
Utö *i.* Sweden **43** 58.56N 18.16E
Utopia Australia **90** 22.14S 134.33E
Utraula India **63** 27.19N 82.25E
Utrecht Neth. **16** 52.04N 5.07E
Utrecht *d.* Neth. **16** 52.04N 5.10E
Utrecht R.S.A. **80** 27.38S 30.19E
Utrera Spain **27** 37.11N 5.47W
Utsira Norway **42** 59.18N 4.54E
Utsjoki Finland **40** 69.53N 27.00E
Utsunomiya Japan **57** 36.40N 139.52E
Utta U.S.S.R. **45** 46.24N 46.01E
Uttaradit Thailand **56** 17.38N 100.05E
Uttarkāshi India **63** 30.44N 78.27E
Uttar Pradesh *d.* India **63** 26.30N 81.30E
Utterson Canada **104** 45.13N 79.20W
Uturoà Is. de la Société **85** 16.44S 151.25W
Uummannarsuaq *see* Farvel, K. Greenland **99**
Uusikaupunki Finland **41** 60.48N 21.25E
Uusimaa *d.* Finland **41** 60.30N 25.00E
Uvalde U.S.A. **111** 29.13N 99.47W
Uvarovichi U.S.S.R. **37** 52.35N 30.44E
Uvat U.S.S.R. **50** 59.10N 68.49E
Uvdal Norway **42** 60.16N 8.44E
Uvéa, Île *i.* N. Cal. **84** 20.30S 166.35E
Uvinza Tanzania **79** 5.08S 30.23E
Uvira Zaïre **79** 3.22S 29.06E
Uvs Nuur *l.* Mongolia **52** 50.30N 92.30E
Uwajima Japan **57** 33.13N 132.32E
Uwayl Sudan **73** 8.46N 27.24E
'Uwaynāt, Jabal al *mtn.* Libya / Sudan **72** 21.54N 24.58E
Uxbridge Canada **104** 44.06N 79.07W
Uxin Qi China **54** 38.30N 108.53E
Uyo Nigeria **77** 5.01N 7.56E
Uyuni Bolivia **124** 20.28S 66.50W
Uyuni, Salar de *f.* Bolivia **124** 20.20S 67.42W
Uzbekistan S.S.R. *d.* U.S.S.R. **9** 42.00N 63.00E
Uzbekskaya S.S.R. *d.* U.S.S.R. **9** 42.00N 63.00E
Uzda U.S.S.R. **37** 53.28N 27.11E
Uzerche France **20** 45.26N 1.34E
Uzès France **21** 44.01N 4.25E
Uzh *r.* U.S.S.R. **37** 51.15N 30.12E
Uzhgorod U.S.S.R. **37** 48.38N 22.15E
Uzunköpru Turkey **34** 41.16N 26.41E

V

Vä Sweden **43** 55.59N 14.05E
Vaagö *i.* Faroe Is. **10** 62.03N 7.14W
Vaal *r.* R.S.A. **80** 29.04S 23.37E
Vaala Finland **40** 64.26N 26.48E
Vaal Dam R.S.A. **80** 26.51S 28.08E
Vaasa Finland **40** 63.06N 21.36E
Vaasa *d.* Finland **40** 62.50N 22.50E
Vác Hungary **37** 47.49N 19.10E
Vaccarès, Étang de *b.* France **21** 43.32N 4.34E
Vadodara India **60** 22.19N 73.14E
Vado Ligure Italy **30** 44.17N 8.27E
Vadsö Norway **40** 70.05N 29.46E
Vadstena Sweden **43** 58.27N 14.54E
Vaduz Liech. **39** 47.09N 9.31E
Vaeröy *i.* Norway **40** 67.40N 12.40E
Vaga *r.* U.S.S.R. **44** 62.45N 42.48E
Vågåmo Norway **41** 61.53N 9.06E
Vaganski Vrh *mtn.* Yugo. **31** 44.22N 15.31E
Vaggeryd Sweden **43** 57.30N 14.07E
Váh *r.* Czech. **37** 47.40N 17.50E
Vahsel B. Antarctica **128** 77.00S 38.00W
Vaiea Niue **84** 19.08S 169.53W
Vaihu I. de Pascua **85** 27.10S 109.22W
Vaijāpur India **62** 19.55N 74.44E
Vailly-sur-Aisne France **19** 49.25N 3.31E
Vairao Tahiti **85** 17.48S 149.17W
Vaison-la-Romaine France **21** 44.14N 5.04E
Vaitupu *i.* Tuvalu **84** 7.28S 178.41E
Vakaga C.A.R. **73** 9.50N 22.30E
Vakarai Sri Lanka **61** 8.08N 81.26E
Vålådalen Sweden **40** 63.09N 13.00E
Valandovo Yugo. **34** 41.19N 22.34E
Valatie U.S.A. **115** 42.25N 73.41W
Valavsk U.S.S.R. **37** 51.40N 28.38E
Val Barrette Canada **105** 46.31N 75.22W
Välberg Sweden **43** 59.24N 13.12E
Valcartier Canada **105** 46.56N 71.27W
Valcheta Argentina **125** 40.40S 66.10W
Valdagno Italy **32** 45.39N 11.18E
Valdavia *r.* Spain **26** 42.24N 4.16W
Valday U.S.S.R. **44** 57.59N 33.10E
Valdayskaya Vozvyshennost *mts.* U.S.S.R. **44** 57.10N 33.00E
Valdecañas, Embalse de *resr.* Spain **27** 39.45N 5.30W
Valdemārpils U.S.S.R. **41** 57.22N 22.35E
Valdemarsvik Sweden **43** 58.12N 16.36E
Valdepeñas Spain **26** 38.46N 3.23W
Valderaduey *r.* Spain **26** 41.31N 5.42W
Valderas Spain **26** 42.05N 5.27W
Valderrobres Spain **25** 40.53N 0.09W
Valdés, Pen. Argentina **125** 42.30S 64.00W
Val des Bois Canada **105** 45.54N 75.35W
Valdez U.S.A. **98** 61.07N 146.17W
Val di Mazara *f.* Italy **32** 37.50N 13.00E
Val di Noto *f.* Italy **33** 36.50N 14.45E
Val d'Isère France **21** 45.27N 6.59E
Valdivia Chile **125** 39.46S 73.15W
Val d'Oise *d.* France **19** 49.10N 2.10E
Val d'Or *town* Canada **102** 48.07N 77.47W
Valdosta U.S.A. **113** 30.51N 83.51W
Valdoviño Spain **26** 43.36N 8.08W
Valença Brazil **126** 22.14S 43.45W
Valença Brazil **123** 13.22S 39.06W
Valença Portugal **26** 42.02N 8.38W
Valençay France **19** 47.09N 1.34E
Valence France **21** 44.56N 4.54E
Valencia Spain **25** 39.28N 0.22W
Valencia *d.* Spain **25** 39.20N 0.45W
Valencia Venezuela **122** 10.14N 67.59W
Valencia, Golfo de *g.* Spain **25** 39.30N 0.20W
Valencia de Alcántara Spain **27** 39.25N 7.14W
Valencia de Don Juan Spain **26** 42.18N 5.31W
Valenciennes France **19** 50.21N 3.32E
Valentin U.S.S.R. **57** 43.09N 134.15E
Valentine Nebr. U.S.A. **110** 42.52N 100.30W
Valentine N.Mex. U.S.A. **109** 30.34N 104.29W
Vale of Evesham *f.* U.K. **13** 52.05N 1.55W
Vale of Pewsey *f.* U.K. **13** 51.21N 1.45W
Vale of York *f.* U.K. **12** 54.12N 1.25W
Valera Venezuela **122** 9.21N 70.38W
Valga U.S.S.R. **44** 57.44N 26.00E
Valguarnera Caropepe Italy **33** 37.30N 14.24E
Valinco, Golfe de *g.* France **21** 41.40N 8.50E
Valjevo Yugo. **31** 44.16N 19.53E
Valkeakoski Finland **41** 61.16N 24.02E
Valkenswaard Neth. **16** 51.21N 5.27E
Valladolid Mexico **117** 20.41N 88.12W
Valladolid Spain **26** 41.39N 4.43W
Valladolid *d.* Spain **26** 41.45N 4.50W
Vall de Uxó Spain **25** 39.49N 0.14W
Valle Norway **42** 59.12N 7.32E
Valle d'Aosta *d.* Italy **30** 45.50N 7.25E
Valle de Cabuérniga Spain **26** 43.14N 4.18W
Valle de la Pascua Venezuela **122** 9.15N 66.00W
Valledupar Colombia **122** 10.31N 73.16W
Valle Edén Uruguay **125** 31.50S 56.09W
Vallegrande Bolivia **124** 18.29S 64.06W
Valle Hermoso Mexico **111** 25.39N 97.52W
Vallenar Chile **124** 28.35S 70.46W
Vallentuna Sweden **43** 59.32N 18.05E
Vallet France **18** 47.10N 1.16W
Valletta Malta **28** 35.53N 14.31E
Valley City U.S.A. **110** 46.57N 97.58W
Valley Falls *town* U.S.A. **108** 42.29N 120.16W
Valleyfield Canada **105** 45.15N 74.08W
Valley Head *town* U.S.A. **114** 38.33N 80.02W
Valley Stream *town* U.S.A. **115** 40.40N 73.42W
Valleyview Canada **100** 55.04N 117.17W
Vallgrund *i.* Finland **40** 63.12N 21.14E
Vallo della Lucania Italy **33** 40.14N 15.17E
Vallon France **21** 44.24N 4.24E
Vallorbe Switz. **19** 46.43N 6.22E
Valls Spain **25** 41.17N 1.15E
Val Marie Canada **101** 49.14N 107.44W
Valmiera U.S.S.R. **44** 57.32N 25.29E
Valnera *mtn.* Spain **26** 43.09N 3.40W
Valognes France **18** 49.31N 1.28W
Valongo Portugal **26** 41.11N 8.30W
Valoria la Buena Spain **26** 41.48N 4.32W
Valparaíso Chile **125** 33.02S 71.38W
Valparaíso Mexico **116** 22.46N 103.34W
Valparaiso U.S.A. **113** 30.30N 86.31W
Valpovo Yugo. **31** 45.39N 18.25E
Valréas France **21** 44.23N 4.59E
Vals, Tanjung *c.* Indonesia **59** 8.30S 137.30E
Valverde Dom. Rep. **117** 19.37N 71.04W
Valverde del Camino Spain **27** 37.34N 6.45W
Vammala Finland **41** 61.20N 22.54E
Vamsadhāra *r.* India **63** 18.21N 84.08E
Van Turkey **64** 38.28N 43.20E
Van Blommestein Meer, W.J. *resr.* Surinam **123** 4.45N 55.05W
Van Buren Ark. U.S.A. **111** 35.26N 94.21W
Van Buren Mo. U.S.A. **111** 37.00N 91.01W
Vancouver Canada **100** 49.20N 123.10W
Vancouver U.S.A. **108** 45.39N 122.40W
Vancouver I. Canada **100** 49.45N 126.00W
Vandalia Ill. U.S.A. **110** 38.58N 89.06W
Vandalia Mo. U.S.A. **110** 39.19N 91.29W
Vanderbilt U.S.A. **104** 45.09N 84.40W
Vandergrift U.S.A. **114** 40.36N 79.34W
Vanderlin I. Australia **90** 15.44S 137.02E
Van Diemen, C. Australia **90** 16.31S 139.41E
Van Diemen G. Australia **90** 11.50S 132.00E
Vandry Canada **103** 47.50N 73.34W
Vänern *l.* Sweden **43** 58.55N 13.30E
Vänersborg Sweden **43** 58.22N 12.19E
Vang Norway **41** 61.10N 8.40E
Vanga Kenya **79** 4.37S 39.13E
Vangaindrano Madagascar **81** 23.21S 47.36E
Van Gölü *l.* Turkey **64** 38.35N 42.52E
Vanier Canada **105** 45.26N 75.40W
Vanimo P.N.G. **59** 2.40S 141.17E
Vankarem U.S.S.R. **51** 67.50N 175.51E
Vankleek Hill *town* Canada **105** 45.31N 74.39W
Vanna *i.* Norway **40** 70.10N 19.40E
Vännäs Sweden **40** 63.58N 19.48E
Vannes France **18** 47.39N 2.46W
Vanoise, Massif de la *mts.* France **21** 45.20N 6.40E
Vanrhynsdorp R.S.A. **80** 31.37S 18.42E
Vansbro Sweden **41** 60.31N 14.13E
Vantaa Finland **41** 60.13N 25.01E
Van Tassell U.S.A. **108** 42.40N 104.02W
Vanthali India **62** 21.29N 70.20E
Vanua Levu *i.* Fiji **84** 16.33S 179.15E
Vanua Mbalavu *i.* Fiji **84** 17.40S 178.57W
Vanuatu Pacific Oc. **84** 16.00S 167.00E
Van Wert U.S.A. **112** 40.53N 84.36W
Vanzylsrus R.S.A. **80** 26.51S 22.03E
Vapnyarka U.S.S.R. **37** 48.31N 28.44E
Var *d.* France **21** 43.30N 6.20E
Var *r.* France **21** 43.39N 7.11E
Vara Sweden **43** 58.16N 12.57E
Varades France **18** 47.23N 1.02W
Varallo Italy **30** 45.49N 8.15E
Varāmīn Iran **65** 35.20N 51.39E
Vārānasi India **63** 25.20N 83.00E
Varangerfjorden *est.* Norway **40** 70.00N 30.00E
Varangerhalvöya *pen.* Norway **40** 70.25N 29.30E
Varano, Lago di *l.* Italy **33** 41.53N 15.45E
Varaždin Yugo. **31** 46.19N 16.20E
Varazze Italy **30** 44.22N 8.34E
Varberg Sweden **43** 57.06N 12.15E
Vardak *d.* Afghan. **62** 34.15N 68.30E
Vardar *r.* Yugo. **34** 41.25N 22.20E
Vardar *r.* *see* Axiós Yugo. **29**
Varde Denmark **42** 55.38N 8.29E
Vardhoúsia Óri *mts.* Greece **35** 38.44N 22.07E
Varel W. Germany **38** 53.24N 8.08E
Varennes Canada **105** 45.41N 73.26W
Varennes France **20** 46.19N 3.24E
Vareš Yugo. **31** 44.09N 18.19E
Varese Italy **30** 45.48N 8.48E
Varese Ligure Italy **30** 44.22N 9.37E
Vårgårda Sweden **43** 58.02N 12.48E
Varginha Brazil **126** 21.33S 45.25W

Vargön to Vilvoorde

Vargön Sweden 43 58.22N 12.22E
Varkhān r. Afghan. 62 32.55N 65.30E
Värmeln l. Sweden 43 59.32N 12.54E
Värmland d. Sweden 43 59.45N 13.15E
Värmland f. Sweden 43 60.05N 13.25E
Värmlandsnäs c. Sweden 43 59.00N 13.10E
Varna Bulgaria 37 43.13N 27.57E
Värnamo Sweden 43 57.11N 14.02E
Varnsdorf E. Germany 38 50.52N 14.40E
Värö Sweden 43 57.16N 12.11E
Várpalota Hungary 37 47.12N 18.09E
Vartofta Sweden 43 58.06N 13.40E
Varvarin Yugo. 34 43.43N 21.19E
Varzo Italy 30 46.12N 8.15E
Varzy France 19 47.22N 3.23E
Vasa see Vaasa Finland 40
Vasai India 62 19.21N 72.48E
Vascão r. Portugal 27 37.31N 7.31W
Vascongadas y Navarra d. Spain 25 42.50N 2.00W
Vashka r. U.S.S.R. 44 64.55N 45.50E
Vasilika Greece 34 40.28N 23.08E
Vasilkov U.S.S.R. 37 50.12N 30.15E
Vaslui Romania 37 46.38N 27.44E
Väsman l. Sweden 43 60.11N 15.04E
Vassar U.S.A. 104 43.22N 83.35W
Västerås Sweden 43 59.37N 16.33E
Västerbotten d. Sweden 40 64.50N 18.10E
Västerdal r. Sweden 41 60.33N 15.08E
Västergötland Sweden 43 58.01N 13.03E
Västerhaninge Sweden 43 59.07N 18.06E
Västernorrland d. Sweden 40 63.20N 17.30E
Västervik Sweden 43 57.45N 16.38E
Västmanland d. Sweden 43 59.53N 16.20E
Västmanland f. Sweden 43 59.47N 15.45E
Vasto Italy 33 42.07N 14.42E
Vasvár Hungary 31 47.03N 16.49E
Vatan France 19 47.05N 1.48E
Váthia Greece 35 36.29N 22.29E
Vatican City Europe 32 41.54N 12.27E
Vaticano, Capo c. Italy 33 38.38N 15.50E
Vatnajökull mts. Iceland 40 64.20N 17.00W
Vatneyri Iceland 40 65.36N 23.59W
Vatomandry Madagascar 81 19.20S 48.59E
Vatra Dornei Romania 37 47.21N 25.21E
Vättern l. Sweden 43 58.24N 14.36E
Vaucluse d. France 21 44.00N 5.20E
Vaucouleurs France 19 48.36N 5.40E
Vaughan Canada 104 43.50N 79.32W
Vaughn Mont. U.S.A. 108 47.35N 111.34W
Vaughn N.Mex. U.S.A. 109 34.36N 105.13W
Vaupés r. Colombia 122 0.20N 69.00W
Vauvert France 21 43.42N 4.17E
Vava'u Group is. Tonga 85 18.40S 174.00W
Vavuniya Sri Lanka 61 8.45N 80.30E
Växjö Sweden 43 56.52N 14.49E
Vaygach U.S.S.R. 50 70.28N 58.59E
Vaygach, Ostrov i. U.S.S.R. 44 70.00N 59.00E
Vecht r. Neth. 16 52.39N 6.01E
Vechta W. Germany 38 52.43N 8.16E
Vecsés Hungary 37 47.26N 19.19E
Veddige Sweden 43 57.16N 12.19E
Vedea r. Romania 34 44.00N 25.20E
Veendam Neth. 16 53.08N 6.52E
Veenendaal Neth. 16 52.03N 5.32E
Vega i. Norway 40 65.39N 11.50E
Vega U.S.A. 111 35.15N 102.26W
Vegarsvatn l. Norway 42 58.50N 8.50E
Veghel Neth. 16 51.37N 5.35E
Vegreville Canada 100 53.30N 112.05W
Veinticinco de Mayo Argentina 125 35.25S 60.11W
Vejen Denmark 42 55.29N 9.09E
Vejer Spain 27 36.15N 5.58W
Vejle Denmark 42 55.42N 9.32E
Vela Luka Yugo. 31 42.58N 16.43E
Velddrif R.S.A. 80 32.47S 18.09E
Velebit Planina mts. Yugo. 31 44.35N 15.00E
Velebitski Kanal str. Yugo. 31 44.40N 14.55E
Velenje Yugo. 31 46.21N 15.06E
Velestinon Greece 35 39.23N 22.45E
Vélez-Málaga Spain 27 36.47N 4.06W
Vélez Rubio Spain 25 37.39N 2.04W
Velhas r. Brazil 126 17.20S 44.55W
Velika Gorica Yugo. 31 45.43N 16.05E
Velika Kapela mts. Yugo. 31 45.20N 15.00E
Velike Lašće Yugo. 31 45.50N 14.38E
Veliki Canal Yugo. 31 45.45N 19.07E
Veliki Vitorog mtn. Yugo. 31 44.07N 17.03E
Velikiye-Luki U.S.S.R. 44 56.19N 30.31E
Velikiy Ustyug U.S.S.R. 44 60.48N 45.15E
Veliko Tŭrnovo Bulgaria 34 43.05N 25.41E
Veli Lošinj Yugo. 31 44.31N 14.30E
Velingrad Bulgaria 34 42.04N 23.58E
Velino, Monte mtn. Italy 30 42.09N 13.23E
Velizh U.S.S.R. 44 55.36N 31.13E
Velletri Italy 30 41.41N 12.47E
Vellinge Sweden 43 55.28N 13.01E
Vellore India 61 12.56N 79.09E
Velsen Neth. 16 52.28N 4.39E
Velsk U.S.S.R. 44 61.05N 42.06E
Velten E. Germany 38 52.41N 13.10E
Veluwe f. Neth. 16 52.17N 5.45E
Velvendós Greece 34 40.15N 22.06E
Vemdalen Sweden 40 62.29N 13.55E
Ven i. Sweden 43 55.54N 12.41E
Venaco France 21 42.14N 9.10E
Venado Tuerto Argentina 125 33.45S 61.56W
Venafro Italy 33 41.29N 14.02E
Venaria Italy 30 45.08N 7.38E
Vence France 21 43.43N 7.07E
Venda Nova Portugal 26 41.40N 7.58W
Vendas Novas Portugal 27 38.41N 8.28W
Vendée d. France 18 46.40N 1.20W
Vendée f. France 18 46.40N 1.10W
Vendée r. France 18 46.30N 0.45W
Vendeuvre-sur-Barse France 19 48.14N 4.28E
Vendôme France 18 47.48N 1.04E
Vendrell Spain 25 41.13N 1.32E
Vendsyssel f. Denmark 42 57.20N 10.00E
Veneto d. Italy 30 45.50N 12.00E
Venev U.S.S.R. 44 54.22N 38.15E
Venezia Italy 30 45.26N 12.20E
Venezuela S. America 122 7.00N 65.20W
Venezuela, Golfo de g. Venezuela 122 11.30N 71.00W
Venezuelan Basin f. Carib. Sea. 127 14.30N 68.00W
Vengurla India 60 15.52N 73.38E
Veniaminof Mtn. U.S.A. 98 56.05N 159.20W
Venice see Venezia Italy 30
Venice U.S.A. 113 27.05N 82.26W
Venice, G. of Med. Sea 30 45.20N 13.00E
Vénissieux France 21 45.41N 4.53E
Venlo Neth. 16 51.22N 6.10E
Vennesla Norway 42 58.17N 7.59E
Venosa Italy 33 40.57N 15.49E
Venraij Neth. 16 51.32N 5.58E
Vent Austria 30 46.52N 10.56E
Vent, Îles du is. Îs. de la Société 85 17.30S 149.30W
Venta r. U.S.S.R. 41 57.24N 21.33E
Ventersdorp R.S.A. 80 26.19S 26.48E
Ventimiglia Italy 30 43.47N 7.36E
Ventnor U.K. 13 50.35N 1.12W
Ventspils U.S.S.R. 41 57.24N 21.36E
Ventuari r. Venezuela 122 4.00N 67.35W
Venus B. Australia 93 38.40S 145.43E
Vera Argentina 126 29.31S 60.30W
Vera Spain 27 37.15N 1.51W
Veracruz Mexico 116 19.11N 96.10W
Veracruz d. Mexico 116 18.00N 95.00W
Verāval India 62 20.54N 70.22E
Verbania Italy 30 45.56N 8.33E
Vercel France 19 47.11N 6.23E
Vercelli Italy 30 45.19N 8.25E
Vercors d. France 21 44.57N 5.25E
Verde r. Argentina 125 42.10S 65.03W
Verde r. Brazil 124 19.11S 50.44W
Verden W. Germany 38 52.55N 9.13E
Verdhikoúsa Greece 34 39.47N 21.59E
Verdon r. France 21 43.43N 5.46E
Verdun Canada 105 45.27N 73.34W
Verdun Meuse France 19 49.10N 5.23E
Verdun T.G. France 20 43.52N 1.14E
Verdun-sur-le-Doubs France 19 46.54N 5.01E
Vereeniging R.S.A. 80 26.40S 27.55E
Vergara Spain 26 43.07N 2.25W
Vergelee R.S.A. 80 25.46S 24.09E
Vergennes U.S.A. 105 44.10N 73.15W
Vergoritis, Límni l. Greece 34 40.45N 21.49E
Vergt France 20 45.02N 0.43E
Verín Spain 26 41.56N 7.26W
Verkhniy Baskunchak U.S.S.R. 45 48.14N 46.44E
Verkhniy Lyulyukary U.S.S.R. 44 65.45N 64.28E
Verkhniy Shar U.S.S.R. 44 68.21N 50.45E
Verkhniy Ufaley U.S.S.R. 44 56.05N 60.14E
Verkhnyaya Taymyra r. U.S.S.R. 51 74.10N 99.50E
Verkhnyaya Tura U.S.S.R. 44 58.22N 59.50E
Verkhovye U.S.S.R. 44 52.49N 37.14E
Verkhoyansk U.S.S.R. 51 67.25N 133.25E
Verkhoyanskiy Khrebet mts. U.S.S.R. 51 66.00N 130.00E
Vermenton France 19 47.40N 3.44E
Vermilion Canada 101 53.22N 110.51W
Vermilion r. Canada 104 46.16N 81.41W
Vermilion U.S.A. 114 41.25N 82.22W
Vermilion Bay town Canada 102 49.51N 93.24W
Vermilion Chutes Canada 100 58.22N 114.51W
Vermillion U.S.A. 110 42.48N 96.55W
Vermont d. U.S.A. 105 43.50N 72.45W
Vernal U.S.A. 108 40.27N 109.32W
Verner Canada 104 46.25N 80.07W
Verneuil France 18 48.44N 0.56E
Vernon Canada 100 50.20N 119.15W
Vernon France 18 49.05N 1.29E
Vernon U.S.A. 111 34.09N 99.17W
Verny France 19 49.01N 6.12E
Vero r. Spain 25 42.00N 0.10E
Vero Beach town U.S.A. 113 27.39N 80.24W
Véroia Greece 34 40.31N 22.12E
Verona Italy 30 45.27N 11.00E
Verónica Argentina 125 35.24S 57.22W
Verrès Italy 30 45.40N 7.42E
Versailles France 19 48.48N 2.08E
Versailles U.S.A. 113 38.02N 84.45W
Vert, Cap c. Senegal 76 14.45N 17.25W
Verteillac France 20 45.21N 0.22E
Vertou France 18 47.10N 1.29W
Vertus France 19 48.54N 4.00E
Vervey Switz. 39 46.28N 6.51E
Verviers Belgium 16 50.36N 5.52E
Vervins France 19 49.50N 3.54E
Vesanto Finland 40 62.56N 26.25E
Vescovato France 21 42.30N 9.26E
Veselí nad Lužnicí Czech. 36 49.11N 14.43E
Vesle r. France 19 49.23N 3.38E
Vesoul France 19 47.38N 6.10E
Vest-Agder d. Norway 42 58.45N 7.00E
Vestbygd Norway 42 58.06N 6.35E
Vesterö Havn Denmark 42 57.18N 10.56E
Vestfjorden est. Norway 40 68.10N 15.00E
Vestfold d. Norway 42 59.20N 10.10E
Vestmanhavn Faroe Is. 10 62.09N 7.11W
Vestmannaeyjar is. Iceland 40 63.30N 20.20W
Vestvågöy i. Norway 40 68.10N 13.50E
Vesuvio mtn. Italy 33 40.49N 14.26E
Vesyegonsk U.S.S.R. 44 58.38N 37.19E
Veszprém Hungary 37 47.06N 17.55E
Vésztö Hungary 37 46.55N 21.16E
Vetka U.S.S.R. 37 52.35N 31.13E
Vetlanda Sweden 43 57.26N 15.04E
Vetluga U.S.S.R. 44 57.50N 45.42E
Vetluga r. U.S.S.R. 44 56.18N 46.19E
Vetovo Bulgaria 34 43.42N 26.16E
Vetralla Italy 30 42.19N 12.03E
Vetren Bulgaria 34 42.15N 24.03E
Vetschau E. Germany 38 51.47N 14.04E
Vettore, Monte mtn. Italy 30 42.49N 13.16E
Veurne Belgium 16 51.04N 2.40E
Vevelstad Norway 40 65.43N 12.30E
Vevey Switz. 19 46.28N 6.51E
Vévi Greece 34 40.47N 21.38E
Veynes France 21 44.32N 5.49E
Vézelise France 19 48.29N 6.05E
Vézère r. France 20 44.53N 0.53E
Vezhen mtn. Bulgaria 34 42.50N 24.20E
Viacha Bolivia 122 16.40S 68.17W
Viadana Italy 30 44.56N 10.31E
Viana Brazil 123 3.13S 45.00W
Viana Portugal 27 38.20N 8.00W
Viana del Bollo Spain 26 42.11N 7.06W
Viana do Castelo Portugal 26 41.42N 8.50W
Viana do Castelo d. Portugal 26 41.55N 8.30W
Viangchan Laos 56 17.59N 102.38E
Viar r. Spain 27 37.36N 5.50W
Viareggio Italy 30 43.52N 10.14E
Viaur r. France 20 44.08N 2.23E
Viborg Denmark 42 56.26N 9.24E
Vibo Valentia Italy 33 38.40N 16.06E
Vibraye France 18 48.03N 0.44E
Vic-en-Bigorre France 20 43.06N 0.05E
Vicente López Argentina 125 34.32S 58.29W
Vicenza Italy 32 45.33N 11.33E
Vich Spain 25 41.56N 2.15E
Vichada r. Colombia 122 4.58N 67.35W
Vichuga U.S.S.R. 44 57.12N 41.50E
Vichy France 20 46.08N 3.26E
Vicksburg U.S.A. 111 32.14N 90.56W
Vico France 21 42.10N 8.48E
Viçosa Alagoas Brazil 123 9.22S 36.10W
Viçosa Minas Gerais Brazil 126 20.45S 42.53W
Vic-sur-Cère France 20 44.59N 2.37E
Victor U.S.A. 114 42.59N 77.24W
Victor Harbour Australia 92 35.36S 138.35E
Victoria Argentina 125 32.40S 60.10W
Victoria d. Australia 93 37.20S 145.00E
Victoria r. Australia 88 15.12S 129.43E
Victoria Canada 100 48.30N 123.25W
Victoria Chile 125 38.13S 72.20W
Victoria Guinea 76 10.50N 14.32W
Victoria Hong Kong 48 22.16N 114.15E
Victoria U.S.A. 111 28.48N 97.00W
Victoria, L. Africa 79 1.00S 33.00E
Victoria, L. Australia 92 34.00S 141.15E
Victoria, Mt. Burma 56 21.12N 93.55E
Victoria, Mt. P.N.G. 90 8.55S 147.35E
Victoria Beach town Canada 101 50.43N 96.33W
Victoria de las Tunas Cuba 117 20.58N 76.59W
Victoria Downs town Australia 90 20.44S 146.21E
Victoria Falls f. Zimbabwe/Zambia 80 17.58S 25.45E
Victoria Harbour Canada 104 44.45N 79.46W
Victoria I. Canada 98 71.00N 110.00W
Victoria L. Australia 92 32.29S 143.22E
Victoria Nile r. Uganda 79 2.14N 31.20E
Victoria River Downs town Australia 90 16.24S 131.00E
Victoriaville Canada 105 46.03N 71.57W
Victoria West R.S.A. 80 31.24S 23.07E
Victorica Argentina 125 36.15S 65.25W
Vidalia U.S.A. 113 32.14N 82.24W
Vidauban France 21 43.26N 6.26E
Videbaek Denmark 42 56.05N 8.38E
Videle Romania 37 44.16N 25.31E
Viderö i. Faroe Is. 10 62.21N 6.30W
Vidigueira Portugal 27 38.13N 7.48W
Vidin Bulgaria 34 43.59N 22.52E
Vidin d. Bulgaria 34 44.00N 22.50E
Vidisha India 63 23.32N 77.49E
Vidöstern l. Sweden 43 57.04N 14.01E
Viechtach W. Germany 39 49.05N 12.53E
Viedma Argentina 125 40.50S 63.00W
Viedma, L. Argentina 125 49.40S 72.30W
Vieira do Minho Portugal 26 41.39N 8.09W
Viella Spain 25 42.42N 0.48E
Vienna see Wien Austria 36
Vienna Md. U.S.A. 115 38.29N 75.49W
Vienna S.Dak. U.S.A. 110 44.42N 97.30W
Vienna Va. U.S.A. 114 38.54N 77.16W
Vienne d. France 18 46.35N 0.30E
Vienne r. France 18 47.13N 0.05E
Vientiane see Viangchan Laos 56
Vieques i. Puerto Rico 117 18.08N 65.30W
Viernheim W. Germany 39 49.33N 8.39E
Viersen W. Germany 38 51.15N 6.23E
Vierwaldstätter See l. Switz. 39 47.00N 8.28E
Vierzon France 19 47.13N 2.05E
Vieste Italy 31 41.53N 16.10E
Vietnam Asia 56 15.00N 108.30E
Viet Tri Vietnam 55 21.20N 105.26E
Vieux-Condé France 16 50.29N 3.31E
Vif France 21 45.03N 5.40E
Vigan France 20 43.59N 3.35E
Vigan Phil. 59 17.35N 120.23E
Vigeland Norway 42 58.05N 7.18E
Vigevano Italy 30 45.19N 8.51E
Vignemale, Pic de mtn. France 20 42.46N 0.08W
Vigneulles-lès-Hattonchâtel France 19 48.59N 5.43E
Vigo Spain 26 42.14N 8.43W
Vigo, Ría de est. Spain 26 42.15N 8.45W
Vigrestad Norway 42 58.34N 5.42E
Vihāri Pakistan 62 30.02N 72.21E
Vihiers France 18 47.09N 0.32W
Vihowa Pakistan 62 31.08N 70.30E
Vijāpur India 62 23.35N 72.45E
Vijayawāda India 61 16.34N 80.40E
Vijosë r. Albania 34 40.37N 19.20E
Vik Norway 40 65.19N 12.10E
Vikajärvi Finland 40 66.37N 26.12E
Viken Sweden 43 56.09N 12.34E
Viken l. Sweden 43 58.39N 14.20E
Vikersund Norway 42 59.59N 10.02E
Vikmanshyttan Sweden 43 60.17N 15.49E
Vikna i. Norway 40 64.52N 10.57E
Vikulovo U.S.S.R. 50 56.51N 70.30E
Vila Vanuatu 84 17.44S 168.19E
Vila da Maganja Mozambique 79 17.25S 37.32E
Vila de Rei Portugal 27 39.40N 8.09W
Vila de Sena Mozambique 79 17.36S 35.00E
Vila do Bispo Portugal 27 37.05N 8.55W
Vila do Conde Portugal 26 41.21N 8.45W
Vila Flor Portugal 26 41.18N 7.09W
Vila Franca Portugal 27 38.57N 8.59W
Vilafranca del Penedès Spain 25 41.21N 1.42E
Vilaine r. France 18 47.30N 2.27W
Vilanculos Mozambique 81 21.59S 35.16E
Vila Nova de Famalicão Portugal 26 41.25N 8.32W
Vila Nova de Fozcoa Portugal 26 41.05N 7.12W
Vila Nova de Gaia Portugal 26 41.45N 8.34W
Vila Nova de Ourém Portugal 27 39.39N 8.35W
Vila Nova do Seles Angola 78 11.24S 14.15E
Vila Real Portugal 26 41.18N 7.45W
Vila Real d. Portugal 26 41.35N 7.35W
Vila Real de Santo António Portugal 27 37.12N 7.25W
Vilar Formoso Portugal 26 40.35N 6.53W
Vila Vasco da Gama Mozambique 79 14.55S 32.12E
Vila Velha Brazil 126 20.20S 40.17W
Vila Velha de Ródão Portugal 27 39.38N 7.40W
Vila Verde Portugal 26 41.39N 8.26W
Vila Veríssimo Sarmento Angola 78 8.08S 20.38E
Vila Viçosa Portugal 27 38.47N 7.25W
Vildbjerg Denmark 42 56.12N 8.46E
Vileyka U.S.S.R. 37 54.30N 26.50E
Vilhelmina Sweden 40 64.37N 16.39E
Vilhena Brazil 122 12.40S 60.08W
Viliga Kushka U.S.S.R. 51 61.35N 156.55E
Viljandi U.S.S.R. 44 58.22N 25.30E
Vilkavišhkis U.S.S.R. 37 54.39N 23.02E
Vil'kitskogo, Proliv str. U.S.S.R. 51 77.57N 102.30E
Vilkovo U.S.S.R. 37 45.28N 29.32E
Villa Adriana site Italy 30 41.56N 12.45E
Villa Angela Argentina 124 27.34S 60.45W
Villa Bella Bolivia 124 10.23S 65.24W
Villablino Spain 26 42.56N 6.19W
Villacañas Spain 27 39.38N 3.20W
Villacarriedo Spain 26 43.14N 3.48W
Villacarrillo Spain 26 38.07N 3.05W
Villacastín Spain 26 40.47N 4.25W
Villach Austria 31 46.36N 13.50E
Villa Clara Argentina 125 31.46S 58.50W
Villa Constitución Argentina 125 33.14S 60.21W
Villada Spain 26 42.15N 4.59W
Villa del Río Spain 27 37.59N 4.17W
Villa de Santiago Mexico 111 25.26N 100.09W
Villadiego Spain 26 42.31N 4.00W
Villa Dolores Argentina 124 31.58S 65.12W
Villafranca del Bierzo Spain 26 42.36N 6.48W
Villafranca de los Barros Spain 27 38.34N 6.20W
Villafranca di Verona Italy 30 45.21N 10.50E
Villagarcía Spain 26 42.36N 8.45W
Villaguay Argentina 125 31.55S 59.00W
Villahermosa Mexico 116 18.00N 92.53W
Villa Hernandarias Argentina 125 31.15S 59.58W
Villa Huidobro Argentina 125 34.50S 64.34W
Villaines-la-Juhel France 18 48.21N 0.17W
Villajoyosa Spain 25 38.30N 0.14W
Villalba Spain 26 43.18N 7.41W
Villalón de Campos Spain 26 42.06N 5.02W
Villalpando Spain 26 41.52N 5.24W
Villa María Argentina 124 32.25S 63.15W
Villamartín Spain 27 36.52N 5.38W
Villa Montes Bolivia 124 21.15S 63.30W
Villandraut France 20 44.28N 0.23W
Villanova Monteleone Italy 32 40.30N 8.28E
Villanueva de Córdoba Spain 26 38.20N 4.37W
Villanueva de la Serena Spain 26 38.58N 5.48W
Villanueva de los Infantes Spain 27 38.45N 3.01W
Villanueva del Río y Minas Spain 27 37.39N 5.42W
Villanueva-y-Geltrú Spain 25 41.14N 1.44E
Villaputzu Italy 32 39.28N 9.33E
Villarcayo Spain 26 42.56N 3.34W
Villard-de-Lans France 21 45.04N 5.33E
Villardefrades Spain 26 41.43N 5.15W
Villar del Arzobispo Spain 25 39.44N 0.49W
Villarobledo Spain 27 39.16N 2.36W
Villarreal Spain 25 39.56N 0.06W
Villarrica Chile 125 39.15S 72.15W
Villarrica Paraguay 126 25.45S 56.28W
Villarrobledo Spain 24 39.16N 2.36W
Villarrubia de los Ojos Spain 27 39.13N 3.36W
Villa San Giovanni Italy 33 38.13N 15.39E
Villa San José Argentina 125 32.12S 58.15W
Villasayas Spain 26 41.21N 2.37W
Villasimius Italy 32 39.09N 9.31E
Villasor Italy 32 39.22N 8.57E
Villavicencio Colombia 122 4.09N 73.38W
Villaviciosa Spain 26 43.29N 5.26W
Villaviciosa de Córdoba Spain 26 38.05N 5.01W
Villazón Bolivia 124 22.06S 65.36W
Villé France 19 48.20N 7.18E
Villedieu France 18 48.50N 1.13W
Villefort France 20 44.26N 3.56E
Villefranche France 21 45.59N 4.43E
Villefranche-de-Rouergue France 20 44.21N 2.02E
Ville Marie Canada 104 47.19N 79.26W
Villena Spain 25 38.38N 0.51W
Villenauxe-la-Grande France 19 48.35N 3.33E
Villeneuve France 20 44.25N 0.42E
Villeneuve-d'Ascq France 19 50.37N 3.10E
Villeneuve-d'Aveyron France 20 44.26N 2.02E
Villeneuve-de-Berg France 21 44.33N 4.30E
Villeneuve-St. Georges France 19 48.44N 2.27E
Villeneuve-sur-Yonne France 19 48.05N 3.18E
Villeroy Canada 105 46.23N 71.53W
Villers Bocage France 18 49.05N 0.39W
Villers-Cotterêts France 19 49.15N 3.05E
Villersexel France 19 47.33N 6.26E
Villers sur Mer France 18 49.21N 0.02W
Villeurbanne France 21 45.46N 4.53E
Villingen W. Germany 39 48.03N 8.27E
Vilnius U.S.S.R. 37 54.40N 25.19E
Vils r. W. Germany 39 48.39N 13.11E
Vilsbiburg W. Germany 39 48.27N 12.12E
Vilshofen W. Germany 39 48.39N 13.12E
Vilvoorde Belgium 16 50.56N 4.25E

Vilyuy to **Wanning**

Vilyuy *r.* U.S.S.R. **51** 64.20N126.55E
Vilyuysk U.S.S.R. **51** 63.46N121.35E
Vimianzo Spain **26** 43.07N 9.02W
Vimmerby Sweden **43** 57.40N 15.51E
Vimoutiers France **18** 48.55N 0.12E
Vimperk Czech. **38** 49.03N 13.47E
Vina *r.* Chad **77** 7.43N 15.30E
Viña del Mar Chile **125** 33.02S 71.34W
Vinaroz Spain **25** 40.28N 0.29E
Vincennes France **19** 48.51N 2.26E
Vincennes U.S.A. **110** 38.41N 87.32W
Vincent U.S.A. **114** 39.23N 81.40W
Vindel *r.* Sweden **40** 63.54N 19.52E
Vindeln Sweden **40** 64.12N 19.44E
Vinderup Denmark **42** 56.29N 8.47E
Vindhya Range *mts.* India **62** 22.45N 75.30E
Vineland U.S.A. **115** 39.29N 75.02W
Vineyard Haven U.S.A. **115** 41.27N 70.36W
Vineyard Sd. U.S.A. **115** 41.25N 70.46W
Vingåker Sweden **43** 59.02N 15.52E
Vinh Vietnam **56** 18.42N105.41E
Vinhais Portugal **26** 41.50N 7.00W
Vinh Long Vietnam **56** 10.15N105.59E
Vinica Yugo. **31** 45.28N 15.15E
Vinita U.S.A. **111** 36.39N 95.09W
Vînju Mare Romania **37** 44.26N 22.52E
Vinkovci Yugo. **31** 45.17N 18.49E
Vinnitsa U.S.S.R. **37** 49.11N 28.30E
Vinson Massif Antarctica **128** 78.00S 85.00W
Vintar Phil. **55** 18.16N120.40E
Vinton U.S.A. **110** 42.10N 92.01W
Vioolsdrif R.S.A. **80** 28.45S 17.33E
Vipava Yugo. **31** 45.51N 13.58E
Vipiteno Italy **30** 46.54N 11.26E
Viqueque Indonesia **59** 8.42S126.30E
Vir *i.* Yugo. **31** 44.18N 15.04E
Virac Phil. **59** 13.35N124.15E
Viramgām India **62** 23.07N 72.02E
Viranşehir Turkey **64** 37.13N 39.45E
Virden Canada **101** 49.51N100.55W
Vire France **18** 48.50N 0.53W
Vire *r.* France **18** 49.20N 1.07W
Vírgenes, C. Argentina **125** 52.00S 68.50W
Virgin Gorda *i.* B.V.Is. **117** 18.30N 64.26W
Virginia U.S.A. **110** 47.31N 92.32W
Virginia *d.* U.S.A. **113** 37.30N 78.45W
Virginia Beach *town* U.S.A. **113** 36.51N 75.59W
Virginia City Mont. U.S.A. **108** 45.18N111.56W
Virginia City Nev. U.S.A. **108** 39.19N119.39W
Virieu-le-Grand France **21** 45.51N 5.39E
Virje Yugo. **31** 46.04N 16.59E
Virovitica Yugo. **31** 45.50N 17.23E
Virpazar Yugo. **31** 42.15N 19.05E
Virrat Finland **40** 62.14N 23.47E
Virserum Sweden **41** 57.19N 15.35E
Virton Belgium **16** 49.35N 5.32E
Virtsu U.S.S.R. **41** 58.34N 23.31E
Virunga Nat. Park Zaïre **79** 0.30S 29.15E
Vis Yugo. **31** 43.03N 16.12E
Vis *i.* Yugo. **31** 43.02N 16.11E
Visalia U.S.A. **109** 36.20N119.18W
Visayan Sea Phil. **59** 11.35N123.51E
Visby Sweden **43** 57.38N 18.18E
Visconde do Rio Branco Brazil **126** 21.00S 42.51W
Viscount Melville Sd. Canada **98** 74.30N104.00W
Visé Belgium **16** 50.44N 5.42E
Višegrad Yugo. **31** 43.47N 19.17E
Viserum Sweden **43** 57.21N 15.34E
Viseu Brazil **123** 1.12S 46.07W
Viseu Portugal **26** 40.39N 7.55W
Viseu *d.* Portugal **26** 40.50N 7.55W
Viseu de Sus Romania **37** 47.44N 24.22E
Vishākhapatnam India **61** 17.42N 83.24E
Viskafors Sweden **43** 57.38N 12.50E
Viskan *r.* Sweden **43** 57.14N 12.12E
Visnagar India **62** 23.42N 72.33E
Viso, Monte *mtn.* Italy **30** 44.40N 7.07E
Visoko Yugo. **31** 43.59N 18.11E
Visp Switz. **39** 46.18N 7.53E
Vissefjärda Sweden **43** 56.32N 15.35E
Visselhövede W. Germany **38** 52.59N 9.35E
Vista U.S.A. **109** 33.12N117.15W
Vistula *r. see* Wisła Poland **37**
Vit *r.* Bulgaria **34** 43.30N 24.30E
Vitanje Yugo. **31** 46.23N 15.18E
Vitarte Peru **122** 12.03S 76.51W
Vitebsk U.S.S.R. **44** 55.10N 30.14E
Viterbo Italy **30** 42.25N 12.06E
Vitigudino Spain **26** 41.00N 6.26W
Viti Levu *i.* Fiji **84** 18.00S178.00E
Vitim U.S.S.R. **51** 59.28N112.35E
Vitim *r.* U.S.S.R. **51** 59.30N112.36E
Vitória Espírito Santo Brazil **126** 20.19S 40.21W
Vitoria Spain **26** 42.51N 2.40W
Vitré France **18** 48.08N 1.12W
Vitry-le-François France **19** 48.44N 4.35E
Vitteaux France **19** 47.24N 4.32E
Vittel France **19** 48.12N 5.57E
Vittoria Italy **33** 36.57N 14.32E
Vittorio Veneto Italy **32** 45.59N 12.18E
Vittsjö Sweden **43** 56.20N 13.40E
Viver Spain **25** 39.55N 0.36W
Viveiro Spain **26** 43.38N 7.35W
Viviers France **21** 44.29N 4.41E
Vivonne Australia **92** 35.58S137.10E
Vivonne France **18** 46.26N 0.16E
Vivonne B. Australia **92** 36.00S137.00E
Vizcaíno, Desierto de *des.* Mexico **109** 27.40N114.40W
Vizcaíno, Sierra *mts.* Mexico **109** 27.20N114.30W
Vizcaya *d.* Spain **26** 43.25N 2.45W
Vizianagaram India **61** 18.07N 83.30E
Vizille France **21** 45.05N 5.46E
Vižinad Yugo. **31** 45.20N 13.46E
Vizinga U.S.S.R. **44** 61.06N 50.05E
Vizzini Italy **33** 37.09N 14.46E
Vlaardingen Neth. **16** 51.55N 4.20E
Vladičin Han Yugo. **34** 42.42N 22.04E
Vladimir U.S.S.R. **44** 56.08N 40.25E
Vladimirets U.S.S.R. **37** 51.28N 26.03E
Vladimir Volynskiy U.S.S.R. **37** 50.51N 24.19E
Vladivostok U.S.S.R. **53** 43.09N131.53E
Vlasenica Yugo. **31** 44.11N 18.56E
Vlieland *i.* Neth. **16** 53.15N 5.00E
Vlissingen Neth. **16** 51.27N 3.35E
Vlorë Albania **34** 40.27N 19.30E
Vlorë *d.* Albania **34** 40.29N 19.29E
Vltava *r.* Czech. **39** 50.21N 14.30E
Vočin Yugo. **31** 45.37N 17.32E
Vöcklabruck Austria **39** 48.01N 13.39E
Vodňany Czech. **39** 49.09N 14.11E
Vodnjan Yugo. **31** 44.57N 13.51E
Voerde W. Germany **16** 51.37N 6.39E
Vogelkop *f. see* Jazirah Doberai Indonesia **59**
Vogelsberg *mts.* W. Germany **38** 50.30N 9.15E
Voghera Italy **30** 44.59N 9.01E
Voh N. Cal. **84** 20.58S164.42E
Vohibinany Madagascar **81** 18.49S 49.04E
Vohimarina Madagascar **81** 13.21S 50.02E
Vohipeno Madagascar **81** 22.22S 47.51E
Voi Kenya **79** 3.23S 38.35E
Void France **19** 48.41N 5.37E
Voiron France **21** 45.22N 5.35E
Voitsberg Austria **31** 47.03N 15.10E
Vojens Denmark **42** 55.15N 9.19E
Vojnić Yugo. **31** 45.19N 15.43E
Volary Czech. **38** 48.55N 13.54E
Volborg U.S.A. **108** 45.50N105.40W
Volcano Is. Japan **84** 25.00N141.00E
Volda Norway **41** 62.09N 6.06E
Volga *r.* U.S.S.R. **45** 45.45N 47.50E
Volgograd U.S.S.R. **45** 48.45N 44.30E
Volgogradskoye Vodokhranilishche *resr.* U.S.S.R. **45** 51.00N 46.05E
Volissós Greece **35** 38.29N 25.58E
Volkach W. Germany **39** 49.52N 10.13E
Volkhov U.S.S.R. **44** 59.54N 32.47E
Volkhov *r.* U.S.S.R. **44** 60.15N 32.15E
Völklingen W. Germany **39** 49.15N 6.50E
Volkovysk U.S.S.R. **37** 53.10N 24.28E
Vollenhove Neth. **16** 52.41N 5.59E
Volnovakha U.S.S.R. **45** 47.36N 37.32E
Volochanka U.S.S.R. **51** 70.59N 94.18E
Volochisk U.S.S.R. **37** 49.34N 26.10E
Volodarsk U.S.S.R. **44** 56.14N 43.10E
Vologda U.S.S.R. **44** 59.10N 39.55E
Volokolamsk U.S.S.R. **44** 56.02N 35.56E
Volonne France **21** 44.07N 6.01E
Vólos Greece **35** 39.21N 22.56E
Volovets U.S.S.R. **37** 48.44N 23.14E
Volsk U.S.S.R. **44** 52.04N 47.22E
Volta *d.* Ghana **76** 7.30N 0.25E
Volta *r.* Ghana **76** 5.50N 0.41E
Volta, L. Ghana **76** 7.00N 0.00
Volta Blanche *see* White Volta U. Volta **76**
Volta-Noire *d.* U. Volta **76** 12.30N 3.25W
Volta Noire *see* Black Volta U. Volta **76**
Volta Redonda Brazil **126** 22.31S 44.05W
Volta Rouge *see* Red Volta U. Volta **76**
Volterra Italy **30** 43.24N 10.51E
Voltri Italy **30** 44.26N 8.45E
Volturno *r.* Italy **33** 41.01N 13.55E
Volvi, Límni *l.* Greece **34** 40.41N 23.23E
Volyně Czech. **38** 49.10N 13.53E
Volzhskiy U.S.S.R. **45** 48.48N 44.45E
Vondrozo Madagascar **81** 22.49S 47.20E
Vónitsa Greece **35** 38.53N 20.58E
Voorburg Neth. **16** 52.05N 4.22E
Vopnafjördhur *est.* Iceland **40** 65.50N 14.30W
Vopnafjördhur *town* Iceland **40** 65.46N 14.50W
Vorarlberg *d.* Austria **39** 47.13N 9.55E
Vóras Óros *mts.* Greece **34** 40.57N 21.45E
Vorderrhein *r.* Switz. **39** 46.49N 9.25E
Vordingborg Denmark **42** 55.01N 11.55E
Voríai Sporádhes *is.* Greece **35** 39.17N 23.23E
Vórios-Evvoïkós Kólpos *b.* Greece **35** 38.45N 23.15E
Vorkuta U.S.S.R. **44** 67.27N 64.00E
Vorma *r.* Norway **42** 60.09N 11.27E
Vormsi *i.* U.S.S.R. **41** 59.00N 23.20E
Voronezh U.S.S.R. **45** 51.40N 39.13E
Voronovo U.S.S.R. **37** 54.09N 25.19E
Voroshilovgrad U.S.S.R. **45** 48.35N 39.20E
Vorpommern *f.* E. Germany **38** 53.49N 13.39E
Vosges *d.* France **19** 48.10N 6.20E
Vosges *mts.* France **19** 48.30N 7.10E
Voss Norway **41** 60.39N 6.26E
Vostochno Sibirskoye More *sea* U.S.S.R. **51** 73.00N160.00E
Vostochnyy Sayan *mts.* U.S.S.R. **52** 51.30N102.00E
Vostok I. Kiribati **85** 10.05S152.23W
Votkinsk U.S.S.R. **44** 57.02N 53.59E
Votkinskoye Vodokhranilishche *resr.* U.S.S.R. **44** 57.00N 55.00E
Votuporanga Brazil **124** 20.26S 49.53W
Vouga *r.* Portugal **26** 40.41N 8.40W
Vouillé France **18** 46.39N 0.10E
Voulou C.A.R. **73** 8.33N 22.36E
Vouziers France **19** 49.24N 4.42E
Voves France **19** 48.16N 1.38E
Voxna Sweden **41** 61.20N 15.30E
Voxna *r.* Sweden **41** 61.17N 16.26E
Voyvozh U.S.S.R. **44** 64.19N 55.12E
Vozhega U.S.S.R. **44** 60.25N 40.11E
Voznesensk U.S.S.R. **23** 47.34N 31.21E
Vrå Denmark **42** 57.21N 9.57E
Vrådal Norway **42** 59.20N 8.25E
Vrakhnéika Greece **35** 38.10N 21.40E
Vrangelya, Ostrov *i.* U.S.S.R. **51** 71.00N180.00
Vranje Yugo. **34** 42.34N 21.54E
Vratsa Bulgaria **34** 43.13N 23.30E
Vratsa *d.* Bulgaria **34** 43.30N 23.30E
Vrbas Yugo. **31** 45.35N 19.39E
Vrbas *r.* Yugo. **31** 45.06N 17.31E
Vrbovec Yugo. **31** 45.53N 16.25E
Vrbovsko Yugo. **31** 45.23N 15.05E
Vrede R.S.A. **80** 27.24S 29.09E
Vredendal R.S.A. **80** 31.40S 18.28E
Vrena Sweden **43** 58.52N 16.41E
Vresse Belgium **16** 49.53N 4.57E
Vrgnmost Yugo. **31** 45.21N 15.52E
Vrhnika Yugo. **31** 45.58N 14.18E
Vries Neth. **16** 53.06N 6.35E
Vrigstad Sweden **43** 57.21N 14.28E
Vrindāvan India **63** 27.35N 77.42E
Vrlika Yugo. **31** 43.55N 16.24E
Vrnograč Yugo. **31** 45.10N 15.57E
Vrondádhes Greece **35** 38.25N 26.08E
Vršac Yugo. **37** 45.08N 21.18E
Vryburg R.S.A. **80** 26.57S 24.42E
Vučitrn Yugo. **34** 42.49N 20.59E
Vught Neth. **16** 51.39N 5.18E
Vukovar Yugo. **31** 45.21N 19.00E
Vulcano, Isola *i.* Italy **33** 38.27N 14.58E
Vŭlchedruma Bulgaria **34** 43.42N 23.16E
Vung Tau Vietnam **56** 10.21N107.04E
Vurshets Bulgaria **34** 43.12N 23.17E
Vyāra India **62** 21.07N 73.24E
Vyatka *r.* U.S.S.R. **50** 55.40N 51.40E
Vyatskiye Polyany U.S.S.R. **44** 56.14N 51.08E
Vyazma U.S.S.R. **44** 55.12N 34.17E
Vyazniki U.S.S.R. **44** 56.14N 42.08E
Vyborg U.S.S.R. **44** 60.45N 28.41E
Vychegda *r.* U.S.S.R. **44** 61.15N 46.28E
Vychodné Beskydy *mts.* Europe **37** 49.30N 22.00E
Vygozero, Ozero *l.* U.S.S.R. **44** 63.30N 34.30E
Vyrnwy, L. U.K. **12** 52.46N 3.30W
Vyshka U.S.S.R. **65** 39.19N 54.10E
Vyshniy-Volochek U.S.S.R. **44** 57.34N 34.23E
Vyšší Brod Czech. **39** 48.37N 14.19E
Vytegra U.S.S.R. **44** 61.04N 36.27E

W

Wa Ghana **76** 10.07N 2.28W
Waal *r.* Neth. **16** 51.45N 4.40E
Waalwijk Neth. **16** 51.42N 5.04E
Wabag P.N.G. **59** 5.28S143.40E
Wabasca *r.* Canada **100** 58.22N115.20W
Wabash U.S.A. **110** 40.47N 85.48W
Wabash *r.* U.S.A. **110** 37.46N 88.02W
Wabeno U.S.A. **110** 45.27N 88.38W
Wąbrzeźno Poland **37** 53.17N 18.57E
Wabush City Canada **103** 52.53N 66.50W
Waco U.S.A. **111** 31.55N 97.08W
Wacouno *r.* Canada **103** 50.50N 65.58W
Wad Pakistan **62** 27.21N 66.22E
Wad Bandah Sudan **73** 13.06N 27.57E
Waddān Libya **75** 29.10N 16.08E
Waddeneilanden *is.* Neth. **16** 53.20N 5.00E
Waddenzee *b.* Neth. **16** 53.15N 5.05E
Wadderin Australia **89** 31.57S118.27E
Waddington U.S.A. **105** 44.52N 75.12W
Waddington, Mt. Canada **100** 51.23N125.15W
Wadena U.S.A. **110** 46.26N 95.08W
Wädenswil Switz. **39** 47.14N 8.40E
Wad Ḥāmid Sudan **72** 16.30N 32.48E
Wadhurst U.K. **13** 51.03N 0.21E
Wādī as Sīr *town* Jordan **67** 31.57N 35.49E
Wādī Ḥalfā' Sudan **64** 21.56N 31.20E
Wadikee Australia **92** 33.18S136.12E
Wādī Mūsá *town* Jordan **66** 30.19N 35.29E
Wad Madanī Sudan **72** 14.24N 33.32E
Wad Nimr Sudan **72** 14.32N 32.08E
Wadsworth U.S.A. **114** 41.02N 81.44W
Wafrah Kuwait **65** 28.39N 47.56E
Wageningen Neth. **16** 51.58N 5.39E
Wager B. Canada **99** 65.26N 88.40W
Wager Bay *town* Canada **99** 65.55N 90.40W
Wagga Wagga Australia **93** 35.07S147.24E
Wagin Australia **89** 33.18S117.21E
Wagon Mound *town* U.S.A. **109** 36.01N104.42W
Wagrien *f.* W. Germany **38** 54.15N 10.45E
Wāh Pakistan **62** 33.48N 72.42E
Wahai Indonesia **59** 2.48S129.30E
Wāḥat Salīmah Sudan **72** 21.22N 29.19E
Wahiawa Hawaiian Is. **85** 21.30N158.01W
Wahiba Sands *des.* Oman **60** 21.56N 58.55E
Wahpeton U.S.A. **110** 46.16N 96.36W
Waiau New Zealand **86** 42.39S173.03E
Waiblingen W. Germany **39** 48.50N 9.19E
Waidhān India **63** 24.04N 82.20E
Waidhofen Austria **36** 47.58N 14.47E
Waigeo *i.* Indonesia **59** 0.05S130.30E
Waihi New Zealand **86** 37.24S175.50E
Waikato *r.* New Zealand **86** 37.19S174.50E
Waikerie Australia **92** 34.11S139.59E
Waikokopu New Zealand **86** 39.05S177.50E
Waikouaiti New Zealand **86** 45.36S170.41E
Wailuku Hawaiian Is. **85** 20.53N156.30W
Waimakariri *r.* New Zealand **86** 43.23S172.40E
Waimate New Zealand **86** 44.45S171.03E
Waimea Hawaiian Is. **85** 20.01N155.41W
Wainganga *r.* India **63** 18.50N 79.55E
Waingapu Indonesia **59** 9.30S120.10E
Wainwright Canada **101** 52.49N110.52W
Wainwright U.S.A. **98** 70.39N160.00W
Waiouru New Zealand **86** 39.39S175.40E
Waipara New Zealand **86** 43.03S172.45E
Waipawa New Zealand **86** 39.56S176.35E
Waipiro New Zealand **86** 38.02S178.21E
Waipu New Zealand **86** 35.59S174.26E
Waipukurau New Zealand **86** 40.00S176.33E
Wairau *r.* New Zealand **86** 41.32S174.08E
Wairoa New Zealand **86** 39.03S177.25E
Waitaki *r.* New Zealand **86** 44.56S171.10E
Waitara New Zealand **86** 38.59S174.13E
Waiuku New Zealand **86** 37.15S174.44E
Wajima Japan **57** 37.24N136.54E
Wajir Kenya **79** 1.46N 40.05E
Waka Ethiopia **73** 7.07N 37.26E
Waka Zaïre **78** 0.48S 20.10E
Wakasa wan *b.* Japan **57** 35.50N135.40E
Wakatipu, L. New Zealand **86** 45.10S168.30E
Wakayama Japan **57** 34.13N135.11E
Wakefield Canada **105** 45.38N 75.56W
Wakefield U.K. **12** 53.41N 1.31W
Wakefield U.S.A. **115** 41.26N 71.30W
Wake I. Pacific Oc. **84** 19.17N166.36E
Wakema Burma **56** 16.36N 95.11E
Wakkanai Japan **57** 45.26N141.43E
Wakonassin *r.* Canada **104** 46.28N 81.51W
Wakre Indonesia **59** 0.30S131.05E
Wakuach, L. Canada **103** 55.37N 67.40W
Walamba Zambia **79** 13.27S 28.44E
Wałbrzych Poland **36** 50.48N 16.19E
Walcha Australia **93** 31.00S151.36E
Walcheren *f.* Neth. **16** 51.32N 3.35E
Wałcz Poland **36** 53.17N 16.28E
Waldbröl W. Germany **16** 50.52N 7.34E
Waldeck W. Germany **38** 51.12N 9.04E
Walden U.S.A. **108** 40.34N106.11W
Waldkirch W. Germany **39** 48.05N 7.57E
Waldorf U.S.A. **114** 38.37N 76.54W
Waldport U.S.A. **108** 44.26N124.04W
Waldron U.S.A. **111** 34.54N 94.05W
Waldshut W. Germany **39** 47.37N 8.13E
Wales *d.* U.K. **13** 52.30N 3.45W
Wales U.S.A. **110** 47.13N 91.41W
Walgett Australia **93** 30.03S148.10E
Walhonding *r.* U.S.A. **114** 40.18N 81.53W
Walikale Zaïre **79** 1.29S 28.05E
Walker U.S.A. **110** 47.06N 94.35W
Walker L. U.S.A. **108** 38.44N118.43W
Walkerton Canada **104** 44.07N 81.09W
Wall U.S.A. **108** 43.59N102.14W
Wallace Canada **104** 45.23N 78.05W
Wallace Idaho U.S.A. **108** 47.28N115.55W
Wallace Nebr. U.S.A. **110** 40.50N101.10W
Wallaceburg Canada **104** 42.36N 82.23W
Wallachia *f.* Romania **37** 44.35N 25.00E
Wallambin, L. Australia **89** 30.58S117.30E
Wallangarra Australia **93** 28.51S151.52E
Wallaroo Australia **92** 33.57S137.36E
Walla Walla Australia **93** 35.48S146.52E
Walla Walla U.S.A. **108** 46.08N118.20W
Wallenpaupack, L. U.S.A. **115** 41.25N 75.12W
Wallingford U.S.A. **115** 41.27N 72.50W
Wallis, Îles *is.* Pacific Oc. **84** 13.16S176.15W
Wallkill *r.* U.S.A. **115** 41.51N 74.03W
Wallowa U.S.A. **108** 45.34N117.32W
Wallowa Mts. U.S.A. **108** 45.10N117.30W
Wallsend Australia **93** 32.55S151.40E
Walmsley L. Canada **101** 63.25N108.36W
Walpole Australia **89** 34.57S116.44E
Walsall U.K. **13** 52.36N 1.59W
Walsenburg U.S.A. **108** 37.37N104.47W
Walsrode W. Germany **38** 52.52N 9.35E
Walterboro U.S.A. **113** 32.54N 80.21W
Waltershausen E. Germany **38** 50.53N 10.33E
Waltham Canada **105** 45.55N 76.57W
Walton N.Y. U.S.A. **115** 42.10N 75.08W
Walton W.Va. U.S.A. **114** 38.40N 81.26W
Walton on the Naze U.K. **13** 51.52N 1.17E
Walton on the Wolds U.K. **12** 52.49N 0.49W
Walvis B. R.S.A. **80** 22.55S 14.30E
Walvisbaai R.S.A. **80** 22.57S 14.30E
Walvis Bay *d.* R.S.A. **80** 22.56S 14.35E
Walvis Bay *town see* Walvisbaai R.S.A. **80**
Walvis Ridge *f.* Atlantic Oc. **127** 28.00S 4.00E
Wamanfo Ghana **76** 7.16N 2.44W
Wamba Kenya **79** 0.58N 37.19E
Wamba Nigeria **77** 8.57N 8.42E
Wamba Zaïre **79** 2.10N 27.59E
Wamba *r.* Zaïre **78** 4.35S 17.15E
Wami *r.* Tanzania **79** 6.10S 38.50E
Wampsville U.S.A. **115** 43.05N 75.42W
Wamsasi Indonesia **59** 3.27S126.07E
Wan Indonesia **90** 8.23S137.55E
Wāna Pakistan **62** 32.17N 69.35E
Wanaaring Australia **92** 29.42S144.14E
Wanaka New Zealand **86** 44.42S169.08E
Wanaka, L. New Zealand **86** 44.30S169.10E
Wan'an China **55** 26.27N114.46E
Wanapiri Indonesia **59** 4.30S135.50E
Wanapitei *r.* Canada **104** 46.02N 80.51W
Wanapitei L. Canada **104** 46.45N 80.45W
Wanbi Australia **92** 34.46S140.19E
Wandana Australia **92** 32.04S133.45E
Wandoan Australia **90** 26.09S149.51E
Wanganella Australia **93** 35.13S144.53E
Wanganui New Zealand **86** 39.56S175.00E
Wangaratta Australia **93** 36.22S146.20E
Wangary Australia **92** 34.30S135.26E
Wangdu China **54** 38.43N115.09E
Wangdu Phodrang Bhutan **63** 27.29N 89.54E
Wangen W. Germany **39** 47.42N 9.50E
Wangerooge *i.* W. Germany **38** 53.46N 7.55E
Wanghai Shan *mtn.* China **54** 41.40N121.43E
Wangianna Australia **92** 29.42S137.32E
Wangjiang China **55** 30.07N116.41E
Wangpan Yang *b.* China **55** 30.30N121.30E
Wangqing China **57** 43.20N129.48E
Wangyuanqiao China **54** 38.24N106.16E
Wani India **63** 20.04N 78.57E
Wānkāner India **62** 22.37N 70.56E
Wankie Nat. Park Zimbabwe **80** 19.00S 26.30E
Wanle Iten Somali Rep. **71** 2.38N 44.55E
Wannian China **55** 28.42N117.03E
Wanning China **55** 18.48N110.22E

Wānow to Wheeler Peak

Wānow Afghan. **62** 32.38N 65.54E
Wantage U.K. **13** 51.35N 1.25W
Wanup Canada **104** 46.24N 80.49W
Wanxian China **55** 30.52N 108.20E
Wanyang Shan *mts.* China **55** 26.01N 113.48E
Wanyuan China **54** 32.04N 108.02E
Wanzai China **55** 28.06N 114.27E
Wanzleben E. Germany **38** 52.03N 11.26E
Wāpi India **62** 20.22N 72.54E
Wapiti *r.* Canada **100** 55.05N 118.18W
Wappingers Falls U.S.A. **115** 41.36N 73.55W
Waqqāş Jordan **67** 32.33N 35.36E
Wārāh Pakistan **62** 27.27N 67.48E
Warangal India **61** 18.00N 79.35E
Waranga Resr. Australia **93** 36.32S 145.04E
Wārāseoni India **63** 21.45N 80.02E
Waratah B. Australia **93** 38.55S 146.04E
Warburg W. Germany **38** 51.29N 9.08E
Warburton *r.* Australia **91** 27.55S 137.15E
Warburton Range *mts.* S.A. Australia **92** 30.30S 134.32E
Warburton Range *mts.* W.A. Australia **88** 26.09S 126.38E
Ward Rep. of Ire. **15** 53.26N 6.20W
Warden R.S.A. **80** 27.49S 28.57E
Wardenburg W. Germany **38** 53.04N 8.11E
Warder *well* Ethiopia **71** 6.58N 45.21E
Wardha India **63** 20.45N 78.37E
Wardha *r.* India **63** 19.38N 79.48E
Ward Hill U.K. **10** 58.54N 3.20W
Wardlow Canada **101** 50.54N 111.33W
Ware U.S.A. **115** 42.16N 72.15W
Wareham U.S.A. **115** 41.46N 70.43W
Waren E. Germany **38** 53.31N 12.40E
Warendorf W. Germany **38** 51.57N 7.59E
Warfordsburg U.S.A. **114** 39.44N 78.15W
Warialda Australia **93** 29.33S 150.36E
Wark Forest *hills* U.K. **12** 55.06N 2.24W
Warkopi Indonesia **59** 1.12S 134.09E
Warkworth New Zealand **86** 36.24S 174.40E
Warley U.K. **13** 52.29N 2.02W
Warmbad Namibia **80** 28.26S 18.41E
Warminster U.K. **13** 51.12N 2.11W
Warm Springs *town* U.S.A. **108** 39.39N 114.49W
Warnemünde E. Germany **38** 54.10N 12.04E
Warner U.S.A. **115** 43.17N 71.49W
Warner Robins U.S.A. **113** 32.35N 83.37W
Warnow *r.* E. Germany **38** 54.06N 12.09E
Waroona Australia **89** 32.51S 115.50E
Warracknabeal Australia **92** 36.15S 142.28E
Warragamba Resr. Australia **93** 33.54S 150.36E
Warragul Australia **93** 38.11S 145.55E
Warrakalanna, L. Australia **92** 28.13S 139.23E
Warrambool *r.* Australia **93** 30.04S 147.38E
Warramutty Australia **92** 30.30S 144.04E
Warrego *r.* Australia **93** 30.25S 145.18E
Warrego Range *mts.* Australia **90** 24.55S 146.20E
Warren Australia **93** 31.44S 147.53E
Warren Ont. Canada **104** 46.27N 80.20W
Warren Ark. U.S.A. **111** 33.37N 92.04W
Warren Mich. U.S.A. **114** 42.28N 83.01W
Warren Minn. U.S.A. **110** 48.12N 96.46W
Warren N.H. U.S.A. **105** 43.56N 71.54W
Warren Ohio U.S.A. **114** 41.14N 80.52W
Warren Penn. U.S.A. **114** 41.51N 79.08W
Warren R.I. U.S.A. **115** 41.43N 71.17W
Warren Vt. U.S.A. **105** 44.06N 72.52W
Warrenpoint U.K. **15** 54.06N 6.15W
Warrensburg Mo. U.S.A. **110** 38.46N 93.44W
Warrensburg N.Y. U.S.A. **115** 43.30N 73.46W
Warrenton R.S.A. **80** 28.07S 24.49E
Warrenton U.S.A. **114** 38.43N 77.48W
Warri Nigeria **77** 5.36N 5.46E
Warrina Australia **92** 28.10S 135.49E
Warriners Creek *r.* Australia **92** 29.15S 137.03E
Warrington U.K. **12** 53.25N 2.38W
Warrington U.S.A. **111** 30.23N 87.16W
Warri Warri Australia **92** 29.00S 141.56E
Warrnambool Australia **92** 38.23S 142.03E
Warroad U.S.A. **110** 48.54N 95.19W
Warrumbungle Range *mts.* Australia **93** 31.20S 149.00E
Warsaw *see* Warszawa Poland **37**
Warsaw Ind. U.S.A. **112** 41.13N 85.52W
Warsaw N.Y. U.S.A. **114** 42.44N 78.08W
Warsaw Ohio U.S.A. **114** 40.20N 82.00W
Warshikh Somali Rep. **71** 2.19N 45.50E
Warszawa Poland **37** 52.15N 21.00E
Warta *r.* Poland **36** 52.45N 15.09E
Warud India **63** 21.28N 78.16E
Warwick Australia **93** 28.12S 152.00E
Warwick Canada **105** 45.56N 71.59W
Warwick U.K. **13** 52.17N 1.36W
Warwick N.Y. U.S.A. **115** 41.16N 74.22W
Warwick R.I. U.S.A. **115** 41.43N 71.28W
Warwickshire *d.* U.K. **13** 52.13N 1.30W
Wasaga Beach Canada **104** 44.31N 80.01W
Wasatch Plateau *f.* U.S.A. **108** 39.20N 111.30W
Wasco Calif. U.S.A. **109** 35.36N 119.20W
Wasco Oreg. U.S.A. **108** 45.35N 120.42W
Washago Canada **104** 44.45N 79.20W
Washburn N.Dak. U.S.A. **110** 47.17N 101.02W
Washburn Wisc. U.S.A. **110** 46.41N 90.52W
Washburn L. Canada **98** 70.03N 106.50W
Wāshim India **62** 20.06N 77.09E
Washington U.K. **12** 54.55N 1.30W
Washington *d.* U.S.A. **108** 47.43N 120.00W
Washington D.C. U.S.A. **114** 38.55N 77.00W
Washington Ga. U.S.A. **113** 33.43N 82.46W
Washington Ind. U.S.A. **112** 38.40N 87.10W
Washington Iowa U.S.A. **110** 41.18N 91.42W
Washington N.C. U.S.A. **113** 35.33N 77.04W
Washington Penn. U.S.A. **114** 40.10N 80.15W
Washington Utah U.S.A. **108** 37.08N 113.30W
Washington Va. U.S.A. **114** 38.43N 78.10W
Washington Crossing U.S.A. **115** 40.18N 74.52W
Wāshuk Pakistan **62** 27.44N 64.48E
Wasian Indonesia **59** 1.51S 133.21E
Wasior Indonesia **59** 2.38S 134.27E
Waskesiu L. Canada **101** 53.56N 106.10W
Waskigomog L. Canada **104** 46.00N 78.59W
Wassen Switz. **39** 46.42N 8.36E
Wassenaar Neth. **16** 52.10N 4.26E
Wasseralfingen W. Germany **39** 48.52N 10.06E
Wasserburg W. Germany **39** 48.04N 12.13E
Wasserkuppe *mtn.* W. Germany **38** 50.30N 9.56E
Wassy France **19** 48.30N 4.57E
Waswanipi Lac *l.* Canada **102** 49.35N 76.40W
Watampone Indonesia **59** 4.33S 120.20E
Watchet U.K. **13** 51.10N 3.20W
Waterbury U.S.A. **115** 41.33N 73.02W
Waterbury L. Canada **101** 58.16N 105.00W
Waterford Canada **104** 42.56N 80.17W
Waterford Rep. of Ire. **15** 52.16N 7.08W
Waterford *d.* Rep. of Ire. **15** 52.10N 7.40W
Waterford U.S.A. **114** 41.57N 79.59W
Waterford Harbour *est.* Rep. of Ire. **15** 52.12N 6.56W
Waterloo Belgium **16** 50.44N 4.24E
Waterloo Ont. Canada **104** 43.28N 80.31W
Waterloo Que. Canada **105** 45.21N 72.31W
Waterloo Iowa U.S.A. **110** 42.30N 92.20W
Waterloo N.Y. U.S.A. **114** 42.54N 76.52W
Waterton Glacier International Peace Park U.S.A./Canada **108** 48.47N 113.45W
Watertown N.Y. U.S.A. **105** 43.59N 75.55W
Watertown S.Dak. U.S.A. **110** 44.54N 97.07W
Watervale Australia **92** 33.58S 138.39E
Water Valley *town* U.S.A. **111** 34.09N 89.38W
Waterville Canada **105** 45.16N 71.54W
Waterville Rep. of Ire. **15** 51.50N 10.11W
Waterville Maine U.S.A. **112** 44.33N 69.38W
Waterville N.Y. U.S.A. **115** 42.56N 75.23W
Waterville Wash. U.S.A. **108** 47.39N 120.04W
Watervliet U.S.A. **115** 42.44N 73.42W
Watford Canada **104** 42.57N 81.53W
Watford U.K. **13** 51.40N 0.25W
Watford City U.S.A. **110** 47.48N 103.17W
Wa'th Sudan **73** 7.24N 28.58E
Wathaman L. Canada **101** 56.55N 103.43W
Watkins Glen U.S.A. **114** 42.23N 76.52W
Watonga U.S.A. **111** 35.51N 98.25W
Watrous Canada **101** 51.40N 105.28W
Watsa Zaïre **79** 3.03N 29.29E
Watson Canada **101** 52.07N 104.31W
Watson Lake *town* Canada **100** 60.06N 128.49W
Watsontown U.S.A. **114** 41.05N 76.52W
Watsonville U.S.A. **108** 36.55N 121.45W
Wattiwarriganna *r.* Australia **92** 28.57S 136.10E
Wattle Vale *town* Australia **92** 30.00S 143.30E
Wattwil Switz. **39** 47.18N 9.06E
Watzmann *mtn.* W. Germany **39** 47.33N 12.55E
Wau P.N.G. **59** 7.22S 146.40E
Wauchope Australia **93** 31.27S 152.43E
Waukaringa Australia **92** 32.18S 139.27E
Waukegan U.S.A. **110** 42.22N 87.50W
Waukesha U.S.A. **110** 43.01N 88.14W
Waukon U.S.A. **110** 43.16N 91.29W
Wauneta U.S.A. **110** 40.25N 101.23W
Waurika U.S.A. **111** 34.10N 98.00W
Wausau U.S.A. **110** 44.58N 89.40W
Wautoma U.S.A. **110** 44.05N 89.17W
Wauwatosa U.S.A. **110** 43.04N 88.02W
Wave Hill *town* Australia **88** 17.29S 130.57E
Waveney *r.* U.K. **13** 52.29N 1.46E
Waverly Ill. U.S.A. **110** 39.36N 89.57W
Waverly Iowa U.S.A. **110** 42.44N 92.29W
Waverly N.Y. U.S.A. **115** 42.00N 76.32W
Wavre Belgium **16** 50.43N 4.37E
Wāw Sudan **73** 7.42N 28.00E
Wāw al Kabīr Libya **75** 25.20N 16.43E
Waxahachie U.S.A. **111** 32.24N 96.51W
Waxweiler W. Germany **39** 50.05N 6.22E
Waycross U.S.A. **113** 31.12N 82.22W
Wayland U.S.A. **114** 42.34N 77.35W
Wayne N.J. U.S.A. **115** 40.03N 75.23W
Wayne W.Va. U.S.A. **114** 38.13N 82.27W
Waynesboro Ga. U.S.A. **113** 33.04N 82.01W
Waynesboro Penn. U.S.A. **114** 39.45N 77.35W
Waynesboro Va. U.S.A. **113** 38.04N 78.53W
Waynesburg Ohio U.S.A. **114** 40.40N 81.16W
Waynesburg Penn. U.S.A. **114** 39.54N 80.11W
Waynesville U.S.A. **113** 35.30N 82.58W
Waynoka U.S.A. **111** 36.35N 98.53W
Wazay Afghan. **62** 33.22N 69.26E
Waziers France **19** 50.23N 3.07E
Wazīrābād Pakistan **62** 32.27N 74.07E
Wear *r.* U.K. **12** 54.55N 1.21W
Weatherford Okla. U.S.A. **111** 35.32N 98.42W
Weatherford Tex. U.S.A. **111** 32.46N 97.48W
Webbwood Canada **104** 46.16N 81.53W
Webera Ethiopia **73** 6.25N 40.45E
Webster Mass. U.S.A. **115** 42.03N 71.53W
Webster N.Y. U.S.A. **114** 43.13N 77.26W
Webster Wisc. U.S.A. **110** 45.53N 92.22W
Webster City U.S.A. **110** 42.28N 93.49W
Webster Groves U.S.A. **110** 38.35N 90.21W
Webster Springs *town* U.S.A. **114** 38.29N 80.25W
Weda Indonesia **59** 0.30N 127.52E
Wedderburn Australia **92** 36.26S 143.39E
Wedgeport Canada **103** 43.44N 65.59W
Wedmore U.K. **13** 51.14N 2.50W
Wedza Zimbabwe **81** 18.37S 31.33E
Weebo Australia **88** 28.01S 121.03E
Weedon Canada **105** 45.42N 71.28W
Weedsport U.S.A. **115** 43.03N 76.34W
Weeho *r.* Canada **100** 63.20N 115.10W
Weelde Belgium **16** 51.25N 5.00E
Weemelah Australia **93** 29.02S 149.15E
Weert Neth. **16** 51.14N 5.40E
Wee Waa Australia **93** 30.34S 149.27E
Wegorzyno Poland **36** 53.32N 15.33E
Wegrów Poland **37** 52.25N 22.01E
Wegscheid W. Germany **39** 48.36N 13.48E
Weichang China **54** 41.56N 117.34E
Weida E. Germany **38** 50.45N 12.04E
Weiden in der Oberpfalz W. Germany **39** 49.41N 12.10E
Weifang China **54** 36.40N 119.10E
Weihai China **54** 37.28N 122.05E
Wei He *r.* Shaanxi China **54** 34.27N 109.30E
Wei He *r.* Shandong China **54** 36.47N 115.42E
Weilburg W. Germany **38** 50.29N 8.15E
Weilheim W. Germany **39** 47.50N 11.08E
Weilmoringle Australia **93** 29.16S 146.55E
Weimar E. Germany **38** 50.59N 11.19E
Weinan China **54** 34.25N 109.30E
Weinheim W. Germany **39** 49.32N 8.39E
Weipa Australia **90** 12.41S 141.52E
Weir *r.* Australia **93** 29.10S 149.06E
Weirton U.S.A. **114** 40.25N 80.35W
Weiser U.S.A. **108** 44.37N 116.58W
Weishan Hu *l.* China **54** 34.40N 117.25E
Weishi China **54** 34.24N 114.14E
Weisse Elster *r.* E. Germany **38** 51.26N 11.57E
Weissenburg in Bayern W. Germany **38** 49.01N 10.58E
Weissenfels E. Germany **38** 51.12N 11.58E
Weisswasser E. Germany **38** 51.30N 14.38E
Wei Xian China **54** 36.21N 114.56E
Weixin China **55** 27.48N 105.05E
Weiya China **52** 41.50N 94.24E
Weizhou *i.* China **55** 21.01N 109.03E
Wejherowo Poland **37** 54.37N 18.15E
Wekusko Canada **101** 54.45N 99.45W
Welbourn Hill *town* Australia **91** 27.21S 134.06E
Weldon U.S.A. **109** 35.40N 118.20W
Weldya Ethiopia **73** 11.50N 39.36E
Welega *d.* Ethiopia **73** 9.40N 35.50E
Welkom R.S.A. **80** 27.59S 26.42E
Welland Canada **104** 42.59N 79.14W
Welland *r.* U.K. **12** 52.53N 0.00
Wellesley Is. Australia **90** 16.42S 139.30E
Wellfleet U.S.A. **115** 41.56N 70.02W
Wellin Belgium **16** 50.05N 5.07E
Wellingborough U.K. **13** 52.18N 0.41W
Wellington N.S.W. Australia **93** 32.33S 148.59E
Wellington S.A. Australia **92** 35.21S 139.23E
Wellington Canada **105** 43.57N 77.21W
Wellington New Zealand **86** 41.17S 174.47E
Wellington *d.* New Zealand **86** 40.00S 175.30E
Wellington Shrops. U.K. **13** 52.42N 2.31W
Wellington Somerset U.K. **13** 50.58N 3.13W
Wellington Kans. U.S.A. **111** 37.16N 97.24W
Wellington Nev. U.S.A. **108** 38.45N 119.22W
Wellington Ohio U.S.A. **114** 41.10N 82.13W
Wellington, Isla *i.* Chile **125** 49.30S 75.00W
Wells U.K. **13** 51.12N 2.39W
Wells Maine U.S.A. **115** 43.20N 70.35W
Wells Nev. U.S.A. **108** 41.07N 114.58W
Wells N.Y. U.S.A. **115** 43.24N 74.17W
Wellsboro U.S.A. **114** 41.45N 77.18W
Wellsburg U.S.A. **114** 40.16N 80.37W
Wells Gray Prov. Park Canada **100** 52.30N 120.15W
Wells L. Canada **101** 57.15N 101.00W
Wells-next-the-Sea U.K. **12** 52.57N 0.51E
Wells River *town* U.S.A. **105** 44.09N 72.06W
Wellston U.S.A. **114** 39.07N 82.32W
Wellsville Mo. U.S.A. **110** 39.04N 91.34W
Wellsville N.Y. U.S.A. **114** 42.07N 77.57W
Wellton U.S.A. **109** 32.40N 114.08W
Welmel *r.* Ethiopia **73** 6.00N 40.20E
Wels Austria **39** 48.10N 14.02E
Welshpool U.K. **13** 52.40N 3.09W
Welwyn Garden City U.K. **13** 51.48N 0.13W
Wem U.K. **12** 52.52N 2.45W
Wembere *r.* Tanzania **79** 4.07S 34.15E
Wenatchee U.S.A. **108** 47.25N 120.19W
Wenchang China **55** 19.37N 110.43E
Wenchi Ghana **76** 7.40N 2.06W
Wendel U.S.A. **108** 40.20N 120.14W
Wendo Ethiopia **73** 6.40N 38.27E
Wendover U.S.A. **108** 40.44N 114.02W
Wenebegon L. Canada **102** 47.25N 83.05W
Wengfengzhen China **54** 34.56N 104.38E
Wenlock *r.* Australia **90** 12.02S 141.55E
Wenquan China **63** 33.13N 91.50E
Wenshan China **55** 23.20N 104.11E
Wensleydale Australia **92** 38.24S 144.01E
Wensleydale *f.* U.K. **12** 54.19N 2.04W
Wentworth Australia **92** 34.06S 141.56E
Wen Xian China **54** 32.52N 104.40E
Wenzhou China **53** 28.02N 120.40E
Weott U.S.A. **108** 40.19N 123.54W
Wepener R.S.A. **80** 29.43S 27.01E
Werda Botswana **80** 25.15S 23.16E
Werdau E. Germany **38** 50.44N 12.22E
Werder E. Germany **38** 52.23N 12.56E
Werdohl W. Germany **38** 51.15N 7.45E
Were Ilu Ethiopia **73** 10.37N 39.28E
Weri Indonesia **59** 3.10S 132.30E
Werne W. Germany **16** 51.39N 7.36E
Wernigerode E. Germany **38** 51.50N 10.47E
Werra *r.* W. Germany **38** 51.26N 9.39E
Werribee Australia **93** 37.54S 144.40E
Werris Creek *town* Australia **93** 31.20S 150.41E
Wertheim W. Germany **39** 49.46N 9.31E
Wertingen W. Germany **39** 48.34N 10.41E
Wesel W. Germany **38** 51.40N 6.38E
Weser *r.* W. Germany **38** 53.15N 8.34E
Wesiri Indonesia **59** 7.30S 126.30E
Weslaco U.S.A. **111** 26.09N 97.59W
Weslemkoon L. Canada **105** 45.02N 77.25W
Wesleyville Canada **103** 49.09N 53.34W
Wesleyville U.S.A. **114** 42.08N 80.01W
Wessel, C. Australia **90** 10.59S 136.46E
Wessel Is. Australia **90** 11.30S 136.25E
Wessington U.S.A. **110** 44.27N 98.42W
Wessington Springs *town* U.S.A. **110** 44.05N 98.34W
West U.S.A. **111** 31.48N 97.06W
West *r.* U.S.A. **115** 42.52N 72.33W
West Australian Basin *f.* Indian Oc. **49** 15.00S 100.00E
West B. U.S.A. **111** 29.15N 94.57W
West Bend U.S.A. **110** 43.25N 88.11W
West Bengal *d.* India **63** 23.00N 88.00E
West-Berlin *d.* W. Germany **38** 52.30N 13.20E
West Branch U.S.A. **104** 44.17N 84.14W
West Bromwich U.K. **13** 52.32N 2.01W
Westbrook U.S.A. **112** 43.41N 70.21W
West Burke U.S.A. **105** 44.38N 71.59W
West Burra *i.* U.K. **10** 60.05N 1.21W
Westby Australia **93** 35.29S 147.27E
West Canada Creek *r.* U.S.A. **115** 43.01N 74.58W
West Caroline Basin Pacific Oc. **84** 5.00N 139.00E
West Chester U.S.A. **115** 39.58N 75.36W
West Des Moines U.S.A. **110** 41.35N 93.43W
Westende Belgium **16** 51.10N 2.46E
Westerland W. Germany **38** 54.54N 8.18E
Westerly U.S.A. **115** 41.22N 71.50W
Western *d.* Ghana **76** 6.00N 2.40W
Western *d.* Kenya **79** 0.30N 34.30E
Western *d.* Zambia **80** 16.00S 23.45E
Western Australia *d.* Australia **88** 24.20S 122.30E
Western Duck I. Canada **104** 45.45N 83.00W
Western Ghāts *mts.* India **60** 15.30N 74.30E
Western Isles *d.* U.K. **14** 57.40N 7.10W
Westernport U.S.A. **114** 39.29N 79.03W
Western Sahara Africa **74** 25.00N 13.30W
Western Samoa Pacific Oc. **84** 13.55S 172.00W
Westerschelde *est.* Neth. **16** 51.25N 3.40E
Westerstede W. Germany **38** 53.15N 7.55E
Westerville U.S.A. **114** 40.08N 82.56W
Westerwald *f.* W. Germany **38** 50.40N 7.45E
West Falkland *i.* Falkland Is. **125** 51.40W 60.00W
West Felton U.K. **12** 52.49N 2.58W
Westfield *r.* U.S.A. **115** 42.05N 72.35W
Westfield Mass. U.S.A. **115** 42.08N 72.45W
Westfield N.J. U.S.A. **115** 40.39N 74.21W
Westfield N.Y. U.S.A. **114** 42.19N 79.35W
Westfield Penn. U.S.A. **114** 41.55N 77.32W
West Fork *r.* U.S.A. **114** 39.28N 80.09W
West Frankfort U.S.A. **111** 37.54N 88.55W
West Frisian Is. *see* Waddeneilanden Neth. **36**
West Germany Europe **38** 50.40N 9.00E
West Glamorgan *d.* U.K. **13** 51.42N 3.47W
Westhampton U.S.A. **115** 40.49N 72.39W
West Haven U.S.A. **115** 41.16N 72.57W
Westhope U.S.A. **110** 48.55N 101.01W
West Indies *is.* C. America **127** 21.00N 74.00W
West Lafayette U.S.A. **112** 40.26N 86.56W
Westland *d.* New Zealand **86** 43.15S 170.10E
West Leyden U.S.A. **115** 43.28N 75.28W
West Linton U.K. **14** 55.45N 3.21W
Westlock Canada **100** 54.09N 113.55W
West Lorne Canada **104** 42.36N 81.36W
Westmeath Canada **105** 45.49N 76.54W
Westmeath *d.* Rep. of Ire. **15** 53.30N 7.30W
West Memphis U.S.A. **111** 35.08N 90.11W
West Middlesex U.S.A. **114** 41.10N 80.27W
West Midlands *d.* U.K. **13** 52.28N 1.50W
Westminster U.S.A. **114** 39.35N 77.00W
Westmoreland Australia **90** 17.18S 138.12E
Westmoreland U.S.A. **115** 42.59N 72.25W
West Nicholson Zimbabwe **80** 21.06S 29.25E
Weston Malaysia **58** 5.14N 115.35E
Weston U.S.A. **114** 39.02N 80.28W
Weston-Super-Mare U.K. **13** 51.20N 2.59W
West Palm Beach *town* U.S.A. **113** 26.42N 80.05W
West Plains *town* U.S.A. **111** 36.44N 91.51W
West Point *town* U.S.A. **111** 33.36N 88.39W
Westport Canada **105** 44.41N 76.26W
Westport New Zealand **86** 41.46S 171.38E
Westport Rep. of Ire. **15** 53.48N 9.32W
Westport Conn. U.S.A. **115** 41.09N 73.22W
Westport N.Y. U.S.A. **105** 44.13N 73.39W
Westport Wash. U.S.A. **108** 46.53N 124.06W
Westray Canada **101** 53.36N 101.24W
Westray *i.* U.K. **14** 59.18N 2.58W
Westree Canada **104** 47.26N 81.34W
West Road *r.* Canada **100** 53.18N 122.53W
West Siberian Plain *f. see* Zapadno-Sibirskaya Ravnina U.S.S.R. **9**
West Springfield U.S.A. **115** 42.06N 72.38W
West Sussex *d.* U.K. **13** 50.58N 0.30W
West Terschelling Neth. **16** 53.22N 5.13E
West Union U.S.A. **114** 39.18N 80.47W
West Virginia *d.* U.S.A. **114** 38.45N 80.30W
West Vlaanderen *d.* Belgium **16** 51.00N 3.00E
West Wyalong Australia **93** 33.54S 147.12E
West Yellowstone U.S.A. **108** 44.30N 111.05W
West York U.S.A. **114** 39.57N 76.46W
West Yorkshire *d.* U.K. **12** 53.45N 1.40W
Wetar *i.* Indonesia **59** 7.45S 126.00E
Wetaskiwin Canada **100** 52.55N 113.24W
Wetteren Belgium **16** 51.00N 3.51E
Wetzlar W. Germany **38** 50.33N 8.29E
Wewak P.N.G. **59** 3.35S 143.35E
Wewoka U.S.A. **111** 35.09N 96.30W
Wexford Rep. of Ire. **15** 52.20N 6.28W
Wexford *d.* Rep. of Ire. **15** 52.20N 6.25W
Wexford B. Rep. of Ire. **15** 52.27N 6.18W
Weyburn Canada **101** 49.41N 103.52W
Weyib *r.* Ethiopia **73** 4.11N 42.09E
Weymouth U.K. **13** 50.36N 2.28W
Weymouth, C. Australia **90** 12.32S 143.36E
Whakatane New Zealand **86** 37.56S 177.00E
Whale Cove *town* Canada **101** 62.11N 92.36W
Whallon *r.* Australia **93** 29.10S 148.42E
Whalsay *i.* U.K. **14** 60.22N 0.59W
Whangarei New Zealand **86** 35.43S 174.20E
Wharfe *r.* U.K. **12** 53.50N 1.07W
Wharfedale *f.* U.K. **12** 54.00N 1.55W
Wharton U.S.A. **111** 29.19N 96.06W
Whataroa New Zealand **86** 43.16S 170.22E
Wheatland U.S.A. **108** 42.03N 104.57W
Wheatley Canada **104** 42.06N 82.27W
Wheaton Md. U.S.A. **114** 39.03N 77.03W
Wheaton Minn. U.S.A. **110** 45.48N 96.30W
Wheeler *r.* Que. Canada **103** 58.05N 67.12W
Wheeler *r.* Sask. Canada **101** 57.25N 105.30W
Wheeler Peak *mtn.* Nev. U.S.A. **108** 38.59N 114.19W

Wheeler Peak to Wyalkatchem

Wheeler Peak mtn. N.Mex. U.S.A. 108 36.34N105.25W
Wheeler Ridge town U.S.A. 109 35.06N119.01W
Wheeler Springs town U.S.A. 109 34.30N119.18W
Wheeling U.S.A. 114 40.05N 80.42W
Whernside mtn. U.K. 12 54.14N 2.25W
Whidbey Pt. Australia 92 34.35S135.07E
Whiskey Gap town Canada 100 49.00N113.03W
Whitburn U.K. 14 55.52N 3.41W
Whitby Canada 104 43.52N 78.56W
Whitby U.K. 12 54.29N 0.37W
Whitchurch Shrops. U.K. 12 52.58N 2.42W
White r. Ark. U.S.A. 111 33.53N 91.10W
White r. Ind. U.S.A. 112 38.29N 87.45W
White r. S.Dak. U.S.A. 110 43.48N 99.22W
White r. Utah U.S.A. 106 40.04N109.41W
White r. Vt. U.S.A. 105 43.37N 72.20W
White, L. Australia 88 21.05S129.00E
White B. Canada 103 50.00N 56.30W
White Cliffs town Australia 92 30.51S143.05E
Whiteface, Mt. U.S.A. 105 44.22N 73.54W
Whitefield U.S.A. 105 44.22N 71.36W
Whitefish Canada 104 46.23N 81.20W
Whitefish U.S.A. 108 48.25N114.20W
Whitefish B. U.S.A. 104 46.40N 84.50W
Whitefish Falls town Canada 104 46.07N 81.44W
Whitefish L. Canada 101 62.41N106.48W
Whitefish Point town U.S.A. 104 46.45N 84.59W
Whitefish Pt. U.S.A. 104 46.45N 85.00W
Whitehall Mont. U.S.A. 108 45.52N112.06W
Whitehall N.Y. U.S.A. 115 43.33N 73.25W
Whitehall Ohio U.S.A. 114 39.58N 82.54W
Whitehall Wisc. U.S.A. 110 44.22N 91.19W
Whitehaven U.K. 12 54.33N 3.35W
White Haven U.S.A. 115 41.04N 75.47W
Whitehorse Canada 100 60.43N135.03W
White L. Canada 105 45.18N 76.31W
White L. U.S.A. 111 29.45N 92.30W
Whitemark Australia 91 40.07S148.00E
White Mountain Peak U.S.A. 108 37.38N118.15W
White Mts. Calif. U.S.A. 108 37.30N118.15W
White Mts. N.H. U.S.A. 105 44.10N 71.35W
Whitemud r. Canada 100 56.41N117.15W
White Nile r. see Abyaḑ, Al Baḩr al Sudan 72
White Otter L. Canada 102 49.09N 91.50W
White Plains town Liberia 76 6.28N 10.40W
White Plains town U.S.A. 115 41.02N 73.46W
Whitesand r. Canada 101 51.34N101.55W
Whitesboro U.S.A. 115 43.07N 75.18W
White Sea see Beloye More U.S.S.R. 44
Whiteshell Prov. Park. Canada 101 50.00N 95.25W
Whitetail U.S.A. 108 48.54N105.10W
White Volta r. Ghana 76 9.13N 1.15W
Whitewater Baldy mtn. U.S.A. 109 33.20N108.39W
Whitfield Australia 93 36.49S146.22E
Whithorn U.K. 14 54.44N 4.25W
Whitianga New Zealand 86 36.50S175.42E
Whiting U.S.A. 115 39.57N 74.23W
Whitley Bay town U.K. 12 55.03N 1.25W
Whitney Canada 104 45.30N 78.14W
Whitney, Mt. U.S.A. 109 36.35N118.18W
Whitney Point town U.S.A. 115 42.20N 75.58W
Whitstable U.K. 13 51.21N 1.02E
Whitsunday I. Australia 90 20.17S148.59E
Whittemore U.S.A. 104 44.14N 83.48W
Whittier U.S.A. 98 60.46N148.41W
Whittlesea Australia 93 37.31S145.08E
Whitton U.K. 12 53.42N 0.39W
Wholdaia L. Canada 101 60.43N104.20W
Whyalla Australia 92 33.02S137.35E
Whyjonta Australia 92 29.42S142.30E
Wiarton Canada 104 44.45N 81.09W
Wichita U.S.A. 111 37.41N 97.20W
Wichita Falls town U.S.A. 111 33.54N 98.30W
Wick U.K. 14 58.26N 3.06W
Wickenburg U.S.A. 109 33.58N112.44W
Wickepin Australia 89 32.45S117.31E
Wickliffe U.S.A. 114 41.36N 81.28W
Wicklow Rep. of Ire. 15 52.59N 6.03W
Wicklow d. Rep. of Ire. 15 52.59N 6.25W
Wicklow Head Rep. of Ire. 15 52.58N 6.00W
Wicklow Mts. Rep. of Ire. 15 53.06N 6.20W
Widdifield Canada 104 46.25N 79.20W
Widen U.S.A. 114 38.28N 80.52W
Widgiemooltha Australia 89 31.30S121.34E
Widnes U.K. 12 53.22N 2.44W
Wiehl W. Germany 38 50.57N 7.31E
Wiek E. Germany 38 54.37N 13.17E
Wieluń Poland 37 51.14N 18.34E
Wien Austria 36 48.13N 16.22E
Wiener Neustadt Austria 36 47.49N 16.15E
Wieprz r. Poland 37 51.34N 21.49E
Wiesbaden W. Germany 39 50.05N 8.14E
Wiesloch W. Germany 39 49.17N 8.42E
Wietze W. Germany 38 52.39N 9.50E
Wigan U.K. 12 53.33N 2.38W
Wight, Isle of U.K. 11 50.40N 1.17W
Wigton U.K. 12 54.50N 3.09W
Wigtown U.K. 14 54.47N 4.26W
Wigtown B. U.K. 14 54.47N 4.15W
Wikwemikong Canada 104 45.48N 81.44W
Wil Switz. 39 47.27N 9.03E
Wilber U.S.A. 110 40.29N 96.58W
Wilberforce Canada 104 45.03N 78.15W
Wilcannia Australia 92 31.33S143.24E
Wilcox U.S.A. 114 41.35N 78.41W
Wilderness U.S.A. 114 38.19N 77.48W
Wildhorn mtn. Switz. 38 46.22N 7.22E
Wildon Austria 31 46.53N 15.31E
Wildrose U.S.A. 110 48.38N103.11W
Wildspitze mtn. Austria 39 46.53N 10.52E
Wildwood U.S.A. 115 38.59N 74.49W
Wilgena Australia 92 30.46S134.44E
Wilhelm, Mt. P.N.G. 59 6.00S144.55E
Wilhelm II Land Antarctica 128 68.00S 89.00E
Wilhelm-Pieck-Stadt Guben E. Germany 38 51.57N 14.43E
Wilhelmshaven W. Germany 38 53.31N 8.08E
Wilkes-Barre U.S.A. 115 41.14N 75.53W
Wilkesboro U.S.A. 113 36.08N 81.09W
Wilkes Land f. Antarctica 128 69.00S120.00E
Wilkie Canada 101 52.25N108.43W
Wilkie Canada 98 52.27N108.42W
Wilkinsburg U.S.A. 114 40.27N 79.53W
Wilkinson Lakes Australia 91 29.40S132.39E
Willandra Billabong r. Australia 92 33.08S144.06E
Willara Australia 92 29.14S144.30E
Willard N.Mex. U.S.A. 109 34.36N106.02W
Willard Ohio U.S.A. 114 41.03N 82.44W
Willemstad Neth. Antilles 122 12.12N 68.56W
Willeroo Australia 88 15.17S131.35E
William, Mt. Australia 92 37.20S142.41E
William Creek town Australia 92 28.52S136.18E
Williams Australia 89 33.01S116.45E
Williams r. Australia 89 32.59S116.24E
Williamsburg U.S.A. 113 37.17N 76.43W
Williams Lake town Canada 100 52.08N122.10W
Williamson U.S.A. 113 37.42N 82.16W
Williamsport Md. U.S.A. 114 39.32N 77.50W
Williamsport Penn. U.S.A. 114 41.14N 77.00W
Williamston U.S.A. 113 35.53N 77.05W
Williamstown N.J. U.S.A. 115 39.41N 75.00W
Williamstown N.Y. U.S.A. 115 43.26N 75.55W
Williamstown W.Va. U.S.A. 114 39.24N 81.27W
Willie's Range hills Australia 92 28.30S144.00E
Willimantic U.S.A. 115 41.43N 72.12W
Willis Group is. Australia 90 16.18S150.00E
Williston R.S.A. 80 31.21S 20.53E
Williston U.S.A. 110 48.09N103.37W
Williston L. Canada 100 55.40N123.40W
Willits U.S.A. 108 39.25N123.21W
Willmar U.S.A. 110 45.07N 95.03W
Willmore Wilderness Park Canada 100 53.45N119.00W
Willochra Australia 92 32.12S138.10E
Willochra r. Australia 92 31.57S137.52E
Willoughby U.S.A. 114 41.38N 81.25W
Willow U.S.A. 98 61.42N150.08W
Willow Grove U.S.A. 115 40.08N 75.06W
Willow Hill town U.S.A. 114 40.06N 77.48W
Willow L. Canada 100 62.10N119.08W
Willowmore R.S.A. 80 33.18S 23.28E
Willow Ranch U.S.A. 108 41.55N120.21W
Willow River town Canada 100 54.06N122.28W
Willsboro U.S.A. 105 44.22N 73.26W
Willunga Australia 92 35.18S138.33E
Wilmette U.S.A. 110 42.04N 87.43W
Wilmington Del. U.S.A. 115 39.44N 75.33W
Wilmington N.C. U.S.A. 113 34.14N 77.55W
Wilmington Vt. U.S.A. 115 42.52N 72.52W
Wilmslow U.K. 12 53.19N 2.14W
Wilpena r. Australia 92 31.13S139.25E
Wilson N.C. U.S.A. 113 35.43N 77.56W
Wilson N.Y. U.S.A. 114 43.19N 78.50W
Wilson's Promontory c. Australia 93 39.06S146.23E
Wilton r. Australia 90 14.45S134.33E
Wilton U.K. 13 51.05N 1.52W
Wilton N.Dak. U.S.A. 110 47.10N100.47W
Wilton N.H. U.S.A. 115 42.51N 71.44W
Wiltshire d. U.K. 13 51.20N 0.34W
Wiltz Lux. 16 49.59N 5.53E
Wiluna Australia 88 26.36S120.13E
Wimmera r. Australia 92 36.05S141.56E
Winam b. Kenya 79 0.15S 34.30E
Winbar Australia 93 30.49S144.50E
Winburg R.S.A. 80 28.30S 27.01E
Wincanton U.K. 13 51.03N 2.24W
Winchendon U.S.A. 115 42.41N 72.03W
Winchester Canada 105 45.06N 75.21W
Winchester U.K. 13 51.04N 1.19W
Winchester Ky. U.S.A. 113 38.00N 84.10W
Winchester N.H. U.S.A. 115 42.46N 72.23W
Winchester Va. U.S.A. 114 39.11N 78.10W
Winchester Wyo. U.S.A. 108 43.51N108.10W
Windber U.S.A. 114 40.14N 78.50W
Windermere l. U.K. 12 54.20N 2.56W
Windfall Canada 100 54.12N116.13W
Windham U.S.A. 114 41.14N 81.03W
Windhoek Namibia 80 22.34S 17.06E
Windom U.S.A. 110 43.52N 95.07W
Windorah Australia 90 25.26S142.39E
Wind River Range mts. U.S.A. 108 43.05N109.25W
Windsor Nfld. Canada 103 48.58N 55.40W
Windsor N.S. Canada 103 44.59N 64.08W
Windsor Ont. Canada 104 42.18N 83.01W
Windsor Que. Canada 105 45.34N 72.00W
Windsor U.K. 13 51.29N 0.38W
Windsor Conn. U.S.A. 115 41.51N 72.39W
Windsor N.Y. U.S.A. 115 42.05N 75.39W
Windsor Vt. U.S.A. 115 43.29N 72.23W
Windsor Locks U.S.A. 115 41.56N 72.38W
Windward Is. C. America 117 13.00N 60.00W
Windward Passage str. Carib. Sea 117 20.00N 74.00W
Winfield Kans. U.S.A. 111 37.15N 96.59W
Winfield W.Va. U.S.A. 114 38.32N 81.53W
Wingen Australia 93 31.43S150.54E
Wingham Australia 93 31.50S152.20E
Wingham Canada 104 43.53N 81.19W
Winifred U.S.A. 108 47.34N109.23W
Winisk Canada 102 55.20N 85.15W
Winisk r. Canada 102 55.00N 85.20W
Winisk L. Canada 102 53.00N 88.00W
Winkler Canada 101 49.11N 97.56W
Winklern Austria 39 46.52N 12.52E
Winneba Ghana 76 5.22N 0.38W
Winnebago, L. U.S.A. 110 44.00N 88.25W
Winnemucca U.S.A. 106 40.58N117.45W
Winnemucca L. U.S.A. 108 40.09N119.20W
Winner U.S.A. 110 43.22N 99.51W
Winnfield U.S.A. 111 31.55N 92.38W
Winnininnie Australia 92 32.35S139.40E
Winnipeg Canada 101 49.53N 97.09W
Winnipeg r. Canada 101 50.38N 96.19W
Winnipeg, L. Canada 101 52.00N 97.00W
Winnipegosis, L. Canada 101 52.30N100.00W
Winnipesaukee, L. U.S.A. 115 43.35N 71.20W
Winnsboro La. U.S.A. 111 32.10N 91.43W
Winnsboro S.C. U.S.A. 113 34.22N 81.05W
Winona Kans. U.S.A. 110 39.04N101.15W
Winona Minn. U.S.A. 110 44.03N 91.39W
Winona Miss. U.S.A. 111 33.29N 89.44W
Winooski U.S.A. 105 44.29N 73.11W
Winooski r. U.S.A. 105 44.30N 73.15W
Winschoten Neth. 16 53.07N 7.02E
Winsen W. Germany 38 53.22N 10.12E
Winsford U.K. 12 53.12N 2.31W
Winslow Ariz. U.S.A. 109 35.01N110.42W
Winslow Maine U.S.A. 112 44.32N 69.38W
Winsted U.S.A. 115 41.55N 73.04W
Winston U.S.A. 108 46.28N111.38W
Winston-Salem U.S.A. 113 36.05N 80.18W
Winsum Neth. 16 53.20N 6.31E
Winter Haven U.S.A. 113 28.02N 81.46W
Winterset U.S.A. 110 41.20N 94.01W
Winterswijk Neth. 16 51.58N 6.44E
Winterthur Switz. 39 47.30N 8.43E
Winthrop Minn. U.S.A. 110 44.32N 94.22W
Winthrop Wash. U.S.A. 108 48.29N120.11W
Winton Australia 90 22.22S143.00E
Winton New Zealand 86 46.10S168.20E
Winton U.S.A. 108 41.45N109.10W
Wipper r. E. Germany 38 51.47N 11.42E
Wirrabara Australia 92 33.03S138.18E
Wirraminna Australia 92 31.11S136.04E
Wirrappa Australia 92 31.28S137.00E
Wirrega Australia 92 36.11S140.37E
Wirrida, L. Australia 92 29.45S134.39E
Wirulla Australia 92 32.24S134.33E
Wisbech U.K. 13 52.39N 0.10E
Wisconsin d. U.S.A. 110 44.30N 90.00W
Wisconsin r. U.S.A. 110 43.00N 91.15W
Wisconsin Dells U.S.A. 110 43.38N 89.46W
Wisconsin Rapids town U.S.A. 110 44.24N 89.50W
Wisdom U.S.A. 108 45.37N113.27W
Wisła r. Poland 37 54.23N 18.52E
Wismar E. Germany 38 53.53N 11.28E
Wisner U.S.A. 110 41.59N 96.55W
Wissembourg France 19 49.02N 7.57E
Wissen W. Germany 38 50.47N 7.43E
Wissmar W. Germany 38 50.38N 8.41E
Wisznice Poland 37 51.48N 23.12E
Witchekan L. Canada 101 53.25N107.35W
Witham r. U.K. 12 52.56N 0.04E
Witherbee U.S.A. 105 44.05N 73.32W
Withernsea U.K. 12 53.43N 0.02E
Witkowo Poland 37 52.27N 17.47E
Witney U.K. 13 51.47N 1.29W
Witsand R.S.A. 80 34.23S 20.49E
Witten W. Germany 16 51.26N 7.19E
Wittenberg E. Germany 38 51.53N 12.39E
Wittenberge E. Germany 38 53.00N 11.44E
Wittenburg E. Germany 38 53.31N 11.04E
Wittenoom Australia 88 22.19S118.21E
Wittingen W. Germany 38 52.43N 10.44E
Wittlich W. Germany 39 49.59N 6.53E
Wittstock E. Germany 38 53.10N 12.29E
Witu Kenya 79 2.22S 40.20E
Witvlei Namibia 80 22.25S 18.29E
Witzenhausen W. Germany 38 51.20N 9.51E
Wiveliscombe U.K. 13 51.02N 3.20W
Wkra r. Poland 37 52.27N 20.44E
Władysławowo Poland 37 54.49N 18.25E
Włocławek Poland 37 52.39N 19.01E
Włodawa Poland 37 51.33N 23.31E
Wodgina Australia 88 21.12S118.48E
Wodonga Australia 93 36.08S146.09E
Woerden Neth. 16 52.07N 4.55E
Wohutun China 54 43.40N123.30E
Wokam i. Indonesia 59 5.45S134.30E
Woking Canada 100 55.35N118.50W
Woking U.K. 13 51.20N 0.34W
Wolcott U.S.A. 114 43.13N 76.49W
Woleai i. Pacific Oc. 84 7.21N143.52E
Wolf r. U.S.A. 110 44.07N 88.43W
Wolfach W. Germany 39 48.17N 8.13E
Wolfboro U.S.A. 115 43.35N 71.12W
Wolf Creek town U.S.A. 108 46.50N112.20W
Wolfe Island town Canada 105 44.12N 76.26W
Wolfen E. Germany 38 51.40N 12.16E
Wolfenbüttel W. Germany 38 52.10N 10.32E
Wolfhagen W. Germany 38 51.19N 9.10E
Wolf Point town U.S.A. 108 48.05N105.39W
Wolfratshausen W. Germany 39 47.54N 11.25E
Wolfsberg Austria 31 46.51N 14.51E
Wolfsburg W. Germany 38 52.25N 10.47E
Wolgast E. Germany 38 54.03N 13.46E
Wolin Poland 36 53.51N 14.38E
Wollaston L. Canada 101 58.15N103.20W
Wollaston Pen. Canada 98 70.00N115.00W
Wollongong Australia 93 34.25S150.52E
Wolmaransstad R.S.A. 80 27.11S 25.58E
Wołomin Poland 37 52.21N 21.14E
Wolseley Australia 92 36.21S140.55E
Wolseley Bay town Canada 104 46.07N 80.22W
Wolvega Neth. 16 52.53N 6.00E
Wolverhampton U.K. 13 52.35N 2.06W
Wolverine U.S.A. 104 45.16N 84.36W
Womelsdorf U.S.A. 115 40.22N 76.11W
Wondai Australia 90 26.19S151.52E
Wongan Hills town Australia 89 30.55S116.41E
Wono Ethiopia 73 8.31N 37.30E
Wonogiri Indonesia 59 7.48S110.52E
Wonosari Indonesia 59 7.55S110.39E
Wonosobo Indonesia 59 7.21S109.56E
Wŏnsan N. Korea 53 39.07N127.26E
Wonthaggi Australia 93 38.38S145.37E
Woocalla Australia 92 31.44S137.10E
Woodbine U.S.A. 115 39.14N 74.49W
Woodbridge U.K. 13 52.06N 1.19E
Woodbridge U.S.A. 114 38.39N 77.15W
Wood Buffalo Nat. Park Canada 100 59.00N113.41W
Woodburn Australia 93 29.04S153.21E
Woodbury U.S.A. 115 39.50N 75.10W
Wooded Bluff f. Australia 93 29.22S153.22E
Woodenbong Australia 93 28.28S152.35E
Woodgate U.S.A. 115 43.32N 75.12W
Woodland U.S.A. 108 38.41N121.46W
Woodlark I. P.N.G. 90 9.05S152.50E
Wood Mts. Canada 101 49.14N106.20W
Woodroffe, Mt. Australia 90 26.20S131.45E
Woods, L. Australia 90 17.50S133.30E
Woods, L. of the Canada/U.S.A. 102 49.15N 94.45W
Woodsfield U.S.A. 114 39.46N 81.07W
Woods Hole U.S.A. 115 41.31N 70.40W
Woodside Australia 93 38.31S146.52E
Woods L. Canada 103 54.40N 64.21W
Woodstock Canada 104 43.08N 80.45W
Woodstock U.K. 13 51.51N 1.20W
Woodstock U.S.A. 115 43.37N 72.31W
Woodstown U.S.A. 115 39.39N 75.20W
Woodsville U.S.A. 105 44.09N 72.02W
Woodville New Zealand 86 40.20S175.52E
Woodward U.S.A. 111 36.26N 99.24W
Wooler U.K. 12 55.33N 2.01W
Woolgangie Australia 89 31.13S120.30E
Woolgoolga Australia 93 30.07S153.12E
Woolibar Australia 89 31.03S121.45E
Wooltana Australia 92 30.28S139.26E
Woomera Australia 92 31.11S136.54E
Woonsocket U.S.A. 115 42.00N 71.31W
Wooramel Australia 88 25.42S114.20E
Wooramel r. Australia 88 25.47S114.10E
Woorong, L. Australia 92 29.24S134.06E
Wooroorooka Australia 93 28.59S145.40E
Wooster U.S.A. 114 40.48N 81.56W
Worb Switz. 19 46.56N 7.34E
Worcester R.S.A. 80 33.39S 19.25E
Worcester U.K. 13 52.12N 2.12W
Worcester U.S.A. 115 42.16N 71.48W
Wörgl Austria 39 47.29N 12.04E
Workington U.K. 12 54.39N 3.34W
Worksop U.K. 12 53.19N 1.09W
Workum Neth. 16 53.00N 5.26E
Worland U.S.A. 108 44.01N107.57W
Worms W. Germany 39 49.38N 8.22E
Wörnitz r. W. Germany 39 48.42N 10.45E
Wörrstadt W. Germany 39 49.50N 8.07E
Wörther See l. Austria 31 46.37N 14.10E
Worthing U.K. 13 50.49N 0.21W
Worthington Minn. U.S.A. 110 43.37N 95.36W
Worthington Ohio U.S.A. 112 40.03N 83.03W
Worthville U.S.A. 112 38.38N 85.05W
Wosi Indonesia 59 0.15S128.00E
Wour Chad 77 21.21N 15.57E
Woutchaba Cameroon 77 5.13N 13.05E
Wowoni i. Indonesia 59 4.10S123.10E
Wragby U.K. 12 53.17N 0.18E
Wrangel I. see Vrangelya, Ostrov U.S.S.R. 51
Wrangell U.S.A. 100 56.28N132.23W
Wrangell Mts. U.S.A. 98 62.00N143.00W
Wrangle U.K. 12 53.03N 0.09E
Wrath, C. U.K. 14 58.37N 5.01W
Wray U.S.A. 110 40.05N102.13W
Wrecks, B. of Kiribati 85 1.52N157.17W
Wrexham U.K. 12 53.05N 3.00W
Wrightville Australia 93 31.36S145.53E
Wrigley Canada 98 63.16N123.39W
Wrocław Poland 37 51.05N 17.00E
Wronki Poland 36 52.43N 16.23E
Wroxeter Canada 104 43.50N 81.07W
Września Poland 37 52.20N 17.34E
Wubin Australia 89 30.06S116.38E
Wuchang China 55 30.21N114.19E
Wucheng China 54 37.12N116.04E
Wuchuan Guangdong China 55 21.21N110.40E
Wuchuan Nei Monggol China 54 41.08N111.24E
Wuda China 54 39.40N106.40E
Wudham 'Alwā' Oman 65 23.48N 57.33E
Wudinna Australia 92 33.03S135.28E
Wudu China 54 33.24N104.50E
Wufeng China 55 30.12N110.36E
Wugang China 55 26.42N110.31E
Wugong Shan mts. China 55 27.15N114.00E
Wuhai China 54 39.50N106.40E
Wuhan China 55 30.37N114.19E
Wuhu China 55 31.25N118.25E
Wüjang China 63 33.38N 79.55E
Wu Jiang r. China 55 29.41N107.24E
Wukari Nigeria 77 7.57N 9.42E
Wulian China 54 35.45N119.12E
Wuliang Shan mts. China 52 24.27N100.43E
Wum Cameroon 77 6.25N 10.03E
Wumbulgal Australia 93 34.25S146.16E
Wuming China 55 23.10N108.16E
Wuning China 55 29.17N115.05E
Wunnummin L. Canada 102 52.50N 89.20W
Wun Rog Sudan 73 9.00N 28.21E
Wunstorf W. Germany 38 52.25N 9.26E
Wuppertal R.S.A. 80 32.16S 19.12E
Wuppertal W. Germany 38 51.16N 7.11E
Wuqi China 54 37.03N108.14E
Wuqiao China 54 37.38N116.22E
Wuqing China 54 39.19N117.05E
Wurno Nigeria 77 13.20N 5.28E
Wurtsboro U.S.A. 115 41.35N 74.29W
Wurung Australia 90 19.14S140.23E
Würzburg W. Germany 39 49.48N 9.56E
Wurzen E. Germany 38 51.22N 12.44E
Wusong China 55 31.20N121.30E
Wutach r. W. Germany 39 47.37N 8.15E
Wutongqiao China 55 29.20N103.48E
Wuwei China 54 38.00N102.59E
Wuxi Jiangsu China 55 31.34N120.20E
Wuxi Sichuan China 55 31.28N109.36E
Wuxing China 55 30.59N120.04E
Wuyi Shan mts. China 55 27.00N117.00E
Wuyuan China 54 41.06N108.16E
Wuzhan China 53 50.14N125.18E
Wuzhi Shan mts. China 55 18.50N109.30E
Wuzhou China 55 23.28N111.21E
Wyalkatchem Australia 89 31.21S117.22E

Wyalong to **Yiyuan**

Wyalong Australia **93** 33.55S147.17E
Wyandotte U.S.A. **114** 42.12N 83.10W
Wyandra Australia **91** 27.15S146.00E
Wyangala Resr. Australia **93** 33.58S148.55E
Wyara, L. Australia **92** 28.42S144.16E
Wye U.K. **13** 51.11N 0.56E
Wye *r.* U.K. **13** 51.37N 2.40W
Wyk W. Germany **38** 54.42N 8.34E
Wymondham U.K. **13** 52.34N 1.07E
Wynbring Australia **91** 30.33S133.32E
Wyndham Australia **88** 15.29S128.05E
Wynne U.S.A. **111** 35.14N 90.47W
Wyoming Canada **104** 42.57N 82.07W
Wyoming *d.* U.S.A. **108** 43.10N107.36W
Wyong Australia **93** 33.17S151.25E
Wyszków Poland **37** 52.36N 21.28E
Wytheville U.S.A. **113** 36.57N 81.07W

X

Xa Cassau Angola **78** 9.02S 20.17E
Xagquka China **63** 31.50N 92.46E
Xainza China **63** 30.56N 88.40E
Xaitongmoin China **63** 29.22N 88.15E
Xai-Xai Mozambique **81** 25.05S 33.38E
Xam Nua Laos **56** 20.25N104.10E
Xangdoring China **63** 32.06N 82.02E
Xangongo Angola **78** 16.31S 15.00E
Xanten W. Germany **38** 51.39N 6.26E
Xánthi Greece **34** 41.08N 24.53E
Xar Hudag China **54** 45.07N114.28E
Xar Moron He *r.* China **54** 43.30N120.42E
Xarrama *r.* Portugal **27** 38.14N 8.20W
Xassengue Angola **78** 10.26S 18.32E
Xau, L. Botswana **80** 21.15S 24.50E
Xebert China **54** 44.02N122.00E
Xenia U.S.A. **112** 39.41N 83.56W
Xequessa Angola **78** 16.47S 19.05E
Xertigny France **19** 48.03N 6.24E
Xhora R.S.A. **80** 31.58S 28.40E
Xiachuan *i.* China **55** 21.40N112.37E
Xiaguan China **52** 25.33N100.09E
Xiamen China **55** 24.30N118.08E
Xi'an China **54** 34.11N108.55E
Xianfeng China **55** 29.41N109.02E
Xiangcheng China **54** 33.50N113.29E
Xiangfan China **55** 32.04N112.05E
Xiangfen China **54** 35.52N111.24E
Xiang Jiang *r.* China **55** 28.49N112.30E
Xiangkhoang Laos **56** 19.21N103.23E
Xiangquan He *r.* China **63** 31.45N 78.40E
Xiangshan China **55** 29.29N121.51E
Xiangtan China **55** 27.50N112.49E
Xiangtang China **55** 28.26N115.58E
Xiangyin China **55** 28.40N112.53E
Xiangyuan China **54** 36.32N113.02E
Xiangzhou China **55** 23.58N109.41E
Xianju China **55** 28.51N120.44E
Xianning China **55** 29.53N114.13E
Xian Xian China **54** 38.12N116.07E
Xianyang China **54** 34.20N108.40E
Xianyou China **55** 25.28N118.50E
Xiao Hinggan Ling *mts.* China **53** 48.40N128.30E
Xiaojiang China **55** 27.34N120.27E
Xiaojiao China **54** 38.24N113.42E
Xiaowutai Shan *mtn.* China **54** 39.57N114.59E
Xiapu China **55** 26.58N119.57E
Xiayang China **55** 26.45N117.58E
Xichang China **52** 27.53N102.18E
Xichou China **55** 23.27N104.40E
Xichuan China **54** 33.15N111.27E
Xifeng China **55** 27.06N106.44E
Xigazê China **52** 29.18N 88.50E
Xiheying China **54** 39.53N114.42E
Xiji China **54** 35.52N105.35E
Xi Jiang *r.* China **55** 22.23N113.20E
Xiliao He *r.* China **54** 43.48N123.00E
Xilin China **55** 24.30N105.03E
Xilókastron Greece **35** 38.04N 22.43E
Ximeng China **61** 22.45N 99.29E
Xin'anjiang China **55** 29.27N119.14E
Xin'anjiang Shuiku *resr.* China **55** 29.32N119.00E
Xincheng Guang. Zhuang China **55** 24.04N108.40E
Xincheng Ningxia Huizu China **54** 38.33N106.10E
Xincheng Shanxi China **54** 37.57N112.35E
Xindu China **55** 30.50N104.12E
Xinfeng Guangdong China **55** 24.04N114.12E
Xinfeng Jiangxi China **55** 25.27N114.58E
Xing'an China **55** 25.35N110.32E
Xingcheng China **54** 40.37N120.43E
Xinghua China **54** 32.51N119.50E
Xingkai Hu *l. see* Khanka, Ozero U.S.S.R. / China **53**
Xingren China **55** 25.26N105.14E
Xingshan China **55** 31.10N110.51E
Xingtai China **54** 37.04N114.26E
Xingu *r.* Brazil **123** 1.40S 52.15W
Xing Xian China **54** 38.31N111.04E
Xingyi China **55** 25.00N104.59E
Xinhe Hebei China **54** 37.22N115.14E
Xinhe Xin. Uygur China **52** 41.34N 82.38E
Xinhua China **55** 27.45N111.18E
Xining China **52** 36.35N101.55E
Xinji China **54** 35.17N115.35E
Xinjiang-Uygur *d.* China **52** 41.15N 87.00E
Xinjie China **54** 39.15N109.36E
Xinjin Liaoning China **54** 39.27N121.48E
Xinjin Sichuan China **55** 30.30N103.47E
Xinle China **54** 38.15N114.40E
Xinlitun China **54** 42.00N122.09E
Xinmin China **54** 42.01N122.48E
Xinning China **55** 26.31N110.48E
Xinshao China **55** 27.20N111.26E
Xin Xian China **54** 38.24N112.47E
Xinxiang China **54** 35.12N113.57E
Xinyang China **54** 32.08N114.04E
Xinyi Guangdong China **55** 22.21N110.57E
Xinyi Jiangsu China **54** 34.20N118.30E
Xinyu China **55** 27.50N114.55E
Xinzheng China **54** 34.25N113.46E
Xinzhu Taiwan **55** 24.50N120.58E
Xiping Henan China **54** 33.23N114.02E
Xiping Zhejiang China **55** 28.27N119.29E
Xique Xique Brazil **123** 10.47S 42.44W
Xi Ujimqin Qi China **54** 44.32N117.40E
Xiuning China **55** 29.48N118.20E
Xiushan China **55** 28.27N108.59E
Xiushui China **55** 29.01N114.37E
Xixabangma Feng *mtn.* China **63** 28.21N 85.47E
Xixia China **54** 33.30N111.30E
Xizang *d.* China **63** 31.45N 87.00E
Xizang *d. see* Tibet *d.* China **52**
Xorkol China **52** 39.04N 91.05E
Xuancheng China **55** 30.59N118.40E
Xuang *r.* Laos **56** 19.59N102.20E
Xuanhan China **55** 31.25N107.38E
Xuanhua China **54** 40.30N115.00E
Xuanwei China **55** 26.16N104.01E
Xuchang China **54** 34.02N113.50E
Xuefeng Shan *mts.* China **55** 27.30N111.00E
Xueshuiwen China **53** 49.15N129.39E
Xugou China **54** 34.40N119.26E
Xunyang China **54** 32.48N109.27E
Xupu China **55** 27.54N110.35E
Xushui China **54** 39.01N115.39E
Xuwen China **55** 20.25N110.20E
Xuyong China **55** 28.17N105.21E
Xuzhou China **54** 34.14N117.20E

Y

Ya Gabon **78** 1.17S 14.14E
Ya'an China **61** 30.00N102.59E
Yaapeet Australia **92** 35.48S142.07E
Ya'bad Jordan **67** 32.27N 35.10E
Yabassi Cameroon **77** 4.30N 9.55E
Yabelo Ethiopia **73** 4.54N 38.05E
Yābis, Wādī al Jordan **67** 32.24N 35.35E
Yablonovyy Khrebet *mts.* U.S.S.R. **51** 53.20N115.00E
Yabrai Shan *mts.* China **54** 39.50N103.30E
Yabrai Yanchang China **54** 39.24N102.43E
Yabrūd Syria **66** 33.58N 36.40E
Yacheng China **55** 18.35N109.13E
Yacuiba Bolivia **124** 22.00S 63.25W
Yādgīr India **60** 16.46N 77.08E
Yadong China **63** 27.29N 88.54E
Yagaba Ghana **76** 10.13N 1.14W
Yagoua Cameroon **77** 10.23N 15.13E
Yagra China **63** 31.32N 82.27E
Yagur Israel **67** 32.44N 35.04E
Yahagi *r.* Japan **57** 34.50N136.59E
Yahisuli Zaïre **78** 0.08S 24.04E
Yahuma Zaïre **78** 1.06N 23.10E
Yaizu Japan **57** 34.52N138.20E
Yajua Nigeria **77** 11.27N 12.49E
Yakchāl Afghan. **62** 31.47N 64.41E
Yakima U.S.A. **108** 46.36N120.31W
Yakmach Pakistan **62** 28.45N 63.51E
Yaksha U.S.S.R. **44** 61.51N 56.59E
Yaku shima *i.* Japan **57** 30.20N130.40E
Yakutat U.S.A. **100** 59.29N139.49W
Yakutat U.S.A. **98** 59.33N139.44W
Yakutat B. U.S.A. **100** 59.29N139.49W
Yakutsk U.S.S.R. **51** 62.10N129.20E
Yala Thailand **56** 6.32N101.19E
Yale U.S.A. **114** 43.08N 82.48W
Yalgoo Australia **89** 28.20S116.41E
Yalinga C.A.R. **73** 6.31N 23.15E
Yallourn Australia **93** 38.09S146.22E
Yalong Jiang *r.* China **52** 26.35N101.44E
Yalpunga Australia **92** 29.04S142.05E
Yalta U.S.S.R. **45** 44.30N 34.09E
Yalu Jiang *r.* China **54** 40.10N124.25E
Yalutorovsk U.S.S.R. **50** 56.41N 66.12E
Yamagata Japan **57** 38.16N140.19E
Yamaguchi Japan **57** 34.10N131.28E
Yamal, Poluostrov *pen.* U.S.S.R. **50** 70.20N 70.00E
Yamanashi Japan **57** 35.40N138.40E
Yamanashi *d.* Japan **57** 35.30N138.35E
Yamandjo Zaïre **78** 1.38N 23.27E
Yaman Tau *mtn.* U.S.S.R. **44** 54.20N 58.10E
Yamaska Canada **105** 46.01N 72.55W
Yamaska *r.* Canada **105** 46.06N 72.56W
Yamato Japan **57** 35.29N139.29E
Yamato-takada Japan **57** 34.31N135.45E
Yamba N.S.W. Australia **93** 29.26S153.22E
Yamba S.A. Australia **92** 34.15S140.54E
Yambéring Guinea **76** 11.49N 12.18W
Yambio Sudan **73** 4.34N 28.23E
Yambol Bulgaria **34** 42.30N 26.30E
Yambol *d.* Bulgaria **34** 42.15N 26.30E
Yamdena *i.* Indonesia **59** 7.30S131.00E
Yamenyingzi China **54** 42.23N121.03E
Yamethin Burma **56** 20.24N 96.08E
Yam HaMelah *see* Dead Sea Jordan **67**
Yam Kinneret *l.* Israel **67** 32.49N 35.36E
Yamma Yamma, L. Australia **90** 26.20S141.25E
Yamoussoukro Ivory Coast **76** 6.51N 5.18W
Yampol U.S.S.R. **37** 48.13N 28.12E
Yamuna *r.* India **63** 25.25N 81.50E
Yamzho Yumco *l.* China **63** 29.00N 90.40E
Yan Nigeria **77** 10.05N 12.11E
Yana *r.* U.S.S.R. **51** 71.30N135.00E
Yanac Australia **92** 36.09S141.29E
Yan'an China **54** 36.45N109.22E
Yanbu'al Baḩr Saudi Arabia **64** 24.07N 38.04E
Yancannia Australia **92** 30.16S142.50E
Yancheng China **54** 33.22N120.05E
Yanchep Australia **89** 31.32S115.33E
Yanchi China **54** 37.47N107.24E
Yanchuan China **54** 36.51N110.05E
Yanco Australia **93** 34.36S146.25E
Yanda Australia **93** 30.18S145.44E
Yanda *r.* Australia **93** 30.22S145.38E
Yandong China **55** 24.02N107.09E
Yandoon Burma **56** 17.02N 95.39E
Yanfolila Mali **76** 11.11N 8.09W
Yangarey U.S.S.R. **44** 68.46N 61.29E
Yangchun China **55** 22.03N111.46E
Yangcun China **55** 23.26N114.30E
Yangjiang China **55** 21.50N111.54E
Yangmingshan Taiwan **55** 25.18N121.35E
Yangqu China **54** 38.03N112.36E
Yangquan China **54** 37.49N113.28E
Yangshan Guangdong China **55** 24.29N112.38E
Yangshan Liaoning China **54** 41.15N120.18E
Yangshuo China **55** 24.47N110.30E
Yangtze *r. see* Chang Jiang China **55**
Yang Xian China **54** 33.10N107.35E
Yangxin China **55** 29.50N115.10E
Yangze China **55** 26.59N118.19E
Yangzhou China **54** 32.22N119.26E
Yanhuqu China **63** 32.32N 82.44E
Yanji China **53** 42.45N129.25E
Yanko *r.* Australia **93** 35.25S145.27E
Yanko Glen *town* Australia **92** 31.43S141.39E
Yankton U.S.A. **110** 42.53N 97.23W
Yanqi China **52** 42.00N 86.30E
Yanshan China **61** 23.36N104.20E
Yanshiping China **63** 33.35N 92.04E
Yanskiy Zaliv *g.* U.S.S.R. **51** 72.00N136.10E
Yantabulla Australia **93** 29.13S145.01E
Yantai China **54** 37.27N121.26E
Yantra *r.* Bulgaria **34** 43.35N 25.37E
Yanxi China **55** 28.11N110.58E
Yanzhou China **54** 35.35N116.52E
Yao Chad **77** 12.52N 17.34E
Yao Japan **57** 34.37N135.36E
Yaopu China **55** 26.05N105.42E
Yaoundé Cameroon **77** 3.51N 11.31E
Yao Xian China **54** 34.52N109.01E
Yap *i.* Caroline Is. **59** 9.30N138.09E
Yapehe Zaïre **78** 0.10S 24.20E
Yapen *i.* Indonesia **59** 1.45S136.10E
Yaqui *r.* Mexico **109** 27.37N110.39W
Yar U.S.S.R. **44** 58.13N 52.08E
Yaraka Australia **90** 24.53S144.04E
Yaransk U.S.S.R. **44** 57.22N 47.49E
Yardea Australia **92** 32.23S135.32E
Yare *r.* U.K. **13** 52.34N 1.45E
Yaremcha U.S.S.R. **37** 48.26N 24.29E
Yarensk U.S.S.R. **44** 62.10N 49.07E
Yargora U.S.S.R. **37** 46.25N 28.20E
Yariga take *mtn.* Japan **57** 36.21N137.39E
Yārīn Lebanon **67** 33.06N 35.14E
Yaritagua Venezuela **122** 10.05N 69.07W
Yarkant He *r.* China **52** 40.30N 80.55E
Yarker Canada **105** 44.22N 76.46W
Yarlung Zangbo Jiang *r. see* Brahmaputra China **63**
Yarmouth Canada **103** 43.50N 66.07W
Yarmūk *r.* Jordan / Syria **67** 32.38N 35.34E
Yaroslavl U.S.S.R. **44** 57.34N 39.52E
Yarqon *r.* Israel **67** 32.06N 34.47E
Yarra *r.* Australia **93** 37.51S144.54E
Yarram Australia **93** 38.30S146.41E
Yarran Range *mts.* Australia **90** 18.08S136.40E
Yarrawonga Australia **93** 36.02S145.59E
Yarrow *r.* U.K. **14** 55.32N 2.51W
Yar Sale U.S.S.R. **50** 66.50N 70.48E
Yartsevo R.S.F.S.R. U.S.S.R. **44** 55.06N 32.43E
Yartsevo R.S.F.S.R. U.S.S.R. **51** 60.17N 90.02E
Yarumal Colombia **122** 6.59N 75.25W
Yasanyama Zaïre **73** 4.18N 21.11E
Yaselda *r.* U.S.S.R. **37** 52.07N 26.28E
Yasen U.S.S.R. **37** 53.10N 28.55E
Yashi Nigeria **77** 12.23N 7.54E
Yashkul U.S.S.R. **45** 46.10N 45.20E
Yasinya U.S.S.R. **37** 48.12N 24.20E
Yasothon Thailand **56** 15.46N104.12E
Yass Australia **93** 34.51S148.55E
Yas'ur Israel **67** 32.54N 35.10E
Yatakala Niger **76** 14.52N 0.22E
Yaté N. Cal. **84** 22.09S166.57E
Yates Center U.S.A. **111** 37.53N 95.44W
Yathkyed L. Canada **101** 62.40N 98.00W
Yatsuo Japan **57** 36.35N137.10E
Yatsushiro Japan **57** 32.32N130.35E
Yaṭṭah Jordan **67** 31.27N 35.05E
Yāval India **62** 21.10N 75.42E
Yavatmāl India **63** 20.24N 78.08E
Yaví, Cerro *mtn.* Venezuela **122** 5.32N 65.59W
Yavne Israel **67** 31.53N 34.45E
Yavne'el Israel **67** 32.42N 35.30E
Yavorov U.S.S.R. **37** 49.59N 23.20E
Yawng-hwe Burma **56** 20.35N 96.58E
Yaxi China **55** 27.35N106.40E
Ya Xian China **55** 18.19N109.32E
Yazd Iran **65** 31.54N 54.22E
Yazmān Pakistan **62** 29.08N 71.45E
Yazoo *r.* U.S.A. **111** 32.22N 91.00W
Yazoo City U.S.A. **111** 32.51N 90.28W
Ybbs Austria **36** 48.11N 15.05E
Yding Skovhöj *hill* Denmark **42** 56.00N 9.48E
Ydsteböhavn Norway **42** 59.08N 5.15E
Ye Burma **56** 15.15N 97.50E
Yea Australia **93** 37.12S145.25E
Yecla Spain **25** 38.37N 1.07W
Yedintsy U.S.S.R. **45** 48.09N 27.18E
Yeeda River *town* Australia **88** 17.36S123.39E
Yefremov U.S.S.R. **44** 53.08N 38.08E
Yegorlyk *r.* U.S.S.R. **45** 46.30N 41.52E
Yegoryevsk U.S.S.R. **44** 55.21N 39.01E
Yegros Paraguay **126** 26.24S 56.25W
Yei Sudan **73** 4.05N 30.40E
Yei *r.* Sudan **73** 7.20N 30.39E
Yeji China **55** 31.51N115.01E
Yelets U.S.S.R. **44** 52.36N 38.30E
Yeletskiy U.S.S.R. **44** 67.04N 64.00E
Yélimané Mali **76** 15.08N 10.34W
Yell *i.* U.K. **14** 60.35N 1.05W
Yellowdine Australia **89** 31.19S119.36E
Yellowhead Pass Canada **100** 52.53N118.25W
Yellowknife Canada **100** 62.27N114.21W
Yellowknife *r.* Canada **100** 62.27N114.19W
Yellow Mt. Australia **93** 32.19S146.50E
Yellow Sea Asia **53** 35.00N123.00E
Yellowstone *r.* U.S.A. **106** 47.55N103.45W
Yellowstone L. U.S.A. **108** 44.25N110.38W
Yellowstone Nat. Park U.S.A. **108** 44.30N110.35W
Yell Sd. U.K. **14** 60.30N 1.11W
Yelma Australia **88** 26.30S121.40E
Yelsk U.S.S.R. **37** 51.50N 29.10E
Yelwa Nigeria **77** 10.48N 4.42E
Yemen Asia **71** 15.15N 44.30E
Yemilchino U.S.S.R. **37** 50.58N 27.40E
Yenagoa Nigeria **77** 4.59N 6.15E
Yenangyaung Burma **56** 20.28N 94.54E
Yen Bai Vietnam **56** 21.43N104.44E
Yendi Ghana **76** 9.29N 0.01W
Yengan Burma **56** 21.06N 96.30E
Yenisey *r.* U.S.S.R. **51** 69.00N 86.00E
Yeniseysk U.S.S.R. **51** 58.27N 92.13E
Yeniseyskiy Zaliv *g.* U.S.S.R. **50** 73.00N 79.00E
Yenshui Taiwan **55** 23.20N120.16E
Yenyuka U.S.S.R. **51** 57.57N121.15E
Yeo, L. Australia **89** 28.04S124.23E
Yeo I. Canada **104** 45.24N 81.49W
Yeola India **62** 20.02N 74.29E
Yeovil U.K. **13** 50.57N 2.38W
Yeppoon Australia **90** 23.08S150.45E
Yeráki Greece **35** 37.00N 22.42E
Yerbent U.S.S.R. **65** 39.23N 58.35E
Yercha U.S.S.R. **51** 69.34N147.30E
Yerepol U.S.S.R. **51** 65.15N168.43E
Yerevan U.S.S.R. **65** 40.10N 44.31E
Yerington U.S.A. **108** 38.59N119.10W
Yermak U.S.S.R. **50** 52.03N 76.55E
Yermitsa U.S.S.R. **44** 66.56N 52.20E
Yermo Mexico **111** 26.23N104.01W
Yermo U.S.A. **109** 34.54N116.50W
Yerolimin Greece **35** 36.28N 22.24E
Yershov U.S.S.R. **45** 51.22N 48.16E
Yertom U.S.S.R. **44** 63.31N 47.51E
Yerushalayim *d.* Israel **67** 31.45N 35.00E
Yerushalayim Israel / Jordan **67** 31.47N 35.13E
Yesa, Embalse de *resr.* Spain **25** 42.36N 1.09W
Yeşil *r.* Turkey **64** 41.22N 36.37E
Yeso U.S.A. **109** 34.26N104.37W
Yessey U.S.S.R. **51** 68.29N102.15E
Yeste Spain **26** 38.22N 2.18W
Yetman Australia **93** 28.55S150.49E
Yeu Burma **56** 22.49N 95.26E
Yeu, Île d' *i.* France **18** 46.42N 2.20W
Yevpatoriya U.S.S.R. **45** 45.12N 33.20E
Yevstratovskiy U.S.S.R. **45** 50.07N 39.45E
Yew Mtn. U.S.A. **114** 38.05N 80.16W
Ye Xian China **54** 37.10N119.56E
Yeysk U.S.S.R. **45** 46.43N 38.17E
Yi *r.* Uruguay **125** 33.17S 58.08W
Yiannitsá Greece **34** 40.46N 22.24E
Yíaros *i.* Greece **35** 37.36N 24.40E
Yibin China **55** 28.42N104.34E
Yibug Caka *l.* China **63** 33.50N 87.00E
Yichang China **55** 30.21N111.21E
Yichuan China **54** 34.25N112.26E
Yidu China **54** 36.45N118.24E
Yifag Ethiopia **73** 12.02N 37.44E
Yiftah Israel **67** 33.07N 35.33E
Yijun China **54** 35.23N109.07E
Yilan China **53** 46.22N129.31E
Yilehuli Shan *mts.* China **53** 51.20N124.20E
Yilliminning Australia **89** 32.54S117.22E
Yilong China **55** 31.34N106.24E
Yimen China **54** 34.21N107.07E
Yinan China **54** 35.33N118.27E
Yinchuan China **54** 38.27N106.18E
Yindarlgooda, L. Australia **89** 30.45S121.55E
Yingcheng China **55** 30.57N113.33E
Yingde China **55** 24.07N113.20E
Yinggehai China **55** 18.31N108.40E
Yingkou China **54** 40.39N122.18E
Yingshan China **55** 31.06N106.35E
Yingshang China **54** 32.42N116.20E
Yingtan China **55** 28.11N116.55E
Yinkanie Australia **92** 34.21S140.20E
Yinning China **52** 43.57N 81.23E
Yin Shan *mts.* China **54** 41.30N109.00E
Yirga Alem Ethiopia **73** 6.52N 38.22E
Yirol Sudan **73** 6.33N 30.30E
Yirwa Sudan **73** 7.47N 27.15E
Yishan China **55** 24.37N108.32E
Yíthion Greece **35** 36.45N 22.34E
Yiwu China **55** 29.18N120.04E
Yi Xian China **54** 41.30N121.14E
Yiyang Henan China **54** 34.30N112.10E
Yiyang Hunan China **55** 28.20N112.30E
Yiyuan China **54** 36.12N118.08E

Yizhang to Zug

Yizhang China **55** 25.24N112.57E
Yizre'el Israel **67** 32.33N 35.20E
Ylitornio Finland **40** 66.19N 23.40E
Ylivieska Finland **40** 64.05N 24.33E
Yngaren *l.* Sweden **43** 58.52N 16.35E
Yoakum U.S.A. **111** 29.17N 97.09W
Yodo *r.* Japan **57** 34.41N135.25E
Yogyakarta Indonesia **59** 7.48S110.24E
Yogyakarta *d.* Indonesia **59** 7.48S110.22E
Yokadouma Cameroon **77** 3.26N 15.06E
Yokkaichi Japan **57** 34.58N136.37E
Yoko Cameroon **77** 5.29N 12.19E
Yokohama Japan **57** 35.27N139.39E
Yokosuka Japan **57** 35.18N139.40E
Yola Nigeria **77** 9.14N 12.32E
Yom *r.* Thailand **56** 15.47N100.05E
Yona Guam **84** 13.25N144.47E
Yonago Japan **57** 35.27N133.20E
Yondok S. Korea **57** 36.26N129.23E
Yongcheng China **54** 33.56N116.22E
Yongchuan China **55** 29.19N105.55E
Yongchun China **55** 25.19N118.17E
Yongdeng China **54** 36.44N103.24E
Yonghe China **54** 36.44N110.39E
Yongnian China **54** 36.47N114.30E
Yongring China **55** 22.45N108.29E
Yongshou China **54** 34.40N108.04E
Yongxiu China **55** 28.58N115.43E
Yonkers U.S.A. **115** 40.56N 73.52W
Yonne *d.* France **19** 47.55N 3.45E
Yonne *r.* France **19** 48.23N 2.58E
York Australia **89** 31.55S116.45E
York Canada **104** 43.41N 79.29W
York U.K. **12** 53.58N 1.07W
York *r.* U.S.A. **113** 37.15N 76.23W
York Nebr. U.S.A. **110** 40.52N 97.36W
York Penn. U.S.A. **114** 39.58N 76.44W
York, C. Australia **90** 10.42S142.31E
Yorke Pen. Australia **92** 35.00S137.30E
Yorketown Australia **92** 35.02S137.35E
York Factory *town* Canada **101** 57.00N 92.18W
York Haven U.S.A. **114** 40.07N 76.43W
Yorkshire Wolds *hills* U.K. **12** 54.00N 0.39W
Yorkton Canada **101** 51.13N102.28W
York Village U.S.A. **115** 43.08N 70.38W
Yoro Honduras **117** 15.09N 87.07W
Yōrō Japan **57** 35.32N140.04E
Yosemite Nat. Park U.S.A. **108** 37.45N119.35W
Yoshino *r.* Japan **57** 34.22N135.40E
Yoshkar Ola U.S.S.R. **44** 56.38N 47.52E
Yos Sudarsa, Pulau *i.* Indonesia **59** 8.00S138.30E
Yŏsu S. Korea **53** 34.46N127.45E
Youghal Rep. of Ire. **15** 51.58N 7.51W
You Jiang *r.* Guang. Zhuang. China **55** 23.28N111.18E
Youkou Ivory Coast **76** 5.16N 7.16W
Youkounkoun Guinea **76** 12.35N 13.11W
Young Australia **93** 34.19S148.20E
Young *r.* Australia **89** 33.45S121.12E
Young Uruguay **125** 32.41S 57.38W
Young U.S.A. **109** 34.06N110.57W
Younghusband, L. Australia **92** 30.51S136.05E
Younghusband Pen. Australia **92** 36.00S139.15E
Youngstown Canada **101** 51.32N111.13W
Youngstown U.S.A. **114** 41.06N 80.39W
Youngsville U.S.A. **114** 41.48N 74.54W
You Xian China **55** 26.59N113.12E
Youyang China **55** 28.52N108.45E
Youyu China **54** 39.59N112.27E
Yoxford U.K. **13** 52.16N 1.30E
Yozgat Turkey **64** 39.50N 34.48E
Ypsilanti U.S.A. **104** 42.15N 83.36W
Yreka U.S.A. **108** 41.44N122.38W
Yssingeaux France **21** 45.08N 4.07E
Ystad Sweden **43** 55.25N 13.49E
Ythan *r.* U.K. **14** 57.21N 2.01W
Ytterhogdal Sweden **41** 62.12N 14.51E
Yu'alliq, Jabal *mtn.* Egypt **66** 30.21N 33.31E
Yuanbaoshan China **54** 42.15N119.14E
Yuan Jiang *r.* China **55** 29.00N111.55E
Yuan Jiang *r. see* Hong Hà China **52**
Yuanling China **55** 28.28N110.15E
Yuanping China **54** 38.42N112.46E
Yuba City U.S.A. **108** 39.08N121.27W
Yūbari Japan **57** 43.04N141.59E
Yubdo Ethiopia **73** 9.00N 35.22E
Yucatán *d.* Mexico **117** 19.30N 89.00W
Yucatan Channel Carib. Sea **117** 21.30N 86.00W
Yucatan Pen. Mexico **116** 19.00N 90.00W
Yucca U.S.A. **109** 34.52N114.09W
Yuci China **54** 37.37N112.47E
Yudino U.S.S.R. **50** 55.49N 48.54E
Yudu China **55** 25.57N115.16E
Yueqing China **55** 28.08N120.57E
Yuexi China **52** 28.36N102.35E
Yueyang China **55** 29.22N113.10E
Yugan China **55** 28.41N116.41E
Yugorskiy Poluostrov *pen.* U.S.S.R. **44** 69.00N 62.30E
Yugoslavia Europe **34** 44.00N 20.00E
Yuhang China **55** 30.25N120.18E
Yuhebu China **54** 37.59N109.51E
Yukon *r.* U.S.A. **98** 62.35N164.20W
Yukon Territory *d.* Canada **98** 65.00N135.00W
Yuleba Australia **90** 26.37S149.20E
Yulin Guang. Zhuang.China **55** 22.38N110.10E
Yulin Shaanxi China **54** 38.11N109.33E
Yuma Ariz. U.S.A. **109** 32.43N114.37W
Yuma Colo. U.S.A. **108** 40.08N102.43W
Yumen China **52** 40.19N 97.12E
Yunan China **55** 23.14N111.35E
Yuncheng China **54** 35.02N111.00E
Yungas *f.* Bolivia **124** 16.20S 65.00W
Yungera Australia **92** 34.48S143.10E
Yungxiao China **55** 23.59N117.27E
Yunkai Dashan *mts.* China **55** 22.30N111.05E
Yunnan *d.* China **52** 24.30N101.30E
Yunta Australia **92** 32.37S139.34E
Yunxi China **54** 33.00N110.22E
Yun Xian China **54** 32.48N110.50E
Yunyang China **55** 30.55N108.56E
Yuqing China **55** 27.12N107.56E
Yuribey U.S.S.R. **50** 71.02N 77.02E
Yurimaguas Peru **122** 5.54S 76.07W
Yuryuzan U.S.S.R. **44** 54.51N 58.25E
Yu Shan *mtn.* Taiwan **55** 23.20N121.03E
Yushkozero U.S.S.R. **44** 64.45N 32.03E
Yushu China **52** 33.06N 96.48E
Yūtō Japan **57** 34.42N137.38E
Yu Xian China **54** 34.10N113.28E
Yuxikou China **55** 31.29N118.16E
Yuyao China **55** 30.03N120.11E
Yuzhno Sakhalinsk U.S.S.R. **53** 46.58N142.45E
Yuzhnyy Bug *r.* U.S.S.R. **37** 46.55N 31.59E
Yuzhong China **54** 35.52N104.02E
Yvelines *d.* France **19** 48.50N 1.50E
Yverdon Switz. **39** 46.47N 6.39E
Yvetot France **18** 49.37N 0.46E

Z

Zaandam Neth. **16** 52.27N 4.49E
Zabid Yemen **72** 14.12N 43.19E
Žabljak Yugo. **31** 43.09N 19.07E
Zābol *d.* Afghan. **62** 32.00N 67.00E
Zābol Iran **65** 31.00N 61.32E
Zāboli Iran **65** 27.08N 61.36E
Zabqung China **63** 31.38N 87.20E
Zabrze Poland **37** 50.18N 18.47E
Zacapa Guatemala **117** 15.00N 89.30W
Zacatecas Mexico **116** 22.48N102.33W
Zacatecas *d.* Mexico **116** 24.00N103.00W
Zadar Yugo. **31** 44.07N 15.14E
Zafra Spain **27** 38.25N 6.25W
Zafriyya Israel **67** 32.00N 34.51E
Zaglivérion Greece **34** 40.36N 23.15E
Zagorá Greece **34** 39.27N 23.06E
Zagorsk U.S.S.R. **44** 56.20N 38.10E
Zagreb Yugo. **31** 45.48N 15.58E
Zāgros, Kūhhā-ye *mts.* Iran **65** 32.00N 51.00E
Zagros Mts. *see* Zāgros, Kūhhā-ye Iran **65**
Zāhedān Iran **65** 29.32N 60.54E
Zaḩlah Lebanon **66** 33.50N 35.55E
Z̧ahrān Saudi Arabia **71** 17.40N 43.30E
Zaindeh *r.* Iran **65** 32.40N 52.50E
Zaïre Africa **78** 2.00S 22.00E
Zaire *d.* Angola **78** 6.30S 13.30E
Zaïre *r.* Zaïre **78** 6.00S 12.30E
Zaječar Yugo. **34** 43.53N 22.18E
Zákas Greece **34** 40.02N 21.16E
Zakataly U.S.S.R. **65** 41.39N 46.40E
Zákinthos *i.* Greece **35** 37.52N 20.44E
Zákinthos *town* Greece **35** 37.47N 20.54E
Zakinthou, Porthmós *str.* Greece **35** 37.50N 21.00E
Zakopane Poland **37** 49.19N 19.57E
Zala *d.* Hungary **31** 46.35N 16.40E
Zalaegerszeg Hungary **31** 46.51N 16.51E
Zalalövö Hungary **31** 46.51N 16.35E
Zalamea de la Serena Spain **26** 38.39N 5.39W
Zalaszentgrót Hungary **31** 46.59N 17.02E
Zalău Romania **37** 47.11N 23.03E
Žalec Yugo. **31** 46.15N 15.10E
Zaleshchiki U.S.S.R. **37** 48.39N 25.50E
Zalingei Sudan **73** 12.54N 23.29E
Zambezi *r.* Mozambique/Zambia **81** 18.15S 35.55E
Zambezi Zambia **78** 13.30S 23.12E
Zambezia *d.* Mozambique **81** 16.30S 37.30E
Zambia Africa **79** 14.00S 28.00E
Zamboanga Phil. **59** 6.55N122.05E
Zambrów Poland **37** 53.00N 22.15E
Zambue Mozambique **80** 15.09S 30.47E
Zamfara *r.* Nigeria **77** 12.04N 4.00E
Zamora Mexico **116** 20.00N102.18W
Zamora Spain **26** 41.30N 5.45W
Zamora *d.* Spain **26** 41.45N 6.00W
Zamość Poland **37** 50.43N 23.15E
Zamtang China **61** 32.26N101.06E
Zaña Peru **122** 7.00S 79.30W
Záncara *r.* Spain **27** 39.18N 3.18W
Zanda China **63** 31.29N 79.50E
Zanesville U.S.A. **114** 39.56N 82.01W
Zanjān Iran **65** 36.40N 48.30E
Zanthus Australia **89** 31.02S123.34E
Zanzibar Tanzania **79** 6.10S 39.16E
Zanzibar I. Tanzania **79** 6.00S 39.20E
Zaouatallaz Algeria **75** 24.52N 8.26E
Zaouiet Azmour Tunisia **32** 36.55N 11.01E
Zaouiet el Mgaïz Tunisia **32** 36.56N 10.50E
Zaozhuang China **54** 34.48N117.50E
Zapadna Morava *r.* Yugo. **34** 43.50N 20.15E
Zapadni Rodopi *mts.* Bulgaria **34** 41.49N 23.58E
Zapadno-Sibirskaya Ravnina *f.* U.S.S.R. **9** 60.00N 75.00E
Zapadnyy Sayan *mts.* U.S.S.R. **51** 53.00N 92.00E
Západočeský *d.* Czech. **38** 49.40N 13.00E
Zapala Argentina **125** 38.55S 70.05W
Zapardiel *r.* Spain **26** 41.29N 5.02W
Zapata U.S.A. **111** 26.52N 99.19W
Zaporozhye U.S.S.R. **45** 47.50N 35.10E
Zapug China **63** 33.17N 80.50E
Zara Turkey **64** 39.55N 37.44E
Zaragoza Spain **25** 41.38N 0.53W
Zaragoza *d.* Spain **25** 41.40N 1.10W
Zarand Iran **65** 30.50N 56.35E
Zaranj Afghan. **62** 31.06N 61.53E
Zárate Argentina **125** 34.05S 59.02W
Zarauz Spain **26** 43.17N 2.10W
Zaraza Venezuela **122** 9.23N 65.20W
Zard Kūh *mtn.* Iran **65** 32.21N 50.04E
Zarembo I. U.S.A. **100** 56.20N132.50W
Zarghūn Shahr Afghan. **60** 32.51N 68.25E
Zari Nigeria **77** 13.03N 12.46E
Zaria Nigeria **77** 11.01N 7.44E
Zárkon Greece **34** 39.37N 22.07E
Zaruma Ecuador **122** 3.40S 79.30W
Zary Poland **36** 51.40N 15.10E
Zarzal Colombia **122** 4.24N 76.01W
Zāskār *r.* Jammu & Kashmir **62** 34.10N 77.20E
Zāskār Mts. Jammu & Kashmir **63** 33.15N 78.00E
Zaslavl U.S.S.R. **37** 54.00N 27.15E
Za'tarī, Wādī az Jordan **67** 32.09N 36.15E
Žatec Czech. **39** 50.18N 13.32E
Zatishye U.S.S.R. **37** 47.20N 29.58E
Zave Zimbabwe **80** 17.14S 30.02E
Zavet Bulgaria **34** 43.46N 26.40E
Zavidovići Yugo. **31** 44.27N 18.09E
Zavitinsk U.S.S.R. **53** 50.08N129.24E
Zāwa Pakistan **62** 28.04N 66.23E
Zawīlah Libya **75** 26.10N 15.07E
Zāwiyat al Amwāt Egypt **66** 28.04N 30.50E
Zāwiyat al Mukhaylá Libya **72** 32.10N 22.17E
Zāyandeh *r.* Iran **65** 32.40N 52.50E
Zaydābād Afghan. **62** 34.17N 69.07E
Zaydī, Wādī az Syria **67** 32.45N 35.50E
Zaysan U.S.S.R. **52** 47.30N 84.57E
Zaysan, Ozero *l.* U.S.S.R. **52** 48.00N 83.30E
Zayzūn Syria **67** 32.43N 35.56E
Zbarazh U.S.S.R. **37** 49.40N 25.49E
Zborov U.S.S.R. **37** 49.40N 25.09E
Zbraslav Czech. **38** 49.59N 14.24E
Zdolbunov U.S.S.R. **37** 50.30N 26.10E
Zduńska Wola Poland **37** 51.36N 18.57E
Zeballos Canada **100** 49.59N126.50W
Zebediela R.S.A. **80** 24.19S 29.17E
Zeebrugge Belgium **16** 51.20N 3.13E
Zeehan Australia **91** 41.55S145.21E
Zeeland *d.* Neth. **16** 51.30N 3.45E
Ze'elim Israel **67** 31.12N 34.32E
Zeerust R.S.A. **80** 25.32S 26.04E
Zefa' Israel **67** 31.07N 35.12E
Zefat Israel **67** 32.57N 35.27E
Zehdenick E. Germany **38** 52.59N 13.20E
Zeila Somali Rep. **71** 11.21N 43.30E
Zeist Neth. **16** 52.03N 5.16E
Zeitz E. Germany **38** 51.03N 12.08E
Zelechów Poland **37** 51.49N 21.54E
Zelengora *mts.* Yugo. **31** 43.20N 18.30E
Zelenodolsk U.S.S.R. **44** 55.50N 48.30E
Zelenogorsk U.S.S.R. **44** 60.15N 29.31E
Zelenokumsk U.S.S.R. **45** 44.25N 43.54E
Zelentsovo U.S.S.R. **44** 59.51N 44.59E
Zelina Yugo. **31** 45.58N 16.15E
Zell W. Germany **39** 50.01N 7.10E
Zella-Mehlis E. Germany **38** 50.39N 10.39E
Zell am Ziller Austria **39** 47.14N 11.53E
Zelts U.S.S.R. **37** 46.38N 30.00E
Zelzate Belgium **16** 51.12N 3.49E
Zembra, Île *i.* Tunisia **32** 37.08N 10.48E
Zemio C.A.R. **73** 5.02N 25.08E
Zemoul, Oued *wadi* Morocco **74** 29.12N 7.52W
Zemun Yugo. **29** 44.51N 20.23E
Zendeh Jān Afghan. **62** 34.21N 61.45E
Zenica Yugo. **31** 44.12N 17.55E
Zenn *r.* W. Germany **39** 49.31N 10.58E
Zenne *r.* Belgium **16** 51.04N 4.25E
Zerbst E. Germany **38** 51.58N 12.04E
Zereh, Gowd-e *l.* Afghan. **62** 29.45N 61.50E
Zergan Albania **34** 41.30N 20.21E
Zetel W. Germany **38** 53.25N 7.58E
Zeulenroda E. Germany **38** 50.39N 11.58E
Zeven W. Germany **38** 53.18N 9.16E
Zevenaar Neth. **16** 51.57N 6.04E
Zevenbergen Neth. **16** 51.41N 4.42E
Zeya U.S.S.R. **51** 53.48N127.14E
Zeya *r.* U.S.S.R. **51** 50.20N127.30E
Zêzere *r.* Portugal **27** 39.28N 8.20W
Zgierz Poland **37** 51.52N 19.25E
Zgorzelec Poland **36** 51.12N 15.01E
Zhailma U.S.S.R. **50** 51.37N 61.33E
Zhanatas U.S.S.R. **52** 43.11N 69.35E
Zhangbei China **54** 41.08N114.44E
Zhanghua Taiwan **55** 24.05N120.30E
Zhangjiakou China **54** 40.47N114.56E
Zhangping China **55** 25.25N117.28E
Zhangpu China **55** 24.06N117.37E
Zhangwu China **54** 42.22N122.31E
Zhang Xian China **54** 34.48N104.27E
Zhangye China **52** 38.56N100.27E
Zhangzhou China **55** 24.57N118.32E
Zhanjiang China **55** 21.08N110.22E
Zhanyu China **54** 44.31N122.40E
Zhao'an China **55** 23.45N117.14E
Zhaoping China **55** 24.06N110.48E
Zhaoqing China **55** 23.02N112.29E
Zhari Namco *l.* China **63** 31.00N 85.30E
Zhashkov U.S.S.R. **37** 49.12N 30.05E
Zhashui China **54** 33.41N109.06E
Zhaxi Co *l.* China **63** 32.10N 85.00E
Zhaxigang China **63** 32.31N 79.33E
Zhdanov U.S.S.R. **45** 47.05N 37.34E
Zhejiang *d.* China **55** 29.00N120.00E
Zheleznodorozhnyy R.S.F.S.R. U.S.S.R. **44** 67.59N 64.47E
Zheleznodorozhnyy R.S.F.S.R. U.S.S.R. **44** 62.39N 50.59E
Zhen'an China **54** 33.24N109.12E
Zhenba China **54** 32.34N107.58E
Zheng'an China **55** 28.30N107.30E
Zhenghe China **55** 27.23N118.51E
Zhengyang China **54** 32.36N114.23E
Zhengzhou China **54** 34.40N113.38E
Zhenhai China **55** 29.58N121.45E
Zhenjiang China **54** 32.09N119.30E
Zhenxiong China **55** 27.27N104.50E
Zhenyuan China **54** 35.42N106.58E
Zherdnoye U.S.S.R. **37** 51.40N 30.11E
Zherong China **55** 27.13N119.52E
Zhidachov U.S.S.R. **37** 49.20N 24.22E
Zhigansk U.S.S.R. **51** 66.48N123.27E
Zhijiang China **55** 27.27N109.41E
Zhitkovichi U.S.S.R. **37** 52.12N 27.49E
Zhitomir U.S.S.R. **37** 50.18N 28.40E
Zhlobin U.S.S.R. **37** 52.50N 30.00E
Zhmerinka U.S.S.R. **37** 49.00N 28.02E
Zhob *r.* Pakistan **62** 32.04N 69.50E
Zhongba China **63** 29.40N 84.07E
Zhongdian China **61** 28.00N 99.30E
Zhongli Taiwan **55** 24.54N121.09E
Zhongning China **54** 37.28N105.41E
Zhongshan Guangdong China **55** 22.31N113.22E
Zhongtiao Shan China **54** 36.00N113.30E
Zhongwei China **54** 37.30N105.15E
Zhoucun China **54** 36.49N117.49E
Zhoushan *i.* China **55** 30.05N122.15E
Zhouzhi China **54** 34.08N108.14E
Zhuanghe China **54** 39.41N123.02E
Zhucheng China **54** 36.00N119.24E
Zhugqu China **54** 33.46N104.18E
Zhuji China **55** 29.43N120.14E
Zhumadian China **54** 32.58N114.02E
Zhuo Xian China **54** 39.30N116.55E
Zhuozi China **54** 40.52N112.33E
Zhuozi Shan *mtn.* China **54** 39.36N107.00E
Zhupanovo U.S.S.R. **51** 53.40N159.52E
Zhuxi China **54** 32.19N109.52E
Zhuzhou China **55** 27.49N113.07E
Ziārat Pakistan **62** 30.23N 67.43E
Ziārat-e Shāh Maqsūd Afghan. **62** 31.59N 65.30E
Žiar nad Hronom Czech. **37** 48.36N 18.52E
Zibo China **54** 36.50N118.00E
Zicavo France **21** 41.54N 9.08E
Ziegenhain W. Germany **38** 50.50N 9.07E
Ziel, Mt. Australia **88** 23.24S132.23E
Zielona Góra Poland **36** 51.57N 15.30E
Ziesar E. Germany **38** 52.16N 12.17E
Ziftā Egypt **66** 30.43N 31.14E
Zigey Chad **77** 14.43N 15.47E
Zigong China **55** 29.18N104.45E
Zigui China **55** 31.01N110.35E
Ziguinchor Senegal **76** 12.35N 16.20W
Zikhron Ya'aqov Israel **67** 32.34N 34.57E
Zile Turkey **64** 40.18N 35.52E
Žilina Czech. **37** 49.14N 18.46E
Zillah Libya **75** 28.33N 17.35E
Zillertaler Alpen *mts.* Austria/Italy **30** 47.00N 11.55E
Zima U.S.S.R. **51** 53.58N102.02E
Zimatlán Mexico **116** 16.52N 96.45W
Zimba Zambia **78** 17.20S 26.25E
Zimbabwe Africa **80** 18.55S 30.00E
Zimbabwe Ruins Zimbabwe **80** 20.30S 30.30E
Zimbor Romania **37** 47.00N 23.16E
Zimi Sierra Leone **76** 7.22N 11.21W
Zimnicea Romania **34** 43.39N 25.21E
Zimniy Bereg *f.* U.S.S.R. **44** 65.50N 41.30E
Zinder Niger **77** 13.46N 8.58E
Zinder *d.* Niger **77** 14.20N 9.30E
Zinga Mtwara Tanzania **79** 9.01S 38.47E
Ziniaré U. Volta **76** 12.34N 1.12W
Zinkgruvan Sweden **43** 58.49N 15.05E
Zinnowitz E. Germany **38** 54.04N 13.55E
Zion Grove U.S.A. **115** 40.54N 76.13W
Zippori Israel **67** 32.45N 35.17E
Žirje *i.* Yugo. **31** 43.40N 15.39E
Ziro India **61** 27.38N 93.42E
Zi Shui *r.* China **55** 28.38N112.30E
Zitong China **55** 31.38N105.11E
Zitsa Greece **34** 39.47N 20.40E
Zittau E. Germany **38** 50.54N 14.47E
Zitundo Mozambique **81** 26.45S 32.49E
Ziway, L. Ethiopia **73** 8.00N 38.50E
Zixi China **55** 27.42N117.05E
Ziyang China **55** 30.02N104.42E
Zizhong China **55** 29.48N104.51E
Zlarin Yugo. **31** 43.42N 15.50E
Zlatar Yugo. **31** 46.06N 16.05E
Zlatograd Bulgaria **34** 41.22N 25.07E
Zlatoust U.S.S.R. **44** 55.10N 59.38E
Zletovo Yugo. **34** 41.59N 22.17E
Zlītan Libya **75** 32.28N 14.34E
Złoczew Poland **37** 51.25N 18.36E
Złotów Poland **37** 53.22N 17.02E
Žlutice Czech. **39** 50.03N 13.10E
Zlynka U.S.S.R. **37** 52.24N 31.45E
Zmeinogorsk U.S.S.R. **50** 51.11N 82.14E
Žminj Yugo. **31** 45.09N 13.55E
Zmiyevka U.S.S.R. **44** 52.40N 36.22E
Znamenka U.S.S.R. **45** 48.42N 32.40E
Żnin Poland **37** 52.52N 17.43E
Znojmo Czech. **36** 48.52N 16.05E
Zobia Zaïre **78** 2.58N 25.56E
Zobue Mozambique **81** 15.35S 34.26E
Zoétélé Cameroon **77** 3.17N 11.54E
Zogno Italy **30** 45.48N 9.40E
Zohreh *r.* Iran **65** 30.04N 49.32E
Zolochev U.S.S.R. **37** 49.48N 24.51E
Zolotonosha U.S.S.R. **45** 49.39N 32.05E
Zomba Malaŵi **79** 15.22S 35.22E
Zonguldak Turkey **64** 41.26N 31.47E
Zong Xian China **55** 30.16N108.01E
Zorita Spain **27** 39.17N 5.42W
Zorzor Liberia **76** 7.46N 9.28W
Zouar Chad **77** 20.27N 16.32E
Zouîrât Mauritania **74** 22.35N 12.20W
Zoutkamp Neth. **16** 53.21N 6.18E
Zrenjanin Yugo. **29** 45.22N 20.23E
Zrmanja *r.* Yugo. **31** 44.15N 15.32E
Zuckerhütl *mtn.* Austria **30** 46.58N 11.09E
Zuénoula Ivory Coast **76** 7.34N 6.03W
Zuera Spain **25** 41.52N 0.47W
Zug Switz. **39** 47.10N 8.31E

Zugspitze *mtn.* W. Germany **39** 47.25N 10.59E
Zuid Beveland *f.* Neth. **16** 51.30N 3.50E
Zuidelijk-Flevoland *f.* Neth. **16** 52.22N 5.22E
Zuid Holland *d.* Neth. **16** 52.00N 4.30E
Zuidhorn Neth. **16** 53.16N 6.25E
Zújar *r.* Spain **26** 39.01N 5.47W
Zújar, Embalse del *resr.* Spain **26** 38.50N 5.20W
Zülpich W. Germany **38** 50.41N 6.39E
Zululand *f.* R.S.A. **80** 27.30S 32.00E
Zumbo Mozambique **80** 15.36S 30.24E

Zungeru Nigeria **77** 9.48N 6.03E
Zunyi China **55** 27.39N 106.48E
Županja Yugo. **31** 45.04N 18.42E
Zurich Neth. **16** 53.08N 5.25E
Zürich Switz. **39** 47.23N 8.32E
Zürichsee *l.* Switz. **39** 47.13N 8.45E
Zuru Nigeria **77** 11.26N 5.16E
Zushi Japan **57** 35.18N 139.35E
Žut *i.* Yugo. **31** 43.52N 15.19E
Zutphen Neth. **16** 52.08N 6.12E

Zuwārah Libya **75** 32.56N 12.06E
Zuwayzā Jordan **67** 31.42N 35.55E
Žužemberk Yugo. **31** 45.50N 14.56E
Zvenigorodka U.S.S.R. **37** 49.05N 30.58E
Zverinogolovskoye U.S.S.R. **50** 48.01N 40.09E
Zvishavane Zimbabwe **80** 20.20S 30.05E
Zvolen Czech. **37** 48.35N 19.08E
Zweibrücken W. Germany **39** 49.15N 7.21E
Zweisimmen Switz. **39** 46.33N 7.22E
Zwettl Austria **36** 48.37N 15.10E

Zwickau E. Germany **38** 50.44N 12.29E
Zwiesel W. Germany **39** 49.01N 13.14E
Zwischenahn W. Germany **38** 53.12N 8.00E
Zwoleń Poland **37** 51.22N 21.35E
Zwolle Neth. **16** 52.31N 6.06E
Zyryanovsk U.S.S.R. **50** 49.45N 84.16E
Zywiec Poland **37** 49.41N 19.12E